The Routledge Handbook of Chinese Discourse Analysis

Chinese is a discourse-oriented language and the underlying mechanisms of the language involve encoding and decoding so the language can be correctly delivered and understood. To date, there has been a lack of consolidation at the discourse level such that a reference framework for understanding the language in a top-down fashion is still underdeveloped.

The Routledge Handbook of Chinese Discourse Analysis is the first to showcase the latest research in the field of Chinese discourse analysis to consolidate existing findings, put the language in both theoretical and socio-functional perspectives, offer guidance and insights for further research and inspire innovative ideas for exploring the Chinese language in the discourse domain. The book is aimed at both students and scholars researching in the areas of Chinese Linguistics and Discourse Analysis.

Chris Shei studied at Taiwan, Cambridge and Edinburgh and has worked at Swansea University since 2003. He teaches and researches in linguistics and translation studies and is particularly interested in the use of computer and web resources for linguistic research, language education and translating. He is the General Editor for two new Routledge series: *Routledge Studies in Chinese Discourse Analysis* and *Routledge Studies in Chinese Translation*.

The Routledge Handbook of Chinese Discourse Analysis

Edited by Chris Shei

LONDON AND NEW YORK

First published 2019
by Routledge
2 Park Square, Milton Park, Abingdon, Oxon OX14 4RN

and by Routledge
52 Vanderbilt Avenue, New York, NY 10017

Routledge is an imprint of the Taylor & Francis Group, an informa business

© 2019 selection and editorial matter, Chris Shei; individual chapters, the contributors

The right of Chris Shei to be identified as the author of the editorial material, and of the authors for their individual chapters, has been asserted in accordance with sections 77 and 78 of the Copyright, Designs and Patents Act 1988.

All rights reserved. No part of this book may be reprinted or reproduced or utilised in any form or by any electronic, mechanical, or other means, now known or hereafter invented, including photocopying and recording, or in any information storage or retrieval system, without permission in writing from the publishers.

Trademark notice: Product or corporate names may be trademarks or registered trademarks, and are used only for identification and explanation without intent to infringe.

British Library Cataloguing-in-Publication Data
A catalogue record for this book is available from the British Library

Library of Congress Cataloging-in-Publication Data
A catalog record for this book has been requested

ISBN: 978-0-415-78979-0 (hbk)
ISBN: 978-1-315-21370-5 (ebk)

Typeset in Bembo
by Apex CoVantage, LLC

Contents

List of figures x
List of tables xiii
List of contributors xvi

    Introduction: Discourse analysis in the Chinese context 1
    Chris Shei

PART I
Approaches to Chinese discourse 19

 1 Chinese conversation analysis: new method, new data, new insights 21
    Kang-Kwong Luke

 2 Critical analysis of Chinese discourse: adaptation and transformation 36
    Weixiao Wei

 3 Sociolinguistic approaches to Chinese discourse 51
    Wei Wang

 4 Analyzing multimodal Chinese discourse: integrating social semiotic and conceptual metaphor theories 65
    Dezheng (William) Feng

PART II
Grammatical aspect of Chinese discourse 83

 5 Conceptual word order principles and Mandarin Chinese grammar 85
    Anna Morbiato

 6 Grammatical constructions and Chinese discourse 102
    Zhuo Jing-Schmidt

Contents

7	Between factuality and counterfactuality: Chinese conditionals in conversations *Yu-Fang Wang and Wayne Schams*	116
8	Information structure in Chinese discourse *Yu-Yin Hsu*	130

PART III
Linguistic elements in Chinese discourse — 145

9	Personal pronouns in Chinese discourse *Xuehua Xiang*	147
10	Aspect in Chinese narrative discourse *Wendan Li*	160
11	The use of modal verbs in political debates *Maria Cheng*	175
12	Zero anaphora and topic chain in Chinese discourse *Ming-Ming Pu*	188

PART IV
Pragmatic aspect of Chinese discourse — 201

13	Politeness and impoliteness in Chinese discourse *Dániel Z. Kádár*	203
14	Pragmatic markers in Chinese discourse *Guangwu Feng*	216
15	The grammaticalization of stance markers in Chinese *Foong Ha Yap and Winnie Chor*	230
16	Language, gesture and meaning *Kawai Chui*	244

PART V
Cognitive aspect of Chinese discourse — 263

17	The psycholinguistics of Chinese discourse processing *Chien-Jer Charles Lin*	265

18	The neurocognitive processing of Chinese discourse *Chiao-Yi Wu and Shen-Hsing Annabel Chen*	280
19	Language impairment in Chinese discourse *Yi-hsiu Lai and Yu-te Lin*	296
20	Discourse, gender and psychologization in contemporary China *Jie Yang*	310

PART VI
Genres of Chinese discourse — 323

21	Chinese business communication *Jiayi Wang*	325
22	Chinese workplace discourse: politeness strategies and power dynamics *Vincent X. Wang*	339
23	Legal discourse studies in the Chinese context *Zhengrui Han and Yunfeng Ge*	352
24	Authoritative classroom discourse: the abuse of power in a Chinese classroom *Bo Wang and Yuanyi Ma*	364

PART VII
Chinese discourse on social media — 377

25	The discourse of Chinese social media: the case of Weibo *Eileen Le Han*	379
26	Chinese censorship of online discourse *Juha A. Vuori and Lauri Paltemaa*	391
27	Don't talk back to your father – online anti-Taiwanese independence nationalist discourse *Ane Bislev*	404
28	Rescuing authoritarian rule: the anti-*Gongzhi* discourse in Chinese cyberspace *Rongbin Han and Linan Jia*	415

Contents

PART VIII
Identity, ideology and control in Chinese discourse 429

29 Discursive construction of national and political identities in China: political and cultural construction of the Chinese nation 431
Qing Cao

30 Ideological patterns in Chinese state media narratives concerning issues of security and sovereignty 444
Lutgard Lams

31 The cultural governance of China's mass media events: how the PRC manages discourses in complex media environments 458
Florian Schneider

32 Identity construction in Chinese discourse 470
Cheng-Tuan Li

PART IX
Chinese discourse and language technology 483

33 Development of computation models for Chinese discourse analysis 485
Hen-Hsen Huang and Hsin-Hsi Chen

34 Chinese spoken dialog system 500
Chung-Hsien Wu and Ming-Hsiang Su

35 Corpus stylistics and Chinese literary discourses: a comparative study of four novels by Shen Congwen and Chang Eileen 519
Zhao-Ming Gao

36 Tracking collective sentiment in Chinese finance-related discourse 536
Samuel W.K. Chan

PART X
The diversity of Chinese discourse 551

37 Code-switching in Singapore Mandarin 553
Cher Leng Lee

38 Studies in Cantonese discourse: two examples 569
John C. Wakefield

| 39 | An introduction to Taiwan Hakka: focusing on its sounds, morph-syntax and social background
Huei-ling Lai | 582 |
| 40 | The dynamics of Southern Min in Taiwan: from Southern Min dialects to "Taigi"
Hui-lu Khoo (Hui-ju Hsu) | 596 |

PART XI
The application of Chinese discourse analysis — 611

41	Discourse analysis in Chinese interpreting and translation studies *Binhua Wang*	613
42	Discourse analysis for Chinese language teaching *Julia Renner*	628
43	Critical cultural discourse analysis: a case study of Chinese official discourse on civil society *Runya Qiaoan*	643
44	A discourse analysis of Macau chefs' accounts of job crafting *Ting Wu*	655

Index — 670

Figures

0.1	Multiword key terms output by CiteSpace based on 4500 abstracts on 'discourse analysis' 1996–2018	4
0.2	A possible speech production model for utterance with sentence final particle	8
0.3	Multiword key terms output by CiteSpace based on 2500 abstracts on '话语分析' 1994–2018	9
1.1	Engagement	28
1.2	Tina's point-and-swipe just before she says '. . . and you'll know'	29
1.3	Tina's circling gesture as she says 'Mother-in-law, man!'	30
2.1	A model of research perspectives and steps for critical discourse analysis	39
4.1	'Chinese dream; spirit of the ox'	72
4.2	'People's heart turns to the Communist Party'	74
4.3	'Children's heart turns toward the CCP'	75
4.4	'Everlasting Chinese civilizations'	76
7.1	Degree of certainty in Chinese conditional markers	123
10.1	Aspect, grounding and temporal progression of the passage in (12)	168
11.1	Modal notions in Chinese	177
16.1	Manual movements produced by the speaker on the left	245
16.2	A writing gesture	245
16.3	Gestural depiction of 'ship'	249
16.4	Gestural depiction of 'chance'	249
16.5	Gestural depiction of 'playing a keyboard musical instrument'	250
16.6	Shape of a mirror: hands configure a rectangle	251
16.7	Length of the sides of a semi-truck: hands move to the sides from center, palms facing each other	251
16.8	Size of a paragraph: hands with thumbs and index fingers spread wide apart to form a large rectangular frame	251
16.9	Bodily location for a dental brace: left hand moves from table to touch the mandible	251
16.10	Pressing the keys on the keyboard of a musical instrument: fingers of both hands go up and down several times	252
16.11	UP IS GOOD: right palm is open and sweeps upward	252
16.12	Gestural depiction of 'going downhill'	253
16.13	Walking direction: left hand moves rightward and upward	254
16.14	Tossing manner: right hand at shoulder level goes forward and downward with force	254
16.15	Shape of the nose: palms with closed fingers come apart in front of nose	254

16.16	DOWN IS QUIET: palms face forward and go downward	254
16.17	Manner of opening a window: hands in fist at chest level curve from the center to the left	255
16.18	Bodily location for glasses: right thumb and index finger forming an open circle go toward the right eye	255
16.19	Rain pouring down as cause of a flood: palms at eye level go down sharply	255
16.20	Swollen face as effect of staying in water: hands with bent fingers are at each side of the face	256
16.21	Pressing a button on a musical instrument: right index finger goes up and down one time	256
16.22	Long glove as the theme of a wearing action: right hand moves up onto left upper arm	256
18.1	Three language-related ERP components: (a) N400, (b) early left-anterior negativity (ELAN), and (c) P600	281
18.2	Brain regions involved in discourse comprehension for Western languages (Ferstl et al., 2008; Xu et al., 2005)	282
18.3	An illustration of the waveform and scalp distribution of the Nref effect for the ambiguity condition and the N400-late positivity components (LPC) for the semantic incoherence and the combined conditions	284
18.4	Brain regions involved in making pragmatic inferences in Chinese (Feng et al., 2017)	292
24.1	Frequency of the speech functions	370
27.1	Xinlang Junshi's version of Liu Leyan's post	409
28.1	Distribution of "*Gongzhi*" mentions (August 2011–September 2015)	419
33.1	Data flow of a learning-based model for Chinese discourse relation recognition	489
33.2	An example of feature extraction. The textual information in the instance (S1) is converted into a vector with word features, punctuation features, and length features	490
33.3	A model for discourse relation recognition based on convolutional neural network (CNN)	491
33.4	Dependency tree of (S1) generated by Stanford CoreNLP. The arrow denotes a dependency in the direction from dependent to governor. The dependency type is labeled with the Universal Dependency tags	493
33.5	Instance of Chinese discourse parsing at the sentence level	495
33.6	The system pipeline for discourse parsing proposed by Wang and Lan (2016)	496
34.1	Principal components of a dialog system	501
34.2	The block diagram of an ASR	502
34.3	Example of the POMDP method	504
34.4	The architecture of the deep RL model	506
34.5	Example of the deep RL method interacting with the user	507
34.6	The architecture of the sequence-to-sequence model	508
34.7	The architecture of the interview coaching system	509
34.8	The dialog state tracking architecture of the interview coaching system	511
34.9	The vector representation of the sentence	511
34.10	Combination of the current answer hidden vector and the historical information	512

Figures

34.11	The flowchart for training the action selection model and the question generation model of the interview coaching system	513
34.12	The framework of Deep Q Network Pre-training of the interview coaching system	513
34.13	The steps in training the action decision model	514
34.14	The flowchart of question generation	515
34.15	Example of action decision and state decision	515
35.1	The SegPoi interface of Chinese NLP tools by Tsui (2018)	522
35.2	The Lancaster Log-likelihood and effect size calculator	523
35.3	The Keyword List function in AntConc	524
35.4	The use of regular expressions in NotePad++ to identify morphological reduplications	524
35.5	The use of regular expressions in NotePad++ to remove any word and the symbol _ that occur before any POS tag	525
35.6	The POS tags after removing all the Chinese words and the symbol _	525
35.7	Concordances of 地 in Chang's corpus	529
36.1	Parse tree of the sentence (S1)	539
36.2	The polarity of a sentence is determined by the propagation of the valences of words from the terminal level up to the root	544
36.3	Fragments of two time series, tracking negative mood and the closing price of HSI, from late March to mid-September in 2016	546
37.1	Main language used at home by primary students from 1980 to 2004 (MOE, 2004)	556
40.1	The conceptualization of the localization process of Taigi	600
41.1	Perspectives for discourse analysis in interpreting and translation studies	616
41.2	Perspectives, paradigms and approaches of discourse analysis in T&I studies	617

Tables

0.1	Top 50 keywords output by WordSmith based on 4500 abstracts on 'discourse analysis' 1996–2018	3
0.2	No. of SFPs found in an FCWR episode and the percentage of utterances containing an SFP	6
0.3	Keywords output by CiteSpace based on 2500 abstracts on '话语分析' 1994–2018	10
2.1	The first 10 collocates for the phrase "critical discourse analysis" by WebCorp	37
2.2	The first 20 key words in our People's Daily corpus with highest keyness values	44
2.3	The first 20 collocates of 台湾 in our People's Daily corpus	45
2.4	Types of expression comprising 台湾-大陆 collocation	46
2.5	The first 20 collocates of (蔡)英文 in our People's Daily corpus	47
2.6	Types of expression formed by 蔡英文 and its collocates	48
3.1	A sample of the running sheets for the program	59
4.1	The social semiotic model of multimodal metaphor analysis	69
4.2	Summary of source domains in the Chinese Dream posters	70
7.1	Frequency of occurrence of conditional clauses in spoken data	120
10.1	Verb categories and situation types	163
10.2	Transitivity features	169
10.3	Transitivity values of the four clauses in (13)	170
11.1	The formality and frequency of modal verbs employed by Ma Ying-jeou and Tsai Ing-wen within the 2012 and 2016 presidential debates	184
12.1	Raw data	196
12.2	Topicality	196
12.3	Referential continuity	197
12.4	Referential persistence	198
12.5	Topic chain and thematic coherence	199
13.1	Historical Chinese forms of (self-)address	208
16.1	The interpretations of the writing gesture without contextual information	246
16.2	The interpretations of the writing gesture with the contextual information about street dance	246
16.3	The semantic information about nominal concepts as represented in gesture	251
16.4	The semantic information about nominal concepts across modalities	252
16.5	The semantic information about motion and state concepts as represented in gesture	254

16.6	The semantic information about action concepts as represented in gesture	255
16.7	The semantic information about verbal concepts across modalities	257
16.8	Semantic redundancy across nominal and verbal concepts	258
21.1	Summary of generic structure (GS)	332
21.2	Key lexical words in the two corpora (keyness calculated using LL)	334
24.1	Four types of exchanges based on Halliday and Matthiessen (2014)	369
24.2	Lexical choices that construe the class leaders' authoritative rule	372
26.1	Typology of formal censorship from the user's point-of-view	395
26.2	The types of images in Baidu.com and Google.com for "Tiananmen/天安门", % (n = 400)	400
28.1	Top 5 Boards with active mentions of "Gongzhi"	418
28.2	The Top 60 Terms Related to "Gongzhi" (excluding stop words)	420
29.1	Western concepts translated into Kanji in Japan	433
34.1	Two types of dialog systems and their associated properties (Skantze, 2007)	501
34.2	The detailed information of the corpus	510
34.3	Actions and slots defined based on the interview corpus	510
35.1	The six types of morphological reduplications and their regular expressions	524
35.2	The number of tokens, types, punctuation marks, type/token ratio, and words per punctuation mark	526
35.3	Keyword lists derived from the corpora by Shen and Chang	527
35.4	LLR test for the six types of morphological reduplications	529
35.5	The keyword lists based on the frequency of POS tags in the two corpora	530
35.6	LLR test of identical pairs of text segments and parallel structures in Shen's and Chang's corpus	531
36.1	Context association features to determine the possible chunk break point between the words 滙控 ("HSBC") and 唾棄 ("cast aside")	542
36.2	Valence of some entries in the dictionaries	543
36.3	Additional rules for estimating the effects of sentence-based polarity in different syntactic structures	544
37.1	Percentage distribution of total population by ethnic group (Singapore Department of Statistics, 2010)	554
37.2	Percentage of major Chinese dialect groups in Singapore (1840 from Seah; 1848; 1911 from Lee, 2003: 272; 2010 from Singapore Statistics 2010)	554
39.1	Consonants in TH	583
39.2	Vowels in TH	584
39.3	Tone systems of SH and HH	585
39.4	Examples of word formation in TM and TH	585
39.5	Examples of different word formation orders in TM and TH	586
39.6	Examples of different compounds in TM and TH	586
39.7	Contrast of 出手 in TM and TH	586
39.8	The distribution of CA and NA across gender and age (N = 158)	590
39.9	Constructions of 当[dong1]	592
40.1	The meanings of Holo of different characters	598
40.2	Examples of Mandarin's influences on Taigi's [ə]/ [ɔ] variation	601
40.3	Examples of Taigi and Mandarin lexical items sharing or using different Han characters 3–1 items sharing Han characters 3–2 items that use different Han characters	602
40.4	Examples of Taigi loanwords transitions from Japanese to Mandarin	602

40.5	Examples of untranslatable Taigi loanwords in Mandarin	603
40.6	Examples of emotional Taigi loanwords in Mandarin	603
40.7	Examples of Taiuan Guoyu pronunciations and the corresponding Mandarin pronunciations	604
40.8	The Taiuan Guoyu terms in (1) and (2) and the corresponding Mandarin terms	605
40.9	Comparisons of the Taiyu Huoxingwen in (3) and their corresponding correct written Taigi	608
40.10	Comparisons of the Taiyu Huoxingwen in (4) and their corresponding correct written Taigi	608
42.1	Pros and cons of CA methodology for SLA research	630
42.2	A conversation opening in a video-based eTandem session	635
42.3	A situation that took place during a one-on-one feedback phase	639
44.1	The top 10 words appearing most frequently in the corpus	657
44.2	The top 10 keywords of the chef interview corpus	658
44.3	The top 10 collocates of 自己 in the chef corpus	658

Contributors

Ane Bislev obtained a PhD in China Studies from Aarhus University in 2006. She currently works as an associate professor at the Department of Culture and Global Studies at Aalborg University. Her research interests include Chinese internet culture and Chinese tourism.

Qing Cao is Associate Professor in Chinese in the School of Modern Languages and Cultures, Durham University, UK. His research interests center on discourse and representation in the mass media with a focus on cross-cultural issues. He is the author of *China under Western Gaze* (2014), lead editor of *Discourse, Politics and Media in Contemporary China* (2014) and 'Brand China' – a special issue of *Critical Arts* (2017).

Samuel W.K. Chan received a M.Sc. degree from the University of Manchester, an M.Phil. degree from the Chinese University of Hong Kong, and a PhD degree from the University of New South Wales, all in Computer Science. He currently works as an associate professor at the Chinese University of Hong Kong. His research interests are in computational linguistics, sentiment analysis and their applications in market prediction. He is one of the architects in developing a Chinese NLP platform, called HanMosaic.

Hsin-Hsi Chen received BS and MS degrees in computer science and information engineering in 1981 and 1983, respectively, and the PhD degree in electrical engineering in 1988, all from National Taiwan University, Taipei, Taiwan. Since August 1995, Hsin-Hsi Chen has been a professor in Department of Computer Science and Information Engineering, National Taiwan University. He served as chair of the department from 2002 to 2005. From 2006 to 2009, he was chief director of Computer and Information Networking Center. He served as associate dean of the College of Electrical Engineering and Computer Science from 2015 to 2018 and served as director of MOST Joint Research Center for AI Technology and All Vista Healthcare from 2018. His research interests are computational linguistics, Chinese language processing, information retrieval and extraction, and web mining. He has published more than 360 papers in these research areas. He won Google research awards in 2007 and 2012, awards of Microsoft Research Asia in 2008 and 2009, NTU EECS Academic Award in 2011, NTU Award for Outstanding Service in 2011 and the MOST Outstanding Research Award in 2017.

Shen-Hsing Annabel Chen is a clinical neuropsychologist, and Professor of Psychology at the School of Social Sciences with joint appointment at LKCMedicine and the Acting Director of the Centre for Research and Development in Learning (CRADLE), at the Nanyang Technological University. She obtained her PhD in Clinical Rehabilitation Psychology from Purdue University and completed a Clinical Psychology Internship at West Virginia University School of Medicine and a post-doctoral residency in Clinical Neuropsychology at the Department of Neurology, Medical College of Wisconsin. She subsequently worked as a post-doctoral research affiliate at the Lucas MRS/I Center in Radiology at Stanford University School of Medicine, before accepting an assistant professorship at the National Taiwan University in the Graduate Clinical Psychology program. She has published widely in top-tier journals in the fields of psychology, neuroscience, and neuroimaging.

Maria Cheng is Associate Professor at the Department of Linguistics and Translation, City University of Hong Kong. She has rich experience in the media industry, including broadcasting, advertising and publishing. She was the launching Editor-in-Chief of the Hong Kong editions of two international magazines *Cosmopolitan* and *Elle*, and is the author of the books *Translation for the Media* and *Essential Terms of Chinese Painting*. She writes and translates extensively with over 300 publications which include SSCI- and CSSCI-listed refereed papers and book chapters on political discourse, news and audio-visual translation studies, trans-editing process, bilingual editing and Chinese painting. She is currently advisor of Guangzhou Jao Tsung-I Academic and Art Academy and Jao Tsung-I Petite Ecole, the University of Hong Kong.

Winnie Chor received her PhD (in Linguistics) on two research scholarships from the University of Sydney, Australia. Winnie's research interests include cognitive semantics, discourse analysis, stance-marking, language change (from the grammaticalization perspective), and Cantonese linguistics (with a focus on particles). She is Assistant Professor in the Department of English, Hong Kong Baptist University. She is the author of the book *Directional Particles in Cantonese: Form, Function, and Grammaticalization*, published by John Benjamins. Her articles appear in journals such as *Journal of Historical Linguistics*, *Language and Linguistics*, and *Journal of Pragmatics*.

Kawai Chui is Professor of Linguistics in the Department of English and a research fellow at the Research Center for Mind, Brain and Learning, National Chengchi University, Taiwan. Her research is mainly concerned with the use of language and gesture in conversational discourse, and the neuro-cognitive processing of speech and gesture. She is also leading a study that investigates semantic specificity across Russian and Mandarin Chinese and its effect on second language acquisition.

Dezheng (William) Feng obtained his PhD from National University of Singapore. He is currently assistant professor at Department of English, The Hong Kong Polytechnic University. His main research area is multimodality, visual communication and critical discourse analysis. His recent papers have appeared in journals such as *Journal of Pragmatics*, *Discourse and Communication* and *Visual Communication*.

Guangwu Feng obtained an MA in Linguistics and English-Language Teaching from the University of Leeds in 2001 and a PhD in Linguistics from the University of Reading in 2006. He currently works as a professor of Linguistics at Guangdong University of Foreign Studies, China. He is the author of *A Theory of Conventional Implicature and Pragmatic Markers in Chinese* (Emerald, 2010). He is also the author of a number of papers published in *Journal of Pragmatics*, *Language Sciences*, and *Pragmatics & Cognition*.

Zhao-Ming Gao received his PhD in language engineering from the University of Manchester Institute of Science and Technology (UMIST) in 1998. He joined the faculty of the Department of Foreign Languages and Literatures at National Taiwan University in 1999, where he currently works as associate professor. Dr Gao has a keen interest in developing corpus-based computational tools and has published extensively on corpus linguistics, computer-assisted translation and intelligent computer-assisted language learning.

Yunfeng Ge obtained a PhD in applied linguistics from Guangdong University of Foreign Studies in 2013. He currently works as an associate professor at the School of Foreign Languages, Shandong Normal University, Jinan, China. His research interests include genre analysis, discourse studies, forensic linguistics, and language and the media. He is the author of *Resolution of Conflict of Interest in Chinese Civil Court Hearings: A Discourse Information Perspective* (Peter Lang, 2018). His papers were recently published in *Discourse, Context and Media, Discourse & Communication*, and *Pragmatics*.

Eileen Le Han is an assistant professor at Michigan State University. She received her PhD in communication at the University of Pennsylvania. Her research is about Chinese digital culture and social media, and mainly focuses on journalism, social activism and collective memories. She has published multiple journal articles in *Critical Studies in Media Communication, Communication, Culture & Critique, International Journal of Communication* and *Memory Studies*. Her book, titled *Micro-Blogging Memories: Weibo and Collective Remembering in Contemporary China* was published in 2016.

Rongbin Han is an assistant professor at the Department of International Affairs, University of Georgia. He received his PhD degree in political science from the University of California, Berkeley. His research interests center on regime transition, media politics and social activism in authoritarian regimes, with an area focus on China. He is the author of *Contesting Cyberspace in China: Online Expression and Authoritarianism Resilience* (Columbia University Press, 2018).

Zhengrui Han obtained a PhD in applied linguistics from City University of Hong Kong and currently works as an associate professor at the College of Foreign Studies, Jinan University, Guangzhou, China. His research interests include genre analysis, professional communication, critical discourse analysis and language and the law. His papers were recently published in the *Journal of Pragmatics, Discourse & Society, Discourse & Communication, Critical Discourse Studies* and *Pragmatics*.

Hen-Hsen Huang received his PhD degree in Computer Science and Information Engineering from National Taiwan University, Taipei, Taiwan, in 2014. His research interests include natural language processing and information retrieval. His work has been published in conferences including ACL, WWW, IJCAI, COLING and CIKM. Dr Huang's awards and honors include the Honorable Mention of Doctoral Dissertation Award of ACLCLP in 2014 and the Honorable Mention of Master Thesis Award of ACLCLP in 2008. He served as PC members of EMNLP 2018, COLING 2018, ACL 2018, NAACL 2018, ACL 2017, COLING 2016, NAACL 2016 and ACL 2015. Dr Huang is currently a postdoctoral fellow in the Department of Computer Science and Information Engineering at the National Taiwan University.

Yu-Yin Hsu obtained her PhD in linguistics from Indiana University in 2013. She currently works as an assistant professor in the Department of Chinese and Bilingual Studies at Hong Kong Polytechnic University. Her research interests include Chinese linguistics, syntactic theory, information structure and its interface areas in syntax and prosody, teaching Chinese as a second language, and psycholinguistic language processing.

Linan Jia is a PhD candidate at the Department of International Affairs, University of Georgia. Her research interests include media politics, authoritarianism, institutional change, and comparative political behavior. Her articles have appeared in the *Journal of Chinese Governance*, *Journal of Contemporary Asia-Pacific Studies* and *Modern China Studies*.

Zhuo Jing-Schmidt received a BA and an MA in German Language and Literature from Peking University in 1992 and 1995, an MA in Germanic Linguistics from UCLA in 1997, and a PhD in General Linguistics from the University of Cologne in 2005. She is currently an Associate Professor of Chinese linguistics at the Department of East-Asian Languages and Literatures, University of Oregon. She researches at the interface of language structure, discourse pragmatics, emotion in language, and Chinese second language acquisition. Her work transcends traditional disciplinary boundaries and she publishes in three languages – English, Chinese and German. She is executive editor of *Chinese Language and Discourse* and is on the editorial board of *Chinese as a Second Language*.

Dániel Z. Kádár is Qihang Chair Professor and Director of the Centre for Pragmatics Research at the Dalian University of Foreign Languages, China. He is also Research Professor of Pragmatics at the Research Institute for Linguistics of the Hungarian Academy of Sciences. He has a long-standing interest in the pragmatics of Chinese, as well as a number of related areas such as Chinese politeness and ritual, intercultural Sino-Western pragmatics and historical Chinese pragmatics. He is author/editor of 23 volumes published with publishing houses of international standing such as Cambridge University Press, and has published a large number of papers in leading academic journals, such as *Journal of Pragmatics* and *Journal of Politeness Research*. Dániel has been active in promoting research on Chinese language use, by acting as Co-Editor-in-Chief (with Xinren Chen) of the peer-reviewed academic journal *East Asian Pragmatics*. His most recent book is *Politeness, Impoliteness and Ritual – Maintaining the Moral Order in Interpersonal Interaction* (Cambridge University Press, 2017). Readers with interest in Dániel Kádár's work are welcome to contact him at: dannier@dlufl.edu.cn.

Hui-lu Khoo (許慧如), also and better known as Hui-ju Hsu, is an associate professor at the Department of Taiwan Culture, Languages, and Literature, National Taiwan Normal University. Hui-lu Khoo is the Taigi Romanization of her name, and Hui-ju Hsu the Mandarin Romanization. Her research interests include language contact, language variation, and sociolinguistics, particularly of Taigi and Taiwan Mandarin.

Huei-ling Lai obtained a PhD in linguistics from the University of Texas at Austin in 1995. She currently works as a distinguished professor of Linguistics at National Chengchi University in Taiwan. Her research interests cover areas from lexical and conceptual semantics, grammaticalization, construction grammar, to metaphor, metonymy and their interactions and applications. She is working on Hakka language from both micro and macro perspectives, with an aim to promote the recognition of Taiwan Hakka in the multiple linguistic and cultural Taiwanese society and in the international realm. She has published papers in *Linguistics, Journal of Pragmatics, Journal of Chinese Linguistics, Language and Linguistics, Concentric: Studies in Linguistics, Taiwan Journal of Linguistics, Language Awareness, International Review of Applied Linguistics in Language*

Contributors

Teaching, Communication and Society, Asian Ethnicity and a book chapter in *The Routledge Handbook of Chinese Applied Linguistics*.

Yi-hsiu Lai obtained a master's degree (with Distinction) in English teaching and learning from the University of Warwick, UK in 2001 and a PhD in Linguistics from the National Kaohsiung Normal University (NKNU), Taiwan in 2006. She currently works as a professor at National University of Kaohsiung (NUK), Taiwan. She was granted the awards "Excellent Young Scholar" in 2013, "Distinguished Research Professor" in 2015 and "Distinguished Professor" in 2017 in NUK. Her research interests include neurolinguistics, discourse analysis and English-language teaching and learning.

Lutgard Lams obtained an MA in Germanic Philology from KU Leuven, an MA in Literary Theory at Carnegie Mellon University, and a PhD in Linguistics from the University of Antwerp. She teaches Pragmatics, Media Discourse Analysis and Intercultural Communication at the Faculty of Arts at the KU Leuven Campus Brussels. Her research interests include political linguistics, authoritarian discourses, framing and Othering in media discourses. She has edited a book on totalitarian/authoritarian discourse and published several articles on Chinese official discourse, European media framing of China, the political linguistics of cross-Strait relations, the interplay between Taiwanese media and elections and discursive practices in Taiwanese presidential discourses and electoral campaigns.

Cher Leng Lee is an associate professor at the Department of Chinese Studies, National University of Singapore. Her research interests include discourse analysis, pragmatics and sociolinguistics. Some publications include "Grandmother's Tongue: Decline of Teochew Language in Singapore" in *Multilingualism in the Chinese Diaspora Worldwide: Transnational Connections and Local Social Realities*, ed. Wei Li, 196–215 (2016), "Compliments and Compliment Responses of Singapore Chinese University Students" *Global Chinese* 1(1), 169–202 (2016), and "English THEN in Colloquial Singapore Mandarin". In *Chinese Discourse and Interaction: Theory and Practice*, eds. Daniel Z. Kadar, Yuling Pan, 77–95. Sheffield: Equinox, 2013.

Cheng-Tuan Li is professor in the Faculty of English Language and Culture at Guangdong University of Foreign Studies, China. His present research concerns the interpersonal pragmatics of identity construction in Chinese and American institutional discourses and is funded by the National Planning Office of Philosophy and Social Sciences in China (18BYY223). His research interests include pragmatics, discourse analysis, identity construction and im/politeness. His recent publications are in the *Journal of Pragmatics* and *Text & Talk* and other top journals of linguistics in China. His address for correspondence is: lichengtuan@163.com

Wendan Li is Professor of Chinese Language and Linguistics in the Department of Asian Studies at the University of North Carolina at Chapel Hill. Her research is in discourse analysis and second language pedagogy of Chinese. She can be reached by e-mail at wli@email.unc.edu

Chien-Jer Charles Lin obtained his PhD in Linguistics and Anthropology from the University of Arizona. He is associate professor of Chinese Linguistics at Indiana University Bloomington, where he directs the Language and Cognition Laboratory. His research interests include processing issues in Chinese linguistics, experimental syntax, sentence and discourse processing, count/mass cognition and the relationship between linguistic typology and thinking.

Contributors

Yu-te Lin received a MD degree from the Medical School, National Yang Ming University in 1994 and a PhD degree in Biological Science from National Sun Yat-Sen University in 2009. In 2010, he went to Keck School of Medicine at the University of Southern California for further training in aging and neurology. Since 2006, he has served as Director of Kaohsiung Alzheimer's Disease Association, Chief of Division of Neurology since 2014, and Director of Center for Geriatrics and Gerontology at Kaohsiung Veterans General Hospital, Taiwan since 2016. He also works as a clinical associate professor at National Defense University. His fields of specialty include dementia, cerebrovascular disease and geriatrics.

Kang-Kwong Luke is Professor of Linguistics at Nanyang Technological University, Singapore. His research interest is in the field of talk and social interaction, using an ethnomethodological and conversation analytic approach. His work focuses on the interface between talk, cognition and interaction and is driven by an interest in what makes communication possible. His publications include *Utterance Particles in Cantonese Conversation*, *Telephone Calls: Unity and Diversity in the Structure of Telephone Conversations across Languages and Cultures*, and two special issues, on 'Turn-continuation in conversation' and 'Affiliation and Alignment in Responding Actions' for *Discourse Processes* and *Journal of Pragmatics*, respectively.

Yuanyi Ma received her doctoral degree from the Hong Kong Polytechnic University. She is a member of the PolySystemic Research Group. Her research interests include Systemic Functional Linguistics, translation studies, discourse analysis and intercultural communication. She is contributor to *The Routledge Handbook of Chinese Language Teaching* and *Perspectives from Systemic Functional Linguistics*.

Anna Morbiato obtained her MA in Technical and Scientific Translation (Chinese, English, Italian) at Ca' Foscari University of Venice in 2010, and a double (cotutelle) PhD in Asian and African studies at Ca' Foscari University of Venice and in Linguistics at the University of Sydney (2018). She currently works as a researcher at Ca' Foscari University of Venice, Department of Asian and North African studies, and collaborates with the School of Languages and Cultures at the University of Sydney.

Lauri Paltemaa is Professor of East-Asian Contemporary History and Politics at the University of Turku. He is the author of *Managing Famine, Flood and Earthquake in China – Tianjin 1958–85* published in 2016 by Routledge. His articles have appeared in journals such as *The China Journal*, *China Information* and *The Modern Asian Studies*. His research interests include Chinese contemporary history, disaster management and social movements in addition to Chinese politics and internet control.

Ming-Ming Pu obtained her PhD in psycholinguistics at the University of Alberta, Canada in 1991 and currently works as a professor of linguistics at the University of Maine, Farmington, USA. Her research interests include cognitive linguistics, Chinese linguistics and comparative discourse analysis. In addition to her book *Discourse Anaphora* (2011), she has published in linguistic journals such as *Discourse Processes*, *Chinese Language Studies*, *Cognitive Linguistics* and *The Canadian Journal of Linguistics*.

Runya Qiaoan obtained her PhD from Masaryk University in 2018, and she currently works at Mendel University and Palacky University in the Czech Republic. Runya studied at Masaryk

University, the University of Toronto, National Chengchi University and Utrecht University. Runya's research interests include civil society and non-governmental organizations, cultural sociology and China-Central Eastern European relations. Her publications include papers and book reviews in international scientific journals, such as *The China Quarterly*, *Journal of Cognition and Culture*, and *Europe-Asia Studies*.

Julia Renner holds an BA/MA in Chinese Studies from the University of Vienna. She has been granted a PhD scholarship by the Austrian Academy of Sciences and is currently pursuing her PhD in linguistics at the University of Vienna. Her research focuses on teaching and learning Chinese as a foreign language and technology-enhanced language learning.

Wayne Schams obtained a PhD in TESOL from National Kaohsiung Normal University, Taiwan, in 2017. He is currently a lecturer in the Department of English at National Pingtung University. His research interests include listening comprehension, vocabulary acquisition, pragmatics, English-Chinese comparative linguistics and issues of discourse and sociolinguistic usage in ESP.

Florian Schneider, PhD, Sheffield University, is Senior University Lecturer in the Politics of Modern China at the Leiden University Institute for Area Studies. He is managing editor of the academic journal *Asiascape: Digital Asia* and the author of *China's Digital Nationalism* (Oxford University Press 2018) and *Visual Political Communication in Popular Chinese Television Series* (Brill 2013), which won the 2014 EastAsiaNet book prize. His research interests include questions of governance, political communication, and digital media in China, as well as international relations in the East-Asian region.

Chris Shei studied at Taiwan, Cambridge and Edinburgh and has worked at Swansea University since 2003. He teaches and researches in linguistics and translation studies and is particularly interested in the use of computer and web resources for linguistic research, language education and translating. He is the General Editor for two new Routledge series: *Routledge Studies in Chinese Discourse Analysis* and *Routledge Studies in Chinese Translation*. Proposals for monographs or edited pieces are received at ccshei@gmail.com on a long-term basis.

Ming-Hsiang Su received his PhD degree in the Department of Computer Science and Information Engineering, National Chung Cheng University, Chiayi, Taiwan. Since 2013, he has been with the Department of Computer Science and Information Engineering at National Cheng Kung University, Tainan, Taiwan, where he is currently a postdoctoral fellow. His research interests include spoken dialog system, personality trait perception, speech emotion recognition, and artificial Intelligence.

Juha A. Vuori is (acting) Professor of International Politics at the University of Turku. He is the author of *Critical Security and Chinese Politics* published in 2014 by Routledge, and co-editor of *Visual Security Studies* published in 2018 by Routledge. His articles have appeared in journals such as *The European Journal of International Relations, Security Dialogue, Surveillance & Society*, and *The Asian Journal of Political Science*. His research interests include critical studies of security, speech-act theory, semiotics, and nuclear weapons in addition to Chinese politics and internet control.

John C. Wakefield obtained his PhD in linguistics from the Department of Chinese and Bilingual Studies at The Hong Kong Polytechnic University. He is currently an associate professor at Hong Kong Baptist University. He served as president of The Hong Kong Linguistic Society from 2016 to 2018. He has two forthcoming books: *English Loanwords in Cantonese: How their Meanings have Changed* (Hong Kong University Press), and an edited volume *Cantonese as a Second Language: Issues, Experiences and Suggestions for Teaching and Learning* (Routledge).

Binhua Wang is professor of interpreting and translation studies and program director of MA Conference Interpreting and Translation Studies in the Centre for Translation Studies at University of Leeds. His research interests lie in various aspects of interpreting and translation studies, in which he has published around 40 articles in refereed CSSCI/Core journals and SSCI/A&HCI journals such as *Interpreting*, *Meta*, *Perspectives* and *Babel* and over a dozen chapters in peer-reviewed collected volumes. He is the author of *A Descriptive Study of Norms in Interpreting* (2013), co-editor of *Interpreting in China: New Trends and Challenges* (2010) and co-translator of the Chinese version of *Introducing Interpreting Studies* (Pöchhacker, 2010).

Bo Wang received his doctoral degree from the Hong Kong Polytechnic University. He is an associate research fellow from the School of International Studies at Sun Yat-sen University, China, and an active member of the PolySystemic Research Group. His research interests include Systemic Functional Linguistics, translation studies, discourse analysis and language typology. He is contributor to *The Routledge Handbook of Chinese Language Teaching*, *The Routledge Handbook of Chinese Translation* and *Perspectives from Systemic Functional Linguistics*. He also works as a translator, and has translated more than 14 books that are published in mainland China.

Jiayi Wang is a principal lecturer at the University of Central Lancashire, UK. Her current research interests include language education, corpus-assisted discourse analysis, pragmatics, and intercultural communication. Jiayi earned a PhD in Applied Linguistics from the University of Warwick, where her research focused on professional (official/business) intercultural communication. Prior to her PhD, she was an international project manager at the Chinese Ministry of Justice. She has published research articles on comparative law, intercultural communication, and foreign- and second-language education.

Vincent X. Wang is an associate professor and NAATI-accredited translator, who teaches translation and comparative language studies at the University of Macau. He has published articles in *Target*, *Translation Watch Quarterly*, *Journal of Language, Literature and Culture* and TESOL-related periodicals, book chapters with Routledge, Brill, and Bookman, and the monograph *Making Requests by Chinese EFL Learners* (John Benjamins).

Wei Wang is Senior Lecturer in Chinese Studies at the University of Sydney. His primary research interests are in the areas of discourse studies, sociolinguistics and translation studies. He is the author of *Media Representation of Migrant Workers: Identities and Stances* (2017) and *Genre across Languages and Cultures* (2007). His publications appear in *Discourse Studies*, *Applied Linguistics Review*, *T & I Review*, *Journal of Multicultural Discourse* and other international academic journals. He also published book chapters with Routledge, Continuum, Benjamins, the University of Michigan Press, Mouton, and Wiley-Blackwell.

Yu-Fang Wang is a professor in the Graduate Institute of Teaching Chinese as a Second/Foreign Language at National Kaohsiung Normal University, Taiwan. Her research interests include discourse analysis, pragmatics, and corpus linguistics, with specific focus on discourse markers. She has published articles in *Cahiers de Linguistique Asie Orientale*, the *Journal of Chinese*

Contributors

Linguistics, Text, Concentric: Studies in Linguistics, Taiwan Journal of Linguistics, Language Sciences, Discourse Studies, the Journal of Pragmatics, Language & Communication, Chinese Language and Discourse, and *Language and Linguistics.*

Weixiao Wei obtained her MA in Foreign Languages and Literatures from Taiyuan University of Technology in 2010. She currently works as a Lecturer at Taiyuan University of Technology in China. Her research interests include discourse analysis, Chinese language teaching and translation studies. She is the first author of 'Chinese Translation in the Twenty First Century' to be published in the *Routledge Handbook of Chinese Applied Linguistics*.

Chiao-Yi Wu is a research scientist at the Centre for Research and Development in Learning (CRADLE) at the Nanyang Technological University. She obtained her PhD in Psychology from Nanyang Technological University and worked as a post-doctoral researcher at the Max Planck Institute for Human Cognitive and Brain Sciences in Germany before joining CRADLE. She is a cognitive neuroscientist with expertise in the neurobiology of language and reading. She uses functional neuroimaging techniques, such as functional magnetic resonance imaging and functional near-infrared spectroscopy, to investigate the neural basis of language and learning in a wide range of population across age and language background. She has published in top-tier journals in the fields of neuroscience and neurobiology of language.

Chung-Hsien Wu received a BS degree in electronics engineering from National Chiao Tung University, Hsinchu, Taiwan, in 1981, and the MS and PhD degrees in electrical engineering from National Cheng Kung University (NCKU), Tainan, Taiwan, in 1987 and 1991, respectively. Since 1991, he has been with the Department of Computer Science and Information Engineering at NCKU. He became the Chair Professor of NCKU in 2017. His research interests include deep learning, affective computing, speech recognition/synthesis, and spoken language processing.

Ting Wu received a PhD in Human Resource Management in 2011 from National Sun Yat-sen University in Taiwan. Her research interests include workplace happiness and work-life balance in strategic human resource management. She currently works as an assistant professor at the School of Business at Macau University of Science and Technology, China.

Xuehua Xiang obtained a PhD in applied linguistics from Pennsylvania State University (USA) in 2006. She currently works as an associate professor at the University of Illinois, Chicago (USA). Her research interests center on discourse analysis, multimodal analysis, pragmatic particles, and second language curriculum development. She is co-author of *Grammar, Meaning, and Concepts: A Discourse-Based Approach to English Grammar*.

Jie Yang is an associate professor of anthropology at Simon Fraser University. She was trained in linguistic anthropology, and her current research centers on psychological/medical anthropology. She has done research on language, privatization, unemployment, new urban poverty, mental health, psychotherapy, and the politics of gender and class in contemporary China. Her research focuses on the emergence of new forms of governance in the context of China's economic restructuring, for example, aesthetic, therapeutic and neoliberal governance. Her first and ongoing project explores the psychological and emotional effects of state-enterprise restructuring on Chinese workers particularly laid-off workers since the 1990s. She has recently started a new project on the mental health of government officials (the phenomenon of *guan xinbing*, "officials' heartache"). She is author of two monographs *Unknotting the Heart: Unemployment and Therapeutic Governance in China* (2015, Cornell University Press) and *Mental Health in China: Change, Tradition, and Therapeutic Governance* (2017, Polity Press). She is editor of *The Political Economy of Affect and Emotion in East Asia* (2014, Routledge).

Foong Ha Yap received her PhD in Applied Linguistics from UCLA. Her research interests include language change, language typology, discourse analysis, and cognitive-functional linguistics. Her (co-)authored works include *Nominalization in Asian Languages: Diachronic and Typological Perspectives* (2011) and a special issue on "Stance-taking and Stance-marking in Asian Languages" in *Journal of Pragmatics* (2015), as well as articles in journals such as *Diachronica, Journal of Historical Pragmatics, Language Sciences, Lingua, Linguistics, Studies in Language, Text & Talk, Discourse & Society,* and *Memory & Cognition*.

Introduction
Discourse analysis in the Chinese context

Chris Shei

About discourse analysis

The first book I read about discourse analysis was Deborah Schiffrin's (1987) *Discourse Markers*. Back in the 1980s, Chomsky's GB theory was mainstream in linguistic research, and luckily for me, Professor Shuanfan Huang, my MA thesis supervisor, was one of those who did not jump on the bandwagon. It took someone as wise as him to see the connection between Schiffrin's work on discourse markers and the Chinese sentence-final particles which had used to be thought of as trivial phatic elements. It took me two years to complete my dissertation entitled *A discourse-functional analysis of Mandarin sentence-final particles* at National Chengchi University, Taiwan in 1991, which is still kept at the library of Cambridge University at the time of writing (my English name was Chi-Chiang Shie in 1991). The story moved on to 1996 when I enrolled in the then Research Centre for English and Applied Linguistics of Cambridge University as an MPhil student where Professor Gillian Brown was the director. Brown and Yule (1983) was another classic core reading for students doing discourse analysis in the late 1980s. Professor Brown saw my MA thesis upon presentation and must have liked it so it found its way into the Cambridge library.

I see working at a university as only a way of earning a living for me, which I think is a better way of using my degrees than throwing parcels in a mail depot or serving at a 'cram school' where telling jokes and entertaining students are more important than teaching. I was lucky and crazy enough to spend 12 years earning one MA, one MPhil and two PhD degrees (one in TESOL and the other in informatics) on scholarships. These allowed me to research and teach in a variety of subjects such as computer-assisted language learning, translation studies, language education, discourse analysis, psycholinguistics and corpus linguistics. I work in linguistics, language technology and translation studies and expanded my interests to media and politics, but I was not deep into any of these, partly due to my disillusionment with what linguistics can do to 'computerize human language'. There is no human-like robot to date like that in the AI movie, or the free speaking *Mother* computer in Alien series. These are science fiction ideals for linguists just as light speed spaceships in Star Wars are for aerospace engineers. A sense of reality of what computers can do in processing human discourse, incidentally, is offered in the language technology section of this handbook. As can be seen, the technicality involved in processing language data is impressive but the ability for machines to understand and produce human language is fairly limited. There are probably no overall principles for language like 'universal grammar' or 'move α'. Language is very untidy, and it is not (currently) possible to program all our knowledge about it neatly into a web of computer algorithms so that a robot can speak like a human being and produce appropriate language on all occasions.

I often wonder what it means to be a linguist. At the end of the day, I thought, we are not Einstein, Stephen Hawking, Donald Trump or even Kim Jong-un. Does it really matter what we do as linguists or social scientists? We probably help keep the wheel turning by providing food for thought for students, teachers, businesspersons, policy makers, politicians and the general public, and we do this today under the same academic rigor faced by a medical doctor. After teaching students what a dental voiceless fricative is and that *The old man the boat* is a 'Garden Path sentence'; after torturing ourselves for months to produce an article on the influence of ideology on educational policy, we feel temporarily safe and retire to the sofa to watch Sky News on YouTube (unless you have paid the TV license fee to watch BBC), thinking about next week's professional review with the head of department. We break our necks to try to gain some funding to outlive our colleagues who have already quit, due to the increasing pressure in the academic world nowadays. Against all the odds, however, linguistics, especially corpus linguistics, cognitive linguistics, applied linguistics and discourse analysis, have made some progress in the past 20 years. Through separate and joint efforts, we have come to understand different facets of language in real contexts. It might not be entirely an impossible dream for robots to talk like human beings in a few hundred years' time, if a substantial number of linguists survive, and if more and more truths about language are uncovered in a piecemeal fashion by various branches of linguistic studies, discourse analysis included.

After having known it for almost 30 years, I found *Discourse Analysis* an incompetent name for what it does, as the discipline is not only concerned with 'analyzing discourse' – whatever that means. It is also a misleading statement that 'discourse analysis deals with language above the sentence'. Rather than the level or size of the linguistic structure in question, it is the dimension of linguistic analysis that makes discourse analysis different from existing disciplines like phonology, morphology or syntax. Discourse analysis is not concerned with 'language above the sentence' only. Instead, it analyzes everything from linguistic tokens (including sounds, words, sentences and anything above) to non-linguistic sounds, images and gestures, which have a bearing on meaning-making in social context. In other words, discourse analysis analyzes language at ALL levels and considers not just the 'mechanics' of language but also the structures of its context including human cognition, social interaction and discourse convention. In that sense, a more appropriate name for discourse analysis may be *Language in Use* although this hardly sounds like a discipline name. In any case, 'discourse analysis' is both a research concept that associates language with its usage and a research methodology that investigates any unit of expression (a word printed on a T-shirt, a sentence written on a billboard, a speech made by the prime minister, etc.) against its background in cognitive and social interactive terms.

To understand what people in this discipline have been writing about in the last two decades, I used the Web of Science citation indexing service, chose the 'topic' search field, keyed in 'discourse analysis' as the search phrase and fetched some 4,500 items dating from 1996 to 2018. This constitutes a two-million-word corpus notably including the titles and abstracts of some 4,500 publications on the topic of 'discourse analysis' from 1996 to 2018. I then used WordSmith 5.0 to create a word list from this corpus of publication details and compared it with the British National Corpus (which served as a reference corpus) and generated a list of keywords from the corpus of 4,500 abstracts centering around the topic of 'discourse analysis'. Table 0.1 shows the top 50 keywords with high 'keyness' values among all the keywords found by WordSmith. From

Table 0.1 Top 50 keywords output by WordSmith based on 4500 abstracts on 'discourse analysis' 1996–2018

No.	Keyword	Freq.	Keyness	No.	Keyword	Freq.	Keyness
1	LANGUAGE	24992	23251	26	CONVERSATION	2110	1325
2	DISCOURSE	19158	18910	27	FUNCTIONAL	1419	1270
3	LINGUISTICS	14296	14076	28	CONTEXT	1939	1257
4	ENGLISH	11586	9315	29	HALLIDAY	1266	1250
5	LINGUIST	8591	8492	30	PRAGMATIC	1357	1249
6	PRAGMATICS	7257	7172	31	CULTURAL	1642	1230
7	ANALYSIS	7571	6472	32	MARKERS	1214	1199
8	SPEECH	6109	5313	33	SPANISH	1586	1198
9	SOCIAL	5363	3462	34	FAIRCLOUGH	1190	1175
10	LINGUISTIC	3619	3382	35	WRITING	2244	1157
11	COMMUNICATION	3298	2425	36	EDUCATION	2215	1143
12	COGNITIVE	2095	2030	37	DISCURSIVE	1101	1087
13	CRITICAL	2454	1970	38	LEARN	1722	1080
14	NARRATIVE	1872	1770	39	STRATEGIES	1238	1068
15	LANGUAGES	2011	1743	40	SYNTAX	1242	1028
16	INTERACTION	1867	1697	41	COGNITION	1054	1027
17	THEORY	2352	1653	42	SCHEGLOFF	1035	1022
18	IDENTITY	2052	1632	43	SEMANTICS	1300	1005
19	METAPHOR	1642	1607	44	TEXTS	1234	980
20	GRAMMAR	1757	1554	45	SOCIOL	984	972
21	POLITENESS	1430	1398	46	TEXT	4583	962
22	LEARNING	1987	1374	47	CULTURE	1398	958
23	SCIENCE	1749	1370	48	MEANING	1378	953
24	TALK	3371	1349	49	MEDIA	1714	948
25	LANGUAGE	1491	1325	50	CLASSROOM	1105	934

this list, we can identify five categories of concepts which are prominent in the span of 22 years of discourse analysis research.

- **General language or linguistic terms**: language, discourse, English, speech, talk, text, grammar, semantics, syntax, analysis
- **Cognitive terms**: cognitive, critical, cognition, learn, learning, metaphor, meaning, identity, theory
- **Interpersonal terms**: social, communication, interaction, conversation, narrative, pragmatics, politeness, functional, strategies, context
- **Genre or institutional terms**: science, education, classroom, media, culture, cultural
- **Author names**: Halliday, Fairclough, Schegloff

These keywords and the concept groups seem to show reasonably clearly what the discourse analysts have been doing in the past 20 years. They build their work based on traditional linguistic branches such as semantics and syntax and extend these into both cognitive and social interactive domains. The most frequently mentioned names of Halliday and Schegloff point out the importance of systematic functional linguistics and conversation analysis in the field. Fairclough's name, on the other hand, is closely associated with critical discourse analysis, which seems to stand out as a prominent subdiscipline of discourse analysis in recent years.

Chris Shei

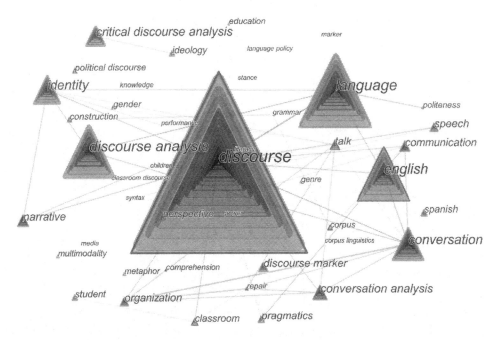

Figure 0.1 Multiword key terms output by CiteSpace based on 4500 abstracts on 'discourse analysis' 1996–2018

To verify the credibility of the WordSmith findings, I double-checked the results with a meta-research tool on citations called *CiteSpace* created by Chaomei Chen (see Chen, 2016 for details). This is an information visualization tool and the same data fed into WordSmith was now processed by CiteSpace to gain the result in Figure 0.1. The keyword analysis facility of CiteSpace can generate multiword keywords from untagged text. Therefore, we see terms like *discourse analysis, conversation analysis, political discourse, classroom discourse, language policy* and so on in Figure 0.1. Interestingly, the phrase *critical discourse analysis* also shows up as a significant triangle only smaller than general terms like *discourse, language* and *conversation*. Compare this phenomenon with Table 0.1 where we find the word *critical* also appearing at No. 13 place in Table 0.1 for a keyness value calculated by WordSmith. This, and the fact that the author name Fairclough shows as No. 34 keyword in Table 0.1, strongly indicates *critical discourse analysis* as a prominent research area in the broadly defined 'discourse analysis' field. Overall, the keywords output by CiteSpace seem to agree with that produced by WordSmith. That is, they concentrate on the basic linguistic, cognitive, interpersonal, and institutional aspects of language analysis. This gives us some ideas as to what discourse analysts have been doing in the past two decades and what the subject *discourse analysis* is probably about.

Chinese discourse analysis

The most obvious interpretation of 'Chinese discourse analysis' is that the data being studied is written or spoken in the Chinese language. The study of Xi Jinping's speech at China's annual parliament is definitely an example of 'Chinese discourse analysis'. However, it can also mean 'discourse analysis (of whatever language) conducted in the Chinese fashion' by which I mean geographically, institutionally and/or ideologically speaking. So, for example, Theresa May's speech on military strikes against Syria may be analyzed differently by British researchers in the UK on one hand, and by Chinese scholars in China on the other hand. This handbook mainly deals with Chinese discourse analysis in the first sense. In some cases, non-Chinese texts written by Chinese individuals or output by Chinese institutions (e.g. China Daily news published in English) can also be taken as 'Chinese discourse' if the focus is on the underlying meaning and ideology rather than on lexical or structural dimensions.

How is Chinese discourse analysis different from the analysis of English discourse? If our understanding so far about what discourse analysis does is correct, then any differences in respect of language, cognition, interaction or social practice will tip the balance and produce somewhat different results and implications when we analyze discourse of a different language generated in a different setting. Judging from the vast differences between Chinese and English languages, cultures and political systems, it should come as no surprise that discourse analysis conducted on both languages will produce very different results. To make this point clear, let us look at a stretch of conversation in Chinese to appreciate how the language plays out in a real situation.

(1)
岳靓：That's my cat
Yue Liang: That's my cat
吴平：很可爱啊！
Wu Ping: It's lovely!
孟非：你喜欢猫吗？
Meng Fei: Do you like cats?
吴平：我有养过一只猫哎
Wu Ping: I used to keep one!
孟非：啊，你看多好啊！有共同爱好，选得很好．
Meng Fei: Wow, you see? How wonderful! They have the same interest. Good choice.

Conversation (1) occurred among three participants on a Reality TV show 非诚勿扰 (*Fei Cheng Wu Rao*, or FCWR, which means literally: 'Do not disturb if you are not sincere'), which is a dating show originating from its English equivalent *Take Me Out*. This was from the April 21, 2018 episode where Yue was one of two female contestants aspiring to have a date with the male suitor Wu. Meng is the host of the show. When Wu is given the choice to see one of the three pieces of information about Yue to decide whether he likes her or not, he chooses to see her 'close roommate', which turns out to be a cat. Thereupon Wu makes a comment in English (presumably because she and Wu both studied and lived in the US before, so she codeswitched to impress Wu with her qualification). Wu responds to this comment with a complement on the cat (How lovely!) After one second's pause, the host of the show asks Wu a question (Do you like cats?). Wu did not answer the question directly but, instead, admitted that he also previously owned a cat. Meng immediately picks up the cue and comments on the compatibility of the likely couple. 'Match-making' is a serious business in China, and the host's enthusiasm and communicative skills in managing the match-making event and conversation are remarkable. For example, he is quick to initiate a new subtopic helpful to the situation and to summarize the talk in a favorable direction.

Linguistically speaking, Meng's final utterance consisted of three clauses: 你看多好啊 ('you see how wonderful'), 有共同爱好 ('have shared interests'), and 选得很好 ('made good choice'). Among them, only the first clause comes with a subject (the generic 'you'). The other two clauses are subjectless. Their hidden subjects, however, need to be inferred from context in order to correctly process the predicates. It is effortless for a Chinese speaker to know the subject of

有共同爱好 to be 'Wu and Yue', the currently matched couple; whereas that for 选得很好 is Wu, who chose the allegedly good information to see. This, however, may not be so easy for a computer or a learner of Chinese as a second language. The second thing to notice is Wu's referring to a historical fact ('I once had a cat') to answer a question about personal inclination ('Do you like cats?'). The maxim of relevance is important here for the listener to make the correct interpretation. No wonder 'cooperative principle' is among the 32 most important keywords in Chinese discourse analysis research as summarized in Table 0.2 below, if 'indirectness' is such a prevalent feature in Chinese conversations. Finally, we notice that as many as four clauses in (1) come with a Chinese sentence-final particle among the six Chinese clauses. They each realize a cognitive and/or social interactive function. For example, the 啊 in 很可爱啊 ('very lovely') reveals the speaker's conviction and emotion about the truth value of the statement. The 吗 in the question 你喜欢猫吗 ('do you like cat') marks the relatively superior position of the speaker to the listener. The 哎 in 我有养过一只猫哎 ('I had a cat before') introduces the information as new, surprising and probably appealing; while the 啊 in 你看多好啊 ('see, how wonderful') again confirms the speaker's belief in and their emotion about the proposition.

Thus, from a simple dialogue we see how concisely and 'effortlessly' Chinese is designed to express semantic, cognitive and social meanings in interpersonal settings. Chinese discourse needs to be approached with an all new language toolkit and from recalibrated cognitive and sociocultural perspectives. The unique findings of Chinese discourse analysis and the insights they bring to the field would certainly be worth the effort.

The study of Chinese discourse does not only promise to enlighten the pragmatics of language but also the psychology of language. Continuing to explore Chinese SFPs, this time from the cognitive perspective, we observe the dialogue in (2).

(2)
孟非：那我想问一下你，你比较喜欢跑车，你也喜欢老爷车吗？
Meng Fei: Then I would like to ask you: I know you like sports cars; what about classic cars?

Table 0.2 No. of SFPs found in an FCWR episode and the percentage of utterances containing an SFP

非诚勿扰 FCWR episode 2013–01–20
Total Chinese characters: 19,522
Total lines of subtitle: 2,590
Average number of characters per line: 7.5

SFP	No. of tokens
了 (*le*, not including 了 as aspect marker)	124
啊 (*a*)	72
呢 (*ne*)	68
吗 (*ma*)	64
吧 (*ba*)	64
呀 (*ya*)	13
嘛 (*ma*)	7
啦 (*la*)	2
Total	414
Percentage number of lines to include an SFP: 414 / 2590 = 0.16 (16%)	

男嘉賓：这个说实话我不太喜欢。当然应该尊敬它们，因为它们是汽车行业的鼻祖啊！

Male guest: To be honest, not really. But they certainly deserve our respect since they are precious assets of the car dealing profession.

孟非：你怎么这么说话呢！怎么能不喜欢丈母娘的职业呢！丈母娘疼姑爷嘛，对不对？

Meng Fei: How can you say that? How dare you dislike mother-in-law's profession? Mother-in-laws are said to cherish their sons-in-law, right?

In (2), Meng Fei, the host of the same show, asks the male suitor if he likes antique cars as the female candidate's mother is a dealer of antique cars. The male suitor does not show preference for these cars, and Meng chastises him (albeit in a joking fashion) for not respecting the profession of his possible mother-in-law. These short exchanges manifest four different SFPs in five instances. Dialogue (2) is of course the result of cherry picking to show the pervasiveness of Chinese SFPs in conversation, especially when interlocutors get more excited at expressing propositional content or pragmatic intentions. However, I have done a more serious calculation of the kinds and number of SFPs used in an episode of FCWR (20 January 2013) and found the result in Table 0.2.

Each line of TV subtitle usually consists of one (or two if very short) Chinese utterances, usually comprising a phrase or a clause. The entire episode of FCWR on 20 January 2013 consists of 2,590 lines of subtitle or roughly the same number of utterances. As Table 0.2 shows, if we divide the overall number of characters counted in the mini FCWR corpus (19,522) by the 2,590 lines, we get an average of 7.5 characters per line, or roughly per utterance. This is a likely number since Chinese clauses are recognized to be short in length, especially more so in spoken Chinese. What is most noteworthy in Table 0.2, however, is the percentage 16%, which means the proportional number of lines in the FCWR corpus that contain an SFP. That is, in every six Chinese utterances, one will come with the marking of an SFP. This is a rough impression gained from the particular FCWR episode, but it highlights an important aspect in spoken Chinese communication – the extensive use of sentence-final particles.

SFPs not only serve pragmatic functions but also carry cognitive implications, especially in the area of language processing. A classic speech production model posited by Levelt (1989) suggests that a speaker starts formulating a sentence from intention and produces a set of speech acts to carry out the intention, which presumably include the pragmatic functions to be fulfilled therein. These speech acts then translate into a set of concepts to be realized by what Levelt calls 'lemmas' with associated syntactic properties to help form a sentence. What is likely here for Chinese language processing is that an SFP could be adopted very early on in speech production when pragmatic functions are determined. The SFP then imposes a restriction on the possible length of a sentence (since the endpoint of an utterance is already determined before everything) among other things. The result is that a sentence which comes with an SFP is often shorter than the average length of a sentence. The idea is graphically presented in Figure 0.2, which shows an SFP generated at the conceptual level 'progresses' to the utterance level directly and feeds back to the syntactic module to produce an 'end-constrained' sentence. The characteristics of such sentence could be 1. being short in length, and 2. having a collocate that habitually co-occurs with the SFP, for example, 好棒 ('very good') with 喔 (wo), 真的 ('really') with 嗎 (ma) and so on. The collocation both facilitates and imposes further constraint on syntactic processing and the final form of the utterance.

The hypothesis that a Chinese sentence with SFP is shorter than a sentence without one is partially borne out by calculating the average number of characters of the 64 utterances marked

A. Sentence without SFP

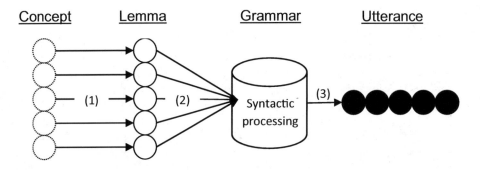

B. Sentence with SFP

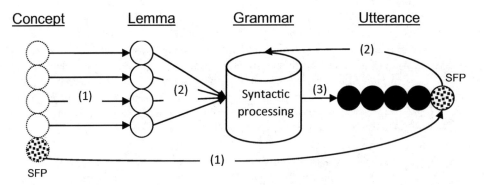

Figure 0.2 A possible speech production model for utterance with sentence final particle

by 吧 (*ba*) in the FCWR corpus mentioned above, which turns out to be 4.1, considerably shorter than the average number of characters of 7.5 for any utterance in the corpus as shown in Table 0.2. A typical usage of 吧 is a tag question like structure such as 對吧 ('Am I not right?') or 是吧 ('Isn't that right?'). The longest utterance with 吧 in the corpus is 这种游戏留着以后带孩子用吧 ('Why don't you keep this kind of game for later use with your children?'). This seems a bit clumsy for an SFP-tagged sentence with a marked subjectless and object-fronted structure. The versatile pragmatic functions of Chinese SFPs and their psycholinguistic implications are just some of the interesting phenomena in Chinese language that promise to offer special insights to discourse analysts worldwide.

To understand what Chinese discourse analysts in China publish about, I looked up the CNKI (China National Knowledge Infrastructure) database with the search phrase 话语分析 (the equivalence of 'discourse analysis' in the Chinese linguistics field). From this search, 2,500 results were found spanning the period of 1994–2018 including details of the publications like author, institution, title, keywords and abstract. These were processed by CiteSpace again to generate the keywords visualization chart in Figure 0.3. The corresponding keyword statistics used to draw the chart are given in Table 0.3.

Introduction

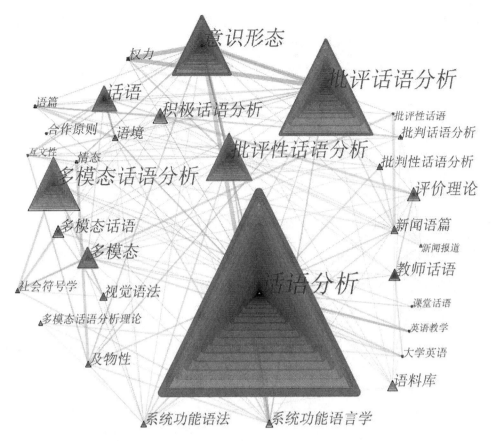

Figure 0.3 Multiword key terms output by CiteSpace based on 2500 abstracts on '话语分析' 1994–2018

From both Figure 0.3 and Table 0.3, we can see that the most significant keywords identified from within the 2500 abstracts of Chinese publications on the topic of 话语分析 ('discourse analysis') between 1994 and 2018 are slightly different from their English counterparts visualized in Figure 0.1. First of all, 批评话语分析 ('critical discourse analysis') stands out to be the second most significant triangle only next to the search phrase 话语分析. This does not include various forms of the same expression in the chart: 批评性话语分析 ('critically oriented discourse analysis'), 批判性话语分析 ('critical-judgmental style discourse analysis') and 批判话语分析 ('critical-judgmental discourse analysis'). This probably means that a lot of people doing discourse analysis in China are doing 'critical discourse analysis'. In support of this view is the prominent triangle of 意识形态 ('ideology') in Figure 0.3 which was not the case for its English counterpart in Figure 0.1.

Secondly, some research methodologies or schools also stand out in Figure 0.3 which was not the case for the English literature, for example, 多模态话语分析 ('multimodal discourse analysis'), 积极话语分析 ('positive discourse analysis'), 评价理论 ('evaluation theory'), 系统功能语言学 ('systemic functional linguistics'), 视觉语法 ('visual grammar') and 社会符号学 ('social semiotics'). Thus, for some reason, the Chinese discourse analysts seem to make a point of emphasizing the theoretical grounds of their research by referring to existing Western linguistic

9

Table 0.3 Keywords output by CiteSpace based on 2500 abstracts on '话语分析' 1994–2018

No.	count	Keywords
1	717	话语分析 (discourse analysis)
2	340	批评话语分析 (critical discourse analysis)
3	226	意识形态 (ideology)
4	205	多模态话语分析 (multimodal discourse analysis)
5	185	批评性话语分析 (critically oriented discourse analysis)
6	110	话语 (discourse)
7	90	多模态 (multimodality)
8	74	积极话语分析 (positive discourse analysis)
9	68	评价理论 (evaluation theory)
10	60	多模态话语 (multimodal discourse)
11	52	教师话语 (teacher discourse)
12	44	系统功能语言学 (systemic functional linguistics)
13	41	语料库 (corpus)
14	38	语境 (context)
15	37	及物性 (transitivity)
16	36	视觉语法 (visual grammar)
17	35	新闻语篇 (media text)
18	34	系统功能语法 (systemic functional grammar)
19	30	批判性话语分析 (critical-judgemental kind of discourse analysis)
20	27	权力 (power)
21	27	合作原则 (cooperative principle)
22	24	批判话语分析 (critical-judgmental discourse analysis)
23	21	社会符号学 (social semiotics)
24	20	情态 (modal)
25	17	语篇 (text)
26	16	大学英语 (college English)
27	16	多模态话语分析理论 (multimodal discourse analysis theory)
28	13	批评性话语 (critical kind of discourse)
29	12	互文性 (intertextuality)
30	11	课堂话语 (classroom discourse)
31	11	英语教学 (English language teaching)
32	11	新闻报道 (news report)

theories. This is understandable since Chinese academic papers are normally shorter than English ones. Many Chinese academic journals in arts and humanities publish papers around 8,000 Chinese characters (e.g. 外语界 *Foreign Language World*, 解放军外国语学院学报 '*Journal of PLA University of Foreign Languages*', 中国翻译 '*Chinese Translators Journal*'), which can translate into as few as half the number (i.e. 4,000) of English words since over half of the Chinese 'words' consist of two characters – for example, 话语分析 (4 Chinese characters) translates into 'discourse analysis' (2 English words). This kind of compact paper offers better accommodation for theoretical thinking than detailed account of evidence-based research.

Finally, 教师话语 ('teacher discourse') and课堂话语 ('classroom discourse') and even 英语教学 ('English teaching') are on the top 32 keywords among 2500 abstracts of Chinese discourse analysis. Analysis of education discourse may therefore be an important genre in Chinese discourse studies which was not seen on the keyword list of English discourse analysis publications.

Introduction

All in all, as discourse analysis is making contribution to the understanding and further harnessing of human language by technology, Chinese researchers and Chinese discourse are actively participating and steadily progressing. In this volume, we put together a substantial set of articles as a fair representation of the current state of Chinese discourse studies globally. These papers explore Chinese words, sentences, information units, dialogues, texts and their discoursal, interpersonal, pragmatic, institutional, political meanings. Hopefully, the materials, methodologies, results and discussions offered in this book can provide guidance and inspirations for novice and experienced researchers alike, as well as generate more research and discussions.

Content of the book

The first part of the book deals with some time-tested research methodologies that have been applied to Chinese discourse analysis. The chapter authored by Kang Kwong Luke explains how **conversation analysis** (CA) works on three principles: naturally occurring data, contextualized analysis, and 'intersubjective perspective,' which means exploring talk from both speaker and listener's points of view. He also clarifies CA does not work on face-to-face conversation only, is not confined to the analysis of talk (but also includes facial expressions, gestures and so on), and does not consider structural aspects of conversation such as turn-taking only (but focuses on the entire range of meaning-making actions). A stretch of talk in Cantonese is used to illustrate how language data are typically annotated in CA and how 'time-sensitive, closely contextualized, form–function analysis' is carried out. Next comes a chapter on **critical discourse analysis** (CDA), a branch of discourse analysis which is quickly growing out of its superordinate discipline. Wei Weixiao's chapter first gives an overview of CDA research in the West including its tenets, working domains and analytical frameworks. It then presents the state of the art CDA research in China, pointing out the reorientation in research focus and agenda and the proliferation of research concepts and methodologies. A case study is then offered to illustrate how corpus-based research can help uncover themes, ideology and power structure underlying Chinese newspaper texts. Sociolinguistics is another well-established discipline which is closely associated with discourse analysis through their shared interest in the social meanings of language. Wei Wang's chapter on **sociolinguistic approaches to Chinese discourse** describes the broad research areas and diverse methodologies covered by the umbrella term 'sociolinguistics'. Wang's review of Chinese sociolinguistics research, however, is limited to three schools of thought: the variationist, the interactional and the sociocultural approach. The chapter offers an extensive study on the construction of Chinese migrant workers' identities by the public media, dividing the discursive practice evidenced in 48 episodes of a TV program into three stages: 'off stage', 'back stage' and 'front stage'. Multiple theories including Foucault's concept of 'abnormality' and Fairclough's foregrounding and backgrounding theory, help support the analysis and interpret the findings. **Multimodal discourse analysis** is a quite fashionable practice in China next only to critical discourse analysis, as manifested in Figure 0.3 and Table 0.3. Dezheng Feng's chapter on the multimodal analysis of Chinese discourse provides some useful background information and theoretical foundation for this relatively new discourse inquiry. Metaphor seems pivotal for this line of research in both theory and analysis. The author developed a 'social semiotic model' and collected 72 posters advocating Xi Jinping's Chinese Dream. Based on multimodal analysis of the titles and images of the posters, they confirm that communication from the party-state has moved from authoritarian coercion to promotion of patriotism, building solidarity on 'multimodal metaphors with rich cultural elements'.

Part 2 of the handbook deals with the grammatical aspect of discourse, that is, how discursive meanings are expressed through grammatical structures. Anna Morbiato's chapter on

conceptual word order principles and Mandarin Chinese grammar links Chinese grammar with cognitive and contextual factors such as time and space. She uses the principle of temporal sequence to explain the relatively fixed word order pattern in Chinese due to its lack of morpho-syntactic changes. The principle of whole-before-part, on the other hand, can be used to explain not only Chinese word formation rules but also discourse-level organization such as the topic-comment structure. Zhuo Jing-Schmidt's chapter on **grammatical constructions and Chinese discourse** defines grammatical construction as a form–meaning pair associating grammatical pattern with conceptual or discourse function. The Chinese *shì . . . de* (是 . . . 的) construction is used to illustrate how a grammatical construction can be utilized to signal lexical, textual and pragmatic contrast and embed conventional implicature, stance, genre and more. The author emphasizes the use of authentic data to help identify the contextual meaning of grammatical constructions. At the clause level, Yu-Fang Wang and Wayne Schams' paper looks at **Chinese conditionals in conversations**, exploring the relationships between different types of conditional constructions and their discourse functions. They found, for example, that sentence-initial conditional clauses often serve an important thematic function, introducing shared information such as the topic for forthcoming discourse. Sentence final conditionals, on the other hand, usually give hearer further elaboration or background information. The fourth chapter in this section written by Yu-Yin Hsu explains the **information structure in Chinese discourse**. 'Information structure', unlike structurally defined linguistic unit like 'noun phrase' or 'sentence', is a discourse-level concept that concerns how a speaker packages information to streamline the text and facilitate understanding. The author mentions zero anaphor and the noun phrase it refers to as an information packaging device in Chinese. In addition, Chinese sentence-final particles (SFPs) are also found to be relevant to the signaling of information status in conversation. For example, the author explains how the appearance of *le* (了) can signal the emergence of a new topic, and another SFP *ne* (呢) is often used to show engagement and contrast in discourse.

Whereas Part 2 deals with the relationship between the structure of language and discursive meaning, Part 3 of the book takes on a few categories of linguistic devices that play a significant role in Chinese discourse. Xuehua Xiang's chapter on **personal pronouns in Chinese discourse** introduces how Chinese pronouns carry out interpersonal functions in various contexts and for different users' needs. In addition to the standard person (first, second, third) and number (singular, plural) sets across all languages, the chapter also introduces some unique Chinese pronominal forms such as the null pronoun, 咱們 (inclusive 'we') and 人家 ('others' or 'me') each having its unique usage and rich connotations. In addition, pronouns in non-Mandarin Chinese varieties (such as Wu, Xiang and Southern Min) are also touched upon in one section to offer interesting comparisons and extra insights. In the chapter **Aspect in Chinese Narrative Discourse**, Wendan Li investigates the rich and complicated discourse meanings expressed by Chinese aspect marking devices. In particular, the author explains the different discourse functions between perfective and imperfective aspect marking in Chinese narrative. Perfective markers like 了 *le* are responsible for 'foregrounding' events and presenting them as the main themes of the story. Imperfective markers such as 在 *zai* and 著 *zhe*, on the other hand, present actions and information as specific details working at the background of the story. Maria Cheng's chapter on **the use of modal verbs in political debates** offers a detailed account of Chinese modal auxiliaries, distinguishing them into three types: those expressing possibility and necessity, permission and obligation, and ability and volition respectively. Like English, many Chinese modals can express multiple meanings and the chapter chooses political discourse to illustrate the different meanings of Chinese polysemous modals. In particular, Ma Ying-jeou and Tsai Ing-wen's uses of modal auxiliaries in presidential debates are quantitatively analyzed to show how both parties use the same or different modals to express their political positions. Ming-Ming Pu's chapter on **zero anaphora and topic chain in Chinese discourse** explores how the topic chain in Chinese text is maintained at the absence of overt reference links (i.e. the 'zero anaphora' phenomenon). The author proposes a 'zero anaphora principle' which claims that a zero anaphor is used to represent the most accessible referent in discourse. The principle also predicts that the zero anaphora or topic chain terminates when a major thematic discontinuity happens. Sections of Chinese narrative discourse support the chapter's claims.

Part 4 consists of four essays that touch upon certain aspects of Chinese pragmatics including politeness, gestures and pragmatic markers. Daniel Kadar's chapter on **politeness and impoliteness in Chinese discourse** offers a useful summary of the historical concept of Chinese politeness concentrating on the rule of elevating others and denigrating oneself. He also explains how this classical concept evolved to become very different practice in contemporary Chinese politeness. Some significant research and publications are mentioned which set norms of Chinese politeness apart from those of the West. For example, 'face' can be understood as 面子 'face, façade' or 臉 'face, dignity' in Chinese. In **Pragmatic markers in Chinese discourse,** Guangwu Feng uses 'pragmatic marker' as an umbrella term for linguistic devices that do not contribute to the propositional content of an utterance but signal speaker's communicative intention instead. Four criteria are given by the author to accurately define what a pragmatic marker is, and then a typology of pragmatic markers is presented with plenty of examples to illustrate their 'conceptual' and 'non-conceptual' usages. Foong Ha Yap and Winnie Chor's chapter on the **grammaticalization of stance markers in Chinese** explains what 'stance marker' means, using Mandarin, Southern Min and Cantonese examples to illustrate their 'subjective' and 'intersubjective' (interpersonal) usages. Grammaticalization here means how a content word like *well* (meaning 'in a good way') becomes a response marker, repair marker or pre-closing device. The authors distinguish three pathways of grammaticalization in Chinese; that is, how some verbs (e.g. 恐怕 'afraid → probably'), nouns and indexicals (e.g. 那 'that → but') developed separately into stance markers. Kawai Chui's chapter on **language, gesture and meaning** introduces readers to six types of gestures: self-adaptors, emblematic gestures, best gestures, deictic gestures, spatial gestures and iconic gestures. Among them, iconic gestures have a semantic relationship with speech and the context of use. The author claims that the use of gestures with hands and arms alongside speech is almost indispensable in everyday communication. Moreover, speech and gestures mostly convey independent information and one cannot be without the other.

Part 5 hosts a group of papers investigating the cognitive and psycholinguistic aspects of Chinese discourse. The chapter on the **psycholinguistics of Chinese discourse comprehension** written by Chien-Jer Charles Lin discusses how speakers understand Chinese discourse using bottom-up processing and top-down prediction. The article explains three aspects of Chinese discourse comprehension using psycholinguistic experimental methods: the processing of information structure, the resolution of anaphoric dependencies and the processing of logical relations. The author demonstrates how the grammar of a discourse-oriented language such as Chinese is influenced by various discourse factors. Closely following is Chiao-Yi Wu and Annabel Chen's chapter on **the neurocognitive processing of Chinese discourse,** which approaches the issue of discourse processing from neurocognitive perspective. Two methods for measuring neuromechanisms underlying linguistic responses are introduced: the neurophysiological method like ERP (event-related potential) and the neuroimaging techniques like fMRI (functional magnetic resonance imaging) while the authors take the reader through many psycholinguistic experiments using these neuroscientific tools. Some discourse processing strategies particular to the Chinese language are discovered using neurophysiological techniques. For example, due to the lack of morpho-syntactic marking, Chinese speakers were found to rely on semantic features even in syntactic processing. Yi-hsiu Lai & Yu-te Lin's chapter on **language impairment in Chinese discourse** offers a relatively rare piece of research on language disorder at the discourse level, in this case, the language of Chinese speakers suffering from Alzheimer's disease (AD). They follow a concise analytical framework which distinguishes between 'discourse-building' and 'discourse-impairing' features. Ten features are identified by the authors where AD patients encountered difficulties when making Chinese sentences in a controlled experimental setting. The authors hope their research can contribute to future treatment of dementia and to the understanding of the difficulties experienced by AD patients. For Jie Yang, author of the chapter **Discourse, gender and psychologization in contemporary China**, 'psychologization' is a process of psycho-political control in which the Chinese government enlists underprivileged women to perform amateurish counseling therapy so as to downplay 'structural forces that generate social problems'. The author also observed a trend of communication in China which directs people's attention from IQ to EQ, especially towards 'affect' or emotion in social interaction. This is manifested in the training of *peiliao* (陪聊 'accompany-talk') where 'talk from the heart' is greatly emphasized. However, for the author, this is just a form of gendered exploitation initiated by the state, which turns to vulnerable individuals for solutions to social problems and public issues created by the regime.

Part 6 hosts four chapters on different genres which are sometimes called 'institutional discourse'. Jiayi Wang's chapter on **Chinese business communication** explains why business Chinese was not a popular genre until China's opening up in 1978 and its transition from planned economy to free markets. The characteristics of modern Chinese business communication are teased out by comparing Chinese sales letters with English ones. It was found, for example, that English sales letters are keen to promote immediate purchase; while Chinese ones concentrate more on building long-term relationship with business partners. Another interesting finding is that the Chinese corporate chairman's statement often starts with political rhetoric such as one echoing the spirit of Xi Jinping's 'China dream'. Vincent Wang's chapter on **Chinese workplace discourse** examines the verbal interactions between managers and their subordinates in Hong Kong workplaces. Discourse analysis shows Hong Kong employees treat their superiors with respect and respond to their requests in prompt and direct ways. However, they sometimes disagree in tacit ways and even reject the manager's request with pertinent lexical choices. The author suggests that the power relations in Chinese workplaces are 'dynamic, interactional and relational'. The chapter on **legal discourse studies in the Chinese context** written by Zhengrui Han and Yunfeng Ge introduces three areas of Chinese legal discourse: legislative discourse, judicial discourse and discourse of legal news reports. Like business communication, legal discourse has undergone dramatic changes since the opening up of China in the late 1970's and the restoration of legal systems after the disruption of the Cultural Revolution in the 1960's. According to the authors, China's citizens are now encouraged to take legal actions to protect their own rights, and judges and arbitrators try their best to make the judgments more 'legally reasonable and reader-friendly'. Another facet of their research reveals how reporters are taking responsibility to offer moral education to the general public by quoting criminals' confessions and reflecting on the consequences of committing crimes. On the educational front, Bo Wang and Yuanyi Ma wrote a chapter on **authoritative classroom discourse** which analyzes the dialogues between two class leaders and their 'subordinates' in a primary school in China. In terms of exchange structure and conversational move, it is shown, for example, that the class leaders often use statements or questions to threaten or blame students. In terms of the lexis used, insulting words are often used by the elementary school class leaders on common students.

According to the authors, this kind of power relationship is an epitome of the state-controlled academic environment.

Part 7 of the book brings up the hot topic of social media discourse in China. The chapter on **discourse of Chinese social media: the case of Weibo** written by Eileen Le Han gives a very inspiring account of how the Twitter-like Chinese social media Weibo experienced a three-stage transformation from being a 'collective witnessing' site where corruptions and wrongdoings were exposed and criticized, to a nationalistic arena where pro-democracy voices were drowned out by both official suppression and voluntary attacks from patriotic netizens, and finally to a social media platform dedicated to earning money. The chapter authored by Juha Vuori and Lauri Paltemaa and entitled **Chinese censorship of online discourse** offers a typology of censorship including both 'overt' (user being aware of the censorship at work) and 'covert' (user unaware of the censorship) methods. Two case studies are presented to illustrate how they work: while overt censorship is applied to the social media platform Weibo where sensitive key words and phrases are regularly censored; covert censorship can be seen in the operation of the Chinese search engine Baidu where only officially approved results are shown to the user. Ane Bislev's chapter on **online anti-Taiwanese independence nationalist discourse** dwells on the tricky issue of Taiwan identity, or what it means to be 'Chinese'. The chapter starts with the recount of an epic adventure where China's netizens had to 'climb over' the Great Firewall to access the usually inaccessible Facebook in order to verbally attack the Taiwan president Tsai Ing-Wen. The issue of how to distinguish between 'anti-Taiwanese' and 'anti-Taiwan independence' is raised against the background of China's nationalistic attacks on Taiwan's people and culture on the web. The chapter on **anti-*gongzhi* discourse in Chinese cyberspace** written by Rongbin Han offers a fresh perspective on the meaning of 'free expression' in China. The chapter describes how the expansion of the internet and the prevalence of social media have enabled 'freer expression' in China although state control is never far away. Liberal-thinking intellectuals (公知) took the first opportunity to thrive, preaching the value of democracy, free speech and more to the general public. However, their assertions were soon refuted, according to the author, not by the state apparatus, but by nationalist netizens voluntarily defending the ideology of the party-state.

Four chapters are presented in Part 8 dwelling on the issues of identity (both national and personal) and ideology and how they translate into governance of the country. Qing Cao's chapter on **discursive construction of national and political identities in China** is predominantly a historical account of identity formation by rival leaders of the Chinese country and regions. It draws from Fairclough's idea that discourse manifests a dialectical relationship with social structures and goes on to explore the 'identity discourses' that characterize different stages of China in recent history as Chinese people and political leaders conceived them. The chapter entitled **Recurrent ideological patterns in Chinese state media narratives** authored by Lutgard Lams works mainly on corpora comprising English texts output by China's news media (i.e. in 'Chinese English') focusing on the reports of three events – Hong Kong handover in 1997, the 2001 US surveillance plane collision, and the 2005 anti-secession law incident in Taiwan. Recurrent linguistic patterns found in these news texts reveal underlying ideological works peculiar to China's official discourse: antagonistic group representations (self vs. other), hegemonic articulations (silencing dissonant voices) and construction of collective imaginaries and myths ('return to the motherland'). **The cultural governance of China's mass media events** written by Florian Schneider uses two high-profile public events – the 2008 Beijing Olympic Games and the 2010 Shanghai World Exposition – to illustrate China's neoliberal approach to media management and cultural governance under Hu Jintao's administration. He argues that by enlisting various stakeholders and distributing discourses under the guidance of the CCP propaganda system, not only the main discourse of China's revival as a great power was established, but the country was also portrayed as a diverse society that could tolerate diverse opinions. Cheng-Tuan Li's chapter on **constructing self-expert identity via other-identity negation in Chinese televised debating discourse** explores the concept of identity as defined by four related disciplines: sociolinguistic approach, psychological approach, the pragmatics approach and the conversation analysis approach. The author draws from the Membership Categorization Analysis framework and uses the concept of 'category-bound' attributes to analyze 120 rounds of TV debates. The result shows 'ingroup-affiliation' and 'outgroup-detachment' strategies to be central to the process of identity construction.

Part 9 consists of five chapters each touching upon one aspect of technology-enhanced discourse studies. Hen-Hsen Huang and Hsin-Hsi Chen's chapter on **development of computation models for Chinese discourse analysis** explains how computational models can be designed to achieve a certain degree of understanding of human discourse. They demonstrate, among other things, how such an easy task as recognizing the logical relationship between two clauses (e.g. contingency, comparison or expansion) can be a very complicated and taxing process to program into a computer. **Chinese spoken dialogue system**, a chapter written by Chung-Hsien Wu and Ming-Hsiang Su, explains the technical details for designing a Chinese spoken dialogue system, including the components of speech recognition, language understanding, dialogue management, language generation and text-to-speech. After explaining each of the main components constituting a dialog system, the chapter also takes the reader through how the dialogue system works by a case study simulating job interview dialogues. Zhaoming Gao's chapter on **computational stylistics and Chinese literary discourses** introduces tools and techniques for corpus-based analysis of Chinese literary texts. The author illustrates the computational study of stylometry (the statistical analysis of literary variations between authors) by showing the lexical, morphological and syntactic differences between two authors arrived at through corpus processing. The procedural account is supported by detailed introductions to various corpus processing tools and functions. The chapter **Tracking collective sentiment in Chinese finance-related discourse** written by Samuel Wai Kwong Chan offers great details in how to use natural language processing techniques to extract sentiment from financial discourse, including Chinese word tagging, sentence parsing and machine learning. The sentiment analysis method developed by the author holds great potential for extending to other areas such as political sentiment analysis and social media analysis for clinical depression.

Part 10 affords the reader a glimpse of non-standard varieties or use of the Chinese language outside mainland China. The chapter **Code-switching in Singapore Mandarin** written by Lee Cher Leng introduces the interesting code-switching phenomenon in Singapore where Mandarin is regularly codeswitched with English, Malay and other Chinese dialect elements. The author analyzes topic areas where code-switching normally happens in Singapore colloquial Mandarin, to whom the speaker is likely to code-switch, and the linguistic structures frequently involved in code-switching in Singapore Mandarin. Huei-ling Lai's chapter on the **introduction of Taiwan Hakka** starts with a historical account of the language variety including its possible origin and how it was suppressed in Taiwan during the KMT's reign after the end of the Chinese civil war in 1950. The author then gives a detailed introduction to Taiwan Hakka's phonetic system and describes the current revival process for the language in Taiwan. This is followed by an introduction to the Taiwan Hakka Spoken Corpus, which is used to present an analysis of degree adverbs in Taiwan Hakka. The chapter **Studies in Cantonese discourse** written by John Wakefield focuses on two aspects of Hong Kong Cantonese: the orthographic issues and the study of sentence final particles (SFPs). The issues of standardization of Cantonese orthography and how representative written Cantonese is of the Hong Kong vernacular are discussed at great length. The other issue, the prevalence of Cantonese SFPs, is interestingly traced back to the richness of lexical tones in Cantonese and the less use of intonation to express pragmatic meanings, thereby putting the burden on SFPs. Huiju Hsu wrote the chapter on the **dynamics of Southern Min in Taiwan**, which offers an in-depth discussion on the identity of Southern Min in Taiwan, its shifting status in Taiwan's language policy and its interaction with the other languages used in Taiwan, notably Mandarin. This chapter also touches upon the very interesting phenomenon of loanwords from and into Taiwan Southern Min as well as the orthographic issues of the language.

The final section of the book consists of four chapters focusing on the application of discourse analysis to translation studies, language teaching and political and social science respectively. The chapter **Discourse analysis in Chinese translation and interpreting studies** authored by Binhua Wang offers a broad coverage of discourse-analytical frameworks applicable to translation and interpreting studies. These include systemic-functional linguistics, critical discourse analysis, pragmatics and conversation analysis, narrative analysis and corpus-based discourse analysis. Julia Renner's chapter on **discourse analysis for Chinese language teaching** works on the basis of conversation analysis (CA) and elaborates on what CA can do to inform Chinese language teaching, that is, for development of teaching materials, teacher training and so on. Some video recorded computer-mediated conversations are used to show how CA can enlighten the modeling of peer-to-peer and teacher-student conversations. Runya Qiaoan attempts to develop a **critical cultural discourse analysis** model in her chapter which introduces a cultural element into the critical discourse analysis (CDA) framework. She completed a general review of Chinese discourse analysis and found CDA to be the most prominent area of research in discourse studies. However, she found existing CDA methodology inadequate in tackling some types of Chinese discourse and proposes a deeper, culture-bases analysis. Her case study includes a deconstruction of Xi Jinping's Chinese Dream slogan. **A discourse analysis of Macau cooks' accounts of job crafting** written by Ting Wu analyzes the interview discourse of 23 chefs from Zhuhai and Macau restaurants. Discourse analysis proves to be a useful tool for uncovering the underlying messages of the cooks' responses to interviewer's questions surrounding the concept and practice of job crafting. Even though the professionals are not aware what they are doing, the analysis of their talks helps link their activities to environmental factors and reveals the cooks' desire to improve the identity and achievement of their work and maintain good relationships with colleagues at workplace.

Acknowledgments

I thank Andrea Hartill for trusting me with this book, and I thank Claire Margerison for her fabulous administrative support. The valuable editorial assistance and general help with my work from Chris Wei in the final stages of the book are highly appreciated. Lutgard Lams, Zhuo Jing-Schmidt and Daniel Z. Kadar have offered extra help in the review of papers. My head of department Tess Fitzpatrick kindly offered a huge amount of administrative and moral support, which is directly relevant to the timely completion of this book. Thanks are also due to Nuria Lorenzo-Dus, Jim Milton, Irene Turner and Vincent W. Chang for their friendship and support. For whatever my work is worth in putting this volume together with immense help from all those admirable contributors, I dedicate this book affectionately to Farn, Shaun and Mei.

References

Brown, G. and Yule, G. (1983) *Discourse Analysis*. Cambridge: Cambridge University.
Chen, C. (2016) *CiteSpace: A Practical Guide for Mapping Scientific Literature*. New York: Nova Science Publishers.
Levelt, W.J.M. (1989) *Speaking: From Intention to Articulation*. Cambridge, MA: The MIT Press.
Schiffrin, D. (1987) *Discourse Markers*. Cambridge: Cambridge University.

Part I
Approaches to Chinese discourse

1

Chinese conversation analysis
New method, new data, new insights

Kang-Kwong Luke

Background

As a new method for the study of talk-in-interaction, Conversation Analysis (henceforth 'CA') has its beginnings in Harvey Sacks' lectures (Sacks, 1992) and a number of key publications by Sacks, Schegloff and Jefferson in the 1960's and 70's (Jefferson et al., 1987; Sacks et al., 1974; Schegloff and Sacks, 1973, etc.). In Sacks' lectures and publications, one finds, for the first time, close observations of how situated talk is designed to be heard in particular ways. One also finds in Sacks' work detailed descriptions of the procedures (or 'ethnomethods' – see Garfinkel, 1967) with which parties-in-interaction jointly achieve intersubjectivity through sequences of turns-at-talk. Scholarly treatments of language prior to Sacks, as seen in the publications of linguists and philosophers of language for example, suffered from a number of theoretical and empirical problems. Theoretically, linguistic signs were conceptualized as codes, and communication as an encoding and decoding process (Saussure, 1959; Russell, 1940). For a variety of reasons, form was given precedence over meaning (Bloomfield, 1933; Chomsky, 1957). Once form is divorced from meaning, it is impossible to put under scrutiny the true relationship between them – how, in detail, meanings and interpretations are constructed by parties to a conversation with the help of forms. Empirically, while 'context' has always been known to be important, in practice more lip service than undivided attention has been paid to it, so much so that one is hard pressed to find a definition or operationally feasible specification of what constitutes 'context'. Add to this the belief that the study of language could proceed profitably by pondering over single sentences in isolation, which furthermore are invented or re-constituted through memory, and the vicious circle is complete.

Sacks' ground-breaking contributions include abandoning the code theory and replacing it with an indexing theory, which maintains a constant and close dialogue between form and function, as well as giving context (and interaction) the central position that it deserves by insisting on the use of naturally occurring data.

My purpose in this chapter is to introduce CA to students of Chinese discourse as a well known but relatively little understood method. My aim is therefore not to offer a literature survey of the entire field of Chinese CA, but to show, through a close analysis of one specimen, some basic principles of CA and how it works in practice.

Conversation analysis: new method

As alluded to above, the CA method is built upon the basis of three essential elements: (1) naturally occurring data, (2) close, contextualized, time-sensitive form-function analysis, and (3) an intersubjective perspective.

Naturally occurring data

Data are deemed 'naturally occurring' if their occurrence is not the outcome of prompting (e.g., interviewing), experimentation, or some other forms of contrivance, i.e., if the text or talk being captured for analysis is produced under natural conditions. CA's insistence on naturally occurring data does not arise out of some romantic notion of naturalness (whereby 'the natural' is deemed superior to 'the artificial'); rather, it is necessitated by a single-minded objective to pin down and subject to close scrutiny, phenomena as they present themselves to us in the form of everyday life experiences. In this regard, as an empirical science, CA is data-driven through and through (as opposed to theory-driven, as in many forms of linguistics, sociology and psychology). Typically, the starting point of CA is a recording (audio or video) of some naturally occurring talk. These recordings are then subjected to repeated, close listening (or watching) and detailed, fine-grained transcription (Jefferson, 2004).

Close, contextualized, time-sensitive form-function analysis

In examining the recordings, using data transcription as an aid, the analyst proceeds slowly and carefully, word-by-word, line-by-line, and moment-by-moment (hence 'time-sensitive'), with her attention focused sharply and squarely on the forms (designs) and functions (actions) of each utterance in the conversation under scrutiny, constantly inviting form and function to interrogate each other by specifying as accurately as possible how a particular design is used to carry out a particular (social) action. This necessarily dense description will be illustrated with reference to a small sample of data in the next section.

An intersubjective perspective

Critical to any measure of success in such an analysis is the adoption of an intersubjective perspective. An intersubjective perspective necessarily involves, and is based upon, an 'emic' perspective (Pike, 1967), i.e., a perspective from *within* the interaction. What's more, 'intersubjective' is used in the present context in opposition to a single, all-encompassing, 'objective' perspective, as assumed by 'the scientist', or an equally single, all encompassing, 'subjective' perspective, as adopted by the non-scientist (e.g., the literary critic or 'the man on the street'). Rather than setting out to uncover or discover a scientific objectivity, or put forward a purely personal or subjective reaction, the CA analyst aims to produce a description of *how* sense is made of forms from *both* the point of view of the speaker *and* the point of view of the hearer (with the roles of 'speaker' and 'hearer' constantly changing, shifting or rotating, from one moment to the next). Any claims resulting from such an analysis are in principle open to verification by others on the basis of inspecting the same piece(s) of data.

To complete this quick sketch of the CA method, a few more comments should now be made as to what CA is *not*. First, in spite of its name, CA's object of study is not confined to everyday, face-to-face conversations. As a method, CA is applicable, and has indeed been applied, to the study of talk and interaction in a variety of non-face-to-face settings – telephone conversations including helplines (Schegloff and Sacks, 1973; Luke and Pavlidou, 2002; Baker et al., 2005), non-verbal activities (e.g., Ivarsson and Greiffenhagen, 2015 on poolskating), video communication (Harper et al., 2017), and media and other texts (Eglin and Hester, 2003).

Second, while talk-in-interaction is indeed one of the main foci of CA work, as a method, CA does not confine itself to the examination of talk in the narrow sense (of the words and structures of a language). Goodwin (1979) and Schegloff (1984) are two early examples of applications of CA to the study of embodiment as it is deployed in the design of actions. More recently, closer and finer reference has been made to the 'attending' features of talk – gaze, facial expressions, hand gestures, body postures; in short, multimodality (e.g., Li, 2014). In order to capture as much of the total communicative situation as possible, analysts are relying increasingly on video-recordings in CA research.

Third, it is sometimes thought that CA is interested primarily in 'structural' issues, such as the mechanisms of turn-taking. Nothing could be further away from the truth. Everything that conversational participants do – every element in the design of their utterances which is deemed, *by the participants themselves*, communicatively meaningful, including not only how turns are taken but also word choice, intonation, prosody, head movements, gestures, facial expressions and the rest, is done in the service of one single goal, namely, the formation and execution of social actions (e.g., greetings, invitations, congratulations, condolences, complaints, consolations, etc.). CA's interest is therefore in action and interaction, which by definition involves meaning and not merely structures or forms.

Finally, and related to the previous point, there appears to be a widespread misconception that CA does not account for, and even positively forbids the use of, 'social' and 'cultural' information 'outside of' the immediate conversational context. Again, this is emphatically not the case. Because of CA's interest in meaning and action, in carrying out an analysis, the analyst must attend to any information necessary for a better understanding of the design or interpretation of an utterance. Whether this knowledge is deemed, from some point of view or other, as 'personal', 'social' or 'cultural', is of no concern to CA. The only thing that matters is whether the relevance of the information to the analytic purpose at hand can be shown to be anchored in the data itself, and not, for example, a figment of the analyst's own imagination (See Hester and Eglin, 1997).

Doing CA: an example

There is no better way to show how the CA method works than by going through an example of data analysis. Through the exemplification, it can be seen what naturally occurring data is like, how it is pre-treated (or transcribed) to facilitate observation and scrutiny, how contextualized, moment-to-moment analysis proceeds and how an intersubjective perspective comes into it.

The piece of data in question is a snippet taken from a video recording of a conversation among three friends, Mandy, Yu, and Tina (all pseudonyms). The conversation took place in the living room of Mandy's apartment (in Hong Kong), and was conducted in Cantonese. In keeping with CA practice, prior to the recording, the participants were given no instructions as to what they should talk about other than "to have a nice chat with one another". As it turned out, one of the first topics that came up was weddings, because Mandy was recently married, and Tina's brother happened to have gotten married also a week or so before.

As we join the conversation, Yu is 'telling Mandy off', in a jocular sort of way, for not wearing a traditional Chinese gown at her wedding. Yu believes, in line with common beliefs in

Kang-Kwong Luke

Hong Kong, that only wives (as opposed to concubines or mistresses) are entitled to proper wedding ceremonies, where they are expected to wear a traditional Chinese wedding gown. In an attempt to drive home her point, Yu puts the following rhetorical question to Mandy: "Only wives can wear the traditional gown. You wouldn't want to be a mistress, would you?", at which point Mandy and Tina both burst out laughing. Tina then offers, in pursuit of the theme of 'wives vs. concubines/mistresses', the following report about her mother in the next turn:

(1) Mother-in-law (SR–C01:0748)

```
1  Tin:   |lei      |tai      |haa       |ngo      aamaa
          你       睇        下        我       阿媽
          you      look     just       my       mum
          You just have to look at my mum,
          |((T starts lifting head))
                 |((T starts looking at M))
                         |((M looks up in the direction of T))
                                 |((T fixes gaze on M))
                                 |((M engages T's gaze))
                 |((T's right hand leaves home position))

2  Tin:   >zeok    dou      |gam       |hang
          着       到        咁        行
          wear     until    so        elaborate
          See how very elaborately she was dressed

3  Tin:                               |((Raises right index finger))
                                      |((Does a swift and vigorous downward-swiping gesture
                                        at M just before 'you', then moves hand back to home
                                        position on final particle 'laa'))

4  Tin:   ☺lei     aa       [zi        laa<
          你       就       知         喇
          you      then     know      FP
          and you'll know,

5  Man:                    [|°Aaiyaa xxx°
                           EXCL
                           Oh...

6  Man:                    |((Widens eye-gaze in show of anticipation for T's next bit of talk))
7  Tin:   (.)    |<LAAILAA::I     wo>       |daailou=
                 奶奶            喔        大佬
                 mother-in-law   FP        Man
                 (She's the) MOTHER-IN-LAW, man!

8  Tin:         |((Raises right hand and does a circling movement with a half-open palm as
                 she widens her smile and says 'mother-in-law', then returns hand to home
                 position))

9  Man:                                   |((M grows smile, straightens up and laughs
                                            just before 'man'))

10 Tin:   =[°zeok    dou      xxx°
           着        到
           dress     till     xxx
           Dressed so xxx
```

24

11 Yu: [|laaiLAA::I   lai-ge-wo: [ho   zanhai
           奶奶   来㗎喔   呵   真係
           mother-in-law   FP   right?   really
           Mother-in-law she really is, isn't she?
           |((looks up from photo-album, gazes at T, puts big smile on face, as she says 'mother-in-law'))
12 Tin: [laailAA::i   wo:
                                                   奶奶   喔
                                                   mother-in-law   FP
                                                   Mother-in-law!
13 Tin: Waa   zoek   dou   sim   dou   aa
           嘩   着   到   閃   到   啊
           EXCL   wear   until   glitter   until   FP
           So dressed up and (how her dresses) glittered!

Data transcription

Before developing an analysis of this piece of data, it will be useful to take a closer look at the transcript, in order to appreciate how much effort has gone into the transcription, and why it is necessary for such a detailed written representation of the video to be made. The way in which the transcription is done, and the symbols that are used for this purpose, are based, as it is now well known, on a set of conventions first devised by Gail Jefferson in the 1960s and 70s. These transcription conventions have become so well established that they are now widely known under the name of 'Jeffersonian transcription', and are adopted by CA practitioners as a field standard.

A look at the data transcript in (1) will reveal a number of readily discernible features. First, the transcription is presented essentially as a *verbatim representation* of the talk as captured on the video recording. Utterances which might otherwise be dismissed as 'false starts', 'repetitions', 'half-finished sentences', or 'trail-offs' are recorded as faithfully as possible, with no prejudice as to why they might have the shape that they do at those points in the conversation. In line 10 of the transcript, for example, Tina can be seen to be going on (from what she has just said in line 7) to say some more about her mother (or, in technical parlance: to produce another turn-constructional unit). But just as she is beginning to construct that next utterance, Yu comes in strongly to proffer an agreement in the form of an understanding display (in line 11). As a result of this overlap, Tina's just-started utterance trails off and is (at least temporarily) abandoned, to make way for Yu's turn. Even though Tina's utterance in line 10 is unclear and incomplete, an attempt is nevertheless made in the transcription to indicate that she did start saying something at that particular juncture in the interaction. As it turns out, this proves to be a good decision, as what Tina ends up saying next (in lines 12 and 13) can now be more accurately described as not simply a continuation of her story about her mother, but as a particular series of actions. First, this involves an attempt to offer an elaboration of the just-told story (line 10), followed by its (temporary) suspension in face of Yu's competing understanding display (line 11), an acknowledgment of and agreement with that display (line 12), and finally an elaboration or extension of the story (line 13). This recognition of the complexity of Tina's actions and their more accurate description would not have been possible if her quiet, unclear and incomplete utterance in line 10 was not carefully noted and recorded in the transcription.

A second noticeable feature is that words that make up the speakers' utterances are represented orthographically rather than phonetically. Thus, the words 'you' and 'look' in line 1, for example, are written in Cantonese Romanization (as 'lei' and 'tai' respectively), with little attempt at rendering them more 'accurately' via (for example) IPA symbols. Indeed, even the tone marks are left out of the syllables (which do, in this language, come with tones, of course). The justification for this is that, as parts of particular words and phrases (e.g., 'tai' and 'haa' as constituents of the word 'tai-haa'), each syllable has an identity that is largely determinate and recognizable *to the conversational participants*, so that its exact phonetic shape (from an 'objective' point of view) is not in question and need not be highlighted as a focus of analytical attention. From time to time, the identity and recognizability of a particular syllable does pose problems to participants, and may create a challenge to communication. When this happens, the transcriber must ensure that the phonetics of the syllable(s) in question should be given closer attention, and recorded carefully with the help of phonetic symbols, if necessary. (See for example Jefferson's (1985) treatment of the different renderings of the definite article 'the' in English conversations.)

A third feature of this kind of transcription is the annotation of a range of prosodic phenomena, including (syllable/word) length (from long to short), pitch (from high to low), loudness (from loud to quiet) and tempo (from fast to slow). Mandy's utterance in line 5, for example, is said quietly, as indicated by a pair of degree signs, as opposed to Tina's utterance in line 7, which is said loudly, as indicate by the use of capital letters. The importance of prosody should go without saying, as prosody and multimodality (or 'embodiment'), such as eye gazes, facial expressions and hand gestures, together constitute the material form of *how* something is said. (See also Brown et al., 2014 and Duranti, 2015 for complementary approaches to prosody and multimodality respectively).

Such multimodal features that 'accompany' talk are described on a separate line below the verbal utterances. Their occurrence is aligned with their corresponding verbal utterances to show the temporal relation between the two, as indicated by the short vertical lines ('|') inserted just before the verbal utterances and the embodiments respectively. An example of this in the transcript is Tina's utterance in line 1. As she begins to utter the second word ('look'), Tina, who has just lifted her head from a downward-looking to a level position in the course of the previous syllable ('you'), now starts looking in the direction of Mandy. At the same time, Tina's right hand starts leaving its home position (which in this case is her lap; see Goodwin, 1981; Schegloff, 1984; Li, 2014) in preparation for a series of gestures, which will be described below.

A final feature which must be mentioned is the careful annotation of inter-turn phenomena including gaps and overlaps. Needless to say, the close attention paid to these details of talk by the transcriber stems from CA's concern with interaction and intersubjectivity. In doing CA work, one's analytic attention is firmly focused, not on single speakers or utterances, but on the construction and interpretation of utterances *in the context of interaction*. The significance of overlapping talk and its resolution (Jefferson, 1973; Schegloff, 2000) can be readily demonstrated with an example from our data excerpt. It can be seen from the transcript that the beginning of Tina's turn in line 12 is said in overlap with the second part of Yu's turn in line 11 (as indicated by the left square brackets placed on the two respective turns at the point where simultaneous talk begins). A closer look at the overlapping talk will reveal that Tina's turn is timed to begin precisely at the point where the first part of Yu's turn ends. Since the 'first part' of Yu's turn is in itself a turn-constructional unit, and thus qualifies as a possible turn, the beginning of Tina's next turn should be properly seen as occurring at a turn-transition relevance place, a 'legitimate' place for turn transitions to take place. Tina's turn in line 12 is thus not an 'interruption', but a 'quick' response to Yu's prior turn. The significance of this instance of overlapping talk can now be stated in terms of 'early start' as a design feature of affiliative agreements (Pomerantz,

1984; Tanaka, 2015; Luke and Tanaka, 2016); in other words, overlapping talk in this particular context, far from posing any hindrance to interaction and communication, is in fact an integral feature in the design of Tina's response as an affiliative agreement.

A final note on data transcription: 'data' and 'transcription' are, needless to say, two different concepts. A transcription is a transcription of some data or other; it is not the data itself. A transcript, however fine and detailed, is never 'complete', and can never replace an audio or video recording. It is meant to serve more as a mnemonic and an aid to the analyst in making finer observations and scrutinizing the data. Thus, in a very real sense, the analysis which is about to be presented, will be developed by reference to the video recording (which unfortunately cannot be shown in this handbook), using the transcript as a tool.

Data analysis

It will not be possible within the space of this short entry to give full justice to the richness of our data, however short or simple it may appear at first sight. In what follows only a very brief sketch of the organization of Tina's telling will be given to show how a piece of data can be analyzed using CA methodology. In terms of its 'content' – what this stretch of conversation is 'about' – 'what happened' can be summarized in just a few words along the following lines. Tina is telling her friends about her mother being elaborately dressed on her brother's wedding day, in keeping with her newly acquired status as a mother-in-law. This 'information' is delivered over the course of a single turn (lines 1–7), following which her two friends, Mandy and Yu, both duly acknowledge receipt of this 'new information'. That pretty much summarizes this brief conversational episode in terms of 'information exchange'.

However, rather than 'content' or 'information', the focus of CA's interest is on action – social action and sequences of actions in interaction. (See Schegloff's [1996] reminder in this connection.) Thus, instead of asking what this piece of discourse is 'about', one asks: What are the participants *doing* (from one moment to the next); specifically, what are their goals at every turn and what means, verbal and non-verbal, are deployed to achieve these goals? This is not to say that CA denies or ignores 'content'. On the contrary: in the case of this data, the fact that Tina is telling her friends about her mother is not in doubt. However, for an accurate account of the interaction to be developed, one cannot simply take this 'content' for granted, but must develop a fine-grained account of the interactional work that goes into the making of that 'content' as a collaborative achievement.

The analytical sketch which will now be given will be organized around three key moments in the continuous flow of interaction that constitutes this episode. Let us refer to them, for convenience, as: (a) engagement; (b) puzzle; and (c) resolution.

(a) Engagement

At the level of interaction, Tina's line 1 is occupied with two main tasks. First, in taking the turn and starting to produce an utterance, Tina has the option of indicating (or not indicating, as the case may be) who her intended addressee is. This being a three-party conversation, there are at least four possibilities: Mandy, Yu, both, or neither. Second, if Tina does indicate her intended addressee, then whoever the addressee(s) happen(s) to be, Tina needs to engage her/their joint attention. Given these interactional 'issues', notice how the beginning of Tina's turn is shaped in such a way as to solicit Mandy's joint attention by using the second-person singular pronoun 'you' (which, in Cantonese – as opposed to English – has a different shape than the plural form), *together with* the formation of an eye-gaze in the course of the first two syllables of her utterance

Tina engaging Mandy as addressee

Figure 1.1   Engagement

(just before 'my mum') from an 'unfocused state' to an eye-gaze with Mandy as the target. A moment's reflection would reveal the critical importance of that combination (of word and eye-gaze): the same verbal utterance ("you just have to") would have a very different effect if Tina's eye-gaze were directed at the other co-participant, Yu, for instance. Notice, further, that having succeeded in making her two co-participants aware of who she intends the upcoming remarks to be addressed to, Tina then quickly moves on to indicate the intended object of joint attention that Mandy is now being invited to co-establish. It turns out that that object of joint attention is not a person or physical object in the surroundings, but Tina's mother as a 'mental object' (i.e., to be retrieved from memory). In preparation for the little story that Tina is about to tell, Mandy is invited to envisage Tina's mother as she 'appears on stage' ("You just have to look at my mum").

(b) Puzzle

Tina's next task (from line 2 onwards) is to give some indication of the nature of her upcoming 'project': What story is she going to tell about her mother, and for what purpose? Having just established a joint focus with Mandy on her mother, Tina now proceeds to 'put her on stage', as she describes how elaborately her mother was dressed on her son's wedding day ("and see how very elaborately she was dressed", said with an enigmatic, wicked smile on Tina's face). Note how the way Tina's mother was dressed is described in a hyperbolical manner using the Cantonese expression *hang* (which may be translated colloquially into English as 'up to her teeth'). This particular word choice is a prototypical example of what Pomerantz calls an 'extreme case formulation' (Pomerantz, 1986). Through such a formulation the mother and her elaborate dresses are presented not simply as a 'fact' but more as a puzzle (line 4: "See how very elaborately she was dressed and you'll know"), a puzzle calling for an explanation and a resolution.

Similar to the seamless integration of verbal ('you') and 'non-verbal' (eye-gaze) resources described in the previous subsection, it can be observed here how a set of hand gestures is choreographed by Tina in such a way as to flow in perfect synchrony with her verbal production. The set of hand gestures in question consists of Tina's right hand first moving away from its home position (back in line 1 as Tina utters the second word in her turn), then gradually forming into the shape of an upward pointing gesture, with her right index finger pointing upwards as she utters "gam" ('very'), in readiness for the final downward swiping movement produced as Tina says "hang" ('up to her teeth') and a quick return of the hand to its original position. The most notable feature of this set of gestures is that it is executed in such a way as to ensure that

Chinese conversation analysis

Tina's first set of gestures

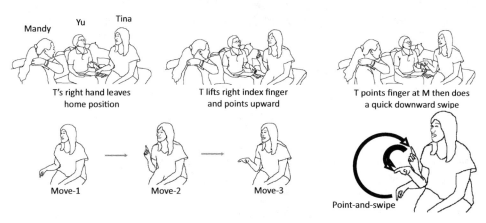

Figure 1.2 Tina's point-and-swipe just before she says '. . . and you'll know'

the climax (the vigorous downward swipe) is reached *just before* Tina utters "lei aa zi laa" ('and you'll know'). This particular format, of a gesture setting the scene for the arrival of a word or expression was first discovered by Schegloff in a now-classical paper on the relationship between words and gestures (Schegloff, 1984).

(c) Resolution

In order to describe the organization of the resolution, one needs to keep an eye on Tina the 'storyteller', Mandy the 'story recipient' and Yu the 'overhearer' (at this point in the telling) *all at the same time.* This task is easier said than done. In truth, the analyst can usually only focus on one person at a time (and often only one modality at a time within the total stream of behavior of a single speaker). For the purposes of exposition, it would be more convenient to comment on the three participants' contributions one after the other. We will therefore proceed by examining, in turn, Tina, Mandy and Yu's verbal and non-verbal contributions during these few moments of interaction (between lines 4 and 12).

As a point of entry into Tina's part in the telling, consider first the syntax of her entire utterance from line 1 to line 7. In essence, the syntactic structure of this utterance can be represented in schematic format as: 'X + and you'll know + Y'. For convenience we may refer to 'X' as part 1, 'and you'll know' as part 2 and 'Y' as part 3 of this construction. As alluded to in the previous section, the delivery of the three-part construction proceeds roughly in the following manner. First, part 1 of the structure is produced to set up a situation with Tina's mother as the main character, who is presented as being in a situation that warrants some accounting or explanation (i.e., being 'dressed up to her teeth'). The speaker (Tina) then executes a pointing-cum-downward-swiping gesture which marks the break between the puzzle and its resolution. In this way, the gesture serves to prepare the scene for the arrival of part 2 (and, arguably, contributes to the heightening of the addressee's involvement by placing more emphasis on 'you'). In terms of its semantic contribution, part 2 clearly serves as a pivot between parts 1 and 3. Its shape ('and you'll know') is such that the element of puzzle in part 1 is now made explicit and brought to the fore.

29

As the telling approaches stage 3 (i.e., resolution), four observations can be made from Tina's point of view. First, at the end of part 2 of her three-part utterance, and just before the start of part 3, a slight but noticeable pause is 'inserted', arguably for (dramatic) effect, as in a lull before the storm. Second, when the resolution finally comes, in a state of full preparedness, as it were, it does so (literally) with a bang: "mother-in-law" is delivered with a sharp up-stepping in pitch and volume as well as a significant elongation particularly of the second syllable (i.e., *LAA::I* in line 7). Third, the strong delivery of the keyword ("mother-in-law") is further buttressed by the addition of an interjection (*dailou* 'man'). Finally, the verbal utterance is accompanied by a series of facial expressions and hand gestures, which at once serves as a form of dramatic enactment (Goffman, 1959) and at the same time further guidance for utterance interpretation. The way these two modalities are integrated is shown in Figure 1.3, where it can be seen how Tina's smile on her face and a circling gesture with her half-open right palm are used at the same time to contextualize the resolution, "(She was the) mother-in-law, man!"

On Mandy's part, her addressee/recipient status was, as we have seen, established right from the start, i.e., near the beginning of Tina's turn (in line 1). If one follows her stream of behavior closely from that point on until the resolution, one can observe how, as Tania's telling progresses, Mandy's response waxes and wanes in fine synchrony with it. Using just a few quick labels we may highlight four stages in Mandy's recipiency: giving attention by engaging in mutual gaze with speaker (line 1), showing interest with facial expression (line 2), heightening anticipation of more to come by a pair of widening eyes and a smile – lines 3–6), and, finally, producing a burst of laughter timed to occur at exactly the moment after "mother-in-law" and before "man", lines 8–9). (Jefferson (1985) on the timing of laughter)

During Tina's telling and Mandy's reception of the story, Yu appears to be attending primarily to a photo-album (of Mandy's wedding), which she is browsing with her head down. Thus, her role, *in the course of Tina's telling of the story*, may best be described as overhearer or secondary recipient. However, as soon as Tina reaches the end of her telling, and at that very moment (just after *daailou* 'man'), Yu looks up at Tina (while Tina is focusing her gaze on Mandy) and delivers a strongly affiliative agreement: "Mother-in-law (she was) indeed!" On the face of it, Yu's utterance appears to be not more than a repetition of Tina's prior turn, using as it does, 'mother-in-law' as the focus. However,

Figure 1.3 Tina's circling gesture as she says 'Mother-in-law, man!'

the sentence-final particle in Yu's turn, *leigowo*, is a very different one from the one that marks the end of Tina's TCU (which is *wo*). The main difference is that, while Tina's particle is used to remind her addressee of the significance of mother-in-laws – 'mother-in-law' being an achievable status only if one is a wife (who has a son that 'brings home' a daughter-in-law), Yu's particle is used to construct an identity statement, i.e., X is Y – in this case, Tina's mother *is* (indeed) a mother-in-law, which makes it a perfect candidate for doing affiliative agreements (On agreements, see Pomerantz, 1984; on affiliative agreements, see Tanaka, 2015; Luke and Tanaka, 2016; on sentence-final particles, see Luke (1990 a,1990b), Wu (2004, 2005).

Conversation analysis of Chinese

Since some initial attempts in the 1990s (Luke, 1990; Chui, 1996; Hopper and Chen, 1996), 'Chinese CA' has come a long way. Not only have there been many more publications and dissertations, in today's CA conferences, presentations and panels featuring the application of CA methods to Chinese data have become something of a commonplace. There have also been special issues devoted to Chinese CA (e.g., Thompson and Wu's special issue for *Chinese Language and Discourse*, 2016) as well as edited volumes (e.g., Li and Ono's edited volume on multimodality in Chinese discourse, 2018). All this points to a promising future, where an even greater contribution can be expected from CA researchers working with Chinese data.

Within the space of this short entry, it is impossible to do this growing literature any justice. The best one can do is make a quick mention of some of these publications as they organize themselves around a number of topics. Of the many topics that have been treated, four stand out in this body of work as ones that have been given the most scholarly attention. These include: repair, particles, telephone conversations and multimodality.

By far the most prominent topic is conversational repair. Following three early efforts at a general characterization of repair in Chinese turn-taking (Chui, 1996; Zhang, 1998; Tao, Fox and Gomez de Garcia, 1999), scholars have carried out more focused studies into particular forms and functions of repair, including repair initiation (Wu, 2006), self-repair (Luke and Zhang, 2010a), and the use of repair in the formulation of modalities (He, 2011). The reason why repair has sparked so much interest is probably due to a more general interest in Chinese syntax, which in some ways works very differently from that of English and other languages. Since repair is closely tied to syntax, an in-depth understanding of repair can produce insights into the workings of syntax.

Within the general topic area of repair there has been a sustained interest in the phenomenon of turn increments, where constituents such as subjects and adverbials are found 'right dislocated' to the end of a turn (as in 买了, 已经 *maile, yijing* '(I've) bought (it), already'.). Earlier attempts at understanding the phenomenon include Luke and Zhang (2010b), Luke (2012), Zhang (2012), Luke, Thompson and Ono (2012), and Lim (2014). Luke and Tanaka (2016) offer a latest account of increments that is interaction-based (as opposed to information-based), using the construction of strong agreements in Cantonese as an example.

For reasons similar to repair, particles, being a distinctive feature of Chinese grammar, have lent themselves particularly well to CA investigations. Luke (1990a, 1990b) represented an early attempt at teasing out the complex relationships between form and function in the use of three Cantonese particles. Wu (2004, 2005) pursued similar concerns in her Mandarin data. More recently, Wu has usefully extended this method to the study of an initial particle (Wu, 2014). Kendrick (2018) applies John Heritage's concept of 'epistemic gradient' to the analysis of the final particle 'ba' in Mandarin.

Another prominent topic has been telephone conversations. Following Hopper and Chen's (1996) study of telephone openings in Taiwan, Luke (2002) presents a first account of topic management in Hong Kong phone calls. This paper is in fact part of an edited volume on telephone conversations across languages and cultures, which offers glimpses of how conversational structures and uses vary from community to community (Luke and Pavlidou, 2002). Subsequently, Sun has contributed two further studies of telephone calls using Mandarin conversational data (2002, 2004).

Multimodality in conversational interaction has fascinated researchers for a long time. Tao (1999) was one of the earliest investigations of postures. Wu (1997) continues this interest in postures but at the same time look at the integration between body movements and the use of particles. Chui (2009) and Yang (2011) represent two among several more contributions to our understanding of the use of gestures and eye gazes in Chinese conversations. Li (2014) is the most recent, and also the most comprehensive, book-length treatment of multimodality in Chinese discourse to date. Useful work has also been done on medical consultations (Yu and Wu, 2015), an area with much promise for CA in Chinese contexts.

Readers interested in delving into this rich literature are referred to an online bibliography entitled 'Conversation Analysis in Chinese', hosted by Lim Ni Eng and freely available on the Internet. It is usefully organized according to themes and topics, and regularly updated. (http://limnieng.wordpress.com/).

Conclusion

In this entry, a brief sketch is made of the theoretical tenets and methodological features of Conversation Analysis. A short video snippet of interaction was presented to show what naturally occurring data is like and how it is transcribed using CA conventions, where considerable attention is paid to the annotation of prosodic and paralinguistic features of talk. In examining the data closely and methodically, moment-by-moment and line-by-line, an attempt was made to show how time-sensitive, closely contextualized, form-function analysis is done, and how the analysis revolves around the intersubjective perspective at its core. Adopting this methodology has made it possible for us to appreciate how, for example, Tina's turn (from line 1 to line7) is constructed using a range of verbal and non-verbal materials and how the utterance comes with a number of design features, each of which is picked and packaged into the turn to serve specific interactional purposes, e.g., word choice ("overly elaborate"), syntax (three-part structure 'X, and you'll know Y'), gaze, gesture and facial expressions (smile). Through these observations we can appreciate how richly textured and finely organized everyday interaction is. Even a 6-second conversational snippet has yielded a wealth of insights that speak to the heart of the linguistic and conversation analysis enterprise: how are meanings produced and constructed through verbal and non-verbal behaviors, and what makes communication possible?

CA is therefore not just another type of discourse analysis, but one where language is subjected to fine-grained analysis in the context of interaction and communication, as demonstrated throughout this entry. In this way, CA offers an empirically grounded way of studying language and interaction which makes it possible for us to integrate linguistic form, from phonetics to syntax and lexis, with meaning production and construction, in Chinese as in other languages.

CA Transcription Conventions (Adapted from Jefferson, 2004, pp. 24–31):

[A left bracket indicates the point of overlap onset
] A right bracket indicates the point at which two overlapping utterances end, if they end simultaneously, or the point at which one of them ends in the course of the other.

=	*Equal signs* indicate no break or gap. *A pair of equal signs*, one at the end of one line and one at the beginning of a next, indicate no break between the two lines.
(0.0)	*Numbers in parentheses* indicate elapsed time by tenths of seconds.
(·)	*A dot in parentheses* indicates a brief interval (± a tenth of a second) within or between utterances.
:: *Colons*	indicate prolongation of the immediately prior sound. The longer the colon row, the longer the prolongation.
.,??	Punctuation markers are used to indicate 'the usual' intonation.
°word°	Degree signs bracketing an utterance or utterance-part indicates that the sounds are softer than the surrounding talk.
word<	A post-positioned left carat indicates that while a word is fully completed, it seems to stop suddenly.
– *A dash*	indicates a cut-off.
> < *Right/left*	*carats* bracketing an utterance or utterance-part indicate that the bracketed material is speeded up, compared to the surrounding talk.
< > *Left/right*	*carats* bracketing an utterance or utterance-part indicate that the bracketed material is slowed down, compared to the surrounding talk.
()	*Empty parentheses* indicate that the transcriber was unable to get what was said. The length of the parenthesized space reflects the length of the ungotten talk.
(word)	Parenthesized words and speaker designations are especially dubious.
(())	Doubled parentheses contain transcriber's descriptions.
☺	smile on face
☹	sad look on face

References

Baker, C., Emmison, M. and Firth, A. (eds.) (2005) *Calling for Help: Language and Social Interaction in Telephone Helplines*. Amsterdam/Philadelphia: John Benjamins.

Bloomfield, L. (1933) *Language*. New York: Henry Holt.

Brown, L., Winter, B., Idemaru, K. and Grawunder, S. (2014) 'Phonetics and Politeness: Perceiving Korean Honorific and Non-Honorific Speech through Phonetic Cues', *Journal of Pragmatics* 66: 45–60.

Chomsky, N. (1957) *Syntactic Structures*. The Hague: Mouton.

Chui, Kawau. (1996) Repair in Chinese Conversation, *Text* 16(3): 343–372.

Chui, Kawai. (2009) Conversational Coherence and Gesture, *Discourse Studies* 11(6): 661–680.

Drew, P., and Heritage, J. (1992) *Talk at Work: Interaction in Institutional Settings*. Cambridge, UK; New York: Cambridge University Press.

Duranti, A. (2015) *The Anthropology of Intentions: Language in a World of Others*. Cambridge: Cambridge University Press.

Eglin, P. and Hester, S. (2003) *The Montreal Massacre: A Story of Membership Categorization Analysis*. Waterloo, ON: Wilfrid Laurier University Press.

Garfinkel, H. (1967) *Studies in Ethnomethodology*. Englewood Cliffs, NJ: Prentice-Hall.

Goffman, E. (1959) *The Presentation of Self in Everyday Life*. University of Edinburgh Social Sciences Research Centre.

Goodwin, C. (1979) 'The Interactive Construction of a Sentence in Natural Conversation', *Everyday Language: Studies in Ethnomethodology*, 97–121.

Goodwin, C. (1981) *Conversational Organization: Interaction between Speakers and Hearers*. New York: Academic Press.

Harper, R., Watson, R. and Licoppe, C. (2017) 'Interpersonal Video Communication as a Site of Human Sociality', *Pragmatics* 27(3): 301–318.

He, Agnes Weiyun. (2011) 'The Role of Repair in Modulating Modal Stances in Chinese Discourse', *Chinese Language & Discourse* 2(1): 1–22.

Hester, S., and Eglin, P. (1997) *Culture in Action: Studies in Membership Categorization Analysis*. Washington, DC: International Institute for Ethnomethodology and Conversation Analysis & University Press of America.

Hopper, R. and Chen, C.-H. (1996) 'Languages, Cultures, Relationships: Telephone Openings in Taiwan', *Research on Language and Social Interaction* 29(4): 291–313.

Ivarsson, J. and Greiffenhagen, C. (2015) 'The Organization of Turn-taking in Poolskate Sessions', *Research on Language and Social Interaction* 48(4): 406–429.

Jefferson, G. (1973) 'A Case of Precision Timing in Ordinary Conversation: Overlapped Tag-Position Address Terms in Closing Sequences', *Semiotica* 9(1): 47–96.

Jefferson, G. (1985) 'An exercise in the transcription and analysis of laughter', in *Handbook of Discourse Analysis*. T.V. Dijk (ed.) London: Academic Press. pp. 25–34.

Jefferson, G. (2004) 'Glossary of transcript symbols with an introduction', in *Conversation Analysis: Studies from the First Generation*. G.H. Lerner (ed.) Amsterdam; Philadelphia: John Benjamins Pub. pp. 13–31.

Jefferson, G., Sacks, H., and Schegloff, E.A. (1987) 'Notes on laughter in the pursuit of intimacy', in *Talk and Social Organization*. G. Button and J.R.E. Lee (eds.) Clevedon, Avon, UK; Philadelphia: Multilingual Matters, c1987. pp. 152–205. Retrieved from http://psycnet.apa.org/psycinfo/1987-98425-006.

Kendrick, K.H. (2018) 'Adjusting Epistemic Gradients: The Final Particle *ba* in Mandarin Chinese Conversation', *East Asian Pragmatics* 3(1): 5–26.

Li, X. (2014) *Multimodality, Interaction and Turn-taking in Mandarin Conversation*. Amsterdam/Philadelphia: John Benjamins.

Li, X. and Ono, T. (eds.) (2018) *Multimodality in Chinese Interaction*. De Gruyter Mouton.

Lim, N.E. (2014) Retroactive Operations: On 'increments' in Mandarin Chinese Conversations, PhD Dissertation, University of California, Los Angeles.

Luke, K.K. (1990a) *Utterance Particles in Cantonese Conversation*. Amsterdam/Philadelphia: John Benjamins.

Luke, K.K. (1990b) 'The Cantonese Particle la and the Accomplishment of Common Understandings in Conversation', *Papers in Pragmatics* 3(1): 39–87.

Luke, K.K. (2002) 'The initiation and introduction of first topics in Hong Kong telephone calls', in *Telephone Calls: Unity and Diversity in the Structure of Telephone Conversations across Languages and Cultures*. K.K. Luke and T.-S. Pavlidou (eds.) Amsterdam: John Benjamins. pp. 171–200.

Luke, K.K. (2012) 'Dislocation or Afterthought? – A Conversation Analytic Account of Incremental Sentences in Chinese', *Discourse Processes* 49(3–4): 338–365.

Luke, K.K. and Pavlidou, T. (2002) *Telephone Calls: Unity and Diversity in Conversational Structure across Languages and Cultures*. John Benjamins Publishing Company.

Luke, K.K. and Tanaka, H. (2016) 'Constructing Agreements with Assessments in Cantonese Conversation: From a Comparative Perspective', *Journal of Pragmatics* 100(July 2016), 25–39.

Luke, K.K., Thompson, S.A., and Ono, T. (2012) 'Turns and Increments: A Comparative Perspective', *Discourse Processes* 49(3–4): 155–162.

Luke, K.K. and Zhang, W. (2010a) 'Insertion as a Self-Repair Device and its Interactional Motivations in Chinese Conversation', *Chinese Language & Discourse* 1(2): 153–182.

Luke, K.K. and Zhang, W. (2010b) 'Retrospective Turn Continuations in Mandarin Chinese Conversation', *Pragmatics* 17(4).

Pike, K. (1967) *Language in Relation to a Unified Theory of the Structure of Human Behavior*. The Hague: Mouton.

Pomerantz, A. (1984) 'Agreeing and disagreeing with assessments: Some features of preferred/dispreferred turn shapes', in *Structures of Social Action*. J.M. Atkinson and J. Heritage (eds.) Cambridge: Cambridge University Press. pp. 57–95.

Pomerantz, A. (1986) 'Extreme Case Formulations: A Way of Legitimizing Claims', *Human Studies* 9(2–3): 219–229.

Russell, B. (1940) *An Inquiry into Meaning and Truth*. New York: W. W. Norton & Company.

Sacks, H. (1992) *Lectures on Conversation, Volumes I and II*. Oxford: Blackwell.

Sacks, H., Schegloff, E.A., and Jefferson, G. (1974) 'A Simplest Systematics for the Organization of Turn-Taking for Conversation', *Language* 50(4): 696–735.

Saussure, F. (1959) *Course in General Linguistics* (C. Bally and A. Sechehaye, Eds., A. Reidlinger, Trans.), New York: Philosophical Library.

Schegloff, E.A. (1984) 'On Some Gestures' Relation to Talk', *Structures of Social Action: Studies in Conversation Analysis* 266–296.

Schegloff, E.A. (1996) *Turn Organization: One Intersection of Grammar and Interaction*.

Schegloff, E.A. (2000) 'Overlapping Talk and the Organization of Turn-Taking for Conversation', *Language in Society* 29: 1–63.

Schegloff, E.A. and Sacks, H. (1973) 'Opening up Closings', *Semiotica*, *8*(4): 289–327.

Sun, H. (2002) 'Display and Reaffirmation of Affect Bond and Relationship: Invited Guessing in Chinese Telephone Conversations', *Language in Society* 31(01): 85–112.

Sun, H. (2004) 'Opening Moves in Informal Chinese Telephone Conversations', *Journal of Pragmatics* 36: 1429–1465.

Tao, H. (1999) 'Body movement and participant alignment in Mandarin conversational interactions', in *Papers from the 35th Regional Meeting of the Chicago Linguistic Society, Vol. II: The Panels*. Chicago: The Chicago Linguistic Society. pp. 125–139.

Tao, H., Fox, B. and Gomez de Garcia, J. (1999) 'Tone-choice repair in conversational Mandarin Chinese', in *Cognition and Function in Language*. Barbara A. Fox, Dan Jurafsky, and Laura A. Michaelis (eds.) Stanford: CSLI. pp. 268–281.

Tanaka, H. (2015) 'Action-Projection in Japanese Conversation: Topic Particles wa, mo, and tte for Triggering Categorization Activities', *Frontiers in Psychology* 6.

Thompson, S.A. and Wu, R.-J.R. (eds.) (2016) 'Special Issue on "Conversation Analysis in Chinese"', *Chinese Language and Discourse* 2016(2).

Wu, R.-J.R. (1997) 'Transforming Participation Frameworks in Multi-Party Mandarin Conversation: The Use of Discourse Particles and Body Behavior', *Issues in Applied Linguistics* 8(2): 97–118.

Wu, R.-J.R. (2004) *Stance in Talk: A Conversation Analysis of Mandarin Final Particles*. Amsterdam: John Benjamins.

Wu, R.-J.R. (2005) '"There is more here than meets the eye!": The Use of Final Ou in Two Sequential Positions in Mandarin Chinese Conversation', *Journal of Pragmatics* 37(7): 967–995.

Wu, R.-J.R. (2006) 'Initiating Repair and Beyond: The Use of Two Repeat-Formatted Repair Initiations in Mandarin Conversation', *Discourse Processes* 41(1): 43.

Wu, R.-J.R. (2014) 'Managing Turn Entry: The Design of EI-Prefaced Turns in Mandarin Conversation', *Journal of Pragmatics* 66: 139–161.

Yang, P. (2011) 'Nonverbal Aspects of Turn Taking in Mandarin Chinese Interaction', *Chinese Language & Discourse* 2(1): 99–130.

Yu, G. and Wu, Y. (2015) 'Managing Awkward, Sensitive or Delicate Topics in Chinese Radio Medical Consultations', *Discourse Processes* 52(3): 201–225.

Zhang, W. (1998) Repair in Chinese Conversation, PhD Dissertation, University of Hong Kong.

Zhang, W. (2012) 'Latching/Rush-Through as a Turn-Holding Device and Its Functions in Retrospectively Oriented Pre-Emptive Turn Continuation: Findings from Mandarin Conversation', *Discourse Processes* 49(3–4): 163–191.

2
Critical analysis of Chinese discourse
Adaptation and transformation

Weixiao Wei

Introduction

At this point in time, as China is reclaiming the world power status and playing an increasingly important role on the global stage, it seems imperative for the world to try to understand the great country through its language, especially the political messages it is sending, which may be dramatically different from those of a Western country in their linguistic nature and underlying principles. In this regard, critical discourse analysis (CDA) seems a useful tool to study Chinese and uncover some of the discourse and power structures underneath the characteristic use of the language. Conversely, the critical study of Chinese discourse in its unique cultural, political and economic background may help recalibrate the ever-evolving field of CDA to the Chinese context and expand its area of concerns and research methodology. In this chapter, we hope to investigate how existing CDA rationale and methodology interact with the Chinese discourse at an era when China is becoming a superpower while its language remains enigmatic and sometimes an object of misunderstanding.

We start this chapter by reviewing some critical discourse studies in the Western tradition including the theoretical frameworks proposed and the research procedures suggested in the academic field. Notably, we refer to Wodak's (2011) Discourse-Historical Approach, Fairclough's (2012) transdisciplinary research methodology, and van Dijk's (2015) socio-cognitive approach while discussing their relevance to the critical analysis of Chinese discourse. We also take Fairclough's view that critical discourse analysis is subsumed in the broader critical social analysis (CSA); therefore, our review includes discourse studies along the wider spectrum of language and social studies, such as multimodal critical discourse analysis, CDA and systemic-functional linguistics, critical metaphor analysis and critical analysis of media discourse.

After describing some of the core ideas of the initial CDA queries, it is important to see their application in the analysis of some social problems (e.g. in media or education discourse) and to introduce some updated theories to more competently tackle newly added research questions. This is what we do in the next section entitled 'domains and orientations'. After that, we investigate the Chinese counterpart of the CDA research communities in the West and see what their contributions are both to the Chinese linguistics field and to the world at large. In the 'Chinese contributions and innovations' section, we discover how CDA is done similarly or differently in the Chinese context regarding research areas, research agendas, and research methodology. It is at this point we find 'positive' discourse analysis (or PDA) particularly relevant.

As an illustration of how critical analysis of Chinese discourse can reveal interesting facts about the thinking patterns and power relations embedded in text, we present a mini corpus-based study drawing from People's Daily news centering around the topic of 'Taiwan'. Using WordSmith 5.0, we isolated a list of keywords with high 'keyness' values, explored some of their concordance lines and collocates, and worked out the main themes developed in the source texts of our corpus. By doing so, we come to understand how cross-strait relations are conceptualized and how the government's messages are delivered through China's official media. On a more theoretical level, we wonder at the end of our discussion whether the nature and queries of CDA need to be modified as a response to the findings presented in this chapter, in particular, regarding the interpretation of the word *critical* and its possible alternatives.

Critical discourse analysis and its Chinese relevance

Using WebCorp (www.webcorp.org.uk/) to look up the phrase 'critical discourse analysis' with *Bing* search engine returns 484 hits at the time of writing. On further processing of the concordance lines for collocates of the phrase, the system returns a result partially shown in Table 2.1. On the basis of this collocational relationship, it seems logical to start the review of CDA in this section by looking at Fairclough and Wodak's works since they are the most mentioned names on the web associated with the key phrase.

A review of the current state of critical discourse analysis is necessarily selective due to the fuzzy and indecisive nature of the subject. Wodak (2011: 38), for example, loosely defined CDA as 'a problem-oriented interdisciplinary research programme, subsuming a variety of approaches'. The same indistinct nature of CDA was echoed by van Dijk (2015: 467) in his caution against the misunderstanding of CDA being 'a special *method* of doing discourse analysis'. Instead, van Dijk recognized CDA as a 'critical perspective', a kind of 'discourse study *with an attitude*' (all emphases original). Fairclough (2012: 19) himself also pointed out that 'CDA is a loosely interconnected set of different approaches'. The heterogeneous nature of CDA paradigm offers flexibility and opportunities for modifying and combining research methods to tackle the problems at hand. In this regard, it seems conducive to the research of Chinese discourse which is fundamentally different from the Western languages and needs markedly different approaches.

Table 2.1 The first 10 collocates for the phrase "critical discourse analysis" by WebCorp

Word	L4	L3	L2	L1	R1	R2	R3	R4	Total
Critical	3	12	1	0	17	34	10	6	83
discourse	12	5	3	1	0	5	2	12	40
Fairclough	5	4	2	0	11	6	6	5	39
Discourse	5	1	9	1	5	11	3	4	39
Methods	0	1	34	0	0	0	3	0	38
analysis	4	8	5	4	0	8	5	2	36
CDA	1	3	0	2	21	1	0	5	33
Wodak	4	2	1	0	5	10	8	2	32
Study	0	0	0	0	0	0	31	0	31
Analysis	5	5	1	8	0	1	7	2	29

Wodak (2011) described a Discourse-Historical Approach (DHA) developed by her and colleagues in Austria as a kind of critical research first to study the anti-Semitism discourse and subsequently applied to the analysis of racism and sexism and organizational discourses. DHA considers four layers of context when analyzing a text: inter-textual relationships, extra-linguistic variables, history of texts and organizations, and institutional frames, exploring how discourses change as a function of socio-political contexts. DHA also identifies five types of discursive strategies which are used to promote 'positive self' and 'negative other': Referential (or Nomination) strategies, Predicational strategies, Argumentation strategies, Perspectivation strategies, and Intensifying/Mitigation strategies. For example, 'Polish thieves' and 'drug dealing black asylum seekers' are examples of nomination strategy. An analogous Chinese term is 日本鬼子 ('Japanese devils') used to refer to Japanese persons in an antagonistic and/or contemptuous way as a result of Japan's historical invasion of China.

Fairclough (2012) explained one version of CDA which emphasizes the transdisciplinary nature of the methodology by 'bringing disciplines and theories together to address research issues' (p. 12). The methodology distinguishes four stages of enquiry: 1. Focus on a social wrong; 2. Identify obstacles to addressing that wrong; 3. Evaluate whether the society 'needs' the social wrong; 4. Suggest possible ways past the obstacles. Fairclough used an extract from Gordon Brown's 2009 speech to illustrate 'the predominance of a flawed economic order' (p. 16) and pondered how CDA can bring about 'shifts in the articulation of genres, discourses and styles in texts' (p. 19) by a combination of linguistic and political-economic analysis, that is, embedding CDA in CPE (cultural political economy) "to explore both the semiotic and the material conditions" (p. 18). In the Chinese context, such a transdisciplinary study can be manifested in, for example, a 'dialectical relationship' as advocated by Fairclough, between Marx's economic theory or Confucianism and linguistic analysis.

van Dijk (2015) introduced another aspect of CDA focusing on the 'discursive reproduction of power' and using 'control' as the keyword. That is, the powerful groups control communicative situations and discourse structures, which then exercise influence on less powerful persons' cognition and ideology affecting their opinions, intentions and actions. In his 'sociocognitive' model, social structures of power are examined through the analysis of the relations between discourse and cognition. van Dijk illustrated how beliefs can be manipulated by discourse structures referring to his own research on dominant discourse on immigration. An example is the use of the word *waves* in media discourse to describe immigrants thereby making the referents more concrete and threatening. In Taiwan media discourse, stereotyped metaphors are often used to refer to certain categories of criminals, such as 毒蟲 (literally 'poison worm', referring to drug users), 色狼 ('sexual desire wolf'), 蛇蠍女 ('snake-scorpion woman'), etc. adding another layer of moral condemnation on top of legal consequences.

The review so far captured three significant threads of CDA expounded by three key figures in the field: Discourse-Historical Approach, CDA as a transdisciplinary approach, and the sociocognitive approach to CDA. Figure 2.1 tentatively integrates the three strands of CDA research into a model of critical discourse analysis to capture its rationale and essence. In this model, text is richly embedded in four layers of textual and social contexts, a situation similar to van Dijk's model of 'discourse structure' being embedded in 'communicative situation'. The entire event, or 'order of discourse' in Fairclough's term, is then used by the powerful groups as a tool to control the less powerful groups. The critical analyst can then follow Fairclough's transdisciplinary approach and study the problems with a four-stage methodology, notably drawing from both linguistic tools and sociological theories to address both the textual and the contextual aspects of the problem.

Critical analysis of discourse

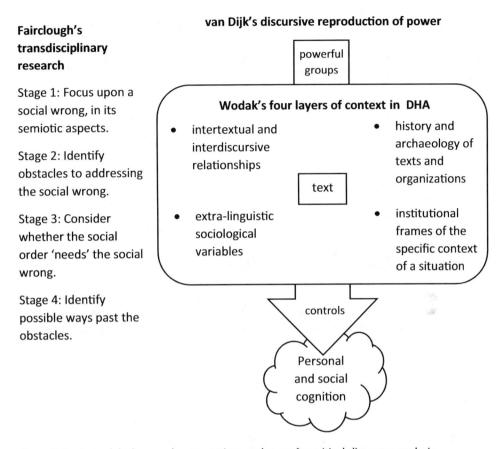

Figure 2.1 A model of research perspectives and steps for critical discourse analysis

The year 2017 has seen the publication of the *Routledge Handbook of Critical Discourse Studies* – the more general term of CDS has been advocated by leading scholars in the field as a more appropriate title than CDA – signifying the independent character of the discipline and the research potential offered by the subject. Retrospectively, many studies that can be recognized as some forms of CDA have more or less followed the model depicted in Figure 2.1 and unearthed many sociocultural and political-economic problems through the study of text (including language and 'other forms of semiosis' in Fairclough's term like body language and images). In the next section, we review some works which have applied CDA methodology in some form to study a variety of social problems. We also look at some new developments of CDA methodology on the theoretical side.

CDA domains and orientations

Media discourse is an obvious area where CDA can actively seek out problems to diagnose and redress due to the unbalanced power structure between media producers (powerful groups) and receivers. The origin of critical analysis of news text is often traced back to Roger Fowler (Fowler et al., 1979; Fowler, 1991) who used Critical Linguistic tools to analyze news texts and showed how ideology work can be embedded in details of language. van Dijk (1988) further presented a linguistic-rhetoric analytical framework for analyzing news, concluding that 'a rhetorical analysis cannot be fully independent of a semantic and ideological analysis of news discourse' (p. 94). For van Dijk, 'ideologies are related to the cognitive representations that underlie news production and understanding' (p. 182). More specifically, in van Dijk's socio-cognitive approach, discourse structures of the news text are linked to the social practice of newsmaking, to the social cognition of news participants and ultimately to the societal structure consisting of class, ethnicity, power, institutions, elite groups, and so on. In other words, the powerful groups control media and use discourse structures to influence personal and social cognition. Meanwhile, the study of news text has moved beyond pure linguistic analysis to the multimodal dimension. Kelsey (2017), for example, examined a piece of Mail Online news involving the use of a video (hence 'multimodal') which showed a woman physically attacking a younger male for using a drone camera on the beach. According to Kelsey, the title of the news 'Crazed woman assaults man for flying drone on beach' supported by the video, provoked a series of reader feedback asserting the belief that men are subjected to mistreatment in society. The news was contextualized in such a way that gender ideology was highlighted at the expense of the equally important issue of privacy and ethics concerning drone filming.

Education is a somewhat surprising area where CDA turns out to be hyperactive in recent years. Across the use of CDA in educational research, two trends have emerged: the first is using CDA methodology to explore ideologies and positions in educational policies, which we can term the 'top-down' approach. Dworin and Bomer (2008), for example, used a linguistic toolkit derived from CDA to analyze a professional development text and revealed how the book utilized a stereotyped 'culture of poverty' to depict the poor as the 'Other' and the author and the teacher-reader as 'We'. The authors think that teachers should learn to recognize when oppressed groups are being represented as deficient and that 'educators must keep a focused commitment to knowing actual people' (p. 118). A more recent example of criticizing educational policy using CDA methodology is Burch (2018) where a 'Special Educational Needs code of practice' was found to be built upon existing ideologies and written to the demands of economy rather to the needs of the children and young people in question. The second trend of educational application of CDA is to use the research methodology at the classroom setting, working with teachers and students involving classroom activities. This is the 'bottom–up' forces that Rogers (2017: 465) believes 'the majority of CDA work in education in the past decade has focused on' with the objective of 'making room for transformational practices'. Rogers used her own experience of working with teacher education students to show how classroom conversation could be analyzed using a reconstructive (as opposed to deconstructive) method to tease out positive discourse practices. In her case study, for example, a multimodal analysis showed a student used laughter to 'bolster the inter-racial alliance' with another student (p. 476).

Because of the flexibility and indecisiveness of the CDA discipline, there seems no boundary for the possible integration between the rudimentary CDA methodology and ideas from other disciplines or within the broadly defined discipline itself (e.g. from other linguistic theories). Bloor and Bloor (2017), for example, explained how systemic functional linguistics (SFL) can offer CDA researchers a good analytical framework with its lexico-grammatical paradigm and other tools such as statistical comparison techniques, Rhetorical Structure Theory and comparisons of lexical density. Another possibility came from narrative analysis, which investigates people's experiences and feelings in society through the interpretation of stories or, as Patton (2002) put it, 'the texts that tell the stories' (p. 118). As CDA focuses on power and language in society, these two independent but thematically related disciplines can merge usefully into a hybrid approach – critical narrative analysis (CNA) to seek a more theoretically and methodologically

Critical analysis of discourse

robust analysis. Stacey et al. (2016), for example, used the framework of CNA to analyze the data collected from focus group discussions by 46 mental health professionals, service users and carers. The objective was to examine how the participants experience decision-making processes and how issues of power and interest are at play during these processes. The result of critical narrative analysis showed all groups, 'while nominally talking about the interests of service users, also spoke about their own interests' (p. 39). The authors concluded that the current literature on SDM (shared decision-making) placing the service user at the center of decision-making processes was just 'political rhetoric' (p. 40).

Hart (2010) offers yet another tool to enhance the ability of CDA to tackle social problems in the cognitive dimension. According to him, there are two missing links in current CDA paradigm that can be filled in by the cognitive approach – Evolutionary Psychology to explain why particular discourse strategies work in political discourse, and Cognitive Linguistics to interpret the working process and effect of linguistic constructions on human cognition. As an example, Hart reveals how manipulation and ideology are embedded in discourse on immigration using his cognitive framework to examine the data. Another new approach created to work with CDA is Piotr Cap's 'proximization' theory, which also focuses on the analysis of discourse strategies intended to, in this case, coerce and legitimize. According to Cap (2014), proximization strategies consist of three dimensions: Spatial, Temporal and Axiological and are mainly applied to 'political discourse soliciting legitimization of interventionist preventive measures against the external threat' (p. 20). Spatial proximization refers to the danger of the enemy force encroaching on home space; temporal proximization, the urgency of required response to the imminent threat; and axiological proximization, the clash between home values and the alien antagonistic values. Cap used G.W. Bush's speech three weeks before the 2003 invasion of Iraq as an example to illustrate how proximization analysis worked. For example, temporal prioritization is realized by invoking America's remote history and 'founding promise', spatial proximization is instantiated by referring to Saddam Hussein's alleged weapons of mass destruction being 'secret and far away' vs people living in 'stable and free nations' and finally, axiological proximization is achieved by making claims such as the world having 'a clear interest in the spread of democratic values'. Thus, we saw how CDA has been usefully applied to analysis of journalism and educational problems. We also knew how CDA methodology can be augmented by related concepts and theories.

Chinese CDA: contributions and innovations

In the previous two sections, we first summarized some core ideas from the initial pool of knowledge in CDA contributed by three prominent figures in the field. We then explored the application of CDA to areas such as journalism, education and politics while introducing some new theories imported to CDA from other branches of linguistics such as systemic functional linguistics, narrative analysis and cognitive linguistics. In this section, we see how the linguistic field in China has been inspired by CDA research in the West, how existing methodology has been adopted and modified to suit the Chinese environment, and how novel CDA agendas have been created to mark CDA 'with Chinese characteristics'.

Mu (2016) looked up the CNKI database with the key phrases 批评话语分析 (critical discourse analysis), 批评语言学 (critical linguistics), 批评性语篇分析 (critical text analysis), 批判性话语分析 (critical-judgmental discourse analysis) and found 1,190 published papers between 1995 and 2015 on these topics. Mu classified these papers into four kinds of CDA research strands: General CDA theory and methodology (20%), CDA as interdisciplinary research (14%), Critical media discourse analysis (49%), Critical analysis of discourses in other fields (17%). According to Mu's categorization, the number of CDA papers produced in China on media

41

discourse is nearly half the total number of papers on CDA over this period. However, 'media discourse' is a large category and can potentially include a variety of topics in news reports or TV shows. Mu's short report did not elaborate on the content of that category. The 'other field' category, on the other hand, was more clearly explained, to include discourses on education, medicine, law and (less obviously) translation. Interestingly, among the 30 top keywords extracted from Mu's corpus of 1,190 CDA papers, only one personal name appears – the former American president 奥巴马 (Obama), which appears 15 times in her corpus. This probably means American political discourse is a prime target of CDA in China.

Zhao (2017) offers a slice of Chinese CDA research in 2016 based on her qualitative review of some seventy papers published in China in that year. Zhao's review provides more information on research topics of Chinese CDA in that period. According to her, Chinese scholars in 2016 investigated a series of social-political issues with 'strong political responsibility' (强烈的政治责任感) and 'up to date international perspective' (富有时代感的国际视野). Zhao especially recommended the research strand dwelling on Xi Jinping's 'China dream' discourse. In particular, the research results presented by an author was said to reveal the national image inherent in the China dream discourse of peace-loving (热爱和平), development-focusing (关注发展) and the determination to bring fortune to its people and the world (造福人民和世界). While, following the well-established and well-respected Chinese convention, Chinese leaders' speech should be carefully and positively evaluated, the national image of China projected in news from international media need be critically examined (except that from Russia where Putin's speech was also positively reviewed). The latter is an important mission pointed out by Zhao who, on one hand, highlights a group of authors' finding that America's mainstream media invariably use 'single-polarized and stereotyped' (单极化和刻板化的) methods to create China's national image in order to 'serve the mainstream emotion and psychological needs of American society' (服务于美国社会的主流情绪和心理需求) and, on the other hand, explains how other authors, using vocabulary categorization, transitivity and metaphor analysis, etc., found the UK Guardian surreptitiously taking a biased view towards China and favoring the Japanese side when reporting the Diaoyu islands dispute. Zhao's paper usefully summarized the political agendas of CDA researchers in China which clearly demonstrate a domestic/socialism (positive) vs foreign/liberalism (critical) distinction.

Outside the dichotomy of domestic versus foreign political discourse analysis, Chinese CDA also works on a variety of other topics to reveal power structures and inequalities underlying social problems. For example, Liu and Li (2017) analyzed discourses about old age on China's newspapers and the social media Weibo. Results show newspapers tend to use more positive phrases to describe old people such as 'dedicatedly serving' (奉献服务) and 'fit as a fiddle' (宝刀未老); whereas social media host more diverse languages about old age including such negative terms as 'burden of society' (社会包袱) and 'old but not respectable' (为老不尊). The authors concluded that unequal social power between the young and the old and the stereotypes created by social media regarding older people are two main factors contributing to conceptualization and ideology of old age. On a more positive note, Chang (2016) did a diachronic study of Chinese obituaries of government officials' deaths posted on *People's Daily* spanning over half a century (1949–2015). She found a simplification procedure in place which gradually lessens the parts on explaining the funeral arrangements and on praise of the dead person over time. To Chang, this demonstrates a dialectical relationship between obituary discourse and society which engendered an ideological change and reduced the occurrence of pompous eulogy and replaced it with more objective statements. This is a sure sign of social progress.

In terms of the synergy of CDA methodology and other analytical frameworks from related disciplines, researchers in China are also very receptive (of novel combinations) and innovative (about their applications). Systemic functional linguistics is a model often used to analyze Chinese discourse in a critical or positive way. Miao (2016), for example, offers further evidence of the textual, cultural and political achievements of Xi Jinping's China Dream proposal based on the three-dimension analysis (ideational, interpersonal, textual) of SFL. Liu and Ma (2016), also worked on the China Dream discourse and focused on how Xinhua News, the official press agency of PRC, disseminate the idea of the China Dream abroad. They applied corpus linguistic techniques and used WordSmith 5.0 to analyze a corpus of 143 news texts. They found that Xinhua's reports on China Dream were too official and overly positive, which may be counter effective. Instead, they highly recommended Xi's multidimensional discourse strategies when promoting China Dream using statistics, storytelling, quotations and personal experiences. Geng and Chen (2016) went one step further to combine multimodal analysis with SFL and created a multidimensional model for analyzing online discourse on a Chinese social media which include text, smiley icons, screenshots, links, documents, video clips and sounds. They cogently concluded that the discourse structures of online communities and the process of communication largely depend on the advance of technology. The progression of technology will continuously change the format of online community discourse. Finally, Zhang and Luo (2017) show an interesting combination of CDA with another linguistic theory who devised a cognitive linguistics framework to analyze a U.S.-China Military Scorecard. However, despite the phrase 'critical cognitive analysis' (批评认知分析) in the title of the paper, there was no critical element in the discussion of intelligence value among the linguistic devices analyzed.

Not only in respect to research topics, research perspectives, and research methodology but also in theoretical grounding of CDA do Chinese publications manifest distinct characters and offer fresh insights vis-à-vis the Western paradigm. Miao and Mu (2016), for example, argued eloquently in Chinese that Marxist philosophy is the theoretical foundation of CDA and Marxist methodology offers 'operational guidance' (操作指南) for critical analysis of discourse. Shi (2016) used the term 'cultural discourse studies' (文化话语研究) as a cover theory for his comparative discourse analysis of 2015 China Defence White Paper vs The National Military Strategy of the United States of America 2015. Written in Chinese for the Chinese audience, Shi's paper schematically showed how American military strategy discourse differs dramatically from the Chinese one. Because of the 'dialectical unity' of Chinese culture and thinking, China's military strategy demonstrates international accommodation (国际包容性) and international harmony (国际和谐性). Because of the culture-thought dualism and Americanism, the nature of the U.S. military strategy is separatism, international expansion and world power. Although the link between culture and discourse is not well developed in this work, the results of the critical discourse studies are interesting and stimulating.

In this section, we saw how CDA was adopted and adapted in the Chinese context, producing a variety of academic works ranging from discussion of CDA's theoretical foundation and creation of new theory, methodology and research questions, to reorientation of the nature of 'criticism' to mostly affirmation of China's official discourse and mostly negative evaluation of Western political or media discourse. These unique characteristics of Chinese CDA should be understood against the sociocultural and political-economic background of China which, perhaps, will shed new light on the future of critical discourse analysis as a global discipline.

Case study

To give a clear idea about how to understand and research Chinese discourse, we report the procedures and results of our study of a media corpus consisting of 1,124,010 Chinese characters extracted from People's Daily news between January 2017 and March 2018 by using the keyword 'Taiwan' to find around 1,118 reports. The relationship between China and Taiwan is an intriguing one and relevant discourses are not yet well-studied. In this research, we adopt an 'open' stance which is neither critical nor positive so that the data can speak for themselves. That is, we mean to present our analysis of the data objectively with a view to generating discussion and without pre-defined political agenda or inclination. We think this is a forward-looking attitude when doing CDA in the Chinese context where political issues under socialism may be conceptualized differently from the West.

To analyze a Chinese corpus, we need to overcome the initial difficulty of word delineation. Because a Chinese text flows in a character-by-character fashion without any marked boundary (such as a space in English text) between 'words' (which are a highly abstract notion in Chinese and not easily definable in mechanical terms), we first need a word boundary detection program to transform the running text into word-by-word format so that a concordancer can meaningfully process the corpus, making word lists and concordance lines, calculating collocation scores and 'keyness' of words and so on. In this case, we used Laurence Anthony's SegmentAnt to transform our corpus into word-segmented text (which was not 100% correct in identifying commonly accepted words due to the limitations of the dictionary used by the software). We then used WordSmith 5.0 to generate the word list and concordance lines needed for the analysis. The Lancaster Corpus of Mandarin Chinese compiled by Tony McEnery and Richard Xiao was used as the reference corpus for generating a word list ordered by the 'keyness' value of individual words.

Table 2.2 shows a list of 20 words which have the highest 'keyness' values among all words contained in our million-character corpus (Note: words and characters related to the mechanics of journalism such as 人民日报, 月, 年 etc. are excluded). This means their presence in the

Table 2.2 The first 20 key words in our People's Daily corpus with highest keyness values

No.	Keyword	Freq.	RC. Freq.	Keyness
1	台湾 (Taiwan)	9538	63	17545.16797
2	两岸 (cross-strait)	3711	45	6628.796387
3	大陆 (the mainland)	3734	57	6580.413086
4	民进党 (Democratic Progressive Party)	1499	0	2853.063965
5	两岸关系 (cross-strait relationship)	1137	0	2163.587402
6	民众 (the public)	1056	19	1836.870483
7	交流 (interflow)	1236	99	1743.078979
8	台北 (Taipei)	957	14	1688.02832
9	台独 (Taiwan independence)	771	0	1466.802002
10	岛内 (inside the island)	754	0	1434.44519
11	当局 (the authority)	972	64	1431.515015
12	蔡 (Cai)	935	56	1403.027466
13	英文 (Ing-Wen, 'English')	789	31	1267.430298
14	台湾同胞 (Taiwan compatriots)	528	0	1004.353821
15	共识 (consensus)	503	12	854.5587769
16	媒体 (media)	452	1	846.4946289
17	九二 (1992)	442	0	840.7218628
18	台商 (Taiwanese merchants)	441	2	815.1791992
19	创业 (entrepreneurship)	470	9	813.411438
20	台胞 (Taiwan compatriots)	426	0	810.2805786

corpus is significant and not random and, from our point of view, are key to understanding what the newspapers try to say to the reader on the topic of 'Taiwan'.

As the corpus consists of 1,118 news reports each containing at least one token of 台湾, it is not surprising that 台湾 is the word that occurs most frequently in the corpus and has the highest keyness value. These 20 keywords can be classified into four conceptual categories:

- Geographical terms: 台湾, 大陆, 两岸, 台北, 岛内
- Political entities: 民进党, 蔡, 英文, 台独, 当局
- Person references: 民众, 台湾同胞, 台商, 台胞
- Cross-strait relation/interaction: 两岸关系, 交流, 共识, 媒体, 九二, 创业

The first thing to notice is that, for anyone familiar with the current China-Taiwan relations, the 'aboutness' of the million-word corpus can be easily grasped through connecting (groups of) words together between the four proposed categories: Taiwan is an island in relation to the mainland across the Taiwan Strait, the relation between the two being defined by 1992 Consensus (i.e. there is only one China). Taiwanese people are mainlanders' compatriots. President Tsai Ing-wen and the Democratic Progressive Party are associated with Taiwan Independence movement.

A further look at collocation of some of the keywords listed in Table 2.2 provides a more complicated view of the themes summarized above. Take, for example, the collocates of the master keyword 台湾 in our corpus. Table 2.3 shows the result calculated by WordSmith 5.0. Likewise, the journalistic words and individual characters are left out in the analysis.

Table 2.3 The first 20 collocates of 台湾 in our People's Daily corpus

No.	Word	With	Total	Total Left	Total Right
1	大陆 (mainland)	台湾	721	353	368
2	民众 (the pubic)	台湾	302	51	251
3	青年 (the youth)	台湾	274	23	251
4	两岸 (cross-strait)	台湾	212	108	104
5	发展 (development)	台湾	195	79	116
6	中国 (China)	台湾	180	66	114
7	经济 (economy)	台湾	167	42	125
8	社会 (society)	台湾	152	29	123
9	问题 (issue)	台湾	141	56	85
10	政治 (politics)	台湾	125	38	87
11	文化 (culture)	台湾	124	51	73
12	创业 (entrepreneurship)	台湾	121	40	81
13	日本 (Japan)	台湾	120	84	36
14	方面 (aspect)	台湾	114	33	81
15	交流 (exchange)	台湾	106	56	50
16	大学 (university)	台湾	103	20	83
17	年轻人 (young persons)	台湾	103	15	88
18	近日 (recently)	台湾	99	50	49
19	学生 (students)	台湾	98	16	82
20	协会 (association)	台湾	95	32	63

We manually scrutinized the concordance lines of the 721 tokens of 大陆 which collocate with 台湾 and classify them into four kinds of expressions based on the semantic content of the text. The four types of expression are each illustrated with a concordance line extracted from the source text shown in Table 2.4 below. Overall, these tell the story of how welcoming China is towards Taiwanese people and what good opportunities have been offered. People in Taiwan are generally passionate about mainland culture and their shared history. Some malevolent politicians in Taiwan, however, are trying to mislead people to separatism. There is only one China and both mainland and Taiwan belong together.

Most of our source texts containing the 台湾-大陆 collocation carry out the first discourse function listed in Table 2.4: to express how welcoming mainland China is to all walks of Taiwanese people to come to the mainland and create a better life. When it comes to the Taiwan–Mainland relationship, however, it is unavoidable to mention the current obstacle to cross-strait reunification: Taiwan's Democratic Progressive Party (DPP). The third type of expression is therefore the exact opposite of the first kind: it attacks the ill-intentioned Taiwanese politicians, specifically those from the DDP (or so-called 'green camp' due to their green party flag) accusing them of the crime of betraying the Chinese nationality and history and trying to mislead innocent Taiwanese people into the wrong path of separation. The most representative icon in

Table 2.4 Types of expression comprising 台湾-大陆 collocation

expression type	example
1. Mainland China offers development opportunities for Taiwanese people	就 在 蔡 英文 施政 陷于 泥沼 之际, 中国 大陆 宣示 要 与 **台湾** 民众 分享 **大陆** 发展 机遇, 并 提供 学习、创业、就业 与 生活 的 同等待遇 (When the Tsai Ing-wen administration led Taiwan into stagnation, Mainland China announced that it would share development opportunities with Taiwanese people and provide equal access to study, entrepreneurship, employment and amenities in life.)
2. Taiwanese people admire Mainland culture and society	我 现在 是 代表 **台湾** 的 画家 来 **大陆** 开 画展, 希望 有朝一日 跟 大陆 的 画家 一起, 共同努力 到 海外 去 宣扬 中华文化 (I represent Taiwanese painters holding an exhibition in Mainland China. I hope one day I will work together with mainland artists and go overseas to promote Chinese culture.)
3. Some Taiwanese politicians are lying and misleading	继续 催眠 普通百姓 。 在 绿营 嘴里, 大陆 什么 都 比 **台湾** 落后 且 相差 数十年, **大陆** 希望 统一 是 为了 分 台湾 的 钱 ([They] continue to hypnotize ordinary people. In the mouth of the green camp, everything in mainland falls decades behind Taiwan. The reason mainland longs for reunification is to divide Taiwan's money.)
4. Both Taiwan and Mainland belong to China	进一步 认识 到 **大陆** 和 **台湾** 不可分割 的 历史 联系, 增进 了 共同 的 中华民族 认同、中华文化 认同 (Further recognizing the inseparable historical connections between the mainland and Taiwan, enabling the identification of common Chinese nationality and Chinese culture.)

Critical analysis of discourse

this category must be the name of the current elected president (not recognized by China as such) of Taiwan, 蔡英文 (Tsai Ing-wen). The name, however, does not appear as a unit in the segmented corpus presumably because it has not been listed in the dictionary of the software yet. The surname 蔡 (Tsai) therefore appears as No. 12 keyword in Table 2.2 and the given name 英文 (Ing-wen or literally 'English') as No. 13 in a separate entry. (The same is true for 九二 in 17 and 共识 in 15, which should have formed a single dictionary entry 九二共识 – the 1992 consensus.) To find out what has been said about 蔡英文 in the People's Daily corpus, we input 英文 as keyword to the Concord application of WordSmith 5.0. Then again, we isolated the first 20 meaningful collocates of the word (蔡)英文, as shown in Table 2.5.

The first 20 words that form a collocational relationship with 蔡英文 in our corpus can be classified into four kinds based on the semantic nature and discourse function they lend to the combination: political affiliation, political action, geographical terms and terms about the general public. Table 2.6 lists the collocates in each category and an example text from the source for each type of expression.

It can be seen from the example texts in Table 2.5, most of the news about 蔡英文 on People's Daily is negative, concentrating on her misjudgment and misdoings about the cross-strait relations and the catastrophic results that follow, including Taiwan's poor economic and international situation and increasing protests from Taiwanese people about the predicament. Overall, our analysis of the corpus seems to project a polarity of two political inclinations manifested in People's Daily news regarding the topic of 'Taiwan' – mainland China's benignity and dedication vs Taiwan government's antagonism and betrayal with the majority of innocent Taiwan people's benefits at stake.

Table 2.5 The first 20 collocates of (蔡)英文 in our People's Daily corpus

No.	Word	With	Total	Total Left	Total Right
1	当局 (the authorities)	英文	54	3	51
2	台湾 (Taiwan)	英文	50	17	33
3	上台 (take office)	英文	37	6	31
4	领导人 (leader)	英文	35	31	4
5	执政 (govern)	英文	30	7	23
6	民进党 (Democratic Progressive Party)	英文	26	12	14
7	民调 (poll)	英文	18	7	11
8	政策 (policy)	英文	18	2	16
9	两岸 (cross-strait)	英文	17	3	14
10	办公室 (office)	英文	17	0	17
11	支持 (support)	英文	17	7	10
12	台当局 (Taiwan authorities)	英文	16	14	2
13	民众 (the public)	英文	16	13	3
14	上任 (take office)	英文	15	1	14
15	民意 (public opinion)	英文	15	5	10
16	抗议 (protest)	英文	14	10	4
17	台独 (Taiwan independence)	英文	14	4	10
18	台湾地区 (Taiwan region)	英文	14	13	1
19	媒体 (media)	英文	13	8	5
20	团队 (team)	英文	13	1	12

47

Table 2.6 Types of expression formed by 蔡英文 and its collocates

expression type	collocates	example
1. political identity/ affiliation	当局, 领导人, 民进党, 办公室, 台当局, 团队 (Taiwan authorities, leader, Democratic Progressive Party, office, Taiwan authorities, team)	日前，台湾地区 **领导人** **蔡** **英文** 过境 美国 旧金山，数百名 来自 大陆 和 台湾 的 侨胞 自发 前往 其所住 酒店 抗议，高喊 " 一个 中国，反对 台独 " (When leader of the Taiwan region Tsai Ing-wen passed through San Francisco, USA, hundreds of overseas compatriots from the mainland and Taiwan spontaneously went to protest outside the hotel and shouted 'There is only one China; against Taiwan independence'.)
2. political action	上台, 执政, 政策, 上任, 台独 (come to power, take office, take power, policy, Taiwan independence)	自 去年 上台 后，**蔡 英文** 始终 拒绝 承认 " 九二 共识 "，导致 两岸关系 陷入僵局，台湾 的 " 国际 空间 " 明显 紧缩 (Since she took office last year, Tsai Ing-wen has consistently refused to recognize the '1992 consensus', resulting in a deadlock in cross-strait relations and a distinct tightening of 'international space' for Taiwan.)
3. geographical term	台湾, 两岸, 台湾地区 (Taiwan, cross-strait, Taiwan region)	民间 不满 **蔡 英文** 两岸 政策 的 比率 明显 上升，其实 都是 社会 舆情 的 真实 流露 (The apparent increase in public dissatisfaction with the cross-strait policy of Tsai Ing-wen is actually a true expression of public sentiment in society.)
4. general public	民调, 支持, 民众, 民意, 抗议, 媒体 (poll, support, the public, public option, protest, media)	上台 短短 一 年间，**蔡 英文** 当局 引来 的 **抗议** 游行 频繁，用 " 遍地 烽火 " 形容 毫不 为 过 (In just one year since she took office, the protests engendered by Tsai Ing-wen's administration have been so frequent it is not exaggerating to see a 'beacon of war' all over the place.)

Conclusion

We have seen how critical discourse analysis works in the Chinese context in terms of its theoretical and methodological advancements and its political orientation in research agendas and perspectives. In China, political stability, social security/harmony and people's welfare are the most important concerns of the government and for the general public. China's official discourses are usually not objects of scholarly discussion except for giving endorsement or minor critiques. This is different from critical discourse studies in the West where political leaders' speeches, for example, are often critically examined to reveal underlying fallacies. The CDA researchers working on political discourse in China are, on the other hand, more concerned with world politics and international relationships, taking into their hands the responsibility to assert China's peaceful intention to the world and point out the discrepancies between the expected and the often exaggerated national image painted by the foreign press. Our case study also demonstrated that, although it is often not possible or desirable to home in on a person or institution and be critical about their discourse in the Chinese context, we can still use the CDA toolkit to uncover the underlying power structures and value systems embedded in texts and leave the research questions open-ended. In that way, the research agenda of critical discourse analysis in China can still be exciting, inspiring and thought-provoking.

Acknowledgment

This research was sponsored by a scholarship awarded to Weixiao Wei by the State Scholarship Fund through a process organized by the China Scholarship Council (CSC). File No. 201706935062.

References

English references

Bloor, M. and Bloor, T. (2017) 'Systemic functional linguistics', in *The Routledge Handbook of Critical Discourse Studies*. John Flowerdew and John E. Richardson (eds.) Oxon: Routledge. pp. 151–164.
Burch, L.F. (2018) 'Governmentality of Adulthood: A Critical Discourse Analysis of the 2014 Special Educational Needs and Disability Code of Practice', *Disability & Society* 33(1): 94–114.
Hart, C. (2010) *Critical Discourse Analysis and Cognitive Science: New Perspectives on Immigration Discourse*. Basingstoke: Palgrave Macmillan.
Dworin, J.E. and Bomer, R. (2008) 'What We All (Supposedly) Know about the Poor: A Critical Discourse Analysis of Ruby Payne's "Framework"', *English Education* 40(2): 101–121.
Fairclough, N. (2012) 'Critical discourse analysis', in *The Routledge Handbook of Discourse Analysis*. James Paul Gee and Michael Handford (eds.) Oxon: Routledge. pp. 9–20.
Fowler, R. (1991) *Language in the News*. London: Routledge.
Fowler, R., Hodge, B., Kress, G. and Trew, T. (1979) *Language and Social Control*. London: Routledge.
Kelsey, D. (2017) 'Journalism and critical discourse studies', in *The Routledge Handbook of Critical Discourse Studies*. John Flowerdew and John E. Richardson (eds.) Oxon: Routledge. pp. 510–524.
Patton, M.Q. (2002) *Qualitative Research & Evaluation Methods*. Thousand Oaks, CA: Sage.
Rogers, R. (2017) 'Critical discourse analysis and educational discourses', in *The Routledge Handbook of Critical Discourse Studies*. John Flowerdew and John E. Richardson (eds.) Oxon: Routledge. pp. 465–479.
Stacey, G., Felton, A., Morgan, A., Stickley, T., Willis, M.E.H., Diamond, B., Houghton, P., Johnson, B. and Dumenya, J. (2016) 'A critical narrative analysis of shared decision-making in acute inpatient mental health care', *Journal of Interprofessional Care* 30(1): 35–41.
van Dijk, T.A. (1988) *News as Discourse*. Hillsdale, NJ: Lawrence Erlbaum.
van Dijk, T.A. (2015) 'Critical discourse analysis', in *The Handbook of Discourse Analysis* (2nd ed.). Deborah Tannen, Heidi E. Hamilton and Deborah Schiffrin (eds.) Chichester, West Sussex: John Wiley & Sons. pp. 467–485.
Wodak, R. (2011) 'Critical discourse analysis', in *Continuum Companion to Discourse Analysis*. K. Hyland and B. Paltridge (eds.) London and New York: Continuum International Publishing Group. pp. 38–53.

Chinese references

Chang, Cui 常翠 (2016) '讣告语体与逝者评价《人民日报》刊发讣告的批评话语析' (The Genre of Obituary and the Evaluation of the Deceased: A Critical Discourse Analysis of the Obituaries in People's Daily), 天津外国语大学学报 *(Journal of Tianjin Foreign Studies University)* 23(2): 15–21.
Geng, Jing-Bei and Chen, Zi-Juan 耿敬北,陈子娟 (2016) '网络社区多模态话语分析 – 以QQ 群话语为例' (Online Community Multimodal Discourse Analysis – Communicative Discourses from QQ Groups), 外语教学 *(Foreign Language Education)* 37(3): 35–39.
Liu, Wen-Yu and Li, Ke 刘文宇,李珂 (2017) '报刊和微博中老年人身份建构差异研究' (A Study on Different Identity Construction of Older People between Newspaper and Weibo),外语与外语教学 *(Foreign Languages and Their Teaching)* 6: 71–80.

Liu, Li-Hua and Ma, Jun-Jie 刘立华,马俊杰 (2016) '一项基于语料库的新华社对外报道中国梦话语研究' (Chinese Dream and the Construction of Discourse Power: A Case Study of Xinhua News Agency's Report of Chinese Dream from a Corpus-based Discourse Approach), 天津外国语大学学报 *(Journal of Tianjin Foreign Studies University)* 23(1): 29–34.

Miao, Xing-Wei苗兴伟 (2016) '未来话语：中国梦的话语建构' (Discourse of the Future: Discursive Construction of Chinese Dream), 天津外国语大学学报 *(Journal of Tianjin Foreign Studies University)* 23(1): 24–28.

Miao, Xing-Wei and Mu, Jun-Fang苗兴伟, 穆军芳 (2016) '批评话语分析的马克思主义哲学观和方法论' (Marxist Philosophy and Methodology in CDA), 当代语言学 *(Contemporary Linguistics)* 18(4): 532–543.

Mu, Jun-Fang穆军芳 (2016) '国内批评话语分析研究进展的科学知识图谱分析' (1995–2015)' (A Scientometric Analysis of Research Advances in China's Critical Discourse Analysis Research (1995–2015), 山东外语教学 *(Shandong Foreign Language Teaching)* 37(6): 146–154.

Shi, Xu施旭 (2016) '国防话语的较量 – 中美军事战略的文化话语研究' (Defense Discourse Contest: A Study of the Cultural Discourse of Sino-U.S. Military Strategy), 外语研究 *(Foreign Languages Research)* 1: 1–10.

Zhang, Hui and Luo, Yi-Li张辉, 罗一丽 (2017) '战略情报话语的批评认知分析 – 认知语法的视角' (A Critical Cognitive Analysis of Strategic Intelligence Discourse – A Perspective from Cognitive Grammar), 外语研究 *(Foreign Languages Research)* 6: 4–10.

Zhao, Peng赵 芃 (2017) '2016年国内批评话语分析研究综述' (A Study of Domestic Critical Discourse of Analysis in 2016), 天津外国语大学学报 *(Journal of Tianjin Foreign Studies University)* 24(4): 72–79.

3
Sociolinguistic approaches to Chinese discourse

Wei Wang

Introduction

Sociolinguistics investigates the relationship between language and society. As its name suggests, it was born as a multidisciplinary field (Coupland, 2016) that might involve disciplines such as linguistics, sociology, psychology, anthropology, education, cultural studies, media studies, etc. It becomes a cover term for segments of different fields, such as variationist sociolinguistics, the social psychology of language, linguistic anthropology, the ethnography of communication, interactional sociolinguistics, linguistic ethnography, sociocultural linguistics, etc. In addition to providing insights to language maintenance and policy making, sociolinguistics also provides researchers with theories and frameworks to deal with language and discourse occurring in diverse social contexts.

The variationist approach of sociolinguistics, first established by Labov (1966, 1972a, 1972b) and his followers, laid the foundation of sociolinguistics as an independent discipline. The key concerns of this approach (i.e. language variation, change, and structure) remain important issues in contemporary linguistics research. Following that, sociolinguistics was extended with the developments of the anthropological approach by Hymes (1974; Gumperz and Hymes, 1972) and interactional sociolinguistics by Gumperz (1982, 2001) among many other approaches. More recently, a sociocultural linguistic approach was initiated by Bucholtz and Hall (2005, 2008) with a view to distinguishing itself from the traditional variationist sociolinguistics, often associated with the quantitative analysis of linguistic features and their correlation to sociological variables. The term 'sociocultural linguistics' is currently used to indicate a broadly interdisciplinary approach to language, culture and society.

The diverse approaches in sociolinguistics can be roughly put in a continuum with 'social' and 'linguistic' orientations at opposite ends. Each approach can be aligned at some point on this continuum. Viewing sociolinguistics as a broad discipline, its linguistic range covers examinations of language variation and change in phonological, lexical, and morphological levels, while its social range extends to research on societal bilingualism or multilingualism, language maintenance and shift, language contact, language ideology, and language planning, etc. In light of their influence on Chinese discourse studies, the discussion below is limited to three sociolinguistic approaches, namely variationist, interactional and sociocultural.

Wei Wang

Variationist approach

Sociolinguists widely attribute the seminal studies of language variation and change in the variationist approach to research conducted by William Labov (1963, 1966, 1969, 1972). Variationist sociolinguistics is concerned with linguistic variation and change in written and spoken language. While linguistic variation is concerned with synchronic differences in speakers' pronunciation, word choice, morphology, or syntax, linguistic change examines the diachronic developments of language. The central idea of this approach is that language varies systematically in accordance with social characteristics of the speakers and the social context in which the language is used. Weinreich and his colleagues (1968: 99–100) argue that linguistic variation is characterized by orderly or 'structured heterogeneity'. That means speakers' choices among variable linguistic forms are systematically constrained by multiple linguistic and social factors. The speakers' language use and the underlying grammatical system also reflect and partially constitute the social organization of the communities to which users of the language belong. This approach aims to uncover the correlation between language variation, especially at phonological, lexical and syntactical levels, and social/cultural factors, such as ethnicity, religion, temporal and spatial differences, gender, age, level of education and occupation.

In terms of research method, variationist sociolinguistics often features large-scale quantitative studies examining the correlation between language forms and language user variables. Contemporary variationist research has also extended its focus from the analysis of traditional aspects of linguistic variation and change, i.e. the phonological, morpho-syntactic, to discourse and pragmatic aspects, while incorporating contemporary quantitative methods and statistical practice.

The variationist approach was first introduced to mainland China in the late 1970s and 1980s (e.g. Zhu, 1985; Chen, 1985), and it has been consistently followed and promoted by a group of Chinese scholars for Chinese discourse studies. Chen's (1999) was the first monograph in Chinese that systematically introduces theories on language variation and change, relevant research methods, and applications of the research. Xu (2006) provided a comprehensive review of the variationist approach in Western contexts, discussing new developments in the field and delineating the potential applications of these theories in Chinese contexts.

Replicating the research of language variation and change in Western contexts, Chinese scholars have investigated variations and changes of Chinese as a result of social and technological development, language contact, and other factors, not only at the lexical level, but also at phonological, syntactic, pragmatic and stylistic levels (e.g. Su, 2010; Xu et al., 2005, 2010; Zhang, 2005). Xu and his colleagues employed this approach to investigate Chinese language variations in the city, for example, the use of *Putonghua*, Nanjing dialect, and other linguistic varieties by people of different genders and age in Nanjing (e.g. Xu and Fu, 2005; Xu and Wang, 2010). Drawing on Labov's 'rapid anonymous observation', they also designed the 'Asking-the-Way' data collection technique to collect street data of linguistic variation by asking people the way in the standard variety (i.e. *Putonghua*) (Xu and Fu, 2005). This study finds that, though most interviewees' 'insider language' (i.e. language used to communicate with family, friends, and all acquaintances) is not Mandarin, nearly 100% of the interviewees accept Mandarin as the daily communication tool, especially as an 'outsider language' to communicate with strangers.

Zhang (2005) examined four phonological variables (i.e. rhotacization, lenition, interdental, full tone) closely linking to the local Beijing Mandarin among Chinese professionals in foreign and state-owned companies in Beijing. Her study demonstrated that professionals in foreign businesses employ linguistic resources from both local and global sources to construct a new cosmopolitan variety of Mandarin, whereas their counterparts in state-owned businesses favor the use of local features. This study shows that the linguistic practice of professionals in foreign companies in the local site of Beijing is inseparable from what is happening in the transnational Chinese community and the global market. They see themselves as belonging simultaneously to Beijing, mainland China, and the international business world. Their sense of flexible belonging is articulated through their linguistic behaviors. This study also indicates that the linguistic variation does not just reflect existing social categories and social change, but is a resource for constructing those categories and participates in social change.

While a considerable amount of previous research in Chinese contexts has largely emphasized linguistic variations and changes in terms of forms, types and the sociocultural reasons behind these variations and changes in scattered social groups and geographical areas, Cao (2013) provided a systematic and comprehensive study which aims to uncover the patterns and structures of these variations and changes, and explore the relationship between these changes and the original Chinese language structure. This endeavor is much in line with the central mission in variationist sociolinguistics. His study examines the emergence of new elements in modern Chinese language in the aspects of vocabulary, semantics and grammar. It reveals that with lexical innovation and deviation from or violation of the rules of the original Chinese language system, the modern Chinese language is in constant progress to forming new norms and patterns because of various social and linguistic factors. These changes have made huge impacts on different levels of traditional Chinese language, but on the other hand, they promote language development through expansion of vocabulary and grammatical systems.

Interactional approach

If we postulate the variationist approach as aligned at the linguistic end of sociolinguistics, the interactional approach is situated in the middle of the socio/linguistic continuum that explores how language is used to create meaning via social interactions. The work drawing on this approach includes research on participants, the norms of interaction and audience, and the social construction of meaning through language choices and changes. Unlike the variationist approach, interactional sociolinguistics, represented by John Gumperz (1982), extends the units of analysis to the larger context of language use and to larger stretches of language use such as conversations and texts. This approach is largely qualitative in nature and aims to combine wider contextual knowledge with linguistic analysis to illuminate the interpretive processes of interaction. Like other branches in sociolinguistics, interactional sociolinguistics bears a strong social/cultural agenda in its linguistic exploration. It aims to demonstrate the connection between 'small-scale interactions' and 'large-scale sociological effects' (Jacquemet, 2011: 475), providing a 'dynamic view of social environments where history, economic forces and interactive processes . . . combine to create or to eliminate social distinctions' (Gumperz, 1982: 29). Scholars in this field also work to identify communication problems as a result of linguistic and cultural diversity and aim to address social issues such as inequality, discrimination, social injustice through examination of language use. Having been developed in an anthropological context of cross-cultural comparison, interactional sociolinguistics has also focused largely on contexts of intercultural miscommunication, including intercultural and inter-group communication, and comparative research.

Although research methods used in interactional sociolinguistic research often blend tools and theories from pragmatics, conversation analysis, politeness and other linguistic theories, interactional sociolinguistics usually makes use of both ethnographic and linguistic methods to investigate language use in interaction (Gumperz, 2001). Ethnographic research is often used at the initial stage of the research to provide insights into the local communication setting; to identify representative data relevant to the research question; and to check whether the analyst's expectations and interpretations are in line with or contrary to the local interlocutors. Following up on that, the researchers examine audio or video-recordings of conversations or other interactions by drawing on various linguistic methods. They analyze linguistic forms such as words, sentences and even the whole text, as well as other subtle cues such as prosody and register what the interlocutors rely on in the communication process. Interactional sociolinguistics has been widely used in investigating linguistic interaction in various social settings and professional domains.

In the field of Chinese discourse studies, interactional sociolinguistics was first introduced as a discourse-analytical approach by Xu et al. (1997) and Xu (2002), followed by a series of introductory and commentary publications in Chinese in the new century. Drawing on interactional sociolinguistics as a developing research field in discourse studies, an increasing number of empirical studies has been conducted to examine Chinese discourse (e.g. Endo, 2013; Pan and Kadar, 2013; Wang, X., 2015; Zhu, 2016). Pan and Kadar (2013) brought together empirical studies that employ diverse methods and analytic frameworks in interactional sociolinguistics in analyzing data sources derived from various Chinese contexts, including mainland China, Hong Kong, Taiwan, Singapore and other overseas Chinese communities. For example, in Pan and Kadar's (2013) collection, Endo (2013) examined the sentential positions and functions of a Chinese expression *wo juede* (我觉得 'I think') and its relation to the epistemic stance that speakers take in conversation. It was found that Chinese speakers modulate social relations with their interlocutors by changing the positions of *wo juede* ('I think') in conversation.

By drawing on interactional sociolinguistics, Wang, X. (2015) examined the supportive verbal feedback such as some interjection or exclamation words like mh (嗯), ah (啊), yeah (对), or some non-verbal feedback signals like nodding, in naturally occurring Chinese conversation with a view to exploring the influence of social factors on supportive verbal feedback. The study investigated the form, pragmatic function and the distribution of verbal supportive feedback in Chinese natural conversations and discussed the interactive mechanism and characteristics of supportive feedback in the Chinese language.

Zhu (2016) investigated extended concurrent speech and guānxì (Chinese: 关系, i.e. relationship) management in Mandarin. Drawing on interactional sociolinguistics (incl. conversation analysis and ethnographic information concerning the participants' relational history, occupation, age, sex and social distance), this study explores extended concurrent speech as a strategy for guānxì management employed by non-familial equal-status Mandarin speakers in everyday practice. Spontaneous mundane conversations (incl. 8 extracts being presented in the article) were analyzed and interpreted with the focuses on central linguistic features and marginalized contextualization cues, which situate inferences in contexts. The participants were found to co-construct extended concurrent speech to maintain or enhance guānxì without any manifestations of negative evaluation. This study suggests the importance of situating research in local and large contexts, and the necessity to examine extended concurrent speech, floor taking and topic switching in different varieties of Chinese language.

In addition, Wu and her colleagues (2016) reviewed and critiqued many sociolinguistic studies on new media during recent decades and proposed future directions for research in this area of inquiry. They call for cross-disciplinary endeavors to be attempted in the theoretical, perspective aspects as well as the methodological aspect in order to better describe, interpret, and predict patterns and development of human interaction in digital times. They also suggest more interactional sociolinguistics and multimodality studies to be conducted in the domain of new media in Chinese language.

Sociocultural linguistics

In the new century, due to disciplinary and methodological distinctions, the term 'sociolinguistics' was often used to only refer to variationist approach in sociolinguistics, that explores the correlation between language forms and language user variables using large-scale quantitative analysis (Shuy, 2003; Spolsky, 2010). In outlining the current developments in sociolinguistic studies and their difference from the traditional variationist approach, Bucholtz and Hall (2005, 2008) advocated the use of the term 'sociocultural linguistics' to highlight the interdisciplinary efforts used to explore the interrelationship between language, individual, culture, and society. In the same vein, scholars in Europe talk about 'linguistic ethnography' (Blommaert, 2005; Rampton et al., 2015) to emphasize the importance of incorporating ethnography into linguistic studies. These two schools, sharing many commonalities, can be regarded as the current efforts to bring together the traditionally separate anthropological and linguistic approaches to language. In the traditional sense, anthropological approaches including interactional linguistics have sought to illuminate culture through investigation of speech events (e.g. Hymes, 1974) and interactional practices (e.g. Gumperz, 1982), whereas the linguistic approach has largely drawn on social information to address issues of linguistic structure, variation and change (e.g. Labov, 1966). In promoting a broadly interdisciplinary sociocultural approach to language and discourse, sociocultural linguistics aims to 'forge an alliance or coalition that fosters dialogue and collaboration between complementary approaches' (Bucholtz and Hall, 2008: 403) in the investigation of language and discourse to illuminate social and cultural processes.

As argued by Bucholtz and Hall (2008: 423), the key strengths of sociocultural linguistics lie in the ethnographic grounding of linguistic anthropology and the rigorous analytic tools of quantitative sociolinguistics and conversation analysis for the detailed investigation of linguistic and interactional structures. Bucholtz and Hall (2008) illustrated sociocultural linguistic approach by re-examining the data collected as part of an ethnographic sociolinguistic study of language, race, and youth culture conducted by Bucholtz in 1995–96 at 'Bay City High School', an ethnically diverse and racially divided urban high school in the San Francisco Bay Area. This study brings the previous ethnographic interview data to the focus of the detailed interactional linguistic analysis. In this data re-examining process, the informal ethnographic interviews used to solicit demographic data information such as name, age, grade level and gender are analyzed in depth by drawing on tools in interactional linguistic analysis. This reanalysis of data yielded rich insights into the students' dilemma in the self-representation of their ethnicity (see detailed analysis in Bucholtz and Hall, 2008: 413–416). It shows that the research interviews in sociolinguistics studies cannot only provide mere background information but also be taken as a medium from which to extract linguistic variables as well as richly contextualized linguistic data in their own right.

Similar to Bucholtz and Hall, Rampton and his UK/Europe-based colleagues described linguistic ethnography (LE) as a 'discursive space' and 'a site of encounter' (Rampton, 2007a, 2007b; Rampton et al., 2015) that brings together scholars with mixed interests and backgrounds in broad alignment with two basic tenets. First, LE scholars assume that the contexts for communication should be investigated rather than assumed. Meaning takes shape within specific social relations, interactional histories and institutional regimes, produced and construed by agents with expectations and repertoires that have to be grasped ethnographically; second, analysis of the internal organization of verbal (and other kinds of semiotic) data is essential to understanding its significance and position in the world. Meaning is far more than just the 'expression of ideas', and biography, identifications, stance and nuance are extensively signaled in the linguistic and textual fine-grain.

Rampton (2007b) illustrates that linguistic ethnography investigates communication within the temporal unfolding of social processes that involve 1) persons, 2) situated encounters, 3) institutions, networks and communities of practice. LE scholars draw on Goffman's perspective (1959, 1967, 1974, 1981) to analyze the whole of what's going on in a communicative event – the physical setting and the participants' positionings, their interactional histories and projects, their institutional and ethnic identities, the topic that they are talking about, their words and their actions.

Scholars drawing on sociocultural linguistics or linguistic ethnography generally hold that language and social life are mutually shaping, and that close analysis of situated language use can provide both fundamental and typical insights into the mechanisms and dynamics of social and cultural practices (Bucholtz and Hall, 2005; Rampton et al., 2015).

In unravelling the intricate relation between language and society, contemporary developments in sociocultural linguistics and linguistic ethnography show increasing interest in small-scale qualitative studies that incorporate ethnographic methods in their socio-cultural linguistic investigation. The following study (Wang, W., 2015) is presented as an example of the small-scale qualitative study that employs the sociocultural approach just described.

Case study

This study examines how identities of migrant workers (i.e. 农民工 *Nongmin Gong*) have been constructed and represented by public media in China. The data for the study were collected from the production and broadcasting process of a TV talk show program in China, called "*China's Nongmin Gong*" (Chinese: 中国农民工), launched by Guizhou Satellite TV (GZSTV) in China in 2007. Drawing on sociocultural linguistic theories on interaction and identity (Bucholtz and Hall, 2005, 2008), and a dramaturgical model of social interaction analysis (Goffman, 1959, 1974), the study explores how the migrant workers' personal life experiences have been transformed into media discourse.

'*China's Nongmin Gong*' is a 40-minute talk show between a host/hostess and one or two migrant worker interviewees, talking about the migrant workers' life experience. It is broadcast once a week by Guizhou Satellite TV (GZSTV), a provincial broadcasting system based in southwestern China, Guizhou province. Located inland in an underdeveloped area of China, this province is a major exporter of migrant workers to other parts of the country every year, which has provided the GZSTV with abundant resources for its coverage of this floating population.

Narrative identities of the migrant workers on this TV program

In discourse studies and sociolinguistics, narrative or storytelling is considered as the 'basic', most 'essential', mode of human communication (Blommaert, 2005: 84). In this talk show program, storytelling/narrative is the key means through which particular aspects of reality and specific facets of the interviewees' identities are co-constructed by themselves and the host/hostess in the program. In doing so, they are constructing a narrative identity by integrating their life experiences into an internalized, evolving story of the self, which provides the individual with a sense of unity and purpose in life (Lorenzo-Dus, 2009; McAdams, 2001). Being identified as typified or outstanding migrants, interviewees are asked to share their life stories on the TV screen. However, they are usually inexperienced media performers, yet are expected to tell 'true stories' about themselves and deliver 'authentic talks' to express their opinions. To achieve this, their participation in the program must be much guided or even manipulated by the television crews, and particularly by the hosts in the studio. Consequently, this study aims at examining the discursive practices used by the public media to achieve this sociolinguistic construction of migrant workers' identities. Their discursive practices are analyzed through three distinctive stages of the production, namely 'off stage', 'back stage', and 'front stage'.

In analyzing the narrative identities of the migrant workers, we also draw on the notion of abnormality, which is attributed to Michel Foucault's *Abnormal* (2003). As noted by Dong (2013), migrants in China are often regarded as 'abnormal individuals', since they cannot be integrated into the normative system in the cities. According to Foucault (2003: 162), the norm is the 'rule of conduct, the tacit law, the principle of order and conformity, against which irregularity, disorder, disorganization, dysfunction, deviation are measured and disqualified'. In this sense, contemporary public discourse in China often regards the migrant worker as someone that deviates from the 'normal' as they have often introduced disorder to, and disruption of, the established normative system in cities (Dong, 2013).

In the context of the public discourse of abnormality around migrant workers, the TV show program '*China's Nongmin Gong*' attempts to provide a counter-discourse (Foucault, 1977) by tempering the perception of abnormality of migrant worker' identities and advocating their normality or even their super-normality. With a view to doing this, this TV program presents to its audience that the migrant workers are as 'normal' as all ordinary people and even 'supernormal' (i.e. better than or exceeding the normal), which is achieved partly through being selected for the TV show.

The data in this study consist of 48 episodes of the '*China's Nongmin Gong*' program broadcast across 2007–2009, and the interviews and observation notes collected through ten days fieldwork by the researcher with the TV crews in 2010. Despite the wide variety of the migrant workers' life experiences showcased in the program, a content analysis of the 48 episodes reveals some common features of their narrative identities that might have made the interviewees exceptional or supernormal. These features include representing the migrant workers as 1) diligent and frugal individuals striving for success; 2) perseverant and confident in face of adversities in life; 3) proactive with visions and strategies. These features in their narrative identities have been well-presented in the TV program through the interviewees' storytelling of their personal experiences.

Discursive practices in the co-construction of identities

The study aims to investigate how the narrative identities of the migrant workers have been represented and manipulated in the media. Drawing on a dramaturgical model of social interaction analysis, interaction between the migrant workers and the TV crew has been analyzed in terms of how they operate as actors performing around the stage (Macionis and Gerber, 2011). The model adopted here has its origin in Goffman's work (1959, 1977), which made an important demarcation between "front stage" and "back stage" behaviors. As the term indicates, "front stage" actions are visible to the audience and are part of the performance. People engage in "back stage" behavior when no audience is present. In this study, 'back stage' refers to the intensive preparation between the TV crew and the migrant worker participants in getting ready for the live 'front stage' performance. 'Off stage' is the term used in this study to refer to the living circumstance of the participants' private life that is distant from the TV studio and it is out of audience sight. The following sections will briefly illustrate the three-stage production of this sociolinguistic construction of identities.

Reaching into the 'off stage' life

Upon being spotted by the media, the interviewees' 'off stage' life is invaded and interfered with by the program crew, who usually pay an on-site visit to the potential interviewees. In this on-site visit, the crew observes, records and interacts with the interviewees and the people around them. Short video clips are shot to focus on some facets of the interviewees' life experience that are considered 'useful' for the program.

At this stage, the interviewees are briefed about the goals and procedures of the TV program. Thus, the migrant workers' 'off stage' life and space, which was previously invisible to the audience, has been accessed by the crew and some aspects of their life are captured for the TV presentation.

'Back stage' preparation

Then, the interviewees are invited to the studio for the 'back stage' preparation of the program. Despite it being claimed a live show, this program makes the participants fully aware of what they should talk about on the show and how they should do it. As a crucial step of the 'back stage', the producer and the program host have a 'lengthy talk' with the interviewee to decide what should be covered at the 'front stage'. The 'lengthy talk' (Chinese: 长谈), so called by the program director, usually takes several sessions over a few days, enabling the program crew to have a thorough understanding of the participants' life, and, more importantly, enabling them to draft a script for the live show on the basis of this 'back stage' interaction.

This script (see an extract in Table 3.1), which serves as a running sheet for the program, covers the key steps of the program and the major points that the program host will bring up. As the professional presenter, the host controls the shape, the length and even the content of the program by following the running sheet with its key questions and points. Below is an extract of such a running sheet with the pre-scripted host's key questions.

'Front stage' performance

The 'reality' talk show interweaves two main sites of the participants: the immediate site of the studio, in which the interview takes place, and the visually marked and dynamic sites from the interviewees' daily life, which have been captured by the pre-recorded video clips. As indicated in Table 3.1, the interviewee in this episode was a music teacher at a rural primary school before migrating to Beijing to become a singer. At the beginning of the program, the host introduced him with a pre-recorded video clip, presenting his background and his school for migrant children. Using the pre-scripted opening remarks and key questions, the host facilitates direct access to the socio-historical world from which the interviewee comes to tell viewers 'true stories' about 'real people'.

As the key player in the reproduction of the migrant workers' life stories, the program host acts as a coaxer who helps the lay participants spell out what the media wants them to say, encouraging them to dwell on certain aspects of their stories and telling the stories in a particular tone of voice. These practices can be simply termed scaffolding in co-construction of the desirable identities of migrant workers for this program. Here scaffolding practices refers to a variety of linguistic practices that the media staff draw on to support presentation of the migrant workers' identities. These include strategies of eliciting, positive feedback, reinforcement, topic change, and, more importantly, foregrounding and backgrounding of specific aspects of the participants' identities. These discursive strategies are discussed below.

ELICITING AND POSITIVE FEEDBACK

Eliciting and positive feedback, commonly employed by the host to introduce the stories or topics, are often manifested in the form of a question, or a statement as a reminder in the live interview.

Sociolinguistic approaches

Table 3.1 A sample of the running sheets for the program

序号 [no.]	环节 [steps]	内容 [content]	要点 [key hints]
1	开场 [opening]	[key lines by the interviewer] 观众朋友，这里是"中国农民工"讲述节目，欢迎收看。欢迎我们节目的嘉宾，来自北京的孙恒，也欢迎来参加我们节目的现场的观众朋友们。先来看一个短片来认识一下今天做客我们节目的嘉宾。[Dear audience, here is the "China's Migrant Workers" program, welcome. Welcome Sun Heng, the participant from Beijing to our program. Also welcome the audience to the site to participate in our program. First, a short film to introduce our guest for our program today.]	
…	…	……	
4	Video clip 2	[Introduction to the school run by Sun Heng] 同心实验学校位于北京朝阳区的金盏乡皮村，距市中心有近两小时的车程。孙恒选择在这里办学校，一是因为地价便宜，二是因为这里聚居着众多的外来打工者，而本地村民只有外来人口的十分之一。[Tongxin Experimental School is located in Pi Village, Jinzhan Township of Chaoyang District, Beijing, about two hours' drive from the city centre. Sun Heng chose here as the location for the school; first because land price is low, second it is inhabited by a large number of migrant workers and local villagers was only one-tenth.] …	
5	演播室访谈 [studio interview]	[key questions by the interviewer] 1. 问：孙恒有没有孩子？他的孩子将来会不会在这里读书。[Q: Does Sun Heng have children? Will his children attend school here in the future?] 2. 问：你怎么想到成立打工青年艺术团的？[Q: What do you think about the establishment of a working youth art ensemble?]	突出那段打工经历给他带来的人生影响 [Highlight the impacts that work experience made on his life] 这个阶段还处于寻找人生道路的迷茫时期 [This stage in his life is the lost time in finding out his life goal.]

Extract 1

1 主持人／你干的是什么工作？[Interviewer/what kind of work do you do?]
2 余大娇／我现在干的是检查员。[Yu Dajiao/I'm now working as an inspector.]
3 主持人／是一个技术性比较高的工作嘛！[Interviewer/ It is a technical job now!]

59

4		余大娇／对。开始因为在里面做事认真、老实，最开始是(普通)员工，最后提到检查员，因为检查员是较好的一个部门。[Yu Dajiao/ Ye. Because I started working with conscientiousness and honesty. At the beginning, I'm a (normal) employee, and was promoted to be an inspector because inspectors are in a good department.]
5		主持人／<u>这个工作是招进去的，还是考进去的？</u> [Interviewer/ You got the job through recruitment or exam?]
6		余大娇／凭自己的实力考进去的，那个厂的效益也是比较好。[Yu Dajiao/ Through an exam with my own strength. The salary in the factory is relatively good.]

In Ext.1, the host deliberately formed the questions about the interviewee's current job by following the eliciting strategy step by step. First (L.1) is the opening question to start the topic; second (L.3) is the elaboration of the topic and positive feedback to what she has done; third (L. 5) is an alternative question (i.e. you got the job through recruitment or a test), exploring how the interviewee got the job. This eliciting strategy aims to highlight two key points regarding the interviewee: 1) the interviewee got a technical job with a higher status due to her '认真、老实' (conscientiousness and honesty); 2) she got the job via passing an exam based on her own capacity. This eliciting strategy enables the host to introduce the topics and guide the interviewees through to spell out the desirable stories.

REINFORCEMENT AND TOPIC CHANGE

Reinforcement, a strategy used to confirm and stress the interviewees' remarks and feelings, was frequently observed in the host's front stage performance. For instance, in the story about Yu Dajiao (details in Ext 1), some questions (underlined in Ext. 2) are found in the host's utterances. Note that these questions are for emphasis or to seek confirmation of the previous remarks rather than to elicit different answers from the interviewee. Here the host purposely repeats or strengthens the interviewees' utterances to draw the attention of the audience.

Extract 2

1 余大娇／一件衣服才十五块。[Yu Dajiao/it is just 15 yuan for each clothes]

   主持人／<u>十五块钱啊!?</u>[Host/ only 15 yuan?!]

2 余海深／开始的话，我一般都是买一下衣服。买的衣服都是很便宜，都是在三四十块钱以下的，都是很便宜的，然后就没有其他的了。[Yu Haishen/ at the beginning, I started with buying some clothes. All the clothing is very cheap, below 30–40 yuan, very cheap, then, buy nothing else.]

   主持人／<u>就没有其他的了?</u>[host/ nothing else?]

Another strategy employed by the host is 'topic change'. It is a discursive technique used by the host to change topics and keep up the pace of the program. In doing so, the host uses hedge phrases or structures, such as 'it seems …' (好像), 'I heard that …' (我听说), 'it is heard that …' (听说) to initiate a new topic when he needs the interviewee to get onto it immediately. For instance,

---

Extract 3

1   主持人／好像你当时思想斗争挺利害的, <u>好像还专门请了一天假去看了一下上海</u>? [Host/ It seems that at that time you were quite conflicted and asked one day leave to visit Shanghai.]

2   主持人／你在那儿, 刚开始去的时候, 也干的是装卸工, <u>后来听说你当队长是自荐的, 自己推荐自己的</u>? [Host/ you were a loader as the start there. Then, it was heard that you self-recommended yourself to be the team leader, self-recommended?]

Here the host uses phrases or sentences to introduce a new topic that he wants the interviewees to talk about next. 'Topic change' here is a technique commonly used by the host to control the pace of the program and to help the interviewees cover the anticipated stories that the program requires them to spell out. It is assumed that in the 'back stage', the host has acquired all the stories that could be told 'on stage', where he is just using this topic change strategy to prompt the new topic on time.

FOREGROUNDING AND BACKGROUNDING

As drawn from Fairclough's work on discourse and social change (1995), foregrounding refers to the practice of emphasizing some concepts or issues in the text, while backgrounding alludes to the practice of playing down concepts or issues in the text. The term 'foregrounding' would overlap in some cases with the term 'reinforcement' and be similar to 'positive feedback'. It is found in this TV program that backgrounding is probably more implicitly presented than foregrounding. However, a distinctive example found in the dataset is in the life story of a migrant worker called Deng Qimao (Extract 4).

Extract 4

主持人／什么错误?你能不能跟我们说一说? [Hostess/what's wrong? Can you tell us about that?]

邓启茂／ . . . 那人就讲了, 弄菜去. 可能就是偷菜了。当时就比较胆怯, 不愿意去。但是人家说你了, 我们天天弄给你吃, 你吃了我们. 你不去弄不行啊, 去的过程当中就被逮着了。 [Deng Qimao/ . . . The man told me to get the veggies. He probably meant stealing. I was a bit shy and unwilling to go. But he said, 'we provide you with food every day. Since you feed on us, you have to go'. So I got caught in the process of doing so.

主持人／<u>等于就是到农民的菜地去摘点菜</u>? [Hostess/ It appears that you <u>picked some vegetables</u> from the farmer's farm?]

邓启茂／到菜地我还没有去摘, 我就在路边站着看他摘。他去摘, 来人了, 他跑了, 把我逮着了。 . . . [Deng Qimao/I haven't picked but standing on the sidewalk, I saw him pick. He picked and the people came. He ran away, and they caught me. . . .]

Here the host attempts to background the interviewee's misconduct of stealing by calling it 'pick veggies from the farm'. While misconduct such as theft and violence have been common complaints by urbanites against migrant workers, the host here deliberately downplays this complaint in order to promote positive images of this population, which might be the key social function of this reality TV talk show program.

Conclusion

This case study revealed how the TV crew drew on diverse discursive strategies and linguistic resources to transform the migrant workers' personal experience to a form suitable for a public media program. As a demonstration of the sociocultural linguistic approach to discourse analysis, this small-scale study employed a wide range of theories and concepts, including sociocultural linguistic theories in identity and interaction, the dramaturgical model of social interaction, Foucault's 'abnormality' and Fairclough's 'foregrounding and backgrounding', to name just a few. This fusion of theories and concepts constructed a theoretical repertoire in addressing the research question of the study, i.e. how the identities of migrant workers have been constructed and represented in public media in China. By employing both ethnographic and linguistic methods, this study exemplified the modern interdisciplinary trend to explore social issues through examination of language use, thus exemplifying the sociolinguistic approach to discourse analysis.

References

English references

Blommaert, Jan (2005) *Discourse*. Cambridge: Cambridge University Press.
Bucholtz, M. and Hall, K. (2005) 'Identity and Interaction: A Sociocultural Linguistic Approach', *Discourse Studies* 7(4–5): 585–614.
Bucholtz, M. and Hall, K. (2008) 'All of the Above: New Coalitions in Sociocultural Linguistics', *Journal of Sociolinguistics* 12(4): 401–431.
Coupland, N. (2016) 'Introduction: Sociolinguistic theory and the practice of sociolinguistics', in *Sociolinguistics: Theoretical Debates*. N. Coupland (ed.) Cambridge: Cambridge University Press. pp. 1–34.
Dong, J. (2013) 'When Modern Public Space Encounters Postmodern Migration: Abnormality and the Making of Migrant Identities', *Sociolinguistic Studies*, 6(2): 239–257.
Endo, T. (2013) 'Epistemic stance in Mandarin conversation: The positions and functions of wo juede (I feel/think)', in *Chinese Discourse and Interaction: Theory and Practice*. Y. Pan and D.Z. Kádár (eds.) London: Equinox. pp. 12–34.
Fairclough, N. (1995) *Discourse and Social Change*. Cambridge: Polity Press.
Foucault, M. (1977) *Language, Counter-Memory, Practice: Selected Essays and Interviews*, ed. with a preface by Donald F. Bouchard; trans. Donald F. Bouchard and Sherry Simon. Oxford: Blackwell.
Foucault, M. (2003) *Abnormal*. New York: Picador.
Goffman, E. (1959) *The Presentation of Self in Everyday Life*. New York: Anchor Books for Doubleday.
Goffman, E. (1967) *Interaction Ritual: Essays in Face-to-face Behavior*. Chicago, London: Aldine Pub.
Goffman, E. (1974) *Frame Analysis: An Essay on the Organization of Experience*. New York: Harper and Row.
Goffman, E. (1981) *Forms of Talk*. Philadelphia: University of Pennsylvania Press.
Gumperz, J. (1982) *Discourse Strategies*, Cambridge: Cambridge University Press.
Gumperz, J. (2001) 'Interactional sociolinguistics: A personal perspective', in *The Handbook of Discourse Analysis*. Deborah Schiffrin, Deborah Tannen and Heidi Hamilton (eds.) Malden, MA: Blackwell. pp. 215–228.
Gumperz, J. and Hymes, D. (eds.) (1972) *Directions in Sociolinguistics: The Ethnography of Communication*. New York: Holt, Rhinehart & Winston.

Hymes, D. (1974) *Foundations in Sociolinguistics: An Ethnographic Approach*. Philadelphia: University of Pennsylvania Press.
Jacquemet, M. (2011) 'Crosstalk 2.0: Asylum and communicative breakdown', in *In Honour of John Gumperz*, Auer and Roberts (eds.). Special issue of *Text and Talk*. 31(4): 475–498.
Labov, W. (1963) 'The social motivation of a sound change', *Word* 19: 273–309.
Labov, W. (1966) *The Social Stratification of English in New York City*. Washington, DC: Center for Applied Linguistics.
Labov, W. (1969) *The Study of Nonstandard English*. Washington, DC: National Council of Teachers of English, 1969.
Labov, W. (1972a) *Sociolinguistic Patterns*. Philadelphia: Pennsylvania University Press.
Labov, W. (1972b) *Language in the Inner City: Studies in the Black English Vernacular*. Philadelphia: University of Pennsylvania Press.
Lorenzo-Dus, Nuria (2009) *Television Discourse: Analyzing Language in the Media*. Basingstoke [England]; New York: Palgrave Macmillan.
Macionis, John J. and Gerber, Linda M. (2011) *Sociology* (7th ed.). Toronto: Pearson Canada.
McAdams, D (2001) 'The Psychology of Life Stories', *Review of General Psychology* 5(2): 100–122.
Pan, Y. and Kádár, D.Z. (eds.) (2013) *Chinese Discourse and Interaction: Theory and Practice*. London: Equinox.
Rampton, B. (2007a) 'Neo-Hymesian Linguistic Ethnography in the United Kingdom', *Journal of Sociolinguistics* 11(5): 584–607.
Rampton, B. (2007b) 'Linguistic Ethnography, Interactional Sociolinguistics and the Study of Identities', *Working Papers in Urban Language & Literacies*, Paper 43. Retrieved from www.kcl.ac.uk/sspp/departments/education/research/Research-Centres/ldc/publications/workingpapers/the-papers/43.pdf
Rampton, B., Maybin, J. and Roberts, C. (2015) 'Theory and method in linguistic ethnography', in *Linguistic Ethnography: Interdisciplinary Explorations*. F. Copland, S. Shaw and J. Snell (eds.). Basingstoke: Palgrave Macmillan. pp. 14–50.
Shuy, R.W. (2003) 'A brief history of American sociolinguistics 1949–1989', in *Sociolinguistics: The Essential Readings*. C.B. Paulston and G.R. Tucker (eds.) Malden, MA: Blackwell. pp. 4–16.
Spolsky, B. (2010) 'Ferguson and Fishman: Sociolinguistics and the sociology of language', in *The Sage Handbook of Sociolinguistics*. R. Wodak, B. Johnstone and P. Kerswill (eds.) Los Angeles: SAGE. pp. 11–23.
Wang, W. (2015) 'Co-construction of Migrant Workers' Identities on a TV Talk Show in China', in *Contemporary Chinese Discourse and Social Practice in China*. W. Wang and L. Tsung (eds.) Amsterdam/Philadelphia: John Benjamins. pp. 125–142.
Weinreich, U., Labov, W. and Herzog, M. (1968) 'Empirical foundations for a theory of language change', in *Directions for Historical Linguistics: A Symposium*. W.P. Lehmann and Y. Malkiel (eds.) Austin: Univ. of Texas Press. pp. 95–195.
Zhang, Q. (2005) 'A Chinese yuppie in Beijing: Phonological Variation and the Construction of a New Professional Identity', *Language in Society* 32: 431–466.
Zhu, Weihua (2016) 'Extended Concurrent Speech and guānxì Management in Mandarin', *Text & Talk* 36(5): 637–660.

Chinese references

Cao, Q. 曹起 (2013) 新时期现代汉语变异研究 *(Research on Variations of Contemporary Chinese Language in the New Era)* (PhD Thesis), Changchun: Jilin University.
Chen, S.陈松岑 (1985) 社会语言学导论 *(Introduction to Sociolinguistics)*. Beijing: Peking University Press.
Chen, S.陈松岑 (1999) 语言变异研究 *(Research on Language Variation)*. Guangzhou: Guangdong Education Press.
Su, J. 苏金智 (2010) '语言接触与语言借用：汉语借词消长研究' (Language Contact and Language Borrowing: The Fluctuating Development of Loan Words in Chinese), 中国语言学报 *(Journal of Chinese Linguistics)* 14: 71–83.
Wang, X. 王晓谦 (2015) 汉语自然会话中的支持性反馈研究 *(A Study of Supportive Feedback in Naturally Occurring Chinese Conversation)*. (PhD Thesis) Beijing: Minzu University of China中央民族大学
Wu, D.D. 吴东英, Li, C. 李朝渊, Feng, J.冯捷蕴 (2016) '新媒体的社会语言学研究：回顾与展望' (Sociolinguistic Studies of New Media: Review and Prospect), 当代语言学 *(Contemporary Linguistics)* 4: 514–531.

Xu, D. 徐大明 (2002) '约翰・甘柏兹的学术思想' (John Gumperz's Academic Thoughts), 语言教学与研究 *(Language Teaching and Research)* 4: 1–6.

Xu, D. 徐大明 (2006) 语言变异与变化 *(Language Variation and Change)*. Shanghai: Shanghai Education Press.

Xu, D. 徐大明 and Fu, Y. 付义荣 (2005) '南京 '问路' 调查' (The Nanjing 'asking the way' Investigation), 中国社会语言学 *(Chinese Sociolinguistics)* 2: 143–150.

Xu, D. 徐大明 and Wang, L. 王玲 (2010) '城市语言调查' (Urban language investigations), 浙江大学学报（人文社会科学版） *(Journal of Zhejiang University (Humanity and Social Sciences Edition)* 6: 134–140.

Xu, D. 徐大明，Tao, H. 陶红印，Xie, T. 谢天蔚 (1997) 当代社会语言学 *(Contemporary Sociolinguistics)*. Beijing: China Social Sciences Press.

Zhu, W.J. 祝畹瑾 (1985) 社会语言学译文集 *(Sociolinguistic Papers in Chinese Translation)*, Beijing: Beijing Press.

4

Analyzing multimodal Chinese discourse

Integrating social semiotic and conceptual metaphor theories

Dezheng (William) Feng

Introduction

Chinese discourse has attracted considerable scholarly attention from communication and discourse researchers during the last decade. For discourse analysis, conspicuously neglected from the existing body of literature is the systematic investigation of multimodal semiotic resources. As multimodality has become the norm in most, if not all, spheres of communication, a large part of meaning is carried by other semiotic resources, such as visual images, facial expressions, gestures, and intonation. Consequently, the exclusive focus on language may lose essential aspects of meaning, and subsequent interpretations of communicative effects, cultural values and ideology may be partial or incorrect. As Kress (2003: 11) points out, 'we cannot now hope to understand written texts by looking at the resources of writing alone. They must be looked at in the context of the choice of modes made, the modes which appear with writing, and even the context of which modes were not chosen'. Similarly, Jewitt (2009: 3) observes that 'speech and writing no longer appear adequate in understanding representation and communication in a variety of fields'. Therefore, it can be argued that studying multimodal discourse is an imperative and logical next step for Chinese discourse research.

This chapter focuses on a strand of multimodal discourse that is currently the most conspicuous in China, namely, the posters of the Chinese Dream campaign. The Chinese Dream is the new political slogan proposed by President Xi Jinping in 2012, and the publicity campaign, which started in 2012 and is still ongoing, is arguably the most pervasive one after the Reform and Opening Up in 1978. Researchers have been explaining the meanings of the term and its social historical contexts (e.g. Bislev, 2015; Mahoney, 2014; Wang, 2014). For example, Mahoney (2014: 15) interprets the 'Chinese Dream' as a discourse that is 'historically and politically situated and contextualized within a number of other ongoing narratives and policies in China'. Wang (2014) argues that the notion of national rejuvenation in the Chinese Dream is a continuation of the story told in previous political slogans such as Jiang Zemin's '三个代表' (The Three Represents) and Hu Jintao's '科学发展观' (Scientific Development). However, while the Chinese Dream matches previous political slogans in many ways, it is different both in content and in strategies of dissemination. In terms of content, 'it is a potentially all-encompassing term that invites multiple interpretations' (Bislev, 2015: 586). In terms of dissemination, instead of dogmatic sermonizing, the Chinese Dream has a more popular appeal and uses modern advertising strategies and traditional Chinese culture in promoting the concept. Aside from political speeches, government documents and news reports, the Chinese Dream is also promoted through TV shows, popular songs, cartoons, publicity films and posters and social media posts. Among them, the '讲文明，树新风' (Improve Manners, Create a New Atmosphere) public service advertisement (PSA) series has been the most prevalent. The PSAs can be found on major news websites (e.g. www.xinhuanet.com, www.gmw.cn, and www.wenming.cn). The posters are also ubiquitous in all Chinese cities, occupying bus stops, train stations, residence building walls, university/school campuses and downtown streets. It is safe to say that most citizens are exposed to these posters on a daily basis. Therefore, investigating the meaning-making mechanisms in them is significant for the understanding of political communication in contemporary China.

This chapter elucidates how the Chinese Dream narratives are constructed through the creative use of text and images in the publicity posters. In particular, it focuses on the use of metaphors, which is a fundamental device in both promotional and political communication (e.g. Charteris-Black, 2004; Forceville, 1996; Semino, 2008), and plays a key role in the posters. In what follows, I will first provide an overview of multimodal discourse analysis and then develop a social semiotic model of multimodal metaphor analysis. The model will be applied to analyzing the Chinese Dream posters. It demonstrates how the integration of social semiotic and conceptual metaphor theories can provide a thorough understanding of the semiotic choices in multimodal discourse as well as why certain choices are made in the specific socio-cultural context.

Overview of multimodal discourse analysis

Multimodal discourse analysis refers to the analysis of texts which contain two or more semiotic resources, or 'modes' of communication. Such resources include paralinguistic features such as intonation, loudness, font and size, non-verbal behaviors such as gestures, facial expressions, and posture, as well as other forms of representation such as painting, music, film and photography. Researchers have been theorizing meaning-making mechanisms in an increasing range of 'modes of communication', for example, photography (Kress and van Leeuwen, 2006), architecture (O'Toole, 1994), music (van Leeuwen, 1999) and film (Bateman and Schmidt, 2011). Among them, visual images have attracted the most scholarly attention as they play a central role in various forms of communication, such as advertising, news, comics, picture books and film. In the current state of the art of multimodal discourse analysis, visual images are mainly analyzed based on two theoretical paradigms: systemic functional linguistics (Halliday and Matthiessen, 2004) and the conceptual metaphor theory (CMT henceforth) (Lakoff and Johnson, 1980). These two theoretical foundations give rise to two approaches to visual analysis: systemic functional visual grammar (e.g. Kress and van Leeuwen, 2006; O'Toole, 1994) and visual/pictorial/multimodal metaphor (e.g. El Refaie, 2003; Forceville, 1996; Forceville and Urios-Aparisi, 2009). I will briefly introduce these two approaches to analyzing visual images.

According to visual grammar, visual images are analyzed in terms of the representation of reality (representational meaning), the interaction between the participants in an image and its viewers (interactive meaning) and the compositional arrangements of different elements (compositional meaning). Representational meaning is analyzed in terms of the 'processes' participants are involved in. Kress and van Leeuwen (2006: 45–113) identified two types of processes, namely, narrative processes and conceptual processes. The distinction between them lies in the ways in which the image participants are related to each other, that is, whether it is based on the 'unfolding of actions and events, processes of change' or based on their 'generalized, stable and timeless essence'. The former mainly includes the depiction of various types of actions and reactions, such as walking, eating, talking, laughing and crying. The latter includes taxonomic relations (i.e. classificational process, such as the books on a library shelf), part-whole relations (i.e. analytical process, as in descriptions of human body parts in biology textbooks), and symbolic relations (i.e. symbolic process, such as the cross for Christianity). Interactive meaning includes contact, social distance and attitude. Contact refers to whether the image participants interact with viewers through gaze. Social distance is constructed by shot distance. Long shot constructs image-viewer relation as distant and close shot constructs the relation as intimate. Attitude includes involvement and power relations, which are realized through frontal/oblique and high/low camera angles. Frontal angle maximally involves viewers with what is represented; whereas oblique angle depicts the visual participants as 'others' or 'strangers'. For vertical angles, symbolic power is typically given to the viewer in high angle representation, and to the represented participants in low angle representation. Compositional meaning relates the representational and interactive meanings into a meaningful whole through information value, salience, and framing (Kress and van Leeuwen, 2006: 177). Information value is realized through the placement of visual elements, such as center or margin, top or bottom. Salience deals with how some elements can be made more eye-catching, more conspicuous than others, through size, sharpness of focus and color contrast (Kress and van Leeuwen, 2006: 202). Framing is concerned with the disconnection and connection of different visual elements.

In the CMT paradigm, metaphor is conceptualized as understanding one thing (which is the target domain) in terms of the other (which is the source domain), and is represented in a Lakoff (1996) formula of A IS B (e.g. LOVE IS A JOURNEY). As a conceptual mapping, metaphor can be realized in both language and other communication modes, such as visual images, gesture and architecture (e.g. Forceville, 1996; Goatly, 2007). Multimodal metaphor researchers have developed theoretical models to identify visual metaphor (e.g. El Refaie, 2003; Forceville, 1996; Feng and O'Halloran, 2013) and have analyzed metaphor in advertising, political cartoons, comics, picture books and films. In Forceville's (1996) seminal work, three types of pictorial metaphor are identified, namely, contextual metaphor, hybrid metaphor and simile. In contextual metaphor, a visually depicted object is compared to something else because of the visual context it appears in. In Forceville's (1996) example in which a shoe is put in the place of a tie in a suit, the metaphor SHOE IS TIE is formed because of the context where it appears. In hybrid metaphor, the source and target are represented as one entity with mixed features. El Refaie (2009) analyzed a cartoon in which George Bush is compared to a baby. This is constructed by depicting Bush crawling on the floor like a baby. In animal protection advertisements, animals are sometimes depicted as human beings (e.g. in clothing, facial expression, and posture) to raise our awareness. In pictorial simile, the target is compared to a source typically through juxtaposition. For example, a cigarette can be put together with a bullet to highlight its danger. Feng and O'Halloran (2013) analyzed an example in which a group of weightlifting athletes are juxtaposed with minivans to suggest that the latter is as strong as the former. Feng and O'Halloran (2013) argued that the three types cannot explain the complex visual realization of metaphor and proposed a model drawing upon Kress and van Leeuwen's (2006) social semiotic visual grammar. Based on that, they argued for the integration of social semiotics and the conceptual metaphor theory in analyzing visual and multimodal discourse, and this chapter is an attempt in this direction.

Dezheng (William) Feng

Towards a social semiotic model of multimodal metaphor analysis

This chapter proposes a model of multimodal metaphor analysis which draws upon key tenets of social semiotics, in particular, the framework of context. Metaphor scholars have long argued that the cognitive semantic approach of Lakoff and Johnson (1980) should be complemented with an analysis of context (e.g. Charteris-Black, 2004; Forceville, 1996). For example, in analyzing pictorial metaphors in advertising, Forceville (1996) distinguishes between contexts within the text and those outside the text. The former refers to 'the immediate, physical surroundings of the advertisement' (Forceville, 1996: 79), and the latter includes anthropological knowledge and cultural knowledge. Particularly relevant to the current study is Charteris-Black's (2004) 'critical metaphor analysis', which involves metaphor identification (recognizing the linguistic manifestations), metaphor interpretation (identifying the underlying conceptual metaphors) and metaphor explanation (explaining why certain metaphors are used in the specific social and communicative context). In what follows, I will provide a brief overview of the social semiotic framework and use it to develop a model of multimodal metaphor analysis.

In social semiotics, context is conceptualized as 'the total environment in which a text unfolds' (Halliday, 1978: 5). Context is stratified into two levels, namely, 'context of situation' and 'context of culture', and a text can only be understood in relation to both levels. A major contribution of Halliday (1978) is his proposal of the three dimensions of context of situation, namely, Field, Tenor, and Mode. Field is concerned with the nature of the social action that is taking place. It can be further divided into first order Field and second order Field. The former refers to the authorial activity and purpose of creating the discourse (e.g. explaining, sharing, or entertaining); the latter refers to the activities within the discourse (i.e. the subject matters). Metaphor is relevant in terms of the domains of experience that are chosen for certain communicative purposes. As Fairclough (1992: 195) points out, 'how a particular domain of experience is metaphorized is one of the stakes in the struggle within and over discourse practices'. Tenor deals with the participants taking part and the nature of the relationship among them in terms of power and distance. Similar with Field, it includes the relation between the author/text and reader (first order) and the relation between participants in the discourse (second order). Metaphors may serve to engage readers' attention, construct solidarity, and reinforce intimacy in this regard (Semino 2008: 32). Mode is concerned with the channel of communication. Following Halliday (1978), I further distinguish between the medium (e.g. print media, television, and face-to-face) and the genre of communication (e.g. advertisement and news).

In social semiotics, context does not only include what happens in the situation, but also 'context of culture', which is the total socio-cultural background enabling and restricting specific situations (Halliday and Hasan, 1989). In the present working model, I distinguish between the concrete, observable socio-cultural events and phenomena (i.e. activities beyond the immediate situation of the discourse) and the abstract, invisible values and ideology. Context of culture at these two levels provides explanations of why certain activities, social relations, and channels of communication are chosen at the level of context of situation.

Moving down to the level of text, a further contribution Halliday (1978) makes is his proposal that each dimension of a social context is realized by the meaning of language, that is, the 'metafunctions'. The ideational function construes the experience of social activities (Field); the interpersonal function enacts social relations (Tenor); the textual function organizes these construals and enactments as meaningful discourse (Mode). For social semiotics, metaphorical mappings are semantic and mainly serve an ideational function by construing something in terms of something else (Semino, 2008: 31). Metaphor analysis at this level is concerned with identifying metaphors and the semantic features that are mapped from the source domain to the target domain. The metafunctions are in turn realized by choices at the level of 'lexicogrammar'. The notion of choice is central in social semiotics, in the sense that the grammar of language is conceptualized as 'resource for making meanings, rather than a code, or a set of rules for producing correct sentences' (Halliday, 1978: 192). Analysis at this level is concerned with the multimodal realization of conceptual metaphors. In print media, where language and images are the semiotic resources available (enabled and restricted by the choice of Mode), a metaphor can be realized purely linguistically or visually. If more than one mode is involved, either as source domain or target domain, a multimodal metaphor is constituted.

The social semiotic model is summarized in Table 4.1. It also includes comparisons with the models of Charteris-Black (2004). Compared with Charteris-Black (2004), the framework provides more explicit modeling of context and the relation between different levels of text and context. In the following section, I will demonstrate how the framework is used to analyze the context, semantics, and multimodal realizations of metaphors in the Chinese Dream posters. The framework enables us to understand fundamental questions such as what metaphors are used to conceptualize the Chinese Dream, how the metaphors are constructed, why multimodal metaphors are used and why these specific metaphors are chosen in the current socio-political context of China.

Analysis of the Chinese dream publicity posters

The data for analysis is 72 posters with metaphors from a total of 272 posters related to the Chinese Dream in the '讲文明，树新风' PSA series. The identification is based on the criteria that a concrete domain of experience (i.e. the source domain) is used to understand the activity of pursuing the Chinese Dream (i.e. the target domain) (and not vice versa), and that at least one identifiable characteristic of the source is mapped onto the target. Only the headlines and the images are considered for the analysis of metaphor for the reasons that the body copies are hardly readable without zooming in on the websites (see further explanation in the analysis of Mode).

The annotation first gives us an overview of the subject matter of the posters (i.e. the second order Field), including both the target domains and the source domains. The target domains are about the process of pursuing the Chinese Dream, and the entities of Chinese people, the Chinese Communist Party (CCP) and China. Each of the elements is conceptualized through one or more source domains, which are summarized in Table 4.2. The process of pursuing the

Table 4.1 The social semiotic model of multimodal metaphor analysis

Charteris-Black (2004)	The social semiotic model		
Metaphor explanation	Context of culture	Visible socio-cultural events and phenomena	Invisible values, ideology and power
	Context of situation	First order – Field: authorial activity – Tenor: author/text-reader relation – Mode: medium of communication	Second order – Field: subject matter – Tenor: character relation in text – Mode: genre
Metaphor interpretation	Discourse semantics	Conceptual metaphors	Semantic features mapped
Metaphor identification	Semiotic resources	Realizations of metaphors in language, images and other semiotic resources	

Table 4.2 Summary of source domains in the Chinese Dream posters

Journey	Animal	Human/family	Plant	Game/sport	Festival
36	25	11	7	6	3

Chinese dream is in most cases conceptualized through the source domain of journey, followed by plant, game/sport, and festival. The source domain of animal is used to conceptualize Chinese people in most cases, and the Chinese Dream in several cases. Human/family and plant are used to conceptualize CCP and China in all cases. This overview is essential because it gives us an idea of what to focus on at the semantic level. Based on the result, I will analyze the metaphors of the two most salient concepts, namely, the process of pursuing the Chinese dream, and the entities of Chinese people and CCP/China. I will start with text analysis, which includes the semantics of the metaphors and their multimodal realizations, and then move on to the analysis of context of situation and context of culture.

Text analysis

(1) Metaphors of pursuing the Chinese dream

The majority of the metaphors are used to conceptualize the process of pursuing the Chinese Dream. I will focus on the two most frequently occurring conceptual metaphors, namely, journey metaphors and animal metaphors.

(A) JOURNEY METAPHORS

Journey metaphors are perhaps the most well known in cognitive linguistics and most common in various types of discourse (e.g. Charteris-Black, 2004; Goatly, 2007; Lakoff and Johnson, 1980; Semino, 2008). The master metaphor underlying half of the posters is PURSUING THE CHINESE DREAM IS A JOURNEY. The source domain of journey entails a number of semantic features that are mapped onto the target.

(i) The journey can be sailing, running, or flying, which conceptualizes the various ways of realizing the Dream. Running is the most frequently represented manner of traveling, appearing 19 times, which suggests the pace of pursuit should be a full-speed race rather than a leisurely walk. This echoes the purpose of the campaign which is to mobilize the general public to join the endeavor.

(ii) The journey requires hard work and other important qualities. The posters use headlines such as '朝夕奔梦' (running towards the Dream from dawn to dark) and '靠着勤劳双手奔向中国梦' (running towards the Chinese Dream through hard work). The qualities are also conceptualized through plants or animals. For example, plum blossom, which comes into flowers in the coldest season, symbolizes dignity and fortitude in the Chinese culture; ox is used to construe determination and firmness. These qualities serve to mobilize Chinese people to work hard and to endure the hardship on the journey.

(iii) The journey is pleasant. First, the roads depicted in most images are wide and smooth, and are surrounded by beautiful scenery, such as sunrise, flowers and trees. The scenery constitutes the two dominant colors of the images, namely, red and green, which symbolize auspiciousness and hope respectively. Second, the journey is full of happiness. Expressions such as '欢欣鼓舞' (dancing with joy) and '欢歌笑语' (happy songs and laughter) are used and the images show people dancing and performing. Happy events, such as weddings and ceremonies, are depicted. Third, people are kind to each other and help each other on the journey. These features complement the hardship discussed in (i) and (ii) and mobilize people by creating a happy atmosphere.

(iv) CCP is guiding the way of the journey. The leadership of CCP is conceptualized through its role as a guide (CCP IS THE GUIDE OF THE JOURNEY). There are two posters devoted to this aspect of meaning, using headlines '圆梦路上党旗高扬' (The CCP flag is hoisted high on the road) and '跟着党奔梦去' (running after CCP towards the Dream). This metaphor naturalizes the leadership of CCP, which is further legitimized by the smoothness and happiness of the journey.

(B) ANIMAL METAPHORS

Animals are a popular source domain in various types of discourse and are extensively used in the posters. The most frequently used animal is the dragon, which appears in 9 posters. Birds also appear in 9 posters, but 2 are used to construe the relation between Chinese people and CCP/China. Other animals include horse, ox, rooster, and duck. Over half of them are mythic animals, like dragon and phoenix, which are totems of the Chinese nation. The animals play two roles: they are the agents pursuing the Dream, and they themselves are the Dream.

(i) CHINESE PEOPLE WHO ARE PURSUING THE CHINESE DREAM ARE ANIMALS. The animals map various positive attributes which are crucial for the journey to Chinese people. Dragon, phoenix and crane are divine animals in Chinese culture and lend auspiciousness to the pursuit of the Dream. Horses symbolize the fast speed on the journey, with images of them galloping full-speed ahead. For the ox, in the poster titled '牛精神' (spirit of the ox) (see Figure 4.1), its attributes of being firm and unyielding are used, as the accompanying poem indicates.

(ii) CHINESE DREAM IS AN ANIMAL. In these cases, the Chinese Dream is compared to a dragon or a bird which can fly. For example, in a poster, the headline is '中国梦飞九天' (the Chinese Dream flies high in the sky) and the image is a flying dragon. The metaphor THE CHINESE DREAM IS A DRAGON construes the divine nature of the endeavor and invokes confidence and pride from the audience. In another example, '放飞中国梦' (let fly the Chinese Dream), the image depicts a woman letting go of a pigeon. This metaphor, CHINESE DREAM IS A PIGEON, suggests that the realization of the Dream lies in the Chinese people's hands. Meanwhile, the pigeon also symbolizes the peaceful nature of the pursuit.

(2) Metaphors of the CCP and China

The second batch of metaphors is concerned with conceptualizing the relation between Chinese people and China/CCP.

(a) CCP/CHINA IS MOTHER and CHINESE PEOPLE ARE CHILDREN. The personification of political parties is a common communication strategy in politics (Lakoff, 1996), but perhaps nowhere in the world is the metaphor exploited to such an extent as in China. The most well-known example is the song lyric 'I compare CCP to my mother. My mother only gave birth to my body, but the light of CCP brightened my heart'. This simile is the slogan in one of the posters (我把党来比母亲), which invokes the lyrics in the mind of all Chinese people.

Figure 4.1 'Chinese dream; spirit of the ox'

The lyrics also capture the semantic features that are mapped from the mother, that is, the spiritual aspect of nurturing the Chinese people, which instills gratitude among them. The mapping between China and mother is even more conventional than that between CCP and mother. The metaphor also highlights the nurturance of 'motherland' and invokes people's love and gratitude.

(b) CCP IS PHOENIX and CHINESE PEOPLE ARE BIRDS. A poster in the data shows the headline '百姓心向共产党' (literally 'people's heart turns toward the CCP') and the image of birds surrounding a phoenix (see Figure 4.2). In Chinese culture, the phoenix is considered the queen of all birds and there is a Chinese idiom '百鸟朝凤' (a hundred birds worship the phoenix). The metaphor construes the sacredness of the CCP and Chinese people's loyalty to it.

(c) CCP IS THE SUN and CHINESE PEOPLE ARE SUNFLOWERS. The poster represents a child and a sunflower, and the headline is '童心向党' (literally 'children's heart turns toward the CCP') (see Figure 4.3). The metaphor is that children follow the CCP just like the sunflower follows the direction of the sun, which construes Chinese people's loyalty to the CCP's leadership. The comparison of the CCP to the sun is traced back to the 1940s and has become a familiar metaphor to all Chinese through the song '东方红' (The East Turns Red).

(d) CHINA IS A PLANT. This metaphor compares China to a big tree with thick, green leaves (see Figure 4.4). The comparison highlights the old history of China on the one hand, and the current prosperity on the other, which serves to trigger a sense of pride, confidence and hope in the audience.

To summarize the semantic analysis, first, metaphors are mainly used to construe the process of pursuing the Chinese dream, and the entities of Chinese people and CCP/China. Second, in terms of the source domains, we see an overall preference toward conventional metaphors, using the well-known domains of experience like journey, animal, plant and family. A particularly noteworthy feature is that the source domains contain rich cultural elements. The domain of journey contains many elements that are unique to the Chinese culture, for example, the red color which is the most auspicious color, and the plum blossom which is regarded as the symbol of the Chinese spirit. Auspicious animals in the Chinese culture such as dragon, phoenix, and horse are used to conceptualize Chinese people and the Chinese Dream. Third, the semantic features that are mapped from the source domains serve to mobilize Chinese people and to instill patriotism in them. These features include ideas that the Chinese Dream project is highly relevant to everybody and requires hard work of all Chinese people, that it is a joyful process, and that it is important to follow the leadership of CCP.

For the realization of the metaphors, the first question is what semiotic resources are used. All the metaphors are multimodal in the sense that both language and images are involved in the mapping. Interestingly, there is no visual metaphor which is constructed purely by visual anomalies, as in print advertisements. That is, language plays a key role in constructing the metaphors. Second, we look at the specific types of mappings. It is found that in most cases the target is in language, while the source is both in language and image (i.e. multimodal, or bimodal, to be precise). The metaphors are typically constructed through colligational anomalies in the headline. This is usually achieved by the collocation of a word which invokes the source domain and a word of the target domain (i.e. dream, CCP, country). The most frequent collocation is '奔梦' (run towards the dream), which appears 19 times. Other anomalies include '荡起梦想' (swing the dream), '中国梦飞九天' (the Chinese Dream flies high in the sky), and '春风又绿中国梦' (the spring breezes turn the Chinese Dream green). In these cases, the images illustrate the linguistic source domains, either through repetition or through collocation. In *repetition*, the image is the visual equivalent of the linguistic item. Most of the ANIMAL metaphors belong to

Figure 4.2 'People's heart turns to the Communist Party'

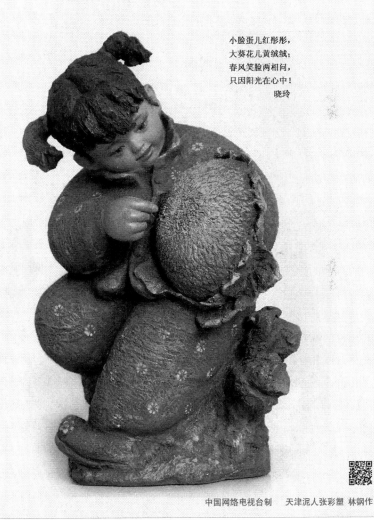

Figure 4.3 'Children's heart turns toward the CCP'

Figure 4.4 'Everlasting Chinese civilizations'

Analyzing multimodal Chinese discourse

this kind, where the image of an animal in drawing or paper-cutting illustrates the word of the animal (e.g. horse, ox, or dragon). In *collocation*, the image and the language are related elements of the source domain. For example, in a poster the image is a boat in a lake, which collocates with the linguistic expression '启航' (sailing). Some ANIMAL metaphors also belong to this type, where the image of an animal collocates with its sound (e.g. 'quack quack' in the case of duck) or behavior (e.g. flying in the case of bird).

In the second type of mapping, a linguistic target is conceptualized through a visual source. Only 6 such cases are found and all of them are used to conceptualize CCP and China, but not the process of pursuing the Chinese Dream. This is presumably because the metaphors for CCP and China are already familiar to the Chinese people and the mappings do not need to be spelled out in language in every case, while the Chinese Dream is a new concept and requires more straightforward linguistic connection. In Figure 4.2, the linguistic target '百姓心向共产党' is conceptualized through the image of birds surrounding a phoenix. In Figure 4.4, the linguistic element is '中华文明生生不息' (everlasting Chinese civilizations), which is understood through the image of a flourishing tree (i.e. CHINESE CIVILIZATION IS A FLOURISHING TREE).

In the third type of mapping, the target is not explicitly represented in language, but is inferred from the theme of the posters or the symbolic meaning of a source domain. The source is visually depicted, which may or may not be represented in language. Figure 4.1 is a typical example, in which the ox is represented visually and linguistically ('牛精神', spirit of the ox), and the target is clearly Chinese people in this context, but it is not represented. Finally, there is a case where the target is represented visually as well as linguistically. As illustrated in Figure 4.3, the child is compared to the sunflower through juxtaposition, while the child is also represented linguistically (童). This is the only case where the target is visual, presumably because other targets are abstract and cannot be visually represented without using metaphors.

To summarize, the realization of the metaphors show a clear pattern. The linguistic mode plays a central role, which is used to represent the target domain in all posters, and is also used to represent the source domain in most cases; the visual mode is used in all posters and only represents the source domain in all cases but one. Most metaphors are constructed by colligational anomalies in the headline. The images illustrate the texts through repetition or collocation, but do not contain anomalies and construct metaphors by themselves as commercial advertisements do. This feature resonates with the preference for conventional metaphors at the semantic level. Both are determined by the contextual requirements of the poster (e.g. the genre, the purpose and the theme), which are discussed in the following subsection.

Analysis of context of situation

Moving up to the level of context, we seek to answer the 'why' questions, including why metaphors are used, why certain metaphors are chosen, and why the metaphors are constructed with visual or multimodal resources. In the social semiotic model, these are motivated by situational and socio-cultural factors, which are discussed in the following two subsections. In this subsection, we look at context of situation, which includes Field, Tenor and Mode. For Field, we look at who are the authors and what they are doing with the posters. For Tenor, we look at what author-reader relation is constructed and how different participants in the posters are related. Lastly, for Mode, we look at the channel and genre of communication.

As explained in the Introduction, instead of dogmatic sermonizing, the Chinese Dream campaign uses modern advertising strategies. This is, first of all, a change of Mode, that is, the channel and genre of communication. First, different from previous campaigns in which the main form of communication was news and pamphlets, the main channels of communication for the Chinese Dream campaign are outdoor posters and websites. Second, the channel of communication motivates the formation of a new genre which blends political propaganda and public service advertising (PSA). The posters belong to the '讲文明，树新风' PSA series and are depoliticized by featuring cultural elements such as traditional Chinese art and auspicious animals. The use of metaphor is a main strategy to construct this genre. However, as previously noted, language plays a primary role and no visual anomalies are used in commercial advertisements, which may suggest that the designers are refrained from capitalizing on visual creativity. Nonetheless, images occupy most of the visual space in all posters, which is the most significant difference with previous language-centered campaign discourse.

The second contextual factor is Field, which deals with authorial activities and subject matters. I have provided an overview of the latter previously based on the coding of metaphors and here I will focus on the former. Authorial activities can be understood by answering the two questions of 'who is the author?' and 'what is he/she doing (i.e. the semiotic activity)?'. All posters acknowledge the producers and creators of the images. The posters are all produced by China Network Television, which is an online platform of China Central Television, and the images are typically created by folk artists of traditional Chinese art, such as painting, sculpting and paper-cutting. This is a significant change from previous campaign texts, which were authored by political leaders and official news reporters and commentators. Accompanying this change is the change of authorial activity and purpose. While political leaders and official reporters are involved in the activities of giving instructions and reporting information, the posters with folk art aim to entertain people and persuade the audience. The change of authorial activity from instructing to persuading echoes current discussions of contemporary ideological work (e.g. Bondes and Heep, 2013; Brady, 2009; Cao, 2014). The abstract concept of pursuing the Chinese Dream is explained through concrete daily experience and vivid pictures.

Finally, Tenor deals with the relation between the authors and the audience (first order) and the relation between characters within the posters (second order). For first order Tenor, we look at who the target audience is and what the author-audience relations are in terms of distance and power. The target audience of the Chinese Dream campaign is broader than that of previous campaigns. As Xi Jinping (2013) explains, the Chinese Dream is for all Chinese people and its realization relies on Chinese people. The producers use the form of PSAs and folk arts to build author-audience solidarity. As the image creators are common people like the audience rather than political leaders, the author-audience relation is equal and close. The posters are very easy to understand and use imageries that are common and unique to the Chinese. In terms of second order Tenor, the main relations depicted are among Chinese people and between Chinese people and CCP/China. As analyzed in the previous section, the relations are naturalized through metaphors (e.g. as mother-children).

The contextual factors above motivate the predominance of visual images and the prevalence of metaphors; at the same time, the contextual requirements are realized by the multimodal metaphors. Therefore, in contextual analysis, we also look at the functions of metaphors in constructing the Field, Tenor and Mode of the discourse. For Field, the use of multimodal metaphors is a fundamental persuasive strategy which serves the purposes of both construing the abstract concept of the Chinese Dream and entertaining the audience through vivid images. For Tenor, they serve to engage the audience's interest and construct author-reader solidarity (cf. Semino, 2008: 32). For Mode, the linguistic element and the visual element are connected through metaphorical mappings to form a coherent discourse and a blended genre of political propaganda and public service advertising.

Analysis of context of culture

We need to further ask what motivates the patterns of Field, Tenor and Mode (e.g. why it uses outdoor posters and why the author-audience relation is equal and close). We also need to answer why particular metaphors are chosen and what ideologies are behind. To address these questions, we need to incorporate the broader socio-cultural context. The historical and political context of the Chinese Dream has been discussed by many researchers (e.g. Mahoney, 2014; Wang, 2014), and in this subsection, I only focus on the factors that are relevant to the explanation of the choices of metaphors and the context of situation.

The Field, Tenor and Mode of the posters reflect the changing manner of political communication from authoritarian coercion to egalitarian solidarity building in recent years (Zhang, 2011). A fundamental driving force is the change of media environment in the age of information technology. By the end of 2016, the number of 'netizens' in China has reached 731 million. In this context, 'the top-down pattern of political communication characterized by dogmatic instructions is proving to be hard to achieve' (Cao, 2014: 3). First, the younger generation has ready access to a wide range of information, especially consumer-driven, entertaining and promotional information, and is simply not interested in dry indoctrinations (cf. Zhang, 2011). Second, new media, especially social media, make bottom-up societal voices easier than ever before, which is breaking the traditional one-way top-down communication and 'has moved China closer to a level playing field of communication' (Cao, 2014: 11). This change is reflected in the choices of Field, Tenor and Mode of the posters as explained in the previous subsection.

Together with the change of political identity is the increasing importance attached to mass persuasion (Brady, 2009; Bondes and Heep, 2013; Zhang, 2011). As Brady (2009: 437) points out, 'China's propaganda system has deliberately absorbed the methodology of political public relations, mass communications, social psychology, and other modern methods of mass persuasion commonly used in Western democratic societies, adapting them to Chinese conditions and needs'. 'The use of culture and entertainment as a vehicle for political messages is one noticeable example of this' (Brady, 2009: 442). This is reflected in the Field of the posters which promote the concept of the Chinese Dream through vivid images and metaphors, rather than impose it on the audience through dogmatic instructions.

We finally look at the socio-cultural factors that motivate the choices of the metaphors. The choice of source domains is related to two implicit aspects of context of culture, namely, ideological functions and Chinese culture. Analysis in this regard is critical in nature as it enables readers to understand the hidden manipulation and ideology behind the metaphors. The metaphors shape the very understanding of the pursuit of the Chinese Dream and the relation between the Party-state and Chinese people, in order to mobilize the general public and to reinforce their loyalty. For example, the role of the CCP is naturalized as the guide for the journey and the relation between the Party-state and people as mother and children. Notably, the metaphors are conventional, 'because with literal language and conventional metaphors the ideology is latent, and therefore all the more powerful' (Goatly, 2007: 29). This also suits the construction of hegemony which requires that the 'connections are natural and automatic' (Fairclough, 1992: 94).

A particular element in the source domains which makes the connections 'natural and automatic' is the use of Chinese culture. As political ideologies have become more pragmatic since 1978, 'the political elites have effectively underpinned a newly formulated value system, substantially with traditional cultures' (Cao, 2014: 178). Chinese culture is, therefore, better appreciated in political communication than before, and the '讲文明，树新风' PSA series campaign is perhaps the largest scale effort to rejuvenate China's cultural traditions (e.g. filial piety and kindness).

To summarize the analysis of context of culture, the choices at the level of text (i.e. the metaphors) and the level of context of situation (i.e. Field, Tenor, and Mode) are motivated by the socio-political reality, cultural values and ideology. At the same time, they serve social and ideological purposes, reproducing, reinforcing and transforming current social practice. The Chinese Dream posters reflect and constitute the mode of political communication from authoritarian coercion to solidarity building and persuasion. In this context, multimodal metaphors with rich cultural elements are employed to construct a desirable version of reality to mobilize the general public and to reinforce patriotism.

Conclusion

Addressing the need of investigating multimodal Chinese discourse, this chapter provides a social semiotic model of multimodal metaphor analysis and applies it to analyzing the currently most widespread type of discourse in China, namely, the publicity posters of the Chinese Dream campaign. The model enables us to analyze metaphors systematically in terms of semantic choices, multimodal realizations, and contexts. In particular, it provides a comprehensive framework for analyzing context by stratifying it into context of situation and context of culture. The analysis of the Chinese Dream posters shows that the metaphors serve to conceptualize essential aspects of pursuing the Chinese Dream to mobilize the Chinese people and to cultivate patriotism. The source domains are mostly familiar things with rich cultural elements, such as the journey, animals and plants. All the metaphors are realized in both language and images, creating multimodal metaphors, and the images mainly illustrate the source domain. At the level of context of situation, the posters reflect interesting new features of the discursive practice which include the medium and the genre of PSA posters (Mode), the activities of promoting and entertaining (Field), and the close and equal author-audience relations (Tenor). These patterns are further explained by the socio-political context of the changing media environment and the changing mode of political communication in contemporary China. Complementing studies in politics and communication, the discourse approach is essentially bottom-up, that is, the critical interpretations of socio-political context are grounded on the systematic analysis of multimodal texts.

I conclude that multimodal discourse needs to be analyzed within context, which includes the Field, Tenor and Mode of communication as well as the broader socio-cultural context. The dialectic relation between text and context determines the complementarity between the analysis of text and the analysis of context. The former provides an empirical basis for the socio-political interpretations, and the latter provides explanations of why certain discursive choices are made. For further studies, a wide range of Chinese discourse can be analyzed from a multimodal perspective, for example, television entertainment shows and news reports, advertisements, social media posts and national/city image publicity films, to name just a few.

References

English references

Bateman, J.A. and Schmidt, K.H. (2011) *Multimodal Film Analysis: How Films Mean*. London: Routledge.
Bislev, A. (2015) 'The Chinese Dream: Imagining China', *Fudan Journal of the Humanities and Social Sciences* 8(4): 585.

Bondes, M. and Heep, S. (2013) 'Conceptualizing the Relationship between Persuasion and Legitimacy: Official Framing in the Case of the Chinese Communist Party', *Journal of Chinese Political Science* 18(4): 317–334.

Brady, A. (2009) 'Mass Persuasion as a Means of Legitimation and China's Popular Authoritarianism', *American Behavioral Scientist* 53(3): 434–457.

Cao, Q. (2014) 'Introduction: Legitimisation, resistance and discursive struggles in contemporary China', in *Discourse, Politics and Media in Contemporary China*. Q. Cao, H. Tian, and P. Chilton (eds.) Amsterdam: Benjamins. pp. 1–21.

Charteris-Black, J. (2004) *Corpus Approaches to Critical Metaphor Analysis*. New York: Palgrave-MacMillan.

El Refaie, E. (2003) 'Understanding Visual Metaphor: The Example of Newspaper Cartoons', *Visual Communication* 2(1): 75–95.

El Refaie, E. (2009) 'Metaphor in political cartoons: Exploring audience responses', in *Multimodal Metaphor*. C.J. Forceville and E. Urios-Aparisi (eds.) Berlin: Mouton de Gruyter. pp. 173–196.

Fairclough, N. (1992) *Discourse and Social Change*. Cambridge: Polity.

Feng, D. and O'Halloran, K.L. (2013) 'The Visual Representation of Metaphor: A Social Semiotic Approach', *Review of Cognitive Linguistics* 11(2): 320–335.

Forceville, C.J. (1996) *Pictorial Metaphor in Advertising*. London: Routledge.

Forceville, C.J. and Urios-Aparisi, E. (2009) *Multimodal Metaphor*. Berlin: Mouton de Gruyter.

Goatly, A. (2007) *Washing the Brain – Metaphor and Hidden Ideology*. Amsterdam: John Benjamins.

Halliday, M.A.K. (1978) *Language as Social Semiotic*. London: Edward Arnold.

Halliday, M.A.K. and Hasan, R. (1989) *Language, Context and Text: Aspects of Language in a Social-Semiotic Perspective*. Oxford: Oxford University Press.

Halliday, M.A.K. and Matthiessen, C.M.I.M. (2004) *An Introduction to Functional Grammar* (3rd ed.). London: Arnold.

Jewitt, C. (2009) 'Different approaches to multimodality', in *The Routledge Handbook of Multimodal Analysis*. C. Jewitt (ed.) Abingdon, Oxon: Routledge. pp. 28–39.

Kress, G. (2003) *Literacy in the New Media Age*. London: Routledge.

Kress, G. and van Leeuwen, T. (2006) *Reading Images: The Grammar of Visual Design* (2nd ed.). Abingdon, Oxon: Routledge.

Lakoff, G. (1996) *Moral Politics: What Conservatives Know That Liberals Don't*. Chicago: University of Chicago Press.

Lakoff, G. and Johnson, M. (1980) *Metaphors We Live By*. Chicago: University of Chicago Press.

Mahoney, J.G. (2014) 'Interpreting the Chinese Dream: An Exercise of Political Hermeneutics', *Journal of Chinese Political Science* 19(1): 15–34.

O'Toole, M. (1994) *The Language of Displayed Art*. London: Leicester University Press.

Semino, E. (2008) *Metaphor in Discourse*. Cambridge: Cambridge University Press.

van Leeuwen, T. (1999) *Speech, Music and Sound*. London: MacMillan.

Wang, Z. (2014) 'The Chinese Dream: Concept and Context', *Journal of Chinese Political Science* 19(1): 1–13.

Zhang, X. (2011) *The Transformation of the Political Communication in China: From Propaganda to Hegemony*. Singapore: Scientific Publications.

Chinese reference

Xi, Jin-Ping 习近平 (2013) '习近平阐释中国梦' (Xi Jinping Interpreting the Chinese Dream), Retrieved from www.xinhuanet.com/politics/mzfxzgm/

Part II
Grammatical aspect of Chinese discourse

5

Conceptual word order principles and Mandarin Chinese grammar

Anna Morbiato

Research on iconicity and word order in Mandarin Chinese (henceforth MC) investigates the correlation between the sequence of linguistic elements in the sentence and the temporal, spatial, and causal characteristics of the events they describe. Such correlations are captured through a number of organizational principles, generally referred to in the literature as *conceptual* or *cognitive* word order principles. Among the most significant principles are the Principle of Temporal Sequence, the Principle of Temporal Scope, and that of Whole-Before-Part. Conceptual principles are of great interest for several reasons: first, they exhibit an iconic nature and show how and to what extent MC word order (henceforth WO) mirrors both universal and culture-specific conceptualizations of space, time and cause-effect logical relations. As such, they are easy to understand and remember, thus providing interesting applications to MC language instruction. Moreover, according to Tai (1985, 1989, 1993), Ho (1993), Hu (1995) and Loar (2011) among others, such principles bear great explanatory power in that they underlie several seemingly unrelated syntactic patterns and constructions. This chapter provides an introduction to organizational principles underlying MC word order, with a specific focus on conceptual (or cognitive) principles, such as the Principle of Temporal Sequence (PTS) and that of Whole-Before-Part (WBP). Specifically, it presents (i) the theoretical approach they are grounded in, (ii) their potential in language description, as compared to grammatical rules, and (iii) their applications to language acquisition and discourse analysis. These principles are shown to operate both at the microlevels of phrase and clause and at higher levels of discourse and text. The discussion avails itself of natural language in use; unless otherwise specified, all examples are drawn from corpora, such as the PKU corpus of Modern Mandarin Chinese, Peking University or Ho's corpus of spontaneous spoken texts (Ho, 1993: 14–6).

Iconicity and word order: the cognitive-functional approach

Research on cognitive principles in MC grounds itself in the cognitive-functional approach to word order (Tai, 1989), which is a synthesis of three functional resources, i.e. the cognitive approach (Lakoff, 1987; Langacker, 1987), the semiotic approach to iconicity (Haiman, 1980, 1985) and the functional approach (Hopper and Thompson, 1980). The basic tenet is that human beings' conceptualization of their experiences of the physical world is 'reflected in the language they speak and imposes constraints on linguistic structures' (Biq et al., 1996: 100). The correlation between the order of sentence elements and the human experience of the events/states they represent goes back to cross-linguistic studies conducted on word order correlates and iconicity in the second half of the last century (Greenberg, 1966; Haiman, 1980). Iconicity refers to 'conceived similarities' between a linguistic form and its meaning/what it describes (Haiman, 1980, 1985; Siewierska, 1988). According to Haiman (1980: 537), 'the structure of language reflects the structure of *thought*, [. . . which] in its turn reflects the structure of reality to an extent greater than it is now fashionable to recognize'.

The cognitive-functional approach offers a number of interesting features and tools, which are capable of capturing correlations and commonalities between different constructions and WO patterns. First, the explanation of linguistic structures avails itself of schemas (or diagrams); schemas generally refer to 'mental representations that code for the kinds of abstract spatiotemporal relations among objects – like paths, containment, contact and support relations – theorized to provide a conceptual base onto which language can be mapped' (Amorapanth et al., 2012: 226). Such schemas are intuitively very easy to understand and memorize, in that 'they occupy an intermediate position between abstract words and concrete percepts in a graded model of representation' (Amorapanth et al., 2012: 226). In Peirce's words, the merit of the diagram 'springs from its being veridically iconic, naturally analogous to the thing represented, and not a creation of conventions' (1931: 4368). Second, this approach offers a different perspective to the study of both cross-linguistic and language-specific features. Cross-linguistic tendencies are seen as revealing universal conceptualization processes due to (i) common needs of human communication and (ii) biological and physiological structures of the human body and their interaction with the physical world. Among the main areas of research is human spatial cognition, namely how space is universally conceptualized through common abstraction schemas (Talmy, 1988). On the other hand, language-specific patterns are regarded as conventionalized conceptual schemas shared by speakers of a specific language; language differences are considered reflections of dissimilar environments, cultures and conventional ways to conceptualize the same situation.

> Due to different socio-cultural experiences, different peoples throughout the world may have different conceptions of physical reality, and those conceptual differences in turn contribute to the unique characteristics of their linguistic behaviors, which are reflected in the structures of human languages.
>
> *(Hu, 1995: 26–27)*

Third, this approach looks at language as a cognitive ability that is not separate from other cognitive functions nor independent of external inputs which speakers get from the environment. Hence, it integrates grammar-internal accounts of linguistic phenomena with system-external, functional explanations, connected to the communicative and socio-cultural context.

However, such an approach also presents some controversial points, specifically connected with the assumption that language reflects how speakers conceptualize reality and events. First, despite an increasing number of studies on the topic, it is difficult to find evidence demonstrating how space and time are cognitively represented in the human brain. Second, neuro-linguistic research to date has provided little empirical evidence regarding how events are conceptualized, and how these conceptualizations are reflected in linguistic structures. Little research has been conducted on the neural organization underlying our use of spatial schemas when thinking about space, and it is not clear whether non-verbal spatial relational information can be stored in the brain independent of language (Amorapanth et al., 2012: 227). Hence, some scholars hold more cautious positions on this point. Levinson (2003: 63), for example, maintains that while 'it is clear that language abstracts from [sensory and motor systems of human cognition] in interesting ways, [...] this abstraction tells us about language, not the underlying cognitive systems'. It is perhaps useful to think of word order principles as conventional linearization patterns shared by speakers in the same speaking community; in other words, they capture common ways in which schemas, which are typically multidimensional, are mapped onto the one-dimensional sequence of linguistic elements, adapting to the linearity of the linguistic sign (Haiman, 1980).

Mandarin Chinese: conceptual principles and their instantiations

In his cross-linguistic investigation on iconicity and typology, Haiman (1985: 68–70) concluded that isolating languages are likely to be more iconic than those displaying a richer morphology. Research conducted by Light (1979), Tai (1985, 1989, 1993), Ho (1993), Hu (1995) and Loar (2011) among others suggests that MC nicely fits this generalization. This section briefly reviews their work, while the following subsections present some of their major insights on the applicability of the PTS, WBP and other conceptual principles to describe WO patterns, alternations and rules.

Among the first linguists to look at the correlation between WO and the temporal/causal characteristics of the described event was Light. His early studies examined the difference between pre- and postverbal interpretations of noun phrases and locatives with respect to their temporal and spatial relations with the verb (as illustrated in example (11) below). The iconic nature of MC grammatical structures was then more thoroughly explored by Tai, who proposed the cognitive-functional approach as a new framework of analysis for WO in MC and singled out a range of cognitive-functional principles underlying grammatical structures and word order restrictions. These include (discussion and examples are provided in sections below):

i   Principle of Temporal Sequence
ii Principle of Temporal Scope
iii Whole-Before-Part
iv Container-Before-Contained
v   Trajector-Landmark
vi Modifier-Before-Modified

Ho (1993), Hu (1995) and Loar (2011) further elaborated the taxonomy of WO principles, integrating notions such as theme, topic and focus along with work on information structure conducted within the Prague School (Functional Sentence Perspective) and American Structuralism (Topic-Comment dichotomy). Functional principles capture WO variations due to communicative needs of language users, who construct a sentence 'from the viewpoint of constructing a message' (Loar, 2011: 7). These functional principles include: the Principle of Topic, whereby elements conveying old information are placed at the beginning of the sentence to act as the topic, anchor or starting point; the Principle of End Focus, whereby new, salient, informationally important information is placed in the focal end position, while informationally predicable elements that are defocused occur earlier in the sentence; the Principle of Communicative Dynamism/Functional Sentence Perspective, which refers to the variation in communicative value between different parts of a sentence (for further discussion and examples see Loar, 2011: 7–12). Other principles mentioned in the literature include those of Semantic Proximity (Haiman, 1983), which captures the fact that semantically/conceptually related constituents are linguistically/syntactically closer, and Referential Precedence, whereby units of high referentiality tend to precede units of low referentiality in a clause and in the internal word order of a NP (Lu, 1998).

While the taxonomies of principles vary with respect to terminology and number of principles (and sub-principles), they all emphasize the interaction between different types of principles: 'any decision on a particular grammatical form is not a matter of applying one principle alone, but the result of the interplay between [sets of principles]' (Loar, 2011: 12). Ho conducted a corpus analysis of natural oral data, analyzing the structure of discourse from three perspectives: thematic structure, information structure and conceptual principles. His study represents a significant contribution, as it demonstrated that a great variety of word order phenomena are in fact instantiations of the interaction of a limited number of conceptual principles. These phenomena include (i) BA and BEI sentences and the restrictions they display with respect to definite vs. indefinite patients/objects; (ii) pre- vs. postverbal position of temporal, locative, manner, and beneficiary phrases; (iii) position of condition, cause, and manner subordinates; and (iv) modifier before modified order. Hu also further explored the interaction between different principles and elaborated a taxonomy categorizing them within three domains, i.e., conceptual, functional, and grammatical:

i   Conceptual domain: Principle of Temporal Sequence, Principle of Temporal Scope, Whole-Before-Part, Container-Before-Contained, Trajector-Landmark;
ii Functional domain: Principle of Communicative Dynamism, Principle of Functional Sentence Perspective, Principle of Perspective Taking, Principle of Focus, Principle of Coherence and Relevance
iii Grammatical domain: Modifier-Before-Head

Importantly, his work also showed that the interaction of these principles effectively explains other WO phenomena, including sentential starting points, pseudo-passives, presentative sentences, paratactic constructions and inverted sentences. Loar further expanded the range of syntactic rules described in terms of organizational principles. Her *Chinese Syntactic Grammar* constitutes an in-depth, detailed analysis of a significant number of grammatical rules in terms of these principles, including the order of different types of adverbials (e.g. position, process, manner, attitudinal), complements (e.g. resultative, directional, potential, duration, degree), the order of clauses in complex sentences, the BA and BEI constructions, existential sentences and locative inversions, 是 … 的 *shì … de*, 连 … 也 *lián … yě* 'even', and other emphatic constrictions, clause order in complex sentences and various instantiations of topic-comment structures.

The Principle of Temporal Sequence

The Principle of Temporal Sequence (PTS) captures the fact that linguistic structures reflect the temporal sequence of states, situations and events that they represent. This type of iconic correlation has been observed to hold crosslinguistically by numerous scholars. In his seminal work on word order patterns and universals, Greenberg (1966: 103) remarked that 'the order of elements in language parallels that in physical experience or the order of knowledge'. Jakobson (1971: 350) observed that the 'temporal order of speech events tends to mirror the order of narrated events in time or in rank': in the sentence *Veni, vidi, vici* 'I came, I saw, I conquered', he maintains, a (near) universal iconic principle forces the order of clauses to correspond in general to the order of events. However, languages differ with respect to (i) the extent to which this principle holds as a word order restriction and (ii) the level of linguistic organization this tendency applies to (i.e., phrase, clause, sentence, discourse). MC has a stronger tendency to hold to this principle in both these respects; according to Tai, PTS subsumes 'a large number of word order rules hitherto regarded as unrelated' (1985: 63). Tai (1985: 50) defined PTS as follows: 'The relative word order between syntactic units is determined by the temporal order of the states that they represent in the conceptual world'.

In what follows, some significant instantiations of this principle in MC are provided, with a focus on the two aspects above, i.e. on PTS (i) as a comparatively more rigid WO restriction and (ii) as a tendency also holding at the microlevels of clause and phrase.

Order of coverbs, verbs and predicates denoting temporally subsequent actions: This principle constrains the relative order of: verbal compounds (1), resultative verbs (2), serial verb/pivotal constructions (3) and sequences of predicates (4). In all instances, the action, state or result denoted by the first verb/predicative element must temporally and logically precede that of the second, and the reverse order is not possible:

1 栽培   甘薯 ...
   zāipéi   gānshǔ
   plant-foster sweet potato
   'Cultivating (lit. planting and fostering) sweet potato ...'

2 早餐   要   吃饱。
   zǎocān   yào   chī bǎo
   breakfast must   eat-(be)full
   'You must be full after eating breakfast'.

3 请   你   开   一下   门。
   qǐng   nǐ   kāi   yīxià   mén
   invite 2SG open   one-bit   door
   'Would you open the door, please?'

4 她   赶紧   上   街   买   晚报。
   tā   gǎnjǐn   shàng   jiē   mǎi   wǎnbào
   3SG   hurriedly go.on   street buy   evening paper
   'She hurriedly went out to buy the evening paper'.

Crucially, in English and in other morphologically richer languages, such as Romance, this principle is less prescriptive, due to the presence of other means of encoding the *consecutio temporum* allowing predicates to occur in reverse temporal order, e.g. verbal tense/mode (2), or other constructions (5):

5 雨   来得快,   走得也很快。 (Ho's corpus)
   yǔ   lái de kuài   zǒu de yě hěn kuài
   rain   come DE quickly   leave DE also very quickly
   'The rain stops as quickly as it comes'.

In the English translations of (2) and (5), the order of the two clauses/predicative elements (underlined) does not correspond to the temporal order of the events they describe. The same order is however not possible in MC: in this case, the PTS is prescriptive.

Order of elements at the clause level: the relative order between verbs and complements is generally dictated by grammatical rules (i.e. complements follow verbs). However, such rules do not capture the reason why in Mandarin certain locative or temporal elements are adjuncts and must precede the verb, as *sān diǎn zhōng* 'at three o'clock' in (6.a), while others are complements and must follow the verb, as *sān ge zhōngtóu* 'for three hours' in (6.b). Crucially, research on Chinese word order acquisition (Jiang, 2009; Morbiato, 2017) has shown that students find this particularly confusing.

6	a	We have a meeting <u>at three o' clock</u>.		(Loar, 2011: 4)
		我们	三点钟	开会。
		wǒmen	sān diǎn zhōng	kāi huì
		1PL	3 hour clock	open meeting
	b	We had a meeting <u>for three hours</u>.		
		我们	开会	开了	三个钟头。
		wǒmen	kāi huì	kāi le	sān ge zhōngtóu
		1PL	open meeting	open LE	3 CL hour

However, this type of rule is readily explainable from a conceptual perspective: the pre- vs postverbal position of time expressions depends on their temporal and causal relation with the verb. Specifically, punctual time expressions are conceptually independent of the action (in Tai's words, they are conceptually pre-existing, hence preverbal). Durative temporal expressions, on the other hand, are a form of measurement of the length of the action described by the verb. Logically, measurement can be carried out only after the action has taken place, and thus time duration expressions like *sān ge zhōngtóu* '3 hours' necessarily follow the verb. Hence, they are complements (and not preverbal adjuncts). Similar considerations hold for other types of complements: resultative (2), frequency (7), quantity and degree (8) complements all give essential information about the action or event in terms of its result or resultative state. Since result (and measurement of result) follows action, it is logical and consistent with the PTS to have such information (underlined) appear after the verb:

7	每年	最少	要	到临汾	去	<u>两趟</u>。
	měi nián	zuì shǎo	yào	dào Línfén	qù	liǎng tāng
	every year	most few	must	arrive Linfen	go	2 CL(time)
	'go(es) to Linfen <u>twice</u> a year at least'.					
8	产品	研究	<u>做得</u>	<u>不够充分</u>。		
	chǎnpǐn	yánjiū	zuò de	bú gòu chōngfèn		
	product	research	do DE	NEG enough adequate		
	'Product analysis was <u>not sufficiently carried out</u>'.					

Again, English WO is not likewise constrained: in both the translations of (2) and (8), expressions encoding a consequence of the action (*bǎo* 'be full' in (2)), and measurement of the action (*bú gòu chōngfèn* 'not sufficiently' in (8)) precede the form denoting the action itself (*chī* 'eat' and *zuò* 'carry out' respectively). For further discussion and examples on complements, see Loar (2011: 115–202). Among the motivations provided for this cross-linguistic difference is that temporal information is provided in languages both by morpho-semantic means (time expressions and verbal tense/consecution temporum) and by word order (whereby the sequence of words corresponds to the sequence of events referenced). Ho (1993: 142) convincingly observed that, in English, Romance and other Indo-European languages, time relations are signaled primarily by the tense system and other inflectional markers, whereas in languages lacking a surface marking system such as MC, information regarding the temporal sequence of events must be encoded through the relative sequence of elements and verbs (which are invariable in form).

Conceptual principles and Mandarin Chinese

The PTS also provides ready and intuitive ways to capture certain restrictions in argument alternations involving the BA construction. Objects cannot be fronted preverbally if they are the result of the action denoted by, for example, creation verbs like 写 *xiě* 'write' or 挖 *wā* 'dig'; object referents for these verbs exist only as a result of the action indicated by the verb, and hence they can only occur after the verb, in line with the PTS:

9 a 挖洞了
      wā dòng le
      dig hole LE
  b *把   洞   挖了
      bǎ   dòng wā le
      BA   hole   dig LE
      Intended meaning: 'Dug a hole'.

When the object of such verbs occurs preverbally, as in (9.c), where it is introduced by the BA morpheme, it is necessarily interpreted as a patient, and not as a resultant object, i.e., as existing before the action takes place, in accordance with the PTS. Specifically, the referent of *dòng* 'hole' in (9.c) is perceived as existing before the digger is requested to finish it, as expressed by the definite article in the English translation:

  c …命令   一个挖掘者   来   把洞   挖完。
      mìnglìng   yī ge wājuézhě lái   bǎ dòng wā wán
      order   one CL digger   come BA hole dig finish
      '(…) ordered a digger to finish digging the hole'.

Word order permutations at the sentence level: In some instances, two sequences of clauses/predicative elements are possible within the same sentence. For example, in the following pair, the two predicates/events *mǎi piào* 'buy ticket' and *jìnqu* 'enter' occur in opposite order. However, this necessarily involves change in meaning: the two events are interpreted as occurring in different sequences, in line with the PTS.

10 a 我们   没有   买票   进去   (60   元/人)。
       wǒmen   méi yǒu   mǎi piào jìnqu   yuán rén
       1PL   NEG   buy ticket enter   60   RMB person
       'We didn't buy the entrance ticket (60RMB/pax)'.
   b 走,   我们   进去   买票   吧!¹
       zǒu   wǒmen   jìnqu   mǎi piào ba
       go   1PL   enter   buy ticket MOD
       'Let's get in and buy tickets'.

As shown in the translations, the different order of the predicates corresponds to the temporal and causal sequence of the events – buy the ticket and/to enter in (10.a) vs. enter and/to buy the ticket in (10.b).

The PTS also helps explain why (and in which cases) only a limited number of prepositions/coverbs can occur after the verb, in addition to their canonical preverbal position. In most grammars, phrases such as *zài mǎbèi shang* in (11.a) are described as prepositional phrases, which need to occur before the main verb. On the other hand, when postverbal, as in (11.b), they are described either as exceptions to the above rule or as resultative complements. In this case,

在 *zài* is regarded as a preposition in (11.a) and as a verb in (11.b); however, this fails to capture the formal parallelism between the two sentences:

11 a   小猴子   在马背上   跳。   (Tai, 1985: 58)
        xiǎo hóuzi   zài mǎbèi shang   tiào
        little monkey (be) at horse-back on jump
        'The little monkey was jumping on the horse's back'.
    b   小猴子   跳   在马背上。
        xiǎo hóuzi   tiào   zài mǎbèi shang
        little monkey jump   (be) at horse-back on
        'The monkey jumped on the horse'.

Nevertheless, if considered in light of the PTS, the different order of the verb *tiào* 'jump' and the locative expression *zài mǎbèi shang* 'on the horse' reflects the temporal sequence of the states/actions they refer to. In (11.a), the location is before the verb, hence the monkey is perceived as being there before it started jumping, while in (11.b), the location is postverbal and hence interpreted as the result of, and thus temporally subsequent to, the action of jumping. Crucially, in the English translations, this is encoded through different tenses (past continuous vs. past simple) and not though WO permutations. The PTS rightly postulates that in MC a locative expression follows a verb if the locality is a result of the action denoted by the verb. This holds true also for other prepositions/coverbs, such as 到 *dào* 'arrive, at', or 给 *gěi* 'give, to' (see Packard 2015 for further discussion on the PTS, iconicity, and asymmetry in MC). The PTS also captures why the postverbal position is generally restricted to result-related prepositions/coverbs (for further discussion see Ho, 1993: 149–154).

There exist other apparent exceptions to the grammatical rule that coverbs/prepositions must occur before the main verb:

12 a   ... 学习   如何   用筷子   吃饭,...
            xuéxí   rúhé   yòng kuàizi   chī fàn
            learn   how   use chopstick eat meal
        '(I) learnt how to eat with chopsticks...'
    b   中国人   吃饭   用筷子,   不用刀叉...
        Zhōngguórén   chī fàn   yòng kuàizi   bú yòng dāochā
        Chinese   eat meal   use chopstick NEG use knife fork
        'Chinese people eat with chopsticks, not with knife and fork'.

However, the interaction of principles readily explains this pattern: the PTS interacts with the Principle of End Focus (Ho, 1993: 99–100), whereby the newest/most salient piece of information is placed towards the end of the sentence. In (12.b), the salient part of the message is *yòng kuàizi* 'use chopsticks'; hence it occurs at the end of the first clause. Crucially, the action of eating (*chī fàn* 'eat meal') is not anchored in time, but denotes a generic, referential and non-predicative activity, thus constituting a frame of validity for the following predication (see next subsection on WBP).

The principles of Temporal Scope, Whole-Before-Part and General-Preceding-Particular

The idea that the general/whole/bigger occurs before the particular/part/smaller has been referred to in the literature in several ways. Tai (1985: 60) defined it with respect to the temporal

Conceptual principles and Mandarin Chinese

scope of events: if 'the conceptual state represented by a syntactic unit X falls within the temporal scope of the conceptual state represented by a syntactic unit Y, then the word order is YX', which he illustrated with respect to the order of temporal expressions:

13 1936 年   12 月   22 日   下午   4 时,   西安   机场。
         nián   yuè   rì   xiàwǔ   shí   Xīān   jīchǎng
         year   month   day   afternoon hour   Xian   airport
    'December 22, 1936 at 4PM, Xian airport'.

However, he then suggested that it relates to a more general scope principle, whereby constituents with a larger scope precede those with a smaller scope in both time and space (Whole-Before-Part). Ho uses the term General-Preceding-Particular, while Hu prefers the label of Container-Before-Contained. Some decades earlier, Householder and Cheng (1967) called it Universe-Scope relation. All the above terms in fact refer to a common schema, which is captured by the following definition by Ho (1993: 165): 'constituents representing a global scope (general or whole) should precede those that represent a smaller scope (particular or specific)'. It is noteworthy to point out that the logical relation between the different items can vary and includes: temporal scope (bigger to smaller temporal spans), spatial scope (bigger to smaller locations/areas), containment (container before contained), partitive relations (whole before part), set-subset-item of a set and body-part (the whole-body comes before the body parts), as well as setting-event/participant relations (whereby the setting precedes the linguistic expression denoting the event/event participants). This principle is of great interest, in that it operates as a word order restriction at essentially all levels of grammatical organization. In what follows, instantiations of this principle are presented at different levels (phrase, clause, and sentence/discourse level).

Phrase level

As shown above, this principle regulates the inner order of temporal phrases such as dates, e.g. 22/12/1936 in (13); similarly, in locative phrases and expressions, e.g. the address in (14), elements are arranged from the biggest to the smallest item (whole–part, or container–contained):

14 北京   朝阳区   金台西路   2号人   民日报
    Běijīng   Cháoyáng qū   Jīntái Xī Lù   2 hào   Rénmín Rìbào
    Beijing   Chaoyang Dst. Jintai West St. 2 n.   People's Daily
    群众工作部
    qúnzhòng gōngzuòbù
    Mass Work Department
    'People's Daily Mass Work Department, 2 Jintai West Road, Chaoyang District, Beijing'.

The principle regulates the sequence of elements in phrases denoting percentages and fractions as well (the whole always precedes the fraction):

15 投资比例   一般   不低于   百   分之   二十五。
    tóuzī bǐlì   yìbān   bù dī yú   bǎi   fēn zhī   èrshíwǔ
    invest ratio normally NEG be lower than   100   part of   25
    'The investment proportion is usually never lower than 25 per cent'.

93

Householder and Cheng's (1967) study on nouns and their modifiers highlights this pattern also within NPs. In (16), the partitive relation within the postverbal NP *nà bā běn shū de sān běn* 'three of the eight books' must respect the sets-subsets sequence:

16 我   已经   读过   <u>那八本书</u>   的   <u>三本</u>。
    wǒ   yǐjing   dú guo   nà bā běn shū   de   sān běn
    1SG   already   read EXP that 8 CL book   DE   3 CL
    'I have already read <u>three</u> of the <u>eight books</u>'.

Crucially, English tends to order elements in the opposite way, i.e. with a part-whole sequence: this is true for dates, addresses and percentages, as translations of the above sentences show. This is an example of a language-specific conceptualization convention. In all the above cases, a part-whole order (as in the English translations) would be ungrammatical in MC.

Clause level: Several scholars have observed that, interestingly, the WBP principle regulates the order between different phrases and expressions within the clause as well. In discussing the Principle of Temporal Scope, Tai points out that time and location adverbials (sentential or preverbal) all set a temporal/spatial scope within which the following predication holds: the temporal scope of the adverbial always contains the time extent in which the action/state denoted by the verb sketches itself, and hence can only occur before the verb, according to the WBP. Preverbal temporal expressions can mark either the beginning or the whole span of the temporal scope within which the action/state of affairs is chronologically located. In Loar's (2011: 54) words, 'all the time-position adverbials, whether denoting a point or a period in time, are ordered before the verbs they modify. They indicate the time when an action begins (a point in time) or happens (a period of time)'.

17 <u>今年</u>   麦子   长得这么高。
    jīnnián   màizi   zhǎng de zhème gāo
    this year   wheat   grow DE so high
    'This year the crop has been growing a lot'.

18 <u>从2007</u>   <u>年起</u>   在   全国   农村地区   推广。
    cóng   nián qǐ   zài   quánguó   nóngcūn dìqū   tuīguǎng
    from 2007   year start   (be) at   whole-country   rural area   spread
    '...since 2007, (it) has been extended to rural areas all over the Country'.

19 <u>《辛丑条约》</u>   订了   以后,   俄国   不肯   退出。
    Xīnchǒu Tiáoyuē   dìng le   yǐhòu   Éguó   bù kěn   tuìchū
    1901 Treaty   conclude   LE after   Russia   NEG consent   withdraw
    'After the 1901 Treaty, Russia did not want to withdraw'.

In (17) the temporal frame within which the state of affairs expressed by the predicate occurs coincides with the time expression *jīnnián* 'this year'. In (18) and (19) the time expressions – the phrase *cóng 2007 nián qǐ* 'since 2007' in (18), and the temporal subordinate *Xīnchǒu Tiáoyuē dìng le yǐhòu* 'after concluding the 1901 Treaty' in (19) – denote the initial point of the time frame of the predication. Similarly, preverbal locative expressions, e.g. *zài mǎbèi shang* 'on the horse' in (11.a), denote a spatial frame within which the action (in this case jumping) takes place: this is why it can, and must, occur preverbally. The schema holds for referential elements as well. For example, when bearing a partitive, set-member or container-contained semantic relation, two or more NPs in the sentence are ordered according to the Whole-Part schema, and the sentence-initial topic always denotes the whole. This is the case in sentences like (20), where the whole (*nà bā běn shū* 'those 8 books') occurs in topic position, while the part (*sān běn*, 'three') occurs postverbally, in focus position.

20 那八本书   我   已经   读过   三本。
    nà bā běn shū   wǒ   yǐjing   dú guo   sān běn
    that 8 CL book   1SG   already   read EXP   3 CL
    'As for the eight books, I have read three of them'.

Householder and Cheng (1967) stressed the parallelism between this type of clause and those like (16), where the whole-part relation is phrase-internal: crucially, in both cases the WBP is an absolute constraint, and no part-whole arrangement is possible. A similar pattern can be observed in sentence (21), where the NP denoting the whole (*shū* 'book') is not modified by a numeral and is interpreted either as having a general reference (books in general) or as referring to a contextually inferable group of elements, denoting the whole ('those books'):

21 书   我   已经   读过   三本。
    shū   wǒ   yǐjing   dú guo   sān běn
    book   1SG   already   read EXP   3 CL
    'As for (those) books, I've already read three'.

This type of sentences has been analyzed in the literature as an instance of *quantifier float*, whereby the quantifier (the numeral-classifier group *sān běn*, 'three') is detached from the head noun (*shū* 'book') and launched in postverbal (focal) position, according to the principle of End Focus. Crucially, both principles (End Focus for new information and General-Preceding-Particular) are respected, resulting in this specific and often not well-understood grammatical structure. Other instantiations of the whole-part schema include the following:

22 吃啊,   快餐   最   便宜。
    chī a,   kuàicān   zuì   piányi
    eat TM   fast-food   most   cheap
    'Talking about food, fast-food is the cheapest option'.

23 他   把   那三个桔子   都   剥了皮。
    tā   bǎ   nà sān ge júzi   dōu   bō le pí
    3SG   BA   that 3 CL tangerine   all   peel LE skin
    'He peeled those three tangerines'.

In (22), often referred to in the literature as a double nominative construction, the semantic relation between the two NPs is that of hypernym (food) vs. hyponym (fast-food) or set-subset, whereas in (23) the semantic relation is that of entity (tangerine) and component (skin). As seen in the examples above, the position of the two NPs can vary with respect to the verb or to morphemes such as 把 *bǎ* and 被 *bèi*: they can be pre- and postverbal, respectively, as in (20) and (21), or all preverbal, as in (22); the first NP can be introduced by BA, as in (23). However, with respect to each other, the order is fixed, as the whole must occur before the part/

component/member of the set: the WBP is an absolute WO constraint. Crucially, in most cases, the whole occurs in topic position. The parallelism between the sentence-initial position, the whole (or universe, or general etc.) and the topic has been pointed out by a number of linguists, including Householder and Cheng (1967), Chafe (1976), Ho (1993), Loar (2011) and Morbiato (2014). Chafe (1976: 50) insightfully defined topics in MC as frame-setters: 'the topic in MC sets a spatial or temporal,' but also an 'individual framework within which the main predication holds'.

The sentence and the discourse level

As seen above, the WBP principle extends to the level of the sentence, and more generally, to the level of discourse organization. On the sentence level, it regulates the relative order of different clauses: specifically, it determines the relative order between subordinate and main clauses, the former providing a background/frame for the latter. The frame can be temporal, spatial, concessional, causal, hypothetical, and so on. Kirkpatrick and Xu (2012) and Ho (1993) observed how clauses can denote a temporal, spatial and conditional scope for what follows, and must be ordered according to the frame-event/participant sequence: that is why such clauses are placed sentence-initially. Chao Yuen-ren (1968: 120) also remarked that all concessive, causal, conditional, temporal and spatial clauses are in the last resort topics (and hence set a frame for the following predication, in the sense of Chafe (1976) mentioned above). The examples he provided include the following:

24 我   死了   丧事   从简
    wǒ   sǐ le   sāngshì   cóngjiǎn
    1SG   die LE   funeral   simple
    TOPIC=FRAME   COMMENT
    'If/when I die the funeral should be simple'.

The clause *wǒ sǐle* '(if/when) I die' clearly provides the temporal/conditional frame for which the following comment *sāngshì cóngjiǎn* 'funeral is simple' holds (the funeral may not be simple if someone else dies). Similar considerations hold for (19), where the temporal subordinate (*Xīnchǒu Tiáoyuē dìng le yǐhòu* 'after concluding the 1901 Treaty') denotes a time frame for the following main clause. Haiman (1978) also highlighted a systematic association between conditionals, topics and topic definitions in terms of frame. In his words: 'Conditionals, like topics, are givens which constitute the frame of reference with respect to which the main clause is either true (if a proposition), or felicitous (if not)' (1978: 564). This is evident in MC in a sentence like the following, where the first sentence is interpreted as the condition (frame) of validity for the second, without any overt concessive marking:

25 你不去,   我去。
    nǐ bú qù   wǒ qù
    2SG NEG go   1SG go
    TOPIC=FRAME   COMMENT
    'If you don't go, I'll go'.

In (26), on the other hand, the frame is temporal 'during the time span when God created animals' (from Ho's (1993) corpus):

26 上帝   造动物，   他   并没有   给动物   这种能力。
    Shàngdì   zào dòngwù   tā   bìng méiyǒu   gěi dòngwù   zhè zhǒng nénglì
    God   create animal 3SG   at.all NEG   give animal   this CL power
    TOPIC = FRAME   COMMENT
    'When God created animals, He did not give them this power'.

Kirkpatrick and Xu also highlighted a commonality between topics, subordinate-main clauses and modifier-modified structures, i.e. they all set a frame of validity for the following part. They talk about 'a sentence whose principal clause is preceded by a clause that sets the framework for it and it follows a modifier-modified sequence' (2012: 111). They also pointed out that Chinese linguists refer to this type of pattern with the term 偏正复句 *piānzhèng fùjù*, literally modifier-modified complex sentence: the term 偏正 *piānzhèng* is traditionally used to describe the modifier-modified relationship in NPs (e.g. adjective- noun NPs) and has been extended to describe sentences that have a 'modifying' clause followed by a 'modified' clause.

Finally, Kirkpatrick and Xu drew a striking parallel between topic-comment, modifier-modified, big-small, whole-part, and the 'because-therefore' or 'frame-main' sequences in extended discourse and texts. According to them, the 'frame-main' and 'whole-part' are common Chinese sequencing patterns of discourse organization. They claim that the 'because-therefore' or 'frame-main' schema has operated in argumentative text since the Western Han period and later became the unmarked rhetorical sequencing in MC. Among the many examples, they discuss the following text from the *Lüshi Chunqiu* (also known in English as Master Lü's Spring and Autumn Annals) highlighting the recursive rhetoric schema [BECAUSE] – <u>THEREFORE</u> or [FRAME] – <u>MAIN</u> (glossing and translation adapted from Kirkpatrick and Xu, 2012: 42):

27 [未有蚩尤之时]，
    wèi yǒu Chīyǒu zhī shí
    not.yet there.be Chiyou PRT time

<u>民固剥林木以战矣</u>，   <u>胜者为长</u>。
mín gù bō línmù yǐ zhàn yǐ   shèngzhě wéi zhǎng
people indeed peel wood CONJ fight PRT   winner become leader
[Before the time of Chiyou], <u>people would whittle pieces of wood to fight</u>, <u>and the winner would become the leader</u>.

[长则犹不足治之]，   故立君。
zhǎng zé yóu bùzú zhì zhī   gù lì jūn
leader though still NEG.sufficient govern PRON   so establish ruler
[The leaders though proved unequal to the task of governing], <u>that is why the position of lord was established</u>.

[君又不足以治之]，   故立天子。
jūn yòu bùzúyǐ zhì zhī   gù lì tiānzǐ
ruler again NEG.sufficient.to govern PRON   so establish emperor
[Lords also proved unequal to the task of governing], <u>that is why the position of Son of Heaven was established</u>.

They further maintain that arguments by analogy and by historical example naturally follow the rhetorical "frame-main" or "because- therefore" sequence, that 'adheres to the fundamental principle of logical and natural sequencing in Chinese' (128). They demonstrate this with examples taken from naturally occurring Chinese discourse and text, which include: a university seminar (informal), a press conference given by the Chinese Ministry of Foreign Affairs (oral, but prewritten), and a summary of a contemporary essay by author Lu Xun (written). Due to space restrictions, other examples of texts they provide cannot be reported here; for further discussion, see Kirkpatrick and Xu.

Applications to Chinese as a second language acquisition

As seen so far, conceptual principles and their iconic schemas are rather intuitive and easy to remember: this offers a wide range of applications for Chinese as a second/foreign language instruction. Both Jiang (2009) and Loar (2011) emphasized the potential of conceptual principles for language pedagogy, in that iconic schemas are easier to memorize and recall compared to grammar rules. Loar (2011: xix) stressed the fact that rules might 'appear to be arbitrary and hard to remember', whereas if the student understands the principle underlying the rules, 'some of the arbitrariness disappears and word order study becomes easier'. Jiang (2009) provided an interesting application of different word order principles to Chinese L2 word order error analysis. Her research involved a cross-sectional study on word order errors committed by English L1 learners of Chinese. She categorized WO errors with respect to the following taxonomy: conceptual errors (violating WO principles such as the PTS or the WBP), grammatical errors (violating rules like modifier-modified order), functional errors (violating information structural rules like given-new order or topic-comment structures) and sociocultural errors. Jiang's (2009) analysis provides a number of interesting results worth mentioning with respect to acquisition of word order in MC. First, the conceptual domain has a much higher error rate than the remaining three domains. Specifically, 79% of word order errors (319/404) fall within this domain. The Principle of Temporal Sequence (PTS) was found to have the widest application range in explaining Chinese L2 word order errors, followed by that of Whole-Before-Part: among the 408 WO errors, 249 (61%) occurred due to the violation of PTS and 70 (17.2%) violated the WBP (Jiang, 2009: 206). Moreover, not only were conceptual WO errors rates the highest, but the conceptual domain also presented an increased tendency in WO errors from level 1 students (6.77) compared to level 3 students (10.45). Examples of word order errors she provided are reported below in the (a) version, whereas the (b) version reports the correct word order:

Violation of PTS:

28 'We spent eighteen years living in the UK'.
    a   *我们   一十八年   住   英国。   *ACTION>MEASURE COMPLEMENT
        wǒmen   yīshíbā nián   zhù   Yīngguó
        1PL   eighteen year   live   UK
    b   我们   住   在英国   十八年。
        wǒmen   zhù   zài Yīngguó   shíbā nián
        1PL   live   (be) in UK   eighteen year

Violation of WBP:

29 'Now I live in Brisbane, Australia'.
    a   *现在   我   住   布里斯本   澳大利亚。   *SPACE FRAME>PART
        xiànzài   wǒ   zhù   Bùlǐsīběn   Àodàlìyà
        now   1SG   live   Brisbane   Australia

b	现在	我	住	澳大利亚	布里斯本。
	xiànzài	wǒ	zhù	Àodàlìyà	Bùlǐsībĕn
	now	1SG	live	Australia	Brisbane

In (28), the temporal duration *shíbā nián* 'eighteen years' measures the durative action of living *zhù*; hence it needs to be postverbal (durative complement), according to the PTS. In (29), *Àodàlìyà* 'Australia' refers to a bigger spatial scope, namely a country, than *Bùlǐsībĕn* 'Brisbane', which is a city in the country; hence the correct order is (29.b), in accordance with the WBP. Jiang hypothesized that the L2 learners' conceptualization of the world is largely based on their L1 and attributes a significant number of word order errors to the fact that 'the learners mapped their L1-based conceptualization onto their L2 structures' (2009: 189). Nonetheless, she stressed the fact that MC language instruction should account for these types of principles as well: 'learners did not seem to be aware of the Chinese word order principles, as their introduction is not a feature of current Chinese language pedagogy'. She further remarked that Chinese textbooks do not introduce the basic Chinese word order principles, especially the conceptual ones: 'the results of this study indicate that it is imperative for the basic Chinese word order principles be included in a CFL curriculum' (Jiang, 2009: 204).

Conclusions

This chapter presented conceptual principles governing word order in MC, with a focus on the Principles of Temporal Sequence and of Whole-Before-Part. The PTS is a cross-linguistic tendency, in that most languages tend to describe states and events in the sequence; however, in MC this tendency is comparatively more consistent, as a result of the lack of morphosyntactic means to encode temporal sequence; hence, it applies to different levels of linguistic organization, as discussed above. On the other hand, the WBP principle is an example of a language- or culture-specific conceptual and organizational principle: while MC necessarily displays the whole-part sequence, in English and other European languages, the part-whole order is more common. An interesting line of research relates this cognitive schema to the cultural or social factors that might have caused this fundamental difference: in this respect, I signal Nisbett and Masuda's (2003) and Nisbett's (2004) studies on the difference between what they call 'East Asian' and 'Western' perception: they conducted surveys and analyzed hystorical, philosophical, social and belief-related factors that contributed shaping and reiforcing different cognitive patterns. Their observations nicely fit and reflect the whole to part and part to whole difference displayed in linguistic data discussed above: East Asians tend to attach importance to the environment, which is seen as unified/whole with the elements it contains, while Westerners tend to focus on individual elements. The PTS and WBP principles account for a number of word order rules and restrictions in MC, including the sequence of preverbal elements (NPs, adverbials sentence-initial elements) and postverbal sequencing (complements in general). In particular, the WBP principle is of great interest, as it holds true both at the micro- and macro-levels of linguistic organization. Moreover, their inherent iconic nature renders them easy to learn and remember; hence, they have interesting applications in disciplines such as MC language teaching, which is still comparatively neglected, both as an area of linguistic research and as a teaching practice.

Acknowledgments

The author would like to acknowledge the support of the China Studies Centre at the University of Sydney through the provision of the 2017 CSC Research Students Support Grant.

Note

1 Source: book 天使的眼泪 https://goo.gl/TL6TDz

References

Amorapanth, P., Kranjec, A., Bromberger, B., Lehet, M., Widick, P., Woods, A.J. and Chatterjee, A. (2012) 'Language, Perception, and the Schematic Representation of Spatial Relations', *Brain and Language* 120(3): 226–236.

Biq, Y.-O., Tai, J.H.-Y. and Thompson, S.A. (1996) 'Recent developments in functional approaches to Chinese', in *New Horizons in Chinese Linguistics*. C.-T.J. Huang and A.Y.-H. Li (eds.) Dordrecht: Kluwer Academic Publishers.

Chafe, W.L. (1976) 'Givenness, contrastiveness, definiteness, subjects, topics, and points of view', in *Subject and Topic*, C. Li (ed.) New York: Academic Press.

Chao, Y. (1968) *A Grammar of Spoken Chinese*. Berkeley: University of California Press.

Greenberg, J. (1966) *Universals of Language*. Cambridge, MA: MIT Press.

Haiman, J. (1978) 'Conditionals Are Topics', *Language* 54(3): 564–589.

Haiman, J. (1980) 'The Iconicity of Grammar: Isomorphism and Motivation', *Language* 56(3): 515–540.

Haiman, J. (1983) 'Iconic and Economic Motivation', *Language* 59(4): 781–819.

Haiman, J. (1985) *Iconicity in Syntax: Proceedings of a Symposium on Iconicity in Syntax, Stanford, June 24–6, 1983*. Amsterdam: John Benjamins.

Ho, Y. (1993) *Aspects of Discourse Structure in Mandarin Chinese*. Lewiston: Mellen University Press.

Hopper, P.J. and Thompson, S.A. (1980) 'Transitivity in Grammar and Discourse', *Language* 56(2): 251–299.

Householder, W.F. and Cheng, L.R. (1967) *Universe-Scope Relations in Chinese and Japanese*. University of California Berkeley Phonology Laboratory, Report number: POLA-2-3.

Hu, W. (1995) Functional Perspectives and Chinese Word Order, PhD Dissertation, Ohio State University, Columbus.

Jakobson, R. (1971) *Selected Writings Vol. 2: Word and Language*. The Hague: De Gruyter.

Jiang, W. (2009) *Acquisition of Word Order in Chinese as a Foreign Language*. Berlin: Mouton de Gruyter.

Kirkpatrick, A. and Xu, Z. (2012) *Chinese Rhetoric and Writing: An Introduction for Language Teachers*. Fort Collins, CO: The WAC Clearinghouse and Parlor Press.

Lakoff, G. (1987) *Women, Fire, and Dangerous Things: What Categories Reveal about the Mind*. Chicago: The University of Chicago Press.

Langacker, R.W. (1987) *Foundations of Cognitive Grammar*. Stanford: Stanford University Press.

Levinson, S.C. (2003) *Space in Language and Cognition: Explorations in Cognitive Diversity*. Cambridge: Cambridge University Press.

Light, T. (1979) 'Word Order and Word Order Change in Mandarin Chinese', *Journal of Chinese Linguistics* 7: 149–180.

Loar, J.K. (2011) *Chinese Syntactic Grammar: Functional and Conceptual Principles*. New York: Peter Lang.

Lu, B. (1998) 'Cong yuyi, yuyong kan yufa xingshi de shizhi' (On the Essence of Grammatical Forms in the Light of Semantics and Pragmatics), *Zhongguo Yuwen* 5(266): 353–367.

Morbiato, A. (2014) 'Cognitive Principles and Preverbal Position in Chinese', *Annali Di Ca' Foscari* 50: 205–224.

Morbiato A. (2017) 'Information encoding, Mandarin Chinese word order and CSLA: A cognitive-functional account', in *Explorations into Chinese as a Second Language. Educational Linguistics, Vol. 31*. I. Kecskes (ed.) Cham: Springer.

Nisbett, R. E., & Masuda, T. (2003). 'Culture and Point of View', *Proceedings of the National Academy of Sciences* 100(19): 11163 LP–11170.

Nisbett, R. E. (2003). *The Geography of Thought: How Asians and Westerners Think Differently– And Why*. New York: Free Press.

Packard J.L. (2015). 'Space, Time and Asymmetry in Chinese', in *Space and Quantification in Languages of China*. D. Xu, and J. Fu (eds.) Cham: Springer.

Peirce, C.S. (1931) *The Collected Papers of Charles Sanders Peirce*, edited by C. Hartshorne and P. Weiss. Cambridge, MA: Harvard University Press.

Siewierska, A. (1988) *Word Order Rules*. London: Croom Helm.

Tai, J.H.-Y. (1985) 'Temporal sequence and word order in Chinese', in *Iconicity in Syntax*. J. Haiman (ed.) Amsterdam: John Benjamins.

Tai, J.H.-Y. (1989) Toward a cognition-based functional grammar of Chinese', in *Functionalism and Chinese Grammar*. J. Tai and F. Hsueh (eds.) South Orange, NJ: Chinese Language Teachers Association.

Tai, J.H.-Y. (1993) 'Iconicity: Motivations in Chinese grammar', in *Principles and Prediction: The Analysis of Natural Language*. M. Eid and G. Iverson (eds.) Amsterdam: John Benjamins.

Talmy, L. (1988) 'Force Dynamics in Language and Cognition', *Cognitive Science* 12(1): 49–100.

6
Grammatical constructions and Chinese discourse

Zhuo Jing-Schmidt

Introduction

Definitions of "discourse" are many, and vary across discipline boundaries (Mills, 1997). This chapter uses the term 'discourse' the way it is generally understood in functionally oriented linguistics, namely language use for communication in social context (Brown and Yule, 1983). While the significance of discourse in linguistic research has increasingly come to be appreciated, its place in linguistics cannot be taken for granted, given the dominance of Formal Linguistics for much of the 20th century. The intensification of interest in discourse in the last three decades was a key part of the functionalist rebellion to Formal Linguistics. Functionalism argues against the existence of syntax as an independent, self-contained structural level (Givón, 1984; Dik, 1997). It insists that grammar be studied in relation to pragmatic functions, discourse context, and discourse structure (Givón, 1979, 1983, 1984, 1989, 1995; Tai and Hsueh, 1989; Dik, 1997; Hopper 2001; Hengeveld and Mackenzie, 2008, 2014, inter alias).

Riding the wave of functionalism, discourse analysis gathered steam in the 1980s, and has now permeated linguistic research. A wide range of grammatical categories have been probed from a discourse perspective, such as word order (Sun and Givón, 1985; Payne, 1992), voice (Shibatani, 1985; Fox and Hopper, 1994), transitivity (Hopper and Thompson, 1980), ergativity (Du Bois, 1987; Cooreman, 1983; Gaby, 2010), tense and aspect (Patard, 2014; Webber, 1988), anaphora (Malt, 1985; Fox, 1987; Givón, 2017), clause combining and subordination (Haiman and Thompson, 1988), to throw a glimpse at the vast literature.

While the above-mentioned research examines grammar from a discourse perspective, research in Conversation Analysis focuses on interaction and how language contributes to this situated social practice. Concerned with grammar as one of many discourse resources, conversation analysts have recognized the need to explore the "mutual bearing of the various organizations of 'language' on the one hand [....] and the organizations of interaction and talk-in-interaction on the other" (Schegloff, 1996: 52). The discourse and grammar interface has become a salient object of research in Discourse and Conversation Analysis (Ochs et al., 1996; Hakulinen and Selting, 2005).

Chinese discourse linguistics is rooted in a functional descriptive tradition as represented by the seminal reference grammars of Wang (1947), Chao (1968), Lü (1980), and Li and Thompson

(1981). These grammars espouse a descriptive framework that emphasizes the meaning and function of grammatical structures and the context of their use. Although discourse does not stand out as a distinct level of description in these reference grammars, due in large part to the analysis of contrived sentence-level examples, their functional approach has foreshadowed and laid the foundation for Chinese discourse grammar.

Grammatical constructions and discourse

The notion of a grammatical construction may seem intuitive and self-evident. However, because it is one of those terms that can be used either in a theory-neutral or in a theory-specific sense, a definition is in order. This chapter adopts the definition of a grammatical construction as proposed in Construction Grammar (Goldberg, 1995, 2006). Within this framework, the boundary between syntax and the lexicon is eliminated. Language is treated as an organized inventory of form-meaning pairs on a continuum from concrete lexical items to abstract sentential patterns. A grammatical construction is a pairing of grammatical patterns with a conceptual or discourse function. In the case of Chinese, a grammatical construction thus defined can be a range of form-meaning pairs varying in size and abstractness. For example, it can be a phrasal pattern such as the numeral-classifier construction [NUM/DEM CLF NP], paired with the function of INDIVIDUATION AND QUANTIFICATION e.g. 一/这个人 'a/this person'. It can be a sentential pattern such as the *ba*-construction [NP$_{subj}$ *ba* NP$_{obj}$ VP] denoting CHANGE BY OBJECT MANIPULATION, or the passive construction [NP$_{subj}$ *bei* (NP$_{obl}$) VP] signaling the AFFECTEDNESS of the patient as a result of an action. It can be a supra-sentential pattern such as the topic-comment construction in the form of [NP$_{topic}$ [(NP$_{subj}$)VP] $_{comment}$], which serves the function of TALKING ABOUT a given topic, e.g. 这本书字太小, literally 'This book font is small'. It can also be a grammatical category that serves a discourse-level function, such as zero anaphora, which pairs a zero form Ø in a particular argument slot of a grammatical construction with the function of TRACKING A CONTEXTUALLY RECOVERABLE REFERENT.

Discourse constraints on grammar

The analysis of the topic-comment construction was one of the earliest attempts to explain Chinese grammar from a discourse point of view. Chao (1968: 69) recognized the typological distinctness of this construction, noting that its adequate description requires the discourse concepts of topic and comment. Following this insight, scholars endeavored to specify the grammatical relations, semantic roles, and the way of information packaging involved in the topic-comment construction (Li and Thompson, 1976, 1981; Tsao, 1987; Shi, 2000). A now classic study of word order variation is Sun and Givón (1985), which refutes the notion that Chinese has undergone a typological shift to SOV by arguing that word order variation is a function of discourse. Presently, the majority of Chinese grammatical constructions have been examined through the lens of discourse. Among the most extensively studied are those that are of typological significance. Zero anaphora, especially zero subject has been shown to be prevalent in Chinese discourse. As an unmarked structure, it serves as the default mechanism of referent tracking (Li and Thompson, 1979; Chen, 1986, 1987; Tsao, 1990). Discourse studies of numeral classifiers have indicated functions related to the referential status and discourse salience of the referent encoded in a numeral-classifier construction, thus rejecting the presumed one-to-one association between noun and classifier (Erbaugh, 1986, 1990, 2002; Sun, 1988). The *ba*-construction, traditionally described as signaling "disposal" (Wang, 1947; Li and Thompson, 1981), has been shown to play a prominent part in dramatizing discourse (Jing-Schmidt, 2005) and expressing subjectivity (Shen, 2002; Jing-Schmidt, 2005). In relation to its discourse functions, the *ba*-construction is known to be selective about genre (Jing-Schmidt and Tao, 2009). Similarly, passive constructions the semantics of which is marked by adversity (Chao, 1968; Li and Thompson, 1981; Liu, 2011) exhibit frequency distributions skewed toward certain genres (Jing-Schmidt and Jing, 2011), and undergo exemplar-based pragmatic innovation in social contexts (Peng, 2017).

Grammar as discursive resource

Scholars interested in talk-in-interaction regard grammatical constructions as linguistic resources that speakers draw on in constructing discourse and managing conversation (Schegloff et al., 1996). Tao and Thompson (1994) showed that there are preferred grammatical constructions in conversation that serve the intended communicative goals. Similarly, Tao (1996) demonstrated discrepancies between nuanced language uses observed in ordinary conversations and the rigidity of sentence grammar, and proposed intonation units as the basic units of conversation analysis. Su (2017) showed that the *ba*-construction is systematically preferred over its structural alternatives in paradigmatic opposition for the purpose of signaling discourse significance. Tao (2000) and Thompson and Tao (2010) showed that even abstract lexical classes such as "demonstrative" and "adjective" exhibit a psychological reality in conversation.

On a methodological note, discourse-oriented analyses of grammatical constructions such as those discussed above, require data on authentic language uses that transcend the boundary of a single sentence. This methodological requirement is based on the very theoretical commitment to the non-autonomy of grammar and the central role played by context in language use. The most important aspects of context, as defined by Cruse (2006: 35), including "(1) preceding and following utterances and/or expressions ('co-text'), (2) the immediate physical situation, (3) the wider situation, including social and power relations, and (4) knowledge presumed shared between speaker and hearer", cannot be adequately explored on intuitively contrived sentence-level data. As will be shown in the section below, it takes contextual analysis of authentic usage data to illuminate the true functions of grammatical constructions in discourse.

The Mandarin Chinese *shì* . . . *de* construction

The *shì* . . . *de* construction in Mandarin Chinese takes the form of [X *shì* Y *de*]. Here, X is the topic, and [*shì* Y *de*] serves as the comment whereby the copula *shì* introduces a nominalized structure [Y *de*]. The Y slot can admit a range of structures. Consider the examples in (1) – (4) as illustrations (adapted from Jing-Schmidt, 2008: 87):[1]

(1) a 书是看的，不是撕的
 shū shì kàn de, bú shì sī de
 book COP look NOM, not COP tear NOM
 'Books are to read, not to tear'.
 b 我是教书的，不是做买卖的
 wǒ shì jiāoshū de, bú shì zuò mǎimai de
 1SG COP teach NOM, not COP do business NOM
 'I am one who teaches, not one who does business'.

(2) a 他是昨天来的
 tā shì zuótiān lái de
 3SG COP yesterday come NOM
 'He came yesterday/It was yesterday that he came'.
 b 这条裙子是妈妈买的
 zhè tiáo qúnzi shì māma mǎi de
 this CLF skirt COP mother buy NOM
 'This skirt, it is mother who bought it'.
 c 汤是用白菜做的
 tāng shì yòng báicài zuò de
 coup COP use Napa.cabbage make NOM
 'The soup, it is made with Napa cabbage'.

(3) a 中国人民是勤劳勇敢的
 zhōngguó rénmín shì qínláo yǒnggǎn de
 China people COP diligent brave NOM
 'The Chinese people are hardworking and courageous'.
 b 你的做法是不对的
 nǐ de zuòfǎ shì búduì de
 2SG ASSOC way COP incorrect NOM
 'Your way of acting is not right'.

(4) a 日本的做法我们是坚决不能接受的
 Rìběn de zuòfǎ wǒmen shì jiānjué bù néng jiēshòu de
 Japan ASSOC way 1PL COP decidedly not can accept NOM
 'We can definitely not accept Japan's way of acting'.
 b 我是爱你的
 wǒ shì ài nǐ de
 1SG COP love 2SG NOM
 'I love you'.

Treatments of this construction fall largely into two camps. One, which I describe as the binary approach, treats the examples in (2) as exemplars of a focus/cleft construction, and those in (3) and (4) as exemplars of an emphatic construction. Representative work in this camp includes Hashimoto (1969), Teng (1979), Ross (1983), Hedberg (1999), Liu et al. (2001), and Lü (2007), among others. The binary approach typically ignores those examples in (1) and other uses that appear atypical of the two presumed distinct types, considering them as derived from the simple copular construction [NP$_1$ shì NP$_2$] via transformation. The other treatment, which I describe as the unitary approach, treats all uses of the construction that share the same surface structure as one single construction, and views it as continuous with the simple copular construction [NP$_1$ shì NP$_2$]. Within this camp, researchers differ in what meaning they postulate for [X shì Y de]. Some adopt the notion of emphasis as the overarching meaning, e.g. Jing-Schmidt (2008), Xu (2014). Others invoke the construct of identification/contrastive focus to account for the meaning of the construction, e.g. Paris (1979), Zhan and Sun (2013), Jing-Schmidt and Peng (2016). In keeping with the definition of a construction as a pairing of a surface form with a function, as discussed in the previous section, I will focus, in what follows, on the unitary approach that is consistent with this definition.

The inadequacy of the emphasis account

The notion of emphasis is also referred to as affirmative attitude or certainty. Its explanatory validity is often taken for granted in the literature. A comparison of (5a), the SVO counterpart of (4b), reintroduced here as (5b), can be instructive:

(5) a 我爱你
    wǒ ài nǐ
    1SG love 2SG
    'I love you'.
   b 我是爱你的
    wǒ shì ài nǐ de
    1SG COP love 2SG NOM
    'I love you'.

In my earlier analysis (Jing-Schmidt, 2008), I made a cognitive semantic argument that emphasis arises from nominalization as conceptual substantiation, the idea that turning a process or property into an entity creates conceptual substance and stability (Langacker, 1987; Seiler, 1993). These conceptual properties render (5b) emphatic about the speaker's feeling for the addressee, whereas its SVO counterpart is a conventional expression of love. From a discourse perspective, the analysis implies that (5a) and (5b) may be used in different contexts. However, this analysis does not specify the nature of those contexts. Critically, one does not say (5b) unless one has reason to believe that the addressee assumes the opposite of the proposition, and wants to refute that assumption. That is, (5b) is meant to preempt or rebut an assumption that is opposite to the proposition. In this function, emphasis is not just insufficient, it is impertinent. While a rebuttal is understandably emphatic, an emphasis is not a rebuttal. This example illustrates the centrality of context to an adequate account of the discourse function of a grammatical construction.

For the same reason, notions such as certainty and subjectivity fall short. Although they signal that speakers are certain and subjective about something and take a stance toward it, they do not specify what their certainty, subjectivity, or stance is up against, which is at the core of many *shì* ... *de* uses. Xu (2014) observed that the dominant type of the *shì* ... *de* construction in her spoken corpus is [*shì* AP *de*], and that the most frequent AP tokens are those that denote subjective judgment. She noted that such tokens are about issues being important or not, ideas or concepts being right or wrong, or situations being the same or different. However, instead of pushing this insight to its logical conclusion about the contrastive nature inherent in these pairs of conceptual opposites, Xu settled with the recognition of "no easily applied measures for these invisible characteristics except for one's own subjective evaluation" (p. 158). The lesson suggested by this example is not so much the lack of contextualized data or a failure to examine the context of use. It is one about the danger of preconceptions. If we do not examine our preconceptions closely and critically against the data, we risk oblivion to our own best insight.

The identification/contrastive focus account

This model of the semantics of the *shì* ... *de* construction maintains that Y as part of the comment [*shì* Y *de*] holds the identification/contrastive focus of the proposition. That is, in all the uses that share the same form, a particular value is presented as new information in contrast to an alternative value with regard to a given variable. The discourse realization of contrast varies in explicitness and across contexts. While contrast is easy to identify in (1) and (2), it seems elusive in (3) and (4), where both the entity in focus and its potential alternatives are more difficult to pin down. Indeed, a fundamental challenge of the unitary account is the gap between the postulated abstract meaning and its functional materializations in discourse. Zhan and Sun (2013) referred to *shì . . . de* construction as a cleft construction, and postulated contrastive focus as its semantics. However, it remains unclear what contrastive focus means in terms of pragmatic function and usage pattern in discourse. In fact, the English-centric notion of cleft reduces the pragmatic scope of the construction, and contradicts the constructionist approach, which by definition views constructions as language-specific form-meaning pairs (Croft, 2001). As such, it prevents the analysis from exploring the rich discursive potentials of the construction.

The problem is in part methodological. A look at the level and units of analysis in previous research suggests that most studies are confined to an analysis of isolated utterances at the sentence level, stripped of their discourse context. There is no clue to the kind of utterances preceding or following the *shì . . . de* construction, to say nothing of how its use is related to the immediate physical situation of the speaker, the wider social and power relation, and the kind of knowledge presumed to be shared between speaker and addressee. In short, there is no indication as to where and when to use this construction. In a series of recent studies, Jing-Schmidt and associates (Jing-Schmidt et al., 2015; Jing-Schmidt and Peng, 2016; Jing-Schmidt, 2016) addressed this problem by looking at larger discourse units based on corpus data. They identified four types of contrast, to which we now turn.

Lexical semantic contrast

The lexical semantic contrast is explicit and readily identifiable as lexical oppositions or alternatives in the focal lexemes, as in (6) and (7), where the lexemes in contrast are underlined in the translation:

(6) 钱是有价的，
qián shì yǒu jià de
money COP have price NOM
政治损失是无法衡量的
zhèngzhì sǔnshī shì wúfǎ héngliáng de
political loss COP impossible measure NOM
'Money is <u>measurable in value</u>, but political loss is <u>immeasurable</u>'.

(7) 第二天的小酥饼竟然出奇地好吃，
dìèr tiān de xiǎo sūbǐng jìngrán chūqíde hǎochī
second day ASSOC small cookie even surprising delicious
'The cookies of the next day were amazingly delicious',
它既不是甜的，也不是咸的，它是椒盐的
tā jì bú shì tián de, yě bú shì xián de, tā shì jiāo-yán de
3SG also NEG COP sweet NOM, also NEG COP salty NOM, it COP pepper-salt NOM
'It is neither <u>sweet</u> nor <u>salty</u>; it is <u>salt-pepper spiced</u>'.

The lexical oppositions we see here are paradigmatic oppositions resulting from the use of two or more *shì . . . de* clauses. Such paradigmatic oppositions explicitly construct a categorical judgment about the entity or entities being talked about. In (6), that judgment pertains to the perceived value of two entities being compared and contrasted. In (7), that judgment picks out one property that uniquely identifies the taste of the cookies in contrast to potential alternative properties. Note also that the lexical opposites are in tandem with grammatical contrast signaled by negation.

Textual contrast

The textual contrast is located outside of the focal element, and is realized as textual (e.g. sequential, temporal, or logical) connectors or combinations thereof, as in (8) and (9):

(8) 每个座席桌上都有一面小镜子，
měigè zuòxí zhuō-shàng dōu yǒu yī miàn xiǎo jìngzi
every seat table-LOC all EXIST one CLF small mirror
一是用来做口形操的，
yī shì yòng lái zuò kǒuxíngcāo de,
one COP use PURP do pronunciation-exercise NOM
二是做微笑服务的，
èr shì zuò wēixiào fúwù de
two COP do smile service NOM
三是用来每天照照看自己的心情的
sān shì yòng lái měitiān zhào-zhào-kàn zìjǐ de xīnqíng de
three COP use PURP everyday look self ASSOC mood NOM
'There is a mirror on each desk, it is <u>first</u> used for pronunciation exercises; <u>second</u>, for customer service with a smile; and <u>third</u>, for monitoring one's mood every day'.

(9) 以前我是不给学生考试范围的，
yǐqián wǒ shì bù gěi xuéshēng kǎoshì fànwéi de,
before 1SG COP not give student test range NOM
但是这次我也随大流和其他老师一样，
dànshì zhècì wǒ yě suí dàliú hé qítā lǎoshī yíyàng
but this.time 1SG also follow big.flow as other teacher same
在考试前把考试的范围和学生说了
zài kǎoshì qián bǎ kǎoshì de fànwéi hé xuéshēng shuō le
LOC exam ahead OM exam ASSOC scope with student say PFV
'<u>In the past</u>, I never gave students any study guide, <u>but this time</u> I followed the other teachers, and told the students what to prepare for before the test'.

Example (8) identifies multiple distinctive functions of an entity and enumerates them by means of overt sequential linking elements, 'first', 'second', and 'third'. In (9), temporal opposites 'before' and 'this time' coordinate with the adversative conjunction 'but' in signaling the contrast between a previous and a current behavior.

Diffuse pragmatic contrast

In the foregoing sections we have seen that the function of the *shì . . . de* construction is not obvious within a single *shì . . . de* clause, in isolation from what is said in the adjacent discourse. Rather, the contrast unfolds across the boundaries of clauses. The same can be said about the designation of pragmatic contrast, only the contextual cues of contrast are subtler and more diffuse, as in (10) – (12).

(10) 有时候人不能由着自己的性子，
 yǒushíhòu rén bù néng yóuzhe zìjǐ de xìngzi
 sometimes person not can indulge self ASSOC nature
 适当地变通一下是必要的
 shìdàng-de biàntōng yíxià shì bìyào de
 appropriately adapt a-little COP necessary NOM
 'Sometimes, one cannot act as they please, it's necessary to adapt a little'.

(11) 大学校园是传播思想、文化和知识的地方，
 dàxué xiàoyuán shì chuánbō sīxiǎng, wénhuà hé zhīshí de dìfāng
 university campus COP disseminate idea, culture, and knowledge ASSOC place
 学生们在校园的公众场合过度亲密，
 xuéshēngmen zài xiàoyuán de gōngzhòng chǎnghé guòdù qīnmì
 students LOC campus ASSOC public place excessively intimate
 显然与大学校园的气氛是不协调的
 xiǎnrán yǔ dàxué xiàoyuán de qìfēn shì bù xiétiáo de
 obviously with university campus ASSOC atmosphere COP NEG compatible NOM
 'The campus of a university is where ideas, cultures and knowledge are disseminated. Students' public displays of affection on campus are obviously incompatible with the academic atmosphere'.

(12) A: 在我眼里，你总是个快乐的人
 zài wǒ yǎn-lǐ, nǐ zǒng shì gè kuàilè de rén
 LOC 1SG eye-LOC, 2SG always COP CLF happy ASSOC person
 'In my eyes, you are always a happy person'.
 B: 唉，那都是我装出来的，蒙人的.
 ài, nà dōu shì wǒ zhuāng-chūlái de, mēng rén de
 Ah, that all COP 1SG pretend-DIR NOM, deceive people NOM
 'Ah, all that is just my pretense, to deceive people'.

In these examples, the *shì . . . de* construction is used as a corrective to counter an assumption located in previous discourse. Structurally speaking, the focused element is structurally diverse and varies in scope. For example, while the contrastive focus in (10) and (11) is the adjective (phrase) immediately following *shì*, e.g. *bìyào* 'necessary' and *bù xiétiáo* 'incompatible', respectively, the contrastive focus in (12) does not coincide with the element immediately following *shì*, which is *wǒ* 'I', but extends over the entire chunk describing agent and action, *wǒ zhuāng-chūlái* 'I pretend', and the purposive verbal phrase *mēng rén* 'deceive people'.

Following from the above discussion, it is simplistic if not incorrect to identify the contrastive focus with the constituent immediately following *shì*, as is commonly suggested (e.g. Zhan and Sun, 2013; Shi, 1994; Teng, 1979; Shi, 2005). The exact element in focus must be identified in discourse context. More generally, the notion of cleft, a language-specific descriptive notion conceived with English grammar in mind, cannot adequately capture the formal characteristics and functional scope of the *shì . . . de* construction. The mismatch between the construct of cleft and the *shì . . . de* construction is due to constraints in English on the cleft-ability of constituents. Specifically, only one element can be clefted in a cleft sentence, and that element has to satisfy the Referential Condition (Hedberg, 1990, 2000).[2] These constraints prohibit the clefting of a wide range of linguistic materials that can be accommodated by the *shì . . . de* construction.

For example, predicates including predicate nominals, predicate adjectives, and predicate verb phrases resist clefting in English (DeClerck, 1988; Emonds, 1976), but have no problem entering the *shì ... de* construction, as the following analysis shows.

Unique value of a variable

When the contrast resides in a constituent put in focus as a unique value of a variable, a sentence is often compared to the English cleft. However, this type of the *shì ... de* construction has a wider range of focus elements than the English cleft. Not only can it single out arguments such as time, place, agent and instrument as focus, it may also focus elements that are not typically considered arguments, e.g. manner. Thus, in addition to the examples in (2), we also observe (13)-(14):

(13) 第二天，当他还在痛苦中时，一只大船向他驶来。
 dièr tiān, dāng tā hái zài tòngkǔ-zhōng shí, yìzhī dàchuán xiàng tā shǐ lái.
 Second day, when 3SG still LOC pain-LOC time, one CLF big-boat to 3SG cruise-DIR
 他得救了。他问：你们是如何知道我在这里的?
 tā déjiù le. tā wèn: nǐmen shì rúhé zhīdào wǒ zài zhèlǐ de.
 3SG get rescue CRS. 3SG ask 2PL COP how know I LOC here NOM.
 'The next day, when he was still suffering, a big boat sailed toward him. He got rescued, and asked: how did you know I was here?'

(14) 想是这样想的，实际做起来却有些出入
 xiǎng shì zhèyàng xiǎng de, shíjiù zuò-qǐlái què yǒu xiē chūrù
 think COP this.way think NOM, realistically do-DIR but EXIST some discrepancy
 'When you think about it, you can think that way, but when you do it in reality, there is some difference'.

The word *rúhé* 'how' asks about the means by which something is accomplished. That is, it seeks a unique value of the variable of means. As the English translation of example (13) indicates, the question word *how* is not typically put in a cleft in ordinary English.[3] This is because *wh*-question words in English undergo left dislocation with added phonological prominence, which marks them as the new information being sought. By contrast, Chinese question words are located in situ, and require overt syntactic marking to stand out as focus. As for (14), the situation is more complex, as it involves both contrastive topic and contrastive focus. The former suggests itself in the contrast between *xiǎng* 'think' in the first clause and *zuò* 'do, act' in the second. The latter suggests itself in what is differentially said about the contrasting topics, namely between *zhèyàng* 'this way' and *yǒu xiē chūrù* 'there is some difference'. Clearly, the two types of contrast, which we see in this *shì ... de* sentence, cannot be simultaneously accommodated in an English cleft sentence.

Conventional implicature, stance, and genre

The contrast that invariably arises from the use of the *shì ... de* construction in various contexts suggests that the construction invariably signals something that it does not explicitly say. Grice (1975) made a distinction between conversational implicature and conventional implicature. The former is a context-dependent inference of a proposition, which can be attributed to general conversational principles. The latter is an inference conventionally associated with a form, although it is not actually said in that form. The notion of conventional implicature bridges the semantics, i.e. what is said, and the pragmatics, i.e. what is meant, of the *shì . . . de* construction, as indicated in (15):

(15) a [X *shì* Y *de*] asserts: FOCUS ON Y AS NEW INFORMATION
 b [X *shì* Y *de*] conventionally implies: REJECT ALL ALTERNATIVES TO Y

By virtue of this conventional implicature, the *shì . . . de* construction is a useful grammatical resource for taking a stance, understood as a "linguistically articulated form of social action whose meaning is to be construed within the broader scope of language, interaction, and sociocultural value" (Du Bois, 2007: 139). As such, this construction is likely preferred in contexts that call for the rejection or correction of assumptions the speaker wishes to rebuff or exclude from their purview. The contrastive contexts discussed previously are just that kind of contexts. The various types of contrast can be seen as ways of contextualizing the exclusive and corrective stance conveyed by the *shì . . . de* construction in interaction, be it evaluation, affective and epistemic positioning, or interpersonal alignment. Jing-Schmidt and Peng (2016) found that the most frequent exemplar of the *shì . . . de* construction in their data from the Chinese Web 2011[4] corpus is 是这样的 *shì zhèyàng de* 'is such that, such is the truth'. It is typically used to introduce a claim of exclusive truth in anticipation of alternative views without explicitly rejecting any such view, as in (16):

(16) 这个世界就是这样的，男性改变世界，
 Zhè-gè shìjiè jiù shì zhèyàng de, nánxìng gǎibiàn shìjiè,
 this CLF world just COP this.way NOM, male change world,
 女性改变男性的世界观
 nǚxìng gǎibiàn nánxìng shìjièguān
 female change male ASSOC worldview
 'The world is such that men change the world while women change men's worldview'.

Jing-Schmidt (2016) found that the most frequent adverbial collocates of this exemplar are 就 *jiù* 'just, simply', 都 *dōu* 'all, universally', and 正 *zhèng* 'exactly', with respective log likelihood values of 148.16, 40.44, and 32.60. All three adverbs serve the function of making unmitigated categorical claims in the sense of Pomerantz (1986), which is consistent with the exclusive and corrective stance conveyed by the *shì . . . de* construction. The collocation strength of 就 *jiù* 'just, simply' in particular, which signals a woeful indifference to alternative judgments, speaks strongly to that stance.

Another evidence of the stance function of the construction is the situation type described by the identification focus. Xu (2014) found that the preferred form of *shì . . . de* takes a stative predicate and is associated with subjectivity. Similarly, Jing-Schmidt and Peng (2016) showed that over 70% of their corpus data fall into what the binary analysis refers to as the emphatic *shì . . . de* construction where the emphatic element denotes a static situation. These results are consistent with the stance-taking potential of the *shì . . . de* construction on account of its conventional implicature.

Because of the stance-taking potential of the *shì . . . de* construction, one would expect it to occur more frequently in a genre that calls for the expression of stance than in one where such expressions are inappropriate. To test this hypothesis, I compared the Beijing Ren (BR) corpus (Zhang and Sang, 1986) and the Shuoming Wen (SW) 'procedural text' sub-corpus of the CCL Corpus of Contemporary Chinese (Zhang et al., 2003) with regard to the relative frequency of the *shì . . . de* construction.[5],[6] The BR is a collection of autobiographical narratives and the SW is a collection of texts in procedural discourse. A statistically significant difference ($X^2 = 7.779$,

$df = 1, p = .005$) was found in the relative frequency of the construction across the genres: While 14.2% of 4,609 tokens of *shì* retrieved from BR are *shì . . . de* uses, only 2.6% of 85,256 tokens of *shì* retrieved from SW are *shì . . . de* uses. The result confirms the expectation that the *shì . . . de* construction is preferred by a genre compatible with the conveyance of stance.

Concluding remarks

This chapter offered a glimpse at the vibrancy of research on the interaction of grammatical constructions and discourse. The critical engagement with recent studies on the Mandarin *shì . . . de* construction illustrated the need to bridge semantics and pragmatics in the study of grammatical constructions by providing explanations of where, when, and why to use them. Such explanations are particularly helpful to learners of Chinese as a second/foreign language (CSL) who do not have access to conventional implicatures for the very reason that such implicatures are not explicitly asserted. Thus, if Chinese linguistics research were to inform CSL teaching and learning, as envisioned by Hu (1999) and Tao (2016), a key task would be to generate systematic, fine-grained and data-driven pragmatic analyses of grammatical constructions that are particularly challenging to CSL learners. On a methodological note, this chapter raised the question about the kind of data necessary to support a theoretical claim in the study of grammatical constructions and discourse. As the case study showed, authentic quantitative data is desirable for its strength in allowing for contextual explorations as well as theoretical generalizations.

Notes

1 Abbreviations used in this chapter include: 1SG = first-person singular, 2SG = second person singular, 3SG = third-person singular, 1PL = first person plural, 2PL = second person plural, 3PL = third-person plural, ASSOC = associative, CLF = classifier, COP = copula, CRS = currently relevant state, DIR = directional, EXIST = existential, LOC = locative, NOM = nominalizer, OM = object marker, PFV = perfective, PN = proper name, PURP = purposive.
2 Given the one-element constraint, as Hedberg (1990) noted, cleft sentence is a useful a test of constituency.
3 In the Biblical language we see something that bears similarity to a cleft sentence, e.g. *And he said unto them, how is it that ye sought me? wist ye not that I must be about my Father's business?* (Luke 2: 49) in the King James Translation. The same sentence is rendered *why is it that ye sought me?* in the Darby Bible Translation. However, this sentence is ambiguous in terms of the grammatical status of *it* and *that*, which is key to whether the sentence is cleft or not.
4 The Chinese Web corpus is part of the TenTen corpora and comprises of over 1.7 billion words. For details, see www.sketchengine.co.uk/zhtenten-chinese-corpus/.
5 The BR corpus is a 500,000-character collection of oral accounts of personal histories by Chinese persons as documented in *Beijing Ren*《北京人》 (Zhang & Sang, 1986).
6 The CCL corpus was chosen for its ability to support syntax-based mass retrieval of the target structure. For this study, a syntax was used that retrieved all tokens of the construction with a maximum of 10 characters between *shì* and *de*. Details on the CCL corpus can be found at http://ccl.pku.edu.cn:8080/ccl_corpus/CCLCorpus_Readme.html.

References

English references

Brown, G. and Yule, G. (1983) *Discourse Analysis*. Cambridge/New York: Cambridge University Press.
Chao, Y.R. (1968) *A Grammar of Spoken Chinese*. Berkeley/Los Angeles: University of California Press.
Chen, P. (1986) Referent Introducing and Tracking in Chinese Narratives, Doctoral dissertation, University of California, Los Angeles.

Cooreman, A. (1983) 'Topic continuity and the voicing system of an ergative language: Chamorro', in *Topic Continuity in Discourse: A Quantitative Cross-Language Study*. T. Givón (ed.) Amsterdam/Philadelphia: John Benjamins. pp. 425–489.
Croft, W. (2001) *Radical Construction Grammar: Syntactic Theory in Typological Perspective*. Oxford: Oxford University Press.
Cruse, A.D. (2006) *A Glossary of Semantics and Pragmatics*. Edinburgh: Edinburgh University Press.
DeClerck, R. (1988) *Studies on Copular Sentences, Clefts and Pseudo-Clefts*. Leuven, Belgium: Leuven University Press.
Dik, S. (1997) *The Theory of Functional Grammar*, 2nd, rev. ed. Berlin: Mouton de Gruyter.
Du Bois, J. (1987) 'The Discourse Basis of Ergativity', *Language* 63(4): 805–855.
Du Bois, J. (2007) 'The stance triangle', in *Stancetaking in Discourse: Subjectivity, Evaluation, Interaction*. R. Englebretson (ed.) Amsterdam: Benjamins. pp. 139–182.
Emonds, J.E. (1976) *A Transformational Approach to English Syntax*. New York: Academic Press.
Erbaugh, M. (1986) 'The development of Chinese noun classifiers historically and in young Children', in *Noun Classes and Categorization*. C. G. Craig (ed.) Amsterdam: John Benjamins. pp. 399–436.
Erbaugh, M. (1990) 'Mandarin Oral Narratives Compared with English: The Pear/Guava Stories', *Journal of Chinese Language Teachers Association* 25(2): 21–42.
Erbaugh, M. (2002) 'Classifiers Are for Specification: Complementary Functions for Sortal and General Classifiers in Cantonese and Mandarin', *Cahiers De Linguistique – Asie Orientale* 31(1): 33–69.
Fox, B. (1987) *Discourse Structure and Anaphora: Written and Conversational English*. Cambridge: Cambridge University Press.
Fox, B. and Hopper, P. (1994) *Voice*. Amsterdam/Philadelphia: John Benjamins.
Gaby, A. (2010) 'From Discourse to Syntax and Back: The Lifecycle of Kuuk Thaayorre Ergative Morphology', *Lingua* 120(7): 1677–1692.
Goldberg, A. (1995) *Constructions: A Construction Grammar Approach to Argument Structure*. Chicago: University of Chicago Press.
Goldberg, A. (2006) *Constructions at Work: The Nature of Generalization in Language*. Oxford: Oxford University Press.
Grice, H.P. (1975) 'Logic and Conversation', *Syntax and Semantics* 3: 41–58.
Givón, T. (1979) *On Understanding Grammar*. New York: Academic Press.
Givón, T. (1983) *Topic Continuity in Discourse: A Quantitative Cross-Language Study*. Amsterdam/Philadelphia: John Benjamins.
Givón, T. (1984) *Syntax: A Functional-Typological Introduction*. Amsterdam/Philadelphia: John Benjamins.
Givón, T. (1989) *Mind, Code, and Context: Essays in Pragmatics*. Hillsdale, N.J.: L. Erlbaum Associates.
Givón, T. (1995) *Functionalism and Grammar*. Amsterdam/Philadelphia: John Benjamins.
Givón, T. (2017) *The Story of Zero*. Amsterdam/Philadelphia: John Benjamins.
Haiman, J. and Thompson, S.A. (1988) *Clause Combining in Grammar and Discourse*. Amsterdam/Philadelphia: John Benjamins.
Hakulinen, A. and Selting, M. (2005) *Syntax and Lexis in Conversation: Studies on the Use of Linguistic Resources in Talk-in-interaction*. Amsterdam: John Benjamins.
Hashimoto, Anne. (1969) 'The Verb 'to Be' in Modern Chinese', *Foundations of Language Supplementary Series* 9(4): 72–111.
Hedberg, N. (1990) Discourse Pragmatics and Cleft Sentences in English, Doctoral dissertation, University of Minnesota.
Hedberg, N. (1999) The Discourse Function of English Clefts and Mandarin *shi . . . de* Constructions. Workshop on the Discourse Function of Clefts. Humboldt University, Berlin, Germany, Oct. 1–3.
Hedberg, N. (2000) 'The Referential Status of Clefts', *Language* 76: 891–920.
Hengeveld, K. and Mackenzie, J. (2008) *Functional Discourse Grammar*. Oxford: Oxford University Press.
Hengeveld, K. and Mackenzie, J. (2014) 'Grammar and Context in Functional Discourse Grammar', *Pragmatics* 24(2): 203–227.
Hopper, P. (2001) 'Grammatical constructions and their discourse origins: Prototype or family resemblance?', in *Applied Cognitive Linguistics I: Theory and Language Acquisition*. M. Putz, S. Niemeier, and R. Dirven (eds.) Berlin: Mouton de Gruyter. pp. 109–129.
Hopper, P. and Thompson, S.A. (1980) 'Transitivity in Grammar and Discourse', *Language* 56(2): 251–299.
Jing-Schmidt, Z. (2005) *Dramatized Discourse*. Amsterdam: John Benjamins.
Jing-Schmidt, Z. (2008) 'Zur Frage der chinesischen *shi-de* Konstruktion: eine konzeptualistische und diskurspragmatische Erklärung', *CHUN Chinesisch Unterricht* 23: 87–112.

Jing-Schmidt, Z. (2016) From Linguistics Theory and Research to Chinese Language Pedagogy. Plenary Speech at the 5th International Symposium on Chinese Applied Linguistics, University of Iowa, April 22–23.

Jing-Schmidt, Z. and Jing, T. (2011) 'Embodied Semantics and Pragmatics: Empathy, Sympathy and Two Passive Constructions in Chinese Media Discourse', *Journal of Pragmatics* 43(11): 2826–2844.

Jing-Schmidt, Z. and Peng, X. (2016) The Identification Focus Construction in Mandarin Chinese. Invited talk at the University of Oregon Linguistics Colloquium, February 26, Eugene.

Jing-Schmidt, Z., Peng, X. and Chen, J.-Y. (2015) Construction Grammar and its Application in Chinese Grammar Pedagogy. Paper Presented on ACTFL 2015. Nov 19–22, San Diego.

Jing-Schmidt, Z. and Tao, H. (2009) 'The Mandarin Disposal Constructions: Usage and Development', *Language and Linguistics* 10(1): 29–58.

Langacker, R. (1987) *Foundations of Cognitive Grammar. Vol. 1. Theoretical Prerequisites*. Stanford, CA: Stanford University Press.

Li, C.N. and Thompson, S.A. (1976) 'Subject and topic: A new typology of language', in *Subject and Topic*. C.N. Li (ed.) New York: Academic Press. pp. 457–489.

Li, C.N. and Thompson, S.A. (1979) 'Third-person pronouns and zero-anaphora in Chinese discourse', in *Discourse and Syntax*. T. Givón (ed.) New York: Academic Press. pp. 311–335.

Li, C.N. and Thompson, S.A. (1981) *Mandarin Chinese: A Functional Reference Grammar*. Berkeley/Los Angeles: University of California Press.

Liu, F. (2011) 'The Bei Passive and Its Discourse Motivations', *Chinese Language and Discourse* 2(2): 198–231.

Malt, B. (1985) 'The Role of Discourse Structure in Understanding Anaphora', *Journal of Memory and Language* 24(3): 271–289.

Mills, S. (1997) *Discourse*. London: Routledge.

Ochs, E., Schegloff, E.A. and Thompson, S.A. (1996) *Interaction and Grammar*. Cambridge: Cambridge University Press.

Paris, Marie-Claude. (1979) *Nominalization in Mandarin Chinese: The Morpheme 'de' and the 'shi . . . de' Constructions*. Université Paris VII, Département de Recherches Linguistiques.

Patard, A. (2014) 'When Tense and Aspect Convey Modality: Reflections on the Modal Uses of Past Tenses in Romance and Germanic Languages', *Journal of Pragmatics* 71: 69–97.

Payne, D. (1992) *Pragmatics of Word Order Flexibility*. Amsterdam/Philadelphia: John Benjamins.

Peng, X. (2017) Linguistic Innovations in Chinese: Internal and External Factors, Doctoral dissertation, University of Oregon.

Pomerantz, A. (1986) 'Extreme Case Formulations: A Way of Legitimizing Claims', *Human Studies* 36(9): 219–229.

Ross, C. (1983) 'On the Functions of Mandarin *de*', *Journal of Chinese Linguistics* 11(2): 214 – 246.

Schegloff, E.A. (1996) 'Turn organization: On intersection of grammar and interaction', in *Interaction and Grammar*. E. Ochs, E.A. Schegloff and S.A. Thompson (eds.) England: Cambridge University Press. pp. 52–133.

Schegloff, E.A., Ochs, E. and Thompson, S.A. (1996) 'Introduction', in *Interaction and Grammar*. E. Ochs, E.A. Schegloff and S.A. Thompson (eds.) Cambridge: Cambridge University Press. pp. 1–51.

Seiler, H. (1993) 'A functional view on prototypes', in *Conceptualizations and Mental Processing in Language*. R.A. Geiger and B. Rudzka-Ostyn (eds.) Berlin: Mounton DeGruyter. pp. 115–140.

Shi, D. (1994) 'The Nature of Chinese Emphatic Sentences', *Journal of East Asian Linguistics* 3(1): 81–100.

Shi, D. (2000) 'Topic and Topic-Comment Constructions in Mandarin Chinese', *Language* 76(2): 383–408.

Shibatani, M. (1985) 'Passives and Related Constructions: A Prototype Analysis', *Language* 61: 821–848.

Su, D. (2017) 'Significance as a Lens: Understanding the Mandarin ba Construction through Discourse Adjacent Alternation', *Journal of Pragmatics* 117: 204–230.

Sun, C. (1988) 'The Discourse Function of Numeral Classifiers in Mandarin Chinese', *Journal of Chinese Linguistics* 16(2): 298–322.

Sun, C. and Givón, T. (1985) 'On the So-called SOV Word Order in Mandarin Chinese: A Quantified Text Study and its Implications', *Language* 61(2): 329–351.

Tai, J.H.Y. and Hsueh, F. (1989) *Functionalism and Chinese Grammar*. South Orange, NJ: Chinese Language Teachers Association.

Tao, H. (1996) *Units in Mandarin Conversation Prosody, Discourse and Grammar*. Amsterdam/Philadelphia: John Benjamins.

Tao, H. (2000) 'The Grammar of Demonstratives in Mandarin Conversational Discourse: A Case Study', *Journal of Chinese Linguistics* 27(1): 69–103.

Tao, H. (2016) 'Integrating Chinese linguistic research and language teaching and learning: An Introduction', in *Integrating Chinese Linguistic Research and Language Teaching and Learning*. H. Tao (ed.) Amsterdam: John Benjamins. pp. xiii–xviii.

Tao, H. and Thompson, S.A. (1994) 'The Discourse and Grammar Interface: Preferred Clause Structure in Mandarin Conversation', *Journal of the Chinese Language Teachers Association* 29(3): 1–34.

Teng, S. (1979) 'Remarks on Cleft Sentences in Chinese', *Journal of Chinese Linguistics* 7(1): 101–114.

Thompson, S.A. and Tao, H. (2010) 'Conversation, Grammar, and Fixedness: Adjectives in Mandarin Revisited', *Chinese Language and Discourse* 1(1): 3–30.

Tsao, F. (1987) 'A Topic-comment Approach to the Ba-Construction', *Journal of Chinese Linguistics* 15(1): 1–53.

Tsao, F. (1990) *Sentence and Clause Structure in Chinese: A Functional Perspective*. Taipei: Student Book Co.

Webber, B. L. (1988) 'Tense as Discourse Anaphor', *Computational Linguistics* 14(2): 61–73.

Xu, Y. (2014) 'A Corpus-based Functional Study of *shi … de* Constructions', *Chinese Language and Discourse* 5(2): 146–184.

Zhan, F. and Sun, C. (2013) 'A Copula Analysis of *shì* in the Chinese Cleft Construction', *Language and Linguistics* 14(4): 755–789.

Chinese references

Chen, P. 陈平. (1987) 汉语零形回指的话语分析 (Discourse Analysis of Zero Anaphora in Chinese). 《中国语文》5: 363–378.

Hu, M 胡明扬. (1999) '中国语言学：一个世纪的回顾和展望' (Chinese Linguistics: A Retrospect of a Century and a Prospect). 世界汉语教学 (*Chinese Teaching in the World*) 2: 31–38.

Liu, Y., W. Pan and Gu, W. 刘月华，潘文娱，故韡. (2001) 实用现代汉语语法 (*New Practical Chinese Grammar*). Beijing: Shangwu Yinshuguan.

Lü, S. 吕叔湘 (ed.) (1980) 现代汉语八百词 (*Eight Hundred Words of Modern Chinese*). Beijing: Shangwu Yinshuguan.

Lü, S. 吕叔湘 (ed.) (2007) 现代汉语八百词 (增订本) (*Eight Hundred Words of Modern Chinese*, expanded edition). Beijing: Shangwu Yinshuguan.

Shen, J. 沈家煊 (2002)如何处置'处置式'：试论把字句的主观性. (*How to Dispose of Disposal Constructions: Subjectivity in the ba-construction*). *Zhongguo Yuwen* 5: 387–399.

Shi, Y. 石毓智 (2005) 论判断，焦点，强调与对比之关系 – "是"的语法功能和使用 条件. [The Relationship of Copula, Focus, Emphasis, and Comparison – The Function and Usage of Shi]. 语言研究 *Studies in Language and Linguistics* 25(4): 43–53.

Wang, L. 王力. (1947) 中国现代语法 *Modern Chinese Grammar*. Shanghai: Zhonghua Shuju.

Zhan, W., Guo, R. and Chen, Y. 詹卫东，郭锐，谌贻荣. (2003) 北京大学中国语 言学研究中心CCL语料库 (规模：7亿字；时间：公元前11世纪-当代) 网址：Retrieved from http://ccl.pku.edu.cn:8080/ccl_corpus

Zhang, X. and Sang, Y. 张欣欣，桑叶 (1986) *Beijing Ren (Chinese Lives)*. Shanghai: Shanghai Literature and Art Publishing Group.

7
Between factuality and counterfactuality
Chinese conditionals in conversations

Yu-Fang Wang and Wayne Schams

Introduction

Conditional constructions are of prime importance in reasoning – both theoretical reasoning about what is true and practical reasoning about what to do. Since they can be used to express abstract conceptual ideas and hypothetical structures, conditionals reflect the human capacity to contemplate various situations and to infer consequences on the basis of known or imaginary conditions (Chou, 2000; Y.-Y. Wang, 2012). Conditional sentences are among the most useful structures in terms of expressing possibilities, guesses, wishes, regrets, and so on (i.e., the so-called subjunctive mood), as well as other abstract notions. They can be used by the speaker or writer to predict a situation that would result from different conditions from those which actually exist, existed in the past, or are likely to exist in the future (i.e., hypothetical expressions). Every language also has its own unique morpho-syntactic system for marking conditionals. Like other Indo-European languages, English has distinct linguistic structures used in conveying hypothetical or counterfactual messages expressed through the form of the verb in conditional sentences.

While English makes grammatical distinctions among the unreal conditionals in the auxiliary verbs and the tense and aspect markers they can or must take, Mandarin Chinese contains no such grammatical distinctions. The type of message that is conveyed by a Mandarin conditional construction is inferred by the hearer from the proposition in the second clause and from his/her knowledge of the world and of the context in which the sentence is expressed (Li and Thompson, 1981: 647). According to Li and Thompson, Chinese conditionals can be classified into three types (i.e., reality, imaginative hypothetical, and imaginative counterfactual) based on the epistemic relationship between the antecedent clause and the consequent clause as well as the speaker's evaluation of reality. They argue that unlike English, although Chinese makes no grammatical distinctions among these three types of conditionals in terms of verb form, the interpreted message is closely related to the context in which it is spoken. For example, the first clause in example (1) below can represent all three types of conditionals:

(1) 如果你看到我妹妹，你一定知道她懷孕了。

(taken from Li and Thompson, 1981: 647)

Reality: 'If you see my younger sister, you'll certainly know that she is pregnant'.

Imaginative hypothetical: 'If you saw my younger sister, you'd know she was pregnant (i.e., I could imagine you seeing her)'.

Imaginative counterfactual: 'If you had seen my younger sister, you would have known that she was pregnant (i.e., you didn't see her)'.

Although some conditional markers, such as 如果 in example (1), can introduce the three types of conditionals, other markers, such as 只有 ('only if') and 只要 ('as long as'), tend to mark factuality or certainty. 只有 is used to indicate that the condition it introduces is necessary for a certain result modified by 才 to take place, implying that there is only one way to achieve the result. When 只要 introduces a clause (i.e., protasis), the clause that follows it (i.e., apodosis) often contains the adverb 就 'then'. Most previous studies (e.g., Lü, 1980 [2007]; Hou, 2004; etc.) argue that 只有 introduces either a necessary or a necessary and sufficient (i.e., unique) condition, while 只要 introduces simply a sufficient one. Consider the following two examples, taken from Lü (2007: 681):

(2) 只有打兩針金黴素，你這病才能好。
'Only if you take two injections will your disease be cured'.

(3) 只要打兩針金黴素，你這病就能好。
'As long as you take an injection, your disease can be cured'.

Example (2) implies that there is no other medicine besides penicillin that can cure the disease, but example (3) denotes that there might be other alternative cures for the disease in addition to penicillin.

To date, much research has been conducted on the unique characteristics of Chinese constructions and recent research has focused more specifically on the functions and uses of Chinese conditionals based on authentic data from cognitive, pragmatic, and discourse perspectives. Su (2005) draws on the Blending Theory (Fauconnier and Turner, 2002) to account for the reasoning processes involved in the interpretation of conditional meaning. She argues that conditionals are employed frequently to link the speaker's knowledge and the addressee's situation in order to create a blend in which the features of two disparate entities are combined. One of the motivations for using a hypothetical statement, as pointed out by Su, is to evoke a frame which is unavailable in the current context. Thus, hypothetical thinking, from the cognitive perspective of conceptual integration, lies in our building of the mental spaces where the irrealis world is conceptualized. In addition to the notion of context, Su also emphasizes pragmatic concerns (e.g., 'intersubjectivity' and 'politeness') in the interpretation of Chinese conditionals. More specifically, intersubjectivity highlights the notion of hearer involvement (Traugott, 2003), illustrating the prototypical function associated with the use of a conditional, that is, mitigating the subjective evaluation of the presupposed ground taken by the speaker. Such mitigation is triggered by the speaker's concern over the hearer's negative face, thus softening the impact of what may have been a face-threatening act (FTA). Similarly, Yang (2007) offers a description of the commonest Chinese conditional constructions, including 如果 'if' conditionals, exceptive (除非 'unless') conditionals, and counterfactual constructions (不是 'not' marked counterfactual conditionals and other negative-stanced conditionals), with the aim of examining the link between conceptual and linguistic structures. She examines the pragmatic use of these Mandarin conditionals, explicating how cognitive structures link to linguistic structure and how mental spaces (Fauconnier, 1985, 1994) are built in various conditional constructions to evoke different reasoning processes. In a cross-linguistic, sentence-level study of the marking and function of conditional clauses, Haiman (1978) claims that conditionals are topics. However, Kuo (2006) points out that the notion of topic lacks consensus among linguists because topic is used in many different ways by linguists who focus on different aspects of communication, such as the message, the speaker, and shared knowledge. Based on this, Kuo explores the roles that Chinese conditionals play in informational structure and in discourse functions, particularly in regard to how conditionals marked by 如, 如果, 要是, 假如, 假設, and 假定 ('if', 'suppose', 'in case that') are used to indicate entity topic, proposition topic, text topic, speaker topic and interaction topic in spoken data. The data suggest that conditionals play different roles in the organization of discourse, for example, repeating, presenting the opposite view, broadening, narrowing down, and expressing polite directives, thus indicating a significant correlation between the information status of conditionals and discourse functions.

Chinese conditional clauses, like English *if*-clauses, tend to precede their matrix clauses and serve as topic (Kuo, 2006; Yang, 2007), except the 除非 clauses which frequently occur following their matrix clauses in spoken Chinese (Wang et al., 2014). Apart from acting as polite directives (Su, 2005; Kuo, 2006), conditionals can be used to carry out FTAs, as shown in example (4):

(4) (A mother, A, is telling her daughter that if she finishes the computer game, Pacman, instead of coming to eat the instant noodles ready for her, she will not have them.)
   A: ..泡麵就涼了,_
   ...(1.1) XX妳<E Pacman E> <X玩 X>完的話,_
   ..然後,_
   ..泡麵也就沒有了.\

(taken from Wang et al., 2014)

   A: 'The instant noodles are ready. XX, if you (do not come immediately) finish Pacman, then there won't be any noodles for you'.

The conditional introduced by 的話 conveys a warning, which can be termed 'a conditional threat' (Limberg, 2009). Thus, conditionals can perform not only face-saving acts, such as polite directives (e.g. Ford and Thompson, 1986; Su, 2005; Kuo, 2006), but also FTAs. In addition, in light of the notion of 'probability' in conditionals (Comrie, 1986), some hypothetical conditionals tend to convey probable situations, while others convey improbable situations, depending on context, in contrast to counterfactual conditionals (i.e., impossible ones). For instance, in example (5) from our spoken data, 的話 appearing after the utterance 沒什麼意外 'no any exception' expresses a probable condition (i.e., a prediction), while the 萬一 utterance conveys a less probable condition (i.e., an exception):

(5) (W and L are classmates. W asks L whether he will stay in the neighborhood around the campus right after spring break.)
   W: ..在你春假完之前,_
   ..你都會在沙鹿哦?/
   L: ..嗯,_
   ..<MRC 對吧 MRC>.\
   W: ..<D 還XXX D>.\
   L: @@
   ..百分之九十九,_
   ..我還不能跟你完全確定啊,_
   ..萬一,_
   ...到時候,_

```
          ..我家裡什麼事,_
          ..要趕回去啦.\
W:    @@@
L:    ..沒啦,_
       ..應該,_
       ...大部分,_
       ..都會在這裡啦,_
       ...嗯,_
       ..沒什麼意外的話.\
```
W: 'Before spring break, will you stay in Shalu?'
L: 'Um, maybe'.
W: '(You) still ...'
L: '99%. I cannot totally be sure. Supposing at that time there are some things at my house, I will go home immediately.'
W: 'Nothing. Most of the time, I will stay here, if there is no exception'.

Some studies (e.g., Wang, 1991; Kennedy, 1998) have categorized conditionals into four semantic categories: factual, predicative, improbable, and counterfactual. However, adopting Comrie's (1986) argument that hypotheticality is a continuum, it seems more appropriate to place different types of conditionals on a continuum between realis and irrealis.

While a large number of studies have been done on the characteristics of Chinese conditional markers in spoken or written discourse (e.g., Su, 2005; Kuo, 2006; Yang, 2007), relatively few have examined the different types of Chinese conditionals in spoken discourse to analyze their discourse-pragmatic functions and distribution of occurrences. In addition, the conditional clause may occur either before or after its matrix clause as manifested in 萬一 and ...的話, respectively, in example (5). These two positions obviously differ in function in terms of managing both the linear flow of information as well as listener attention while being guided through the discourse. A systematic analysis of them based on large-scale spoken data has yet to be done, which is the focus of the present study. Taking the view that the way in which information is arranged within an utterance or clause is affected by the patterns of the constructions within the discourse as a whole, the present study attempts to explore the functions of these different types of Chinese conditionals in daily conversation. This chapter addresses the following questions:

(1) What are the characteristics of the different types of Chinese conditional clauses (e.g., factual, predicative, improbable, and counterfactual), especially the conditional markers?
(2) What are the various types of conditional clauses in relation to the initial and final positions with respect to their matrix clauses? What discourse-pragmatic functions do they perform in spoken Chinese discourse?

The conditional clauses in initial vs. final placement in the data

The present study adopts Conversation Analysis as the theoretical framework for a spoken corpus containing daily conversations in order to examine different types of conditionals. The spoken corpus in this study contains naturally occurring two-party or multi-party conversations. The diverse parties in these conversations include students, colleagues and housewives, and the situations occur in home, school and work settings. The total length of the recordings comprising all the data is 90 hours, 37 minutes and 25 seconds, and the data were recorded via audio cassettes and transcribed into intonation units, that is, sequences of words combined under a single

Table 7.1 Frequency of occurrence of conditional clauses in spoken data

Conditional Marker	Initial conditional	Final conditional	No main cl.	Total (%)
…的話	202	4	4	210 (14.25%)
如果(說)…(的話)	880	28	31	**939 (63.7%)**
若…(的話)	20	0	0	20 (1.36%)
只要	120	13	1	134 (9.09%)
只有	12	0	0	12 (0.81%)
要是…(的話)	39	0	0	39 (2.65%)
要不是	3	0	0	3 (0.20%)
假如(說)…(的話)	35	1	2	38 (2.58%)
假設	10	1	0	11 (0.75%)
除非	25	23	4	52 (3.53%)
萬一…(的話)	10	1	1	12 (0.81%)
一旦	4	0	0	4 (0.27%)
Total (%)	1360 (92.3%)	71 (4.8%)	43 (2.9%)	1474 (100%)

unified intonation contour and usually preceded by a pause (Cruttenden, 1989; Du Bois et al., 1993). The conditional data in the corpus were categorized into the following three types with respect to their positions in relation to their main clauses: (i) the conditional clause preceding the main clause (i.e., the initial conditional); (ii) the main clause preceding the conditional (i.e., the final conditional); and (iii) no main clause. The data in our study yielded a total of 1474 valid tokens of conditional clauses, a summary of which is given in Table 7.1.

In our spoken data, the most common condition marker is 如果, comprising 63.7% of the total, while 的話, which appears in the clause-final position and can also occur with other markers, is the second most common marker (i.e., 14.25%) followed by 只要 (9.09%). Table 7.1 also indicates that conditional clauses tend to occur before their main clauses. Out of the entire data, there are 1360 instances in the preposed position with respect to their associated utterances but just 71 in the post-posed position, accounting for 92.3% and 4.8%, respectively. There is a strong tendency for conditional clauses to occur initially. However, in contrast with the other conditional clauses, 44.23% (23 out of 52) of the 除非 clauses appear after their main clauses and are thus different from the others in terms of their distribution.

Probability signaled by Chinese conditional markers

Unlike English, Chinese is a typical analytic language in which lexicon and context are more important than morphology. Our data suggest that the illocutionary force of a conditional is encoded at lexical, syntactic and discourse levels (i.e., conditional markers and the sequence of a conditional and its main clause).

As mentioned earlier, a conditional sentence that expresses an implication is also called a factual conditional sentence. A factual conditional is used to make statements about the real world and often refers to general truths when the time being referred to is now or always and the situation is real and possible. The clauses introduced by 只有 and 只要 pertain to factual conditionals. As noted in previous studies (e.g., Lü, 1980 [2007]; Hou, 2004; etc.), 只有 often occurs with 才, and 只要 is accompanied by 就. However, our data show that 只要 can also occur with 都, as shown in example (6).

(6) B: ..只要好聽我都唱呀,_
 ..男生女生我都唱呀._
 B: 'As long as the song sounds nice, I will sing it. No matter whether it is sung by a male or female singer, I will sing it'.

Although the conditionals introduced by both 只有 and 只要 are usually factual conditionals, the certainty that the 只有 clause expresses is stronger than that of the 只要 clause, for the former is a necessary condition and must co-occur with the adverb 才 in its matrix clause, while the latter signifies a sufficient condition and can co-occur with 就 or 都 in its matric clause. Besides, 只要 can appear after its matrix clause (Table 7.1) and the logical relationship between the condition and the result is not as strong as it is in 只有, which more often occurs before its main clause.

Among Chinese conditional markers, only 的話 occurs in the clause-final position and can mark a factual, probable, possible, or counterfactual clause. In spoken Chinese, 的話 can serve as a topic marker or as a conditional marker. The semantic and functional similarities between topic marking and conditional marking have been well documented crosslinguistically (Haiman, 1978). 的話 also tends to co-occur with other conditional markers to establish an imaginative situation in discourse.

如果 is the most common conditional marker in Chinese spoken discourse and, as pointed out by Li and Thompson (1981), it can preface a factual, probable, possible, or counterfactual clause (see example (1) above). However, it more often marks a factual or probable conditional, which expresses general truths and sometimes can be replaced by the temporal marker 當 'when'. In addition, as seen in example (7), 如果 can occur with 只要 to indicate that the possibility of occurrence in a given situation is very high.

(7) (C, a graduate student majoring in English and working part-time as an English teaching assistant, tells her classmate that seemingly any graduate student in their English department can teach the Aural and Oral English courses, if there is an opportunity.)
 C: ..其實是好像,_
 ..只要,_
 ..是研究生,_
 ..如果妳,_
 ..想要教啊,_
 ..應該都有機會,_
 C: 'Actually, it seems that as long as you are a graduate student, if you want to teach (Aural and Oral English), you might have an opportunity'.

Here, replacing 如果 with other conditional markers such as 要是 or 假如 would sound odd.

Like 如果, 要是 can also introduce different types of conditionals and the time frame of the hypothetical situation may be in the past, present or future. However, it tends to preface an improbable or counterfactual situation, as shown in example (8):

(8) (F and E are classmates. F compliments E on winning the award for best actor in their department's drama contest last year.)
 F: ..你還得到那個什麼獎去了,_
 ..最佳演員是不是?/
 E: ..不過,_
 ..那是僥倖啦,_
 ..對啊/

F: ..不過,_
..那也是很厲害啊,_
..要是我就沒有辦法了.\

F: 'You got the award for best actor, right?'
E: 'But, I was lucky! Yeah'.
F: 'Well, you were terrific. If I were you, I would not have gotten the award'.

The conditional clause marked by 要是 conveys a counterfactual situation in the speaker's present time. The most common expression in conversation is 要是我(是)... 'if I were ...' in the spoken data. Its negative counterpart 要不是 is used specifically to convey counterfactuality, as manifested in example (9):

(9) (M and F thank two of their classmates for lending them their handouts to help them prepare for exams.)
M: ..尤其是沈感瑛寶典,_
..最好用了.\
F: ..對啊.\
..要不是靠你們兩個,_
..我哪有今天啊.\
..所以我感激你們的大恩大德,_

M: 'The handouts written by Shen Ganying are very useful and helpful'.
F: 'Right. If I had not relied on you two, how would I have become the person I am? So I am grateful to you for your great kindness'.

Here, the 要不是 clause refers to a past event and it is used to counter reality. The time frame of the hypothetical situation could be either past or present, and the time frame of the condition does not always correspond to that of the consequence.

While 要是 and 要不是 conditional clauses are often used to indicate counterfactuality, 假如, 假設 and 假使, which all contain the morpheme 假 'fake', often introduce a less probable or counterfactual situation, as shown in example (10):

(10) (B's friend is going to B's house for a long stay while B is out. B tells her how to use the gas stove and the oven in the kitchen.)
B: ..然後妳記得喔,_
..這樣是開的,_
..然後這樣是完全沒有鎖的,_
..然後如果妳還沒有要走的話,_
..就先用這個鎖著,_
..然後假如說你要走了,_
..就先用這個.\

B: 'And remember, this is open, and this is completely locked. If you are still not going to leave, just use it to lock. If you want to leave, then you first use it'.

In example (10), A is going to stay at B's house when B is not at home. Before leaving, B tells A how to use the gas in the kitchen. B employs both 如果 and 假如 in the excerpt. Since A is going to stay at B's house, B uses 如果 to indicate her staying (a situation which is going to occur) and to indicate the less probable situation of her leaving. Here, 如果 marks a more

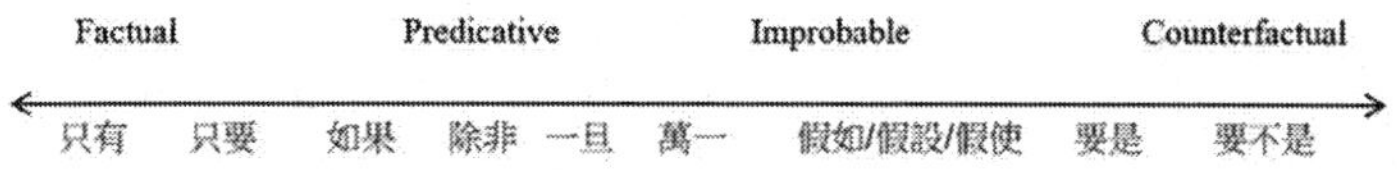

Between factuality and counterfactuality

Factual	Predicative	Improbable	Counterfactual
只有　　只要	如果　除非　一旦　萬一	假如/假設/假使	要是　　要不是

Figure 7.1 Degree of certainty in Chinese conditional markers

probable condition than 假如. Hence, the degree of certainty in the use of 如果 is higher than it is when 假如 is used. 假如 and its variants (假設 and 假使) are used to refer to unreal situations.

Although conditionals can express the speaker's (un)desirability (Akatsuka, 1985, 1986), the markers 只有, 只要, 如果, 假如, 假設 and 假使 are not necessary to do so. However, the predicative conditionals introduced by 除非 ('unless'), 一旦 ('once') and 萬一 (literally 'one out of ten thousand') are necessary. That is, 除非, 一旦 and 萬一 are related to the speaker's (un)desirability about a situation which may occur in the future. Hence, they are often called 'predicative conditionals'. A predictive conditional concerns a situation that is to some degree dependent on a possible future event. The consequence is normally also a statement about the future, although it may also be a consequent statement involving the present or past. Among the three, 除非 occurs more often than the other two in spoken discourse (see Table 7.1), and it is often followed by a matric clause introduced by 不然/要不然 or 否則 'otherwise', as manifested in example (11):

(11) (B tells his recipient that nowadays it is hard to teach high school students.)
　　B: ..除非你很有]魅力啊,_
　　　　..啊不然真的是很難帶,_
　　B: 'Unless you are very attractive, otherwise, it would be very difficult to manage the students'.

除非, similar to English *unless*, refers to the conditional part of the sentence, whereas 不然 refers to the result part of the sentence. 除非 is often used to code the premise for the desired condition to come true. The clauses marked by 除非, 一旦 and 萬一 are used to refer to the present or future where the situation is likely to be real. In other words, it refers to a possible condition and its probable result. However, the possibility of occurrence (i.e., certainty) in situations where these three are used is, ranging from highest to lowest, 除非, 一旦 and 萬一, respectively.

On the whole, the data show that Chinese conditional markers are used by the speaker as signposts (Sperber and Wilson, 1986/1995) to guide the hearer into an imaginary scenario. If the conditional markers are arranged on a continuum between the two extremes of factuality and counterfactuality, 只有 would be on the factuality end, followed by 只要. These would be followed by 除非, 一旦, and 萬一. 假如, 假設 and 假使 indicate a less probable situation, and 要是 does as well but, akin to its negative counterpart 要不是, tends to mark counterfactuality. Figure 7.1 summarizes the degree of certainty to which these Chinese conditionals correlate.

The functions of conditionals in spoken Chinese

The initial conditionals

In the English spoken data in their study, Ford and Thompson (1986) found that initial condition clauses mainly perform five functions in terms of their connection with prior discourse: exploring options, providing polite requests, illustrating, contrasting, and assuming. Although the initial conditional clauses in our data are rather versatile in their functions, they can fall naturally into seven types: the five types proposed by Ford and Thompson (1986), plus conditionals indicating counterfactuality that express gratitude (see example (9) above) and warnings or threats, that is, the so-called 'conditional threat' (Limberg, 2009). Although the initial conditional clauses can be categorized into these seven types, all of them are used to create the backgrounds for subsequent utterances and to present pieces of information as given, implying that such information is to be treated as shared background for the discourse that follows.

Firstly, initial conditional clauses, like their English counterparts, are commonly utilized when presenting options, as suggested by Ford (1993: 42). In particular, they are used to present options that follow from points reached in prior discourse. An example of presenting an option through an initial 如果 clause can be seen below in example (12):

(12) (W asks Y how many people are in her family. Y answers that there are ten in total, including her and her husband.)
W: ..你們家有多少人?/
Y: ...(2.4)還沒結婚的ho,_
..我大哥,_
..二姊,_
..然後就是爸爸,_
..媽媽了.\
Z: ..四個.\
Y: ..然後他們,_
..如果,_
..我姊姊,_
..姊夫和,_
..兩個孩子都回來,_
..就八個.\
W: ..哦.\
Y: ..加上我們兩個就十個.\
W: 'How many members are there in your family?'
Y: 'As for unmarried, there are my eldest brother and my second elder sister. And my dad and mom'.
Z: 'Four people'.
Y: 'And they, if my elder sister, brother-in-law, and their two children visit us, there will be eight'.
W: 'Oh'.
Z: 'There are ten in total, including us'.

W asks Y how many members there are in her family. Y answers the question from the standpoint of those members who are married and those who are unmarried by presenting an option that is introduced by a conditional.

Secondly, an initial conditional clause may also express a polite request. Ford and Thompson (1986) argue that "the fact that conditionals can encode polite directives may be due to a combination of the softening effect of hypotheticality and the fact that conditionals seem to imply an option with alternatives" (1986: 365). This function can be seen in example (13):

(13) (Z and his wife treat their visitors to some snacks. However, one of their visitors says that she is full.)

Z: ..你如gu –
..妳**如果**吃不下,_
..沒有關係.\
Z: 'If you – If you cannot eat (it) anymore, it doesn't matter'.

Here again, this example involves an option. Z makes a suggestion to one of his guests during dinner. When Z observes that W is full and cannot eat more, he offers a snack to W. This option is conveyed through an initial conditional clause, which then frames the following clause (i.e., the solution to the possible problem).

Thirdly, some conditionals can be used to show a contrast to material presented in prior talk. Unlike the first type which only presents options, a contrasting conditional restates and contradicts what preceded it in discourse, as shown in example (14):

(14) (S is talking about the difficulty her friend, Lujun, a news reporter, encounters on her job in terms of an interpersonal relationship.)
S: ..以綠君的個性她也不可能去逃.\
..可是,_
..**如果**,_
..妳叫她不要介意,_
..那又很難.\
S: 'It's impossible for Lujun to escape (from the situation). But, if you persuade her to not mind it, that will be difficult, too'.

This type of conditional usually co-occurs with contrastive markers, such as 可是 'but' as seen in example (14). It is clear that this initial conditional clause of contrast presents an assertion that is the opposite of, or is an option competing with, some assertion(s) made in previous talk.

In a fourth example, another use of an initial conditional in the spoken data is to provide an illustration of a particular case or idea under discussion. For instance, in example (15), A cites an example, introduced by an initial conditional clause and its main clause, in order to make his question (i.e., 'Do you know how he (an umpire) rules an obstruction foul?') clearer to the hearer:

(15) (A and B are talking about a basketball game on TV.)
A: ..你知道他怎麼=判阻擋犯規嗎?/
..舉個例,_
..我**如果**站在這裏,_
..你過來衝我,_
..撞我的話,_
..你這樣是帶球犯.\
B: ..這樣是帶球的那個犯規.\
A: 'Do you know how he rules an obstruction foul? Let me cite an example. If I stand here and you dribble the ball and run into me, then you foul. It's a foul'.
B: 'In such case, it is the one who dribbles the ball who fouls'.

Fifth, in addition to the four types of initial conditionals, they can be used to present options or possibilities involving the presentation of information that is to be treated as shared. This kind of conditional evokes the speaker's knowledge or the knowledge that is supposedly shared by speaker and hearer, as shown in example (16).

(16) (M is in charge of managing the janitors in his department. He is writing their job descriptions and telling them to his colleague.)
   M: ..我現在是希望說,_
      ...把這些東西很^明確的寫下來,_
      ..把它印出來.\
      ...那這樣的話,_
      ..誰要是沒做好,_
      ..那我就說,_
      ..ey.是你要做的.\
   M: 'Now I hope that (I) can write down these (job descriptions) in detail and print them out. If someone does not carry them out well, I will point out that it's his/her duty'.

Notice that the conditional clause, along with its main clause, expresses an alternative that is relative to the topic 'then if such is the case' in example (16). In this excerpt, although the information conveyed in the initial conditional clause is not mentioned in prior discourse, the speaker uses the initial conditional clause to state the basis for his reasoning, where the content of the clause being presented is, at least temporarily, given or shared. This type of initial conditional is used to recapitulate an assumption made from a prior utterance.

Our data suggest that initial conditionals can be used not only to express polite directives (Su, 2005; Kuo, 2006) but also to perform FTAs. This type of initial conditional is called a 'conditional threat' and is considered an impolite speech act, as seen in example (17):

(17) (O, a little girl, tells A, her mother, that if her father, who is going on a business trip, does not phone her, she will not talk to him anymore.)
   O: ..五月十號之前,_
      ..沒有接到他的電話的話,_
      ..我就跟他^絕交.\
   A: ..他說他這兩天非常忙.\
   O: 'If I do not get a phone call from him by May 10th, I will not talk to him anymore'.
   A: 'He said that he is very busy during these two days'.

Such a conditional threat is usually conveyed through initial conditionals which indicate factuality, meaning that the possibility of following through with the threat is very high and therefore serves as a warning. Since the logical relationship between the conditional and its main clause is strong in order to indicate the speaker's perlocutionary force, 如果 or 的話 is more appropriate than 假如/假設/假使 or 要是.

The final conditional clauses

After investigating English final adverbial clauses, Ford claimed that "in addition to representing the editing of a speaker's talk based on her/his own thought process, such final adverbial clauses may also be the products of speaker-recipient negotiation specifically aimed at achieving interactional ends" (1993: 102). Ford refers to such clauses as *post-completion extensions* (henceforth PCEs). PCEs may be prompted by a recipient's response or by a perceptible pause in the negotiation at a point where a response would be appropriate. A speaker may add a PCE to help avoid any obvious sign of interactional trouble, even in the absence of a pause or a response from the recipient. For instance, the final conditional clause in example (18), triggered by Speaker C, acts as an elaboration of her question in her preceding turn:

(18) (C and S discuss the difficulties that Christians might encounter in their work.)
    C: ..像這種困難--
       ..我就想說,_
       ..像這種困難,_
       ..我們怎樣去面對啊._
       ((6 IUs are omitted here))
    S: ...怎麼去面對._
    C: ..對啊,_
       ..像我們面對這種困難.\
       ..如果,_
       ..弟兄姊妹有這種困難.\
    C: 'Like this kind of difficulty which I am thinking about, how do we deal with it?'
    S: 'How to deal with them?'
    C: 'Yeah, like the problems we are facing. I wonder if our (Christian) brothers and sisters encounter such problems'.

At the beginning, C asks S how they can deal with such difficulties and then turns to another girl to say hello while that girl is passing by her and S. After greeting the girl, C observes that S is still mulling over her question and has not yet answered her. It seems that S is having difficulty answering or does not quite understand C's question, so C repeats the question and adds a final conditional clause as an elaboration. The PCE is an extension prompted by the lack of a response.

In contrast, the PCE in example (19) below is not prompted by the recipient but seems to be a speaker-based attempt to elaborate on his/her own turn. Borrowing Ford's term, we refer to this as a "self-edit" (Ford, 1993: 121). That is, the PCE in example (19) which is prefaced by a conditional clause arises from the speaker's editing (i.e., elaboration).

(19) (G consults B, a medical intern, about her eye problem.)
    G: ..然後真的是結膜炎怎麼辦.\
    B: ..結膜炎,_
       ..結膜炎事實上沒有什麼.\
    G: (0)沒有關係,_
       ..是不是?/
    B: ..對.\
    G: ..不會變瞎子?/
    B: ..<@ 不會 @>.\
       ..<@ 不會 @>.\
       ..除非是那種=很^可怕細菌感染,_
    G: 'And if I get conjunctivitis, what should I do?'
    B: 'Conjunctivitis is actually nothing (serious)'.
    G: 'It doesn't matter. Right?'
    B: 'Right'.
    G: 'I won't go blind, (if I get it)'.
    B: 'You won't, unless you are infected with some kind of terrible bacteria (in your eyes)'.

G consults B, a medical intern, about her eye problem. G worries that she might develop conjunctivitis due to inflammation in her eyes. B tells her that conjunctivitis is not a serious enough disease to cause blindness. He then adds further explanation (i.e., that conjunctivitis causes blindness only in the case of a serious bacterial infection in the eyes), which is introduced by a conditional clause.

To summarize, final conditional clauses, in comparison with initial ones, are not involved in discourse-organizing work but rather are local in scope, merely providing semantic qualification or grounding for their main clauses. The final conditional clauses in our data serve as general introducers of background or motivating information. Very often they also appear in environments where a recipient is in need of further elaboration. They can also introduce material that is more predictably necessary for some information to be clear. From our data, it can be seen that the conditional markers, especially 除非, often do extra work when there is an interactional warrant for elaboration or additional explanation.

Conclusion

The results of our study show that conditional clauses are prevalent initially and that different Chinese conditional markers are used by the speaker as signposts to guide the hearer into an imaginary world between factuality and counterfactuality. We have shown that different Chinese conditional markers can signal different types of conditionals and serve as contextualization cues that aid the hearer in understanding the degree of possibility expressed in the propositions they signal.

The conversation data in this study also reveal that conditionals, like topics, tend to occur initially in conversations. As pointed out by Ford (1993: 133), it is their hypotheticality which makes conditional clauses particularly useful in presenting a piece of information that is given or shared in forthcoming discourse. The prototypical use of conditional clauses in conversation is to prepose them before the material they link (i.e., the matrix clause) through which discourse-structuring functions introduce and establish the background for the associated modified material. In particular, initial conditionals can be used in directives, assertives, commissives and expressives (Searle, 1969). Our data reveal that factual conditionals tend to be used to perform assertives (e.g., assertions, claims, etc.), predicative conditionals are typically used to carry out commissives (e.g., warnings, threats, etc.), improbable conditionals are more commonly used in giving directives (e.g., advice, suggestions, etc.), and counterfactual conditionals are generally used more in communicating expressives (e.g., regret, gratitude, etc.).

References

Akatsuka, N. (1985) 'Conditionals and the Epistemic Scale', *Language* 61(3): 625–639.
Akatsuka, N. (1986) 'Conditionals are discourse-bound', in *On Conditionals*. E.C. Traugott et al. (eds.) Cambridge: Cambridge University Press. pp. 333–351.
Chou, C.-L. (2000) 'Chinese Speakers' Acquisition of English Conditionals: Acquisition Order and L1 Transfer Effects', *Second Language Studies* 19(1): 57–98.
Comrie, B. (1986) 'Conditionals: A typology', in *On Conditionals*. E.C. Traugott et al. (eds.) Cambridge: Cambridge University Press. pp. 77–99.
Cruttenden, A. (1989) *Intonation*. Cambridge: Cambridge University Press.
Du Bois, J.W., Schuetze-Coburn, S., Paolino, D. and Cuming, S. (1993) 'Outline of discourse transcription', in *Talking Data: Transcription and Coding Methods for Language Research*. Jane A. Edwards and Martin D. Lampert (eds.) Hillsdale, NJ: Lawrence Erlbaum. pp. 45–89.
Fauconnier, G. (1985) *Mental Spaces: Roles and Strategies*. Cambridge, MA: MIT Press.
Fauconnier, G. (1994) *Mental Spaces: Aspects of Meaning Construction in Natural Language*. Cambridge: Cambridge University Press.
Fauconnier, G. and Turner, M. (2002) *The Way We Think: Conceptual Blending and the Mind's Hidden Complexities*. New York: Basic Books.

Ford, C.E. (1993) *Grammar in Interaction: Adverbial Clauses in American English Conversations*. Cambridge: Cambridge University Press.
Ford, C.E. and Thompson, S.A. (1986) 'Conditionals in discourse: A text-based study from English', in *On Conditionals*. E.C. Traugott et al. (eds.) Cambridge: Cambridge University Press. pp. 353–372.
Haiman, J. (1978) 'Conditionals Are Topics', *Language* 54: 564–589.
Hou, X. (ed.). (2004) *Xiandai hanyu xuci cidian [Dictionary of Modern Chinese Function Words]*. Peking: Peking University Press.
Kennedy, G. (1998) *An Introduction to Corpus Linguistics*. London & New York: Longman.
Kuo, C.-H. (2006) The Information Status and Discourse Functions of Conditionals in Mandarin Chinese, PhD Dissertation of Georgetown University.
Li, C.N. and Thompson, S.A. (1981) *Mandarin Chinese: A Functional Reference Grammar*. Berkeley: University of California Press.
Limberg, H. (2009) 'Impoliteness and Threat Response', *Journal of Pragmatics* 41: 1376–1394.
Lü, S. (1980/2007) *Xiandai Hanyu Babai Ci [800 Words in Modern Chinese]*. Hong Kong: Commercial Press.
Searle, J.R. (1969) *Speech Acts*. Cambridge: Cambridge University Press.
Sperber, Dan and Wilson, Deirdre. (1986/1995) *Relevance: Communication and Cognition*. Oxford: Blackwell.
Su, I.-W. (2005) 'Conditional Reasoning as a Reflection of Mind', *Language and Linguistics* 6(4): 655–680.
Traugott, E.C. (2003) 'From subjectification to intersubjectification', in *Motives for Language Change*. R. Hickey (ed.) Cambridge: Cambridge University Press. pp. 124–139.
Wang, S. (1991) *A Corpus Study of English Conditionals*. Unpublished MA Thesis. Victoria University of Wellington.
Wang, Y.-F., Chen, J.-G., Treanor, D. and Hsu, H.-M. (2014) 'Exclusivity, Contingency, Exceptionality and (Un)desirability: A Corpus-based Study of Chinese *chufei* ('unless') in Spoken and Written Discourse'. *Language & Communication* 37: 40–59.
Wang, Y.-Y. (2012) The Ingredients of Counterfactuality in Mandarin Chinese, PhD Dissertation of the Hong Kong Polytechnic University.
Yang, F.-P. (2007) A Cognitive Approach to Mandarin Conditionals, Unpublished PhD Dissertation. Berkeley: University of California.

8
Information structure in Chinese discourse

Yu-Yin Hsu

Introduction

Important tasks for language researchers have included uncovering not only how language works, but what it is, and what it is for (Firth, 1935). In addition to deciding what to say, interlocutors must make choices about how to phrase their utterances. In natural languages, information structure and discourse are held to be universal, and linguistic forms to dynamically reflect and relate informational content to discourse context. Several concepts related to this view will be discussed in this chapter, which is divided into two parts. First, it provides an overview of theories of discourse analysis and information structure in general. Then, it presents the framework and core concepts it adopts, and goes on to explore the universal and Chinese-specific principles of – and structural constraints on – identifying the information statuses of noun phrases. How information packaging interacts with structure and discourse will also be discussed.

Discourse analysis

In various research domains including psychology, social science, and linguistics, discourse analysis is a general term for the study of language in use. According to Gee (2014: 18), "[d]iscourse concerns how various sentences flowing one after the other relate to each other to create meanings or to facilitate interpretation". Brown and Yule (1983) and Halliday (1985) deemed discourse a multidimensional process; and texts, products of that process. Because "discourse is inaccessible in its entirety but traces of it are found in texts" (Ainsworth, 2017: 5), discourse analysis focuses on intertextuality and records of naturally occurring utterances.

Some studies, adopting the viewpoint that language is an integrated communicative phenomenon, have adopted a macro view: looking at language use in broader contexts, and its impact on social interaction and social practices (e.g., Davies and Harré, 1990). The micro view, on the other hand, focuses on how various levels of linguistic structure help develop the meanings of utterances in specific contexts, and on the cognitive factors behind discourse structure, such as coherence, information management, event integration and rhetorical structure (e.g., Chafe, 1976; Halliday, 1985).

Researchers interested in linguistic structure and organization tend to view grammar as a tool that speakers and writers use to package and deliver specific information (Givón, 1983; Kuno, 1972). One of the most studied linguistic phenomena is the reference resolution of noun phrases. Such phrases can be presented in three forms – zero anaphor, personal pronoun, and simple noun – and can be replaced with pronouns when their referents can be understood from the context. Additionally, noun phrases can sometimes be left unpronounced (i.e., zero anaphora, marked as Ø in the following examples) when their identity or referent can be understood from preceding contexts. In (1), for example, the pronoun *he* refers to *John* (marked by the same co-index *i*), and the unpronounced noun phrase (Ø) is co-indexed with *he* and therefore means *John*. The noun phrase *the car* refers to *a Mercedes*, as indicated by the co-index subscript *j*.

(1)
John$_i$ told me that he$_i$ went to Germany and Ø$_i$ bought a Mercedes$_j$.
The car$_j$ cost him over $40,000.

The same phenomenon occurs in Chinese, albeit with the difference that multiple co-occurring zero anaphors are commonly found in a Chinese paragraph. The example paragraph in (2) contains several unpronounced noun phrases (Ø, i.e., zero anaphors), the identity of which relies on the preceding text. In this example, the subscript *i* refers to 那輛車 ('that car') in (2a), and the subscript *j* refers to the narrator 我 ('I') in (2c). The phenomenon presented here, i.e., cross-sentence coreference of zero anaphors (Ø) and their referents, is often referred to as "topic chains" (Dik, 1997; Tsao, 1979).

(2)
(a) 那輛車$_i$太貴， (b) Ø$_i$顏色也不好， (c) 我$_j$不太想買Ø$_i$。
(d) 昨天Ø$_j$去開了一下Ø$_i$， (e) Ø$_j$還是不喜歡Ø$_i$。

(a) *nà-liàng-chē*   *tài*   *guì,*   (b) Ø   *yánsè*   *yě*   *bù*   *hǎo,*
that-classifier-car   too   pricey   color   also   not   good
(c) *wǒ*   *bù*   *tài*   *xiǎng*   *mǎi*   Ø.
I   not   really   want   buy
(d) *Zuótiān*   Ø   *qù*   *kāi-le*   *yī-xià,*   (e) Ø   *háishì*   *bù*   *xǐhuān*   Ø.
yesterday   go   drive-PERFECT   a-bit   still   not   like

'That car is too pricey, and its color is not good either, so I don't really want to buy it. I went to test-drive it yesterday, but I still don't like it'.

Considerable research attention has been devoted to the resolution of pronouns and zero anaphors in Chinese (e.g., Li and Thompson, 1976; Shi, 1989). This leads scholars to ask: How do hearers know which referent to search for to correctly identify the interpretation in an example such as in (2)? And what makes a unit a "topic"? In turn, such questions have led researchers to consider a broader question: Why and how do people organize information to express themselves in a certain way, but not in another? In addition to the relationships between words' and utterances' meanings and their associations in various contexts, researchers are interested in the general principles that enable speakers to formulate and convey specific aspects of information (Birner and Ward, 1998). Accordingly, the next section discusses some general concepts and approaches used to study information structure.

Information structure

Any form of organization that reflects the purpose and the content of what speakers wish to share is termed "information structure" (Halliday, 1967) or "information packaging" (Chafe, 1976). It strongly affects how speakers refer to the persons and other entities involved in an event, and thus frequently influences choices of linguistic structure by means of morphological marking, pitch accent, and word order alternation (Lambrecht, 1994; LaPolla, 1995). The following two sections discuss information management in relation to the roles of the concepts of *old* and *new* in information structure, before proceeding to a discussion of terminology such as theme/rheme, topic/comment, and focus/background, with particular reference to how *focus* and *topic* are defined in Rooth's (1992) framework of alternative semantics.

Information management

Scholars have devoted considerable attention to how the order of the constituents in an utterance is governed by the oldness or newness of the information they provide. Many languages use different linguistic forms for previously known and previously unknown information. For example, when an entity is introduced for the first time, English speakers use an indefinite article to refer to it (e.g., 'a fox'), whereas if it has been mentioned before, or is known to all participants in a conversation, it is referred to using a definite article (e.g., 'the fox') or a pronoun (e.g., 'it'). Except for the known/unknown distinction made in the noun phrases, the sentences in (3) describe the same event, and speakers can make their own decisions about which pattern of response is more felicitous.

(3)
    a   A fox chased the rabbits.
    b   The rabbits were chased by a fox.

For Chafe (1976), information structure arises from interlocutors' packaging of information in response to immediate communicative needs. He further used the term *common ground* to refer to information that changes continuously, yet is mutually known and shared by the parties to a communicative event. Speakers' contributions of information to a discourse are packaged in ways that correspond to common ground at the moment they are uttered. *Old/given information* refers to knowledge that the speaker assumes the addressee possesses at the time of the utterance, while *new information* is what the speaker assumes to be newly introduced into the addressee's consciousness.

In Prince's (1981) more refined view, the old/new dichotomy can be further categorized into five information types: discourse-old/new, hearer-old/new, and inferable. For example, in the sentence in (4a) (Prince, 1992: 305), the first occurrence of *the door* is hearer-old (as indicated by the definite article *the*), and its second occurrence is discourse-old and thus hearer-old. In (4b), however, *the door* is discourse-new, although if a speaker chooses to say (4b), s/he probably assumes that the hearer already knows which door is being referred to (i.e., *the door of the Bastille*). Therefore, *the door* in (4b) is considered inferable by the hearer, and is hearer-old.

(4)
    a   He passed by the door of the Bastille, and the door was painted purple.
    b   He passed by the Bastille, and the door was painted purple.

Prince further specified that discourse-old is information that has been evoked in preceding contexts, and that hearer-old information is believed by the speaker to be in the hearer's conscious knowledge. When a speaker introduces an entity, s/he often assumes that the hearer can infer its existence "based on the speaker's beliefs about the hearer's beliefs and reasoning ability" (Prince, 1992: 304). Thus, what is new in the discourse does not have to be new knowledge to the hearer (cf. Firbas, 1966): a view that is adopted in the discussion that follows.

Information status and alternative semantics

Although discrepancies exist, the terminology that scholars use to describe units of information structure generally addresses two major differences: first, between the part that is related to the discourse purpose and the part that further advances the discourse (e.g., topic and comment, or theme and rheme); and second, between the part that helps emphasize or differentiate a subpart of sentence content, and the potential alternatives to that subpart that the discourse makes available (e.g., background and focus).

The basic concepts that these terms represent are exemplified in a paragraph such as (5) (Arnold et al., 2013).

(5)
    The little brown worm wiggled under the lettuce. A few moments later, he emerged from the ground for his dinner. It was arugula that he ate.

Because the subject *The little brown worm* includes the definite article *the*, it is assumed to carry old information that the speaker believes the hearer possesses. The pronoun *he* in the second sentence refers to *the worm*, expressing a topic denotation of this discourse and forming a topic chain. And in the final sentence, *arugula* was introduced into the discourse for the first time through a cleft sentence (i.e., a focus structure; cf. Teng, 1979), in which *that he ate* refers to what the sentence is about, serving as the background of the focus, *arugula*.

Of the theme/rheme dichotomy, Halliday (1985: 38) noted that "theme" can usually be adopted as the starting point of information (e.g., *The little brown worm* in (5)), whereas "rheme" refers to what the sentence is about (e.g., *wiggled under the lettuce*). When a theme unit also expresses old information, it is often referred as a topic.

Similarly, Givón (1990) emphasized that a topic is a functional notion at the discourse level, and is important 'if it remains "talked about" or "important" during a number of successive clauses' (Givón, 1990: 902). Taking structural relations into consideration, Lambrecht (1994: 118) proposed that when a referent "is interpreted as the topic of a proposition in a given situation, the proposition is construed as being about this referent". When a sentence does not contain specific morphosyntactic, prosodic or semantic clues that mark a unique information structure, the subject of a sentence often may function as a topic, and its predicate as a comment about this topic.

Focus can be defined by the structures that express a special type of information, and by the interpretations that focused units express based on the context. For Lambrecht (1994), *focus structure* was a grammatical system marking "focus" information in contradistinction to "presupposition", with the latter being information that the speaker assumes to be already salient to and/or inferable from the discourse context (i.e., part of the common ground; cf. Vallduví, 1990). Lambrecht categorized focus structure into three types: predicate focus (6), narrow focus (7), and sentence focus (8) (see also *neutral description* in Kuno, 1972 and *thetic structure* in Sasse,

1987). The part marked in bold in speaker B's utterances in these three examples indicates the focus unit of those sentences.

(6)
    A: How's your car?
    B: My car/It **broke down**.

(7)
    A: I heard your motorcycle broke down?
    B: **My car** broke down.

(8)
    A: What happened?
    B: **My car broke down**.

Whereas the first two types require a presupposition, the focus structure in (8) requires little or no presupposition because the focus is the entire sentence.

    Kamp's (1981) discourse-representation theory proposes that people first identify a presupposition in the sentence that it is introduced in, and then accommodate or evaluate that presupposition via discourse. In the two sentences in example (9) (Russel, 1905), *The present king of France* induces a presupposition of the existence of a person who is the king of France. If this phrase is introduced in a positive context (9a), the presupposition is false, whereas if it is introduced in a negative context (9b), it survives.

(9) a The present king of France is bald.
      b It is not the case that the present king of France is bald.

Rooth (1992) proposed that the function of focus is to cause the hearer to search for an appropriate set of alternatives. In this view, the B sentences in (6–8) have the same ordinary semantic value (i.e., the same truth-condition), but they exhibit different focus semantic values; and each focus domain signals its own unique set of relevant alternatives. For example, (6B) presupposes that *something happened to B's car*, and the focus alternatives are a set of possible associations with B's car, including *breaking down*. Example (7B) presupposes that *something broke down*, and the focus alternatives are individual entities, including *my car*. In (8B), the set of focus alternatives includes a set of appropriate propositions. The speaker asserts that *my car broke down* is the right proposition among the alternatives.

    For purposes of the present chapter, focus will refer to a language unit that, first, prompts the hearer to search for an appropriate set of alternatives, and second, signals or asserts that just one of those alternatives is suitable to the discourse at hand. The next section provides a general explanation of information structure in Chinese contexts before proceeding to a discussion of two Chinese-specific phenomena: zero anaphora and sentence final particles, 了 ('le') and 呢 ('ne').

Information structure in Chinese discourse

Beginning with Hockett (1958) and Chao (1968), linguists have debated whether Chinese sentences should be understood through a subject-predicate partition or a topic-comment partition (Li and Thompson, 1976). Generally, when a sentence in Chinese does not contain specific morphosyntactic or prosodic marks that signal a unique information structure, units that express old information appear earlier, and those that carry new information, later (Teng, 1977). In such cases, the subject of a sentence tends to express the discourse topic, whereas the predicate functions as a comment about this topic (Chao, 1968). Chinese languages do not have articles akin to *the* and *a* in English, and does not employ morphological marking to signal the referents of noun phrases in a sentence. Therefore, whether information is hearer-old/new is not marked in the way that it is in English, and the distinction between topic and subject is also less obvious than in morphologically rich languages. However, two Chinese element types are sensitive to information packaging and discourse functions, and are discussed in the following two subsections.

Zero anaphora

Zero anaphors are pervasive in the formation of topic chains in Chinese discourse (Chu, 1998; Tsao, 1979). According to Chu (1998), a topic chain is formed in three stages: introduction, selection, and continuation. Example (10) shows that both the subject (長安 'Chang-an City') and the object (名歌女 'famous female singer') can be newly introduced, and that in principle, both can function as the topic. In this example specifically, there is a good reason for the city to serve as a topic, since it is historically prominent as China's largest city during the Tang dynasty, and appeared in many literary works. However, because an animate subject is required by the predicate in (10b), 聰慧過人 ('be extraordinarily smart'), the hearer can confirm that the sentence's initial zero anaphor (Ø) refers to the singer rather than the city as the topic. Such an association between a topic and its (multiple) zero anaphors is known as a topic chain (see Tsao, 1979).

(10)
    (a)   長安$_i$ 有   個名歌女$_j$,
          Cháng'ān   *yǒu*   *gè-míng-gēnǚ,*
          Chang-an.city   have   CLASSIFIER-famous-female.singer
    (b)   Ø$_j$ 聰慧   過人。
          cōnghuì   *guò-rén.*
          smart   extraordinary
    'There was a famous female singer in Chang-an [who] was extraordinarily smart'.

The topic of a discourse can be changed. In (10), for example, one can make a statement such as (10c), in which the zero anaphor refers back to the city rather than to the singer.

(10)
    (c)   此外,   Ø$_i$ 還   有   個美麗的名舞女!
          cǐwà,   Ø   *hái*   *yǒu*   *gè-měilì.de-míng-wǔnǚ*
          besides   still   have   CLASSIFIER-beautiful-famous-female.dancer
    'In addition, [there] was also a beautiful, famous female dancer'.

Notably, (10c)'s object ('a beautiful, famous female dancer') is indefinite, and occurs in the regular postverbal object position (see LaPolla, 1995 on post-verbal position as a non-topical position). In addition, it contrasts with the 'famous female singer' of the previous discourse context (i.e., (10a)) and adds new information. In turn, the information updated in (10c) provides an appropriate context for shifting the topic of the discourse from the singer to its other relevant noun phrase, the city.

Yu-Yin Hsu

Sentence final particles 了 *and* 呢

Most linguistic studies of sentence final particles (SFPs) in Chinese have focused on their grammatical functions within sentences (e.g., Chao, 1968). In addition to the illocutionary force that they express, and their semantic and syntactic functions, SFPs have specific discourse functions. For instance, in the discourse in (11) (from Chang, 1986), the SFP 了 is used when a topic chain ends. The passage in question was adopted from a personal letter, so the unpronounced subject (Ø_i) in (11a) is interpreted as *us*. According to Chang (1986) and Chu (1998), when the SFP 了 occurs in a passage (e.g., at the ends of (11a) and (11b)), its occurrence signals the emergence of a new topic. For example, a change of topic chain occurs in (11b) (interpreted as the narrator, *I*), and this new topic continues in (11c). Then, in (11d), a new referent is introduced, i.e., 你的大名 ('your name').

(11)
 (a) 一轉眼，Ø_i 又快兩年沒見面了。 (b) 這次會議Ø_j 著實忙了一陣。
 (c) Ø_j現在總算可以略為喘口氣了。 (d) 你的大名_k已列入會議名單。

 (a) *Yī-zhuǎn-yǎn,*　　　Ø　*yòu*　*kuài*　*liǎng-nián*　*méi*　*jiànmiàn*　*le.*
　　One-turn-around　　　　again　almost　two-year　　not　　meet　　　SFP
　　'Time flies. Again, [we] haven't met for almost two years'.
 (b) *Zhè-cì-huìyì*　　　　　Ø　　　　*zhuóshí*　　　*máng-le*　　　　*yī-zhèn.*
　　This-CLASSIFIER-meeting　　　　indeed　　　busy-PERFECT　　a-while
 (c) Ø *xiànzài*　　*zǒngsuàn*　*kěyǐ*　*lüèwéi*　　　　*chuǎn-kǒuqì*　*le.*
　　　now　　　finally　　　can　　approximately　relieve-breath　SFP
　　'During this meeting, [I] was indeed pretty occupied, and now [I] finally can take a break'.
 (d) *Nǐ.de-dàmíng*　*yǐ*　　　*lièrù*　　*huìyì-míng.dān.*
　　your-name　　already　list　　　meeting-name.list
　　'Your name has already been placed on the list of this meeting's attendees'.

The SFP 呢 also has discourse functions in addition to its syntactic and semantic ones. Considering discourse and relevance (cf. Roberts, 1996), Chu (2006) argued that one important function of 呢 is to highlight – or indeed enhance – the relevance of a conversation. In discourse (12), in addition to the literal meaning of (12B), the presence of 呢 is intended to boost the hearer's sense of the relevance of the discourse, as indicated in the fragments in bold in the B sentences.

(12)
 A: 他-家　很　窮，你　就　不　要　跟　他　來往　了。
　　Tā-jiā　*hěn*　*qióng,*　*nǐ*　*jiù*　*bù*　*yào*　*gēn*　*tā*　*láiwǎng*　*le*
　　his-home　very　poor　　you　then　not　want　with　him　be-friend　SFP
　　'He is from a very poor family; you'd better not be friends with him anymore'.
 B: 他-家　有　三-頭-牛　呢！
　　Tā-jiā　*yǒu*　*sān-tóu-niú*　*ne*
　　his-home　have　three-CLASSIFIER-cattle　SFP
　　'**For your information**, they have three head of cattle!'

Interestingly, Chu (2006) noted that there seems to be a certain level of strength difference concerning the function of relevance that 呢 brings to the discourse. For example, if 呢 were omitted from (12B), that sentence could not be a felicitous response in its conversational context, instead becoming a statement of fact that is irrelevant to the conversation. And if 呢 were omitted from (13B), below, it would sound too abrupt, making speaker B sound rude and unwilling to participate in the conversation. Based on observations such as these, Chu proposed that the SFP 呢 has two major discourse functions: to show contrast with a preceding context, and to show a willingness to continue the conversation.

(13)
A:	老李	怎麼	還	沒有	來？
	Lǎolǐ	*zěnme*	*hái*	*méiyǒu*	*lái*
	Laoli	how.come	yet	not	come

'How come Old Li is not here yet?'

B:	他	老	早	就	來-了	呢。
	Tā	*lǎo*	*zǎo*	*jiù*	*lái-le*	*ne*
	he	old	early	already	come-PERFECT	SFP

'He came a **long** time ago'.

Information statuses of Chinese noun phrases

This section's aims are threefold. First, it demonstrates that Chinese noun phrases that occur in a non-canonical, preverbal position can express different types of information status reflecting various discourse needs. Second, it shows that such interpretational flexibility is structurally constrained, as demonstrated by two types of existential sentence. And third, it presents a method for identifying the differing information statuses of noun phrases, along with how such discourse knowledge helps with processing the resolution of anaphors and topic chains in a wider context.

Why is a pronoun sometimes used, rather than a zero anaphor? Why must a full noun phrase sometimes be used instead of a pronoun or a zero anaphor? Why do certain noun phrases intervene in an established topic chain, while other phrases do not? To answer these questions, let us first consider a phenomenon referred to as *preposed objects*.

The canonical word order of modern Chinese is subject-verb-object (SVO) (Li and Thompson, 1981).

(14)
小明	讀-了	那-本-書。
Xiǎomíng	*dú-le*	*nà-běn-shū*
Xiaoming	read-PERFECT	that-CLASSIFIER-book

'Xiaoming has read that book'.

In some sentences, however, two noun phrases occur before the verb. Sentences such as (15) are referred to as using preposed-object construction because the object (in this case, 那本書) occurs in a non-canonical, preverbal position (cf. (14)). Various structural terms have been proposed to describe this type of sentence, such as a secondary topic (e.g., Paul, 2002) or a focus (e.g., Tsai, 1994).

(15)
	小明	那-本-書	沒-讀-完。
	Xiǎomíng	*nà-běn-shū*	*méi-dú-wán*
	Xiaoming	that-CLASSIFIER-book	not-read-PERF
a	Topic/Subject	Secondary-topic	
b	Subject	Focus	

'Xiaoming has not finished reading that book'.

Whether a preposed object expresses a topic or a focus can be made clearer via consideration of the discourse in which it occurs (Hsu, 2008, 2012). Given that a *wh-* interrogative expression and its answers express a focus, the sentence in (16B) that contains the preposed object, 一篇論文 'one paper', answers the question in A, and thus represents a narrow focus (cf. Lambrecht, 1994).

(16)
    A: 小明   什麼   讀完-了?
          Xiǎomíng   *shénme*   *dúwán-le*
          Xiaoming   what   read-PERF
          'What has Xiaoming finished reading?'
    B: 他   [一-篇-論文]FOCUS   讀完-了。
          Tā   *yī-piān-lùnwén*   *dúwán-le*
          he   one-CLASSIFIER-paper   read-PERF
          'He has finished reading a paper'.

This focus denotation cannot be expressed by a zero anaphor, as shown in example (16B'), below – even if the speaker is holding papers in his/her hand while uttering this sentence.

(16)
    B': *他   [Ø]FOCUS   讀完-了。
          Tā   *dúwán-le*
          he   read-PERF
          'He has finished reading [the paper]'.

However, in other discourses, the preposed object might function as a topic; and when it does, the preposed object 論文 can be expressed by a zero anaphor (Ø), as in (17B'), unlike the narrowly focused preposed object in discourse (16).

(17)
    A   [說到   論文]TOPIC,   這-篇-的-內容   很   簡單。
         shuōdào   *lùnwén*   *zhè-piān-de-nèiróng*   *hěn*   *jiǎndān*.
         speaking.of   paper   this-CL-DE-content   very   simple
         'Speaking of papers, the content of this one is very easy'.
    B   沒錯!   我   [論文]TOPIC   已經   讀完-了。
         méicuò!   *wǒ*   *lùnwén*   *yǐjīng*   *dúwán-le*
         indeed   I   paper   already   read-PERF
         'Indeed, I have already finished reading the paper'.
    B'   沒錯!   我   [Ø]TOPIC   已經   讀完-了。
         méicuò!   *wǒ*   *yǐjīng*   *dúwán-le*
         'Indeed, I have already finished reading [the paper]'.

The fact that both a topic and a focus co-occur tends to uphold the claim that structurally, there are two positions between the subject and the predicate, with the topic phrase always preceding the focus phrase (Hsu, 2008; Paul, 2002). Topic/focus characteristics are clearly distinguished in discourse. Consider the example in (18): both topic and focus phrases occur in the answer (18B), and in (18B'), the topic can be replaced by Ø. However, if we were to use a zero anaphor to refer to a focus unit, the sentence would become infelicitous, as in (18B").

(18)
    A: 小明　　　[水果]_{TOPIC}　[什麼]_{FOCUS}　最-常　　吃?
        Xiǎomíng　shuǐguǒ　　　shénme　　zuì-cháng　chī
        Xiaoming　fruit　　　　　what　　　most-often　eat
        'Speaking of fruit, what does Xiaoming eat most often?'
    B: 他　　　[水果]_{TOPIC}　[蘋果]_{FOCUS}　最-常　　吃。
        Tā　　shuǐguǒ　　　píngguǒ　　zuì-cháng　chī
        he　　fruit　　　　　apple　　　most-often　eat
        'Speaking of fruit, he eats apples most often'.
    B': 他　　　[Ø]_{TOPIC}　　[蘋果]_{FOCUS}　最-常　　吃。
        Tā　　　　　　　　píngguǒ　　zuì-cháng　chī
        he　　　　　　　　apple　　　most-often　eat
        '[Speaking of fruit,] he eats apples most often'.
    B": *他　　[水果]_{TOPIC}[Ø]_{FOCUS}　最-常　　吃。
        Tā　　shuǐguǒ　　　　　　　zuì-cháng　chī
        he　　fruit　　　　　　　　most-often　eat
        '[Speaking of fruit,] he eats [apples] most often'.

It is noteworthy that substantially less discussion has been devoted to the fact that contrastiveness does not always concern focus. According to Lambrecht (1994: 291), contrastiveness "is not a category of grammar but the result of . . . general cognitive processes" referred to as "conversational implicatures". For example, a phrase that involves alternatives to and partitions of the previously mentioned topic, is referred to as a contrastive-topic (CT) phrase (Hsu, 2012; cf. Büring, 1997, 2003; Lee, 2003). In other words, in the immediate discourse, there are other entities about which a comment *could* be made, but the speaker selects one or some of these alternative topics. In (19), for example, the intended topic concerns cities in the United States. The nouns *Chicago* and *NYC* express CTs because they partition the previously mentioned 美國的城市.

(19)
    A: 你　　去-過　　美國的-城市　　　嗎?
        Nǐ　　qù-guò　　Měiguó.de-chéngshì　ma
        you　go-EXP　　US-city　　　　　　Q.PART
        'Have you been to cities in the US?'
    B: 我　[芝加哥]_{CT}　去-過　　了，　但是　　[紐約]_{CT}　還　　沒。
        Wǒ　Zhījiāgē　　qù-guò　le,　dànshì　Niǔyuē　　hái　méi
        I　　Chicago　　go-EXP　ASP　but　　　NYC　　　still　not
        'I have been to Chicago, but I have not been to NYC yet'.

Interestingly, the same sentence shown in (19B) can express a different information structure when used in a different discourse. In (20), for instance, the preposed objects *Chicago* and *NYC* serve to correct information, and thus are considered contrastive foci (CFs).

(20)
    A: 美美　　說　　你　　去-過　　紐約。
        Měiměi　shuō　nǐ　　qù-guò　Niǔyuē
        Meimei　say　　you　go-EXP　NYC
        'Meimei says that you've been to NYC'.

B: (其實) 我 [芝加哥]_CF 去-過-了, 但是 [紐約]_CF 還 沒。
    Qíshí wǒ Zhījiāgē qù-guò-le, dànshì Niǔyuē hái méi
    actually I Chicago go-EXP-ASP but NYC still not
    'I have been to Chicago, but I have not been to NYC yet'.

These examples again show that the same sentence may be used to express different types of information packaging, to reflect different discourse needs; and that identifying the relevant information statuses of noun phrases helps one to understand both why and when zero anaphora can be used.

However, it is not true that every sentence allows noun phrases this flexible accommodation of information. For instance, sentence structures can constrain information packaging. In this context, it is important to consider Chinese existential sentences, which allow a freer word order, as shown in (21).

(21) a (在) 院子裡 有 一-隻-狗。
      Zài yuànzi-lǐ yǒu yī-zhī-gǒu
      in yard-inside exist one-CLASSIFIER-dog
      'In the yard, there is a dog'.
    b 有 一-隻-狗 在 院子裡。
      Yǒu yī-zhī-gǒu zài yuànzi-lǐ
      exist one-CLASSIFIER-dog in yard-inside
      'There is a dog in the yard'.

Li and Thompson (1981: 509) noted that sentences such as (21) exhibit a grammatical difference from one another in terms of the definiteness of the locative phrases, e.g., 院子裡. However, LaPolla (1995) argued that the locative phrases in both sentences in (21) are definite and identifiable, and differ chiefly with respect to the information roles they play within those sentences. In (21a), 院子裡 serves "to anchor the new referent in the discourse" (LaPolla, 1995: 311); and in (21b), the noun phrase 一隻狗 'a dog' is a referent newly introduced into the discourse, and the locative phrase serves as an assertion about it. As such, the sentences in (21) involve distinct types of information packaging. This becomes clearer when the sentences are examined in discourse:

(22) a 院子裡 有 軍人_i, 但是 Ø_i 不 多。
      Yuànzi-lǐ yǒu jūnrén dànshì bù duō
      yard-inside exist soldier but not many
      'There are soldiers in the yard but not many'.
    b *院子裡_i 有 軍人, 但是 Ø_i 又 寬 又 大。
      yuànzi-lǐ yǒu jūnrén dànshì yòu kuān yòu dà
      yard-inside exist soldier but also wide also big
      'There are soldiers in the yard, but [the yard is] wide and big'.

According to LaPolla (1995), a so-called existential presentative sentence such as the first clause in (22) introduces a new entity into the discourse (i.e., 'soldier'). In this example, 院子裡 is simply an identifiable location, not a topic or focus – meaning, for instance, that a zero anaphor cannot be co-indexed with 院子裡, as shown in (22b).

According to LaPolla, Chinese has another type of existential sentence that involves possessors, and differs fundamentally from the type of existential sentence discussed above. In this second type, the preverbal possessor subject (e.g., 王冕 in (23)) is the topic, and the predicate after it expresses focus. This analysis gains some support from the discourse: for example, the noun phrase after the verb (父親 'father') in (23) cannot serve as the antecedent for the following pronoun and zero anaphor in (24), despite readers recognizing that (23) describes 'Wangmian's father'. This suggests that 父親 is not located in a topic position.

(23)

[王冕]TOPIC   [死-了   父親$_i$]FOCUS。
Wángmiǎn   *sǐ-le*   *fùqīn*
Wangmian   die-PERFECT   father
'Wangmian's father died'.

(24)

*他$_i$ 辛辛苦苦   把   孩子   養-大,   Ø$_i$ 卻   無法   享福。
Tā   *xīnxīnkǔkǔ*   *bǎ*   *háizi*   *yǎng-dà*   *què*   *wúfǎ*   *xiǎngfú*
he   painstakingly   BA   child   raise-big   but   cannot   enjoy-life
'He strove to raise his children, but [he] had no chance to enjoy his life'.

Notably, (23)'s proposition can be expressed by a different sentence with a possessive noun phrase. As shown in (25a), the possessive noun phrase 'Wangmian's father' can be the antecedent of the pronoun and the zero anaphor in contexts that follow, such as (25b).

(25)

    a   [王冕.的-父親$_i$]TOPIC   [死-了]FOCUS。
          Wángmiǎn.de-fùqīn   *sǐ-le*
          Wangmian.DE-father   die-PERFECT
          'Wangmian's father died'.

    b   他$_i$辛辛苦苦把孩子養-大, Ø$_i$卻無法享福。 (=(24))
          'He strove to raise his children, but [he] had no chance to enjoy his life'.

In light of the discussion so far, one may wonder how the resolution of zero anaphora in a larger discourse may be accounted for. Accordingly, let us consider the example in (26) (texts from *Sinica Corpus*, Chen et al., 1996, modified for this discussion). The referents introduced in (26a) are 一位已經退休的同事 ('a retired colleague') and 其他同事們 ('other colleagues'). First, it should be recalled that the 有 'exist' existential construction introduces new referents into the discourse. Here, the new referent 'a retired colleague' – functioning as a subject – provides a new topic. The noun phrase 大家 in (26b) is marked with the subscript *j*, which indicates that it refers to the previously mentioned 其他同事們. Because of this intervening referent, the pronoun 他 is needed in (26b) to refer back to 'a retired colleague'; and because that pronoun is present, the following Ø in (26b) can be referred to and co-indexed with it. In (26c), a new referent is introduced by a full noun phrase 他的兒子 in a copula sentence, marked with the subscript *k*, and serves as the topic for the following zero anaphors. Because of this intervening sentence (26c), which forms a new topic chain based on the noun phrase 'his son', (26d) needs a

141

fully expressed noun phrase (i.e., 這位原來該享清福的同事) to clearly refer back to the previously mentioned topic, i.e., the retired colleague.

(26)
- a 有一位已經退休的同事ᵢ最近一直向其他同事們借錢。
  'There is a retired colleague who has been trying to borrow money from other colleagues recently'.
- b 大家很納悶。他ᵢ已經退休了，Øᵢ怎麼需要做這種事?
  'Everyone wonders why. He is already retired. Why would [he] need to do such things?'
- c 原來是他ᵢ的兒子ₖ正在創業，Øₖ與人投資，但Øₖ經營不善，Øₖ欠了一大筆錢。
  'It turned out that it is because of his son, who is running a new business, [and] has been investing [in] it with friends, but [his son] is not good at business, and now, owes a lot of money'.
- d 如今，這位原來該享清福的同事ᵢ只好到處奔走，Øᵢ為兒子ₖ籌錢。
  'Now, this colleague who was originally supposed to enjoy life after retirement has no choice but to go hither and thither and to help collect money for his son'.

Clearly, the interrelationships of information statuses and language forms, and the role of information partitioning, are as complex in Chinese, as they are in other languages. In the next section, I briefly conclude this chapter.

Concluding remarks

Based on a detailed consideration of Chinese examples in light of the existing literature on information structure and discourse, this chapter has suggested that information structure and its associated discourse functions result from constituents' dynamic reflections of information statuses in their various contexts. Concepts related to information packaging have a universal quality; and yet, they are constrained by language-specific factors. The Chinese language does not employ much morphological marking for informational purposes, but several of its language phenomena are still sensitive to informational considerations. As demonstrated in this chapter, some categorical divisions of informational concepts (e.g., topic vs. focus, and old vs. new) are encoded through specific structural planning in discourse. While much theoretical research on information structure has emphasized the syntactic, prosodic or semantic felicity of information concepts within a sentence, a wider-lensed examination of the types of contexts in which whole sentences become felicitous will more systematically advance our understanding of inter- and intra-language phenomena and their characteristics.

References

English references

Ainsworth, S. (2017) 'Discourse analysis/methods', in *The International Encyclopedia of Organizational Communication*. Craig R. Scott and Laurie Lewis (eds.) John Wiley & Sons, Inc. pp. 1–14. DOI: 10.1002/9781118955567.wbieoc061.

Arnold, J.E., Kaiser, E., Kahn, J.M. and Kim, L.K. (2013) 'Information Structure: Linguistic, Cognitive, and Processing Approaches', *Wiley Interdisciplinary Reviews: Cognitive Science* 4(4): 403–413.

Birner, B.J. and Ward, G. (1998) *Information Status and Noncanonical Word Order in English*. Amsterdam & Philadelphia: John Benjamins Publishing Company.

Brown, G. and Yule, G. (1983) *Discourse Analysis*. Cambridge: Cambridge University Press.

Büring, D. (1997) *The Meaning of Topic and Focus: The 59th Street Bridge Accent*. London & New York: Routledge.
Büring, D. (2003) 'On D-Trees, Beans, and B-Accents', *Linguistics and Philosophy* 26(5): 511–545.
Chafe, W. (1976) 'Givenness, contrastiveness, definiteness, subjects, topics, and point of view', in *Subject and Topic*. C. Li (ed.) New York: Academic Press. pp. 25–56.
Chang, V.W. (1986) The Particle Le in Chinese Narrative Discourse. Unpublished University of Florida PhD Dissertation, Gainesville, FL.
Chao, Y.R. (1968) *A Grammar of Spoken Chinese*. Berkeley: University of California Press.
Chen, Keh-Jiann, Chu-Ren Huang, Li-Ping Chang, Hui-Li Hsu. (1996) 'SINICA CORPUS: Design Methodology for Balanced Corpora', *Proceedings of Language Information and Computation (PACLIC 11)*: 167–176.
Chu, C.C.-H. (1998) *A Discourse Grammar of Mandarin Chinese* (Vol. 6). New York: Peter Lang.
Davies, B. and Harré, R. (1990) 'Positioning: The Discursive Production of Selves', *Journal for the Theory of Social Behaviour* 20(1): 43–63.
Dik, S.C. (1997) *The Theory of Functional Grammar, Part I: The Structure of the Clause*, K. Hengeveld (ed.) Berlijn/New York: Mouton de Gruyter.
Firbas, J. (1966) 'Non-Thematic Subjects in Contemporary English', *Travaux Linguistiques de Prague* 2: 239–256.
Firth, J.R. (1935) 'The Technique of Semantics', *Transactions of the Philological Society. Philological Society* 34(1): 36–73.
Gee, J. (2014) *An Introduction to Discourse Analysis: Theory and Method* (4th ed.). New York: Routledge.
Givón, T. (1983) *Topic Continuity in Discourse: A Quantitative Cross-language Study*. Amsterdam & Philadelphia: John Benjamins Publishing Company.
Givón, T. (1990) *Syntax: A Functional-typological Introduction, Vol. 2*. Amsterdam & Philadelphia: John Benjamins Publishing Company.
Halliday, M.A.K. (1967) 'Notes on Transitivity and Theme in English: Part 2', *Journal of Linguistics* 3(2): 199–244.
Halliday, M.A.K. (1985) *An Introduction to Functional Grammar*. Baltimore: University Park Press.
Hockett, C.F. (1958) *A Course in Modern Linguistics*. New Delhi: Oxford And Ibh Publishing Co.
Hsu, Y.-Y. (2008) 'The Sentence-Internal Topic and Focus in Chinese', *Proceedings of the 20th North American Conference on Chinese Linguistics*.
Hsu, Y.-Y. (2012) 'Two Functional Projections in the Medial Domain in Chinese', *Concentric: Studies in Linguistics* 38(1): 93–136.
Kamp, H. (1981) 'A theory of truth and semantic representation', in *Formal Methods in the Study of Language*. J. Groenendijk, T. Janssen and M. Stokhof, J. Groenendijk (eds.) Amsterdam: Mathematisch Centrum. pp. 277–322.
Kuno, S. (1972) 'Functional Sentence Perspective: A Case Study from Japanese and English', *Linguistic Inquiry* 3(3): 269–320.
Lambrecht, K. (1994) *Information Structure and Sentence Form: Topic, Focus, and the Mental Representations of Discourse Referents*. Cambridge: Cambridge University Press.
LaPolla, R.J. (1995) 'Pragmatic relations and word order in Chinese', in *Word Order in Discourse*. P. Downing and M. Noonan (eds.) Amsterdam & Philadelphia: John Benjamins Publishing Company. pp. 297–329.
Lee Chungmin. (2003) 'Contrastive topic and proposition structure', in *Asymmetry in Grammar*. Vol. 1. A. Di Sciullo (ed.) Amsterdam/Philadelphia: John Benjamins Publishing Company. pp. 345–371.
Li, C.N. and Thompson, S.A. (1976) 'Subject and topic: A new typology of language in subject and topic', in *Subject and Topic*. C.N. Li (ed.) New York: Academic Press. pp. 457–489.
Li, C.N. and Thompson, S.A. (1981) *Mandarin Chinese: A Functional Reference Grammar*. Berkeley & Los Angeles & London: University of California Press.
Paul, W. (2002) 'Sentence-Internal Topics in Mandarin Chinese: The Case of Object Preposing', *Language and Linguistics Compass* 3(4): 695–714.
Prince, E. (1981) 'Toward a taxonomy of given-new information', in *Radical Pragmatics*. P. Cole (ed.) New York: Academic Press. pp. 223–255.
Prince, E.F. (1992) 'The ZPG letter: Subjects, definiteness, and information-status', in *Discourse Description: Diverse Analyses of a Fund Raising Text*. W. Mann and S. Thompson (eds.) Amsterdam/Philadelphia: John Benjamins Publishing Company. pp. 295–325.
Roberts, C. (1996) 'Information structure in discourse: Towards an integrated formal theory of pragmatics', *Working Papers in Linguistics-Ohio State University Department of Linguistics*: 91–136.
Rooth, M. (1992) 'A Theory of Focus Interpretation', *Natural Language Semantics* 1(1): 75–116.

Russell, B. (1905) 'On Denoting', *Mind; a Quarterly Review of Psychology and Philosophy* 14(56): 479–493.
Sasse, H.-J. (1987) 'The Thetic/categorical Distinction Revisited', *Linguistics and Philosophy* 25(3): 511–580.
Shi, D. (1989) 'Topic Chain as a Syntactic Category in Chinese', *Journal of Chinese Linguistics* 17(2): 223–262.
Teng, S.-H. (1977) *A Basic Course in Chinese Grammar: A Graded Approach through Conversational Chinese*. San Francisco: Chinese Materials Center.
Teng, S.-H. (1979) 'Remarks on Cleft Sentences in Chinese', *Journal of Chinese Linguistics* 7(1): 101–114.
Tsai, W.-T.D. (1994) 'On Nominal Islands and LF Extraction in Chinese', *Natural Language and Linguistic Theory* 12(1): 121–175.
Tsao, F.-F. (1979) *A Functional Study of Topic in Chinese*. Taipei: Student Book Co.
Vallduví, E. (1990) The Information Component, PhD Dissertation, University of Pennsylvania.

Chinese reference

屈承熹 Chu, C.C.-H. (2006) '汉语篇章语法：理论与方法' (Mandarin Chinese Discourse Grammar: Theory and Practice), 俄语语言文学研究 (*Russian Language and Literature Studies*), 13(3): 1–15.

Part III
Linguistic elements in Chinese discourse

9
Personal pronouns in Chinese discourse

Xuehua Xiang

Introduction

Personal pronouns are essential in the grammatical systems of any language. Carrying out referential functions, personal pronouns also bear regional differences, differ in usage and meaning in the oral vs. written registers, and vary according to situations of use. The usage and evolution of personal pronouns are deeply intertwined with the social activities in everyday life. The social contexts that give rise to specific characteristics of personal pronouns continue to shift and evolve engendering new changes in the ways we communicate and interact with one another.

Chinese personal pronouns: a discourse-grammatical sketch

The Chinese personal pronoun system is relatively simple from a typological point of view,[1] exemplifying what Greenberg (1963: 96) calls a three-way person differentiation (first, second and third) and a two-way number differentiation (singular, plural). The interrogative form of personal pronouns is the uniform 谁 *shéi* 'who'. The possessive form is the combination of a pronoun and the possessive marker 的-*de* (e.g., *wǒ-de* 'my, mine'). Chinese personal pronouns do not mark syntactic positions; the same form occurs in the subject as well as the object positions. This relatively straightforward morphological system is illustrated below based on Standard Mandarin Chinese in Mainland China.

- *wǒ, nǐ, tā* (first, second, third person, singular)
- *wǒ-men, nǐ-men, tā-men* (first, second, third-person, plural).[2]
- *wǒ-de, nǐ-de, tā-de* (first, second, third person, singular, possessive)
- *wǒmen-de, nǐmen-de, tāmen-de* (first, second, third person, plural, possessive)
- *shéi* (interrogative)
- *shéi-de* (interrogative, possessive)

Beyond this core system, Chinese uses a set of lexical items for reciprocal, reflexive, and generic person references. Below is a list of such referential words, comprising a lexical category that Yip and Rimmington (2004) call "pro-words" (56).

- [reciprocal pronouns 'each other'] 彼此 *bǐcǐ*, 互相 *hùxiāng*
- [reflexive pronoun 'self'] 自己 *zìjǐ*, 本身 *běnshēn*, 本人 *běnrén*, 自个儿 *zìgěr*
- [generic reference 'all'] 大家 *dàjiā*, 诸位 *zhūwèi*, 各位 *gèwèi*, 大伙儿 *dàhuǒr*
- [generic third-person 'other(s)'] 别人 *biérén*, 人家 *rénjia*

(Zhu, 1999: 98)

Gender is not marked in pronouns in spoken Chinese. The spoken third person *tā* is gender-neutral. In modern written Chinese, however, the third-person *tā* has three forms, i.e., the masculine 他 *tā*, the feminine 她 *tā*, and the non-human 它 *tā*. This three-way gender and human vs. non-human distinction is a recent development influenced by the "Written Vernacular Chinese Movement" (白话文运动 *Báihuàwén Yùndòng*) in the decades following the anti-imperialist "May Fourth Movement" (五四运动 *Wǔsì Yùndòng*) that broke out in 1919. The grammar and style of written Chinese underwent radical shifts in this period due to large quantities of literary works being translated from European languages into Chinese (Chen, 1999). As European languages mark gender in their pronoun systems, the Chinese translations had to incorporate various written forms to accommodate the gendered pronouns in the original texts in an *ad hoc* fashion. Gradually, 他, 她 and 它 find their way to become the standard forms in written Chinese in Mainland China. A more elaborate system is retained in Taiwan Mandarin which additionally uses 牠 for animals and 祂 for deities and spiritual beings (Shei, 2014: 52). The same process of diversification and standardization occurred with the second-person pronoun as well. The second-person pronoun *nǐ* retains a standard, gender-neutral written form 你 in Mainland China while it has two variants, the gender-neutral 你 and the feminine 妳, in Taiwan Mandarin.

Register variation

Register-specific personal pronouns have long been a tradition in spoken and written Chinese. The singular second-person pronoun 您 *nín* marks deference and social distance (Zhu, 1999: 96). To illustrate, below is an extract from the Q&A section of a public lecture by 李敖 (Lǐ Áo), a well-known writer in his 70s at the time of this lecture. A member of the audience uses the deferential *nín* 'you' throughout his question and Lǐ Áo uses the unmarked 你 *nǐ* 'you' in his response.

(1) 观众:李敖先生, 您好, . . . 您作为当初的也算是一个同学, 从这个角度, 您想对您现在的这些同学说什么？谢谢。
李敖:我现在对年轻的北京四中的小朋友们所说的话就是, . . . 在你一天24小时的时间里面, 哪怕是抽出一个小时或者半个小时, 是属于你真正自己的时间, 做你自己真正想做的事情, 可能是最好的。
Audience: Mr. Lǐ Áo, greetings to you (*nín*). . . . You (*nín*) were a pupil once. From this viewpoint, what would you (*nín*) want to say to the pupils in front of you (*nín*) today? Thank (you).
Lǐ Áo: What I'd like to say to the kids from Beijing No. 4 Middle School is that . . . in the 24 hours of your (*nǐ*) days, even if it's only for one hour or half of an hour, that truly belong to you (*nǐ*), do what you (*nǐ*) yourself truly want to do, (that) is perhaps the best.

In this interactional context, Lǐ Áo is higher in social status and older than his addressee. The setting is also formal. These contextual factors warrant the audience's use of the deferential *nín*, along with other markers of deference such as the address term 李敖先生, the greeting at the beginning of the question, and the remark of gratitude at the end. Lǐ Áo doesn't use explicit politeness forms, but his answer is sincere and courteous, appropriate for the context.

Marking formality and deference, *nín* has also become a marker of the service and business register. In formal business and service settings, customers are typically addressed with *nín*. Example (2) illustrates:

(2) a 您当前位置 'your (*nín*) current location' (a sign on an e-commerce website)
    b 正在努力为您加载视频 '(We are) working hard to load the video for you (*nín*)' (automatically generated message on a media site when a video is loading)
    c 您何时进入公司？您现在所在的部门？ 'When did you (*nín*) join the company? What is your (*nín*) current department?' (questions on a company's internal survey)

In speech contexts where deference or formality are not relevant, using *nín* may be interpreted as intentionally distant or even ironic. For example, this formulaic expression, 您说的比唱的还好听 'What you (*nín*) say is even better than singing', presents an incongruity between the deferential pronoun *nin* and the ironic compliment. Such incongruity violates the Quality maxim for cooperative interaction (i.e. to mean what one says) (Grice, 1975) and may thus be interpreted as mockery.

On the other hand, certain pronouns mark informality and group solidarity. In the Northern Mandarin dialects of Mainland China, the pronoun 咱*zán* and its plural form 咱们*zánmen* 'we, us' refer to a "we" group that includes both the speaker and the direct addressee. In contrast, the plural pronoun *wǒmen* in these dialects refer to a "we" group that excludes the direct addressee. A speaker thus has two variants to designate a "we" group, namely, the addressee-inclusive *zán* or *zánmen* and the addressee-exclusive *wǒmen*. Speakers of these dialects can use these two variants to signal affiliative or disaffiliative stances toward the immediate addressee (Zhao, 1987). For example, the following lines are from the classic three-act play 茶馆 'Teahouse' 老舍 (Lǎo Shě's 1956/2014) in the Beijing Mandarin Vernacular. The scene is set in 1898, the tumultuous year of "Hundred Days' Reform". The patrons at the teahouse were in their daily ritual of conversation over tea.

(3) a (Wáng Lìfā is the cautious manager of the teahouse. He entreats his patrons to refrain from discussing politics.)
       Wáng Lìfā: 诸位主顾，咱们还是莫谈国事吧！ (*zánmen*: addressee-inclusive)
       'Gentlemen, let's not discuss affairs of state, shall we?'
    b (Two special agents are eavesdropping on the conversation. They approach to arrest the patrons for slandering the government. One of the patrons, Master Sōng, protests.)
       Master Sōng: 哥儿们，我们天天在这儿喝茶。王掌柜知道，我们都是地道老好人！ (*wǒmen*: addressee-exclusive)
       'Buddies, we have tea here every day. Manager Wáng knows, we're harmless good people'.

In Example 3(a), using *zánmen*, the manager positions himself as an ingroup member with his patrons. In Example 3(b), speaking to the special agents, Master Sōng uses the addressee-exclusive *wǒmen* to protest his innocence.

Null pronoun

The null pronoun is a salient typological feature of Chinese as well as other Asian languages (e.g., Japanese, Korean). The null pronoun refers to the subject or object syntactic position unoccupied by an overt linguistic element, as illustrated by the symbol ∅ in Example (4).

(4) Ø去哪儿？(compare: 你去哪儿？)
    'Where are (Ø) going? (compare: Where are you going?)'

From a syntactic perspective and based on a non pro-drop language (e.g. English), one may form the impression that the null pronoun is a reduced variation of an overt pronoun, even a structural anomaly. However, using natural spoken discourse, Tao (1996) demonstrated that the null pronoun is an independent, natural and very basic form of Spoken Chinese Grammar.

A range of communicative factors motivates the use of the null pronoun as compared to an overt pronoun. These factors range from the speaker and the hearer's shared understanding of the identity of the referent, the accessibility of the referent in the communicative context, politeness strategies, textual coherence considerations, as well as register and style. For example, in a conversation, the immediate speaker and addressee are contextually salient referents. The null pronoun is more appropriate than an overt "I" or "you" for self- and addressee- reference (as in example 4). Example (5) is extracted from a television news piece showing an interview with the Head Coach of the Chinese Women's Volleyball Team after the team has just won an Olympics Game.

(5) 1 Reporter: 为什么Ø 这么给我们惊喜呢？
    2 Coach: 呃, 我觉得Ø 还是队员打得比较英勇吧。Ø打好每个球。
    1 Reporter: Why do (you) give us such a wonderful surprise?
    2 Coach: Um, I think (it) is because the team fought bravely. (The team) hit each ball.

In Line 1, the reporter uses the null pronoun to address the coach and the addressee-exclusive *wǒmen* 'we' to represent himself along with the viewers in front of the television. The reporter's question positions the coach as the focal point of attention whose identity is salient and understood by all, warranting no explicit mention. The coach uses two null pronouns in her response. The first instance refers to the topic at hand, i.e. the reason for her team's successful game. Since the topic has just been activated in the prior turn, an overt reference to it is not necessary; the null pronoun helps to create a cohesive question-and-answer sequence. Further, instead of positioning herself at the center of attention, the coach mentions her team, and uses the null pronoun to refer to her team, positioning them as the most salient referent at the moment of interaction. These discourse-level motivations for the null pronoun will be discussed in more detail in a later section.

Reflexive pronoun 自己 *zìjǐ* 'self, -self'

Zìjǐ is a reflexive pronoun that either occurs alone ("bare *zìjǐ*") or with another pronoun ("compound *zìjǐ*") (Xiang, 2003). Example (6) illustrates these two variants.

(6) a 自己做错了, 要有勇气承认. (bare *zìjǐ*)
       '(If) self has done wrong, (self) should have the courage to admit it'.
    b 你自己做错了, 要有勇气承认. (compound *zìjǐ*)
       '(If) you yourself have done wrong, (you) should have the courage to admit it'.
                                                            (adapted from Zhu, 1999: 96)

Zhu (1999: 96) suggested that bare *zìjǐ* signals a generic reference similar to the English indefinite pronoun "one". In Example 6(a), the wrongdoing described in the first clause is not attributed to a specific person; bare *zìjǐ* here merely marks a "Subject of Consciousness" (cf. logophoricity as discussed in Zribi-Hertz, 1989).

Using television and radio interview data, Xiang (2003) illustrates that bare *zìjǐ* expresses empathy, which enables the interviewer to probe the interviewee's private thoughts without appearing ostensibly intrusive. To illustrate, Example (7) is excerpted from a talk show with a female celebrity guest. Immediately preceding the segment, the guest and the host, along with the studio audience, watched a video clip depicting the guest in her multiple roles of public personality, mother, daughter and wife. The following is the first question after the video clip.

(7) Interviewer: 你对自己其实一直也困惑着。(bare *zìjǐ*)
    Interviewee: 我觉得我现在有很多困惑。。
    Interviewer: In fact, you have always felt bewildered about (your)self.
    Interviewee: I feel that I have much bewilderment now.

Here the host initiates a sensitive topic, that is, underneath the guest's public persona as a confident and successful career woman, she is burdened by the demands of her multiple social roles. Using *nǐ* in the subject position and bare *zìjǐ* in the object position in the phrase 对自己 'about (one's) self', the host is able to conjecture about the addressee's private emotion, inviting the guest to reveal more.

Compound *zìjǐ*, in contrast, signals an emphatic overtone, juxtaposing the referent of *zìjǐ* vis-à-vis other people. Example (8) is excerpted from a radio interview with the Chinese Women's Gymnastic Team captain regarding her team's underwhelming performance at a recent Olympic Game.

(8) 很多人都认为中国女队呢, 应该有机会要不拿冠军, 要不都拿亚军, 还是差那么一点点。那你自己作为其中的一份子来看呢, 就觉得中国女队老是排在第三, 在哪方面才能冲上去呢？
    'Many people think that the Chinese Team should win the Gold Medal, or at least the Silver Medal, (yet the team) still missed (the top medals). You yourself as a member of the team, the Chinese Women's Team has always ranked third. In what aspects can the team move up?'.

(Xiang, 2003: 504)

The compound reflexive pronoun juxtaposes the team captain's viewpoint with the discontent of the general public. The communicative effect is that the addressee is put in a position to have to speak critically of her team, obligated to defend and justify its performance.

人家 *Rénjia*

Rénjia literally means "person's family" and is viewed in traditional grammar as a non-specific third-person reference (Chao, 1968). *Rénjia* appears to be interchangeable with 别人 *biéren* 'other people' at the sentential level, illustrated by Example (9):

(9) a 你一个人说了, 人家(*rénjia*)/别人(*biéren*)没意见啊？
      'You said it all by yourself. Won't others have objections?'
    b 人家(*rénjia*)/别人(*biéren*) 越夸, 他说得越起劲儿。
      'The more others praise (him), the more he enjoys talking'.

(Adapted from Zhu, 1999: 98)

In these invented examples without an actual interactional context, both *rénjia* and *biéren* appear to refer to a non-specific third person and interchangeable. However, in natural discourse, *rénjia* is not interchangeable with *biéren* without significantly altering the speaker's meaning. Unlike *biéren* which refers to a generic 'other', the referent of *rénjia* can refer to a specific, definite individual, as illustrated by Example (10) from a television interview with an actor.

(10) 1   Interviewer：你在中戏上学的时候,就是说有一年整个都没跟老师说过话,是吗？
    2   Interviewee：对,我们的班主任。 其实这老师特别好。
    3   Interviewer：干嘛不理人家？
    1   Interviewer: When you studied in Zhong Xi (The Central Academy of Drama), you didn't talk to (your) teacher for a whole year. Is this true?
    2   Interviewee: Yes, (it was) our class teacher. Actually this teacher was really nice.
    3   Interviewer: Why didn't (you) talk to *rénjia* (the teacher)?

In Example (10), it is apparent from context that the referent of *rénjia* is specific and mutually understood. Using the non-specific *rénjia* to refer to a specific, known third person creates a "gossip" effect. Liu (2001) suggests that the rhetorical effect of *rénjia* is such that its referent is neither central to the communication nor conscious of the fact that he or she is being discussed. In Example (10), using *rénjia*, the host focuses on eliciting more storytelling from the famed actor and his college teacher's identity is part of the backdrop.

Speakers may also use the third-person *rénjia* for self-reference. In this regard, *rénjia* is very similar to *lang5* 'person, people' in Taiwan Min and *yàhn/yàhndeih* 'person, people' in Cantonese. Example (11) illustrates these dialectal variations for self-reference in remarkably similar ways.[3]

(11) a   (A singer is thrilled by a surprise appearance of her former, somewhat estranged mentor at her concert. The singer uses *rénjia* to refer to herself and to request a hug from the mentor.)
         Singer: (to mentor) 让人家抱一下嘛。 (turning to the audience) 来,你们帮我求他。
         '(To mentor) Let <u>someone</u> (i.e., me) give (you) a hug. (To audience) Come on, you guys, help me ask him'.
     b   Cantonese plural *yàhndeih*
         Yàhndeih pacháu āma. 人哋怕醜吖嘛.
         'Well, <u>some people</u> are shy'. (i.e. I am shy).
         (Matthews and Yip, 1994: 79; Chinese orthography is rendered by current author)
     c   Taiwan Min *lang5*
         Lang5 ma7 m7 cai1 e7 an1 ne1 a.
         人也不知道會這樣啊. / 人嘛乜知會按呢啊.
         '<u>Someone</u> (i.e., I) didn't expect it to turn out like this'.
         (Hsieh, 2009: 116; Taiwan Min orthography and English translation are rendered by current author)

In all three instances, using the third-person *rénjia* (and its dialectal equivalents) for self-reference, the speaker shifts his or her role from a speaking subject to an objective third-party individual. Xie (2009) calls this function "焦点转移" or "focus shifting" (116). Xie (2009) notes that such self-reference typically occurs in contexts where some negativity is perceived, such as a face-threatening act (11a), an embarrassing emotion (11b) or a past occurrence that had a negative consequence (11c). This indirect self-reference is similar in function to a number of other means of indirect self-reference, all of which tend to be used more commonly by females. Xie shows that in Taiwan Min, while males tend to refer to themselves with the standard first-person singular form *gua2* 我 'I'; women tend to use the aforementioned generic third person as well as the plural first person or the second person (e.g., li2 你 'you', gun2 阮 'you', lan2 咱 'we'). The correlation between these indirect self-reference styles and gender identity remains to be further explored.

Diversity across dialects

The personal pronoun systems of Chinese dialects appear to be similar in terms of marking a three-way distinction in person (first, second and third) and a two-way distinction in number (singular and plural). These commonalities notwithstanding, the diversity of personal pronouns across Chinese dialects is not to be overlooked.

The range of personal pronouns in the non-Mandarin varieties of Chinese provides crucial clues for understanding the historical development of the Chinese language. For example, common across several Southern Min dialects (such as Taiwanese Min), the plural forms of the personal pronouns are realized by suffixing a nasal segment to the singular pronoun stem, e.g. 我 gua3 (first-person singular) vs. 阮 guan3/gun3 (first personal plural), 汝 li3 (second-person singular) vs. 恁 lin3 (second-person plural) (Mei, 1999: 2). In the Wu dialects (Li, 2001), the plural first-person 阿拉 aklak 'we' originally consisted of the first-person singular form and a location word. This lexical origin is also seen in the Xiang dialects where the plural suffix is 里 li, originally meaning "residence, place" (Wu, 2005: 121). These similarities not only provide some evidential basis for constructing the typological relationships between Chinese regional dialects. They also provide interesting, albeit circumstantial, clues regarding the cultural bases of Chinese grammatical categories (e.g., the Chinese society's residence-based social structure seems to correlate well with using a place marker to mark plural personal pronouns).

Personal pronouns and notions of self

The notion of self in the traditional Chinese society is heavily relational (Pan and Kádár, 2011). Distinct from the Western Cartesian model of an independent individual, in the traditional Chinese society, an individual is positioned in intricate social networks based on family and blood relations, workplace relations, as well as relationships based on age, gender, and class. As social structures change, personal pronouns, in form and usage, continue to evolve as well.

Lee (2012) examined the use of four variations of the first-person pronoun in the Analects of the Confucius (论语 Lúnyǔ, 551–479 BC): 朕 zhèn, 予 yǔ, 我 wǒ, 吾 wú. The discourse distributions of these pronouns are not syntactically determined; they are influenced by the specific topics in focus and the relationship between the social agents evoked in the writing. In the Analects, 朕 is used solely by the emperor, indexing absolute supreme power. 予 occurs in contexts of "sacred subject matter", where the speaker interacts with heaven or the divine such as in ritualistic texts. 我 denotes a 'public self', neutral and without deference to social hierarchy; thus it is able to represent a speaking subject as well as to mark generic indefinite reference (similar to the English indefinite pronoun "one"). 吾 is used in contexts where the speaker evokes a "private self", as occurs in texts of private speech and self-reflection. These four pronouns serve distinctive communicative functions. Lee's analysis provides us with interesting insight that the concept of self was multifaceted and socially constituted even two millenniums ago.

Notions of self are also manifested in practices of politeness. Pan and Kádár (2011) demonstrated dramatic disparities between the Chinese historical and contemporary politeness practices and such disparities were directly and indirectly caused by the colonization of China by foreign imperialist powers in the 19th century, which led to further socio-political movements that deeply altered the Chinese interactional-pragmatic norms. In classical Chinese, the discursive means of politeness included a large repertoire of personal pronouns and ritualistic address terms such as 小人 'lit. small person, i.e., this worthless person' vs. 高君 'high lord', 小女 xiǎonǚ 'lit. small woman, i.e., worthless daughter' vs.千金 'lit. thousand gold, i.e., venerable daughter', 仆 'your servant', 弟子 'your pupil' vs. 先生 'teacher', etc. These linguistic expressions elevate the addressee's status and downplay one's own. The series of social transformation in subsequent decades, from the Written Vernacular Movement in the 1910s-20s, the founding of the P.R. China in 1949, the Cultural Revolution in the 1960s-70s and the Open Door and Economic Reforms of recent decades, effectually rendered these traditional hierarchy-based referential terms obsolete in Mainland China, disappearing altogether in most domains of use.

In recent years, a new orthographical representation of the third-person singular pronoun, written as TA, ta or Ta, has become a common usage on the Internet. To illustrate, a running topic (marked by the hashtag symbol #) on the Chinese microblog platform, 微博 Wēibó, is "#对ta说你要好好的#" '#Tell ta to be good and well#'. Another topic on a comparable web blog platform, 腾讯微博 Tencent Wēibó, is "#2016我想对TA说#" '#2016 I want to say to TA#'. Tens of thousands of people participated in these topics, writing messages to a significant other whose gender was kept unspecified using ta/Ta/TA. The reasons for this new form are complex. In the past two decades, the Chinese society has gained more awareness of gender equality and the rights of the LGBTQ (lesbian, gay, bisexual, transgender, queer) communities. The gender-neutral Ta provides a linguistic tool to not only communicate effectively, but also to defy the traditional binary gender categories. Compared to the Written Vernacular Chinese movement which ushered in gender-specific pronouns in written Chinese a century ago, this new gender-neutral pronoun came into everyday use under very different social circumstances, indexing a new kind of metalinguistic awareness.

Personal pronouns in text and talk

Sentence-level conceptions of personal pronouns, such as syntactic constraints and co-referencing, are inadequate models to account for how personal pronouns work in discourse and interaction. The use of personal pronouns is complex and varied, textually, cognitively and socially, illustrated below.

Personal pronouns and information structure

Pronouns play a significant role in creating discourse cohesion (Halliday and Hasan, 1976). In discourse, pronouns replace a noun phrase while maintaining its referent in focus. Example (12) illustrates:

(12) A: 那场电影你觉得怎么样?
         'How did you feel about that movie?'
     B: ∅一点都不喜欢∅.
         '(I) didn't like (it) a bit'.

(adapted from Li and Thompson, 1981: 658)

In Example (12), the focal referents are the addressee and the movie, initially referenced in the form of a full noun phrase (那场电影) and the second-person pronoun 你. In B's response, both the person reference and reference to the movie occur in the form of a null pronoun, since their identities are now shared.

Referential expressions also reflect how the speaker or writer constructs the world symbolically for their interlocutor or reader. To illustrate, the following is an extract from the narration in the documentary film, 舌尖上的新年 'A Bite of China-Celebrating the Chinese New Year' (Chen, 2016).

(13) 这是一年中最重要的时间节点。从农历腊月开始,整整一个半月,<u>几乎所有中国人</u>会放下手中的一切, Ø专心致志地投入到一种忙碌而甜蜜的状态。<u>他们</u>用四季所得精心炮制年味。Ø敬天地, Ø礼神明, Ø寄托对家人的情结, Ø抒发对岁时的感怀。
'This is the most important time of the year. From the beginning of the twelfth lunar month, for a full one and half months, <u>almost all of the Chinese people</u> would put away everything in (their) hands, Ødevote (themselves) to a busy and sweet state. <u>They</u> create the New Year flavors with the bounties of the four seasons, Ø respect heaven and earth, Ø perform rituals, Ø find subsistance in the caring of their loved ones, Ø express their feelings toward time and age'.

The key subject throughout this excerpt is the Chinese people, a collective entity. Its reference initially occurs in the form of a full NP, then pronouns (including the null pronoun) once the referent is clearly established. These pronoun choices, alternating between full references and overt or null pronouns, jointly create a rhythmic phonological pattern contributing to the formal and poetic style of the narration. The choice of the third-person plural (compared to the first-person plural *wǒmen* 'we') reflects the documentary genre of the film favoring the stance of an objective observer and commentator. The choice of the masculine orthographic variation for the third-person plural reference 他们 (compare to the feminine variation 她们) reflects the long-rooted patriarchal gender bias in pronoun use, not only in Chinese, but widespread across cultures (Lakoff, 1973).

Personal pronouns as window into consciousness

Chafe (1994: 41) theorizes that the main functions of language are to convert "unique experience into something familiar and manageable" and to offer "a way to narrow the chasm between independent minds". Referential expressions are important tools for both functions. Compared to a full noun phrase, personal pronouns presume a certain degree of hearer/reader familiarity with the referent. Because personal pronouns position the referent as "shared/known" to the reader/addressee, in literary works, the writer can use personal pronouns to construct a world where the protagonists are presumably known or accessible to the reader/listener. The following is the very beginning of the novel 半生缘 *Half a Lifetime Romance* written by 张爱玲 (Eileen Chang, 1948/2016). The very first word of the novel is a third-person pronoun.

(14) <u>他</u>和曼桢认识, 已经是多年前的事了。Ø算起来倒已经有十四年了 -- Ø真吓人一跳！Ø马上使<u>他</u>连带地觉得<u>自己</u>老了许多。
'<u>He</u> and Mànzhēn had met a long time ago. Working it out, (he) realized it had been fourteen years since then. Quite a shock! (It) made <u>him</u> feel, suddenly, that (he him)<u>self</u> has gone much older'. (translation is adapted from Chang, 1948/2016).

In ordinary conversations, speakers usually do not start a new topic with *tā* without having established a context where the identity of *tā* is known or accessible to the addressee. In creative works such as Example (14), the writer uses *tā* to evoke/force a shared/accessible status of *tā*, transporting the reader immediately into the narrated world, into the mind of the protagonist.

Zhang (2002) examined the use of personal pronouns in the novel 小饭店 'Little Restaurant' written by 王安忆 Wáng Ānyì. Zhang demonstrated that personal pronouns are instrumental in the novel to portray the segregated life of rural migrant workers in the megacity of Shanghai. The story starts with the second person *nǐ* and *nǐmen*, which directly address the reader, bonding with them and inviting them to scrutinize the world of migrant workers at a distance (e.g., 你们从这里走过, 推开这座简易房屋的小饭店的门, 朝里望去, 会想, 人怎么能够这样生活？ 'You pass by this place, push open the door of this makeshift little restaurant, look inside, and (you) will think: how can humans live like this?' (Zhang, 2002: 147).

In the novel, no proper nouns or other personal identifiers are used to refer to the migrant workers. Migrant workers are only referenced with group labels, such as the third-person plural *tāmen*, 打工妹 'working girls', 外来妹们 'outsider girls', 小姐们 'misses' (Zhang, 2002: 153). Zhang's analysis demonstrates that personal pronouns not only function to create textual cohesion through repeated, synonymous references to the same individuals; they also reflect the ways people see the world around them, filtered through ideological lenses.

Personal pronoun in face-to-face interaction

The first-person and second-person pronouns are deictic, that is, the referent of *wǒ* 'I, me' is not fixed; it corresponds to the speaking subject at each specific moment of utterance and shifts as the speaking subject shifts. Similarly, the referent of *nǐ* 'you' corresponds to the immediate addressee at each specific moment of speaking (Bühler, 1990).

However, this straightforward mapping of 'I' to the speaker and 'you' to the interlocutor falls short of accounting for the diverse range of uses these two pronouns instigate in face-to-face interaction. Based on naturally occurring data, Biq (1991) identified four functions of *nǐ* in interaction: 1) the traditional referential meaning, namely, referring to the addressee; 2) the impersonal *nǐ* referring to a generic being (cf. generic 'you' in English, Quirk et al., 1985); 3) the dramatic *nǐ* where the speaker adopts the voice of another person in ventriloquy; 4) the metalinguistic *nǐ* which has no propositional content; it functions to elicit the addressee's attention, and occurs in formulaic phrases such as 你说 *nǐ shuō* 'you say', 你知道 *nǐ zhīdào* 'you know', 你看看 *nǐ kànkàn* 'you see', 你想想看 *nǐ xiǎngxiǎng kàn* 'you think about it', 你比方说 'you for example, i.e. for example'. Below is an extract to illustrate the impersonal as well as the metalinguistic uses of *nǐ*.

(15) (TV interview with a businessman)
Businessman: 一个亿很快就到了, 十亿也到, 一百亿也到了, 但<u>你知道</u>, 超过10亿, 超过一个亿的时候, 财富对一个人已经没什么价值了。实际上在一个亿或者到十个亿, 尤其在这么年轻的时候, <u>你</u>会有一种失落, 有一种茫然, <u>你</u>会觉得人生失去了意义.

'Very soon (the goal) of 100 million was reached, (then) a billion was reached, 10 billion was reached. But <u>you know</u> (metalinguistic), when it's beyond a billion, beyond 100 million, wealth is no longer of value to an individual. In fact, at the point of 100 million or a billion, especially at such a young age, <u>you</u> (impersonal) will feel a sense of loss, a sense of bewilderment, <u>you</u> (impersonal) will feel that life has lost its meaning'.

In this example, the first instance of *nǐ* occurs in a formulaic expression to call for the addressee's attention. This metalinguistic function is evidenced by its placement right at the moment where the speaker shifts from a narration to a metacognitive comment on the effect of sudden wealth on young minds; the contrastive conjunction 但 'but' coincides with this topical shift. The second instance of *nǐ* reflects what Biq identifies as the impersonal *nǐ*. However, building on Biq (1991), Hsiao (2011) suggested that such case exemplifies deictic role-shift: that is, such instances of *nǐ* 'you' are not impersonal; on the contrary, they appeal to the addressee's empathy. By saying "你会有一种失落, 有一种茫然", the speaker is referring to his own state of mind. But instead of using the canonical first-person pronoun *wǒ*, by using *nǐ* 'you', the speaker extends the relevance of such feeling to the addressee. Hsiao relates this type of referential role-switch to Hannah Arendt's (1958) rumination that, through speaking and interacting, humans relate their personal experiences to the wider world transcending physical, spatial and temporal divides. The canonical referents of *nǐ* 'you' and *wǒ* 'I' can be switched because humans are capable of seeing the world beyond their egotistic center, a skill essential for cooperative survival.

Conclusion

This paper has illustrated that personal pronouns are much more than a grammatical system. In discourse, personal pronouns do much more than refer to a real-world referent. Speakers' pronoun choices are based on a wide range of linguistic, social, psychological, aesthetic and pragmatic factors. In this chapter, the discussions are largely based on Mandarin Chinese in Mainland China. It goes without saying that we need much more research on referential practices in less commonly studied Mandarin and non-Mandarin Chinese varieties situated in specific cultures, regions and communities.

One generalization we can draw about the Chinese pronoun system is that it offers a rich repertoire for speaking with indirection: bare *zìjǐ*, null pronoun, and *rénjia*, in their respective ways, provide nuanced ways where the speaker could avoid explicit designation of a person to an event, feeling or situation. Further research is needed to explore the relationship between pronoun systems and speech styles across gender, region and communicative context.

As societies continue to evolve and change, the linguistic resources we draw upon to communicate will also change. Computer- and mobile-device mediated communication is rapidly changing the ways we connect and interact with each other. The Chinese language, including its writing system, its genre practices, as well as people's politeness routines and interactional norms are changing rapidly due to these new digital mediums. Naturally, our senses of group solidarity, social distance, power and social hierarchy will also change. The use and change of personal pronouns in the age of digital communication is a fascinating and indispensable area of research.

Notes

1 Throughout this chapter, the word "Chinese" refers to Mandarin Chinese by default. However, the Chinese language encompasses a wide range of varieties across temporal, spatial and sociocultural spans.
2 The plural marker 们 *-men* is not a fully productive suffix. The restrictions on the use of 们 *-men* include the semantic features of animate and human (Shei, 2014: 51).
3 In this chapter, Mandarin Chinese pronouns and their examples are presented using the Simplified Chinese writing system and the Pinyin Romanization system. Pronouns and examples from other Chinese varieties (e.g., Cantonese and Taiwanese Min) are represented using the orthographic systems originally used in the articles from which the examples are taken. In some cases, additional orthographic variations are added by the current author for the reader's interest.

References

English references

Arendt, H. (1958) *The Human Condition*. Chicago, IL: University of Chicago Press.
Biq, Y.-O. (1991) 'The Multiple Uses of the Second Person Singular Pronoun Ni in Conversational Mandarin', *Journal of Pragmatics* 16: 307–321.

Bühler, K. (1990) *Theory of Language: The Representational Function of Language* (Donald Fraser Goodwin, Trans., 1934). Amsterdam and Philadelphia: John Benjamins.

Chafe, W. (1994) *Discourse, Consciousness, and Time: The Flow and Displacement of Conscious Experience in Speaking and Writing*. Chicago, IL: The University of Chicago Press.

Chao, Y.R. (1968) *A Grammar of Spoken Chinese*. Berkeley, CA: University of California Press.

Chen, P. (1999) *Modern Chinese: History and Sociolinguistics*. Cambridge, MA: Cambridge University Press.

Greenberg, J.H. (1963) 'Some universals of grammar with particular reference to the order of meaningful elements', in *Universals of Human Language*. J.H. Greenberg (ed.) Cambridge, MA: MIT Press. pp. 73–113.

Grice, P. (1975) 'Logic and conversation', in *Syntax and Semantics*, Volume 3: *Speech Acts*. P. Cole and J. Morgan (eds.) New York: Academic Press. pp. 41–58.

Halliday, M.A.K. and Hasan, R. (1976). *Cohesion in English*. London: Longman.

Hsiao, C.-H. (2011) 'Personal Pronoun Interchanges in Mandarin Chinese Conversation', *Language Sciences* 33: 799–821.

Lakoff, R. (1973) 'Language and Woman's Place', *Language in Society* 2(1): 45–80.

Lee, C.L. (2012) 'Self-Presentation, Face and First-Person Pronouns in the Analects', *Journal of Politeness Research* 8: 75–92.

Li, C.N. and Thompson, S. (1981) *Mandarin Chinese: A Functional Reference Grammar*. Berkeley, CA: University of California Press.

Liu, C.-S.L. (2001) 'Antilogophoricity, Sympathy and the Sympathetic Antilogophor Renjia', *Journal of East Asian Linguistics* 10: 307–336.

Matthews, S. and Yip, V. (1994) *Cantonese: A Comprehensive Grammar*. London: Routledge.

Pan, Y. and Kádár, D.Z. (2011) *Politeness in Historical and Contemporary Chinese*. London and New York: Continuum

Quirk, R., Greenbaum, S., Leech, J. and Svartvik, J. (1985) *A Grammar of Contemporary English*. London and New York: Longman.

Shei, C. (2014) *Understanding the Chinese Language: A Comprehensive Linguistic Introduction*. London and New York: Routledge.

Tao, H. (1996) *Units in Mandarin Conversation: Prosody, Discourse, and Grammar*. Philadelphia: John Benjamins.

Wu, Y. (2005) *A Synchronic and Diachronic Study of the Grammar of the Chinese Xiang Dialects*. Berlin and New York: Mouton de Gruyter.

Xiang, X. (2003) 'Multiplicity of Self in Public Discourse: The Use of Personal References in Two Radio Sports Shows', *Language Sciences* 25: 489–514.

Zhang, X. (2002). '"Them" and "Us" in Shanghai Today', *International Journal of the Sociology of Language* 158: 141–161.

Zhao, H. (1987) 'The Chinese Pronoun Zan and Its Person and Social Deictic Features', *Journal of Chinese Linguistics* 15(1): 152–176.

Zribi-Hertz, A. (1989) 'Anaphor Binding and Narrative Point of View: English Reflexive Pronouns in Sentence and Discourse', *Language* 65: 695–727.

Yip, P. and Rimmington, D. (2004) *Chinese: An Essential Grammar*. New York: Routledge.

Chinese references

Chang, E. 张爱玲 (1948/2016) 半生缘. (*Half a Lifetime Romance*, Trans. K. Kingsbury). New York: Anchor Books.

Chen, Xiaoqing 陈晓卿 (2016) 舌尖上的新年 (*A Bite of China-Celebrating the Chinese New Year*). 爱奇艺/中国国际电视总公司.

Hsieh, Shelley Ching-yu 謝菁玉. (2009) 台語的'我': 第一人稱指涉詞的運用及其社會意義 ("I" in Taiwanese Southern Min: The Application and Social Implication of the Speaker Identity), 台湾语文研究 (*Journal of Taiwanese Languages and Literature*) 3: 109–127.

Lǎo Shě 老舍. (1956/2014) '茶馆 (Teahouse: A play in three acts. Translated by Ying Ruocheng)' in *The Columbia Anthology of Modern Chinese Drama*. X. Chen (ed.) New York: Columbia University Press. pp. 334–384.

Li, Rulong 李如龙. (2001) 汉语方言的比较研究 (*A Comparative Study of Chinese Dialects*). 北京: 商务印书馆 (The Commercial Press).

Mei, T.-L. 梅祖麟 (1999) '幾個臺灣閩南話常用虛詞的來源' (The etymologies of some grammatical particles in Southern Min) in *Contemporary Studies on the Min Dialects*. P. Ting (ed.) *Journal of Chinese Linguistics Monograph* No. 14: 1–41.

Zhu, Dexi 朱德熙. (1999) 朱德熙文集第一卷 (*Works of Zhu Dexi, Volume 1*). 北京: 商务出版社 Beijing: The Commercial Press.

10
Aspect in Chinese narrative discourse

Wendan Li

Introduction

Aspect is a grammatical category that expresses how a situation denoted by a verb phrase is presented or viewed with regards to its temporal feature. Commonly occurring and widely discussed aspectual distinctions include perfective and imperfective, durative and non-durative, inceptive and completive, and progressive and non-progressive aspects. These distinctions are commonly expressed in languages. This chapter takes a discourse – functional approach to the study of aspect by examining its role in Chinese narrative structure. Focus is given to the perfective and imperfective aspect. It shows that aspect, as a grammatical phenomenon, functions as a grounding device in narrative discourse. The perfective aspect, which presents events in their entirety, records and highlights major events, putting them in the foreground; these events form the main developmental line of a story. The imperfective aspect, which presents ongoing and unbounded events, demotes situations into the background. These clauses play a supporting role in the thematic development of the story, adding descriptions, elaborations and comments. Aspectual choices thus reflect the narrator's decision to package the information and tell a story from a certain perspective in order to achieve a particular goal.

Aspect can be studied in a sentence-based approach or a discourse-oriented approach. Traditional analysis of aspect describes the meaning and functions of aspectual devices at the clause or sentence level. Up to the present, most studies of Chinese aspect have been done at this level, focusing on the use and function of grammatical aspectual markers, such as – *zhe* 着, *-le* 了 and – *guo* 过. A discourse approach, which the present chapter takes, examines the role of aspectual devices in a larger context, taking multiple sentences or clauses, episodes or even an entire story into consideration. In this chapter, the section "Aspectual Devices" demonstrates how perfective and imperfective aspects are indicated in Chinese. The section "Aspect and Temporal Advancement in Narrative" examines the role of aspect in temporal advancement in narrative text. The section "Aspect and Narrative Grounding" looks at aspect and other related features of the clause and discourse, such as grounding, transitivity and clause type. The last section offers concluding remarks. Excerpts of actual narrative discourse (fiction) are used for illustration. Sources of the excerpts are indicated at the end of each item by author's last name and page number of the work. English translation of the excerpts are taken from published sources (See "sources of examples" in appendixes).

Aspectual devices

A consensus in aspectual analysis is that aspectual meaning of a sentence is compositional – a result of the interactions of categories both within the grammar and among grammar, lexicon, and semantics (Verkuyl, 1972). The discussion in this section adopts Smith's (1997) two-component view and her terminology of *viewpoint aspect* and *situation aspect* as the descriptive framework.

Viewpoint (grammatical) aspect markers

Grammatical markings on the main verb indicate viewpoint aspect. For this reason, it is also referred to as *grammatical aspect*. It indicates "different ways of viewing the internal temporal constituency of a situation" (Comrie, 1976: 3). The *perfective aspect* presents a bounded situation as a single unanalyzable whole. The beginning, middle, and end of the situation are rolled into one. No attempt is made to divide it into individual phases. It is, in a sense, an outside view of a situation. The *imperfective aspect*, by contrast, looks inside a situation and focuses on a specific part, typically without endpoints. In (1) is an English example from Comrie (1976: 4) to show their differences. Clauses are letter-marked for discussion.

(1) (a) *John **read** a book yesterday;* (b) *while he **was reading** it,* (c) *the postman came.*

To see the point here, some features of English need to be looked at first. English is a language without overt aspectual marking. Aspectual information is conveyed through tense. Dynamic verbs in the past tense typically encode the perfective aspect. This can be seen in (1a), in which the event of John's book reading is presented in its entirety without distinguishing various internal phases. By contrast, the progressive tense in (1b) conveys the imperfective aspect; it focuses on the middle portion of the event exclusively, saying that it was at a certain point during John's reading that the postman arrived. Therefore, in (1), the event of John's reading is presented from two aspectual viewpoints.

In Chinese, aspect is grammatically marked by aspectual morphemes. The perfective marker *-le* following a dynamic verb indicates the perfective aspect. The imperfective aspect involves a group of markers, including the progressive *zai* 在, the durative *-zhe*, the experiential *-guo*, and the inceptive *-qilai* 起来 (Smith, 1997; Xiao and McEnery, 2004).[1] The example in (2) contrasts the imperfective and the perfective aspects. In (a), the verb *he* 'drink' followed by the imperfective marker *-zhe* presents an ongoing event of drinking; in (b), the verb *dian* 'nod' followed by the perfective marker *-le* presents a complete and bounded event as a single unanalyzable whole.[2]

(2) (a) 傅家杰默默地独自喝着酒, (b) 点了点头。 (Chen [1981] 57)
    (a) *Fu Jiajie momodi duzi he-zhe jiu,* (b) *dian-le-dian tou.*
    (a) Fu Jiajie silently by himself drink-ZHE wine (b) nod-LE-DUPL head
    'Jiajie, who was silently sipping wine on his own, nodded his head'.

Chinese aspect has a unique feature: The use of grammatical markers is not obligatory. In fact, most clauses in narrative discourse do not use aspectual markers. The clauses in (3), for example, narrate three events in temporal sequence. The clauses are all interpreted as perfective, but only one -*le* is used in (a) (shown in bold). In the other two clauses, -*le* could be used in the positions indicated by the underlined blanks, but is not.

(3) (a) 母亲拧开了仿古台灯, (b) 从书架上拿出___一个包装好的礼品盒, (c) 递给___柳璀。 (Hong [2009] 9)

    (a) *Muqin   ning-kai-**le**   fanggu   taideng*, (b) *cong   shujia-shang na-chu*
    (a) mother switch-open-LE antique.style lamp (b) from bookshelf-on bring-out
    Yige   baozhuang-hao de   lipinhe (c) *di-gei Liu Cui.*
    one.CL wrap-good   MOD gift.box (c) pass-to Liu Cui.
    'She switched on the mock antique table lamp and took a well-wrapped gift box off the bookshelf, which she passed to Liu'.

The nonobligatory use of grammatical aspectual markers, especially – *le*, is discussed in most major works on Chinese aspect (Chao, 1968; Smith, 1997; Xiao and McEnery, 2004). A statistical study observed that only 21.55% of the clauses in narrative discourse use aspect markers (Yang, 2002). Smith (1997: 279), who made a similar observation, commented that "the most important pragmatic fact about the viewpoint morphemes of Mandarin is their optionality". The question is then raised: When -*le* is not used in a perfective clause, how is the aspectual information conveyed? A logical answer to the question points to the compositional view of aspect, which takes situation aspect into account.

Situation aspect

While viewpoint aspect is the grammatical marking on the verb, *situation aspect* is conveyed by the lexical content of the verbal predication. It concerns the inherent nature of situations, e.g., whether a situation is dynamic or static, durative or non-durative, telic or atelic. In Chinese, several lexical categories contribute to the expression of situation aspect including verb types, resultative verb complements (RVC), expressions of event quantification, and prepositional phrases (PP) with a bounding effect.

Verb categories and aspectual meaning

Verbs represent different situation types and convey important aspectual information. The study of verb categorization has found that things and situations in the world are perceived and categorized according to their underlying temporal features related to the passage of time. People in different cultures perceive situations in similar ways. Table 10.1 shows a common verb categorization that has been validated crosslinguistically (Comrie, 1976; Smith, 1997; Vendler, 1957). The five situation types are characterized by feature descriptions. They are divided broadly into either states or events. Events comprise all non-stative situations. *Situation* is a cover term that includes states and events as well as their subcategories.

    The feature *dynamic* refers to the amount of energy involved in maintaining a situation. Whereas events are sustainable only with a constant input of energy, states require no energy to maintain and remain static over time. This crucial feature distinguishes events from states. However, note that "states can also start, and cease. The start or end of a state is dynamic" (Comrie, 1976: 50). The feature *durative* refers to whether a situation is carried out with a clear transitional

Aspect in narrative discourse

Table 10.1 Verb categories and situation types

Situation types	Feature descriptions			Examples
	Dynamic	Telic	Durative	
States	–	–	+	有 *you* 'have', 知道 *zhidao* 'know', 高兴 *gaoxing* 'happy', 喜欢 *xihuan* 'like'
Events				
Activities	+	–	+	告诉 *gaosu* 'tell', 跑步 *paobu* 'jog', 走 *zou* 'walk', 推车 *tuiche* 'push a cart'
Accomplishments	+	+	+	走回家 *zou-hui jia* 'walk-back home', 带来 *dai-lai* 'carry-come (bring)', 学会 *xue-hui* 'study-know (having learned)', 长大 *zhang-da* 'grow-big'
Achievements	+	+	–	打破 *da-po* 'hit-break', 看见 *kanjian* 'look-see', 睡着 *shui-zhao* 'sleep-attain'
Semelfactives	+	–	–	咳嗽 *kesou* 'cough', 敲 *qiao* 'knock', 踢 *ti* 'kick'

phase between onset and completion. This feature further divides events into those that are punctual (achievements and Semelfactives) and those that are not (activities and accomplishments). The feature *telic* specifies whether an event or action has an endpoint. Situation types with an inherent endpoint, result, or conceptual boundary are said to be telic, while those without are atelic. This feature further differentiates activities and accomplishments.

The temporal profile of the situation types contributes to aspectual meaning. *States and activities* do not have an endpoint. They are atelic (unbounded) and, therefore, imperfective. Activities, being dynamic and durative, may appear in the progressive aspect. Accomplishments and achievements, being telic (bounded with an endpoint), are most likely perfective (Sasse, 2002). *Semelfactives* are punctual and atelic; additional information in context is needed to determine whether they encode a perfective or imperfective situation.

Note that telic verbs in Chinese (accomplishments and achievements as shown in Table 10.1) are complex in structure. They consist of two parts: an activity verb followed by a "bounding expression" that gives the event an endpoint. The verb *xue-hui* 'having learned' in Table 10.1 expresses the activity *xue* 'study' bounded by its end result *hui* 'know (how to)'. Similarly, *kanjian* 'having seen' records the event *kan* 'look' bounded by its result *jian* 'see'. In Chinese, bounding expressions play an important role in the expression of perfectivity. Here we examine a few subcategories: RVCs, expressions of event quantification and PPs with a bounding effect.

Resultative verb complements (RVC)

An RVC is the second part of a two-element verbal compound. The first element is an activity verb; the RVC that follows it can be a verb (*ting-dong* 听懂 'listen-understand'), an adjective denoting the result of the action (*he-zui* 喝醉 'drink-drunk'), or a word indicating the direction of a motion (*zhan-qilai* 站起来 'stand-up').[3] RVCs are abundant and frequently used in Chinese. The V-RVC sequence and the relationship between the two components demonstrate rich syntactic and semantic features. For this reason, RVCs constitute one of the particularities of the Chinese language and as such they have been widely studied (Chao, 1968; C. Li and Thompson, 1981).

RVCs contribute to perfectivity in a different way from the perfective marker *-le*. While – *le* indicates event boundedness in an abstract way, RVCs, with lexical content, provide specific

163

information not only about event endpoints but also about the types of boundaries involved (e.g., completion, termination, direction of motion, or resultative state).

Expressions of event quantification

Activities can also be bounded by quantifying expressions indicating the length of time an activity lasts, the number of times it takes place, or the distance a motion covers. In (4a), the expression *yixia* 'a bit' shows that the event of *youyu* 'hesitate' lasted a very short time. See W. Li (2012) for additional examples of event quantification.

(4) (a) 我犹豫了一下, (b) 走了进去。 (Liang [1991] 278)
    (a) *Wo youyu-le-yixia*, (b) *zou-le-jinqu*.
    (a) I hesitate-LE-a.bit (b) walk-LE-in
    'I hesitated and then walked in'.

Verb duplication is another means of event quantification. It limits the designated activity to a short duration or a light degree. The same meaning is sometimes expressed in English by the phrase 'take a (noun)', e.g., *zou zou* 走走 (walk DUPL) 'take a walk' and *kan kan* 看看 (look DUPL) 'take a look'. For past events, the perfective marker *-le* can be attached to the first verb, i.e., between the duplicated syllables, as shown in (5).

(5) 她笑着摇了摇头, (Bingxin [1983] 274)
    Ta xiao-zhe **yao-le-yao** *tou*,
    she smile-ZHE shake-LE-shake head
    'Smiling, she shook her head'.

Prepositional phrases with a bounding effect

Prepositional (or coverb) phrases (PP) are bounding expressions when they follow the main verb of the clause. In the examples here, they are linked to the verb by a hyphen. Three major prepositions are used for this function: *Zai* 在-PP, illustrated in (6b), denotes the location of a participant as a result of the event; *gei* 给-PP, shown in (7), expresses the recipient of a transferred object; and *dao* 到-PP, as in (8), indicates the destination of a motion.

(6) (a) 我舀了盆凉水, (b) 轻轻放在他脚旁。 (Liang [1991] 248)
    (a) *wo yao-le pen liang shui*, (b) *qingqing fang-zai ta jiaopang*.
    (a) I scoop-LE a.pot cold water (b) lightly put-ZAI his feet.side
    'I fetched a pot of cold water and quietly put it by his feet'.

(7) 掌秤的女人把鱼倒给她, (A. Wang [1999] 117)
    Zhangcheng de nüren ba yu dao-gei ta,
    handle.scale MOD woman BA fish pour-to her
    'The woman at the scales handed her the fish',

(8) (a) 远把她送到房门口, (b) Ø道了晚安, (c) Ø便转身去了。 (Bingxin [1983] 242)
    (a) *Yuan ba ta song-dao fangmenkou*, (b) Ø *dao-le wan'an*,
    (a) Yuan BA her see-to door.way (b) Ø say-LE good.night

(c) Ø   bian   zhuanshen   qu-le.
(c) Ø   then   turn   go-LE
   'Yuan saw her to her cabin, wished her good night, and left'.

PPs are a complex phenomenon in modern Chinese, not only because of the various developmental histories of prepositions but also because of their current multiple functions. They can appear either before or after the main verb, depending on their functions. But only those in the postverbal position play a bounding role. In this position, they can be understood as playing the dual role of an RVC and a preposition (W. Li, 2012).

The pervasive use of bounding expressions shows that Chinese has a strong tendency to code events' endpoints explicitly (W. Li, 2014a). Bounding expressions can work either in conjunction with the grammatical marker -le or in the absence of -le to convey perfectivity. This provides an answer to the question regarding the nonobligatory use of perfective marker -le. Looking back at example (3) that narrates a series of past events, we can see that the verb in (3a) *ning* 'switch' is followed by both the RVC -*kai* 'open' and -le. In (3b) and (3c), the verbs are not grammatically marked by -le, but they are followed by a bounding expression, i.e., the RVC -*chu* 'out' and the RVC/preposition -*gei* 'to'. They are perfective nonetheless.

Situation aspect and viewpoint aspect converge at the clause level to bring together grammatical and semantic information for aspectual interpretation: A situation's temporal schema is made semantically available by situation aspect, including the inherent features of the verb and the features conveyed by other constituents. The viewpoint aspect then puts the entire situation in perspective, depending on the need of the discourse. Note that all these devices that convey event bounding in Chinese – -le, RVCs, event quantifying expressions and PPs – occur after the verb. The iconicity principle of word order is in full effect here. Because grammatical aspect and situational aspect can work in conjunction or separately to convey perfectivity, they give the perfective constructions unusual range and flexibility.

Aspect and temporal advancement in narrative

The narration of events in a story typically progresses along a temporal line. For this reason, temporal dynamism is a vital feature of narrative discourse. Labov (1972: 360) defined "the minimal narrative" as "a sequence of two clauses, which are *temporally ordered*: that is, a change in their order will result in a change in the temporal sequence of the original semantic interpretation". Discourse analysis has revealed that perfective verbs have the capacity of recording sequences of actions in extended discourse. By so doing, they also advance narrative time.

In narrative discourse, events' temporal locations are often implicit and, by default, in the past. When two perfective clauses are temporally ordered with respect to each other and no explicit time expression is used to indicate temporal progress, the endpoint of the first event serves as the *temporal juncture* that specifies the beginning of the following event. As the events unfold in sequence, the reference time advances one step at a time from the endpoint of the first event to a point *just after* the second event (Hopper, 1979a, 1979b; Labov, 1972; Labov and Waletzky, 1967).

In (9) is an example with two narrative clauses in (a) and (b), both in the perfective aspect. In (a) the event *qu* 'go' is bounded by -le. The endpoint of this event is the temporal juncture between this event and the next one in (b). As the next event is also perfective due to -le, time moves forward to a point just after the second event. The two clauses are thus interpreted as recording consecutive events in temporal sequence. The English translation uses past tense verbs to present the events perfectively.

(9) (a) 她去了浴室， (b) 迅速洗了一个澡。 (Hong [2009] 104)
    (a) *Ta qu-le yushi,* (b) *xunsu xi-le yige zao.*
    (a) she go.to-LE bathroom (b) quickly wash-LE one.CL shower
    'She went into the bathroom and had a quick shower'.

In a similar fashion, the passage in (10) consists of three clauses, (a) – (c), describing three events in temporal order. All the clauses are perfective. The endpoint of the first event in (a), indicated by both – *le* and the RVC – *qilai*, is the temporal juncture between the first two events. In (b), the event *tuo* 'take off' is bounded by the RVC *-xia* 'down'. Narrative time advances to the point just after the second event. The same pattern is repeated in (c), where the endpoint of the activity *gua* 'hang' is specified by the RVC (or preposition) *zai*. Narrative time again moves forward. This pattern can also be observed in earlier examples (3), (4), (6), and (8).

(10) (a) 她站了起来， (b) Ø帮丈夫脱下西装, (c) Ø挂在衣柜里。 (Hong [2009] 163)
    (a) *Ta **zhan-le-qilai**,* (b) *Ø bang zhangfu **tuo-xia** xizhuang,* (c) *Ø **gua zai** yigui-li*
    (a) She stand-LE-up (b) Ø help husband take-down jacket (c) Ø hang ZAI wardrobe-in
    'She stood up to help her husband out of his jacket and hung it up in the wardrobe'.

We can see from these examples that temporal sequence is a vital feature of narrative discourse. In Chinese, temporal advancement is achieved in perfective clauses through a two-step procedure: First, the verb denotes a dynamic event. After that, *-le*, a bounding expression, or both, indicate the endpoint of the event and the temporal juncture. As a series of perfective clauses unfold, the two steps alternate like footsteps, nudging time forward. Very often, such clauses form a topic chain, as in (3), (4), (8) and (10), where the topic NP, e.g., *ta* 'she' in (10a), appears only once in the first clause and referred to in subsequent clauses by a zero anaphora (indicated by Ø). The tightly knit structure reflects the close relationship of the events iconically.

Aspect and narrative grounding

Analyses of narrative discourse have also found that aspect is an important device to indicate the grounding structure of the narrative. Grounding is a universal phenomenon in narrative discourse: Events and entities are not recorded as equally important. Rather, they show a grounding structure: Those that are perceived as more salient and important to the plot development are foregrounded. They tend to be dynamic events that form the main storyline. A common analogy is that foregrounded events form the backbone or skeleton of the story. They succeed one another in the same order as they occur in the real world and move the narrative time forward. With regards to aspect, independent clauses in the perfective aspect are found to be an important means of recording foregrounded events in narrative text.

In comparison, situations that are less salient and less important are backgrounded. They tend to be ongoing events designated by imperfective verbs, or durative, habitual or stative situations off the main storyline. Backgrounded clauses are not temporally ordered. They are concurrent with each other or with foregrounded events. Thematically, they play a supporting role by adding descriptions of participants, scene-setting material, and evaluative commentary that does not immediately and crucially contribute to the main storyline. When grouped together, they do not yield a satisfactory summary of the narrative. Grammatically, backgrounded clauses may use imperfective aspect markers, state verbs, or have no aspectual marking (but with an imperfective or stative interpretation).

Research has found that the correlation between perfectivity, foregrounding and sequenced events is universal. Aspect is a device that facilitates temporal sequencing and the foregrounding-backgrounding distinction. The discussion in the last section has shown that action sequencing and plot advancement are the most characteristic functions of perfective verbs. For this reason, narrative discourse is rich in aspectual features (Fleischman, 1990; Hopper, 1979a, 1979b; Reinhart, 1984; Smith, 1997, 2003; Tomlin, 1985, 1987; Wallace, 1982).

In the above section, examples such as (9) and (10) demonstrate foregrounded narrative clauses that moves narrative time forward. To provide a contrast, (11) is a typical example of backgrounded text. The excerpt describes the setting of a new shopping street. Clause (a) uses a state verb, *jiao* 'has the name of'. Clause (b) has an adjectival predicate *hen jingzhi* 'very exquisite'. The next three clauses, (c), (d) and (e), are existential constructions describing durative situations (W. Li, 2014b). The verbs in the last two clauses are also marked by the imperfective marker – *zhe*. All these situations are ongoing and concurrent; no – *le* or bounding expressions are used. Time is static.

(11) (a) 新的中心大街雅名叫浣纱路， (b) 两面的店面房子很精致， (c) 有好几家商店和公司正开张， (d) 摆着大大小小的花篮， (e) 门厅里贴着红字金字横竖对联。
(Hong [2009] 24)
(a) *Xinde zhongxin dajie yaming   jiao Huanshalu,* (b) *liangmian de dianmian*
(a) new center street elegant.name call Huanshalu, (b) both.side MOD front.store
fangzi   hen jingzhi, (c) *you   haojijia shangdian he gongsi zheng*
building very exquisite (c) exist a.few.CL store   and company in.progress
kaizhang, (d) *bai-zhe dadaxiaoxiaode hua lan,* (e) *mentingli tie-zhe*
open (d) display-ZHE large.and.small flower bascket (e) lobby.in put-ZHE
hongzi   jinzi   hengshuduilian.
red character gold character couplet
'The high street in the center of town had the elegant name of "Rinsing Silk Road". The storefronts facing the street were exquisite. Quite a few shops and businesses had just opened; there were flowers outside and red and gold characters displayed on the posters just inside the doors to welcome new customers'.

The excerpt in (12) has a combination of foregrounded and backgrounded clauses, so their features can be compared. Clauses (a), (d) and (e) are perfective, presenting foregrounded events in temporal sequence. This sequence is interrupted by (b) and (c) that provide background descriptions of the participant, *nüshi* 'woman'. They are stative and durative situations off the temporal storyline.

(12) (a) 他给我介绍了一位女士， (b) 她是贵族遗裔， (c) 住在最清静高贵的贵族区 – 第七区。 (d) 我前天去见了她， (e) 也看了房子 … (Bingxin [1983] 265)
(a) *Ta gei wo jieshao-le   yiwei   nüshi,* (b) *ta shi guizu   yiyi,*
(a) he to me introduce-LE one.CL woman (b) she be aristocratic descendent
(c) *zhu-zai zui   qingjing gaoguide guizuqu   – diqiu.* (d) *wo qiantian qu jian-le ta,*
(c) live-be most quiet   high-class noble.area the.7th.district (d) I the.other.day go see-LE her
(e) *ye   kan-le fangzi …*
(e) also see-LE house
'He introduced to me a certain woman in town, a lady of aristocratic bloodline who lives in the high-society part of town, the seventh arrondissement. I went to see her the other day and saw her house'.

Figure 10.1 is a schematized view of (12) that visualizes the contrast between foregrounded and backgrounded situations. The long horizontal line shows the direction of temporal progression. Foregrounded perfective clauses, (a) and (d)–(e), appear above this temporal line. The short lines with an arrow indicate the sequence of events and temporal advancement from one event to the next. Backgrounded clauses, (b) and (c), are below the temporal line. Their situation time overlaps with each other and surrounds the event time in the figure.

The next excerpt in (13) also combines foregrounding and backgrounding, although in a different pattern. Imperfective (backgrounded) clauses are in (a)–(b) and perfective (foregrounded) clauses in (c)–(d). Clause (a) is irrealis (*bingwei* 'not'), another feature of backgrounding. Clause (b) is marked by the imperfective marker *zai* (progressive).[4] No – *le* or bounding expression is used and no temporal advancement in these two clauses. By contrast, the activity described in (c), *zou* 'walk', is bounded by the RVC/preposition *ru* 'into;' the event in (d), *guan* 'close', is bounded by the RVC *diao* 'off'. These two events are temporally sequenced and the narrative time moves forward. Thus, in this passage, (a)–(b) provide background descriptions for the perfective and foregrounded narration of main storyline events in (c)–(d).

(13) (a) 风沙并未减轻, (b) 呼呼地在玻璃窗外狂叫。 (c) 母亲走入卧室, (d) 把大彩电关掉。
(Hong [2009] 9)

(a) *fengsha bingwei jianqing,*   (b) *huhudi   zai bolichuang-wai kuangjiao.*
(a) sand.storm not   quiet.down   (b) howling   ZAI window-outside swirl
(c) *muqin **zou-ru** woshi,*   (d) *ba da caidian **guan-diao**.*
(c) mother walk-into bedroom   (d) BA big color.TV close-off

'The sandstorm was raging as fiercely as ever, howling madly against the window panes. Liu's mother went into the bedroom and turned off the large television'.

So far, we have examined grounding as a bi-level structure, i.e., foreground and background, based on aspectual features of the clause and the sequentiality of events. We can see that grounding is not marked by any special device. Rather, it is indicated by a cluster of semantic and morpho-syntactic features of the clause, including temporal sequence and aspect. However, grounding is not a dichotic notion. Because of the multiple factors involved and the complexity of discourse, foregrounding and backgrounding can be seen in relative degrees.

To account for this phenomenon, researchers have found a high correlation between grounding and transitivity of the clause (Hopper and Thompson, 1980). High transitivity is correlated with foregrounding; low transitivity with backgrounding. A clause's degree of transitivity is determined by 10 features shown in a-j in Table 10.2. For each feature, clauses can be ranked high or low. The more features in which a clause is ranked high, the more transitive and foregrounded the clause is. Hopper and Thompson (1980) scored clauses in three English narrative texts using these transitivity features. They found that foregrounded clauses averaged 8.0 points out of 10; backgrounded clauses scored 4.1. The likelihood for a clause to receive a foregrounded interpretation is proportional to the height of that clause on the scale of transitivity.

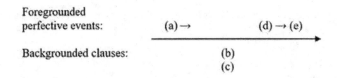

Figure 10.1   Aspect, grounding and temporal progression of the passage in (12)

Aspect in narrative discourse

Table 10.2 Transitivity features

Features	High	Low
a. Participants	two or more, agent & object	one
b. Kinesis	action	non-action
c. Aspect	telic	atelic
d. Punctuality	punctual	non-punctual
e. Volition	volitional	non-volitional
f. Affirmation	affirmative	negative
g. Mode	realis	irrealis
h. Agency	highly potent agent	low-potency agent
i. Affectedness of object	totally affected	not affected
j. Individuation of object	highly individuated	not individuated

Note: Adapted from Hopper and Thompson (1980).

Here, as an illustration, the four clauses in (13) were scored using the ten transitivity features. Table 10.3 shows the result.[5] For each feature, the "high" ranking for a feature is represented by "1" and the "low" by "0". The transitivity value for each clause is the sum of the 10 numbers, shown on the last line.

As can be seen in Table 10.3, the clauses (13c) and (13d) received high scores in ranking; their average transitivity value is a perfect 10. Because they are high in transitivity, they are foregrounded. By contrast, (13a) and (13b) rank low for most of the transitivity features; the average of their transitivity values is only 2.5. The low transitivity values indicate that they are backgrounded. This result verifies the correlation between the transitivity features of the clauses and their grounding features discussed earlier.

Taking a closer look at the ten transitivity features, one would find that the correlation between high transitivity and foregrounding is only natural. The features in fact define the two prototype notions of events and states with contrasting attributes. Prototypical events are highly transitive. They are kinetic activities initiated by a human agent acting volitionally and causing a change in a patient. Such events are salient in both the physical and the perceptual worlds; they tend to be foregrounded. Stative predications, on the other hand, are low in transitivity. They are low in multiple dimensions: kinesis, agency, punctuality and volitionality. They are backgrounded. The gradient transition between the prototypes is reflected in the gradient degrees of transitivity and grounding.

Clause type is another factor that interacts with aspect to determine degrees of grounding. To illustrate this point, we look at two phenomena. One is subordination; the other has to do with word order. We will see that, even when a clause uses a perfective verb form, features at the clause or sentence level, such as subordination and peripheral word order, may override the verb form and change the aspectual interpretation and, consequently, the grounding status of the clause.

It is well established crosslinguistically that subordination is a backgrounding device (Labov, 1972; Labov and Waletzky, 1967; Reinhart, 1984; Thompson, 1983; Tomlin, 1985). Even when the verb is perfective in form, subordination may put the clause in background. Take (14) as an example. The four clauses in this excerpt are all perfective in form; they present the events in temporal sequence. The verbs in (a)-(c) are followed by RVCs, and the one in (d) by an RVC/preposition *gei*. However, the clauses are not equal in grounding status. While (a), (c) and (d) are foregrounded, the clause in (b) is a subordinate structure due to *hou* 'after', which puts the clause

Table 10.3 Transitivity values of the four clauses in (13)

Features	(a)	(b)	(c)	(d)
a. Participants	0	0	1	1
b. Kinesis	1	1	1	1
c. Aspect	0	0	1	1
d. Punctuality	0	0	1	1
e. Volition	0	0	1	1
f. Affirmation	0	1	1	1
g. Mode	0	1	1	1
h. Agency	0	1	1	1
i. Affectedness of object	0	0	1	1
j. Individuation of object	0	0	1	1
Total transitivity value	1	4	10	10

in background – in relative terms. Presumably, a larger context (e.g., at the paragraph level) would include stative clauses. A grounding analysis of the larger unit would then reveal that (b) has a lower degree of foregrounding compared to (a), (c) and (d) because of its subordination, although it is still foregrounded to some degree compared to the stative predications due to its high kinesis, aspect, punctuality, volitionality and agency.

(14) (a) 他掏出镀金名片夹，(b) Ø弹开后，(c) Ø轻轻拈起一张，(d) Ø恭敬地递给柳 璀。

(Hong [2009] 72)

(a) *ta tao-**chu** dujin mingpianjia,*   (b) *Ø tan-**kai**   hou,*
(a) he fish-out gilt business.card.case, (b) Ø flick–open after
(c) *Ø qingqingde nian-**qi**   yi   zhang,*   (d) *Ø gongjingde di-**gei** Liucui.*
(c) Ø lightly   pick-up one piece   (d) Ø respectfully pass-to Liucui

'He reached into his jacket and drew out a gilt business card case. Flicking it open, he whisked out a card and presented it to Liu with both hands'.

The second point regarding clause type is that perfective verbs require the canonical SV(O) word order for their foregrounding interpretation, as can be seen in (3), (4), (8), (9) and (10). When word order deviates from SV(O), the grounding status of the clause may be changed. W. Li (2014a, 2018) examined a variety of clause types in peripheral word order, e.g., notional passive and existential sentences, and demonstrated that, when word order deviates from SV(O), the clauses tend to designate stative situations with no temporal advancement, even when the verb is perfective in form. See (15) for an example. The excerpt describes a successful eye surgery and the state of the eye as a result.

(15) (a) 手术极其顺利，(b) 最后一针缝好了。(c) 最后的一个结扎上了。(d) 那移植上去的圆形材料，严丝合缝地贴在了病人的眼珠上。 (Chen [1981] 101)

(a) *Shoushu   jiqi   shunli,*   (b) *zuihou yizhen feng-hao-le.*   (c) *zuihoude yige*
(a) operation extremely smooth (b) last suture stitch-good-LE (c) last   one.CL
jie   zha-shang-le. (d) *na yizhi-shangqu de   yuanxing cailiao, yansihefengde*
knot tie-up-LE   (d) that transplant-on MOD round   material precisely
tie-zai-le bingrende yanzhu-shang.
fit-ZAI-LE patient's eye.ball-on

'The operation went extremely smoothly. The last suture was put in place, the final stitch knotted, and the donor cornea had been precisely fitted into the patient's eye'.

This discussion focuses on the three clauses in (15b)–(15d). These clauses use dynamic verbs in the perfective form, i.e., *feng-hao* 'stitch-good' in (15b), *zha-shang* 'tie-up' in (15c) and *tie-zai* 'fit-into (a locative PP)' in (15d). However, the clauses are not in the canonical SVO word order. The agent of the dynamic actions, i.e., the eye surgeon, is not overtly encoded. Instead, the patient noun phrases, *zuihou yi zhen* 'the last suture', *zuihoude yige jie* 'the final knot' and *yuanxing cailiao* 'the donor cornea', are used as the subject and the clauses express passive meaning. Such clauses are commonly known as notional passives (or pseudo-passives) (Cheng and J. Huang, 1994; Shi, 1997, 2000). As passive clauses, they do not designate dynamic actions per se but, rather, the state of the patient NPs as the result of the actions. The clauses are overlapping in time; no temporal advancement is observed. If (15b)–(15d) are rated on the transitivity scale in Table 10.2, they would be low in participants, kinesis, agency, punctuality, and volitionality. Their low transitivity values are reminiscent of their backgrounded status, despite the perfective verb form used.

Observations such as these led to the view that clause types and constituent order are key in distinguishing between event and state designations in Chinese. The canonical SVO clauses with the perfective verb form designates prototypical events – complete events, including endpoints. The word order iconically depicts the flow of energy from the source and initiator of the action to the recipient. A deviation from the canonical SVO entails a deviation from the prototypical event.

Concluding remarks

We have seen in this chapter that aspectual meaning of a sentence is compositional, involving the interactions of categories within the grammar and among grammar, lexicon, and semantics. Both grammatical marking and lexical expressions contribute to aspectual information. The two-component approach to aspect not only details the various devices, but also explains the discretionary use of grammatical marking, which has been a thorny issue. Bounding expressions subcategorized in this chapter contribute to the analysis of situation aspect. An adequate account of perfectivity in Chinese should recognize their roles both in individual sentences and at the discourse level.

This chapter has also demonstrated that aspect is tied intimately with the dynamics of narrative discourse. The perfective aspect is a device to identify temporally sequenced and bounded events in the foreground as the main storyline. It is responsible for moving narrative time forward. Imperfective events and states, unbounded and durative, are backgrounded; they play a supporting role without advancing time. The discourse view of aspect shows that part of syntax is pragmatically motivated, and that grammatical forms have discourse functions.

Aspectual information can be processed at different levels. The perfective form in the verb phrase, for example, can work with other features of the clause to determine the aspectual interpretation at the clause level. Factors outside of the verb phrase, such as subordination and word order, may override the perfective verb form and alter the aspectual interpretation of the clause.

Aspectual choices and the related grounding distinctions have direct psycholinguistic and pragmatic implications: They allow the writer (or speaker) to present situations from different angles and talk about situations in more than one way. Reality does not occur in the narrative form. In order to create narrative, the narrator first decides on a communicative intent and a particular perspective to present the story. Then, he or she isolates certain elements out of the unbroken, seamless web of past events and fits them into the construct. A narrative is thus a configuration of events that has texture, focus and perspective in order to achieve a communicative goal. The narrator can manipulate the foreground-background distinction according to his or her communicative intent. Depending on the goal, the same incidents can be narrated, or grounded, differently by different narrators (Fleischman, 1985; Labov and Waletzky, 1967; Ong, 1981). This, at the receiving end, guides the reader or hearer in a direction of interpretation. The writer-reader interaction is manipulated through the medium of the text (Peer, 1986). This central point is borne out by studies of car-accident narratives, for example, given by the two parties involved in an accident, or the narratives of football commentators for opposing teams.

The psycholinguistic and pragmatic aspects of grounding, of which aspect is an important part, are reflected in more recent studies of subjectivity, intentionality, and stance in discourse production and interpretation. Herman, for example, drawing on treatments of intentionality in cognitive science, demonstrated that narrative production and interpretation require adopting the heuristic strategy of "the intentional stance" (2008: 233). Narratives are told for particular reasons – in the service of communicative goals. Grounding and intention always go hand in hand. In fact, narrative is a means by which humans learn to take up the intentional stance in the first place, and later practice using it in the safe zone afforded by story worlds (see also Caracciolo, 2012; Fitsmaurice, 2004; Traugott, 2012). Subjectivity is recognized by any study of narrative discourse. Language users have tacit knowledge of both the available devices in the language and their functions.

All these being said, it is also worth noting that the perfective aspect does not always correspond to foregrounding. The same can also be said about imperfective aspect and backgrounding. Marked uses do occur. The imperfective, for example, can be used to move events forward, as it entails the beginning of the situation in question. Subordination may also advance narrative time (Ramsay, 1987). It is important to keep this in mind in empirical studies.

The discourse function of aspect in Chinese is an area widely open for further investigation. Remaining issues include aspectual interpretation at different levels and the need for a broader vision and scope of analysis. Studies in this area will provide additional ground for a better understanding not only of aspectual choices in grammar but also of their semantic and pragmatic functions and their relation with other grammatical structures and communicative intent.

Notes

1 Smith (1997) also treated resultative verb complements and verb reduplication as markers of the perfective viewpoint. Here, these two categories are treated as "event-bounding expressions" in the component of situation aspect.
2 In Chinese, there is a homonymous *le* used in the sentence-final position, unhyphenated in notation, to indicate "change of state" (Li and Thompson 1981). That *le* is not covered in this description. Also excluded from this description is the zero aspect, i.e., the absence of aspectual marking in a phrase where there is aspectual meaning (See Smith 1997).
3 Note that the RVC *-qilai*, indicating direction of motion, is different from the inceptive aspectual marker, as in *chang-qilai* 唱起来 sing-QILAI 'start singing'.
4 This preverbal *zai* can be interpreted as a locative preposition and a progressive aspect marker simultaneously.
5 The ranking of individual clauses based on these features is not always a straightforward matter. See Hopper and Thompson (1980) for discussion. W. Li (2014c) is another study of grounding in Chinese using this scale.

References

Caracciolo, M. (2012) 'On the Experientiality of Stories: A Follow-up on David Herman's "Narrative theory and the intentional stance"', *Partial Answers: Journal of Literature and the History of Ideas* 10(2): 197–221.
Chao, Yuen-Ren (1968) *A Grammar of Spoken Chinese*. Los Angeles: University of California Press.

Cheng, L. and Huang, J.C.-T. (1994) 'On the argument structure of resultative compounds', in *In Honor of William S.-Y. Wang: Interdisciplinary Studies on Language and Language Change*. M.Y. Chen and O.J.-L. Tzeng (eds.) Taipei: Pyramid. pp. 187–221.

Comrie, B. (1976) *Aspect: An Introduction to the Study of Verbal Aspect and Related Problems*. Cambridge: Cambridge University Press.

Fitsmaurice, S. (2004) 'Subjectivity, Intersubjectivity and the Historical Construction of Interlocutor Stance: From Stance Markers to Discourse Markers', *Discourse Studies* 6(4): 427–448.

Fleischman, S. (1985) 'Discourse Function of Tense-aspect Oppositions in Narrative: Toward a Theory of Grounding', *Linguistics* 23: 851–882.

Fleischman, S. (1990) *Tense and Narrativity: From Medieval Performance to Modern Fiction*. London: Routledge.

Herman, David. 2008. 'Narrative Theory and the Intentional Stance', *Partial Answers: Journal of Literature and the History of Ideas* 6(2): 233–260.

Hopper, P.J. (1979a) 'Some Observations on the Typology of Focus and Aspect in Narrative Language', *Studies in Language* 3: 37–64.

Hopper, P.J. (1979b) 'Aspect and foregrounding in discourse', in *Discourse and Syntax (Syntax and Semantics 12)*. T. Givón (ed.) New York: Academic Press. pp. 213–241.

Hopper, P.J. and Thompson, S.A. (1980) 'Transitivity in Grammar and Discourse', *Language* 56: 251–299.

Labov, W. (1972) *The Transformation of Experience in Narrative Syntax: Language in the Inner City: Studies in the Black English Vernacular*. Philadelphia: University of Pennsylvania Press.

Labov, W. and Waletzky, J. (1967) 'Narrative analysis: Oral versions of personal experience', in *Essays on the Verbal and Visual Arts*. J. Helm (ed.) Seattle, WA: University of Washington Press. pp. 12–44.

Li, C.N. and Thompson, S.A. (1981) *Mandarin Chinese: A Functional Reference Grammar*. Los Angeles: University of California Press.

Li, Wendan (2012) 'Temporal and Aspectual References in Mandarin Chinese', *Journal of Pragmatics* 44: 2045–2066.

Li, Wendan (2014a) 'Perfectivity and Grounding in Mandarin Chinese', *Studies in Language* 38(1): 128–170.

Li, Wendan (2014b) 'The Pragmatics of Existential-Presentative Constructions in Chinese: A Discourse-based Study', *International Journal of Chinese Linguistics* 1(2): 244–274.

Li, Wendan (2014c) 'Clause Structure and Grounding in Chinese Narrative Discourse', *Chinese Language and Discourse* 5(2): 99–145.

Li, Wendan (2018) *Grounding in Chinese Written Narrative Discourse*. Leiden: Brill.

Ong, W.J. (1981) 'Oral Remembering and Narrative Structures', *Georgetown University Round Table on Languages and Linguistics* 1981: 12–24.

Peer, W. van (1986) *Stylistics and Psychology: Investigations of Foregrounding*. London: Croom Helm.

Ramsay, V. (1987) 'The functional distribution of preposed and postposed IF and WHEN clauses in written discourse', in *Coherence and Grounding in Discourse*. R.S. Tomlin (ed.) Amsterdam: John Benjamins. pp. 383–408.

Reinhart, T. (1984) 'Principles of Gestalt Perception in the Temporal Organization of Narrative Texts', *Linguistics* 22: 779–809.

Sasse, H-J. (2002) 'Recent Activity in the Theory of Aspect: Accomplishments, Achievements or Just Non-progressive State?', *Linguistic Typology* 6: 199–271.

Shi, Dingxu (1997) 'Issues on Chinese Passive', *Journal of Chinese Linguistics* 25(1): 41–70.

Shi, Dingxu (2000) 'Topic and Topic-comment Constructions in Mandarin Chinese', *Language* 76(2): 383–408.

Smith, C.S. (1997 [1991]) *The Parameter of Aspect* (2nd ed.). Dordrecht: Kluwer.

Smith, C.S. (2003) *Mode of Discourse: The Local Structure of Text*. Cambridge: Cambridge University Press.

Thompson, S.A. (1983) 'Grammar and discourse: English detached participial clause', in *Discourse Perspectives on Syntax*. F. Klein-Andreu (ed.) New York: Academic Press. pp. 43–65.

Tomlin, R.S. (1985) 'Foreground-Background Information and the Syntax of Subordination', *Text* 5: 85–122.

Tomlin, R.S. (ed.) (1987) *Coherence and Grounding in Discourse (Typological Studies in Language 11)*. Amsterdam: John Benjamins.

Traugott, E.C. (2012) 'Intersubjectification and Clause Periphery', *English Text Construction* 5(1): 7–28.

Vendler, Z. (1957) 'Verbs and Times', *The Philosophical Review* 66: 143–160.

Verkuyl, H.J. (1972) *On the Compositional Nature of the Aspects*. Dordrecht: Reidel.

Wallace, S. (1982) 'Figure and ground: The interrelationships of linguistic categories', in *Tense-Aspect: Between Semantics and Pragmatics*. P. Hopper (ed.) Amsterdam: John Benjamins. pp. 201–223.

Xiao, R. and McEnery, T. (2004) *Aspect in Mandarin Chinese: A Corpus-based Study*. Philadelphia: John Benjamins.

Yang, Jun (2002) The Acquisition of Temporality by Adult Second Language Learners of Chinese, Doctoral dissertation, University of Arizona, Tucson, AZ.

Sources of examples

Bingxin 冰心 (1983) 《冰心选集》 (*Selected Works of Bingxin*). Vol. 1. Sichuan: Sichuan Renmin Chubanshe, English translation by Jeff Book.

Chen, Rong 谌容 (1981) 《人到中年》 (*At Middle Age*). Tianjin: Baihua Wenyi Chubanshe, English translation by Margaret Decker.

Hong, Ying 虹影 (2009) 《孔雀的叫喊》 (*Peacock Cries at the Three Gorges*). Xi'an: Shanxi Shifan Daxue Chubanshe, English translation by Mark Smith and Henry Zhao.

Liang, Xiaosheng 梁晓声 (1991) 《非礼节性的"访问"》 (*Selected Works of Liang Xiaosheng*). Sichuan: Wenyi Chubanshe, English translation by Liu Shicong and Christine Ferreira.

Wang, Anyi 王安忆 (1999) 《王安忆小说选》 (bilingual version) (*Selected Stories by Wang Anyi*). Beijing: Chinese Literature Press and Foreign Language Teaching and Research Press, English translation by Michael Day and Howard Goldblatt.

11
The use of modal verbs in political debates

Maria Cheng

Introduction

Language is not only a means of interpersonal communication, but also a vital instrument of political communication. Politics, being the science and art of government, involves the expression of convictions and opinions by different parties; political communication, therefore, plays an important role in the transmission of information between political institutions, politicians, the news media and members of the public, which may in turn affect the attitudes, perceptions and behaviors of each of these parties. Language is interrelated with politics and power as a medium for initiating, justifying, legitimizing and coordinating action; reconciling differences, negotiating conflict, and affirming diversity; as well as for achieving recognition and gaining power through discussion and persuasion in the political process (Wodak and Forchtner, 2017). The use of language in politics, thus, provides a rich source of insights on how language is used by those who wish to gain, exercise and keep power (Beard, 2000).

Political debate, one important domain of political forums, displays the characteristics of political discourse, acting as a vehicle for the exchange of reasoned views and for offering alternative proposals to solve legislative, governance or societal problems; and it inevitably involves arguments on contentious topics and the expression of dissension by different parties and/or nations. Because of the distinctively antagonistic nature of political action, political debates exhibit speakers' propensity for persuasive discourse. Politicians manipulate the power of deliberative language, adopting an articulated format to handle controversial issues, to express their views on certain contentious topics, to reveal their beliefs and values, and to mask their true intentions, and carefully control their language to fulfill certain political purposes. Cheng (2016) posits that politicians, in addition to their major linguistic strategies, make tactical use of modality to frame arguments and propositions to fulfill their persuasive objectives.

Considering the significant role of the Chinese language in the international arena and politics, this chapter will investigate the use of Chinese modal verbs in political debates. First, this chapter will explore the nature of and use of language in political debate. Second, it will examine how the peculiar features of modality reveal a speaker's knowledge and judgment concerning a specific event and his/her attitudes towards a given proposition. Third, it will clearly express the use of Chinese modal verbs in political debates. Lastly, it will sketch how different political parties in Taiwan articulate their positions on key issues in presidential debates.

Maria Cheng

Political debate and modality: conceptual foundations

Debate, in the views of Patterson and Zarefsky (1983) and Pfau, Thomas and Ulrich (1987), is a purposeful process of argument for opposing sides in a conflict to obtain a decision in favor of one or both sides from a presumably neutral third party. Political debate is a common formal activity seen in discussions on government policy and proposals for new laws, as well as in discussions on topical issues seen in international bodies or parliamentary governments. Examples of the latter include the annual General Debate of the United Nations General Assembly and the debates held in the Houses of Parliament in London and the United States Congress in Washington, D.C. In modern history, presidential debates have been an integral part of the overall culture of political debate, and televised presidential debates are an efficient means of campaign communication for candidates to address the same sets of issues and to outline their respective election manifestoes (Cheng, 2016). In a presidential debate, the contestants adhere to a formalized set of rules, in which they present their propositions and arguments while reinforcing their preferred images. They seek to affect voters' attitudes and perceptions, to change voters' voting intentions and to solicit favorable support, all in order to secure a greater number of votes than their opponent(s) in the election (Benoit et al., 2003; Geer, 1988). Framing an argument in a favorable way to win the adherence of listeners, especially potential voters, is essential in presidential debates. Politicians tactically manipulate rhetorical strategies or make persuasive use of modality to frame facts, beliefs and political choices (Jerit, 2008; Sniderman and Theriault, 2004) to influence and mobilize voters behind their respective policy positions.

Modality, encompassing the interpersonal meanings of a speaker's expression, is a device for indicating a speaker's attitudes concerning the validity, possibility, necessity, predictability, desirability, inclination, volition, obligation, permission and evaluation of an event (Halliday, 1970; Johannesson, 1976). Generally speaking, modality may be described along two axes: epistemic and non-epistemic. Lyons (1977) categorizes modality into two types: epistemic modality reveals the possibility or necessity of the truth of a proposition, while deontic modality is concerned with obligation or permission of acts. Palmer (2001) suggests instead a binary distinction between propositional modality and event modality, with the former illustrating a speaker' attitude towards a proposition and the latter comprising deontic and dynamic modality. Epistemic modality and evidentiality are proposition-oriented and reflect a speaker's grounds for a speech act, whereas deontic modality is considered event-oriented. Halliday and Matthiessen (2013), on the other hand, classify modality in terms of modalization (i.e. probability and usuality) and modulation (i.e. obligation and inclination), and divide modality into three categories of high (*must, ought to, need, have to*), median (*will, would, shall, should*) and low values (*may, might, can, could*). Gonzalvez-Garcia (2000) further explains that modalization, as epistemic modality, expresses concepts of possibility, necessity and prediction, whereas modulation (deontic modality) indicates permission, obligation and volition concerning the proposition of the discourse. Foley and Valin (1984) have also distinguished between the roles of the core operators and peripheral operators of non-epistemic modals and epistemic modals. The category of epistemic modality reflects a speaker's estimation of reality, possibility and necessity. This type of modality denoting the likelihood of a particular state of affairs may be either subjective or objective. It is therefore regarded as a type of peripheral operator whose functions are external to the core layer of a clause. In contrast, non-epistemic modality is concerned with ability, volition, permission and obligation, and functions as a core operator, which is internal to the core layer and qualifies the relationship between a core argument and the predicate.

The basic modal verbs functioning as pragmatic markers in English are: *will, would* (future prediction, intention, promise or likelihood); *can, could* (ability, possibility, request, permission);

may, might (possibility, request, permission); *shall* (intention, prediction, willingness, volition); and *should, must* (obligation, logical judgement, necessity). There are also the additional modal verbs of *need to, dare, ought to, have to* and *used to*. Politicians extensively and strategically make use of modal verbs in political settings.

The notion of Chinese modality

In Chinese, modality (Cheng, 2016) can be realized through three types of linguistic devices. First, it may appear in the preceding modal verbs or modal adjective, such as 必須 (*bixu*, "must"), 應該 (*yinggai*, "should"), 能夠 (*nenggou*, "can"), indicating a speaker's judgment or attitude. Second, modal adverbs may be placed at the beginning of a sentence or between the subject and the predicate, for example, 一定 (*yiding*, "definitely"), 可能 (*keneng*, "probably"), 無疑 (*wuyi*, "undoubtedly"), in which case they take on evaluative roles reflecting the speaker's opinion or attitude. Third, modal particles, for instance, 的 (*de*), 呢 (*ne*), 啊 (*a*), 呀 (*ya*), may be placed at the end of a sentence or at a pause in the middle of it, and are a salient pragmatic feature in Chinese for the expression of moods; some may also have a mitigating or politeness effect on the speech act.

Similar to the use of modality in English, Chinese modal verbs (called "modal auxiliaries", by Chinese grammarians before the 1990s) and adverbs (or "modal adjuncts") help the hearer to understand the speaker's feelings, attitudes and judgments, and enable the speaker to influence and guide the hearer's attitudes and behaviors. The concept of modality is, however, controversial in Chinese grammar (e.g. Lü, 1979) and typological descriptions of the concept may vary from a dozen (Hu, 1981; Huang and Liao, 2007) to more than 50 (Ma, 2005) depending on the temporal and geographical differences, and the usage and scope of the linguistic means addressed.

Figure 11.1, applying the theoretical and conceptual frameworks of modality in English, exhibits the major properties of Chinese modality.

Epistemic modality is concerned with a speaker's knowledge and estimations about the uncertainty of an event, ranging from possibility (Excerpts 1–3) to necessity (4–5).

(1) 會 (*hui* "may"), e.g. 聽了司長這番話, 很多人**可能會**覺得特區政府在扶貧工作上確實花了不少氣力 ("After listening to these words of the Chief Secretary, many **may** think that the SAR Government has devoted a lot of efforts to poverty alleviation").

(2) 能/能夠 (*neng /nenggou* "can"), e.g. 對於行政長官的承諾, 很多人都質疑現時的房屋政策是否**能夠**落實 ("As for the pledges made by the Chief Executive, many people query if the prevailing housing policy **can** be implemented").

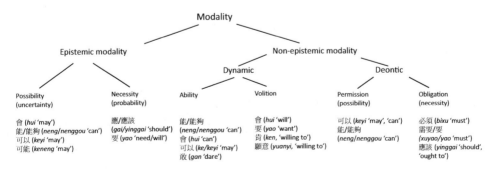

Figure 11.1 Modal notions in Chinese

(3) 可能 (*keneng* "may"), e.g. . . . 但這可能是 "周期性" 的問題 (". . . but the construction peak at present **may** just be a cyclical phenomenon").

(4) 要/需要 (*yao/xuyao* "need/will"), e.g. 近年患有失智症的長者越來越多, 如果他們可以在熟悉的社區安老, 無須重新適應環境, 必然會大大減少不必要的走失等問題。 ("In recent years the number of elderly people with dementia has been on the increase. If elderly people can live in the communities they know well, they **need not** adapt to new environments. Then the incidence of elderly persons going astray will thereby certainly be greatly reduced").

(5) 該/應該 (*gai/yinggai* "should"), representing a speaker's judgments about the probability of the factual status of a proposition that something will (not) happen, e.g. 我相信, 如果有了這個認知和文化的話, 這些情況<u>應該</u>不會出現。 ("I believe that if we can foster such an understanding and culture, it **should** be possible to avoid many such behaviours").

Non-epistemic modality involves *dynamic* modality, indicating <u>ability</u> (i.e. 能/能夠 "can", 會 "can", 可以 "may", 敢 "dare") and representing a speaker's judgements of capability or willingness (Excerpts 6); or <u>volition</u> (會 "will", 要 "want", 肯 "willing to", 願意 "willing to") and conveying a speaker's judgment about the need to do something (Excerpts 7–8).

(6) 所以, 我很希望行政長官<u>能夠</u>改變和社會、學生、泛民議員的溝通方式, 促進社會和諧 ("Hence, I greatly hope that the Chief Executive **can** change his way of communicating with the community, students and the pan-democrat Members for the sake of promoting social harmony").

(7) 在課程修訂及優化, 均<u>會</u>特別強化, 亦要加強幼稚園的管治和透明度 . . . ("In reviewing and refining the curriculum, we **will** enhance the governance and transparency of kindergartens").

(8) 還有青年內地交流資助計劃 . . . 等措施, 亦引起了社會不少討論和爭議, 未必有很多人<u>願意</u>參與。 ("There are also initiatives like the Funding Scheme for Youth Exchange in the Mainland . . . , although there are still many arguments in the community, and many people may not be **willing to** participate in them").

These two categories of dynamic modality pertain to a participant-internal modality and denote the speaker's capability and willingness to perform an action.

Another type of non-epistemic modality is *deontic* modality, which indicates a speaker's judgments about <u>permission</u> (可以 "may, can"; 能/能夠 "can") (Excerpts 9–10) or <u>obligation</u> (必須 "must"; 需要/要 "must", 應該 "should, ought to") (Excerpts 11–12).

(9) 胡志偉議員, 你<u>可以</u>動議你的修正案 ("Mr Wu Chi-wai, you **may** move your amendment").

(10) 現在各項修正案已經被否決, 剩下來便只有我提出的原議案, 我希望各位同事<u>可以</u>支持這項象徵式的議案 ("Now all amendments have been vetoed, and only the original motion that I have proposed remains. I hope my Honorable colleagues **can** support this symbolic motion").

(11) 因此, 功能界別的選舉方法<u>必須</u>改革 ("Hence, the election method for the FCs **must** be reformed").

(12) 年青人**應該**積極裝備自己、擴闊視野, 把握"一帶一路"的機遇, 放眼國際 ("Young people **should** equip themselves and broaden their horizons, seizing the opportunities brought by the Belt and Road Initiative and looking beyond Hong Kong").

These two categories of deontic modality are a type of participant-external modality.

Owing to the salient grammatical features of the Chinese language, polysemous modal expressions can occur, depending on their contextual meanings. For example, 會 "will/would", "can", or "may", and 要 "will", "need", or "must" both bear more than one subtype of modal meaning. The modal verb 會 is usually translated as "shall/will" and is widely understood to represent a type of future tense in Chinese. It acts as an epistemic modality for "may/might" in utterances where the speaker expresses his/her opinion or attitude regarding uncertainty, while it indicates dynamic modality for "can" when it is concerned with the "ability" of the speaker, and it also acts as an approximate equivalent to "will" to indicate a speaker's volition. In contrast, the modal 要, carries the same meaning of epistemic modality as 需要 "need" when it is concerned with necessity, but may act as a type of dynamic modality "will", in which case it represents the "volition" or "inclination" of the speaker, i.e. what the speaker 想 "want[s]" and 願意 "will, [is] willing to" do. Finally, it can express deontic modality when used to indicate one's need of obligation, in which case it is equivalent to 必須 "must".

The use of Chinese modal verbs in presidential debates

Political debate is a distinctive domain of argumentation for proposals for action (Kock, 2017). In democratic societies, presidential debate is a critical issue-based political activity for presidential aspirants to account for their campaign promises. At the same time, it provides an opportunity for the electorate to gain an understanding of the traits and image of each of the candidates (McKinney and Carlin, 2004), as well as to increase their knowledge of current issues and to assess the salience of those issues in making their voting choice. With the persuasive objectives of political discourse, candidates tend to use deliberative rhetoric to stipulate their proposed policies, anticipate the future, assert their respective positions, affirm their judgements or loyalties, or disavow undesirable behaviors. The subtly articulated use of modality in their arguments enables candidates to express necessity and possibility, permission and obligation, as well as their ability and volition to create a better country.

This section, by taking modality to be a semantic system encompassing the interpersonal meanings of a speaker and signaling the degree and nature of a speaker's commitment to the truth of a proposition or to the occurrence of an event, therefore, applies the aforementioned understanding of Chinese modality to an investigation of its usage in political discourse. The three major aspects of modality outlined above, namely possibility and necessity, permission and obligation, and ability and volition, will be discussed with reference to the arguments made by two presidents-elect in Taiwan, Ma Ying-jeou of the Kuomintang (KMT) and Tsai Ing-wen of the Democratic Progressive Party (DPP) in the 2012 and 2016 debates respectively.

Possibility and necessity

Presidential debates are a type of audition for the candidates for national leadership. Such debates are a part of the presidential campaign in which candidates seek to inform and impress the electorate with their specific policies, as well as to force rival parties to understand one's own positions. Benoit et al. (2003) suggests that during debates candidates discuss different issues and takes positions to appeal to other groups of voters who may have disparate concerns from those of committed partisans. Propositions made during debates are mostly based on the candidates' estimations about the uncertainty of an event and judgments about the probability of the factual status of a proposition. The use of epistemic modality as a rhetorical tool thus functions as a set of peripheral operators to support the candidates' arguments for their speculations and judgments about the possibility and necessity that something will (not) happen. Such modality helps candidates to achieve their persuasive goals by emphasizing a consecutive interpretation of their ability and accomplishments, as well as to solicit the electorate's support through specific requests and demand.

In Chinese, the modal verbs expressing epistemic possibility and speculation, and denoting uncertainty are 會 ("may, might, would"), 能/能夠 ("can, could"), and 可以 ("may, might"). During presidential debates, candidates usually make use of counterfactual conditional sentences to illustrate a speculative situation to warn their rivals or the electorate, and to imply a commitment to the truth of the propositions that they utter. The predictability underscored by truth modality acts to turn the hearers' opinion to the speaker's advantage and may vary in strength along a scale from low confidence to absolute confidence (see Excerpts 13–15).

(13) 各位鄉親正確的選擇，<u>會</u>帶來黃金十年；錯誤的選擇，<u>會</u>帶來十年的倒退。
"Should you all make the correct choice, it **will** bring about a golden decade, while the wrong choice **might** bring about a decade of regression". (Ma Ying-jeou, 2012 Taiwan Presidential Debate)

(14) 這個九二共識是擱置爭議、共創雙贏最好的辦法。如果你不承認它，兩岸關係<u>會</u>陷入不確定的狀態，甚至<u>會</u>倒退。
"The 1992 Consensus is the best means of putting aside disputes and creating a win-win situation. If this is not recognized, cross-Strait relations **would** fall into a state of uncertainty, and even retrogression". (Ma, 2012)

(15) 台灣畢竟是一個民主社會，民主一定<u>會</u>有政黨輪替……
"Taiwan, after all, is a democratic society, democracy **will** <u>definitely</u> have interparty rotation…". (Tsai Ing-wen, 2016)

In (13) and (14), KMT presidential candidate Ma Ying-jeou employed the median-value epistemic modal verb 會 ("will/would/might") to project a plausible future resulting from the electorate's choice and predicting a possible calamity for cross-strait relations in the absence of the "1992 Consensus". He argued using this modality to convince the electorate that his vision was the relevant choice. While in (15), Tsai Ing-wen of the DPP suggested a choice of power rotation. The degree of possibility is implicit in Chinese due to the absence of inflectional change in the language. In the case of 會, whether the word should be represented by "will", "would" or "might" in English will depend on the specific decoding of the message and speaker's tone. In addition, Tsai, in (16) and (17), also made a tactical use of low-value epistemic modal verbs 可以 ("may") and 能 ("can/could") to present both her position and her viewpoints on the uncertainty of the cross-strait issue and Taiwan's economic policies. In (16), she chose to use a conciliatory tone, with 可以, to express her openness concerning the cross-strait relationship.

(16) 九二年並沒有九二共識，九二共識是在2000年才出來的名詞，這是一個名詞的使用跟詮釋的問題，這個我們大家都<u>可以</u>坐下來談。
"There was no '1992 Consensus' in 1992; the term was only coined in 2000. Yet, we **may** sit down and discuss its use and interpretation". (Tsai, 2016)

(17) 經濟政策是一個很嚴肅、很艱鉅的問題。如果靠修法就**能**解決低薪的問題, 靠加薪就**能**讓我們整個的景氣回來, 經濟就**能**往前, 那我想世界上經濟問題就不會那麼複雜；那現在全世界陷入的經濟困境, 就**能**迎刃而解。

"Economic policy is a very serious and complicated issue. If we **could** solve the problem of low wages just by revising the law, and we **could** bring about a booming economy and move forward just through a wage increase, then I think the economic problems in the world would not be so complicated. If all of that were true, then we **could** solve the economic dilemma faced all around the world". (Tsai, 2016)

These five low- to median-value modals of possibility reflect the uncertainty of the propositions and function as mediation operators between the speaker's knowledge and estimations, preserving some leeway for both the candidates and the electorate.

Necessity modality is another aspect of epistemic modality that is important in presenting a candidate's arguments. In Chinese, the modals 應該 ("should") and 要 ("need to, will") suggest a certain degree of probability, and they may be employed conjunctively to encode the necessity of a certain state (Excerpts 18 and 19). In the statements below, the modal 要 denotes a requirement for the qualities of a leader, whereas 應該 is a statement of what *should* be the case as opposed to what the present state is. Both discursive strategies of necessity modality reflect the subjective views of the candidates.

(18) 各位鄉親, 台灣人民一定**要**選擇一個有能力、有經驗、能夠衝破金融風暴的好手, **要**選擇一個清廉正直、始終如一的總統。

"Fellow compatriots, the people of Taiwan definitely **need to** choose [a leader] who has ability, experience and can break through the financial turmoil; you **need to** choose an incorruptible president with consistent integrity". (Ma, 2012)

(19) 人心不安的社會也**應該要**來改。

"The level of discontent in society **should** also be improved". (Tsai, 2016)

Ability and volition

Appropriate portrayal of candidates' personal character traits is essential in a presidential election, as voter perceptions of the candidates' personal qualities, leadership ability and ideals are important influences voter decisions. As summarized in Figure 11.1 above, dynamic modals involve ability (能夠 "can", 會 "can", 可以 "may", 敢 "dare") and volition (會 "will", 要 "want", 肯 "willing to", 願意 "willing to"). These two categories of dynamic modality are intentionally highlighted by the candidates (see Excerpts 20–25) to acclaim or attack an opponent in the presidential debates.

(20) 我們一個國家的領導人, 一定要有一個能力, **能夠**穩定兩岸關係......這個情況下, 我提出來不統、不獨、不武是最好的政策。

"The leader of this country must have the **ability** to [must be the one who **can**] stabilize the cross-Strait relationship. . . . Under these circumstances, I have proposed that we should adopt the 'Three Noes' policy of no unification, no independence and no war". (Ma, 2012)

Drawing on evidence from past accomplishment as support for his position, Ma touted his own ability by employing the modal 能夠 "can". He further challenged the ability of his rival in the 2012 presidential debate by using another dynamic modal, 敢 "dare". His use of the modal in an interrogative utterance reaffirms his support of his proposed "Three Noes" policy.

(21) 蔡主席，我**敢**說，不統、不獨、不武；你**敢不敢**說同樣的話？
"Chairperson Tsai, I **dare** to say, 'no unification, no independence, and no war'. Do you **dare** to say the same thing?" (Ma, 2012)

The concepts of ability and volition both fall within the same category of dynamic modality. According to Palmer (1979), the volitional modal "will" implies future actuality. In Chinese, the modal 會 "will" also concerns a speaker's or subject's volition, determination, insistence and offering of promises, as in (22) or (23). Tsai fully utilized the median-value modal 會 attributing to her discussion of proposed social measures and exhibiting her ability and volition (as in 22). The 會 in an "if" clause (23) indicates Ma's volition to assure and convince the voters. In particular, the conjugated use of the positive and negation of the dynamic modal emphasizes the speakers' commitment that the stronger volition should be expressed through negation, as in these two examples.

(22) 我堅持務實穩健的改革，我**會**照顧現在依賴退休金過日子的人，**不會**造成他們生活安定上的衝擊。
"I **will** adhere to a pragmatic and moderate reform and **will** take care of those who are now relying on pensions, and this reform **will not** have any impact on their livelihood". (Tsai, 2016)

(23) 如果還有努力的空間，我**不會**放棄，我**還會**繼續向前邁進，譬如說，像失業率、像經濟成長，還有八年到三萬美金，我**還會**繼續努力。
"I **won't** give up if there is room for our efforts, and I **will** continue to move forward, say, in respect of the unemployment rate, economic growth, as well as attaining per capita GDP of US$ 30,000 within eight years. I **will** continue to strive for this". (Ma, 2012)

In addition to Ma's use of the dynamic modal 敢 "dare", he further employed a tactful rhetorical use of other modal verbs 願意 "willing to/would" and 肯 "willing to" in greater discrepancy to attack and acclaim, as exhibited in Excerpts (24) and (25).

(24) 我們**願意**回到民進黨執政的時候，那種社會混亂的台灣嗎？
我們**願意**回到民進黨執政的時候，八年台海緊張關係的台灣嗎？
我們**願意**退到民進黨執政的時候，貪污腐敗、鎖國退步的情況嗎？
我們沒有人**願意**。
"My fellow, **would** we [are we **willing to**] rather live again in a Taiwan of economic downturn as happened during the DPP's 8-year rule? ... **Would** we rather return to the kind of social chaos during the DPP's 8-year rule? ... **Would** we rather return to 8-year strained relations across the Taiwan Strait during the DPP's rule? None of us **would**". (Ma, 2012)

(25) 日本為甚麼**肯**到台灣來簽投資協議？跟ECFA有絕大的關係：因為日商在台灣投資之後，就可以利用ECFA的協議減稅，把這個產品賣到大陸去⋯⋯。
"Why is Japan **willing to** come to Taiwan to sign an investment agreement with us? There is a great relationship with ECFA: Japanese companies can use the framework of the ECFA tax cut to sell this product to the mainland if they invest in Taiwan". (Ma, 2012)

Permission and obligation

Lyons (1977) postulates a distinction between epistemic modality and deontic modality, in that the former is possibility-based whereas the latter is necessity-based. Building on this distinction, Van der Auwera and Plungian (1998: 81) opine that "deontic modality identifies the enabling or compelling circumstances external to the participant as some person(s), often the speaker, and/or some social or ethical norm(s) permitting or obliging the participant to engage in the state of affairs". The deontic modals, according to Fowler (1991), indicate a speaker's judgements about permission (i.e. statements in which the speaker grants or withholds permission as expressed by *may*) and obligation (i.e. statements in which the speaker stipulates that the audience *ought to*, *should* or *must* perform certain actions). These two subtypes of deontic modality, according to Martin and White (2005), are associated with relationships of power and control.

The Chinese modals indicating a speaker's judgment about permission are represented by 可以 "may, can", and 能夠 "can", while 必須, 需要 or 要 "must", and 應該 "should, ought to" are concerned with obligation deriving from external factors. As this kind of deontic modal explicitly grounds the demand of the speaker, such modality is generally employed in presidential debates to explain and clarify a speaker's opinions, beliefs or values. The deontic modal 必須, interchangeably with 需要, 要, or 必須要, not only expresses the candidates' strong views about a proposition, but also the candidates' political obligations and manipulations, as well as his/her strong commitments. As indicated in Excerpts (26) and (27), both candidates attempt to let the electorate know the urgency of an issue and seek their approval and support.

(26) 各位鄉親，台灣**必須要**一個清廉正直、始終如一的總統，台灣繼續向前行，台灣才會贏。
"Fellow compatriots, the people of Taiwan **must/have to** have an incorruptible and consistent president with integrity so that Taiwan can continue to march forward and win". (Ma, 2012)

(27) 所以領導人**必須要**團結這個國家，**必須要**包容 ....。
"Therefore, the leader **must** unite this country, and **must** be inclusive". (Tsai, 2016)

Apart from the above use of the high-value modal 必須要, which acts as a compelling force, another median-value deontic modal, 應該, is also used in an attempt to gain the audience's consent. This modal, which generally occurs with its core meaning of a subjective obligation, is not necessarily weaker, but reflects a scale of certainty concerning whether the proposition has a good chance or just some chance of realization. As in Excerpt (28), it may be used as a defensive strategy for what the speaker has achieved. In addition, this modal – expressing an imperative suggestion but avoiding a strong feeling of coercion – generally works out as a more effective means of persuading people to act voluntarily in a desired way. In (29) below, the DPP candidate Tsai has tried to use this modal to uphold the belief of her party and to seek consent from the electorate.

(28) 而我們現在所做的每一個政策都是如此，我們跟大陸簽了十六個協議，每一個都是公開的。... 因此透明化，其實我們已經在實踐，我們的做法，**應該**是目前最適當的。
"And every policy we are setting is being done in this way: we have signed 16 agreements with the Mainland, all of which are open to the public. ... In fact, we are practicing a kind of transparency in government affairs, and such practice **should** be seen as the most appropriate at present". (Ma, 2012)

(29) 任何人，都不**應該**低估，我們人民捍衛自由和民主的意志。
"No one **should** underestimate the will of our people to defend freedom and democracy". (Tsai, 2016)

Permission, representing a speaker's granting of the possibility that something may occur, does not imply that he/she will make the event occur. Unlike the comparatively compelling tone seen in the modality about obligation, this deontic modality is concerned with requests, as represented here by 可以 "can, may" and 能夠 "can".

Excerpt (30), making use of an antithesis, evinces the common behavior of a candidate making a request and asks for the electorate's support.

(30) 請給國民黨一個機會下台反省，請給民進黨一個機會，讓進步的力量**可以**過半，讓我們來證明，立法院**可以**不一樣，**可以**為這個國家的改變作出貢獻。
"Please offer the Kuomintang a chance to step down for self-examination, and give the DPP an opportunity to prove the power of progress **can** carry than half (of the vote). Let us prove that the Legislative Yuan **can** make a difference and that we **can** contribute to changing this country". (Tsai, 2016)

On the other hand, use of the interrogative 可以 is also shown to be a strategy for attack in the cross-examination portion of a presidential debate (Excerpt 31).

(31) 您也說過，國民黨的中華民國是流亡政府，您現在競選的，是不是一個流亡政府的總統？您標榜高格調的選舉，可是卻用陳盈助事件來抹黑我，**可不可以**請您出來說清楚？
"You have said that the Kuomintang's Republic of China is a government in exile. May I know if you are currently running for the presidency of a government in exile? You have also flaunted the integrity of this election, but you have tried to discredit me for meeting with Chen Ying-chu [a gambling leader]. **Can** you clarify what you mean?" (Ma, 2012)

Table 11.1 The formality and frequency of modal verbs employed by Ma Ying-jeou and Tsai Ing-wen within the 2012 and 2016 presidential debates

	Modality	Ma (2012)	Tsai (2016)	Frequency	Frequency Ranking
High value	要 yào ("must")	104	149	253	1
	必須 bìxū ("have to, must")	14	29	43	5
	需要 xūyào ("need")	12	12	24	7
Median value	會 huì ("will")	68	117	185	2
	應該 yīnggāi ("should/ought to")	17	21	38	6
Low value	能; 能夠 néng; nénggòu ("able, can/could")	74	62	136	3
	可以 kěyǐ ("may/might")	36	77	113	4
	可能 kěnéng ("may/might, possible")	13	10	23	8
	願意 yuànyì ("willing")	16	3	19	9
	敢 gǎn ("dare")	10	0	10	10
	肯 kěn ("willing")	3	1	4	11
Frequency		367	481	848	

Among the major Chinese modal verbs, the modals most frequently employed in the Taiwanese presidential debates include (in order of frequency) 要 ("will, must, have to"), 會 ("will, would"), 能夠 ("can, could") and 可以 ("may, might"). The discursive strategies of modality of each of the two presidents-elects, as an incumbent-party candidate or as a challenger, are shown in Table 11.1.

The high-value modal 要 ("will, must, have to") is most frequently employed by both presidents-elect Ma Ying-jeou and Tsai Ing-wen in the presidential debates and is used to assert their respective propositions and express their obligations to reinforce their level of credibility. In addition, Tsai, as a challenger, chose to use the median-value modal 會 to attribute probability to her discussion of policy issues and to indicate her volition, while Ma instead made use of the low-value modal 能夠 to underscore his previous accomplishments and ability as the incumbent-party candidate.

Conclusion

The aim of this chapter has been to gain insight into the categorization of modal meanings in Chinese. The chapter began by first examining the relationship between language and politics in political debates. The chapter then investigated the salient features of Chinese modal verbs as a means of revealing a speaker's knowledge and judgements concerning an event and his/her attitudes towards a proposition. Third, the chapter enunciated the application of these Chinese modal expressions in political debates. Fourth, the chapter sketched how different political parties in Taiwan articulate their positions on pertinent issues in presidential debates.

This chapter has scrutinized the properties of three types of Chinese modality, namely epistemic, deontic, and dynamic modality, in expressing a speaker's attitude, judgement or assessments of possibility and necessity; ability and volition; and permission and obligation respectively. The salient features of Chinese modality were identified, particularly in the use of monosyllabic and disyllabic modal verbs paired with negation to accentuate the level of assertiveness.

Verbs of high-value modality including 要, 需要 and 必須 convey obligative and directive assertiveness, reinforcing the speaker's credibility or informing the addressees of the speaker's or ingroup's values. This modality reflects the speaker's ideology and helps politicians to shape the political cognition and behaviors of the hearers. Nonetheless, its impact is double-edged, as it may express integration or differentiation to the addressees depending on the context. The assertive commitment to a steadfast enactment of one's values or position may even induce an antagonistic feeling between the speaker and the addressee.

Verbs of median- and low-value modality, such as 會, 應該, 可以 and 能夠 expressing weaker commitment, on the other hand, communicate a comparatively positive tone and soften a confrontation in preparation for a resolution. These modalities, bearing commissive, directive or optative functions to reflect a speaker's attitudes, beliefs and values, volition or obligation, are manipulated persuasively in political discourse, and especially in presidential debates, to evince the speaker's position and viewpoint on a stated proposition so as to influence the judgements or gain the support of an audience.

The interpersonal meaning of the arguments made by the presidents-elect in the 2012 and 2016 Taiwan Presidential Elections, as exemplified through the provided excerpts, reveal the multifaceted advantages and deficiencies of modality in political debate. Persuasiveness is potently deployed through the speaker's intentional modality choices. In particular, the polysemous high-value modal 要 ("will, need, want, must") and the median-value modal 會 ("will, can, may") indubitably reflect the art of the political action of debate, which can be corroborated in the presidential debates. In the cases of epistemic possibility and necessity, the modal 會 implies the uncertainty of an event, as manipulated by the speakers, whereas the same modal functioning as a dynamic modal indicates ability or volition, and is used by speakers to underscore their judgements of capability or to acclaim their prior accomplishments. This modal is a persuasive tool employed by speakers to express their volition and commitment to solicit the support of the hearer, and a stronger sense of volition is expressed through the conjugated use of a positive and a negation of this dynamic modal. On the other hand, the modal 要 exhibits the speaker's volition and judgement of necessity, but overuse of obligative and direct assertiveness in a debate (as evidenced in Table 11.1) may not offer any advantage for the speaker to gain support and power.

References

English references

Beard, A. (2000) *The Language of Politics*. London: Routledge.
Benoit, W.L., Hansen, G.J. and Verser, R.M. (2003) 'A Meta-Analysis of the Effects of Viewing U.S. Presidential Debates', *Communication Monographs*, 70(4): 335–350.
Cheng, M. (2016) 'The Power of Persuasion: Modality and Issue Framing in the 2012 Taiwan Presidential Debates', *Discourse & Society*, 27(2): 172–94 (First published on December 23, 2015).
Foley, W.A. and Van Valin, R.D., Jr. (1984) *Functional Syntax and Universal Grammar*. Cambridge: Cambridge University Press.
Fowler, R. (1991) *Language in the News*. London: Routledge.
Geer, J.G. (1988) 'The Effects of Presidential Debates on the Electorate's Preference for Candidates', *American Politics Quarterly*, 16: 486–501.
Gonzálvez-Garcia, F. (2000) 'Modulating Grammar through Modality: A Discourse Approach', *Elia* 119–135.
Halliday, M.A.K. (1970) *Explorations in the Functions of Language*. London: Edward Arnold.
Halliday, M.A.K. and Matthiessen, C.M.I.M. (2013) *Introduction to Functional Grammar* (4th ed.). London and New York: Routledge.
Jerit, J. (2008) 'Issue Framing and Engagement: Rhetorical Strategy in Public Policy Debates', *Political Behavior* 30: 1–24.
Johannesson, N.L. (1976) *The English Modal Auxiliaries: A Stratificational Account*. Stockholm: Almqvist and Wiksell International.
Kock, C. (2017) 'Dialectical Obligations in Political Debate', *Informal Logic* 27(3): 223–247.
Lyons, J. (1977) *Semantics*, Vol. 2. Cambridge: Cambridge University Press.
Martin, J.R. and White, P.R.R. (2005) *The Language of Evaluation*. London and New York: Palgrave Macmillan.
McKinney, M.S. and Carlin, D.B. (2004) 'Political campaign debates', in *Handbook of Political Communication Research*. L.L. Kaid (ed.) Mahwah, NJ: Erlbaum.
Palmer, F.R. (1979) *Modality and the English Modals*. London: Longman.
Palmer, F.R. (2001) *Mood and Modality*. Paddyfield: Cambridge University Press.
Patterson, J.W. and Zarefsky, D. (1983) *Contemporary Debate*. Boston: Houghton Mifflin.
Pfau, M., Thomas, D.A. and Ulrich, W. (1987) *Debate and Argument: A Systems Approach to Advocacy*. Glenview, IL: Scott, Foresman.
Sniderman, P.M. and Theriault, S.M. (2004) 'The structure of political argument and the logic of issue framing', in *Studies in Public Opinion: Attitudes, Nonattitudes, Measurement Error, and Change*. W.E. Saris and P.M. Sniderman (eds.) Princeton, NJ: Princeton University Press.
Van der Auwera, J. and Plungian, V.A. (1998) 'Modality's Semantic Map', *Linguistic Typology* 2(1): 79–124.
Wodak, R. and Forchtner, B. (eds.) (2017) *The Routledge Handbook of Language and Politics*. London: Taylor & Francis.

Chinese references

Hu, Yushu 胡裕樹 (1981) 現代漢語 (*Modern Chinese*). Shanghai: Shanghai Education Press.
Huang, B.R. 黃伯榮 and Liao, X.D. 廖序東 (2007) 現代漢語 (*Modern Chinese*), (4th ed.). Beijing: Higher Education Press.

Lü, SX 呂叔湘 (1979) 漢語語法分析問題 (*Issues of Grammatical Analysis in Chinese*), Beijing: Commercial Press.

Ma, QZ 馬慶株 (2005) 漢語動詞和動詞性結構 (*Chinese Verbs and Verbal Structures*), Beijing: Language Institute Press.

Ma, Ying-jeou. (2012). '2012 總統辯論實況' (Taiwan Presidential Debates), www.youtube.com/watch?v=5qTo7TSeZPs (first half) and www.youtube.com/watch?v=Vxv9lDj1yx0 (second half).

Tsai, Ing-wen. (2016). '2016 總統大選電視辯論' (2016 Televised Taiwan Presidential Election), www.youtube.com/watch?v=Je8f4yfDUxo (first half) and www.youtube.com/watch?v=7Hn7nNAJ0IY (second half).

12

Zero anaphora and topic chain in Chinese discourse

Ming-Ming Pu

Introduction

The study of anaphora has long been the focus of considerable research in various fields because of its importance to our understanding of the relationship between language and cognition. This chapter explores one particular anaphoric form – zero anaphora – in Chinese discourse, and discusses central issues concerning when and how speaker/writers decide to use a zero anaphor, among several available linguistic forms, to refer to an entity in an ongoing discourse so that their hearer/readers can uniquely and quickly identify the referent of the ellipsis, and what motivates them to do so in the reference tracking process.

We take a cognitive-functional approach to the study of zero anaphora in narrative discourse because on the one hand narrative is a universally pervasive form of language with which people transmit and understand personal and vicarious experiences in relation to identity and social life, and on the other hand narrative serves various social and communicative functions, in terms of which language is best understood. We argue, specifically, that zero anaphora is strictly rule-governed, the use of which in Chinese (and in natural language in general) is constrained by cognitive activities of attention and focus, and motivated by the functional or discourse correlates of these cognitive activities. An established referent currently in focal attention is cognitively most accessible, which manifests itself in discourse as highly topical, (referentially) continuous and thematically most coherent with the preceding information. In other words, it is most accessible in discourse representation as well. The high degree of discourse accessibility warrants the use of zero anaphora, commonly found in a TOPIC CHAIN, which is the most prevalent device coding a maximally coherent discourse unit and ultimately responsible for the general occurrence and distribution of zero anaphora in Chinese discourse.

Prior research on zero anaphora

Zero anaphora, "one of the most natural, universal, ancient and functionally-coherent grammatical devices in the tool-kit of natural language" (Givón, 2017: 3), has attracted ample attention in diverse fields of linguistic inquiry over the past few decades. In GB framework zero anaphora has been examined from a syntactic perspective, based on which languages are classified typologically into three types: Pro-drop, partial-pro-drop, and non-pro-drop. Pro-drop languages such as Italian permit a null subject that is controlled by rich agreement. Non-pro-drop languages such as English do not permit a null subject due to their lack of rich agreement, and partial-pro-drop languages such as Finnish permit null subjects in certain restricted environments. The Chinese language permits a null subject but lacks rich agreement governing it, and J. Huang (1984) argues that such a null subject is controlled by either an overt NP in the superordinate clause (i.e., a pronominal) or a null topic co-indexed with a salient referent in the discourse (i.e., a variable).

In the tradition of functional linguistics, on the other hand, research on zero anaphora has focused on considerable cross-linguistic comparisons among rigid-and flexible-order languages from a discourse perspective, showing that one of the most important universal characteristics of zero anaphor is to signal referential continuity in discourse (see Givón, 1983a, *inter alia*). More recently, Givón (2017) challenges the GB account of pro-drop phenomenon and provides an extensive account of zero anaphora crosslinguistically in terms of discourse-functional distribution and diachronic development, which demonstrates that zero anaphora is not only ubiquitous in all mature grammars but also arises diachronically from paratactic zeros or various pronominal precursors. In the research of Chinese zero anaphora, some studies (Li and Thompson, 1979; Chen, 1986) contend that semantic and pragmatic factors such as conjoinability between consecutive clauses or identifiability of referents are crucial for the occurrence of zero anaphora in discourse while others (S. Huang, 2013; Li, 2005; Tsao, 1990) focus on 'topic prominency' and argue for the close relationship between discourse-pragmatic factors and the use of anaphora.

The studies from both formal and functional traditions have shed light on the structure and mechanisms of Chinese zero anaphora and made significant contributions to our understanding of its communicative logic and importance in the Chinese grammar. Nonetheless, the GB treatment, though including the discourse notion of *topic*, has remained at the clause and sentence level, and hence hardly captures the nature of *discourse* zero anaphora and its well-governedness at the level of discourse in natural language, while the functional approaches have rarely recognized and explored the importance of cognitive underpinnings of this linguistic phenomenon, and hence come short of providing a full account of its occurrence and distribution as well as its governing principles.

A cognitive-functional framework

This chapter argues that anaphora is a cognitive and discourse phenomenon. On the one hand, if the human mind is capable of dealing with only a limited number of entities at a time (i.e., working-memory constraints), this limitation would certainly play a part in determining the nature of the 'rules' for reference tracking in natural language. In discourse processing, on the other hand, an anaphor should not be regarded simply as a word that substitutes for, or refers back to, another word or words in a clause or sentence, but as a process where references are managed in a developing structure to maintain local and global topics and achieve coherence between interlocutors.

From a cognitive perspective, the use of discourse anaphora is constrained by cognitive activities, especially the storage, capacity and processing of working memory, as abundant literature has demonstrated (Ariel, 1994; Chafe, 1994; Givón, 1983b; Gundel et al., 1993; Tomlin and Pu, 1991, *inter alia*). The cognitive basis underlying reference tracking is best described by Oberauer (2002: 412) in a concentric working-memory model with its structure and process. To put it briefly, the model consists of three functionally distinctive yet interconnected regions: A focus of attention at the center surrounded by a capacity-limited region of direct access, with an activated part of long-term memory outside the two inner areas. During information processing, the region of direct access forms a selection set of elements from the activated part of long-term memory that are needed for an ongoing task, and the one memory item/chunk selected within the selection set enters the focus of attention at any given moment of processing.

Oberauer's concentric model helps illustrate the relationship between memory representations of referents and their encoding in discourse. It makes great processing sense that in reference tracking, an entity currently in the focus of attention would be coded by a most attenuated syntactic form (e.g., an ellipsis) because it is selected for the upcoming cognitive task and most accessible in our mental representation of discourse, a referent that is in the region of direct access (i.e., among a selected set of activated elements in long-term memory) would be coded by a more attenuated form (e.g., a lexical pronoun) because it is held available for the ongoing operation and more accessible, and a referent that is currently inactive tends to be coded by a least attenuated form (a full NP) because it is presently in the background unrelated to the ongoing task and less accessible.

What increases or decreases activation levels of a referent in our mental representation, however, depends largely on the discourse, pragmatic and semantic properties of the referent. For example, in a span of discourse where information flows smoothly, cognitive resources may be devoted mostly to activations of referents, whereas in discourse where information flow is disrupted, limited cognitive resources would have to be shared between bridging the information gap and activating referents. Hence discourse coherence would promote activation processes while thematic discontinuity would hinder the process. From a functional perspective, discourse anaphora is mainly a hearer-oriented process, where the speaker must constantly make assessment about the hearer's cognitive status on a particular referent and choose an appropriate anaphoric form base on that assessment. Every anaphor constitutes a specific tacit instruction to operate on the mental discourse representation that the hearer is constructing in collaboration with the speaker. Since anaphor resolution seems in general to be a regular, routine, and automatic process in discourse comprehension, the hearer must be sensitive to or constantly seeking, albeit mostly subconsciously, the signals and cues provided by the speaker on discourse structure, upon which anaphora is interpreted.

The close tie between discourse anaphora and the storage, capacity and processing of working memory has been abundantly documented in the literature of discourse analysis and psycholinguistics (Chafe, 1994; Gernsbacher, 1990; Givón, 1983b, 2017; S. Huang, 2013; Pu, 2011; Tomlin and Pu, 1991). It has been shown in psycholinguistic experiments that the syntax of reference is a function of memory and attention statuses: Zero anaphora (in Chinese) and unstressed lexical pronouns (in English) are used to maintain references when attention sustains and full NPs are used to introduce or reinstate references when attention is disrupted (Pu, 2011; Tomlin and Pu, 1991). Similarly, Chafe (1994) and Gundel et al. (1993) posit that if the activation status of a referent determines its syntactic coding, i.e., what is 'in focus' would be coded by a less explicit anaphor and vice versa. In the same vein, S. Huang (2013: 157) proposes an accessibility scale for anaphora in Chinese discourse, where zero anaphor is the highest on the hierarchy, coding the most accessible referent across clauses.

Furthermore, anaphora is tied to discourse structure, which manifests mental representation of discourse. Due to cognitive constraints, an entire discourse must be chunked into sizable and comprehensible thematic units in discourse organization, which are related thematically to one another linearly and hierarchically to maintain discourse coherence. Within a discourse unit where information flows smoothly, a referent would be more accessible; across a unit boundary where information flow is disrupted, the same referent would be less accessible due to limited cognitive resources devoted to setting up the new unit (Gernsbacher, 1990).

Thus, in discourse comprehension, an anaphoric form serves a dual function, i.e., signaling the cognitive status of its referent and constituting a specific tacit instruction to whether it resides within or across units and how it is related to the same or a different referent in prior discourse. Indeed, paragraph or episode structure of discourse has been found to manifest mental representations of discourse underlying the reference tracking system in general: Unstressed pronouns and/or zero anaphora to code a given referent within a paragraph, and full noun phrases to code the same referent across a paragraph boundary (Black and Bower, 1979; Hinds, 1977; Longacre, 1979).

Zero anaphora principle

Three-pronged discourse accessibility

Based on the relationship between memory constraints and linguistic coding, it is clear that discourse anaphora is a function of cognitive accessibility: The more accessible the referent, the less coding form it requires. Cognitive accessibility is, in turn, facilitated by discourse accessibility of three aspects: topicality, referential continuity and thematic coherence (c.f., Ariel, 1994; Givón, 1983a *inter alia*). Topicality signals the thematic importance of the referent, referential continuity describes the persistence of the referent, and thematic coherence indicates the flow of information. The three aspects are distinct but interrelated in the reference tracking system. For example, a topical referent that appears for the first time in discourse lacks referential continuity, and the same referent that re-appears after a thematic break is referentially continuous but thematically less coherent. On the other hand, only a referent of high topicality would persist over a span of discourse, and this referential continuity may contribute to the thematic coherence of the discourse unit. A referent is most accessible in discourse processing only when it is a topic and persists through a highly coherent span of discourse.

Hence, we propose a general ZERO ANAPHORA PRINCIPLE, arguing for the crucial relationship between zero anaphora and the three-pronged discourse accessibility:

> A zero anaphor encodes a referent or entity of high discourse accessibility, viz., the referent must be topical, referentially continuous, and resides in a maximally coherent discourse unit. Once the high accessibility is impaired, zero anaphora would be terminated.

Theoretical constructs

Of the three variables of discourse accessibility, topicality and referential continuity are well-defined notions in the literature of functional linguistics (Givón, 1983b; Gundel, 1985; Du Bois, 1985, *inter alia*), but the concept of thematic coherence that is key to discourse unit is less clear. Therefore, defining and identifying thematic coherence and discontinuity are crucial to our investigation of whether zero anaphor distribution in Chinese discourse is governed by the proposed principle. This section focuses on the theoretical constructs of thematic coherence and discontinuity, with special attention to *topic chain*, the most prevalent discourse structure where zero anaphors occur.

Degree of coherence in discourse

A discourse unit is generally considered as a semantic unit subsumed under a macro-proposition, or a major prosodic segment consisting of one or more clauses or 'intonation units' (Chafe, 1994;

Givón, 2017; van Dijk and Kintsch, 1983). Although paragraphs have been proposed as discourse units in written discourse (Hinds, 1977; Longacre, 1979, *inter alia*), they vary considerably in size, scope and temporal-spatial dimension. We contend, however, that a paragraph is often comprised of more than one macro-units that are interrelated to contribute to the paragraph-level theme, and each macro-unit, in turn, consists of one or more core discourse units, within which the incoming information coheres seamlessly with the previously presented information. Cognitively, each core unit may be regarded as an "activated cluster of knowledge within which speakers navigate with more limited, fully activated foci of consciousness" (Chafe, 2002: 259). Structurally, such a unit may consist of one, or most commonly, a sequence of clauses that often, but not always, marked at the end of the unit by the punctuation of a period or semi-colon in written discourse, and by a long pause of over 100 milliseconds (Givón, 2017: 282), a change in pitch baseline, or distinctive final pitch contour and final change in voice quality (Chafe, 1994) in spoken discourse. In terms of reference tracking, such a unit commonly centers on an entity that is typically topical, human, agentive, and coded as subject/topic, and focuses narrowly on a certain state, event or action of the entity.

In Chinese oral and written discourse, a core unit involving reference tracking is usually one of the five kinds and typically represented by topic chains: (1) portraying or characterizing the topical referent, (2) describing a particular state of affairs of the topical referent, (3) sequencing tight-knit foreground actions or events involving the topical referent, (4) indicating a simultaneous state of events, and (5) connecting and compressing important past (or possibly future) experiences or events of the topical referent as a coherent whole. The following examples illustrate each of the five kinds of core discourse units.

(1) 段去尘为人正派，Ø对工作要求严格，Ø在待人方面又很随和，Ø同什么人都能说上话，Ø从来不摆架子。
'Duan Quchen was a decent man, demanding as far as work was concerned but congenial in dealing with people. He could strike up a conversation with anyone, and never appear arrogant or remote'.

Passage (1) exemplifies the first type of maximally coherent unit, which portrays or characterizes a topical referent with no deviation from this central theme. The unit is realized structurally in a topic chain with five clauses: The topical referent is introduced by a proper name *Duan Quchen* as subject/topic of the first clause, and then coded repeatedly as null subject for the rest of the passage.

(2) 女儿长大了，Ø会做菜了，Ø懂得替母亲分担家务了。
The daughter had grown up, learned to cook and share housework with her mother.

Passage (2) exemplifies the second type of core unit coded in a topic chain, which describes a particular state of affairs of the topical referent, *daughter*, i.e., her maturity in terms of sharing household chores with her mother.

(3) 她匆匆地抄起几本书，Ø塞到书包里，Ø又匆匆地走出宿舍楼，沿着一条林荫道，Ø走向校门。
'She quickly picked up a few books, put them into the bag, hurried out of the dormitory building, and walked toward the campus gate along a tree-lined boulevard'.

Passage (3) exemplifies the third type of core unit, which depicts a close-knit action sequence indispensable to the advance of the storyline. Such a sequence of actions or events is usually foregrounded and tightly packed in a succession of clauses, the order of which commonly mirrors the order of the developing action or event process. The action sequence such as (3) typically occurs continuously within the same time frame and in the same location, and a topic chain is again used to represent the core unit.

(4) 维杨见她躺在床上, Ø 心里一边叫'不好', Ø 一边也有些不悦, Ø 心想: . . .
Seeing her lie in bed, Wei Yang felt guilty but at the same time a bit upset, thinking: . . .

Passage (4) exemplifies the fourth type of core unit, which indicates that the actions or events happen at the same time or accompanying each other or one another. In (4), what the referent, *Wei Yang*, saw, felt and thought of occurs simultaneously. Even though the act of "seeing" may lead to the referent's feeling and thinking, it doesn't mean that the events encoded in the passage happen one after another. The simultaneity of actions/events is best represented by topic chains in Chinese discourse, as shown in (4).

(5) 他在小客栈宿了一宵, Ø第二天拉了个同乡去大世界开开眼, Ø给他的屋里人买了半打美女牌香皂, Ø在哈哈镜前乐了一阵, Ø也就带着一种'总算去过了'的安慰下船回程了。
'He stayed in a small inn overnight, visited the Grand World the next day with a fellow villager, had a good laugh in front of the distorting mirrors, bought half a dozen Beauty-brand toilet soaps for his wife, and then boarded the ship to return home with a satisfying feeling of 'been-there-done-that'.

Passage (5) exemplified the fifth type of core unit, which provides a succinct recount of major past experiences or events of a topical referent, *he*. These events, usually occurring over a period of time in different locales, are also foreground information important to the development of the story, and commonly coded compactly in a topic chain as if they had occurred sequentially in a short time frame, although they may or may not mirror the natural order of events.

The above discussion shows that a typical topic chain represents a core discourse unit (i.e., a maximally coherent thematic unit), which manifests sustained attentional effort on the part of the speaker/writer. Zero subject used in topic chains such as (1–5) is prevalent in Chinese discourse and seems to be a grammaticalized phenomenon. In a quantitative study, Pu (1997) shows that zero subject accounts for 94% of all zero anaphors in her text data. Li's (2005: 112) topic chain results confirm Pu's finding: 93% of all zero anaphors in her study are null subjects.

Thematic discontinuity

This subsection examines the other part of the ZERO ANAPHORA PRINCIPLE, i.e., thematic discontinuity that breaks maximum coherence and terminates the use of a topic chain. In other words, between core units zero anaphora is no longer sufficient to code a referent even if it has been a topical referent in the preceding core unit because focal attention is being diverted and limited cognitive resources are devoted to building a new unit. At this juncture of discourse, a more explicit anaphoric form is required for the coding of the referent so as to 'start over', so to speak, with discourse production and comprehension.

While major thematic discontinuity between macro-units is often characterized by salient breaks in discourse such as changes of topic, place, time, object or possible world (van Dijk and Kintsch, 1983: 204), and marked by a definite NP of some sort to reinstate a known referent (Chafe, 1994; Givon, 1983b; Hinds, 1977; Longacre, 1979), minor thematic discontinuity between core units are more subtle, five of which we identify as common in Chinese discourse: (1) local topic change (switch references), (2) interruption in close-knit action/event sequence, (3) thematic shift, (4) desired effect for emphasis, and (5) weakened topicality.

The first type is illustrated in passage (6), which describes a topical referent's ('the daughter') internal thoughts at the moment, i.e., her indignation of and resentment at her father who betrayed her mother during the Cultural Revolution. It consists of three core units: (a) setting the 'verdict', (b) providing reason, and (c) giving further support and the resolution.

(6) (a) 她不能宽恕这无情无义的父亲。(b) 是他夺去了自己金色的童年，Ø 把幼小的女儿投向苦难的深渊。(c) Ø 为了孤苦无助的妈妈，她更不能宽恕这个哭哭啼啼的人。
'She couldn't forgive this heartless father. It was he who deprived her of a golden childhood and threw the baby daughter into an abyss of endless suffering. She could forgive this crying man even less for the sake of her lonely and defenseless mother'.

From (a) to (b) there is a switch of reference: The secondary referent, *father*, coded as direct object in (a), is promoted to the 'focus' position in (b) by a cleft structure, whereas the topical referent, *daughter*, is being 'demoted' (as a direct object). As the *daughter* reorients her thoughts back to her own resolution in (c), another switch of reference occurs with *she* back to the topic/subject position, even though the semantic-pragmatic information would've sufficiently revealed who the referent was, had its coding form been a zero subject. Note that in the first clause of (c), a cataphor (rather than an anaphor) is used that refers forward to the topical referent in the following clause. The cataphoric use of zero anaphora has various distinct discourse functions, one of which is to mark discontinuity in the flow of discourse information (Li, 2005).

The second type of minor discontinuity is represented by a minor break in a close-knit action or event sequence, e.g., a time or location change in the action or event sequence centering on a topical referent. For example,

(7) (a) 邹心萍跳下马车，Ø向拖拉机走去。(b) 她进入驾驶室，Ø把拖拉机开到路边，Ø灭了火，Ø却不立即下来。
'Zou Xinping jumped off the horse carriage and Ø walked to the tractor. *She* entered the cab, Ø drove the tractor to the roadside, Ø killed the engine, Ø but didn't disembark right away'.

Although passage (7) describes an action sequence, the activity occurs in two places, i.e., outside the tractor (a) and inside it (b). The location change represents a minor discontinuity in the flow of information and triggers the use of a lexical pronoun for *Zou Xinping*, even though *she* is the only referent in the passage.

The third type of minor discontinuity is represented by thematic shifts in the flow of information, which are often transitions in the narration from a topical referent's physical activities to her/his state of mind, from the portrayal of the referent's appearance to his/her internal thoughts, or between foreground and background information of the storyline, etc. Such a shift would disrupt maximal coherence in the information flow and thus terminates a topic chain. For example,

(8) (a) 曾惠心顶着穿心刺骨的寒风，Ø用劲地推着小车，Ø歪歪斜斜地行进在崎岖不平的土路上。(b) 她感不到冷...
'Zeng Huixin braved the cold wind, Ø pushed the cart with all (her) strength, and Ø staggered along the rugged dirt road. *She* didn't feel cold...'

The first three clauses in (a) describing an ongoing event involving the topical referent, *Zeng Huixin*, coded by a topic chain. Though still about the same referent, (b) shifts from what she did to what she felt while *pushing the cart in the rugged dirt road*, where a lexical pronoun is used to start a new unit.

The fourth type of minor discontinuity is one created by the writer to achieve certain emphatic effects. This often occurs in a core unit where the flow of information is highly coherent, but the writer tries to break this continuity by repeatedly using an explicit anaphor for a topical referent so as to emphasize certain attributes or qualities. For example,

(9) (a) 因为她是记者；(b) 因为她深深地同情那些被冤屈的人；(c) 因为她痛恨生活中的一切丑恶 –
'Because *she* was a journalist; because *she* sympathized deeply with those who suffered injustice; because *she* was indignant over all ugliness in life'.

In (9) the topical referent is coded by a chain of lexical pronouns to emphasize the reasons why *she* has been intensely involved in a case described in the preceding discourse. This overuse of resources would make the reader linger over the 'anomaly' of the reference, thus fulfilling the writer's goal to emphasize each reason specified in (a-c).

The fifth type of minor thematic discontinuity involves double topics in a discourse unit. Although human referents are mostly the center of narratives and figure prominently as topics of discourse, important non-human entities, almost always occurring for the first time as a grammatical object, may be topicalized to mark its significance in advancing the storyline. As the topicalized object is placed in the topic (or clause-initial) position, the human topical referent, though still the clause-subject, would have to be 'demoted' to non-topic position. This change of focus, albeit temporary, weakens the topical status of the human referent and creates minor referential discontinuity, where a zero anaphor would not be adequate to code the human referent that is being bumped out of focus at the moment. For example,

(10) (a) 最近一段时间他$_i$一直在写一个故事$_j$，(b) 这故事$_j$他$_i$构思了很久，Ø$_j$ Ø$_i$ 早就想写，Ø$_j$ Ø$_i$ 可是一直没有时间写。
'He had been writing a story recently, the story *he* had conceived for a long time, wanted to write long ago but had no time to write'.

In (10) *this story* (这故事), the direct object of (a) is an important entity of the discourse segment and is topicalized and preposed to clause-initial position in (b) to promote its importance. At the moment of topic shift (from *he* to *this story*), a new unit starts and a lexical pronoun is used to code the topical referent. Once the new topic (*this story*) is established at the beginning of (b), the human referent, the controller and manipulator of the inanimate entity, reenters focal attention, and a double-topic chain is used to code both the human referent and *this story* throughout the core unit of (b).

Data analysis and discussion

This section reports a quantitative text analysis on zero anaphora in Chinese discourse to test the viability and validity of the zero anaphora principle proposed in §4.1. The database consists of 40 pages of narrative text from four short stories by two male (Jin Ou, 2002; Ma Busheng, 2002) and two female authors (Chi Li, 1995; Fang Fang, 2001). The raw data tallies all anaphoric forms, i.e., full noun phrases (including proper names, bare NP and modified NP), lexical pronouns and zero anaphors, each of which refers to an 'antecedent' at least once in the discourse context. All three types of referential forms are examined because the analysis of the distribution of zero anaphora is meaningful only when it is compared to that of the other forms in terms of discourse accessibility.

The raw data points from each of the four authors are summarized in Table 12.1. The distribution patterns of references are very comparable among them, and no statistically significant difference is found in the general distribution of the three types of anaphoric forms (ANOVA: $F = 4.25, p > 0.05$). Hence, the subsequent analyses are performed on the pooled data.

The focus of the data analysis is to measure the strength of the three-pronged discourse accessibility, i.e., topicality, referential continuity and thematic coherence of the three types of referential forms, especially that of zero anaphora, which is proposed to be the most accessible of the three in discourse processing.

Topicality

The first parameter to measure is 'topicality', which signals the thematic importance of the referent. It can be assessed with regard to humanness, givenness, and syntactic position of a given anaphor because topical referents are typically human, definite, referential and grammatical subjects (Du Bois, 1985).

Table 12.2 shows the results of topicality for all referential forms, where 'H' stands for human and 'S/T' for those that occupy either the syntactic position of subject (S) or being

Table 12.1 Raw data

Author	NP Nr	%	Pronoun Nr	%	Zero Nr	%	Total
Chi	64	47.76	15	11.19	55	41.05	134
Fang	141	40.63	55	15.85	151	43.52	347
Jin	107	37.28	78	27.18	102	35.54	287
Ma	124	45.26	41	14.96	109	39.78	274
Total	436	41.84	189	18.14	417	40.02	1042

Table 12.2 Topicality

	Topical S/T H	NonH	Non-S/T H	NonH	Non-topical S/T H	NonH	Non-S/T H	NonH	Total
NP	215	30	74	37	9	6	13	52	436
%	49.31	6.88	16.97	9.49	2.06	1.38	2.98	11.93	
Pron	125	2	52	8	0	0	0	2	189
%	66.14	1.06	27.51	4.23	0.00	0.00	0.00	1.06	
Zero	348	41	8	20	0	0	0	0	417
%	83.45	9.83	1.92	4.80	0.00	0.00	0.00	0.00	
Total	688	73	134	65	9	6	13	54	1042
%	66.03	7.01	12.86	6.24	0.86	0.57	1.25	5.18	

topicalized (T) and take clause/sentence-initial position, although the two positions often coincide in the coding of a topical human referent.

It is obvious that zero anaphora ranks the highest in the category of topicality: 83.45% of all tokens encode topical, human referents that are in S/T position, while 66.4% of pronoun tokens and only 49.31% of NP tokens encode such referents. Since the pronoun and zero anaphora are almost non-existent in the 'Non-topical' category, statistical tests are performed only on the 'Topical' tokens: One X^2-test shows a significant difference among the distribution of the three types of references ($X^2 = 11.80\star$, p < 0.001), and so does another X^2-test between that of pronoun and zero anaphora ($X^2 = 105.65\star$, p < 0.001).

Referential continuity

The second parameter to measure is referential continuity, which can be assessed in terms of referential distance, i.e., how many clauses intervene between an anaphor and its 'antecedent', and referential persistence, i.e., how many clauses the anaphor persists after its first mention in a span of discourse.

With regard to referential distance, the data is organized into relevant categories such as 'first mention (FM)' (whether a token is mentioned for the first time in discourse), 'over the boundary (OB)' (whether a token is used across a paragraph boundary), 'one clause (RD = 1C)' (a token refers to its antecedent in the preceding clause), 'two clauses (RD = 2C)' (one clause intervenes between a token and its antecedent), and so on. Table 12.3 shows the results of referential continuity.

The table reveals several interesting results. First, all first mentions of referents are made with full NPs, as expected. Second, major discourse boundaries, i.e., paragraph boundaries in written text, are marked overwhelmingly by full NPs (133 of 142 tokens, 93.66%), rarely by pronouns (9 of 142 tokens, 6.34%), and never by zero anaphora, as predicted in the present study, because thematic discontinuity, as a new discourse unit starts, increases cognitive demand and diverts focus of attention, where a minimal marking form, i.e., zero anaphora, would not be preferred. Third, although zero anaphora accounts for 63.55% of all tokens that have a minimal referential distance, i.e., RD = 1, almost all zero tokens (415 of 417; 99.53%) are 'marked' RD = 1 because they encode highly accessible referents that are currently in focus, or well within reach, so to speak.

With regard to referential persistence, all referents that are mentioned continuously in the subsequent clause (C = 2) or clauses (C > 2) are included in the analysis, and every such reference is tallied in terms of its first referential form (1st RF) and subsequent forms as well as how many

Table 12.3 Referential continuity

	FM	OB	RD = 1C	RD = 2C	RD = 3C	RD > 3C	Total
NP	76	133	107	41	28	51	436
%	100.00	93.66	16.39	53.95	80.00	85.00	
Pron	0	9	131	33	7	9	189
%	0.00	4.34	20.06	43.42	20.00	15.00	
Zero	0	0	415	2	0	0	417
%	0.00	0.00	63.55	2.63	0.00	0.00	
Total	76	142	653	76	35	60	1042
%	100.00	100.00	100.00	100.00	100.00	100.00	

clauses the first reference persists in discourse. There are altogether 148 referents that persist over as few as two and as many as eleven clauses. Table 12.4 summarizes the persistence results.

Table 12.4 shows that while the first mention is coded overwhelmingly by NPs (85.14%) and rarely by pronouns (13.51%), zero anaphora is by far the most preferred form to code the subsequent mentions of a referent (63.25% on average against NPs and pronouns, and 99.5% of all zero tokens). Even with the explicit referential forms (NP + Pron) combined, the difference between the distribution of zero anaphora and explicit references for each condition (i.e., C = 2, C = 3, C = 4 and C > 4) is statistically significant ($X^2 = 8.02\star$, $p < 0.005$; $X^2 = 10.57\star$, $p < 0.005$; $X^2 = 13.29\star$, $p < 0.001$ $X^2 = 19.50\star$, $p < 0.001$, respectively).

The persistence results in Table 12.4 further verify that the primary function of zero anaphora is to encode referents already in focus and thus highly accessible. Once a referent is made topic and focused on in discourse, it tends to persist and be encoded by a topic chain.

Thematic coherence

The third parameter to measure is thematic coherence, which indicates the flow of information with regard to whether the incoming information highly coheres (within a core discourse unit) or discontinues from the previously presented information (between core discourse units) in a span of discourse. We assessed thematic coherence by first tallying all topic chains in the data and then examining whether these topic chains are characterized by any of the five types of maximum thematic coherence described in §4.2.1 and whether they are terminated because of any of the five types of thematic discontinuity described in §4.5.2. There are 187 topic chains with varying lengths (from two to eleven clauses) found in the 40 pages of data, and the results are summarized in Table 12.5: The first two rows tally the number and percentage in terms of topic chain lengths, the next two rows count the number and percentage in terms of thematic coherence types (CT), and the last two total the number and percentage in terms of thematic discontinuity types (DT).

Table 12.5 shows that more than half (61.5%) of all topic chains are longer than two clauses and the majority (93.05%) represent the five types of maximum coherence. On the other hand, once a thematic discontinuity of any kind occurs, the topic chain breaks and zero anaphora ceases to appear. Indeed, the data show that the majority of the topic chains are terminated because of discontinuity type 1 and type 3 (i.e., local topic change/switch references and thematic shift respectively). The results again strongly support the ZERO ANAPHORA PRINCIPLE in that a topical referent in a core discourse unit is likely to be encoded by a topic chain as high

Table 12.4 Referential persistence

	1st RF	C = 2	C = 3	C = 4	C > 4	Total
NP	126	7	11	15	74	233
%	85.14	15.56	15.94	14.56	17.05	
Pron	20	6	10	18	97	151
%	13.51	13.33	14.49	17.48	22.35	
Zero	2	32	48	70	263	415
%	1.35	71.11	69.57	67.96	60.60	
Total	148	45	69	103	434	801
	100%	100%	100%	100%	100%	

Table 12.5 Topic chain and thematic coherence

Topic Chain	C = 2	C = 3	C = 4	C > 4			Total
	72	58	29	28			187
	38.50	31.02	15.51	14.97			100%
Coherence	CT1	CT2	CT3	CT4	CT5	Other	Total
	28	43	57	8	38	13	187
	14.97	23.00	30.48	4.28	20.32	6.95	100%
Discontinuity	DT1	DT2	DT3	DT4	DT5	Other	Total
	90	12	70	12	3	0	187
	48.13	6.42	37.43	6.42	2.00	0.00	100%

thematic coherence is established and maintained, while zero anaphora is strongly rejected once the high degree of coherence is disrupted.

Conclusion

The present study explores processes and factors governing the use of zero anaphora in Chinese discourse from a cognitive-functional perspective. It proposes a ZERO ANAPHORA PRINCIPLE and argues that a zero anaphor or a topic chain is used to encode a most accessible referent in discourse, which is highly topical and typically persists over a core discourse unit. The principle predicts that the end of a core unit due to minor or major thematic discontinuity triggers the termination of a zero anaphor or topic chain. The study examines further what constitutes a core discourse unit and what represents minor or major thematic discontinuity, with qualitative and quantitative text data from Chinese narrative discourse. The text results have given solid support to the validity of the principle and shown that the use of discourse anaphora of all types in general is very much a function of the three-pronged discourse accessibility as represented by topicality, referential continuity and thematic coherence.

The present study concludes that anaphor use and interpretation is an integral part of discourse organization and coherence constrained by cognitive activities, and establishing and maintaining discourse topics in a shared mental representation is key to successful reference tracking. To that extent, we argue that the use of zero anaphor is more of a universal characteristic and less of a dividing parameter between topic- and subject-oriented or pro-drop and non-pro-drop languages. Although the universality of zero anaphora in a diversity of languages constitutes an empirical hypothesis subject to further research and refinement.

References

Ariel, M. (1994) 'Interpreting Anaphoric Expressions: A Cognitive versus a Pragmatic Approach', *Journal of Linguistics* 30: 3–42.
Black, J.B. and Bower, G.H. (1979) 'Episodes as Chunks in Narrative Memory', *Journal of Verbal Learning and Verbal Behavior* 18: 109–118.
Chafe, W. (1994) *Discourse, Consciousness, and Time: The Flow and Displacement of Conscious Experience in Speaking and Writing*. Chicago: University of Chicago Press.
Chafe, W. (2002) 'Searching for Meaning in Language: A Memoir', *Historiographia Linguistica* 29: 245–261.
Chen, P. (1986) *Referential Introducing and Tracking in Chinese Narratives*, Unpublished PhD Thesis. UCLA.
Chi, L. (1995). 'Cold or hot, it's good we're alive', in *Collected Works of Chi Li*. Nanjing: Jiangsu Literature and Art Publishing House.

Du Bois, J.W. (1985) 'Competing motivations', in *Iconicity in Syntax*. J. Haiman (ed.) Amsterdam: John Benjamins.

Fang, F. (2001). 'Paper wedding', in *Selected Chinese Fictions*. Wuhan: Changjiang Literature and Art Publishing House.

Gernsbacher, M.A. (1990) *Language Comprehension as Structure Building*. Hillsdale, New Jersey: Lawrence Erlbaum.

Givón, T. (1983a) 'Topic continuity and word order pragmatics in Ute', in *Topic Continuity in Discourse*. T. Givón (ed.) Amsterdam: John Benjamins.

Givón, T. (ed.) (1983b) *Topic Continuity in Discourse*. Amsterdam: John Benjamins.

Givón, T. (2017) *The Story of Zero*. Amsterdam: John Benjamins.

Gundel, J.K. (1985) 'Shared Knowledge and Topicality', *Journal of Pragmatics* 9(1): 83–107.

Gundel, J., Hedberg, N. and Zacharski, R. (1993) 'Cognitive Status and the Form of Referring Expressions in Discourse', *Language* 69: 274–307.

Hinds, J. (1977) 'Paragraph Structure and Pronominalization', *Papers in Linguistics* 10: 77-99.

Huang, S. (2013) *Chinese Grammar at Work*. Amsterdam: John Benjamins.

Huang, J. C-T. (1984) 'On the Distribution and Reference of Empty Pronouns', *Linguistic Inquiry* 15(4): 531-574.

Jin, O. (2002). 'The War of a Fish', in *Award-winning Short Stories*. Yinchuan: Ningxia People's Press.

Li, C.N. and Thompson, S.A. (1979) 'Third-person pronouns and zero-anaphora in Chinese discourse', in *Syntax and Semantics: Discourse and Syntax*. T. Givon (ed.) New York: Academic Press.

Li, W. (2005) *Topic Chains in Chinese: A Discourse Analysis and Applications in Language Teaching*. Muenchen: LINCOM Europa.

Longacre, R.E. (1979) 'The paragraph as a grammatical unit', in *Syntax and Semantics: Discourse and Syntax*. T. Givón (ed.) New York: Academic Press.

Ma, B.S. (2002). 'Ha Yidao', in *Award-winning Short Stories*. Yinchuan: Ningxia People's Press.

Oberauer, K. (2002) 'Access to Information in Working Memory: Exploring the Focus of Attention', *Journal of Experimental Psychology: Learning, Memory, and Cognition* 28(3): 411–421.

Pu, M.-M. (1997) 'Zero anaphora and grammatical relations in Mandarin', in *Grammatical Relations: Typological Studies in Language 35*. T. Givón (ed.) Amsterdam: John Benjamins.

Pu, M.-M. (2011) *Discourse Anaphora: A Cognitive-Functional Approach*. LINCOM studies in theoretical linguistics 47. München: LINCOM Academic Publishers.

Tomlin, R.S. and Pu, M-M. (1991) 'The Management of Reference in Mandarin Discourse', *Cognitive Linguistics* 2(1): 65-93.

Tsao, F.F. (1990) *A Functional Study of Topic in Chinese: The First Step towards Discourse*. Taipei: Student Book Co.

van Dijk, T. and Kintsch, W. (1983) *Strategies in Discourse Comprehension*. New York: Academic Press.

Part IV
Pragmatic aspect of Chinese discourse

13
Politeness and impoliteness in Chinese discourse

Dániel Z. Kádár

Introduction

Politeness and impoliteness can be defined in many (often significantly different) ways. Since politeness research has become one of the most popular areas in pragmatics (see an overview in Culpeper et al., 2017), it would be unproductive to attempt to claim that there is a single authoritative definition of these phenomena, and this chapter provides a simple and relatively broad working definition for politeness and impoliteness, in order to aid the reader:

> *Essentially, politeness is not limited to conventional expressions by means of which polite intentions are indicated, or which display the status of the addressee, but it also encompasses all kinds of interactional behaviour through which one indicates that one takes the feelings of the other as to how they want to be treated in account. In a similar fashion, impoliteness covers interactional behaviour through which offence is caused.*

Readers with further interest in technical definitions of (im)politeness are advised to consult Kádár and Haugh (2013).

Politeness and impoliteness have been stereotypically regarded as a key aspect of Chinese language and discourse. As Pan and Kádár (2011) argue, when it comes to the Chinese, observers tend to describe interactional practices in extremes, either as overtly polite or impolite. It is obvious that these are simply stereotypes, and many 'lay' language users – both cultural insiders and outsiders – tend to describe politeness and impoliteness (henceforth '(im)politeness') in terms of some stereotypes across languages and cultures. Yet, when it comes to Chinese, there is such a contradiction between the above-mentioned lay stereotypes that one cannot afford simply to ignore them as 'ordinary' culturally-situated perceptions of interpersonal behavior. The Chinese are often either represented (or represent themselves) as 'super-polite' or as surprisingly rude by Western standards. This is all the more the case because these stereotypes dominate metadiscourses surrounding instances of culture shock that emerge in encounters between Chinese and foreigners (Loi and Pierce, 2015): retrospective accounts of Chinese interactional behavior (i.e. metadiscourse) tend to describe the Chinese as either a rude mass of people who ignore others, or as extremely generous and nice. It is only sufficient here to consider discussions

Dániel Z. Kádár

on Chinese tourists, and foreign tourists' experiences in China. In such accounts, Chinese interpersonal behavior tends to be represented by using extremes (see e.g. Siu et al., 2013 as an interesting example). In addition, the Chinese tend to describe themselves in a similar fashion, as either inheritors of an ancient (and often mystified) system of politeness, or in very critical terms (cf. Pan and Kádár, 2011). For instance, many Chinese newspaper headlines have been published on the 'intolerable' public behavior of Chinese masses in encounters with foreigners. As this chapter points out, these stereotypes can be pinned down to the specific history of Chinese (im)politeness. It is due to the specific development of Chinese (im)politeness that there is a cluster of seemingly contradictory norms of Chinese (im)politeness.

To explain these contradictions, along with a historical overview, a summary of Chinese discourse and (im)politeness is needed to examine Chinese academic 'metadiscourse(s)' *on* (im)politeness. More specifically, as Chinese academic discourses on politeness have a long history and also have had significant influence on (and received similar influence from) Western academia, perhaps no account of Chinese (im)politeness can be complete without an overview of the history of such academic discourses. Another point that deserves attention in an overview of this scope is the way in which the field is currently developing: research on this area has recently ventured into highly innovative areas.

Note that the present chapter does not transliterate examples by using the Latin *pinyin* alphabet, but uses *pinyin* only for in-text words and expressions. In addition, due to its historical focus, this chapter uses traditional characters. It is also important to point out that this chapter pursues an interest in the phenomenon of (im)politeness instead of 'face'. Conventionally, in particular in politeness research before the 2000s, face – a technical term that denotes a person's self-appreciation – and politeness had been perceived as inseparable phenomena. This perception comes from the high-impact framework of Brown and Levinson (1987), according to which the main goal of politeness is to minimize threats to the interlocutor's face, hence conveying polite intention. However, recent research such as Bargiela-Chiappini's (2003) authoritative work has revealed that face and (im)politeness are not inherently related, and politeness and face research have become independent areas (cf. Kádár and Haugh, 2013). Yet, as 'face' is an etic construct in Western academia with roots in Chinese culture, and also because it has played a key role in Chinese academic discussions on (im)politeness, this chapter discusses this notion as an important academic metalexeme, i.e. a technical term used about (perceptions of) discursive behavior.

The history of Chinese (im)politeness

Until approximately the 20th century, the Chinese had no equivalent for the English metalexeme 'politeness' – this is not a surprising fact if one considers that in many European cultures equivalents of 'politeness' are relatively new from the historical pragmatician's point of view (cf. Kádár and Culpeper, 2010). The Chinese used the word *li* 礼/禮 in reference to behavior that covers – amongst other things – interpersonal behavior; this word can roughly be translated as 'ritual', and it has a broad, semi-religious meaning, as the following extract from the Han Dynasty (206 B.C. – 220 A.D.) character etymological dictionary, the *Shuowen jiezi* 說文解字 illustrates:

禮，[...] 所以事神致福也。
Li [is...] through which spirits are served [in order to] give wealth.

*(*Liji 禮記, Reprint Edition: 4)

That is, the interpretation of *li* was originally 'religious rite or sacrifice' in ancient times. From many dictionaries, e.g. the *Guhanyu dacidian* 古漢語大辭典 (2000: 1899), it becomes clear that *li* gained its later '(linguistic) politeness' meaning from this original interpretation: through a sacrificial act, humans express respect (*jing* 敬) towards the spirits.

Such descriptions of *li* date back to ancient times, and *li* itself is one of the key principles of Confucianism: it is pertinent here to refer to the *Book of Rites* (*Liji* 礼记 'The Book of Rites'), which is a Classic of the Confucian Canon. However, it is rather ambitious to claim that politeness research (on the concept of *li* as a native lexeme *for* politeness) itself has a 1,000 years of history, as some Chinese sources such as Yuan (1994) argues. These sources relatively rarely discuss *li* beyond a particular aspect of politeness behavior, namely, ritual and ceremonial interaction in a limited number of institutional scenarios. While such discussions boosted the occurrence of etiquette literature in a narrower sense – i.e. the description of etiquette rules in more ordinary settings – such literature occurred only in the second millennium B.C. (Kádár, 2007), and it was the 20th century when the Chinese coined the modern word *limao* 礼貌 for interpersonal politeness.

It was also only the 20th century when Chinese scholars started to conduct academic research on interpersonal discursive notions, such as the above-mentioned concept/metalexeme of Chinese 'face'. Research on 'face' started with Hu's (1944) ground-breaking paper, which was soon followed by another related publication by Yang (1945). These studies were far more revolutionary than one would normally assume. Before Hu and Yang, few native Chinese wrote on 'face' because, in Confucianist thinking, which traditionally emphasizes morality and rituality over emotions, the emotive-psychological concept of 'face' is regarded as relatively 'unimportant' (see Zhai, 1994). In terms of technical definitions of 'politeness' (Section 1), the concept of *li* is relatively loosely related to politeness, insofar as one interprets this phenomenon as a way of constructing and maintaining interpersonal relationships in ordinary (non-ceremonial) settings. It was roughly the 1930s when Chinese 'face' received wider quasi-scholarly attention beyond in-passim descriptions by native scholars and foreign travelers. First, in 1932, the famous writer Lin Yutang 林語堂 (1895–1976) published an essay with the title *Lian yu fazhi* 臉與法治 ('Face and Ruling'). This essay was followed in 1934 by another essay, *Qiejie-ting zawen* 且介亭雜文 ('Various Essays from the Qiejie Pavilion'), by another literary celebrity Lu Xun 魯迅 (1881–1936). Both Lin's and Lu's essays are heavily loaded with cultural nationalism, and they introduce 'face' as a national value of the Chinese people. It is exactly because of their nationalism that these essays are most interesting documents because they reflect a then-new worldview in China, according to which 'face' is a potential cohesive social force that was supposed to be able to save the Chinese nation from the decline caused by the 19th century colonization of the country. During the period of 'Westernization' (Ruhi and Kádár, 2011) 'face', for the first time, received attention alongside *li* 禮 ('politeness ritual') and other traditional notions of socio-morality. Lu Xun wrote the following noteworthy words on *face*:

面子是中國精神的綱領。
'Face' (*mianzi*) is the quintessence of the Chinese spirit.

Turning back to Hu (1944) and Yang (1945), it is an interesting fact that these works on the so-far unexplored 'face' phenomenon were published only a decade after the two nationalistic and political essays.

When it comes to the history of Chinese (im)politeness, one needs to treat claims for historical legacy critically. This, however, does not mean that politeness was insignificant in historical China – i.e. imperial China before the birth of the Republic in 1911. It is simply that a) instead of using Classical sources on *li*, the operation of historical Chinese politeness (and impoliteness) can be more reliably reconstructed by researchers looking into corpora of vernacular (in

Chinese: *jindai hanyu* 近代汉语) sources, such as novels, which represent interactions between ordinary people. Second, it is an ambitious attempt to define exactly how long historical Chinese politeness can be traced back in history. What can be argued with certainty is that by the Song Dynasty (960–1279) the Chinese had a system of interpersonal politeness (and impoliteness) behavior, which was in use until 1911. In what follows, let us overview the main characteristics of this system.

As Gu's (1990) ground-breaking study points out, the arguably most salient historical Chinese norm of politeness behavior was the notion that one needs to denigrate oneself and elevate the other. This norm is prevalent in discursive practices that one can reconstruct by using historical Chinese written sources. It is important to refer here to the historical pragmatic argument (Jucker, 2008) that using historical data is inherently problematic to some extent, in the respect that any historical sources that we use only represent a fragment of colloquial language use, and usually were filtered through the interpretation of the learned elite. Thus, arguing that the Chinese only expressed politeness through practices of elevation and denigration would be – to say the least – overly ambitious. When it comes to the long history of Chinese discourse and politeness one needs to admit some defeat: compared with the immense amount of Chinese written sources, we know very little about the supposedly complex ways through which the Chinese built up and maintained their interpersonal relationships via language use. On the other hand, the study of historical evidence allows us, at least, to gain insight into the dominant norms of interpersonal interaction, and it is safe to argue that these norms are centered on the notion that one needs to symbolically display one's own and the other's social status vis-à-vis denigration and elevation. 'Symbolic' means that one not only acknowledges the rank of the other, but also symbolically elevates it on a social scale, and at the same time denigrates one's own rank; this symbolic element is what conveys the message of politeness. At the same time, this system was highly indexical (Agha, 2007), in the respect that the interactants were normatively constrained to undertake such symbolic elevation/denigration within the boundaries of their actual social status.

The symbolic elevation/denigration character of historical Chinese politeness manifested itself in the form of a large lexicon of forms of address and self-address, by means of which the speaker denigrated him/herself and everything that belonged to them (including e.g. family members and objects) and elevated the other and the other person's belongings. For example, the term *xiaoren* 小人 (lit. 'small person', i.e. 'this worthless person') denigrates the speaker and *gaojun* 高君 ('high lord') elevates the speech partner. *Xiaonü* 小女 (lit. 'small woman', i.e. 'worthless daughter') denigrates the speaker's daughter and *qianjin* 千金 (lit. 'thousand gold', i.e. 'venerable daughter') elevates the addressee's daughter. Interestingly, indirect honorific terms of address also exist in reference to inanimate entities such as the house of the speaker/writer (e.g. *hanshe* 寒舍, lit. 'cold lodging') and that of the addressee (e.g. *guifu* 贵府, lit. 'precious court').

No quantitative study has been carried out so far to estimate the number of such honorific forms in Chinese, but it can be argued without the risk of exaggeration that there were several thousand terms of address (see Ji, 2000) – although it is fair to add that many of these forms existed only in writing, and the majority of the population supposedly used a very limited lexical inventory. This extensive number was supposedly due to the above-discussed constraint of undertaking symbolic elevation/denigration within the boundaries of one's actual social status: as the author of this chapter pointed out in Kádár (2007), members of various social classes made use of specific inventories of elevating/denigrating forms of (self-)address when they spoke to people with their own status, and another set when they interacted with people of higher social standing (denigration and elevation did not apply for interaction with lower-ranking interactants).

In order to illustrate the discursive operation of elevating forms of address and denigrating self-address, it is worth citing here a number of examples from historical Chinese vernacular sources. Owing to limitation of space, these examples do not illustrate how these forms of (self-) address operated within and across social levels; for a more detailed discussion on this latter point see Pan and Kádár (2011).

這家童去了半載。一日回來，見了小塘說：「小人到家把書信與大爺看了 . . . 」(【升仙傳】第三回)
This young male servant was away for a half year. One day he came back and when he saw Little Tang he said: "This humble person came home in order to give this letter to Your Highness . . ."

(Shengxian zhuan, Chapter 3)

賈珍感謝不盡，只說：「待服滿後，親帶小犬到府叩謝。」(【紅樓夢】第三十回)
Jia Zhen was expressing his gratitude endlessly, saying: "Please wait until the time of the mourning is over and [I will] personally bring [my] worthless son to [your] noble dwelling to respectfully say thanks to you."

(Honglou meng, Chapter 30)

這日正有親友鄰里來慶賀，外面家人來回說，說有國清寺方丈性空，給員外送來一份厚禮，親來賀喜。員外 接進來。性空說：「員外大喜。令郎公可平安？」(【濟公全傳】第一回)
On this day the relatives and neighbors came to congratulate; a family member who was receiving the guests said that Xingkong Abbot of the Guoqing Temple came to congratulate in person and brought a generous celebration gift to the squire. The squire invited him in. Xingkong said: "[I wish you] great happiness, Squire. Is the Young Lord in good health?"

(Jigong quan-zhuan, Chapter 1)

In the first example the speaker refers to himself as *xiaoren* 小人 ('this worthless person') and elevates his interlocutor as *daye* 大爺 (lit. 'great grandfather', i.e. 'Your Highness'); this extract exemplifies the use of direct elevating/denigrating forms of address. In the second extract, the speaker refers to his son as *xiaoquan* 小犬 (lit. 'small dog', i.e. 'my worthless son'), which illustrates indirect self-denigration, i.e. when one denigrates one's intimates (and, consequently, oneself). Furthermore, the speaker refers to the other's home as *fu* 府 (lit. 'court', i.e. noble dwelling), which is an example of the elevation of a non-animate belonging of the recipient (his home). In the third example the Abbot refers to the addressee's son as *linglang-gong* 令郎公 (lit. 'ruling young lord', 'Young Lord'), which is thus an example of the indirect elevation of the addressee's family member.

Owing to the important role of family in Chinese society, this system of direct and indirect honorific (self-)addressing had different lexicons for familial and non-familial settings. That is, different forms of address were used towards family members and non-family addressees, and the category of familial forms of address also had different subcategories: patriarchal and matriarchal relatives, as well as the relatives of one's spouse, were addressed/referred to by different lexicons.

The system of historical Chinese honorific forms of address are summarized by Table 13.1, cited from Pan and Kádár (2011):

Dániel Z. Kádár

Table 13.1 Historical Chinese forms of (self-)address

Term of address	Example
direct elevating	*daren* 大人 (lit. 'great man', Your Honor)
direct denigrating	*xiaoren* 小人 (lit. 'small man', this humble person)
indirect elevating (ref. animated entity)	*zun-furen* 尊夫人 (lit. 'revered lady', your wife)
indirect denigrating (ref animated entity)	*yuqi* 愚妻 (lit. 'foolish wife', humble wife)
indirect elevating (ref. unanimated entity)	*guifu* 貴府 (lit. 'precious court', your home); *yayi* 牙意 (lit. 'refined opinion', your opinion)
indirect denigrating (ref. unanimated entity)	*hanshe* 寒舍 (lit. 'cold lodging', my humble home); *biyi* 鄙意 (lit. 'humble opinion')
quasi-familial elevating	*xianxiong* 賢兄 (lit. 'wise elder brother')
quasi-familial denigrating	*yuxiong* 愚兄 (lit. 'this foolish elder brother of yours')

It is worth noting in passing that this large inventory of self- and other-address had its rude equivalent, even though there is significantly less information available about such forms. For instance, one could denigrate a Buddhist monk by calling him *tulü* 禿驢 ('hairless donkey'), hence denigrating his social status, and refer to oneself as *laoye* 老爺 ('this venerable gentleman'), which is a form used by default towards bureaucrats, and in the self-elevating use, it symbolically increases the speaker's claimed social status.

Along with terms of address, another important historical lexical tool for elevation and denigration is the group of honorific verb forms, i.e. forms that deferentially describe the actions of the speaker and the addressee. The following extract illustrates the operation of these verbal forms:

數行奉佈，希即命駕！(【雪鴻軒尺牘】與謝丙南)
[I write these] few lines to respectfully inform [you of this matter, and I] sincerely hope [you will] immediately prepare for travel.
 (*Letters from Snow Swan Retreat, Letter to Xie Bingnan*)

In this letter subscription the author uses the forms *fengbu* 奉佈 (lit. 'offering a declaration respectfully with two hands', i.e. respectfully inform somebody about a matter) and *mingjia* 命駕 (lit. 'ordering chariot', i.e. prepare for travel). The first form deferentially lowers the status of the speaker/writer, while the second one elevates that of the addressee (a relatively poor person) by deferentially comparing his departure to that of a high-ranking person who gives orders to his chariot driver(s) before a journey.

Elevating/denigrating verb forms are less frequent in the data studied than terms of address. This is perhaps partly because the use of verb forms necessitated a good command of Classical Chinese literature: explorations of vernacular texts seem to suggest that honorific verbs were popular among the educated elite, while in the data studied, lower-educated speakers rarely apply these forms. Another, related, reason is that these forms are considerably more frequent in letters and other monologic genres than in novels and similar dialogic genres. Due to the 'written style' of these forms, in dialogic interactions they are used only in relatively formal contexts or interactions of significant power difference.

If one examines the history of Chinese politeness, it becomes evident that this system largely disappeared during the 20th century: if one examines modern Chinese communication, one can find isolated lexical items with roots in historical Chinese, but as a system denigration/elevation lost its lexical importance. Historical research (see Pan and Kádár, 2011) has revealed that this perhaps unprecedented change was due to the fact that the norms of historical Chinese politeness were subject to major challenges. That is, after China became a semi-colony during the 19th century, the Chinese had become increasingly critical of their historical heritage, and following the birth of the Republic of China a large portion of the archaic lexicon disappeared from everyday language use. Since the very essence of the historical system is the emphasis of differences between the interactants, it is a logical consequence that it was strongly criticized during modern reform attempts. Also, with the disappearance of ancient differences between certain social classes, historical norms of politeness – which aimed to maintain this order – had to disappear. Thus it can also be argued that historical Chinese politeness, due to the fact that it embodied Confucian class ideologies, was vulnerable to large-scale ideological and subsequent social changes during the 20th century.

While such ideological changes bear the responsibility for the gap between historical and contemporary Chinese politeness, this historical change raises an interesting question: Chinese seems to represent a unique case, in that elevating/denigrating expressions of deference did not entirely disappear from other Asian languages that were subjects to major ideological reforms, such as North Korean (cf. Anderson, 1948). Honorifics and other historical forms of deference are not disappearing in the North Korean language – rather, they have even become intensified in a specific but recurring discursive domain, namely the exaltation of the Kims who have ruled the country in the fashion of a royal dynasty. Also, while there is not much information available on the speech style of ordinary North Koreans, it is certain that honorifics and other forms of deference are quite popular in official interactions in the North Korean Communist Party. This fact makes it necessary to consider the question as to how ideological changes could cause major changes in Chinese politeness. That is, without denying the influence of ideologies, we need to look into the characteristics of Chinese verbal expressions that represented the norms of historical Chinese politeness.

The examination of this problem reveals that the resistance of languages such as Korean – and the vulnerability of Chinese – is due to *grammaticalization* (or the lack of it). In Korean and Japanese, honorifics are not confined to the word level as in Chinese but they are systematically built into the grammar. Speakers of Korean and Japanese (two languages with somewhat similar honorific systems) can eliminate many ostentatious (or 'feudal') expressions from everyday speech, but it is not easy to discard 'common' honorifics in these languages because honorific forms and inflections are profoundly built in as a well-defined subsystem of the grammar (Lee, 1990). So, certain interactional situations necessitate the use of 'proper' honorific inflection and deferential forms, and deferential style is thus not necessarily a volitional choice (Ide, 1989).

Norms and practices of Chinese (im)politeness

The contrasting stereotypes that surround Chinese (im)politeness become logical if one considers these stereotypes in light of historical developments: the lack of a once-profound honorific system and related phenomena explains why cultural outsiders find Chinese discursive practices strikingly void of 'traditional' elements. However, this is just one side of the coin: if one examines modern Chinese norms of politeness, it becomes evident that in modern China there are various interactional norms that differ from Western understandings of politeness (although it also is problematic to make generalizations about the 'West'). Such differences do not imply that the Chinese are any 'less polite' than others. It is relevant here to recall the working definition of politeness, as a phenomenon that implies taking the other's perceived feelings as to how (s)he wants to be treated into account. An overview of modern Chinese politeness reveals that this sense of being polite to the other applies to a different cluster of interpersonal relationships in China than in the West. It is also worth noting that the norms of Chinese politeness have changed a lot due to the active Westernization of the country (see He and Wie, 2016), and many of the conventional cross-cultural differences described here have disappeared to some extent.

As Pan's (2000) authoritative study reveals, many of the Sino-Western discursive practices in terms of politeness are due to the Chinese normative distinction between inside and outside relationships. Different rules are applied in an inside as opposed to an outside relationship when choosing politeness behavior. Ingroup members are treated with elaborate face-exaggerating behavior showing respect or involvement according to the hierarchical structure between the interlocutors. Outsiders are treated with an even higher degree of respect (although the degree of this respect may change according to a person's country of origin and other factors), but only as far as they are related in some sense to the speaker or their group – e.g. if someone visits a Chinese university as a guest lecturer, they can expect to be treated with extreme reverence as an outsider. On the other hand, by default, the Western moral value of treating strangers with respect does not straightforwardly apply to Chinese culture: one is not supposed to invest energy into communicating with or being nice to strangers. While many Westerners find the Chinese extremely *haoke* 好客, i.e. friendly towards strangers, a Chinese person is normally not expected to be polite in stranger relationships that occasion the moral perception for the need of 'civility' in western cultures. For example, if someone steps on another person's foot on a Chinese train, one may not apologize (unless the other gets injured). In a similar fashion, one does not have to wave hands as a sign of thank you for a car if the driver lets you cross the road. This lack of connectedness to strangers – which existed in historical China as well (Kádár, 2007) – is a logical way of social life in a country of China's size, and it has to be noted again that it is only a norm, which individuals may or may not follow, depending on their social status, education, habitus and so on. Yet, it is important to be aware of this norm (and related moral implications) because it is the main motivating factor behind the above-discussed contrasting stereotypes.

When it comes to the practices of modern Chinese politeness, the main question is what Chinese discourse offers instead of honorifics and respectful communication – the rest of this section focuses on this problem. In modern Chinese, deferential forms of address have remained relatively important in certain areas of life such as business, in which work titles express deference. In contemporary China, there are many fewer terms of address in comparison with historical times, and their application is governed by complex unwritten rules. Most importantly, many Chinese try to avoid using formal terms of address when interacting with strangers in contexts that necessitate some deference. For instance, when asking one's way, (a) is preferred to (b):

(a) 請問，辦公室在二樓嗎？
 Please let me ask, is the office on the second floor?
(b) 先生，請問，辦公室在二樓嗎？
 Sir/Mister, please let me ask, is the office on the second floor?

While it is possible to address a male stranger as *xiansheng* 先生 'mister', speakers of Chinese may usually avoid such an address form, which may count as over-polite for a simple question.

In addition to forms of address used towards group outsiders, familial or kinship terms of address have always been an important inventory in Chinese vocatives, partly because of the value and importance placed on family and familial relationships in Chinese culture (see Liu, 1988). Kinship terms of address are often used with non-kin and close relationships such as those of close friends and neighbors. In addition, kinship terms of address gained popularity in informal social interactions, as expressions conveying a friendly and polite attitude.

Along with forms of address, particles (e.g. *ya* 呀, *a* 啊, *aiya* 哎呀) play a special role in politeness practice in contemporary Chinese. Lee-Wong's (2000) empirical study shows that some sentence final particles in Mandarin can be used as politeness hedges to reduce the illocutionary force of direct requests.

Another key aspect of Chinese interactional politeness behavior can be captured in the order of speaking and turn-taking. In the Chinese context, interactants who are acquainted with each other, such as in the workplace, among friends, and in a family situation, need to observe the unspoken rule of who speaks first in a given situation. For example, in a dyadic interaction such as student-teacher interaction, the one in a lower position initiates the greeting, but not the topic of conversation. When a student and a teacher meet on campus, the student normally greets the teacher first. The teacher returns the greeting, but the teacher is the person who introduces a new topic in the conversation (Scollon and Scollon, 1991).

In addition to the above manifestations of politeness, a fundamental aspect of Chinese discursive politeness is the employment of small talk (e.g., conversation on topics other than those related to the intended action). Zhang (1995) noticed that small talk was a central component of Chinese indirectness when redressing a face-threatening-act such as a request. Small talk even became part of ritual greetings in daily life. For example, expressions like *Chi le ma?* 吃了嗎？ ('Have you eaten?') and *Ni qu nar?* 你去那兒？ ('Where are you going?') tend to be interpreted as conventionalized formulae in small talk, rather than genuine questions. The following example from the monograph of Pan and Kádár (2011) illustrates the operation of small talk; here a Chinese professor gave her name card to one of the authors, Yuling Pan. Pan looked at the card and read out her university "Wuhan Technology University", the professor said:

對，我是從武漢來的。你下次回國，一定來武漢玩。
Yes, I am from Wuhan. When you go visit China next time, definitely visit Wuhan.

One can notice a few interesting points here. First, the professor did not use any honorific terms or deferential expressions. Instead, she used a phatic expression (an invitation) to show her friendliness and politeness. This conventionalized invitation serves the function of an English polite expression 'Very nice to meet you' in this context.

It is beyond the scope of this chapter to overview practices of modern Chinese politeness beyond this detail, but this summary is sufficient to reveal that stereotypes about 'rudeness' in Chinese culture should be treated critically, even in cases when such stereotypes represent Chinese metadiscursive trends. As Kádár and Haugh (2013) point out, in many cultures people tend to moralizingly complain about the 'lack' of politeness in society, and Chinese is not an exception to this trend. This does not mean that there is no rudeness in Chinese and that cultural insider/outsider stereotypes are completely unfounded. Apart from the complexity of discursive practices due to the above-discussed insider/outsider distinction, in China there is an actual perceived social need for educating about politeness behavior. In addition, in Chinese there is a relatively rich lexicon of swearwords, which is largely ignored by the technical literature. There might be several reasons for this lack, and the most likely explanation is the native perception that the study of such expressions, and impoliteness in a broader sense, would reflect negatively on Chinese people (see also Section 5).

The history of Chinese (im)politeness research

(Im)politeness represents an important aspect of Chinese discourse; but in a similar fashion, discourse on Chinese (im)politeness, i.e. academic metadiscourse triggered by the study of Chinese data represents a fundamental contribution to the research of (im)politeness (see Hyland, 2005 on this discursive understanding of metadiscourse). This section overviews this point, by highlighting three studies, which have been selected predominantly on the basis of their academic impact on the field of Chinese sociopragmatics and discourse studies.

The concept of *li* received some attention in the cultural anthropological sinological research of the 20th century (Liu, 2003). Apart from anthropologists, Chinese linguistic politeness has been also touched on by various linguists such as Lü (1985). The first genuinely influential work from the politeness researcher's point-of-view was written by Yueguo Gu (1990). Gu's study, which has remained the most widely cited publication on Chinese politeness to date, made a ground-breaking dual contribution to the field. First, it is perhaps the first pragmatics-based research that overviews Chinese politeness per se in it describes the concept of self-denigration and other-elevation by using Chinese data in an accessible way for readers who are not fluent in the language. Second, it contributed to then-ongoing discussions on the applicability of Brown and Levinson's (1987) politeness framework. In order to understand this contribution, it is worth noting that Brown and Levinson (1987) argued that politeness can be described across languages and cultures by using universal concepts such as face and conflict avoidance. This argument has gained popularity and various scholars used culture-specific data (including data drawn from Chinese and Japanese) to approve the validity of the Brown and Levinsonian framework. Gu (1990), however, challenged this then-dominant framework by relying on Leech's (1983) approach, which captures politeness behavior in (culturally) dominant maxims. He argued that Chinese cannot be described by using universals, as the phenomenon of elevation and denigration is saliently different from Western norms of politeness. While it is possible to question the validity of this argument, considering that denigration/elevation exists across languages and cultures, including historical Western cultures (see an overview in Kádár and Culpeper, 2010), Gu pointed out one of the major weaknesses of the Brown and Levinsonian framework and has generated a major debate on culture-specificity in the field.

Another important contribution to the field is Mao's (1994) seminal study. Mao revisited Brown and Levinson (1987) from an alternative angle, by focusing on their concept of 'face' as a universal motivator behind politeness behavior. Mao pointed out that using such a concept in a Western interpretation is problematic when it comes to cultures such as the Chinese, in which 'face' can be expressed by using various metalexemes, such as *mianzi* 面子 for 'front' or 'light' face, which can be lost without a major interactional crisis, and *lian* 脸 for 'back' and 'heavy' face, which cannot be lost without serious personal and interpersonal effect. Along with contributing to politeness theory, Mao's work has generated a long-standing interest in metalexical research in the field.

Chen's (2001) cross-cultural research revealed an interesting, and possibly universal characteristic of politeness (partly) by using data from Chinese culture, namely, that politeness is not necessarily directed only to someone else, but at the same time, it also helps the speaker to build up and maintain a particular self-image. While this work does not criticize the Brown and Levinsonian framework, it brings another noteworthy innovation to the field, by pointing out that understandings of politeness as an other-oriented phenomenon may be influenced by Western epistemologies.

Current areas of research

After the 2000s, there have been various attempts to integrate Chinese politeness research into 'mainstream' politeness research, by using Chinese data as a testing ground for Western theories. It is worth pointing out Haugh and Hinze (2003) amongst such attempts. By using metapragmatic data drawn from Chinese and Japanese cultures, this paper points out the complexities of theorizing politeness in East-Asian languages and the importance of metapragmatics in such theorization. The previously cited monograph by Pan and Kádár (2011) is an attempt to overview Chinese politeness by using frameworks rooted in post-2000 politeness research. Kádár (2012) use Chinese data to contribute to ongoing theoretical discussions in politeness research.

One of the most significant areas in the field to explore is Chinese politeness in intercultural communication. This topic has played a central role in various high-impact publications, such as Spencer-Oatey's (2000/2008) edited volume, and the authoritative work of Gao and Ting-Toomey (1998). Yet, as Kádár and Pan (2010) point out, many gaps have remained in this area, which has become increasingly important, considering the global role of China in politics and finance. In particular, there has been insufficient focus on Chinese discourse and (im)politeness in the post-2010 period. Although a number of scholars like He and Wei (2016) have addressed this issue, it still remains a relatively gray area. A forthcoming book project by Wang and Kádár (2019) aims to fill this gap.

Another dominant area of research has been the study of Chinese (im)politeness in various channels and modes of interaction, such as computer-mediated communication. This research has been initiated supposedly by Ma's (1996) early study. Since then Chinese (im)politeness and internet has become a highly popular area, even though research on Chinese impoliteness – which is perhaps more prevalent than politeness when it comes to the realm of the internet (Locher, 2010) – has remained understudied. Further research is needed to examine the characteristics of Chinese impoliteness across various modes of interpersonal communication. It is hoped that the ground-breaking work of scholars in Mainland China – where this area has recently gained momentum – will fill this knowledge-gap. Representative research in this area include Chaoqun Xie's work (currently co-editing *Internet Pragmatics* with Fransisco Yus), and Wei Ren's research (who has delivered noteworthy research on Chinese e-language; see Ren ed. forthcoming).

There are various sociocultural factors that have been actively studied in the field, such as gender and age, in terms of politeness. Chinese gender and politeness has been studied not only by feminist scholars but also by linguists, e.g. Farris (2000). In a similar fashion, scholars such as He (2012) have studied the ways in which age and generational gaps affect the perception and use of politeness in Chinese society. Yet, considering the immense size of Chinese society, there is clearly a need for more research on the relationship between (im)politeness and social variables.

Acknowledgments

I would like to express my gratitude to the two Referees who have provided extremely useful and constructive feedback on this chapter. I am also indebted to Chris Shei for being a wonderful and supporting editor. I would like to acknowledge the research support of MTA Lendulet

(LP2017–5) research grant of the Hungarian Academy of Sciences, which has made it possible for me to carry out the present research.

References

English references

Agha, A. (2007) *Language and Social Relations*. Cambridge: Cambridge University Press.
Anderson, P.S. (1948) 'Korean Language Reform', *The Modern Language Journal* 32: 508–511.
Bargiela-Chiappini, F. (2003) 'Face and Politeness: New (Insights) for Old (Concepts)', *Journal of Pragmatics* 35(10/11): 1453–1469.
Brown, P. and Levinson, S.C. (1987) *Politeness: Some Universals in Language Usage*. Cambridge: Cambridge University Press.
Chen, R. (2001) 'Self-politeness: A Proposal', *Journal of Pragmatics* 33(1): 87–106.
Culpeper, J., Haugh M. and Kádár, D.Z. (2017) 'Introduction', in *The Palgrave Handbook of Linguistic (Im)politeness*. J. Culpeper, M. Haugh and D.Z. Kádár (eds.) Basingstoke: Palgrave Macmillan.
Farris, C.S.P. (2000) 'Cross-sex peer Conflict and the Discursive Production of Gender in a Chinese Preschool in Taiwan', *Journal of Pragmatics* 32(5): 539–568.
Gao, G. and Ting-Toomey, S. (1998) *Communicating Effectively with the Chinese*. Thousand Oaks: Sage.
Gu, Y. (1990) 'Politeness Phenomena in Modern Chinese', *Journal of Pragmatics* 14: 237–257.
Haugh, M. and Hinze, C. (2003) 'A Metalinguistic Approach to Deconstructing the Concepts of "face" and "politeness" in Chinese, English and Japanese', *Journal of Pragmatics* 35(10/11): 1581–1611.
He, Y. (2012) 'Different Generations, Different Face? A Discursive Approach to Naturally Occurring Compliment Responses in Chinese', *Journal of Politeness Research* 8(1): 29–51.
He, Z.R. and Wei, R. (2016) 'Current Address Behavior in China', *East Asian Pragmatics* 1(2): 163–180.
Hu, H. (1944) 'The Chinese Concept of "face"', *American Anthropologist* 46(1): 45–64.
Hyland, Ken. (2005) 'Metadiscourse', in *The International Encyclopedia of Language and Social Interaction*. London: Wiley. pp. 1–11.
Ide, S. (1989) 'Formal Forms and Discernment: Two Neglected Aspects of Universals of Linguistic Politeness', *Multilingua* 8/2–3: 223–248.
Jucker, A.H. (2008) 'Historical Pragmatics', *Language and Linguistics Compass* 2(5): 894–906.
Kádár, D.Z. (2007) *Terms of (Im)Politeness: On the Communicational Properties of Traditional Chinese Terms of Address*. Budapest: Eotvos Lorand University Press.
Kádár, D.Z. (2012) 'Historical Chinese Politeness and Rhetoric: A Case-study of Epistolary Refusals', *Journal of Politeness Research* 8(1): 93–110.
Kádár, D.Z. and Culpeper, J. (2010) 'Introduction', in J. Culpeper and D.Z. Kádár (eds.) *Historical (Im)Politeness*. Bern: Peter Lang. pp. 9–36.
Kádár, D.Z. and Haugh, M. (2013) *Understanding Politeness*. Cambridge: Cambridge University Press.
Kádár, D.Z. and Pan, Y. (2010) 'Chinese Face and Im/politeness: An Introduction', *Journal of Politeness Research* 8(1): 1–10.
Lee, H.-B. (1990) 'Differences in Language Use between North and South Korean', *International Journal of the Sociology of Language* 82: 71–86.
Lee-Wong, S.M. (2000) *Politeness and Face in Chinese Culture*. Frankfurt am Main: Peter Lang.
Leech, Geoffrey. (1983) *Principles of Pragmatics*. London: Longman.
Liu, M.X. (2003) 'A Historical Overview of Anthropology in China', *Anthropologist* 5(4): 217–223.
Locher, M. (2010) 'Introduction: Politeness and Impoliteness in Computer-mediated Communication', *Journal of Politeness Research* 6: 1–5.
Loi, K-L. and Pierce, P.L. (2015) 'Exploring Perceived Tensions Arising from Tourist Behaviours in a Chinese Context', *Journal of Travel and Tourism Marketing* 32(1/2): 65–79.
Ma, R. (1996) 'Computer-mediated conversations as a new dimension of intercultural communication between East Asian and North American college students', in *Computer-mediated Communication: Linguistic, Social and Cross-cultural Perspectives*. S. Herring (ed.) Amsterdam: John Benjamins, 173–186.
Mao, L.M.R. (1994) 'Beyond Politeness Theory: "Face" Revisited and Renewed', *Journal of Pragmatics* 21(5): 451–486.
Pan, Y. (2000) *Politeness in Chinese Face-to-Face Behaviour*. Stamford: Ablex.
Pan, Y. and Kádár, D.Z. (2011) *Politeness in Historical and Contemporary Chinese*. London: Bloomsbury.

Ren, W. (ed.) (2017). *Special Issue of Discourse, Context and Media, Dedicated to Chinese*.
Ruhi, Ş. and Kádár, D. (2011) '"Face" across Historical Cultures: A Comparative Study of Turkish and Chinese', *Journal of Historical Pragmatics* 12(1–2): 25–48.
Scollon, R. and Scollon, S.W. (1991) 'Topic Confusion in English-Asian Discourse', *World Englishes* 10: 113–125.
Siu, G., Lee, Y.S. and Leung, D. (2013) 'Residents' Perceptions towards the "Chinese Tourists' Wave" in Hong Kong. An Exploratory Study', *Asia Pacific Journal of Tourism Research* 18(5): 446–463.
Spencer-Oatey, H. (ed.) (2000/2008) *Culturally Speaking: Culture, Communication and Politeness Theory*. London: Bloomsbury.
Wang, J. and Kádár, D.Z. (2019 forthcoming). *The Changing Faces of Im/Politeness in Modern Chinese*. Edinburgh: Edinburgh University Press.
Yang, M.C. (1945) *A Chinese Village: Taitou, Shantung Province*. New York: Columbia University Press. Kegan Paul reprint, 1967.
Zhang, Y.Y. (1995) 'Indirectness in Chinese requesting', in G. Kasper (ed.) *Pragmatics of Chinese as Native and Target Language*. Honolulu: University of Hawaii Press, 69–118.

Chinese references

Ji, C.H 吉常宏 (ed.). (2000) *Hanyu chengwei dacidian* 漢語稱謂大辭典 (*A Comprehensive Dictionary of Chinese Addressing Terms*). Shijiazhuang: Hebei jiaoyu chubanshe.
Liu, Z.F. 劉再復. (1988) *Chuangtong yu Zhongguoren* 傳統與中國人 (*Tradition and the Chinese*). Hong Kong: Joint Publishing.
Lü, S-X. 呂叔湘. (1985) *Jindai hanyu zhidaici* 近代漢語指代詞 (*The Pronouns of Vernacular Chinese*). Shanghai: Xuelin chubanshe.
Yuan, T. 袁庭棟. (1994) *Guren chengwei mantan* 古人稱謂漫談 (*An Introduction into Historical Address Forms*). Beijing: Zhonghua shuju.
Zhai, X. 翟学位. (1994) *Mianzi, renqing, guanxi-wang* 面子、人情、关系网 (*Face, Emotions and Connection-Networks*). Zhengzhou: He'nan renmin chubanshe.

14
Pragmatic markers in Chinese discourse

Guangwu Feng

Introduction

In Chinese, there is a class of linguistic expressions, which have been generally characterized as semantically non-truth-conditional and syntactically peripheral. Prototypical members are connectives like 所以 'so' (see Zhang, 2010; Tang, 2015). In some studies, (e.g. Feng, 2010), parenthetical expressions like 不幸的是 'unfortunately', and sentence-final particles like 了 *le* are also included. A multiple array of terms have been used for them, but it seems to be narrowing down to 'pragmatic markers'. Pragmatic markers (henceforth PMs) in English have been the subject of intense investigation, but a principled and systematic description of PMs in Chinese discourse has hitherto not been undertaken. This chapter attempts to do so.

Why 'pragmatic marker'?

'PM' and 'discourse marker' (and a variety of others) have been competing for roughly the same class of expressions. Fraser (1996) assigns each of them a different range of reference. On his account, the former is an umbrella term encompassing all linguistically encoded clues which do not contribute to the propositional content of the sentence but signal the speaker's potential communicative intentions. Under the umbrella are (i) basic markers (e.g., sentence mood and performative expressions) which signal more or less specifically the force of the basic message of the sentence, (ii) commentary markers (e.g., fortunately) which comment on some aspect of the basic message, (iii) parallel markers (e.g., titles, vocatives) which signal an entire message in addition to the basic message of the sentence, and (iv) discourse markers (e.g., therefore) which mark the relationship between the message they introduce and the foregoing message.

Following Fraser (1996, 1999, 2006), I take discourse markers (henceforth DMs) as a subset of PMs. But a DM is connective in nature, while a PM is not necessarily so. This agrees with the general understanding that a discourse is a unit of text consisting of more than one segment above sentence level, and a DM is a cohesive device functioning to create local or global coherence (see Schiffrin, 1987; Risselada and Spooren, 1998). I opt for the term 'PMs' for the linguistic expressions under scrutiny not merely because many of them occur with single utterances, but primarily because they do not affect the truth conditions of the sentence that hosts

Defining PMs

A PM is a linguistic expression which (i) does not affect the truth conditions of the proposition(s) to which it is attached, (ii) operates on the proposition(s) of the matrix clause, (iii) is syntactically dispensable from the matrix clause, and (iv) is semantically parasitic on the propositional content of the matrix clause.

Non-truth-conditionality

A PM does not affect the truth conditions of the propositional content. Non-truth-conditionality is necessary (though not sufficient) for determining whether an expression is a PM. Consider, for instance, 令人惊讶 'amazing' in (1).

(1) a 令人惊讶的是，那个孩子十二岁上了大学。
 'Amazingly, the child entered university at the age of 12'.
 b 令人惊讶的是那个十二岁的孩子。
 'What was amazing is that 12-year-old boy'.
 c 那个孩子十二岁上大学令人惊讶。
 'It was amazing that the child entered university at the age of ten'.

All the sentences in (1) contain the lexical item 令人惊讶. But in (1a), it does not affect the truth/falsity of the whole sentence. In other words, the truth/falsity of (1a) depends on whether or not there is a child in the world and the child entered university at the age of 12 rather than whether or not the speaker is amazed. In (1b), the same expression affects the truth/falsity of the sentence. The sentence will be false if what is amazing is not the 12-year-old boy but somebody (or something) else. In (1c), the expression also matters for its truth/falsity. It is true, provided that there is such a child in the world and his entry into university at the age of 12 did amaze people. Therefore, only in (1a) does the lexical item 令人惊讶 acquire the status as a PM. The distinction between (2a) and (2b) can be made in a parallel manner.

(2) a 她很疲倦，这样她就去睡觉了。
 'She was very tired. So she went to bed'.
 b 我想也是这样。
 'I think so too'.

The expression 这样 'so' in (2a) is non-truth-conditional, whereas it is truth-conditional in (2b). To put it more precisely, the truth/falsity of (2a) depends solely on whether or not the two propositions ("She was very tired" and "she went to bed") are true rather than whether or not the consequential relationship between them holds. The same lexical form in (2b) affects the truth conditions of the utterance once its reference is fixed. Therefore, 这样 is a PM in (2a) while a mere demonstrative pronoun in (2b).

Propositional scope

A PM operates on the proposition of the sentence with which it occurs rather than a sentence constituent. Some PMs indicate the speaker's commitment or attitude to the proposition, while others foreground the speaker's conception of the connection between the propositions (stated, implied or observed).

(3) 遗憾的是，王洪回家了。
'Unfortunately, Wang Hong went home'.

(4) 教授八十，可是妻子才三十。
'The professor is 80 years old, but his wife is only 30'.

(5) 王洪是教授啊。
'He is a professor'.
In (3), 遗憾的是 'unfortunately' makes a comment on the proposition that Wang Hong has gone home. In (4), 可是 'but' links two propositions: 'The professor is 80' and 'The professor's wife is 30'. In (5), 啊 *a* operates on the proposition that Wang Hong is a professor.

Syntactic dispensability

A PM is syntactically dispensable. Direct evidence is the fact that to remove a PM does not render ungrammatical the sentence to which it is attached. For instance, when 幸运的是 'fortunately' in (6) and 吧 *ba* in (7) are removed, the grammaticality of the sentences remains unaffected and their propositions untouched.

(6) 幸运的是，张华换了下一个航班。
'Fortunately, Zhang Hua changed to the next flight'.

(7) 王洪是教授吧。
'(I think) Wang Hong is a professor'.

There is indirect evidence in these examples. The first piece of such evidence is the fact that the negation of the sentence does not apply to the PM. For instance, (8) does not yield the interpretation that it is not fortunate that Zhang Hua did not change to the next flight.

(8) 幸运的是，张华没换下一个航班。
'Fortunately, Zhang Hua did not change to the next flight'.

The second piece of indirect evidence is the fact that a PM does not enlarge the possibilities for semantic relationship between the segments with which it is associated. In other words, when a PM is omitted, the relationship may still be there. For example, (9) and (10) may well be understood roughly the same way.

(9) 其他同学去西藏，但我去海南。
'Other students are going to Tibet. But I am going to Hainan'.

(10) 其他同学去西藏，我去海南。
'Other students are going to Tibet. I am going to Hainan'.

Semantic dependency

A PM depends on the propositional content of the matrix clause. In other words, it cannot stand by itself.

(11) a ★然而
   But
   b 希腊没有一流的球星，然而他们赢得了奖杯。
   'Greece has no first-class football stars, but they won the trophy'.

(12) a ★幸运的是
   Fortunately
   b 幸运的是，张华遇到了好老师。
   'Fortunately, Zhang Hua has met a good teacher'.

As marked, the PM 然而 'but' in (11a) is grammatically incomplete because it has no propositions to connect. The same expression in (11b), by contrast, indicates a contrastive relation between the two propositions stated. (12a) is incomplete as the PM 幸运的是 has nothing to comment on, while (12b) indicates the speaker's comment on the proposition. Semantic dependency is even more obvious with sentence-final PMs like 了 *le*, 啊 *a*, 嘛 *ma*, and 呢 *ne* etc.

Expressions that are not PMs

Given that PMs enjoy the above properties, the following categories of linguistic expressions which are usually included in the domain of PMs can be counted out.

Utterance modifiers

First comes the category generally referred to as 'utterance modifiers' (e.g., Bach, 1999), and alternatively as 'pragmatic adverbs' (e.g., Bellert, 1977), 'style disjuncts' (e.g., Hoye, 1997), 'speech-act adverbials' (e.g., Cinque, 1999), and 'speech-act predicationals' (e.g., Ernst, 2002). Members of this category include 老实说 'honestly speaking', 客气地说 'politely speaking', 严肃地说 'seriously speaking'. An utterance modifier specifies the way the speaker presents the propositional content. Therefore, they are truth-conditional, for the user of an utterance modifier can be said to have not spoken in the way/manner specified by the adjective.

Domain adverbials

Domain adverbials such as 经济上讲 'economically', 化学角度讲 'chemically', 政治角度讲 'politically', and 逻辑角度讲 'logically' are excluded from the domain of PMs on the basis of the following two facts. Firstly, a domain adverbial does not comment on a proposition, but rather specifies the domain with respect to which the proposition is said to hold. For example, the inherent import of 经济上讲 restricts the truth of the upcoming proposition within the domain of economy. Secondly, a domain adverbial affects the truth conditions of its host clause. When it is used with a proposition, the truth value of the proposition is valid only within the given domain.

Temporal connectives

The third category excluded from the domain of PMs includes temporal connectives such as 然后 'then', 最后 'finally', 最先 'at first', 此前 'before that', 后来 'after that', 与此同时 'at the same time' and ordinals such as 第一 'first', 第二 'second', and so on and so forth. They are truth-conditional because they describe the actual sequence of events or the sequential order of narration. Subtypes include succession (e.g., 后来 'after that'), simultaneity (e.g., 与此同时 'meanwhile'), and anteriority (e.g., 此前 'before that'). The truth/falsity of these sequences narrated can be checked in the same way the truth/falsity of world affairs is checked.

Second-person forms

The fourth category excluded from the domain of PMs constitutes what we call second-person forms such as 你说 'you say' and 告诉我 'tell me'. They are so called for the reason that they contain the second-person pronoun 你 'you' in the syntactic subject position or object position. Instead of marking the speaker's comment on the proposition expressed, a second-person form serves to explicitly announce what sort of effect the speaker intends to have on the hearer or "to oil the wheels of conversational exchange" (Fitzmaurice, 2004: 428). It is a locutionary performative belonging to a kind of meta-language. Unlike a PM, it is devoid of comment on the proposition. It has, instead, an interactive discourse function, which is indexed by a second-person marking. Commonplace examples include 你想 'you think', 你说说看 'tell me/us', 你想想 'you think', 我警告你 'I warn you', 你听我说 'listen to me', 我奉劝你 'I advise you' and 我问你 'I ask you'.

A typology of PMs in Chinese Discourse

PMs in Chinese can be generally classified into two types: conceptual and non-conceptual. This general typology is made on the basis of the inherent semantic import of PMs. A conceptual PM encodes certain conceptual information. For example, 幸运的是 'fortunately' invokes the concept [FORTUNATE]. Syntactically, they are claimed to be the highest class of adverbs or the most peripheral elements, often referred to as modal adverbs or adverbs of mood or modal adjuncts. Non-conceptual PMs encode no conceptual messages. Grammatically, they are conjunctions or sentence-final particles.

Conceptual PMs

A conceptual PM makes observable the speaker's opinion about what he is saying. They are compositional, multi-categorical and multi-functional.

Conceptual PMs can be semantically simple, or interact with other words to form a complex, and therefore can be analyzed compositionally. For instance, 十分 'very' can be added to 遗憾的是 'unfortunately' to render it into a complex PM. The grasp of the concept of a PM is related to the grasp of the meaning of its parts.

Conceptual PMs are coded in a range of lexical categories and grammatical constructions (e.g., single adverbs, adjective phrases, noun phrases, prepositional phrases, finite subordinate clauses). Examples are 确实 'actually', 非常不幸 'very unfortunately', 毫无疑问 'no doubt' and 我想 'I think'. Besides, many conceptual PMs are formed by an adjective plus 的是 *deshi*. Many of them can be prefixed with 令人/让人 *lingren/rangren*. For example, 遗憾的是 has a variant 令人遗憾的是.

The lexical form does not function exclusively as a PM. In other words, the homophonous form can function truth-conditionally in other contexts, as shown in the utterances in (13).

(13) a 希腊非常幸运地避开了法国。
         'Greece was fortunate to have avoided France'.
      b 非常幸运，希腊避开了法国。
         'Fortunately, Greece avoided France'.

The expression 非常幸运 (feichangxingyun, 'very fortunately') in (13a) is an adverb phrase functioning as an adverbial modifying the main verb. In (13b), the same expression is a PM operating syntactically upon the whole proposition. It is structurally marginal with its semantics reduced to a degree at which its contribution is irrelevant to the truth/falsity of the whole sentence.

Conceptual PMs should be posited as a heterogeneous pragmatic class as they belong to different grammatical categories such as adverbs (e.g., 确实), adjective phrases (e.g., 非常不幸), noun phrases (e.g., 毫无疑问) and finite clauses (e.g., 我想). Their various formal realizations can be exemplified by (14)-(17).

(14) 确实，他取得这样的成绩很不容易。
'Indeed, it is not easy at all for him to have achieved this'.

(15) 非常不幸，他五岁失去双亲。
'Very unfortunately, he lost his parents at the age of five'.

(16) 毫无疑问，今天姚明是火箭的第一功臣。
'Undoubtedly, Yao Ming is the hero of the Rockets today'.

(17) 我想，他在图书馆看书。
'He is reading in the library, I think'.

Structurally, conceptual PMs do not occur naturally with questions demanding information. This is because to use such a question implies that the speaker is not sure whether the propositional content is true or not, but the use of a conceptual PM presupposes the speaker's commitment to its factuality. This contradiction will render the whole sentence awkward. For example, to change (14)-(17) into questions will result in awkward utterances, as shown by (18)-(21).

(18) ?确实，他取得这样的成绩很不容易吗？
'Indeed, is it difficult for him to have achieved this?'

(19) ?非常不幸，他五岁失去双亲吗？
'Very unfortunately, did he lose his parents at the age of five?'

(20) ?毫无疑问，今天谁是火箭的第一功臣吗？
'Undoubtedly, who is the hero of the Rockets today?'

(21) ?我想，他在哪里看书呢？
'I think, where is he reading?'

Conceptual PMs enjoy a high degree of mobility within the sentences where they occur. They can occur initially, medially or finally with a comma in writing and a pause in speech. This can be illustrated by the occurrences of 我想 in (22).

(22) a 我想，他现在在图书馆看书。
'I think, he is reading in the library at the moment'.
b 他现在，我想，在图书馆看书。
'He is, I think, reading in the library at the moment'.
c 他现在在图书馆看书，我想。
'He is reading in the library at the moment, I think'.

In simple sentences, wherever it occurs, a conceptual PM takes into scope the whole sentence to which it is attached. However, in complex utterances the position of the marker does affect the scope and consequently the meaning of the whole utterance.

(23) a 他现在图书馆，但不是看书，我想。
'He is now in the library, but he is not reading, I think'.
b 他现在图书馆，我想，但不是看书。
'He is now in the library, I think, but he is not reading'.
c 他现在图书馆，但我想，不是看书。
'He is now in the library, but I think, he is not reading'.

(23a) is ambiguous. The marker at the sentence-final position can take either the whole sentence or just the second segment into its scope. The same marker in (23b) takes only the first segment into scope, while in (23c) it takes only the second segment into scope. Different positions give rise to different interpretations.

Epistemic conceptual PMs and evaluative conceptual PMs

Semantically, conceptual PMs can be grouped into two subtypes: epistemic and evaluative.

An epistemic PM is an indication of the speaker's commitment to the degree of certitude of the proposition.

(24) 也许，阿尔法狗比柯洁强大。
'Perhaps, AlphaGo is stronger than Ke Jie'.

(25) 毫无疑问，阿尔法狗比柯洁强大。
'Undoubtedly, AlphaGo is stronger than Ke Jie'.

The PM 也许 (yexu, 'perhaps') in (25) indicates the speaker's lack of confidence in the proposition that AlphaGo is stronger than Ke Jie. The PM 毫无疑问 'no doubt' in (25) indicates that the speaker is committed to the truth of the same proposition.

Structurally, epistemic conceptual PMs fall into two subcategories: epistemic clausal PMs and epistemic adverbial ones. The former displays four formal properties: (i) They do not co-occur with aspect particles 着 *zhe*, 'progressive', 了 *le*, 'perfective' and 过 *guo*, 'simple past'; (ii) They do not co-occur with time adverbial expressions; (iii) The verb involved cannot be repeated within the same phrase; (iv) They cannot be negated by 不 'not'. Let me illustrate them with 我看.

This PM is morphologically formed with the first-person pronoun 我 'I' and the verb 看 ' see' which literally means 'to look' or 'to view'. However, when the verb is combined with 我 and followed by a propositional clause, it no longer indicates a physical event of sight.

(26) a 我看着母亲的照片。
'I was looking at Wang Hong's picture'.
b 我看，这件事不难办。
'This matter is not difficult to handle, I think'.

Semantically, the lexeme italicized in (26a) encodes the action of looking at a picture of the speaker's mother. It expresses a sense perception. Syntactically, it is a predicate verb. The same lexeme loses its literal meaning in (26b). Combined with the first-person pronoun 我, it gains the status as a PM indicating the speaker's mental state with respect to the proposition expressed. A simple test for the difference is to see if it can take an aspect particle or if the single lexeme 看 can be repeated. If yes, it is a simple subject-predicate structure. Otherwise, it is a PM.

(27) a 我看了母亲的照片。
       'I have taken a look at my mother's picture'.
    b 我看看母亲的照片。
       'I took a look at my mother's picture'.
    c ★我看了这件事不难办。
       'I have seen that this matter is not difficult to handle'.
    d ★我看看这件事不难办。
       'I took a look that this matter is not difficult to handle'.

(27a-b) are fully acceptable sentences, where the lexeme 看 is a verb of perception, which takes an aspect particle or is repeated. In this circumstance, a combination of the verb with the first-person pronoun 我 loses its status as a PM, but gains the status as a subject-predicate structure, which requires a concrete object. (27c-d) are unacceptable because 看 as a verb of perception in each of them is followed by an epistemic concept rather than a concrete object.

When an epistemic clause co-occurs with a time adverbial, it loses its status as a PM too. For instance, when 我想 'I think' is inserted by a time adverbial (e.g., 我当时想 'I then thought' it merely reports a mental action at a certain time in the past. Other prototypical members of epistemic clausal PMs include 我猜想 'I guess', 我相信 'I believe' 我怀疑 'I doubt' and a spectrum of others.

Epistemic adverbial PMs mark the speaker's degree of commitment to the truth of the proposition. They can be further divided into two types according to the degree of commitment: those which indicate the speaker's certainty, and those that mark the speaker's reservation or doubt. Prototypical members of the first type include 其实 'actually', 当然 'certainly', 的确 'indeed', 肯定 'definitely', 确实 'indeed', 显然 'obviously' and so on. Examples of the other type include 大概 'probably', and 也许/或许 'perhaps'.

An evaluative PM is essentially the speaker's indication of his attitude, feeling, value judgement, or expectation with regard to the proposition expressed. A noticeable formal property of evaluative PMs is that they are composed of an adjective stem and a combination of an adjective marker 的 de with the copula 是 shi, as shown in (28).

(28) 惊呀的是，奥斯塔彭科获得了冠军。
     'Amazingly, Ostapenko got the championship'.

Semantically, an evaluative PM presupposes the truth of the proposition expressed, while an epistemic one does not. For instance, the use of 惊讶的是 'amazingly' in (28) presupposes that Ostapenko got the championship, while the use of 我看 in (29) does not presuppose that Liu Xiang's success is due to his coach.

(29) 我看，刘翔的成功归于他的教练。
     'Liu Xiang's success is due to his coach, I think'.

Evaluative PMs can be subcategorized into event-oriented and agent-oriented types. The two types can be formally distinguished. When the evaluation carried by the PM is oriented to the event narrated, it can be prefixed with 令人/让人 'making people' or 令我/让我 'making me'. For example, (28) above can be changed to (30) without any alteration of its meaning.

(30) 令人惊呀的是，奥斯塔彭科获得冠军。
'Amazingly, Ostapenko won the championship'.

By contrast, when the evaluation is oriented to the agent with respect to what he/she has done, the marker cannot be prefixed with 令人/让人 or 令我/让我. For example, the prefix 令人 renders (31) unacceptable.

(31) *令人不幸的是，郑洁比赛中受伤了。
'Unfortunately, Zheng Jie got hurt in the middle of the match'.

Agent-oriented PMs have two arguments, one being the agent, which is usually the subject of the sentence, and the other being the event represented by the immediate discourse. The agent is judged as such (what the adjective specifies) with respect to the event narrated. For instance, in (32a), Zhang Hua is judged clever as far as that he sold the house a month ago. Agent-oriented PMs must have the agent involved as the subject of the sentence and that the event concerned must be under the agent's control (he is able to choose to do or not to do it). This explains why (32b-c) sound odd.

(32) a 聪明的是，张华一个月前把房子卖了。
'Cleverly, Zhang Hua sold the house a month ago'.
b ?聪明的是，房子一个月以前就卖了。
'Cleverly, the house was sold two years ago'.
c ?聪明的是，张华必须把房子卖了。
'Cleverly, Zhang Hua has to sell the house'.

The oddity of (32b) results from the fact that the agent to whom the PM is oriented does not appear in the subject position. (32c) is awkward because 必须 'must' indicates an obligation, which is outside the control of the agent, Zhang Hua.

Non-conceptual PMs

Non-conceptual PMs are non-compositional, i.e., they do not interact with other words and thus defies compositional analysis; they enjoy a stable form, i.e., they cannot be semantically simple or complex; they play no part in sentence formation and are not subsumed in regular grammatical frameworks. (Shei, 2014: 204). Non-conceptual PMs fall into two categories according to their positions in a discourse: inter-sentential and sentence-final PMs. The former category (traditionally called clausal conjunctions or discourse connectives) indicate the speaker's conception of a relation between propositions, while the latter (traditionally called sentence-final particles or mood particles) indicate the speaker's response to the proposition encoded in the sentence to which it is attached.

Inter-sentential PMs

Inter-sentential PMs can be grouped into contrastive, elaborative, and inferential ones. A contrastive PM indicates a sort of contrast between the two propositions it is in construction with. The contrast is either between two literally expressed propositions as instantiated in (33) or between two implications as exemplified in (34) or between an implication and a literally expressed proposition as illustrated in (35).

(33) 张华月收入两万，可是他还在叫穷。
'Zhang Hua's monthly income is 20,000, but he still says he is poor'.

(34) 北京是冬天，可是悉尼是夏天。
'It is winter in Beijing, but it is summer in Sydney'.

(35) 她五十岁了，可是依然很漂亮。
'She is already 50, but she is still very beautiful'.

The contrast in (33) is between Zhang Hua's having a monthly income of 20,000 and his saying that he is poor. Both propositions are literally expressed. Suppose (34) is uttered as a reply to someone in Beijing who is packing a lot of winter clothes for a trip to Sydney. The conceived contrast is between two implications: one needs heavy clothes in Beijing, but one does not need them in Sydney. In (35), the contrast is between an implication that a woman over 50 is normally no longer beautiful and a literally expressed proposition that the woman concerned is beautiful.

Structurally, two subtypes of contrastive PMs can be distinguished by their locations: the first type occurs with the second segment, while the other type is with the first segment. The most typical member of the first type is 但/但是 'but', which has as its variants 可/可是 ke/keshi, 然而 raner, 却 que, 只是 zhishi, 不过 buguo, 就是 jiushi, 哪里知道 nalizhidao, 不料 buliao, and 反之 fanzhi etc. Typical examples of the other type are 虽然 'although' and its variant 尽管 jinguan. Whichever type is used, the speaker puts at the end the segment which carries greater conversational weight. In some cases, either type suffices to mark a contrast, in others, the two types co-occur as shown in (36).

(36) a 他天天锻炼，但是身体还是不好。
'He does physical exercises every day, but he is still not in good health'.
b 虽然他天天锻炼，但是身体还是不好。
'He does physical exercises every day, but he is still not in good health'.

In some circumstances, 但是, 可是, and 然而 can be used interchangeably with 却 (que), as shown in (37).

(37) a 他学了十年英语，却不能和英国人交谈。
'He has learned English for ten years, but he cannot talk with English people'.
b 他学了十年英语，但是不能和英国人交谈。
'He has learned English for ten years, but he cannot talk with English people'.

In other cases, 却 cannot be used interchangeably with 但/但是, 可是, and 然而. For example, when the second segment starts with its own syntactic subject or an adverbial of time or place etc., 却 need occur after them and cannot be replaced by 但/但是. The utterances in (38) and (39) are illustrative of the distinction.

(38) a 他身上有缺点，我却喜欢和他在一起。
'He has shortcomings, but I like staying with him'.

  b ★他身上有缺点，我但是喜欢和他在一起。
    'He has shortcomings, but I like staying with him'.
  c 他身上有缺点，但是我喜欢和他在一起。
    'He has shortcomings, but I like staying with him'.

(39) a 他平时口才很好，这会儿却结结巴巴。
    'He is normally very eloquent, but he is stammering at this moment'.
  b ★他平时口才很好，这会儿但结结巴巴。
    'He is normally very eloquent, but he is stammering at the moment'.
  c 他平时口才很好，但是这会儿结结巴巴。
    'He is normally very eloquent, but he is stammering at the moment'.

However, 但/但是 and 却 can be used in collaboration in the second segment. 但/但是 occurs at the beginning, 却 still occurs after the subject or the adverbial of time/place.

(40) 他身上有缺点，但是我却喜欢和他在一起。
   'He has shortcomings, but I like staying with him'.

(41) 他平时口才很好，但是这会儿却结结巴巴。
   'He is normally very eloquent, but he is stammering at the moment'.

An elaborative PM indicates that the speaker thinks that the proposition to which it is attached is elaborative/conclusive of or more important than the previous proposition. Members of this type include 并且 *bingqie*, 再说 *zaishuo*, 加之 *jiazhi*, 更有甚者 *gengyoushenzhe*, 而且 *erqie*, 比如 *biru*, 也就是说 *yejiushishuo*, 总之 *zongzhi*, 总而言之 *zongeryanzhi*, 一句话 *yijuhua*, 同样 *tongyang* and 同理 *tongli*.

  An elaborative PM is anaphoric in nature. In other words, its use presupposes a previous proposition. For example, 同理 requires a previous proposition to which the upcoming proposition is analogous, 比如 requires a previous proposition of which the upcoming proposition is an example or instance. This is why both (42a) and (42b) sound incomplete.

(42) a 同理，文件也要备份。
    'Analogously, a copy of the files needs to be made'.
  b 再说，张华是剑桥毕业的。
    'In addition, Zhang Hua graduated from Cambridge'.

An inferential PM indicates an inferential relation between the propositions involved. The most typical member of this type is 所以 'so'. It can be used either on its own or in collaboration with 因为 'because' or its single-syllable variant 因 (yin), which introduces the premise.

(43) a 她要挣钱，所以很勤劳。
    'She needs to make money, so she works hard'.
  b 因为她要挣钱，所以很勤劳。
    'She works hard because she needs to make money'.
  c 她要挣钱，所以她很勤劳。
    'She needs to make money, so she works hard'.
  d ★她要挣钱，她所以很勤劳。
    'She needs to make money, so she works hard'.

    e   她因为要挣钱，所以很勤劳。
          'She works hard because she needs to make money'.

As indicated, (43d) is ungrammatical. This is because syntactically, 所以 has to precede the subject of the clause, while 因为 can occur either before or after the subject of the clause to which it is attached. 所以 (especially when occurring in collaboration with 因为) is basically used to describe an actual cause-effect relation, but it can also be used to show the speaker's own epistemic conception (as is the case with all the sentences in (43)). Because of this, 因为 can be emphasized by emphatic adverbs such as 就是/正 'just', or corrected by 而是 'but', or negated by 不是 'not'.

(44) a   就是因为我想孩子，我才回家。
          'I went home just because I missed my child'.
     b   不是因为我想孩子，我才回家，而是因为孩子想我。
          'I went home not because I missed my child, but because my child missed me'.

Unlike 所以, 既然 … 就 'therefore' tends to emphasize the subjective aspect of the inferential relation. 既然 introduces the reason. It can occur either before or after the subject, 就 introduces the inference. It precedes the subject when the clause in which it occurs has a subject.

(45) a   既然你想出国读书，就得省钱。
          'Since you want to go abroad to study, you have to save money'.
     b   你既然想出国读书，你就得省钱。
          'Since you want to go abroad to study, you have to save money'.
     c   *你既然想出国读书，就你得省钱。
          'Since you want to go abroad to study, you have to save money'.

Another notable distinction between 因为 and 既然 is that the latter can be followed by a question, while the former cannot.

(46) a   既然他都认错了，为什么还打他？
          Now that he has admitted the mistake, why are you still beating him?
     b   *因为他都认错了，为什么还打他？
          'Because he has admitted the mistake, why are you still beating him?'

Sentence-final PMs

There is no complete consensus as to the number of sentence-final PMs. Shei (2014) lists 11 primary sentence-final PMs, not including their variants. Cheung (2017) discusses six. The most commonly used PMs of this type are 了le, 呢ne, 啊a, 呀ya, 吗ma and 吧ba. Almost all of them can occur with questions, where they are question markers. Only when they occur with declarative sentences do they gain the status as PMs.

    The sentence-final PM 呢 indicates the speaker's notice of a change of state, i.e. from p to ¬P or vice versa. The change of state is obvious when we compare the two sentences in (47),

(47) a   王洪是教授。
          'Wang Hong is a professor'.
     b   王洪是教授了。
          'Wang Hong has turned professor'.

Both (47a) and (47b) are truth-conditionally equivalent, but in (47a), the speaker just states the fact that Wang Hong is a professor, while in (47b) the speaker, in addition to the fact that Wang Hong is a professor, indicates he has noticed the change of Wang Hong's academic position.

The PM 了 can be used to show the speaker's assumption that what is asserted is contrary to his or the hearer's expectation.

(48) a 你不用来上课。
        'You do not need to come to class'.
     b 你不用来上课了。
        'You do not need to come to class'.

In (48b), the speaker does not only assert that the hearer does not need to come to class, but also indicates, with the use of 了, that it is contrary to the hearer's expectation that he needs to go to class. It is more accurate to be uttered when the hearer is normally expected to come to class, but somehow the speaker thinks that he does not need to come anymore.

Similar to 了, 呢 indicates that what is stated is contrary to the hearer's belief or expectation. The point is clear in the following dialogue.

(49) A: 王洪什么也没有。
         'Wang Hong has nothing'.
     B: 他有别墅呢！
         'He has a house'.

Here B does not only assert that Wang Hong has a house, but also suggests that this is contrary to A's belief that Wang Hong has nothing valuable. This explains why it sounds very natural as a response to an assertion that Wang has nothing worthwhile.

The sentence-final PM 啊 and its variant 呀 indicate the speaker's surprise about the statement made and suggests that the information is very important.

(50) 王洪是老师啊/呀！
     'Wang Hong is a teacher!'

By uttering (50), the speaker asserts that Wang Hong is a teacher, and at the same time suggests that she is surprised by that fact or there is something contrary to what he expects of a teacher, and this something is very relevant to the current topic of discussion. For instance, (50) is a perfect response when Wang Hong sets a good (or bad) example as a teacher in a certain circumstance.

The PM 吧 indicates the speaker's uncertainty about the factuality of the statement made. This can be clearly illustrated when we change (50) into (51).

(51) 王洪是老师吧。
     'Wang Hong is a teacher'.

By uttering (51), the speaker states the fact that Wang Hong is a teacher and at the same time suggests, by using 吧 at the end, that he is not certain about it. He hopes to get confirmation from the hearer.

Contrary to 吧, 嘛 indicates that the speaker is sure of the statement made or he thinks that the information is obvious to both interlocutors.

(52) 他是孩子嘛。
'He is a child'.

By using 嘛 in (52), the speaker is suggesting that the fact that the person concerned is a child is beyond doubt and at the same time blaming the hearer for his overlooking this fact. It can serve, for example, as a response when someone is blaming the child for some mischief.

Conclusion

I have in this chapter offered a detailed and systematic description of PMs in Chinese discourse. I started with an explanation of why the term 'PM' is opted for. I then offered a definition for PMs followed by a discussion of their general characteristics. Bearing in mind the definition and the general properties, I have excluded from the domain of PMs some expressions which have been generally counted as PMs and suggested some ways of identifying the distinction. The kernel of the chapter is concerned with a typology of PMs. A valid distinction between conceptual and non-conceptual types is made on the basis of their semantic import. Specific characteristics (morphological, syntactic, semantic and pragmatic) of each type (and subtypes) have been presented.

References

Bach, K. (1999) 'The Myth of Conventional Implicature', *Linguistics and Philosophy* 22: 327–366.
Bellert, I. (1977) 'On Semantic and Distributional Properties of Sentential Adverbs', *Linguistic Inquiry* 8: 337–351.
Cheung, C. (2017) *Parts of Speech in Mandarin: The State of the Art*. Singapore: Springer.
Cinque, G. (1999) *Adverbs and Functional Heads: A Cross-linguistic Perspective*. Oxford: Oxford University Press.
Ernst, T. (2002) *The Syntax of Adjuncts*. Cambridge: Cambridge University Press.
Feng, G. (2010) *A Theory of Conventional Implicature and Pragmatic Markers in Chinese*. Bingley: Emerald Group Publishing Limited.
Fitzmaurice, S. (2004) 'Subjectivity, Intersubjectivity and the Historical Construction of Interlocutor Stance: From Stance Markers to Discourse Markers', *Discourse Studies* 6: 427–448.
Fraser, B. (1996) 'Pragmatic Markers', *Pragmatics* 6: 167–190.
Fraser, B. (1999) 'What Are Discourse Markers?', *Journal of Pragmatics* 31: 931–952.
Fraser, B. (2006) 'Towards a theory of discourse markers', in *Approaches to Discourse Particles*. Kerstin Fischer (ed.) Amsterdam: Elsevier. pp. 189–204.
Hoye, L. (1997) *Adverbs and Modality in English*, London: Longman.
Risselada, R. Spooren, W. (1998) 'Introduction: Discourse Markers and Coherence Relations', *Journal of Pragmatics* 30: 131–133.
Shei, C. (2014) *Understanding the Chinese Language: A Comprehensive Linguistic Introduction*. London: Routledge.
Schiffrin, D. (1987) *Discourse Markers*. Cambridge: Cambridge University Press.
Tang, R. (2015) *On the Pragmaticalization of Chinese Pragmatic Markers*. Bejing: China Science Publishing.
Zhang, Wenxian, (2010) *On the Connective Functions of Chinese Connectives*. PhD Thesis, Beijing University.

15
The grammaticalization of stance markers in Chinese

Foong Ha Yap and Winnie Chor

1. Introduction

Every utterance we make signals our stance – toward someone, something, someplace, some event or situation or some idea. Essentially, our stance is the expression of our beliefs, perspectives, evaluations, and attitudes and can be expressed explicitly (e.g. *I don't like this*) or implicitly (e.g. *I guess this will do*). It can be detected, not only at the clausal level as just shown, but also at the lexical (e.g. *awful*) and phrasal (e.g. *not quite what I expect*) levels as well (Xing, 2006). Naturally, for a more comprehensive assessment of a speaker's stance, we will need to evaluate numerous utterances – sometimes on multiple occasions, and in various contexts, and on a broader scale at the discourse level as well. The focus of this chapter is on stance markers that have emerged as a result of frequent and conventionalized usage, often involving pragmatic implicature. Among the stance markers to be discussed in this chapter are epistemic, evidential and attitudinal markers. We will focus on three major pathways for the emergence of these stance markers in Chinese, namely, the verbal, nominal and indexical pathways.

2. Stance markers and discourse

Stance markers are used not only to express the speaker's subjective views, judgments and intentions. They are also often used to signal the speaker's alignment or disalignment with other interlocutors – that is, they often also serve an interpersonal or 'intersubjective' function (see Traugott, 2010). For this reason, stance markers play an important role in the negotiation of speaker's and hearer's footing (i.e. their positioning relative to the message and to others) in the course of interactive talk.

Stance markers can be found in a variety of positions within an utterance. Some stance markers occur in utterance-initial position, with many of them having developed from discourse markers, as in the case of Mandarin disagreement marker *nà* 那 'but' (which is derived from distal demonstrative 'that') shown in (1). This is not surprising, given that discourse markers often occur at turn-transition points in a conversation, and thus are in an ideal position to signal the speaker's evaluation of what was said in the previous turn, and to then signal his/her expectation of how the subsequent turn(s) would unfold (Yang, 2017).

(1) 那你還是去看一看醫生吧，雖然你說已經好多了。
  Nà *nǐ* *háishì* *qù* *kàn* *yi* *kàn* *yīshēng* *ba,*
  NA 2SG still go see one see doctor SFP,
  suīrán *nǐ* *shuō* *yǐjīng* *hǎoduō* *le.*
  though 2SG say already better SFP
  '**But** you'd better still go and visit the doctor, though you said you are already better'.

Some stance markers in clause-initial position have also developed from complement-taking verb constructions, among them cognition verbs such as *wǒ juéde* 我覺得 'I think', which often give rise to epistemic readings, as in (2a), and perception verbs such as *(wǒ) tīngshuō* (我)聽說 '(I) hear', which frequently yield evidential readings (see further discussion in §3.1.2). Some of these stance markers can also occur in utterance-medial and utterance-final positions, as illustrated with *wǒ juéde* in (2b) and (2c) respectively. The Chinese language is known to be rich in utterance-final mood particles, with some particles (e.g. *de*) combining with other particles (e.g. *la* and *ba*) to form complex sentence final particles such as *dela* 'I'm sure' and *deba* 'I suppose' in (3) (see Yap et al., 2017).

(2) a 我覺得他不會成功的。
   wǒ ***juédé*** *tā* *bú* *huì* *chénggōng* *de*
   1SG think 3SG NEG FUT succeed   SFP
   '**I think/Probably** he will not succeed'.
  b 他，我覺得不會成功的。
   tā, ***wǒ*** ***juéde*** *bú* *huì* *chénggōng* *de*
   3SG 1SG think NEG FUT succeed   SFP
   'He, **I think/probably**, will not succeed'.
  c 他不會成功的，我覺得。
   tā *bú* *huì* *chénggōng* *de,* ***wǒ*** ***juéde***
   3SG NEG FUT succeed   SFP 1SG think
   'He will not succeed, **I think/probably**'.

(3) 他不會成功的啦/的吧。
  tā *bú* *huì* *chénggōng* ***dela/deba***
  3SG NEG FUT succeed   SFP
  'He will not succeed (***I'm sure /I suppose***)'.

Most stance markers have their origin as a lexical or grammatical item. Via different pathways of grammaticalization, they have evolved into stance markers indicating different shades of speaker meanings. For instance, in (1), *nà* is no longer a deictic demonstrative meaning 'that', but is more appropriately understood as a stance marker indicating the speaker's disagreement with the assessment of the situation as suggested by the addressee in the prior turn (in this case, the addressee's assessment that she is now already better). As a versatile indexical, the deictic demonstrative *nà* has grammaticalized into a stance marker, such that the *nà*-prefaced turn could now indicate the speaker's disagreement with what was said in a prior turn. In (2), *wǒ juéde* has extended its function from a complement-taking construction with the meaning 'I have a particular opinion' to an epistemic phrase indicating probability, and often further used as a pragmatic hedge with politeness and solidarity-enhancing functions. In (3), we see nominalizer *de* often combining with other particles to form complex sentence final particles that convey subtle differences in the speaker's subjective and intersubjective stance (e.g. *dela* to convey certainty and *deba* to convey a supposition rather than an assertion).

3. Sources of stance markers

Stance markers in the Sinitic language family are derived from a rich variety of sources. In the subsections that follow, we briefly illustrate three robust grammaticalization pathways, namely, the verbal pathway (§3.1), the nominal pathway (§3.2) and the indexical pathway (§3.3).

3.1 Verb-based stance markers

3.1.1 Stance markers derived from serial verb constructions

A common source for stance markers in Chinese is the serial verb construction, where the second verb (V_2) in a V_1-V_2 construction often evolves into a marker of aspect, tense and/or mood, the latter often broadly construed to include a wide range of speaker's subjective and intersubjective stance. We will illustrate this with the Mandarin verb *liǎo* 了 'finish'. The completive verb *liǎo*, attested in Old Chinese as seen in (4a), has developed into both a perfective and perfect aspect marker *le*, as shown in (4b) and (4c) respectively, as well as an interactional sentence final particle *le* (4d). This interactional particle *le* comes with a realis interpretation that often conveys a ring of finality and closure to a discourse topic at the end of a speaker's turn of talk and in this way helps to open up the conversational floor for a next-speaker turn (see Lu and Su, 2009).

(4) a 晨起早掃，食了洗滌
    chén   qǐ   zǎo   sǎo,   shí   liǎo   xǐdí
    morning get.up   early   sweep   eat   finish wash
    '(One should) get up in the morning, sweep (the house) and wash (clothes) after finishing the meal'.
    (*Quanhanshu*, Eastern Han, 25–220 AD, PKU Center for Chinese Linguistics Corpus)

b 我買了一本書。
    wǒ   mǎi   le   yī   běn   shū
    1SG   buy   LE   one   CL   book
    'I (have) bought one book'.

c 他過來了。
    tā   guòlái   le
    3SG   come.over LE
    'He has come over'.

d E: [你]們也是用中文就對了.
    nǐmen   yěshì   yòng   zhōngwén   jiù   duì   le.
    2PL   also   use   Chinese   PRT   right   LE
    'You also use Chinese, right?'

J: (0) 對.
    duì
    right
    語意學他們是用中文.
    yǔyìxué   tāmen   shì   yòng   zhōngwén
    semantics   3PL   FOC   use   Chinese
    'Yeah. They teach semantics in Chinese'.

(Lu and Su, 2009: 162–163; re-glossed)

The grammaticalization of stance markers

As a marker of next-speaker turns, *le* frequently occurs as part of addressee-engaging expressions such as *jiù duì le* 'right?', in response to which the next speaker often produces brief reactive tokens such as *duì* 對 'yeah'/'right', as seen in (4d). In other words, *le* is often used as a marker of the speaker's intersubjective (i.e. interpersonal) stance. Also worth noting here is that the semantic extension of *le* from serial verb to aspect marker and sentence final particle is accompanied by syntactic scope expansion as well: [_Serial.verb_ V *liǎo*] > [_Postverbal.aspect_ V-*le*] > [_(Inter)subjective.stance_ [_Finite.clause_ (NP) VP] *le*].

3.1.2 Stance markers derived from complement-taking verb constructions

Complement-taking verbs (with or without the first-person matrix subject 'I/We') are also good sources for (inter)subjective speaker-stance markers. Consider the English *I think* construction (5a), which is lexically already inherently subjective. Not surprisingly, inherently subjective constructions involving the mental state of the speaker as in the case of *I think* often develop into an epistemic marker (5b-d), and in the process often triggering the insubordination of the complement clause (*he's going to win*) into a new finite main clause, with *I think* in the matrix clause reinterpreted as the speaker's subjectivity marker, namely, epistemic hedging and/or pragmatic softening (see, for example, Thompson and Mulac, 1991; Kärkkäinen, 2003). The use of *I think* as an epistemic marker allows the speaker to hedge his/her claims for a wide range of reasons, including going beyond the subjective function of expressing the speaker's guarded inference, uncertainty and/or anxiety (5b-c) to the intersubjective function of downgrading the strength of the speaker's epistemic claim and thereby enhance solidarity with the addressee (5d).[1] From a syntactic perspective, it is worth noting that the utterance-final position is ideally suited for the socio-interactional purpose of shifting turns of talk, which includes building rapport with the addressee.

(5) a **I think** *(that) he's not going to win.*
  b **I think** [UNSTRESSED] *he's not going to win.* [= 'Probably, he's not going to win'.]
  c *He,* **I think**, *is not going to win.* [= 'He probably is not going to win']
  d *He's not going to win,* **I think**. [= 'He's not going to win, probably'.]

Similar constructions have also been observed in Chinese. The epistemic markers *wǒ juéde* and *(wǒ) kǒngpà* (我)恐怕 'I'm afraid' have also evolved into a sentence final epistemic marker indicating the speaker's attenuated degree of commitment to the proposition (Endo, 2010; Lim, 2011; Yap et al., 2014). We elaborate further using *kǒngpà*, as shown in (6).

(6) a 恐怕他不會成功的。
  kǒngpà tā bú huì chénggōng de
  afraid 3SG NEG FUT succeed SFP
  '**I'm afraid/Probably** he will not succeed'.
  b 他恐怕不會成功的。
  tā **kǒngpà** bú huì chénggōng de
  3SG probably NEG FUT succeed SFP
  'He **probably** will not succeed'.
  c 他不會成功的,**(?恐怕)**。
  tā bú huì chénggōng de **(?kǒngpà)**
  3SG NEG FUT succeed SFP probably
  Intended meaning: 'He will not succeed, **probably**'.

233

Note that whereas *wǒ juéde,* as seen earlier in (2c), is sometimes used in utterance-final position in tag-like fashion, the use of *kǒngpà* as an utterance tag in (6c) is marginal. This is partly because the verbal semantics of 'fear' in *kǒngpà* is still lexically transparent and the use of *kǒngpà* is largely restricted to adversative contexts, where overt expression of the speaker as an affectee is preferably avoided for taboo reasons.

While mental/psych verbs such as 'think' and 'be afraid' often yield epistemic and inferential readings, perception verbs such as 'hear' and utterance verbs such as 'say' typically yield instead hearsay evidential readings, as shown in (7a-b). Hearsay evidential uses of these utterance verb constructions often also serve as an indirect hedging strategy, allowing the speaker to distance himself/herself from full responsibility for an epistemic claim by borrowing the voice of others. In Chinese, as illustrated in (8a) and (8b), these complement-taking verbs with a hearsay evidential function can appear with or without the first-person subject *wǒ* ('I') in the matrix clause. Crucially, even without overt expression of the first-person subject (= speaker), a subjective reading still obtains. There are also variations in the way the speaker weighs his/her epistemic commitment to the source of information. As seen in (8c), hearsay expressions sometimes explicitly express a/some third-person referent(s) (e.g. using *rénmen* 人們 'people' or *tāmen* 他們 'they') as the source of information; these constructions with third-person sources often imply that although some/most people think a certain way (e.g. that so-and-so will win the contest), the speaker himself/herself thinks otherwise, or the outcome turns out otherwise. The construction is more marked than expressions which do not explicitly single out what other people say, as it expresses the speaker's disalignment to the norm.

(7) a {*I hear/see*} *he's not going to win.*
 b {*People say/They say*} *he's not going to win.*

(8) a 我聽說他不會贏。
 wǒ   tīngshuō   tā   bú   huì   yíng
 1SG   hear.say   3SG   NEG   will   win
 '**I hear/see** he is not going to win'.
 b 聽說他不會贏。
 tīngshuō   tā   bú   huì   yíng
 hear.say   3SG   NEG   will   win
 '**It is said** (< (I) hear (people) say) he is not going to win'.
 c 人們說/他們說他不會贏。
 rénmen   shuō/   tāmen   shuō   tā   bú   huì   yíng
 people   say/   3PL   say   3SG   NEG   will   win
 '**People say/ They say** he is not going to win'.

3.1.3 Stance markers derived from versatile transfer verb constructions

An interesting stance-marking strategy that has thus far not been observed in other languages is the Chinese 'speaker affectedness' marker in expressions such as *Huā gěi sǐ le* 花給死了 'The flowering plant, alas, has withered and died' (Chen and Yap, 2018). The grammaticalization of the 'give' verb *gei* into a speaker affectedness marker involves a valence-reducing process. As shown in the Mandarin Chinese examples in (9a-d), the 'give' verb (9a) can develop into a causative verb meaning 'let' or 'allow' (9b) (see Lord et al., 2002). As seen in (9c), the 'give' verb can also be reinterpreted as a case marker for defocused agents in passive constructions (e.g. *gěi xiāofángyuán* 給消防員 'by the firefighters') (see Hashimoto, 1988; Yap and Iwasaki,

2003). Of particular interest here, and rather rare in the languages of the world (attested thus far only within the Sinitic language family, typically observed among speakers of Mandarin and Southern Min varieties, as shown in (9d) and (9e-f) respectively), the 'give' verb can further be used as a speaker affectedness marker (Chen and Yap, 2018). Matthews et al. (2005) and Lin (2011) discuss this function of the 'give' morpheme in terms of adversity marking, while Huang (2013) identifies it as a case marker for 'phantom (i.e. covert or implicit) affectees' that include an affected speaker. This grammaticalization process involves the extended use of the 'give' verb from a causative (3-place predicate) construction to a passive (2-place predicate) construction in virtually all Chinese varieties, and further to an unaccusative (1-place predicate) construction in only some Chinese varieties (Huang, 2013; Chen and Yap, 2018).

(9) a Lexical verb 'give' (Mandarin Chinese)
他給了我一個機會。
tā **gěile** wǒ yīgè jīhuì
3SG GIVE-PFV 1SG one.CL chance
'He **gave** me a chance'.

b Light verb 'give' in causative construction (Mandarin Chinese)
你應該給他上學。
nǐ yīnggāi **gěi** tā shàngxué
2SG should GIVE 3SG go.to.school
'You should **let** him go to school'.

c 'Give' as case marker of defocused agent (Mandarin Chinese)
火給（消防員）滅了。
huǒ **gěi** *(xiāofángyuán)* miè-le
fire GIVE (firemen) extinguish-PFV
'The fire was extinguished **(by the firefighters)**'.

d 'Give' as a 'speaker affectedness' marker (Mandarin Chinese)
金魚給它死了。
jīnyú **gěi** *(tā)* sǐ-le
goldfish GIVE 3SG die-RVC
'**Alas**, the goldfish has died. (Someone must have overfed it and I'm upset)'.

e 'Give' as a 'speaker affectedness' marker (Hui'an Southern Min)
金魚與伊死去。
$kiəm^1hu^2$ **$khɔ^{5-4}$** i^1 si^3khu^0
goldfish GIVE 3SG die-RVC
'**Alas**, the goldfish has died. (That's unfortunate and I'm upset)'.

f 'Give' as a 'speaker affectedness' marker (Hui'an Southern Min)
金魚與伊死去。
$kiəm^1hu^2$ **$khɔ^{5-1}$** si^3khu^0
goldfish GIVE.3SG die-RVC
'**Alas**, the goldfish has died. (That's unfortunate and I'm upset)'.

The narrative for the emergence of the 'speaker affectedness' marker is worth a closer look. Essentially, as seen in (9d), the versatile and semantically bleached 'give' morpheme can still retain traces of its causative function that we see in (9b), such that in mainland Mandarin Chinese varieties, native speakers often associate the third-person pronoun *tā* (3SG) in (9d) with an implicit causer, which often gives rise to interpretations with a tinge of blame assignment (e.g. '*Someone/Something* caused the boat to sink').

235

In Southern Min varieties such as Hui'an, on the other hand, the 'give' morpheme in (9e-f) tends to lean more towards a case-marking function, more specifically as a case marker for affected participants. As noted in Chen and Yap (2018), the Hui'an third-person pronoun *i¹* (3SG) as seen in (9e-f) is far more grammaticalized than its Mandarin counterpart *tā* (3SG) in (9d), in that it is highly pleonastic and could refer not only to singular third-person referents (3SG) but also to plural third-person referents (3PL), as well as to second person referents (2SG). This highly pleonastic Hui'an third-person pronoun *i¹* can thus refer to a wide variety of referents that are affected by the adversative event, among them the affected patient and affected others in the discourse, *including the speaker himself/herself*. Thus, in subtle contrast to Mandarin speakers as shown in (9d), Hui'an speakers as shown in (9e-f) are more inclined to focus on the adversative outcome than on an implicit causer.

Overall, for both the Mandarin and Southern Min varieties, it is largely due to the underspecified status of the third-person pronoun (sometimes explicitly expressed but often elided as in the case of Mandarin *tā* in (9d) or phonologically incorporated as in the case of Hui'an *i¹* in (9f)) that the speaker-affected 'give' construction has come to also express the subjective stance of the speaker.

3.2 Noun-based stance markers

It has often been observed that stance markers often share the same form as nominalizers derived from general nouns. This syncretism has been attested in many language families, among them Tibeto-Burman (see Matisoff, 1972; Noonan, 1997; Bickel, 1999; Watters, 2008; DeLancey, 2011; Morey, 2011; *inter alia*), Japanese and Korean (e.g. Fujii, 2000; Horie, 2008; Rhee, 2008, 2011), as well as Chinese (e.g. Yap et al., 2010; Yap et al., 2017). Crosslinguistically, the grammaticalization trajectory takes the following path: general noun > nominalizer > stance marker (Yap and Grunow-Hårsta, 2010; *inter alia*). Below we will focus on how noun-based stance markers emerge from copula-elided constructions.

As seen in (10), from Mandarin Chinese, nominalization constructions such as *wǒ zuótiān mǎi de* 我昨天買的 'the one that I bought yesterday' are frequently used in copula constructions (10a.i), where the head-final nominalizer (in this case *de* 的, which is etymologically derived from the noun *dǐ* 底 meaning 'base, foundation, bottom'), can end up in utterance-final position and be reinterpreted as a sentence final mood particle (10a.ii). Such reanalysis is facilitated by the nominalizer being situated in utterance-final position, where it can easily host the utterance-final prosody of the speaker (see Yap et al., 2010). Given that copula constructions such as (10a) are focus constructions with assertive force, the default mood reading associated with sentence final particle (SFP) *de* is assertive as well. Reanalysis of head-final nominalizer (NMLZ) *de* to sentence final mood particle (SFP) *de* is also made easier in Chinese because the language allows for subject and copula elision, as seen in (10b).

(10) a 這個是<u>我昨天買的</u>。
       zhège   *shì*   *wǒ*   *zuótiān*   *mǎi*   ***de***
       this.CL   COP   1SG   yesterday   buy   NMLZ/SFP
       (i)   'This is [**what** I bought yesterday]'. (< 'This is [**that which** I bought yesterday]'.)
       (ii)   '[This is what I bought yesterday] ***de*** (=*you can take my word for it*)'.
   b 我昨天買的。
       wǒ   *zuótiān*   *mǎi*   ***de***
       1SG   yesterday   buy   NMLZ/SFP
       (i)   '(This is) **something (that)** I bought yesterday'.
       (ii)   '(This) I bought yesterday'./'I bought this yesterday'.

Elision of the matrix subject and copula, as in (10b), yields a stand-alone nominalization construction that is reinterpreted as the new main clause. This syntactic restructuring phenomenon is widely attested crosslinguistically, and involves a process known as 'insubordination' (Evans, 2007; Evans and Watanabe, 2016). Basically, we see a subordinate complement clause (in this case, a *de*-type nominalization construction in the form [Complement.clause [*wǒ zuótiān mǎi* _] *de*] '[that which [I bought yesterday]]') which is reanalyzed as an independent finite structure, with nominalizer *de* reinterpreted as a sentence final mood particle (SFP) and hence the finiteness marker for the new insubordinated clause (i.e. [New.main..clause [[*wǒ zuótiān mǎi* _] _] *de*]] 'I bought (it) yesterday'). This reanalysis is highlighted in (10') below.

(10') [Subject *zhège* [Copula/Focus *shì* [DE-type.nominalization.construction [*wǒ zuótiān mǎi* _] *de*]
→ [DE-type,insubordinated.clause [DE-type.nominalization.construction [*wǒ zuótiān mǎi* _] _] *de*]

This insubordination process is facilitated by the frequent association of copula *shì* and nominalizer *de* in copula-based focus constructions (often also called the *shì . . . de* focus construction). That is, through frequent association in emphatic contexts, nominalizer *de* comes to acquire the assertive force of the *shì . . . de* focus construction. At the same time, given its utterance-final position by virtue of its being a head-final nominalizer within the *shì . . . de* construction, *de* also gets to host the speaker's utterance-final assertive prosody. Both conditions facilitate the syntactic scope expansion that gives rise to the reanalysis of nominalizer *de* as a sentence final mood particle. In sum, the resulting *de*-type insubordinated clause is 'anchored' in the discourse by the speaker's illocutionary force, typically assertive, with the head-final nominalizer *de* reinterpreted as a finiteness particle. In most Chinese varieties, utterance-final *de* is typically reinterpreted as an assertive mood particle, as seen in (10b.ii). In some northern Mandarin varieties, this finite particle is additionally used as a past tense marker as well (see Simpson and Wu, 2002; Cheng and Sybesma, 2005).

Other types of semantic prosodies are also possible for utterance-final *de*, depending on contextual and prosodic cues. For example, a rising prosody can help induce either a dubitative (subjective) or confirmation-seeking (intersubjective) reading, as in (11a.i) and (11a.ii) respectively. The ambiguity between a nominalizer and a sentence final mood particle reading for utterance-final *de* is still noticeable in some constructions, as seen in (11b) below.

(11) a 我昨天買的？
  *wǒ   zuótiān   mǎi   **de**?*
  1SG   yesterday   buy   NMLZ/SFP
  (i) 'Is **THIS** what I bought yesterday?' (≠ *wǒ shì zuótiān mǎi **de**?*)
  (ii) 'Did I buy this **YESTERDAY**?' (= *wǒ shì zuótiān mǎi **de**?*)
  b 我昨天去的？
  *wǒ   zuótiān   qù   **de**?*
  1SG   yesterday   go   NMLZ/SFP
  (i) 'Is it [**that** I went (there) yesterday]?' (nominalizer/complementizer *de* reading)
  (ii) '[Did I go there yesterday?]' (sentence final particle *de* reading)

Noun-based nominalizers and stance markers such as Mandarin *de* are frequently derived from general nouns referring to people, objects or places. The semantic generality of such nouns makes them highly versatile, and easily grammaticalizable into nominalizers via a relativization process (e.g. '(some)one/(some)thing that VPs'). They can go further into stance markers via an insubordination process, as illustrated in (11a) above, where nominalizer *de* in '(This is) *the thing*

(=*what*) I bought yesterday?' is reanalyzed as a sentence final dubitative-interrogative marker in '*This is the thing* I bought yesterday?' or '*Did* I buy this yesterday?'. A similar insubordination reanalysis applies to (11b).

Nominalizer-derived stance markers also often combine with other utterance-final particles to yield a more specific stance interpretation (Yap et al., 2017). For example, as seen in (12), nominalizer-derived stance marker *de* can combine with another mood particle *ba* 吧 to yield a complex sentence final particle that marks the speaker's insistent but still uncertain and speculative stance.[2] A few other examples were also noted earlier (recall example (3) in §2).

(12) 人活到七十三歲，
rén   huó   dào   qīshísān   suì
'People live   to   73   years'.
總有些什麼秘密的吧。
*zǒng   yǒu   xiē   shénme   mìmì   **deba***
always   have   some   what   secret   SFP
'People who have lived for 73 years must have some secret'.
(*Canxue Zixuan Ji*, PKU Center for Chinese Linguistics Corpus; cited in Yap et al., 2016)

3.3 Indexical-based stance markers

Indexicals such as demonstratives and possessive markers have also been found to be good sources for the development of stance markers (see, for example, Nagaya, 2011 on the pragmatic uses of demonstratives *ang* and *yung* in Tagalog and Brosig, Gegentana and Yap, forthcoming on the subjective and intersubjective uses of postnominal possessives in Mongolian). This section explores how demonstratives in Chinese can also be employed as stance markers to externalize the speaker's subjective evaluations and thoughts. Mandarin Chinese *nà* and Cantonese *go²di¹* 嗰啲 'that.CL' constructions will be used as illustrative examples.

In Mandarin Chinese, *nà* is a deictic demonstrative used to indicate an entity that is distant from the speaker, as opposed to *zhè* 這 'this' which indicates a proximal orientation. As seen in (13), *nà* can be used to refer to an entity that has already been mentioned earlier in the text – i.e. for anaphoric referent tracking.

(13) 那是他媽媽。
Nà   *shì*   *tā*   *māma.*
that   COP   3SG   mother
'That is his mother'.

In recent work on spontaneous conversations, Yang (2017) suggests that from this demonstrative function, *nà* has grammaticalized into a connective linking the prior turn to the following turn. Upon further grammaticalization, this linker *nà* has further evolved into a stance marker that indicates the speaker's perspective towards the assessment previously made by the addressee. As shown in (14) below, reproduced from (1), *nà* has totally lost its function as a demonstrative, but is used instead as a stance marker to indicate the speaker's disagreement towards the assessment made earlier – that is, even though the addressee is already feeling better (and the situation might have been improved and the addressee might not need another visit to the doctor), the speaker still believes, on the contrary, that the addressee should still go visit the doctor as a precautionary measure. In effect, we see *nà* extending its use as a deictic marker from the spatio-temporal domain to the socio-interactional domain.

(14) 那你還是去看一看醫生吧，雖然你說已經好多了。 (=1)
   Nà   nǐ   háishì   qù   kàn   yī   kàn   yīshēng   ba,
   NA   2SG   still   go   see   one   see   doctor   SFP,
   suīrán   nǐ   shuō   yǐjīng   hǎoduō   le.
   though   2SG   say   already   better   SFP
   '**But** you'd better still go and visit the doctor, though you said you are already better'.

In some Chinese varieties, classifier-demonstratives have also developed into stance markers. In Cantonese, the distal demonstrative-classifier *go²di¹* 'that + classifier' has extended beyond its deictic functions (e.g. *go²di¹ zaap⁶zi³* 嗰啲雜誌 'those magazines' (i.e. the magazines that are distal to the speaker at the time of speaking)) to further develop into a negative attitudinal marker. Consider (15) and (16) below in which classifier-demonstrative *go²di¹* yields a (self-)deprecatory reading.

(15) 係呀，喺 hotels.com 嗰啲 book
   hai⁶   aa³   hai²   hotels.com   **go²di¹**   book
   yes   PRT   at   hotels.com   that.CL   book
   'Yes, I made the booking at those (websites) like hotels.com'. (OpenU Corpus)

(16) 冇呀，住 hostel 嗰啲咋嘛
   mou⁵   aa³   cyu⁶   hostel   **go²di¹**   zaa¹maa³
   NEG   PRT   stay   hostel   that.CL   PRT
   'No, I was just staying in hostels, those types (of inexpensive accommodations)'. (OpenU Corpus)³

In (15) and (16), *go²di¹* functions as a pronoun, referring to slightly cheaper hotel booking websites such as hotels.com as opposed to more expensive travel agencies in (15), and to affordable hostels as opposed to luxury hotels in (16). The deprecatory readings in these classifier-demonstrative *go²di¹* constructions arise from the definite but non-specific reading of pronominal *go²di¹*. Note that in these two examples, the speaker has actually made use of the website *hotel.com* and has stayed in a hostel; thus, the additional use of classifier-demonstrative *go²di¹* seems unnecessary if the speaker's intention is simply to provide information since *hotels.com* is a proper noun and hence already inherently definite and specific. As it turns out, the presence of *go²di¹* adds a negative evaluative reading to the utterances in (15) and (16). That is, rather than being deployed merely as a demonstrative pronoun that replaces a referent identifiable to both interlocutors (speaker and hearer), *go²di¹* has gained a negative overtone to refer to something trivial or unimpressive. Alongside with its pronominal function, *go²di¹* additionally conveys a negative evaluation, similar to expressing the meaning "nothing significant, it is just like those (not very important) things". This trivialness reading emerges from the original use of *di¹* as a collective classifier for a substance in small quantities.

Extending from this deprecatory non-specific reference, *go²di¹* can further be used by the speaker to replace anything that is treated by the speaker as a taboo topic. For example, the speaker can utter (17) to mean that he works in the funeral industry – something that tends to be talked about euphemistically in society.

(17) 我做嗰啲
   ngo⁵   zou⁶   **go²di¹**
   1SG   do   that.CL
   'I do those (kind of) things'. (Yap and Chor, 2016)

This negative bias can be accounted for in terms of the distal meaning of demonstrative *go²* 'that', which pragmatically has come to also refer to social and psychological distance, yielding a sense of indirectness – and by extension, politeness, or otherwise 'feigned politeness' – that can help to attenuate face threats when negative attitudes are being expressed.

The use of demonstrative-classifier constructions such as *go²di¹* to express the speaker's negative attitude is not an isolated phenomenon observable only in Yue dialects such as Cantonese. In fact, this negative attitudinal usage is even more prominent in Xiang varieties. In the Wugang Xiang dialect, for example, the [DEM + CL *di* + N] constructions are used not only to evaluate others negatively but sometimes also for self-deprecation, with the latter function also used to attenuate potential face threats to others (see Deng et al., 2017). An interesting question for future research is whether all or only some Sinitic varieties recruit their demonstrative-classifier constructions for the expression of the speaker's negative attitudinal stance.

4. Conclusion

In this chapter, we have focused on stance-taking, a phenomenon known to be pervasive in human communication, with speakers frequently signaling their stance in both explicit and implicit ways. More specifically, we have identified the development of a number of stance markers in Chinese, paying special attention to their source and grammaticalization pathway(s), and also to the subjective and intersubjective meaning(s) that these stance markers add to our utterance. The three types of source categories identified focused mainly on the verbal, nominal and indexical pathways.

Among the verbal pathways, serial verb constructions and complement-taking verb constructions were found to be frequent sources for stance markers with epistemic, evidential, attitudinal and other (inter)subjective stance readings. An example from among the serial verb constructions is the 'finish'-type verbs in V₂ position, which in the case of Mandarin *le* has developed into a perfect(ive) aspect marker that is often further recruited to serve as an addressee-oriented interactional particle, often used to signal completion of the speaker's turn and at the same time implicitly solicit agreement from the addressee, particularly in potential turn-transition points in a conversation. In the case of complement-taking verbs such as the 'think'-type and 'hear/say'-type verbs (e.g. Mandarin *wǒ juéde* and *tīngshuō*), reanalysis of these cognition-perception-utterance verbs as epistemic and evidential stance markers further paves the way for their use as pragmatic hedges for politeness and solidarity-enhancing work in interactional talk.

Rather rare (and possibly unique) crosslinguistically, transfer verbs in some Chinese varieties have developed into speaker affectedness markers; this semantic extension, observable in Mandarin and Southern Min varieties, emerged through a process of valence underspecification. As illustrated in the Mandarin example *huā gěi sǐ le* 'The flowering plant, alas, has withered away and died', the trivalent verb *gěi* 'give' in this unaccusative (1-place predicate or monovalent) construction does not overtly display its full range of arguments (giver, transferred object, and goal/recipient) yet still makes room for the implicit presence of covert arguments, with the affected speaker being among these 'phantom' referents.

Within the nominal domain, general nouns often develop into nominalizers, some of which further develop into utterance-final stance markers (e.g. Mandarin sentence final mood particle *de*). In many languages, indexicals such as demonstratives also often develop into stance markers (see, for example, Adachi, 2016 on the paradigmatic use of demonstratives as sentence final mood particles in Vietnamese). In some Chinese varieties, we further see an interesting development in which the distal demonstrative combines with a classifier to yield negative attitudinal readings such as in the Cantonese *Nei^5 jau^6 heoi^3 (go^2)di^1 gam^2 ge^3 dei^{6}fong^1 aa^4* 你又去(嗰)啲噉嘅地方呀'(Don't tell me) you are going to (those) kinds of places again?!'. The negative evaluation in this type of demonstrative-classifier construction arises from the psychological-distancing effect of the distal demonstrative *go^2* 'that' and is further reinforced by the trivial value associated with classifier *di^1*. Also worth noting is that versatile distal demonstratives can also develop into stance markers in utterance-initial position, as seen in the case of Mandarin discourse marker *nà*, which is used at conversational turn-transition points to signal speaker disagreement.

To conclude, we often see how resourceful speakers can be in coming up with different stance-marking strategies to express their subjective and intersubjective footing when interacting with others. Crosslinguistically, what is common in the development of these strategies is the strong tendency for stance constructions to emerge from more concrete physical (e.g. referential and spatio-temporal) domains and then further extend to more abstract psychological and socio-pragmatic domains. With reference to previous studies, both diachronic and typological, we have shown how various types of constructions in Chinese have likewise extended their range of functions from the more concrete to the more abstract domains. In some cases, these semantic extensions were accompanied by syntactic reanalyses via robust grammaticalization pathways such as verb serialization and insubordination of complement clauses; in other cases, the extensions traverse less frequently attested pathways, among them the inducement of negative attitudes from classifier-demonstratives and the emergence of speaker affectedness readings from valence-reduced transfer verb (e.g. 'give') constructions. Whether widely attested or rarely attested, the emergence of these stance markers also form part of the robust tendency observed in numerous grammaticalization phenomena, whereby extended use of a given form leads to semantic generalization and semantic bleaching, which paradoxically paves the way for pragmatic strengthening, as the semantically underspecified form comes to be increasingly associated with its context-of-use (see Traugott, 1995 on subjectification and intersubjectification phenomena). From a cognitive perspective, the availability of these various stance-marking strategies co-contribute to the formation of our fairly stable and at the same time permeable, malleable and renewable language systems, which makes it easier for us to meet our expressive needs at both psychological and socio-interactional levels.

Acknowledgments

We gratefully acknowledge funding support from the Research Grants Council of Hong Kong through the project entitled "Valence-reducing Phenomena and the Emergence of Markers of Speaker Affectedness" (RGC General Research Fund Project No. 154055/14H; HKPU B-Q45F). We wish to thank the editor and anonymous reviewers for their comments, and to also express special thanks to Weirong Chen, Serena Deng, Shoichi Iwasaki, Tak-Sum Wong for helpful discussions in the writing of this paper.

Notes

1 English also has a highly grammaticalized (albeit literary and archaic) form *methink(s)* with a strong subjective evaluative reading, as seen in (i) below. This subjective evaluative marker is characterized by the absence of finite properties, as seen in its non-nominative form (*me* instead of *I*), and the fusion of the non-nominative subject (*me*) and the complement-taking verb (*think*), yielding *methink* or *methinks*.

(i) a **Methink** *it Grete Skill.* (15th century Scottish English; cited in Williams & McClure 2013)
 b **Methinks** *the answer to this can be summed up in three letters,...*
 c *The lady doth protest too much,* **methinks**. (Shakespeare's *Hamlet*; late 16th century)

2 With falling intonation, *ba* signals the speaker's speculative and uncertain stance, as in (i); however, with rising intonation, *ba* serves a confirmation-seeking function, as in (ii):

Nǐ   jīntiān   huì   qù   ***ba***.
2SG   today   will   go   SFP
(i) 'You will go, **I suppose**'.
(ii) 'You will go today, **am I right?**'

3 The OpenU Corpus is a Cantonese Corpus consisting of 10 short conversations (40 minutes each) developed under the project *Epistemic Modulation and Speaker Attitude in Cantonese: A Discourse-Pragmatic Perspective*, funded by the Research Grant Council of Hong Kong (FDS #UGC/FDS16/H07/14, PI: Dr Winnie Chor).

References

Adachi, M. (2016) *Demonstratives as Sentence-final Particles in Vietnamese*. Manuscript, Tokyo University of Foreign Studies.

Bickel, B. (1999) 'Nominalization and focus in some Kiranti languages', in *Topics in Nepalese Linguistics*. Y.P. Yadava and W.W. Glover (eds.) Kathmandu: Royal Nepal Academy. pp. 271–296.

Brosig, B., Gegentana and Yap, F.H. (forthcoming). 'Evaluative Uses of Postnominal Possessives in Mongolian', *Journal of Pragmatics*.

Chen, W. and Yap, F.H. (2018) 'Pathways to Adversity and Speaker-affectedness: On the Emergence of Unaccusative "give" Constructions in Chinese', *Linguistics* 56(1): 19–68.

Cheng, L.L.-S. and Sybesma, R. (2005) 'Classifiers in four varieties of Chinese', in *The Oxford Handbook of Comparative Syntax*. G. Cinque and R. Kayne (eds.) Oxford: Oxford University Press. pp. 259–292.

DeLancey, S. (2011) 'Finite structures from clausal nominalization in Tibeto-Burman', in *Nominalization in Asian Languages: Diachronic and Typological Perspectives*. F.H. Yap, K. Grunow-Hårsta and J. Wrona (eds.) Amsterdam: John Benjamins. pp. 343–360.

Deng, Y., Yap, F.H. and Chor, W. (2017) Negative Evaluative Uses of Demonstrative-classifier *di* in Wugang Xiang. Paper Presented at the 15th International Pragmatics Conference (IPrA), 16–21 July, Belfast.

Endo, T. (2010) Expressing Stance in Mandarin Conversation: Epistemic and Non-epistemic Uses of wo juede, Unpublished doctoral dissertation, Department of Asian Languages and Cultures, UCLA.

Evans, N. (2007) 'Insubordination and its uses', in *Finiteness: Theoretical and Empirical Foundations*. I. Nikolaeva (ed.) Oxford: Oxford University Press. pp. 366–431.

Evans, N. and Watanabe, H. (2016) *Insubordination*. Amsterdam: John Benjamins.

Fujii, S. (2000) 'Incipient decategorization of MONO and grammaticalization of speaker attitude in Japanese discourse', in *Pragmatics and Propositional Attitude*. G. Andersen and T. Fretheim (eds.) Amsterdam: John Benjamins. pp. 85–118.

Hashimoto, M.J. (1988) 'The structure and typology of the Chinese passive construction', in *Passive and Voice*. M. Shibatani (ed.) Amsterdam: John Benjamins. pp. 329–354.

Horie, K. (2008) 'The grammaticalization of nominalizers in Japanese and Korean', in *Rethinking Grammaticalization: New Perspectives*. M.J. López-Couso and E. Seoane (eds.) Amsterdam: John Benjamins. pp. 169–187.

Huang, C.J. (2013) 'Variations in non-canonical passives', in *Non-Canonical Passives*. A. Alexiadou and F. Schäfer (eds.) Amsterdam: John Benjamins. pp. 95–114.

Kärkkäinen, E. (2003) *Epistemic Stance in English Conversation: A Description of its Interactional Functions, With a Focus on I Think*, Amsterdam: John Benjamins.

Lim, N.E. (2011) 'From subjectivity to intersubjectivity: Epistemic marker *wo juede* in Chinese', in *Current Issues in Chinese Linguistics*. Y. Xiao, L. Tao and H.L. Soh (eds.) Cambridge: Cambridge Scholars Press. pp. 265–300.

Lin, H. (2011) 'Pure Unaccusatives with HOO I in Taiwan Southern Min', *Lingua* 121: 2035–2047.

Lord, C., Yap, F.H. and Iwasaki, S. (2002) 'Grammaticalization of "give": African and Asian Perspectives', in *New Reflections on Grammaticalization*. I. Wischer and G. Diewald (eds.) Amsterdam: John Benjamins. pp. 217–235.

Lu, L.W. and Su, L.I-W. (2009) Speech in Interaction: Mandarin Particle *le* as a Marker of Intersubjectivity. Manuscript, National Taiwan University, Taipei, Taiwan.

Matisoff, J. (1972) 'Lahu nominalization, relativization, and genitivization', in *Syntax and Semantics, Volume 1, Studies in Language Series*. J. Kimball (ed.) New York: Seminar Press. pp. 237–257.

Matthews, S., Xu, H. and Yip, V. (2005) 'Passive and Unaccusative in the Jieyang Dialect of Chaozhou', *Journal of East Asian Linguistics* 14(4): 267–298.

Morey, S. (2011) 'Nominalization in Numhpuk Singpho', in *Nominalization in Asian Languages*. F.H. Yap, K. Grunow-Hårsta and J. Wrona (eds.) Amsterdam: John Benjamins. pp. 289–331.

Nagaya, N. (2011) 'Rise and fall of referentiality: articles in Philippine languages', in *Nominalization in Asian Languages*. F.H. Yap, K. Grunow-Hårsta and J. Wrona (eds.) Amsterdam: John Benjamins. pp. 589–626.

Noonan, M. (1997) 'Versatile nominalizations', in *Essays on Language Function and Language Type*. T. Givón, J. Bybee, J. Haiman and S.A. Thompson (eds.) Amsterdam: John Benjamins. pp. 373–394.

Rhee, S. (2008) 'On the rise and fall of Korean nominalizers', in *Rethinking Grammaticalization: New Perspectives*. M.J. Lopez-Couso and E. Seoane (eds.) in collaboration with T. Fanego. Amsterdam: John Benjamins. pp. 239–264.

Rhee, S. (2011) 'Nominalization and stance marking in Korean', in *Nominalization in Asian Languages: Diachronic and Typological Perspectives*. F.H. Yap, K. Grunow- Hårsta and J. Wrona (eds.) Amsterdam: John Benjamins. pp. 393–422.

Simpson, A. and Wu, Z. (2002) 'Agreement, Shells and Focus', *Language* 78: 287–313.

Thompson, S.A. and Mulac, A. (1991) 'The Discourse Conditions For the Use of the Complementizer that in Conversational English', *Journal of Pragmatics* 15(3): 237–251.

Traugott E.C. (1995) 'Subjectification in grammaticalisation', in *Subjectivity and Subjectivisation: Linguistic Perspectives, Vol. 1*. D. Stein and S. Wright (eds.) Cambridge, UK: Cambridge University Press. pp. 31–54.

Traugott, E.C. (2010) 'Grammaticalization', *Historical Pragmatics* 8: 97.

Watters, D. (2008) 'Nominalization in the East and Central Himalayish Languages of Nepal', *Linguistics of the Tibeto-Burman Area* 31(2): 1–43.

Williams, J.H. and McClure, J.D. (2013) *Fresche Fontanis: Studies in the Culture of Medieval and Early Modern Scotland*. Cambridge Scholar Publishing.

Xing, J.Z. (2006) 'Mechanisms of Semantic Change in Chinese', *Studies in Language* 30(3): 461–483.

Yang, Y. (2017) 'Turn Initial *na* "that": The Emergence of a Stance Marker in Mandarin Chinese Conversations', Paper Presented at the 15th International Pragmatics Conference (IPrA), 16–21 July, Belfast.

Yap, F.H. and Chor, W. (2016) Implicit Deicticity and Negative Attitudinal Marking: The Case of Nei di and Go di [Demonstrative + Classifier] Constructions in Cantonese Discourse. Paper Presented at the 26th Annual Meeting of the Southeast Asian Linguistics Society (SEALS-26), 26–28 May, Manila, the Philippines.

Yap, F.H., Choi, P.-L. and Cheung, K.S. (2010) 'De-lexicalizing *di3*: How a Chinese locative noun has evolved into an attitudinal nominalizer', in *Formal Evidence in Grammaticalization Research*. A. Van linden, J-C. Verstraete and K. Davidse (eds.) Amsterdam: John Benjamins. pp. 63–91.

Yap, F.H., Deng, Y. and Caboara, M. (2017) 'Attitudinal Nominalizer(s) in Chinese: Evidence of Recursive Grammaticalization and Pragmaticization', *Lingua* 200: 1–21.

Yap, F.H. and Grunow-Hårsta, K. (2010) 'Non-referential Uses of Nominalization Constructions: Asian Perspectives', *Language and Linguistics Compass* 4(12): 1154–1175.

Yap, F.H. and Iwasaki, S. (2003) 'From Causative to Passive: A Passage in Some East and Southeast Asian Languages', in *Cognitive Linguistics and Non-Indo-European Languages*. E. Casad and G. Palmer (eds.) Berlin: Mouton de Gruyter. pp. 419–446.

Yap, F.H., Yang, Y. and Wong, T-S. (2014) 'On the development of sentence final particles (and utterance tags) in Chinese', in *Discourse Functions at the Left and Right Periphery: Crosslinguistic Investigations of Language Use and Language Change [Studies in Pragmatics 12]*, K. Beeching and U. Detges (eds.) Leiden, The Netherlands: Brill. pp. 179–220.

16
Language, gesture and meaning

Kawai Chui

Introduction

We speak; we gesture. A variety of gestures occur naturally when people talk to each other. First, self-adaptors are self-touching movements which can be meaningful in interaction. For instance, a simple touch of the nose could mean that someone was not being truthful. Such movements do not bear a direct semantic relationship with the utterance. Emblematic gestures, on the other hand, are meaningful in their own right. They have socially agreed-upon standards of well-formedness and are produced in much the same way across the users of a particular language, like waving the hand for 'goodbye' or making the okay gesture for 'approval'. The emblematic meaning may or may not be associated with speech (Ekman and Friesen, 1969; Goldin-Meadow, 1999; Kendon, 1984, 1995, 2004; McNeill, 1992, 2005). Beat gestures, however, are bound to utterance. They are typically small up and down or back and forth flicks of one or both hands that occur along with the rhythm of speech (McNeill, 1992; McClave, 1994). Beat gestures have no semantic association with speech, but can be used to emphasize portions of the speech content (Efron, 1941, 1972; Wagner et al., 2014). McNeill (1992: 15) found that in narrative discourse, "the occurrence of beats is related to discourse structure, when there are shifts among the narrative, metanarrative, and paranarrative levels of discourse". Next, deictic gestures have to do with pointing to linguistic referents in the immediate speech environment. Spatial gestures are used to allocate gesture spaces symbolically to the linguistic referents. Finally, iconic gestures bear a direct semantic relationship with speech (McNeill, 1992, 2000). The meaning conveyed by iconic gestures mainly rests upon context. Consider Figure 16.1. The speaker on the left, who first had the arms crossed under the chest, moved the hands to the front; then, the hands in lightly formed fists, the left one slightly above the right, moved in a curve from the center to her right periphery. It is difficult to comprehend what such gesture means in the interaction without the presence of speech, despite the fact that the hand movements are conspicuous, noticeable, and produced in the center space (see the Gesture Space in McNeill, 1992).

Example 1 as follows is the linguistic context for the occurrence of the gesture in Figure 16.1. The participants were chatting about an incident related to a hornet's nest. The person on the right (F1) first brought up the fact of a hornet's nest being built outside the window of her room. The speaker on the left (F2) responded that the nest could be seen by opening the

Language, gesture and meaning

Figure 16.1 Manual movements produced by the speaker on the left

window. During this response, a gesture was produced at the time that the speaker uttered the question about opening the window in Line 3: The speaker's hands started to rise and extend outward with closed fingers during the uttering of the second pronominal 你 and the question form 要不要 'want-NEG-want' for a period of 499 milliseconds. The movement was done in preparation for the next gestural stroke, in which the enactment of the open-the-window action for 673 milliseconds synchronized with the uttering of the main verb 打開來 'open'. Afterward, the arms and hands returned to their original position under the chest. The gesture as a whole depicts the manner of the opening of a window in the context of having a hornet's nest outside the window of a room.

(1) 1 F1: ..就是我有朋友來..我都會跟他說
    2   ..eh 你看..我房間窗戶有蜂窩耶
          'When my friends came, I would tell them, "You see, my room . . . the window . . . (outside) the window of my room, there is a beehive"'.
    3 F2: ..是虎頭蜂的唷..你要不要打開來看看
          'It is a hornet's nest. Do you want to open (the window) and have a look (at it)?'

The dependence on context for the understanding of iconic gestures can further be attested by a survey of people's interpretation of a gesture in the absence of speech. A naturally occurring gestural instance from the NCCU (National Chengchi University) Corpus of Spoken Taiwan Mandarin depicts the idea of writing answers in the context of school exams. As shown in Example 2, the speaker on the left was saying that the students did not write the type of answer that was expected, but rather their MSN addresses and telephone numbers instead. At the same time, he extended his right index finger to enact the holding of a pen at the moment of producing the first syllable of the word 考卷 'exam paper'. He then moved the right hand leftward to meet the left hand. See Figure 16.2. These manual movements realize the idea of students writing answers on exam papers in the context of examination.

Figure 16.2 A writing gesture

(2) M: ..考卷上**都不是答案**..都是學生的那個 **MSN** 跟電話這樣
      'On the exam papers, it was not answers but students' MSN and phone numbers'.

The video clip, which only contained this particular gesture, was presented without sound and without information about the context to a group of 24 college students of a general education course in 2017, to examine the effect of the lack of contextual information on people's understanding of this iconic gesture. The students were requested to write down an interpretation of the gesture. Only half of the participants interpreted the manual action as being in relation to writing. The other half did not associate the gesture with writing, as indicated by some of the responses in Table 16.1.

The same video was also viewed by another group of 29 college students of a general education course without sound, but the students were informed that the participants in the video were talking about 街舞 'street-dance'. A completely different set of responses was obtained. Only six responses (20.7%) were related to writing; four were ideas not relevant to writing and dance (13.8%). The remaining majority (65.5%) were associated with what people could do with street dance, as exemplified in Table 16.2. The results of the survey provide evidence in support of the close relationship between iconic gestures and the context of use.

Self-adaptors, emblems, beats, deictic, spatial, and iconic gestures are all common manual movements in interaction. How frequently do people use them when they speak? In terms of the clause which consists of a predicate and its argument(s), a dataset of eleven conversational excerpts that total 224 minutes of talk yielded 6,383 clauses. Beat and/or self-touching gestures occurred 65% of the time on average. For those gestures that are semantically related to speech, an average of 18% of all the clauses included emblematic, deictic, spatial, and/or iconic gestures.

Iconic gestures in particular have received much attention from researchers because of their close semantic relation with speech. Gestures of this type also bear a wide variety of functions in speech communication. They can facilitate speech production (Rime and Schiaratura, 1991),

Table 16.1 The interpretations of the writing gesture without contextual information

Original response	Translation
分享切牛排的技巧	Share the skill of how to cut steaks
他在教怎麼做料理	He is teaching how to cook something
表達某種很長的東西	Express that a particular thing is very long
表達延綿不絕持續的意思	Express the meaning of continuity
解釋他說的話	Explain what he is talking about
讓對方能更加理解他所訴說的情境	Have the addressee better understand the situation he is talking about
引起對方注意，有助於溝通	Get the attention of the addressee for better communication
使發言者的話語更顯張力	Show the intensity in the speech of the speaker

Table 16.2 The interpretations of the writing gesture with the contextual information about street dance

Original response	Translation
討論舞步	Discuss dance steps
街舞的基本動作	The basic movements of street dance
街舞動作的形式與意義	The form and meaning of the movement of street dance
介紹其中一種街舞的形式	Introduce the form of a kind of street dance
地板的旋轉動作	The rotating movement on the floor
以肢體律動的方式表現情感	Use bodily rhythm to show feelings
邀觀眾一起投入舞蹈	Invite the audience to join in the dance together

lexical retrieval (Krauss et al., 2000), problem-solving (Alibali et al., 1999), remembering more (Goldin-Meadow et al., 2001), organizing the speaker's thinking for speaking (Alibali et al., 2000), establishing conversational coherence (Chui, 2009) and accomplishing common ground in conversational interaction (Clark and Krych, 2004). There has also been a large body of experimental and neuroimaging research on the processing of iconic gestures (such as Özyürek et al., 2007; Holle et al., 2008; Straube et al., 2012; Dick et al., 2014; Chui et al., 2018). These previous studies present converging evidence that speech and gesture are integrated during language processing, no matter whether the two modalities convey the same or different information (see the review in Özyürek, 2014). However, despite the wide range of gesture studies, the empirical investigation of the use of gesture in real-time interaction is still scarce. Regarding the semantic relation between speech and iconic gesture, the two modalities can overlap in the representation of meaning, but gesture can also convey a meaning that makes the linguistic meaning more specific, creates a version of an object being referred to, or depicts the shape, size and spatial characteristics or relationships of an object (Kendon, 2004). In Taiwan Mandarin conversational discourse, gestures were found to convey attitudinal, script-evoked, and topical information about the associated speech events (Chui, 2008). In relation to different conceptual frames, gestures could depict information about roles, role relations, and scripts (Chui, 2012a). Finally, the study of the linguistic-gestural representation of motion events demonstrated modal specificity as the path information was found to be preferred in gesture, but a preference between manner and path was not apparent in speech (Chui, 2012b). All of these results are evidence that a speaker may talk about something while making a gesture about something else simultaneously. In this study, the focus of interest is on the representation of meaning in speech and iconic gesture about the same nominal or verbal concept, so as to understand the extent of the semantic redundancy between speech and gesture, and modal specificity in the communication of meaning.

This chapter addresses the following questions concerning the cross-modal representation of meaning: Do speech and gesture tend to convey an identical or different semantic information? Do they demonstrate modal specificity in the representation of meaning, in that there is a preference for different types of information about nominal and verbal concepts to be expressed by different modalities? A sizable amount of linguistic-gestural instances associated with nouns or verbs from Taiwan Mandarin conversational data constitutes the dataset for the study.

In the next section, the data and methodology are introduced. Then, the analysis of the representation of meaning about the same concept across the modalities is presented, followed by the general discussion of the findings and the conclusion.

Data and methods

The data for this study consisted of everyday face-to-face conversations among adult native speakers of Mandarin contained in the NCCU Corpus of Spoken Taiwan Mandarin.[1] The participants were recruited to hold a conversation with their friends, family members or colleagues who knew each other well. All of the participants were paid, and they were informed that they were participating in research on conversation, but gestures were not mentioned. For each recording, the participants chose a place where they could talk in a leisurely manner, such as a classroom, students' lounge, dorm room, or living room. They recorded themselves using a digital video camera on a tripod for approximately an hour. The participants were free to find and develop topics of common interest. One stretch of talk, at a time when the participants were comfortable in front of the camera, of about twenty to forty minutes from the total length of each talk, was then selected for transcription. The data are available online with written consent from the participants (Chui and Lai, 2008; Chui et al., 2017). For the present study, the speech and the gesture data were gathered from eleven conversational excerpts consisting of 16 female and 8 male participants (age range = 17–29) for a total length of 224 minutes of talk.

In order to investigate the distribution of semantic information between speech and gesture, the study focuses on the expression of lexical concepts. The selection of the data was done according to the following criteria. First, a lexical concept is encoded as a nominal referent or as a predicate in the utterance. Second, each lexical constituent is accompanied by an iconic gesture, which conveys semantic information related to the same nominal or verbal concept. Two coders worked independently to identify the linguistic-gestural instances that met the above conditions.

For every instance of the gesture, the coders first identified the boundary of a gesture with respect to three major phases: 'preparation', 'stroke', and 'retraction' (McNeill, 1992, 2005). During the preparation phase, the hand(s) move(s) from a resting position to the location of the beginning point of the gesture stroke. The stroke phase bears the main part of the meaning of the gesture, after which the hand(s) start(s) to return to a resting position. The stroke is obligatory, while both preparation and retraction are optional. It is within the stroke phase that the configuration of the gesture is characterized by considering the major gestural features: the position of the arm and hand in the gesture space, the hand shape, the palm-finger orientation, and, if any, the movement and the direction (cf. Kendon, 2004; McNeill, 1992, 2005; Wagner et al., 2014). The understanding of the meaning in the gesture rests on the overall realization of these features and the associated speech. For instance, the characterization of the gesture in Figure 16.1 was that the female speaker's arms and hands rose from the chest level to shoulder level, and the hands in fist in front of the chest curved from the center space to her right side. This configuration as a whole enacted the manner of the action related to the associated verb 'open'. Further, the gestural meaning was put into words. The inter-analyst reliability between the two coders for the identification and analysis of the linguistic-gestural instances, the gesture phases, the gestural features, and the meaning of the gesture was about 90% on average. Reanalysis was done in the cases where there was disagreement. Data for which no consensus was reached were not included in the study. Agreement was reached on 222 linguistic-gestural instances for use in the study with a comparable distribution between N and V of 102 lexical nouns and 120 lexical verbs.

Linguistic-gestural representation of meaning

This section discusses how speech and gesture represent the meaning of the same lexical concept. The points under consideration are whether the two modalities tend to convey an identical or distinct semantic information across nouns and verbs, and whether there is modal specificity in such semantic representation.

Nominal concepts

The dataset includes 102 nominal instances of concrete concepts such as 鏡子 'mirror' and 船 'ship', or abstract concepts like 順序 'sequence' and 機會 'chance'. Sixty-five instances (63.7%) were depicted by the object gesture, which configures a boundary for a nominal referent. Despite the variation in the ways in which a bounded area could be formed, the use of a cupped hand was the most common way to enact a boundary (Chui, 2017). Consider the pair of examples below. In Example 3, the male speaker was talking about a whale crashing into a ship. At the time that the speaker produced the referent 那個 'that' 船 'ship', his left hand at face level started

Language, gesture and meaning

to descend and formed the boundary of a ship in a cupped shape with fingers loosely apart and curled in the center space (Figure 16.3).

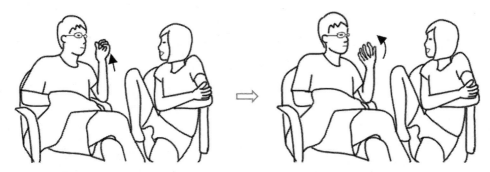

Figure 16.3 Gestural depiction of 'ship'

(3) M: ..那個船就被撞翻
   'The ship was then turned over'.

Example 4 is about teachers giving students chances to try many things at school. In the utterance, the female speaker produced the abstract referent 機會 'chance', which was simultaneously depicted by an object gesture, as the female speaker turned the left palm upward and formed a cupped shape in the center space (Figure 16.4).

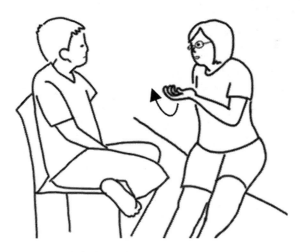

Figure 16.4 Gestural depiction of 'chance'

(4) F: ...很多老師其實都給我們機會
   'Actually, many teachers gave us chances'.

The linguistic-gestural instances in Examples 3 and 4 demonstrate semantic redundancy between the two modalities. In the data, there are 33 nominal instances (32.4%) where both the NP forms and the object gestures correspond in representing the nominal concepts as entities. In the majority of cases (67.6%), the two modalities convey distinct information. Example 5 is an instance showing that gesture and speech are complementary in expressing related but non-redundant semantic information. In Figure 16.5, the speaker on the left was talking about a scene in a pub in a movie, where there was a live band. At the time that he produced the demonstrative 那種 'that-kind', his hands came together in front of the chest. While uttering the nominal referent 現場 'live' 樂隊 'band', the fingers of his hands moved up and down several times for the depiction of the pressing of the keys on the keyboard of a musical instrument. Here, the clausal utterance states the existence of a live band in the pub, whereas the accompanying iconic gesture depicts a different aspect of meaning about the same concept of 'live band' – that a member of the band was playing a musical instrument with a keyboard.

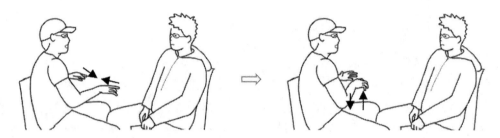

Figure 16.5 Gestural depiction of 'playing a keyboard musical instrument'

(5) M: ..就是在 pub 裡面..然後有那種現場樂隊
'That is, in the pub, there is a live band'.

For the understanding of modal specificity in the representation of meaning, the study separated the semantic information expressed by the two modalities for analysis. Table 16.3 lists the various types of semantic information represented in gesture. In our data, gestures are used to depict the semantic traits of referents, including the shape of a mirror (Example 6), the length of a semi-truck (Example 7), the size of a paragraph (Example 8) or the bodily location of the speaker's dental brace (Example 9). Gestures are also used to express information about what people do with the referents, like a live band playing music in Example 10. Last, gestures also convey alternative metaphorical thoughts about the referents, like the gesture depicting UP IS GOOD while speech expressing FRONT IS GOOD for the referent of the top three priorities in selecting a choice of university in Example 11.

On the part of speech, the semantic information about the nominal concepts includes size (e.g. 這麼一大段 'such a big paragraph'), color (e.g. 那種綠色管子 'that kind of green (fume exhaust) tube'), trait (e.g. 很模糊的世界 'a very vague world'), value (e.g. 一百塊的那個芒果塔 'the mango tart that costs $100 dollars'), material (e.g. 塑膠的那個 'the plastic one (glove)'), quantity (e.g. 一些陸地 'some pieces of land'), sequence (e.g. 前三志願 'the top three priorities'), possessor (e.g. 他的方向 'its direction (the direction of the examination))', location (e.g. SOGO 裡面的商圈 'the shopping district in (the area of) Sogo'), and activity related to the referent (e.g. 學習的東西 'the thing to learn').

Table 16.4 presents the statistics concerning the types of semantic information conveyed by each modality, excluding semantic redundancy, as indicated by the use of bare nominal forms

Table 16.3 The semantic information about nominal concepts as represented in gesture

(6)   Speech – A weird person
        F: . . 啊有一面鏡子在那邊
            'There is a mirror there'.

Figure 16.6 Shape of a mirror: hands configure a rectangle.

(7)   Speech – A dead whale on a semi-truck
        M: . . 就他在拖板車
            'It (a dead whale) was on a semi-truck'.

Figure 16.7 Length of the sides of a semi-truck: hands move to the sides from center, palms facing each other.

(8)   Speech – Weekly journal
        F: . . 就寫了這樣這麼一大段
            '(He) then wrote a big paragraph like this'

Figure 16.8 Size of a paragraph: hands with thumbs and index fingers spread wide apart to form a large rectangular frame.

(9)   Speech – A dental brace affects speaking
        F: . . 因為我現在有牙套
            'Because I am having a dental brace now'.

Figure 16.9 Bodily location for a dental brace: left hand moves from table to touch the mandible.

(*Continued*)

Table 16.3 (Continued)

(10)   Speech – A live band at a bar
       M: . . 然後有那種現場樂隊
           'Then, there is a live band'.

Figure 16.10 Pressing the keys on the keyboard of a musical instrument: fingers of both hands go up and down several times.

(11)   Speech – University entrance exam and priorities
       F: . . 大概前三志願 . . 考細心
           'Probably, (you must be) careful (in the exam in order to enter a university which is one of your) top three priorities'.

Figure 16.11 UP IS GOOD: right palm is open and sweeps upward.

* The speech associated with a gesture is in boldface.

Table 16.4 The semantic information about nominal concepts across modalities

	Speech		Gesture	
Quantity	16	35.6%	–	0.0%
Activity	7	15.6%	9	23.1%
Possessor	6	13.3%	–	0.0%
Trait	6	13.3%	–	0.0%
Shape/size/length	3	6.7%	21	53.8%
Bodily location	2	4.4%	6	15.4%
Sequence	2	4.4%	–	0.0%
Color	1	2.2%	–	0.0%
Material	1	2.2%	–	0.0%
Value	1	2.2%	–	0.0%
Metaphor	–	0.0%	3	7.7%
Total:	45	100.0%	39	100.0%

(57.8%, 59 out of 102) and the use of object gestures (63.7%, 65 out of 102). Some instances expressed more than one type of information, like the nominal 'the top three priorities' simultaneously conveying sequence and quantity about the referent 志願 'priorities', or the gesture for 'pillar' indicating both its shape and length at the same time. Different types of information about the same instance were separated for tabulation. The range of the meaning being represented is wider in speech than in gesture, and information about quantity is most commonly brought up in speech. Manually, information about dimension with respect to the shape, size, or length of the referents tend to be represented in gesture.

To summarize, in 32.4% of cases, speech and gesture overlap in meaning, and both represent the nominal concepts as entities. For the majority of such cases, the nominal referents are encoded in speech as objects and enacted by the object gestures. When the two modalities represent different types of information, modal specificity in the distribution of meaning is in evidence, in that speech tends to encode information about quantity, while gesture largely enacts information about dimension. The next section will show that the distribution of meaning about verbal concepts also patterns diversely across modalities.

Verbal concepts

There are 120 linguistic-gestural instances of verbal concepts in the dataset. Cases where the modalities convey identical information take up only 23 instances (19.2%), among which 22 of them concern motion events represented by path verbs such as 下山 'go downhill' in Example 11. The speaker on the left was talking about seeing two students who were going downhill. In the utterance, the speaker produced the path verb 下山 and moved the right hand downward at an angle to the left simultaneously (Figure 16.12). One instance of semantic redundancy is about the explosion of the body of a dead whale that was lying in a semi-truck and made the cars on the street become red. The change of color is encoded by the verb 變成 'become' and enacted correspondingly by moving the hand from one spatial position to another.

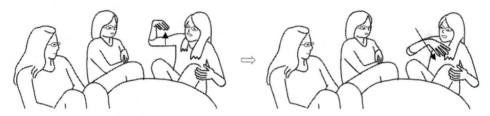

Figure 16.12 Gestural depiction of 'going downhill'

(12) F: …對啊就開車下山呐..然後他們兩個走路
'Right, we drove downhill, and then they both walked'.

In 80.8% of the verbal instances, speech and gesture represent distinct meanings. As in Example 1, about opening a window to see a hornet's nest, the speaker uttered the verb 'open', while her hands enacted the manner of opening a window (Figure 16.1).

Three types of verbal concepts were distinguished for the investigation of semantic non-redundancy across the linguistic and gestural modalities, namely 'motion', 'state', and 'action'. The first two types, which total 22 cases in the dataset, constitute a minority (22.7%). First, as shown in Table 16.5, a manner verb can co-occur with an orientational gesture to indicate the direction of a motion event, such as 走路 'walk' and the moving of the left hand of the speaker to the right in Example 13. Manner gestures also co-occur with manner verbs, but with more contextual details manually, such as where the verb 丟 'throw', which occurs with the manner gesture of throwing a water bottle with force, as in Example 14. Second, a state verb can co-occur with a gesture, which enacts different characteristics of the theme of being involved in a state, such as where the predicate 寬 'be wide' occurs with the gesturing of the shape of the nose as in Example 15. Last, the metaphorical thought of some stative concepts

Table 16.5 The semantic information about motion and state concepts as represented in gesture

(13)　　Speech – Encountering two students
　　　　F: . . 然後他們兩個**走路**
　　　　　　'Then, they both walked'.

Figure 16.13　Walking direction: left hand moves rightward and upward.

(14)　　Speech – An action against a person
　　　　M: . . 他在旁邊直接拿那個..水瓶**去丟**他
　　　　　　'Standing at the side, he took the water bottle directly and threw (it) at him'.

Figure 16.14　Tossing manner: right hand at shoulder level goes forward and downward with force.

(15)　　Speech – The appearance of a person
　　　　F: . . 然後鼻子這裡就..就很**寬**這樣子
　　　　　　'Then, the nose here was then, then, very wide'.

Figure 16.15　Shape of the nose: palms with closed fingers come apart in front of nose.

(16)　　Speech – A troubled student
　　　　F: . . 總之讓他**安靜**
　　　　　　'Anyway, (it was necessary to) make him quiet'.

Figure 16.16　DOWN IS QUIET: palms face forward and go downward.

* The speech associated with a gesture is in boldface.

Language, gesture and meaning

can also be conveyed in gesture, such as BE QUIET IS DOWN for the state of quietness 安靜 in Example 16.

The third type of verbal concepts has to do with action events, which constitute the large majority of the verbal concepts in the dataset (80.6%, 75 out of 93). Different aspects of action are depicted manually. See Table 16.6. One major aspect is manner, such as the action of opening

Table 16.6 The semantic information about action concepts as represented in gesture

(17) Speech – Hornets
F2: ...是虎頭蜂的唷..你要不要打開來看看
'It is a hornet's nest. Do you want to open (the window) and have a look at it?'

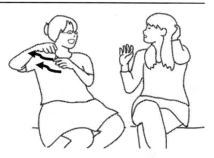

Figure 16.17 Manner of opening a window: hands in fist at chest level curve from the center to the left.

(18) Speech – Wearing glasses
F: ...以前..小時候戴眼鏡
'In the past, as a child, (I) wore glasses'.

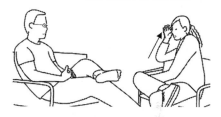

Figure 16.18 Bodily location for glasses: right thumb and index finger forming an open circle go toward the right eye.

(19) Speech – City flood
F: ...對..就會裝水
'Right, right, (the city) will be filled with water'.

Figure 16.19 Rain pouring down as cause of a flood: palms at eye level go down sharply.

(Continued)

255

Table 16.6 (Continued)

(20) Speech – Staying in water
  M: . . 泡在水裡面
    '(She) soaked in water'.

Figure 16.20 Swollen face as effect of staying in water: hands with bent fingers are at each side of the face.

(21) Speech – Music and dance
  M: . . 你就放音效
    'You then played the sound effects'

Figure 16.21 Pressing a button on a musical instrument: right index finger goes up and down one time.

(22) Speech – Dealing with hornets
  F: . . 然後就是穿這
    'Then, that is, (he) wore this (glove)'.

Figure 16.22 Long glove as the theme of a wearing action: right hand moves up onto left upper arm.

* The speech associated with a gesture is in boldface.

the window of a room 打開來 which is paired with the gestural information about the way by which the window of the room was opened (Figure 16.17). Another aspect is concerned with the bodily location with which an action is associated, like the thumb and index finger forming an open circle and moving to the right eye performed along with the utterance of the predicate 戴眼鏡 'wear glasses' in Example 18. The other aspects of meaning include the cause, the effect or result, the means, and the characteristics of the theme being involved with an action. In

Table 16.7 The semantic information about verbal concepts across modalities

		Speech		Gesture	
Motion					
I	Manner-path	3	3.1%	–	0.0%
II	Manner	6	6.2%	4	4.1%
III	Direction	–	0.0%	5	5.2%
State					
IV	State	13	13.4%	–	0.0%
V	Theme	–	0.0%	9	9.3%
VI	Metaphor	–	0.0%	4	4.1%
Action					
VII	Action	75	77.3%	–	0.0%
VIII	Manner	–	0.0%	57	58.8%
IX	Theme	–	0.0%	8	8.2%
X	Effect	–	0.0%	3	3.1%
XI	Means	–	0.0%	3	3.1%
XII	Location	–	0.0%	2	2.1%
XIII	Cause	–	0.0%	2	2.1%
	Total:	97	100.0%	97	100.0%

Example 19, the cause of Taipei City being filled with water 裝水 was rain pouring down very heavily, as configured by the hands at head level going downward sharply. In Example 20, the result of a person soaking in water 泡 'soak' was a swollen face as depicted by the slightly bent fingers at each side of the speaker's face. Example 21 has to do with playing some sound effects 放音效, and the means by which the sound effects were produced was expressed by moving the right index finger down one time as if pressing a button on a machine. Finally, the action of wearing a glove 穿 'wear' in Example 22 is accompanied by a gesture depicting the length of the glove by having the right hand move up onto the left upper arm.

For each of the modalities to convey distinct meanings varies by the type of verb. Table 16.7 presents the frequency distribution of various types of semantic information. Modal specificity is discussed only in relation to action events due to the small numbers for motion (I – III) and state (IV – VI). Semantically, the action verbs are generic, whereas the gestures provide more specific information about manner, the cause and the effect/result of an action, the instrument, the location, and the theme involved with an action, among which the information about manner in gesture predominates.

In summary, speech and gesture overlap in meaning in merely 19.2% of the verbal cases. The rate of semantic redundancy is low as speech and gesture tend to represent different information. Meanings in speech are largely generic, but meanings in gesture exhibit a wide variety of semantic information about different and varied types of verbal concepts. Modal specificity in the communication of meaning is, again, borne out.

General discussion and conclusion

For the understanding of how the meaning of the same concept is represented simultaneously across speech and gesture in conversational discourse, the current study employed a dataset of 222 lexical instances, each simultaneously accompanied by an iconic gesture. In this section, given the quantitative and qualitative results presented above, the issues regarding the extent of the semantic redundancy between the two modalities, and modal specificity in the communication of meaning are discussed accordingly.

Do speech and gesture tend to convey an identical or different meaning?

There were 102 nominal concepts and 120 verbal concepts for the study. These two types of concepts demonstrate a similar tendency in the representation of meaning by virtue of speech and gesture. As shown in Table 16.8, the two modalities mostly convey distinct information. The chi-square value does not indicate a significant difference between nominal and verbal concepts in representing identical or different meanings (X^2 (1) = 1.7793, p – value = .182233). Overall, the semantic redundancy across the modalities is low, 26% on average. That is, most of the time, speech does not provide a complete view of the message that the speaker intends to convey in face-to-face communication.

Do speech and gesture demonstrate modal specificity in the representation of meaning?

The representation of nominal and verbal meanings across modalities provides evidence of modal specificity. First, regarding the identical information, nominal concepts are consistently represented as entities, coded in the bare NP form and configured as the object gesture. Verbal concepts, on the other hand, are mainly concerned with directions, and are coded in words as (manner-)path verbs or directional verbs and depicted manually by moving the hand(s) in the corresponding directions.

Modal specificity is borne out when speech and gesture represent distinct meanings. The types of semantic information about nominal concepts were found to be more diverse in speech than in gesture, with information about quantity being the type of information most frequently expressed in words. In gesture, however, it is common for the manual configurations to present semantic information about the characteristics of the entities including shape, length, and size. For the range of semantic information about action concepts, on the other hand, the linguistic meanings are more generic, whereas the gestural meanings are more specific, with manner information being expressed commonly in the manual modality.

Altogether, the study presented two empirical facts about the cross-modal distribution of meaning, which are essential to understanding the cognitive relationship between language and gesture (McNeill, 1992, 2005; de Ruiter, 2000; Kita and Özyürek, 2003). First, the fact that speech and gesture can convey meaning about the same concept supports McNeill's (1992, 2005) claim that the minimal idea unit of the speaker is a combination of linguistic and gestural elements, and that the two modalities are conceptually linked in an early processing stage of speech-gesture production. Another empirical fact is that cross-modal semantic redundancy is low, and that it is common for the two modalities to represent distinct information. If the

Table 16.8 Semantic redundancy across nominal and verbal concepts

	Nominal concepts	Verbal concepts
Identical information across modalities	31 (30.4%)	27 (22.5%)
Different information across modalities	71 (69.6%)	93 (77.5%)

various types of unsaid gestural information, whether about nominal or verbal concepts, were represented in words, the original utterances would have to be changed or new utterances be added in words. Thus, the processing of the linguistic and gestural meanings in a later stage is separate. The remaining question as to whether the linguistic and gestural meanings are processed in parallel (de Ruiter, 2000) or with bidirectional interaction (Kita and Özyürek, 2003) awaits future investigation.

The results of the study also raise the question as to why speakers produce distinct information across modalities. Three reasons were proposed by Alibali et al. (2009). The first has to do with difficulties that speakers may encounter in speaking. No evidence for such proposition was found in this study, since 93.7% of all the instances were produced without hesitation pauses or self-repairs. The second reason is that "[speakers] may have multiple ideas activated at the moment of speaking, and they express one in speech, and the other(s) in gesture". This reason accounts for our finding of low cross-modal semantic redundancy where only 30% of the nominal cases and 22% of the verbal cases had speech and gesture convey the same meanings. The third reason is that certain types of semantic information are more readily expressed by gestures than in words, which accounts for our results that the gestural representation specific to nominal concepts has to do with dimensional information, while the gestural representation specific to action concepts has to do with manner information.

In conclusion, the use of hands and arms along with speech is indispensable and prevalent in everyday communication (McNeill, 1992, 2000; Goldin-Meadow, 1999; Kendon, 2004). Gestures with noticeable and discernible manual configurations are communicative and convey meaning along with speech. This chapter has provided empirical findings about the clear distinction between nominal and verbal concepts in the cross-modal representation of meaning, the extent of cross-modal semantic redundancy, and modal specificity in the manifestation of meaning. Just like language, gesture is a crucial part of communication.

Appendix

Appendix: Speech transcription conventions

:	speaker identity
...	medium pause
..	short pause

Acknowledgments

This research was supported by grants from the Ministry of Science and Technology, Taiwan, ROC (MOST103–2410-H-004–180 -MY3). I am very grateful to the anonymous reviewers for their helpful comments and suggestions on this article.

Note

1 Permissions were obtained from all of the participants to use the audio-visual data from The NCCU Corpus of Spoken Taiwan Mandarin for research. The data can be accessed online at http://spoken taiwanmandarin.nccu.edu.tw/ or at TalkBank http://talkbank.org/access/CABank/TaiwanMandarin.html

References

Alibali, M.W., Bassok, M., Solomon, K.O., Syc, S.E. and Goldin-Meadow, S. (1999) 'Illuminating Mental Representations through Speech and Gesture', *Psychological Science* 10(4): 327–333.

Alibali, M.W., Kita, S. and Young, A. (2000) 'Gesture and the Process of Speech Production: We Think, Therefore We Gesture', *Language and Cognitive Processes* 15: 593–613.

Alibali, M.W., Evans, J.L., Hostetter, A.B., Ryan, K. and Mainela-Arnold, E. (2009) 'Gesture–Speech Integration in Narrative: Are Children Less Redundant Than Adults?' *Gesture* 9(3): 290–311.

Chui, K. (2008) 'Complementary Gestures and Information Types', *Language and Linguistics* 9(1): 1–22.

Chui, K. (2009) 'Conversational Coherence and Gesture', *Discourse Studies* 11(6): 661–680.

Chui, K. (2012a). 'Gestural Manifestation of Knowledge in Conceptual Frames', *Discourse Processes* 49(8): 599–621.

Chui, K. (2012b) 'Cross-linguistic Comparison of Representations of Motion in Language and Gesture', *Gesture* 12(1): 40–61.

Chui, K. (2017) 'Entity Metaphor, Object Gesture, and Context of Use', *Metaphor and Symbol* 32: 30–51.

Chui, K. and Lai, H.L. (2008) 'The NCCU Corpus of Spoken Chinese: Mandarin, Hakka, and Southern Min', *Taiwan Journal of Linguistics* 6(2): 119–144.

Chui, K., Lai, H.L. and Chan, H.C. (2017) 'The Taiwan spoken Chinese corpus', in *Encyclopedia of Chinese Language and Linguistics*. R. Sybesma (ed.) Boston, MA: Brill. pp. 257–259.

Chui, K., Lee, C-Y., Yeh, K-Y. and Chao, P-C. (2018) 'Semantic Processing of Self-adaptors, Emblems, and Iconic Gestures: An ERP Study', *Journal of Neurolinguistics* 47: 105–122.

Clark, H.H. and Krych, M.A. (2004) 'Speaking while Monitoring Addressees for Understanding', *Journal of Memory and Language* 50(1): 62–81.

De Ruiter, J.P. (2000) 'The production of gesture and speech', in *Language and Gesture*. D. McNeill (ed.) Cambridge: Cambridge University Press. pp. 284–311.

Dick, A.S., Mok, E.H., Beharelle, A.R., Goldin-Meadow, S. and Small, Steven L. (2014) 'Frontal and Temporal Contributions to Understanding the Iconic Co-speech Gestures that Accompany Speech', *Human Brain Mapping* 35(3): 900–917.

Efron, D. (1941) *Gesture and Environment*. New York: King's Crown Press.

Efron, D. (1972) *Gesture, Race and Culture*. The Hague: Mouton.

Ekman, P. and Friesen, W.V. (1969) 'The Repertoire of Nonverbal Behavior: Categories, Origins, Usage, and Coding', *Semiotica* 1(1): 49–98.

Goldin-Meadow, S. (1999) 'The Role of Gesture in Communication and Thinking', *Trends in Cognitive Science* 3: 419–429.

Goldin-Meadow, S., Nusbaum, H., Kelly, S. and Wagner, S. (2001) 'Explaining Math: Gesturing Lightens the Load', *Psychological Science* 12: 516–522.

Holle, H., Gunter, T.C., Rüschemeyer, S.A., Hennenlotter, A. and Iacoboni, M. (2008) 'Neural Correlates of the Processing of Co-speech Gestures', *Neuroimage* 39(4): 2010–2024.

Kendon, A. (1984) 'Some uses of gesture', in *Perspectives on Silence*. D. Tannen and M. Saville-Troike (eds.) New Jersey: Ablex Publishing Corporation. pp. 215–234.

Kendon, A. (1995) 'Gestures as Illocutionary and Discourse Structure Makers in Southern Italian Conversation', *Journal of Pragmatics* 23: 247–279.

Kendon, A. (2004) *Gesture: Visible Action as Utterance*. Cambridge: Cambridge University Press.

Kita, S. and Özyürek A. (2003) 'What Does Cross-Linguistic Ariation in Semantic Coordination of Speech and Gesture Reveal? Evidence for an Interface Representation of Spatial Thinking and Speaking', *Journal of Memory and Language* 481: 16–32.

Krauss, Robert M., Chen, Yihsiu and Gottesman, Rebecca F. (2000) 'Lexical gestures and lexical access: A process model', in *Language and Gesture*. D. McNeill (ed.) Cambridge: Cambridge University Press. pp. 261–283.

McClave, E. (1994) 'Gestural Beats: The Rhythm Hypothesis', *Journal of Psycholinguistic Research* 23(1): 45–66.

McNeill, D. (1992) *Hand and Mind: What Gestures Reveal about Thought*. Chicago: The University of Chicago Press.

McNeill, D. (2005) *Gesture and Thought*. Chicago: The University of Chicago Press.

McNeill, D. (ed.) (2000) *Language and Gesture*. Cambridge: Cambridge University Press.

Özyürek, A. (2014) 'Hearing and Seeing Meaning in Speech and Gesture: Insights from Brain and Behaviour', *Philosophical Transactions of the Royal Society B: Biological Sciences* 369(1651).

Özyürek, A., Roel, M.W., Sotaro, K. and Hagoort, P. (2007) 'On-Line Integration of Semantic Information from Speech and Gesture: Insights From Event-related Brain Potentials', *Journal of Cognitive Neuroscience* 19(4): 605–616.

Rime, B. and Schiaratura, L. (1991) 'Gesture and speech', in *Fundamentals of Nonverbal Behavior*. R. S. Feldman and B. Rime (eds.) New York: Cambridge University Press. pp. 239–281.
Straube, B., Green, A., Weis, S. and Kircher, T. (2012) 'A Supramodal Neural Network for Speech and Gesture Semantics: An fMRI Study', *PLoS ONE* 7: e51207.
Wagner, P., Malisz, Z. and Kopp, Stefan. (2014) 'Gesture and Speech in Interaction: An Overview', *Speech Communication* 57: 209–232.

Part V
Cognitive aspect of Chinese discourse

17
The psycholinguistics of Chinese discourse processing

Chien-Jer Charles Lin

Introduction

Verbal experiences are heavily contextualized. Speech sounds are embedded in words, words in sentences and sentences in text and utterances. Discourse, which is made of interrelated clauses, conveys messages that motivate and unify grammatically defined units such as phrases and sentences. The goal of discourse processing research has been to unravel how interpretations of linguistic expressions beyond words and sentences are achieved and how they serve communicative functions in textual and social contexts. This chapter provides an overview of Chinese discourse processing, highlighting two important abilities of human language comprehension: the ability to *integrate* linguistic materials and the ability to *make predictions*. Linguistic composition involves accessing the grammatical and semantic properties of lower-level linguistic units to form larger units. Representations that have been constructed and temporarily stored in the working memory need to be integrated with materials that show up at a later point of the discourse. Discourse prediction, on the other hand, involves incrementally using information from earlier linguistic units and higher linguistic levels to predict how an utterance may unfold. With these two abilities, propositions are composed, the logical connections between propositions are established, and mental models about discourse content can be constructed.

Elements of discourse processing

The goal of discourse comprehension is to arrive at interpretations of linguistic message at the highest communicative level. This process involves constructing propositions, which are usually composed of participants and events, building dependencies across linguistic constructs, and weaving propositions into a coherent mental model (Kintsch, 1998). To do so, one needs to identify the content of clauses, compose propositional content by relating events and actions with nominal referents that participate in an event, establish logical relations and construct a discourse representation. Discourse cohesion and coherence are maintained by following a conventionalized flow of information regarding discourse statuses (e.g. focus, topic, newness, and givenness), connecting through logical markers (e.g. *because, although*) and building anaphoric dependencies using devices such as pronouns, which connect nominal referents in different propositions to retain topic-continuity.

Discourse comprehension encompasses all aspects of language processing: from prosodic perception to syntactic parsing, and from lexical ambiguity resolution to establishing logical relations across sentences. In language processing, linguistic units range from smaller units like phonemes, syllables, and words to higher-level units like phrases, clauses, passages, and texts. Discourse processing involves both a bottom-up process – using smaller units as building blocks to compose higher-level units – and a top-down process – using higher-level constructs and general knowledge to inform the identification and interpretation of lower-level units.

Due to limited attention and memory, linguistic message is packaged into manageable chunks of actions and events, which involve protagonists that participate in them. Three types of information are established at the discourse level. First, attention is given to what the predication is about. Namely, what is the *topic* or *focus* of the message? Nominal entities that are the topic or focus of a proposition receive higher levels of activation and are more accessible for integration and reactivation. Referent tracking associated with pronouns, reflexives and zero anaphora is directly related to the attentional state of nominal entities and information statuses. Second, nominal entities and propositions are connected following an iconic progression of information. The principle of given before new, for example, establishes grounding relations between nouns. Third, logical relations such as causation and concession connect propositions and form discourse representations.

Before using Mandarin Chinese to illustrate each of these elements of discourse processing, I briefly introduce common experimental methods in language processing. Psycholinguists working on discourse comprehension adopt both online reading experiments and offline acceptability ratings. These experimental measures help contrast processing costs associated with linguistic materials that are at issue. Since discourse comprehension is an ongoing temporal process, online measures that are sensitive to the fluctuation of processing cost in different parts of a discourse allow researchers to pinpoint where processing difficulties ensue. Experimental methods that measure the time taken to read particular parts of discourse such as the self-paced reading paradigm, and instruments that record eye movements while reading texts are useful measures that can reveal processing costs associated with specific parts of a text. Using these measures, longer reading/fixation times and greater numbers of eye fixations and regressions in a textual region indicate greater processing difficulty. Non-invasive recordings of brain activities using electroencephalography (EEG) further provide data of how the brain responds to linguistic materials. Common event-related potential (ERP) signatures for sentence and discourse processing include N400 – a negative deflection peaking around 400 milliseconds post-stimulus onset and typically associated with unexpected or incongruent continuations of discourse (Kutas and Federmeier, 2000), and P600 – a late positive deflection peaking around 600 milliseconds post-stimulus onset and typically associated with integration and reanalysis effects in discourse (see Swaab et al., 2012 and Kaan, 2007 for a comprehensive overview of the EEG methodology). Production studies typically use different types of contexts in a dialogue format to motivate certain types of responses and measure the acoustic and other linguistic properties of the speech produced.

Information structure and noun phrase prominence

Nouns present participants of actions and events around which discourse content is centered. The information status of a nominal entity is among the most important driving forces in organizing discourse. Key notions related to information structure include whether a noun phrase (NP) is a topic or a focus, how it is contrasted with other NPs, and whether a proposition provides given or new information. Different degrees of prominence are usually assigned to nominal entities based on their information statuses, which determine the accessibility of these NPs in discourse. Information structure is thus closely associated with the prominence of linguistic entities and propositions. Compared with unmarked NPs, NPs that are topics or focuses are usually stronger candidates for retrieval and reactivation.

Topic

Topic can be understood as what a sentence or an utterance is about and is usually based on information already shared by interlocutors. Being a language that is "topic-prominent" (Li and Thompson, 1981), Chinese relies heavily on the information status of noun phrases for determining word orders. As the basic word order of Chinese is SVO, deviations from the basic word order usually indicate the special status of an NP. The grammaticalized position for a topic NP in Chinese is at the left periphery of a clause. If an object appears before a subject as in the order of OSV, the object is typically taken to be at the topic position. Since a subject NP can already appear at the clause-initial position, it is not easy to determine its information status based on word order. A topicalized NP can additionally be marked by a pause or by a discourse marker such as *a* or *ne* following it.

Topics can be indexed by prosodic marking (Wang and Xu, 2011), its position in a sentence, and sometimes a topic-identifying question like *what about X* in (1).

(1) Question:
 李四/張三　　怎麼　了?
 Lisi/Zhangsan　how　ASP
 'What about Lisi/Zhangsan?'

Hung and Schumacher (2012) designed an EEG study to test whether language users are sensitive to informational conflicts between a topic established by a question and a topic established by word order information. In an OSV sequence like (2), Zhangsan, appearing in the clause-initial periphery position, is established as the topic of the sentence. When this sentence follows a question that identifies a different NP (e.g. Lisi) as the topic, a greater and more sustained N400 was observed than when a consistent NP (e.g. Zhangsan) is identified as the topic in the question.

(2) Answer:
 張三　　李四　毆打　了
 Zhangsan　Lisi　beat　ASP
 'Zhangsan, Lisi beat (him).'

Not all NPs are equally likely to serve as topics. Topicalized NPs are more likely to be animate personal nouns, and they tend to be given entities that have appeared in the previous context than being newly introduced. While greater surprisal reflected by N400 has been observed when the topic NP established by a question is different from the topicalized NP at a clause-initial position, only when the topic NP was inanimate was an additional late positivity found (Hung and Schumacher, 2014), suggesting that inanimate NPs are less expected in topic positions. The animacy of an NP thus provides as a pivotal cue for topic identification in Chinese discourse.

Focus

While topic is about given information shared by interlocutors, focus provides information that is new to the discourse. In standard Chinese, focus is prosodically manifested by syllable lengthening and raised or expanded pitch ranges (Xu, 1999). Focused items display more distinct pitch contours and less tonal coarticulation with neighboring syllables (Chen and Gussenhoven, 2008), while post-focus regions of a sentence are typically compressed in pitch ranges (Chen, 2010). Focus NPs are not always easy to identify. In general, responses to *wh*-questions can be taken as the focus of a sentence. In the question-answer pair (3–4), the question in (3) seeks information about the object of *eating*, thus placing the focus on the object NP 'cake' in (4). With the same answer (4), a question like (5) would place the focus on the subject NP, *Anan*, thus marking the subject NP as the focus.

(3) 諳諳　吃掉　什麼?
    Anan　eat up　what
    'What did Anan eat?'

(4) 諳諳　吃掉　蛋糕
    Anan　eat up　cake
    'Anan ate a cake'.

(5) 誰　吃掉　蛋糕?
    Who　eat up　cake
    'Who ate a cake?'

Focus NPs draw greater attention in processing. Greater surprise (i.e. an enlarged N400) is induced when an anomaly is located at the focused position of the sentence, e.g. when it is part of the focal response to a wh- question, than when the anomaly appears in a non-focal position (Wang et al., 2009). As an example, the semantic anomaly in (6) is due to the object NP *watch* not being an edible object of the verb *eat up*. When this sentence follows a question like (3), which places focus on the object NP, the surprisal is greater than when the sentence follows a question like (5), which places focus on the subject NP. Such greater tolerance of a semantic anomaly in a non-focal position is referred to as a *semantic illusion*.

(6) 諳諳　吃掉　手錶
    Anan　eat up　watch
    'Anan ate a watch'.

A special kind of focus related to selecting a referent from potential candidates in the background is called *contrastive focus*, where the focused NP is contrasted with the unselected NPs. With contrastive focus, it is presupposed that multiple referents already exist in the background, and that an assertion is selectively applied to a subset of the candidate NPs, and not the rest. In standard Chinese, contrastive focus can be structurally manifested by using the focus marker *shi* in the cleft construction *shi . . . (de)* 'it is . . . who' where the NP following *shi* is the focus as illustrated by (7).

(7) Mandarin cleft construction:
    是　諳諳 [focus]　吃掉　蛋糕　的
    SHI Anan　eat up　cake　DE
    'It was Anan who ate up the cake'.

The psycholinguistics of discourse processing

Contrastive focus presupposes multiple referents present in the background. When there is only one active referent available in the background like (8), where contrastive focus is not motivated, further predication about this referent requires no contrast. When the context provides two referents like (9), the referential presupposition for contrastive focus is licensed.

(8) Context with one character:
 諳諳　去　看　電影
 Anan　go　see　movie
 'Anan went to see a movie'.

(9) Context with two characters:
 諳諳　和　壹壹　去　看　電影
 Anan　and　Yiyi　go　see　movie
 'Anan and Yiyi went to see a movie'.

Thus, after a context with two active referents like (9), a sentence with the focus marker *shi* (as in 10) is processed with greater ease (i.e. shorter eye-fixation time) than a sentence without a focus marker like (11) (Chen and Yang, 2015). However, focus markers do not facilitate processing when there is only one referent in the context like (8).

(10) Critical sentence with contrastive focus marker:
 是　諳諳　買了　票
 shi　Anan　buy-ASP　ticket
 'It was Anan who bought the ticket'.

(11) Critical sentence without contrastive focus marker:
 諳諳　買了　票
 Anan　buy-ASP　ticket
 'Anan bought the ticket'.

Restrictiveness and relative clauses

Related to the cleft construction and focus-marking using the emphatic marker *shi* is the relative clause construction, which serves the restrictive function of picking out a referent from a set of candidates in contexts like (12), where multiple referents of similar properties need to be contrasted. A sentence with a restrictive relative clause like (13) picks out a referent from the set of two candidates in the context using contrastive information provided in the embedded clause. Restrictive relative clauses are therefore closely tied to the referential presupposition in the context. They focus on a referent from the candidates and contrast this referent with other unselected referents.

(12) 台上　有　兩位　語言學家
 stage-on　have　two-CL　linguist
 'There are two linguists on the stage'.
 其中　一位　研究　關係子句
 among them　one-CL　study　relative clauses
 'One of them studies relative clauses'.
 另一位　研究　聲調
 the other one　study　tone
 'The other one studies tones'.

269

(13) 研究　　關係子句　　的　　那個　　語言學家　　喜歡　　喝　　咖啡
　　　study   relative clause   DE   that-CL   linguist   likes   drink   coffee
　　　'The linguist who studies relative clauses likes to drink coffee'.

Relative clause constructions have been particularly useful for studying contextual influences on structural expectations (Crain and Steedman, 1985). In English, sentences with reduced relative clauses like *the horse raced past the barn fell* are problematic for comprehension (Bever, 1970). Readers tend to misread such sentences and demonstrate difficulty in recovering from the misreading. Using contexts that present multiple referents (i.e. *horses*) before the relative clauses, however, this misreading can be reduced, suggesting that when the presupposition regarding contrastive referents of a restrictive relative clause is satisfied, readers are better at correctly parsing an ambiguous sequence as a reduced relative clause.

　　Chinese relative clauses present a similar challenge regarding the possibility of being misread (Lin and Bever, 2011). Being prenominal, the embedded clause of a Chinese relative clause construction is not morphologically marked and therefore can be initially mistaken as a main clause. Reanalysis often takes place in the post relative clause region, such as on the relativizer *de* or the head noun, which mark the prenominal clauses as clausal modifiers. A referential context like (12), which presents multiple referents that can be further contrasted, increases the expectation of a restrictive relative clause like (13). By contrast, when relative clauses appear after contexts like (14), where only one referent is present, they are not referentially motivated and are comprehended with longer reading time in the disambiguating regions (Hsu et al., 2006; Lin, 2015).

(14) 台上　　有　　一個　　語言學家
　　　stage-on   have   one-CL   linguist
　　　'There is a linguist on the stage'.
　　　他　　研究　　關係子句
　　　he   study   relative clauses
　　　'He studies relative clauses'.

Since Chao (1968), the position of a relative clause in relation to a determiner-classifier sequence such as *na-ge* 'that-CL' has been taken to potentially distinguish a restrictive relative clause from a non-restrictive one in standard Chinese. Relative clauses that precede a determiner-classifier sequence like (13) are considered restrictive while those that follow a determiner-classifier sequence like (15) are considered non-restrictive.

(15) 那個　　研究　　關係子句　　的　　語言學家　　喜歡　　喝　　咖啡
　　　that-CL   study   relative clause   DE   linguist   likes   drink   coffee
　　　'The linguist who studies relative clauses likes to drink coffee'.

Comparing relative clauses that appear before and after the determiner-classifier sequence, Lin (2015) found shorter reading time on relative clauses that appear after the determiner-classifier sequence than those that appear before the sequence, suggesting relative clauses that appear before the determiner-classifier sequence are more marked. He further compared the *production* of these two kinds of relative clauses by presenting them after contexts like (12) and (14). Even though both kinds of relative clauses can be used to pick out a referent in a context with contrastive referents, native speakers are more likely to place a relative clause before the determiner-classifier sequence when the context provides multiple referents that need to be contrasted like (12). Similarly, the reading time is shorter when these sentences follow a context

Information flow: given before new

Finally, an important property of organizing discourse information related to topic and focus is whether information has been established as shared knowledge or is being presented as new information. Topic is usually based on shared knowledge that has already been introduced while focus tends to be new information. In terms of information organization, old information tends to be presented earlier to lay ground for focused information. In Chinese, where SVO is the basic word order, this means old information tends to appear in the subject position while new information tends to appear in the predicate position. Using relative clauses, which provide shared background information for predication, Lin (2015) found that restrictive relatives like (13) are better expected in subject positions than in object positions. Similar findings have been reported in English (Gibson et al., 2005), so this organizational preference has been attested crosslinguistically.

Regarding prosodic marking, Chinese speakers tend to increase word durations and heighten pitch levels to indicate prosodic prominence and accentuation. Words that carry old information tend to be deaccented while words that carry new information tend to be accentuated. When a prosodic cue is inappropriately assigned, that is, when words carrying old information are accentuated but words carrying new information are deaccented, native speakers respond to such anomalous prosodic assignment with an enlarged N400, suggesting that prosodic cues for accentuation are directly associated with the processing of information structure (Li et al., 2008).

Anaphors and tracking referents in discourse

An important task in discourse comprehension is to keep track of the noun phrases that have entered the discourse. In natural language, nominal referents do not appear in their complete forms (i.e. full noun phrases) each time they are mentioned. Three kinds of anaphoric expressions are useful for referring to a referent that has appeared earlier: *pronouns* such as *ta* 'he, she', *zero anaphoras*, which are phonologically empty, and *reflexives* such as *ziji* 'self'.

Anaphoric expressions are important pronominal devices for maintaining coherence in discourse. They establish dependencies within and across clauses by centering on nominal expressions that are focal points in a discourse. While both are bound by antecedent NPs for interpretation, reflexives and pronouns are distinguished by where their antecedent NP can be located. A reflexive pronoun like *ziji* has to be bound by a subject NP within the same clause as in (16); a non-reflexive pronoun such as *ta* 'he/she' cannot be bound by a local subject NP but has to be coreferential with a non-local NP in discourse as in (17). A pronoun and a reflexive are therefore complementarily distributed regarding which NP in the sentential context they can co-refer with.

(16) 諳諳$_i$　對　壹壹$_j$　讚美　自己$_{i/*j/*k}$
　　　Anan　to　Yiyi　praise　self
　　　'Anan$_i$ praised herself$_{i/*j/*k}$ in front of Yiyi'.

(17) 諳諳$_i$　對　壹壹$_j$　讚美　他$_{*i/j/k}$
　　　Anan　to　Yiyi　praise　he/she
　　　'Anan praised him/her in front of Yiyi'.

Note that when these clauses are complements of a verb like *shuo* 'say' in Chinese, as in (18–19), the upper subject can bind both the embedded reflexive pronoun (18) and the non-reflexive pronoun (19). Thus, in (18), both the upper subject and the local subject serve as the potential antecedent of *ziji*. This property, shared by East-Asian languages, contrasts with the exclusive local binding in English where only the local subject NP can bind a reflexive pronoun (Tang, 1989).

(18) 媽媽ₘ 說 諳諳ᵢ 對 壹壹ⱼ 讚美 自己_{m/i/*j/*k}
     Mama say Anan to Yiyi praise self
     'Mom said Anan praised herself in front of Yiyi'.

(19) 媽媽ₘ 說 諳諳ᵢ 對 壹壹ⱼ 讚美 他_{m/*i/j/k}
     Mama say Anan to Yiyi praise him/her
     'Mom said Anan praised her in front of Yiyi'.

Processing reflexives

As illustrated by (16) and (18), the structural position of an antecedent NP is important for the interpretation of reflexives: only a subject NP, not an NP inside an adjunct phrase, can be interpreted as the antecedent of a reflexive. An important question in discourse processing concerns how one identifies the antecedent NP of a reflexive pronoun. Are all NPs appearing before *ziji*, including *Mama*, *Anan*, and *Yiyi* in (18) considered as potential candidates of *ziji*'s antecedent, or are only the structurally appropriate subject NPs (i.e. *Mama* and *Anan*) considered when the processor looks for an antecedent for *ziji*?

Research on this topic consistently found greater binding effect and stronger retrieval of a local subject NP than that of a distant subject NP, suggesting a stronger dependency between a reflexive pronoun and its antecedent within the *local* clausal domain (Gao et al., 2005; Li and Zhou, 2010). The syntactic position of an NP plays an important role for retrieval as a subject NP inside the local clause is more quickly retrieved as the antecedent of *ziji* than a more distant and structurally higher subject NP (Dillon et al., 2014; Liu, 2009). The NPs in non-subject positions are also activated in the search for the antecedent NP, producing an interference effect when the intervening NPs share semantic features such as animacy with the correct antecedent (Chen et al., 2012). In sentences like (20), where a non-subject NP (i.e. *Anan*) inside an adjunct clause is not regarded as a possible antecedent NP for *ziji* syntactically, an interference effect owing to the animacy feature shared between the correct antecedent *mom*, and the intervening NP *Anan* induces a longer retrieval time at *ziji* than when the intervening NP is an inanimate noun, suggesting that in processing reflexive dependencies, all preceding NPs are active, regardless of their syntactic positions, and may pose a semantic interference effect for retrieving the grammatically correct antecedent NPs.

(20) 媽媽ᵢ [在 諳諳ⱼ 唱 歌 的 時候]_{Adv-P} 讚美 自己_{i/*j}
     Mama at Anan sing song DE time praise self
     'Mom praised herself (at the time) when Anan was singing'.

In addition to processing preferences based on the locality of structural positions and the semantic properties of the NPs preceding the reflexive, the semantics of the main verbs also interacts with the interpretation of reflexives (Shuai et al., 2013). When a sentence contains two reflexives like (21), these two reflexives tend to be coreferential and preferably bound by the local subject (i.e. *Yiyi*). However, when the matrix verb is an attitude verb like *huaiyi* 'suspect', the preferred

The psycholinguistics of discourse processing

interpretation becomes assigning the first subject NP *Anan* as the antecedent of the second *ziji* and the local subject NP as the antecedent of the first *ziji*.

(21) 諳諳　說　壹壹　把　自己　的　書　給　自己　的　朋友
Anan　say　Yiyi　BA　self　DE　book　give　self　DE　friend
'Anan said Yiyi gave her friend her book'.

(22) 諳諳　懷疑　壹壹　把　自己　的　書　給　自己　的　朋友
Anan　suspect　Yiyi　BA　self　DE　book　give　self　DE　friend
'Anan suspected Yiyi gave her friend her book'.

The various threads of research on reflexive processing reviewed in this section show that the processor's search for an antecedent NP is subject to a locality effect; that is, antecedent NPs in the local clause are preferred to those in the non-local clause. The processor keeps track of both the syntactic and the semantic properties of all the NPs that appear before a reflexive pronoun. While the syntactic knowledge that a reflexive should be bound by a subject NP dictates the interpretation of a reflexive all NPs, regardless of their syntactic positions remain active candidates and produce intervening effects if they share semantic features with the target NP. Even the meaning of a verb influences the interpretation of reflexives and produces preferences over the possible dependency combinations. Reflexive processing thus continues to be an exciting research arena for studying the intricate relations between syntax, semantics, and processing in discourse comprehension.

Processing pronouns

Different from reflexives, a pronoun can be bound by any antecedent NPs that are *not* in the same local clause. In (23), the third-person pronoun *ta* (ambiguous in its phonetic form regarding gender in Standard Chinese) can refer to the subject NP (i.e. *Anan*) or the object NP (i.e. *Yiyi*) of the previous clause. Within the same clause, as in (19) repeated below, however, *ta* cannot be coreferential with the subject NP in the same local clause.

(23) 諳諳　昨天　弄哭　了　壹壹$_i$。他$_{i/j}$　...
Anan　yesterday　make cry　ASP　Yiyi　s/he
'Anan$_i$ made Yiyi$_j$ cry yesterday. S/he$_{i/j}$ ...'

(19) 媽媽$_m$　說　諳諳$_i$　對　壹壹$_j$　讚美　他$_{m/*i/j/k}$
Mama　say　Anan　to　Yiyi　praise　him/her
'Mom said Anan praised her in front of Yiyi'.

Like reflexives, the coreferential dependency between a pronoun and an antecedent NP has been of central importance for processing theories as it sheds light on how NPs are represented in the working memory and how they are later retrieved for the interpretation of anaphoric expressions. Several factors are instrumental for accessing NPs and predicting coreferential preferences. First, syntactic positions such as subjects are more accessible in subsequent discourse (Cheng and Almor, 2017; Chen et al., 2000; Simpson et al., 2016; Xu and Zhou, 2016; Yang et al., 2003); that is, the pronoun in (23) is more likely to be coreferential with the subject NP *Anan* than the object NP *Yiyi*. This effect is independent of the thematic role of the NPs as the subject NP, not the agent NP, in a passive sentence like (24) is still the preferred referent of *ta*.

(24) 壹壹ᵢ 昨天 被 諳諳ⱼ 弄哭 了。 他ᵢ/ⱼ ...
　　 Yiyi yesterday BEI Anan make cry ASP s/he
　　 'Yiyiᵢ was made cry by Ananⱼ yesterday. S/heᵢ/ⱼ ...'

Second, NP accessibility is influenced by how much attention an NP receives in discourse. NPs that are topics or focuses receive greater attention and are more accessible than those that are not. When (24) is preceded by a question like (25), which places *Anan* as the focus of the sentence, this focus NP becomes the preferred antecedent of *ta* even though it is not at a syntactically prominent (subject) position (Xu and Zhou, 2016; Xu, 2015).

(25) 壹壹ᵢ 被 誰 弄哭 了?
　　 Yiyi BEI who make cry ASP
　　 'By whom was Yiyiᵢ made cry?'

Likewise, NPs that appear in topic positions are more likely to be the antecedent of a pronoun. Comparing (26) and (27), *Anan* in (27) is at a pre-adverbial topic position and therefore, more likely to be the antecedent of the pronoun *ta* than *Anan* in (26), which is at an unmarked post-adverbial position.

(26) 因為 諳諳ᵢ 昨天 弄哭 了 壹壹ⱼ, 他ᵢ/ⱼ ...
　　 because Anan yesterday make cry ASP Yiyi s/he
　　 'Because Ananᵢ made Yiyiⱼ cry yesterday, s/heᵢ/ⱼ ...'

(27) 諳諳ᵢ 因為 昨天 弄哭 了 壹壹ⱼ, 他ᵢ/ⱼ ...
　　 Ananᵢ yinwei zuotian nongku le Yiyiⱼ taᵢ/ⱼ ...
　　 Anan because yesterday make cry ASP Yiyi s/he
　　 'Because Ananᵢ made Yiyiⱼ cry yesterday, s/heᵢ/ⱼ ...'

Third, language users pay attention to semantic features such as gender and social status on the NPs and pronouns for anaphor resolution. While gender is not phonetically marked in standard Chinese, the male and female third-person pronouns are distinguishable in writing, with different semantic radicals indicating gender markedness. Language users are sensitive to mismatches between pronouns presented visually and stereotypical genders associated with professions (Qiu et al., 2012; Su et al., 2016; Xu et al., 2013) and can use the stereotypical gender information of proper nouns and professional nouns to limit the potential referents of a pronoun (Yang et al., 2003). In addition to gender, second-person pronouns in standard Chinese can be marked based on the social statuses of the interlocutors. The respectful form *nin*, instead of the default form *ni*, is used to address a person that has a higher social status. When the pronouns are inappropriately used, an N400 has been observed (Jiang et al., 2013).

Finally, subject pronouns that are unpronounced (i.e. empty) due to pro-drop have the same preference of being coreferential with a subject NP in the previous clause, in particular in a passive clause like (24). Thus, (28a) serves as a preferred continuation than (28b) (Yang et al., 2003).

(28) 壹壹ᵢ 昨天 被 諳諳ⱼ 弄哭 了
　　 Yiyi yesterday BEI Anan make cry ASP
　　 'Yiyiᵢ was made cry by Ananⱼ yesterday.'
　　 a proᵢ 一直 覺得 很 傷心
　　 　 pro constantly feel very sad
　　 　 '(She) constantly felt very sad'.

b pro_j 一點也不   覺得   做錯事   了
   pro   not at all feel   make mistake ASP
   '(She) did not feel that she made a mistake at all'.

Causal and concessive relations in discourse

Besides dependencies between lexical items, clauses are logically connected. Causal relation, as one of the most fundamental logical relations, can be indicated by *yinwei* 'because' as in (29). Its plausibility is contingent on the conditional presupposition indicated by *ruguo* 'if' in (30).

(29) 因為   累   了   壹壹   馬上   睡著   了
      because tired   ASP   Yiyi   right away   fall aslpeep ASP
      'Because she was tired, Yiyi fell asleep right away'.

(30) 如果 累   了   就   容易   睡著
      if   tired   ASP   then   easily   fall asleep
      'If one is tired, one falls asleep easily'.

By contrast, concessive relations indicated by *suiran* 'although' or *jinguan* 'even though' such as (31) involve the reversal of the consequence portion of the conditional presupposition of (30).

(31) 諳諳   沒   睡著,   儘管   她   累   了
      Anan   not   fall asleep   even though   she   tired   ASP
      'Anan did not fall asleep, even though she was tired'.

While both causal relations and concessive relations invoke the presupposition of a conditional relation like (30), concessive relations are more complicated due to invoking the *reversal* of a conditional proposition (Lyu and Lin, 2018; Xu et al., 2017). Studies using EEG found distinctive neural patterns associated with violations of logical expectations in concessive relations such as (32) and causal relations such as (33) (Xu et al., 2015). While both violations invoke a larger N400, a causal violation like (33) invokes an additional P600. A concessive violation like (32) additionally invokes a larger negativity at a later point after the violation.

(32) 諳諳   睡著   了,   儘管   她   累   了
      Anan   fall aslpeep   ASP   even though   she   tired   ASP
      'Anan fell asleep even though she was tired'.

(33) 諳諳   沒   睡著,   因為   她   累   了
      Anan   not   fall aslpeep   because   she   tired   ASP
      'Anan did not fall asleep because she was tired'.

Different causal connectors such as *yinwei* 'because' and *suoyi* 'therefore' direct attention to different parts of a causal relation and produce preferences for anaphor resolution. *Yinwei* as in (34) directs greater attention to the causer while *suoyi* as in (35) directs more attention to the undergoer (Cheng and Almer, 2017). Therefore, causal adverbials like *yinwei* preferably introduces the causer as the subject of the following clause while resultative adverbials like *suoyi* preferably introduces the event undergoer as the subject.

(34) 諳諳ᵢ   弄哭   了   壹壹ⱼ   因為   他ᵢ/ⱼ   ...
     Anan   make cry   ASP   Yiyi   because   s/he
     'Ananᵢ caused Yiyiⱼ to cry. Because sheᵢ₌ⱼ ...'

(35) 諳諳ᵢ   弄哭   了   壹壹ⱼ   所以   他ᵢ/ⱼ   ...
     Anan   make cry   ASP   Yiyi   therefore s/he
     'Ananᵢ caused Yiyiⱼ to cry. Therefore sheᵢ<ⱼ ...'

Production of Chinese discourse

Like all other aspects of psycholinguistic research, research of Chinese discourse processing is unproportionally focused on the receiving end than on the production end. Production studies, nevertheless, provide an important complementary perspective about human language processing. It is generally accepted that discourse production and discourse comprehension are two sides of the same coin as they operate under similar cognitive and linguistic influences. In comprehending natural discourse, one attempts to reconstruct the linguistic message and intention of the speaker/writer using both lexical knowledge and knowledge about information organization. In producing discourse, similar knowledge is used to generate utterances that can be decoded by the hearers.

Research on discourse production has thus far explored factors such as information structure, semantic saliency, and the allocation of attention. A significant series of research has been done on the acoustic encodings associated with information structure, in particular focusing on how different types of focuses are realized by prosody (see Chen et al., 2015 for a comprehensive review). Focus associated with new information as established in (3–4) is marked with greater pitch ranges and longer durations (Chen and Braun, 2006). While corrective focus, as illustrated by (36), is also realized with greater pitch ranges and longer word durations, the differences are more drastic and the intensity are greater for corrective focus than focus-marking new information (Ouyang and Kaiser, 2015). These findings support distinctive acoustic underpinnings for different types of focuses, demonstrating how prosodic features of speech production can reflect distinctive information statuses of discourse elements.

(36) A: Did Lyla buy bananas?
     B: She bought mangos[contrastive focus].

Regarding anaphors in discourse, Pu (1995) investigated the production of pronominals by speakers of Mandarin and speakers of English in a story production experiment, where participants narrated episodes of stories that were divided into unnatural sections. In both languages, she found a universal semantic saliency effect on anaphor use: human NPs are more likely to be pronominalized than non-human and inanimate NPs. Furthermore, episodic boundaries create a need for relocating attention; therefore, the use of full NPs significantly increases at episode boundaries while the use of pronominals appear within episodes. These results suggest full NPs are associated with attention resetting while the use of pronominals is associated with retaining within-discourse coherence.

Conclusion

Correctly interpreting linguistic message in discourse has been among the most challenging goals of linguistic communication. Constructing a discourse model involves not only knowing what is said but also what is meant between the lines. In a mentally constructed discourse model, participants of events are identified and predicated. Attention is distributed and constantly shifted among nominal referents based on the flow of information. Nominal referents can be *topics* that an utterance is about, newly introduced information in discourse, or part of the focal or at-issue information in response to a question. Different degrees of prominence are allotted to referents based on their information status in discourse. Such prominence is directly related to the accessibility of nouns in anaphor resolution. NPs receiving greater attention such as topic and focus are more salient and more accessible. Identifying referents for anaphors such as pronouns and reflexives involves using syntactic knowledge about anaphoric binding, being sensitive to semantic features such as gender and animacy, and keeping track of the information statuses of potential referents in discourse. Propositions in discourse are further organized based on foregrounding, backgrounding, temporal sequencing, and logical relations (e.g. causal and conditional relations).

This chapter reviewed processing research on each of the above-mentioned aspects in Chinese, showing that language users attribute different degrees of attention to NPs based on their information statuses, and use both syntactic and semantic knowledge to track referents and establish logical relations between clauses. Being a discourse-oriented language, Chinese grammar is influenced by discourse factors on various fronts. Future research on Chinese discourse processing will continue to deepen our understanding of the common mechanisms in information organization, the interactions between discourse and different aspects of Chinese grammar, and how discourse markers and connectors serve to create a mental model of discourse in Chinese.

References

English references

Bever, T.G. (1970) 'Cognitive basis for linguistic structures', in *Cognition and the Development of Language*. Hayes, J.R. (ed.) New York: Wiley.
Chao, Y.R. (1968) *A Grammar of Spoken Chinese*. Berkeley, CA: University of California Press.
Chen, H.-C., Cheung, H., Tang, S.L. and Wong, Y.T. (2000) 'Effects of Antecedent Order and Semantic Context on Chinese Pronoun Resolution', *Memory and Cognition* 28: 427–438.
Chen, L. and Yang, Y. (2015) 'Emphasizing the Only Character: Emphasis, Attention and Contrast', *Cognition* 136: 222–227.
Chen, Y. (2010) 'Post-focus F0 Compression – Now You See It, Now You Don't', *Journal of Phonetics*. 38: 517–525.
Chen, Y. and Braun, B. (2006) 'Prosodic realization in information structure categories in standard Chinese', in *Speech Prosody 2006*. R. Hoffmann and H. Mixdorff (eds.) Dresden: TUD Press.
Chen, Y. and Gussenhoven, C. (2008) 'Emphasis and Tonal Implementation in Standard Chinese', *Journal of Phonetics* 36: 724–746.
Chen, Z., Jäger, L. and Vasishth, S. (2012) 'How structure-sensitive is the parser? Evidence from Mandarin Chinese', in *Empirical Approaches to Linguistic Theory: Studies of Meaning and Structure*. B. Stolterfoht and S. Featherston (eds.) Berlin: De Guyter Mouton.
Cheng, W. and Almor, A. (2017) 'The Effect of Implicit Causality and Consequentiality on Nonnative Pronoun Resolution', *Applied Psycholinguistics* 38: 1–26.
Crain, S. and Steedman, M. (1985) 'On not being led up the garden path: The use of context by the psychological parser', in *Natural Language Parsing: Psychological, Computational, and Theoretical Perspectives*. D.R. Dowty, L. Karttunen and A.M. Zwicky (eds.) New York: Cambridge University Press.

Dillon, B., Chow, W.-Y., Wagers, M., Guo, T., Liu, F. and Phillips, C. (2014) 'The Structure-Sensitivity of Memory Access: Evidence from Mandarin Chinese', *Frontiers in Psychology* 5: 1025.

Gibson, E., Desmet, T., Grodner, D., Watson, D. and Ko, K. (2005) Reading Relative Clauses in English. *Cognitive Linguistics* 16: 313–353.

Hsu, C.-C.N., Hurewitz, F. and Phillips, C. (2006) 'Contextual and syntactic cues for processing head-final relative clauses in Chinese', in *The 19th Annual CUNY Conference on Human Sentence Processing*. New York, NY: City University of New York.

Hung, Y.-C. and Schumacher, P.B. (2014) 'Animacy Matters Erp Evidence for the Multi-Dimensionality of Topic-Worthiness in Chinese', *Brain Research* 1555: 36–47.

Jiang, X., Li, Y. and Zhou, X. (2013) 'Is it Over-respectful or Disrespectful? Differential Patterns of Brain Activity in Perceiving Pragmatic Violation of Social Status Information During Utterance Comprehension', *Neuropsychologia* 51: 2210–2223.

Kaan, E. (2007) 'Event-related Potentials and Language Processing: A Brief Overview', *Language and Linguistics Compass* 1: 571–591.

Kintsch, W. (1998) *Comprehension: A Paradigm for Cognition*. Cambridge university press.

Kutas, M. and Federmeier, K.D. (2000) 'Electrophysiology Reveals Semantic Memory Use in Language Comprehension', *Trends in Cognitive Sciences* 4: 463–470.

Li, C.N. and Thompson, S.A. (1981) *Mandarin Chinese: A Functional Reference Grammar*. Berkeley, CA, University of California Press.

Li, X., Hagoort, P. and Yang, Y. (2008) 'Event-related Potential Evidence on the Influence of Accentuation in Spoken Discourse Comprehension in Chinese', *Journal of Cognitive Neuroscience* 20: 906–915.

Li, X. and Zhou, X. (2010) 'Who Is Ziji? ERP Responses to the Chinese Reflexive Pronoun during Sentence Comprehension', *Brain Research*, 1331: 96–104.

Lin, C.-J.C. (2015) 'Focusing on contrast sets: Motivating Mandarin Chinese restrictive relative clauses in comprehension and production', in *The 28th Annual CUNY Conference on Human Sentence Processing*. University of Southern California, Los Angeles CA.

Lin, C.-J.C. and Bever, T.G. (2011) Garden path and the comprehension of head-final relative clauses', in *Processing and Producing Head-final Structures*. H. Yamashita, Y. Hirose and J.L. Packard (eds.) New York: Springer.

Liu, Z. (2009) 'The Cognitive Process of Chinese Reflexive Processing', *Journal of Chinese Linguistics* 37: 1–27.

Lyu, S. and Lin, C.-J.C. (2018) 'Plausibility and topichood in processing Chinese concessives', in *Joint Meeting of the 26th Annual Conference of International Association of Chinese Linguistics (IACL-26) & the 20th International Conference on Chinese Language and Culture (ICCLC-20)*. University of Wisconsin-Madison, WI.

Ouyang, I.C. and Kaiser, E. (2015) 'Prosody and Information Structure in a Tone Language: An Investigation of Mandarin Chinese', *Language, Cognition and Neuroscience* 30: 57–72.

Pu, M.M. (1995) 'Anaphoric Patterning in English and Mandarin Narrative Production', *Discourse Processes* 19: 279–300.

Qiu, L., Swaab, T.Y., Chen, H.-C. and Wang, S. (2012) 'The Role of Gender Information in Pronoun Resolution: Evidence from Chinese', *PloS One* 7: e36156.

Shuai, L., Gong, T. and Wu, Y. (2013) 'Who Is Who? Interpretation of Multiple Occurrences of the Chinese Reflexive: Evidence from Real-Time Sentence Processing', *PloS One* 8: e73226.

Simpson, A., Wu, Z. and Li, Y. (2016) 'Grammatical Roles, Coherence Relations, and the Interpretation of Pronouns in Chinese', *Lingua Sinica*, 2: 2.

Su, J.-J., Molinaro, N., Gillon-Dowens, M., Tsai, P.-S., Wu, D.H. and Carreiras, M. (2016) 'When "he" can also be "she": An ERP Study of Reflexive Pronoun Resolution in Written Mandarin Chinese', *Frontiers in Psychology* 7: 151.

Swaab, T.Y., Ledoux, K., Camblin, C.C. and Boudewyn, M.A. (2012) 'Language-related ERP components', in *Oxford Handbook of Event-Related Potential Components*. S.J. Luck and E.S. Kappenman (eds.) Oxford: Oxford University Press.

Tang, C.-C.J. (1989) 'Chinese Reflexives', *Natural Language & Linguistic Theory* 7: 93–121.

Wang, B. and Xu, Y. (2011) 'Differential Prosodic Encoding of Topic and Focus in Sentence-initial Position in Mandarin Chinese', *Journal of Phonetics* 37: 502–520.

Wang, L., Hagoort, P. and Yang, Y. (2009) 'Semantic Illusion Depends on Information Structure: Erp Evidence', *Brain research* 1282: 50–56.

Xu, X. (2015) 'The Influence of Information Status on Pronoun Resolution in Mandarin Chinese: Evidence from ERPs', *Frontiers in Psychology* 6: 873.

Xu, X., Chen, Q., Panther, K.-U. and Wu, Y. (2017) 'Influence of Concessive and Causal Conjunctions on Pragmatic Processing: Online Measures from Eye Movements and Self-paced Reading', *Discourse Processes* 1–23.

Xu, X., Jiang, X. and Zhou, X. (2013) 'Processing Biological Gender and Number Information during Chinese Pronoun Resolution: ERP Evidence for Functional Differentiation', *Brain and Cognition* 81: 223–236.

Xu, X., Jiang, X. and Zhou, X. (2015) 'When a Causal Assumption is Not Satisfied by Reality: Differential Brain Responses to Concessive and Causal Relations during Sentence Comprehension', *Language, Cognition and Neuroscience* 30: 704–715.

Xu, X. and Zhou, X. (2016) 'Topic Shift Impairs Pronoun Resolution During Sentence Comprehension: Evidence from Event-related Potentials', *Psychophysiology* 53: 129–142.

Xu, Y. (1999) 'Effects of Tone and Focus on the Formation and Alignment of F0 Contours', *Journal of Phonetics* 27: 55–105.

Yang, C.L., Gordon, P.C., Hendrick, R. and Hue, C.W. (2003) 'Constraining the Comprehension of Pronominal Expressions in Chinese', *Cognition* 86: 283–315.

Chinese reference

Gao, L., Liu, Z. and Huang, Y. 高立群, 刘兆静, 黄月圆 (2005) "自己"是谁？– 对约束原则的实验研究 (Who Is "ziji": An Experimental Study about the Binding Principle). 语言科学 *(Linguistic Sciences)* 4: 39–50.

18

The neurocognitive processing of Chinese discourse

Chiao-Yi Wu and Shen-Hsing Annabel Chen

Introduction

We encounter discourse frequently in verbal communication as well as in text reading. The comprehension of spoken or written texts surpasses lexical meanings of single words and transcends syntactic structures of sentences. It involves sensitivity to suprasegmental cues that hint on coherence between sentences within the given context or even beyond. Discourse comprehension, therefore, requires not only the immediate analysis of the input but also the integration between the input and the information from a variety of linguistic and non-linguistic domains within the context (e.g., discourse cues, one's prior knowledge).

There are growing interests in studying how the human brain produces and comprehends language. Probing into the neural underpinnings of language processing provides further information to characterize the complex mechanisms as it can reveal subtle changes in response to language inputs, which may not be easily distinguished by explicit behaviors. In addition to behavioral measures, the study of discourse comprehension can especially benefit from neurophysiological (e.g., event-related potentials, ERPs) and neuroimaging (e.g., functional magnetic resonance imaging, fMRI) techniques as they can be used to delineate the rapid, interactive, and intricate processes involved at the neural level. Both ERPs and fMRI provide non-invasive and complementary ways to study the neurobiological basis of discourse processing.

The ERPs are averaged electrical fluctuations in the brain that are time-locked to a particular event (e.g., the onset of a critical word). It can be measured by electroencephalography (EEG), a method to record electrical activity in the brain. The ERP waveforms are described according to the direction of voltage deflections (P for positive and N for negative) and latency. For instance, the N400 and P600 components are two prominent language-related components that have been associated with semantic and syntactic anomalies, respectively (Kutas and Van Petten, 1994). The N400 component denotes the negative peak in the ERP waveform that occurs at around 400 ms after the stimulus onset (Figure 18.1a), and the P600 component refers to the positive peak that occurs at around 600 ms after the stimulus onset (Figure 18.1c). Another language-related component is the early left-anterior negativity (ELAN) component, which is a negative shift in the ERP waveform occurring early after stimulus onset in the left anterior

The neurocognitive processing

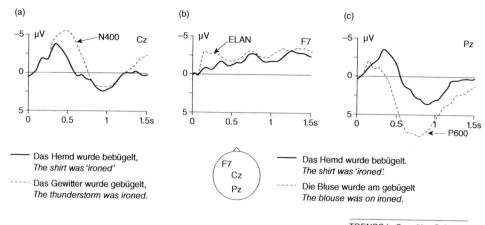

Figure 18.1 Three language-related ERP components: (a) N400, (b) early left-anterior negativity (ELAN), and (c) P600. Each plot represents the ERP waveforms recorded from the electrodes in different areas of the brain (Cz, F7, and Pz). Negative voltage is plotted above and positive voltage below the zero baseline. The solid lines represent the ERP waveforms for the correct conditions, and the dashed lines for the incorrect conditions with semantic and syntactic violations.

(Reprinted with permission from Friederici (2002). Copyright Elsevier.)

part of the brain (Figure 18.1b). It has been associated with detecting word-category errors in sentence processing (Friederici, 2002).

The fMRI technique measures brain activities by detecting changes in the blood flow that are coupled with neural activities. When a brain region is in use, neural activities are accompanied by changes in blood flow in the nearby vessels. This is called hemodynamic response. The signals measured by fMRI are induced by the changes in the level of oxygenated and deoxygenated hemoglobin in the blood flow, which are used to infer neural activities in particular brain areas. Functional MRI has been widely used to examine language processing. Although the definitive functions of the brain regions are still a matter of debate, studies have consistently reported the left fronto-temporal perisylvian cortex as the core language-related areas, including the inferior frontal gyrus, the posterior superior temporal gyrus/sulcus, and the posterior middle temporal gyrus in the left hemisphere (Friederici, 2011). These regions are depicted in Figure 18.2.

Neuroimaging techniques are often evaluated in terms of temporal resolution and spatial resolution. Temporal resolution refers to the precision of measurements with respect to time, and spatial resolution describes the extent to which a brain region can be accurately identified and differentiated from other regions. The ERP technique has very good temporal resolution to the order of milliseconds. In other words, ERPs can detect signal changes in milliseconds. However, the spatial resolution of ERPs is so low that it is difficult to identify the precise location of the sources of ERP responses. Rather, the locations that generate the ERP components are usually depicted with coarse areas. For instance, a frontally distributed N400 component refers to an N400 component that is distributed in the frontal regions of the brain. On the contrary, fMRI offers good spatial resolution to the scale of millimeters and provides nice contrasts between different tissues in the brain. While fMRI is useful in identifying the brain regions that are engaged by external stimuli, it has lower temporal resolution due to the slow hemodynamic responses

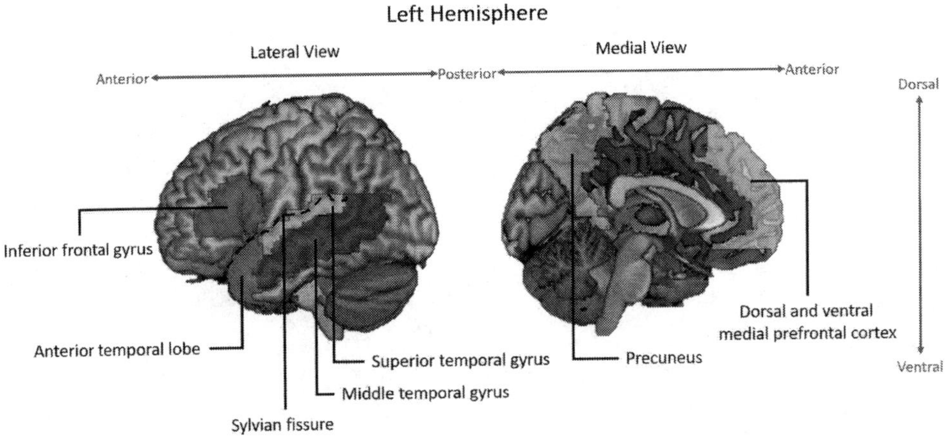

Figure 18.2 Brain regions involved in discourse comprehension for Western languages (Ferstl et al., 2008; Xu et al., 2005). Regions are shown in the left hemisphere. A color version of the figure is available online.

that usually peak at 4–6 s after the stimulus onset. That is, there are a few seconds delay between the onset of neural activity and the measured fMRI signals.

In this chapter, we aim to synthesize a review on the current understanding of the neural basis underlying Chinese discourse processing. First, we will provide an overview of the existing neurocognitive evidence for discourse comprehension that is primarily obtained from languages other than Chinese. Next, we will focus on the research on Chinese discourse processing, followed by a comparison with the neural evidence for discourse processing in other languages. The majority of the existing studies on the neural mechanisms of Chinese discourse processing utilized ERPs to investigate the rich temporal dynamics in discourse comprehension. Hence, the review in this section is mainly supported by the available ERP studies of the Chinese language. The research on Chinese discourse processing can be classified into three categories that examine the effects of syntactic structure, discourse structure and prosodic structure on discourse comprehension. Based on the review, some implications will be discussed and directions for future investigations will be raised to establish the knowledge of the neurocognitive processing of Chinese discourse comprehension.

Discourse processing in the brain

When engaged in discourse, we are dealing with a tremendous amount of information within a short time period. We need to recognize the upcoming words, retrieve the meanings, decode the phrase or sentence structure, and moreover, we evaluate the relationship between the words and the given context. This process is not only bottom-up but also top-down in an interactive way by which our prior knowledge can influence how we interpret the discourse (Aryadoust, 2017).

The cognitive process of discourse comprehension

Based on the inputs, readers and listeners construct three levels of representation for discourse comprehension: (1) the surface level – the representation of the exact words conveyed; (2) the propositional level or textbase — the representation of the underlying meanings of words conveyed; (3) the level of situation or mental model — the representation of information built by individuals that may or may not be directly conveyed by the discourse (Sparks and Rapp, 2010). Beyond these, the interpretation of discourse is influenced by variations in individuals' prior knowledge, language abilities, goals and more.

Different models have been proposed to account for how discourse contexts influence information retrieval from memory and how the retrieved information influences comprehension (Sparks and Rapp, 2010). The memory-based view suggests that this is an automatic and passive process, where the current context activates relevant information in memory. Conversely, the constructionist view favors a directed and active process that involves a strategic search of relevant information in memory according to the context. However, more and more studies have provided evidence to support a combined process, where both memory-based retrieval and constructionist search are necessary in discourse comprehension. Hence, an integrated model has been put forward. According to this model, text content interacts with readers' prior knowledge in two stages. At the first stage, the context input broadly activates concepts in memory that might be retrieved by the reader later. At the second stage, the reader strategically searches the activated concepts to find the most related information for further processing.

Discourse comprehension, unequivocally, is a dynamic process that has high demands on cognitive resources and working memory. The human brain is simultaneously dealing with a variety of processes at different levels and it is extraordinarily sensitive to any violations during these processes. For instance, since the course of discourse encompasses more than one sentence over time, one of the essential cognitive processes is to link the concepts across the discourse by reference making. Referential ambiguity may arise, however, when individuals are unable to locate a correct referent for an input entity from available candidates within the course of discourse. Several neurophysiological and neuroimaging studies investigating the neural dynamics and signature of referential ambiguity have shed light on the neurocognitive basis of discourse processing.

Neurophysiological effects

Language comprehension engages rich temporal dynamics of the neural activity as various linguistic and non-linguistic information has to be processed rapidly. The temporal dynamics can be nicely captured by neurophysiological measures, such as ERPs. A number of ERP studies have observed a sustained negative deflection of the ERP waveform occurring between 300 and 400 ms after the onset of the word that causes referential ambiguity within discourse (Hagoort, 2008). This sustained negativity shift of the ERP waveform is referred to as the Nref effect by Nieuwland and Van Berkum (2008b), and it is the most consistent response to referential ambiguity. The Nref effect is primarily distributed in the anterior part of the brain (see Figure 18.3 for an illustration of the Nref effect). The early onset of the referential ERP component suggests that referential processing within discourse may occur immediately and incrementally on a word-by-word basis.

Another effect that has been discussed is the N400-late positivity components (LPC). The N400 component is a negative-going potential, usually observed after semantics-related events, emerging at around 200–250 ms and reaching the maximal amplitude at around 400 ms after stimulus onset (Kutas and Hillyard, 1980). The LPC is the waveform that belongs to the positive deflection following the N400 component. The N400-LPC effect has been observed when semantic incoherence occurs in discourse (Nieuwland and Van Berkum, 2008a; see Figure 18.3 for an illustration of the N400-LPC effect).

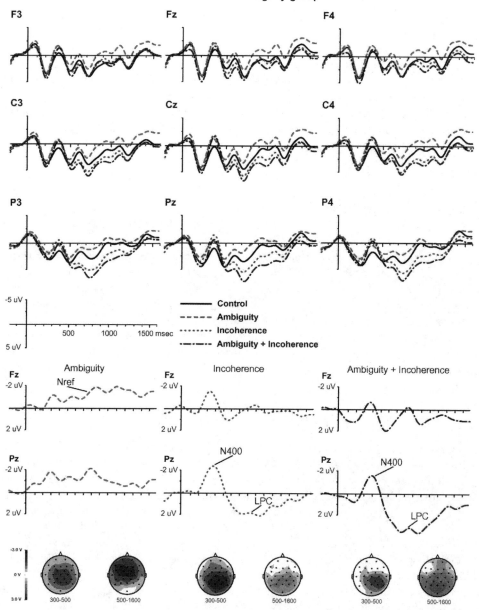

Figure 18.3 An illustration of the waveform and scalp distribution of the Nref effect for the ambiguity condition and the N400-late positivity components (LPC) for the semantic incoherence and the combined conditions. Fz and Pz are the electrode positions. Negative voltage is plotted above and positive voltage below the zero baseline. A color version of the figure is available online.

(Reprinted with permission from Nieuwland and Van Berkum (2008a). Copyright Elsevier.)

Neuroanatomical correlates

To understand the peculiarities of discourse-level processing, Xu et al. (2005) compared word-level, sentence-level, and narrative-level processing using fMRI within one study. All three levels were found to activate the core language areas in the left perisylvian cortex including the inferior frontal and the posterior middle temporal regions. As processing complexity increased from words to sentences to narratives, brain activation in the perisylvian areas increased and spread over to extrasylvian areas. Compared to sentence-level processing, narrative processing recruited greater activation not only in the left-lateralized perisylvian areas but also in bilateral extrasylvian regions including the dorsal and ventral medial prefrontal cortices and precuneus (depicted in Figure 18.2). In particular, the medial prefrontal cortex has been implicated in the theory-of-mind process – the ability to understand that others might have different mental states (e.g., knowledge, intention, purposes) from one's own – which is necessary for the listeners to be able to interpret the actions and thoughts of the characters in the narrative. The precuneus was attributed to linking the contextual information with the listener's prior knowledge in order to build up a situation model for the narrative, and it might be associated with episodic memory retrieval. The involvement of the fronto- and parieto-medial cortices in discourse processing has been reported in other neuroimaging studies. In one fMRI study, it was found that referential ambiguity recruited greater activation in the medial prefrontal and parietal regions, which were associated with evaluation and inference procedures (Nieuwland et al., 2007). A meta-analysis on neuroimaging studies demonstrated that for coherent text comprehension, the fronto-medial cortex coactivated with the parieto-medial cortex in the processing of inferences (Ferstl et al., 2008).

Ferstl et al. (2008) conducted a quantitative meta-analysis of 23 neuroimaging studies on text comprehension, including studies using fMRI or positron emission tomography (PET), with visual or auditory presentation, regardless of language. They identified an extended language network for text comprehension. In addition to the left inferior frontal and superior temporal regions serving for core language processing, they found consistent engagement of the bilateral anterior temporal lobes (depicted in Figure 18.2) for coherent text comprehension, independent of the compared baseline. Some researchers have suggested that the anterior temporal lobes are responsible for integrating words into the semantic context of the discourse (Perfetti and Frishkoff, 2008).

Linking neurophysiological and neuroanatomical evidence

Researchers have attempted to link the neurophysiological effects with the neuroanatomical correlates that have been associated with referential processing according to the location of signals and their proposed functional roles. On the one hand, the Nref effect has been observed in discourse with referential ambiguity (Nieuwland and Van Berkum, 2008b), and the dorsomedial prefrontal region showed increased activation in referential ambiguity conditions or when inferencing processes were engaged between sentences (Nieuwland et al., 2007). The Nref effect detected by ERP has a frontal distribution in the brain, and has corresponded to the dorsomedial prefrontal activity measured by fMRI. These processes, subserved by the Nref effect and the dorsomedial prefrontal activity, may be associated with the evaluation of alternative referents in order to restore referential coherence from ambiguity (Perfetti and Frishkoff, 2008).

On the other hand, the anterior temporal lobes showed increased activity for connected discourse compared to isolated words, and have been taken to reflect increased demands of semantic processing for connected discourse. The neural activity in the anterior temporal lobes has been linked to the semantics-relevant N400 effect that is sensitive to the level of difficulty in discourse-level semantic integration. Taken together, the anterior temporal lobes and the N400 effect may be associated with semantic processing and integration in discourse processing (Perfetti and Frishkoff, 2008).

Neural correlates of Chinese discourse processing

Neurocognitive research on Chinese discourse processing only emerged a decade ago. Much of our current understanding about the neural correlates of Chinese discourse processing originated from the ERP studies that have investigated the neurophysiological effects of different factors on Chinese discourse comprehension. Some studied the effect of local syntactic anomalies on referential processing (Yu et al., 2015). Others examined the effect of discourse structure on semantic integration in discourse, in terms of discourse distance (Yang et al., 2015), topicality (i.e., topic-maintained or topic-shifted; Yang et al., 2013), and contextual influences (e.g., givenness and animacy) on topic-worthiness (Hung and Schumacher, 2012; Hung and Schumacher, 2014). Still others assessed the effects of prosodic structure, including prosodic prominence and prosodic boundaries, on spoken discourse comprehension (Li et al., 2011; Li et al., 2008a; Li et al., 2008b; Li et al., 2010). We will review the neurophysiological evidence from these studies in the following section.

Effects of syntactic structure

At the local sentence level, Yu et al. (2015) investigated whether referential processing would be blocked (the blocking hypothesis), or delayed (the repair hypothesis) or would proceed (the independent hypothesis) when semantic/syntactic anomalies were present. The results showed a sustained Nref effect in referential ambiguity conditions, but this effect was absent when the noun phrase was semantically/syntactically incoherent (i.e., in the incoherent and referentially ambiguous condition like (1)).

(1) 小明有两个弟弟。其中一个弟弟很胖，另一个很瘦。那个很弟弟昨天刚来过。(Yu et al., 2015)
'Xiaoming has two brothers. One of the brothers is very fat, and the other very thin. That **very** brother just came yesterday.'

In (1), referential ambiguity emerged as it was not clear which brother of the two just came yesterday. The word in bold, 'very' (很), induced local semantic/syntactic incoherence as an adjective (either fat or thin) was missing. For this condition, the Nref effect would have been expected due to referential ambiguity, but it was not observed when there was semantic/syntactic incoherence. The results indicate that referential processing is blocked by failure in syntactic phrase structure building, incoherent semantic processing, or both, thus supporting the blocking hypothesis.

Effects of discourse structure

Beyond sentences, the discourse structure has significant influences on semantic integration within the discourse context. Yang et al. (2015) examined the effects of discourse distance and semantic congruency on semantic integration in discourse. The discourse distance was varied by intervening one or three sentences between the lead-in and the target sentences. Semantic congruency was manipulated in the target sentence, where the critical word might be semantically congruent or incongruent with the prior context. Their results showed that the semantically incongruent conditions elicited a more negative-going N400 effect compared to the semantically congruent condition, for both short- and long-distance discourse. In other words, the amplitude of the N400 effect was greater for the semantically incongruent condition than the congruent condition. The semantic congruency effect reflected by the N400 component indicates that the incoming word is immediately integrated into the wider discourse context for semantic interpretation (Hagoort and van Berkum, 2007). The semantically incongruent conditions were also found to induce a greater P600 effect compared to the semantically congruent condition, but this was only observed for the long-distance and not the short-distance discourse. This result implied that readers needed increased processing costs to resolve semantic anomalies and make reinterpretation within a larger discourse context. Taken together, their findings suggest that discourse distance influences semantic integration. Although distance does not influence the initial memory-based processing in which the incoming words are accessed and integrated with the context, it does influence the later constructionist process in which reinterpretation and reconstruction are initiated to reach global coherence within a discourse.

In addition to discourse distance, the topic structure – whether the topic is maintained or shifted along the unfolding of discourse – also modulates semantic integration in the discourse context. In a study by Yang et al. (2013), the topic structure (topic-maintained or topic-shifted) and semantic congruency of the critical word were manipulated to investigate whether semantic integration was influenced by topic structure. Topic structure was varied in the intervening sentences, and semantic congruency was realized in the critical words in the target sentences. They found that incongruent words elicited a larger N400 effect than congruent words for both topic structures. However, this congruency effect reflected by N400 had different scalp distribution with respect to the topic structures. It was widely distributed over the scalp for the topic-maintained condition, whereas it was only present in the right hemisphere and stronger at the central and posterior sites for the topic-shifted condition. As suggested by the authors, semantic integration is more fully implemented when the topic is maintained during the discourse, whereas it interferes when the topic is shifted. The extent to which semantic integration is accomplished for the topic-maintained and topic-shifted structures may explain the broad and restricted distribution of the N400 effect, respectively. In the window of 450–600 ms after the onset of the critical word, the incongruent words also elicited a larger late positivity effect (i.e., the ERP waveform shifted towards the positive deflection) than congruent words only in the topic-shifted condition but not in the topic-maintained condition. The selective late positivity effect was attributed to the increasing discourse complexity for the topic-shifted condition as readers may need to recruit more resources to update the semantic representation of a discourse when encountering a semantic anomalous word with a new topic. This study provides clear evidence demonstrating that discourse structure influences not only the initial stage of semantic integration of the upcoming words with the wider context but also the later stage of the updating of discourse representation.

In Chinese, the topic of a given context is usually determined at the sentence-initial position. Using question-answer pairs, Hung and Schumacher (2012) investigated whether referential processing at the sentence-initial positions and non-sentence-initial positions were governed by topicality and givenness. For topicality, the words at the sentence-initial position of the target sentence were either a continuation of the topic in the question (Topic-Continuity), the discontinuation of the previous topic (Topic-Shift), or an introduction of a new topic (Novel-Topic). Givenness was determined by whether the words at the non-topic positions were new (Topic-New) or given (Topic-Given) entities following topic questions, or new entities preceded by non-topic questions (NonTopic-New). For instance, keeping the target sentence structure identical in (2), the authors varied the subjects in the questions to generate different conditions. In (2a), the topic 'Lisi' (李四) in the question was maintained in the answer, and the word at the non-topic position in the answer was a new concept 'Zhangsan' (张三). On the contrary, in (2b) the topic 'Zhangsan' (张三) in the question was shifted to 'Lisi' (李四) in the answer, while it was repeated at the non-topic position. The question in (2c) did not introduce any topics, so the words in the answer were both novel concepts.

(2) Context question: (Hung and Schumacher, 2012)
    (2a) Topic position: Topic-Continuity; non-topic position: Topic-New
        李四怎么了？
        'What happened to Lisi?'
    (2b) Topic position: Topic-Shift; non-topic position: Topic-Given
        张三怎么了？
        'What happened to Zhangsan?'
    (2c) Topic position: Novel-Topic; non-topic position: NonTopic-New
        怎么了？
        'What happened?'
Target sentence:
    李四殴打了张三。
    '**Lisi** beat **Zhangsan**.'

At the sentence-initial position, topic typicality modulated the ERP waveform and showed a biphasic pattern composed of the N400 and the late positivity effects (refer to the N400-LPC waveform in Figure 18.3). The largest N400 effect was elicited by Topic-Shift words, followed by Novel-Topic, and smallest by Topic-Continuity, which was thought to reflect expectation-based processing rather than pure semantic processing or repetition. Between 500 and 700 ms after the onset of the target word, Topic-Shift words evoked the largest positivity compared to Novel-Topic and Topic-Continuity. The late positivity was related to the maintenance and updating of discourse information. Interestingly, a biphasic N400-late positivity pattern was also observed at the non-topic positions, and the effect was larger for the conditions with new information (Topic-New and NonTopic-New) than that with old information (Topic-Given). Based on the findings of differential modulations on the biphasic N400-late positivity pattern, the authors conclude that referential processing is subject to position-specific demands – while it is mainly modulated by topicality at sentence-initial positions, information processing is guided by givenness at the non-topic positions.

Besides sentential position and givenness, other factors such as animacy also contribute to topic-worthiness. An element that is given/old and animate is considered more topic-worthy, that is, it has higher value in being the topic of the context. In the next study by Hung and Schumacher (2014), they explored to what extent animacy and givenness interacted with each other in referential processing. The results revealed that at the sentence-initial positions, the expectation-based N400 effect was modulated by givenness regardless of animacy, where the topic-shift conditions elicited more negative-going N400 effects than topic-continuity conditions. However, the late positivity effects were elicited by shifted topics with inanimate features but not those with animate features. This is a highlighted finding as it suggests that the updating mechanism is not only sensitive to the information status but also to animacy, and more importantly, animacy outweighs givenness in determining topic-worthiness of the entities within a discourse. At the non-initial sentence positions, by contrast, the biphasic N400-late positivity effects were not influenced by animacy at all but only by givenness, with new information eliciting more negative N400 and larger late positivity than given information. Consistent with the previous study (Hung and Schumacher, 2012), the current findings provide further neurocognitive evidence to support the position-specific account for referential processing.

Effects of prosodic structure

When the lexical entities and discourse structures are kept constant, another suprasegmental factor that hints on the grouping, emphasis or pitch contour of lexical elements could also influence spoken discourse comprehension. This factor is prosody. The temporal grouping of lexical items in an utterance is referred to as prosodic boundary. Making a particular word prominent by increasing the intensity or raising the pitch is referred to as accentuation. Another feature that varies the rising or falling of pitch contours is intonation. All together, prosodic boundary, prosodic prominence (e.g., accentuation), and intonation constitute three prosodic features that impact semantic integration in discourse processing.

To explore the neurodynamics of the interaction between prosody and the information state of the critical words given by the previous discourse context, Li et al. (2008a) studied the neurophysiological effects of accentuation (i.e., whether the critical word is accented or deaccented) and givenness (i.e., whether the critical word has been introduced in the prior context or not). It is generally agreed that speakers tend to place accentuation on new information within a discourse; however, semantic anomalies may occur when old information is accented. The N400 effect was found and its amplitude was modulated by both accentuation (accented words greater than deaccented words) and givenness (new words greater than old words). Furthermore, there was a significant interaction between accentuation and givenness for the N400 effect. The accented words elicited greater N400 effects than the deaccented words for both new and old information, and the amplitude difference was larger for the old information compared to new information. Since the accented new information still elicited larger N400 effect than the deaccented new information, the amplitude difference of the N400 effect cannot be simply explained by semantic anomalies. Instead, the authors suggest that the N400 effect is sensitive to the information status of the words as signaled by accentuation and can be attributed to the semantic integration load induced by the upcoming words.

In Chinese, a tonal language, the processing of prosodic cues could be complicated by lexical tones. Whereas lexical tones determine lexical meanings of words, pitch accent influences the information status of words, which therefore affects semantic integration within a broader context. Given these different functions, several intriguing questions emerge. How do Chinese speakers differentiate changes in lexical tones from those in pitch accent? Does the brain have differentiated responses to these two features? Li et al. (2008b) tried to answer these questions by examining brain responses to lexical tone and pitch accent in online speech comprehension. In (3) below, the first two sentences provided context information including the introduction and the question, followed by one of the target sentences (3a-d). The underlined words were the critical words, and the words in brackets were the accented words. Tones were manipulated at the words in bold, which resulted in two words with different meanings (e.g., 'flower' 花 [hua1] and 'picture' 画 [hua4]). Other words were identical across four conditions.

(3) Introduction: (Li et al., 2008b)
现在正是玫瑰盛开的季节。
'Now, it is the season when roses are in full blossom.'

Question:
明天小秦去买什么把房间装饰一下？
'Tomorrow what is Xiaoqin going to buy to decorate the room?'
- (3a) Appropriate accentuation and appropriate tone:
  明天小秦去买(花)装饰房间。
  'Tomorrow <u>Xiaoqin</u> is going to buy (**flowers**) to decorate the room.'
- (3b) Appropriate accentuation and inappropriate tone:
  明天小秦去买(画)装饰房间。
  'Tomorrow <u>Xiaoqin</u> is going to buy (**pictures**) to decorate the room.'
- (3c) Inappropriate accentuation and appropriate tone:
  明天(小秦)去买花装饰房间。
  'Tomorrow (<u>Xiaoqin</u>) is going to buy **flowers** to decorate the room.'
- (3d) Inappropriate accentuation and inappropriate tone:
  明天(小秦)去买画装饰房间。
  'Tomorrow (<u>Xiaoqin</u>) is going to buy **pictures** to decorate the room.'

Their results showed that both lexical tone and pitch accent violations elicited an N400 effect that was distributed in the central-posterior part of the brain. There was no interaction between the effects of lexical tone and pitch accent. More critically, the brain responses to the combined violation (3d) was additive, which was equivalent to the sum of the effects of only the lexical tone violation (3b) and only the pitch accent violation (3c). Furthermore, the effect of lexical tone violation occurred 90 ms earlier than that of pitch accent violation. The time delay may reflect different functional roles of lexical tone and pitch accent in that lexical tone determines lexical access immediately whereas pitch accent influences information structure of the discourse at a higher level.

The grouping of words in an utterance – prosodic boundary – can influence syntactic structure and hence semantic integration in discourse comprehension as well. Li et al. (2010) investigated the effect of prosodic boundaries on syntactic parsing in spoken discourse processing. Using ambiguous sentences consisting of a verb, a first noun, an auxiliary, and a second noun, they manipulated the location of prosodic boundaries to create two types of phrases consisting of identical words but different syntactic parsing and meanings. One type of sentences has the prosodic boundary before the second noun, which creates the modifier-noun construction (MNC, 4a). The other type has the prosodic boundary before the first noun, leading to the narrative-object structure (NOS, 4b).

(4) Question: (Li et al., 2010)
- (4A) MNC context:
  村长正在安慰惦记谁的父母？
  'Which parents is the village head comforting, the parents missing whom?'
- (4B) NOS context:
  村长心里一直惦记着谁的父母？
  'Whose parents is the village head missing?'

Answer:
- (4a) MNC:
  惦记<u>水手的</u>/父母
  'The parents who miss the <u>sailor</u>.'
- (4b) NOS:
  惦记/<u>水手的</u>父母
  'Miss the <u>sailor</u>'s parents'

The critical words were set at the first nouns in the answers, namely 'sailor' (水手) underlined in (4a–b). Using questions that probed either type of phrase structure, they manipulated the presence or absence of prosodic boundary (indicated by slash) before the critical word to generate consistent or inconsistent answers. For example, an answer with the absence of prosodic boundary before the critical word (4a) would be an inconsistent answer to a NOS question (4B), which elicited a larger left anterior negativity (LAN) effect compared to the consistent MNC discourse context (4A). The LAN effect was an early negative peak in the ERP waveform that was distributed in the frontal-central regions of the brain. On the contrary, for the answer with the presence of prosodic boundary (4b), the MNC discourse context (4A) would be inconsistent and elicited a broadly distributed negative effect in the ERPs, which may be a combination of the LAN and N400 effects. The LAN effect induced by inconsistent conditions reflect that prosodic boundaries influence syntactic parsing (Friederici, 2002).

As demonstrated in the aforementioned studies, prosodic prominence modulates the information status of the accented word for semantic integration (Li et al., 2008a), while prosodic boundaries influence syntactic parsing (Li et al., 2010). In a later study, Li et al. (2011) investigated how prosodic prominence and prosodic boundaries interacted with each other in discourse comprehension. Keeping the answer (target sentence) constant for all conditions, they created four types of questions to induce different violations including coherent context, simple prosodic prominence violation, simple prosodic boundary violation, and combined prosodic prominence-boundary violation. The simple prosodic prominence violation elicited a frontal-central negativity effect (occurring at 270–510 ms after the critical word) that peaked in the frontal lobe, suggesting that prosodic prominence immediately modulates the information status of the words for online semantic integration in the discourse. The semantic integration process may involve reference establishment, thus eliciting the Nref-like effect. The simple prosodic boundary violation evoked a broadly distributed negativity effect (at 270–510 ms and 510–660 ms). Consistent with the previous study (Li et al., 2010), such a broad negativity effect with an early onset was suggested to reflect that prosodic boundaries have impacts on syntactic parsing and immediately influence the integration or grouping of a word into the syntactic structure. The combined prosodic prominence-boundary violation elicited a similar negativity effect as that of the simple prosodic prominence violation. Interestingly, they found an interaction between prosodic prominence violation and prosodic boundary violation in the time window of 270–510 ms, whereby the amplitude of the negativity effect of prosodic boundary violation was increased by the addition of prosodic prominence violation, whereas the size of the prosodic prominence violation effect was not different from that with additional prosodic boundary violation. This finding demonstrates an asymmetrical interaction between prosodic prominence and prosodic boundary during discourse comprehension, which may highlight an important characteristic for the Chinese language. Whereas the processing load of syntactic parsing determined by prosodic boundary was increased by additional prosodic prominence violation, semantic integration modulated by prosodic prominence was not affected by additional prosodic boundary violation. This may indicate that the lack of morpho-syntactic features in Chinese bias Chinese speakers to rely more on semantic features even in syntactic processing, but less on syntactic structure for semantic processing.

Discourse processing in Chinese vs. other languages

According to the studies reviewed so far, neuroscientific research on Chinese discourse processing seems to pay attention to different but not entirely exclusive aspects from those in other languages. While a large body of studies examined referential and inferential processing in other languages, studies in Chinese investigated how syntactic anomalies, discourse structure, and prosodic features influence semantic integration within the discourse. It should be noted, however, that these discourse cues also have impacts on referential processing to some extent, which is essential for reaching global coherence to enhance semantic comprehension in the discourse context. For instance, a topic-shifted structure would impede referential processing as the listeners would face challenges linking the new topic back to the prior context.

Accumulating neurophysiological evidence has revealed similar ERP components for discourse processing in Chinese and in other languages. In general, when it is unclear which referents from the prior context the critical word is referred to, referential ambiguity arises and elicits the Nref effect (e.g., Nieuwland and Van Berkum, 2008a; Yu et al., 2015; Figure 18.3). When contextual cues (e.g., topic maintenance, topic-worthiness) or non-contextual cues (e.g., prosodic prominence, prosodic boundaries) alter the discourse structure, difficulties in semantic comprehension elicit either the N400 effect or the biphasic N400-late positivity effects (e.g., Hung and Schumacher, 2012; Nieuwland and Van Berkum, 2008a; Figure 18.3). The N400 effect has been suggested to reflect increased processing costs for semantic integration, while the late positivity effect has been attributed to higher demands in updating information and reconstructing coherence in the discourse context.

On the other hand, the rather limited number of fMRI studies on Chinese discourse processing rendered cross-language comparisons on the neuroanatomical representations of discourse difficult. Nevertheless, a recent study by Feng et al. (2017) may provide some hints. They investigated the neural substrates underlying the processing of indirect replies with various contextual relevance. Their findings were in keeping with those from previous studies on inferential processing in other languages (e.g., Bašnáková et al., 2014). The authors showed that understanding indirect replies activated not only the fronto-temporal language network including bilateral inferior frontal gyri (IFG) and middle temporal gyri (MTG), but also the theory-of-mind related network including the right temporo-parietal junction (rTPJ), dorsomedial prefrontal cortex (dmPFC) and precuneus (as illustrated in Figure 18.4). The core language network was associated with semantic processing and the understanding of the implicated meanings given the context. The activation in rTPJ, dmPFC and precuneus was recruited for the processing of pragmatic inferences as the listener had to mentalize and infer the speaker's aim and intention – an operation overlapping with theory of mind processing. Furthermore, they revealed the functional interplay between the core language network and the theory of mind

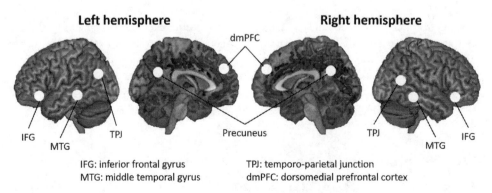

Figure 18.4 Brain regions involved in making pragmatic inferences in Chinese (Feng et al., 2017).

network by showing higher functional coupling between rTPJ and dmPFC with bilateral IFG and MTG for indirect replies compared to direct replies. This study demonstrates that processing of pragmatic inferences in Chinese engages similar brain regions as those in other languages.

Although the evidence so far seems to suggest a universal neural network for discourse processing, some linguistic features specific to Chinese need to be taken into account for discrepant findings between studies. For example, the tonal features of Chinese may be an additional factor to tease apart when researchers examine the effect of prosodic prominence on discourse processing (Li et al., 2008b). Moreover, the lack of morpho-syntactic structures in Chinese has been suggested to encourage Chinese speakers to rely more on semantic cues than on syntactic cues in language comprehension. This preference may result in differential neuroanatomical and neurophysiological representations for discourse comprehension (Li et al., 2011). More direct cross-language comparison studies would be required to elucidate the similarities and differences in discourse processing between Chinese and other languages.

Conclusions and future directions

In light of the vigorously growing body of research, a picture depicting the neurocognitive basis of Chinese discourse processing has begun to surface. It has come to our understanding that interactive networks of brain activity are engaged during discourse comprehension. Within these networks, the core language-relevant regions are sensitive to the information status of discourse cues and the integration of discourse cues for semantic interpretation. Meanwhile, the fronto- and parieto-medial cortices are responsible for the processing of references and pragmatic inferences. These two networks communicate with each other to enable a global comprehension for discourse. The neuroanatomical representations of discourse processing correspond to the neurophysiological findings revealed by ERPs. The semantic integration processes elicit the N400 effect or the biphasic N400-late positivity effects, while referential processing is associated with the Nref effect. Going beyond traditional behavioral observations, the neuroscientific techniques (e.g., ERP, fMRI) have allowed us to reveal the temporal and spatial dynamics underlying discourse processing with higher resolution.

The understanding of the neural mechanisms underlying discourse processing has important implications for clinical populations. Although most neuropsychological assessments of language abilities focus on core language domains (e.g., phonology, semantics, syntax), referential and inferential processing in discourse also plays an essential role in natural language. The identification of the neuroanatomical and neurophysiological correlates of discourse processing in addition to those for core language processing is especially informative. The findings would not only inform neurosurgeons in pre-surgical planning about whether the ability of discourse processing may be compromised by brain surgery, but also help them to provide prognoses about language recovery after brain damage or surgery. For instance, when planning to remove a tumor located at the dorsomedial prefrontal cortex, neurosurgeons would consider whether the ability to make references or pragmatic inferences may be affected resulting in disabilities in discourse processing.

Given the language-specific characteristics (e.g., Chinese relies more on semantic than on morpho-syntactic cues in language comprehension), it is critical to elucidate whether discourse processing in Chinese share the similar neurocognitive mechanisms as the other languages. The investigations of other language domains have implicated that the universal language network may be modulated by language-specific characteristics (Tan et al., 2005; Wu et al., 2012). In this regard, cross-language comparison or bilingual research will shed light on the peculiarities of the neurocognitive basis of Chinese discourse processing in comparison with other languages.

Finally, we have learnt from ERP studies that the biphasic N400-late positivity effects play an important role in Chinese discourse comprehension as they are sensitive to various types of discourse cues (e.g., contextual references, topicality, prosodic prominence, prosodic boundary). However, the brain areas that serve the processing of these cues remained to be identified by neuroimaging studies. Future fMRI studies are required to delineate whether the discourse cues indeed modulate brain activity in semantic and syntactic regions reflecting interference in semantic integration and syntactic parsing, or they engage other brain regions that interact with the semantic and syntactic networks for discourse comprehension. The information gained from neurophysiological and neuroimaging studies will supplement behavioral observations, which together will enable a holistic understanding towards a neurocognitive model of Chinese discourse processing.

References

Aryadoust, V. (2017) 'An Integrated Cognitive Theory of Comprehension', *International Journal of Listening*: 1–30.

Bašnáková, J., Weber, K., Petersson, K.M., van Berkum, J. and Hagoort, P. (2014) 'Beyond the Language Given: The Neural Correlates of Inferring Speaker Meaning', *Cerebral Cortex*, 24(10): 2572–2578.

Feng, W., Wu, Y., Jan, C., Yu, H., Jiang, X. and Zhou, X. (2017) 'Effects of Contextual Relevance on Pragmatic Inference during Conversation: An fMRI Study', *Brain and Language*, 171: 52–61.

Ferstl, E.C., Neumann, J., Bogler, C. and von Cramon, D.Y. (2008) 'TheExtended Language Network: A Meta-analysis of Neuroimaging Studies on Text Comprehension', *Human Brain Mapping*, 29(5): 581–593.

Friederici, A.D. (2002) 'Towards a Neural Basis of Auditory Sentence Processing', *Trends in Cognitive Sciences*, 6(2): 78–84.

Friederici, A.D. (2011) 'The Brain Basis of Language Processing: From Structure to Function', *Physiological Reviews*, 91(4): 1357–1392.

Hagoort, P. (2008) 'The Fractionation of Spoken Language Understanding by Measuring Electrical and-Magnetic Brain Signals', *Philosophical Transactions of the Royal Society B: Biological Sciences*, 363(1493): 1055–1069.

Hagoort, P. and van Berkum, J. (2007) 'Beyond the Sentence Given'. *Philosophical Transactions of the Royal Society B: Biological Sciences*, 362(1481): 801–811.

Hung, Y.-C. and Schumacher, P.B. (2012) 'Topicality Matters: Position-Specific Demands on Chinese Discourse Processing'. *Neuroscience Letters*, 511(2): 59–64.

Hung, Y.-C. and Schumacher, P.B. (2014) 'Animacy Matters: ERP Evidence for the Multi-Dimensionality of Topic-Worthiness in Chinese', *Brain Research*, 1555: 36–47.

Kutas, M. and Hillyard, S. (1980) 'Reading Senseless Sentences: Brain Potentials Reflect Semantic Incongruity'. *Science*, 207(4427): 203–205.

Kutas, M. and Van Petten, C.K. (1994) 'Psycholinguistics electrified: Event-related brain potential investigations', in *Handbook of Psycholinguistics*. San Diego, CA: Academic Press.

Li, X., Chen, Y. and Yang, Y. (2011) 'Immediate Integration of Different Types of Prosodic Information during On-line Spoken Language Comprehension: An ERP Study', *Brain Research*, 1386: 139–152.

Li, X., Hagoort, P. and Yang, Y. (2008a) 'Event-related Potential Evidence on the Influence of Accentuation in Spoken Discourse Comprehension in Chinese', *Journal of Cognitive Neuroscience*, 20(5): 906–915.

Li, X., Yang, Y. and Hagoort, P. (2008b) 'Pitch Accent and Lexical Tone Processing in Chinese Discourse Comprehension: An ERP Study', *Brain Research*, 1222: 192–200.

Li, X., Yang, Y. and Lu, Y. (2010) 'How and When Prosodic Boundaries Influence Syntactic Parsing under Different Discourse Contexts: An ERP Study', *Biological Psychology*, 83(3): 250–259.

Nieuwland, M.S., Petersson, K.M. and Van Berkum, J.J.A. (2007) 'On Sense and Reference: Examining the Functional Neuroanatomy of Referential Processing', *NeuroImage*, 37(3): 993–1004.

Nieuwland, M.S. and Van Berkum, J.J.A. (2008a) 'The Interplay between Semantic and Referential Aspects of Anaphoric Noun Phrase Resolution: Evidence from ERPs', *Brain and Language*, 106(2): 119–131.

Nieuwland, M.S. and Van Berkum, J.J.A. (2008b) 'The Neurocognition of Referential Ambiguity in Language Comprehension', *Language and Linguistics Compass*, 2(4): 603–630.

Perfetti, C.A. and Frishkoff, G.A. (2008) 'Chapter 16 – The neural bases of text and discourse processing', in *Handbook of the Neuroscience of Language*. San Diego: Elsevier.

Sparks, J.R. and Rapp, D.N. (2010) 'Discourse Processing – Examining Our Everyday Language Experiences', *Wiley Interdisciplinary Reviews: Cognitive Science*, 1(3): 371–381.

Tan, L.H., Laird, A.R., Li, K. and Fox, P.T. (2005) 'Neuroanatomical Correlates of Phonological Processing of Chinese Characters and Alphabetic Words: A Meta-Analysis', *Human Brain Mapping*, 25(1): 83–91.

Wu, C.-Y., Ho, M.-H.R. and Chen, S.-H.A. (2012) 'A Meta-analysis of fMRI Studies on Chinese Orthographic, Phonological, and Semantic Processing', *NeuroImage*, 63(1): 381–391.

Xu, J., Kemeny, S., Park, G., Frattali, C. and Braun, A. (2005) 'Language in Context: Emergent Features of Word, Sentence, and Narrative Comprehension', *NeuroImage*, 25(3): 1002–1015.

Yang, X., Chen, S., Chen, X. and Yang, Y. (2015) 'How Distance Affects Semantic Integration in Discourse: Evidence from Event-Related Potentials', *PLoS ONE*, 10(11): e0142967.

Yang, X., Chen, X., Chen, S., Xu, X. and Yang, Y. (2013) 'Topic Structure Affects Semantic Integration: Evidence from Event-Related Potentials', *PLoS ONE*, 8(12): e79734.

Yu, J., Zhang, Y., Boland, J.E. and Cai, L. (2015) 'The Interplay between Referential Processing and Local Syntactic/Semantic Processing: ERPs to Written Chinese Discourse', *Brain Research*, 1597: 139–158.

19
Language impairment in Chinese discourse

Yi-hsiu Lai and Yu-te Lin

Introduction

Over the past few decades, multiple cognitive deficits have been used to characterize persons with Alzheimer's disease (AD). The most significant features among these deficits, including semantic impairments and progressive memory loss, have been widely examined (Brandt and Rich, 1995; Sebastian et al., 2001). Sebastian et al. (2001), for instance, examined the performance of 40 AD persons in the Brown-Peterson task and analyzed a pattern of errors, as compared with 55 elderly controls. The results showed that AD persons performed with lower scores in the three retention intervals than the healthy controls. But non-significant interaction was identified between group and interval. They argued for the similar rate of forgetfulness in the two groups and highlighted the problems in the central executive as well as in updating the working memory. Some earlier studies in psycholinguistics looked into the qualitative differences in prose discourse of persons with AD (see Abeysinghe et al., 1990; Lyons et al., 1994). Abeysinghe et al. (1990) was one of the pioneer reports on the nature of semantic memory impairment in AD persons. Three semantic tasks, including word association, definition, and associate rank ordering were implemented. Compared with healthy controls, the AD persons were more likely to give repetitious or unrelated responses. Additionally, the AD persons were unable to offer meaningful associates in the definition task and they were significantly impaired in identifying semantic associates of words. The results suggested that the AD persons were characterized by semantic memory deterioration and that semantic deficits were shown in the early stages of AD.

The discourse analysis of AD persons is another way to investigate possible cognitive impairments. Discourse analysis of a particular clinical population or AD persons can offer crucial information on how their linguistic abilities are affected (Cherney, 1998; Dijkstra et al., 2004). Discourse analysis is used as a tool to identify the underlying cognitive and linguistic processes that cause impairment to discourse. Thus, there is no doubt that examining the abilities of persons with AD to communicate is important to developing remedial treatment to this population. As Martin and McDonald (2003: 451) stated, the ability to communicate in commonly acceptable language depends on both an intact language system and 'knowledge of the specific communicative context, knowledge about the co-conversant(s), and general knowledge of the world'. Combining sentences into a consistent and meaningful discourse requires not only lexical and syntactic skills but also 'knowledge of discourse structure and rules for appropriate language use' (Huppert et al., 1994: 346). Facilitating strategies (i.e., achieving coherence, conciseness, elaboration and appropriate pronominal reference) and cognitive resources are more important than lexical or syntactic skills in maintaining coherent discourse (Dijkstra et al., 2002a, 2002b, 2004).

A higher frequency of indefinite and empty words as well as aborted phrases in AD persons was observed in early AD discourse studies, as compared with healthy counterparts (see Kempler, 1991; Ripich and Terrell, 1988). Ripich and Terrell (1988), for example, investigated discourse patterns in the use of propositions and cohesion devices. Six AD persons and six healthy elderly participated in the topic-centered interviews in the study. Compared to the healthy controls, AD persons made significantly more use of words and conversational turns, making those interviews more lengthy as well as interactive. A pattern of cohesion disruptions in AD persons was found. The results suggest that incoherence may be attributed to being unable to take the conversation partner's perspective in developing thematic structure. Hence, Ripich and Terrell (1988) argued that AD persons' incoherent speech results not only from the linguistic impairments, but also from the discourse impairments. Also, Kempler and Goral (2008) note that AD persons have trouble recalling names and words by using conceptually related words (e.g., "dog" for "horse"), or substituting pro-forms (e.g., "he", "it"). To yield appropriate pronouns, we need sufficient memory capacity to match with the earlier information in the discourse and to figure out the preceding antecedents. AD persons, however, are often reported to be impaired with memory capacity and semantic memory (Baddeley, 1996; Orange and Purves, 1996), which cause them to face greater difficulty in their oral performance. As Orange and Purves (1996) highlight, AD cognitive impairments and their conversational performance are closely linked in some conversational features, such as topic and repair. AD speech is often characterized by digression from the topic, irrelevant responses to questions, disturbed semantic cohesion and inappropriate conversational repair. The finding of degraded or lost meaning elements in semantic and episodic memories, especially specific subordinate concepts and word-finding difficulties, may help account for the discourse and memory-based related problems encountered by AD persons when interacting with others.

Discourse features: discourse-building vs. discourse-impairing

In recent years, a series of studies on English-speaking AD discourse were carried out by Dijkstra et al. (2002a, 2002b, 2004). They described discourse in conversations on the basis of two features, namely discourse-building features and discourse-impairing features. The former facilitate the continuation of conversations, while the latter impedes the communicative purpose of conversations. According to Dijkstra et al. (2002a, 2002b), 'cohesion, coherence, and conciseness' are regarded as discourse-building features; on the contrary, 'revisions, aborted phrases, empty phrases, repetitions, indefinite words, and disruptive topic shifts' are classified as discourse-impairing features. Cohesion occurs in discourse in which the understanding of an element relies on that of another element (Ripich et al., 2000). Cohesion refers to combining discourse components in the form of references, surface indicators of nexuses between and within sentences, ellipsis, substitutions, conjunctions and lexical markers (Dijkstra et al., 2004; Liles and Coelho, 1998). Coherence can be defined both locally and globally. The former defines it as a representation of how closely an utterance (sentence) concerns the content and theme of the next preceding utterance. The latter regards it as the close connection between a general topic and an utterance (Laine et al., 1998). The theme is well-maintained with global coherence. Conciseness denotes the addition of information without excessive detail. It demonstrates the efficiency of information, high information content (Shadden, 1998) and the relationships of discourse (Ripich and Terrell, 1988; Shadden, 1998).

Unlike the discourse-building features, discourse-impairing features impede the development of conversation via errors, incompleteness, vagueness, repetitions, aborted phrases, empty phrases (phrases that have no meanings), indefinite words (non-specific words, for example, 'thing' and 'stuff'), as well as disruptive topic shifts (Garcia and Joanette, 1997). Improper restatements of ideas or intact repetitions of words are known as repetition, which often occurs in the discourse of persons with AD (Bayles and Tomoeda, 1991). Ulatowska and Chapman (1991) defined disruptive topic shifts as a tangent or excursive discourse from a given topic. The English discourse profiles of 30 sanatorium AD patients and 30 healthy older adults were compared in the study of Dijkstra et al. (2004). A total of 60 transcripts of interview-style conversations were analyzed. The results revealed that compared to the adults with dementia, healthy adults utilized more discourse-building features, for example, coherence and cohesion. On the contrary, the conversations of persons with AD showed more discourse-impairing features, such as empty phrases and disruptive topic shifts, than the conversations of healthy adults. A decrease in the memory of persons with AD was reflected from their discourse features.

Following the framework proposed by Dijkstra et al. (2002a, 2002b, 2004), we examined the discourse features of Chinese-speaking older adults with and without AD (Lai, 2014). Forty interview transcripts were analyzed. Discourse patterns were examined in light of discourse-building features and discourse-impairing features. Semantic and pragmatic aspects in oral revisions were also discussed. The results indicated that fewer discourse-building features but more discourse-impairing features were found in the conversations of older adults with dementia compared to the healthy controls. Discourse-impairing variables possessed more predictive power of degrees of dementia than did the discourse-building variables. Especially, revision and no global coherence could reliably predict the severity of dementia for the Chinese-speaking AD population.

No matter how much research interest in the AD discourse patterns has grown, open questions still exist. The research in the correlation between discourse features and the severity of AD has been a less investigated area. The knowledge of how and what severity of discourse variables distinguish healthy older adults from those with a moderate degree of Alzheimer's dementia would be beneficial to the aging society. Furthermore, few studies have addressed the cognitive mechanism in the discourse of Chinese-speaking AD persons. Hence, Mandarin Chinese-speaking AD older adults' discourse patterns remain worthy of further examination. Describing AD impaired discourse patterns can also provide recommendations and advice to Chinese families as well as professional caregivers.

Language performance of Chinese-speaking AD persons

Compared to those in the Western literature, linguistic studies on Chinese-speaking AD persons have been relatively ignored and limited (see Jhang, 2011; Liu, 2005, 2010; Wang, 2010). In the past decade, increasing attention has been attached to the cognitive mechanism in Mandarin Chinese-speaking AD persons' discourse. We have conducted a series of relevant studies (see Lai, 2013, 2014, 2017a, 2017b, 2017c; Lai et al., 2009; Lai and Lin, 2012; Lai and Lin, 2013).

In the earlier research (Lai et al., 2009), we examined the linguistic patterns of Chinese-speaking AD persons. We collected speech samples of picture descriptions from 30 AD patients and 32 older adults as the control group. The study analyzed conceptual-semantic and syntactic errors. The discussions focused on the perspectives of semantic and syntactic preservation. The results showed that AD persons communicated with less information and had more semantic errors. Despite these impairments, they not only continued to use an abundance of structures, but also employed similar syntactic structures to those of the control group. Multiple regression analyses were used to examine the severity of dementia and linguistic attributes. The findings regarding semantic-conceptual deterioration in light of relative structural preservation in AD supports the modularity of grammar and the separation of structural operations from semantic-conceptual ones (Chomsky, 1972; Jackendoff, 1972), and the empirical data from persons with focal brain lesions (Grodzinsky, 1990; Moscovitch and Umilta, 1990). Thus, it can be concluded that "the psychological reality of linguistic domains can be either impaired or preserved and that the modularity of grammar hold true with respect to language breakdown in AD and in focal brain lesion" (Lai et al., 2009: 474).

Lai and Lin (2013) is a follow-up study to our earlier paper (Lai et al., 2009). Speech samples were collected from 20 AD older adults, 20 control older adults and 20 control non-older adults in Taiwan. A category fluency task and a picture naming task were implemented to further explore the factors in action-object semantic disorders for AD persons and the possible category effect. Semantic categories, for example, nouns and verbs, have been known to correlate significantly with semantic memory deficits. Object/noun naming versus action/verb naming by AD persons has been conducted to examine semantic category effects, but findings in the Western literature have not gone undisputed. Some studies report that the verb production is better preserved than the noun production. Others claim that object naming is less impaired than action naming. Still others argue that both nouns and verbs were impaired and feature-based semantic representations help explain the impairment. Lai and Lin's (2013) category fluency task was composed of two different semantic categories, namely objects (or nouns) and actions (or verbs). Participants were asked to report as many items within a category as possible in one minute. Thirty black-and-white pictures, including 15 object and 15 action pictures, were adopted as instruments for the naming task. Action fluency refers to the score of correct responses in the category of action in one minute, also called the action naming task. Similarly, the score of correct responses in the category of noun in one minute (the object naming task) is referred to as noun fluency. Variables such as frequency, age of acquisition, or familiarity were contained in each picture. Frequency differences can be found between nouns and verbs in the pictures. Also, the predictive power of semantic variables for the severity of Alzheimer's dementia was examined. The results of the category fluency task revealed that the AD participants made a significantly smaller number of informative items, demonstrating the content of information was seriously deteriorated. For the healthy controls, category effect was only significant in the fluency task; no significant category effect was observed in the AD participants. The results of multiple regression analysis further demonstrated that action fluency, action naming, and frequency of pictures could reliably predict the severity of dementia. This finding regarding the nature of semantic disorders echoed the argument that semantic-lexical disorders resulted mainly from a loss of information in semantic representations (Abeysinghe et al., 1990). The content of information stored in AD participants, compared with the controls, was found to be seriously deteriorated. This further empirically supported the loss of information hypothesis, in which semantic-lexical disorders come mainly from a loss of information in the semantic representation. This study additionally contributed to the predictive power of semantic variables and of pictorial variables concerning the severity of Alzheimer's dementia.

Discourse markers produced by Chinese-speaking older adults with and without AD also were examined in Lai and Lin (2012). Early reports of Chinese discourse markers focused mainly on the use of specific markers, *hao* 'okay', *danshi* 'but', *keshi* 'but', *buguo* 'but', and *na(me)* 'then' (Miracle, 1991), *meiyou* 'no' (Wang et al., 2007), *ranhou* 'then', *jieguo* 'result', *ne* 'question', *na* 'that', and *dui bu dui* 'yes or no' (Green, 2011). A typology of Chinese pragmatic markers is presented in Feng (2008). On the basis of the inherent semantic import, Chinese pragmatic markers are described in a principled and systematic way. Based on Feng's framework (2008), we analyzed two types of Chinese discourse markers, namely conceptual ones and non-conceptual ones. The former are further divided into two subtypes: epistemic (e.g., *haoxiang* 'seem', *dagai* 'probably', *keneng* 'possible') and evaluative markers (e.g., *eryi* 'that is all', *zhishi* 'merely', *shizai* 'really'). We divided the latter into three subtypes: contrastive (e.g., *dan(shi)* 'but', *keshi* 'but', *buguo* 'but', *suiran* 'though'), elaborative (e.g., *haiyou* 'and', *na* 'and then', *lingwai* 'in addition') and inferential markers (e.g., *suoyi* 'so', *yinwei* 'because'). Two kinds of discourse, the descriptive discourse and the narrative discourse, and two major types of Chinese discourse markers were discussed. We highlighted issues concerning what discourse markers are frequently adopted by these two groups and which types of discourse markers significantly differentiate these two groups. Speech samples were collected from 30 persons with AD and 30 control older adults in Taiwan. Their ages ranged from 61 to 85 years old. Each participant individually described a picture (i.e., the descriptive discourse) and answered questions regarding his/her personal life and experience (i.e., the narrative discourse).

The results showed less frequency and less variation in the AD discourse markers than in those of the controls. These AD participants, in spite of uttering the same markers as the controls, did not fully manipulate the functions of markers used by the controls. Examples of contrastive markers, *danshi* 'but' and *suiran* 'though', marking a contrast between two propositions, clearly show the tremendous differences between the AD discourse and the control discourse. In the AD discourse, *danshi* 'but' is adopted mainly to reveal the fact that the AD individuals identify a contrast between two utterances. But, they sometimes fail to specify the definite propositions (e.g., 就是上有 XX 但是 XXXX 'The above is XX, but XXXX'. and 我知道但是說不出來 'I know that but I can't name it') (Lai and Lin, 2012: 1998). The control individuals, by contrast, used *danshi* 'but' with specific contrasting propositions (e.g., 現在應該是吃的比較清淡，但是偶爾也會跟一些好朋友，像我明天我老婆的生日，就要跟我朋友，幾對3, 4對朋友去吃大餐 'We have light meals now, but sometimes I have big meals with some good friends. For example, I will have a big meal with three or four couples for my wife's birthday tomorrow'.) or with another logical marker *suiran* 'though' (e.g., 雖然已經走了四五年了，但是一直都在我腦海裡面，久久都不能退去 'Though he was dead for four or five years, he has been in my mind without disappearing for a long time') (Lai and Lin, 2012: 1999).

Additionally, following Romero-Trillo's (2001) Specificity Index of Functions (SIf), we found the AD and control participants performed with tremendous differences concerning the use of markers in the realization of functions. For the AD participants, the overall use of markers realizing functions ranged from the medium level to the low level of specificity without any high specificity of functions. The zero value of SIf in three categories in the descriptive discourse (i.e., inferential, contrastive, and evaluative markers) manifested the fact that the AD individuals, suffering from cognitive deficits, were relatively impaired in manipulating these functions. By contrast, the control participants adopted the discourse markers to realize functions ranging from the medium level to the high level of specificity (i.e., inferential and contrastive markers in the narrative discourse) without the use of the low specificity. In brief, the dementia factors played an essential role in the AD persons' overall use of markers to realize a function. The major findings contribute to the specific patterns of discourse markers produced by the AD persons in terms of marker variety and marker function.

A case study of Chinese-speaking AD discourse

This chapter offers a follow-up report of our previous studies (Lai et al., 2009; Lai, 2014) and further elaborates the language impairments in Chinese-speaking AD discourse. The AD discourse in the present chapter was produced by native speakers of Mandarin Chinese in Taiwan. They were clinically diagnosed as probable AD, not from other types of dementia, according to the NINCDS-ADRDA criteria (McKhann et al., 1984) after standardized dementia assessment.

The AD discourse-building and discourse-impairing features mainly follow the framework of Dijkstra et al. (2002b). Discourse-building features, including explicit information units, local coherence, global coherence, cohesion, proper pronouns, and appropriate conjunctions, are instrumental in the continuation of conversations. Information units refer to the explicit contents, such as action, actors, places, or objects, in participants' utterances. Specific examples are presented in Lai (2014).

On the contrary, discourse-impairing features impede the communicative purposes of conversations (Dijkstra et al., 2002b). One of discourse-impairing features is word-finding difficulty, which occurs when the speaker pauses for a certain period of time. When subjects repeat a word or phrase immediately, it is identified as repetition. Non-specific words, for example, "thing" or "stuff", are called indefinite words. Empty phrases are defined as utterances with little or no content. No cohesion comprises the lack of referential cohesion, temporal cohesion, as well as causal cohesion. No local coherence refers to the meanings or topics of two successive sentences not being coherently related. When there is no correlation between an utterance and the topic, it is marked as having no global coherence. No global coherence is also explained as disruptive topic shifts (Ulatowska and Chapman, 1991), which is identified when speakers generate tangents or digressions from the topic.

Revisions occur when utterances are monitored, troubles are detected, and corrections are made. The AD participants make revisions when monitoring their utterances, detecting problems, and correcting ideas or rephrasing words (Lai, 2014). In the current analysis, revision refers to "self-revision", which is adapted from "self-repair" (Levelt, 1983). Revision is made not merely to replace an error, but to achieve the appropriateness and clarity of the message. To further probe the possible differences in the revised patterns of these two groups, revised forms are further analyzed in two linguistic categories, "semantic aspects" (Geluykens, 1994) and "pragmatic aspects" (Slobin, 1975). In the semantic aspects, revision is mainly derived from Replacement.[1] Revision usually follows two principles: the Clarity Principle and the Expressivity Principle (Slobin, 1975)[2] in the pragmatic aspects. The former refers to the purposes of clarification, confirmation, and explanation, which pleads the intelligibility and clarity of a message. The latter concerns the expressive and aesthetic aspects of the message and includes the purposes of emphasis, agreement, and disagreement.

In this section, we focus primarily on ten discourse features where the AD patients differed significantly from the control group. They are word-finding difficulty, indefinite words, repetitions, revision (in the semantic aspect)-replacement, revision (in the pragmatic aspect)-emphasis, revision (in the pragmatic aspect)-clarification, revision (in the pragmatic aspect)-explanation, no local coherence, no global coherence and empty phrases. Specific examples of each type are presented below.

1. Word-finding difficulty

One of the most common language impairments in Chinese AD discourse is word-finding difficulty. AD participants failed to specify the names of objects or places. It is sometimes referred to as the phenomenon of anomia and is frequently reported in the research on AD discourse (Condret-Santi et al., 2013; Lai et al., 2009). Examples below demonstrate that AD persons encounter a serious problem finding appropriate words in their discourse.

(1) 大人在   洗   洗   洗   碗   啦!   洗   那個 . . .
    adult at wash   wash   wash   bowl   PRT!   Wash   that . . .
    "The adult is washing the dishes! Washing that . . . ."

(2) 這個 . . .   這個、這個是 . . . 一   個什麼?   ㄟ,   一   個什麼,XXXX
    this . . .   this . . . this COP . . . a   what?   SP,   a   what, XXXX
    "This . . . this . . . this is . . . is a what? Argh, a what? XXXX"

(3) 這 . . . 倉 . . . 這個 . . .   是 . . . 倉庫
    this CANG this . . .   COP warehouse
    "This . . . ware . . . this . . . is . . . warehouse".

2. Indefinite words

Indefinite words refer to such non-specific words as "thing" or "stuff" in English, or "dong-xi" in Chinese. Word-finding difficulties in AD discourse are also reflected in the speaker's use of indefinite words. AD participants tended to use such indefinite words as "thing" or "stuff" to replace the specific terms, manifesting word-finding difficulties in their discourse. As demonstrated in several studies (see Dijkstra et al., 2004; Ripich and Terrell, 1988), inappropriate use of such empty words as "thing" or "do" is commonly found in AD discourse. Examples of indefinite words in Chinese AD discourse are shown below.

(4) 這個是   那個 . . . 放   東西的   櫃子   嘛!
    this COP   that . . . put   stuff DE   wardrobe   PRT
    "This is the . . . wardrobe where we put things!"

(5) 她好像   要   去   去   拿   凳子   站起來   要拿   東西
    3s like   want   go   go   take   chair   stand up   want take   stuff
    "She seems to go to get the chair and climb up to fetch something".

(6) 小、小孩,   他 . . . 在拿   東西的意思   拿   東西 . . .
    little, little child,   3s . . . at take   stuff DE meaning   take   stuff . . .
    "The child . . . He is taking something. Taking something . . ."

3. Repetitions

Repetitions are commonly found when AD participants fail to find specific words appropriate for the context. Repeating words or phrases, for example, *shen-me shen-me* 'what . . . what . . .' and *zhe-ge zhe-ge zhe-ge* 'this . . . this . . . this', is highly related to the process of word-finding difficulties.

(7) 他 . . . 手上   拿   著   拿   著   什麼   什麼   東西
    he . . . hand up   take   DUR   take   DUR   what   what   stuff
    做什麼   我不   知道
    do what   I NEG   know
    "He . . . his hand is holding some, something. I don't know what he is doing".

(8) 這個   櫃櫃子   好像是   我們   開出來   放東西
    this   ward-wardrobe   like COP   we   open   put stuff
    "This wardrobe, wardrobe is like something we open and put something in".

(9) 這個　　這個　　這個　　他爬在　　上面　　　阿
　　 this　　 this　　 this　　 he crawl　at upside　PRT
　　 "This, this, this ... he is crawling on it".

4. Revision in the semantic aspect-replacement

AD participants sometimes make revisions when monitoring their utterances, detecting problems and correcting ideas or rephrasing words (Lai, 2014). In the semantic aspects, revision is mainly a result of replacement. For instance, *shi xiao* '小孩' and *xiao peng you* '小朋友' both refer to children.

(10) 這個　　　是小孩　　　這個是　　小朋友!
　　　this　　　COP child　　this COP　kid
　　　"This is a child; this is a kid".

(11) 這　　是　　什麼　　東西　　這是　　　碟...　　盤...　　碟子啊!
　　　this　COP　what　　stuff　　this COP　plate...　dish...　plate PRT
　　　"What is this? This is a plate ... dish ... plate!"

5. Revision in the pragmatic aspect-emphasis

As for the pragmatic aspects, revision includes three purposes: emphasis, clarification and explanation. The first one deals with the expressive aspects of message, which follows the Expressivity Principle (to be expressive). The other two concern the clarity and intelligibility of the message, which deals with the Clarity Principle (to be clear) (Slobin, 1975). In the AD discourse, more attention is given to the emphatic aspects of the message, *wan la wan la* 'bowl', as illustrated below.

(12) 這　　這　　都　　是　　廚房　　的　　碗　　啦!　　碗　　啦!
　　　this　this　all　COP　kitchen　DE　bowl　PRT!　bowl　PRT!
　　　"These, these are bowls in the kitchen! Bowls!"

(13) 櫥櫃　　　啊!　　櫥櫃　　　啊!
　　　wardrobe　PRT!　wardrobe　PRT!
　　　"Wardrobe! Wardrobe!"

6. Revision in the pragmatic aspect-clarification

Clarification is the second purpose of making revisions in the pragmatic aspect. AD participants sometimes revise to clarify the message; for instance, *xiao hai* 'child' is revised as *xiao nü hai* 'little girl' to clarify the gender of the child.

(14) 這個　　小孩　　這個　　是　　　小女孩
　　　this　　child　　this　　COP　little girl
　　　"This is a child. This is a little girl".

(15) 這個　　好像是　　　灶子　　大概　　　灶　　　東西　　吧
　　　this　　seem COP　stove　　probably　stove　　stuff　　PRT
　　　煮　　　菜　　　　的　　東西　　地方　　吧
　　　cook　vegetable　DE　stuff　　place　　PRT
　　　"This is somewhere like kitchen, the place where we cook".

303

7. Revision in the pragmatic aspect-explanation

Explanation is the third purpose of making revisions in the pragmatic aspect. In the AD discourse, they sometimes explain their earlier utterances to improve the clarity of the messages. As presented below, the utterance *xi chu fang yong di* 'place in the kitchen for washing' is revised as *chu fang yong de tai zi* 'the counter in the kitchen' to make the message much more intelligible.

(16) 一個   大人   兩個   小孩   啊   一個   男生   一個   女生
     one   adult   two   children PRT one   boy   one   girl
     小   嘿   小朋友   就是   了啦
     little PRT   kid   that is PRT PRT
     "An adult, two children, a boy and a girl, little ... they are little kids".

(17) 這像...   好像是   一個洗   廚房   用地...
     this like... like COP CL wash   kitchen place...
     廚房用   的   檯子   啊！
     kitchen DE   counter   PRT!
     "This.... seems like a ... place in the kitchen for washing ... the counter in the kitchen".

8. No local coherence

No local coherence occurs when the meanings or themes of two consecutive sentences are not coherently related. The following examples clearly illustrate that the AD discourse is impaired, due to being not coherently associated.

(18) (Q: 你看這個是蚊帳還是房間裡面的窗子?):
     (when asked: you see this COP mosquito net or room in DE window?):
     房間的......這是   圓圈......這個   也是   圓圈
     room DE...this   COP circle...this also   COP circle
     "(When asked: what do 2s reckon? Is this a mosquito net or a window in the room?): The room ... this is circle ... this is also circle".

(19) 一個   小孩...   個   大人！   這個   跟   年輕   的！
     one   child...   CL   adult!   this   and   young   DE!
     "A child ... adult! This one and a younger one!"

9. No global coherence

No global coherence is identified when an utterance is irrelevant to the topic. This is also referred to as disruptive topic shifts (Ulatowska and Chapman, 1991) by which tangents or digressions from the topic are produced. For example, when asking what the adult is doing, one AD participant answered, *ta na ge hao xiang shi pan zi shen me dong xi* "That looks like a plate or something". This finding echoes the previous finding that Chinese-speaking AD persons utter a higher mean of external comments than healthy controls (Lai et al., 2009). These implausible details, although syntactically correct, are inappropriate statements when considering the topic. This discourse feature has often been identified in the narrative discourse of demented persons.

(20) (Q: 啊 它 出去 這 像 什麼?):
     (when asked: PRT it outside this like what?):

外面	應該	是...	有	窗戶	啊!
outside	probably	COP...	have	window	PRT!

"(When asked: What does this look like outside?):
It seems like... there is a window outside!"

(21) (Q: 那 大人在做 什麼事?):
(when asked: then adult at do what thing?):

他那個	好像是	盤子什麼	東西
3s that	like COP	plate what	stuff.

"(When asked: What is the adult doing then?): That seems like a plate or something".

10. Empty phrases

Empty phrases are any utterances that have little or no content. In our earlier report (Lai et al., 2009), Chinese-speaking AD persons made more syntactic errors than did the healthy controls in unintelligible sentences. Examples of empty phrases are presented below.

(22)
房子	像是...	房子	也	有...	人家xxxxxxxx	這個...	這個	房子
house	like COP	house	also	have	people xxxxxxxx	this...	this	house

"The house seems like... the house also... he xxxxxxxx this... this house".

(23)
這邊的	就是	那個話	xxxxxx	就	溢	出來了!
here DE	that is	that word	xxxxxx	then	flow	out PRT

"This one is that... xxxxxx it flows out!"

(24)
看	有	像	廚房	也是	比較	有	xxxxxx
look	have	like	kitchen	also COP	more	have	xxxxxx

"Look! It seems like a kitchen, and has more xxxxxx".

Discussion

In the above section, ten discourse features significantly differing from healthy discourse are exemplified and discussed. First of all, word-finding difficulties, indefinite words, and revisions frequently occur in Chinese AD discourse. Chinese indefinite terms (e.g., *dong-xi* 'thing') or deixis without specific referents (e.g., *zhe-ge* ... 'this ...' or *na-ge* ... 'that ...') are examples of word-finding difficulties. Discourse of AD persons often contains inappropriate use of empty words such as "thing" or "do", as has been demonstrated in several studies, for example, Dijkstra et al. (2004) and Ripich and Terrell (1988).

Additionally, this chapter is in line with the finding that AD persons produce more disruptive topic switches and unintelligible sentences, being tangents or deviations from the topic (Ulatowska and Chapman, 1991). It is found that AD persons generate less global coherence by either producing more circumlocutionary comments or more empty phrases. They seem to digress from the task at hand, and their speech appears to be less informative and succinct. This tendency may show a coping mechanism applied by these AD persons to overcome the problems in the communication task or in the testing circumstance. Less coherent discourse produced by AD persons is also confirmed in the analysis of discourse markers (Lai and Lin, 2012). Compared with the controls, the AD persons were relatively impaired in relating two propositions and less frequent in adopting non-conceptual markers to specify cohesive relations between two messages. Non-conceptual markers, including contrastive (e.g., *dan(shi)* 'but', *keshi* 'but', *buguo* 'but', *suiran* 'though'), elaborative (e.g., *haiyou* 'and', *na* 'and then', *lingwai* 'in addition') and inferential markers (e.g., *suoyi* 'so', *yinwei* 'because'), refer to 'lexical items which indicate the speaker's personal conception of the relations holding between propositions' (Feng, 2008: 1707). In brief, the ability to use these markers as conjoining discourse elements decreases more significantly in the AD persons than in the controls.

This chapter makes substantial contribution to the existing theory related to the associations between revision and cognitive capacity. Revision can be reviewed as a kind of repair (Paltridge, 2006), which requires a higher-level processing task. In order to make a revision, individuals have to first get acquainted with the possible errors and come up with alternatives for revision. Persons with AD are frequently found to make fewer revisions than healthy controls owing to the brain damage, which makes them fail to successfully repair their utterances. Compared with healthy older adults, the AD persons' ability to revise was relatively diminished, and this finding agrees with previous studies (Bryan and Maxim, 2006; McNamara et al., 1992). Additionally, in line with the claim of the capacity theory in working memory (Baddeley, 1996), AD persons often suffer from more cognitively demanding processes (as in the process of making revision). From a cognitive perspective, AD disruptions in topic management or in repair have been mainly interpreted as the impaired working-memory models, especially in processing more cognitively demanding tasks.

Furthermore, this chapter is contributive to the specific repair patterns made by Chinese-speaking AD persons. In the further analysis of repair patterns in semantic and pragmatic aspects, Chinese-speaking AD persons semantically refer to replacement as a labor-saving and effectual way to solve problems of semantic vagueness or ambiguity. From the pragmatic point of view, AD persons apply both the Principle of Expressivity (i.e., emphasis) and the Principle of Clarity (i.e., clarification, explanation) but with different degrees compared with the healthy controls. As discussed in Lai (2014), healthy Chinese-speaking participants used revision mainly to maintain meaning clarity. Unlike the control group, the Principle of Expressivity (i.e., Emphasis) is preferred in the AD group. For the AD participants, the first priority of pragmatic function is to emphasize.

Conclusion

This chapter introduces the characteristics of Chinese AD speakers in terms of their discourse-level performance regarding two features: discourse-building and discourse-impairing features. The former makes a contribution to the continuation of conversations, while the latter impedes the communicative purpose of conversations. Specific examples of Chinese-speaking AD impaired discourse, discourse-impairing features in particular, are demonstrated, and the major findings are summarized.

Finally, the current chapter has the potential to enhance the understanding of Chinese AD impaired discourse and to offer helpful directions for the clinical treatment of dementia in the future. The conversational partners should notice the difficulties that AD persons suffer. To facilitate the communication with AD persons, attention given to their impaired discourse features and appropriate assistance offered in communicating with them should be of great help.

Acknowledgments

The researchers would like to thank three national institutions, Ministry of Education (MOE), Ministry of Science and Technology (MOST) and Kaohsiung Veterans General Hospital

(KVGH), for offering research grants to support the experiments. Also, many heart-felt thanks are given to the participants of the experiments and to the support of their families. The data collection would not have been completed without their enthusiastic participation and cooperation.

Notes

1 According to Fromkin et al. (2010), semantic aspects mainly include: Replacement (when there is a shift in meaning), Broadening (when the meaning becomes more encompassing), and Narrowing (when the meaning becomes less encompassing). Two of them, Broadening and Narrowing, are rarely found in AD discourse, and are thus excluded from this chapter.
2 Slobin (1975) proposed four principles to demonstrate how people use language: the Expressivity Principle (to be expressive), the Clarity Principle (to be clear), the Economy Principle (to be quick and easy), and the Processibility Principle (to be humanly processible in ongoing time). In the current chapter, only the Clarity Principle and Expressivity Principle are discussed in detail because these two are the main principles in studying conversations (Wei, 2003).

References

Abeysinghe, S.C., Bayles, K.A. and Trosset, M.W. (1990) 'Semantic Memory Deterioration in Alzheimer's Subjects: Evidence From Word Association, Definition, and Associate Ranking Tasks', *Journal of Speech and Hearing Research* 33: 574–582.
Baddeley, A.D. (1996) 'Exploring the Central Executive', *The Quarterly Journal of Experimental Psychology* 49: 5–28.
Bayles, K.A. and Tomoeda, C.K. (1991) 'Caregiver Report of Prevalence and Appearance Order of Linguistic Symptoms in Alzheimer's Patients', *The Gerontologist* 31: 210–216.
Brandt, J. and Rich, J.B. (1995) 'Memory disorders in the dementias', in *Handbook of Memory Disorders*. A.D. Baddeley and B.A. Wilson (eds.) New York: John Wiley. pp. 243–270.
Bryan, K. and Maxim, J. (2006) *Communication Disability in the Dementias*. London: Whurr.
Cherney, L.S. (1998) 'Pragmatics and discourse: An introduction', in *Analyzing Discourse in Communicatively Impaired Adults*. L.R. Cherney, B.B. Shadden and C.A. Coelho (eds.) Gaithersburg, MA: Aspen Publishers. pp. 1–8.
Chomsky, N. (1972) *Studies on Semantics in Generative Grammar*. The Hague, the Netherlands: Mouton & Company.
Condret-Santi, V., Barbeau E.J., Matharan, F., Le Goff M., Dartigues J.-F. and Amieva H. (2013) 'Prevalence of Word Retrieval Complaint and Prediction of Dementia in a Population-based Study of Elderly Subjects', *Dementia and Geriatric Cognitive Disorders* 35: 313–321.
Dijkstra, K., Bourgeois, M., Burgio, L. and Allen, R. (2002a) 'Effects of a Communication Intervention on the Discourse of Nursing Home Residents with Dementia and their Nursing Assistants', *Journal of Medical Speech-Language Pathology* 10: 143–157.
Dijkstra, K., Bourgeois, M., Petrie, G., Burgio, L. and Allen-Burge, R. (2002b) 'My Recaller Is on Vacation: Discourse Analysis of Nursing Home Residents with Dementia', *Discourse Processes* 33: 53–74.
Dijkstra, K., Bourgeois, M., Allen, R. and Burgio, L. (2004) 'Conversational Coherence: Discourse Analysis of Older Adults With and Without Dementia', *Journal of Neurolinguistics* 17: 263–283.
Feng, G.W. (2008) 'Pragmatic Markers in Chinese', *Journal of Pragmatics* 40: 1687–1718.
Fromkin, V., Rodman, R. and Hyams, N. (2010) *An Introduction to Language*. USA: Thomson/Heinle.
Garcia, L.J. and Joanette, Y. (1997) 'Analysis of Conversational Topic Shifts: A Multiple Case Study', *Brain and Language* 58: 92–114.
Geluykens, R. (1994) *The Pragmatic of Discourse Anaphora in English: Evidence from Conversational Repair*. Berlin: Mouton de Gruyter.
Green, K. (2011) *The Use of Pragmatic Markers in Native and Non-native Chinese Oral Narrative*, Unpublished master's thesis. Fu Jen Catholic University, Taiwan.
Grodzinsky, Y. (1990) *Theoretical Perspectives on Language Deficits*. Cambridge, MA: MIT Press.
Huppert, F.A., Brayne, C. and O'Connor, D.W. (1994) *Dementia and Normal Aging*. Cambridge: Cambridge University Press.
Jackendoff, R.S. (1972) *Semantic Interpretation in Generative Grammar*. Cambridge, MA: MIT Press.

Jhang, A.-D. (2011) *The Study of Naming Abilities in Patients with Alzheimer's Disease*, Unpublished master's thesis. National Taipei University of Nursing and Health Sciences, Taiwan.

Kempler, D. (1991) 'Language changes in dementia of the Alzheimer type', in *Dementia and Communication*. R. Lubinski, J.B. Orange, D. Henderson and N. Stecker (eds.). Philadelphia, Hamilton: B.C. Decker Inc. pp. 98–114.

Kempler, D. and Goral, M. (2008) 'Language and Dementia: Neuropsychological Aspects', *Annual Review of Applied Linguistics* 28: 73–90.

Lai, Y.H. (2013) *Language Processing in Chinese-speaking Seniors with Alzheimer's Disease*. Taipei: The Crane Publishing.

Lai, Y.H. (2014) 'Discourse Features of Chinese-Speaking Seniors With and Without Alzheimer's Disease', *Language & Linguistics* 15(3): 411–434.

Lai, Y.H. (2017a) *Alzheimer's Disease: A Study of Temporal Parameters*. Taipei: The Crane Publishing.

Lai, Y.H. (2017b) Language Processing of Seniors with Alzheimer's Disease: From the Perspective of Temporal Parameters. Paper Presented at *ICLPNM 2017: 19th International Conference on Language Processing and Neural Mechanisms*, July 4–5, Singapore, SG.

Lai, Y.H. (2017c) Psychological Processing in Mandarin Chinese: Dementia Effects, Category Effects and Task Effects. Paper Presented at *The 3rd International Conference on Education, Psychology and Society*, July 25–27, Okinawa, Japan.

Laine, M., Laakso, M., Vuorinen, E. and Rinne, J. (1998) 'Coherence and Informativeness of Discourse in Two Dementia Types', *Journal of Neurolinguistics* 11: 79–87.

Lai, Y.H. and Lin, Y.T. (2012) 'Discourse Markers Produced by Chinese-speaking Seniors with and without Alzheimer's Disease', *Journal of Pragmatics* 44: 1982–2003.

Lai, Y.H. and Lin, Y.T. (2013) 'Factors in Action-object Semantic Disorder for Chinese-speaking Persons with or without Alzheimer's Disease', *Journal of Neurolinguistics* 26(2): 298–311.

Lai, Y.H., Pai, H.H. and Lin, Y.T. (2009) 'To be Semantically-Impaired or to be Syntactically-Impaired: Linguistic Patterns in Chinese-speaking Persons with or without Dementia', *Journal of Neurolinguistics* 22(5): 465–475.

Levelt. W.J.M. (1983) 'Monitor and Self-Repair in Speech', *Cognition* 14: 41–104.

Liles, B.Z. and Coelho, C.A. (1998) 'Cohesion analysis', in *Analyzing Discourse in Communicatively Impaired Adults*. L.R. Cherney, B.B. Shadden and C.A. Coelho (eds.). Gaithersburg, MA: Aspen. pp. 65–84.

Liu, H.-Y. (2005) A Comparative Study of Ability and Disability of Situated Discourse by Chinese Alzheimer Seniors and Normal Aging People, Unpublished doctoral dissertation. Beijing Foreign Studies University, China.

Liu, H.-Y. (2010) *Exploring Chinese Alzheimer Patients' Situated Discourse Abilities and Disabilities: A Contrastive and Corpus-based Approach*. 2010 The Third International Conference on Multicultural Discourses (August 27–29). China: Hangzhou.

Lyons, K., Kemper, S., LaBarge, E., Ferraro, F.R., Balota, D. and Storandt, M. (1994) 'Oral Language and Alzheimer's Disease: A Reduction in Syntactic Complexity', *Aging and Cognition* 1: 271–281.

Martin, I. and McDonald, S. (2003) 'Weak Coherence, No Theory of Mind, or Executive Dysfunction? Solving the Puzzle of Pragmatic Language Disorders', *Brain and Language* 85: 451–466.

McKhann, G., Drachman, D., Folstein, M., Katzman, R., Price, D. and Stadlan, E.M. (1984) 'Clinical Diagnosis of Alzheimer's Disease: Report of the NINCDS-ADRDA Work Group under the Auspices of the Department of Health and Human Services Task Force on Alzheimer's Disease', *Neurology* 34: 939–944.

McNamara, P., Obler, L.K. and Au, R. (1992) 'Speech Monitoring Skills in Alzheimer's Disease, Parkinson's Disease and Normal Aging', *Brain and Language* 42: 38–51.

Miracle, W.C. (1991) Discourse Markers in Mandarin Chinese, Unpublished doctoral dissertation. The Ohio State University, USA.

Moscovitch, M. and Umilta, C. (1990) 'Modularity and neuropsychology: modules and central processes in attention and memory', in *Modular Deficits in Alzheimer-Type Dementia*. M.F. Schwartz (ed.). Cambridge, MA: MIT Press. pp. 1–58.

Orange, J.B. and Purves, B. (1996) 'Conversational Discourse and Cognitive Impairment: Implications for Alzheimer's Disease', *Journal of Speech-Language and Audiology* 20: 139–150.

Paltridge, B. (2006) *Discourse Analysis: An Introduction*. London: Continuum.

Ripich, D.N., Carpenter, B.D. and Ziol, E. (2000) 'Conversational Cohesion Patterns in Men and Women with Alzheimer's Disease: A Longitudinal Study', *International Journal of Language and Communication Disorders* 35: 49–64.

Ripich, D.N. and Terrell, B.Y. (1988) 'Patterns of Discourse Cohesion and Coherence in Alzheimer's Disease', *Journal of Speech and Hearing Disorders* 53: 8–15.

Romero-Trillo, J. (2001) 'A Mathematical Model for the Analysis of Variation in Discourse', *Journal of Linguistics* 37: 527–550.

Sebastian, M.V., Menor, J. and Elosua, R. (2001) 'Patterns of Errors in Short-term Forgetting in AD and Ageing', *Memory* 9: 223–231.

Shadden, B.B. (1998) 'Sentential/Surface-level analysis', in *Analyzing Discourse in Communicatively Impaired Adults*. L.R. Cherney, B.B. Shadden and C.A. Coelho (eds.). Gaithersburg, MA: Aspen. pp. 35–64.

Slobin, D.I. (1975) 'The more it changes ... on understanding language by watching it move through time', in *Papers and Reports on Child Language Development*. Berkley: University of California. pp. 1–30.

Ulatowska, H.K. and Chapman, S.B. (1991) 'Discourse studies', in *Dementia and Communication*. R. Lubinski, J.B. Orange, D. Henderson and N. Stecker (eds.). Philadelphia, Hamilton: B.C. Decker Inc. pp. 115–132.

Wang, H.-Y. (2010) *The Abilities of Retrieving Nouns and Verbs in Chinese Speaking Parkinson's and Alzheimer's Diseases*, Unpublished master's thesis. National Tsing Hua University, Taiwan.

Wang, Y.F., Tsai, P.H. and Ling, M.Y. (2007) 'From Informational to Emotive Use: Meiyou ('no') as a Discourse Marker in Taiwan Mandarin Conversation', *Discourse Studies* 9: 645–669.

Wei, S.-T. (2003) *Socio-pragmatic Analysis of Repair in Mandarin Conversation*, Unpublished master's thesis. National Cheng-chi University, Taiwan.

20
Discourse, gender and psychologization in contemporary China

Jie Yang

Introduction

This chapter analyzes the evolving discourse surrounding and contributing to the establishment of a new female-centric profession in China, *peiliao* "陪聊 chatting companion". I argue that this profession, in which women provide warmth, comfort and care for suffering people in their homes, distills several key features of Chinese discourse. While practical in that *peiliao* reemploys women workers laid off from state-owned enterprises as a result of privatization and downsizing (see Yang, 2007, 2013), on a deeper level, the profession reinforces a gendered discourse about the appropriate (female) agents of care amidst mounting distress. It also provides a related discourse emphasizing productivity and social harmony in China. This gendered discourse of care and productivity reflects the new relationship between language and gender in China amidst the country's economic restructuring.

In this chapter, I adopt a Foucauldian approach to discourse analysis, engaging both signs and practices as expressions of power dynamics. In addition to the meaning of a given discourse, this approach – for example, critical discourse analysis (hereafter CDA) – emphasizes language's contribution to power inequalities. CDA is derived from Foucault's genealogical work, where power is linked to the formation of discourse within specific historical periods (Given, 2008). For CDA analysts, discourse is socially constitutive as well as socially conditioned. CDA focuses on how the social world, as expressed through language, is affected by various sources of power (Fairclough, 1992). This form of analysis engages flexible techniques and theories to produce insights into the role of discourse in reproducing (or resisting) social and political inequality, abuses of power or domination. The analysis is not limited to specific structures of text or talk, but rather, systematically relates these to structures of the socio-political context, studying both opaque and transparent structural relationships of dominance, discrimination, power and control as manifested in language.

As for gender, I adopt a poststructural approach. Instead of seeing gender as a binary or opposition and analyzing gendered difference in language use, I examine how incorporating a gender dimension in research makes difference in revealing new power dynamics and inequality (see McElhinny, 2007). In this sense, gender is considered as a basic principle structuring practices, institutions and society. I engage gender as a mode of analysis that may reveal (new) modes of exploitation and injustice, as well as new forms of contestation. My overall project has been to undertake a contextualized analysis of the relationship between discourse and gender in China's psychoboom. In this work, I attend to the ways in which women (especially underprivileged women) are mobilized to contribute to the governmental promotion of happiness and wellbeing. Such state promotion has multiple goals, chief among them to relieve the consequences of economic restructuring and privatization since the 1990s. I highlight how the new psycho-politics essentialize gendered differences, reinforce women's attachment to the domestic sphere and intensify exploitation of women's emotional labor.

In what follows, I zero in on an example of psycho-politics that reveals new developments in the relationship between discourse and gender through analysis of the work of *peiliao*. In studying the language and work life of a group of women taking part in *peiliao* or *peitan* – chatting companions who do companionable counseling – I focus on their training by government-sponsored counselors and subsequent application of this training in their work. I attempt to conceptualize the role of gender in China's psychoboom. In this case, underprivileged women are asked to play the role of the vanguard in promoting and performing psychotherapy. I also attempt to complement a discursive approach with an analysis of affective or bodily modes of communication. With this dual approach, I seek to tease out a Chinese notion of psycho-politics that diverges from biopower by emphasizing how the body, and, in particular, the heart – the basis of cognition, virtue and sensation – can become a site of control and value extraction.

Gender and psychologization in post-Mao China

During Mao's era, under "state feminism", women's liberation and equality was to be achieved through their mobilization into the workforce and eradication of Confucian ideas about women's work. The discourse centered on women's duty to contribute to and conform with socialist ideals. This process also entailed women conforming to masculine norms and standards (see Rofel, 1999; Yang, 1999). Biological differences between men and women were downplayed, and women were called upon to do "whatever men can do", thus maximizing their labor for socialist ends (Yang 2007). Since China's reforms began in 1979, the discourse, and along with it, gender ideology, has been significantly transformed: far from ignored, innate, biological sex differences are now emphasized in media and government programs. The state now promotes a naturalized, even essentialized, view of gender in which hyperfemininity and domestic femininity are being popularized. Women are not only encouraged to reproduce the labor force, but also to undertake underpaid (or unpaid) domestic and service-sector work. The more women who do so, the lower the overall cost of operating a capitalist economy and the greater its profit margins. One of the most obvious effects of this shift has been women's retreat from the public sector to the domestic sphere, which has widened the income gap between husbands and wives, lowering women's status, and diminishing their control over their own lives, marriages and reproductive events.

Essentializing discourse and gendered ideology are further advanced through the psychologization process, an important aspect of China's psychoboom. In China since the 1980s, resonating with the country's reform-era depoliticization of social life and growing emphasis on the self (Kipnis, 2012; Kleinman et al., 2011), there has emerged a "psychoboom" – a notable increase in the use of psychology, psychometrics and psychotherapy in social life (Kleinman, 2010; Huang, 2014). This psychoboom has also heralded a process of psychologization; that is, addressing social experience in personal and psychological terms or through psychological modes of thinking, and deploying psychologically inflected discourse to resolve social ills.

Psychologization is a devolved, mass movement, which however can be co-opted by government initiatives and propaganda (see Yang, 2015, 2018) to conceal structural roots of distress.

One major component of this psychoboom and psychologization is a vast collection of psychological self-help literature, which many people now turn to as a remedy for distress and which is gender-specific. This literature and associated media, including books, websites, and counseling services, tend to essentialize gender and attribute certain psychological traits to each of the sexes.

For example, Chinese counselors see a sense of security as vital to women's physical and mental health, and yet acknowledge a lack of security as epidemic among women in the country (Li, 2016). Accordingly, women suffer from stress, anxiety, and depression, which can affect other aspects of their health and their identities as well. The well-known Chinese counselor Li Zixun (2016) promotes essentializing views of men's and women's emotional lives. Men, he argues, are keen to use reason, power and violence to control and even break apart the world, while women use their water-like emotions to repair the world. Li contends that women accommodate the maintenance of male interest and affection. If men represent the "natural" power of human beings via aggression, dominance and expansion, then women represent humanity's inner nature, via management, governance and tolerance.

This discourse follows a typical media pattern opposing women to men in China, with men as the foil and standard, and women developing psychological traits to serve men's interests, as well as, by extension, those of the family and state. The implied pedagogy for women is "how to become a woman whom a man cannot live without", and "a woman who makes her husband flourish". In this pedagogy, women also learn how to become "wise mothers" and "virtuous wives" and make a whole family happy, healthy and successful, implicitly contributing to a harmonious society. The current discourse reinforces the value of sacrifice, docility and submissiveness for women at the very moment that China has relaxed its one-child family policy since 2015, and many women are debating whether to interrupt their work lives to have a second child. The discourse of the "feminine, happy, and well-adjusted mother", is thus available and a tempting substitute for the old, Maoist promotion of masculinized women and socialist laborers. The choice for women is not easy.

Within the psychoboom, awareness has also grown of a widespread mental health "crisis", with millions of Chinese people suffering from depression and anxiety (see Yang, 2018).[1] The new profession of *peiliao* thus redresses a chronic shortage of professional counselors in China. Unlike other psychological caregivers who empathize or sympathize through imagining the situation of another who suffers, laid-off women turned *peiliao* are encouraged by their trainers to appropriate their direct experience of unemployment in their current care work.

Peiliao: affect and "companionable counseling"

The profession of *peiliao* resembles "*baomu* 保姆, housemaid", but its preliminary training in positive psychology is supposed to enable practitioners to conduct basic counseling. Informally, *peiliao* has been practiced since the mid-1990s, when laid-off women and rural migrants began retraining as domestic workers at state-led re-employment programs or paid-by-the-hour job centers (Wang, 2003; Yang, 2007). Indeed, being trained as a *peiliao* or possessing basic psychological knowledge has been increasingly looked upon by job centers as the minimal qualification for almost all of the new women's "professions".[2] However, *peiliao* was slow to gain recognition as a "profession", due, in part, to the assumed link between women's companionship and sex: many professional counselors consider *peiliao* to rest on shaky moral ground. They suspect that *sanpei* (sex workers at night clubs) are also *peiliao*, and that the reverse might also occur. In Shanghai, due to the fear of *peiliao* becoming sex work, the profession only got official approval in early 2010 and requires more significant formal training. To obtain a license requires 400 hours of academic studies or training in social psychology, education psychology, crisis intervention skills, and psychological care techniques. Elsewhere, including Beijing and Shandong province, where I have conducted research, *peiliao* training is much less rigorous, and the profession has yet to be officially approved.

Despite the mental health crisis mentioned above, public support in China for increased mental health care is not sufficient. China has only 2.4 formally trained counselors per 1 million people – in contrast with the United States, which has 3,000 counselors per 1 million people (Han and Zhang, 2007). One solution in China has been to create more informal counselors, including *peiliao*, who after being trained in techniques of basic nursing, domestic work and counseling or positive psychology, go to care for the young, the old, the sick, the dying, or the depressed wherever those individuals live.

Based on research conducted in two working-class communities in Changping, Beijing and Zhangqiu, Shandong Province, I argue that the rise of *peiliao* results from and is deep-rooted in the discourse of psychologization. This discourse tends to erase the structural forces that have produced mass unemployment, especially among women, as well as the resulting widespread distress, while emphasizing the psychological and moral traits of individuals. The government seizes upon this discourse to nurture the potential and growth of the individual for value extraction. This trend has opened up a new arena of politics in China and a subtle, though hegemonic form of control. When retraining women as *peiliao*, arms of the state responsible for the re-employment programs in effect exploit women's emotional and psychological labors for their own ends – to alleviate the consequences of economic restructuring and advance market development. The women's training as *peiliao* not only re-inscribes these women's pain (arising from their own unemployment history), but also naturalizes their psychological labor as part of their moral virtue as women. This both downplays their work's social and economic value, and requires them to conduct a uniquely embodied, affective form of labor in service of transmitting happiness to clients. As a new category of work without legal regulation, institutional protection, or even consistent descriptions of the work entailed, those who practice *peiliao* are open to discrimination and exploitation in such a deregulated job market.

Laid-off women are trained by job counselors or psychosocial workers as *peiliao*s. They were often asked to use embodied and holistic approaches to deal with their clients' problems – that is, to apply what they have learned to their new companion domestic work. One theme is how they use affect/emotion including both cognition and bodily sensation (see below) – embodied knowledge of pain and suffering from their own unemployment experiences – to "counsel" their clients and transmit happiness and positive psychology.

Discourse and affect

The notion of affect plays a key role in the counseling, training and reorientation women receive to become *peiliao*, and in the actual "counseling" they offer their clients. This is part of a larger story in which affect has been linked to gendered political discourse in China. Today, there is greater emphasis on the utility of affect in communication in China in both institutional and everyday interactions. Chinese researchers report that, in general, what matters most in communication is to properly express one's emotions: 70 percent of successful communication between people relies on appropriate emotional management, and just 30 percent of communication lies in the content (see also Feng, 1996; Lee, 2011; see Wallis, 2018 on how affect creates potential for agency among female Chinese domestic workers). Thus, not only talk or discourse, but also affect and feeling have been linked with communicative efficiency.

In the literature there have been diverse and multiple genealogies and definitions of affect (see McElhinny, 2010; Gregg and Selgworth, 2010). For example, Brian Massumi (2002) distinguishes affect and emotion clearly, defining the former as bodily sensation that can be felt but cannot be captured by language, while the latter as something that can be captured by narration. However, feminist scholars often use emotion and affect interchangeably (see Gorton, 2007 for a review of works on this use). Echoing this feminist definition, my approach to affect resembles Sianne Ngai's work, in which the differences between affect and emotion are a matter of degree:

> [A]ffects are less formed and structured than emotions, but not lacking form or structure altogether; less "sociolinguistically fixed," but by no means code-free or meaningless; less "organized in response to our interpretations of situations," but by no means entirely devoid of organization or diagnostic powers.
>
> *(Ngai, 2005: 27)*

Following many feminist scholars who see affect as both cognition and bodily sensation (Ahmed, 2004), I see affect as a felt quality that gives meanings and imaginative potential to social, political and economic transformations. It is the force or energy that circulates and mediates within, between, and around bodies and worlds, organizing or structuring social, economic and political activities. It is bodily, but cannot be entirely contained or embodied. It has its own autonomy but can be partially captured by language. The turn to affect in communication is manifest in the recent focus in China on the discourse of EQ (Emotional Quotient; in Chinese *qingshang*) and HQ (Happiness Quotient; in Chinese *fushang* or *leshang*). In 2013, President Xi Jinping, during his visit to the Psychology Center at Beijing Normal University, went so far as to state explicitly that EQ is more important nowadays (in terms of team work or nurturing docility) than IQ for the market economy, and that psychology is crucial to help people improve their EQ.

Indeed, in China, amidst economic restructuring and privatization, the tertiary service industry has been prioritized in order to advance a market economy. In this industry, communication and talk are key to success – and to truly communicate means appropriately expressing one's emotions (*ganqing*) or sentiment. Positive emotions, such as pleasantness and happiness, are highly valued. Beyond just high EQ or HQ, one must cultivate the ability of *rangren shufu*, "让人舒服 (making people feel comfortable)" in communications. This encompasses both feeling and talk and is implicitly gendered. Below, I track the evolution of the approach to training *peiliao* as it keeps apace with this discourse of care through positive communication.

Ruan shili "soft strength": from EQ/HQ to heart-based holistic labor

In addition to nursing and domestic management, training of laid-off women for *peiliao* focuses on improving their psychological quality (*xinli suzhi*, 心理素质) or heart-attitude (*xintai* 心态), which is thought to help them recover from their own traumatic experience with unemployment (see Yang, 2015 on unemployment as trauma), while helping them help others who suffer, in their new capacity as housemaids. This training is mainly based on Western psychotherapy, complemented with elements of Chinese cultural tradition (i.e., doctrines of Confucianism or Buddhism). In 2009, I observed *peiliao* training that centered on recasting certain moral traits (such as *laoshi* "老实 honest or down-to-earth") that were once nurtured in the socialist work-unit system as psychological traits. These traits were promoted as a tool for the women's new companionable counseling. To some trainees, however, this essentialized and impoverished their subjectivities (see Yang, 2015).

Later, in 2013, I observed a shift in training toward the discourse of *qingshang* EQ and *leshang/fushang* HQ, which were perceived by trainers as enhancing the women's employability. For example, at the "Sunshine Sisters Job Center" in Zhangqiu, Shandong Province a counselor lectured on *leshang* HQ (happiness quotient). He explained,

> *Leshang* not only refers to the degree of one's own optimism but also one's ability to turn the negative situation into something positive and blessing affecting others to become optimistic. *Leshang* is more powerful and effective than IQ and EQ in bringing people hope and success. Even if we may not succeed at work or in life, *leshang* can guarantee us to be happy and enjoy life.

> 乐商不仅指一个人的乐观度，而且指一个人把逆境转为顺境成为别人的祝福。 乐商比智商和情商更能有效的给人带来希望和成功。 即便我们在工作生活中不成功， 乐商也能给我们幸福让我们享受生活。

This counselor used funny stories to illustrate the power of HQ and positive emotions, stressing that, "positive emotions like happiness not only divert people's attention from pain and suffering but also heal them. That is why when you counsel people you need to use your *leshang* to transmit happiness". For this counselor, IQ may be innate, but EQ and HQ can be trained and learned. In general EQ and HQ aim to cultivate a subject who is rational, strategic and manipulative in terms of managing their own emotional states, which in turn affects those around them. Having studied government happiness campaigns, it seemed clear that this trainer had absorbed a psychologizing discourse advanced by the state. This discourse highlighted the special role of women in creating and maintaining happiness. He believed it was his role to help shape *peiliao* in this function.

Not many of my informants found the notion of HQ useful or appropriate in their work, as they believe that the concepts of optimism and positive psychology do not suit the Chinese mentality, which they think is a kind of resilience based on enduring bitterness and suffering. One exception may be a *peiliao* surnamed Ling in Changping. She found positive emotions instrumental to her care work, but not very helpful in helping her cope with her own psychological suffering. Ling was employed as a housemaid and *peiliao* to care for a woman in her early 70s. The old woman has a daughter with epilepsy who was, at that point, childless. The woman was concerned that her son-in-law would ignore and eventually, after her death, kill her daughter during a seizure in order to gain her inheritance. Her daily ritual was to pour out her worries over her daughter's future to Ling. Ling told me how she counseled her.

> I said to her, what you're worrying about may never happen. Why not use the same energy of worrying to hope for the best. . . . Worry is not good for your health either. She would repeatedly ask me to consult lawyers how to write a will to guarantee that her son-in-law regardless of the situation must treat her daughter well. I think she is not good-natured and depressed. Her negative outlooks are poisonous and unbearable. But to make money to feed my kid, I have to endure this. Days spent with this lady were gloomy and long.

> 我说你现在担心的可能永远不会发生， 为什么不用你来担心的精力往好处想。。。担心也不利于健康。她反复叫我去咨询律师怎样立遗嘱才能保证她女婿无论如何 都必须对她女儿好。我觉得她

> 人不好也抑郁。她太负面，这种世界观有毒，让人无法忍受。但是为了赚钱养孩子，我不得不忍受。跟这个老太太在一起的日子漫长又昏暗。

Ling pathologizes her employer by invoking both the language of positive psychology and psychomedical illness categories. She sometimes found concepts of positive psychology helpful to cheer up her employer, but she had to engage traditional Chinese wisdom of life-nurturing and cultivating her heart in order to detach herself from the woman's negative influence and keep her own sanity. Like many other informants she considered the heart as the moral core. She hoped such heart cultivation could not only help her cope with stress but also nurture her peacefulness and amiable persona (*xinping qihe*), which in turn she hoped would appease her disgruntled employer. For her, the heart is both affected and affective.

Still later, in 2016, at many job centers for domestic workers and *peiliao* in both Beijing and Zhangqiu, I noted a new discourse promoting an even more holistic training that emphasized the role of the heart in conveying warmth and authenticity and to, as mentioned earlier, "make people comfortable" (*rang ren shu fu*). "Making people feel comfortable" is widely treated as a form of *ruan shili* "软实力 (soft strength or soft power)". It was not only a *peiliao*'s language, but also her whole presence that could be soothing, therapeutic and uplifting to clients. Another job counselor in Changping, Beijing explained, "How to make people comfortable requires not only your language but also your heart and your whole presence that are calm and pleasant". This notion of *ruan shili* by highlighting both linguistic and bodily practices, differs from the concept of soft power by Joseph Nye. Nye (2004) defines it as "twisting minds not twisting arms" through "reasoned persuasion". With an emphasis on "minds", Nye's notion of soft power operates mainly as a cognitive process (Nye, 2008). But the notion of *ruan shili* demands the whole-bodied, holistic labor, which sets a high ethical and moral standard for these underprivileged women and intensifies the exploitation of their labor (including both physical and emotional labor).

One job counselor in Changping discussed how to use one's presence as a holistic, therapeutic resource to make people comfortable, for example, through bodily practices. He instructed trainees on how to *cha yan guan se*, "study the color of their clients' faces to read their hearts", and suggested that *peiliao* must "look straight on" (make eye contact with clients) while offering their own experiences of psychological suffering as a gateway for the clients to express theirs. This training differs starkly from that of typical maids, who are expected to have only "peripheral vision" – more of a surreptitious glance than a steady gaze (Sun, 2009). Arguably, this added mission of connecting directly with clients puts *peiliao* at greater risk for exploitation. Quite a few informants complained that as paid-by-the-hour maids they were expected to work efficiently, cleaning, cooking and washing for clients, but without looking rushed or stressed in order to make their clients comfortable. However, this required balanced and intensified physical and emotional strength.

Discourse and the heart

In the summers of 2009 and 2013, at a series of training sessions offered by a well-known counselor surnamed Ma at a job center in Changping, Beijing, I observed how Ma approached the question of heart. In one session, Ma discussed the relationship between talk and the heart, stating, 讲话就像用心画画，心是作者，舌头是画笔，题目是各种颜料和画具。一副好画取

决于心。 "Talk is like painting a picture in one's heart. The heart is the author. The tongue is the brush. The topics are the various colors and painting materials. A good painting relies on the heart". For Ma, talk encompasses complex processes centered on the heart, involving the tongue, the creative moment of painting, and the resulting pictorial image that talk makes. The product of the talk is a picture in the heart that can be seen and read, that is, affective. When Ma said, "一副好画取决于心 (A good painting relies on the heart)," he meant that talk entails ethical and moral connotations. We can also see this statement as acknowledging how talk participates in the dynamic and sometimes contradictory currents of discourse. The heart guides the speaker through this process, thereby rendering discourse moral, physical and textual.

Indeed, Ma's illustration of the heart and talk relationship, as well as other instructions, suggest that the heart has both the freedom to act and constrains action. Spontaneous bodily reactions (including linguistic practices) are regulated by high moral reflection of the heart. The heart is the moral core necessary to achieve equanimity; a state of equilibrium in which one is not shaken by external disturbances. But this notion of the heart has ambiguous and contradictory connotations, which is also manifested in Ma's hybrid training pedagogy. Despite being one of the most fundamental components of being and subjectivity, pointing inward, the heart affects the external world too, but only through cultivating its inner moral core to achieve a high ethical and moral standard. As Ma stressed, "真心话更有感染力 (When one's talk comes from the heart, it will be affective)". This is premised on the Confucian notion of *ren* (compassion or benevolence) and the premise that human beings are innately good. However, in reality, this inward, linear, and causal relationship between talk and the heart, while deeply psychologizing talk and its speaker, seldom develops efficiently. While the heart guiding talk could accommodate external relationships and the flow of discourse, talk can deviate from, or fail to express the desire of the heart because of social and political contexts and structural relationships between interlocutors involved in the delivery of speech.

I see the heart/talk relationship as resonating with Goffman's conceptualization of speaking. Goffman (1981) takes apart the role of speaker into three functional nodes in a communication system: animator, author and principal. The animator is the sounding box, the body engaged in the performance of speaking. The author is the subject who encodes speech and sets the sentiments being expressed. The principal is not only the speaker of words, but also the subject who commits to what she says. In the training of *peiliao*, by emphasizing the significance of the heart in generating and regulating speech, Ma seemed to encourage women to combine the three modes of speaking to make their companionable counseling heart-felt, whole-bodied, empathic and affective.

Based on this language and heart dynamic, Ma addressed concerns among *peiliao* about underpayment by instructing the women to simply "use/show your hearts without worrying about payment or possible mistreatment". "*peng chu ni de xin, rang tamen kanzhe gei* 捧出你的心，让他们看着给［钱］ (Focusing on your work and moral integrity – that is, your heart, you will not be mistreated)". Again, this is based on his Confucian understanding of human nature. The underlying message is that if *peiliao* are mistreated, it is because their own work ethic was lacking, or due to moral failure. One way to share their hearts in their counseling work, according to Ma, is to share their own means of coping with a recent traumatic experience of job loss. This constructs empathy and helps clients cope with their distress. Ma viewed empathy as an interactive, corporal and experiential process. In my own observations of him, Ma rarely made direct reference to positive psychology. Rather, he had embedded that discourse, along with the government-backed discourse of HQ, into his views of the heart. In this way, Ma synthesized discourses that supported government objectives, while delivering indigenously tinged wisdom. The synthesis of psychologizing discourse with indigenous notions seems to be the ideal vehicle for promoting the individualistic orientation that the Chinese government seeks, especially among women caregivers. Ma emphasized personal, experiential narratives as the central construct for bridging the gap between self and others, as well as understanding others. However, while he stressed how the heart serves as the core of one's subjectivity and the author of talk, he still taught *peiliao* how to manipulate their experiential narrative in order to address shifting needs of their clients, which helped them construct a sense of plasticity of their selves.

The cultivation of a plastic self among *peiliao* and the hybridity of Ma's pedagogy also manifested in his other ways of communicating empathy. Following Carl Rogers's person-centered therapy, Ma encouraged *peiliao* to minimize their own speaking agency, while emphasizing the self and heart of the client, which slightly contradicted his previous teaching on *peiliao*'s whole-bodied speech style, but was still heart-based – this time, focusing on the client. Ma suggested that counselors give clients full speakerhood and agency and help them narrate and realize their "true" selves. Ideally, the speech of the counselor becomes part of the client's own voice, helping the client feel accepted and unique by stressing how they thought, felt and spoke. According to Ma, feelings of acceptance and uniqueness are key to deep caring. The primary tenet of this therapy is the principle of *jiena* (acceptance); that is, full acceptance of the client as a unique human being. You must see her heart, not just what she says and does. It is worth noting that this orientation differs from traditional communist ideological orientation, which often denies individuality.

However, many *peiliao* find it hard, in actual "counseling" to apply this heart-to-heart, deeply psychologized, moralized approach to people and events, and to assess when to share their own hearts and when to channel their clients' own heart sharing. One informant, Xu, a 48-year-old single mother, gave an example.

> When my employer's daughter eloped with her boyfriend, she was so enraged and devastated that for several days she couldn't eat or sleep and kept sighing in front of me, often with tears welled in her eyes. At some point, I couldn't help sharing my experience with my own daughter who had also run away with a person I didn't like. But much to my surprise, without allowing me to finish my story, she stopped me and said, "you know what, we are not to compare who is more miserable." She then withdrew to her bedroom. I later realized what she wanted at that moment – maybe just to have someone to listen to her. She had no interest or mood to hear other people's stories. Or she doesn't treat me as an equal who has the ability to experience things similarly. If I were her peer, I doubt she would interrupt me this way.

> 当我雇主的女儿跟她男朋友私奔后，我雇主特别生气特别沮丧她好几天不吃不睡，含着眼泪在我面前不停唉声叹气。 在某个时候， 我实在忍不住就跟她说了我女儿与一个我不同意的人私奔的事，但是出乎我意料的是， 没让我说完她就打断了我，说 "你知道吗，我们不是在比较谁更不幸。" 她然后退回她房间。 我后来意识到她在那一刻需要什么。 或许她只需要有人听她倾诉 她没兴趣也没心情去听别人的故事。 或者她没把我看成一个能和她有相同境遇的人。 如果我和她平级， 我怀疑她会那样打断我说话。

Xu's account challenged the kind of training she received in two ways: one, instead of proffering her own embodied knowledge of dealing with distress and suffering caused by job loss to empathize with clients, she invoked her experience as a mother, not only because it related to the situation of her client, but also because it challenged the reduction and psychologization of her rich subjectivity by job counselors and the media portrayal of laid-off women. Second, while she has good motivations, her talk failed to express what her heart intended to achieve (*haoxin wu hao bao* "好心无好报. A kind heart nevertheless cannot achieve what it intends to"). For many *peiliao*, sharing one's heart through personal narrative is not automatic; it requires not only skill and strategy, but also depends on socio-political factors, including the heart and mood of the employer, the spatio-temporality of the event unfolding in the conversation, and, ultimately the structural/class relationship between them and their employers. I would argue that these structural relationships are supported by key discourses, deepened in media, about the identities of laid-off women. Xu complained that it was this kind of ambivalence in her daily (class-based) power struggle with her employers, and the constant, subtle calculation of how to narrow the incongruence between the efficacy of her talk and her heart's desire that exhausted her (heart) most (*xin lei* 心累, literally translated as "heart exhaustion"). Presumably one can recover from physical exhaustion easily through rest but it is difficult to recover from the exhaustion of the heart as heart-exhaustion entails a complexity of anxiety, uncertainty and insecurity. Such heart-exhaustion reflects the depth, fluidity and contingency of *peiliao*'s psychological and affective labor.

These women's heart-based and highly contextualized psychological labor both converges and diverges from the Marxist-feminist notion of affective labor. Affective labor refers to labor that does not produce a physical commodity or object, but rather, aims to evoke/transform certain affective states in others through the regulation of one's own affective condition. The concept has been deployed by feminist scholars in order to extend existing notions of labor (as the production of material goods) to include the unwaged, affective work provided by women in the domestic sphere. More contemporarily, the concept of affective labor has been extended by scholars like Michael Hardt and Arlie Hochschild. Hardt (1999) suggests that in the transformation from an industrial to a service and informational economy, affective labor has become not only directly productive of capital, but located at the very pinnacle of the hierarchy of laboring forms. Economic sectors, from health care to the entertainment industry, are increasingly relying upon the regulation and production of affect. Through her notions of global care chains and emotional surplus value, Hochschild (2012) uncovers how affective energies have become integrated into the global circulation and exchange of goods, values, and services. In China, women's affective labor is mobilized to help develop the service industry through the prevalent psychologizing and essentializing discourse with the advent of the psychoboom.

Conclusion: language, gender and psychologization

This chapter has studied the relationship between language, gender and the new psycho-political economy in China. The analysis of underprivileged women's psychological and affective labor engages the linguistic, bodily and moral dimensions of their performance.

Linguistic practice, a key component of *peiliao*'s companionable counseling, represents a state of transition, ambivalence and in-betweenness. It is neither typical counseling/talk therapy, as it is not conducted in professional settings, nor workplace language, as *peiliao* is not considered by its practitioners as a profession or proper work, but rather, as a transitional, temporary survival strategy before they can pursue something more lasting or formal. The language of *peiliao* is supposedly derived from the heart, and expresses the heart, here seen as the fundamental component of one's subjectivity. The congruence between language and heart putatively constitutes the work ethics and subjectivities of *peiliao*, who are mobilized by counselors and the government to address social, moral and psychological distress. In this sense, both language and the heart constitute a force that downplays the social and political contexts in which the talk is produced. These women are given only the minimum skills to carry forward constructs of newly psychologized subjectivities, and a lack of power, legal or institutional support puts both these women's employment and their own wellbeing at risk.

The work of *peiliao* is a result and component of the recent psychologization and moralization of social issues in China. Psychologization downplays or masks structural forces that generate social problems, including mass unemployment and widespread social distress. To some extent, underprivileged women are mobilized to serve as a proxy for structural change, and gender is used to express class-based issues. In other words, this trend of psychologization reforms those on the margins of society, skews their employment trajectories towards political and economic ends that benefit the state, a process that resonates with the notion of therapeutic governance (see Yang, 2018), which focuses on citizens' sense of self and emphasizes emotions as a source of truth. In this form of governance, control appears as activities of therapy, heart-based psychotherapeutic "care", and permissive empathy. To relieve the economic burden on the state generated by unemployment, the Chinese government, viewing marginalized women specifically through a gendered lens, has deployed both the unemployment and mental health crises as motivators for rendering a kind of psychological control, one that propagandizes and normalizes the role of women as *peiliao*. In exerting this control, the government supports the notion that it is "natural" for a caring woman to take a job like *peiliao*. Shifting gender ideology and Chinese cultural discourse not only constitutes it but further justifies and naturalizes it. In taking on their new job, *peiliao* serve both families and the state. In this sense, gender is central in the trend toward psychologization. However, as this analysis shows, the attention to gender and language also highlights the contradictions and tensions involved in this psychologization, which is a deeply political process.

The attention to language and gender constitutes a process to track new political forms of engagement, for example, the role women's heart work plays in the psychologizing discourse. For job counselors, the heart, as the moral core, is the very site for generating and constraining emotions and affective labor, as well as an inner healing resource. The emphasis on cultivating the heart for establishing equilibrium to cope with stress broadens and deepens the power of experts (job trainers) and the state to intrude into people's lives more thoroughly than typical psyche-based therapies. Through cultivating the heart's moral core, this therapeutic intervention reduces solutions to complex social issues to individual moral and psychological practices. However, for *peiliao*, their affective holistic labor may derive from the heart but is constrained by their limited social circumstances.

The analysis of the daily linguistic practice and gendered, holistic labor of *peiliao* reveals a process in which underprivileged women are cultivated as moralized and psychologized subjects who play a vanguard role in promoting and performing "psychotherapy." Their work is a bridge between expertise and the masses, and fills the psychological and moral vacuum created by the decline in acceptance of communism and the new market economy. The analysis of their labor bears witness to how they confront and resist the impoverishment of their subjectivities. This confrontation between the women and the attempt to reduce their subjectivities compels people to interrogate China's current governing, which turns to the private and internal lives of the individual for solutions to public issues as a means of shunning state culpability for creating social problems and widespread social distress.

The emphasis on gender over class in China, and the push for marginalized women to embody the feminine ideal and the emerging therapeutic ethos help explain the background for the abuse suffered by *peiliao* (apart from their obvious structural lack of power). They are positioned as both "counselors" (class status) and "female company" (caring, sexualized, low status);

both subject positions are united in *peiliao*, which creates paradoxical effects on these women's identities and new vulnerabilities to gendered exploitation in the job market (see Yang, 2013). For laid-off women workers, whose livelihoods and psychological wellbeing were destroyed by economic restructuring, expert and government promotion of gendered discourse and gendered practices regarding their psychological labor sets up the conditions for real conflict. The women must make a new living that requires heart work, which nevertheless cannot enable them to regain a full sense of self.

Notes

1 A 2009 survey by the Chinese Disease Control Center reported that over 100 million of the 1.3 billion Chinese suffer some form of mental illness (7.7 percent); within that group, over 16 million suffer severe mental illness (Chen Zewei 2010) (16 percent). About 190 million Chinese are said to be in need of professional counseling or psychiatric treatment (Shao 2016) – a figure that is bigger than the statistics offered by the above 2009 survey but aligns with global predictions: the World Health Organization estimates that by 2020 mental illness will account for one quarter of the overall health burden in China (Shao 2016).

2 These new female-centric professions also include *dou xiao shi* "逗笑师 (an assistant to make young children smile)" while being photographed at photography studios, *daole* "导乐 (an assistant who guides women through labor in informative and pleasant manners)", and *yuesao* "月嫂 (a live-in nanny who assists mothers to care for their newborns)".

References

English references

Ahmed, Sara. (2004) *The Cultural Politics of Emotion*. London: Routledge.
Fairclough, Norman. (1992) *Discourse and Social Change*. Cambridge: Polity,
Given, Lisa, M. (2008) *The Sage Encyclopedia of Qualitative Research Methods*. London: Sage. p. 249.
Goffman, Erving. (1981) *Forms of Talk*. Pennsylvania: University of Pennsylvania Press.
Gorton, Kristyn. (2007) 'Theorizing Emotion and Affect: Feminist Engagement', *Feminist Theory* 8(3): 333–348.
Gregg, Melissa and Selgworth, Gregory J. (2010) *The Affect Theory Reader*. Durham: Duke University Press.
Han, Buxin and Zhang Kan. (2007) 'Psychology in China', *Psychologist* 20: 737–736.
Hardt, Michael. (1999) 'Affective Labor', *Boundary* 26(2): 89–100.
Hochschild, Arlie, R. (2012) *The Managed Heart: Commercialization of Human Feeling*. Berkeley: University of California Press.
Huang, Hsuan-Ying. (2014) 'The emergence of the psycho-boom in contemporary urban China', in *Psychiatry and Chinese History*. Howard Chiang (ed.). London: Pickering & Chatto. pp. 183–204.
Kipnis, Andrew (2012) *Chinese Modernity and the Individual Psyche*. New York: Palgrave Macmillan.
Kleinman, Arthur. (2010) 'The Art of Medicine: Remaking the Moral Person in China: Implications for Health', *The Lancet*, 375(9720): 1074–1075.
Kleinman, Arthur, Yan, Yunxiang, Jun, Jing, Lee, Sing, Zhang, Everett, Tianshu, Pan, Fei, Wu and Jinhua, Guo. (2011) *Deep China: The Moral Life of the Person*. Berkeley: University of California Press.
Lee, Sing. (2011) 'Depression: Coming of Age in China', in *Deep China: The Moral Life of the Person*. Arthur Kleinman, Yunxiang Yan, Jing Jun, Sing Lee, Everett Zhang, Pan Tianshu, Wu Fei and Guo Jinhua (eds.) Berkeley: University of California Press. pp. 177–212.
Massumi, Brian. (2002) *Parables for the Virtual: Movement, Affect, Sensation Parables for the Virtual: Movement, Affect, Sensation*. Durham: Duke University Press.
McElhinny, Bonnie. (2007) 'Introduction', in *Words, Worlds, Material Girls: Language, Gender and Global Economies*. Berlin: Mouton. pp. 1–36.
McElhinny, Bonnie. (2010) 'The Audacity of Affect: Gender, Race, and History in Linguistic Account of Legitimacy and Belonging', *Annual Review of Anthropology* 39: 309–328.
Ngai, Sianne. (2005) *Ugly Feelings*. Cambridge and London: Harvard University Press.

Nye, Joseph. (2004) *Soft Power: The Means to Success in World Politics*. New York: Public Affairs.
Nye, Joseph S. Jr. (2008) 'Foreword', in *Soft Power Superpowers: Cultural and National Assets of Japan and the United States*. Watanabe Yasushi and David McConnell (eds.) New York: M.E. Sharpe. pp. ix–xiv.
Rofel, Lisa. (1999) *Other Modernities: Gendered Yearnings in China after Socialism*. Berkeley: University of California Press.
Sun, Wangning. (2009) 'Mapping Space for the Maid: Metropolitan Gaze, Peripheral Vision and Subaltern Spectatorship in Urban China', *Feminist Media Studies* 9(1): 57–71.
Wallis, Cara. (2018) 'Domestic Workers and the Affective Dimensions of Communicative Empowerment', *Communication, Culture & Critique* 11(2): 213–230. DOI: 10.1093/ccc/tcy001.
Wang, Zheng. (2003) 'Gender, employment and women's resistance', in *Chinese Society: Change, Conflict and Resistance*. Elizabeth J. Perry and Mark Selden (eds.) New York: Routledge Curzon.
Yang, Jie. (2007) '"Reemployment Stars": Language, Gender and Neoliberal Restructuring in China', in *Words, Worlds, Material Girls: Language, Gender and Global Economies*. Bonnie McElhinny (ed.) Berlin: Mouton de Gruyter.
Yang, Jie. (2013) '*Peiliao* "Companion to Chat": Gender, Psychologization and Psychological Labor in China', *Social Analysis* 57(2): 41–58.
Yang, Jie. (2015) *Unknotting the Heart: Unemployment and Therapeutic Governance in China*. Ithaca, NY: Cornell University Press.
Yang, Jie. (2018) *Mental Health in China: Change, Tradition, and Therapeutic Governance*. Cambridge: Polity Press.
Yang, Mayfair Meihui. (1999) *Spaces of Their Own: Women's Public Sphere in Transnational China*. Minneapolis: University of Minnesota Press.

Chinese references

Chen, Zewei 陈泽伟. (2010) 'Resolving the Pain/Threats Posed by the Mentally Ill', *Outlook Weekly*. May 31: 36–37.
Feng Jicai 冯骥才. (1996) *Ten Years of Madness: Oral Histories of China's Cultural Revolution*. San Francisco: China Books.
Li Zixun 李子勋 (2016) 'Women and Psychology', WeChat: *Li Zixun*. March 16, 2016 (in Chinese).
Shao, Jingjun 邵景军. (2016) 'Psychological Health Should Become an Important Criterion for Appointing Cadres', *Chinese Cadres Tribune* 3: 16–18.

Part VI
Genres of Chinese discourse

Other pragmatic functions mentioned were the intensifying involvement in a story (Nishimura 1995; see also Kim 2003) or CS in order to fill lexical gaps.

A relatively new field of research in CS involving Japanese pays attention to the linguistic accommodation of the addressee. Japanese scholars of CS can in general be said to have been more addressee-oriented in comparison to North-American scholars. One of Nishimura's descriptions for the motivation for CS is addressee-oriented. Speakers switch to Japanese for "native Japanese" persons like Nishimura herself, or for addressees who use more Japanese.

Scholars of Japanese CS never questioned the bilingual identities of speakers, as the canonical studies in the US had already affirmed that CS indexed bilingual identity. Poplack (1980) concluded that the reason why the speakers who were more competent in both languages in her data switched more often was due to their desire to express their belonging to both the English-speaking and the Spanish-speaking communities. Poplack's finding had a large impact to reverse the ideology that CS is a sign of incompetence in the languages involved in CS. Azuma (1997) also observes that bilingual speakers with high proficiency frequently engaged in CS. Unfortunately, these insights backfired in Japan, as some misinterpreted these findings in a way that only full bilinguals would engage in CS and that anything else was merely a "search for words". However, it is not the competence in both languages that promotes CS but the belonging to two communities of practice.

In Japan, the Korean community is of particular interest when studying CS. As the Korean population in Japan and their migration patterns diversified, studies of Korean speakers started to look at different CS patterns across different groups of migrant Koreans. These groups involved students, newcomer workers and returnees (individuals who had spent part of their youth in Japan and then moved to Korea). They found that students from Korea studying in Japan and Koreans brought up in Japan have indeed different language choice patterns (Yoshida 2005; Kwak 2013). Linguistic competencies are seen to be the main factor for this. Also, the more proficient speakers are in both languages, the more complex that CS becomes. A good way to better grasp these complexities is to apply methods of conversation analysis. In Europe, scholars started to include this to the study of CS from the 1990s onwards, and this trend was also picked up in Japan. A conversation analysis approach to the language use of a teenage "multiethnic Japanese"[2] friendship group in an international school in Japan confirmed that CS is part of bilingual youths' practice of bi-ethnic membership (Greer 2007, 2010). This finding underlined once more that it is not ethnicity as such that creates sense of community but that language practices play a crucial role thereby.

Studies mentioned so far sketched a speech community with speakers across a horizontal axis in terms of social power. Analyzing verbal interactions can also reveal existing hierarchies within a community. In Japan, minority languages are often marginalized and considered less valuable among speakers of these languages themselves, but this does not mean that minority languages are always the inferior code. For example, students at Korean schools share the habit of using Korean to elders in the community and they also use it for greetings. Choosing Korean over Japanese in such contexts is considered a sign of respect. We can see here how language use is intricately linked with social roles.

The topic of social roles is taken up by Iwata (2011) who applies Goffman's frame analysis to study language use at a dinner table in an English-Japanese bilingual family that is based in Japan. This study pays particular attention to gender and family roles. The mother often switches from Japanese to English in order to invite the father who does not speak a lot of Japanese into the conversation. His lower proficiency in Japanese notwithstanding, the father took more controlling frames than the mother, while the mother acted often as a communication facilitator, telling children to repeat in English what they said before in Japanese. In this way, the father became a "language monitor" who took a more controlling role in the conversations, while the mother remained the subordinate facilitator and mediator of conversation by switching to English (Iwata 2011).

Language transgressions

In the following, I refrain from using meta-language that has been developed entirely on western case studies for discussions of phenomena occurring in Japanese society. "Transgression" as defined by Heinrich (2017) refers to culturally neutral ways to discuss similarities between case studies such as "crossing" in England, "Kiezdeutsch" in Germany or "dialect cosplay" in Japan. Transgression is an etic term, while crossing or dialect cosplay are emic categories.

Crossing

Many CS works presented in the previous section studied speakers switching between languages with others who share the same repertoires and were members of the same community. Language crossing, on the other hand, refers to linguistic behavior where speakers "cross" into languages that are not socially recognized as part of speakers' repertoire (Rampton 1995, 1999). Unlike CS, speakers tend to have limited knowledge of the language they cross into. Unlike CS, crossing cannot be explained in a purely pragmatic framework like Gumperz (1982) does, because it involves a transgression in terms of social boundaries.

Following the tradition of British and American sociolinguistics, where categories of race and ethnicity have played a central role, Rampton studied student interactions in a multiethnic secondary school in England. He found that crossing occurred mostly in "moments and events where normal social relations are suspended" (Rampton 1999: 54). In such moments, boundaries of race and ethnicity were an issue. Pupils crossed not to mock the particular social group associated with a language, but they crossed in order to transcend social boundaries and in this way establish a sense of solidarity. For example, in one instance, a South-Asian male pupil refers to the Anglo female teacher in Caribbean creole in her absence to make other pupils laugh. According to Rampton, these instances invoke a sense of solidarity among the pupils and constitute a challenging move towards the institutional system of school and the dominating Anglo society. Crossing is thus not a racially hostile interaction. It served to reassure peer solidarity and to create spaces where participants challenge or mock the predominant ideologies connected to language, ethnicity and identity.

Dialect cosplay

Crossing in terms of race or ethnicity has not been reported in Japanese sociolinguistic academia, but we find in Japan many young people engaging in linguistic transgressions by using tokens of dialects they do not speak. Such partial knowledge of dialects is common among younger Japanese, as different dialects along with regional stereotypes are ubiquitous in the Japanese media (anime, manga, TV, etc.). Tanaka's (2011) book, *Hōgen kosupure no jidai* (The Age of Dialect Cosplay), calls attention to the fact that young people today have added elements of non-native dialect items to their language repertoire. A quarter of the 127 college students in Tokyo that Tanaka surveyed reported to use what she calls "fake dialect" (*nise hōgen*) when texting, i.e., they used elements of dialects with which they had not been socialized. The most commonly used fake dialect was that of the Kansai region. Students also reported using northern Kanto, Tohoku, Kyushu, Chugoku and other dialects, suggesting that an extensive and creative repertoire exists among them. Most dialect elements consisted of clause final or sentence-final forms. Dialects were strategically "put on and off" (Tanaka 2011: 3) according to the situation. Using fake dialects allowed students to exploit regional stereotypes for communicative purposes and to create informal settings. Tanaka notes that the users attach positive values to dialectal elements. Speakers use these "mainly to expand their repertoire of expression and have fun, regardless of their regional origin" (Tanaka 2011: 10). Furthermore, young people choose different "styles" to perform characters (*kyara*) associated with the dialect in order to diverge from their bare self (*su no jibun*). These stylized expressions evoke stereotypical features of those imagined to speak the specific dialect in question, and this evocation is used as a strategy in conversation (Tanaka 2011: 16). Unlike Rampton's crossing, young Japanese employ these dialects casually, without putting their own regional identity or identity as a standard language speaker at risk. They do not question, challenge or express affinity or hostility towards regional identities. Such use of dialect features is also not part of linguistic accommodation.

Is dialect cosplay "crossing" for fun?

What then is similar between crossing and dialect cosplay, and what is different? First of all, both phenomena investigate how participants diverge from the language or language variety they mainly use and with which they are associated. Crossing was observed in a particular social group in the school that Rampton studied, while the extent of responses that Tanaka gathered in her survey suggests that dialect cosplay was shared by a larger group of people than just school friends. Whereas Rampton's participants did not exploit linguistic elements to invoke stereotypes, Tanaka's participants did so. Rampton's data was ethnographic and allowed to study face-to-face interaction in a particular social context, whereas dialect cosplay is more like a genre that is crucially based in texting. Both Tanaka and Rampton see the use of non-native repertoires as non-discriminating. Due to the standardization process, young people in Japan may no longer encounter diverse regional varieties in their everyday interactions. However, such variety continues to exist in texts or in audiovisual media, and it is from there that it enters into young people's repertoires. In Japan, discussions about ethnolinguistic boundaries are difficult to define, but in Yamashita's (2016) study of language in a mosque in the Kanto area, we find a variety of instances where Pakistani pupils switch to a second language variety of Japanese – a variety that resembles the speech of their parents' generation.

Role language, fictional styles and registers

Role language (*yakuwarigo*) is another field of research in Japan that studies linguistic forms associated with stereotypical speakers.[3] Such imagined speakers are prevalent in fiction, and language is used for the differentiation of and "building up" of fictional characters (Kinsui 2003). The most famous such role language is *rōjingo* (old men's language). It is very close to *hakasego* (PhD or scientist language). *Hakasego* is often assigned to male scientists with gray hair in a white doctor's lab coat. The first person pronoun is *washi*, and the sentence-final form *-ja* is used. Role-language forms often manifests through particular sentence-final particles that are called *kyara gobi* (social character final particles). It goes without saying that in real-life "old men" or "scientists" have never used such language. From historical evidence, Kinsui (2003) assumes that the prestige and power that certain western dialect speakers (some of whom had *washi* and *-ja* forms in their repertoire) had during the Meiji Period (1868–1912) led to the association between these linguistic elements and these specific roles. Other known sets of linguistic elements that Kinsui (2003) identified as role language include *joseigo* (women's language, a generic term for all different subsets of women) and *kuruwa kotoba* (language of courtesans and prostitutes dating back to Edo Period, literally "language of the red-light districts"). Kinsui approaches the study of role language in two ways. One is to trace back the origin of such role language by using historical language documents. The other is to look at its use by past or present fictional characters. His research is based on written data that includes comics, newspapers, chronicles, diaries but also classic literature. He hardly examines spoken or interactional data, as he is more comfortable to postulate that the image created by role language is the product of writers and other artists (Kinsui, personal communication).

If one extends role language to all fictional registers that are associated with a particular gender, age or occupation, we can find many more roles than those identified by Kinsui. Role language, as a fictional register, can also be used in everyday social interactions. For example, in (5), two Pakistani boys shift to "teacher register" in Japanese. It is debatable whether teacher register here is made up on the spot or is part of a set role language. However, it is evident that the two boys share the same indexical association between the linguistic forms and the imagined character associated with them. Since their roles in the classroom are that of students, the boys are engaging here in a linguistic transgression. This shift challenges the authority of the teacher by appropriating the language associated with the teacher.

(4)
01 Bilquis: Wait, I'll get the marker.
02   <Mrs. Bilquis leaves the room>
03 Imran: <whispers> *jibun no sutoresu kotchi ni butsukechattan da yo* ([Mrs. Bilquis has]) burst out her own stress at us)
04 Imran: <stops whispering, changes his tone> *dame da zo, kimī* (Hey yooou, you shouldn't do that)
05 Khareem: *yūki ga areba nandatte dekiru* (with courage, you can accomplish anything)
06 Imran: *sō sō* (exactly)

(Adapted from Yamashita 2016: 266)

Mrs. Bilquis scolds the class, and after returning to teaching, she leaves the classroom to grab a pen for the whiteboard (line 01). Imran whispers that Mrs. Bilquis was getting at them, and that she was in a bad mood. Then Imran lowers the pitch and utters the phrase (line 03) where the sentence-final form *-zo* and the word *kimi* index masculinity and communication between peers, or from superior to inferior. *Kimi* is not the second person pronoun used by the pupils either. They use *omae* to each other, and they usually address the teachers by *sensei* (teacher). Both are socio-pragmatically appropriate in Japanese. In some rare cases they use *anata* (formal, polite form), which is marginally acceptable. *Kimi*, on the other hand, indexes a superior position, a register associated with male superiors – be it seniors or teachers. In line 04, Khareem adds in a lower pitch voice what sounds like a teacher admonishing pupils, taking after what Imran has said. In so doing, the pupils are crossing into a fictional "senior register" which they usually do not use. They use it in the absence of the teacher in order to challenge her authority.

Usually, protagonists of manga and anime are portrayed as speakers of Standard Japanese, because the standard language facilitates readers' self-identification with the protagonists (Kinsui 2003: 51). At the same time, dialects are sometimes employed as role language in order to invoke regional stereotypes. For example, Kansai dialect can be used to express "crudeness" or "openness", or to portray a character for being "a gourmand" or "talkative", etc. (Kinsui 2003: 82–83). Fictional dialect speakers tend to have an inferior status vis-à-vis the protagonist. More recently, we can witness this allocation of linguistic features to change. In present-day manga and anime, also protagonists occasionally switch to dialect. In addition, not all dialects use is employed to index stereotypes. Yuri Katsuki, the protagonist of the immensely popular anime series *Yuri!!! On Ice* (henceforth YOI) occasionally uses his native Kyushu dialect. Other Kyushu-born characters in YOI, especially by older characters, also use this dialect. That is to say, the protagonist Yuri and various sub-characters share the same dialect. It is arguable whether the Kyushu dialect is used to stress the stereotyped "bossiness" of Kyushu men, because Yuri uses Kyushu dialect from the start of the series when he is still portrayed as unconfident. In this case, the use of the Kyushu dialect is merely an indication of his geographical origin, rather than a means to define his character by linking language use to social stereotypes. Dialects may be assigned to characters in order to stress a geographical connection or to evoke an association with regard to their personal character. Ultimately, the interpretation of this rests with the audience, and they may come up with different conclusions according to their own language repertoires and language uses.

We can see that the association between dialect and regional stereotypes is opaque in the example of Michele Crispino, a fictional Italian figure skater in the YOI series. Crispino uses *washi* as his first person pronoun, and often uses *-ja* and *-jaken* as clause final forms. While both *washi* and *-ja* are also part of the *rōjingo* (old men role language), the use of *-jaken* indicates that Crispino is not using *rōjingo* but rather Hiroshima dialect. Hiroshima dialect is less well known, making it harder for the audience to come up with a stereotyped association for his character on the basis of his language use. Let us therefore consider reactions that were posted on Twitter where YOI viewers discuss Michele Crispino's use of Hiroshima dialect. We can notice altogether six different types of interpretation.

(5)
(a) Confusion: The viewers try to voice out and/or interpret the unconventional assignment of the Hiroshima dialect to someone not associated with Hiroshima, e.g., "Why is he using Hiroshima dialect when he is from Italy?"
(b) General positive evaluation: "Interesting mix", "initially surprised but now I got used to it and came to like it"
(c) Positive evaluation by associating it with one's own linguistic identity: e.g., "I like that someone is speaking my dialect"
(d) Interpretation – Reading the ideological analogy of standard/non-standard dichotomy, e.g., "My friend who lives in US told me that Italian-American English sounds like Hiroshima dialect", "maybe people from Naples, southern Italy, correspond with people from Hiroshima, in the western part of Japan"
(e) Authenticity judgment and approval/disapproval: Viewers use their linguistic knowledge to evaluate the authenticity of the dialectal forms, often accompanied with affective evaluation, e.g., "it sounds authentic", "I hate it because it sounds fake"
(f) Others: "As an Okayama person, it bugs me as I wonder whether it is Okayama dialect or Hiroshima dialect?" "I didn't realize it was a dialect until certain point", "I was wondering why he was speaking like an old man"

We see that Hiroshima dialect does not evoke one set stereotype shared among all viewers. If the author meant to utilize an existing stereotype to index a particular character, then this strategy has failed. However, it is significant that the use of dialect invokes a lot of fan discussions and creates some sort of mystery to be discussed among fans. Once the stereotype attached to Hiroshima dialect speakers is detached from the regional background of the character, users are even free to show an affinity to an Italian character because he speaks the same dialect as they do (see 5(c)). The stereotype associated with Hiroshima dialect does not come into play here. There is also the possibility that Michele is assigned Hiroshima dialect/old men role language in order to stress the gap between the assumed "Italian stereotype", and the way Michele is actually portrayed in the series. During an inner monologue, he describes himself (in dialect) as "Italian but introvert". Meanwhile, in his "biographical information" on the official website of the series he states to be "a prudish virgin, contrary to the stereotype of Italian guys" (*itaria otoko no imēji o kutsugaesu kōha na dōtei*) and confesses to have a sister complex. It could therefore well be that the artist intended to portray him as "unsexy" or "conservative for his generation" and towards this end assigned him a dialect that shares features with old men role language. At the same time, there is also the possibility that the artist wanted to create an "interesting character" that has an unexpected mismatch between how viewers would assume him to be and how he actually is. This unexpectedness clearly shows in some of the reactions shown above. In Japan, dialects can thus be employed to create contested and layered meanings, even to foreign characters that have no geographical association to Japanese dialect areas. This unexpectedness reflects well how young Japanese associate themselves with dialects but also how anime and manga are consumed today. Anime and manga are not a unilateral production, flowing from author to the audience. Character design is more important than ever, because viewers, especially the fervent ones, also purchase limited edition products and reproduce the anime-content through secondary creation (*niji-sōsaku*), multiplying thereby the fandom (we will return to this further below). The portrayal of fictional characters today is an open, ambivalent and layered enterprise. Authors may in fact be exactly playing with these features to create multiple meanings that then become topics of discussion and resource in the fans' secondary reproductions of popular culture.

Race, ethnicity and Japanese language

Let us next consider examples of racial and ethnic forms of Japanese language that are perceived to various extent as fictional and that circulate in the Japanese-speaking media. Despite the transgression and emancipation from a one-on-one relationship between language and ethnicity that we discussed in previous sections, not all association between language and ethnicity is lost in Japan.

Aruyo kotoba

We find in Japan also role language that points at ethnic groups. *Aruyo kotoba* is a role language that is often used for Chinese and other exotic foreign characters (Kinsui 2003). Kinsui traces its origins to the *aruyo* form used in the 1878 textbook *Exercises in the Yokohama Dialect* by Bishop of Homoco.[4] Many phrases in the book have a pidgin feel to them because they lack verb inflexion. Either *aruyo* or *arimas* is attached to the dictionary verb form (*-ru* form), which is an ungrammatical construction. Kinsui (2003) doubts that there actually existed a person such as "Bishop of Homoco" and speculates that the book may have been supposed to be a joke. This notwithstanding, Kinsui notes that the use of *aruyo* can be observed in comics in the utterances of Chinese characters since the 1950s. *Aruyo* is simply added to the Standard Japanese predicate parts and auxiliary verbs are simplified. Most if not all readers of such books today are aware that second language Japanese speakers of Chinese origin do not speak like this.

English as a foreign-role language and stylization of "whiteness"

Besides role language, race or ethnicity can also be indicated by certain uses of English. English can be stylized through modification in orthography, phonetic articulation and intonation to evoke associations on the speaker. Black or white characters in fictions sometimes switch to English in otherwise entirely Japanese works of fiction. This, too, is a kind of "role language". It assigns and emphasizes racial or ethnic traits in order to underline the personality of a given character. If we stick to our example of YOI, we find there the Canadian figure skater Jean Jack "JJ" Leroy whose signature phrase is, in English, "It's JJ style". This phrase is used without phonological adaptation to Japanese. It may be seen as a display of narcissist over-confidence, an image that loosely connects to stereotypes of white men in Japan. Another example is Viktor Nikiforov, a Russian coach, who uses English words such as "amaaazing" (with a prolonged second vowel) also without any phonological adaptations to Japanese. One interpretation of this would be that the audience expects that Viktor and the Japanese protagonist skater Yuri cannot communicate in Japanese. However, Asian characters (Chinese, Korean, Thai, Kazakh) with whom Yuri would not be using Japanese either do not use this kind of phrase, or anything similar.

In written language, katakana script is often used for this type of "racialized Japanese". Users of language transcribed in katakana are often "white", less often "black" and far less Asians (Asians can traditionally be assigned *aruyo kotoba*). In spoken Japanese, such racial linguistic stylization is often expressed though American English articulation of Japanese. The Japanese moraic structure is abandoned in place of a syllable-based pronunciation. Vowels are lengthened or over-emphasized and the pitch accent is altered. For example, in Standard Japanese, the polite form of the copula *desu* is produced with a sharp falling intonation in affirmative, and the second vowel /u/ is devoiced. Meanwhile, in the stylized "white Japanese", the last syllable is voiced and lengthened. Such stylized "white Japanese" appears widely in animated series, TV dramas, TV advertisements, comedy performances, movies or as recorded voices of "white" Christian missionaries that can heard through loudspeakers on streets across Japan.[5]

Mock Korean

The spread of SNS has also opened up spaces for everyone to develop and share new virtual ethnolects, and the assignment of race and ethnicity via language does not only occur in neutral, "fun" or fictional contexts. These strategies are also used for discriminating motives. Racist and extreme rightist groups and individuals in Japan have targeted Resident Koreans in Japan as targets of hate speech and racist public demonstrations (see Taka 2015 for an overview). The fictional sentence-final form *-nida* (written in katakana) is commonly used as an element to create a fictional Korean ethnolect that is employed for derogatory purposes. It is mainly used on online discussion boards (such as the notorious 2ch discussion board), blogs, as well as kinds of tweets that engage in hate speech. *Nida* is likely to be derived from the Korean verb ending (*-mnida*). There is no evidence that Korean speakers have ever used *-nida* as a sentence-final form when speaking in Japanese (mock Korean in italics).

In (6) we see an example from such use from the 2ch discussion board.

(6)
uri wa sanryū kokka *nida*
(*We* are a third-class nation *nida*)

In example (6), *uri* and *nida* were written in katakana characters. Both are not Japanese words. *Uri* is a first person pronoun in Korean, which is used either as a subject or as a possessive marker. Korean phrases *uri mal* and *uri nara*, respectively, refer to "our (Korean) language" and "our (Korean) nation". Racist users are thus degrading Koreans by using *uri* – a term Koreans use with pride – in a derogatory sense.

Makoto Sakurai of the ultranationalist Japan First Party has been involved in numerous anti-Korean demonstrations, and he also ran for the Tokyo mayor election in 2016. He often uses *-nida*, when quoting, dubbing or voicing his opponents in sentences that are otherwise entirely in Standard Japanese. In (7) we have one of his tweets on a randomly chosen day.

(7)
Sukoshi zutsu desu ga yo no nagare ga kawari-tsutsu arimasu. Payoku-gawa wa "heito supīchi o tomeru-nida" to wameki chirashimasu ga, nihonjin wa baka de wa arimasen.
Albeit in small steps, the tide is changing. The "payoku" side screams out "stop the hate speech *nida*", but Japanese people aren't stupid [...]

(12 December 2016)

The word *payoku* which rhymes with *sayoku* (left wing) is rightist jargon to refer to "liberals" who are seen to be "siding" with resident Koreans. Hostility is expressed in the use of their own jargon, *payoku* and *-nida*. People referred to as *payoku* in this tweet include all Japanese who are not on Sakurai's side. Hence, while in (6) *-nida* was assigned to Koreans through direct indexicality, *payoku* in (7) is an example where it is assigned to leftists though indirect indexicality (Ochs 1992).

Mediatized translinguistic practices

Despite the monolingual stereotype of Japanese society, using or mixing two different languages is not an exclusive practice of bilinguals. Many "monolingual" Japanese speakers make use of (partial) knowledge of English and other languages in their social networks. Tokens from other languages are incorporated into everyday casual interaction, and this language use leaves traces in media. Previously, this kind of language use has been overlooked and has been simply labeled as "jargon" or studies as short-lived "buzzwords". Some may consider it to be the result of an influence of or aspiration for English, but there is actually no evidence for this. With the recently increased interest in and awareness of translanguaging (Garcia and Li Wei 2014), it is better understood how Japanese employ bits and pieces of foreign languages without being full-fledged users of these languages.

As is the case with loanwords, English is the most common source for linguistic items used in translinguistic practices in Japan. As English is taught in compulsory education, many Japanese have a large repertoire of English words and everyday interaction and discourses on Japanese media are full of these translinguistic practices. This phenomenon has existed for several decades by now, but these translinguistic practices have been made more visible and become frequent with the rise of SNS in the past two decades.

Translinguistic buzzwords of the past

English influence on buzzwords, product names, advertisements, popular songs, daily interactions, TV programs, dishes on the menu, etc. are a common sight in Japan. One of the famous buzzwords of 1970s and 1980s, that is before the fervent discussions on globalization started, was *naui*, meaning "trendy". It is a combination of the English adjective "now" and the Japanese adjective ending *-i*. The mid-1990s saw another popular mixed phrase – *choberiba*, a clipped version of *chō berī baddo* (super very bad), where *chō* is Japanese (extremely) while *berī baddo* is the English ("very bad" adapted to Japanese articulation). *Choberiba* became an iconic phrase of the then booming *gyaru* (gal) subculture, i.e., trend-setting urban teenage girls. These buzzwords were seen as deviant, but fun to use. They were never considered as signs of "bilingualism" or associated with "knowledge of English". It basically had nothing to do with English, or English-speaking culture. The media, especially TV, highlighted such language use, and while such buzzwords became widely known, they were still strongly associated with teenage girls.

Karaoke nau!

The introduction of SNS made translinguistic practices in everyday interactions more visible. It also showed how people other than teenage girls engage in creating and using neologisms. More than 25 million people use Twitter in Japan. It is so popular that Japanese tweets resulted in the crash of Twitter's servers when over 20,000 tweeted "Happy New Year" precisely at midnight in 2013. In the same year, 140,000 people tweeted "*barusu*" in one second, exactly at the time the word was uttered in a TV screening of an all-time favorite animation film of Japan.[6] This set a Twitter world record at the time. When there are earthquakes or severe weather conditions, many Japanese users use Twitter to report on it and to collect information.

The "pre-SNS buzzwords" *naui* and *choberiba* were adjectives and adverbs. They were easy to use without violating either the grammar of Japanese or English because adjectives precede nouns in both languages. Things have changed. Today, we find translinguistic words which express time, finality or intention on Twitter or elsewhere that are often "violating" both English and Japanese grammar. Mediatized translinguistic practices are more widely spread today, too. They are no longer limited to or associated with young people or *gyaru*. Forms such as *nau* (now), *wazu* (was), *dan* (done) and *wiru* (will) are widely used to share the temporal flow of everyday life through SNS. They are written in hiragana, i.e., not marked as loanwords by choosing katakana. These terms usually follow names of places such as school, hospital, geographical locations, names of restaurants, events such as reunions, concerts, festivals or activities such as karaoke, shopping, golf, homework, etc. Examples of such language use are listed in (8).

(8)
Place names (Tokyo): *Tōkyō wazu, Tōkyō nau, Tōkyō dan, Tōkyō wiru*
Nouns (*shukudai*, homework): *shukudai wazu, shukudai nau, shukudai dan, shukudai wiru*
Events (*raibu*, live concert): *raibu wazu, raibu nau, raibu dan, raibu wiru*

Tōkyō wazu and *Tōkyō dan* means the user is about to leave Tokyo or has left Tokyo, respectively. *Tōkyō nau* means the user is already or has just arrived in Tokyo, while *Tōkyō wiru* indicates that someone is on the way or planning to go to Tokyo.

The words "violate" the grammars of both Japanese and English to some extent. First of all, *dan* (done) is not a word-to-word translation of *owatta* (finished), which would be used in an entirely Japanese utterance. "Done" corresponds more closely to Japanese *shita* (did/done). Furthermore, *dan* (done) is in English the past participle of the verb "to do" and this form does not appear without auxiliary verb (e.g., have done) independently. However, phrases where "done" follows a noun without an auxiliary verb can be seen in informal writings (e.g., "conference done!"). Meanwhile, the verbs in these tweets come at the end, following Japanese syntax. Many Japanese speakers may be familiar how "done" is used in English when one is finished with doing something. We find the same pattern with *wazu* (was). Many Japanese speakers would use *kaeru* (going back) or *kaette-kita* (came back) when reporting their return. The verb forms *ita* and *imashita* (was) sound more objective, and distant physically and temporally, and of course an utterance such as "Tokyo was" in English is incomplete and basically devoid of meaning.

We can also find *nau*, *wazu*, *dan* and *wiru* after long nominal clauses such as in (9).

(9)
Ōe ana no otakara eizō ni me o kagayakaseru shōgatsu dan
The New Year holidays where (one) indulges in exclusive clips from broadcaster Ōe are over.
(Posted on Twitter by a user on 1 January 2012)

These expressions do not seem to be "one-off calques", but have become part of unmarked language in SNS, where users report their momentary locations and activities through simple written text, often without addressing any particular individual. Note also, that such expressions do not occur in spoken bilingual interactions. Many users that apply these terms never tweet in English. Also, the use of these terms does not have the usual social or pragmatic motivations we can find in classic CS studies. At the time of writing, such practices had been online on various SNS platforms for at least six years, and they have not become obsolete. This does not seem to be a linguistic fad. What we have, instead, is a blurring of boundaries between monolingual and bilingual language use, and this points directly to the elasticity and flexibility of linguistic forms and language use in contemporary Japanese society.

Transliterated foreign language terms and phatic communication

In the age of SNS, foreign words, phrases or linguistic items are not replacements of their Japanese equivalents. They are semiotic resources that are used to construct identities and to engage in phatic communication (Bucholtz and Hall 2004; Otsuji and Pennycook 2010; Pennycook and Otsuji 2015). They are used as icons of solidarity and affinity in networks of users that are often not in face-to-face contact. The forms can have several meanings, and they can spread through different means.

Russia is a prominent country for figure skating, and some Japanese figure-skating fans, of which there are many in Japan, use certain phrases in the languages where famous figure skaters are from. Use of Russian such as *davaj* (let's go) can be observed in face-to-face communication among fans, but also in SNS. Such language use became notably more widely spread when YOI was broadcast on TV and the Internet. This fictional series centers on the Japanese male figure skater Yuri Katsuki who is competing at the international level. The broadcast of this series coincided with the real Grand Prix competition season in 2016, and it gained almost three million tweets in the first two months of its airing. Real-life international figure skaters across the globe also tweeted about this series, which brought it further attention among figure-skating fans and anime fans. Yuri Plisetsky (the protagonist's rival) and Viktor Nikiforov (the protagonist's coach) are important characters in the series. They usually speak in Japanese, but since they are Russian, they sometimes also utter Russian words such as *vkusno* (delicious) or *davaj!* (let's go!). On SNS fans started to use these expressions widely, and transliterated them in katakana as *fukūsuna* and *dabāi/davāi*, respectively. We can tell that these posts refer to YOI, because users also make several linguistic and iconic references to the series. Some account names include the phrases *dabāi/davāi* or *fukūsuna* itself, and/or use the Cyrillic alphabet. Some users tweeted *fukūsuna* along photos of food they were eating that day. Many photos happen to be *katsu-don* (pork cutlet bowl – Yuri Katsuki's favorite dish) or Russian dishes such as *pirozhki* (the "comfort food" that Yuri Plisetsky's grandfather prepares for him in the series). Fans identify themselves through such semiotic resources, and use them for expressing and sharing their affection for the series with others. It goes without saying that users know that these words are Russian, and that these expressions are also not used to communicate with Russians. These terms are used to share an affinity towards this anime series, and these terms come in handy as emblems of their appreciation and as a means to identify as a fan.

Outlook

In Japan, we do not find much discussion on race and ethnicity, because Japan is thought of as a racially and culturally homogeneous country. Ethnic and cultural diversity does of course exist in Japan (Fujita-Round and Maher 2017), and Japanese society is in fact further diversifying at the present. As an effect thereof, the once undisputed dichotomy between "Japanese" and "non-Japanese" is becoming fuzzier, and this raises the question of how to deal with this in sociolinguistic research. Rather than applying western notions of racial and cultural diversity to the case of Japan, and of uncritically linking them with mainstream sociolinguistic ideas and terminology, one needs to examine how diversity actually relates to and manifests in contemporary Japanese society. An entirely new way to approach this topic is that of "metroethnicity" (Maher 2005) and "metrolingualism" (see Otsuji and Pennycook 2010; Pennycook and Otsuji 2015). These "metro" ideas emerged in academic discourse as a means to make sense of how speakers actually use the different linguistic resources that are available to them. It stresses that metrolingualism and metroethnicity is not necessarily only a means of self-representation, neither is it simply about transgressing social and linguistic boundaries. Similar in line, but with more focus on the creativity of linguistic forms is the concept of "translanguaging" (Garcia and Li 2014). Meanwhile, focusing on the flexibility and the diversity of language use alone does not eliminate issues of racism or linguicism as we could see above. For this reason, the study of such phenomena needs also to be critical. There are other problems of methodology. Metrolingualism involves ethnography, but the study of texting and written language does not match well with ethnography. Analyzing texting in the narrow confines of "role language" and "dialect cosplay" blocks the expansion of these phenomena to also include, for example, issues of language and social justice.

With the strong bias in linguistics towards spoken language, we have not yet attained a method that is up-to-date with the study of communication in contemporary society. A good point of departure to expand the field is media studies and language ideology. In many examples of mediatized translinguistic phenomena, we saw various social and semiotic associations being created by users of SNS platforms. Some linguistic forms may be fun, casual and friendly like in the case of dialect cosplay, others are hostile and dehumanizing as in the case of "mock Korean". From a linguistic perspective, the crossover between spoken language, texting and written language calls for more attention. Here, too, we can already find a range of approaches to start with (e.g., Iwasaki 2015; Sadanobu 2011). Applying these is important to create a new vision of linguistic and sociolinguistic study, one that is inclusive of all languages and individuals in Japan and, what is more, that deals with language as it is actually used in the real world in which we currently live.

Notes

1. Jeju-Korean refers to Jeju language, a Koreanic language spoken in the Jeju Province in South Korea. Jeju was one of the three main provinces of origin for colonial migration of Korean laborers to Japan. In her discussion on code-switching, Kim (2003) includes Jeju-Korean under Korean, but make notes of some Jeju-specific forms.
2. Greer uses the term "multiethnic Japanese" to refer to the participants in his study. For a review and discussion on various terms used to refer to people with both non-Japanese origins and Japanese origins, see Okamura (2013, 2016).
3. The issue of assigning different varieties in translations has been previously discussed by Hiramoto (2009), and the topic of "over-feminization" in translated works and dubbed TV dramas is discussed by Nakamura (2013).
4. Honmoku is still a name of a district in Yokohama City today.
5. A representative example of this can be found online by searching "*peñ kaikoku shite kudasai*" on Google. The results refer to a popular audio comedy (source unknown) acting as Matthew C. Perry, the Commodore of the United States Navy who pressured Japan to open its doors in mid-nineteenth century. Two examples of what is meant here by "voices of white Christians on streets and in unexpected places" come immediately to mind. One is the "Christian style" marriage ceremony in Japanese wedding halls, where a Caucasian man takes the role of the priest marrying the couple. The second are tape-recorded religious speeches. Such speeches can at times be heard on streets via loud speakers.
6. *Barusu* is an incantation in the popular animation film *Tenkū no shiro rapyuta* (*Castle in the Sky*), directed by Hayao Miyazaki in 1986. The two protagonists, Pazu and Sheeta, recite this at the climax of the story, as they decide to destroy the flying castle rather than handing it over to the villain, Colonel Muska. During the 2011 screening of this film on TV, Twitter recorded 25,088 tweets of *barusu* in one second, making it a world record. In a 2013 TV screening, this multiplied and arrived at 143,199 tweets per second (*The Economist* 2013).

References

Azuma, Shoji (1997) Lexical Categories and Code-Switching. A Study of Japanese/English Code-Switching in Japan. *The Journal of the Association of Teachers of Japanese* 31(2): 1–24.

Blom, Jan-Petter and John J. Gumperz (1972) Social Meaning in Linguistic Structure. Code-switching in Norway. In: *Directions in Sociolinguistics. The Ethnography of Communication*. John J. Gumperz and Dell Hymes (eds), 407–434. New York: Holt, Rinehart and Winston.

Bucholtz, Mary and Kira Hall (2004) Language and Identity. In: *A Companion to Linguistic Anthropology*. Alessandro Duranti (ed.), 369–394. Blackwell: Malden.

Flores, Tanya L. and Aja Williams (forthcoming) Japoñol: Spanish-Japanese Code-Switching. *Indiana University Linguistics Club Working Papers*.

Fujita-Round, Sachiyo and John C. Maher (2017) Language Policy and Education in Japan. In: *Encyclopedia of Language and Education*. Stephen May and Teresa McCarthy (eds), 393–404. Cham: Springer.

Garcia, Ofelia and Li Wei (2014) *Translanguaging. Language, Bilingualism, and Education*. Basingstoke: Palgrave Macmillan.

Greer, Tim (2007) Accomplishing Identity in Bilingual Interaction. Codeswitching Practices among a Group of Multiethnic Japanese Teenagers. PhD thesis, University of Southern Queensland.

——— (2010) Switching Languages, Juggling Identities. A Sequence of Multilingual, Multi-party Talk. *Pragmatics and Language Learning* 12: 43–65.

Gumperz, John J. (1982) *Discourse Strategies*. Cambridge: Cambridge University Press.

Heinrich, Patrick (2017) New Presentations of Self in Everyday Life. Linguistic Transgressions in England, Germany and Japan. In: *Identity and Dialect Performance*. Reem Bassiouney (ed.), 381–407. London: Routledge.

Hiramoto, Mie (2009) Slaves Speak Pseudo-Tōhoku-ben. The Representation of Minorities in the Japanese Translation of Gone with the Wind. *Journal of Sociolinguistics* 13(2): 249–263.

Inoue, Miyako (2003) Speech without a Speaking Body. "Japanese Women's Language" in Translation. *Language & Communication* 23(3): 315–330.

Iwasaki, Shoichi (2015) A Multiple-grammar Model of Speakers' Linguistic Knowledge. *Cognitive Linguistics* 26(2): 161–210.

Iwata, Yuko (2011) The Invisible Mother. Gender Socialization in a Bilingual Family. In: *Proceedings of the 6th Biennial International Gender and Language Conference*. Claire Maree and Kyoko Satoh (eds.), 138–149. Tokyo: Tsuda College.

Kim, Miseon (2003) Majiriau kotoba – zainichi korian issei no konyō kōdo ni tsuite [Mixed Language. Mixed Behavior among First Generation Koreans in Japan]. *Gengo* 32(6): 46–52.

Kinsui, Satoshi (2003) *Vācharu nihongo – yakuwarigo no nazo* [*Virtual Japanese. The Mystery of Role Language*]. Tokyo: Iwanami.

Kwak, Eun-Sim (2013) Kannichi bairingaru no kōdo suitchingu ni kansuru kenkyū [A Study on Code Switching among Korean-Japanese Bilinguals]. PhD thesis, Chung-Ang University (South Korea).

Maher, John C. (2005) Metroethnicity, Language, and the Principle of Cool. *International Journal of the Sociology of Language* 175/176: 83–102.

Myers-Scotton, Carol (1993) *Social Motivations for Codeswitching. Evidence from Africa*. Oxford: Clarendon Press.

——— (1997) *Duelling Languages. Grammatical Structure in Codeswitching*. Oxford: Oxford University Press.

Nakamizu, Ellen (2000) Zainichi burajirujin jakunensō ni okeru nigengo heiyō [Bilingual Language Use among Young Brazilians in Japan]. In: *20seiki firudo gengogaku no kiseki – Tokugawa Munemasa sensei tsuito kinen ronbunshū*. Hen'i Riron Kenkyūkai (ed.), 67–77. Tokyo: Hen'i Riron Kenkyūkai.

——— (2003) Kōdo kirikae o hikiokosu no wa nani ka [What Triggers Behavioral Switches?]. *Gengo* 32(6): 53–61.

Nakamura, Momoko (2013) *Honyaku ga tsukuru nihongo – hiroin wa "onna kotoba" o hanashitsuzukeru.* [*Japanese Made Through Translation. Heroines Continue to Speak "Women's Language"*]. Tokyo: Hakutakusha.

Nanba, Kazuhiko (2014) Kōdo suitchingu – gengogakuteki sokumen [Codeswitching. Linguistic Aspects]. In: *Bairingarizumu nyūmon*. Masayo Yamamoto (ed.), 115–133. Tokyo: Taishūkan.

Nishimura, Miwa (1995) A Functional Analysis of Japanese/English Code-switching. *Journal of Pragmatics* 23(2): 157–181.

——— (1997) *Japanese/English Code-switching*. New York: Peter Lang.

Ochs, Elinor (1992) Indexing Gender. In: *Rethinking Context. Language as an Interactive Phenomenon*. Alessandro Duranti and Charles Goodwin (eds), 335–358. Cambridge: Cambridge University Press.

Okamoto, Shigeko and Janet S. Shibamoto-Smith (2016) *The Social Life of the Japanese Language*. Cambridge: Cambridge University Press.

Okamura, Hyoue (2013) "Konketsu" o meguru gensetsu – kindai nihon jisho ni arawareru sono dōigo o chūshin ni [Discourses on "konketsu". With Focus on Synonyms in Modern Japanese Dictionaries]. *Intercultural Studies Review (Kokusai bunkagaku)* 26: 22–47.

——— (2016) "Hāfu" o meguru gensetsu – kenkyūsha ya shiensha no chojutsu o chūshin ni [Discourses of "hāfu". With a Focus on Writings of its Researchers and Supporters]. In: *Jinshu shinwa o kaitai suru* [*Dismantling the Race Myth*] (volume 3). Kohei Kawashima and Yasuko Takezawa (eds), 37–67. Tokyo: University of Tokyo Press.

Otsuji, Emi and Alistair Pennycook (2010) Metrolingualism. Fixity, Fluidity and Language in Flux. *International Journal of Multilingualism* 7(3): 240–254.

Pennycook, Alistair and Emi Otsuji (2015) *Metrolingualism. Language in the City*. London: Routledge.

Poplack, Shana (1980) Sometimes I'll Start a Sentence in Spanish Y TERMINO EN ESPAÑOL. Towards a Typology of Code-switching. *Linguistics* 18: 581–618.

Rampton, Ben (1995) *Crossing. Language and Ethnicity Among Adolescents*. London: Longman.

——— (1997) Cross-talk and Language Crossing. Indian English, Interactional Sociolinguistics and Late Modernity. *Southern African Journal of Applied Language Studies* 5(2): 1–20.

——— (1999) Crossing. *Journal of Linguistic Anthropology* 9(1/2): 54–56.

Sadanobu, Toshiyuki (2011) *Nihongo shakai nozoki kyara kuri* [*Characters in the World of Japanese Language*]. Tokyo: Sanseidō.

Taka, Fumiaki (2015) *Reishizumu o kaibō suru – zainichi korian e no henken to intānetto* [*Analyzing Racism. The Internet and Prejudices against Zainichi Koreans*]. Tokyo: Keisō Shobō.

Tanaka, Yukari (2011) *Hōgen kosupure no jidai* [*The Age of Dialect Cosplay*]. Tokyo: Iwanami.

The Economist (2013) "The Economist Explains. How Did a Japanese Anime Film Set a Twitter Record?" In: *The Economist* (13 August). Available online at: www.economist.com/the-economist-explains/2013/08/20/how-did-a-japanese-anime-film-set-a-twitter-record (accessed 14 May 2017).

Woolard, Katheryn A. (2004) Codeswitching. In: *A Companion to Linguistic Anthropology*. Alessandro Duranti (ed.), 73–94. Malden: Blackwell.

Yamashita, Rika (2014) Mosuku kyōshitsu ni okeru zainichi pakisutanjin jidō no kōdo suitchingu [Code Switching in a Mosque School Classroom by Pakistani Pupils in Japan]. *The Japanese Journal of Language in Society* 17(1): 61–76.

——— (2016) *Zainichi pakisutanjin jidō no tagengo shiyō – kōdo suitchingu to sutairu shifuto no kenkyū* [*Multilingualism of Pakistani Children in Japan. A Study of Code Switching and Style Shift*]. Tokyo: Hitsuji Shobō.

Yoshida, Sachi (2005) Nigengo no nōryoku to kōdo suitchingu – kankoku-kei minzoku gakkō no kōkōsei o taishō to shite. [Bilingual Proficiency and Code Switching Patterns among South Korean High School Students in Japan] *Japanese Journal of Language in Society* 8(1): 43–56.

15
LANGUAGE AND SOCIAL RELATIONS

Zi Wang

Introduction

Language is pervasive in our human world of social activities. Our acts of using language entail not only aspects of writing and speaking for simple communication, but also to do something and be someone (Austin 1962; Gee 2014). Language use is thus a social behavior as it constitutes social actions and identities, as well as enacting social relations among interlocutors (Searle 2010). Although languages and societies differ in the ways in which such interactions among language, identities and social relations occur, the underlying mechanisms apply, and the Japanese language is no exception. So, how does the Japanese language constitute social actions and relations? First and foremost, it should be noted that there exists no overarching, identifiable field of study in Japanese sociolinguistics in this regard. Since the early post-war days of formal linguistic research, disparate studies anchored in several major research pillars contributed to our understanding of the linguistic construction of social relations in Japan. In this chapter, I review developments across various periods and strands of (socio)linguistic research on the Japanese language and its "social life", focusing on different aspects of language use and the bringing into existence of diverse types of social relations. First, I iterate the pervasiveness of the linguistic constitution of social relations in the Japanese language. Then, I discuss the modern origins of Japanese sociolinguistic research and identify the different research foci that brought about the connection between language use and the construction of social identities and relations. In the process, I trace the dominant research approaches and methodologies in the Japanese sociolinguistic scene, the emergence of ethnomethodology and discourse analysis in western literature, and their inroad into Japanese sociolinguistics. I supplement this discussion with recent studies that have incorporated theoretical and methodological aspects of social constructionism, ethnomethodology and discourse analysis in order to demonstrate that a much wider perspective could be adopted than has hitherto been the case in Japanese sociolinguistics.

In this chapter, I call the practice of using language to enact social identities and relations "discursive practice/strategy". Here, the term "discourse" is understood as instances of spoken and written language use. However, the aim of this chapter is to provide an overview of Japanese sociolinguistics in the study of language use and the constitution of social relations. Therefore, I will not delve into surveying the development of "discourse analysis", although parts of its research agenda overlap with and inform sociolinguistics, in which case due mention will be given.

The linguistic constitution of social relations: Discursive practices, social constructionism and the Japanese language

It has been established that the Japanese social hierarchical system is well encoded in the language, be it in the grammar of forms of address or in the different ways of utilizing honorifics (Mühlhäusler and Harré 1990). If fine social distinctions between speakers are overtly expressed in language choice (Mühlhäusler and Harré 1990), then the appropriate language use by interlocutors is the constitution of social relationships between them in an interaction (Jørgensen and Phillips 2002). Since sociolinguistics can be broadly conceived as the study of social functions and significance of speech factors, i.e., the interaction and intersection of language and society (Paulston and Tucker 2003; Reisigl 2013), the examination of language use (as discursive practice) and its constitution of social relations should occupy a central place in the research agenda. This could in turn contribute to our understanding of how language use acts to ascribe meanings to physical facts to turn them into social facts, thus bringing into being the social world of identities and relations, as well as how changes in discursive practices facilitate social change. To achieve this, we need to adopt a social constructionist perspective on language and society. Although there is no single description that could fully define all approaches of social constructionism, there does exist a kind of "family resemblance" (Burr 2003: 2), or "common tenets" adopted by researchers engaged in social constructionist works (Fairhurst and Grant 2010: 173). That is, all are critical of taken-for-granted knowledge and recognize that our knowledge of the world is not an objective reflection of the world "out there" but is a product of how we categorize the world. Such products of knowledge are created and maintained by social processes, in particular, social interactions. Hence, with the above-mentioned premises, social constructionism argues that people use language in interactions to constitute taken-for-granted social facts by representing natural or physical facts with ascribed meanings. Such social facts (of which various types of social relations and identities are a major element) constitute the constructed social worlds which are then experienced by people as objectivized and pre-given (Berger and Luckmann 1990[1966]; Burr 2003; Fairhurst and Grant 2010). Thus, social constructionist research has, as the focus of inquiry, social interactions and above all the use of language. The following sections survey origins and developments of Japanese sociolinguistics, reveal the emergence of research informed by and/or reflecting social constructionist thoughts, and put contemporaneous western sociolinguistics into perspective.

From language life to sociolinguistics: Early theoretical origins

Before sociolinguistics established itself as a branch of scientific inquiry in the West, scholars in Japan had already been examining language in its social context under the label of *gengo seikatsu* (language life) since the pre-World War Two era. Although the research agenda of "language life" lacked clearly defined paradigms, research objects and methodologies, it nonetheless espoused an important and relevant perspective in this nascent age of Japanese language studies – language should be seen as a part of (human) life (Heinrich 2002). This implied an acknowledgement of the social nature of language, and a recognition that concrete instances of Japanese language use by individual speakers should be the central focus of research. With the above-mentioned perspective notwithstanding, research in this orientation did not bear much fruit in the early years. In this section, I explain the reason for this apparent lack of fruition and discuss subsequent research developments that dealt with the issue of language use and social relations in the post-war years.

The main theoretical framework under "language studies" up until the early post-war years was proposed by Tokieda Motoki (1941), who viewed language use as acts of perception and expression. In this paradigm, language should not be detached from the individual speaker and studies of language use should also focus on the physical and psychological sides on the part of interlocutors. Theoretical works investigating the speaker subject, addressee and communication contexts emerged in the 1940s and 1950s under this dominant framework. However, before they could gain a foothold in the academic tradition of "language life", the momentum stopped in the 1960s after Tokieda passed away. At the same time, the empirical tradition of language research developed at and practiced by the National Language Research Institute (henceforth, NLRI) began to gain wider acceptance (Heinrich 2002).

The age of empirical research: Data revealing the constitutive nature of language on social relations

It was also in the post-war years at the NLRI that saw the introduction of statistical methods into Japanese linguistics (Heinrich 2002). Some attribute this to influences from American structural linguistics with a positivist approach focusing on large-scale sampling, hypotheses formulation and testing, as well as a reliance on quantitative analytical methods (Sibata 1999). Such a natural science-like research methodology has been a cornerstone of the different sub-areas of sociolinguistics research at least until the 1990s and early 2000s. Often conducted without a clearly defined supporting theoretical and conceptual framework, data collected through these methods nonetheless pointed toward the ways in which language could have been used by speakers to construct social relations (though initial research aims were different). In what follows, I examine some of these results from various research foci.

Language standardization

An early achievement in the study of language use and social relations came from a survey project in one of the designated sub-fields of Japanese sociolinguistics, that of language standardization. The survey in question was the second phase (conducted in 1971) of a 20-year project by the NLRI. First launched in 1951, the large-scale project aimed to survey phonetic and phonological variables in the Tsuruoka local speech in Yamagata Prefecture, with respect to the standard variants based on the Japanese used in the Kanto region. The second phase of the study was primarily meant to explore diachronic changes among original respondents, but researchers found out that speakers could be classified into two groups in regard to standardization: (1) those who used a combination of standard forms and dialects in most contexts, and (2) those who used standard forms and dialects distinctively in different situations (Shibamoto 1987). The significance of this finding is that one could speculate the existence of a relationship between speaker identity and strategies for language use. This was, therefore, one of the first empirical results in post-war Japanese sociolinguistics that revealed the active nature of human agency in discursive practices and the constitution of social identities under corresponding social circumstances. Unfortunately, the respective backgrounds of speakers who fell into these two groups of language users were not recorded, and nor were the contexts in which such strategies were used, so that speculations could not be turned into concrete sociolinguistic generalizations (Shibamoto 1987).

Honorifics research

In addition to language standardization research, the field of honorifics research also saw a series of studies which explored various aspects of language use and social relations in Japanese sociolinguistics. A pioneering and influential figure is Sibata Takesi, who published a series of articles – both theoretical/conceptual and empirical – in the late 1970s (some of the studies mentioned had been conducted at even earlier dates).[1] In an article entitled "The Language Life of the Japanese" (1977), Sibata advanced the argument that honorific usage was a linguistic apparatus employed by interlocutors to underpin the in-out (*uchi-soto*) distinction among them (Sibata 1999). Seen in this light, honorifics were considered by Sibata as discursive practices of speakers to construct social distance, and by extension, enact interpersonal relations.

In another conceptual paper on "Honorifics and Honorifics Research" (1979), Sibata discussed the concept of "treatment" among interlocutors, that is, the idea that speakers *treat* superiors or strangers and inferiors and intimates as such by using linguistic devices of different forms (the respective endings of *de gozaimasu, desu* and *da*). Instead of labeling them as polite (as part of honorifics) and plain forms, Sibata proposed to call them "treatment words", which are defined as "special linguistic forms used differently according to the social and psychological distances existing between listeners, third parties and the speaker" (Sibata 1999: 92). By extension, the linguistic behavior of speakers' utilization of such forms was referred to as "treatment behavior". In this regard, Sibata's works find resonance in those of western social theorists and philosophers of language such as Austin (1962), Searle (2010) and Parker and Sedgwick (1995), in pointing out that certain types of utterances under certain circumstances are also performing actions (of treating someone as a superior, stranger, inferior or intimate). In addition, insofar as the use of the "treatment words" to create social distances among interlocutors is concerned, similarities are also found in the western discourse-analytic perspective which posited that to say something (i.e., to use language) is also to do (i.e., to perform an action) and to be (i.e., to take on an identity) (Gee 2014). A culmination of honorifics research in the 1970s and 1980s focusing on interpersonal relations was presented by Ide (1982). She concluded that there were three basic rules that determined politeness in Japanese speech: (1) be polite to people of higher social status, (2) be polite to people of power, and (3) be polite to elderly people. However, these three rules succumb to the imperative that one should always be polite in formal situations, implying that, for instance, a more powerful and older superior should in effect be polite to his younger inferior at the latter's wedding ceremony. Though not explicitly expressed this way, Ide's research has, in essence, underscored the dialectical relationship between discursive language use and social contexts, identities and relations, and how they co-construct, constitute and shape each other. Taken together, these works were among the first to contain social constructionist elements in post-war Japanese sociolinguistics.

Meanwhile, the NLRI (whose name changed to the "National Institute for Japanese Language" in 2001, and from 2009 has been officially known as the "National Institute for Japanese Language and Linguistics", or NINJAL for short) continued to conduct large-scale empirical surveys.[2] Such large-scale sampling, as is characteristic of many projects carried out by the NLRI, displayed rich *descriptive power*: the data show not only the linguistic strategies employed by speakers to enact social identities and relations, but also variations in such strategies across regional, age, and gender groups. On the other hand, however, the *explanatory power* of this kind of study is limited in the sense that we cannot tell from such data the specific social circumstances under which diverse types of social relations and identities come into play, or the profiles of the actors involved, nor their rationale for selecting particular discursive strategies.

The emergence of discourse analytic and ethnomethodological approaches in the West and their inroad into Japanese sociolinguistics

The aforementioned inadequacies are, in fact, not peculiar to Japanese sociolinguistics in the study of language use and social relations. In western academia, turning points and concomitant methodological innovations emerged only with the advent of the "third wave" of variationist sociolinguistics (for a concise overview, refer to Eckert 2012). In essence, this was represented by a transition "from a view of variation as a reflection of social identities and categories to the linguistic practice in which speakers place themselves in the social landscape through stylistic practice" (Eckert 2012: 93–94). This also signaled the beginning of sociolinguistics research on language use and social relations and identities. The concept of "human agency" was recognized as having an important role in speech, that is, the idea that speakers actively use language in a variety of ways (as discursive practices) to foreground and background a multitude of identities and establish social relations.

Since the early stages in this "third wave" in the West, scholars who were interested in language and social relations in society (which almost invariably involved the notion of power and power relations) have made contributions under the general label of discourse analysis, whose present form comprises an increasing number of approaches, and within some approaches, sub-branches.[3] In most sociolinguistics literature, "discourse" is considered as language use in social contexts, and by extension, "discourse analysis" as a method to analyze such language use (Reisigl 2013: 68). The initial relationship between discourse analysis and sociolinguistics was one of subordination. Discourse analysis was seen as a method of sociolinguistics, employed to study utterances in social contexts. There are contentions over whether discourse analysis is a sub-branch of sociolinguistics, a research method of sociolinguistics or a research "package" in its own right, encompassing transdisciplinary perspectives, methodologies and research methods. One's perspective on the relationship between discourse analysis and sociolinguistics also varies according to one's own scientific culture as well as which branch of discourse analysis is concerned (Reisigl 2013). As this chapter is not a survey of the development of discourse analysis, it suffices to say that, as far as the present topic at hand is concerned, the critical language study (which later developed into the main branch of critical discourse analysis, CDA) promoted by Fairclough (1988, 1992) drew significant theoretical inspirations from sociolinguistics in the development of a research agenda that not only examines single correlations between language (as in linguistic features like accents) and society, but also, and more importantly, looks for deeper causal relations and not-so-static styles (Reisigl 2013). This approach coincides with the emergence of the third wave of sociolinguistics and brings the connection between language and social relations to the fore – social relations and "objects" have a materiality that is conditioned by human knowledge, and this materiality is influenced by social constructions *performed* by social subjects (Fairclough 2006: 12). To put it differently, language use is regarded as a social practice – the performance of social actions in different contexts – to co-construct identities, power and interpersonal relations.

There exists yet another complementary development, but not originating from (socio) linguistics. In his 1967 work *Studies in Ethnomethodology*, Harold Garfinkel (1991) established ethnomethodology as a field of inquiry in sociology. This conceptual framework offered a new way of dealing with sociological issues – to examine daily routines and activities of social actors by putting the analytical lens on individuals, and to look at the ways in which people knew how to behave and conduct themselves in their respective social roles (Allan 2011; Yamazaki et al. 2006). On the basis of Garfinkel's ethnomethodology, Harvey Sacks developed conversation analysis in the 1960s in order to explore structures and organizations in individuals' conversations and find recurring patterns of social interactions. The development of conversation analysis has enabled ethnomethodologically informed or inspired scientific inquiries to spread beyond the confines of sociology into fields as diverse as anthropology, psychology and (socio)linguistics in the West (Yamazaki et al. 2006).

Such a research landscape in western social sciences in general, and in sociolinguistics in particular, was made possible through a novel combination of theoretical and methodological approaches. Theoretically, this new research approach in the West often entails a certain degree of constructionism and a focus on power relations among social actors constituted in and through talk (discourse). Methodologically, there has been a corresponding shift to qualitative methods aimed at complementing the quantitative methods and their hitherto explicit focus on analyzing language out of its social context. Hence, audio (at times also visual) recording of real-life conversations in a variety of contexts for conversation analysis, participant observation and the gathering and analysis of official written texts and documents have been incorporated into the toolkit of data collection methods.

In Japanese sociolinguistics, however, neither ethnomethodologically informed ethnography nor discourse analysis has been incorporated into the package of research methods prior to the early 2000s (Yukawa and Saito 2004). A handful of works situated in ethnomethodology that utilized conversation analysis did appear in the 1990s. For instance, Nishizaka examined the ways in which being Japanese could be achieved in interactions, and found that cultural identities were "constituted in and through the actual course of the interaction" (Nishizaka 1995: 301). However, such research for the most part was disseminated through non-sociolinguistic academic media and situated either in philosophy or in general sociology. This could have been the main reason for the initial lack of cohesive and comprehensive sociolinguistic studies combining theoretical and empirical traditions (hitherto in "opposition") that would shed light on the discursive construction of social relations and identities of real people's talk in their everyday lives.

Methodological innovations (but research still dispersed in diverse areas)

Even though there has not been an explicitly advocated critical turn in linguistics research in Japan, there still seemed to be a turning point where contrasts to earlier works in Japan, such as those by Sibata, were observed. Concretely, there has been a decreasing reliance on quantification of large data sets and statistical significance in favor of more analytic rigor in smaller, selected settings in the qualitative tradition.

More recently, there has been a surge of foreign scholars in Japan and Japanese researchers trained or based abroad taking up the study of language use as discursive practices in the co-construction of social relations. Such studies usually find a certain degree of conceptual resonance in constructionism and/or ethnomethodology, while adopting rigorous conversation analysis as part of their analytical toolkit. One such study is Backhaus's (2009) paper on "Politeness in Institutional Elderly Care in Japan: A Cross-cultural Comparison" which, albeit with politeness as its main focus, dealt with groups of speakers leading institutionalized ways of life and doing institutional talks. Conflicts arising from diverging institutional roles and delicate changes of social relations between care givers (members of staff) and care receivers (elderly residents) in nursing homes are enacted through linguistic interaction. Conversation analysis is employed to highlight the ways in which linguistic behavior creates social actions and strengthens specific relational roles. Methodologically, Backhaus's (2009) work employed conversation analysis to explore language use and social relations of control and submission in a specific institutional context. This study includes a detailed record of the backgrounds of speakers involved as well as an analysis is also substantiated by the researcher's participant observations in the institutional life of elderly care. The result is not only an illumination on the dynamics of discursive strategies and their construction of social relations and identities, but also de-essentialized culture. Specific forms of institutional talk might find resonance in the same institutional contexts in societies with seemingly different cultures (and languages), thus giving rise to similar discursive strategies of social relation and identity construction.

Also anchored in politeness research, but with an explicit focus on the plain (*da*) and polite (*desu/masu*) forms of talk, Enyo's (2013, 2015) works on meanings and contexts of different Japanese speech styles and the ways in which they construct identities represent some of the latest additions to this field in Japanese sociolinguistics. Speech styles (understood by Sibata as "treatment words") could, depending on contexts, construct interactants' identity along hierarchical orders in a university movie club (Enyo 2013, 2015). Based largely on social constructivism and frame analysis (Goffman 1986), such recent studies gathered real-time, "naturally occurring" conversation data and utilized conversation analysis, much in line with contemporary practices in western literature. In these works, extensive conversation analysis and close observations by the researcher on both the contexts of talk and interlocutors have been used in the research process. As a result, it became possible to move beyond the conventional wisdom that "polite forms" (*desu/masu*) were exclusively used by subordinates to show respect and plain forms (*da*) were used by superiors in return, and show that such forms are not only discursive strategies to index social positions, but also constitute social roles in specific (formal and informal) contexts.

By way of illustration, Enyo (2015) examined language use and the construction of social identities and hierarchical relationships while taking into account biographical information of interlocutors (age, status, functions) and the nature of communication context (official, informal) in a university movie club.

(1)
1 Okada   *nee, ()*   *kon' aida*   *itsu*   *kaet-ta?*
          hey   the other day   when   return-PST
          Hey, hey, ((unclear utterance)) when did [you] leave the other day?

2 Takatoshi *boku*   **des-u** *ka?*
             I(MAS)   COP Q
             Me?

3 Okada   *un,*   *itsu=no*   *ma=ni ka*   *i-na-katta*   *no, tonari-ni.*
          yeah   when=GEN   duration=INE Q   exist-NEG-PST   MODP next=LOC
          Yeah, [you] disappeared [from the seat] next [to me], without [me] knowing when.

4 Takatoshi *hachiji:*   *sugi gurai*   **des-u**   *yo*
             8 o'clock   past about   COP(POL)-MPST   JP
             [It was] a little past 8 o'clock.

(Taken and adapted from Enyo 2015: 352)

In the above Example 1, we can clearly see how the use of the *desu/masu* form of talk constructs the hierarchical relationship between seniors and juniors in Japanese group dynamics. As the author observed, this conversation occurred in an informal context and in a chat between Okada, a graduate student, and Takatoshi, a sophomore from the movie club. In lines 1 and 3, Okada used the plain form in asking a question and making a remark directed toward Takatoshi (see underlined text). In response, Takatoshi answered in both instances (lines 2 and 4) with the *desu/masu* form (see text in bold). This, as Enyo reveals,

> is a prototypical case of non-reciprocal use of speech styles, which would be commonly interpreted as showing their *senpai-kōhai* [senior-junior, ZW][4] relationships. Their contrastive use of sentence-ending forms contributes to the construction of their *senpai-kōhai* relationships.
>
> (Enyo 2015: 352–353)

It is important to bear in mind that these instances are but one possible choice: a similar interaction could well have taken place even if Takatoshi had also used the plain form in response to Okada's questions. The fact that Takatoshi chose to do otherwise reflects his adoption of the *desu/masu* form as a discursive strategy, and the ways in which language use is constitutive of social relations thus become apparent.

In formal contexts, language use can also be constitutive of social identities and relationships, albeit of different natures other than simply to show a hierarchical relationship. This is also well documented in Enyo's study:

(2)
1 Yōhei *ano kontentsu=ga   yowa-i   n   ja na-i   **des-u** ka*.
　　　　um content=NOM weak-NPST NOMLZ COP NEG=NPST COP()POL-NPST Q
　　　　Um, aren't [our plans on] contents [of the event] weak?
2 Hiroshi *(.) yoku yut-te   kure-**mashi-ta**.*
　　　　well say-PCP give-POL-PST
　　　　Well said.

(Taken and adapted from Enyo 2015: 356)

In the excerpt above, Enyo observed that both interlocutors, Yōhei and Hiroshi, are junior students attending a sales meeting in the movie club (Hiroshi acting as the discussion leader). The interaction was examined through Goffman's (1986) concept of frame, i.e., the excerpt above represents the frame of on-stage talk (Enyo 2015). Therefore, when Hiroshi solicited Yōhei's opinion on the weaknesses of the movie club (not shown in the excerpt), the latter formulated a response in the *desu/masu* form. Hiroshi, in turn, replied by positively evaluating this response, also in the *desu/masu* form. This interaction could have taken place in the plain form as well, but both speakers used the *desu/masu* form. This highlights the fact that a discursive strategy has been used by the interlocutors to bring into existence the different identities they had at the moment – as discussion leader for Hiroshi, and as a participant contributing to the discussion for Yōhei. In this sense, their language use enacted the formal relationship between them in the context of an on-stage talk (Enyo 2015).

The collection of data and subsequent analyses with this level of richness and robustness in explanatory power are achieved through a research approach that combines theoretical frameworks (constructivism, framing, etc.) and qualitative methods including participant observation and meticulous conversation analysis. Such studies not only showed the ways in which language use constructs social identities and relations, but even more importantly, how such research could be done. These aforementioned examples by Backhaus (2009) and Enyo (2015) illustrate that, by combining theory and (qualitative) empirical research, what emerges from the data could also be used to refine theory. This no doubt portrays a rather ideal picture of a research package with theoretical, methodological and empirical connection and consistency.

Besides contributions from the study of honorifics, research in language and gender has also provided much momentum in the analysis of language use and the co-construction of identities and interpersonal relations. The works I discuss below all have the explicit research aim of exploring the ways in which language constitutes aspects of the social relationship of gender.

In her book, *Gender, Language, and Culture: A Study of Japanese Television Interview Discourse*, Tanaka (2004) was one of the first to combine sociolinguistic and communication theories of gender, age and the genre of interview discourse, with the specific method of conversation analysis on a limited data scale (contrary to large-scale surveys and studies in the early days). This work "shows how participants interact through language and project their identities as defined by role, age, gender and relationship in the context of the [television] interview" (Tanaka 2004: 1). The research rationale was that conversation analysis would be employed to examine the ways in which interlocutors use language to construct gender identities and relations in the institutional talk of television interviews. However, one weakness in this study was that, as the data analysis progressed, the author seemed to have simply assumed a natural dichotomy of male and female speech and directly assigned some of what she observed in the data to either one of these categories. To cite but one example, on the use of the final particle *no* in questions, the transcript of a section of recorded interview showed a female host using the particle. From this the author concluded that *no* was "a final particle used mainly by women" (Tanaka 2004: 67). Such an essentialization of gender represents the typical research paradigm in the first and second waves of interactional sociolinguistics, though the researcher had set out to locate her research in the third wave in analyzing language use and its constructions of social relations by giving the central role to human agency and interactional contexts rather than pre-determined social categories to which speakers belonged.

The edited volume by Okamoto and Smith (2004: 4) on Japanese language, gender and ideology emphasized "the importance of examining local linguistic practices of real speakers as social agents" and how such practices are context-dependent. Works in this volume, whose broad scope covered areas such as media discourse, farm women discourse, speeches of middle-aged mothers, high schoolers and men from Kanto and Kansai regions, avoided pre-determined and static categorizations of relationships between language and social categories. Rather, they analyzed, from a gender perspective, a "speaker's active involvement in language choice as a performative strategy for creating the desired social context, *in particular identities and relations*" (Okamoto and Smith 2004: 6, emphasis added). This could be seen as adopting a "grounded approach" in that conclusions on how discursive practices co-constructed gender identities and relations were drawn only after having examined actual speech data.

As an example in the edited volume, in Miyazaki's (2004) study of the social worlds of boys and girls in a Japanese junior high school (for pupils aged 13 to 15), interviews in which participants were asked to describe their own and their peers' use or non-use of different types of first person pronouns were conducted and constituted the main source of data. This was further supplemented by the author's observations of the informants' daily interactions. Taken together, the collected data were then used to further the argument that conventional gendered speech is but a set of normative, ideological presuppositions and does not necessarily relate to the gender of a speaker. This is evidenced by the fact that many girls reported the use of a supposedly coarse, manly and other-deprecatory first person pronoun *ore*, while there were cases of a boy reportedly using *atashi*, commonly thought to be a rather feminine pronoun. This study was thus able to reveal the widespread misconceptions on the gendered language use of first person pronouns and the related identity constructions. In terms of data collection methods,

Miyazaki (2004) also relied on interviews with informants to gather self-reported language use and their perceived interpersonal relations. A word of caution on this is that, researchers seeking to employ this method should be aware of potential problems in self-reported language use. In these instances, people think through carefully before they respond, whereas in actual linguistic and social interactions, speakers hardly go through the same process of reflection before uttering something. Reliance on self-reported language use as the main data source should always be qualified, and if possible, accompanied by supplementary verification methods like participant observation, just like Miyazaki (2004) did.

In yet another study (not specifically situated in any sociolinguistic research focus) that examined the discursive construction of hierarchical social relationships between senior and junior secondary school club members, a combination of participant observation, recordings, and interviews was used (Wang 2018). The data revealed similar patterns across the different clubs observed in that the ways in which people addressed each other form an important constituent part of the relationships between them. Wang observed that, no matter which school/club, a junior member was always expected to, and did, address his/her seniors with the suffixes *-senpai* or *-san*. Subsequent recordings further illustrated that the juniors' use of such polite suffixes was accompanied by their use of *desu/masu* forms of talk and other aspects of honorific language to varying degrees (Wang 2018). This was almost never reciprocated by seniors, unless in on-stage, official talk (not unlike Enyo 2015's findings). Because of the qualitative nature of this study, it is easy to answer the question of "who uses what kind of language to whom, when, and why?", i.e., to place data in the social contexts in which they occurred. More interestingly, informants also revealed in interviews that they used such respectful language not only when talking to their seniors, but also when talking *about* them (Wang 2018). This represents yet another stark illustration of the ways in which language use constitutes social relations.

These works arguably represent the state of the art in this field in Japanese sociolinguistics, in that they build on established concepts ("treatment words" and human agency in language use) and adopt meticulous conversation analysis and observations in their empirical studies of various aspects of the discursive construction of social relations. Taken together, such existing studies, as mentioned thus far, facilitate our understanding of language use and social relations in a variety of contexts, and at times even with cross-national perspective.

Another achievement is that a majority of Japanese and foreign academic staff based in Japan, as well as Japanese scholars based abroad, have been publishing most of their works in the English language (Gottlieb 2010). Evidently, this also includes works related to this field, thus making the existing literature extremely accessible to an international audience. This fact alone is commendable as it is not always the case in non-English language academic cultures.

However, comprehensive and organized works, such as those cited above, still represent a minority within this field. More often than not, published works in this area, especially (but not exclusively) those originally published in Japanese, are either solely theoretical or solely empirical. A quick survey of Japanese publications on discourse analysis and discursive constructions of social relations reveal studies that remain largely on the theoretical and conceptual level. For instance, some recent works such as those by Hayashi (2008) – *Approaches to Discourse Analysis: Theory and Practice* – simply explained different aspects of studying discursive practices in social contexts, at most with very short extracts of fictive or second-hand, often out-of-context data. On the other hand, surveys by the National Institute for Japanese Language and Linguistics (Kokuritsu Kokugo Kenkyūjo 2002) on honorifics did reveal the tendency to use honorifics as a part of discursive practice to enact social relations, but they were of a purely empirical nature with virtually no theoretical foundations or efforts in theory-building; and this is despite the existence of theoretical and conceptual works such as those by Sibata (1999) and Ide (1982). The issue at hand is not so much that there should not be purely theoretical discussions or purely empirical surveys on language use and social relations, but rather that the disconnect between theory and empirics in many publications means that very few works have actually been able to demonstrate how to study discursive practices and the construction of social relations. This trend hampers further development in both theoretical advancements and empirical methods in the field in Japanese sociolinguistics.

Outlook

Despite the aforementioned solid foundations on the theoretical and conceptual levels of language use and the construction of social relations, as well as recent works with much analytic rigor, there still remain several lacunae which should be filled by future research. These could be further divided into two broad and related categories: (1) content-based research and (2) institutional and organizational improvements.

In terms of theoretical perspectives, methodology and research aims, it has been observed that most of the existing works to date are situated within the trinity of "standard language-gender-honorifics". While the aim here is not to discourage such practices in future research, what is at stake is the fact that, by adhering to rigid research frameworks set out in post-war sociolinguistic research, and by trying to (forcefully) locate research on discursive constructions of social relations in one or more of the topics under the above-mentioned research framework, one risks missing out on the "broader picture" of language use in society at large and its dynamic constitutions of social relations. How are relations and hierarchy played out in institutional contexts such as police interrogations, doctor-patient interactions and job interviews? And what about in informal conversations among intimate family members and friends? If we divert our attention away from the dominant research agenda in Japanese sociolinguistics, could we still study language use and its construction of social relations? A dearth of theoretically founded empirical work in these areas suggests that more interaction and cooperation among scholars from the separate disciplines of sociolinguistics, sociology and those with an interest in discourse analysis are not just desired, but also needed. This would not only advance the present state of research, but also produce works that show, in a systematic manner, how one could actually study the discursive constructions of social relations.

In order for the above-mentioned development to take place, changes at the institutional and organizational levels are necessary. The three relevant established associations, namely the Japan Association of Sociolinguistic Sciences (JASS), the Pragmatics Society of Japan (PSJ) and the Japanese Association for Ethnomethodology and Conversation Analysis, could, for example, initiate winter/summer schools for graduate students, propose degree-granting programs in discourse and society, and launch interdisciplinary journals or conferences, by collaborating with each other and with universities. As mentioned earlier, ethnography and discourse analysis have only recently made inroads into the methodological scene of Japanese sociolinguistic inquiry. This should be further promoted, because new methodological developments consisting of a combination of ethnographic and variationist techniques would pave the way for a continued and sustained development in theoretical and empirical innovations.

List of transcription conventions

(.)   unmeasured micropause
()   unclear utterance
(()) commentary

[]   omitted elements from translation
:   sound stretch
?   rising intonation
,   continuation of tones, such as slightly rising intonation
.   falling intonation (full stop)

Notes

1 A collection with annotations was published in Sibata (1999), all articles cited here are from this volume.
2 For instance, see Kokuritsu Kokugo Kenkyūjo (2002) for a survey of honorifics in schools, with thousands of respondents from Tokyo, Osaka and Yamagata revealing how they felt the need to mind their language and expressions in interactional contexts such as extracurricular club activities where status asymmetry existed.
3 For an overview of broadly defined discourse approaches, refer to Jørgensen and Phillips (2002). For a fine overview of how a single approach of critical discourse analysis could be further sub-divided, refer to Reisigl (2013). Note, however, that these are by no means the only ways to classify the approaches.
4 The terms *senpai* and *kōhai* refer to seniors and juniors respectively. In this context, seniority is largely defined by age and experience in the university movie club, and the asymmetrical status is manifested through different forms of talk.

References

Allan, Kenneth (2011) *Contemporary Social and Sociological Theory. Visualizing Social Worlds* (second edition). Thousand Oaks: Pine Forge.
Austin, John L. (1962) *How to Do Things with Words*. Oxford: Oxford University Press.
Backhaus, Peter (2009) Politeness in Institutional Elderly Care in Japan. A Cross-cultural Comparison. *Journal of Politeness Research. Language, Behaviour, Culture* 5(1): 53–71.
Berger, Peter L. and Thomas Luckmann (1990[1966]) *The Social Construction of Reality. A Treatise in the Sociology of Knowledge*. New York: Anchor Books.
Burr, Vivien (2003) *Social Constructionism* (second edition). London: Routledge.
Cave, Peter (2004) Bukatsudo. The Educational Role of Japanese School Clubs. *The Journal of Japanese Studies* 30(2): 383–415.
Eckert, Penelope (2012) Three Waves of Variation Study. The Emergence of Meaning in the Study of Sociolinguistic Variation. *Annual Review of Anthropology* 41(1): 87–100.
Enyo, Yumiko (2013) Exploring senpai-kōhai Relationships in Club Meetings in a Japanese University. PhD thesis, Department of Linguistics, University of Hawai'i at Manoa.
——— (2015) Contexts and Meanings of Japanese Speech Styles. A Case of Hierarchical Identity Construction among Japanese College Students. *Pragmatics* 25(3): 345–367.
Fairclough, Norman (1988) *Language and Power*. Harlow: Longman.
——— (1992) *Discourse and Social Change*. Cambridge: Polity Press.
——— (2006) *Language and Globalization*. London: Routledge.
Fairhurst, Gail T. and David Grant (2010) The Social Construction of Leadership. A Sailing Guide. *Management Communication Quarterly* 24(2): 171–210.
Garfinkel, Harold (1991) *Studies in Ethnomethodology. Social and Political Theory*. Cambridge: Polity Press.
Gee, James P. (2014) *An Introduction to Discourse Analysis. Theory and Method* (fourth edition). Abingdon: Routledge.
Goffman, Erving (1986) *Frame Analysis. An Essay on the Organization of Experience* (revised edition). Boston: Northeastern University Press.
Gottlieb, Nanette (2010) Sociolinguistics in Japan. In: *The Routledge Handbook of Sociolinguistics around the World*. Martin J. Ball (ed.), 89–97. London: Routledge.
Hayashi, Takuo (2008) *Danwa bunseki no apurōchi – riron to jissen* [*Approaches to Discourse Analysis. Theory and Practice*]. Tokyo: Kenkyūsha.
Hebert, David G. (2012) *Wind Bands and Cultural Identity in Japanese Schools*. Dordrecht: Springer.
Heinrich, Patrick (2002) Gengo seikatsu. The Study of Language Life in Japan, 1945–1995. *Historiographia Linguistica* 29(1): 95–119.

Ide, Sachiko (1982) Japanese Sociolinguistics. Politeness and Women's Language. *Lingua* 57: 357–85.

Jørgensen, Marianne and Louise Phillips (2002) *Discourse Analysis as Theory and Method*. London: SAGE.

Kokuritsu Kokugo Kenkyūjo (2002) *Gakkō no naka no keigo 1 – ankēto chōsa-hen* [*Honorifics in Japanese Schools 1. Results from Questionnaires*]. Tokyo: Sanseidō.

Miyazaki, Ayumi (2004) Japanese Junior High School Girls' and Boys' First-person Pronoun Use and their Social World. In: *Japanese Language, Gender, and Ideology. Cultural Models and Real People*. Shigeko Okamoto and Janet Shibamoto-Smith (eds), 256–274. Oxford: Oxford University Press.

Mühlhäusler, Peter and Rom Harré (1990) *Pronouns and People. The Linguistic Construction of Social and Personal Identity*. Oxford: Blackwell.

Nishizaka, Aug (1995) The Interactive Constitution of Interculturality. How to be a Japanese with Words. *Human Studies* 18(2/3): 301–326.

Okamoto, Shigeko and Janet Shibamoto-Smith (eds) (2004) *Japanese Language, Gender, and Ideology. Cultural Models and Real People*. Oxford: Oxford University Press.

Parker, Andrew and Eve K. Sedgwick (1995) *Performativity and Performance*. New York: Routledge.

Paulston, Christina B. and Richard G. Tucker (2003) *Sociolinguistics. The Essential Readings*. Malden: Blackwell.

Reisigl, Martin (2013) Critical Discourse Analysis. In: *The Oxford Handbook of Sociolinguistics*. Robert Bayley, Richard Cameron and Ceil Lucas (eds), 67–90. Oxford: Oxford University Press.

Searle, John R. (2010) *Making the Social World. The Structure of Human Civilization*. Oxford: Oxford University Press.

Shibamoto, Janet S. (1987) Japanese Sociolinguistics. *Annual Review of Anthropology* 16: 261–278.

Sibata, Takesi (1999) *Sociolinguistics in Japanese Contexts* (translated, edited and introduced by Tetsuya Kunihiro, Fumio Inoue and Daniel Long). Berlin: Mouton de Gruyter.

Tanaka, Lidia (2004) *Gender, Language and Culture. A Study of Japanese Television Interview Discourse*. Amsterdam: John Benjamins.

Tokieda, Motoki (1941) *Kokugogaku genron* [*A Course in Linguistics of the National Language*]. Tokyo: Iwanami.

Wang, Zi (2018) Understanding Japanese Society. An Ethnographic Study of the Discursive Construction of Hierarchy in Japanese School Clubs. PhD thesis, Duisburg-Essen University.

Yamazaki, Kei'ichi, Kawajima Rie and Kuyuoka Hideaki (2006) "Esunomesodorojīteki na kenkyū o ikani okonauka [How to Conduct Ethnomethodological Research]. *Human Interface* 8 (4): 223–228.

Yukawa, Sumiyuki and Masami Saito (2004) Cultural Ideologies in Japanese Language and Gender Studies. A Theoretical Review. In: *Japanese Language, Gender, and Ideology. Cultural Models and Real People*. Shigeko Okamoto and Janet Shibamoto-Smith (eds), 23–37. Oxford: Oxford University Press.

16
POLITENESS

Yasuko Obana

Introduction

Politeness exists in every speech community. It is customarily defined as a tool for smooth and conflict-free communication, which conforms to its etymology in Latin, *polit-us*, meaning "polished, refined", or *polire*, meaning "to smooth, to polish" (the Oxford English Dictionary). This definition of "politeness" encompasses much broader ranges of social actions than we expect because it not only includes the good manners and refined behavior we find in an etiquette book, but also refers to other acts aimed at smooth communication such as swear words among close buddies to strengthen their bond, mock impoliteness or teasing to a close friend to display their solidarity and even imperatives that demand the other to act willingly (e.g., "Marry me!" or "Kiss me!"). Politeness also refers to linguistic as well as non-verbal features, e.g., *aizuchi* (back channel cues), body language, dress code and so on. It is culture-specific, and even within the same culture it differs from one social group to another. Furthermore, politeness is not a set of prescribed rules. A recent trend in politeness research advocates that politeness is not a static product but a result of discursive effects in given contexts and with listeners' judgments; thus, the same utterance may be judged as polite or impolite, depending on its contexts and the listener's stance. The discursive approach was initiated by Eelen (2001), and followed by Watts (2003), Mills (2003) and Locher and Watts (2005), among others. To this extent, politeness includes all sorts of social interactions that maintain our interpersonal relationships.

The above-mentioned applies to all languages, and Japanese is no exception. Mention of Japanese politeness immediately calls to mind honorifics or *keigo*. Due to its formal and conventionalized image, *keigo* is often considered "ritualistic" (e.g., Ide 2006; Kádár 2013; Kádár and Mills 2013). However, a closer look at honorific phenomena in reality reveals that honorifics can be manipulated, and may dynamically change in accordance with given contexts and the interactants' stances, enhancing the quality of communication. In this chapter, I discuss the characteristics of honorifics, first, their status in pragmatic principles, and second, their effective manipulation in interaction. I then go on to discuss how politeness strategies are built up in the world of honorifics. I call such strategies "honorific strategies". Honorifics do not contribute to the semantic content of an utterance but rather function as merely "indexing" a social or psychological distance. In other words, they function as the grammatical conversion of what has already been strategically constructed, and it is honorific strategies that contribute to designing the linguistic architecture and the content of an utterance. Therefore, it is worth introducing examples of honorific strategies by comparing them with English politeness strategies. Honorific strategies in many ways conform to one's *tachiba* (literally, one's "standing-place") (Obana 2009; Haugh and Obana 2011), while English politeness strategies primarily aim at "face-saving" as claimed by Brown and Levinson (1978, 1987).

Since this chapter is about "politeness", I do not discuss other effects of honorific use such as showing conflict, anger, "irony" (Okamoto 1999) and the speaker's "weak and vulnerable psychology" (Maynard 2001), which occur at the time of speech level shifts, particularly shifts from plain to *masu/desu* forms, i.e., verb endings changed from plain forms to addressee honorifics. These effects are indeed extracted by taking advantage of the basic nature of honorifics, i.e., distance, in certain contexts; however, they are beyond the scope of this chapter.

Japanese honorifics

This section first attempts to clarify the status of Japanese honorifics in pragmatic principles by reviewing previous studies on honorifics. Second, by examining the origin of honorifics, it illustrates how these forms are preserved and extensively used in modern Japanese. Finally, further dynamic ways of honorific use in modern Japanese are introduced.

The status of Japanese honorifics in pragmatic principles
Honorifics as wakimae

Brown and Levinson's (1978, 1987) groundbreaking face theory enabled "politeness" to become a central topic in pragmatics, sociolinguistics and politeness research and the last three decades has witnessed flourishing discussions as well as vigorous controversies.[1] One of the frequently debated topics is the status of Japanese honorifics. Ide (1989, 1992, 2006), for example, argues against Brown and Levinson's claim that Japanese honorifics constitute negative politeness strategies, and contends that Japanese honorifics are not strategies but social norms to which speakers are obliged to adhere. According to Ide, Brown and Levinson's strategic politeness originates in the speaker's individual choices, i.e., "volition", while honorifics are regulated by *wakimae* (discernment), i.e., "the practice of polite behavior according to social conventions" (Ide 1989: 230).

Ide's *wakimae* was questioned by Eelen (2001) and Kádár and Mills (2013) on the grounds that *wakimae* belongs to "politeness 1", which is "an everyday concept" (Eelen, 2001) or "a second-order folk theoretic concept" (Kádár and Mills 2013). This, the authors claimed, cannot be discussed on the same plane as "volition", which is categorized as "politeness 2", meaning "an academic concept" (Eelen 2001) or "a theoretical concept" (Kádár and Mills, 2013). Thus, it has been questioned whether it is valid to contrast between *wakimae* and volition as Ide claims (e.g., Pizziconi 2003; Kádár and Mills 2013). Furthermore, the concept of *wakimae* is not a unique property of Japanese honorifics, but applies to a variety of social actions regardless of languages (Pizziconi 2003; Obana 2016a, 2017). This is because *wakimae* portrays the appropriate knowledge of social skills one has experienced and learned; in other words, it is proficiency of know-how.[2] This means that Brown and Levinson's (1978, 1987) strategies such as thanking, apologizing and appreciating when used appropriately also constitute a part of *wakimae*. Therefore, *wakimae* is not restricted to honorifics but is relevant to politeness strategies and many other polite behaviors.

Researchers investigating speech level shifts largely support the discursive approach, and thus argue against the *wakimae* approach because "the notion of *wakimae* presupposes a priori given social rules and a static speaker-hearer relationship with no agency being given to the speaker or hearer" (Cook 2011: 3658). Shibamoto-Smith (2011) calls Ide's (2006) idea of Japanese honorifics "Japanese linguistic ideology" and a "static view". Saito (2010: 3272) describes the reality of honorific use as more fluid, noting that "the use of honorifics and plain forms is not strictly informed by social norms or social rules as proposed by scholars such as Ide, but rather their use is more diverse and context-bound, and hence does not only reflect socio-cultural ideology". This view is shared among numerous researchers on speech level shifts, unveiling a variety of socio-pragmatic purposes and meanings honorific terms offer (e.g., Barke 2011; Cook 1996a, b, 1997, 2008, 2011; Geyer 2008; Ikuta 1983; Ishizaki 2000; Makino 2002; Maynard 2001, 2004; Megumi 2002; Okamoto 1999; Saito 2010; Shibamoto-Smith 2011). Therefore, honorifics can be manipulated for effective communication, and their use is quite diverse and volatile.

Honorifics as a negative strategy

Those who support Brown and Levinson's (1978, 1987) categorization of honorifics as a negative politeness strategy share a common view that the use of honorifics creates a certain distance whereby the speaker avoids intervening in the hearer's territory (Chinami 2005; Fukuda and Asato 2004; Kumai 2009; Moriyama 2010; Takiura 2005, 2008; Usami 2001). It is indeed true that honorifics function to create distance, but it does not necessarily follow that they are to be categorized as a negative politeness strategy, because honorifics and Brown and Levinson's strategies have a fundamental difference in the process of construction. That is, honorifics are the grammatically converted (or honorific-marked) forms that have already been strategically constructed; in other words, honorific forms present a double layer in their linguistic architecture (Obana 2016a, 2017). For example,

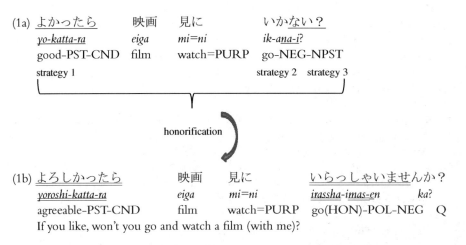

If you like, won't you go and watch a film (with me)?

Utterance (1a) is an invitation to watch a film to a close friend, for instance, expressed through the use of a plain non-past negative verb form *ikanai* ("not go"). It is strategically constructed with *yokattara* ("if you like") as a tentative invitation (strategy 1), -*nai* (not) as a pessimistic hope (strategy 2), and an interrogative for giving options (strategy 3). Utterance (1b), on the other hand, is an invitation to someone the speaker most likely does not know well. Linguistically, it is the conversion of utterance (1a) with honorific markings on *yokattara* yielding *yoroshikattara*, and with plain form *iku* ("to go") converted to its honorific equivalent *irassharu* plus an addressee honorific *-masu* ending. However, the content of utterance (1b) remains the same as that of (1a); that is, the speaker's goal (invitation), the strategies (tentative invitation, pessimistic hope and giving options) to achieve the goal, and the syntactic architecture of the utterance remain exactly the same between utterances (1a) and (1b). This means that utterance (1b) holds a double-layered structure – a strategically constructed unit with honorific markings on it.

Brown and Levinson's (1987) strategies focus on how the content of an utterance may affect the hearer, and how an appropriate strategy is employed to avoid a potential face-threatening act (FTA). Negative politeness strategies are therefore defined as strategies that mitigate potential FTAs because the speaker's goal (e.g., a request) expressed in the content of the utterance potentially threaten the hearer's negative face, i.e., imposes on the hearer's desire for autonomy. By contrast, honorifics or precisely honorific markings are themselves not responsible for the content of an utterance or its potential FTA, nor do they constitute a strategy for FTA mitigation. These arrangements are already completed when constructing the basic structure of an utterance. Honorific markings occur when the speaker measures a social or psychological distance from the hearer; therefore, they function merely as "marking" or "indexing" such a distance (of course, both strategic planning and honorific marking are operationalized at the same time in reality).

I have demonstrated that honorifics, or more precisely honorific markings, serve as the grammatical conversion of what has already been strategically constructed, and pragmatically function to index distance whether it is social or psychological. In spite of their complex and multifarious systems, honorifics never contribute to the semantic content of an utterance, but merely perform as "relation-acknowledging devices" (Matsumoto, 1988). Simply put, they show the other interactant what social (or psychological) relationship one recognizes or intends to have in a given interaction. The next question is where "distance" comes from. The following subsection explains that "distance" is derived from the origin of honorifics. It also illustrates that many pragmatic effects the origin possessed (e.g., enhancing gratitude, showing attentiveness and carefulness) are well preserved in modern Japanese.

The origin of honorifics

In the introduction, the definition of "politeness" was provided; it aims at smooth and conflict-free communication. This means that friendliness, kindness and even swear words can achieve politeness in given contexts. However, the term "to be polite" is not exactly isomorphic between Japanese and English. This term is translated as *reigi tadashii* (respect-ritual correct) and *teinei na* (neat, civil) in Japanese. For example, Ide et al. (1992) report via a questionnaire survey of native speakers of Japanese and English that the Japanese "polite" behavior does not necessarily imply "friendliness", which is commonly accepted as "polite" in English. Obana and Tomoda (1994) also found through interviews with native speakers of English and Japanese that *reigi tadashii* and *teinei na* are strongly associated with the use of *keigo* and accordingly with "aloof interactions, concern for keeping public face and formal settings" (Obana and Tomoda 1994: 47). Pizziconi (2007) confirms the findings above with a more elaborate and extensive survey. This means that the term "politeness" in English covers a much wider range of social actions than its equivalent in Japanese, and that Japanese politeness is predominantly associated with honorific use.[3]

Why then are honorifics closely related to aloofness and formality? It is because honorific use creates "distance" whether it is social or psychological (e.g., Ikuta 1983; Kabaya 2003; Kumai 2003; Takiura 2005), and this can be traced back to the origin of honorifics.

The origin of Japanese honorifics is in the ritual prayers used in the act of praising and worshipping gods and goddesses in animism, which later developed as Shintoism.[4] Asada (2001, 2005, 2014) examined ancient documents and found that the first written honorifics appeared in *norito* (literally, "words of celebration"), a prayer for gods and goddesses. Because people believed gods and goddesses resided in all kinds of sentient and non-sentient things in nature, they created special language (honorifics) to refer to spirits at a higher level, keeping them at a distance, putting them on a pedestal, and deifying them as superior beings. This is because they believed that natural disasters occurred due to gods' and goddesses' wrath, birth and death were in their hands, and happy occasions such as recovery from illness and abundant harvests were their blessings. Thus, honorifics originate in humans' awe of gods and goddesses, but at the same time, honorific use enhanced humans' gratitude, showed their careful approach to gods/goddesses as well as attentiveness with offerings.[5]

Because Shintoism was developed to dignify emperors/empresses as descendants of gods/goddesses, honorific use was extended to human beings, first, to emperors/empresses, and second, to their family members and court nobles. When samurai (members of the warrior class) dominated the society from the thirteenth century onwards, honorifics began to be used more extensively. Over the centuries, complex social classes evolved, which accordingly shaped more elaborate honorifics.

Although honorifics today are quite different in form, style and purpose from those in the past, modern honorifics maintain an original feature that has transcended historic changes – distance. Social status and age differences, which readily prompt honorifics, indicate a social distance. Formal public situations are social settings in which the speaker, whether he/she is older or higher in status than the audience, creates aloofness and hence formality in effect by using honorifics in order to enhance the ceremonial ambience of the occasion. Honorific use toward customers implies that customers are put on a pedestal to avoid *narenareshisa* (too much familiarity); a respectful distance creates a comfortable zone for customers. At the same time, the original purpose of honorific use in Old Japanese still persists when honorifics are used effectively in a given context: treating the other like a god/goddess. This is the reason why higher-ranked people, customers and the audience at a ceremony, upon receiving honorifics, feel they are treated deferentially as if they were deified.

The origin of honorifics in modern Japanese

The origin of honorifics persists in a variety of social practices in modern Japanese. It is not just "distance" that has been preserved, but other emotional motivations such as gratitude, regret, tentativeness and thoughtfulness. These were once directed toward gods and goddesses, and can be displayed in modern Japanese by using honorifics. For example, close friends normally do not use honorifics with each other, but may use honorifics when they show their "profound gratitude", when they "sincerely apologize", when they "tentatively" ask a favor, or when they have to be "careful" in approaching each other. Honorifics used in such situations function as enhancing the speaker's emotion and attitude toward the other.

Obana (2016b) examined 18 pairs of university friends' mobile phone conversations[6] (thus, they use plain forms as the basic speech level), in which one requests that the other to participate in recording their conversation for 20 minutes and informs the other that each participant will receive a book token worth 500 yen as a reward. Obana found that addressee honorifics (*desu/masu* forms as the verb ending) occurred quite frequently when the conversation was related to the request situation.[7] For instance,

(2) JFC05: お願いがあって電話したん<u>ですけど</u> …
o-negai=ga   at-te   denwa shi-ta   n   <u>des-u</u>   kedo …
HON-request=NOM have-PCP phone do-PST   NMLZ   COP(POL)-NPST   but
I wanted to ask you a favor and so contacted you.

              JF – Japanese female,
              C – Correspondent (the person who initially contacted his/her friend)
              05 – File number 5
                                  (Obana 2016b: 269, Japanese writing added)

Utterance (2) is a direct preliminary to the request and contains *desu*, an addressee honorific. The speaker becomes tentative because the subsequent request may inflict a threat, and this triggers the occurrence of *desu* as the speaker's "careful approach" to her friend.

Another example is:

(3) JMC01:<u>よろしくお願いします</u>。
       <u>yorossiku</u>   <u>o-negai</u>   <u>shi-mas-u</u>.
       well   HON-request   do-POL-NPST

    JMR01: はい、分かり<u>まし</u>た。
       hai,   wakar-<u>imashi</u>-ta.
       OK   understand-POL-PST

  JMC01: <u>すみません</u>。
       <u>sum-imasen</u>.
       sorry-POL

       JMC01: Thank you [for your agreement].
       JMR01: OK, I accept [my job].
       JMC01: Thanks.
       JM – Japanese male, R – Respondent (the person who received the call)
                                  (Obana 2016b: 271, Japanese writing added)

Example (3) shows that after JMR01 accepted JMC01's request, JMC01 confirmed the request with the formula, *yoroshiku onegai shimasu*, which follows JMR01's equally formal confirmation, and then JMC01 expressed thanks. The three utterances are all honorific-marked, underlined parts in example (3).

The formulaic *yoroshiku onegai shimasu* is a well-established ritual, here with the meaning "I wish to leave the decision (or the requested job) to you", showing the speaker's humble stance towards the other (Obana 2012b). When this formula is used at the end of the request, it indicates the confirmation of the request and at the same time shows the speaker's gratefulness for the other's acceptance of the request. This gratitude is further enhanced by using the addressee honorific *-masu* form, which implies that the speaker is approaching the other cautiously but in gratitude. This sudden formality led the other to equally responding formally by uttering *hai, wakarimashita*, which gives rise to a ceremonial solemnity as if his promise were an official contract. The last utterance, *sumimasen*, is an apologetic expression, showing gratitude with the feeling of indebtedness (Coulmas 1981), which is quite formal compared with its equivalent *gomen ne* in the abrupt form. The formal expression enhances the speaker's gratitude.

As the examples of honorific use in close relationships above indicate, the origin of honorifics is well preserved in modern Japanese. Honorific use can, if not always, show the speaker's respect and awe toward the other; appreciation, gratitude and tentativeness can therefore be enhanced by using honorifics, i.e., creating a certain distance with honorifics does in fact honor the other with admiration, thoughtfulness or attentiveness.

Role change and honorific change

It is commonly believed that "the appropriate use of Japanese honorifics can signal the speaker's relative rank in a given interaction" as "politeness [...] shows verbally one's sense of place or role in a given situation according to social conventions" (Kádár and Haugh 2013: 21). While this may be true in many conventional and thus predictable situations to which the interactants can readily adjust themselves, there are equally many other situations where one's role or place is not fixed but changes fluidly, bringing on dynamic changes of honorifics (as mentioned earlier, our discussion is limited to politeness with honorific use). In the previous subsection, we have seen effects of honorific use between close friends who normally do not use honorifics, in achieving politeness by showing the speaker's respect and awe to a friend. This subsection looks at examples in which one's role changes cause honorific variations.

A typical example of role changes is when close colleagues, who normally do not use honorifics to each other, may use them at a formal meeting. Obana (2016b) creates the term "task-based roles" to explain that honorifics in the meeting are the implementation of their task-roles as meeting attendees while they are basically close colleagues as their social role-identity (Obana 2012a). Roles are multi-layered and the most suitable role to each situation emerges on the surface, causing speech level changes to suit each situation.

The task-based role above is brought about by a public and formal situation that obliges the colleagues to use honorifics. Task-based roles can also be created by choice. For example, a female interviewer in her late 30s interviewed 23 people aged from 20 to their 70s. Each interview lasted 20 to 30 minutes, extracting information about the interviewee's family members, friends and hobbies. Eight interviewees out of 23 are the interviewer's close friends, and the others were introduced via her friends and parents, so she met them for the first time at the time of the interview. Looking at the transcription of all the interviews, I have noticed that speech levels used by the interviewees are not significantly different whether the interviewees are strangers or close friends to the interviewer. The interviewer could have changed her speech levels according to whom she was facing. However, she and her close friends decided to act formally as public task-based roles throughout the interview (and there was no prior specific instruction as to how interviews should be conducted except for the types of questions the interviewer should make). For example,

(4)
    Ami: XXさんとはよく行き来なさいますか。英語学校以外に。
        XX-san=to=wa   yoku   iki-ki-nasa-imas-u   ka,
        XX-HON=COM=TOP   often   go-come-do(HON)-POL-NPST   Q
        eigo   gakkoo   igai=ni.
        English   school   except=ADV
    Yoko: はい。お近くなの、ご近所なので、よくお顔を会わせますし、あの、何かのおりには、お茶を飲んだりすることもあります。

```
hai.     o-chikaku      na        no,        go-kinjo              na=node,
yes      HON-near       COP       MODP       HON-neighborhood      COP=since
yoku  o-kao=o               awase-mas-u         si, ano, nanika=no     ori=ni=wa,
often HON-face=ACC       meet-POL-NPST       CNJ well some=GEN chance=LOC=TOP
ocha=o          non-dari              su-ru         koto=mo          ar-imas-u.
tea=ACC         drink-for.instance do-NPST          occasion=too     exist-POL-NPST
```

Ami: Do you often see XX outside the English class?
Yoko: Yes. [She lives] nearby. As [we are] neighbors, [we] often bump into [each other], and occasionally [we] have tea together.

Example (4) shows that Ami, the interviewer, is a close friend to Yoko since their college time. As Ami started formally, Yoko responded equally, and never used plain forms or any peer language (*tameguchi*) during the interview. The underlined parts in Yoko's utterance include an honorific prefix (in, *go-kinjo*; *ochikaku nano* was wrong and rephrased as *gokinjo nanode*), formal expressions (*o-kao o awase-*, happen to see; *ori*, chance) and addressee honorifics.[8] Yoko is fully aware of her task-role as an interviewee, and plays her role throughout the interview.

Roles can be psychological as well as social. For example, the same senior-junior relationship does not necessarily maintain the same level of honorifics. When the interaction goes into sensitive issues at work such as the junior's special request that she/he wants the senior to grant, the junior may approach the senior with more formal expressions. When the interaction shifts to a casual talk such as the next golf competition with the company members, the junior may use the lowest level of honorifics. This type of different levels of honorifics implies that while the junior is aware of his/her social relationship with the senior (thus the junior uses honorifics), the more official their interaction is, the more (psychological) distance the junior puts between them and the more cautiously she/he approaches the senior. On the other hand, when the interaction moves on to non-official matters, the junior, while maintaining honorifics to some extent, may safely lower honorific levels in order to be closer to the senior. This shows that the speaker in fact knows how to manipulate honorifics and attempts to approach the senior with varied levels of honorifics.

An interesting honorific use is reported by Ōkubo (2009), in which a wedding MC (Master of Ceremonies) keeps changing honorifics from humble to deferential forms when referring to the same people. This is because the MC takes different roles to suit the ongoing situation. Ōkubo does not refer to "roles" but uses the term *daiben* (speaking by proxy). For instance, when talking to the guests, the MC takes a role on behalf of the bride and groom, using humble styles when talking about the behavior of the couple. When the MC asks the bride and groom to take a certain action, he uses deferential styles in referring to their behavior. That is, the different roles the MC takes prompt different honorific styles even when the same person refers to the same people. For example,

(5) これよりお二人、…すべてのテーブルにご挨拶に伺います。
```
    kore=yori          o-futari, …          subete=no            teeburu=ni
    now=from           HON-couple           all=GEN              table=LAT
    go-aisatu=ni                            ukaga-imas-u.
    HON-greeting=PURP                       visit(HON)-POL-NPST
```
Now, the couple will come to (your) tables to offer a greeting (to you).

(Ōkubo 2009: 170)

(6) じゃ、これがんばって一口でお召し上がりください。
 ja, kore ganbat-te   *hitokuchi=de*   *o-meshiagari-kudasa-i.*
 OK this make.effort-PCP one.mouthful=INSTR eat(HON)-give(HON)-IMP
 OK, please try to eat this in a single mouthful.

(Ōkubo, 2009: 166)

In example (5), the MC uses a humble style when talking about the couple's behavior, indicating that the MC takes the role of the couple and speaks to the guests on their behalf. In example (6), the MC, using a deferential style, asks the groom to bite a piece of cake, which has been cut out of the wedding cake. In this case, the MC is playing his social role as an MC, and exalts the groom, a central figure at the ceremony.

In this section, I have illustrated that, although honorifics do not directly contribute to the semantic content of an utterance, they can be manipulated quite dynamically to suit each moment or situation in interaction, generating a multiplicity of pragmatic effects and even revealing the speaker's psychological motivations.

Honorific strategies: The implementation of one's *tachiba*

Brown and Levinson (1987) claim that politeness arises from face-saving strategies, i.e., strategies designed not to humiliate or embarrass the other. Thus, directive speech acts such as requests, negotiations, offers, refusals, advice and suggestions are basically all potential face-threatening acts (FTAs) which the speaker may mitigate by employing various politeness strategies. Therefore, the more potential FTAs are predicted in approaching the other, the more cautious strategies are employed. This often precedes the speaker's social position in English-speaking societies. For example, a request is essentially a benefit to the speaker at the cost of the hearer, thus, potentially an FTA. Therefore, one may use an indirect form with an interrogative to mitigate the potential threat and save the other's negative face. This strategy is quite common regardless of whether the speaker is junior or senior to the hearer. This implies that, in English politeness, the consideration of a potential FTA takes priority over the interactants' social positions.

Japanese honorific strategies, on the other hand, are often the result of how the speaker perceives his/her *tachiba* in a given situation (Obana 2009; Haugh and Obana 2011). *Tachiba* refers to a variety of social stances one takes in interaction, including one's social rank or position, task, responsibility, capacity and situation where one is placed.[9] For example, if one is entitled to make a request on the basis of one's *tachiba* (e.g., a traffic controller at a car park [= *tachiba*] asking drivers to park their car at a certain space), one may use a polite but imperative form (*-te kudasai*, please do). When one's *tachiba* is strongly recognized, it takes priority over the content of an utterance, and strategies that suit one's *tachiba* are employed.

It should be noted that we are dealing with how linguistic politeness is formed, not how society is run. It is not denied that English-speaking countries do function according to the social position each member of the community has. Therefore, *tachiba* itself is not unique to Japanese society; it exists in every society.[10] However, the term is worth employing in explaining Japanese strategies because *tachiba* is by priority exercised, and linguistically reflected as a recurring pattern. In a similar way, FTAs do exist and should carefully be handled in Japanese society, too. However, when one's *tachiba* is strongly recognized, it holds priority over the consideration of FTAs. The following subsection introduces examples of honorific strategies that contrast markedly with English strategies. The asterisked examples in the following, which are not acceptable as honorific strategies in Japanese, are all from errors made by learners who are English speakers.

Praising a senior's professional performance

Praising is normally considered warm approval of the other, expressing one's respect to the other. It is commonly observed in both English and Japanese and is categorized by Brown and Levinson (1987) as a positive politeness strategy that aims to "exaggerate (interest, approval, sympathy with H [Hearer Y.O.])".

However, praising the other's professional performance and achievement needs great care in the honorific world because "praising" is a kind of evaluation, and evaluation is the result of judging the other by one's own yardstick. Because a junior's *tachiba* does not allow him/her to judge and state his/her evaluation of the domain of his/her senior's profession, direct praising as in examples (7) and (8) is not appropriate.

(7) ＊社長のスピーチ、上手だったと思います。
　　＊*shachoo=no　　　spīchi, jōzu　　　dat-ta　　　to　　　omo-imas-u.*
　　　president=GEN　speech adept　　COP-PST QT　think-POL-NPST
　　　Sir, (your) speech was adept, I think.

(8) ＊先生の書かれた本、分かりやすくて、よくまとまっています。
　　＊*sensee=no　　　kak-are-ta　　　hon,　　　wakari-yasuku-te..*
　　　teacher=GEN　　write-HON-PST　book　　understand-easy-PCP
　　　yoku　　matomat-te　　i-mas-u.
　　　well　　organize-PCP　RES-POL-NPST
　　　Professor, (your) book is easy to follow and well organized.

Examples (7) and (8) are not acceptable because the words underlined contain evaluations as a result of the junior's judgment, even though the utterances themselves are positive politeness strategies. The junior's face-to-face evaluation of their senior's performance is not socially accepted because it interferes in the senior's *tachiba* as a guide and mentor to his/her junior, and that being so, it is not the junior's *tachiba* to evaluate or judge the senior's work. A simple solution to this is to use *subarashii* (wonderful), which is open-handed praising, imposing the least judgmental undertones. Another strategy is to praise the other's performance by stating either how much one was moved or what benefits one received from it. In other words, one should refer to what benefits one received from the other's performance rather than directly access and evaluate the other's performance. Hence, example (7) can be changed to:

(9) 社長のスピーチ、感動しました。
　　shachoo=no　　　spīchi　　　kandō　　　shi-mashi-ta.
　　president=GEN　speech　　impression　　do-POL-PST
　　Sir, (I) was impressed by (your) speech.

Example (8) can be changed to:

(10) 先生の書かれた本から多くを学ばせてもらいました。
　　sensee=no　　　kak-are-ta　　　hon=kara　　　ooku=o
　　teacher=GEN　　write-HON-PST　book=ABL　　much=ACC

manab-ase-te	mora-imashi-ta.
learn-CAUS-PCP	receive-POL-PST

(I humbly) learned a lot from the book you wrote, Sir.

It should be noted that strategies such as examples (9) and (10) are limited to the senior's "professional" performances. Compliments on other things such as the senior's property (e.g., "your house is wonderful", "you are well-dressed") and hobbies (e.g., "you are good at golf") can be made without reserve.

Offer and suggestion to a senior

Brown and Levinson (1987) suggest the following two positive politeness strategies, which may be expressed via offers and suggestions:

Strategy 1: Notice, attend to Hearer (his interests, wants, needs, goods)
Strategy 9: Assert or presuppose Speaker's knowledge of and concern for Hearer's wants

These strategies imply that, by asking the other what he/she wants or what the other wants one to do, one can save the other's positive face and satisfy the other's needs/wants. For example, "Would you like me to help you?" to a friend, "Perhaps you would like to have a look at our pamphlet and consider our offer?" to a potential customer on phone inquiry, "Are you hungry? Would you like to have lunch now?" to a traveling companion, are all appropriate in English-speaking societies because asking what the other wants is a generous gesture, implying that one is willing to be accommodating to the other.

Offers and suggestions in the world of Japanese honorifics, on the other hand, do not involve the inquiry of what the other wants, but tend to take a direct approach by clearly stating what one can do for the other. The junior's *tachiba* does not allow him/her to verbalize or ask what is possibly on the senior's mind. As discussed earlier, honorifics are the linguistic evidence of a social or psychological distance between the speaker and the other person. Therefore, this "distance" deters the junior from entering into the senior's mind. Asking whether or not the senior wants help, for example, not only ignores such a distance but may also give the senior the impression that the junior is reluctant to help the senior. In fact, asking about the other's wants does not exist in Japanese unless the speaker and the other interactant are family members or very close friends. Obana (2000: 252–254) calls such members "absolute *uchi* (in-group) members", and *V'* + *tai* (verb stem plus auxiliary meaning "want") cannot occur with honorifics because *-tai* belongs to the speaker and his/her absolute *uchi* members. Therefore, example (11), which is a common error made by learners, is not acceptable.

(11) *お手伝いしていただきたいですか。

*o-tetsudai	shi-te	itadak-ita-i		des-u	ka?
HON-help	do-PCP	receive(HON)-want-NPST		COP(POL)-NPST	Q

Would you like (me) to help (you)?

Considering the junior's *tachiba*, honorific strategies in offer situations should indicate what the junior will do. Therefore, example (11) can be changed to:

(12) お手伝いします。
    o-tetsudai   *shi-mas-u.*
    HON-help   do-POL-NPST
    (I) will help (you).

Example (12) is a direct offer with a humble style *o-V-suru* together with an addressee honorific *-masu*. A more polite offer is:

(13) お手伝いさせてください。
    o-tetsudai   *sa-se-te*   *kudasa-i.*
    HON-help   do-CAUS-PCP   give(HON)-IMP
    Let (me) help (you).

By using a causative morpheme *-se* (*-seru* is the original form), the speaker takes a lower stance as if getting the senior's permission, although the offer is imposed with the polite but imperative form *kudasai*.[11]

Offers such as the one in example (12) indicate what the speaker intends to do for the senior. In this case, the offer should be direct and almost imposing. However, if an offer involves the senior's response, it should be made with an interrogative, but without asking what is on the senior's mind. For instance,

(14) そろそろ12時ですが、お昼でもいかがですか。
    sorosoro *juuni-ji*   *des-u*   *ga,*   *o-hiru*   *demo*
    soon   twelve-o'clock COP(POL)-NPST CNJ   HON-lunch or.something
    ikaga   *des-u*   *ka.*
    how(HON)   COP(POL)-NPST Q
    It's almost noon. How about lunch or something like that?

Example (14) shows that by explaining a fact (it's almost noon), the speaker implies it is lunch time (assuming the senior must be hungry), and then, suggests lunch in an interrogative style. In this utterance, there is no mention of what is on the senior's mind (e.g., "aren't you hungry?") and no question of what the senior wants to do (e.g., "would you like to have lunch?"). The junior's *tachiba* allows him/her to refer only to what the junior can do (e.g., suggesting) by giving options (e.g., asking what the senior thinks about the suggestion).

I have demonstrated a few examples of honorific strategies that are contrastive with English strategies.[12] English politeness strategies are based on the mitigation of potential FTAs and consideration of how the content of an utterance might affect the other interactant. On the other hand, Japanese honorific strategies assign priority to one's *tachiba* when it is strongly recognized in a given context.

Conclusion

In this chapter, I have introduced current trends concerning Japanese politeness and added my own idea of how to grasp Japanese honorifics in pragmatic principles. In spite of the richness and complexity of honorific forms and styles, their function is merely the indexing of a social or psychological distance without being involved with the semantic content of an utterance. On the other hand, honorific use creates an enormous diversity of pragmatic effects due to their fluid and dynamic changes in each moment of the ongoing interaction.

I have also discussed honorific strategies, which I believe are worthy of more attention in politeness research. I have chosen a few examples that are quite contrastive with English politeness strategies. In the non-honorific world, many Japanese politeness strategies follow the way in which English strategies are constructed, i.e., by considering potential FTAs. However, certain honorific strategies are by priority based on one's *tachiba*, which gives rise to the generation of different types of strategy from those found in English.

Notes

1 Brown and Levinson's theory focuses on "face" as one's social image, and politeness is strategically employed in order to save face. Positive strategies (e.g., thanking, agreement, praising) save one's positive face, i.e., one's wants to be approved, and negative strategies (e.g., indirect requests, hedges, apologizing) and save one's negative face, i.e., one's wants to be unimpeded. Therefore, strategies aim to avoid potential face-threatening actions (FTAs).
2 *Wakimae* originates in Old Chinese, meaning "dividing or separation" such as cutting meat, and in modern Japanese, it applies to social behavior, indicating that one knows how to behave (by distinguishing appropriate from inappropriate actions).
3 Perhaps this is a reason why nowadays *poraitonesu* (politeness) is used to incorporate a more variety of social actions (e.g., Usami 2001; Takiura 2005, 2008). In a similar way, *hairyo hyōgen* (literally, "expressions of consideration") is preferred by some other scholars (e.g., Miyake 2011; Noda et al. 2014; Yamaoka et al. 2010).
4 Shinto means "the way of Gods". Its mythology is described in the *Kojiki* (Records of Ancient Events) which was written in the eighth century, attempting to claim that emperors and empresses are descendants of gods and goddesses.
5 Asada (2001: 185–186) notes that Japanese gods and goddesses are quite different from the western God as the former are more like humans, conducting good as well as bad and even mischievous deeds. They do not demand humans adhere to their precepts but merely bring about what they can do (e.g., natural disasters). Therefore, people in the old days believed that by using honorifics with offerings they could negotiate anything with gods and goddesses.
6 The corpus comes from a part of the data collected by Mayumi Usami and her team at Tokyo University of Foreign Studies, compiled as *BTS ni yoru tagengo hanashi kotoba kōpasu* (Multilingual conversation corpus by Basic Transcription System).
7 Examples (2) and (3) are traditionally categorized as speech (plus-) level shifts as they occur occasionally in the context which is organized with plain forms as the basic speech level (e.g., between close friends, family members). Speech level shifts are often discussed separately from the so-called "conventional" honorifics. However, Obana (2016a, b, 2017) finds a parallel between them, which forms two ends of a continuum; that is, speech level shifts are derived from, or take advantage of, "conventional" honorifics, and are used as speaker strategies to express temporary psychological changes.
8 The prefix *o-* in *o-cha* (tea) is apparently an honorific prefix, but categorized as women's language, which is used by women regardless of their social/psychological relationship with the other interactants.
9 In this discussion, I follow the way in which Obana (2009) and Haugh and Obana (2011) analyzed Japanese strategies by using the term *tachiba*. However, strictly speaking, *tachiba* is a subcategory of "roles" referred to earlier since roles include social stances (*tachiba*) as well as psychological motivations, both of which are instrumental in determining honorific forms and strategies.
10 Holmes and Stubbe (2003) provide examples of English interaction in which negotiating with the boss at work inevitably invites polite devices such as *hedging* and *attenuation*. They also noticed social statuses are verbally emphasized during the interaction, entailing juniors' *tachiba*.
11 This is from *kudasaru* + imperative; the former is honorific-marked on *kureru* = giving from higher to lower positions.
12 For further examples, see Obana (2009). Haugh and Obana (2011) also discuss *tachiba* strategies in the non-honorific world as well as those in the honorific world.

References

Asada, Hideko (2001) *Keigo de toku nihon no bōydo, fubyōdo* [*Equality and Non-equality in Japan Revealed via Honorifics*]. Tokyo: Kōdansha Shinsho.

――― (2005) *Keigoron – uta kara keigo e* [*On Honorifics. From Poetic Prayers to Honorifics*]. Tokyo: Bensei Shuppan.

――― (2014) *Keigo no genre oyobi hatten no kenkyū* [*Studies on the Principles of Honorifics and their Development*]. Tokyo: Tōkyōdō Shuppan.

Barke, Andrew (2011) Situated Functions of Addressee Honorifics in Japanese Television Drama. In: *Situated Politeness*. Bethan L. Davies, Michael Haugh and Andrew J. Merrison (eds), 111–128. London: Continuum.

Brown, Penelope and Stephen Levinson (1978) Universals in Language Usage. Politeness Phenomena. In: *Questions and Politeness*. Esther N. Goody (ed.), 56–311. Cambridge: Cambridge University Press.

――― (1987) *Politeness. Some Universals in Language Usage*. Cambridge: Cambridge University Press.

Chinami, Kyōko (2005) Nihongo no poraitonesu – sono seidoteki sokumen to goyōron sokumen [Japanese Politeness. Its Institutional and Pragmatic Aspects]. *Kyushu University Korean-Japanese Language and Culture Studies* 6: 35–66.

Cook, Haruko Minegishi (1996a) Japanese Language Socialization. Indexing the Modes of Self. *Discourse Processes* 22: 171–197.

――― (1996b) The Use of Addressee Honorifics in Japanese Elementary School Classrooms. In: *Japanese/Korean Linguistics* (volume 5). Noriko Akatsuka, Shoichi Iwasaki and Susan Strauss (eds), 67–81. Stanford: CSLI Publications.

――― (1997) The Role of the Japanese masu Form in Caregiver-child Conversation. *Journal of Pragmatics* 28: 695–718.

――― (2008) Style Shifts in Japanese Academic Consultations. In: *Style Shifting in Japanese*. Kimberly Jones and Tsuyoshi Ono (eds), 9–38. Amsterdam: John Benjamins.

――― (2011) Are Honorifics Polite? Uses of Referent Honorifics in a Japanese Committee Meeting. *Journal of Pragmatics* 43: 3655–3672.

Coulmas, Florian (1981) Poison to your Soul. Thanks and Apologies Contrastively Viewed. In: *Conversational Routine*. Florian Coulmas (ed.), 69–91. The Hague: De Gruyter.

Eelen, Gino (2001) *A Critique of Politeness Theories*. Manchester: St. Jerome.

Fukuda, Atsushi and Noriko Asato (2004) Universal Politeness Theory. Application to the Use of Japanese Honorifics. *Journal of Pragmatics* 11: 131–146.

Geyer, Naomi (2008) Interpersonal Functions of Style Shift. The Use of Plain and masu Forms in Faculty Meetings. In: *Style Shifting in Japanese*. Kimberly Jones and Tsuyoshi Ono (eds), 39–70. Amsterdam: John Benjamins.

Haugh, Michael and Yasuko Obana (2011) Politeness in Japan. In: *Politeness in East Asia*. Daniel Z. Kádár and Sarah Mills (eds), 147–175. Cambridge: Cambridge University Press.

Holmes, Janet and Maria Stubbe (2003) *Power and Politeness in the Workplace*. London: Longman.

Ide, Sachiko (1989) Formal Forms and Discernment. Two Neglected Aspects of Universals of Linguistic Politeness. *Multilingua* 2: 223–248.

――― (1992) On the Notion of wakimae. Toward an Integrated Framework of Linguistic Politeness. In: *Mosaic of Language. Essays in Honor of Professor Natsuko Okuda*. Mejiro Linguistic Society (ed.), 298–305. Tokyo: Mejiro Linguistic Society.

Ide, Sachiko (2006) *Wakimae no goyō-ron* [*The Pragmatics of wakimae*]. Tokyo: Taishūkan.

Ide, Sachiko, Beverly Hill, Yukiko M. Carnes, Tsunao Ogino and Akiko Kawasaki (1992) The Concept of Politeness. An Empirical Study of American English and Japanese. In: *Politeness in Language. Studies in its History, Theory and Practice*. Richard J. Watts, Sachiko Ide and Konrad Ehlich (eds), 299–323. Berlin: Mouton de Gruyter.

Ikuta, Shoko (1983) Speech Level Shift and Conversational Strategy in Japanese Discourse. *Language Science* 5: 37–53.

Ishizaki, Akiko (2000) Denwa renraku no kaiwa ni okeru supīchi reberu shifuto [Speech Level Shifts in Information Delivery in Telephone Conversation]. *Gengo bunka to nihongo kyōiku* 19: 62–74.

Kabaya, Hiroshi (2003) Hyōgen kōi no kanten kara mita keigo [Honorifics from the Viewpoint of Expressive Behaviour]. In: *Asakura nihongo kōza, keigo* [*Asakura Japanese Lectures: Honorifics*]. Yasuo Kitahara and Yasuto Kikuchi (eds), 53–72. Tokyo: Asakura Shoten.

Kádár, Z. Dániel (2013) *Relational Rituals and Communication. Ritual Interaction in Groups*. Basingstoke: Palgrave Macmillan.

Kádár, Z. Dániel and Michael Haugh (2013) *Understanding Politeness*. Cambridge: Cambridge University Press.

Kádár, Z. Dániel and Sara Mills (2013) Rethinking Discernment. *Journal of Politeness Research* 9(2): 133–158.

Kumai, Hiroko (2003) Taigū hyōgen no shosokumen to sono hirogari [Various Aspects of Expressions of How to Treat People and their Broader Usages]. In: *Asakura nihongo kōza, keigo*. Yasuo Kitahara and Yasuto Kikuchi (eds), 31–52. Tokyo: Asakura Shoten.

——— (2009) Nihongo no politeness to taijin kōdō ni kansuru ichikōsatsu [A Study on Japanese Politeness and Acts in Personal Relationship]. *Bulletin of the Center for International Exchanges, University of Shizuoka* 3: 1–26.

Locher, Miriam and Richard J. Watts (2005) Politeness Theory and Relational Work. *Journal of Politeness Research* 1(1): 9–34.

Makino, Sei'ichi (2002) When Does Communication Turn Mentally Inward? A Case Study of Japanese Formal-to-informal Switching. In: *Japanese /Korean Linguistics* (volume 10). Noriko M. Akatsuka and Susan. Strauss (eds), 121–135. Stanford: CSLI Publications.

Matsumoto, Yoshiko (1988) Reexamination of the Universality of Face. Politeness Phenomena in Japanese. *Journal of Pragmatics* 12: 403–426.

Maynard, Senko K. (2001) *Koisuru futari no kanjō kotoba – dorama hyōgen no bunseki to nihongo-ron* [*Emotional Language between the Two in Love. Analysis of Expressions in Dramas and Japanese Language*]. Tokyo: Kuroshio Shuppan.

——— (2004) *Danwa gengogaku* [*Discourse Linguistics*]. Tokyo: Kuroshio Shuppan.

Megumi, Maeri (2002) The Switching between desu/masu Form and Plain Form. From the Perspective of Turn Construction. In: *Japanese/Korean Linguistics* (volume 10). Noriko M. Atatsuka and Susan Strass (eds), 206–234. Stanford: CSLI Publications.

Mills, Sara (2003) *Gender and Politeness*. Cambridge: Cambridge University Press.

Miyake, Kazuko (2011) *Nihongo no taijin kankei ha'aku to hairyo gengo kōdō* [*How Interactional Relationships are Grasped in Japanese and Entailed in Considerate Linguistic Behavior*]. Tokyo: Hitsuji Shobō.

Mori'izumi, Satoshi (2009) Face Concern and Requests in Japan. Exploring the Effects of Relational Closeness and Social Status. *Journal of Intercultural Communication Research* 38(3): 149–174.

Moriyama, Yukiko (2010) Gendai nihongo no keigo no kinō to poraitonesu [The Functions of Japanese Honorifics and Politeness]. *Nihongo nihonbungaku* 22: 1–19.

Noda, Hisashi, Yoshiyuki Takayama and Kobayashi Takashi (eds) (2014) *Nihongo no hairyo hyōgen no tayōsei* [*Diversity of Japanese Expressions of Consideration*]. Tokyo: Kuroshio Shuppan.

Obana, Yasuko (2000) *Understanding Japanese. A Handbook for Learners and Teachers*. Tokyo: Kuroshio Shuppan.

——— (2009) Politeness Strategies in Japanese Honorifics. Contrasts between English and Japanese in Strategic Planning. *Gengo to bunka* 12: 39–53.

——— (2012a) Politeness as Role-identity. Application of Symbolic Interactionism. *Gengo to bunka* 15: 1–16.

——— (2012b) Re-examination of yoroshiku onegaishimasu. The Routine Formula as the Linguistic Implementation of one's tachiba-role. *Journal of Pragmatics* 44: 1535–1548.

——— (2016a) Nihongo no keigo sai-sai-kō – yakuwari aidentiti no kanten kara [Re-re-examination of Japanese Honorifics. From the Viewpoint of Role-identity]. *Gengo to bunka* 19: 31–46.

——— (2016b) Speech Level Shifts in Japanese. A Different Perspective – the Application of Symbolic Interactionist Role Theory. *Pragmatics* 26(2): 247–290.

——— (2017) Japanese honorifics re-re-visited. *Journal of Politeness Research* 13(2): 4–31.

Obana, Yasuko and Takako Tomoda (1994) The Sociological Significance of "Politeness" in English and Japanese Languages. Report from a Pilot Study. *Japanese Studies Bulletin* 14(2): 37–49.

Ōubo, Kanako (2009) Sonkeigo, kenjōgo no kinō ni kansuru kōsatsu – kekkon hirōen no shikai no hatsuwa o rei ni [On the Functions of Deferential and Humble Terms. Examples from the Wedding MC's Utterances]. *Shakai gengo kagaku* 12(1): 162–173.

Okamoto Shigeko (1999) Situated Politeness. Manipulating Honorific and Non-honorific Expressions in Japanese Conversation. *Pragmatics* 9: 51–74.

——— (2009) Politeness and Perception of Irony. Honorifics in Japanese. *Metaphor and Symbol* 17: 119–139.

Pizziconi, Barbara (2003) Re-examining Politeness, Face and the Japanese Language. *Journal of Pragmatics* 35: 1471–1506.

——— (2007) The Lexical Mapping of Politeness in British English and Japanese. *Journal of Politeness Research* 3(2): 207–241.

Saito, Junko (2010) Subordinates' Use of Japanese Plain Forms. An Examination of Superior-subordinate Interactions in the Workplace. *Journal of Pragmatics* 42: 3271–3282.

Shibamoto-Smith, Janet (2011) Honorifics, "Politeness", and Power in Japanese Political Debate. *Journal of Pragmatics* 43: 3707–3719.

Takiura, Masato (2005) *Nihon no keigoron* [*On Japanese Honorifics*]. Tokyo: Taishūkan.

——— (2008) *Poraitonesu nyūmon* [*Introducing Politeness*]. Tokyo: Kenkyūsha.

Usami, Mayumi (2001) Disukōsu poraitonesu to iu kanten kara mita keigo shiyō no kinō [The Functions of Honorific Use from the Viewpoint of Discourse Politeness]. *Gogaku kenkyū shoronshū* 6: 1–29.

Watts, Richard J. (2003) *Politeness*. Cambridge: Cambridge University Press.

Yamaoka, Masanori, Isao Makihara and Masaki Ono (2010) *Komyunikēshon to hairyo hyōgen* [*Communication and Expressions of Consideration*]. Tokyo: Meiji Shoin.

17
IMPOLITENESS

Yukiko Nishimura

Introduction

Impoliteness, as Culpeper (2011) has pointed out, lacks a single universally accepted definition. In this review, I will treat impoliteness as a cover term for a wide range of offensive language, from lexical insults and other "bad words" to verbal face-threatening acts that violate expected norms for appropriate use of language in a given context. This chapter also looks at related phenomena in which seemingly impolite language does not cause offense, such as ritual insults (Labov 1972) and the yelling of curse words at festivals. Social psychologist Okamoto (2016) identifies contemporary directions in Japanese research on impoliteness in both online and offline interactions that include stereotyping, verbal assault and abuse, sexual and other types of harassment. Following Okamoto, this chapter provides a selective overview of impoliteness, with particular focus on impoliteness online. I will first explore pioneering lexical work on impoliteness, and then consider early descriptive studies and research utilizing the Japanese conceptual/analytical framework of *taigū hyōgen* (treatment expressions). Cyberbullying and domestic violence as reported in women's blogs are addressed afterwards as examples of online impoliteness. Two very different contexts for impoliteness, parliamentary debates and online discussion forums, are then considered. Taking the perspective of cultural anthropology, the final part of this chapter discusses current cultural contexts in which apparently rude language functions in potentially positive ways.

In sharp contrast to the extensive literature on politeness in Japanese sociolinguistics, impoliteness has yet to receive a comparable degree of attention. This is evident, for example, in Minami's (1974) more than 60-page-long chapter on *keigo* (honorifics) in which abusive expressions are discussed in just eight lines on "minus *keigo*". Although *keigo* does not correspond to politeness, nor abusive language to impoliteness, Minami's treatment is suggestive of the imbalance between politeness and impoliteness research in Japan. Except for a few lexicographic works on bad, vulgar and abusive language (Maeda 1962; Tsutsui 1967), research on impoliteness can be viewed as originating with psychologist Hoshino (1971), who first challenged the marginal treatment of this topic.

Hoshino (1971) considered the indifference of Japanese language experts of topics deemed unworthy of study, one of these topics being impoliteness. The underlying assumption was that speakers should not use "bad" language, as many of these linguists were also language instructors teaching "good" Japanese. Another reason for the neglect, Hoshino states, is that while *keigo* has an elaborate linguistic system embedded in the Japanese language system, the range of comparable linguistic features in "minus *keigo*" is relatively limited. For these reasons, Hoshino conjectures, the study of impoliteness did not draw much scholarly interest among Japanese linguists. Subsequently, vocabulary associated with impoliteness was explored by specialists in other fields, for example, social scientists (Konno 1988; Uchino 1990; Kobayashi 2016), journalists (Okuyama 1996; Matsumoto 1996), but also poets such as Kawasaki (2003).

In the broader academic landscape, sociolinguistics was recognized as a new interdisciplinary field in Japanese research communities in the 1970s. In Hoshino's (1974) comments on the first Japan–US joint sociolinguistics conference held in Hawai'i in 1970, he summarized the research trends, methods and objectives in US-based sociolinguistics. Among Japanese sociolinguists the focus was on areas other than impoliteness, which may also be a reflection of western research trends at the time. Yet, as later scholars have noted (e.g., Arai 1981; Nishio 2015), Hoshino's early studies had in fact paved the way for future sociolinguistic and interdisciplinary studies of impoliteness. From the perspective of international research trends, Hoshino's foresight is especially noteworthy. In their overview of the history of impoliteness research, the earliest works cited by Culpeper and Hardaker (2017: 206–208) date to the 1980s. Hoshino predates these works by almost one decade.

In the field of sociolinguistics, there are at least three reasons why impoliteness research is important. (1) The spread of technologically mediated communication has expanded the potential scope of impoliteness, e.g., through cyberbullying; (2) an understanding of impoliteness is important for language learners in a globalized world; and (3) work originating in Japanese socio-cultural contexts can motivate advances in impoliteness research elsewhere.

In technologically mediated communication in contemporary Japan, there is an increasing need to deepen and expand our understanding of impolite linguistic and interactional behavior online. Under the "cloak of anonymity" (Lakoff 2005: 32), users of discussion boards, chat rooms and social media can interact in ways that hurt others, as a way to "get power and vent negative feelings" (Beebe 1995: 154). This can be especially alarming for school children and their parents, who are hurt by cyberbullying (Kanō 2016), some to the extent that they commit suicide (Ogiue 2008: 21). While websites attempt to maintain appropriate and healthy interactions and reject anti-social behavior, offensive and discriminatory expressions survive in subtly disguised ways, on unofficial sites privately managed by students and in other social media outlets.

In applied Japanese sociolinguistics and in teaching Japanese as a foreign or a second language, impoliteness is also significant (Hoshino 1989). The lack of accumulated research in the area of impoliteness can limit teachers (Kuki 1971; Hajikano, Kumatoridani and Fujimori 1996). Not treating impoliteness in Japanese language textbooks and references may well be a reflection of language experts' orientation toward politeness rather than impoliteness. In local communities where globalization is unfolding rapidly, however, more people are interacting with others from different cultural and linguistic backgrounds. Impoliteness is part of their lives, and it can even result in having people lose their jobs (Tanaka 1999: 42). Under these circumstances, researchers and teachers should be able to provide insight to language learners also with regard to impoliteness in order that they can successfully function in Japanese speech communities.

Research on impoliteness in Japanese can contribute both to Japanese sociolinguistics and a growing literature on the topic worldwide. Contrary to the relative lack of interest among Japanese sociolinguists, western scholars have been very productive on this topic in the last decade (e.g., Bousfield 2008; Culpeper 2011). Culpeper, Haugh and Kádár (2017: 6) stress that the study of (im)politeness is "thoroughly multidisciplinary", and that it extends from pragmatics and interactional sociolinguistics to diverse fields such as management, health, law, politics and humor. Impoliteness research on Japanese socio-cultural contexts has much to contribute, especially when anthropological perspectives are considered.

Early approaches to impoliteness
Lexical studies

Before any analysis or theorization of a phenomenon can be undertaken, it is necessary to first review the data we currently have at hand. Impoliteness research in Japanese sociolinguistics began with descriptive collections of vocabulary associated with impoliteness, and then moved on to studies of the psychological and social processes involved in verbalizing negative reactions to unpleasant situations within the framework of *taigū hyōgen* (treatment expressions), an approach to the study of (im)politeness originally developed in Japanese linguistics.

Inspired by US scholars' sociolinguistic research on and approaches to language use and behavior at the aforementioned Japan–US 1971 sociolinguistics conference in Hawai'i, Hoshino (1971) recognized the need for working on impolite language and speakers' behavior in society. In this sense, his research on impoliteness can be seen as having being influenced by western academic works of sociolinguistics in the 1970s, even before pragmatic research on politeness had become a prominent topic there (e.g., Lakoff 1973; Brown and Levinson 1978).

Hoshino (1971) pointed to Tsutsui's (1967) classification of impoliteness vocabulary into 16 categories, including, e.g., imaginary being (*akuma*, devil), person (*furyō*, delinquent), profession (*yabu isha*, quack doctor), animal (*yajū*, beast) or bird (*hiyokko*, greenhorn), among others. He also provided another impoliteness list based on a classification of English swearwords, e.g., ancestral (*amae no kāsan debeso*, literally "your mom has a protruding navel"), religious (*bachi atari*, cursed), anatomical (*hage*, bald), excretory (*kuso kurae*, literally "eat shit") and sexual (*baita*, whore). In contrast to English, which has swear words originating from Christianity, Hoshino cited Tsurumi's (1954) observation that the Japanese language lacks swear words related to the emperor or to Shintoism, let alone to Christianity. It does, however, have swear words originating from Buddhism (e.g., *chikushō*, literally "a (sub-human) brute", but functioning as a curse word in the sense of "damn it"). One characteristic feature of Japanese curse words, according to Tsurumi (1954), is the abundant use of excretory vocabulary such as *kuso* (shit), which can be productively used both as a prefix and suffix, e.g., *kuso gaki* (brat).

Hoshino (1971) further categorized impoliteness by target (i.e., self, addressee and absent referent) and situation (i.e., privately or in the presence of others). His list of motives for impoliteness included: (1) attacking others when frustrated, accompanied by anger and hatred; (2) attacking without hostility; and (3) using abusive expressions as banter without hostility or hatred. Judging from his impact on subsequent researchers, it is no exaggeration to say that Hoshino is the founder of impoliteness research in Japan, and that he foresaw comparative cultural developments in an interdisciplinary field of study.

Following Hoshino (1971), Asada (1979) conducted surveys on various groups, in particular, boys and girls from elementary, middle and high school. Respondents were asked to list abusive expressions. They were also asked to whom they would use these expressions and their accompanying emotions. The results revealed age and gender differences, not only in the form and content of abusive expressions, but also with regard to the respondents' emotions. Older respondents tended to criticize the behavior and character of their seniors (parents and teachers). Boys tended to use abusive expressions more light-heartedly as an indication of solidarity and were not bothered too much when abuse was thrown at them, while girls uttered abusive expressions when attacking others and suffered psychologically when they were targeted. Certain lexical items such as *namaiki* (sassy) were mainly used toward one's juniors. Asada's study is one of the very few works dealing with impoliteness, especially among school children. Her work is valuable both for its empirical findings, and for advancing research on forms and uses of impolite language.

Impoliteness as "minus treatment expressions"

Also inspired by Hoshino (1971), Nishio (1998, 2001, 2005, 2007, 2015) works on impoliteness departing from the Japanese approach of *taigū hyōgen* (treatment expressions), which can presumably be both polite and impolite. *Taigū hyōgen* literally refers to expressions that are used when interacting with others and describing situations (Agency for Cultural Affairs 1971). Kikuchi (1997: 36–42) identifies six types of such expressions: (1) vertical treatment of others as up/above or down/below; (2) polite or impolite; (3) formal or informal; (4) elegant or vulgar; (5) like or dislike; and (6) a person received or did not receive a favor. Within the first type, treating the other as someone in an up/above position constitutes the main bulk of *keigo* (honorifics). Type (2) refers to the sentence-ending forms *-masu* and *desu* as polite, and the verb-root form *da* as neutral. Also, while the request *kaite kudasai* (please write) is polite or neutral, *kake* (write!) in the imperative form is seen as rude. Type (3) can be exemplified with men's first person pronouns, e.g., *watakushi* is formal, *watashi* neutral, *boku* informal, and *ore/oira* rough, while *washi* sounds arrogant. Regarding Type (4), *o-hana* (flower), in which the beautifying prefix *o-* is attached to *hana* (flower), is elegant, while *hana* without the prefix is neutral; *shiri* (butt) is neutral, while *ketsu* (arse) is vulgar. Type (5) is concerned with speakers having a good, favorable impression/feeling of the situation or a negative one. For example, *shinu* (die) is neutral, while *kutabaru* (kick the bucket) expresses the situation negatively. Finally, regarding Type (6), *dareka ga kuru* (someone is coming) is neutral, while *dareka ga kite kureru* (someone is coming [for me]) implies that a favor is received. Based on such distinctions, Nishio argues that the concept of *taigū hyōgen* can be utilized also for impoliteness research, focusing on the negative terms, which he calls "minus treatment expressions".

Nishio characterizes impoliteness as "minus" *taigū hyōgen* within Japanese linguistics based on a review of previous work on *taigū hyōgen* dating all the way back to 1901 (Nishio 2015: 29–54). He recognizes two types of minus *taigū hyōgen*, one that affects interpersonal relationships and one that does not. He furthermore criticizes previous impoliteness research for simply collecting abusive expressions and for not considering the social and psychological factors involved in such language use (Nishio 2001: 71). A speaker may risk aggravating social relations with others by uttering negative evaluations, and may therefore restrict such utterances in order to maintain harmonious social relations. Nishio posits three stages in the social and psychological process of producing minus *taigū hyōgen*: (1) the speakers evaluate the situation negatively; (2) they choose to express a negative evaluation; and (3) they use specific linguistic expressions to this end.

In order to investigate how restrictions in verbalizing negative reactions may affect linguistic output, Nishio (1998) analyses 480 utterances in surveys, asking what expressions to use with interlocutors of different relations in particular situations. Examining younger and middle-aged men and women, he finds that while younger respondents indicate negative evaluations in rough linguistic forms, middle-aged speakers tend to express negative evaluations in more indirect ways. Nishio finds that restrictions in the choice of linguistic expressions vary from person to person, and in cases where there are strong restrictions on certain linguistic forms (e.g., direct imperative forms), speakers may employ other, less direct forms that still serve their expressive intentions.

Nishio's (2005) discussion of the auxiliary verb *yoru* among young people in the Osaka area contributed to the refinement of the *taigū hyōgen* system. Nishio (2005: 50) writes that "the treatment expression system of the Kansai dialect expresses not only human relations but also speakers' emotions". From this he argues for a new theoretical perspective for the categorization of treatment expression systems. Nishio's (2015) approach is not influenced by western impoliteness research originating with the seminal work of Culpeper (1996). His work is important for focusing on the social and psychological processes taking place when being impolite in interaction. Using inductive sociolinguistic methodology, Nishio tackles a research gap by addressing a range of understudied phenomena of impoliteness in both Standard Japanese and regional dialects.

Impoliteness research online

Early analyses of impolite terms typically relied on lexicographic or questionnaire-based methods. More recent research has focused on occurrences of impoliteness in actual language use, both online and offline. In this section, research based on data from social media and blogs will be discussed to explore how and why speakers engage in impoliteness.

Online bullying

In view of the many reported cases of cyberbullying, a number of scholars have studied how to detect and extract abusive language online, e.g., by searching for particular expressions such as *maji uzai* (totally annoying) or *shine!* (die!). Ishizaka and Yamamoto (2010, 2011) focus on the language used on Japan's largest bulletin board system, Channel 2. Matsuba et al. (2009) work on detecting harmful content including abuse, obscenity and violence on informal school sites, which help website administrators to check and patrol these sites. While a Ministry of Education, Culture, Sports, Science and Technology survey (MEXT 2015) reports 7,898 cases of cyberbullying in total, a decline by 890 from the previous year, Takahashi (2015) warns that cyberbullying has shifted from schools' informal websites to social media outlets such as Line on smartphones, making the content basically invisible to outsiders.

The abusive language used in cyberbullying is therefore a form of impoliteness that is extremely difficult to detect and to study. When found, it is furthermore hard to analyze it without its larger background and context. As an example of the language used in cyberbullying, an excerpt from Twitter may be considered here. The excerpt was made available by Kanō (2011, 2016), a specialist working with victims for the prevention of cyberbullying. Posted from the Twitter account aruaru@_WeHateThisGirl, we find an example of cyberbullying where the target's physical traits and personality are attacked (Kanō 2016: 194–195).

(1) jibun   igai=wa   minna   busu
    self   except=TO   everyone ugly
    [The target says] everyone except her is ugly.

(2) ashi=ga   shin-u   hodo   kusa-i
    feet=NOM die=NPST to the extent stink-NPST
    [Her] feet are so stinky [everyone] would almost die.

(3) kuchi=o   hirak-eba   jiman   banashi
    mouth=ACC open=PROV bragging story
    When she opens her mouth, she brags.

The attacker and the victim, both ninth-grade female students, were in the same extracurricular club in a six-year private high school. The victim had been ignored in class by the bullies for about three years prior to these tweets. In this particular case, the victim saw the tweets and was shocked. Although the tweets were anonymous, she could guess the bully's identity. While this short excerpt illustrates the kind of language used in cyberbullying, a full understanding would require analysts to adopt an ethnographic approach. Obtaining detailed information about the people concerned and the background of the post can thus be a barrier to researching such sensitive issues. Geyer (2008) adopts an ethnographic approach to the study of a Japanese school and, though interested in politeness phenomena rather than cyberbullying, her methodology (interviews with students and attendance of faculty meetings) offers a model for future researchers.

Impoliteness and verbal abuse of women

Another area that deserves attention in impoliteness research is verbal attacks against women. It occurs in a number of forms in contemporary society. One of the most invisible forms is emotional abuse by intimate partners, or "moral harassment" (Hirigoyen 2000). Moral harassment refers to regular emotional abuse and domestic bullying. The term originates from the French *harcèlement moral*, as articulated by Marie-France Hirigoyen, a psychiatrist and psychoanalyst specializing in mobbing and mental abuse.

In my own research, I have examined how harassed Japanese women describe their sufferings from, and reactions to, moral harassment. I have thereby employed qualitative analyses on the language and the style of posts collected from Japan's largest blog (Nishimura 2016). Bloggers describe impoliteness addressed to them retrospectively and give their assessments of it, including descriptions of the emotional consequences on them. Methodologically, publicly available blog posts are advantageous for impoliteness research, because they often include reflections or metapragmatic comments on impoliteness events (Culpeper 2012: 1131), in addition to bloggers' profile information about approximate age, gender, job, years of married life, children, etc. This greatly helps readers – including linguists – to understand what bloggers write about and why, as both the background information and the verbal content supply context for each post.

With regard to linguistic aggression against women, Anderson and Cermele (2016) examine and compare two different kinds of data, one from Tweets surrounding an analysis of imbalanced gender representation in electronic gaming, and the other from petitions by victims seeking legal protection from courts of law. There are notable similarities in women's descriptions of harassment between the petition files examined by Anderson and Cermele (2016) and the blog posts in my own studies. In both cases, victims describe what their intimate partners said and did, even though the context and purposes of their descriptions are different. Anderson and Cermele (2016: 115) classify aggression into the following eight categories, all of which can also be applied to my Japanese blog data:

Categories	Examples from Japanese moral harassment blog corpus
Appearance	*honekawa* (skin and bones)
Sex part	*mune o misero* (show me your breasts/tits)
Overt gender insult	*babā* (old hag), *shikome* (ugly woman)
Violence threats	*kodomo ga dekinai gen'in o tsukitome te, warui hō ga shine. Dakara omae ga shine.* (Let's find out the cause of not having a child, and the responsible one can die. So you're gonna die.)
Non-gendered insult	*munō* (incompetent), *dekisokonai* (defective [unable to give birth])

Patriarchal control	*yashinatte yatteru* (I'm doing you the favor of feeding you)
Command	*kansha shiro* (be thankful), *shaberu na, kiero* (don't talk, get lost)
Unspecified	*omae ga warui* (you're to blame)

Notice that different approaches are also possible. Anderson and Cermele (2016) went on to compare the number and percentages of occurrences, while Nishimura (2016) investigated posts qualitatively and found that moral harassment typically takes the form of rejecting communication, e.g., *damare* (shut up), telling blatant lies, blaming the woman, e.g., *omae no sei da* (it's your fault), and exhibiting distrust and contempt. Most victims described their experiences and how they dealt with it in a rather reserved tone. Some victims who had overcome their hardships hoped that their blogs might help others in similar situations. Still others vented their feelings in their blog, an emotional outlet that they secretly used. While fearful of being discovered by their harassing (ex)-husbands, they blog to process their ordeal and to maintain psychological stability. Deeply rooted masculine ideologies of power and dominance over women were evident throughout the bloggers' descriptions of men's language and behavior. In studying how victims of moral harassment put their experience into words, such types of study are addressing an entirely new field of impoliteness towards women in Japanese socio-cultural contexts.

As the research on cyberbullying and abuse of women has shown, individuals in a weaker position become targets of impoliteness and other disparaging or threatening types of language use. The victims of such abuse have typically suffered in silence and, as noted above, it can be difficult for linguists to gain access to this kind of data. However, bringing their experiences to light – whether through blogging or by sharing it with counselors and other authority figures – may be an important step toward empowering the targets of cyberbullying.

Impoliteness in communities of practice

The following section will discuss studies utilizing a widely recognized theoretical framework for investigating (im)politeness in political discourse first, and then discusses impoliteness as manifest in online discussion forums.

Political discourse

Among Japanese scholars working on language in politics (e.g., Matsuda 2008; Azuma 2005; 2007, 2010), Yanagida (2013) discusses impoliteness in political discourses. He thereby adopts a discursive approach in a post-Brown and Levinson framework (see e.g., Eelen 2001; Watts 2003) from the perspectives of critical discourse analysis (Fairclough and Wodak 1997) and media and cultural studies (van Dijk 1997; Hall 1980). Yanagida (2014) stresses the "socio" rather than "linguistic" aspects of sociolinguistics, focusing on societal concerns such as the reproduction of inequality and discrimination. These are areas explored by western critical discourse analysts, but not yet very prominent in Japanese sociolinguistics.

In his discussion of parliamentary debates, Yanagida (2013) employs the notion of "face-work" (Goffman 1967) or interactional commitments between the speaker and the interlocutor, noting that face can be enhanced, maintained or aggravated when interacting with others. Extending Harris's (2001) analysis of British parliamentary debates to the House of Representatives in Japan, Yanagida observes that the highly controlled turn-taking system in which the speaker allocates the floor to a member of parliament causes "preferred turn" sequences such as compliment-self-deprecation to be broken (Pomerantz 1984); the preferred second turn cannot follow sequentially. Similarly, a questioner can aggravate the face of an interlocutor, who is obliged to respond to the assigned question even if it will result in a loss of face. Yet within the institutional constraints of the parliament, it is possible for the respondent to counter-attack a questioner. Thus, interactions involving face-work in parliamentary debates are different from ordinary conversations, and different norms of interaction have evolved there as a result.

The speeches Yanagida (2013) examines are formally recorded and archived, and no irregular utterances can be found in the transcripts. Heckling, however, actually exists, and it can influence the flow of debates. Though not included in the official records of the debates, instances of heckling can be seen in video recordings on sites such as YouTube, which is another data source for the study of impoliteness. These videos are interesting not only from the viewpoint of face-work, but also with regard to the (in)appropriateness of utterances, which sometimes include discriminatory and sexist remarks. For example, Yanagida (2017) reports the case of a female member of the Tokyo Metropolitan Parliament who was advocating women's issues, while being heckled by male members of parliament who told her to get married, and asked whether she could have children. When she subsequently tweeted about this and this incident became reported in newspapers, a flood of protests followed. Although speaking without permission is forbidden by the rules of parliament, interruptions are often tolerated in practice. But when the content of heckling is impolite, i.e., deemed offensive, it can unleash public outrage. Turning our attention from parliamentary debates, let us next consider at a different type of community, an online community of practice having its own interactional norms for participants.

Internet discussion forums

Extending western research on impoliteness in face-to-face interactions, I have studied Japanese online interactions and the different norms with respect to impoliteness on two discussion forums (Nishimura 2010). The data were drawn from Channel 2, Japan's largest anonymous discussion forum/bulletin board system, and Yahoo! Japan BBS (hereafter, Yahoo), another large-scale discussion forum, where participants post opinions on a multitude of topics pseudonymously. For comparative purposes threads on the same topic, namely studying English, were chosen for both Channel 2 and Yahoo. In general, the style used on Yahoo is polite, with -*masu* and *desu* honorifics, while Channel 2 uses an informal style with plain verb roots and *da*. The differences between the two forums are not limited to the language used by participants, but also include the management of the websites. Channel 2 is an unregulated site, where core members take care of deleting inappropriate posts, while Yahoo is regulated by its parent site Yahoo! Japan, which has explicitly stated rules on the language that is allowed. When someone responds to another's posts, an automated message from the Yahoo system employs *desu/masu* polite endings. Channel 2 does not have such an automated message system, but simply uses an arrow or angle bracket to indicate to whom a message is responding.

The differences in language norms on the two forums are illustrated in examples (4) and (5) below. On Yahoo, where there had been active postings and discussion about the merits of studying English abroad, one poster (A) disparaged another poster (B) for having made comments that were said to be jumbled and irrelevant, concluding:

(4)   *nidoto*   *koko=ni*   *chikazuk-u-na!!!*
       again   here=LAT   come near-IMP=NEG
       Never come around here again!!!

In (4), A uses a bare, direct imperative form. This "impolite" post silenced discussion for the next ten days on this thread.

In contrast, on Channel 2 bare imperative forms, such as *kiero* in the following example, also on the topic of studying abroad, appear more frequently and do not seem to bother anyone, as illustrated in (5):

(5) XX   *uke-ru*   *to*   *ka*   *iu*   *onna*
    XX [name of university]   take-NPST   QT   Q   say   woman
    maji   *de*   *uza-i*   *kara*   *kie-ro*
    serious ADV   annoying=NPST   because   disappear-IMP
    The woman who says she'll apply to XX must disappear, because she's really annoying.

After the post in (5), the discussion of studying abroad continued without a break on Channel 2. From the interactional patterns of Channel 2 and Yahoo, it appears that what is regarded as normal on Channel 2 is seen as impolite on Yahoo.

Within the larger Japanese speech community, Channel 2 is an online subcultural "community of practice" (Wenger 1998) with a specific linguistic repertoire (Nishimura 2003, 2008), which may be viewed as rude, impolite and even abusive from the viewpoint of mainstream language practices. Such sub-cultures have been the object of anthropological studies, which are considered in the next section.

Anthropological approaches to the study of impoliteness

This section will consider Japanese cultural contexts where impoliteness functions in positive ways.

A subcultural community of idols and fans

In the context of certain fan cultures, impoliteness serves to signal bonds and affection among idol group members and their fans. According to Galbraith and Karlin (2012: 2), the term "idol" in Japan refers to "highly produced and promoted singers, models, and media personalities [...]. [They] can be male or female, [...] and are not expected to be greatly talented at any one thing, for example singing, dancing, or acting." Wikipedia (2017b) lists 160 female idol groups in Japan in the 2010s, including one called *Surū sukiruzu* (literally, "Through Skills"). They are referred to as *nonoshiri aidoru*, which combines *nonoshiri* (cursing each other) and *aidoru* (idol) joined together. *Surū sukiruzu* was created in January 2013 by comedian Tamaura Jun, who was unable to ignore disparaging tweets he received and tweeted back at his attackers. From his experience of not being able to ignore abuse, he formed an idol group consisting of members with the skills to ignore all insults and abuse thrown at them. *Surū* is used here in the sense of "ignoring" as in "going 'through' a stop sign". Tamura's concept is that this is the world's first idol group that can be abused – abuse from fans/followers is transformed into support for them. Thus, each member of the group has a curse word, for example:

(6) *babā* (old hag), *onchi* (tone deaf), *usotsuki* (liar), *herahera* (stupid), *ponkotsu* (useless), *mesu buta* (female pig), *kuso gaki* (fucking brat)

When they appear on stage, fans shout at them *kaere* (go home). This is a strong, direct imperative which, as we've seen above, could have negative consequences if used in a different community of practice. To understand the idols' response in (7), it is important to know that in

Japanese, the ritual formula to be uttered before eating a meal is the honorific verb *itadakimasu* (I'm going to eat, I shall dine) and the corresponding formula following a meal is the honorific *gochisō-sama* (thanks for the [delicious] meal). When their fans yell *kaere*, the idols respond as follows.

(7) *minna no sutoresu itadakimasu, surū sukiruzu desu.*
We're going to eat everyone's stress (all the stress you can give us). We're Through Skills.

At the end of the performance, they say:

(8) *Minna no sutoresu, gochisō-sama, surū sukiruzu deshita.*
Thank you for all your [delicious] stress. This has been Through Skills.

The lyrics of one of their songs begin with *nonoshitte* (please curse us). This is an artificially created, small-scale fan/idol community, and it is not clear to what extent their linguistic practices qualify as "anti-language" – a primarily metaphorical kind of language used as a mode of resistance in a subculture created as an alternative to the dominant society (Halliday 1976: 570). However, it can at least be said that some linguistic features of the community can be regarded as part of a social dialect, which is "not necessarily associated with caste or class; [it] may be religious, generational, […] and perhaps other things too" (Halliday 1976: 580). Further research is necessary to obtain more information about the characteristics of language use in this and other such subcultural groups in Japan.

Akutai matsuri or "curse festivals"

The ritual use of abusive language in Japan has also been researched in other contexts. Hoshino (1971: 39), in his discussion of an interdisciplinary approach to impoliteness, mentions curse festivals, which exemplify Japan's unique perspective on impoliteness. Among many related festivals in Japan, the one organized at the Atago Shrine in Kasama City in Ibaraki Prefecture is relatively well documented (Ibaraki Prefecture Board of Education 2010). Wikipedia (2017a) also describes this festival, and the account that follows is based on these two sources.

According to the Ibaraki Board of Education, various origins have been proposed for the curse festival. One source claims that it was started in the middle of the Edo Period (1603–1868) by officials in order to hear villagers' complaints and allow farmers to vent their anger. Other sources say the festival was intended to purge evil spirits and illnesses. Be that as it may, on the day of the festival in November, 13 adult men, already chosen and dressed as *tengu* (goblins), place offerings at 18 sacred places along the way to the shrine. The climax occurs at Atago Shrine, where the 13 *tengu* throw *mochi* (rice cakes) to those who have gathered. Since uttering curses is regarded as a way to purge *kegare* (defilement), people hurl curses at the *tengu* during the festival. Some participants yell *tengu no baka yarō!* ("damn fools, *tengu*!") and steal the *mochi* offerings, which are said to bring good luck.

Prior to 1941, only men participated in the festival and it was at night, so participants could utter curses freely, without fear of negative consequences. The festival was suspended during WWII. When it was revived after the war, it was held during the day, and visitors were not as wild and vocal as before. During a recent festival, no adults cursed at the *tengu*, although they did take the offerings. The significance of uttering curses to purge evil seemed no longer to be shared among visitors. One participant who experienced the pre-war festival recalled that any curses could be uttered, as one could not see others' faces in the dark (Asahi Shinbun 2014). However, more recent festivals show a somewhat different pattern.

Mainichi Shinbun (2015) reports that participants at the 2015 festival said that they enjoyed yelling curses out loud, as there are no opportunities to do so in everyday life, and Tokyo Shinbun (2016) reported similar opinions. Another change is that the number of participants in this festival has increased. Due to the city's effort to promote the festival as a recreational event, the festival attracted 200 participants in 2011, but 1,000 in 2013 and even more in later years.

It is interesting to observe the changes over time in the meaning of the curses. The act of cursing was originally directed toward a mythical being. Since the curses were not targeted at fellow people, participants could, in principle, utter curses out loud, without being concerned about harming their relations with others. When the festival was held during the day and the participants could see one another, they could no longer curse freely, even though other participants were not the target of the curses. This was at the time when there were not as many visitors to the festival. At recent festivals, however, participants shout curses during the day as an act of recreation and enjoyment when they are encouraged to curse by city megaphones. These changes can be interpreted by considering the context for uttering curses. People can curse when they are anonymous and cannot be identified, as in the night-time festivals, and when there are many people they do not know around them, as in the huge crowds at the recent festivals. Thus, the curse festival sheds light on the role of anonymity in understanding impoliteness in Japan.

Future directions in research on impoliteness

This chapter has explored studies of impoliteness in Japanese sociolinguistics, beginning with Hoshino's (1971) pioneering work. Although Hoshino laid the foundation for research on impoliteness, the area remained largely unexplored for 30 years afterwards. In the late 1990s, Nishio's treatment of impoliteness in terms of "minus treatment expressions", an original Japanese research framework, represented an important advance. From these early milestones to recent studies of online impoliteness, most sociolinguists have focused on linguistic rather than on societal issues. But research on cyberbullying and verbal abuse of women suggests that sociolinguistics can have a role in raising awareness of the ways in which individuals are victimized linguistically, and perhaps also in helping to empower victims of such abuse and to break the pattern of silence.

Japanese research on online forums and parliamentary debates explores impoliteness in the context of communities of practice. A key finding of this type of research is that different communities have different norms and interactional patterns with respect to impoliteness. What is consistent across these differences is that particular ways of using language, from the choice of verb forms in online forums to the content of heckling in parliament, can be sources of negative reactions when community norms are violated.

A promising area of research on impoliteness in Japan is the study of cultural contexts in which seemingly abusive language, such as insults and cursing, is a powerful source of bonding within a specific community of practice. Idols and their fans create a subcultural community of insiders where meanings of words are reversed with respect to the use in Japanese society. At the curse festival, participants also enjoy reversing social norms by yelling curses at mythical beings in an anonymous crowd. In the pre-war version of the festival, it was the cover of darkness that gave participants the freedom to curse without fear of being identified. The same anonymity often characterizes online communication today, encouraging some participants in online forums to criticize others without sticking to expected norms of politeness and, in the worst case, allowing cyberbullies to verbally attack their victims.

Though this chapter has covered several areas of research on impoliteness, many others remain unexplored, for example, irony (Okamoto 2007). Impoliteness can be conveyed through implicit, nuanced use of language, even tactfully or cunningly using polite auxiliaries in certain contexts (Yonekawa 1999). Such aspects of impoliteness in interaction warrant further research. As Culpeper and Hardaker (2017) mention, another important area for future study is "criminal linguistic behavior such as threats and hate speech", a growing area of concern both in on- and offline communication.

There are many other avenues for future research. These include how norms of impoliteness change diachronically within or across Japanese speech communities (e.g., Endō 2005); whether men's and women's perceptions of impoliteness differ, and if so, how (e.g., Mills 2005); how Japanese children acquire impolite linguistic behaviors and learn to restrict them through the process of socialization; how impoliteness spreads geographically across Japan (e.g., Matsumoto 1996); and how impoliteness is manifested in verbal performance and art forms such as *kabuki*, *rakugo* and *manzai*, as well as other forms of entertainment (see e.g., Culpeper 2005). It is hoped that this review of impoliteness will encourage scholars to contribute to this area of research, not only to fill a gap in Japanese sociolinguistics but, more importantly, to illuminate aspects of a phenomenon that is fundamental to any society.

References

Agency for Cultural Affairs (1971) *Taigū hyōgen* [*Treatment Expressions*]. Tokyo: Ministry of Finance Printing Bureau.
Anderson, Kristin L. and Jill Cermele (2016) Public/Private Language Aggression against Women. Tweeting Rage and Intimate Partner Violence. In: *Exploring Language Aggression against Women*. Patricia Bou-Franch (ed.), 107–126. Amsterdam: John Benjamins.
Arai, Yoshihiro (1981) Akutai kōi ron – senryaku-teki sōgo sayō to shite no akutai [A Study on Abusive Behavior. Abuse as Strategic Interaction]. In: *Kōza nihongogaku. Keigo-shi* [*Japanese Linguistics Series. History of Honorifics*]. Kenji Morioka, Yutaka Miyaji, Hideo Teramura and Yoshiaki Kawabata (eds), 66–87. Tokyo: Meiji Shoin.
Asada, Yoshiko (1979) Warukuchi no shakai gengogaku-teki ichikōsatsu [A Sociolinguistic Study of Abusive Language]. In: *Hidden Dimensions of Communication*. Fred C. C. Peng (ed.), 103–123. Hiroshima: Bunka Hyōron Shuppan.
Asahi Shinbun (2014) Fukuramu kankōkyaku, shibomu basei Kasama "akutai matsuri" asu kaisai [Growing Tourists, Shrinking Curses at Kasama's Curse Festival, to be Held Tomorrow]. In: *Asahi shinbun* (20 December).
Azuma, Shoji (2005) *Rekidai shushō no gengoryoku o shindan suru* [*Diagnosing the Language Ability of Successive Prime Ministers*]. Tokyo: Kenkyūsha.
——— (2007) *Gengogakusha ga seijika o maru hadaka ni suru* [*A Linguist Exposes Politicians*]. Tokyo: Bungei Shunjū.
——— (2010) *Senkyo enzetsu no gengogaku* [*Linguistics Analysis of Election Speeches*]. Tokyo: Minerva Shobō.
Beebe, Leslie. M. (1995) Polite Fictions. Instrumental Rudeness as Pragmatic Competence. In: *Linguistics and the Education of Language Teachers. Ethnolinguistic, Psycholinguistics and Sociolinguistic Aspects*. James E. Alatis, Carolyn A. Straehle, Brent Gallenberger and Maggie Ronkin (eds), 154–168. Georgetown: Georgetown University Press.
Bousfield, Derek (2008) *Impoliteness in Interaction*. Amsterdam: John Benjamins.
Bousfield, Derek and Miriam Locher (eds) (2008) *Impoliteness in Language. Studies on its Interplay with Power in Theory and Practice*. Berlin: Mouton de Gruyter.
Brown, Penelope and Stephen Levinson (1978) Universals in Language Usage. Politeness Phenomena. In: *Questions and Politeness. Strategies in Social Interaction*. Esther N. Goody (ed.), 56–310. Cambridge: Cambridge University Press.
Culpeper, Johnathan (1996) Towards an Anatomy of Impoliteness. *Journal of Pragmatics* 25: 349–367.
——— (2005) Impoliteness and Entertainment in the Television Quiz Show "The Weakest Link". *Journal of Politeness Research* 1(1): 35–72.

——— (2011) *Impoliteness. Using Language to Cause Offence*. Cambridge: Cambridge University Press.
——— (2012) Epilogue (Im)politeness. Three Issues. *Journal of Pragmatics* 44: 1128–1133.
Culpeper, Johnathan and Claire Hardaker (2017) Impoliteness. In: *The Palgrave Handbook of Linguistic (Im) politeness*. Johnathan Culpeper, Michael Haugh and Daniel. Z. Kádár (eds), 199–225. London: Palgrave Macmillan.
Culpeper, Johnathan, Michael Haugh and Daniel. Z. Kádár (eds) (2017) *The Palgrave Handbook of Linguistic (Im)politeness*. Basingstoke: Palgrave Macmillan.
Eelen, Gino (2001) *Critique of Politeness Theories*. Manchester: St Jerome Press.
Endō, Orie (2005) Sabetsugo, fukaigo no rokujū-nen [Sixty Years of Discriminatory and Displeasing Words]. In: *Hyōgen to buntai*. Akira Nakamura, Masa'aki Nomura, Mayumi Sakuma and Chizuko Komiya (eds), 437–455. Tokyo: Tōkyōdō.
Fairclough, Norman and Ruth Wodak (1997) Critical Discourse Analysis. In: *Discourse as Social Interaction*. Teun A. van Dijk (ed.), 258–285. London: Sage.
Galbraith, Patrick W. and Janson G. Karlin (2012) Introduction. The Mirror of Idols and Celebrity. In: *Idols and Celebrity in Japanese Media Culture*. Patrick W. Galbraith and Janson G. Karlin (eds), 1–32. Basingstoke: Palgrave Macmillan.
Geyer, Naomi (2008) *Discourse and Politeness. Ambivalent Face in Japanese*. London: Continuum.
Goffman, Erving (1967) *Interactional Ritual. Essays on Face-to face Behavior*. New York: Pantheon Books.
Hajikano, Are, Tetsuo Kumatoridani and Hiroko Fujimori (1996) Fuman hyōmei sutorateji no shiyō keikō – nihongo bogo washa to nihongo gakushūsha no hikaku [Usage Tendency of Dissatisfaction Expression Strategies. Comparison between Japanese Native Speakers and Japanese Learners]. *Nihongo kyōiku* 78: 128–139.
Hall, Stuart (1980) Encoding/Decoding. In: *Culture, Media, Language. Working Papers in Cultural Studies, 1972–79*. Stuart Hall, Dorothy Hobson, Andrew Lowe and Paul Willis (eds), 117–127. London: Unwin Hyman.
Halliday, M. A. K. (1976). Anti-languages. *American Anthropologist* 78(3): 570–584.
Harris, Sandra (2001) Being Politically Impolite. Extending Politeness Theory to Adversarial Political Discourse. *Discourse and Society* 12(4): 451–472.
Hirigoyen, Marie-France (2000) *Stalking the Soul. Emotional Abuse and the Erosion of Identity*. New York: Helen Marx Book.
Hoshino, Akira (1971) Akutai mokutai kō – akutai no shosō to kinō [Thoughts on Abusive Language. Aspects of Abusive Language and its Functions]. *Kikan jinruigaku* 2(3): 29–52.
——— (1974) Shakai gengogaku to iu shinbunya [A New Field Called Sociolinguistics]. *Gendai no esupuri kotoba to shinri* 85: 19–29.
——— (1989) Mainasu keigo to shite no keihigo, bago, akukō [Insulting, Abusive and Offensive Words as Minus Honorifics]. *Nihongo kyōiku* 69: 110–120.
Ibaraki Prefecture Board of Education (2010) Akutai matsuri [Curse Festivals]. Available online at: www.edu.pref.ibaraki.jp/board/welcome/soshiki/soshiki/bunka/maturi/akutai.pdf (accessed 26 June 2017).
Ishizaka, Tatsuya and Kazuhide Yamamoto (2010) Ni-channeru o taishō to shita waruguchi no chūshutu [Extraction of Abusive Expressions Focused on Channel Two]. *The Proceedings for the 16th Annual Meeting of the Association for Natural Language Processing*. Available online at: www.anlp.jp/proceedings/annual_meeting/2010/index.html (accessed 2 March 2018).
——— (2011) Webbu-jō no hibō chushō o arawasu bun no jidō kenshutsu [Automatic Detection of Sentences Expressing Slander on the Web]. *The Proceedings for the 17th Annual Meeting of the Association for Natural Language Processing*. Available online at: www.anlp.jp/proceedings/annual_meeting/2011/index.html (accessed 2 March 2018).
Kanō, Hiroko (2011) Netto ijime o kaiketsu suru kagi no arika [Locations of Keys to Solve Internet Bullying. *Gendai no esupuri* 526: 5–15.
——— (2016) *Netto ijime no kōzō to taisho/yobō* [*Structure of and Preventive Measures for Internet Bullying*]. Tokyo: Kaneko Shobō.
Kawasaki, Hiroshi (2003) *Kagayaku nihongo no akutai* [*Shining Abusive Words in Japanese*]. Tokyo: Shinchō Bunko.
Kikuchi, Yasuto (1997) *Keigo* [*Honorifics*]. Tokyo: Kōdansha.
Kobayashi, Kenji (2016) *Saishin sabetsugo, fukaigo* [*The Newest Discriminatory Words and Displeasing Words*]. Tokyo: Ningen Shuppan.

Konno, Toshihiko (1988) *Bessigo – kotoba to sabetsu* [*Discriminatory Words. Language and Discrimination*]. Tokyo. Akashi Shoten.

Kuki, Hiroshi (1971) *Cursing Words in Japanese, with some Reference to English. A Tentative Report in Sociolinguistics* (=Working Papers in Anthropology Archaeology Linguistics Maori Studies 25). Auckland: University of Auckland.

Labov, William (1972) *Language in the Inner City. Studies in the Black English Vernacular*. Philadelphia: University of Pennsylvania Press.

Lakoff, Robin. T. (1973) The Logic of Politeness, or Minding your P's and Q's. *Chicago Linguistics Society* 9: 292–305.

——— (2005) Civility and Discontents. Or, Getting in your Face. In: *Broadening the Horizon of Linguistic Politeness*. Robin T. Lakoff and Sachiko Ide (eds), 23–43. Amsterdam: John Benjamins.

Maeda, Isamu (1962) *Warui kotoba gehin na kotoba* [*Bad Words, Vulgar Words*]. Tokyo: Tōkyōdō.

Mainichi Shinbun (2015) Akutai matsuri – issei ni "ōbaka yarō" [Curse Festival. "Damn Fools" Shouting all Together]. In: *Mainichi shinbun* (20 December). Available online at: http://mainichi.jp/articles/20151221/k00/00m/040/039000c (accessed 20 June 2017).

Matsuba, Tatsuaki, Fumio Masui, Atsuo Kawai and Naonori Isu (2010) Gakkō hi kō shiki saito ni okeru yūgai jōhō kenshutsu [Extraction of Harmful Information on Informal Sites of Schools]. *The Proceedings for the 16th Annual Meeting of the Association for Natural Language Processing*. Available online at: www.anlp.jp/proceedings/annual_meeting/2010/index.html (accessed 2 March 2018).

Matsuda, Kenjirō (2008) *Kokkai kaigiroku o tsukatta nihongo kenkyū* [*Japanese Language Study Utilizing the Minutes of Parliament Debates*]. Tokyo: Hitsuji Shobō.

Matsumoto, Osamu (1996) *Zenkoku aho baka bunpu kō – haruka naru kotoba no tabiji* [*A Study on Nationwide Spread of aho and baka. The Wonderful Journey of Words*]. Tokyo: Shinchōsha.

MEXT = Ministry of Education, Culture, Sports, Science and Technology (2015) *Heisei 26 nendo jidō seito no mondai kōdō to seito shidōjō no shomondai ni kansuru chōsa kekka ni tsuite* [On Survey Results Regarding Problems in Instructing Pupils and Students with Problem Behavior]. Available online at: www.mext.go.jp/b_menu/hōdō/27/09/__icsFiles/afieldfile/2015/10/07/1362012_1_1.pdf (accessed 18 June 2017).

Mills, Sara (2005) Gender and Impoliteness. *Journal of Politeness Research* 1(2): 263–280.

Minami, Fujio (1974) *Gendai nihongo no kōzō* [*The Structure of Contemporary Japanese*]. Tokyo: Taishūkan.

Nishimura, Yukiko (2003) Establishing a Community of Practice on the Internet. Linguistic Behavior of Online Japanese Communication. *Berkeley Linguistics Society* 29: 337–348.

——— (2008) Japanese BBS Websites as Online Communities. (Im)politeness Perspectives. *Language@Internet* 5. Available online at: www.languageatinternet.org/articles/2008/1520 (accessed 22 February 2018).

——— (2010) Impoliteness in Japanese BBS Interactions. Observations from Message Exchanges in two Online Communities. *Journal of Politeness Research* 6(1): 33–55.

——— (2016) Impoliteness in Diary Blogs by Japanese Victims of Moral Harassment. Three Case Studies of Harassers' Words in Context. (Paper presented at The 4th Linguistic Im/politeness, Aggression and Rudeness Conference, Manchester Metropolitan University, Manchester, 12–16 July 2016.)

Nishio, Junji (1998) Mainasu taigū kōdō no hyōgen sutairu – kisei sareru gengo kōdō o megutte [Styles of Utterance in Language Behaviour Using Minus Treatment Expressions. On Language Behaviour with Restrictions]. *The Japanese Journal of Language in Society* 1(1): 19–28.

——— (2001) Mainasu taigū hyōgen no shosō [Aspects of Minus Treatment Expressions in Language Behaviour]. *Nihongogaku* 20(4): 68–77.

——— (2005) The Nature of YORU, the Auxiliary Verb of the Minus Treatment Expression Used by Young People in the Kansai Region Centring on Osaka. *The Japanese Journal of Language in Society* 7(2): 50–65.

——— (2007) Nonoshiri to sono shūhen no gengo kōdō [Abusing and its Related Linguistic Behaviours]. In: *Kotoba no komyunikēshon – taijin kankei no retorikku*. Shin'ichirō Okamoto (ed.), 194–208. Kyoto: Nakanishiya.

——— (2015) *Mainasu no taigū hyōgen kōdō – taishō o hikuku waruku atsukau hyōgen e no kisei to hairyo* [*Language Behaviour of Minus Treatment Expressions. Restrictions and Considerations for Expressions that Treat Objects Low and Bad*]. Tokyo: Kuroshio Shuppan.

Ogiue, Chiki (2008) *Netto ijime – webbu shakai to owari naki "kyara sensō"* [*Cyberbullying. Web Society and Never-ending Character Wars*]. Tokyo: PHP Shinsho.

Okamoto, Shin'ichirō (2007) An Analysis of the Use of Japanese hiniku. Based on the Communicative Insincerity Theory of Irony. *Journal of Pragmatics* 39: 1143–1169.

——— (2016) *Akui no shinrigaku – waruguchi, uso, heito supīchi* [*Psychology of Malice. Abuses, Lies and Hate Speech*]. Tokyo: Chūō Kōronsha.

Okuyama, Masurō (1996) *Bari zōgon jiten* [*Dictionary of Abusive Words*]. Tokyo: Tōkyōdō.

Pomerantz, Anita (1984) Agreeing and Disagreeing with Assessments. Some Features of Preferred/Dispreferred Turn Shapes. In: *Structures of Social Action. Studies in Conversation Analysis*. J. Maxwell Atkinson and John Heritage (eds), 57–101, Cambridge: Cambridge University Press.

Takahashi, Akiko (2015) Kodomo o oitsumeru "LINE ijime" – "netto ijime" no ima ["LINE Bullying" Corners Children. Current Situations of Cyberbullying]. *CNET Japan*. Available online at: https://japan.cnet.com/article/35072933/ (accessed 18 June 2017).

Tanaka, Katsuhiko (1999) Keigo wa nihongo o sekai kara tozasu [Japanese Honorifics Closes the Language from the World]. *Gengo* 28(11): 41–47.

Tokyo Shinbun (2016) "Baka yarō" donari usa harasu – Kasama Atago jinja de "akutai matsuri" ["Damn fool" People Shout for Diversion. Kasama City's Atago Shrine Held its Curse Festival]. In: *Tōkyō shinbun* (20 December). Available online at: www.tokyo-np.co.jp/article/ibaraki/list/201612/CK2016122002000170.html (accessed 20 June 2017).

Tsurumi, Shunsuke (1954) *Taishū geijutsu* [*Popular Art*]. Tokyo: Kawade Shobō.

Tsutsui, Yasutaka (1967) Akukō zōgon bari zanbō shiron [A Study on Slurs, Abuses, Curses and Swear Words]. *Kotoba no uchū* (August): 23–30.

Uchino, Masayuki (1990) *Sabetsu-teki hyōgen* [*Discriminatory Expressions*]. Tokyo: Yūhikaku.

van Dijk, Teun A. (1997) What is Political Discourse Analysis? In: *Political Linguistics*. Jan Blommaert and Chris Bulcaen (eds), 11–52. Amsterdam: John Benjamins.

Watts, Richard J. (2003) *Politeness*. Cambridge: Cambridge University Press.

Wenger, Etienne (1998) *Communities of Practice. Learning, Meaning, and Identity*. Cambridge: Cambridge University Press.

Wikipedia (2017a) Akutai matsuri (Kasama shi) [Curse festival (Kasama City)]. Available online at: https://ja.wikipedia.org/wiki/%E6%82%AA%E6%85%8B%E7%A5%AD%E3%82%8A_(%E7%AC%A0%E9%96%93%E5%B8%82) (accessed 15 June 2017).

——— (2017b) Josei aidoru gurūpu. [Female idol group]. Available online at: https://ja.wikipedia.org/wiki/%E5%A5%B3%E6%80%A7%E3%82%A2%E3%82%A4%E3%83%89%E3%83%AB%E3%82%B0%E3%83%AB%E3%83%BC%E3%83%97#2010.E5.B9.B4.E4.BB.A3 (accessed 24 June 2017).

Yanagida, Ryogo (2013) Seiji no gengo to in/poraitonesu – kokkai tōben ni okeru feisuwāku o tegakari ni [Language in Politics and Im/politeness. Face-work in Parliamentary Debates in Japan]. *Ōsaka Daigaku gengo bunkagaku* 22: 83–94.

——— (2014) Poraitonesu no seiji, seiji no poraitonesu – danwateki apurōchi kara mita rigai/kanshin no hihan-teki bunseki [Politics of Politeness, Politeness of Politics. Critical Analysis of Interests and Concerns from a Discursive Approach]. PhD thesis, Osaka University.

——— (2017) Poraitonesu to rigai/kanshin – Tōkyō togikai yaji mondai o tegakari ni [Politeness and Interest. With a Clue of Hecklings Issues at Tokyo Metropolitan Parliamentary Debate]. *Kotoba to shakai* 19: 178–201.

Yonekawa, Akihiko (1999) Hiba hyōgen mo kawari yuku [Abusive Expressions are also Changing] *Gengo* 28(11): 30–33.

18
GENDERED SPEECH

Yumiko Ohara

Introduction: Historical background

In recent years, many have shown concern about a "deterioration" of Japanese. Much of this concern has focused on women's language. Observers lament such changes because they believe that it represents the loss of unique characteristics only seen in Japanese. Others welcome such changes and regard it as a sign of a "decrease in sexism" in Japanese society. This chapter discusses issues related to the use and perception of gendered language. More specifically, it addresses the following questions:

(1) How has gendered language been studied?

(2) Is it true that gender-based differences have decreased recently?

In attempting to seek answers to these questions, another problem inevitably arises.

(3) What is the nature of so-called "women's language"? Is it an actuality, a social construct, or both?

A scholarly focus on everyday language use developed in Japan earlier than it did in the West. In the US and in Europe, sociolinguistics and the sociology of language became well-defined fields of inquiry in the 1960s, and from this period on sociolinguistics spread across many parts of the world. In Japan, the examination of language use in daily life, or to use the term developed by Japanese scholars, *gengo seikatsu* (language life), was already well in place in the 1930s (Heinrich 2002, 2015; Sibata 1999). In 1948, the National Institute for Japanese Language (*Kokuritsu Kokugo Kenkyūjo*) was established, and its journal *Gengo seikatsu* started its publication in 1951. While gender along with other biographical information was sometimes considered in *gengo seikatsu* research, mostly through surveys on language use, it did not initially occupy a prominent role in Japanese sociolinguistics.

There is consensus that academic work on gendered language precedes *gengo seikatsu* research. Kikuzawa (1929) is often seen as the starting point. Early research points out gendered speech from the Muromachi Period (1336–1573) until the end of the Edo Period (1603–1868) focusing on two types of speakers, *nyōbo* (court ladies) and *yūjo* (prostitutes, literally "play ladies"). For instance, *Ama no mokuzu* (Mermaid Seaweed), compiled in 1420, which describes events and customs at the Imperial Palace, the households of high elites and the court, is listed as the first record of words used by court ladies (Shiraki 1970). It lists 17 such words. Many researchers agree that this was the first work documenting gender differences in Japanese (e.g., Kikuzawa 1933; Kunida 1964; Mashimo 1948; Shiraki 1970). Another historical account, *Ōjōrō onna no koto* (Names and Customs of High-ranking Court Ladies), believed to have been written between 1449–1473, includes a section titled *Nyōbo kotoba* (Court Ladies' Language). It lists 115 lexical items (Shiraki 1970). *Oyudononoue no nikki* (Collection of Diaries on the Daily Life in the Imperial Court) is a diary written from 1477 to 1826 by court ladies. It is thought that they took turns making a record of events and established customs. According to Shiraki (1970), it contains around 350 instances of *nyōbo kotoba*. A Japanese–Portuguese dictionary (Doi 2013[1603]) is another early work that contains 120 words of women's language (Shiraki 1970). Kunida (1964) offers an extensive look at the development of *nyōbo kotoba*, rationalizations for its occurrence, how it permeated general usage and also its relationship with contemporary women's language.

The main reason for the creation of *nyōbo kotoba* was to obscure negative connotations by replacing or modifying existing words. The objective of *yūjo* speech is deemed to be different. *Yūjo* were found in *yūri* (literally "play land") and this language use was referred to as *yūrigo* (literally "play land language"). The main reason for the creation of *yūrigo* was to conceal the local dialects used by women brought to *yūri* from various parts of Japan. *Yūrigo* contributed to the appeal of the *yūjo* and the *yūri* (Yuzawa 1964), and Mashimo states that:

> *Yūrigo* never fails to express stronger respect, politeness, and humility especially on the sentence final forms. Despite their [the *yūjo* Y.O.] apparent insightfulness and classiness, they were in actuality objects of monetary exchange and therefore needed to show their awareness of deference to their customers in their language behavior.
>
> *(Mashimo 1966: 3)*

Similar points on the origin and the effects of *yūrigo* have been made by Shiraki (1970) and Yuzawa (1964). The latter is an extensive collection of *yūrigo* that includes polite and courteous verbs and their conjugations.

Some claim that these two specific ways of speaking had a strong influence on the Japanese language. According to Kunida (1964), *nyōbo kotoba* is extremely important for the origin of women's language. He links it directly to later occurrences of women's language. Concerning his own work, Mashimo (1966) states that what might simply appear as a study of *yūrigo* should actually be regarded as a general history of women's language in the Edo Period. He claims that doing so allows for emphasizing the influence of *yūjogo* on later occurrences of women's language. Furthermore, according to Mashimo (1966), much of the modern literary work adopted *yūri*, which was then the only place of entertainment for male commoners. It is stated that almost all genres of literature that sought to write about *yūri* included *yūjo* into their storylines, and this is seen as an important reason why it is necessary to study *yūjogo* as a part of women's language in general.

Concerning more recent views, many surveys have shown that honorifics and gendered language are considered to be two particularities specific to Japanese, and that these features often serve as sources of pride for speakers of Japanese (e.g., Bunkachō 2016; Horii 1990; Kindaichi 1957). By closely examining the study of gendered language, its history, construction and focus, we can deepen our understanding of various issues such as language attitudes, language ideology, language policy, and language and identity. In the following section, I examine the major developments in the study of gendered language from these perspectives. I do so by discussing the so-called "difference approach", the "dominance approach", the "discernment approach", the "historical approach", the "sociophonetic approach", and an approach that focuses on "men's speech". I will juxtapose research within and outside of Japan and show how they relate to one another. I continue with a discussion of the concepts of "sex" and "gender" that have been central in research conducted in the US and Europe, and consider then its influence on exploration of the Japanese language.

Approaches to the study of women's language: Sex, gender, gender role

Our understanding about the social world is based on the division of human beings according to perceived attributes. In particular, attributes such as "age", "nationality", "ethnicity", "sex" and various physical characteristics that isolate, separate and categorize people appear to be so "obvious" that they need no explanation. After all, the act of categorization based on these attributes is an integral part of our day-to-day experiences. Among the attributes that factor into categorizing people, "gender" is perhaps the most pervasive (e.g., Echlund, Lincoln and Tansey 2012; Howard 2000; West and Zimmerman 1987). Starting with newborn babies and the names we give them, concepts and differentiation based on gender permeate our life. The problem thereby is that we base our expectation of people's behaviors on their assumed sex, and we attempt to understand and sometimes even judge them accordingly in our daily interactions.

It was not until the 1970s that scholars started to closely examine the interplay between "linguistic behavior" and "gender". An important contribution to the study of "language and gender" was the distinction between "sex" and "gender". Many earlier works departed from John Money's transgender studies (e.g., Money, Hampson and Hampson 1955a, 1955b), which defined "sex" as referring to physical characteristics and "gender" to psychological ones. Oakely (1972) illuminated the problem of equating biologically determined facts with social concepts and expectations based on sex. In one of the most quoted phrases in gender studies, de Beauvoir (1974[1949]: 295) writes: "One is not born, but rather becomes, a woman", an expression which precisely captures the contrast between biological and social influences on identity. It was now maintained that sex was meant to refer to innate and biological differences while gender referred to behavior that was socially acquired.

Also, studies of intersex and transgender individuals (Garfinkel 1967; Kessler and McKenna 1978) challenged the essentialist view of sex and gender. Employing ethnomethodology, Kessler and McKenna (1978) indicated that human bodies are not dichotomized in terms of women's and men's bodies, but that there is a great deal of variability between them. As they note (Kessler and McKenna 1978: vii), "a world of two 'sexes' is a result of the socially shared, taken-for-granted methods which members use to construct reality". Kessler (1990, 1998) provides further evidence for the social and medical construction of two genders and sexes. Additional works by Bing and Bergvall (1996) and Butler (1990) further paved the way to see sex and gender as continua. Furthermore, this kind of work resulted in a theorization of gender as culturally appropriate, idealized performances of femininity and masculinity. Gender is something we accomplish everyday (Garfinkel 1967), or in the words of West and Zimmerman (1987: 125), "gender is a routine accomplishment embedded in everyday interaction".

Research on Japanese produced several notable case studies that show how gender is accomplished through language. Ogawa and Smith (1997) analyze the grammar of six gay men in Osaka and Tokyo in the 1990 movie *Rasen no sobyō* (*Rough Sketch of a Spiral*), the first Japanese documentary about gay men. They examined first person, second person and third person reference terms as well as sentence-final particles. The self- and other-referencing practices of a couple from Osaka were found to be similar to stereotypical heterosexually gendered couples, while others were found to use various forms. Concerning sentence-final particles, the subjects mostly used neutral to masculine particles. They did not follow the language use of stereotypical heterosexual gendered couples. In the same volume, Valentine (1997: 97) showed that "[t]he identification of lesbians and gay men in Japan has to be understood in terms of the predominant conflation of sex, gender and sexuality". He traced the concepts of "queer", "otherness" or "general oddness" and also gave a historical account of homosexual eroticism in Japan. Furthermore, he examined foreign and native terms referring to heterosexuals and transgenders. Abe (2004) is a rare sociolinguistic study of lesbians in Japan. She also examines the language practices of transgendered individuals (Abe 2010). In both studies, the focus is placed on how lesbians and gay men construct their identities through linguistic practices.

In Japan, neither the reexamination of the differences between sex and gender nor the rethinking of gender identities of intersex individuals had an immediate effect. Initially, differences between sex and gender as well as gender identities did not warrant much debate. However, there are some recent changes in this area. For instance, Nishino (2015) and Yoshizawa (2016) make important contributions on gender identities and the conceptualization of "gender identity disorder". The influence of this research has yet to be seen in research where gender and Japanese language intersect.

Deficient, difference and dominance approaches

Research viewing gender as a social category has explored how language is used to create, display and reinforce gender and gender identities. In particular, the publication of Robin Lakoff's (1975) *Language and Women's Place* increased the awareness of how deeply language is related to female and male identities, and it also gave a glimpse into the possibilities of examining language and gender from a critical perspective. Lakoff's criticisms was focused on her observation that women were disadvantaged, because they were restricted to using language that was (often) different from that employed by men. Lakoff's work set the stage for a wave of research that explored how and why women's speech differs from that of men, including studies which saw the differences in terms of male dominance (e.g., Fishman 1978; Thorn and Henley 1975; Zimmermann and West 1975) and those which posited cultural forces as the source of difference (e.g., Maltz and Borker 1982; Tannen 1986, 1990).

Lakoff (1975) had a tremendous international influence on the study of gender and language. However, the reception of her work by Japanese scholars was mixed. Some refuted the assertion that women's language is "deficient" in comparison to male speech. Discussion will first focus on research that follows the ideas of Lakoff (1975). However, it is not necessarily clear just how the different approaches – "deficient" and "difference and dominance" – diverge from one another. For instance, Coates talks about the differences between these two approaches as follows:

> The first – the difference approach – emphasizes the idea that women and man belong to separate sub-cultures. The linguistic differences in women's and men's speech are interpreted as reflecting these different sub-cultures […]. The second – the dominance approach – sees women as an oppressed group and interpret linguistic differences in women's and men's speech as a reflection of men's dominance and women's subordination.
>
> *(Coates 1986: 12)*

Concerning the deficient approach, the focus was on men's language use as the norm, and therefore, "non-male speech" was seen as deficient. These differentiations, however, might not be practical, due to the fact that Lakoff's (1975) work itself has been sometimes viewed as an example of the "dominance approach", and at other times as an example of the "deficient approach" (Uchida 1992). This is comprehensible, given the fact that Lakoff's work is multi-layered. On the one hand, it is "deficient" because it views women's language use as compared to men's, which was assumed to be standard. On the other hand, it considers "differences" being caused by social inequality between sexes.

Jugaku (1979) is an early study that takes an approach similar to Lakoff. Jugaku described the influence of the concept of "femininity", sometimes dictating every aspect of women's lives and lifestyle choices. She asserts that "femininity" was how community, work, school and society at large perceived women. She argued for "feminine" as a concept constructed through aspects of Japanese language, and she also felt that the "femininity" of language becomes an essential part of language itself. Analyzing sentence types used in contemporary texts such as magazines as well as the use of Chinese characters in classic texts such as *Genji monogatari* (*The Tale of Genji*), Jugaku's work exposed dominant language ideologies of each historical period.

Katsue Akiba-Reynolds translated Lakoff (1975) into Japanese (Reynolds 1985a) and also showed in her own research on various syntactic restrictions in Japanese based on the gender of the speaker (Reynolds 1985b). This work showed how gender-based restriction spread into declaratives, copula deletion and imperative forms, all of which results in women's speech being perceived as "less assertive" and "more tentative", in a nutshell, as "more polite". Since many of the earlier claims on gender differences concentrated on preferred use of certain nouns and adjectives in English (e.g., "divine", "lovely", a wider range of color terms), Reynolds' study made a significant contribution toward understanding the scope of gender differences in different languages. Reynolds (1991) demonstrates that more than 200 years of feudalism had left a lasting mark on contemporary Japanese society and language. This work also noted that these normative rules are not always followed by women, and that the distinctions between women's and men's language use is not necessarily clear-cut. Furthermore, she discussed the use of the male self-referential personal pronoun, *boku* (I) by young females – a use that was considered by some as unthinkable and as posing a serious threat to Japanese society and language. Others saw this use as a sign of young women going through a transformative phase that does not cause any "damage" to the overall language structure. She also discussed the avoidance of using *shujin* (literally "master") to refer to women's husbands. All in all, her work illustrated quite effectively rarely analyzed aspects of Japanese language by female speakers.

Shibamoto (1985) is another influential work on gendered language in Japan, analyzing syntactic features in interviews conducted in the late 1970s. Her focus was on syntactic differences in casual discourse. Her work was revolutionary, as most previous studies had simply relied on researchers' own perceptions of femininity and masculinity. Furthermore, the majority of gendered differences studied prior to Shibamoto's work had examined lexical differences, sentence-final particles or honorific forms. However, Shibamoto found clear gender differences in the deletion of case markers and noun phrases in her extensive data, as females engaged more in these practices than males did.

Wakimae (discernment)

A series of studies by Sachiko Ide represent the majority of work conducted on *wakimae*, for which the closest English equivalent might be "discernment" (Hill et al. 1986; Ide 1989). Ide (1989: 230) defines *wakimae* as showing "verbally and non-verbally one's sense of place or role in a given situation according to social conventions". The concept of *wakimae* in language behavior follows earlier Japanese works such as the study of *nyōbo kotoba* (Kikuzawa 1929; Shiraki 1970) and *yūjogo* (Kunida 1964; Yuzawa 1964). The application of this approach to the analysis of women's language is based on the concept of *isō* (phase) as developed by Kikuzawa (1933) and Mashimo (1969). According to Ide (2006), *isōgo* (*isō* = phase, *-go* = language / word) is different from the notions of "register" or "social dialect" as developed in the West. It refers to the differentiated use of language according to the social or occupational categories that a person belongs to, for example monks, merchants, scholars, court ladies and prostitutes as advocated by Kikuzawa (1933). Ide claims that studying Japanese language in this way is appropriate to Japanese tradition. Furthermore, she maintains that it is important to grasp women's language as *isōgo*, and not see it in comparison to men's language. She argues that the *isōgo* of *nyōbo* and *yūjo* have had a significant influence on contemporary women's language, echoing earlier works discussed in the introduction (e.g., Kunida 1964; Mashimo 1966). According to Ide (2003: 233) *yūjo* "were much respected professionals" and together with *nyōbo*, represented high culture. Both directly relate to present-day women's language. Furthermore, Ide claims that the perception of women's language based on the perspective of *isōgo* gives women's language in Japan positive assessment, as opposed to viewing it negatively as in the western deficient approach.

Ide's views share some features with the "difference approach" advocated by Tannen (1986, 1990), in that gendered differences are seen to originate from the fact that women and men occupy different social roles. Ide and others further developed the concept of social role into a theory of *wakimae*, claiming that discernment is a crucial concept in women's language. Ide also maintains that there are different behavioral rules according to *isō* and that people understand and behave linguistically and extra-linguistically according to these. These rules, in turn, are based on categories of belonging. As a result thereof, Ide et al. (1986, 1991, 2003) argue that women's use of language is more polite than men's due to the fact that

> housewives are engaged in socially oriented, more private activities, whereas men are more frequently involved in efficiency-oriented activities. Since it is a general tendency to use more polite speech in social interaction than in workplace interaction, it is natural for both men and women to use polite speech in ways that reflect this general distinction.
>
> *(Ide 2003: 228)*

It is asserted that "the source of women's more polite speech is the difference in their role rather than a difference in their status" (Ide 2003: 228). It is then elaborated that women's speech conveys the demeanor of "'good manners' (a feature associated with prestigious status, cf. Goffman 1967)" (Ide 2003: 228). Ide and Yoshida (1999) furthermore maintain that honorifics and gender differences can be fully explained by the concept of discernment. Ide repeatedly argues for the employment of a native way of examining Japanese language (e.g., Ide 1989, 1993, 1997, 1999, 2003, 2006, 2011), and to be sure, there are many who charge that sociolinguistics itself suffers from a preoccupation with western perspectives and shows an undue emphasis on English (e.g., Coulmas 2005; Smakman 2015). It is indeed necessary to investigate how people themselves view their language and language use. I will return to this point later.

Historical approaches

Let us first discuss the historical approach to women's language. Ide and Yoshida assert that there is a need for an historical approach to gender-related language issues in Japanese society […]. The studies of gender and language of contemporary Japanese that are based on the perspectives of gender research that have originated in Western research fails to do justice to the issue as it is generally understood in Japanese society.

(Ide and Yoshida 1999: 479–480)

Most of the past 80 years of research on gendered language in Japan have focused on the differences between linguistic segments used by women and men. Endo (1997) offers a historical overview of Japanese illustrating how women were involved in literary activities from ancient mythologies, but also noting that women's involvement stopped around the twelfth century when men started to monopolize political power. Her work provided evidence of historical language behavior and attitudes that people held toward women's language use. It showed that in classic literature such as in the *Kojiki* (*An Account of Ancient Matters*) and in the *Manyōshū* (*Collection of a Myriad Leaves*) few gendered differences were found (see also Shiraki 1970). In addition, when the *Genji Monogatari* (*The Tale of Genji*) was written in the early eleventh century, no profound differences can be found between the ways women and men talked (Kunida 1964; Mashimo 1969). During the Kamakura Period (1185–1333) and the Muromachi Period (1392–1573) the Imperial Court was established, and this led to the rise of *nyōbo kotoba*. As shown above, it was Kikuzawa (1929), a specialist on *nyōbo kotoba*, who introduced gendered language into academia (e.g., Inoue 2004; Nakamura 2014a, 2014b; Washi 2000, 2004). Kikuzawa (1929: 67) listed four feminine characteristics of the language of court:

(1) speak politely,
(2) use beautiful and elegant words,
(3) speak indirectly, and
(4) avoid clumsy Chinese words.

Kikuzawa (1933: 75) then went on to list "characteristics of women's language which are beautiful, soft, and graceful" and also asserted that "these are characteristics of our national language" (see also Inoue 2004; Nakamura 2014a).

"National language scholars" (*kokugo gakusha*) such as Kikuzawa played an active role in connecting emotional sentiments with forms of speech in Japan. This is shown effectively in the work of Inoue (2004) and Washi (2000). Inoue (2004: 57–58) challenges the widely held conception of a Japanese woman's language "with unbroken historical roots in an archetypical Japanese past, and inescapably linked with an equally traditional and archetypical Japanese womanhood". Just as writing in the *genbun itchi* style (unifying speech and writing) helped to carefully craft Standard Japanese at the end of the nineteenth century (Heinrich 2005; Nomura 2007), the concept of women's language was also developed and constructed during this phase of language modernization (Nakamura 2014). Washi (2000) further examined the role played by the National Language Association which was established in 1937 in selecting and propagating specific forms, including nouns and polite language, as "correct" women's language. Washi (2000: 59) asserts that "the aim of the authorities was to subordinate women as a good wives and mothers to men" by establishing the idea of a "correct" women's language.

Nakamura (2007) asserts that the influence of Kikuzawa (1929) on subsequent works was enormous. This is already evidenced by the frequency with which the characteristics mentioned above were repeated as aspects of Japanese women's language over and over again. As an example, Nakamura mentions Yoshida's (1935: 149) claim that men are "intellectual" and "logical" and women are "emotional" and "sensitive". As an effect, women's language is seen as "graceful" and "elegant". The latter are qualities that also serve to characterize Japanese women in general. The ideological nature of these assertions was analyzed by Endo (2008). What separates her work from others is a comparison of *nyōbo kotoba* word formation with word formation processes by contemporary young female Japanese. Despite the difference in time, both word formation processes are found to be identical. However, as noted above, *nyōbo kotoba* is deemed "beautiful" and "elegant" (e.g., Kikuzawa 1929; Yoshida 1935), while the language used by the contemporary youth is considered "corrupted" and "rude". It is entirely the merit of Endo to have debunked such widespread attitudes as being completely ideological and as lacking a scholarly and empirical basis.

Sociophonetic approaches

It is asserted that the biological distinction between women and men involves differences in language behavior. A frequently used example to illustrate this is anatomical differences regarding the larynx size and the vocal cord length. These differences seemingly account for variance in the pitch of people's voices (e.g., Hirano, Sato and Yukizane 1997). Similar to musical instruments, thinner and shorter vocal chords produce higher fundamental frequencies, i.e., higher pitch. It is argued that women produce higher fundamental frequency due to their thinner and shorter vocal tracts, as compared to those of men. At the same time, researchers found that differences in pitch between genders are greater than could be expected based on physical differences alone (e.g., Mattingly 1966; Sach, Lieberman and Erickson 1973), and that there are also cross-linguistic differences (e.g., Simpson 2009). All of this indicates that anatomy alone cannot account for these pitch differences. In earlier research, the high pitch used by Japanese women had been explained by physiological difference (Onishi 1981) or by natural characteristics and personality (Shiraki 1970) such as a "greater expression of emotionalism" (Mashimo 1969, cited in Shibamoto 1985), or as being rooted in the language structure itself (Yamazaki, Hideko and Hollien 1992).

Loveday (1986) provides a first attempt to examine gender-dependent differences in pitch in Japanese on the basis of experiments. He compared Japanese pitch to that of British English from a sociolinguistic perspective. His study employed ten informants, five native speakers of Japanese and five native speakers of British English. All were asked to play a role in a pre-scripted conversation and to read it out in both languages. The conversation included politeness formulae such as greetings and expressions of gratitude. The fundamental frequency of these utterances was analyzed. The results showed that Japanese males restricted themselves to the use of lower ranges (120 Hz) in comparison to English males, and also that there were greater range differences between Japanese females (100–150 Hz) and males (20–50 Hz), than between English females and males. He concluded that these differences rest in rigid expectations of sexual and social roles between Japanese and English society and that these roles cause the differences across the two languages.

In another study of pitch, Ohara (1992) studied six female and six male native speakers of Japanese who read aloud semantically neutral sentences in English and their translated versions in Japanese. All of the female subjects employed a significantly higher pitch when speaking Japanese, and they also used a wider range of pitch. On the other hand, the male informants did not show any statistically significant differences across languages. Ohara (1992: 474) argues that Japanese females were conforming to social expectations concerning pitch behavior since "people modify their pitch in order to convey a particular image or to conform to stereotyped expectations prescribed by their society". Using naturally occurring conversation at work, Ohara (2004) also found that pitch and femininity are mediated by politeness. Although both female and male subjects used varying pitch in conversations between themselves, only female subjects used a higher pitched voice when speaking to customers as compared to talking to acquaintances.

Some studies directly bring gender ideologies of language to the forefront. Ohara (1997) studies assumptions of how Japanese women speak. This is a follow-up study to her earlier work (Ohara 1992) that showed systematic pitch differences between Japanese women and men. She found that only Japanese women (but not men) raise their pitch when speaking in Japanese as compared to speaking in English. Therefore, Ohara (1997) chose to focus on examining the social value attached to "feminine" pitch. She investigated the relationship between pitch and perceived attributes, including "cuteness", "directness", "beautifulness", "kindness", "elegance", "politeness", "softness", "selfishness" and "intelligence". The results showed that the higher the pitch, the more "soft", "cute", "kind", "polite", "elegant" and "beautiful" a woman was perceived to be. On the other hand, the lower the pitch, the "stronger", more "selfish", "intelligent" and "direct" a person was seen to be.

There have also been studies comparing pitch behavior and perception between Japanese speakers and Dutch speakers. Van Bezooijien (1995) tested pitch in its correlation with physical and psychological power between Dutch and Japanese speakers. Eight female subjects for Japanese and Dutch, respectively, were asked to produce speech samples (reading neutral descriptions of a house). The obtained data was modified to yield lower and higher pitched versions, and these samples (lower, original and higher) were then used in a listening experiment. The listening subjects were 30 Japanese and 30 Dutch female and male university students, and they rated the speech in terms "short-tall", "weak-strong", "dependent-independent", "attractive-non-attractive" and "modest-arrogant" binaries. They were also asked to rate the ideal woman and man on the categories "tall", "strong", "independent" and "arrogant". The results showed that higher pitched voices were associated with shorter, weaker and more dependent individuals in both languages but that differentiation between the imagined "ideal woman" and "ideal man" was greater among the Japanese than among the Dutch. Van Bezooijen (1995, 1996) was able to illustrate that pitch, like other aspects of language such as lexicon and syntactic variations or non-linguistic factors such as clothes, hairstyles, way of sitting, etc., are a means to project a specifically gendered image. In another study, van Bezooijen (1996) employed native speakers of Dutch, Flemish and Japanese who read out a semantically neutral description of a house. There were eight females per language. Obtained speech samples were manipulated to produce three different versions (low, intermediate and high pitch). Thirty university students in the Netherlands, 15 females and 15 males, served as listening subjects. It was found there were no gender differences between female and male subjects. There were also no significant differences among the different languages. The experiment showed, however, that

> lower pitched voices suggest a less feminine type of person (more independent, more arrogant, more prestigious, more insensitive, more rational), whereas higher pitched voices evoke a more feminine type of person (more dependent, more modest, less prestigious, more sensitive, more emotional).
>
> *(van Bezooijen 1996: 764)*

Yuasa (2008) conducted a cross-cultural analysis based on voice pitch in Japanese and US English spontaneous conversations. She started with a description of gendered pitch behavior found in novels and etiquette manuals. She then empirically analyzed the relation of attitudinal characteristics, namely, "politeness" and "emotional involvement" in voice pitch. Her work demonstrated that voice pitch was used to express gender and that pitch range indicates differences across two languages when speaking with familiar and non-familiar interlocutors. She also found that both female and male Japanese speakers used a restricted pitch range when speaking with those familiar to them as compared to people with whom they were not familiar.

Media studies

Gendered language and its social significance were carefully designed to maintain social order from the Meiji Period (1868–1912) onwards. Literature in the Meiji Period helped establish gendered language and disseminate it to the public (e.g., Endo 1997; Nakamura 2007; Washi 2000). Over time, not only literary works but also media outlets such as newspapers, TV, radio, dictionaries, movies or anime have greatly contributed to the creation, maintenance and dissemination of gendered speech in Japan.

Endo and her associates analyzed how dictionaries were in the service of reinforcing common-sense assumptions on gender (Endo 1980, 1984, 1985, 1993). Generally speaking, men appear far more often in example sentences. Women, if they appear at all, are typically used as the object of actions rather than the agents of actions. Furthermore, dictionaries consistently employ adjectives for women that highlight their physical appearance and desirability, while men are framed as strong and capable.

Tanaka Kazuko also contributed to gender analysis in the media. Tanaka (1984) and others (Tanaka and Josei to Shinbun Media Kenkyūkai 1990, 2006; Tanaka and Morobashi 1996; Tanaka and Josei Zasshi Kenkyūkai 1989) analyzed expressions in three major newspapers in Japan. They thereby challenged the notion that men are the standard gender. The idea of man as standard can be consistently seen in the use of female prefixes (*josei kanshi*). Female prefixes, underlined in the following, are elements used to show that the referent is a woman as for example in *joshi chūgakusei* (female junior high school student) or *joi* (female doctor). As noted by Tanaka, there is no such thing as "male prefixes", and this absence reveals the unmarked nature of men's speech. Satake (2003) supported this observation by showing that although the prefix *onna-*, which connotes a more offensive meaning, is nowadays used less frequently, many instances of prefixes with *josei-* as in *josei chiji* (female governor) remain. It is argued that the more offensive sounding prefix *onna-* was replaced by *josei-*, but that the use of gender-marking prefixes still continues.

There are etiquette and manner books from the Edo Period (1603–1868) that include assertions about how women should speak (Endo 1997; Nakamura 2007). Such books exist also in contemporary Japan. Okamoto (2010) points out that the vast majority of these books target female readers. Furthermore, almost all of these books promote ideal feminine ways of speaking, namely "polite", "beautiful", "elegant", "kind" and "courteous". This is consistent with findings by Ohara (2002) who asserts that language in self-help books is seen as a tool for allowing women to be loved and to be beautiful.

There are also critical analyses of TV and anime studies. Mizumoto's (2006) examination of TV dramas and Satake's (2003) focus on TV anime both found similar results. Contrary to how people actually use Japanese, TV drama and anime give exaggerated versions of gendered speech, thereby strengthening dominant language ideological views on women's language. Women's language use on TV conforms to stereotypical views of gendered speech. Mizumoto, Fukumori and Takada (2008) distributed questionnaires and received responses from 80 drama writers (only one-fifth of whom were women), who indicated that they purposefully used feminine sentence final particles when they want to emphasize a character's femininity.

Research at the discourse level has shown how language use in the media assists the construction of popular images of femininity. Okamoto and Shibamoto (2008) describe how the use of general stylistic features that are considered the norm for Japanese women's language creates an indexical link to ideologies of femininity. They argue not that the linguistic forms themselves are gendered, but that their interpretations are ideological, and that these interpretations create rather complex connections on the part of listeners to perceived feminine features such as "gentleness", "politeness" and "refinement". This complex process of indexicality, they argue, allows for more varied language use on the part of women and also for contestations of gender ideologies. Ohara and Saft (2003) and Saft and Ohara (2009) show how some participants in Japanese daytime talk shows attempt to negotiate and contest the expression of gender ideologies. At the same time, they also describe how gender ideologies may be expressed within social interaction in ways that favor men and disadvantage women. They illuminate how gender ideologies are employed by participants on talk shows to construct certain behaviors such as adultery as normal for men and other behaviors, for example maintaining a beautiful physical appearance, as part of the normal expectations for women.

Studies on men's speech

The vast majority of gendered speech in Japanese has focused on women. SturtzSreetharan (2004, 2006, 2009) argues that studies of women's language typically assume men's language to be a stable baseline of comparison. As an effect, women's speech is described in terms of how it differs from men's speech, for example, that it is "more polite" or "less vulgar". Since empirical studies of men in conversational interaction is rare, it is unquestionably assumed that men's speech is what women's speech is not. In other words, men's speech is assumed to be normative and unmarked. SturtzSreetharan has been pioneering studies that actually study the real language behavior of Japanese men in casual conversation. For instance, using data collected in 1979 in the Kanto area – with subjects described as native-speaking middle-class men in their 30s and 40s – she demonstrated that these men engaged in talk about many different topics, including personal and emotional topics such as in-laws, extramarital affairs, children, care for aging parents and their relationships with their wives (Sturtz 2002). She showed that these men also exhibited various supportive and collaborative conversational strategies such as latching, overlapping and verbal insertions that assist in the development of these topics, despite the fact that these supportive strategies have been claimed to be used mostly by women (e.g., Fishman 1978, Lakoff 1975, Tannen 1990).

SturtzStreetharan also criticized research on Japanese gendered speech for concentrating too much on women's speech and on Standard Japanese. Consequently, SturtzStreetharan (2004, 2006, 2009) used conversational data by Japanese males who speak Kansai dialect. The ages of her informants ranged from 19 to 68 years, and their occupations varied, ranging from university students, white-collar workers and white-collar retirees. The focus of Sturtz (2004) was on sentence-final particles. The data of her study showed that only the youngest group, university students, used the most masculine forms, *-zo* and *-ze*, while the most frequently used forms by all men were actually gender-neutral forms.

SturtzStreetharan (2006) used the same naturally occurring casual conversational data-set as above – with participants who were male and friends with each other – to investigate the use of the polite *-masu* verb ending. It turned out that the youngest speakers produced the least amount of this polite form, followed by the oldest group, while the middle-aged group produced it most frequently. First and second person pronouns are the focus in SturtzStreetharan (2009). Results show that the most common use is the non-occurrence (pronoun drop). It was also found that the younger speakers use the stronger form *ore* while older males use the less-masculine *boku*. This finding is in line with her previous studies, indicating the youngest speakers using more masculine syntactic forms and sentence-final particles.

SturtzStreetharan (2004: 84) succeeded in demonstrating that her research "challenges the model of 'the generic Japanese man'". Her work indicates, in contrast to what the literature states, that men do not generally use strongly masculine forms that include sentence-final particles, morphology, syntax and first and second person pronouns. In addition, her research suggests that men employ conversational strategies that have supportive discourse functions. All in all, her work challenges the stereotypical assumption of men being mainly engaged in impersonal topics and competition for the floor.

Outlook

This chapter gave an overview of Japanese gendered speech from the 1930s to the present. It showed that gendered speech has been studied from diverse perspectives with distinct focuses that include the lexicon, sentence-final particles, syntax, phonetics, discourse and media as well as ideology. So is Japanese women's language dwindling as some scholars and the general public suspect (e.g., Bunkachō 2016)? To answer this a question, Satake (2012) provides a compelling argument. Examining headlines on language use in newspapers from 1949–1999, she persistently found criticism on "recent changes" in women's language, most notably that it was losing its distinct feminine characteristics and was becoming more similar to men's speech. She concluded that during these 50 years the same comment about the masculinization of women's language had been continuously repeated, and that these comments were indicative of the socially expected norms of how women should speak. Kumagai (2016) also discusses the existence of this common-sense assumption about women's language among the public and scholars, and following Endo et al. (2004), she criticizes attempts to reconstruct gendered speech on radio and TV shows despite the existence of notable differences in how people actually talk. Reynolds (1990) also discusses the alleged "recently" emerging use of *boku* by young female students by reminding her readers that Jugaku (1979) already talked about this "recent trend" 40 years ago.

How gendered language has been studied is largely based on how it is perceived. The idea that women and men use different linguistic forms (e.g., personal pronouns and sentence-final particles) is a topic that is often too easily discussed. Gottlieb asserts that language practices are actually language policies because they have a significant influence on language ideologies:

> This is true not only in the overt domain of language policy but also in the covert, i.e., in the domain of the unstated but nevertheless completely understood expectations which frame the use of language in particular situations and are accepted as the prescriptive norm.
>
> (Gottlieb 2012: 3)

According to a language attitude survey by the Agency for Cultural Affairs (Bunkachō 2016), women's language and honorifics are seen as integral parts of beautiful Japanese (*utsukushii nihongo*).

The concept of women's language is today also frequently presented in translation, in manga and in robots. There are studies demonstrating that robots are gendered according to normative assumptions. Japan possesses the largest number of industrial robots across the globe. In fact, Japan owns over half of all industrial robots worldwide. Japan also leads in the creation of robots (Robertson 2010). The field of robotics is well-funded and enjoys much support in Japan. Prime Minister Abe Shinzo has expressed his desire to "make robots a key pillar of our growth strategy"

(Tobe 2014). The field of robotics is working to develop human-like robots (humanoids). Japanese humanoid roboticists are aiming to manufacture bio-compatible materials such as artificial muscles and tissues, and they are also incorporating common-sense assumptions about gender into these humanoids. Robertson (2011: 4) argues that "[h]ow robot-makers gender their humanoids is a tangible manifestation of their tacit understanding of femininity in relation to masculinity, and vice versa". More recent humanoids talk in a "gendered" manner that includes a breathy, high pitched and girlish voice (Robertson 2011). If roboticists are reinforcing the stereotypes of women in gynoids and gendering robots as asserted by Robertson (2010, 2011), it would be insightful to study the speech of these humanoids. Likewise, it would also make the study of the effects of their linguistic behavior on humans an interesting area of research.

Let's return to the argument presented at the start, that is, the claim that "recent changes" in gendered speech could reflect an "improved nature of sexism" in Japan. Current Prime Minister Abe Shinzo's "'womenomics' – a policy of opening top political and business positions to women" (Schieder 2014: 53) is intricately interrelated with the actual situation of contemporary Japanese women. However, the reality for regular women involves a persistent institutionalized sexism with a decrease in job security and an increase in dead end jobs (Allison 2013), resulting in growing singlehood (Yoshida 2016) as well as in a feminization of poverty (Schieder 2014). From this perspective, attributing changes in gendered speech to the "decrease in sexism" in Japan is problematic for two reasons. For one, as demonstrated above through the work of Reynolds (1990), Jugaku (1979) and Satake (2012), this supposedly "recent change" has been with us for a long period of time. Second, it is actually the ideologies of the gendered speech that we are dealing with (e.g., Endo et al. 2004; Heinrich 2012; Nakamura 2014a, 2014b; Ohara 1992; SturtzStreetharan 2009). It is imperative for scholars, first of all, to be aware what phenomena they are actually dealing with, whether it is the "ideology of language" or "actual language usage", in order to make significant contributions and meaningful advancements in this field.

References

Abe, Hideko (2004) Lesbian Bar Talk in Shinjuku, Tokyo. In: *Japanese Language, Gender, and Ideology. Cultural Models and Real People*. Shigeko Okamoto and Janet S. Shibamoto (eds), 205–221. Oxford: Oxford University Press.

——— (2010) *Queer Japanese. Gender and Sexual Identities through Linguistic Practices*. New York: Palgrave Macmillan.

Allison, Anne (2013) *Precarious Japan*. Durham: Duke University Press.

Bing, Janet and Victoria Bergvall (1996) The Question of Questions. Beyond Binary Thinking. In: *Rethinking Language and Gender Research. Theory and Practice*. Victoria Bergvall, Janet Bing and Alice Freed (eds), 1–30. London: Longman.

Bunkachō (2016) Heisei 27-nendo "kokugo ni kansuru yoron chōsa" no kekka no gaiyō [Summary of the Results of the Public Opinion Poll on National Language]. Available online at: www.bunka.go.jp/koho_hodo_oshirase/hodohappyo/pdf/2016092101_besshi.pdf (accessed 13 February 2017).

Butler, Judith (1990) *Gender Trouble. Feminism and Subversion of Identity*. New York: Routledge.

Coates, Jennifer (1986) *Women, Men, and Language. A Sociolinguistic Account of Sex Differences in Language*. London: Longman.

Coulmas, Florian (2005) *Sociolinguistics. The Study of Speakers' Choice*. Cambridge: Cambridge University Press.

de Beauvoir, Simone (1974[1949]) *The Second Sex*. New York: Random House.

Doi, Tadao, Takeshi Morita, Minoru Chonan (eds) (2013[1603]) *Hōyaku nippo jisho* [Japanese Translation, Japanese–Portuguese Dictionary]. Tokyo: Iwanami.

Ecklund, Elaine Howard, Anne E. Lincoln and Cassandra Tansey (2012) Gender Segregation in Elite Academic Science. *Gender & Society* 26: 693–717.

Endo, Orie (1980) Josei o arawasu kotoba [Words to Express Women]. *Kotoba* 1: 19–54.

―――― (1985) *Kokugo jiten ni miru josei sabetsu* [*Sexism in Japanese Dictionaries*]. Tokyo: San'ichi Shobō.
―――― (1997) *Onna no kotoba no bunkashi* [*The Cultural History of Women's Language*]. Tokyo: Gakuyō Shobō.
―――― (2001) *Onna to kotoba* [*Women and Language*]. Tokyo: Akashi Shoin.
―――― (2008) The Role of Court Lady's Language in the Historical Norm Construction of Japanese Women's Language. *Gender and Language* 2(11): 9–24.
Endo, Orie, Taku Kimura, Takashi Sakurai, Chieko Suzuki and Haruko Hayakawa (2004) *Senjichū no hanashi kotoba* [*Spoken Language during the War*]. Tokyo: Hitsuji Shobō.
Fishman, Pamela M. (1978) Interaction. The Work Women Do. *Social Problems* 25(4): 397–406.
Garfinkel, Harold (1967) *Studies in Ethnomethodology*. Englewood Cliffs: Prentice-Hall.
Gottlieb, Nanette (2012) *Language Policy in Japan. The Challenge of Change*. Cambridge: Cambridge University Press.
Heinrich, Patrick (2002) Gengo seikatsu. The Study of Language Life in Japan, 1945–1995. *Historiographia Linguistica* 29(1/2): 95–119.
―――― (2005) Things you Have to Leave Behind. The Demise of "Elegant Writing" and the Rise of genbun itchi Style in Meiji-period Japan. *Journal of Historical Pragmatics* 6(1): 113–32.
―――― (2012) *The Making of Monolingual Japan. Language Ideology and Japanese Modernity*. Bristol: Multilingual Matters.
―――― (2015) The Study of Politeness and Women's Language in Japan. In: *Globalising Sociolinguistics. Challenging and Expanding Theory*. Dick Smakman and Patrick Heinrich (eds), 178–193. London: Routledge.
Hill, Beverly, Sachiko Ide, Shoko Ikuta, Akiko Kawasaki and Tsunao Ogino (1986) Universals of Linguistic Politeness. Quantitative Evidence from Japanese and American English. *Journal of Pragmatics* 10: 347–371.
Hiramoto, Mie and Andrew Wong (2005) Another Look at "Japanese Women's Language". A Prosodic Analysis. *Proceedings from the Annual Meeting of the Chicago Linguistics Society* 41(1): 111–123.
Hirano, Minoru, Kiminori Sato and Kei'ichiro Yukizane (1997) Male-female Difference in Anterior Commissure Angle. In: *Speech Production and Language*. Shigeru Kiritani, Hajime Hirose and Hiroya Fujisaki (eds), 11–17. Berlin: Mouton de Gruyter.
Horii, Reiji (1990) *Onna no Kotoba* [*Women's Language*]. Tokyo: Meiji Shoin.
Howard, Judith A. (2000) Social Psychology of Identities. *Annual Review of Sociology* 26: 367–393.
Ide, Sachiko (1989) Formal Forms and Discernment. Two Neglected Aspects of Universals of Linguistic Politeness. *Multilingua* 8(2/3): 223–234.
Ide, Sachiko (ed.) (1993) *Sekai no joseigo, nihon no jogseigo* [*Women's Languages in the World, Women's Language in Japan*] (= Special Issue of *Nihongogaku* 12). Tokyo: Meiji Shoin.
―――― (ed.) (1997) *Joseigo no sekai* [*The World of Women's Language*]. Tokyo: Meiji Shoin.
―――― (2003) Women's Language as a Group Identity Marker in Japanese. In: *Gender Across Languages. The Linguistic Representation of Women and Men* (volume 3). Marlis Hellinger and Hadomud Bußmann (eds), 227–238. Amsterdam: John Benjamins.
―――― (2006) *Wakimae no goyōron* [*The Pragmatics of Discernment*]. Tokyo: Taishūkan.
Ide, Sachiko and Kishiko Ueno (2011) Honorifics and Address Terms. In: *Pragmatics of Society*. Gisle Andersen and Karin Aijmer (eds), 439–470. Berlin: de Gruyter Mouton.
―――― (2011) Roots of the wakimae Aspects of Linguistics Politeness. Modal Expressions and Japanese Sense of Self. In: *Pragmaticizing Understanding*. Michael Meeuwis and Jan-Ola Östman (eds), 121–138. Amsterdam: John Benjamins.
Ide, Sachiko and Naomi McGloin (1991) *Aspects of Japanese Women's Language*. Tokyo: Kuroshio Shuppan.
Ide, Sachiko, Tsunao Ogino, Akiko Kawasaki and Shoko Ikuta (1986) *Nihonjin to amerikajin no keigo kōdō* [*The Linguistic Politeness of Japanese and Americans*]. Tokyo: Nanundo.
Ide, Sachiko and Megumi Yoshida (1999) Sociolinguistics. Honorifics and Gender Differences. In: *The Handbook of Japanese Linguistics*. Natsuko Tsujimura (ed.), 444–480. Malden: Blackwell.
Imai, Terumi (2010) An Emerging Gender Difference in Japanese Vowel Devoicing. In: *A Reader in Sociophonetics*. Dennis R. Preston and Nancy Niedzielski (eds), 177–187. New York: de Gruyter Mouton.
Inoue, Miyako (2004) Gender, Language, and Modernity. Toward an Effective History of "Japanese Women's Language". In: *Japanese Language, Gender, and Ideology. Cultural Models and Real People*. Shigeko Okamoto and Janet S. Shibamoto (eds), 57–75. Oxford: Oxford University Press.
Jugaku, Akiko (1979) *Nihongo to onna* [*Japanese Language and Women*]. Tokyo: Akashi Shoten.
Kessler, Suzanne. J. and Wendy McKenna (1985[1978]) *Gender. An Ethnomethodological Approach*. Chicago: Chicago University Press.

Kessler, Suzanne J. (1990) The Medical Construction of Gender. Case Management of Intersexed Infants. *Signs* 16(1): 3–26.

——— (1998) *Lessons from the Intersexes*. New Brunswick: Rutgers University Press.

Kikuzawa, Sueo (1929) Fujin no kotoba no tokuchō ni tsuite [On Characteristics of Women's Language]. *Kokugo kyōiku* 14(3): 66–75.

——— (1933) *Kokugo kagaku kōza (3). Kokugogaku kokugo isōron* [*Course in National Language Science (volume 3). The Phasic Theory of National Language*]. Tokyo: Meiji Shoin.

Kindaichi, Haruhiko (1957) *Nihongo* [*The Japanese Language*]. Tokyo: Iwanami Shoten.

Kumagai, Shigeko (2016) Rethinking the Discourse on "Women's Language" is Dwindling. *Jinbun ronshū* 67(1): 111–128.

Kunida, Yuriko (1964) *Nyōbo kotoba no kenkyū* [*The Study of the Language of Court Ladies*]. Tokyo: Kazama Shobō.

Lakoff, Robin (1975) *Language and Women's Place*. New York: Harper & Row.

Loveday, Leo (1986) *Explorations in Japanese Sociolinguistics*. New York: John Benjamins.

Maltz, Daniel L. and Ruth Borker (1982) A Cultural Approach to Male-female Miscommunication. In: *Language and Social Identity*. John J. Gumperz (ed.), 196–216. Cambridge: Cambridge University Press.

Mashimo, Saburo (1969[1948]) *Fujingo no kenkyū* [*The Study of Women's Language*]. Tokyo: Tōkyōdō Shuppan.

——— (1966) *Yūrigo no kenkyū* [*The Study of Language Used in Red-light Districts*]. Tokyo: Tōkyōdō Shuppan.

Mattingly, Ignatius (1966) Speaker Variation and Vocal Tract Size. *Journal of the Acoustical Society of America* 39: 1219.

Mizumoto, Terumi (2006) Terebi dorama to jisshakai ni okeru josei bunmatsushi shiyō no zure ni miru jendā firutā [The Gender Filter as Seen in Discrepancies in Women's Use of Sentence-final Forms in Television Dramas versus Real Society]. In: *Nihongo to jendā*. Nihongo Jendā Gakkai (ed.), 73–94. Tokyo: Hitsuji Shobō.

Mizumoto, Terumi, Sugako Fukumori and Kyōko Takada (2008) Dorama ni tsukawareru josei bunmatsushi – kyakuhonka no ishiki chōsa yori [Feminine Sentence Ending Forms Used in Dramas. From Attitude Survey of Drama Writers]. *Nihongo to Jendā* 8. Online available at https://gender.jp/journal/backnumber/no8_contents/mizumoto/ (accessed 26 March 2019).

Money, John, Joan G. Hampson and John L. Hampson (1955a) An Examination of Some Basic Sexual Concepts. The Evidence of Human Hermaphroditism. *Johns Hopkins Hospital Bulletin* 97: 301–319.

——— (1955b) Hermaphroditism. Recommendations Concerning Assignment of Sex, Change of Sex, and Psychological Management. *Johns Hopkins Hospital Bulletin* 97: 284–300.

Nakamura, Momoko (2007) *"Onna kotoba" wa tsukurareru* [*"Women's Language is Constructed"*]. Tokyo: Hitsuji Shobō.

——— (2014a) Historical Discourse Approach to Japanese Women's Language. Ideology, Indexicality, and Metalanguage. In: *Handbook of Language, Gender, and Sexuality* (second edition). Susan Ehrlich, Miriam Meyerhoff and Janet Homes (eds), 378–395. Malden: John Wiley & Sons.

——— (2014b) *Gender, Language and Ideology. A Genealogy of Japanese Women's Language*. Amsterdam: John Benjamin.

Nishino, Aki (2015) Seibetsu iwa o yūsuru mono no shakaiteki seibetsu ikō ni kansuru shinrigakuteki kenkyū [Psychological Study on Gender Shifting of those who Possess Differing Gender Identity]. PhD thesis, Mejiro University Tokyo.

Nomura, Takashi (2007) Meiji sutandādo to genbun itchi. Genbun itchi o chūshin ni [Standard in Meiji and genbun itchi. Focusing on genbun itchi]. *Language, Information, Text* 14: 35–67.

Oakely, Ann (1972) *Sex, Gender, and Society*. London: Temple Smith.

Ogawa, Naoko and Janet S. Shibamoto (1997) The Gendering of the Gay Male Sex Class in Japan. In: *Queerly Phrase. Language, Gender, and Sexuality*. Anna Livia and Kira Hall (eds), 402–415. Oxford: Oxford University Press.

Ohara, Yumiko (1992) Gender-dependent Pitch Levels in Japanese and English. In: *Locating Power. Proceedings of the Second Berkeley Women and Language Conference*. Kira Hall, Mary Bucholtz and Birch Moonwomon (eds), 469–477. Berkeley: Berkeley Women and Language Group.

——— (1997) Shakai onseigaku no kanten kara mita nihonjin no koe no kōtei [Japanese Pitch from a Sociophonetic Perspective] In: *Joseigo no Sekai*. Sachiko Ide (ed.), 42–58. Tokyo: Meiji Shoin.

——— (2002) Ideology of Language and Gender. A Critical Discourse Analysis of Japanese Prescriptive Texts. In: *Critical Discourse Analysis. Critical Concepts in Linguistics*. Michael Toolan (ed.), 273–286. London: Routledge.

───── (2004) Prosody and Gender in Workplace Interaction. Exploring Constraints and Resources in the Use of Japanese. In: *Japanese Language, Gender, and Ideology. Cultural Models and Real People*. Shigeko Okamoto and Janet S. Shibamoto (eds), 222–239. Oxford: Oxford University Press.

Ohara, Yumiko and Scott Saft (2003) Using Conversation Analysis to Track Gender Ideologies in Social Interaction. Toward a Feminist Analysis of a Japanese Phone-in Consultation TV Program. *Discourse & Society* 14(2): 153–172.

Okamoto, Shigeko (1995) "Tasteless" Japanese. Less Feminine Speech among Young Japanese Women. In: *Gender Articulated. Language and the Socially Constructed Self*. Kira Hall and Mary Bucholtz (eds), 297–325. New York: Routledge.

───── (2010) Kotoba bijin ni naru hō. Josei no hanashikata o oshieru jitsuyōsho no bunseki [How to Become a Language Beauty. Analysis of Self-help Books that Teach Women how to Talk]. *Nihongo to jendā* 10: 1–24.

Okamoto, Shigeko and Janet S. Shibamoto (2008) Constructing Linguistic Femininity in Contemporary Japan. Scholarly and Popular Representations. *Gender and Language* 2(1): 87–112.

Onishi, Masao (1981) *A Grand Dictionary of Phonetics*. Tokyo: Phonetic Society of Japan.

Reynolds, Katsue A. (1985a) *Gengo to sei – eigo ni okeru onna no ichi* [*Language and Gender. Women's Place in English*] (translation of Robin Lakoff, *Language and Women's Place*). Tokyo: Yūshindō.

───── (1985b) Female Speakers of Japanese. *Feminist Issues* 5(2): 13–46.

───── (1991) Female Speakers of Japanese in Transition. In: *Aspects of Japanese Women's Language*. Sachiko Ide and Naomi H. McGloin (eds), 127–144. Tokyo: Kuroshio Shuppan.

Robertson, Jennifer (2010) Gendering Humanoid Robots: Robo-sexism in Japan. *Body & Society* 16(2): 1–36.

───── (2011) Gendering Robots. Posthuman Traditionalism in Japan. In: *Recreating Japanese Men*. Sabine Frühstück and Anne Walthall (eds), 284–310. Berkeley: University of California Press.

Sachs, Jacqueline, Philip Lieberman and Donna Erickson (1973) Anatomical and Cultural Determinants of Male and Female Speech. In: *Language Attitudes. Current Trends and Prospects*. Roger W. Shuy and Ralph W. Fasold (eds), 74–84. Washington D.C.: Georgetown University Press.

Saft, Scott and Yumiko Ohara (2009) Men's Adultery as Sickness. Metaphor, Gender Categories and the Discursive Construction of Gender Differences on Japanese Television Consultation Programs. *Critical Inquiry in Language Studies* 6(3): 113–147.

Satake, Kuniko (2003) Terebi anime no rufu-suru "onna kotoba/otoko kotoba" kihan [Norms for "Women's Language and Men's Language Disseminated by TV Anime]. *Kotoba* 24: 43–59.

───── (2012) Joseigo no keisei to suitai [Formation and Dwindling of Women's Language]. *Nihongogaku* 31(7): 44–55.

Schieder, Chelsea Szendi (2014) Womenomics vs. Women. Neoliberal Cooptation of Feminism in Japan. *Meiji Journal of Political Science and Economics* 3: 53–60.

Shibamoto, Janet. S. (1985) *Japanese Women's Language*. New York: Academic Press.

───── (2003) Gendered Structures in Japanese. In: *Gender Across Languages. The Linguistic Representation of Women and Men* (volume 3). Marlis Hellinger and Hadumod Bußmann (eds), 201–225. Amsterdam: John Benjamins.

Sibata, Takesi (1999) *Sociolinguistics in Japanese Contexts* (translated, edited and introduced by Tetsuya Kunihiro, Fumio Inoue and Daniel Long). Berlin: Mouton de Gruyter.

Shiraki, Susumu (1970) Nihongo ni okeru joseigo no seiritsu to sono haikei no kōsatsu [The Study of the Formation and Background of Women's Language in Japanese]. *Kokubungaku kenkyū* 6 : 155–166.

Simpson, Adrian P. (2009) Phonetic Differences between Male and Female Speech. *Language and Linguistics Compass* 3(2): 621–640.

Smakman, Dick (2015) The Westernizing Mechanisms in Sociolinguistics. In: *Globalizing Sociolinguistics. Challenging and Expanding Theory*. Dick Smakman and Patrick Heinrich (eds), 16–36. London: Routledge.

Spender, Dale (1980) *Man Made Language*. New York: Routledge & Kegan Paul.

Sturtz, Cindi (2002) "Uwaki tte iu no wa attemo ii-n janai ka?" Japanese Men's Conversations Up-close and Personal. *Japanese Studies* 22(1): 49–63.

SturtzStreetharan, Cindi (2004) Students, sarariiman (pl.), and Seniors. Japanese Men's Use of "Manly" Speech Register. *Language in Society* 33(1): 81–107.

───── (2006) Gentlemanly Gender? Japanese Men's Use of Clause-final Politeness in Casual Conversations. *Journal of Sociolinguistics* 10(1): 70–92.

───── (2009) Ore and omae. Japanese Men's Uses of First- and Second-person Pronouns. *Pragmatics* 19(2): 253–278.

Tanaka, Kazuko (1984) Shinbun ni miru kōzōka sareta seisabetsu hyōgen [The Structured Sex Discriminated Expressions Seen in Newspapers]. In: *Masukomi to sabetsugo mondai*. Ei'ichi Isomura and Yasunori Fukuoka (eds), 198–201. Tokyo: Akashi Shoten.

Tanaka, Kazuko and Josei to Shinbun Media Kenkyūkai (1990) Shinbun shimen ni arawareta gendā. Seisabetsu hyōgen no ryōteki bunseki o chūshin ni [Gender that Appeared on Newspapers. Focusing on Quantitative Studies of Sexist Expressions]. *Kokugakuin hōgaku* 28(1): 87–119.

——— (2006) Shinbun ni oite josei wa dono yō ni hyōgen sareteiru ka, shinbun shimen ni arawareta jendā dai-yonkai chōsa o chūshi ni [How are Women Expressed on Newspapers, Gender that Appeared on Newspapers, Focusing on the Fourth Investigation]. *Kokugakuin hōgaku* 43(4): 69–162.

Tanaka, Kazuko and Josei Zasshi Kenkyūkai (1989) *Josei zasshi o kaidoku suru* [*Analyzing Women's Magazines*]. Tokyo: Kakiuchi Shuppan.

Tanaka, Kazuko and Taiki Morobashi (eds) (1996) *Jendā kara mita shinbun no ura omote* [*The Front and Back of Newspapers Seen from the Perspective of Gender*]. Tokyo: Gendai Shokan.

Tannen, Deborah (1986) *That's not What I Meant*. New York: Morrow.

——— (1990) *You Just Don't Understand. Women and Men in Conversation*. New York: Virgo Press.

Thorne, Barry and Nancy Henley (eds.) (1975) *Language and Sex. Difference and Dominance*. Rowley: Newbury House.

Tobe, Frank (2014) Japan's New Robotics Push. Funding and Deregulation. The Robot Report. Tracking the Business of Robotics. Available online at: www.therobotreport.com/news/japans-new-robotics-push-funding-and-deregulation (accessed 2 February 2017).

Uchida, Aki (1992) When "Difference" is "Dominance": A Critique of the "Anti-power-based" Cultural Approach to Sex Differences. *Language in Society* 21(4): 547–568.

Valentine, James (1997) Pots and Pans. Identification of Queer Japanese in Terms of Discrimination. In: *The Gendering of the Gay Male Sex Class in Japan*. Anna Livia and Kira Hall (eds), 95–114. Oxford: Oxford University Press.

van Bezooijen, Renee (1995) Sociocultural Aspects of Pitch Differences between Japanese and Dutch Women. *Language and Speech* 38(3): 253–265.

——— (1996) The Effect of Pitch of the Attribution of Gender-related Personality Traits. In: *Gender and Belief System. Proceedings of the Berkeley Women and Language Conference*. Natasha Warner, Jocelyn Ahlers, Leela Bilmes, Monica Oliver, Suzanne Wertheim and Melina Chen (eds), 755–766. Berkeley: Berkeley Women and Language Group.

Washi, Rumi (2000) Japanese Female Speech and Language Policy. On the Meaning of the Relationship between the National Language Association and the Leaders of Female Educators during the Total War. *Journal of Gender Studies* 3: 59–69.

——— (2004) "Japanese Female Speech" and Language Policy in the World War II Era. In: *Japanese Language, Gender, and Ideology. Cultural Models and Real People*. Shigeko Okamoto and Janet S. Shibamoto (eds), 76–91. Oxford: Oxford University Press.

West, Candace and Don H. Zimmerman (1987) Doing Gender. *Gender & Society* 1(2): 125–151.

Yamazawa, Hideko and Harry Hollien (1992) Speaking Fundamental Frequency Pattern of Japanese Women. *Phonetica* 49(2): 128–140.

Yoshida, Akiko (2016) *Unmarried Women in Japan. The Drift into Singlehood*. London: Routledge.

Yoshida, Sumio (1935) Fujin no kotoba [Language of Women]. In: *Kotoba no kōza dai-ni shū*. Japan Broadcasting Corporation Publishing (ed.), 145–156. Tokyo: NHK Shuppan.

Yoshizawa, Kyosuke (2016) "Seidōitsu shōgai" gainen no fukyū ni tomonau toransu gendā kaishaku no henka [The Changes Promoted by Spread of the Concept "Gender Identity Disorder"]. Available online at: http://teapot.lib.ocha.ac.jp/ocha/bitstream/10083/58416/1/193-202.pdf (accessed 14 February 2017).

Yuasa, Ikuko, P. (2008) *Culture and Gender of Voice Pitch. A Sociophonetic Comparison of the Japanese and Americans*. London: Equinox.

Yuzawa, Kokichiro (1964) *Kuruwa kotoba no kenkyū* [*The Study of Language Used in Red-light Districts*]. Tokyo: Meiji Shoin.

Zimmerman, Don H. and Candace West (1975) Sex Role, Interruptions and Silences in Conversation. In: *Language and Sex. Differences and Dominance*. Barrie Thorn and Nancy Henley (eds), 105–129. Rowley: Newbury House.

PART IV

Language problems and language planning

19
LANGUAGE POLICY AND PLANNING

Ruriko Otomo

Introduction

Language policy and planning (LPP) has constituted one of the prominent sociolinguistic fields in Japan, as shown in several well-established English references (e.g., Carroll 2001; Gottlieb 2011). This notwithstanding, few attempts have been made to provide an introductory yet comprehensive overview on the disciplinary trends and developments. The aim of this chapter is, therefore, to organize intellectual contributions made in the context of Japan in line with the scholarly progress of LPP. It is not meant to be an exhaustive list of LPP research concerning Japanese (imperial) territory, and/or languages in linguistic, historical and socio-political relationship to Japan. This chapter rather attempts to be one of heuristics for LPP researchers to reflect on their past and current works, and identify the potential direction toward which their current and future research can move. Such a reflective mode of analysis is a much-needed practice, since consideration of researchers' reflexivity and subjectivity has been recognized as LPP researchers' moral responsibility (Ramanathan 2011; Lin 2015) as well as an essential opportunity to discover and develop new and alternative understandings of any research project (Alvesson and Sköldberg 2000).

Researchers' self-reflection is also likely to broaden the potential of LPP studies in general. The present social climate marks the changing role of nation-states which are long considered as the de facto and often exclusive policymaking authority, while witnessing the emergence of other alternative forms of control and technologies of order (Gee, Glynda and Lankshear 1996; Bauman 1998). This contemporary societal condition allows new forms of language policy to emerge, requiring LPP researchers to focus on multiple manifestations of policy representation, discourse and knowledge about language. Thus, the complex nature of language policy that is intricately linked with historical, economic, socio-political and educational issues is highlighted, giving research opportunities not only for LPP researchers, but also for those whose research interests are thought to have had little relevance to LPP.

This chapter is organized as follows. I begin with outlining the theoretical progress of the LPP discipline, which is roughly divided into three phases; classical, critical and what I will call here in absence of an established term, "new-wave". Then, I turn my attention to LPP works done in the context of Japan, mapping them onto the three phases provided above. The final section offers a summary on the LPP genealogy map with a call for further research in the new-wave direction.

Overview of three developmental stages in the field of LPP

This section summarizes the theoretical development of LPP. As any development cannot be documented in a clear-cut linear manner, the LPP scholarship has been transformed gradually through several changes and has been characterized by periods of reflection and critique (Johnson 2013; Johnson and Ricento 2013; Nekvapil 2011; Ricento 2000; Tollefson 2011). However, I introduce three major phases in which theoretical moves are relatively observable, and discuss changing views and approaches toward language planning and policymaking.

Classical LPP work in the early 1960s was characterized by such themes as "decolonization, structuralism and pragmatism" (Ricento 2000: 197). Many scholars, usually trained in structural linguistics, joined language planning projects and became involved as experts in policymaking in order to solve language problems affecting newly independent nations and to modernize those countries through language reforms (see, for example, Fishman, Ferguson and Das Gupta 1968). A similar approach was also applied to older, established nations such as France and Turkey (Fishman 1972) which sought national unity under the banner of one-language, one-nation and one-culture. During this formative period of LPP, language forms and language functions were at issue. Based on Haugen (1966), Kloss (1966) categorized these two aspects as "corpus planning" and "status planning" respectively. Corpus planning deals with cultivation of language itself (e.g., standardization of grammar and orthography, dictionary making) while status planning attaches functional and symbolical meanings to language (e.g., national language and official language). Researchers such as Ferguson (1968), Haugen (1966) and Kloss (1966) created fundamental frameworks and typologies to account for types, approaches, goals and processes of language planning and language policy.

This early period of LPP was charged with hopes and expectations that language planning and policymaking had a high potential to help to modernize and develop what was then called "third-world nations" (see Tollefson 2011). However, in the 1970s and 1980s, these aspirations faded due to unwanted results. Some LPP scholars found the early LPP frameworks naïve and inadequate in their ability to address social, political, historical and cultural factors that influence processes and outcomes of language policy and language planning (Johnson and Ricento 2013; Ricento 2000). Johnson and Ricento (2013: 10) identified three major advancements of this reflective period, "a broader focus on activity in multiple contexts and layers of LPP"; "attention to language planning for schools"; and "increased focus on the socio-political and/or ideological nature of LPP", all of which provide a springboard for the emergence of the next phase of LPP, that is, the critical approach.

With the rise of critical theory in other academic disciplines, an application of critical theory to the field of LPP marked an influential turn in the theoretical evolution and has remained a seminal approach up to today. Critical language policy (Tollefson 2006) depicts a more delicate and contextualized social world and draws attention to a close relationship between language and politics, economy and history in society. For instance, Tollefson's historical-structural approach (1991) accounts for socio-political, historical and ideological influences on language planning and policymaking. He argued that power, ideology and social structure constitute the basis on which dominant social groups make choices about language. Therefore, these issues have considerable effects on language policy as well as on the conditions under which it is planned. The historical-structural approach distinguishes itself from the earlier approach, i.e., "the neo-classical approach" in Tollefson's terminology, which saw language planning and policymaking as an ideologically neutral and problem-oriented activity.

While critical language policy has had a great deal of impact in the body of LPP scholarship, it has also faced criticism. For example, Davis (1999: 70) pointed out its inability of addressing "current conditions and methods for determining or documenting language plans" (1999: 70) and "the actual needs and purposes of language and literacy within speech communities" (1999: 71). In addition to critical LPP's deterministic attitude and methodological limitation, others (Hornberger and Johnson 2007; Liddicoat and Baldauf 2008; Ricento and Hornberger 1996) have also stated that the conceptualization of power in critical language policy downplays the importance of agency, that is "the role of individuals and collectives in the processes of language use, attitudes and ultimately policies" (Ricento 2000: 208).

Greater awareness of agency has pushed the field forward, resulting in the emergence of new-wave LPP research in the recent decade. While acknowledging the advances of critical language policy, a number of scholars have argued for more attention to "agents, levels and processes" (Ricento and Hornberger 1996: 408) and started looking at local contexts, agency, interpretation and implementation in language planning and policymaking. Therefore, this approach often combines the integration of so-called "top-down" and "bottom-up" approaches, analyzing authoritative language policy documents as well as local policy implementation efforts, paying more attention to the oft-ignored meso-level of policy activities, such as local government and school as an intermediate institution.

A genealogy of Japanese LPP studies

According to the three paradigms elucidated above, this section organizes language planning and policymaking activities and research literature on language varieties existing in Japan, in various Japanese diasporas in the past and at present, and in myriads of Japanese-speaking communities across the globe. In Japanese LPP academia, two terms have been used to name the scholarly approach and define their subject of analysis. *Kokugo/gengo mondai* (national language/language problem) has been used not only as a deictic term to problematize a particular aspect of language structure and use but also as a disciplinary name for a collection of LPP inquires; see, for instance, *Kokugo Nenkan* (Japanese Language Studies Annual Survey) organized by the *Kokuritsu kokugo kenkyūjo* (National Institute for Japanese Language and Linguistics, NINJAL for short). While *gengo seisaku* (language policy) appears somewhat as a flexible and handy option to many LPP scholars, *gengo kanri* (language management) has been keenly adopted, most likely due to the influence of Jiří Václav Neustupný and his associates' contributions to language studies in Japan in general, and their theorization, namely language management theory, in particular (Neustupný 1995; Nekvapil 2006).[1] This theoretical framework illuminates language issues arising in daily interaction and literacy activities so as to inform language policymaking, implementation and evaluation, and eventually to bridge the gap between policy makers and language users.

In order to take account of these diverging approaches existing in the Japanese scholarly context, the following sections refer to a set of scholarships that have paid attention to "language policing" (Blommaert et al. 2009). This term is understood here as an amalgam of reflections and associated actions of various kinds of actors, from the state to the individual, who normatively regulate or navigate civil/institutional/individual language life under a certain circumstance and with a certain ideological baggage. In other words, the open concept of language policy is adopted, shifting attention from a rather dominant, static concept of language policy (e.g., documented and represented in policy "papers") to performance and action involved in the processes of language policy.

Classical LPP

The nineteenth century saw the emergence of classical language planning and policymaking activities in Japan (Gottlieb 1995; Carroll 2001). The early activities were initiated due to increased contact with external forces. The end of national isolation in the mid-nineteenth century initiated the formation of diplomatic relationship with countries other than China and the Netherlands. It was followed by the participation in a series of wars and the experience of post-war US occupation. The national priorities of these times were given to catching up with or surpassing other countries through industrialization, unification and democratization of the nation. Language and education reforms were conceived of as an important means to realize these goals, generally following the precedent model of one-language-one-nation that had been implemented in many European countries (Sanada 2001).

Under this socio-political condition, classical LPP scholarship evolved as an effort in modern nation building. The national necessities caused some individuals and groups to make early efforts for language planning, for example, on writing. Writing style was one of the most hotly debated topics, and it resulted in the *genbun itchi undō* (Movement to unify spoken and written language) of the late nineteenth century to the early twentieth century (see Twine 1978, for details). Since the writing style and orthography of the time was too divergent from actual speech, closing the gap between written and spoken language featured high on the national and societal agenda. While some literary individuals adopted creative writing styles, others made explicit proposals, arguing for the exclusive use of either kana, Latin alphabet or a limited use of kanji (Seeley 1991). After WWII, writing surfaced once again as a crucial problem to be solved, albeit loaded with a different motivation. At the time, the democratization and reconstruction of Japan was a major goal for a range of policy measures, including language reforms. Several advocates, including those who would have been the target of ultranationalist reprisal otherwise, began to use the catchphrase of "democracy" and "rationalization" in order to argue for their ends. Their proposals included the replacement of Japanese in favor of French, the increase in the use of horizontally written kana, the romanization of orthography for mass education and circulation of print media, the reduction in the number of kanji and the reworking of kana use in order to match it with the modern standard pronunciation (Gottlieb 1995).

The (re)construction of *keigo* (honorifics) was also discussed among classical LPP scholars. Yamashita (2009) has critically outlined the chronology of *keigo* studies and their influence on norm constructions. He pointed out that pre-war scholars, such as Matsushita Daizaburō and Yamada Takao, assisted the reinforcement of an essentialist ideology to form the standard/national language, by particularizing and beautifying *keigo* as a representation of "tender-hearted" Japanese culture and nationals. Yamashita (2009) also explained that researchers in 1990s continued to exert policing effects on (some) people's language use and attitudes by presenting *keigo* as something beautiful, useful and unique to Japan.

It was not only corpus planning, but also status planning that served the national and societal interest. Yasuda (2000) introduced Tatebe Tongo and Matsumoto Junichirō as two early LPP researchers, whose research interest overlapped with the national agenda for modernization as well as for colony management. They attempted to theorize language planning and policymaking in a systematic manner, organizing function, type, activities and regulatory organizations for Japan and its colonial territories. As Yasuda (2000) alluded, their simplistic visions about the relationship between language and society illustrate well the mindset of LPP scholars of the time. For example, Tatebe mentioned that "one should not leave language change to nature"[2] (Tatebe 1918: 46, cited in Yasuda 2000: 43), leaving thus no doubt about the importance and the ability of language policy in controlling and managing language. He also affirms the close-knit relationship between language and nation, by writing that "the national language protects the nation, the national language cultivates the nation, the national language expands the nation" (Tatebe 1918: 24, cited in Yasuda 2000: 44).

Likewise, Matsumoto built on the link between nation and language, while arguing that national language policymaking begins with standard selection. This step was considered as the sine qua non of "organically running communal life of the nation that integrates vast foreign parts and local regions, and a variety of social classes" (Matsumoto 1942: 3, cited in Yasuda 2000: 45). Yet, according to Yasuda (2000), Matsumoto believed that the language of the socially advantaged bears the criteria of universality – hence its status of "standard" – while automatically assuming a sociolinguistic sacrifice from the side of the socially disadvantaged. Here, Matsumoto not only elaborated the inevitable connection between language and governance, but also normalized the inequality between the language of the establishment and the rest (e.g., regional varieties and vernacular languages in the former colonies). In sum, Tatebe and Matsumoto typify classical LPP scholars, showing their uncritical appreciation of the making and spread of the national language on the one hand, and being overly positive and confident about the efficacy of language policy to make a promising contribution to the nation.

Other scholars, such as Shioda Norikazu, can also be considered a classical LPP scholar, not because his work was a mere documentation of language policy events and issues, but because he maintained the belief of an ideologically neutral position of LPP research. Shioda (1973) acknowledged the political issues over language by referring to examples in which language functions as an apparatus of discriminatory practices around the world. Yet, the preface of his book clarifies his own stance as follows:

> In most cases, these issues, including script and language issues, are discussed in relation to the relevant worldview and specific philosophy, always resulting in various and complex interpretations. In this regard, this book is to organize and examine language and script issues in Japan by refraining as much as possible from approaching the issue from a particular philosophical perspective.
>
> (Shioda 1973: 5)

Shioda's approach can represent classical attitude permeated throughout the circle of post-war Japanese (socio)linguists who were "instilled to consider it a taboo to investigate the relationship between [language] and society" (Sanada 2006: 1, cited in Masiko 2014: 8). His view differs from Tatebe and Matsumoto who proposed their LPP theories to support Japan's national progress. By contrast, Shioda attempted to undertake "purely scientific and objective" LPP studies which were free of interference from any social values and ideological orientation.

Classical LPP scholarship and activities were not limited to prominent individuals and interest groups, but included government bodies. Carroll (2001) listed three major language planning and policymaking organizations under the jurisdiction of the Ministry of Education, Science and Culture (now renamed as Ministry of Education, Culture, Sports, Science and Technology) and described their responsibilities as follows:

> The National Language Council discusses and makes policy decisions; the National Language Section is responsible for day-to-day administration and implementation of policy; and the National Language Research Institute carries out the background research.
>
> (Carroll 2001: 41)

While Carroll (2001) rightly acknowledged that these three organizations cannot account for the full range of governmental interventions for language planning and policymaking, they are indeed powerful players on Japan's language policymaking table as well as prolific research institutes. Some of their intellectual contributions exemplify classical LPP scholarship in Japan.

Unarguably, it was the National Language Council (*Kokugo Shingikai*) which demonstrated heightened concerns to language issues and was heavily committed to the language standardization process. Along its unique organizational restructuring and developmental path (see Yasuda 2007 for details), the Council conducted numerous linguistic surveys to make the relevant policy recommendations. For example, the predecessor of the Council, the National Language Investigative Committee (*Kokugo chōsa i'inkai*) raised the following major research goals:

(1) "to investigate pros and cons of kana, Latin alphabet, and others in order to adopt the phonographic system for writing",
(2) "to do relevant research in order to adopt the *genbun itchi* system",
(3) "to investigate the phonological system of the national language", and
(4) "to select the standard by surveying dialects".

(Shioda 1973: 46)

Like Tatebe and Matsumoto's views, the Committee's research projects were pursued to "serve the immediate need of mainstream education" (Shioda 1973: 46) with the ultimate motive to advance national development. In fact, these research agendas, particularly the extensive dialectology research, served the establishment of the national language. According to Lee (1996), for example, the third research goal was set to prepare pronunciation redress training for dialect speakers, while the fourth was meant to be an inspection of the "enemy" base in order to eliminate the dialects. The Council's subsequent involvement in consolidating the legitimate foundation for language standardization would later crucially contribute to the emergence of the critical LPP approach in Japan (see below).

After the restructuring of the central government in 2001, the last Council was dissolved and integrated into the Agency for Cultural Affairs (*Bunka-chō*) where the National Language Section (*Kokugo-ka*) has long been institutionalized. However, the Council's relocation makes little change to the interdependent relationship between the Council and the Section. The Council (renamed as Subdivision on National Language of the Council for Cultural Affairs, or *Bunka shingikai kokugo bunkakai*) lays the groundwork for the Section by discussing language-related issues and making relevant proposals. There are subcommittees and working groups that deal with specific items such as honorifics, kanji and language education, to name a few.[3]

On the other hand, the Section acts on the Council's directives and promotes the finalized decisions, including the list of commonly used kanji (*jōyō kanji-hyō*), and usage of kana and romanization, in the form of official guidelines as well as in general reference works available to the public. Added to the policy dissemination function, the Section serves also as a research institution, focusing on Japanese language education. It launches various programs for teacher education and community-based language education, produces education materials, and it teams up with private educational institutions, testing organizations, universities, academic societies and the National Language Research Institute.

While sometimes outsourcing its research work to external bodies, the Section has been conducting survey research on the situation of, and needs for Japanese language education in local communities since 1967. The primary purpose of their research is said to provide basic information on these matters. Their motivation hints at a vision of classical LPP scholarship. For instance, the overview of a survey study conducted in 1999, titled "The Future Advancement of Japanese Language Policy: Aiming for the New Development of Japanese Language Education", includes the following "rosy" statement:

> Amidst of the acceleration of globalization, it is of extreme importance to actively engage in external cultural transmission and to deepen external understanding of our nation. Thus, overseas Japanese language education becomes the foundation of such external cultural transmission as well as the *face* of our national culture.
> *(Agency for Cultural Affairs, 1999, emphasis in the original)*

The optimism expressed in the quote demonstrates the long-held essentialist belief of one-nation-one-culture-one-language that has been running not only through commercial learning materials (Kumagai 2014; Kubota 2014) but also through the policy discourse on the promotion of Japanese language education and culture abroad (Yamamoto 2014). This ideological undercurrent has also undergirded the Ministry of Foreign Affair's (MOFA) Japanese language promotion strategy, indicating a practical and expedient motivation to mobilize human resources with Japanese language ability (*nihongo jinzai*) to compensate for the declining working population and for the shrinking economy (Hashimoto 2018). In a similar vein, research on Japanese language education overseas has continuously been conducted by the Japan Foundation, a Ministry of Foreign Affairs affiliated governmental hub for Japanese language education, which is likely to fall into the category of classical LPP orientation (Ichinose 2012, 2014).

Lastly, the National Language Research Institute (currently abbreviated as NINJAL) conducts many kinds of language-related research that generally focuses on data gathering in a quantitative manner (as represented in a growth of corpus-oriented projects, for example), and involves mostly descriptive and theoretical research on the Japanese language. Yet, they do also conduct research incorporating applied linguistics and sociolinguistic elements, too, as shown in their current mission of promoting research "application in various fields such as Japanese language education, natural language processing, etc." (NINJAL 2009a). According to Ide (1986: 232), their research was conducted based on their identification of language problems and the outcomes are produced to "predict future speech behavior", showing thus much confidence in deliberately transforming language structure and uses.

This buoyant optimism continues up to today. One of the ongoing research project strands states its mission as "to improve the international presence of Japanese language studies as well as the Japanese language per se" (NINJAL 2009b), a statement that resembles closely that of the Section's remark just quoted above. Their quantitative-focused approach may assist them to sustain their ideologically neutral stance for language studies. However, especially when their mission statement reflects the national agenda and their research is designed to make implications for language education and language use in society, their contributions, too, are likely to produce a profound policing effect.

As reviewed above, early language planning and policymaking activities and much of the research undertaken by the government bodies can be categorized to be part of classical LPP. The general aim has been to produce deliberate, mechanical and expert-led changes and influences, with particular attention to corpus planning (e.g., script reforms), status planning (e.g., establishment of a standard language) and increasingly, acquisition planning (e.g., overseas promotion of Japanese language education). Such an approach often downplays the importance of actual sociolinguistic conditions, failing to address or to acknowledge the ideological linkages between language, history and power.

Critical LPP

According to Masiko (2014), the critical approach in the field of sociolinguistics and LPP in Japan was largely inspired by western critical inquiries that situate language in the social context, investigating its role in imperialism, gender and class discrimination, and in other forms of inequality. As a concerted reaction to the dominant classical approach, critical scholars in Japan squarely take issues that have been under-addressed, underestimated and neglected, drawing attention primarily to the interrelation between language and historical, socio-political and economic circumstances, and the consequences they entailed. Early critical sociolinguists, most notably Tanaka Katsuhiko, paved way for such an approach, having a greater and long-lasting influence on the ways other scholars approached language issues. Tanaka (1981: 216) explicitly expressed the emancipatory vision of the critical paradigm that aims at "clarifying underlying elitist anti-humanitarian characteristics behind commonly-believed prejudice about language".

Critical LPP researchers are also scrutinizing underlying motivations and philosophies of classical LPP scholarship and activities. Classical researchers are often involved in the actual creation of policy because their research results are employed to define, identify and/or solve what they conceive to be "language problems" (e.g., the Council's undertakings in relation to language standardization). On the other hand, critical LPP scholarship attends to language policy with more awareness of one's own positionality. The researchers interrogate and examine the conditions under which certain policies are created and enacted. In other words, they raise such questions as how and by whom are language problems identified for what purposes and on what grounds and in what ways are such policies designed to resolve or fix those problem? Today, critical LPP has proved itself as a popular and rigorous approach in Japan, as shown in the continued growth in the number of contributions particularly in the following areas: (1) the establishment of *kokugo*, (2) its relation to indigenous languages, (3) to Japanese former colonies and (4) the presence of English.

The national language, or *kokugo*, has been one of the most widely studied topics among critical LPP researchers. The subject of analysis often lies in Japan's modern language project, focusing on the mechanism of how the creation of *kokugo* was imbued with the imperialistic motivation to enhance national unity, and to consolidate and expand the Japanese empire. Many scholars critique the Council's language standardization and the development and reproduction of the one-language-one-nation myth, most notably promoted by a Japan's first modern linguist Ueda Kazutoshi and later elaborated by his pupil Hoshina Koichi and others (for details, see Lee 1996; Yasuda 2000). By employing historical document analysis, these scholars revealed that the commonly held myth is a social fabrication, playing a powerful role in rationalizing the creation and dissemination of the national/standard language in the context of Japan's territorial unification, expansion and sovereignty at the expense of subordinating and abandoning vernacular languages, such as Ryukyuan, Ainu and the languages in the former colonies, all existing well before the idea of standard language/national language was invented and enforced in the form of language education policy.

While many researchers of Ryukyuans and Ainu do not always frame their research as LPP, the trajectories of these indigenous languages cannot be explained without referring to language policies. Critical investigations were made to examine the central government's language policy initiatives, such as the establishment of educational institutions and the introduction of materials for *kokugo* instruction, and the enactment of legislation such as the Protective Act for the Ainu in Hokkaido (*Hokkaidō kyū-dojin hogo-hō*) in 1899. Critical LPP research has pinpointed that these largely coercive cultural, ethnic and linguistic assimilation measures not only empowered the myth of national and linguistic homogeneity, but also prompted language shift among speakers of Ryukyuan languages (Anderson and Heinrich 2014) and of Ainu (DeChicchis 1995; Maher 2001).

With regards to the language policies in the former colonies of Japan, critical LPP scholars historically trace the policy process, while investigating language ideologies and beliefs embedded in the policy discourse and in the actual implementation at the same time. Shi's seminal work (2003) on Japan's wartime language policies is one such example. He carefully illustrated the development and deployment of language policy with empirical historical evidence, while exploring ideologies that upheld the spread of Japanese over the occupied territories, such as *kotodama* (language sprit) and the fabricated hierarchy between the language of suzerain (*kokugo*/Japanese) and those of subordinate territories such as Chinese and Korean (see also Lee 1996; Yasuda 2000 for a similar approach).

Critical insights are found equally useful for investigating policies regarding foreign language education, most notably, English. Due to its lasting presence in Japanese society in general and in the policy discourse in particular, English-in-education policies have been scrutinized by many investigators. For example, the policy document analysis has been rigorously conducted to identify underlying ideologies such as the utilitarian value of English (Kubota 2002), native speaker superiority (Hashimoto 2013), and an earlier-is-better myth that promises good learning outcomes (Jones 2004). These ideologies were effectively employed to announce and embark on the following policy provisions: de facto status of English as the foreign language in the education curriculum, almost exclusive recruitment of native (often American) English-speaking teachers, active usage of commercially available English tests, valorization of inner circle English accents in the government-approved textbooks and introduction of English language education for primary school. In addition, critical LPP scholars have addressed the complex representation of English in the policy discourse (Hashimoto 2000, 2009, 2012; Liddicoat 2007). They pointed out that the English language, on the one hand, is represented as a vital tool for Japanese citizens to participate in the global and cosmopolitan sphere that eventually boosts Japan's cultural and economic competitiveness, while English is at the same time also portrayed as a potential threat to the national unity and identity (see also Yamagami and Tollefson 2011). The analysis not only shows the resistant and impervious nature of modernist ideology and the persistent ethnolinguistic identity, but also exposes the hidden nationalistic agenda and cultural essentialism behind these policies. In other words, critical LPP scholars have revealed that Japan's English language education policy is not simply a matter of pedagogy per se but can be a matter of basically any other issues, such as the promotion of patriotism.

In sum, the contribution of critical LPP scholarship in Japan is two-fold. First, it illuminates the significance of power and ideologies in language policy, covering a variety of policing activities undertaken in different times and spaces for different target groups with varying sociopolitical and economic ramifications. In other words, critical scholars are explicit about their position, claiming that there is no ideologically and politically neutral stance in the making as well as in the research of language policies. The second accomplishment of critical LPP is to illustrate and explain linkages among Japan's language policies. The application of the historical-structural approach (Tollefson 1991) offers an analytical lens to examine policies that differ in time of enactment/revision, intensity, effective span, means of enforcement, target population and consequences. Critical LPP scholars not only demonstrate these differences, but also identify the connections among them. For example, Yasuda (1997) and Oguma (2000) underlined the ideological link behind two separate initiatives behind the establishment and spread of national/standard language – the suppression of indigenous language varieties in Japan and that of the languages in Japan's former colonies. The former was motivated to form and advance the state system and management, and to achieve national unity through nurturing the ethnolinguistic identity, while the latter was a clear representation of domination over and control of the colonies. Yet, these scholars argued that these seemingly different motivations were in fact complementary, anchored in the idea of *kokugo* that naturalizes the link between language, nation, citizenship and pride. With this equation model, the central government succeeded in circulating the idea that knowledge of and proficiency in *kokugo* represents the scale of one's civilization and demonstrates one's willingness to become a Japanese citizen as well as one's loyalty for their colonial master. At the same time, Japan's encroachment on overseas territories gave a legitimate basis to achieve the solid status of the standard language within Japan, since one unified language was considered appropriate in the management of the colonies and the indoctrination of the people.

New-wave LPP

Although the recently emerging approach is conveniently termed here "new-wave" LPP, it is rather difficult to draw a cut-off line between the critical and the new-wave approaches. The latter appears not as a countermove against the critical approach but rather as an attempt to take better advantage of its theoretical and methodological advances and robustness. To do so, LPP researchers are encouraged to adopt, at least, three perspectives. First, they display sensitivity to an ever-growing number of sociolinguistic issues, enabling them to identify and situate their topic of investigation in a dynamic matrix where meanings associated with language are being newly made or re-made under the condition of socio-political, economic and technological changes. Such sensitivities are not exclusive to new-wave scholarship. For example, the aforementioned work by Shi (2003) on Japan's wartime language policy in the former colonies is not closed to a specific spatiality and temporality. Linking the past and the present, he demonstrates how the powerful ideologies of the colonial times are connected to the current sociolinguistic reality of Japan (see also Yasuda 2011 for the similar effort in connecting Japan's monolingual and homogenous mindset with the present-day discourse about multilingualism and immigration in Japan).

A greater focus on sociolinguistic dynamics not only transcends time boundaries but also opens up and expands arenas for scholarly investigation. With regard to *keigo* studies, an urgent need for moving beyond the prescriptive research tradition is emphasized (Yamashita 2009) and gradually realized by looking at *keigo* usage in situ rather than treating it as a norm (for example, Okamoto and Shibamoto-Smith 2016). These works signal a contemporary direction for the research of corpus planning and status planning. There is also an upsurge of academic interest in diversified language communities in and outside of Japan such as children learning Japanese as a second language (e.g., Kamiyoshi 2014), multilingual Filipino mothers looking after their children's bilingual language education in Japan (e.g., Takeuchi 2016), and Japanese volunteers teaching Japanese in rural communities in Japan (e.g., Morimoto 2009) and in Japanese diaspora (e.g., Motobayashi 2015, 2016). Paying greater attention to their personal/communal narratives and practices, these studies shed light on the link between their interactional and educational decisions and experiences and the conditions under which a certain language policy takes shape. In other words, the new-wave researchers are interested in discovering various forms of language planning and policymaking participation among individuals/groups/corporations, which have emerged out of the technological, socio-political and economic changes in society, or which had been simply under-investigated in the LPP light.

Second, the concept of language policy has been appropriated as something open and elastic rather than closed and static. Language policy is no longer captured solely as a concrete, visible product crafted through a step-by-step procedure, implemented in a geographically confined area during a historically bounded timespan. While certainly acknowledging this kind of conventional manifestation and formation of policy, the new-wave scholarship welcomes the renewed conceptualization of language policy as an iterative, complex, often fractured process. They do not assume a teleological linearity but acknowledge many complexities in the policy process in which multiple interests are at stake, multiple voices are heard, and a number of often conflicting ideologies are in competition (see Shannon 1999; Lo Bianco 2001 for examples).

One way of making it possible to describe these complex processes could be the employment of ethnography in LPP research. In the context of Japan, Kanno's ethnographic study (2008) of five different schools, for instance, has revealed the mechanism of schooling that produces varying policing effects not only on children's access to bilingual education but also on their future life direction. Her monograph has succeeded in demonstrating the potential and strength of ethnography in language-in-education policy studies. Informed by the ethnography of language policy (Johnson 2009), Otomo (2017) investigates the Economic Partnership Agreement signed between Japan and Southeast Asian countries in which the Japanese language plays a crucial role in determining life and professional trajectories of migrant healthcare workers. In addition to the policy archival analysis in which the hidden agendas and motivations behind the expert/authority-led planning and policymaking activities were identified, she conducted field research in an elderly care home. Her on-site observation delineates the local power hierarchy in which language policy arbiters (Johnson and Johnson 2015) exert far greater determining and binding power than the codified language policy.

Finally, the new-wave researchers are urged to reflect their own norms, beliefs, actions and research ethics (Pérez-Milans and Tollefson 2018). Ethnography not only enables them to engage deeply with local "linguistic culture" (Schiffman 2006), but also lays a solid base on which they can critically act on their discoveries and insights. Although critical LPP entails activism for social justice as a major feature (Tollefson 2002), the central theme of critical scholarship has almost always been on the relationship between language, power and inequality. This tendency generally applies to Japanese academia; however, Ryukyuan scholars are spearheading this direction. They have achieved the liberation of Ryukyuan languages from the dialectological tradition, creating a springboard for revitalizing/documenting the Ryukyuan languages, and politicizing the long-disregarded language issues (Heinrich and Sugita 2009; Heinrich 2014). These activities are not only inspired by a critical vision of discriminatory practices and language endangerment, but also by constant reflection about their own standpoint and responsibility as researchers, which broadly resonates Tokugawa's (1999) expectation for researchers' engagement in language studies. Ethnographically informed knowledge certainly opens one important window into which LPP researchers take a new step forward to exercise their criticality at this next level.

Concluding remarks

This chapter has aligned a body of LPP works in the context of Japan with the general progress outlined in the field, roughly categorized into three paradigms: the classical, the critical and the new-wave. Classical LPP works in Japan, and elsewhere, all had a similar outlook in terms of their agenda – developing national language policies for their respective modernization projects – and of their research focus on reforms on language structures and the socio-political positioning of languages. In Japan, classical LPP scholarship appeared not only as an effort to create a nation on the basis of one single language but also as a product and legacy of such a national project, notably accomplished in two forms: (1) the codification of a Tokyo variety, its elevation and spread as the standard language in Japan and its colonial empire, and (2) the elimination and/or subordination of all other language varieties.

Western (socio)linguistics scholarship had stimulated the development of critical LPP scholarship in Japan, marking a departure from the overly optimistic, often nationalistic and naïvely claimed neutral attitude of the classical LPP paradigm. Critical researchers point out that the classical LPP scholarship has served the interests of powerful and already-privileged groups, while discriminating and suppressing others who are socially, politically and economically powerless and disadvantaged. This line of research therefore pays significant attention to power issues and inequality involved in policymaking and its implementations. In other words, they question commonly acknowledged assumptions and values about language (i.e., language ideologies) that often support a certain provision while blocking others. In Japan, critical scholars have examined historical, socio-political and economic conditions under which a given language variety (e.g., *a Tokyo variety*) is chosen and gets preferential treatment over others (e.g., *kokugo*) and its consequences (e.g., language extinction).

In Japan, a growing number of researchers have begun to adopt the new-wave perspective, an emerging scholarly attempt to overcome the limitation of critical LPP and capitalize on its advances. With their heightened awareness of agency, these researchers have come to regard a variety of individuals as policy makers, and to consider language policy as "processual, dynamic, and in motion" (McCarty 2011: 2). While adopting locally attuned methodologies such as ethnography to tease out the intricacies that policy entails, these scholars pay closer attention to the changing societal conditions under which a language policy is taking effect, is being revised, and how a new form of language policy comes into being.

This chapter is generally supportive of the new-wave scholarly venture. Today, it still receives limited attention especially in Japan where the static concept of language policy has been dominant for so long. The wide-open concept of language policy probably upsets some scholars whose focus solely remains in the identification of what they perceive to constitute a "language problem" to be fixed and/or removed through purposeful planning and thorough implementation attempts, or a text-based analysis of a codified set of language policy documents per se. Indeed, the new-wave LPP requires researchers to make considerable intellectual efforts at reworking their previous assumptions and breaking their own conceptual boundaries. Yet, I believe that such a transformative exercise is an excellent opportunity for furthering the theoretical enrichment of the field as well as to better fulfill our moral duties as researchers.[4] Language planning and policymaking is often not a matter of language per se but what language means in a particular societal context, which is inseparable from intra- and international politics, economic and social problems, including education, health, social welfare, employment and public safety. The new-wave perspective has the great potential of illuminating and enhancing this multidisciplinary nature of LPP. By moving in this direction, we can continue to shed light on a language policy that is changing its form, function and associated social conditions, and that governs far-reaching domains with varying binding power in order to achieve social justice through our research conducts.

Notes

1 The utility of the term "*gengo seisaku*" (language policy) has been witnessed not only by the number of scholarly publications with "*gengo seisaku*" included in the titles, but also by the NINJAL's publication. While its database organizes published LPP work under the name of *gengo/kokugo mondai*, an electronic yearbook published by NINJAL in 2009 had a subsection heading titled "*gengo seisaku*" (NINJAL 2009c).
2 All translations from Japanese publication in English are mine.
3 In the recent decade, the Council's committee and working groups are relatively inactive. Yet, their activities (and inactivity) merit scholarly attention, providing ample resources both for critical and new-wave LPP investigation.

4 Paying greater awareness to one's moral and research ethics is not an entirely new call. For example, Ruiz's (1984) important categorization of LPP orientation, (1) language-as-problem, (2) language-as-right and (3) language-as-resource, has firmly set the tone for the emergence of the new-wave LPP literature (McCarty 2016).

References

Agency for Cultural Affairs (1999) Kongo no nihongo kyōiku shisaku no suishin ni tsuite – nihongo kyōiku no aratana tenkai o mezashite [The Future Advancement of Japanese Language Policy. Aiming for the New Development of Japanese Language Education]. Available online at: www.bunka.go.jp/tokei_hakusho_shuppan/tokeichosa/nihongokyoiku_suishin/nihongokyoiku_tenkai/ (accessed 12 February 2018).

Alvesson, Mats and Kay Sköldberg (2000) *Reflexive Methodology. New Vistas for Qualitative Research.* London: Sage Publications.

Anderson, Mark and Patrick Heinrich (eds) (2014) *Language Crisis in the Ryukyus.* Newcastle upon Tyne: Cambridge Scholars Publishing.

Bauman, Zygmunt (1998) *Globalization. The Human Consequences.* Cambridge: Polity Press.

Blommaert, Jan, Helen Kelly-Holmes, Pia Lane, Sirpa Leppänen, Máiréad Moriarty, Sari Pietikäinen and Arja Piirainen-Marsh (2009) Media, Multilingualism and Language Policing. An Introduction. *Language Policy* 8(3): 203–207.

Carroll, Tessa (2001) *Language Planning and Language Change in Japan.* Richmond: Curzon.

Chua, Siew Kheng Catherine and Richard B. Baldauf Jr. (2011) Micro Language Planning. In: *Handbook of Research in Second Language Teaching and Learning* (volume 2). Eli Hinkel (ed.), 936–951. London: Routledge.

Davis, Kathryn A. (1999) The Sociopolitical Dynamics of Indigenous Language Maintenance and Loss. A Framework for Language Policy and Planning. In: *Sociopolitical Perspectives on Language Policy and Planning in the USA.* Thom Huebner and Kathryn A. Davis (eds), 67–97. Amsterdam: John Benjamins.

DeChicchis, Joseph (1995) The Current State of the Ainu Language. In: *Multilingual Japan.* John C. Maher and Kyoko Yashiro (eds), 103–124. Clevedon: Multilingual Matters.

Ferguson, Charles. A. (1968) Language Development. In: *Language Problems of Developing Nations.* Joshua A. Fishman, Charles A. Ferguson and Jyotirindra Das Gupta (eds), 27–35. New York: John Wiley & Sons.

Fishman, Joshua. A. (1972) *Language in Sociocultural Change.* Stanford: Stanford University Press.

Fishman, Joshua. A., Charles A. Ferguson and Jyotirindra Das Gupta (eds) (1968) *Language Problems of Developing Nations.* New York: John Wiley & Sons.

Gee, James Paul, Glynda Hull and Colin Lankshear (1996) *The New Work Order. Behind the Language of the New Capitalism.* Boulder, Colorado: Westview.

Gottlieb, Nanette (1995) *Kanji Politics. Language Policy and Japanese Script.* London: Kegan Paul International.

—— (2011) *Language Policy in Japan. The Challenge of Change.* Cambridge: Cambridge University Press.

Hashimoto, Kayoko (2000) Internationalisation is "Japanisation". Japan's Foreign Language Education and National Identity. *Journal of Intercultural Studies* 21(1): 39–51.

—— (2009) Cultivating "Japanese Who Can Use English". Problems and Contradictions in Government Policy. *Asian Studies Review* 33: 21–42.

—— (2012) The Japanisation of English Language Education. Promotion of the National Language within Foreign Language Policy. In: *Language Policies in Education* (second edition). James W. Tollefson (ed.), 175–190. London: Routledge.

—— (2013) The Construction of the "Native Speaker" in Japan's Educational Policies for TEFL. In: *Native-speakerism in Japan. Intergroup Dynamics in Foreign Language Education.* Stephanie Ann Houghton and Damian J. Rivers (eds), 159–168. Bristol: Multilingual Matters.

—— (2018) Cool Japan and Japanese Language. Why Does Japan Need "Japan Fans"? In: *Japanese Language and Soft Power in Asia.* Kayoko Hashimoto (ed), 43–62. Basingstoke: Palgrave Macmillan.

Haugen, Einar (1966) *Language Conflict and Language Planning. The Case of Modern Norwegian.* Cambridge: Harvard University Press.

Heinrich, Patrick (2014) Don't Leave Ryukyuan Languages Alone. A Roadmap for Language Revitalization. In: *Language Crisis in the Ryukyus.* Mark Anderson and Patrick Heinrich (eds), 295–321. Newcastle upon Tyne: Cambridge Scholars Publishing.

Heinrich, Patrick and Yuko Sugita (2009) Kiki gengo kiroku hozon to gengo fukkō no tōgō e mukete [Towards an Integration of Language Documentation and Language Revitalization]. *Shakai gengo kagaku* 11(2): 15–27.

Hornberger, Nancy H. and David Cassels Johnson (2007) Slicing the Onion Ethnographically. Layers and Spaces in Multilingual Language Education Policy and Practice. *TESOL Quarterly* 41(3): 509–532.

Ichinose, Shunsuke (2012) Kokusai kōryū kikin no nihongo kyōiku seisaku tenkan ni tsuite – "nihongo kyōiku sutandādo" no kōchiku o megutte [Japan Foundation's Policy Shift in Japanese Language Education with Reference to the Establishment of "Standards of Japanese Language Education"]. *Kobe Kokusai Daigaku kiyō* 82: 6–73.

―――― (2014) Kokusai kōryū kikin no retorikku ga nihongo kyōiku kara mienaku suru mono [What Makes Japan Foundation's Rhetoric Invisible in the Field of Japanese Language Education]. *Kobe Kokusai Daigaku kiyō* 87: 53–70.

Ide, Sachiko (1986) The Background of Japanese Sociolinguistics. *Journal of Pragmatics* 10: 281–286.

Jernudd, Bjorn H. (1993) Language Planning from a Management Perspective. An Interpretation of Findings. In: *Language Conflict and Language Planning*. Ernst Håkon Jahr (ed), 133–142. Berlin: Mouton de Gruyter.

Johnson, David Cassels (2009) Ethnography of Language Policy. *Language Policy* 8(2): 139–159.

―――― (2013) *Language Policy*. Basingstoke: Palgrave Macmillan.

Johnson, David Cassels and Eric J. Johnson (2015) Power and Agency in Language Policy Appropriation. *Language Policy* 14(3): 221–243.

Johnson, David Cassels and Thomas Ricento (2013) Conceptual and Theoretical Perspectives in Language Planning and Policy. Situating the Ethnography of Language Policy. *International Journal of the Sociology of Language* 219: 7–21.

Jones, Mark (2004) Conflicting Agendas. The Implementation of English Language Classes in Japanese Primary Schools. In: *Global English and Primary Schools. Challenges for Elementary Education*. Penny Lee and Hazita Azman (eds), 129–149. Melbourne: CAE Press.

Kamiyoshi, Uichi (2014) How Japanese Education for Young People Has Been Discussed. A Critical Analysis from a Relational Viewpoint. In: *Rethinking Language and Culture in Japanese Education. Beyond the Standard*. Shinji Sato and Neriko Musha Doerr (eds), 128–142. Bristol: Multilingual Matters.

Kanno, Yasuko (2008) *Language and Education in Japan. Unequal Access to Bilingualism*. Basingstoke: Palgrave Macmillan.

Kloss, Heinz (1966) Types of Multilingual Communities. A Discussion of Ten Variables. *Sociological Inquiry* 36: 7–17.

Kubota, Ryuko (2002) Impact of Globalization on Language Teaching in Japan. In: *Globalization and Language Teaching*. David Block and Deborah Cameron (eds), 13–28. London: Routledge.

―――― (2014) Critical Teaching of Japanese Culture. In: *Rethinking Language and Culture in Japanese Education. Beyond the Standard*. Shinji Sato and Neriko Musha Doerr (eds), 218–237. Bristol: Multilingual Matters.

Kumagai, Yuri (2014) On Learning Japanese Language. Critical Reading of Japanese Language Textbook. In: *Rethinking Language and Culture in Japanese Education. Beyond the Standard*. Shinji Sato and Neriko Musha Doerr (eds), 201–217. Bristol: Multilingual Matters.

Lee, Yeounsuk (1996) *Kokugo to iu shisō* [*An Ideology Called National Language*]. Tokyo: Iwanami.

Liddicoat, Anthony J. (2007) Internationalising Japan. Nihonjinron and the Intercultural in Japanese Language-in-education Policy. *Journal of Multilingual Discourses* 2: 32–46.

Liddicoat, Anthony. J. and Richard B. Baldauf Jr. (2008) Language Planning in Local Contexts. Agents, Contexts and Interactions. In: *Language Planning in Local Contexts. Agents, Contexts and Interactions*. Anthony J. Liddicoat and Richard B. Baldauf Jr. (eds), 18–41. Clevedon: Multilingual Matters.

Lin, Angel M. Y. (2015) Researcher Positionality. In: *Research Methods in Language Policy and Planning. A Practical Guide*. Francis M. Hult and David Cassels Johnson (eds), 21–32. Malden: Wiley-Blackwell.

Lo Bianco, Joseph (2001) Policy Literacy. *Language and Education* 15(2/3): 212–227.

Maher, John. C. (2001) Akor Itak – Our Language, Your Language. Ainu in Japan. In: *Can Threatened Language Be Saved?* Joshua A. Fishman (ed), 323–349. Clevedon: Multilingual Matters.

Masiko, Hidenori (2014). Nihon no shakai gengogaku wa nani o shitte kita no ka, doko e ikō to shiteiru no ka [What has Japanese Sociolinguistics Done thus Far? Where Is it Going Next?]. *Shakai gengogaku* 14: 1–23.

McCarty, Teresa. L. (ed.) (2011) *Ethnography and Language Policy*. London: Routledge.

―――― (2016) "Language Planning is Social Planning". Reflections on the Language Planning Contributions of Richard Ruiz. In *Honoring Richard Ruiz and his Work on Language Planning and Bilingual Education*. Nancy H. Hornberger (ed.), 1–14. Bristol: Multilingual Matters.

McKenzie, Robert. M. (2010) *The Social Psychology of English as a Global Language. Attitudes, Awareness and Identity in the Japanese Context*. London: Springer.

Morimoto, Ikuyo (2009) Chi'iki nihongo kyōiku no hihanteki saikentō [Critical Reconsideration on Community Japanese Education]. In: *"Tadashisa" e no toi – hihanteki shakai gengogaku no kokoromi [Inquiring "Correctness". An Attempt in Critical Sociolinguistics]*. Kayoko Noro and Hitoshi Yamashita (eds), 215–247. Tokyo: Sangensha.

Motobayashi, Kyoko (2015) Language Teaching as Foreign Policy. Japanese Language Teachers in Japan's International Cooperation Program. PhD dissertation, University of Toronto.

Motobayashi, Kyoko (2016) Language Teacher Subjectivities in Japan's Diaspora Strategies. Teaching My Language as Someone's Heritage Language. *Multilingua* 35(4): 441–468.

Nekvapil, Jiří (2006) From Language Planning to Language Management. *Sociolinguistica. International Yearbook of European Sociolinguistics* 20: 92–104.

——— (2011) The History and Theory of Language Planning. In: *Handbook of Research in Second Language Teaching and Learning* (volume 2). Eli Hinkel (ed.), 871–887. London: Routledge.

Neustupný, Jiří Václav (1995) Nihongo kyōiku to gengo kanri [Japanese Language Education and Language Management]. *Handai nihongo kenkyū* 7: 67–82.

NINJAL (2009a) General Description. Available online at: www.ninjal.ac.jp/english/info/aboutus/ (accessed 12 February 2018).

——— (2009b) Institute-based Projects. Available online at: www.ninjal.ac.jp/english/research/project-3/institute/ (accessed 12 February 2018).

——— (2009c) Kokugo nenkan 2009-nendo ban denshi ban [Japanese Language Studies Annual Survey and Bibliography 2009 Electronic Publication]. Available online at: www.ninjal.ac.jp/publication/catalogue/files/kokugonenkan/kokugonenkan2009.pdf (accessed 12 February 2018).

Oguma, Eiji (2000) Nihongo no gengo teikoku shugi [Japan's Linguistic Imperialism]. In: *Gengo teikoku shugi to wa nani-ka [What Is Linguistic Imperialism?]*. Nobutaka Miura and Keisuke Kasuya (eds), 55–65. Tokyo: Fujiwara Shoten.

Okamoto, Shigeko and Janet S. Shibamoto-Smith (2016) *The Social Life of the Japanese Language. Cultural Discourses and Situated Practice*. Cambridge: Cambridge University Press.

Okubo, Yuko (2014) A Consideration of the Discourse on Mother Tongue Instruction in Japanese Language Education. A Case Study of the Practices of Japanese Language Classes for Chinese Returnees and Vietnamese Residents. In: *Rethinking Language and Culture in Japanese Education. Beyond the Standard*. Shinji Sato and Neriko Musha Doerr (eds), 143–171. Bristol: Multilingual Matters.

Otomo, Ruriko (2017) Japan's Economic Partnership Agreement as Language Policy. Creation, Interpretation, Appropriation. PhD dissertation, The University of Hong Kong.

Pérez-Milans, Miguel and James W. Tollefson (2018) Language Policy and Planning. Directions for Future Research. In: *The Oxford Handbook of Language Policy and Planning*. James W. Tollefson and Miguel Pérez-Milans (eds), 727–742. Oxford: Oxford University Press.

Ramanathan, Vaidehi (2011) Researching Texting Tensions in Qualitative Research. Ethics in and around Textual Fidelity, Selectivity, and Translations. In: *Ethnography and Language Policy*, Teresa L. McCarthy (ed), 255–270. London: Routledge.

Ricento, Thomas (2000) Historical and Theoretical Perspectives in Language Policy and Planning. *Journal of Sociolinguistics* 4(2): 196–213.

Ricento, Thomas and Nancy H. Hornberger (1996) Unpeeling the Onion. Language Planning and Policy and the ELT Professional. *TESOL Quarterly* 30(3): 401–427.

Ruiz, Richard (1984) Orientations in Language Planning. *NABE Journal* 8: 15–34.

Sanada, Shinji (2001) *Hyōjungo no setsuritsu jijō [The Circumstances of Standard Language Formation]*. Tokyo: PHP.

Sanada, Shinji (2006) *Shakai gengogaku no kadai [The Tasks of Sociolinguistics]*. Tokyo: Kuroshio.

Seeley, Christopher (1991) *A History of Writing in Japan*. Leiden: Brill.

Schiffman, Harold (2006) Language Policy and Linguistic Culture. In: *An Introduction to Language Policy. Theory and Method*. Thomas Ricento (ed), 111–125. Oxford: Blackwell.

Shannon, Sheila. M. (1999) The Debate on Bilingual Education in the US. Language Ideology as Reflected in the Practice of Bilingual Teachers. In: *Language Ideological Debates*. Jan Blommaert (ed), 171–201. Berlin: Mouton de Gruyter.

Shi, Gang (2003) *Shokuminchi shihai to nihongo [Management of the Colonies and Japanese]*. Tokyo: Sangensha.

Shioda, Norikazu (1973) *Nihon no gengo seisaku no kenkyū [A Study on Language Policies of Japan]*. Tokyo: Kuroshio Shuppan.

Takeuchi, Miwa (2016) Transformation of Discourse. Multilingual Resources and Practices among Filipino Mothers in Japan. *International Journal of Bilingual Education and Bilingualism* 19(3): 235–248.

Tanaka, Katsuhiko (1981) *Kotoba to kokka* [*Language and State*]. Tokyo: Iwanami Shoten.
Tokugawa, Munemasa (1999). Taidan – werufea ringuisutikusu no shuppatsu [Interview. The Inauguration of Welfare Linguistics]. *Shakai gengo kagaku* 2(1): 89–100.
Tollefson, James. W. (1991) *Planning Language, Planning Inequality. Language Policy in the Community.* London: Longman.
Tollefson, James W. (2002) Introduction. Critical Issues in Educational Language Policy. In: *Language Policies in Education. Critical Issues.* James. W. Tollefson (ed.), 3–15. Mahwah: Lawrence Elbaum Associates.
Tollefson, James W. (2006) Critical Theory in Language Policy. In: *An Introduction to Language Policy. Theory and Method.* Thomas Ricento (ed.), 42–59. Malden: Blackwell Publishing.
Tollefson, James W. (2011) Language Policy and Planning. In: *The Cambridge Handbook of Sociolinguistics.* Rajend Mesthrie (ed.), 357–376. Cambridge: Cambridge University Press.
Twine, Nanette (1978) The genbunitchi Movement. Its Origin, Development, and Conclusion. *Monumenta Nipponica* 33(3): 333–356.
Yamagami, Mai and James W. Tollefson (2011) Elite Discourses of Globalization in Japan. The Role of English. In: *English in Japan in the Era of Globalization.* Philip Seargeant (ed.), 15–37. Basingstoke: Palgrave Macmillan.
Yamamoto, Saeri (2014) *Sengo no kokka to nihongo kyōiku* [*The Post-war State and Japanese Language Education*]. Tokyo: Kuroshio Shuppan.
Yamashita, Hitoshi (2009) Nihon no yomikaki nōryōku no shinwa – sono inpei kinōno kaimei to mondai kaiketsu no tame no kenkyūni tsuite [Myth of Japanese Literacy. Revealing its Cover-Up Function and Study for Solving a Problem]. *Shakaigengogaku* 9: 195–211.
Yasuda, Toshiaki (1997) *Teikoku nihon no gengo hensei* [*Language Regimentation in Imperial Japan*]. Tokyo: Sangensha.
Yasuda, Toshiaki (2000) *Kindai nihongo gengo-shi sai-shikō* [*Reconsideration of the History of Modern Japanese*]. Tokyo: Sangensha.
Yasuda, Toshiaki (2007) *Kokugo shingikai – meisō no 60-nen* [*The National Language Council. A Wandering of Sixty Years*]. Tokyo: Kōdansha.
Yasuda, Toshiaki (2011) *"Tagengo shakai" to iu gensō* [*A Fantasy Called "Multilingual Society"*]. Tokyo: Sangensha.

20
SCRIPT AND ORTHOGRAPHY PROBLEMS

Hidenori Masiko (Translated from Japanese by Yumiko Ohara)

Introduction

The concurrent use of several scripts in the Japanese writing system is the basis for a large range of problems concerning writing and orthography in contemporary Japanese. Morphosyllabic kanji, syllabic hiragana and katakana are combined into a writing system to which also the Roman alphabet and Arabic numerals are frequently added. Leaving out any of the three main scripts involved would be perceived as "odd" writing and therefore not be practicable at the present. This kind of constraint represents yet another factor that contributes to the difficulties of writing in Japan.

There is a long-held and widespread belief that post-war Japan has little educational disparity and an unmatched high rate of literacy, and that this is an achievement of its education system. There are also many who have criticized such declarations, pointing out that there are actually a number of problems with Japan's self-praise of claiming a literacy rate of 99% (e.g., Abe 2015; Kadoya and Abe 2010; Sumi 2012; Yamashita 2011). There are many reasons why the literacy rate in Japan is considerably lower than this. One of the reasons is the difficulty to employ the various scripts appropriately and the orthographic problems that result thereof. Japan's autochthonous linguistic diversity also results in a range of problems, most evidently when it comes to the choice of script for other languages of Japan (Ainu, Ryukyuan, Hachijo), or the representation of place names and personal names of Japan's linguistic minorities (Ogawa 2015). All of this calls for a comprehensive discussion of problems of script and orthography in Japan. I will discuss first the problems of using kanji in Japan, followed by a discussion of kana and finally of Latin script.

Kanji problems

The majority of Japan's script and orthography problems are rooted in the concurrent use of three distinctive scripts, two of which are phonetic (hiragana and katakana) and one of which is both phonetic and semantic (kanji). There are other such writing systems in the world, for example in South Korea, but the situation there is less complex than that of Japan. For example, when using the kanji <金> (gold) for a personal name, it is always read as *kim* in Korean, and when it is used as a term for the metal it is always read *kum*. On the other hand, there are endless examples in Japan where the mapping of sounds onto kanji is very complicated, and therefore requires a lot of practice. To start with, there are Sino-Japanese readings of kanji (*on-yomi*), and there are Japanese readings (*kun-yomi*). Furthermore, there are often several *on-* or *kun*-readings of one and the same kanji. The kanji <生>, for example, is notorious for having a great number of readings that readers must learn to map on the script character in question according to the context. In example (1), the underlined part indicates the reading that must be mapped onto the script symbol <生> in order to produce different words that employ this kanji.

(1)
生きる *ikiru* (to live)
生まれる *umareru* (to be born)
生卵 *namatamago* (raw egg)
生娘 *kimusume* (virgin)
一生 *isshō* (life time)
生活 *seikatsu* (life)

To add to the difficulties, there are also customary readings (2) that rely only on historical conventions in addition to (3) varied readings that can only be discerned from context.

Some typical examples of the first case can be seen in the following proper nouns.

(2)
<長谷> (*hase / nagatani*), <東海林> (*shoji*), <飛鳥> (*asuka*), <角田> (*kakuda / kakuta / tsunoda / sumida / sumita / kadota*), <北京> (*pekin*), <南京> (*nankin*), <東京> (*tōkyō*), <西京> (*saikyō*)

Varied readings that can only be read out according to the context include the following examples:

(3)
<明日> (*asu / myōnichi*, tomorrow), <日本> (*nihon / nippon / hinomoto*, Japan), <開眼> (*kaigan*, be able to see, to understand / *kaigen*, enlightenment), <工夫> (*kufū*, to device / *kōfu*, laborer)

There are also instances where these two cases co-occur (4). The readings mapped onto the kanji compounds in question are underlined.

(4)
<清水区> (*shimizu-ku*, Shimizu Ward) / <清水寺> (*kiyomizu-dera*, Kiyomizu Temple), <大山> (*ōyama / daisen*), <浅草> (*asakusa*) / <浅草寺> (*sensō-ji*, Sensōji Temple, <鶴舞駅> (*tsumumai-eki*, Tsumumai train station) / <鶴舞公園> (*tsumuma-kōen*, Tsumuma Park)

Concerning the distinction between <清水区> (*shimizu-ku*) and <清水寺> (*kiyomizudera*), it is impossible to know which reading is appropriate, *shimizu* or *kiyomizu*, unless one has access to the contextual information based on the geographical knowledge of the area, i.e., the ward of Shimizu or the temple of Kiyomizu. Similarly, <東京浅草浅草寺> (*tōkyō asakusa sensōji*, Sensōji Temple in Asakusa, Tokyo) as well as <名古屋市鶴舞駅下車鶴舞公園> (*nagoya-shi tsumumai-eki gesha tsumuma-kōen*, Tsumuma Park, getting off from Tsumumai Station in Nagoya City) cannot be read correctly without having particular knowledge of these areas in question. In Japan place names using the same kanji compounds can be read differently according to their locality. Due to their semantic function, kanji are at times quite opaque with regard to their phonetic representation. To summarize, if context is established or known, then a sound can be mapped on a kanji. Seen the other way around, sounds cannot always be mapped onto kanji without such knowledge. It is also unclear whether a kanji compound refers to a proper name or a common noun, but this distinction has consequences on how it is actually read.

Such complicated conventions for writing and reading might seem bizarre to people who are not familiar with the Japanese writing system. Unsurprisingly, therefore, great importance is given to the acquisition of kanji in the Japanese education system. There is a testing service called Japan Kanji Aptitude Testing (*nihon kanji nōryoku kentei*) where people pay to be tested. Participants of this test are thus provided with a certificate for the ability to write and read their first language. Furthermore, it is not uncommon to have a section on kanji in a college entrance exam in order to verify the level with which the candidates are able to write and read kanji. This is noteworthy, because it points to the fact that even at the age of 18 years some individuals seeking university admission may not be able to write and read kanji appropriately for entering tertiary education. The basis of functional literacy in Japan is the ability to use approximately 2,000 kanji designated for daily use (*jōyō kanji*), in addition to a fundamental knowledge of kanji that are used 100% phonetically, that is irrespective of the semantic content of the script symbol. Knowledge of the written representation of words via these "called-upon kanji compounds" (*ateji*) is seen as another fundamental part of the knowledge required for everyday life. However, the reality is that even many high school graduates have difficulty achieving such a level of functional literacy without the help of dictionaries. Misused or miswritten words are seen as a "lack of education" or as a "lack of care", and it may trigger negative reactions. As an effect, many Japanese feel quite nervous about their writing and reading abilities.

An often-heard self-accusation among Japanese adults is to have lost the ability to write kanji. This is said to be the result of no longer writing kanji by hand, due to the spread of kanji input through smartphones, computers, keyboards, touch panels, etc. in every aspect of life outside school. As a result, even students at Japanese elite universities feel uncomfortable when it comes to handwriting kanji. Many report difficulties in doing so without the help of electronic devices. Just as with other languages, computer technology suggests and revises spelling mistakes in Japanese. There is in particular a strong anxiety about possible mistakes when it comes to kanji that have many strokes (Matsumoto 1997). I, too, often experience a sense of uneasiness when I have to write something on the blackboard during university lectures.

The above-illustrated difficulties and insecurities point out that kanji as a cultural apparatus supporting everyday life is not without problems, and so far we have only discussed the difficulties of Japanese first language speakers. It goes without saying that exchange students, recently arrived migrants from non-kanji using countries, experience enormous difficulty and often find themselves restricted, alienated and rejected through kanji writing. Ezaki (2010), for instance, reports difficulties experienced by residents in Japan from English-speaking countries. It is a well-known fact that kanji constitute a formidable cultural barrier for foreign trainees, interns, foreign nurses and nursing care worker candidates who enter Japan on the basis of Economic Partnership Agreements (Otomo 2016). Also, terms such as *gaijin* or *gaijin-san* (Mr./Ms. Foreigner), which are widely used by many Japanese to refer to foreign nationals, indicate a great psychological distance between Japanese and foreign nationals. This terminology refers to "Cultural Others", and this otherness crucially includes staying outside the world of Japanese kanji writing and reading. Cultural Others lack both the experience and the psychological burden that comes along with learning and skillfully using the Japanese writing system. Seen this way, the writing system in Japan is a cultural resource that is prone to result in social exclusion and discrimination.[1]

The mixed semantic–phonetic character of kanji has also contributed to the recent and unexpected trend of "glittering names" (*kirakira nēmu*), that is to say, mapping unusual readings onto kanji in order to create "glittering" or "sparkling" names (Nishizawa 2016). Remember

that, for example, a family name written <角田> can be read as either *kakuda, kakuta, tsunoda, sumida, sumita* or *kadota*. One literally has to ask the person having the name <角田> how to pronounce it. While family names are usually not up for choice and change, first names are, and we find in contemporary Japanese society a newfound liberty to create new readings of kanji used in personal names. The personal name for newborns is entirely up to the decision of the parents. The Family Registration Law states only the following provisions (Japanese Law Translation 2007):
Article 50

(1) For the given name of a child, characters that are simple and in common use shall be used.
(2) The scope of characters that are simple and in common use shall be defined by Ordinance of the Ministry of Justice.

The Ordinance for Enforcement of the Family Register Act that regulates "the scope of characters that are simple and in common use" states the following (Japanese Law Translation 2012).
Article 60
Characters that are plain and in common use as referred to in Article 50, paragraph (2) of the Family Register Act shall be the following:

(1) the kanji characters set in the national list of kanji characters in common use (Cabinet Notice No. 2 of 2010) (where a kanji character accompanies an alternative kanji character in parentheses, it shall be limited to the kanji character outside the parentheses).
(2) the kanji characters set forth in Appended Table 2.
(3) katakana or hiragana characters (excluding obsolete kana characters).

To sum up, the legal regulations on Japanese personal names involves only two rules, namely that some kanji cannot be used for naming and that script other than kanji, hiragana and katakana cannot be used. The trend of *kirakira-nēmu* is based on this liberal regulation. As long as one uses common kanji, the way names are actually read out is entirely up to the parents. This can result in extremely creative readings and names. One popular "sparkling name" in 2015 was for instance <皇帝> *shīzā*, the Japanese pronunciation of "Caesar". The mapping of *shīzā* onto <皇帝> is completely ad hoc. If one follows the (dominant) Sino-Japanese reading <皇帝> would be pronounced *kōtei* (emperor). However, parents who followed the trend of "sparkling names" ignore such conventions and read it as *shīzā* (Caesar) because Caesar was an emperor. In other words, the semantic side of kanji takes precedence and totally eclipses the phonological function of the script symbols in question. Consider some more examples where names of Japanese anime and pop culture have come to be used for personal names.

(5)
<光宙> (光 = light + 宙 = sky) is read as *pikachū*, not in conventional Sino-Japanese as *kōchū*
<愛猫> (愛 = love + 猫 = cat) is read as *kitī* (Hello Kitty), not in conventional Sino-Japanese as *aibyō*
<今鹿> (今 = now + 鹿 = deer) is read as *naushika*, not in conventional Sino-Japanese as *konka*

There is by now an entire generation of people with *kirakira-nēmu* in Japan. The oldest of them are today in their twenties. They have arrived at a stage in their life when they engage in job-hunting activities or have to undergo rituals such as exchanging business cards. Afraid of being discriminated by personnel management due to their unusual names, some are considering adapting nicknames in place of their sparkling personal names. While prejudice based on personal names is not desirable, their parents' choice of such names is widely seen as an act of thoughtlessness if not as an outright sign of a lack of common sense. As a matter of fact, the derogatory term *DQN nēmu* (read as *dokyun nēmu*) has recently spread in Japan. The term is part of Internet slang and refers to individuals of poor knowledge and intelligence. It was coined and spread through a reality TV show where people were made to look foolish for their ignorance on specific matters. There can be no doubt in the fact that having a sparkling name involves a range of social problems.

Another seemingly minor point on which, however, much attention is attached concerns the strict rules on stroke order when teaching and learning kanji in school. In present-day Japan, we can find two opposing camps on this matter. One of them has basically a blind faith in a set stroke order. One specific strike order is seen as a "natural movement" by the hand and the resulting kanji are declared to be "well-formed" and "beautiful". The opposite camp sneers at such beliefs. For instance, some consider that the kanji <必> (certainty) has a set stroke order (top to down, left to right), while others believe that there are two established ways to write it, and that there is no rational ground to insist on any of the two as being "correct". Many linguists are in the latter camp, and so is actually the Japanese Ministry for Education, Culture, Sports, Science and Technology. However, the majority of schoolteachers in Japan subscribe to a prescriptive stroke order. In this context, it is interesting to note that high school students have documented and actually tested the consistency of 200 teachers' judgment and found that there are great inconsistencies in what teachers themselves were proclaiming to be the "correct stroke order" (Kyōiku no Mado 2013; Masiko 2009).

Problems of the Japanese writing system also involve the script style of kanji (*kanji jitai*). As soon as somebody reads texts published before 1945, they must inevitably deal with historical styles of kanji and kana (*kyū-jitai*) and with irregular script style (*i-jitai*). A good example how script style can be problematic in contemporary Japan can be seen in the scandal surrounding Moritomo Gakuen in 2017. A part of the scandal was that a kindergarten administered by Moritomo Gakuen provided education that was based on extreme right-wing thoughts, which involved, for example, the recitation of the Imperial Rescript on Education (*kyōiku chokugo*), a text that reflects and symbolizes ideologies of the imperial system (Economist 2017). In addition, the planned establishment of an elementary school by Moritomo Gakuen had to be canceled. The bone of contention in this case was the name of the planned elementary school, <瑞穂の國記念小學院> *mizuho no kuni kinen shōgakkōin* (Wikipedia 2018). The problem was that the name of the school was written in the old script style, i.e. <國> (*kuni*, country) was used instead of the simplified and commonly used form of <国>. Likewise, <學> (*gaku*, study) was used instead of <学>. These old kanji forms were eliminated after WWII, but they remain the preferred style by right-wing individuals or groups in contemporary Japan. The reason for this is that the new script style has been implemented during the post-war script reforms under Allied Occupation (1945–1952). Reactionary groups see the abolition of the old script style therefore as a symbol of Japan's defeat to the Allied Forces, and insist that old script styles such as <國> and <學> are the only legitimate and correct forms.

Other than reflecting imperialistic attitudes and ideologies, there are a number of other problems that derive from using the old script style. One of the biggest thereof is the complex differentiation of kanji used for family names. In family names, old style kanji are often maintained. The name Watanabe, for instance, the fifth most common family name in Japan, is said to have 65 different kanji forms and combinations, including the most common <渡辺> but also variation such as <渡邊> or <渡邉>. Saitō, which is the 15th most common last name, has 31 different variations including <斎藤> and <斉藤>. To be sure, these two family names are exceptional examples, but the comparison with romanization is nevertheless illustrative. When using the Latin Alphabet, the family name could be written in capital letters as <WATANABE> or it could simply be transcribed as <Watanabe>, while one has with the second name additionally the possibility to indicate the vowel length through macron or not, arriving thus at <Saitō> or <Saito>. Having more than a dozen variants for a name only involving two characters in a writing system composed of thousands of characters is obviously problematic. Such a writing convention also represents a heavy burden on visually impaired people. Those with weak eyesight need to consistently pay close attention in order to distinguish between the different characters, styles and variants. Also, the selection of the appropriate kanji with touchscreen or keyboard input is anything but easy.

On the other hand, supporters of the established writing conventions stress that only the semantic features of kanji allow for distinguishing the large number of homophones in Japanese. Somewhat ironically, a great number of Japanese playwrights are ardent supporters of kanji despite the fact their plays function on stage without using kanji. Thus, the conditions that linguists term "homophonic collision", that is, misunderstanding due to the use of homophones, will not occur as long as there is a shared context between the actors and the audience (see Murakami and Hotta 2011; Wydell, Patterson and Humphreys 1993).

If kanji compounds appear in completely different contexts, such as <下顎> *kagaku* (lower jaw) and <歌学> *kagaku* (study of 31-syllable traditional poems), they do not cause any misunderstandings. However, since Japanese has a great number of homonyms, there are indeed cases of confusion. For example, the following homonym pairs can appear in very similar context, and they can therefore not be distinguished on the basis of this context. Homonyms like the following are frequently used:

(6)
    <科学> *kagaku* (science) <化学> *kagaku* (chemistry)
    <工学> *kōgaku* (engineering) <光学> *kōgaku* (optics)
    <私立> *shiritsu* (private) <市立> *shiritsu* (public)
    <遍在> *henzai* (omnipresence, ubiquity) <偏在> *henzai* (unevenly distributed)

Note that one of these examples actually represents antonyms, <遍在> (omnipresence, ubiquity) and <偏在> (unevenly distributed). If a scriptwriter were to seek a comedic reaction by employing the homonym pair <遍在> and <偏在>, it will most likely not work, because it would either confuse the audience or require an additional explanation.

Another problem with kanji homonyms is that different kanji can have the same reading. For instance, words such as *hakaru* (to measure), *utsuru* (to be reflected; intransitive form of the verb *utsusu*, to reflect), *tomaru* (to be stopped; intransitive from of *tomeru*, to stop) and *atsui* (to be hot, to be thick) are written with a number of different kanji. The different kanji are believed to express a distinctive meaning in totally homophonic words. It is therefore necessary to choose the correct kanji according to an intended meaning. Distinctions such as that of *hakaru* and *utsuru* explained below are seen to constitute basic knowledge of the Japanese language, and it is expected that adult Japanese know these differences.

(7)
<図る> *hakaru* (to plan, to attempt)
<謀る> *hakaru* (to plan, to plot)
<計る> *hakaru* (to measure time or quantity)
<測る> *hakaru* (to measure length or area)
<量る> *hakaru* (to measure weight)

(8)
<映る> *utsuru* (to be reflected)
<移る> *utsuru* (to move residence or to be transferred)
<写る> *utsuru* (to be taken in a picture or video)
<遷る> *utsuru* (to be contagious, to be infected, to elapse, to move)

These homonyms do not necessarily have clear-cut semantic differences. For instance, <図る> and <謀る> (*hakaru*) share the meaning "to plan", and <計る>, <測る> and <量る> (*hakaru*) all mean "to measure". There is semantic continuity and overlap across these kanji, but this notwithstanding, some Japanese claim that not maintaining these distinctions and separate uses would imply a destruction of tradition. Others again prefer to write these words in hiragana, e.g., <はかる> *hakaru*, <うつる> *utsuru* and thereby effectively avoid all problems that come along with having to choose the adequate kanji for the intended meaning. These conflicting stances and practices for how to deal with such words and their written representation will in all likelihood not be settled any time soon. In the entrance exam systems for schools and universities, these distinctions are expected to be known, since conservatives generally control these systems. On the other hand, individual choices and styles are respected in professional writing. One therefore encounters the same words sometimes written in kanji and sometimes in written kana, depending on who writes and for what purpose. As a result, search engines on the Internet must be prepared for several different written representations of one and the same word.

Kana problems

Script problems in Japan are not only limited to kanji. There are also a number of difficulties with regard to kana. Kana were derived from kanji, and there were two principal ways this was done. Some kana represented modifications of kanji while others were simplified representations. Put briefly, the modified kanji developed into hiragana, while the simplified selection became katakana. Consider an example. The hiragana <い> (*i*) is a modified form of the kanji <以> while the katakana <イ> (*i*) is a simplified form of the kanji <伊>. Some problematic issues with kana derive from the fact that both scripts derived from kanji. As an effect, their contrasts are not always easy to spot. Among the hiragana, <あ/め/ぬ>, <お/ね/れ/わ>, <き/さ/ち>, <ほ/ま> and <い/じ> sometimes appear similar and also a number of katakana have similar forms: <ア/マ/ス/ヌ>, <ラ/フ/ク/ワ/ウ/ケ>, <チ/テ>, <ノ/ソ/シ/ツ> or <リ/ル/レ>. In particular when quickly written by hand, it can become difficult to distinguish them.

The above-mentioned problems are not the only problem of hiragana and katakana. Although Japanese orthography it is not as arbitrary as, for example, that of English, contemporary Japanese has a few inconsistencies between sounds and their written representation. For example, in order to produce the family name, <亀井> *kamei* (<亀> *kame* and <井> *i*) and the noun <加盟> *kamei* (<加> *ka* and <盟> *mei*, "affiliation"), we need to input in both cases *kamei* in a word processor in order to convert it into the respective kanji combinations. However, their pronunciation actually differs. The first one is pronounced *kamei* and the second one *kamē*, and this may well cause confusion in the input of the words in question via keyboards or touchscreens. Consider another example. In order to have <王子> *ōji* (prince) by means of text-input kanji conversion, you have to either enter *ouji* or *ouzi* in order to represent the long vowel *ō*, but if you want to write <大路> *ōji* (large road), then you need to enter *ooji* or *oozi*, that is, the long vowel needs to be input as *oo*, although the pronunciation for <王子> and

<大路> is exactly the same. These are inconsistencies that are based on the fact that the orthography does not exactly match with the spoken language. Another example of such difficulties is the script input necessary for creating the kanji <通り> *tōri* (street). It requires the input *toori*, and neither *touri* nor *douri* (also "street" in spoken language) can be converted into <通り>. Furthermore, although the kana <は> *ha*, <へ> *he* and <を> *wo* are used for the representation of case particles, the pronunciation of these case particles is *wa*, *e* and *o*, respectively. As a result, when enumerating the particles, we write <てにをは> *teniwoha*, but when used as particles the pronunciation becomes *teniowa*. Hence, a sentence such as <家へは帰らない> *ie e wa kaeranai* (I will not return home) must be input as *ie he ha kaeranai*.

Before the end of WWII, the discrepancy between writing and pronunciation was much larger than it is today. What is pronounced *kōyūyōna* ("like this"), was then written <かういふやうな> *kauihuyauna* with the kanji equivalent being <斯う云ふ様な>. The postwar script reforms improved the correspondence between orthography and pronunciation, and they facilitated the conventions of kanji use. Today, "like this" is written as <こうゆうような> in kana and <こう言う様な> in kanji. This notwithstanding, no exact one-to-one correspondence between spelling and pronunciation exists today, and some people actually read <こう言う様な> as *kōiu*. That is to say, they fail to read the kana-kanji combination as an idiomatic expression and instead assign each character its conventional reading. While <言う> alone is read as *iu*, it is always read as *yū* when preceded by <こう> (*kō*) or <そう> (*sō*). Hence, <こう言う> (*kōyū*) needs to be read in the exact same way as <交友> (friend), <交遊> (companionship) or <公有> (public ownership). In effect, computer-mediated input of Japanese script is not without problems, and other than <こう言う>, there are a number of other words and expressions that require an idiomatic input of sounds. Japanese orthography remains arbitrary even after the post-war reforms, and while hiragana and katakana are portrayed as phonological script systems in contemporary Japanese, they, too, are not without discrepancies. Japanese orthography also requires the conventional use of smaller-sized fonts and lower-set kana in order to express all the sounds that exist in Standard Japanese. This results in notations such as, for example, <きゃ> *kya*, <きゅ> *kyu*, <きょ> *kyo*, <しゃ> *sha*, <しゅ> *shu* or <しょ> *sho*. In addition, the small *tsu* <っ> in hiragana and <ッ> in katakana is used to represent gemination, for example, in <カット> *katto* (cut). These conventions are often difficult to distinguish since the difference between normal fonts and smaller fonts is often minimal, and hence proofreaders and editors tend to have a hard time distinguishing them.

The difficulties of the Japanese writing system are most evident in the use of hiragana in addition to kanji in order to indicate the reading of kanji. In other words, two notations are used at the same time to represent a word. What is called *okurigana* (literally "accompanying letters") in Japanese refers to small-fonts kana written above the kanji. *Okurigana* are used to indicate either difficult or unconventional readings, but also to distinguish different meanings (via different readings) of one and the same kana-kanji combination. For example, you cannot distinguish on the basis of the orthography whether <行った> represents *itta* (gone) or *okonatta* (done). Also, there are two possible readings for <入った>, namely *itta* and *haitta*. These two possible readings and meanings are indistinguishable, unless the reader can specify the context.

Latin alphabet problems

When political and cultural leaders in the Meiji period (1868–1912) adopted a national language policy in order to modernize Japanese, the possibility of a Japanese writing system based in the Latin alphabet (*rōmaji*) was also vividly discussed (see Yamada 1942). This possibility re-emerged in the education and script reforms that followed Japanese defeat in WWII. In particular, the General Head Quarter of the Allied Forced pushed for such reforms during the occupation period (Unger 1996). Although there were twists and turns throughout the history of modern Japan, it is no exaggeration to say that a *rōmaji*-based writing system for Japanese is today hardly considered an option in Japanese society. This notwithstanding, romanized Japanese is widely used in Japan, be that in school education, in the linguistic landscape or in written documents. Two orthographies coexist for writing Japanese in Latin letters. One is the official Kunrei style and the second the much more widely used Hepburn style. The Kunrei style, literally "Cabinet-ordered" style, is more appropriate to the Japanese phonological system (which is why it is used for linguistic analysis). Despite its unofficial status, the Hepburn style, created by US missionary James Curtis Hepburn in the late nineteenth century is the de facto standard for writing documents, or for writing in the linguistic landscape. In educational settings, both Kunrei style and Hepburn style are used in parallel, and in practice both conventions often get mixed as a result. Surprisingly, the situation is not seen to require a solution, and Japanese language policy does not address mixed and idiosyncratic uses.

The Hepburn style is regarded to best represent sounds of Japanese to western foreigners, but it does not strictly conform to the phonological system of Standard Japanese. Consider as an example, the *sa*, *ta* and *ha* lines of the kana syllabaries. According to Hepburn style romanization, they are written as:

(9)
<sa shi su se so>
<ta chi tsu te to>
<ha hi fu he ho>

The inconsistencies are obvious, and it becomes more obvious, yet, if we contrast it to the Kunrei style representation of the same lines.

(19)
<sa si su se so>
<ta ti tu te to to>
<ha hi hu he ho>

The Kunrei style is highly systematic and consistent. However, Japanese educators seem to be indifferent to this fact, and they tend to prefer the Hepburn style.

There is no consistent policy on *rōmaji* orthography within the government. The Ministry of Education, Culture, Sports, Science and Technology stipulated in its regulations on *rōmaji* (Cabinet Notice No. 1, 12 September 1954) that "only when international relations and other conventional practices are inadequately amenable, spelling conventions which are stated in graph 2 [Hepburn style H.M.] can be used". However, by attaching a proviso with the Hepburn style, the ministry in effect tolerates deviations from its own regulations, and in practice Kunrei style is completely ignored by most ministries in Japan. The Ministry of Education, Culture, Sports, Science and Technology itself has not maintained a consistent position on this issue, and Hepburn style is used in many contexts where it is hard to see how "international relations and other conventional practices are inadequately amenable". Personal names are a case in point. It seems that bureaucrats have no doubt that, for example, my own names should be transcribed as <Hidenori Mashiko> in Latin script, that is, following the conventions of the Hepburn orthography and the western name order. However, it is questionable why one would need to choose a convention whose single benefit is to better accommodate western foreigners, in particular English speakers. The Kunrei-style romanization as <Masiko Hidenori>, on the other hand, follows the Japanese custom of putting the family name first, and it adequately represents the Japanese phonological system. In order to reduce problems for foreigners not accustomed with the Japanese name order, misunderstanding can be minimized by capitalizing the family name as <MASIKO>. However, such transcriptions of personal names remain the exception in Japan today.

The Japanese government, including the Ministry of Education, Culture, Sports, Science and Technology, has never set a consistent position toward romanization. It has adopted a laissez-faire attitude also when it comes to issues such as official documents, regulations or transcriptions of Japanese names. In practice, one frequently encounters idiosyncratic mixtures of Hepburn style and Kunrei style, and nobody seems to care. At present, there are no opportunities to receive systematic guidance on basic principles how to transcribe Japanese in the Latin alphabet, despite the fact that such input is indispensable in everyday life in Japan. In this way, a mixture of indifference and unawareness continues to endlessly reproduce problems of Latin script orthography.

Outlook

With regard to writing, contemporary Japan constitutes a particular cultural space. Issues of writing systems and orthography present barriers and difficulties for a vast array of different individuals, ranging from newly arrived foreigners, Japanese who grew up overseas, visually impaired, or people not skilled with IT applications, individuals who drop out the Japanese education system – for whatever reason, etc. This notwithstanding, the major part of the Japanese population is unaware or insensitive to these problems. Japanese society appears to have accepted actual practices and problems involved in writing in Japan. It seems that the long training required to learning how to write in Japan results also in approving of a writing system that is marred with difficulties and problems. Learning to deal with the Japanese writing system is an inevitable part of youth in Japan. All those who did not go through these experiences are inevitably seen as cultural outsiders. There are no serious considerations to change the current situation. While Japanese society is sometimes said to show a sense of inferiority towards the West, we cannot find any traces of such sentiment with regard to the Japanese writing system. On the contrary, when it comes to writing, Japanese society sticks to stubborn exclusionism and takes pride in this stance.

Note

1 One might be led to think that data processing in Japanese is difficult and expensive due to the above-mentioned complexity and problems. There is in fact a consensus that the distinction of proper names and common nouns in data processing is a problem, and that addressing this problem requires time and money. It is also clear that the delay in the popular spread of personal computers and word processing machines had resulted from data processing problems caused by the complexity and arbitrariness of kanji. These difficulties had already been foreseen by a visionary publication half a century ago (Umesao 1969). For details on kanji, technology and computers at the time, see Gottlieb (2000).

References

Abe, Yasushi (2015) *Kotoba no bariafuri – jōhō hoshō to komyunikēshon no shōgaigaku* [*Disability Studies of Guaranteeing Information Accessibility and Communication*]. Tokyo: Seikatsu Shoin.
The Economist (2017) An Ultranationalist Kindergarten for Japan. Available online at: www.economist.com/asia/2017/03/04/an-ultranationalist-kindergarten-in-japan (accessed 11 July 2018).

Ezaki, Makoto (2010) Strategic Deviations. The Role of Kanji in Contemporary Japanese. *Japanese Language and Literature* 44(2): 179–212.
Gottlieb, Nanette (2000) *Word Processor Technology in Japan. Kanji and the Keyboard*. London: Routledge.
Japanese Law Translation (2007) Family Register Act. Available online at: www.japaneselawtranslation. go.jp/law/detail/?id=2161&vm=04&re=01 (accessed 11 July 2018).
Japanese Law Translation (2012) Ordinance for Enforcement of the Family Register Act. Available online at: www.japaneselawtranslation.go.jp/law/detail/?ky=商業登記&page=8&la=01&re=01 (accessed 11 July 2018).
Kadoya, Hidenori and Yasushi Abe (eds.) (2010) *Shikiji no shakai gengogaku* [*Sociolinguistics of Literacy*]. Tokyo: Seikatsu Shoin.
Kyōiku no Mado (2013) Kibishii kanji tesuto o kōkōsei ga kokuhatsu [High School Students Criticize Harsh Kanji Tests]. Available online at: http://blog.livedoor.jp/rve83253/archives/1773903.html (accessed 11 July 2018).
Masiko, Hidenori (2009) "Kanji tesuto" ga ukibori ni suru ideorogī [Ideology Revealed by "Kanji Tests"]. *Shakai gengogaku* 9: 283–297.
Matsumoto, Hitoshi (1997) Iwayuru "tadashii hitsujun" no gensō [The Illusion of the So-called "Correct Stroke Order']. *Kodai Forum* 29(2). Available online at: http://home.hiroshima-u.ac.jp/forum/29-2/hitujyun.html (accessed 11 July 2018).
Murakami, Jin'ichi and Haseo Hotta (2011) Japanese Speaker-independent Homonyms Speech Recognition. *Procedia. Social and Behavioral Sciences* 27: 306–13.
Nishizawa, Amelie (2016) The Surprising Trend of kirakira-names in Japan. Available online at: http://cotoacademy.com/japanese-kira-kira-names (accessed 11 July 2018).
Ogawa, Shinji (ed.) (2015) *Ryūkyū no kotoba no kakikata* [*How to Write in Ryukyuan Languages*]. Tokyo: Kuroshio Shuppan.
Otomo, Ruriko (2016) New Form of National Language Policy? The Case of the Economic Partnership Agreement (EPA) in Japan. *The Asia-Pacific Education Researcher* 25(5): 735–742.
Sumi, Tomoyuki (2012) *Shikiji shinwa o yomitoku – "shikijiritsu 99%" no kuni, nihon to iu ideorogī* [*Deciphering the Myth of Literacy. Japan as an Ideology of a County with "99% Literacy Rate"*]. Tokyo: Akashi Shoten.
Umesao, Tadao (1969) *Gijutsu seisan no gijutsu* [*Technology for Intellectual Production*]. Tokyo: Iwanami.
Unger, Marshall J. (1996) *Literacy and Script Reform in Occupation Japan*. Oxford: Oxford University Press.
Wikipedia (2018) Mizuho no kuni [Mizuho no Kuni Elementary School]. Available online at: https://en.wikipedia.org/wiki/Mizuho_no_Kuni (accessed 11 July 2018).
Wydell, Taeko N., Karalyn E. Patterson and Glyn W. Humphreys (1993) Phonologically Mediated Access to Meaning for Kanji. Is a Rows still a Rose in Japanese kanji? *Journal of Experimental Psychology. Learning, Memory, and Cognition* 19(3): 491–514.
Yamada, Fusakazu (1942) *Gengo kankei kankō shomoku* [*A Bibliography of Linguistic Works*]. Osaka: Private Publication.
Yamashita, Hitoshi (2011) Japan's Literacy Myth and its Social Functions. In: *Language Life in Japan*. Patrick Heinrich and Christian Galan (eds), 94–108. London: Routledge.

21
LITERACY AND ILLITERACY

Takeshi Nakashima

Introduction

Until recently, Japanese sociolinguistics has paid little attention to literacy and illiteracy. That does not mean that there was no research, though. Studies on literacy and illiteracy are dotted across disciplines and have taken educational, historical and linguistic approaches. This chapter gives an overview about all these strands, how they developed and how they have mutually influenced one another.

Research on this topic falls into two broad fields: one is concerned with school-age children, and the other with teaching literacy to adults. Both fields feature distinct academic attitudes. In the case of education for school children, literacy tends to be understood as reading and writing skills that are necessary for participation in everyday life. Emphasis is placed on functional aspects of literacy. As an effect of a global theoretical shift, initiated and spread by surveys and activities of the OECD (e.g., OECD 2000; Rychen and Salganik 2003), the study of literacy in children has gradually expanded to include "competencies" in a wider sense. Teaching literacy to adults, on the other hand, remains deeply connected with issues of illiteracy and stigma.

There are many more illiterate people in Japan than is generally thought. Enormous efforts to empower illiterate people have been carried out through the teaching of reading and writing skills (Yamashita 2011). The main perspective that has framed such efforts is "critical literacy", which has resulted in a "literacy movement" (*shikiji undō*). Research along the lines of critical literacy coexists with a historical approach to literacy and illiteracy. Here the central question is that of determining the literacy rate in the context of the Japanese history of education. The major difficulty thereby is thus to define the border between literate and illiterate. Such decisions are always affected by definitions of literacy. We will discuss this point further below.

A good overview on literacy from the perspective of Japanese linguistics in the early 1990s is Shimamura (1991), and for an international overview during the same period Moro (1991) is the best source. Comparing these two works is helpful in order to identify the particularities and trends of literacy studies. Moro introduces ethnographic studies on literacy in North America, focusing on Freire's literacy model. His review covers critical viewpoints on literacy. Shimamura, on another hand, discusses past surveys from the beginning of the Meiji Period (1868–1912) onwards, but no attention is given to critical aspects and the plurality of literacy in this work. A comparison of the works by Moro and Shimamura makes clear that there is no single and undisputed approach to literacy studies in Japan.[1]

Distinguishing literates and illiterates

There exist a number of works examining literacy and illiteracy in Japan from the early modern period (1603–1868) onwards (see, e.g., Tone 1981; Yakuwa 1992; Umihara 1998). A common feature of these works is that they attempt to identify the rate of literacy. This topic has been a central concern in historical studies on education in Japan. Non-Japanese researchers have made an important contribution to this field, too. Attention is placed on the pre-modern schooling system, and is different to that of the West at the time. These works conclude that there existed comparatively favorable literacy conditions in early modern Japan. Passin (1965) and Dore (1964), for example, state that the literacy skills of Japanese in the Edo Period (1603–1868) were higher than had initially been estimated, and that the existence of temple schools (*terakoya*), a private style of schooling that was common at the time, had been a major factor for the high literacy rate. Both also claim that these literacy skills were of great importance for Japan's modernization. As a consequence of these positive evaluations of pre-modern literacy in Japan, some conclude that the literacy rate in Japan had been the highest in the world at this time. This remains an unproved assessment, though.

As a matter of fact, recent studies have expressed some doubts about the high rate of literacy in pre-modern Japan. In this context, the difficulty of calculating the exact percentage of literate people has been repeatedly underlined. Kimura (2014) states that statistical approaches to estimate the rate of literacy in early modern Japan cannot be accurate due to the simple fact that there existed no accurate demographic data of that time. Rubinger (2007) criticized the practice of equating temple school enrollment with literacy. In order to shed more light on pre-modern literacy and illiteracy, researchers have started paying more attention to primary source materials such as handwriting (Umemura 2014). As Ōguro (2015) points out, this shift away from temple school enrollment towards the study of historical written documents is influenced by western approaches where signatures on marriage certificates are used for estimating historical literacy rates (see e.g., Stone 1969). In employing such a philological approach, Yakuwa (2011) and Kawamura (2014) study the literacy rate of the early Meiji Period (1868–1912) for specific regions of Japan (Yamaguchi Prefecture, Okayama Prefecture and Wakayama Prefecture). In order to overcome the binary of literate versus illiterate, both studies also classify the state of literacy into more specific categories. Accordingly, the illiterate strata (*hi-shikijisō*) of society is defined as being unable to read and write their name, the rudimentary literate strata (*seimei-tō jicho kanōsō*) are those who are able to do so and the functional literate strata (*jitsuyōteki shikijisō*) refers to those who are capable to read and write public documents. These efforts notwithstanding, the problem remains that the basis on which individuals are classified into categories such as literate, functional literate and illiterate is arbitrary.

Literacy studies from an educational perspective

Research on literacy from a historical perspective in Japan has gradually shifted to functional reading and writing skills as a reaction to international research trends. In this paragraph, some of the major developments are summarized.

From the start, the term "literacy" has meant the ability to read and write. Following the establishment of public education in the US in 1883 (Willinsky 1990), the concept of literacy has been linked with the process of modernization. William Gray's (1956) seminal work on functional literacy was presented to UNESCO, and this led to an expansion of what we understand today as "literacy" to include the occupational and technical knowledge that is necessary to participate in society. In the 1950s, literacy came to be seen as a basic set of skills of reading and writing which are required in order to functionally participate in society. Institutions such as UNESCO promoted and spread this approach into what was then called the "Third World" through massive literacy campaigns. However, a number of studies have criticized this concept of functional literacy for its hegemonic status and the ideologies that inform it (e.g., Baynham 1995; Gee 1996; Street 1984; Stuckey 1991). Looking at the work of Goody (1968), Olson (1977) and Ong (1982), they disapprove of the dichotomy between speech and writing (i.e., orality and literacy). They do not accept that literacy is a "neutral set" of reading and writing skills unaffected by actual circumstances. Furthermore, they reject the idea that acquisition of literacy has the effect of improving universal cognitive skills to think logically and abstractly. Street (1984) called such universal literacy detached from social situations an "autonomous model" of Literacy with a big "L and a single y". Writing "Literacy" with capital L and the singular y implies its generality or independence from social context and emphasizes its "standard" image that differs from the actual existence of the plural of "literacies".

The concept of literacy has turned into a broader concept, including now also access and use of information, the selection of more suitable information, and critically thinking about the meaning of documents within their specific contexts. This approach informs for example the PISA studies on literacy.[2] The latest, and currently dominant, understanding of literacy in educational pedagogy is that of a human ability, which also includes emotion and affect. A number of efforts by OECD policies have influenced this understanding of literacy. In particular the research project called DeSeCo (Definition and Selection of Competencies) has focused on how to cultivate the necessary abilities for functioning in real-life situations beyond school settings.

Discussions on more narrowly defined concepts of literacy are nowadays basically absent in Japanese educational studies.[3] One of the causes for this is that literacy has been seen as a "self-evident" ability in Japan, which is why Japanese educators and researchers have embraced new perspectives such as the theory of critical literacy (Freire 1970), critical pedagogy (Giroux 1988, 1992) or the differences between functional literacy and cultural literacy (Hirsh 1987). There now exist works such as Uechi's (2003), giving detailed descriptions about Giroux's critical pedagogy, Hayakawa (1994) elaborating the emancipative aspects of Giroux's theory and Koyanagi (2010) stressing that economic growth was the precondition for the emergence of the concept of functional literacy in the 1960s. More recently, the "competencies concept", which has sprung up as an effect of the nascent knowledge society, has been much discussed in Japan (e.g., Matsuo 2016).

There is dissent among researchers in Japan, whether or not literacy ought to be seen as a bundle of competencies (see e.g., Satō 2003; Higuchi 2010). Matsushita (2010) first advocated approaching literacy in the way that PISA does. She underlined that literacy included a critical viewpoint and the individual context. Her study was simultaneously a critique of Honda (2008), who had explicitly contradicted the competencies concept and had criticized it as an exploitation of human emotions for demands of the labor market. However, according to Matsushita (2014) this tendency can be seen in all approaches to functional literacy since the 1960s. That is to say, functional literacy is always informed by an ideology to develop individuals as human capital for societal development. Already this brief summary illustrates that discussions on literacy are part and parcel of discussions of politics and power. While politics and power have been included and discussed in the Japanese context from early on, little attention has actually been placed on discussing literacy of languages other than Japanese, or literacy of foreign residents in Japan. Furthermore, literacies of people with disabilities (e.g., the Deaf) have rarely been discussed.

The *shikiji* perspective

Discrimination against outcast people, the so-called "*buraku*", has existed in Japan since at least the early modern period (Teraki 2016: 82). *Buraku* (literally "settlement") refers to areas where social outcast people were forced to live. As a result of their social and geographic exclusion, the *buraku* have experienced particular problems with regard to literacy. The modern public education system, inaugurated in 1872, initially refused admission to *buraku* children in public schools.[4] Until today, academic achievements and access to higher education remain below average. Around 10% of the *buraku* community is estimated to be illiterate, and in particular among elderly *buraku* illiteracy is high (Nabeshima 1997). Illiteracy among the *buraku* is interconnected with the fact that their human rights have often not been respected. This is also the case with the permanent Korean residents in Japan (*zainichi*). This situation results in the reproduction of social inequality and stigma, a topic to which we will return further below.

In reviewing the issue of the stigma and illiteracy, Roberts and Street (1997) report that to many "illiteracy" is paramount to "ignorance, stupidity, cognitive deficit, etc." (Roberts and Street 1997: 174–175). In Japan, too, illiteracy is linked with humiliation. The long-standing discrimination of *buraku* and *zainichi* persists partly due the fact that the stigma and humiliation of illiteracy remains. Sumi (2012: 198–206) illustrates the case of a woman who could not write her name in a hospital and was publicly ridiculed by nurses, and also a case of an illiterate man who had to change work because he could not compile conference materials. Up to today, the employment rate of members of the *buraku* community is comparatively low, and white-collar employees of this group remain a rarity (Ishimoto 1997: 72). Furthermore, since many of them have family names that are indicative of their *buraku* background, many continue to suffer discrimination in the labor market and also with regard to marriage (Honda 1992: 51).

Leaders of the *buraku* liberation movement have for a long time engaged in teaching literacy for empowerment. They believe that literacy could be the main breakthrough to escape their humiliating situation. In this *buraku* liberation context, "literacy" is generally called *shikiji* (literally "knowing letters"). The distinct character of *shikiji*, as compared with *riterashī* (literacy), is that *shikiji* is a concept created by the *buraku* liberation movement. *Shikiji* connotes their desperate desire to learn how to read and write (see Uchiyama 1991; Uesugi 2016). The basis of *shikiji* can clearly be traced back to Freire's work (1970) on critical literacy; *kaihō* (emancipation) and *henkaku* (transformation) are key concepts that have been directly inspired by his work and figured prominently as foregrounded in the *shikiji* approach (see Hirasawa 1983; Mori 1991). The *shikiji* movement encourages learners to identify and analyze what has prevented them from learning how to read and write. This analysis also applies to other minority groups in Japan such as the permanent Korean residents mentioned above.

Recent studies argue that until recently there has been one main master-narrative that defines all *shikiji* efforts. That is, researchers were always interested in the experiences of the illiterates being oppressed. The aim of learning to be literate was initially "liberation and emancipation", even though there might have been learners who did not fully subscribe to this idea. The current paradigm includes also other narratives, and it focuses on participant observation in specific local communities in order to broaden our understanding of illiterate experiences in Japan. Yamane (2009), for example, depicts how a second generation resident Korean illiterate woman joins a *shikiji* class in order to make friends (rather than to simply accomplish literacy). This kind of fieldwork enables us also to see that illiterate people have specific strategies to overcome the literacy problems linked with their daily lives. Literacy strategies of illiterate resident Koreans in Japan emerge as social networks that facilitate the circulation of common information. Ethnographic studies have shown how illiterate resident Koreans manage daily life without reading, for example by memorizing shapes and pictures on public signs. Using colors, shapes and pictures as a substitute for letters is an important strategy to survive as illiterates in a literate society. Sumi (2012) notes the existence of social networks in his work on written materials of formerly illiterate *buraku* individuals. He adopts in his work the idea of a "literacy event" as proposed by Heath (1982: 93) and defined as "any occasion in which a piece of writing is integral to the nature of participants' interactions and their interpretive processes". Heath's seminal study demonstrated that literacy is best understood in the context of social practice and needs to be embedded in a certain community and specific situation.

The Deaf in Japan have experienced similar discrimination as the *buraku* and *zainichi*. The Deaf have specific literacy skills. Most teachers of Deaf schools are hearing, and they usually do not know Japanese Sign Language until they start teaching there. Such lack of skills on the side of the teachers is known to contribute to lower-than-average academic achievement of Deaf children in school (Nakashima 2013). In his study of daily uses of Japanese literacy by Deaf, Nakashima (2016) found that some have a low regard for themselves because they compare their own literacy with the unachievable objective of the literacy as defined by hearing Japanese. Due to such self-abasement, many are reluctant to participate in literacy-mediated communication with the hearing. In order to solve communication problems mediated by Japanese literacy, Deaf people utilize their social network in similar ways as hearing illiterates do. Nakashima (2016) proposes also a reciprocal relationship between the Deaf and the hearing in Japan. In referring to Fingeret's (1983) work on the lives of illiterate people in the US, he discusses how illiterate people need not always be seen to require help, but that they can also provide help to literates in specific situations.

Illiteracy does not necessarily equate with unhappiness or being oppressed. This becomes evident in examining the ethnographic approaches to literacy focusing on everyday practices. Heath (1982), Fingeret (1983) and other researchers promoting an ethnographic approach to the study of literacy and illiteracy pay attention to specific situations and communities. They focus on "plurality", "local" and "practice", resulting thereby in new literacy studies that have also exerted influence on current Japanese research. This notwithstanding, some theoretical weaknesses remain. Despite best efforts to acquire letters, many formerly illiterate individuals will not achieve the same level of literacy as those who attained literacy at an early age. Therefore, a wide diversity in their use of literacy remains. We may say that they possess a "vernacular literacy". For example, kanji with additional kana annotation and exclusive use of hiragana are a prominent feature in materials circulated and used in *shikiji* workshops (Uchiyama 1991). Also, the Deaf usually make adjustments in their literacy use. In case they communicate exclusively among Deaf through written language, they pay attention to the literacy level of their conversational partners and adopt a suitable literacy variation that can at times be quite different from the "standard literacy" style (Nakashima 2016). Such "vernacular use" of literacy remains, however, subject to stigmatization in Japan. It may be interpreted as "childish writing".

The widespread belief that the dominant literacy style of mixing kanji, hiragana and katakana is the best and quasi "natural way" of writing entails a devaluation of non-standard uses of literacy. It does not acknowledge that a plurality of literacies exists in Japanese society. Literacy studies within the *buraku* liberation movement among the Korean residents also reinforce the idea of full literacy by trying to make the *buraku* and the *zainichi* maximally literate, instead of critically reflecting on the ideological concept of "full literacy". Some present studies try to debunk this ideology. Kadoya (2010) problematized the *shikiji* movement by discussing theoretical confusions within the movement. For example, while *shikiji* movement leaders try to protect the illiterate from social discrimination, they reproduce dominant ideologies on the writing system and portray society as being characterized through a set literacy proficiency. As a result, the possibility of not using literacy criteria has never been discussed within the movement. In order to adjust this and to direct further *shikiji* movement activities in a new direction, Kadoya proposes first taking a critical look at ideologies connected to literacy skills.

Focusing on the exclusive function of literacy

Stuckey's (1991) seminal book *The Violence of Literacy* was translated into Japanese by Kikuchi Kyūichi in 1995. In sharing Stuckey's perspectives on literacy, Kikuchi (1995) insists that literacy crucially involves issues of authority and power. Both Stuckey and Kikuchi point out the negative influences of subscribing to the idea of a "single literacy". They criticize the privileged position of western-style school literacy, which is protected and promoted by powerful institutions. Kikuchi's work is important, because he shows how literacy serves also as a tool for social control. Literacy, he maintains, monopolizes the construction of social knowledge. This view has gradually spread across Japanese sociolinguistics.

Sunano (2012) studies the hegemonic power of the idea of a single literacy and analyzes it as a mechanism of social exclusion. He distinguishes between three categories of literacy comprehension: (1) literacy as a project of the modern age, (2) literacy as an ideological device, and (3) literacy as a mechanism of exclusion. Consider these three perspectives in more detail:

(1) To start, literacy is a product of the modern age that has laid the foundation for the construction of "citizen". Hence, literacy is linked to concepts of enlightenment such as "freedom", "citizen" and "democracy", that is, key ideas used to break free from the limits of feudal society. In order to accomplish discourse in the public sphere under democratic values, acquiring literacy became seen as a precondition for the existence of modern societies. By looking at literacy though such "modernist lenses", western-style schooling comes to be seen as the central institution responsible for spreading literacy.

(2) The idea of literacy as an ideological device presents literacy as a product of the modern age where people are integrated into the nation in order to control them. Sunano identifies critical literacy as an important concept in order to overcome the limits of the idea of standard literacy.

(3) Last, literacy as a mechanism of exclusion highlights the existence of a demarcation line by literacy. When literacy is connected to a writing system too complicated for ordinary people to learn, then the establishment can monopolize it. In other words, literacy becomes a tool to control illiterate people. This is how literacy functioned in feudal societies. Literacy as a product of the modern age appears to disrupt this mechanism of excluding people. However, contrary to what most people think, the exclusivity characteristic of literacy remains intact in modern societies. The idea of "single literacy", owned and controlled by the establishment, is part and parcel of such mechanisms of exclusion.

From these three points of view, the stigma of being illiterate emerges as the result of social rejection through the exclusionary function of literacy. It can also be connected to the global tendency of stigmatizing the illiterate, an idea that UNESCO and other institutions inadvertently reproduce through some of their campaigns. In spite of their philanthropic efforts, negative connotations are inherent in slogans such as "eradication of illiteracy". The excluding function of literacy is not resolved in this way. It continues to do its work. We have already seen that Japanese literacy functions in a way to exclude some *buraku* and *zainichi*. Moreover, Japanese literacy, as a single dominant literacy system, has also been an instrument of oppression and control of Japan's indigenous minorities such as the Ainu and the Ryukyuans. Next, we will discuss concrete examples demonstrating how literacy results in exclusion in Japanese contexts.

The total literacy myth in Japan

The contemporary Japanese writing system is beyond doubt very difficult. The number of general use of kanji is presently limited to 2,136 characters. However, many more kanji are used in daily life. Most kanji have at least two pronunciations, further complicating the Japanese script. It is therefore not surprising to find a mistranslation of "illiteracy" such as "*man-mou*" in Barton and Lee (2011: 599) – it should be transcribed as "*monmō*". Literacy in Japanese is widely associated with the ability to read, write and remember an enormous number of kanji, and *monmō* literally means "sentence-blindness" as Barton and Lee correctly note. Thus, we can see a deep tie between illiteracy and disability already in the term *monmō*. This notwithstanding, literacy studies in Japan have avoided discussing the literacy of people with disabilities. It is no exaggeration to say that people with disabilities have been excluded from literacy studies.

In order to gain a more comprehensive understanding of the exclusion through literacy and disabilities, Sumi (2010) flatly rejects the popular myth that the literacy rate of Japan stands at 99%. The main pillar of this myth is a survey conducted after WWII under US occupation. Results of an extensive literacy survey conducted in 1948 were published by a Research Committee for Literacy as a report titled *Nihonjin no yomikaki chōsa* (Survey on the Literacy of Japanese) (Yomikaki Chōsa I'inkai 1951). It consisted of 90 questions that included hiragana, katakana and kanji, both used independently and intermixed. The survey was conducted among 21,008 Japanese, who had been invited to participate in this survey by postcards using kanji and kana mixed orthography, between the ages of 15 and 64 years across 270 municipalities. The results showed that 4.4% had perfect scores, while 1.7% had scored zero. These 1.7% serve as the basis to claim that 99% of the Japanese population is literate, which is surprising given that the report itself states that "the literate criteria is only fulfilled by a perfect score" (Yomikaki Chōsa I'inkai 1951: 332). If this procedure had been applied, the literacy rate according to this survey would have been 4.4%, an equally inappropriate result. What matters for our discussion here is simply that the "total literacy myth" was built upon a problematic survey methodology (written invitations) and a one-sided interpretation of the results (everyone who did not score zero is literate).

At the time the survey was conducted, there was an intense debate on the Japanese language and its writing system (*kokugo kokuji mondai*). Some placed a high value on the phonographic writing system and argued to abolish kanji altogether, while others advocated the continued use of kanji. Needless to say, those in support of maintaining kanji used the results of the literacy survey to advance their cause. They created the 99% literacy myth (Yamashita 2011). This myth then spread around the world. Consider a statement by the International Bureau of Education and UNESCO (1964: 92) two decades after the survey: "The problem of illiteracy has been solved completely. Modern Japanese is usually transcribed in Japanese syllabaries (48 phonetic letters) and kanji (1,850 words, ideographs for the most part). A person is considered as illiterate if he is unable to read and write these words and letters at all." This was the official statement made at an international conference on public education by the Japanese Ministry of Education.

However, different language ideological positions led to different interpretations of the survey results. It is for this reason that Sumi (2010) returns to a discussion of the 1948 survey in order to examine the effects of this myth on parts of Japanese society. However, Sumi stresses that this official position cannot be tenable already for the fact that this number obviously excludes people with mental or physical disabilities. In 1948, to start, people with disabilities were not enrolled in the education system. School attendance of children with disabilities was virtually ignored then, and many disabled children remained illiterate their entire life as a result of not attending school. What is more, disabled people were not even considered in discussions on illiteracy. They were eliminated from the Japanese education system and their literacy problems were hidden in order to maintain the literacy myth, so that the Japanese government could boast about the efficiency of the Japanese education system. The literacy myth purposefully excludes people with disabilities from discussions on literacy, and the literacy survey of 1948 has been used as the scholarly stamp of approval of this myth (Yamashita 2009: 204). Three points are hidden in this way: (1) the number of illiterate Japanese is higher than claimed, (2) some individuals are illiterate as a result of social and institutional discrimination, and (3) Japanese society is discriminative, and this is not critically reflected upon.

The social model perspective on illiteracy

Above, I reviewed research showing the exclusionary character of literacy and its negative effects on people with disabilities. Shifting the point of view on how reading and writing relates to physical individuality further makes clear that there is yet another way in which literacy affects people with disabilities.

Let us start this discussion by acknowledging that no human body is exactly the same. Differences include those who read written letters with their eyes and those who read Braille with their hands. Deaf people usually prefer communication through sign language to oral conversation. In principle, if one insists on one specific way of communication, this will inevitably affect those who prefer to communicate differently. In this context Kadoya (2012) points out that a unitary style of communication potentially rejects considering alternatives. The same logic can be applied to literacy. The practice of considering "standard literacy" only, and to take it for granted, creates problems for certain groups of people. Standard literacy is the quasi-hallmark of non-disabled people. Especially for individuals with mental disabilities, it is very difficult to come close to standard literacy. The exclusion through literacy has severe impacts on their lives (Koga 2006).

Abe (2010) criticizes mainstream sociolinguistics for not having discussed the diversity of the human body. Hence, mainstream sociolinguistics can be said to be concerned with the study of "normal bodies". In order to guarantee access to information for all, one needs to consider "plural media" and various styles of literacy. In addressing this point, Masiko (2002) proposes a "universal design of media" departing from considerations of information accessibility for all. People who have difficulty understanding dominant literacy, e.g., people with disabilities but also a large number of foreigners, need different media to cater to their specific needs. A universal design of literacy pays justice to this problem by trying to prepare as many literacy media as possible, thereby weakening the reproduction of social inequality though literacy. In this way, it encourages critical thinking about the existing literacy system, too. Framing literacy in the context of information accessibility is a new and welcome approach. On the basis of departing from "standard literacy", individuals with disabilities are bound to be seen as "illiterate" or "not fully literate", and the resulting reflex of this is "to train them" to come as close as possible to the standard of non-disabled people or first language speakers. This is where "standard literacy" fails to acknowledge the differences that exist between individuals of a given society. Undoing this mechanism requires a shift away from "disability" towards "social responsibility" guided by the principle of guaranteeing information accessibility for all.

Kadoya (2012) has provided a crucial contribution to this end. Inspired by research in the field of disability studies, he developed a "social paradigm" and applied it to the case of literacy studies in Japan. In departing from the so-called "social model", he stresses that literacy and illiteracy should not be seen as a personal responsibility, but as a socially created problem. The old strategy of "catching up" is thereby exposed as inappropriate. It does not resolve the problems but contributes to the exclusion of illiterates, because the catch-up strategy places standard literacy and standard literate people above all others. It demands that illiterate people change, but some cannot change and others have limits to the degree they can change. Empowering illiterates by teaching them a set of literacy skills may help to some extent, but many may not benefit at all.

The benefit of adopting a disability studies view on literacy and applying its social model lies in the fact that it highlights the limits of mainstream approaches. Accepting different levels of literacy implies that those not experiencing difficulties should modify their own norms and expectations of literacy. The social model approach has the potential to restructure common knowledge on literacy and to enhance the valuation of vernacular literacies. While theoretical aspects of the social model are relatively well examined in Japanese sociolinguistics now, little attention has been given to empirical studies that depart from such a perspective so far. It is important to expand the study on the social model beyond theoretical discussions. One example where this is being done is the development and use of *yasashii nihongo* (Plain Japanese). Plain Japanese has originally been created for informing foreign residents in Japan in cases of natural disasters, but it is applicable in other domains, too. Abe (2013) examines Plain Japanese from the perspective of maximal information dissemination, and Oka (2013) employs it for the education of the Deaf. More research taking such a direction should follow henceforth.

Outlook

In this chapter various approaches to the study of literacy and illiteracy were discussed. Each approach has developed independent theoretical perspectives, but there are also a number of correspondences between them. One notable overlap is the recent attention given to ethnographic studies. The existence of personal experiences illustrates a number of important issues related to literacy and illiteracy. However, the new narratives remain still somewhat isolated at the present. Another notable trend is that the educational approaches to literacy based on the competencies concept by the OECD are in decline. In particular the criticism that PISA literacy first and foremost promotes "literacy for work" is hard to refute. It underlines the limits of such an approach. More attention should be given to reflect upon these limits instead of uncritically spreading this type of idea on literacy across the world. Not being critical is to ignore nonstandard varieties of literacy, which are often very different from the type of literacy promoted by PISA. This chapter has shown that vernacular literacy makes important contributions to the daily lives of many people.

Adopting the social model of disability studies to sociolinguistic studies has been another notable recent trend in Japan. This, too, constitutes an important initiative to gain a more critical and comprehensive grasp on literacy and illiteracy. This paradigm shift is a unique Japanese development, but it may also be fruitfully applied to other countries, languages and writing systems. A future desiderate in literacy studies is to strengthen the link with disability studies on the one hand, and to integrate these results more strongly into Japanese sociolinguistics, on the other hand. It is thereby important to be sensitive to the symbolic violence caused by dominant literacy. Every unitary type of literacy inevitably includes aspects of and produces exclusion. Universal design practice promotes plural media of communication and this constitutes an important new discussion in order to find solutions to this dilemma. However, suitable media and styles of literacy for specific persons differ unlimitedly. What is more, these needs are constantly changing and shifting. This is why the observation of communities of practices and modification of literacies are vital for universal design practices. Ethnographic approaches are important to understanding these shifts and changes. Involving scholars of neighboring disciplines into universal design practices is highly desirable, too. Taken together, all these new initiatives should then feed back into our understanding of literacy and illiteracy in theoretical terms.

Notes

1 It is basically impossible to outline all of literacy-related studies in Japan in this chapter. The present review includes few discussions of the linguistic assimilation of the Ainu people, of Ryukyuans, people in former Japanese colonies and the problems of literacy and illiteracy that their assimilation entailed. Itagaki (1999) considering literacy survey in Korea at Japanese colonial age and Tomita (2003) studying one in Taiwan are informative references on this field.
2 PISA (Program for International Student Assessment) is an international achievement test to fifteen-year students. Reading, mathematical, and scientific literacy are the objects for comparative investigation. PISA literacy is characterized by use of information, and recently places emphasis on problem-solving skills (OECD 2004).
3 The sole exception to this trend is research associated the Buraku Liberation Movement (*Buraku kaihō undō*). *Buraku* refers to a group of discriminated people in Japan. Even after the inauguration of Japan's modern public education system in 1872, *buraku* were at times refused entry to local public schools (Yasukawa 1998), causing illiteracy among them. In addition, discrimination in marriage has been continuous (Komori 1997). The Buraku Liberation Movement seeks to end such discrimination, thereby placing importance on teaching literacy (Uchiyama 1991; Motoki 1991).
4 According to Yasukawa (1998: 83–93), there were some private *buraku* schools in Meiji Period (1868–1912), supported by the *buraku* community. They were severely underfunded.

References

Abe, Yasushi (2010) Tegaki moji e no manazashi – moji to karada no tayōsei o megutte [Eyes for Handwriting Letters. About Letters and Diversity of Human Body]. In: *Shikiji no shakai gengogaku*. Hidenori Kadoya and Yasushi Abe (eds), 114–158. Tokyo: Seikatsu Shoin.
——— (2013) Jōhō hōshō to yasashii nihongo [Guaranteeing Information and Plain Japanese]. In: *Yasashii nihongo wa nani o mezasuka – tabunka kyōsei shakai o jitsugen suru tame ni*. Isao Iori, Yeonsuk Lee and Atsushi Mori (eds), 279–298. Tokyo: CoCo Shuppan.
Barton, David and Mary Hamilton (1998) *Local Literacies. Reading and Writing in One Community*. London: Routledge.
Barton, David and Carmen Lee (2011) Literacy Studies. In: *The SAGE Handbook of Sociolinguistics*. Ruth Wodak, Barbara Johnstone and Paul Kerswill (eds), 598–611. London: SAGE.
Baynham, Mike (1995) *Literacy Practices. Investigating Literacy in Social Contexts*. New York: Longman.
Dore, Ronald Philip (1964) *Education in Tokugawa Japan*. Berkeley: University of California Press.
Fingeret, Arlene (1983). Social Network. A New Perspective on Independence and Illiterate Adults. *Adult Education Quarterly* 33(3): 133–146.
Freire, Paulo (1970) *Pedagogy of the Oppressed*. New York: Continuum.
Gee, James. Paul (1996) *Social Linguistics and Literacies* (second edition). London: Routledge.
Giroux, Henry Armand (1988) *Teachers as Intellectuals. Toward a Critical Pedagogy of Learning* . South Hadley: Bergin and Garvey.
——— (1992) *Border Crossing. Cultural Workers and the Politics of Education*. London: Routledge.
——— (2001) Literacy, Ideology and Politics of Schooling. In: *Theory and Resistance in Education. Toward a Pedagogy for the Opposition*. Henry A. Giroux (ed.), 205–231. Westport: Bergin and Garvey.
Goody, Jack and Ian Watt (1968) The Consequences of Literacy. In: *Literacy in Traditional Societies*. Jack Goody (ed.), 53–84. Cambridge: Cambridge University Press.
Gray, William Scott (1956) *The Teaching of Reading and Writing*. Paris: UNESCO.
Gray, William Scott and Bernice Rogers (1956) *Maturity of Reading*. Chicago: University of Chicago Press.

Hayakawa, Misao (1994) Henkakuteki riterashī no tenbō [Foresight of Transformative Literacy]. In: *Amerika kyōiku no bunkateki kōzō*. Takeo Taura (ed.), 146–162. Nagoya: Nagoya Daigaku Shuppan.

Heath, Shirley Brice (1982) Protean Shapes in Literacy Events. Evershifting Oral and Literate Traditions. In: *Spoken and Written Language. Exploring Orality and Literacy*. Deborah Tannen (ed.), 91–117. Norwood: ABLEX.

Higuchi, Tomiko (2010) Riterashī gainen no tenkai – kinōteki riterashī to hihanteki riterashī [Development of Literacy Concepts. Functional Literacy and Critical Literacy]. In: *Atarashii nōryoku wa kyōiku o kaeruka – gakuryoku riterashī konpitenshī*. Kayo Matsushita (ed.), 80–107. Kyoto: Mineruva Shobō.

Hirasawa, Yasumasa (1983) Shikiji undō ni okeru kokusai rentai ni mukete – Paulo Freire to kaihō kyōiku no shisō [For International Solidarity on Literacy Movement. Paulo Freire and Thought of Liberation Education]. *Buraku kaihō kenkyū* 33: 111–35.

Hirsh, Eric Donald (1987) *Cultural Literacy. What Every American Needs to Know*. New York: Houghton Mifflin.

Honda, Yuki (2008) *Kishimu shakai [Creaking Society]*. Tokyo: Sōfūsha.

Honda, Yutaka (1992) *Dōwa kyōiku o shiru – sabetsu no genjitsu ni fukaku manabu [Knowing of Dōwa Education. Learning on the Real Condition of Discrimination]*. Tokyo: Emutei Shuppan.

International Bureau of Education Geneva and UNESCO (1964) *Literacy and Education for Adults. Research in Comparative Education*. Paris: UNESCO.

Ishimoto, Kiyohide (1997) Shūrō [Employment]. In: *Konnichi no buraku sabetsu – daisanpan kakuchi no jittai chōsa kekka yori*. Buraku Kaihō Kenkyūjo (ed.), 68–87. Osaka: Kaihō Shuppansha.

Itagaki, Ryuta (1999) Shokuminchi-ki chōsen ni okeru shikiji chōsa [Literacy Survey in Colonial Korea]. *Ajia afurika gengo bunka kenkyū* 58: 277–316.

Kadoya, Hidenori (2012) Shikiji jōhō no yunibāsaru dezain to iu kōsō – shikiji gengoken shōgaigaku [Vision of Universal Design of Literacy and Information. Literacy, Language Rights, Disability Studies]. *Kotoba to shakai* 14: 141–59.

——— (2010) Nihon no shikiji undō saikō [Reexamination of the shikiji Movement in Japan]. In: *Shikiji no shakai gengogaku*. Hidenori Kadoya and Yasushi Abe (eds), 25–82. Tokyo: Seikatsu Shoin.

Kawamura, Hajime (2014) Meiji shonen no shikiji jōkyō – Wakayama-ken no jirei o chūshin to shite [The Literacy State in the First Years of Meiji. Mainly the Case of Wakayama Prefecture]. In: *Shikiji to manabi no shakai-shi – nihon ni okeru riterashī no shosō*. Yasuhiro Ōto and Tomohiro Yakuwa (eds), 309–345. Kyoto: Shibunkaku Shuppan.

Kikuchi, Kyūichi (1995) *Shikiji no kōzō – shikō o yokuatsu suru moji bunka [Structure of Literacy. Literate Culture Oppressing Thought]*. Tokyo: Keisō Shobō.

Kimura, Masanobu (2014) Zen-kindai nihon ni okeru shikiji-ritsu suitei o meguru hōhōronteki kentō [A Methodological Study for the Presumption about the Literacy Rate before the Modern Period in Japan]. In: *Shikiji to manabi no shakai-shi – nihon ni okeru riterashī no shosō*. Yasuhiro Ōto and Tomohiro Yakuwa (eds), 25–46. Kyoto: Shibunkaku Shuppan.

Komori, Tetsuo (1997) Kekkon [Marriage]. In: *Konnichi no buraku sabetsu – kakuchi no jittai chōsakekka yori*. Buraku Kaihō Kenkyūjo (ed.), 136–139. Osaka: Kaihō Shuppansha.

Koyanagi, Masashi (2010) *Riterashī no chihei [Horizon of Literacy]*. Okayama: Daigaku Kyōiku Shuppan.

Masiko, Hidenori (2002) *Kotoba no seiji shakaigaku [Political Sociology of Language]*. Tokyo: Sangensha.

Matsuo, Tomoaki (2016) Chishiki shakai to konpitenshī gainen o kangaeru – OECD kokusai kyōiku shihyō (INES) jigyō ni okeru rironteki tenkai o chūshin ni [Exploring the Knowledge-based Society and the Concept of Competencies. Focusing on its Theoretical Development in the OECD Indicators of Education Systems (INES) Project]. *Kyōikugaku kenkyū* 83(2): 16–27.

Matsushita, Kayo (2010) Atarashii nōryoku gainen to kyōiku – sono haikei to keifu [Concept of New Abilities and Education. Its Background and Genealogy]. In: *Atarashii nōryoku wa kyōiku o kaeruka – gakuryoku riterashī konpitenshī*. Kayo Matsushita (ed.), 1–42. Kyoto: Mineruva Shobō.

——— (2014) Pisa riterashī o kainarasu – gurōbaruna kinōteki riterashī to nashonaru na kyōiku naiyō [The Taming of PISA Literacy. Global Functional Literacy and National Educational Content]. *Kyōikugaku kenkyū* 81(2): 14–27.

Mori, Mimoru (1991) Riterashī kenkyū no dōkō to kadai – ninchi nōryokuron kara kenryokuron e [Trend and Issues of Literacy Studies. From Cognitive Ability Theory to Power Relation Theory]. In: *Kokusai shikiji jūnen to nihon no shikiji mondai*. Nihon Shakai Kyōiku Gakkai (ed.), 38–48. Tokyo: Tōyōkan Shuppan.

Motoki, Ken (1991) Kokusai shikijinen to nihon no shikiji mondai [International Literacy Year and Literacy Problems in Japan]. In: *Kokusai shikiji jūnen to nihon no shikiji mondai*. Nihon Shakai Kyōiku Gakkai (ed.), 2–18. Tokyo: Tōyōkan Shuppan.

Moro, Yūji (1991) Sekai no shikiji kenkyū [Literacy Studies in Foreign Countries]. *Nihongogaku* 3: 56–63.
Nabeshima, Yoshirō (1997) Kyōiku [Education]. In: *Konnichi no buraku sabetsu – kakuchi no jittai chōsakekka yori*. Buraku Kaihō Kenkyūjo (ed.), 96–119. Osaka: Kaihō Shuppansha.
Nakashima, Takeshi (2013) Rōgakkō ni okeru rōji to kyōshi no kankeisei to teigakuryoku [Relationship between Deaf Children and Teacher and Low Academic Achievement on School for the Deaf]. *Shakai gengogaku* 13: 85–112.
――― (2016) Rōji no nihongo riterashī jissen – yomikaki no esunogurafī [Japanese Literacy Practice of Deaf Children. Ethnography of Literacy]. *Shakai gengogaku* 16: 1–35.
OECD (2000) *A Contribution of the OECD Program Definition and Selection of Competencies. Theoretical and Conceptual Foundations. Definition and Selection of Key Competencies*. Paris: OECD.
――― (2002) *Reading for Change. Performance and Engagement Across Countries. Results from PISA 2002*. Paris: OECD.
――― (2004) *The PISA 2003 Assessment Framework. Mathematics, Science and Problem Solving Knowledge and Skills*. Paris: OECD.
Ōguro, Shunji (2015) Shohyō. Ōto Yasuhiro Yakuwa Tomohiro (hen) (2014) Shikiji to manabi no shakaishi – nihon ni okeru riterashī no shosō [Book Review: Ōto Yasuhiro, Yakuwa Tomohiro (eds) (2014) Social History of Literacy and Learning. Various Aspects of Literacy in Japan]. *Shakai gengogaku* 15: 195–203.
Oka, Norie (2013) Rōji e no nihongo kyōiku to yasashii nihongo [Japanese Language Teaching to Deaf Children and Plain Japanese]. In: *Yasashii nihongo wa nani o mezasuka – tabunka kyōsei shakai o jitsugen suru tame ni*. Isao Iori, Yeonsuk Lee and Atsushi Mori (eds), 299–319. Tokyo: CoCo Shuppan.
Olson, David Richard (1977) From Utterance to Text. The Bias of Language in Speech and Writing. *Harvard Educational Review* 47: 257–281.
Ong, Walter Jackson (1982) *Orality and Literacy. The Technologizing of the Word*. London: Methuen.
Passin, Herbert (1965) *Society and Education in Japan*. New York: Teachers College and East Asian Institute, Columbia University.
Roberts, Celia and Brian Street (1997) Spoken and Written Language. In: *The Handbook of Sociolinguistics*. Florian Coulmas (ed.), 168–186. Oxford: Blackwell.
Rubinger, Richard (2007) *Popular Literacy in Early Modern Japan*. Honolulu: University of Hawai'i Press.
Rychen, Dominique Simone and Laura Salganik Hersh (2003) *Key Competencies for a Successful Life and a Well-functioning Society*. Göttingen: Hogrefe & Huber.
Satō, Manabu (2003) Riterashī no gainen to sono saiteigi [Concept of Literacy and Its Redefinition]. *Kyōikugaku kenkyū* 70(3): 2–11.
Shimamura, Naomi (1991) Nihon no shikiji kenkyū [Literacy Studies in Japan]. *Nihongogaku* 3: 47–55.
Stone, Lawrence (1969) Literacy and Education in England 1640–1900. *Past and Present* 42: 69–139.
Street, Brian (1984) *Literacy in Theory and Practice*. Cambridge: Cambridge University Press.
Stuckey, Elspeth (1991) *The Violence of Literacy*. Portsmouth: Boynton/Cook Heinemann.
Sumi, Tomoyuki (2010) Shikijiritsu no shinwa – nihonjin no yomikaki nōryoku chōsa 1948 no saikenshō [Myth of the Literacy Ratio. Reexamination of the Japanese Reading and Writing Proficiency Survey of 1948]. In: *Shikiji no shakai gengogaku*. Hidenori Kadoya and Yasushi Abe (eds), 159–99. Tokyo: Seikatsu Shoin.
――― (2012) *Shikiji shinwa o yomitoku – shikijiritsu 99 pāsento no kuni nihon to iu ideorogī [Deciphering the Literacy Myth. Ideology as Japan, 99 Percent of Literacy Ratio]*. Tokyo: Akashi Shoten.
Sunano, Yukitoshi (2012) Kindai no aporia to shite no riterashī [Literacy as an Aporia of Modern Age]. *Kotoba to shakai* 14: 4–42.
Teraki, Nobuaki (2016) Kinsei shakai to kawata chōri mibun (kinsei buraku) no seiritsu [Early Modern Society and Formation of Kawata Chōri Position, Early Modern Buraku]. In: *Nyūmon hisabetsu buraku no rekishi*. Nobuaki Teraki and Midori Kurokawa (eds), 71–99. Osaka: Kaihō Shuppansha.
Tomita, Akira (2003) Nihon tōchi-ki taiwan de no sensasu to kana no yomikaki chōsa [Census and Literacy Survey of Kana in Colonial Taiwan]. *Shakai gengogaku* 3: 43–57.
Tone, Keizaburō (1981) *Terakoya to shomin kyōiku no jisshōteki kenkyū [An Empirical Study on Terakoya and Education to Ordinary People]*. Tokyo: Yūzankaku Shuppan.
Uchiyama, Kazuo (1991) Hisabetsu buraku no shikiji undō – sono rekishi to kadai [Literacy Movement of the Buraku People. Its History and Tasks]. In: *Kokusai shikiji jūnen to nihon no shikiji mondai*. Nihon Shakai Kyōiku Gakkai (ed.), 49–62. Tokyo: Tōyōkan Shuppan.
Uechi, Kanji (2003) Hihanteki kyōikugaku ni okeru riterashī [Literacy in Critical Pedagogy]. *Kyōikugaku kenkyū* 70(3): 35–45.

Uesugi, Takamichi (2016) Riterashī to shikiji no gainen seiri [Organizing Concepts of Literacy and shikiji]. *Buraku kaihō kenkyū* 205: 8–21.

Umemura, Kayo (2014) Kinsei nōmin no jichokaō to shikiji ni kansuru ichi kōsatsu – chūsei makki kinsei shoki Ōmi no kuni katsuragawa myōōin shiryō o chūshin to shite [A Study on the Self-writing Kaō and Literacy of Peasants in the Early Modern Period. From the End of the Middle Age to the Beginning of the Early Modern Period, Mainly about the Written Material, Katsuragawa Myōōin Shiryō of Ōmi]. In: *Shikiji to manabi no shakaishi – nihon ni okeru riterashī no shosō*. Yasuhiro Ōto and Tomohiro Yakuwa (eds), 177–208. Kyoto: Shibunkaku Shuppan.

Umihara, Tōru (1998) *Kinsei no gakkō to kyōiku* [*School and Education in the Early Modern Period*]. Kyoto: Shibunkaku Shuppan.

Willinsky, John (1990) *The New Literacy. Redefining Reading and Writing in the Schools*. London: Routledge.

Yakuwa, Tomohiro (1992) Shiga-ken Ika-gun ni okeru 1898-nen no shikijiritsu [The Literacy Rate of 1898, the Case of Ika-gun, Shiga Prefecture]. *Niigata Daigaku kyōiku gakubu kiyō* 34(1): 47–61.

Yamane, Miki (2009) Zainichi chōsenjin ni totte no yakan chūgaku – raifusutōrī kara no apurōchi [Night Junior High School for the Permanent Korean Residents in Japan. Approach from Lifestory]. *Ryukoku Daigaku keizaigaku ronshū* 49(1): 197–218.

Yamashita, Hitoshi (2009) Nihon no yomikaki nōryoku no shinwa – sono inpei kinō no kaimei to mondai kaiketsu no tame no kenkyū ni tsuite [Myth of Japanese Literacy. Revealing its Cover-Up Function and Study for Solving a Problem]. *Shakai gengogaku* 9: 195–211.

——— (2011) Japan's Literacy Myth and its Social Functions. In: *Language Life in Japan*. Patrick Heinrich and Christian Galan (eds), 94–108. London: Routledge.

Yasukawa, Junosuke (1998) Tennōsei kyogaku taisei to hisabetuburaku – sabetsu to hakugai no kyōiku [Educational Structure under the Imperial System and Discriminated Buraku. Education of Discrimination and Persecution]. In: *Nihon kindai kyōiku to sabetu – burakumondai no kyōikushiteki kenkyū*. Junosuke Yasukawa (ed.), 81–242. Tokyo: Akashi Shoten.

Yomikaki Chōsa I'inkai (1951) *Nihonjin no yomikaki chōsa* [*On the Literacy Research in Japanese*]. Tokyo: Tokyo University Press.

22
JAPANESE LANGUAGE SPREAD IN THE COLONIES AND OCCUPIED TERRITORIES

Toshiaki Yasuda (Translated from Japanese by Yumiko Ohara)

Introduction

In less than 100 years, Japan transformed itself from a secluded country into a modern nation-state, colonized parts of East Asia, occupied large parts of Southeast Asia, and lost WWII, along with all of its colonies. In this period of time, Japanese was spread first between Japan's autochthonous minorities, then in the colonies, and finally also in the areas controlled by Japanese military.

Japan's period of isolation ended abruptly in 1853 when US Commodore Mathew Perry demanded to open Japanese ports for trade. Soon afterwards, industrialization and modernization became the new goals of the Japanese nation. The expansion of the Japanese territory into Hokkaido and Ryukyu began soon after the confrontation with foreign nations in the last decades of the nineteenth century. This was then followed by a campaign to conquer more territories in Asia and the Pacific. The time span of 1895–1945 is often described as the era of Japanese imperialism (Beasley 1987), but the Japanese colonies were also considered to be some kind of extension of the Japanese nation-state, and they were therefore under direct control of the Japanese government. In order to examine the spread of the Japanese language in these territories, we need to consider events that took place in the colonies and in those parts of East Asia that came under control of the Japanese government. This area was referred to as the "Greater East Asia Co-Prosperity Sphere". Besides the colonies (Taiwan, Korea, the South Pacific Mandate), it included Manchukuo in northeastern China (1932–1945), which was under control of a Japanese puppet government, and Southeast Asia, which was under Japanese military administration of Japan from 1941 to 1945.[1]

Let us start by considering first the state of language education in the Japanese territories and in the Greater East Asia Co-Prosperity Sphere. Ōide Masahiro, a scholar of Japanese language education, wrote in 1943 that Japanese language education in Taiwan and Korea had been successful. He warned, however, that the methods used in these colonies could not be applied to other regions, because they had specifically been developed for "imperial subjects". He therefore thought that a successful application of the methods for Manchukuo was doubtful, and he considered it strictly out of the question that they were employed across the Greater East Asia Co-Prosperity Sphere (Ōide 1943). Although it is not clear what Ōide meant by "successful language education", some important insights emerge from his statements. First, it is obvious that the spread of Japanese was seen as a non-negotiable necessity. Second, since Ōide had been an educator, his remarks reflect the actual situation in these territories. He bluntly states that Taiwan and Korea were part of the "Japanese territory", and that Japanese language education in those regions was part of assimilating the population as national subjects. The parts of China and Southeast Asia that were under Japanese military control had differed from this pattern. It is for this reason that the spread of Japanese languages needed to be based on different principles there. In discussions about the Japanese language spread, we obviously need to be aware about regionally differentiated principles, terms and concepts.

The national language, *kokugo* in Japanese, refers to the role of Japanese in various institutions (judiciary, education, military, media, etc.). The whole institutional system linked to and operated by *kokugo* aims to unify citizens. Just as the national flag and the national anthem, the national language, too, is symbolically loaded. Speaking *kokugo* played (and plays) a crucial role and functioned as one of the central pillars for unifying "the nation". Note in this context, however, that "national language" denotes two different concepts. On the one hand, it designates the "language of a nation" in general. On the other hand, it functions as a proper noun and is synonymous to "the Japanese language". While *kokugo* in the first sense is technical meta-language, *kokugo* in the second sense is an ideologically loaded term. In order to not fall into the trap of confusing the two, we need to be aware of the institutionalization of *kokugo* in modern Japan and of the role it subsequently came to play. The institutionalization of national language in Japan is usually seen to have started in the first decade of the twentieth century. However, in reality we can think that the national language was established a bit later, in the early 1930s when the Japanese government set up a puppet state in Manchukuo. In Manchukuo, domination through language was employed in a different way. We will return to this further below.

Given that the view that Japanese language spread was considered essential for the governance of territories outside of Japan, the respective colonial governments and a whole range of other governmental organizations compiled detailed statistics. Judging by the numerical data assembled in this way, Japanese language use was reported to amount to some 30% in Korea in 1943, while in Taiwan, according to the statistics of 1941, it had reached 57%. Such numbers reflected the percentage of students enrolled or graduated from Japanese language educational institutions. It included also people who had completed adult courses in Japanese. These numbers do not give us any information about the level of competence that had been attained in this way, though. This is one of the reasons why there were continuous discussions among educators and policy makers at the time about appropriate methods to increase "the spread of Japanese".

The history of education is one of the fields that includes investigations on Japanese language spread. However, it took several decades after the war before research was launched into the oppressive and assimilative aspects of national education. In the immediate post-war years, any sense of Japan as an oppressor remained weak. It was not until 1967 that a first publication emerged that portrayed education in East Asia by Japan as part of an "ethnic suppression" campaign (Ozawa 1967). It took another five years before a first work appeared that critically addressed the Japanese educational system in colonial Taiwan and Korea (Hirotani and Hirokawa 1973). Before that, we find only one comprehensive volume on language policy in modern Japan (Toyoda 1964), where the author reports on various discourses on policies, their actual objectives and consequences. Reflecting the influence of decolonization in the 1950s and 1960s, and taking a critical stance towards language policy in territories controlled by Japan, Toyoda (1964) drew attention to the fact that efforts of modernization and independence by various polities in East Asia had been obstructed by Japanese policies. Toyada's work was largely ignored at the time, possibly also due to the fact that he was not a university professor but worked as a high school teacher. It took until the 1990s to see the history of Japanese language education picking up the issue of Japanese language spread in the colonies (e.g., Kimura 1991; Seki 1997). None of these early works went much beyond the insights that had already been gained by Toyoda. On the contrary, some revisionist tendencies can be attested in the works published in the 1990s. This was most likely due to the fact that Japanese-as-a-foreign language teachers, and not specialists of educational history, conducted this type of research then. Their work is characterized by somewhat partial and uncritical views on the history of Japanese language spread.

Sociolinguistics research at the time paid no attention to Japanese language spread in the colonies, and it also showed no awareness about it. The seminal sociolinguist Sibata Takesi (1975), for example, declared in a work published in English that there were no issues of bilingualism or problems related to minority languages in Japan. This remark is of course inconsistent with the sociolinguistic situation of Japan. His statement reflects the ideology of Japan as an ethnically and linguistically homogeneous nation-state, but it takes only a brief look at modern sociolinguistic history to understand that his view was not based on empirical fact. It is quite dubious whether there had ever existed a society without bilingual issues. In this way, the start of sociolinguistics in Japan shows neglect of historical and of social awareness. When dealing with issues of Japanese language spread or the creation and spread of standard language, Japanese sociolinguistics confined itself to theoretical discussions of language policy frameworks. They restricted themselves to what could be called "single nation sociolinguistics" (e.g., Shibuya 1992). As a matter of fact, these works are more a continuation of Japanese philology than "sociolinguistics" in the strict sense of the word.[2]

This situation started to change in the 1990s, and we can witness the emergence of critical perspectives towards the various institutions involved in colonialism then. It led to conscious questionings of oppressive and violent aspects related to issues touching on the nation-state and on ethnicity. This shift of attention is related to the collapse of the cold war system, the reunification of Germany and the collapse of the Soviet Union. These events led to reconsiderations about the role of the modern nation-state in various fields of study, also in Japan. The eight volumes on *Modern Japan and the Colonies* produced by publishing house Iwanami Shoten (1992–1993) are a representative example of this trend.

Later in the 1990s, research that departed from the aforementioned study of Toyoda (1964) expanded his study of colonial domination (e.g., Shi 1993). Also, an analysis of language ideology and modernity was published in Japanese in 1996, and was translated afterwards into English (Lee 2010). It is worth noting here that young, foreign scholars from formerly colonized regions produced this work. Shi and Lee drew on the work of Tanaka Katsuhiko, and he also guided them in their PhD studies in Japan that would result in these publications. Tanaka had previously discussed the relation of language and state in Mongolia (Tanaka 1981). His discussions entailed an in-depth criticism on the logic of a one-nation historical narrative, and it was this critical perspective that his students Shi, Lee and others started to apply on the case of Japan. Although sociolinguistic methodology remained marginal in these works, such publications were seminal contributions to the study of Japanese language spread in the colonies. What is more, these works also influenced Japanese sociolinguistics research outside the field, and we can subsequently find novel attention to how historical data and discussions could be used in sociolinguistics. These publications and the studies they inspired made clear that sociolinguists could not ignore historical issues of Japanese language spread.

Japanese language policy in historical perspective
The making of national language

Thinking about the motivation for Japanese language spread implies reconsidering the relationship between nation-state and national language (Yasuda 1998). A concern for language policy in modern Japan emerged during the Sino-Japanese War (1894–1895), when we find attempts to facilitate Japanese language spread by establishing the concept of "national language". Japanese as a national language was then linked with and involved in national development and national indoctrination. It also served as a rationale to eliminate the variation within the language and language diversity existing in Japan (Heinrich 2012).

The creation of the term national language (*kokugo*) is intimately related to the work of Japan's first linguistic professor, Ueda Kazutoshi, who collaborated closely with various sections responsible for language policy at the Ministry of Education. Although the need for a Japanese standard language had been seen as an urgent desideratum already in the nineteenth century, concern for linguistic unification under the roof of national language took several decades to realize. When Ueda took up his activities in shaping language education in school, the legal system, military service and the introduction of the telegraph had also been established. Language came to play an important function in these new domains. In other words, the foundations had been laid to have these modern institutions function through national language.

In the speech delivered by Ueda (2011[1895]), "National language and the state", immediately after the end of his studies in Germany and France (1890–1894), he advocated the idea of a "national language" for Japan. He famously stated that the national language in Japan was as old as the imperial family, he equated national language to "blood that flows through the nation", and concluded that through this "blood" national unity could be realized. In the collection of his speeches and essays that he subsequently published under the title *Kokugo no tame* (*For the National Language*), Ueda (2011[1895]) stated in the inlay "Japanese is the bulwark of the imperial family and the nation's affectionate mother". We can recognize therein his intention to intimately relate the Japanese national language to the Japanese state and the Japanese nation. Ueda sought to have an institutionalized national language play the role of a "mother" in people's lives. Furthermore, by presenting national language through the metaphor of the mother, he provided for a naturalization of the language spread process (see Lakoff and Johnson 1980; Neagu 2013). Having constructed these ideological connections between national language, nation and state, he raised the rhetorical question "are we taking enough care of the Japanese language?" Ueda pointed out the lack of an unequivocally recognized grammar, of a unified writing system, and a of standardized variety of the national language. As a first step towards filling these gaps, he proposed to create a unified spoken and written national language, as only such a kind of language could be used for uniting all Japanese nationals under the roof of a national language (Yasuda 2006a).

Ueda's ideas fell on fertile grounds. When he started promoting his idea of Japanese as a national language, the entire country experienced a dramatic surge in national pride as an effect of Japanese victory in the Sino-Japanese War of 1894–95. This led to stronger appeals of developing a national institution in charge of establishing a standard language. Reacting to these calls, a National Language Research Committee (*Kokugo chōsa i'inkai*) was established at the Ministry of Education in 1902. The Committee worked on this task until it was dissolved in 1913. Ueda, and other members of the Committee, crucially contributed to the formation of a standard language, and they established, among other things, a state-supported grammar of modern colloquial Japanese. Ueda also set up, and became the first chairperson of, the National Language Research Laboratory (*Kokugo kenkyūshitsu*) at Tokyo Imperial University in 1897. There, he engaged his graduates in research for the creation of a national language, and he also trained all those who would later be involved in the formulation of language policy. In short, Ueda was influential in establishing research organizations and in the institutionalization of the Japanese language. Due to his activities, national language (*kokugo*) was established as an elementary school subject in 1900. This in turn prepared the ground for the popularization of his national language framework, and the spread of knowledge about national language history and its standard variety.

The national language, dialects, minorities

The standard variety of the national language had to be learned by all national citizens who lived in the so-called "inner territory" (*naichi*). Inner territory identifies the area under control of the Meiji state at the time when Japan's first constitution was proclaimed (Honshu, Shikoku, Kyushu, Hokkaido and Okinawa). Karafuto (Shakalin) was added in 1943. *Naichi* can be considered as a legally united region in which the perception of forming one homogenous ethnic group took root, despite all evidence to the contrary in the form of Ainu and the Ryukyuan languages. It was this ideological stance that opened the possibility to unilaterally impose the national language across the entire Japanese nation. While diversity in language and ethnicity remained, and therefore contradicted national language ideology, the inferiority in terms of number and the marginal position of Japan's indigenous minorities in Japanese society meant that they were subordinated by the majority. As an effect, all minorities came under strong pressure to assimilate themselves.

Examples of such assimilation can be seen in Hokkaido and Okinawa, territories that were included into the state before the promulgation of the Meiji Constitution of 1889. Even though a barrier was constructed between the Ainu and the Japanese in the form of a Law for the Protection of Hokkaido's Native Inhabitants (*Hokkaidō kyūdojin hogohō*), in the institution of Native Primary Schools (*Kyūdojin shōgakkō*) and of many other activities, the acquisition of the Japanese language was of utmost importance, and it became mandatory for everyone (Ogawa 1997). In Okinawa, there was always the question of how to deal with the difference between the Ryukyuan languages and (Standard) Japanese. The more the differences between the two became noticeable, the more pressure was imposed on efforts of Ryukyuan "dialect correction". Repressions grew also against intellectuals who considered the Ryukyuan languages as worthy of preservation.[3] Despite the fact that the same uniform standard language education was implemented in Hokkaido and in Okinawa, these two regions cannot be easily compared. The many differences between them originate from very different and distinct historical trajectories (see Kondō 2006). In addition, the concept of "dialect" emerged only in discussions of its relationship with the standard language in the modern period. All language that was not Standard Japanese was now seen as "dialect", and the existence of dialect was regarded as an impediment to the homogenization efforts of the nation-state. At the same time, we see the emergence of a belief that "ancient language resides in dialects". Accordingly, dialects were portrayed to constitute an important link of the present to the past. Due to this connection, all perceived "dialects" were related to the national language. The result of this view was that "dialects" of the Ryukyuan languages were regarded as particularly "strong dialects", and they were thus earmarked for strenuous efforts of "dialect correction" (Yasuda 1999).

Japanese language in colonies

The organization of modern state institutions, the formation of a normative language consciousness inside Japan coincided historically with the annexation of Japan's first colonies of Taiwan (1895–1945) and Korea (1910–1945).[4] It is for this reason that, after some initial difficulties, the very same policy of creating "Japanese citizens" among Ainu and Ryukyuans through Japanese national language was implemented also in the colonies. This notwithstanding, a number of legal differences between Japan and its colonies remained. The idea that the Japanese language was the carrier of a Japanese "national spirit" was prominent among Japanese colonizers, and this led them to believe that "learning Japanese" was paramount to "becoming Japanese". Dialects were looked down upon, because they deviated from the newly created standard language. Following the same logic, the different languages spoken in the colonies, but also Ainu and Ryukyuan inside Japan, were seen with contempt. It was generally believed that Japan's mission consisted of turning "primitive people" into "civilized people". Japanese was perceived to embody "civilization". Bringing "civilization" to the "uncivilized" was a demonstration of being modern.

Some polities under Japanese rule had themselves taken initiatives to create national language systems themselves. Particularly in Korea, we can find attempts to set up institutions that were meant to develop a Korean standard language. These efforts came to an abrupt end under Japanese colonial rule. In Taiwan, the future role of teaching classical Chinese in public school was intensively debated in 1900. Classical Chinese was downgraded to a facultative subject, and this marked the first step for spreading Japanese in the same way as it had been done in Japan. While specific language policies were implemented in Japan and in each of its colonies, we can see in all policy efforts of transforming people and the social institutions governing them through the spread of Japanese (Inaba 1999; Satō 2000; Morita 1987; Cai 1977; Chen 2001). The longer colonial domination continued, the more time came to be devoted to Japanese language education in the curriculum. Already the above-mentioned Ōide (1943) had noted that the colonies were considered to be part of the Japanese national territory. Hence, the implementation of school education similar to that of Japan was seen as the ultimate objective. This approach was called assimilation education (*dōka kyōiku*), but while education was claimed to be egalitarian, schools were actually divided according to ethnicity. This trend was particularly evident in primary education. The ideal of treating everyone alike in school education was already undermined by the fact that education started at different periods of time. Compulsory education was introduced in Japan in 1872 but was not introduced in Taiwan until 1943. The people in the colonies did not receive the same treatment as the Japanese. They were considered being equal only in ideology, while in reality various restrictions were imposed on them.

Language spread increased with the duration of Japanese language education. As an effect, proficiency was higher for men than for women, and higher in urban centers as compared to rural areas. In the case of Taiwan, Japanese was more widely spread among the Han Chinese majority as compared to Taiwan's indigenous minorities. We need to be careful when discussing such numbers though. There were many cases where pupils were officially enrolled in school but were actually unable to attend (especially girls). Such pupils nevertheless found entry into the statistical data. Recently, more detailed insights into the extent of Japanese language spread and Japanese proficiency have been gained through studies correlating gender and school withdrawal rates (Kim 2005), through research on language education among the indigenous minorities (Kitamura 2008), and through studies on adult education (Fujimori 2016). We understand from these works that the social and institutional role of Japanese had been politically constructed in a way that Japanese could be used as official language in public domains. Initially, the various indigenous languages were ignored in the private domains, as long as the colonial subjects were learning Japanese. The bilingualism that emerged from Japanese language spread received no attention and was not suppressed. This was already due to the fact that an implementation of colonial policies would not have been possible without the support of the indigenous languages.

The situation changed in the 1930s. With Japan's further expansion into foreign territories, the strategic importance of Taiwan and Korea grew. In concurrence with an "imperialization" movement of local inhabitants, the governmental directives became more radical. Campaigns calling for "complete understanding of the national language" and "everyday use of the national language" aimed at the diffusion of Japanese in all domains (see Kondō 1996). Requests for a "unified national language" that sought to completely eliminate all languages other than Japanese began to appear (Yasuda 2011a). This turn in policy was also motivated by the necessities of mobilizing all colonial subjects into Japan's ongoing war efforts. This included a conscription system for the colonies. In this situation, the perception grew that bilingualism was "abnormal" and thus undesirable. Bilingualism was seen as a transitional step to reach Japanese monolingualism.

Japanese language spread in Manchukuo

The language policy of the Manchukuo, officially independent but actually a puppet state of Japan, was of a different nature than that in the (other) colonies.[5] The usual argument for Japanese language spread in the colonies was that Japanese was the language of modernity, and the language of Japanese citizens. In Manchukuo, however, this logic was difficult to apply in view of the fact that the state had been founded on the pretext of national self-determination (*minzoku jiketsu*). Departing from the Japanese slogan of *gozoku kyōwa* (harmony of the five races), language policy in Manchukuo took multiple languages into consideration. However, contrary to the above slogan, language policy in Manchukuo did not aim at maintaining or creating a "harmony" between the various languages. Rather, languages were ranked on a hierarchical scale, with Japan occupying the top position as the alleged lingua franca of East Asia.

The history of Japanese language spread in Manchukuo can be divided into two periods, with the mid-1930s as the dividing line (Yamamuro 1993). Before that, the spread of Japanese was not actively pursued, in part due to practical reasons such as a shortage of Japanese language teachers. Because all state institutions had been based on the Chinese language after the establishment of the Republic of China in 1912, there were major difficulties to make Japanese the sole language of administration. Hence, the status of autochthonous languages in Manchukuo was acknowledged to some extent. There were also some individuals who questioned the necessity of Japanese language spread in Manchukuo. All of this changed in the second half of the 1930s. Especially after the outbreak of the Sino-Japanese War in 1937, the status of the Manchu steadily declined. With Japanese advancements in mainland China in full swing, Manchukuo became increasingly Japanized and this crucially entailed Japanese language spread. In order for Japanese to replace Chinese as the sole language of administration, attempts were made to downgrade other languages spoken there (Chinese, Manchu, Mongolian, Korean, etc.). The following changes can be noticed with regard to spreading Japanese in the institutional system: (a) use of Japanese in official documents, (b) more importance to Japanese language skills in the promotion system of public officials (which led to the implementation of a Japanese language proficiency test examination), (c) the establishment of an agency for language policy, and (d) the inclusion of Japanese in the curriculum (together with Manchu and Mongolian) after 1938. Bilingualism remained to be institutionally recognized, but Japanese was now clearly seen to be the main language of Manchukuo.

In Manchukuo, the Japanese government gave Japanese people the opportunity to learn different languages – a stark contrast to the situation in Japan's official colonies. However, also in Manchukuo, there was no doubt that Japanese was unchallenged in its importance in all matters touching on public administration, jurisprudence and education. A system was established that obliged everyone to learn Japanese, and this in turn made sure that Japanese would become the central pillar of state administration. This reveals the puppet-state nature of Manchukuo. On the other hand, we see less emphasis on Japanese language spread and an increased awareness that the only way to lend prestige to Japanese in Manchukuo was through institutional rather than ideological support.

In Manchukuo, the center was administered through Japanese, but in the periphery Chinese and Mongolian retained much of their importance. In order to reduce this antagonism, the idea of large-scale diffusion of Japanese language took a backseat, and Chinese started to be transliterated with katakana. This writing system was called "Manchu kana". It was developed by the Manchukuo Committee for the Research on National Language and Welfare (*Manshūkoku minseibu kokugo chosā i'inkai*) and implemented in 1944. It sought to increase the literacy rate through the adoption on katakana. At the same time, it was meant to serve as a steppingstone for a more thorough Japanese language spread in the future. Although Manchu kana were short-lived, their implementation can be seen as a sign of more ambitious language spread intentions in Manchukuo, and by that as a desire to close the gap to the language policy in the Japanese colonies. We recognize in this also an effort to undermine all previous efforts of language modernization by the Republic of China in Manchukuo.

Japanese language diffusion in Southeast Asia

The control of Southeast Asia by the Japanese military was influenced by military intentions and war strategies. We find in this region attempts to maintain at least one local language to accompany Japanese for military administration.[6] There are differences in this approach due to the divergent strategic importance of the respective occupied territories, but we nonetheless find the same attempts of developing nationalism through an indigenous language across Southeast Asia. In the Philippines, for example, it was initially stipulated that Japanese and Tagalog were to function as official languages. Even the use of English was recognized for a while, but after the declaration of Philippine "independence" in 1943, the adoption of Japanese as the official language ended.[7] Also in the Dutch East Indies a system was created to teach Japanese in schools together with Indonesian. It seems, however, that Japanese served mainly as a tool to diffuse Indonesian. It can be said that this strategy aimed to distance the various countries from their former hegemonic suzerains (the US and the Netherlands). Attempts to develop Japanese into the lingua franca of East Asia became increasingly prominent after the outbreak of the Sino-Japanese War. Japanese was henceforth sought to be used for communication across the various regions and, at the same time, as a means to foster closer relations with Japan.

The military authorities of every occupied region discussed plans how to best teach Japanese with the Japanese Council for Construction of Greater East Asia. See Kurasawa (1997) on matters of occupation policy; Ishii (1994) on educational policy; Tani (2000) and Matsunaga (2001) for Japanese language spread policy. There were two main reasons for considering such an imposition of Japanese in Southeast Asia. First, Japanese was the language of Japan, that is, the leading state of the Greater East Asia Co-Prosperity Sphere and, second, Japanese was seen as indispensable for acquiring a "Japanese spirit".

In August 1942, the Japanese cabinet approved a document titled "Japanese language spread in the southern regions". It outlined a language policy for the spread of Japanese as the lingua franca of the Greater East Co-Prosperity Sphere, i.e., for all East Asia. In this document, the Japanese Ministry of Education sided with requests made by military forces to train and dispatch Japanese language education staff across this region. Such training courses were held eight times, lasting about six weeks, and some 300 individuals were trained and dispatched each time (Akashi 1992). One year later, in September 1943, the cabinet approved a document titled "On the due dissemination of the Japanese language in the southern regions". It established that Japanese was to be spread throughout the entire Greater East Asia Co-Prosperity Sphere. The objective was to strengthen the unity of the various ethnic groups and to diffuse Japanese culture by teaching Japanese language skills deemed necessary for everyday life. This plan was without doubt extremely ambitious (and in all likelihood not realizable). It asked to focus on discipline in Japanese language teaching methods. Japanese teachers were reminded of their role as representatives of the Japanese nation. They were required to constantly train their personality, and to study local languages and customs in order to better comprehend local inhabitants. In particular, the idea of "Japanese language education as discipline" is worthy of attention. It reveals a language ideology that claims an indivisible bond between "Japanese language education" and "ceremonial education", i.e., being obliged to bow in the direction of the imperial palace or to show respect to the Japanese flag. Fostering this type of discipline was a major factor behind the decision to teach Japanese also in Southeast Asia. In contrast to the Japanese colonies, a suzerain language already existed there, and these languages (Dutch, English) had in parts already functioned as mediums of modernity. Given this situation, it was practically impossible to suddenly replace them by Japanese. Also, "bringing modernity" to these regions could not justify mandatory learning of Japanese there. This left language planners with no other argument than of claiming that Japanese was the language of "the leading country" in East Asia and the embodiment of the "Japanese spirit".

In the colonies, we find intentions to spread spoken and written language similar to that used in mainland Japan. By contrast, we can see a tendency to accept a compromised and simplified variety of Japanese in Southeast Asia. It goes without saying that this was a controversial topic at the time, but such confrontations of opinions only resulted in yet more state control over the language spread activities. The number of controversies over the control of the Japanese language, and its ideal forms, increased in the last years before the war ended, and no final decision was made on this aspect of Japanese language spread.

Language spread policy differs both across regions and periods of time. These differences were also shaped by international reactions to Japanese expansionism and by national independence movements in East Asia. At the time of Japan's colonization of Taiwan and Korea, it was commonly taken for granted that ethnic independence movements of colonies were not to be supported, and this included the view that indigenous languages should not be modernized and developed. In the case of Manchukuo, we find some considerations for ethnic self-determination embedded in the ideology of *gozoku kyōwa* (harmony of the five races) and this also manifested with regard to language. Despite an unwavering claim of Japanese language supremacy, considerations for the Chinese language were relatively important there.

In the 1940s, national movements gained strength in the colonies. In places where Japan exerted military occupation in Southeast Asia, it had to show consideration for such movements from the onset. Japanese language spread policies also differed slightly in the reaction to these movements, according to their popularity and the military importance of the regions in question. When the Japanese government had to acknowledge languages other than Japanese, it arbitrarily decided which language constituted the "native language" for the population. In the colonies, however, no concessions were made to the national movements, despite the continuous growth of these movements. On the contrary, regulations and language policies became increasingly suppressive and coercive.

Japanese language use and language awareness

Japanese language spread has also been studied from the perspective of the "receiving end" of Japanese language policy. The reactions of those who studied Japanese in the colonies and regions under Japanese military control and the outcomes of such language learning have been investigated. It is difficult to reconstruct what kind of Japanese was spoken at a time when no audio data was recorded. This notwithstanding, studies have been conducted to analyze what kind of Japanese was used by interviewing elderly people who had received Japanese language education in their childhood (e.g., Kai 2013). Other studies focus on the history of Japanese language teaching (e.g., Gōzu 2002). Cultural anthropologists, again, have interviewed ethnic minorities in Taiwan (e.g., Kamizuru 2006). While these are important contributions to the field, none of these studies can of course provide for accurate reconstructions. One ultimately needs to be aware of the many changes that happened after 1945. This is not simply a linguistic matter. The colonial domination of Japan cannot be directly judged on the basis of present-day attitudes, evaluations and recollections. Doing so would mean to relativize Japanese colonization and military control, and in so doing distort these historical events (Makino 2011).

There is yet another approach to shed light on Japanese language policy in the colonies and the occupied areas. This strand of research analyses documents written by teachers who tried to have their students speak "proper Japanese", and who recorded "mistakes" as reference data for future corrections. By paying attention to this type data, it is possible to uncover some characteristics of the Japanese that was used by students in the colonies. These documents constitute insightful material for sociolinguists. We can recognize therein students' first language interferences on Japanese, but also traces of Japanese dialects spoken by Japanese teachers (Yasuda 2011a). For example, the pronunciation of /d/ as /r/ is indicative of an influence of Southern Ming ("Taiwanese"), while manifestations of /s/ as /ʃ/ is seen as an influence of Kyushu dialects on the part of the teachers. It is well known that many teachers in Taiwan originated from Kyushu. Such data hints at the diversity of the Japanese language spoken by the Japanese people and the colonial subjects at the time. Uniformity in language may have been fervently desired by policy makers, but it was far from being achieved. We also find the creation of new patterns that had not existed in mainland Japanese. Some scholars do not regard these new uses as "mistakes" but interpret them the development of ethnic dialects of Japanese (Yasuda 2011a). It is also possible to suppose that Pidgin Japanese emerged in some places of language contact, but it is no longer possible to adequately investigate this due to the lack of linguistic data. Tackling the issue of language contact in the colonies and the occupied territories from the other end, Sakurai (2015) studied partly acquired Chinese spoken by Japanese abroad. Japanese troops were regularly dispatched to mainland China, including Manchukuo, ever since the outbreak of the Sino-Japanese War in 1894. The "Chinese-like language" that emerged as a consequence was not something that could be called "Chinese" in the strict sense, as speakers were not able to express complex matters or use the language productively. Nonetheless, we know that Chinese language tokens were widely used by soldiers. The existence of these Chinese tokens testify both that contact existed between Japanese and Chinese, but also that such contact was superficial and one-sided (Sakurai 2015).

Although it has basically become impossible to conduct research on issues relating to language awareness on the side of the Japanese colonizers, some insights can be gained based on notes made by individuals. The records left by Hiroyuki Murakami (1904–1951) during the colonial period are such an example. Murakami had majored in psychology at Tokyo Imperial University. After graduation, he went on to teach Japanese ("national language") in vocational schools in colonial Korea. He asked his students in which contexts they used Japanese and Korean, and also inquired whether they thought that place names or personal names written in kanji should be read in Japanese or in Korean. While conducting this kind of research, Murakami felt that it was impossible for Japanese language to deeply diffuse in colonial society. He also realized that the actual spread of Japanese did not correspond to the objectives formulated by the colonial administrators (Yasuda 2011b).[8] The logic that "civilization" was best attained through learning Japanese was also undermined by a study conducted by Chen (2001). It showed that people in colonial Taiwan tended to acquire only specific knowledge through the Japanese language, rather than assimilating themselves into the Japanese nation. This is an important finding. It points to the necessity to examine in more detail the idea of "bringing civilization through Japanese" and how individuals or society as a whole reacted to this policy.

Japanese language as a "heritage" in East Asia

For a comprehensive consideration of Japanese language spread, it is necessary to consider the specific functions of Japanese in Taiwan, Korea, mainland China and in the occupied territories, also after the end of Japanese colonization or military domination there. Japanese as "national language" was initially established as an institutional system and as a means to construct a Japanese nation-state. Because it constituted a system, it was possible to transplant it to the colonies just as the case had been with other systems, e.g., the legislative system.

There exists, in general, the possibility to appropriate colonial systems during decolonization. We can see this, for example, in the adaptation of former colonial languages as official languages in decolonizing states. In the case of Japan, however, no single country or region where Japanese had been spread adopted Japanese as an official language. The case of the Ryukyu Islands, under US control from 1945 to 1972, constitutes an interesting case thereby. There were considerations at this time to use Ryukyuan for education, but these ideas were short-lived, and it was decided to continue school education as it was conducted in mainland Japan (Heinrich 2004). The reversion to Japan in 1972 also meant an uncontested reversion to the Japanese language.

There are cases in which we can find some kind of legacy of Japan's colonization. For example, after declaring independence in 1948, the Republic of Korea used a considerable part of the Korean textbook that had been compiled during the colonial period. What changed was that they were now used as textbooks of Korean as a "national language". In other words, the structure of the system created by Japan was adopted, just the language changed from Japanese to Korean (Park 2013). In Taiwan, during the period of unrest and confusion that followed the seizure of power by the Koumintang Party, Taiwanese utilized Japanese as a means to differentiate between those who had been in Taiwan during the colonial period and those who fled from Mainland China to Taiwan after 1949 (Chen 2005). In this case, Japanese was not adopted to create some new state system, but used to distinguish one political group from another. The position of the Japanese language undoubtedly changed during these days of unrest and change in Taiwan. In Japan, this phenomenon is often misunderstood as a sign of "Taiwanese attachment to Japanese". In other words, it is mistaken for a positive affirmation of Japanese colonial governance, and it even evokes a sense of nostalgia in some quarters. This is an issue that should henceforth be studied more comprehensively, and a field of study that should be conducted more carefully.

Somewhat similar are studies maintaining that a new sense of order and discipline was spread through Japanese language education. The influence of Japanese language education on the lives in the colonies and the occupied territories can be studied through interviews of individuals who had received Japanese language education in Southeast Asia under Japanese military control (e.g., Matsunaga 2008). These interviews often conclude that Japanese language education contributed to the development of skilled people. However, one needs to take these insights with a grain of salt. Usually only individuals with a certain degree of success in life are interviewed, and they tend to recognize in retrospect their past education as a positive contribution. Relating Japanese language education before 1945 to postcolonial life courses relativizes childhood experiences and memories. Caution is needed when placing such testimonies in the context of the "history of Japanese language education". Without historical awareness, such research is at risk of producing superficial and uncritical results.

Note for instance that it took many decades before Japanese was taught again in each of the former colonies. In the Republic of Korea, the Japanese language started only being taught during the Park Chung-hee regime in the 1960s (Kim 2008), and in the People's Republic of China, Japanese language education was suppressed at the time of the Cultural Revolution (Honda 2012). These examples remind us that the memories of the Japanese domination and of Japanese language education are closely related.

Conclusions

Simply tracing data and discourses concerning Japanese language spread does not directly constitute research. Since the history of imperial modern Japan and the diffusion of the language are interconnected, both language and politics must be approached critically. As a matter fact, Japanese language spread emerged only as a field of research when critical studies of colonial domination became possible in Japan. The history of Japanese language spread invites reflections on what a multilingual society is. Despite much evidence to the contrary, the idea of Japan being home to a single ethnic group and a monolingual society remains prominent. However, there exists no society without some degree of multilingualism. Multilingualism can therefore also be considered as being something "normal" also in the case of Japan. The point of "who interprets what and how" is largely defined by the historical context. It is therefore unsurprising to find that one and the same multilingual situation may be interpreted differently (Yasuda 2006b). Already the belief of some sociolinguists that multilingualism "has arrived" in Japan from outside (e.g., Kawahara and Yamamoto 2004) serves as a reminder to critically examine the social and historical understanding of sociolinguists.

What about the history of Japanese language education, then? Within this field we find a tendency to perceive language education as a matter of didactic and technique, and to thus focus on issues such as whether or not a given method is effective. As mentioned earlier in this chapter, Ōide (1943) argued already more than 70 years ago that Japanese language education in the colonies served the aim of assimilating colonial subjects as national subjects. This point is easily forgotten over technical discussions. More reflection is needed how to conduct research into the history of the Japanese language (*nihongo kyōiku-shi*). On the other hand, the history of national language education (*kokugo kyōiku-shi*) ignores language education in colonies completely, despite the fact that Japanese was taught there as "national language". Likewise, "national language education" for the Ainu and Ryukyuans remains a controversial topic. These issues, too, deserve careful structural and historical considerations.

What can be learned from this when we look forward? In a multilingual setting, a language policy should be formulated, deliberated and implemented by persons and institutions with a grasp on the present sociolinguistic situation. Such a language policy would require a fundamentally new ideology to start with. Multilingualism does not determine a language policy. A language policy interprets, regulates and reformulates a multilingual situation. To spread Japanese to the colonies meant to unilaterally promote multilingualism there. Imposing the exclusive use of Japanese in the colonies was an effort to eliminate this multilingualism. It rejected both social and individual bilingualism. By looking back on the history of modern Japanese language policies, we recognize that multilingualism was never determined by language policy, but also that language policies never used multilingualism as a resource. Political objectives determined by the historical context were always given priority. It is for this reason that Japanese language policy is to be included in the list of examples where multilingualism is at the mercy of politics, both in the past and in present-day Japan.

Notes

1 The designation "Greater East Asia Co-Prosperity Sphere" was used as a slogan to unify the vast regions that make up this region (see Yasuda 2006).
2 The same holds true for research on the so-called "national language script reform".
3 The global historical setting facilitated these developments. All these events unfolded in the last period in which it was possible for world powers to acquire colonies, and Japan became one of those latecomer powers.
4 A detailed discussion can be found in Yasuda (1997), especially in chapter 3.
5 For more thorough discussion, refer to Yasuda (1997), especially chapter 4.
6 Imperial Japan occupied the Commonwealth of the Philippines from 1942 until the surrender of Japan in 1945.
7 Discovering more individuals like Murakami might be an important topic for future research.
8 The implications of this case are significant for our discussions of Japanese language spread, but are too complex to be discussed here (for more details, see Kondō 2006).

References

Akashi, Yōji (1992) Gunseika shingapōru, himaraya ni okeru nihon no kyōiku seisaku [Eductional Policy of Japan under Military Government in Singapore and the Himalaya]. *Kokuritsu Kyōiku Kenkyūjo kiyō* 121: 237–266.
Beasley, William G. (1987) *Japanese Imperialism, 1894–1945*. Oxford: Oxford University Press.
Cai, Maofeng (1977) *Chūgokujin ni taisuru nihongo kyōiku no shiteki kenkyū* [*An Historical Study on Japanese Language Education for Chinese People*]. Unpublished manuscript.
Chen, Peifeng (2001) *"Dōka" no dōshō imu – nihon tōchika taiwan no kokugo kyōikushi saikō* [*Cohabitation with Having Different Dreams of "Assimilation". Reconsidering the History of Japanese Language Education in Taiwan under Japanese Rule*]. Tokyo: Sangensha.
――― (2005) Taiwan ni okeru futatsu no kokugo "dōka" seisaku – kindaika minzokuka taiwanka [Two-language Assimilation Policy in Taiwan. Modernization, Nationalization, Taiwanization]. *Kotoba to shakai* (supplementary volume) 2: 41–64.
Fujimori, Tomoko (2016) *Nihon tōchika taiwan no "kokugo" fukyū undō – kokugo kōshūjo no seiritsu to sono eikyō* [*Taiwan's "National Language" Dissemination Movement under Japanese Rule. The Establishment and Influence of a National Language Training Center*]. Tokyo: Keiō Gijuku Daigaku Shuppan.
Gōzu, Miho (2002) Kanzokukei taiwanjin kōnensō no nihongo shiyō – gengo seikatsushi chōsa o tsūjite [Japanese Language Use of Elderly Taiwanese. Research on the History of Language Use]. *Shinshū Daigaku ryūgakusei sentā kiyō* 3: 25–44.
Heinrich, Patrick (2004) Language Planning and Language Ideology in the Ryukyu Islands. *Language Policy* 3: 153–179.
――― (2012) *The Making of Monolingual Japan. Language Ideology and Japanese Modernity*. Bristol: Multilingual Matters.
Hirotani, Takio and Toshiko Hirokawa (1973) Nihon tōchika no taiwan chōsen ni okeru shokuminchi kyōiku seido no hikakushiteki kenkyū [A Comparative Historical Study on the Colonial Education System in Taiwan and Korea under Japanese Rule]. *Hokkaidō Daigaku kyōiku gakubu kiyō* 22: 19–92.
Honda, Hiroyuki (2012) *Bunkaku kara "kaikaku kaihou" ki ni okeru chūgoku chōsen zoku no nihongo kyōiku no kenkyū* [*A Study on Japanese Language Education of Chinese and Korean Ethnic Groups at the Time of the "Reform and Openness" from Cultural Revolution*]. Tokyo: Hitsuji Shobō.
Inaba, Tsuguo (1999) *Kyū-kankoku no kyōiku to nihonjin* [*Japanese Education in Former Korea and Japanese People*]. Fukuoka: Kyushu University Press.
Ishii, Hitoshi (1994) *Daitōa kensetsu shingikai to nanpō gunseika no kyōiku* [*Greater East Asia Construction Council and Education under the Southern Military Administration*]. Nagoya: Nishinihon Hōki Shuppan.
Kai, Masumi (2013) *Taiwan ni okeru kokugo toshite no nihongo shūtoku – taiwanjin no nihongo shūtoku to gengo hoji, soshite sono hoka no shokuminchi to no hikaku kara* [*The Acquisition of Japanese as a National Language in Taiwan. Taiwanese's Japanese Language Acquisition and Language Retention in Comparison with the other Colonies*]. Tokyo: Hitsuji Shobō.
Kamizuru, Hisahiko (2006) Jigazō keisei no dōgu toshite no "nihongo" – taiwan shakai no "nihon" o ikani kangaeru-ka [Japanese Language as a Device for Constructing a Self-image. How to Consider "Japan"

in Taiwanese Society]. In: *Sengo taiwan ni okeru "nihon" – shokuminchi keiken no renzoku, henbō, riyō*. Masako Igarashi and Yūko Mio (eds), 187–216. Tokyo: Fuyōsha.

Kawahara, Toshiaki and Tadayuki Yamamoto (2004) *Tagengo shakai ga yattekita – sekai no gengo seisaku Q&A* [*The Multilingual Society Has Arrived. Q&A about Language Policies around the World*]. Tokyo: Kuroshio Shuppan.

Kim, Hyeonsin (2008) *Ibunka-kan komyunikēshon kara mita kankoku kōtō gakkō no nihongo kyōiku* [*Japanese Language Education at Korean High School from the Viewpoint of Intercultural Communication*]. Tokyo: Hitsuji Shobō.

Kim, Puja (2005) *Shokuminchi-ki chōsen no kyōiku to jendā – shūgaku fushūgaku o meguru kenryoku kankei* [*Education and Gender in Colonial-period Korea. Power Relationships Regarding School Attendance and Non-attendance*]. Yokohama: Seori Shobō.

Kimura, Muneo (1991) *Nihongo kyōiku no rekishi* [*History of Japanese Language Education*] (volume 15). Tokyo: Meiji Shoin.

Kitamura, Kae (2008) *Nihon shokuminchika no taiwan senjūmin kyōikushi* [*History of Taiwan's Aborigines Education under the Japanese Colonial Domination*]. Sapporo: Hokkaido University Press

Kondō, Ken'ichirō (2006) *Kindai okinawa ni okeru kyōiku to kokumin tōgō* [*Education and National Mobilization in Modern Okinawa*]. Sapporo: Hokkaido University Press.

Kondō, Masami (1996) *Sōryokusen to taiwan – nihon shokuminchi hōkai no kenkyū* [*Total Warfare and Taiwan. A Study on Japanese Colonial Collapse*]. Tokyo: Tōsui Shobō.

Kurasawa, Aiko (1997) *Tōnan ajia-shi no naka no nihon senryō* [*Japanese Occupation in Southeast Asian History*]. Tokyo: Waseda University Press.

Lakoff, Goerge and Mark Johnson (1980) *Metaphors We live By*. Chicago: University of Chicago Press.

Lee, Yeonsuk (2010) *The Ideology of Kokugo. Nationalizing Language in Modern Japan* (translated by Maki Harano Hubbard). Honolulu: University of Hawai'i Press.

Makino, Atsushi (2011) *Mitomeraretai yokubō to kajō na jibun katari – soshite iawaseta tasha kako to tomoni aru watashi e* [*Desire to Be Accepted and Excessive Self-talking. And Others Who Happen to Be Present. To My Past Self*]. Tokyo: Tokyo University Press.

Matsunaga, Noriko (2001) *Nihon gunseika no maraya ni okeru nihongo kyōiku* [*Japanese Language Education in Malaya under Japanese Military Government*]. Tokyo: Kazama Shobō.

––––––– (2008) *"Sōryokusen" ka no jinzai yōsei to nihongo kyōiku* [*Personnel Training during the Total War and Japanese Language Education*]. Fukuoka: Hana Shoin.

Morita, Yoshio (1987) *Kankoku ni okeru kokugo kokushi kyōiku – chōsen ōchōki nihon tōchiki kaihōgo* [*National Language and National History Education in Korea. Korean Dynastic Period, Japanese Rule Period, after Liberation*]. Tokyo: Hara Shobō.

Neagu, Maria-Ionela (2013) *Decoding Political Discourse. Conceptual Metaphors and Argumentation*. London: Palgrave Pivot.

Ogawa, Masahito (1997) *Kindai ainu kyōiku seidoshi kenkyū* [*A Study on the History of Modern Ainu Education System*]. Sapporo: Hokkaidō Daigaku Tosho Kankōkai.

Ōide, Masahiro (1943) *Nihongo fukyū no genjō to shōrai – kyōju no kon'nansei to sono taisaku ni tsuite* [*The Current Situation and Future of Japanese Language Diffusion. On the Difficulties of the Professors and their Countermeasure*]. Unpublished manuscript.

Ozawa, Yūsaku (1967) *Minzoku kyōiku-ron* [*National Education Theory*]. Tokyo: Meiji Tosho Shuppan.

Park, Jeonglan (2013) *"Kokugo" o saiseisan suru sengo kūkan – kenkokuki kankoku ni okeru kokugoka kyōkasho kenkyū* [*Postwar Free Space for "National Language" Reproduction. A Study on the National Language Textbooks in Korea in its Founding Period*]. Tokyo: Sangensha.

Sakurai, Takashi (2015) *Senjika no pijin chūgokugo – "kyōwago" "heitaishinago" nado* [*Pidgin Chinese during the War. Manchukuo Dialect, Soldiers' Chinese Language and Others*]. Tokyo: Sangensha.

Satō, Yumi (2000) *Shokuminchi kyōiku seisaku no kenkyū chōsen 1905–1911* [*A Study on the Education Policy in the Colonies. Korea 1905–1911*]. Tokyo: Ryūkei Shosha.

Seki, Masa'aki (1997) *Nihongo kyōikushi kenkyū josetsu* [*An Introduction to the Study of the History of Japanese Language Education*]. Tokyo: Suriēnettowāku.

Shi, Gang (1993) *Shokuminchi shihai to nihongo – taiwan, manshūkoku, tairiku senryōchi ni okeru gengo seisaku* [*Colonial Rule and Japanese Language. Language Policy in Taiwan, Manchukoku and the Continental Occupied Areas*]. Tokyo: Sangensha.

Sibata, Takesi (1975) On Some Problems in Japanese Sociolinguistics. Reflections and Prospect. In: *Language in Japanese Society*. Fred C. C. Peng (ed.), 159–173. Tokyo: University of Tokyo Press.

Shibutani, Katsumi (1992) Gengo keikaku [Language Planning]. In: *Shakai gengogaku*. Shinji Sanada, Katsumi Shibuya, Masakata Jinouchi and Seiju Sugito (eds), 159–183. Tokyo: Hōfūsha.

Tanaka, Katsuhiko (1981) *Kotoba to kokka* [*Language and State*]. Tokyo: Iwanami Shoten.

Tani, Yasuyo (2000) *Daitōa kyōeiken to nihongo* [*Greater East Asia Co-Prosperity Sphere and Japanese Language*]. Tokyo: Keisō Shobō.

Tanigawa, Ken'ichirō (ed.) (1970) *Waga okinawa – hōgen ronsō* [*Our Okinawa. Dialect Debate*]. Tokyo: Mokujisha.

Toyoda, Kunio (1964) *Minzoku to gengo no mondai – gengo seisaku kenkyū no kadai to sono kōsatsu* [*The Problem of Ethnicity and Language. Issues of Language Policy Research and Considerations about them*]. Tokyo: Kinseisha.

Ueda, Kazutoshi (2011[1895]) *Kokugo no tame* [*For the National Language*]. Tokyo: Heibonsha.

Yamamuro, Shin'ichi (1993) *Kimera – manshūkoku no shōzō* [*Chimera. A Portrait of Manchukuo*]. Tokyo: Chūkō Shinsho.

Yasuda, Toshiaki (1997) *Teikoku nihon no gengo hensei* [*Language Regime in Imperial Japan*]. Yokohama: Seori Shobō.

——— (1998) *Shokuminchi no naka no "kokugogaku"* [*"National Language Studies" in the Colonies*]. Tokyo: Sangensha.

——— (1999) *Kokugo to hōgen no aida – gengo kōchiku no seijigaku* [*Between Japanese Language and Dialect. Politics of Language Construction*]. Tokyo: Jinbun Shoin.

——— (2006) *"Kokugo" no kindaishi – teikoku nihon no kokugo gakusha-tachi* [*Modern History of National Language. Japanese Language Scholars in Imperial Japan*]. Tokyo: Chūkou Kōron Shinsha.

——— (2011a) *Karera no nihongo – taiwan "zanryū" nihongo-ron* [*Their Japanese. Taiwan "Residual" Japanese Language Theory*]. Tokyo: Jinbun Shoin.

——— (2011b) Gengo seisaku wa dono yō ni nichijō o shihai suru no ka – Murakami Hiroyuki no giron o chūshin ni [How Language Policies Regulate Everyday Life. Focusing on Murakami Hiroyuki's Discussion]. *Nichigo nichibungaku kenkyū* 79(1/2): 47–68.

23
AINU LANGUAGE SHIFT

Takayuki Okazaki

Introduction

This chapter provides an overview of Ainu language research as well as preservation and revitalization initiatives from the past to the present. It describes the distinctive socio-political and historical context that has shaped Ainu language research and Ainu language shift and outlines achievements and challenges of the revitalization movement.

While comprehensive sociolinguistic research on Ainu language shift in general has in its earlier stage been conducted and published in English by scholars such as DeChicchis (1995) or Maher (2001), in recent years researchers and educators more directly involved in Ainu language revitalization added to such research, both in Ainu (e.g., Kitahara 2012; Ota 2014; Narita 2015) as well as in Japanese (Okuda 2010; Kitahara 2011; Satō 2012; Nakagawa 2013).

Two decades have passed since DeChicchis (1995) described the Ainu language situation. DeChicchis as well as those who followed, Maher (2001), Gottlieb (2005), Martin (2011), Teeter and Okazaki (2011) and Heinrich (2012), attempted to capture the historical shift of Ainu language in sociolinguistic terms. Since they published their findings in English, they found a wider readership that included sociolinguists not specialized in Ainu or Japan. In recent years, new and more detailed reports on the current situation of the Ainu language have contributed to our understanding of Ainu language shift.

In the Japanese academic community, Ainu language shift has been addressed by research in descriptive linguistics and educational history. Descriptive linguists have made various contributions including the compilation of dictionaries and grammatical analyses, but have also collected and partly archived linguistic data through extensive fieldwork with Ainu language speakers. Many of these researchers have recently also taken up the role of reporting on the Ainu language situation.

Historians, especially in the field of modern education such as Ogawa (1991) and Hirose (1996), have provided detailed accounts of the social situation of Ainu people and have shown how Ainu language and culture was systematically "devastated" in educational institutions in the Meiji Period (Ogawa 1991: 314).

Until recently, the majority of research on the Ainu language has not been in the Ainu language itself. Three recent academic papers written bilingually in Ainu and Japanese (Kitahara 2012; Ota 2014; Narita 2015) can be found in the journal *Kotoba to shakai* (*Language and Society*).

This journal often includes bilingual articles in Ryukyuan, Japanese and migrant community languages in Japan. An Ainu language educator, Tetsuhito Ōno, reported in Japanese on the Ainu language situation from the first issue in 1999 to the sixth issue in 2002. Although it has been more common to publish research on Ainu in Japanese and English, it is noteworthy that Ainu language speakers are working to address the lack of academic writing on Ainu also in Ainu. Such a practice presents readers with opportunities to witness active Ainu language use, which increases the awareness about the Ainu language and may, for some, spur more interest into the language. Furthermore, Ainu learners can study Ainu by reading these articles. Key themes that have been repeatedly discussed in the journal *Kotoba to shakai* are recording the number of Ainu speakers, historical analysis on language shift and recent efforts, advancements and problems of Ainu language revitalization.

On counting speakers

To grasp the current sociolinguistic situation and how it has come about, it is vital to give an overview of discussions on the number of Ainu speakers, as well as on the history of contact with other speech communities.

Though it is understandable that those newly acquainted with Ainu situations seek to know the number of speakers or the number of Ainu people as such for a quick reference, both Ainu and researchers in the field are reluctant to provide such information. Ainu people and scholars of Ainu alike have described the difficulties in giving an exact figure for the number of Ainu speakers (DeChicchis 1995; Kitahara 2011; Maher 2001; Nakagawa 2013; Okuda 2010; Satō 2012; Teeter and Okazaki 2011). This is due to the varying definitions of what it means to be a "speaker" and to the political issues that accompany this question.

Ainu speakers

When UNESCO (2009) declared that Ainu was "critically endangered" and estimated that it had 15 remaining speakers, this announcement sent shockwaves through the Ainu community. This is also due to the fact that Ainu and scholars of Ainu had themselves not been able to ascertain an exact figure. Nakagawa (2013: 70) notes that Ainu language researchers have a history of discovering new Ainu language speakers, even though they, too, try to estimate the number of speakers. Ultimately, Nakagawa attributes this situation to the social environment in Japan, where many Ainu feel it may be best to hide their identity. This has repercussions also on a number of other issues, such as the relationship between researchers and Ainu, the timing of their encounters or whether people remember having been exposed to Ainu language in their childhood. Even if researchers visit an Ainu with the same purpose, they might well receive different responses and treatments in comparison to another researcher.

It is widely known that being identified as Ainu can leave a person vulnerable to social and economic discrimination in Japan. This trend is multiplied by the idea that not just the person in question, but also those associated with them may feel to be at risk of discrimination. A 2006 poll conducted by the Hokkaido prefectural government (Hokkaidō Kankyō Seikatsu-bu 2006) found the number of the Ainu population to stand at 23,782. However, responses to these prefectural polls are voluntary and those who want to hide their Ainu identity in public tend not to participate (Kitahara 2011). Moreover, many Ainu who live outside of Hokkaido were not polled. According to Maher (2014), the Hokkaido Ainu Association (2013) estimated the population to be 50,000.[1] Cultural Survival (2001), on the other hand, estimates the population to be as large as 200,000. These difficulties of determining an exact number for the Ainu population also confuses the issue surrounding accurate figures for the number of Ainu speakers.

Ainu language vitality has forcibly weakened as an effect of a Japanese assimilatory education that started at the end of nineteenth century. While there are very few Ainu today who acquired Ainu in the family, Okuda (2010) nevertheless claims that there is a significant number of young Ainu who can express themselves in Ainu. Some of them can have free conversations and understand long and complex Ainu stories. He argues that even though such individuals may not be considered "native speakers", they can be considered "active speakers" of Ainu.

Given the current situation of Ainu second language learning, it is imperative to problematize the use of the term "native speaker". When Ainu language specialist Nakagawa (2009) was invited to speak to the Advisory Council for Future Ainu Policy, formed by the Cabinet Secretariat of Japan, he suggested using the word "native" in quotation marks. If the circumstances would allow, Nakagawa argued, Ainu would have normally acquired Ainu as their native language. He argues that all can learn Ainu as their "native" language, regardless of the speaker's age or social circumstances. Ideally, the definition of "native speaker" should be stretched enough to encompass differing levels of fluency. For similar reasons Sawai (1998) criticizes the use of categories such as "endangered" or "minority" language when discussing Ainu language, because these terms have a negative impact.

Political implications of being an Ainu speaker

While not denying the academic significance of the question of how many Ainu speakers there are, Ainu linguist Satō (2012) states that the question is still all too easily asked. He argues that this heavily nuanced question remains poorly understood. While most speakers of Japanese or English have never had to hide their ability to speak their respective languages, Ainu speakers agreeing to participate in research or disclosing information have to consider the possibility of having their privacy violated. If they decide to participate in research, they also need to consider the impact on their immediate family and relatives. Satō (2012) maintains that in present-day Japanese society "being an Ainu speaker" is a delicate piece of personal information that needs to be treated carefully.

Even being an Ainu language learner can be a political choice for an Ainu person. In a paper in Sakhalin Ainu, Kitahara (2012: 297) describes the concerns that accompany Ainu when they chose to study the Ainu language:

> Sianno haciko ohta neanpe hanke ahci tura ekihi nee koroka, icaakasnocise ohta ahun ohta otuye. Nee teh yaytuymaaste ike, ramurenkayne sinenehpone neera an pe ka kii easkay pahno poro koh, aynu weekaari ohta oman kuru ka an koroka, pookoro koh poo eyaynuahte kusu suy otuye hemaka. Ene teh, neera an yahka eyaycaakasno kuru neanpe sianno yuhke ramu koro kuru nee ike, porosereke poo reske hemaka teh, monrayki hemaka teh eh.

> Taken by their grandparents (to Ainu language classes) in their infant age, they come to study Ainu language. However, their learning is discontinued when they enter school. When they become old enough to keep a certain distance from others and act with their own will, some people come to Ainu-related activities, but when they have children, they tend to be away considering the influence on their children. It takes exceptionally strong will to continue studying, and it is often the case that people restart their study after raising children or retiring from work.

> *(Translated by the author)*

From this statement, it becomes apparent that many Ainu feel that it is better to avoid attending Ainu language classes in their youth in order to not be associated with Ainu by non-Ainu. Narita (2015) describes how as a non-Ainu teacher he interacted with Ainu children and families in Tokyo. Knowing that the students at his parent-child study of Ainu language class were in a situation where they could not openly say they were Ainu or studying Ainu at their own school, he emphasized the need to create a safe space where students could feel secure and enjoy speaking and learning Ainu.

The portrayal of Ainu as a minority language has propagated the conception that there are not many speakers. Sawai, for example, elucidates how the act of giving the Ainu language "a death sentence", so to speak, has influenced conceptions of its vitality:

> Many people still do not doubt that Japan is a monolingual nation. Thus, here we see a paternalistic illusion; that other languages do not exist in the monolingual nation, or if they do, like Ainu, they are declared to be "minority languages". They are said to be endangered, or vanishing, too far gone to be revived because of the small number of native speakers left. Speakers are being given the countdown.
>
> *(Sawai 1998: 187)*

The existence of the Ainu language, she argues, is viewed as incompatible with a Japanese language dominant society; this type of framing obscures the complicated reality of its actual use.

Language shift

The Ainu language was once spoken from the southern part of Sakhalin, through the Kurile Islands and present-day Hokkaido to the northern part of Tohoku in Honshu. While the language is often widely categorized into three groups, Sakhalin Ainu, Kurile Ainu and Hokkaido Ainu, each of these groups constitutes many varieties. In Ainu, the word *ainumosir* is used to describe the land where humans live, as opposed to *kamuymosir* where the gods or divine spirits live. *Yaunmosir* is used to describe what is now called Hokkaido. While Tohoku Ainu had been spoken until the middle of the eighteenth century and Kurile Ainu spoken until the beginning of the last century, it is assumed that there are no speakers left for each of these respective Ainu dialects (Nakagawa 2013).

Both Kurile Ainu and Sakhalin Ainu (or *enciw*) experienced dramatic reconfigurations of their lifestyles by the Japanese imperial government, adversely affecting the use of Ainu. Both Russia and Japan sought to assimilate Ainu into their respective states.[2] In 1875, the Sakhalin-Kurile Exchange Treaty (Treaty of Saint Petersburg) was signed by Japan and Russia, making Sakhalin Russian territory and the Kurile Islands Japanese territory. In 1884, Japan forcefully relocated 97 Ainu who lived in Shumshu, the closest island to the Russian territory in the Kamchatka Peninsula. The island is 1,058 kilometers away from Shikotan, the island of the Kurile Archipelago that is closest to Hokkaido (Kitahara 2011). In addition to the high cost of travel to Shumshu, Japanese colonists were also concerned that Shumshu Ainu would become "Russianized" due to their close relationships with people in the Kamchatka Peninsula (Kuwabara 2015).

On the other hand, the southern part of Sakhalin became Russian territory in 1875 but Japanese territory after the Russo-Japanese War in 1905. After WWII it became again territory of the Soviet Union: 841 of the 2,400 Enciw (Ainu) were relocated by the Japanese government, first to Soya in Hokkaido in 1875, and then more inland to Tsuishikari one year later. The relocated Enciw could not continue their livelihood that had been based on fishing and many died from diseases such as cholera and smallpox (Ogawa 2013; Inoue 2016). Many of those who survived moved back to Sakhalin and became referred to as "Tsuishikari Ainu". However, when Japan surrendered at the end of WWII, they and their descendants chose to move to Hokkaido (Tangiku 2011). Tamura (2008) has studied their motives for leaving their indigenous land of Sakhalin. These reasons included that their lifestyles had been "Japanized" through education, marriage and work, and that some wanted to be reunited with family members who had served in the Japanese army. Others preferred to not live in a socialist political system.

Inoue (2016) reports that following the end of WWII, more than one thousand Enciw were evacuated from the island of Sakhalin between 1945 and 1948, mostly to Hokkaido, but also to other parts of Japan. Since they were being discriminated against by Japanese, these evacuees attempted to blend into Japanese society, and many decided not to pass on their culture and language to their children. The reportedly last Sakhalin Ainu speaker, Take Asai (born in 1902), passed away in 1994 (Murasaki 2001).

Ainu in Hokkaido

Research on the history of Ainu language shift has focused primarily on the policies of the Meiji Period (1868–1912). It is generally understood that the colonial policies of the Meiji government severely damaged the Ainu language. However, Tezuka (2006), and other researchers of education history, state that one of the biggest impacts on Ainu had been the policies of the feudal Matsumae Domain, the governors of a fief in modern-day Hokkaido who had established their rule there in the late sixteenth century, led to an exploitation of Ainu and to restrictions of Ainu ways of living.[3] The Matsumae Domain prohibited Ainu from using Japanese, while the Tokugawa Shogunate promoted the use of Japanese among Ainu. Tezuka (2006) sees these contradictory policies on language use having little influence on Ainu language. More crucial for language loss was the fact that the Matsumae Domain restricted where and with whom Ainu could trade. According to the so-called *basho ukeoi-sei* (subcontracted trade system), merchants contracted by the Matsumae Domain relocated Ainu, mainly young males but also females and children (Ogawa 1991) from their homes to work at fisheries and other businesses all over Ezo-chi, as Hokkaido was called in the Tokugawa Shogunate.[4] Ainu who worked there were basically treated like slaves. In addition, violence against female Ainu, exposure to unfamiliar diseases, malnutrition and hunger led to Ainu population decrease (Walker 2006). Ogawa (1991) reports that the number of Ainu living on the western part of Ezo-chi decreased by half in the short timespan between 1822 and 1854. Not only the population, but also Ainu lifestyles were threatened by these policies. This created an environment where Japan's future colonial policies would become devastating (Tezuka 2006).

Most researchers concur that Ainu continued to suffer severe harm throughout the Meiji Period. This is the period when the survival of the Ainu language was most threatened. While the violence perpetrated by Edo Period (1603–1868) merchants had considerably weakened Ainu communities, Nakagawa (2013) estimates that in 1869 almost all the 16,000 recorded Ainu were fluent speakers of Ainu. After the end of the Tokugawa Shogunate, the government of the Meiji state set up a Colonization Commission (*Kaitakushi*) in August 1869 with the mandate of colonizing Ezo-chi, which would henceforth be renamed as "Hokkaido" on that occasion. All Ainu land was incorporated into the territory of the Meiji state.

A series of administrative orders by the Colonization Commission proved to have severe ramifications for Ainu. An 8 October 1871 order encouraged settled agriculture; Ainu would receive agricultural tools if they settled down and cultivated land (Kuwabara 2015). Other orders included the prohibition of Ainu traditions such as female tattooing, male piercing and *kasomante*, a funeral rite where Ainu burn the house in which the deceased had lived. The last article of this order also called for Ainu to learn spoken and written Japanese. These orders were made several times throughout the Meiji Period, leading Heinrich (2012) to conclude that the efforts to spread the Japanese language amongst Ainu in the first 30 years of the Meiji era were unsystematic and poorly organized, and that they only became more stringent from 1899 onwards.

The first attempts of teaching Japanese culture and language started right after the Kaitakushi administrative orders of 1871. According to Hirata (2009), Kiyotaka Kuroda, then director of the Kaitakushi, sought to accelerate Ainu assimilation into Japanese society by separating Ainu from their living environment and by educating them separately. The first plan towards this end was to recruit 100 Ainu and to teach them agriculture in Tokyo. After their return from Tokyo, they should then become leaders of their respective communities, promote agriculture among Ainu and help make them loyal subjects to the Japanese government. However, only 35 young Ainu could be recruited for this plan. They came from Ishikari, Sapporo, Otaru and Yoichi in Hokkaido to Zojoji in Tokyo in 1872 (Hasegawa 2008; Kanō and Hirose 2008). Three more Ainu joined them from Yoichi and Etorofu Island in 1874. The age of the Ainu participating in this project ranged from 13 to 38 (Ueno 2011). Their school in Tokyo was called Hokkaido Aborigine Education Center (*Hokkaidō dojin kyōikusho*) and was affiliated to the Kaitakushi Temporary School. They were taught in the same building as those who were studying to work for the Kaitakushi, and all their teachers came from Kaitakushi Temporary School. After arriving in Tokyo, it was decided that they should learn reading, writing and math in Japanese, in addition to receiving agriculture training (Hirata 2009). Since Ainu traditionally had been an oral language, and the teachers in Tokyo did not understand the Ainu language or culture, it was extremely difficult for the Ainu students to learn how to read and write Japanese. These difficulties were further enhanced by the fact that they read texts about the geography and history of Japan, which was unfamiliar to them. In such circumstances the Kaitakushi education did not achieve any of its expected outcomes. It ended in tragedy.[5] By the spring of 1874, four of the 38 Ainu had died from sickness, three returned to their villages because of sickness, and one ran away. Out of the remaining 30, 25 requested to go back to their communities, and only five decided to continue their education at the Kaitakushi Temporary School.

Nakagawa (2013) argues that what made the number of Ainu speakers decrease so rapidly is not so much the government's authoritarian assimilatory policies but rather the policies that ignored the existence of Ainu. While not directly related to language, Maher (2001) regards Article 7 of the Land Regulation Ordinance (*Jishokisoku*) to be a watershed moment for Ainu communities as all Ainu land was confiscated, considering Hokkaido to be *terra nullis*, rather than acknowledging Ainu's historic presence and thus de facto "ownership" of the territory in colonial terms. In efforts to colonize the newly annexed territory of Hokkaido, the land was subsequently distributed to companies and hundreds of thousands of people who were actively recruited from the Japanese mainland (*honshū*). Article 15 of the 1877 Hokkaido Land Certificates Publishing Regulations (*Hokkaidō jiken hakkō jōrei*) regulated remaining mountains, forests and uncultivated areas to the auspices of the colonial government (Maher 2001). Due to this article, Ainu were no longer able to freely enter into the mountains and forests where they had hunted and collected wood and mountain vegetables for sustenance. In 1889 deer hunting was banned, and in 1898 salmon fishing for private use was also banned. This was a further blow to Ainu's ability to obtain two of their main staple foods (Nakagawa 2013). Ogawa (1991) also reports 18 major incidents of forceful relocation of at least 420 families within Hokkaido from 1870 to 1900. One of the reasons for these forceful relocations was to move Ainu out of the newly developing city centers.

Such authoritarian measures which lacked any consideration of Ainu existence and their lifestyles were accompanied by a paternalistic concern for Ainu due to their perceived helplessness. Hence emerges a discourse to "rescue" Ainu from their misery and impoverishment. The poverty-stricken Ainu were to be taught how to work in settled agriculture, but they were often given barren land to do so. Denied of their livelihood and robbed of their living space, the ability for Ainu to continue passing down their knowledge and ways of life to their children was severely impaired. Thus, at the early stage of the Meiji Period, assimilation was carried out more via the destruction of the basis for Ainu livelihood rather than through systematic education or linguistic policies.

The Hokkaido Former Aborigines Protection Act (*Hokkaidō kyūdojin hogohō*) is seen by most researchers as having been one of the most devastating edicts in terms of the negative impact on Ainu language, culture and people, marking it a critical turning point in the government's policy towards Ainu. Though several Ainu schools had been established in the 1880s, school attendance remained low then. It barely reached 9% in 1886 (Ogawa 1991: 261). The background for the adoption of this act was the idea that Ainu needed to "be saved". Though not acknowledging that their misery was government-inflicted, the impoverishment of Ainu had become known to the wider Japanese public, as more and more Japanese immigrated to Hokkaido and witnessed the circumstances in which they lived. Also, the media in- and outside of Hokkaido reported on Ainu. In addition, scholars of anthropology and linguistics became interested in Ainu, whom they framed as a "rare" and "dying" people. They organized lectures and exhibitions, which amplified the image of Ainu as undeveloped and savage people (Ogawa 1991). Thus, the idea of "rescuing" Ainu became a topic for many people, including those engaged in national politics.

Japanese policy makers were concerned that Christian schools would be preferred over Japanese government schools for Ainu (Ogawa 1991). John Bachelor, a missionary active in spreading Christianity in Hokkaido since 1877, led the Church Missionary Society. After several years of trial and error, the Airin Christian School for Ainu was established in 1887 with the assistance of the Kannari family in Horobetsu (Frey 2007). By 1896 the Church Missionary Society had established eight schools (Ogawa 1991), and set up an additional four in subsequent years (Frey 2007).[6] Through this Christian education, Ainu was learned using the Latin alphabet, and it is reported that they preferred the Christian education to that offered by the Japanese government. Ogawa (1991), for instance, reports that while not one Ainu attended the public school in Shiranuka in 1900, the school established by the Church Missionary Society in the same town had 27 Ainu students.

In the 1890s, the impoverished state of many Ainu and the best ways of how to "rescue" them was debated in the Diet leading to the passage of the Former Aborigines Protection Act in the 13th Imperial Diet. The act had two main pillars, settling Ainu into farms and assimilating Ainu through education. Agriculture was considered the best way to "save" Ainu from poverty, and the act mandated that each family was to be allocated five hectares of land to be used for farming, although in reality families only received an average of two hectares of often unfertile land (Siddle 1996). Because many Ainu did not read Japanese, they were not aware that this land would be confiscated within 15 years if they failed to cultivate it. Furthermore, many were tricked into forfeiting their land by Japanese and consequently were made to work under Japanese landlords. Using Japanese thereby became a necessity (Nakagawa 2013).

The provision of education to Ainu, which is referred to as Ainu education (*Ainu kyōiku*) in the Japanese literature, was introduced through the Articles 7 and 9 of the act. It specified that Ainu children were to be provided free education via schools built in Ainu communities. Two years later, Ainu education was further systematized with the 1901 Hokkaido Regulation for the Education of Former Aborigine Children (*Kyūdojin jidō kyōiku kitei*). It declared that three schools were to be established every year for the following seven years in order to reach a total of 21 additional schools (Ueno 2011). This regulation also stipulated that Ainu and Japanese students were to be taught separately. This notwithstanding, all of the classes were taught in Japanese. The curriculum consisted of classes in ethics, national language (Japanese), math, physical education (de facto, songs in Japanese), sewing and agriculture. This curriculum served as the vehicle through which Ainu were to be taught how to live in accordance with Japanese lifestyles, customs and ethics. The latter crucially included emperor worship and patriotism. Ainu education was provided with the assumption that Ainu were unsanitary, disorderly and immature (Ueno 2011; Ogawa 1991). Although the regulation did not prohibit the use of Ainu, and teachers did use some Ainu they knew in order to manage the classes, using Ainu in school became strongly discouraged. Around the 1890s, some Ainu started to find it necessary to receive this education and sincerely wanted schools to be established. Scholars contend that this is mainly because they were deprived of their land and because their former lifestyle had been destroyed, leaving them therefore with no option but to assimilate. Ogawa (1991: 261) reports that attendance in schools reached almost 30% by 1898, 70% by 1904 and exceeded 90% by 1910.

Ogawa (1991) argues that characterizing the formal education provided under the Former Aborigines Protection Act as assimilatory education or education to integrate Ainu is insufficient, as Ainu were intentionally not provided the same quality of education as their Japanese contemporaries. In analyzing the enactment of the Former Aborigines Protection Act and the Hokkaido Regulation for the Education of Former Aborigine Children, and by scrutinizing the syllabus and method of teaching, he emphasizes that a simplified and inferior education played a key role in the destruction of the indigenous language, culture and lifestyle, and that this had indeed been the aim from the onset. Ueno (2011) also contends that only Japanese knowledge and values were included in the curriculum for all subjects, textbooks and activities in school. Through this education, the idea that Ainu were inferior and Japanese were superior was imprinted in the minds of Ainu. Ueno (2011) suggests that this led to Ainu abandoning their language.

Based on fieldwork with Ainu who had been born around 1900, Nakagawa (2013) reports these individuals were often told that Ainu is a "dirty" language and they do not need to learn it. Kaizawa (1998, quoted in Ogawa and Yamada 1998: 119) noted in 1931, "today few young Ainu understand me if I talk to them in Ainu. Now, only the elderly speak Ainu among themselves, but most of them speak Japanese to young Ainu".

In terms of Ainu attempts to reverse the language shift, the first Ainu publication by an Ainu was published in 1913. Yamabe Yasunosuke, the author, used the Japanese katakana syllabary for writing Ainu and the Japanese linguist Kindaichi Kyōsuke translated it into Japanese (Ishihara 2004). Another Ainu, Chiri Yukie, published 13 *kamuy yukar* in Ainu in Latin alphabet in 1923 and translated them into Japanese for a book titled *Ainu shinyōshū* (*A Collection of Ainu Deity Epics*).[7] In the introduction, Chiri expressed her deep sorrow about the loss of the Ainu language and the effects of colonization:

> Our ancestors left us the language, sayings and beautiful words they used to communicate their daily ups and downs. Is it, too, disappearing along with other "weak dying things"? Oh, what an incredibly tragic waste!
>
> *(Chiri 1978: 4)*

Kitahara (2011) provides a useful summary of other efforts to record the Ainu language, including oral literature, prayers, autobiographies and poems (also Ainu poems written in Japanese styles), as well as linguistic works such as dictionaries and language textbooks.

Takayuki Okazaki

Recent developments in Ainu language revitalization

More than 20 years ago, DeChicchis (1995) expressed hope about the future of the Ainu language in view of television documentary coverage of Ainu, increases in Ainu language classes both in the local Ainu communities and at universities, the availability of recorded materials of *yukar* and other oral literature and the revival of various Ainu ceremonies.

> With thousands of Ainu singing and praying and greeting each other, and teaching their children these Ainu songs and prayer and greetings, it is also a safe bet that the Ainu language is not about to die.
>
> *(DeChicchis 1995: 118–119)*

This chapter was written at a time when Ainu activism gained momentum, and Ainu were calling for their rights to be recognized as an indigenous minority in Japan and abroad. At the community level, more and more Ainu language classes were established, following the pioneering school established by Kayano Shigeru in Nibutani in 1983. DeChicchis identified 11 schools in Hokkaido in his paper, and this number would eventually grow to 14 schools. These schools were all funded by the Hokkaido Ainu Association (Teeter and Okazaki 2011). At the national level, Kayano Shigeru became the first Ainu parliament member of Japan in 1994. Ainu sought international pressure as well in order to have their voices heard in Japan. In 1992, Nomura Gi'ichi, who led Hokkaido Utari Association for 32 years as an executive director, represented Ainu people at the Opening Ceremony of the International Year of the World's Indigenous People at the United Nations General Assembly calling for the rights of indigenous peoples to be recognized in Japan and in the world (Hokkaido Ainu Association 2016).[8]

These initiatives as well as the Ainu New Law Proposal by the Hokkaido Utari Association adopted in the general assembly in 1984 to replace the Former Aborigines Protection Act culminated in the enactment of an Ainu Culture Promotion Act in 1997. Although it includes Ainu language as one of the core cultural elements to be promoted, most linguists are critical of this act. They criticize it because it ignores most of the Ainu New Law Proposal, including the protection of human rights, the establishment of indigenous seats in Parliament, the promotion of industrial activities led by Ainu, the creation of a fund for Ainu self-reliance and the formation of a central consultative body for Ainu policy. In addition, its definition of "Ainu culture" is extremely narrow and does not reflect the current lifestyle and economy of Ainu.

Okuda (2001) emphasizes that the Ainu culture promotion policies that resulted from this act are restricting Ainu activities to the image of traditional culture, which is often fixed, limited and detached from contemporary Ainu life. What is more, it is often characterized as contradistinctive from Japanese culture. Since the act does not specify how Ainu language education should be carried out, Tezuka (2006) claims that Ainu language education was purposefully left out of the act. Nakagawa (2013) mentions that while it is clear that the biggest cause of the decline of Ainu language and culture is that Ainu were deprived of their economic foundation, the Ainu Culture Promotion Act fails to address the causes, and it also does not consider indigenous rights. He goes on to argue that without a revitalization of the economic foundation of Ainu, the fundamental problem remains how to plan for and implement language and culture revitalization. Although Satō (2012) praises several language activities that resulted directly from the act, he also states that the act only recognizes the presence of Ainu "culture", but does not recognize Ainu as indigenous people or grant them indigenous rights. He thus concludes the act provides no assistance for those Ainu who decided not to be involved in Ainu "culture" as defined in the act. This view is shared by Okuda (2010) who states that those policies coming out of the act have directed the energies of Ainu youth towards the types of traditional cultural activities defined in the act, diverting attention and energy away from other kinds of activism such as political or emancipative movements.

In order to implement the Ainu Culture Promotion Act the Foundation for Research and Promotion of Ainu Culture (henceforth, FRPAC) – a government agency that funds Ainu cultural activities including language revitalization – was established. With regard to language, FRPAC funds the following projects.

1. Training of instructors (three-day long intensive courses, three times per year).
2. Advanced language classes (in five locations, on four weekends a year).
3. Parent-child study of Ainu language projects (in six locations, twice a month for a total of 72 hours).
4. Introductory Ainu classes (in seven locations, twice a month for a total of 40 hours).
5. The annual Ainu speech contest *itak=an ro*.
6. The STV weekly Ainu Radio program (7–7:15 am, every Sunday).

The evaluation of FRPAC projects on Ainu language varies. Maher (2014) compares the Ainu language situation with that of Celtic languages. He is generally positive about FRPAC activities, seeing it as an effective organization for the support and realization of the Ainu language. Satō (2012) writes extensively on each of the activities supported by FRPAC, highlighting the many difficulties encountered in different locations. His account is extremely insightful, because he was a member of FRPAC's Ainu language education improvement committee between 2008 and 2009 and has insider information into the various projects. Although he understands that every project relies largely on the willingness of participants to sacrifice their time, money and energy, he nevertheless considers that many of the FRPAC projects have come to be successful. Okuda (2010), on the other hand, is critical towards the FRPAC activities, writing that those who are active and fluent in Ainu language had studied the language and gained their fluency before the Ainu Culture Promotion Act was enforced. While he acknowledges that the number of young Ainu willing to learn the language has increased, he knows of no young Ainu who can freely converse, tell Ainu stories without memorization or understand stories that they hear for the first time. Nakagawa (2013) also points out the fact that none of these projects are actually creating active Ainu language speakers. The three-day intensive instructor-training project, for example, is held six times in two years, which is merely 18 days long. This does not improve the language proficiency of the participants dramatically, nor their ability to teach Ainu. However, Nakagawa is adamant that these Ainu learners need "space" to meet and maintain their motivation to do something for the language. Quite a few learners study Ainu by themselves. Such users are usually isolated across Hokkaido and the Japanese mainland. In fact, those who completed the instructor-training project requested that they want to participate again in such a project, and this desire led to the creation of the three-day follow-up sessions that are held every August since 2010. It is for such reasons that Nakagawa sees it necessary to create many more such spaces to nurture these kinds of human resources.

Though most researchers do not mention it, it is important to note that FRPAC outsources an apprentice-training program to the Ainu Museum in Shiraoi (Foundation for Research and Promotion of Ainu Culture 2016). This gives several apprentices accommodation and stipends for three years, allowing them to learn various aspects of Ainu livelihood, including the Ainu language. Currently, Ainu language classes are offered for eight hours a week and their third cohort will have graduated in March 2017.

After Ainu were recognized as an indigenous people of Japan in 2008 (Winchester 2009), the Advisory Council for Future Ainu Policy (*Ainu seisaku no arikata ni kansuru yūshikisha kondankai*) was formed by the cabinet and tasked to develop future Ainu policies. In its fifth meeting, Nakagawa (2009) was invited to talk about the future of Ainu language learning. On this occasion, he underlined the importance of improving the prestige and status of the Ainu language and towards this end recommended the following steps to be taken:

(1) raising public awareness on Ainu culture and history by the central government.
(2) educating teachers on Ainu language and history.
(3) establishing a national Ainu language research institute.
(4) making the publications by Ainu related agencies bilingual in Ainu and Japanese.
(5) creating language learning "spaces" as mentioned above.
(6) creating a system to publish and distribute more textbooks and other language related books.
(7) and establishing a language archiving system.

The Council's final report in 2009 stated the following:

> The nation has a responsibility to consider methods to restore the Ainu culture. Strong consideration is needed for policies that respect Ainu culture and spirituality, particularly the revitalization of the Ainu language.
> *(Advisory Board for Future Ainu Policy 2009: 28)*

Note, however, that the report does not offer any concrete recommendations on language education when it comes to future suggestions. Nothing is done beyond praising the current FRPAC efforts and suggesting that FRPAC-funded Ainu language projects be enhanced (see Teeter and Okazaki 2011 for a discussion). Okuda (2010) concludes that it is the intention of the government to make an appeal to the public that they have shown their respect to Ainu people, but they do not support the creation of an environment to improve Ainu people's status.

In similar fashion, the Council for Ainu Policy Promotion formed by the central government in 2010 appears to have little interest in Ainu language education. Their discussion over the last seven years has primarily been concerned with the creation of a Symbolic Space for Ethnic Harmony (*Minzoku kyōsei no shōchō to naru kūkan*) near Lake Poroto in Shiraoi. The most recent report on the Symbolic Space by the Council for Ainu Policy Promotion (2016) states that the Symbolic Space will be a national center for revitalizing Ainu culture. It is scheduled to be open in 2020 on the occasion of the Tokyo Olympics, with a National Ainu Museum (*Kokuritsu ainu minzoku hakubutsukan*) and a National Ethnic Harmony Park (*Kokuritsu minzoku kyōsei kōen*) as major facilities. The purposes of the Symbolic Space are:

(1) A hub to create and transmit history, tradition and culture by Ainu.
(2) A hub to promote the understanding of Ainu in Japan and abroad.
(3) A hub for national network for Ainu culture revitalization.
(Council for Ainu Policy Promotion 2016)

In the report, Ainu language is sometimes mentioned but never focused on. Ainu will merely be one of the languages for multilingual signs at the exhibitions and their multilingual websites to disseminate information. Together with craftwork and traditional lifestyles, Ainu language lessons will only be made available to groups of visitors including students with school trip as an experiential learning activity. It seems that Ainu language education is again left off the agenda. However, according to Kitahara (2012), Honda Yūko, a former vice-president of

Sapporo University and member of the Council for Ainu Policy Promotion, suggested that the Symbolic Space should have a place where children can gather such as a day-care center for those who work at the space.[9] Honda, an expert on Ainu language, stresses thereby the importance of exposure to Ainu from early on. Kitahara (2012) goes on to say that one of the students at Sapporo University is studying Ainu and at the same time training to receive the necessary qualifications to become a nursery teacher.

Regardless of whether Ainu language policy addresses actual Ainu language revitalization or not, Ainu language teachers and learners have been working hard to create a better learning environment for themselves. One of the recent and often cited initiatives by researchers is the *urespaa* ("nurturing each other" in Ainu) project at Sapporo University. Headed by the above-mentioned professor Honda, this project offers full tuition waivers to several Ainu students each year who study Ainu culture and language. This project started in 2010.

Grassroots level initiatives are also important. Ota (2014), in addition to his classes in Asahikawa and Urakawa, reports on his Internet activities which include teaching the Ainu language through the social networking service Mixi, writing novels, interactive broadcasting where he discovered *utar* (comrades), and announcing new vocabulary on Twitter. Katayama (2016) also discusses the importance of the online Ainu community including a network formed through a video-sharing website called *nikoniko dōga* with live streaming of lessons as well as a time-shift function allowing busy people to see lessons at any time and at any place. Though recognizing the effectiveness of the Internet and utilizing emails and chatting in Ainu, Kitahara (2012) stresses the significance of child education, especially surrounding children with music and children's books in Ainu.

Ainu teachers have also tried to learn from the approaches of other indigenous peoples. In the past five years, Ainu language educators visited Aotearoa/New Zealand several times and also invited Maori educators to Ainumosir in order to learn about ways to revitalize Ainu. One of the methods that resonated strongly with these educators was Te Ataarangi, a method developed by Katerina Mataira and Ngoi Pewhairangi in the 1970s. This method has made a great impact on Maori language revitalization, especially among adults who could not speak Maori (Te Ataarangi 2014). With the help of Maori Te Ataarangi specialists, Ainu language teachers and learners in Nibutani, Shiraoi, Akan and Tokyo have applied the approach to teaching Ainu. According to Erana Brewerton, the Te Ataarangi expert who visited Ainumosir, one of the important concepts of this approach is to create a space for learners to feel safe and secure as many Maori who could not speak Maori had a deep sense of *whakama* (embarrassment or shame) (Okazaki 2015). Sekine Kenji of Nibutani teaches weekly classes using this approach and developed a curriculum for beginner level lessons. Also learning from Maori approaches, a weekend immersion camp has been put into practice by Ainu language teachers. Students and teachers spend a whole weekend together in such camps and try to only speak in Ainu in a large meetinghouse (*marae* in Maori) sharing cooking and sleeping together under one roof.[10]

Outlook

Japanese treatment of Ainu from as early as the Edo Period (1603–1868) impacted Ainu language acquisition, resulting in a language shift in the Ainu communities. Education provided in Japanese served as a powerful force that resulted in cultural and linguistic assimilation. From the report by the Council for Ainu Policy Promotion, it appears highly likely that Ainu language revitalization will be largely left out of the picture. However, concerted efforts at grassroots levels are serving to unite those interested in speaking and studying the Ainu language.

Understanding the socio-political and socioeconomic history is central to analyzing the current state of the Ainu language. Researchers and supporters must be careful to not contribute to paternalism and linguicism in their scholarly work on the Ainu language. It should be kept in mind that Ainu language revitalization is a personal affair and a lengthy history of colonization continues to shape Ainu identity and Ainu language use. Okuda (2001) argues that it is not sufficient for researchers to simply respond to the speakers' wishes or help Ainu language revitalization. While one of the public interests that linguistic research is directly related to is documenting Ainu language and oral literature as a common asset of humanity, the other one is maintaining Ainu identity and eradicating ethnic discrimination. Furthermore, as a basic public interest, one must remember not to prevent each Ainu from achieving their own ways and objectives of self-realization (Okuda 2001).

Another common theme that has emerged in this chapter was the need for the creation of safe spaces for Ainu language use and learning. Some of the examples of spaces for language use and learning have been discussed throughout this chapter. Katayama (2016) emphasizes members of the Internet community she was in felt safe with only Ainu participants sharing their stories and backgrounds. Narita (2015) also reports the case where Ainu children did not feel safe as a non-Ainu male came to the classroom and took photos without permission. In her fieldwork, Martin (2011: 86) also notes that the language class she observed "provides a safe environment for the development of a sense of belonging in which being Ainu is socially acceptable".

Looking at a bigger picture of Japanese society as a whole, Kitahara (2011) problematizes that it has been seen to be unorthodox to use Ainu in Japanese society. Nakagawa (2013) also suggests that Japanese society needs to change in a way that no one feels strange about someone speaking Ainu as a language of Japan. Thus, the issue of language ideology is an important one. Kitahara (2011) is hopeful that the recent acceptance of multilingualism in Japanese society will create a better environment for Ainu language use as well. Thus, one of the important roles of sociolinguistics research is to report what is happening in Japan in terms of multilingualism. Additional work is also needed by sociolinguists on how they can support this language revitalization to work in a manner that is empowering and transformative.

In addition to issues of language ideology, the accumulated knowledge of sociolinguistics, as well as future research can be useful in recommending ways to create more space for language use, develop language and teaching materials, increase language awareness and change language policies. Though it is erroneous to assume that language revitalization efforts of other languages can directly be transferred to the Ainu language situation, they are, nevertheless, informative in terms of what could happen to Ainu language. Tezuka (2006), for example, introduces different language acts from Welsh, Basque, Saami and Estonian, which stipulate the obligation of the government and the right for education.

Nakagawa (2013) thinks that the number of Ainu language learners in their 20s and 30s is increasing, which he sees as unique compared with other so-called endangered languages. He sees that the key to Ainu language revitalization is the state of Japanese society in the future. If future Japanese society can be a place where people do not exclude others and where various peoples can coexist with respect for each other's cultures, he considers it possible to revitalize Ainu. Sociolinguists have an important role to play in shaping such a future.

Notes

1 Hokkaido Ainu Association was the name used when it was established in 1930 until 1961 and from 2009 onwards. The name Hokkaido Utari Association was used between 1961 and 2009. The more

vague term *utari* was preferred due to fear of discrimination. If the word Ainu was used people feared they would be discriminated against.
2 Though the term "Sakhalin Ainu" is more commonly used, the word *enciw* is often preferred. In Sakhakin Ainu, *enciw* was used when Ainu referred to themselves. Inoue (2016) estimates that it was necessary for the Sakhalin Ainu and their descendants relocated to Hokkaido after the WWII to use *enciw* to distinguish themselves from the Hokkaido Ainu.
3 The domain of the Matsumae family was granted control over the area around Matsumae in the southern end of modern-day Matsumae Peninsula of Hokkaido by Hideyoshi Toyotomi, who conquered Japan in 1590. The Matsumae domain also was given control over all trade between Japanese and Ainu upon its incorporation into the Tokugawa Shogunate in 1604.
4 *Ezo-chi* was the word used by Japanese to refer to the area where Ainu lived until the Meiji Restoration. Upon annexation of *Ezo-chi* in August 1869, the Japanese government renamed it Hokkaido (literally, "northern sea circuit").
5 It is also important to note that in losing 38 Ainu young adults, the families and communities from which they came suffered economically and mentally as they lost their main productive members in the village.
6 Frey (2007) also reports that these Christian schools closed in 1900s due to governmental control over them through regulations including the 1899 Regulations for Private School (*shiritsu gakkō-rei*), forbidding religious teaching in schools. Funding and staffing issues also contributed to their closure.
7 *Kamuy yukar* are Ainu deity epics that have been passed on generation after generation.
8 As mentioned above, *utari* was used instead of Ainu between 1961 and 2009.
9 She spent long years as an assistant to Kayano Shigeru to teach Ainu language to children in Nibutani.
10 *Marae* is a meeting place that includes a big meetinghouse that holds important ceremonies and meetings, and hosts cultural activities including language lessons, sleepovers and other activities.

References

Advisory Council for Future Ainu Policy (2009) *Ainu seisaku no arikata ni kansuru yūshikisha kondankai hōkokusho* [*Advisory Council for Future Ainu Policy Report*]. Tokyo: Naikaku.

Chiri, Yukie (1978) *Ainu shinyōshū* [*A Collection of Ainu Deity Epics*]. Tokyo: Iwanami Bunko.

Council for Ainu Policy Promotion (2016) "Minzoku kyōsei shōchō kūkan" kihon kōsō [The Basic Concept for "Symbolic Space for Ethnic Harmony"]. Available online at: www.kantei.go.jp/jp/singi/ainusuishin/index_e.html#policy_overview (accessed 14 February 2017).

Cultural Survival (2001) Japan's Ainu Seek Help to Preserve their Native Culture. Available online at: www.culturalsurvival.org/publications/cultural-survival-quarterly/japans-ainu-seek-help-preserve-their-native-culture (accessed 14 November 2016).

DeChicchis, Joseph (1995) The Current State of the Ainu Language. In: *Multilingual Japan*. John C. Maher and Kyoko Yashiro (eds), 103–124. Clevedon: Multilingual Matters.

Foundation for Research and Promotion of Ainu Culture (2016) Heisei 28-nendo jigyō keikakusho [2016 Annual Project Plans]. Available online at: www.frpac.or.jp/about/files/H28%20事業計画書.pdf (accessed 15 April 2017).

Frey, Christopher J. (2007) Ainu Schools and Education Policy in Nineteenth-century Hokkaido, Japan. PhD thesis, Indiana University.

Gottlieb, Nanette (2005) *Language and Society in Japan*. Cambridge: Cambridge University Press.

Hasegawa, Osamu (2008) Sinrit mosir koicarpa e no michi [The Path towards Conducting Ceremonies for our Ancestors]. In: *Tokyo Icarpa he no michi*. Tokyo Ainu-shi Kenkyūkai (ed.), 7–38. Tōkyō: Gendai Kikakushitsu.

Heinrich, Patrick (2012) *The Making of Monolingual Japan. Language Ideology and Japanese Modernity*. Bristol: Multilingual Matters.

Hirata, Miki (2009) Karigakkō fuzoku "Hokkaidō dojin kyōikujo" ni okeru ainu kyōiku no jittai – kyōkasho kara miru Meiji shoki no ainu kyōiku seisaku [The Actual Situation of Ainu Education at "Hokkaido Aborigine School" Affiliated with Colonization Commission Tentative School. Ainu Education Policies in the Beginning of Meiji Period through Textbooks]. *Hokkaido University Graduate School of International Media* 5: 29–42.

Hirose, Ken'ichiro (1996) Kaitakushi karigakkō fuzoku Hokkaidō dojin kyōikujo to kaitakushi kanen e no ainu no kyōsei shūgaku ni kansuru kenkyū [A Study on How Ainu Youth were Forced to Attend

Kaitakushi Ainu School and National Farms in Tokyo]. *Hokkaido University Annual Reports on Educational Science* 72: 89–119.

Hokkaido Ainu Association (2016) Inauguration Speech at the UN General Assembly. Available online at: www.ainu-assn.or.jp/english/inaugu.html (accessed 15 February 2017).

Hokkaidō Kankyō Seikatsu-bu (2006) Ainu seikatsu jittai hōkokusho [Report on Living Conditions of Ainu People]. Sapporo: Hokkaidō Kankyō Seikatsu-bu.

Inoue, Koichi (2016) A Case Study on Identity Issues with Regard to Enchiws (Sakhalin Ainu). *Journal of the Center for Northern Humanities* 9: 75–87.

Ishihara, Makoto (2004) Ainu minzoku jishin ni yoru chosaku ni tsuite [On Publications by Ainu People]. In: *Heisei 16-nendo ainu bunka fukyū keihatsu seminā hōkukoshū*. Foundation for Research and Promotion of Ainu Culture (ed.), 18–25. Sapporo: Foundation for Research and Promotion of Ainu Culture.

Kaizawa, Tōzō (1998) Ainu no sakebi [A Call by the Ainu]. In: *Ainu minzoku no kindai no kiroku*. Masahito Ogawa and Shin'ichi Yamada (eds), 373–389. Tokyo: Sofukan.

Kanō, Yuichi and Ken'ichiro Hirose (2008) Kaitakushi ni yoru Tōkyō de no Ainu kyōiku [Ainu Education in Tokyo Conducted by the Colonization Commission]. In: *Tokyo Icarpa e no michi*. Tōkyō Ainu-shi Kenkyūkai (ed.), 39–142. Tokyo: Gendai Kikakushitsu.

Kitahara, Jirōta M. (2011) Ainu go keishō no genjō [The Current Situation of Ainu Language Transmission]. In: *Kikiteki na jōkyō ni aru gengo hōgen no jittai ni kansuru chōsa kenkyū jigyō*. NINJAL (eds), 91–7. Tokyo: NINLAL.

—— (2012) Aynu itah eyaycaakasno [Studying Ainu Language]. *Kotoba to shakai* 14: 276–304.

Kuwabara, Masato (2015) Meiji ishin to ainu minzoku [Meiji Restoration and Ainu People]. In: *Ainu minzoku no rekishi*. Akira Sekiguchi, Hiroshi Tabata, Masato Kuwabara and Tadashi Takizawa (eds), 139–162. Tokyo: Yamakawa Shuppan

Maher, John. C. (1997) Linguistic Minorities and Education in Japan. *Educational Review* 49(2): 115–127.

—— (2001) Akor Itak – Our Language, Your Language. Ainu in Japan. In: *Can Threatened Languages be Saved? Reversing Language Shift, Revisited*. Joshua. A. Fishman (ed.), 323–349. Clevedon: Multilingual Matters.

—— (2014) Reversing Language Shift and Revitalization. Ainu and the Celtic Languages. *Shakai gengo kagaku* 17(1): 20–35.

Martin, Kylie (2011) Aynu itak. On the Road to Ainu Language Revitalization. *Hokkaido University Media and Communication Studies* 60: 57–93.

Murasaki, Kyōko (2001) Katafuto ainugo to denshōsha [Karafuto Ainu Language and Succeesors]. In: *Heisei 13-nendo Ainu bunka fukyū keihatsu seminā hōkukoshū*. Foundation for Research and Promotion of Ainu Culture (ed.), 22–9. Sapporo: Foundation for Research and Promotion of Ainu Culture.

Nakagawa, Hiroshi (2009) Ainugo gakushū no mirai ni mukete. Kangaekata to annai [Guidelines on How to Think about the Future of the Ainu Language]. In: *Ainu seisaku no arikata ni kansuru yūshikisha kondankai (dai 5 kai) shiryō 2*. Tokyo: Naikaku.

—— (2013) Ainugo [Ainu language]. *Nihongogaku* 32(10): 62–75.

Narita, Hidetoshi (2015) Sisam utar aynuitak eyayhonokka katu ene an i an wa ene ku=yaynu i [On Japanese Studying Ainu Language]. *Kotoba to shakai* 17: 190–208.

Ogawa, Masahito (1991) "Ainu gakkō" no setchi to "Hokkaidō kyūdojin hogohō" / "kyūdojin jidō kyōiku kitei" no seiritsu [A Historical Study on "Ainu School" (an Elementary School in the Ainu Community). The Forming Process of the Educational System for Ainu Children]. *Hokkaido University Annual Reports on Educational Science* 55: 257–325.

—— (2013) Tsuishikari gakkō no rekishi. Hokkaidō ni kyōseijū saserareta Karafuto ainu no kyōikushi [History of the Tsuishikari School. From the Viewpoint of the History of the Education for the Children of the Sakhalin Ainu Forcibly Relocated]. *Japanese Journal of Educational Research* 80(3): 309–321.

Okazaki, Takayuki (2015) Te ataarangi to maorigo fukkō [Te Ataarangi and Maori Language Revitalization]. *Konton* 12: 48–65.

Okuda, Osami (2001) Ainu go fukkō undō no genjō to ainu go kenkyūsha no sekinin [Present Situation of Ainu Language Revival Movement and the Responsibility of Researchers]. *Journal of Chiba University Eurasian Society* 4: 103–110.

—— (2010) Ainugo shiryō no hozon to katsuyō [Preservation and Utilization of Ainu Language Materials]. *Kokubungaku. Kaishaku to kanshō* 75(1): 44–48.

Ota, Mitsuru (2014) Aynuitaksiknuka kusu ku=ki p [My Efforts to Revitalize Ainu]. *Kotoba to shakai* 14: 276–304.

Satō, Tomomi (2012) Ainugo no genjō to fukkō [The Current Situation of Ainu Language and its Revitalization]. *Gengo kenkyū* 142: 29–44.

Sawai, Harumi (1998) The Present Situation of the Ainu Language. *Studies in Endangered Languages*. In: Kazuto Matsumura (ed.), 177–189. Tokyo: Hitsuji Shobō.

Siddle, Richard (1996) *Race, Resistance and the Ainu of Japan*. London: Routledge.

Tamura, Masato (2008) Karafuto ainu no "hikiage" [Salvage of Sakhalin Ainu]. In: *Nihon teikoku o meguru jinkō idō no kokusai shakaigaku [Transnational Sociology of Human Migration around Japanese Empire]*. Shinzō Araragi (ed.), 463–502. Tokyo: Fuji Shuppan.

Tangiku, Itsuji (2011) Aru nivufujin no senzen to sengo [Pre and Post World War II of some Nivkh]. *Wako University Bulletin of the Faculty of Human Studies* 4: 129–143.

Te Atararigi (2014) Learning Principles. Available online at: www.teataarangi.org.nz/?q=about-te-ataarangi/methodology (accessed on 16 January 2014).

Teeter, Jennifer L. and Takayuki Okazaki (2011) Ainu as a Heritage Language of Japan. History, Current State and Future of Ainu Language Policy and Education. *Heritage Language Journal* 8(2): 96–114.

Tezuka, Yoritaka (2006) Ainugo-shi gaikan. Gengo, shakai, seifu [An Overview of Ainu Language History]. In: *I/yay-pakasnu. Ainugo no gakushū to kyōiku no tame ni*. Katsunobu Izutsu (ed.), 87–110. Asahikawa: Hokkaidō Kyōiku Daigaku.

Ueno, Masayuki (2011) Ainugo no suitai to fukkō ni kansuru ichikōsatsu [A Study of the Decline and Revival of the Ainu Language]. *Bulletin of Saitama Gakuen University* 11: 211–224.

UNESCO (2009) UNESCO Interactive Atlas of the World's Languages in Danger. Available online at: www.unesco.org/culture/ich/index.php?pg=00206 (accessed on 16 January 2017).

Walker, Brett L. (2006) *The Conquest of Ainu Lands. Ecology and Culture in Japanese Expansion, 1590–1800*. Berkley: University of California Press.

Winchester, Mark (2009) On the Dawn of a New National Ainu Policy. The "'Ainu' as a Situation" Today. *The Asia-Pacific Journal*, 41(3) Available online at: http://apjjf.org/-Mark-Winchester/3234/article.pdf (accessed on 12 April 2017).

24
LANGUAGE SHIFT IN THE RYUKYU ISLANDS

Mark Anderson

Language shift

Language shift is the disappearance of a subordinate "retreating" language through the emergent effect of changing language choices to a dominant "replacing" language on a societal level. It is brought about by a complex interplay of factors, including aspirational language attitudes on the part of minority language speakers themselves as well as changing political and economic circumstances. But ultimately the stage for language shift is set when a community speaking lower status language X (in this case a Ryukyuan language) comes into contact and is dominated by a more powerful community speaking language Y (in this case Japanese). Language shift theory incorporates the concept of "domains", that is, different situational, relational and topical contexts of language use such as administration, media/literature, religion, entertaining arts, education, work, neighborhood and home/family. Language shift progresses as people begin to use the replacing language either in domains where the retreating language was formerly used or in new domains created in the process of modernization. A language becomes "endangered" when language choices change in the home/family domain, a phenomenon Dorian (1981) refers to as linguistic "tip" to reflect the metaphorical tipping of the balance of scales.

For over a century, Ryukyuans have been successfully convinced that their languages are in fact dialects (*hōgen*) of Japanese and this, coupled with a misguided concept of national identity (Clarke 2015: 631), has led the Ryukyuan languages to become endangered after intergenerational transmission was lost in the 1950s. These languages have been assessed at grade 2 ("severely endangered") on the UNESCO Language Vitality and Endangerment Scale and are forecast to disappear within the next few decades unless drastic action is taken in pursuance of language shift reversal (Ishihara 2014: 161).

Over the past decade or so there has been growing acceptance of the Ryukyuan languages' status as languages in their own right. This was in part due to UNESCO's formal recognition of six separate languages in the Ryukyu Archipelago – those of Amami, Kunigami, Okinawa, Miyako, Yaeyama and Yonaguni (Moseley 2009). Although these are sometimes still referred to as Japanese dialects and studied as such within the dialectologist tradition, the title of this chapter necessarily takes a standpoint by virtue of its reference to "language" as opposed to "dialect". Scholars today generally see what is happening across the Ryukyus as a straightforward example of language shift from Ryukyuan languages to Japanese, whereas previously the situation was characterized as a case of dialect leveling, to use Trudgill's (1986) term, from one Japanese dialect to another.

The recognition of Ryukyuan languages as sister languages of Japanese within the Japonic language family is not a trivial matter. It has implications for approaches towards Ryukyuan language revitalization and for the academic study of both Ryukyuan languages and Japanese. Such a recognition is important in the context of this volume because it represents a commitment to the idea of Japan as a multilingual country and defines Japanese sociolinguistics not as "sociolinguistic aspects of the Japanese language" but as "sociolinguistic aspects of the languages of Japan". This chapter self-consciously frames discussion in the latter perspective. It is deemed important to do so given the rapid loss of linguistic diversity in the Ryukyus and in Japan as a whole, and for the sake of potential efforts to reverse language shift.

Ryukyuan sociolinguistics

Sociolinguistic research on Ryukyuan languages began in the 1960s, rooted firmly in the tradition of Japanese dialectology. Whereas previous research by the likes of Hattori Shirō, Hirayama Teruo and Nakamoto Masachie had been purely descriptive and focused on geographical boundaries between regional dialects in terms of lexicon, grammar and accent, some scholars began to shift their attention to language use and functions. Notable early examples in the literature are Narita's (1960) paper on bilingualism in Okinawa and his (1964) study on Okinawan "language life" (*gengo seikatsu*); Shinzato's (1963) article on language policy; and Hokama's articles on Okinawan language education (1964) and language history (1968).[1]

Over the next two decades, Ryukyuan studies with a sociolinguistic focus would be comparatively rare, but there were some important contributions made during this time such as Motonaga's (1979) study of young people's language in Okinawa and Yabiku's (1987) article on local varieties of Japanese spoken in Okinawa, both of which influenced subsequent investigations into substratum effects. To a limited extent during this period there was also scholarly interest in language change in a broader range of Ryukyuan varieties such as Yonaguni (Nagata 1983) and Okinoerabujima (Kigawa 1986). The publication of these studies clearly reflected a gradual realization that language use was seen to be changing at the time, even if the gravity of the situation was not appreciated. All of these articles from the 1960s to the 1980s, being pre-Internet age, are now difficult for scholars to access, particularly if research is being conducted outside Japan. Many of them are from journals that are now out of print and only sold second-hand. If they can be bought through popular online shops like Amazon, international shipping is generally unavailable. Luckily, all of the above studies were republished as part of a large-scale compilation of research into Japanese dialects, the final seven volumes of which were devoted to the Ryukyus (Inoue et al. 2001). Most of the articles appear in the sociolinguistic research section of Volume 30 (the third Ryukyuan volume), but even that has become more difficult to obtain over the last few years (for example, the one copy existing in Australia was recently put into library storage without even being considered for inclusion in a rare books collection).

The year 1990 saw the publication of Shibatani's *Languages of Japan*, and while the use of the plural "languages" in its title signified something of a change of mindset, the book only took account of two languages – Japanese and Ainu – and Ryukyuan languages were discussed in a relatively short section (Shibatani 1990: 189–196) as "Ryukyuan dialects", standing in contrast to "mainland dialects". It was not until the publication of Maher and Yashiro's (1995) *Multilingual Japan* – a direct response to Shibatani's book – that Ryukyuan varieties were presented unambiguously as "vernacular languages" rather than mere dialects of Japanese (Matsumori 1995: 19). Weiner (1997) continued this trend shortly thereafter with the publication of *Japan's Minorities: The Illusion of Homogeneity*, which dealt broadly with cultural diversity in Japan rather than focusing on language only and continued the discourse in a similar vein to Maher and Yashiro's work, presenting Japan as a multicultural society including Ryukyuan people as well as *burakumin*, Korean and Taiwanese immigrants, Ainu and so on. These publications were perhaps an inevitable consequence of a growing interest in endangered languages in the international community since the 1960s, starting with Joshua Fishman's many contributions to the literature over several decades, and including a number of important and oft-cited edited books towards the end of the twentieth century (e.g., Dorian 1989; Brenzinger 1992; Grenoble and Whaley 1998).[2]

More recently, mostly in the last decade, sociolinguistic research into Ryukyuan languages has witnessed an (albeit belated) expansion and generated more interest among scholars who have gone on to specialize in particular areas within the discipline. This research has been spearheaded by Patrick Heinrich, who has played a large part in galvanizing scholars all over the world into collaborative projects such as conferences and the publication of edited books, perhaps the most important and ambitious of which is the *Handbook of Ryukyuan Languages* (Heinrich, Miyara and Shimoji 2015). Bolstered by UNESCO's recognition of six Ryukyuan languages in 2009, Heinrich has been consistently vocal in his opposition to the use of the term "dialect" to refer to what he points out are essentially unroofed *abstand* languages (Heinrich 2014), literally "languages by distance" using Kloss' (1967) terminology. Although most sociolinguistic research on Ryukyuan languages is being conducted in this "endangered language" or "Ryukyuan linguistics" paradigm, the dialectologist tradition lives on and, whether or not one agrees with the traditional perspective, the scholars involved continue to provide interesting and useful linguistic insights.

The aim of this chapter is to focus on various scholars' findings on Ryukyuan language shift, regardless of political bent, and to summarize any insights that are relevant to Japanese sociolinguistics. There are two main sections, the first relating to diachronic studies focusing on the language shift process and its causes (organized chronologically), and the second covering synchronic studies of the linguistic behavioral and social psychological effects of language shift. This chapter concludes by summarizing what scholars interested in language endangerment can learn from the Ryukyuan case, and a final section points to some gaps in the literature on Ryukyuan language shift which may be addressed in the future.

The language shift process and its causes

This section summarizes the Ryukyuan language shift process in two parts – the period of Japanese language spread in the public domains from the Meiji Period until after WWII, and the post-war era of broken intergenerational transmission and subsequent decline of Ryukyuan languages in private domains.

Education and punishment: The engineering of subtractive bilingualism

First let us consider the most important findings in the literature on the beginnings of the language shift process and its progression through a phase when children were brought up as productive bilinguals in a Ryukyuan L1 and Japanese L2 until after the Pacific War. Below is an explanation as to what caused the first generation of bilinguals to emerge in the Ryukyus during the Meiji Period and how the subsequent L1 devalorization process and active promotion of L2 created the right conditions for eventual intergenerational transmission loss of Ryukyuan languages in the home/family domain.

The language shift process commenced shortly after the annexation of the Ryukyu Kingdom by Meiji Japan in 1872 with the establishment of Okinawa Prefecture in 1879. The northernmost islands of the Ryukyu Kingdom had already been ceded to the Shimazu Clan of the Satsuma domain in 1609 but the kingdom had remained intact in order to avoid conflict with China, and the languages of the archipelago had been maintained. Now the Ryukyuan people were a minority nested within the larger Japanese nation-state. At this time, the former Ryukyu Kingdom was viewed with suspicion and Ryukyuans were seen as foreign by the rest of Japan, in part due to the kingdom's previous tributary relationship with China but also because of the language barrier (Clarke 2015: 632). Ryukyuan languages and Japanese are mutually unintelligible.

In these early stages, Okinawa Prefecture was run rather like a colony (Shinzato 1963: 44), with modern institutions such as local governmental administration, military, post offices, banks, the police and military initially staffed by personnel from the mainland, more specifically from Kyushu (Fujisawa 2000: 226–247). Administration, education and media/literature had existed on a small scale in the Ryukyus before annexation, but now expanded rapidly and underwent complete reorganization as part of the modernization process. Administration systems changed, schools were built and new local newspapers, books and magazines were printed. Japanese was the language of choice in these so-called "public domains" as well as any context in which written language was required (Heinrich 2015b: 616–618). Furthermore, Japanese adopted the role of lingua franca for communication between speakers of different languages of the Ryukyu Islands. As the language of the royal court, the Shuri variety had had the potential to perform this function, but the demise of the aristocracy and the assimilationist push by the Meiji government now precluded this possibility (Clarke 2015: 633). Japanese was imagined as a historically shared language and on this basis it symbolized the nation. Since Ryukyuan languages differed so obviously from Japanese, it was seen as necessary to enforce the use of Japanese in the Ryukyus while at the same time suppressing local languages. It was this dual process of language spread and shift that would eventually result in language endangerment (Heinrich 2012a).

In the years immediately following the abolition of the Ryukyu Kingdom, Ryukyuans referred to Japanese as *yamatuguchi* (Yamato language) and in practice this was the variety spoken in Kagoshima, Kyushu, since Japanese was not yet standardized (Shinzato 1963: 43). Hokama Shuzen, one of Okinawa's most influential linguists, traces the spread of Japanese in the late nineteenth and early twentieth centuries and identifies four periods in the spread of Japanese language: times when Japanese was known as *Tōkyō no kotoba* (Tokyo language), *futsūgo* (normal language), *hyōjungo* (standard language) and *kyōtsugo* (common language) (Hokama 1971: 52–61). Ryukyuan linguistics is fortunate to be well documented in terms of educational practices during the period when Japanese was being spread in schools. Researchers have worked extensively with primary evidence such as school textbooks, local newspapers, interviews with elderly retired teachers, and even records of published school chronicles from every elementary school in Okinawa Prefecture. These studies have allowed us to build up a detailed picture of the progression of events in connection with language spread and language shift. See for example Kondō's (2006) summary of his previous work with school records, and Maeda's (2010) article on the Amamian experience.

In the early 1880s after annexation by Imperial Japan, the pre-standardized "Tokyo language" was introduced into what would become the first ever primary school curriculum for Okinawa Prefecture (Yoshimura 2014: 33). At this time, Japanese was learnt by rote memorization rather than acquired in context. A bilingual textbook called *Okinawa taiwa* (Okinawa Conversation) was used in class, and children learnt Japanese through oral translation drills from Okinawan to Japanese and vice versa (Kondō 2014: 56). There were such severe communication problems between teachers from the mainland and Okinawan students that interpreters were required in the classroom (Yoshimura 2014: 33). For these children, school must have been an alienating experience, especially after the bilingual textbook was abolished in favor of a monolingual one written in literary style Japanese (written register) in 1888. However, Japanese had not yet gained a foothold in the community in terms of valorization, and the local language was still used as a teaching aid in class by both teachers and students. After students graduated, they forgot the literary Japanese they had learnt at school and did not use it in their everyday lives (Yoshimura 2014: 36). Thus, children who went to school during this period would constitute the last generation of monolinguals in their local language before societal bilingualism set in. When this generation later grew up and started families, they would struggle to understand the Japanese their own children were speaking to them.

The period from 1897 to 1935 was when Japanese language was more widely spread through school education under the name *futsūgo* (normal language) (Hokama 1971). There was a heightened sense of national pride around this time owing to Japan's victories in the Sino-Japanese War in 1895 and in the Russo-Japanese War in 1905, and nationalism began to be promoted through textbooks written in non-literary style Japanese (spoken register). This played a major role in "Japanizing" the Okinawan population (Yoshimura 2014: 41). At this time, bilingual education was transitional; that is, local languages were only used to facilitate the transition to a stage where children were ready to learn through the medium of Japanese.[3] In this system, pupils were receiving monolingual education in Japanese by their third year in primary school (Kondō 2004: 29).

By the beginning of the twentieth century, most of the teachers were Japanese-educated locals. The use of local languages in class had been phased out, and Japanese antonyms and synonyms were being used instead for concept checking (Yoshimura 2014: 43–44). Teachers blamed their students' lack of proficiency in Japanese on bilingual teaching methods, and hence after 1904 Japanese-medium monolingual education was reinforced through strict playground monitoring and in Japanese conversation classes after school (Yoshimura 2014: 47–48). In the absence of bilingual education, then, it can be assumed that the devalorization of Ryukyuan languages as a cognitive tool (i.e., an organizer of knowledge) led to subtractive bilingualism in this generation of children. In the literature on bilingual education, subtractive bilingualism, a term coined by Lambert (1981), refers to an imbalanced type of bilinguality[4] in children whose lack of mother tongue support at school leads to a delay in their cognitive development and erosion of the home language.[5]

Monolingual education became formalized through the introduction of more suppressive measures focused on assimilating Ryukyuans. In 1907, the Ordinance to Regulate the Dialect (*hōgen torishimari-rei*) was declared in an attempt to ban Ryukyuan languages outright from schools. In accordance with the Meiji government's ideology of a homogeneous, monolingual society, individual teachers began to use punitive measures in the classroom such as the *hōgen fuda* (dialect tag), a placard hung around a student's neck with the intention of causing humiliation for speaking the local vernacular, in order to bring about an end to discrimination by forcing children to abandon what was regarded as a divergent "dialect" of Japanese (Itani 2006; Kondō 2006). There is evidence that this harsh correction method led to further devalorization of Ryukyuan languages in the minds of children at this time: some children began using Japanese when interacting with each other or even when addressing their parents, thereby necessitating translation by older children (Masiko 1991: 152).[6]

During the depression of the 1920s, Japanese came to be valorized and Ryukyuan languages further devalorized in the community as emigration to mainland Japan increased and Okinawans suffered discrimination on account of their linguistic differences (Kondō 2014: 63). In these times of economic hardship known as the "cycad hell" (*sotetsu jigoku*), Okinawans sought to emigrate overseas, particularly to work on coffee plantations in Brazil, but one condition imposed on migrants by the Japanese Ministry of Foreign Affairs in 1926 was a good understanding of Standard Japanese (Yoshimura 2014: 49–50).[7] With this incentive, Japanese monolingualism was strictly enforced in schools as part of a promotion of nationalism and teachers were instructed to help in raising parents' awareness of the need for their children to speak Japanese. At this time, the use of local languages at home and in the community was blamed for children's poor reading skills in Japanese (Kondō 2014: 65–67). This societal valorization of Japanese literacy as a means to social integration and upward mobility further contributed to individual children's perception of local languages as lacking value.

The result of this devalorization of Ryukyuan languages through teacher-supported policing and punishment was the emergence of the first generation of so-called "early consecutive/sequential bilinguals" in the Ryukyus; that is, by the time these children reached school age, their form-function mappings for everyday language had already been established in their local language and Japanese was subsequently acquired as a second language from the age of six.[8] However, since Ryukyuan languages have never had a standardized orthography (Heinrich 2012b; Ogawa 2015), the school-starters were, like their parents, illiterate in their L1. This had serious implications for the first few years of their schooling. It meant that primary communicative skills in Japanese – their second language – had to be acquired at the same time as literacy, which involves dealing with decontextualized language. Consequently, Ryukyuan children were disadvantaged from the very outset when compared to their peers in mainland Japan whose mother tongue was a variety of Japanese.

It must be stressed that Ryukyuan languages were still maintained in the home/family domain at this time, otherwise children could not have become proficient in their local language. Furthermore, although the same Japanese-medium teaching methods lasted until the 1930s, Ryukyuan languages were being maintained in everyday interaction between Okinawans in the neighborhood domain outside school in the community throughout this period. Indeed, the fact that schoolchildren were reportedly observed taking time to translate mentally from their L1 to L2 before speaking to teachers (Kondō 2014: 68) constitutes evidence that they were L1 dominant, at least in their early years. Ryukyuans are well known for their longevity and there are many of this generation still alive today, although they are now all elderly. In Anderson's (2009, 2014b) typology of speaker types, they are called "full speakers", that is, those bilinguals aged 80+ (born before the mid-1930s) who are considered by younger generations to have full command of the spoken language.[9]

The fact that full speakers attained a relatively high level of L2 proficiency in addition to maintaining their L1 (Ōsumi 2001: 72) may perhaps be explained by the similarity between Ryukyuan languages and Japanese, which is arguably likely to facilitate positive L1 transfer. While bilinguals of this generation exhibit noticeable signs of L1 interference and distinctively Ryukyuan pronunciation when speaking Japanese, it is clear that they have been able to compensate for any early linguistic or learning difficulties over the course of their lifetime as their exposure to Japanese has increased during the process of language shift. However, it is unknown whether these seemingly balanced bilinguals are in fact now Japanese-dominant in old age and, if so, to what extent. Since there are no longer any speakers monolingual in their local language for comparison, relative proficiency between L1 and L2 could be established through (self-)evaluation scales, word association, and response time tests for processing and automaticity, something that has never been attempted in Ryukyuan linguistics. If such psycholinguistic tests are to be carried out on full speakers, they clearly need to be conducted very soon.

The 1930s saw an intensification of the campaign to spread Japanese and eradicate Ryukyuan languages, fueled by a new wave of nationalism. In 1931, new measures were introduced to promote the use of Japanese in the community as part of the Movement to Enforce the Normal Language (*futsūgo reikō undō*). By the end of the 1930s, Japanese had been standardized and was now known as *hyōjungo* (standard language), a name which implied a higher status language to which to aspire. Accordingly, the movement was renamed the Movement to Enforce the Standard Language (*hyōjungo reikō undō*). Criticism from mainland folklorist Yanagi Muneyoshi (also known as Yanagi Sōetsu) triggered the well-known "dialect debate" (*hōgen ronsō*) between Yanagi's supporters and the Okinawa Prefectural Department of Education (see Clarke 1997; Heinrich 2013). This played out in the media for just over a year before fizzling out.

By the beginning of WWII, Japanese thus already dominated in public domains and the use of Ryukyuan languages was mainly restricted to private domains. The language education campaign continued during WWII with the prefectural government sponsorship of teacher training in Standard Japanese, focusing on "correct" pronunciation. In addition, teachers and pupils organized orientation events on Japanese language and etiquette for local residents as well as debating, presentation and story-telling circles (Kondō 2014: 72–73; Hokama 1971: 84–89). These efforts were evidently not far-reaching enough to cause Japanese to replace Ryukyuan languages in the neighborhood domain, but from a social psychological point of view, they led to further devalorization of Ryukyuan languages in the minds of individual child bilinguals born from the mid-1930s onwards.

In April 1945, during the Battle of Okinawa at the end of WWII, the Japanese military issued an order to execute Ryukyuan language speakers on the presumption that they were spies working for the United States (Heinrich 2015a: 601). Many more would die as an effect of being trapped between the frontline moving up and down the island during a merciless battle that lasted for 82 days. By the end of the battle, one-quarter of the total Ryukyuan population had been wiped out, and this sudden decline in the absolute number of Ryukyuan speakers and the hardships experienced by survivors set the stage for language abandonment in the following decade while under US occupation.

The tipping point: Language loss and broken intergenerational transmission

The post-war period was a critical point in the history of Ryukyuan languages. In 1946, Japanese imperial administrative rights over Okinawa were terminated, and Ryukyuans were encouraged to use their local language. The US military recommended that the Okinawa Advisory Council reinstate public education in Ryukyuan languages. However, in the absence of suitable textbooks and a pan-Ryukyuan lingua franca, these recommendations were not followed and local teachers revived the corrective methods used by teachers drafted from the mainland in previous decades. The aforementioned Movement to Enforce the Standard Language was continued with renewed vigor, constituting an important phase of Ryukyuan language shift which is described in detail in Masiko (2014). Japanese further encroached in elite domains such as the arts and academia: for example, Okinawan plays had to be translated into Japanese, and Japanese terms were used in formal lectures on account of the lexical paucity of specialist vocabulary in Ryukyuan languages (Masiko 2014: 91).

Between 1950 and 1972, anti-US sentiment became the driving force behind a popular Movement for Return to the Fatherland (*Sokoku fukki undō*), characterized by a heightened sense of Japanese nationalism (Heinrich 2015a: 602). It was this shift in Ryukyuans' identity from "being Ryukyuan" to "being Japanese" that was to seal the fate of Ryukyuan languages (Clarke 2015), and it was felt particularly strongly in the Amami island group owing to their early reversion to Japan in 1953. An important effect of this psychological shift was Japanese language spread into the service industry and other industries where formal speech was required. In banks and post offices previously staffed by mainland Japanese personnel, Okinawan-born shopkeepers and bank clerks began to use Japanese with their customers (Ōsumi 2001: 75). This societal change in language choice would eventually lead to language loss – specifically register reduction – in Ryukyuan languages owing to the underuse and undermodeling of honorific and humble forms (Anderson 2009: 265).

The generation of productive bilinguals who were entering the workforce in the 1950s after leaving school were the first speakers of Ryukyuan languages who lacked the opportunity to acquire certain styles of their local language (Anderson 2014b: 113–115). They did not have the community reinforcement required for maintenance of full proficiency in the kind of formal language people would be likely to use with strangers in shops, for example. As a consequence, they became dominant in their L2 – Japanese, in contrast to the previous generation who tended more towards a more balanced bilinguality or perhaps L1 dominance (full speakers). The level of exposure required for a balanced form of bilinguistic development was simply unavailable now that Japanese had all but replaced Ryukyuan languages in formal contexts outside the private domain.[10]

Furthermore, as people in the community increasingly expected to be addressed in Japanese in the street, new members of the workforce were unable to receive feedback on their use of their L1 and consequently lacked confidence, experiencing some degree of L1 attrition as the years passed. To this day they lack adequate Ryukyuan-speaking and Ryukyuan-valorizing networks of the type enjoyed by previous generations and hence also situational contexts in which their local language can be used and positive language attitudes reproduced.[11] Anderson (2009, 2014b) refers to this generation of bilinguals, born between the mid-1930s and the mid-1950s, as "rusty speakers".[12]

The first generation of rusty speakers led the way in introducing Japanese to the home domain when they reached childbearing age (Anderson 2014b: 118), thus heralding the beginning of linguistic "tip" into the so-called "moribund" phase of language shift, a term used by Krauss (1992) to refer to the stage at which the retreating language is still "alive" in the community despite the cessation of intergenerational transmission from parent to child. The tip phase saw the emergence of the first acquirers of Japanese as a mother tongue. This process of drastic social change was driven by women as innovators in language choice – in response to the enduring discrepancy in academic results between Okinawa and the mainland, an assimilation movement was begun by female teachers in collaboration with mothers in the region. In other words, the Ryukyuans' shift to a Japanese identity was due not only to anti-American sentiment but also to an inferiority complex vis-à-vis Japanese mainlanders (Masiko 2014: 86–87).

As a result of triangulating data from synchronic studies of language repertoires across the different generations with first-hand reports from the period in question, scholars agree that Japanese replaced Ryukyuan languages in the home/family domain in the mid-1950s (e.g., Anderson 2009: 252; Heinrich 2015b: 621; Ōsumi 2001: 73). Seen from a speaker-oriented perspective, this means that the first child-bearers among the rusty speakers, being L2-dominant bilingual teenagers mostly living in abject poverty in temporary camps, now raised their children to speak Japanese for the sake of future social mobility, and full speaker parents probably followed their example given the importance of in-group conformity in Japanese society (Anderson 2014b: 117–121). Of course, the Japanese spoken in the home was not the standard version but a local-accented variety that incorporated a Ryukyuan substratum.[13] Nevertheless, Japanese was seen as a means to minimize potential discrimination and maximize job opportunities for this new generation. Heinrich (2015b: 622) points out that the timing of the tip phase differed from region to region across the Ryukyu Archipelago and that these local differences are not well documented in the literature. Regardless of the timing, however, all the Ryukyuan languages are now in a moribund state, and none has been transmitted to children in the home for many decades now.

Anderson (2014b) examines the progression of the tip phase in Okinawan and finds that informal registers of Ryukyuan languages were still commonly spoken in the neighborhood domain until the 1990s; that is, they could be heard in casual conversations between friends and relatives in the street (Anderson 2014b: 125).[14] Informal registers were also maintained to an extent in the work domain, mainly in industries such as fishing, farming and construction (Heinrich 2015b: 617). Hence, the first generation of non-acquirers of Ryukyuan languages in the home/family domain would develop into semi-speakers.[15] In the case of Okinawan, this generation of semi-speakers, born between about 1950 and the mid-1980s (Anderson 2014b: 106), were able to pick up some of their local language as their L2 through varying degrees of exposure to it in their local neighborhood depending on their parents' social network (Anderson 2014b: 127). Their skills were learnt when overhearing bilinguals in conversation with each other, or when being addressed by older friends and relatives in their extended family who would sometimes code-switch into their L1 knowing that they would be understood. According to Agarie et al. (1983), this exposure varied by region and the mother's language use at home had a particularly strong influence on the degree of acquisition. For some semi-speakers, these Ryukyuan language skills would be reinforced at work in later life.

But this situation would only last for one generation. Semi-speakers reached childbearing age and began to have children of their own at around the time of Okinawa's reversion to Japanese rule in 1972. Without productive bilingual proficiency, these semi-speaker parents had no choice but to raise their children as monolingual Japanese speakers, and late childbearing rusty speakers may have followed this parental trend (Anderson 2014b: 128). Consequently, there were few opportunities for children to interact with bilinguals and this lack of exposure led to the emergence of a generation of non-speakers of Okinawan. These children were to all intents and purposes monolingual, having virtually no productive or receptive abilities in their local language with the exception of a limited number of special expressions remaining in the substratum. Meanwhile, the advent of television in the 1960s had had the effect of raising the perceived status of Japanese and now provided children with a model of Standard Japanese to contrast the variety spoken by their parents (Sugita 2015: 512; Heinrich 2015b: 625). When the first generation of non-speakers of Okinawan entered the workforce in the 1990s, people accommodated to them linguistically and language shift in the work domain was all but complete, leaving the religion and entertaining arts as the only domains where Ryukyuan languages are still maintained, and even these are now under threat, albeit for different reasons (Heinrich 2015b: 624; Gillan 2015: 697; Anderson 2014a: 10–11). On Okinawa Island, all generations since the 1970s have been raised as monolingual Japanese speakers, unable to understand or speak the language of their ancestors.

On the basis of the above findings, Anderson (2009: 283–284) predicts that the Okinawan language will cease to be spoken with its full range of lexicon and registers by the 2030s; the language as it is spoken by bilinguals today will disappear with its speakers by the 2050s; and by the 2080s, receptive skills will be virtually non-existent and accuracy in transcription and translation of archived recordings will be unverifiable. It has not yet been investigated whether the progression of the moribund phase in the other Ryukyuan languages spoken in Amami, Kunigami, Miyako, Yaeyama, and Yonaguni corresponds directly to that of Okinawan, but surveys by Niinaga, Ishihara and Nishioka (2014) for the Northern Ryukyus and Aso, Shimoji and Heinrich (2014) for the Southern Ryukyus suggest that the patterns of shift must have been similar. Based on survey data on language choices collected in 2005–2006 and first analyzed in Heinrich (2007), Heinrich (2015b: 623) points out that the Miyako language may have maintained comparatively high vitality for some time, while Yaeyama and Yonaguni were first to become seriously endangered, the neighborhood domain having been maintained in Yonaguni only because of outmigration and a consequent aging population. Further qualitative data is needed to add richer detail to what we know about historic patterns of shift from these quantitative studies. In the diaspora (Hawai'i, Brazil, Peru and Bolivia, among other places), language shift has taken place in a parallel process as English, Portuguese and Spanish have replaced the Ryukyuan languages among the immigrant population. Sociolinguistic aspects of the diaspora have been studied most prolifically by Miyahira Katsuyuki and Peter Petrucci (Miyahira and Petrucci 2007, 2011, 2015; Petrucci and Miyahira 2010, 2014).

Efforts towards revitalization of Ryukyuan languages across the Ryukyu Archipelago are now quite well documented thanks to an increasing amount of research in this area in recent years. Such studies have discussed the activities of prefecture-wide organizations such as the Society for Okinawan Language Revitalization (*Okinawa fukyū kyōgikai*) as well as various local projects (Hara 2005; Heinrich 2005a, 2005b; Hara and Heinrich 2015; Ishihara 2016; Anderson 2014a; Heinrich 2017; Heinrich and Ishihara 2017). Moreover, in the literature written in both English and Japanese there is now a clearly outlined theoretical "roadmap" to language shift reversal (Heinrich 2014; Shimoji and Heinrich 2014; Heinrich and Sugita 2009). In brief, this involves redressing the existing power imbalance through status planning and institutional support in the administration, education and media domains in the first stages so that a firm foundation is provided for subsequent attempts at reinstating intergenerational transmission in the home/family domain. It has been stated unambiguously that if strategies are not pushed in the recommended direction then the languages will certainly become extinct.

The impact of language shift

So far, the historical progression of language shift has been discussed in chronological order. This next section focuses on literature pertaining not to the process of language shift but rather to its observable effects on the language repertoires, behaviors and attitudes of the Ryukyuan people.

The linguistic behavioral dimension

To date there have been several surveys of language choices, language use and language proficiency in Okinawa. Sociolinguistic research of this type began with Narita (1964) and Teruya (1976), and these were followed by a series of studies in the 1980s which would prove to be highly influential (Motonaga 1981; Agarie et al. 1983; Nagata 1983, 1984; Nagata et al. 1985; Agarie et al. 1985; Kigawa 1986). Somewhat conveniently for scholars in this field, all of these studies were later republished in books that included collections of previous papers alongside more recent work (Motonaga 1994; Nagata 1996; Inoue et al. 2001). Other important survey analyses include Ōno (1995) and Heinrich (2007).[16] A comparison of the synchronic cross-generational data from these studies lends support to the diachronic accounts of declining Ryukyuan language use and proficiency as well as Japanese language spread during the moribund phase of language shift discussed in the previous section. The specific findings of each study should, however, be treated with due caution as such self-reports are vulnerable to response bias. Furthermore, these survey reports are now decades old and are therefore unlikely to reflect the situation in current Okinawan society. Perhaps in response to the need for updated information, this area of research has recently seen a revival, and the latest quantitative studies have used much larger samples and sophisticated software for data analysis (e.g., Sasaki et al. 2014).

Another strand of Ryukyuan sociolinguistic research has focused on the ways in which Ryukyuans mix elements of local languages with Japanese as a consequence of language shift (see Anderson, this volume). Of particular interest is the range of local varieties of Japanese, the features of which differ by region, generation and gender (Nagata 1996; Takaesu 1994; Kinjō and Shō 2000). These discourse modes are essentially dialects of Japanese with a Ryukyuan substratum, and in the literature they have often been known by names such as *uchinaa yamatuguchi* (Okinawan Japanese) and *ton-futsūgo* (Amamian "Sweet Potato" Japanese). These varieties incorporate non-standard particle and aspect usage, a limited number of words retained or borrowed back from Ryukyuan languages, and hypercorrection and phonosyntactic transfer in the case of older speakers.

Language loss (i.e., language attrition on a societal level) is an area that has thus far been neglected in Ryukyuan sociolinguistics. Language loss in the Ryukyus manifests itself as the obsolescence of certain registers (see Anderson 2014b; Nagata et al. 1985, reworked in Nagata 1996: 147–157) as well as superstrate influence in the form of phonological, grammatical and lexical interference from Japanese (see Karimata 2012). However, it is difficult to ascertain what exactly has been lost from the languages (e.g., registers, phonemes, lexical items) when bilinguals are nowadays speaking mostly Japanese or code-switching extensively in conversation. Researchers perhaps ought to be cautious in making assumptions about Japanese code-switches and insertions being due, for example, to language attrition, although such suggestions have been tentatively made in the literature (e.g., Anderson 2009: 188). Indeed, it may be safer to rely on self-reporting through qualitative analysis of speakers' meta-conversations about lacking L1 proficiency (e.g., Anderson 2009: 196). Another method used in the literature is quantitative analysis of surveys that elicit production of Ryukyuan lexical items across different generations. Nagata's surveys in Amami-Ōshima and Kikaijima, for example, showed noticeable gaps in the lexical knowledge of rusty speakers as compared with full speakers (Nagata 1996: 118–122). Ryukyuan language attrition would ideally be investigated through experimental methods (e.g., evaluation scales, word association, and response time tests), but such studies do not yet exist in the literature.[17]

The social psychological dimension

Next, let us consider studies of language attitudes and beliefs, which are perhaps best investigated using survey methods. This sociolinguistic aspect of Ryukyuan languages has begun to receive more attention from scholars and local governmental bodies. Much of this research has taken a quantitative approach using questionnaires, but there are also some qualitative studies. For example, Matsuno (2004) discusses language attitudes among inhabitants of Henna Village based on responses from interview participants, while Anderson (2014a) summarizes evidence pertaining to attitudes revealed in interview transcripts from a series of (2001) *Okinawa Times* articles and in quotes from recordings of natural conversation taken by the author. The findings of both studies indicate a mixture of positive and negative attitudes towards Ryukyuan languages and their revitalization: Okinawans emphasize the importance of preserving the languages on the basis of their association with traditional culture while failing to recognize the value of language maintenance for use across a range of functions in everyday life.

In terms of quantitative research, the earliest surveys to incorporate items eliciting language attitudes were Teruya (1976), Motonaga (1981) and Agarie et al. (1983). Overall, these showed that, although stigmatization and active repression of Ryukyuan languages had diminished over time, Ryukyuans continued to show ambivalence towards their local languages while recognizing the high status and utility of Standard Japanese. These studies were followed by Ōno's

(1995) survey report, which included a section on attitudes towards Okinawa-substrate Japanese in relation to Okinawan and Standard Japanese. More recently, a major contribution has been made by Ishihara Masahide, who conducted a survey on language attitudes and practices in 2010 and 2011, and later published the results as part of a broader study assessing Ryukyuan languages on UNESCO's (2003) language vitality and endangerment scale (Ishihara 2014). Ishihara asked participants to respond to 5-point Likert-type scale items eliciting the proportion of their everyday use of Ryukyuan languages in relation to Japanese; their desire to speak their local language in the future and for their children and grandchildren to be able to speak it; and whether they thought that it would be maintained. His findings revealed a gap between participants' stated desire to speak their local language and their negative expectations about whether this would actually be achieved. Ishihara's sample was intentionally limited to specific subsections of the population selected via convenience sampling, namely performers of traditional Okinawan music (around 600 participants) and performing arts students at Haebaru High School, the University of the Ryukyus and Okinawa International University (around 470 participants), and his findings therefore lack generalizability to the Ryukyuan population as a whole. Furthermore, Ishihara's analysis explicitly assumes that the participants' stated desire to speak their local language includes a positive attitude towards future reinstatement of language transmission.

Other major surveys of language attitudes have been conducted by the Okinawa Prefectural government and organizations concerned with Ryukyuan language revitalization. One prominent example was administered by the Department of Culture, Tourism and Sports and involved 1,500 participants aged 20–70 (Okinawa-ken 2013). Over 80% of respondents considered local languages to be "friendly-sounding" and "needed in everyday life". Furthermore, it was reported that many Okinawans consider it important to teach local languages in schools. Such studies tend to reveal that participants generally agree with language maintenance initiatives in principle, but are unenthusiastic about actively participating in activities that would foster proficiency in local languages.

What is needed in future studies of language attitudes in the Ryukyus is a suitable questionnaire with good construct validity using items that have been refined through consultation and pilot testing. The survey could seek to elicit participants' attitudes towards revitalization of Ryukyuan languages as well as their beliefs about the language's vitality and utility. Statistical analyses could then be performed on the data to identify whether language attitudes/beliefs are predicted by age, gender or place of residence (city/village). At present there are conflicting accounts as to whether Okinawans living in rural areas are more conservative than their city-dwelling counterparts in terms of their attitudes/beliefs towards their heritage language. Anecdotal evidence would seem to suggest that this is the case, but close examination may reveal more negative attitudes among inhabitants of rural villages in comparison to city people. It is not uncommon to hear native Okinawans saying that they would like their language to be "saved" (Anderson, 2014a), but this apparent positive attitude does not appear to be reflected in language choices and linguistic behavior. A firm understanding of local attitudes towards language revitalization is necessary in determining the best approach to language planning since, as Ishihara (2014: 156) points out, attitudes may indicate the likelihood of success in language maintenance.

Concluding remarks

Dorian (1977) introduced to sociolinguists the "Problem of the semi-speaker in language death", but this chapter has shown that, at least in the Ryukyuan case, the seeds of language shift were sown long before the emergence of generations of non-acquirers of the retreating language. The fertile ground on which language shift took place turns out to have been the rusty speakers, who were not only deprived of adequate social networks and social spaces in which their L1 acquisition could continue, but were also denied access to bilingual education and L1 literacy skills development during childhood. Since their L1 was not valorized by their schools and community networks, dominance in their L2 was an inevitable outcome. As Japanese had been established as the only viable language of power and modernity, by the time these rusty speakers reached childbearing age, they were led to believe that they had no choice but to embrace a Japanese identity and raise their own children to speak Japanese as their mother tongue.

Of particular relevance here is Landry, Allard and Henry's (1996) extension of the concept of subtractive bilingualism from the individual to the group. It is clear that the main factors leading to language shift in Okinawa were the onset of subtractive bilingualism in a whole generation of schoolchildren in combination with a collective shift in identity in response to external sociopolitical and socioeconomic forces. This generation's L2 dominance allowed them to raise their children as Japanese speakers. If the majority had anticipated language shift and been in favor of counteracting it at the time, reversal of the process might have been possible if the following had been put into practice:

(1) Challenging of negative attitudes towards Okinawan through careful status planning (valorization process).
(2) Development of orthography and introduction of home literacy programs where parents encourage valorization of L1 as a cognitive tool by reading to children in Okinawan since, according to Hamers and Blanc (2000: 217), "oral use of the language for everyday activities does not seem to be enough to foster language maintenance and balanced bilinguality in the next generation".
(3) Dissociation of literacy from Japanese language acquisition (necessary L1 form-function mappings attained before L2).
(4) Education of the community about the natural developmental curve of early consecutive bilinguals (e.g., delayed lexicon acquisition and code-switching tendencies) and the pitfalls of the "bilingual handicap" myth (Cummins 1981).

What can be learnt from the Okinawan situation? Based on psycholinguistic theories pertaining to early consecutive bilinguality, it is suggested here that the alarm bell for societal language shift before the loss of intergenerational transmission of the L1 at home may be the presence of subtractive bilingualism in individual schoolchildren, that is, cognitive delay due to a lack of L1 support and development at school. Minority communities should be alert to early signs of subtractive bilingualism in schoolchildren because, as Hamers and Blanc (2000: 328) suggest: "A subtractive form is a negative asset not only for the individual but also for the group, and indeed for society as a whole." This is being recognized in some parts of the world where language shift is at an earlier stage and intergenerational transmission at home is still intact. In the Algerian Kabyle Berber region, for example, efforts are being made to encourage valorization and development of the L1 by creating extracurricular material for interactive and engaging Kabyle-medium classes in subjects like astronomy. For this purpose, careful status and corpus planning has been necessary. In addition, signs written in Berber language have been displayed on walls and doors around schools (field notes). Through these methods, it is hoped that potential rusty speakers of Kabyle Berber could be turned into full speakers who value their L1 as a cognitive tool. Unfortunately, though, the introduction of these kinds of language revitalization measures in schools in the Ryukyus would be much more difficult in view of the fact that intergenerational transmission of local languages was lost decades ago.

Research desiderata

Since the gaps in the literature have already been discussed, they will be summarized in list form below. The areas of sociolinguistic inquiry where it has been suggested in the literature that more research is needed can be divided into two main disciplines – those which focus on the sociological aspects of language shift, and those which have a more social psychological or psycholinguistic emphasis.

Sociological

(1) The progression of language shift phases in languages other than Okinawan, i.e., Amami, Miyako, Yaeyama and Yonaguni.
(2) Language use in different kinds of workplace.

Social psychological or psycholinguistic

(1) Language attitude surveys (questionnaires on language revitalization analyzed by age, gender and place of residence).
(2) Language attrition and bilingual proficiency in individuals (experimental measurement of processing and automaticity).

Acknowledgements

I would like to thank Patrick Heinrich and Anikó Hatoss for their comments on early drafts. I am indebted to Anikó Hatoss for her guidance in psycholinguistic perspectives on bilingualism applicable to the Ryukyuan context, and to Jae Yup Jung for his insights into language attitudes and beliefs.

Notes

1. *Gengo seikatsu* (language life) is a term used in Japanese sociolinguistics to denote socio-cultural aspects of language use, such as style/register according to context and language change negotiated by speakers through linguistic practice (see Heinrich and Galan 2011).
2. Fishman (1964) was an important initial landmark publication relating to language maintenance and shift.
3. See Fishman and Lovas (1970) for further explanation of transitional bilingual education.
4. Hamers and Blanc (2000) make a useful distinction between "bilinguality", linguistic competence as a property of an individual, and "bilingualism", the use of two languages on a societal level.
5. A similar situation often obtains among immigrant ethnic minority children in multicultural countries who are subject to so-called "submersion" in L2 (no L1 support at school) and whose academic results are compared unfavorably with those achieved by monolingual children from the dominant culture.
6. See Peck (1978) for a discussion of such child–child discourse in L2 acquisition.
7. Famine forced Ryukyuans to resort to eating the cycad plant, which is toxic without proper preparation.
8. This age has been described as a "landmark for distinguishing between native-like and near-native attainment [in L2]" (Hyltenstam 1992).
9. The term "full speaker" was first introduced in Sasse (1992: 61–62) to reflect the speaker's high level of proficiency in the retreating language.
10. According to Pearson et al. (1997), a balanced form of bilinguistic development requires 40–60% exposure to each language.
11. See Milroy (1980) for a discussion of social networks as norm-enforcement mechanisms.
12. The term "rusty speaker" was first introduced in Menn (1989: 345) to reflect the gradual attrition experienced by members of this speaker subgroup through lack of practice. This attrition could itself

be a motivation for frequent code-switching when interacting with other rusty speakers (Anderson 2009: 189). The extent of L1 attrition in Ryukyuan rusty speakers is unknown but could be tested in future research using methods developed by experimental psychologists.

13 It must be noted that the term "substratum/substrate" is not used in quite the same sense as in creole linguistics; rather, it should be interpreted in Batibo's (1992: 92) sense of residual retention of words and expressions from the retreating language in speakers' use of the replacing language.

14 The Okinawan language, known in Okinawa as *Uchinaaguchi*, is the Ryukyuan language spoken in the southern part of Okinawa Island and surrounding islets.

15 The term "semi-speaker" was first introduced by Dorian (1977) to denote people who display a fair degree of receptive proficiency but lack productive skills in the retreating language.

16 This (2007) report on a questionnaire survey conducted in 2005/2006 was later summarized in Heinrich (2015b: 622–623).

17 Nagata (1996: 162) suggests that older survey participants have demonstrated slow recall times for Ryukyuan vocabulary.

References

Agarie, Nariyuki (ed.) (1983) *Okinawa ni okeru gengo seikatsu oyobi gengo nōryoku ni kansuru hikaku/sokuteiteki kenkyū* [*A Comparative/Descriptive Study of Language Life and Language Proficiency in Okinawa*]. Nakagusuku: Okinawa Gengo Shinri Kenkyūkai.

Agarie, Nariyuki, Yoshitake Ōshiro, Yasuharu Agarie, Moriyasu Motonaga, Kiyoharu Ishikawa and Taketoshi Takuma (1983) Chūgakusei no gengoseikatsu to hōgen rikaido – ryūkyū hōgenken ni oite [Everyday Language and Dialect Comprehension of Junior High School Students: Concerning the Ryukyuan Dialect Area]. *Ryūkyū Daigaku hōbungakubu kiyō* 26: 1–38.

Agarie, Yasuharu, Nariyuki Agarie, Yoshitake Ōshiro, Moriyasu Motonaga, Kiyoharu Ishikawa and Taketoshi Takuma (1985). Ryūkyū hōgen kiso goi no nan'ido to chūgakusei no hōgen rikaido [Scale Analysis of Basic Vocabulary of Ryukyu Dialects and Dialect Comprehension of Junior High School Students]. *Ryūkyū Daigaku kyōikugakubu kiyō* 28(2): 215–236.

Anderson, Mark (2009) Emergent Language Shift in Okinawa. PhD thesis, Department of Japanese Studies, University of Sydney.

——— (2014a) Revitalisation Attempts and Language Attitudes in the Ryukyus. In: *Language Crisis in the Ryukyus*. Mark Anderson and Patrick Heinrich (eds), 1–30. Newcastle upon Tyne: Cambridge Scholars Publishing.

——— (2014b) Language Shift and Language Loss. In: *Language Crisis in the Ryukyus*. Mark Anderson and Patrick Heinrich (eds), 103–139. Newcastle upon Tyne: Cambridge Scholars Publishing.

Asō, Reiko, Michinori Shimoji and Patrick Heinrich (2014) Sakishima no gengo kiki to gengo sonzokusei [Language Endangerment and Vitality in Sakishima]. In: *Ryūkyū shogo no hoji o mezashite*. Michinori Shimoji and Patrick Heinrich (eds), 144–158. Tokyo: CoCo Shuppan.

Batibo, Herman M. (1992) The Fate of Ethnic Languages in Tanzania. In: *Language Death. Factual and Theoretical Explorations with Special Reference to East Africa*. Matthias Brenzinger (ed.), 85–98. Berlin: Mouton de Gruyter.

Brenzinger, Matthias (ed.) (1992) *Language Death. Factual and Theoretical Explorations with Special Reference to East Africa*. Berlin: Mouton de Gruyter.

Clarke, Hugh (1997) The Great Dialect Debate. The State and Language Policy in Okinawa. In: *Society and the State in Interwar Japan*. Elise K. Tipton (ed.), 193–217. London: Routledge.

——— (2015) Language and Identity in Okinawa and Amami. Past, Present and Future. In: *Handbook of the Ryukyuan Languages*. Patrick Heinrich, Shinsho Miyara and Michinori Shimoji (eds), 631–647. Boston: de Gruyter Mouton.

Cummins, James P. (1981) The Role of Primary Language Development in Promoting Educational Success for Language Minority Students. In: *Schooling and Language Minority Students. A Theoretical Framework*. Charles F. Leyba (ed.), 3–49. Los Angeles: California State University.

Dorian, Nancy C. (1977) The Problem of the Semi-speaker in Language Death. *International Journal of the Sociology of Language* 12: 23–32.

——— (1981) *Language Death. The Life Cycle of a Scottish Gaelic Dialect*. Philadelphia: University of Pennsylvania Press.

——— (ed.) (1989) *Investigating Obsolescence. Studies in Language Contraction and Death*. Cambridge: Cambridge University Press.

Fishman, Joshua A. (1964) Language Maintenance and Language Shift as a Field of Inquiry. *Linguistics* 9: 32–70.
Fishman, Joshua A. and John Lovas (1970) Bilingual Education in Sociolinguistic Perspective. *TESOL Quarterly* 4: 215–222.
Fujisawa, Ken'ichi (2000) *Kindai okinawa kyōiku-shi no shikaku* [*Perspectives on the Modern History of Education in Okinawa*]. Tokyo: Shakai Hyōronsha.
Gillan, Matt (2015) Ryukyuan Languages in Ryukyuan Music. In: *Handbook of the Ryukyuan Languages*. Patrick Heinrich, Shinsho Miyara and Michinori Shimoji (eds), 685–702. Boston: de Gruyter Mouton.
Grenoble, Lenore A. and Lindsay J. Whaley (eds) (1998) *Endangered Languages. Current Issues and Future Prospects*. Cambridge: Cambridge University Press.
Hamers, Josiane F. and Michel H. A. Blanc (2000) *Biliguality and Bilingualism* (second edition). Cambridge: Cambridge University Press.
Hara, Kiyoshi (2005) Events for Regional Dialect and Cultural Development in Japan and Europe. *International Journal of the Sociology of Language* 175/176: 193–211.
Hara, Kiyoshi and Patrick Heinrich (2015) Linguistic and Cultural Revitalization. In: *Handbook of the Ryukyuan Languages*. Patrick Heinrich, Shinsho Miyara and Michinori Shimoji (eds), 649–665. Boston: de Gruyter Mouton.
Heinrich, Patrick (2005a) Language Loss and Revitalization in the Ryukyu Islands. *The Asia-Pacific Journal – Japan Focus*, November 10, 2005. Available online at: http://apjjf.org/-Patrick-Heinrich/1596/article.html (accessed on 3 June 2017).
——— (2005b) What Leaves a Mark Should no Longer Stain. Progressive Erasure and Reversing Language Shift Activities in the Ryukyu Islands. *Refereed Papers from the 1st International Small Islands Cultures Conference* (Kagoshima University Centre for the Pacific Islands, 7–10 February 2005). Available online at http://sicri-network.org/ISIC1/j.%20ISIC1P%20Heinrich.pdf (accessed on 3 June 2017).
——— (2007) *Look Who's Talking. Language Choices in the Ryukyu Islands* (=LAUD Working Papers 691). Essen: Duisburg-Essen University.
——— (2012a) *The Making of Monolingual Japan. Language Ideology and Japanese Modernity*. Bristol: Multilingual Matters.
——— (2012b) Not Writing as a Key Factor in Language Endangerment. The Case of the Ryukyu Islands. In: *Literacy for Dialogue in Multilingual Societies. Proceedings of Linguapax Asia Symposium 2011*. John Maher, Jelisava Dobovsek-Sethna and Cary Duval (eds), 39–52. Tokyo: Linguapax Asia.
——— (2013) Hōgen ronsō. The Great Ryukyuan Languages Debate of 1940. *Contemporary Japan* 25(2): 167–187.
——— (2014) Don't Leave Ryukyuan Languages Alone. A Roadmap for Language Revitalization. In: *Language Crisis in the Ryukyus*. Mark Anderson and Patrick Heinrich (eds), 296–322. Newcastle upon Tyne: Cambridge Scholars Publishing.
——— (2015a) Japanese Language Spread. In: *Handbook of the Ryukyuan Languages*. Patrick Heinrich, Shinsho Miyara and Michinori Shimoji (eds), 593–611. Boston: de Gruyter Mouton.
——— (2015b) Language Shift. In: *Handbook of the Ryukyuan Languages*. Patrick Heinrich, Shinsho Miyara and Michinori Shimoji (eds), 613–630. Boston: de Gruyter Mouton.
——— (2017) Revitalization of the Ryukyuan Languages. In: *Handbook of Endangered Languages*. Leanne Hinton, Leena Huss and Gerald Roche (eds), 455–463. London: Routledge.
Heinrich, Patrick and Christian Galan (eds) (2011). *Language Life in Japan*. London: Routledge.
Heinrich, Patrick and Masahide Ishihara (2017). Ryukyuan Languages in Japan. In: *Heritage Language Policies around the World*. Corinne A. Seals and Sheena Shah (eds), 165–184. London: Routledge.
Heinrich, Patrick, Shinsho Miyara and Michinori Shimoji (eds) (2015) *Handbook of the Ryukyuan Languages*. Boston: de Gruyter Mouton.
Heinrich, Patrick and Yūko Sugita (2009) Kiki gengo kiroku hozon to gengo fukkō no tōgō e mukete [Towards an Integration of Language Documentation and Language Revitalization]. *Shakai gengo kagaku* 11(2): 15–27.
Hokama, Shuzen (1964) Okinawa no gengo kyōikushi – Meiji ikō [The History of Language Education in Okinawa Since the Meiji Restoration]. *Gengo seikatsu* 155: 64–73.
——— (1968) Okinawa no gengoshi [The Language History of Okinawa]. *Bungaku* 36(1): 15–33.
——— (1971) *Okinawa no gengoshi* [*The Language History of Okinawa*]. Tokyo: Hōsei University.
Hyltenstam, Kenneth (1992) Non-native Features of Near-native Speakers. On the Ultimate Attainment of Childhood L2 Learners. In: *Cognitive Processing in Bilinguals*. Richard J. Harris (ed.), 351–368. Amsterdam: Elsevier.

Inoue, Fumio, Kōichi Shinozaki, Takashi Kobayashi and Takuichirō Ōshiro (eds) (2001) *Ryūkyū hōgen-kō* [*Ryukyuan Dialect Studies*] (7 volumes). Tokyo: Yumani Shobō.

Ishihara, Masahide (2014) Language Vitality and Endangerment in the Ryukyus. In: *Language Crisis in the Ryukyus*. Mark Anderson and Patrick Heinrich (eds), 140–168. Newcastle upon Tyne: Cambridge Scholars Publishing.

—— (2016) Language Revitalisation Efforts in the Ryukyus. In: *Self-determinable Development of Small Islands*. Masahide Ishihara, Ei'ichi Hoshino and Yoko Fujita (eds), 67–82. Singapore: Springer.

Itani, Yasuhiko (2006) *Okinawa no hōgen fuda* [*The Dialect Tag in Okinawa*]. Naha: Border Ink.

Karimata, Shigehisa (2012) Ryūkyū rettō ni okeru gengo sesshoku kenkyū no tame no oboegaki [Notes on Research into Language Contact in the Ryukyu Archipelago]. *Ryūkyū no hōgen* 36: 17–38.

Kigawa, Yukio (1986) Okinoerabujima ni okeru kansai hōgen to zenkoku kyōtsūgo no eikyō – ankēto chōsa no kekka kara [The Influence of Kansai Dialect and Standard Japanese in Okinoerabujima. From the Results of a Questionnaire Survey]. *Tōdai ronkyū* 23: 1–18.

Kinjō, Naomi and Makiko Shō (2000) Okinawa no daigakusei no seikatsugo no jittai – wakamono no uchinaayamatuguchi [The State of Okinawan University Students' Everyday Language. Young People's Okinawan Japanese]. *Southern Review* 15: 25–39.

Kloss, Heinz (1967) Bilingualism and Nationalism. *Journal of Social Issues* 23(2): 39–47.

Kondō, Ken'ichirō (2004) Okinawa-kenyō jinjō shōgaku dokuhon shiyō-ki (1897–1904) no Okinawa ni okeru hyōjungo kyōiku jisshi to sono ronri [The Practice and Rationale of Standard Language Education during the Period of Use of the Elementary School Textbook for Okinawa (1897–1904)]. *Kokugoka kyōiku* 56: 26–33.

—— (2006) *Kindai okinawa ni okeru kyōiku to kokumin tōgō* [*Education and National Mobilization in Modern Okinawa*]. Sapporo: Hokkaido University Press.

—— (2014) Japanese Language Education in Modern Okinawa until 1945. In: *Language Crisis in the Ryukyus*. Mark Anderson and Patrick Heinrich (eds), 54–81. Newcastle upon Tyne: Cambridge Scholars Publishing.

Krauss, Michael E. (1992) The World's Languages in Crisis. *Language* 68(1): 4–10.

Lambert, Wallace E. (1981) *Bilingualism and Language Acquisition*. New York: Academy of Science.

Landry, Rodrigue, Réal Allard and Jacques Henry (1996) French in South Louisiana. Towards Language Loss. *Journal of Multilingual and Multicultural Development* 17(6): 442–468.

Maeda, Tatsurō (2010) Keiken to shite no imin to sono gengo. Amamijin to shimaguchi o jirei ni [Immigration as an Experience and the Role of Language. The Case of Amamians and their Language]. *Kotoba to shakai* 12: 129–53.

Maher, John C. and Kyoko Yashiro (eds) (1995) *Multilingual Japan*. Clevedon: Multilingual Matters.

Masiko, Hidenori (1991) Dōka sōchi to shite no kokugo – kindai Okinawa bunka-ken no hyōjungo shintō ni okeru junkyo shūdan hendō, chishikijin, kyōiku shisutemu [The State Language as an Assimilation Apparatus. The Changes of Reference Group, Intellectuals and the Educational System in the Penetration of the Standard Language into the Ryukyu Cultural Zone]. *Kyōiku shakaigaku kenkyū* 48: 146–165.

—— (2014) The Politics of the Movement to Enforce Standard Japanese under the US Occupation. In: *Language Crisis in the Ryukyus*. Mark Anderson and Patrick Heinrich (eds), 82–102. Newcastle upon Tyne: Cambridge Scholars Publishing.

Matsumori, Akiko (1995) Ryūkyuan. Past, Present, and Future. In: *Multilingual Japan*. John C. Maher and Kyoko Yashiro (eds), 19–45. Clevedon: Multilingual Matters.

Matsuno, Yūko (2004) A Study of Okinawan Language Shift and Ideology. MA thesis, University of Arizona.

Menn, Lise (1989) Some People Who Don't Talk Right. Universal and Particular in Child Language, Aphasia and Language Obsolescence. In: *Investigating Obsolescence. Studies in Language Contraction and Death*. Nancy C. Dorian (ed.), 335–346. Cambridge: Cambridge University Press.

Milroy, Lesley (1980) *Language and Social Networks*. Oxford: Blackwell.

Miyahira, Katsuyuki and Peter R. Petrucci (2007) Going Home to Okinawa. Perspectives of Heritage Language Speakers Studying in the Ancestral Homeland. In: *Identity and Second Language Learning. Culture, Inquiry, and Dialogic Activity in Educational Contexts*. Miguel Mantero (ed.), 257–282. Charlotte: Information Age Publishing.

—— (2011) Reaching Out with Chimugukuru. Positioning Okinawan Identity at the Fourth Worldwide Uchinaanchu Festival and Beyond. In: *Re-Centering Asia: Histories, Encounters, Identities*. Jacob Edmond, Henry Johnson and Jacqueline Leckie (eds), 285–309. Leiden: Global Oriental.

────── (2015) Uchinaaguchi as an Online Symbolic Resource within and across the Okinawan Diaspora. In: *Handbook of the Ryukyuan Languages*. Patrick Heinrich, Shinsho Miyara and Michinori Shimoji (eds), 554–573. Boston: de Gruyter Mouton.

Moseley, Christopher (ed.) (2009) *Atlas of the World's Languages in Danger* (third edition). Paris: UNESCO.

Motonaga, Moriyasu (1979) Okinawa ni okeru jidōseito no kotoba [Young People's Language in Okinawa]. *Ryūkyū daigaku kyōiku gakubu kiyō* 23(1): 37–52.

────── (1981) Okinawa ni okeru jidōseito no gengo seikatsu to gengo ishiki [The Language Life and Language Attitudes of Young People in Okinawa]. *Okinawa gengo kenkyū sentā shiryō* (volume 30). Nishihara: University of the Ryukyus.

────── (1994) *Ryūkyū-ken seikatsugo no kenkyū* [*Studies in the Everyday Language of the Ryukyus*]. Tokyo: Shunjūsha.

Nagata, Takashi (1983) Yonaguni no gengo henka [Language Change in Yonaguni]. *Gengo no sekai* 1(2).

────── (1984) Yonaguni hōgen no kyōtsūgoka – shakai gengogakuteki kenkyū [Standardization of the Yonaguni Dialect – Sociolinguistic Research]. *Gengo no sekai* 2(1).

────── (1996) *Ryūkyū de umareta kyōtsūgo* [*Regional Varieties of Japanese that have Emerged in the Ryukyus*]. Tokyo: Ōfū.

Nagata, Takashi, Aoi Tsuda, Atsuko Nagao, Hae Kyong Shinn, Yō Matsumoto, Masayuki Iwahashi, Maki Tsutsumi, Chiyoko Nemoto and Kenjirō Matsuda (1985) Okinawa-ken Ōsato ni okeru kyōtsūgoka [Language Standardization in Ōsato, Okinawa Prefecture]. *Sophia Linguistica* 18: 131–143.

Narita, Yoshimitsu (1960) Okinawa ni okeru bilingualism ni tsuite [Concerning Bilingualism in Okinawa]. *Kokugogaku* 41: 86–93.

────── (1964) Okinawa no gengo seikatsu [Language Life in Okinawa]. *Jinbun shakai kagaku kenkyū* 2: 137–153.

Niinaga, Yūto, Masahide Ishihara and Satoshi Nishioka (2014) Kita-ryūkyū shogo (amamigo, kunigamigo, okinawago) no sonzokuryoku to kikido [Language Endangerment and Vitality in the Inner (Northern) Ryukyuan Languages]. In: *Ryūkyū shogo no hoji o mezashite*. Michinori Shimoji and Patrick Heinrich (eds), 96–142. Tokyo: CoCo Shuppan.

Ogawa, Shinji (2015) Orthography Development. In: *Handbook of the Ryukyuan Languages*. Patrick Heinrich, Shinsho Miyara and Michinori Shimoji (eds), 575–589. Boston: de Gruyter Mouton.

Okinawa-ken (2013) *Shimakutuba kenmin undō suishin jigyō kenmin ishiki chōsa* [*Prefectural Campaign for the Promotion of Community Languages. A Prefecture-wide Survey of Language Attitudes*]. Naha: Okinawa Prefecture.

Ōno, Makio (1995) Chūkan hōgen to shite no uchinaa yamatoguchi no isō [Aspects of Okinawan Japanese as an Interdialect Form]. *Gengo* 24(12): 178–191.

Ōsumi, Midori (2001) Language and Identity in Okinawa Today. In: *Studies in Japanese Bilingualism*. Mary Noguchi and Sandra Fotos (eds), 68–97. Clevedon: Multilingual Matters.

Pearson, Barbara Z., Sylvia C. Fernández, Vanessa Lewedeg and D. Kimbrough Oller (1997) The Relation of Input Factors to Lexical Learning by Infant Bilinguals. *Applied Psycholinguistics* 18: 41–58.

Peck, Sabrina (1978) Child-child Discourse in Second Language Acquisition. In: *Second Language Acquisition*. Evelyn M. Hatch (ed.), 383–400. Rowley: Newbury House.

Petrucci, Peter and Katsuyuki Miyahira (2010) Language Preservation in a Transnational Context. One Okinawan Community's Efforts to Maintain Uchinaaguchi in São Paulo, Brazil. *Romanitas* 4(2). Available online at: http://romanitas.uprrp.edu/vol_4_num_2/petrucci_miyahira.html (accessed on 3 June 2017).

────── (2014) Community Efforts to Maintain Uchinaaguhi in São Paulo. In: *Language Crisis in the Ryukyus*. Mark Anderson and Patrick Heinrich (eds), 255–278. Newcastle upon Tyne: Cambridge Scholars Publishing.

Sasaki, Kayoko, Makiko Shō, Yukiko Karimata and Kanji Tanaka (2014) Kōkōsei no okinawago shiyō ni tsuite no chōsa/kenkyū – kiete iku kotoba no naka de nani ga nokotte iku ka? [*Survey Research on the Use of the Okinawan Language among High School Students. What will Remain of the Disappearing Language?*]. Nishihara: University of the Ryukyus.

Sasse, Hans-Jürgen (1992) Language Decay and Contact-induced Change. Similarities and Differences. In: *Language Death. Factual and Theoretical Explorations with Special Reference to East Africa*. Matthias Brenzinger (ed.), 59–80. Berlin: Mouton de Gruyter.

Shibatani, Masayoshi (1990) *The Languages of Japan*. Cambridge: Cambridge University Press.

Shimoji, Michinori and Patrick Heinrich (eds) (2014). *Ryūkyū shogo no hoji o mezashite* [*In Pursuance of Ryukyuan Language Maintenance*]. Tokyo: CoCo Shuppan.

Shinzato, Keiji (1963). Okinawa ni okeru hyōjungo seisaku no kōzai [The Pros and Cons of Language Standardization Policy in Okinawa]. *Gengo seikatsu* 142: 43–9.

Sugita, Yuko (2015) Local Language Varieties and the Media. In: *Handbook of the Ryukyuan Languages*. Patrick Heinrich, Shinsho Miyara and Michinori Shimoji (eds), 511–530. Boston: de Gruyter Mouton.

Takaesu, Yoriko (1994) Uchinaa yamatuguchi – sono onsei, bunpō, goi ni tsuite. [Okinawan Japanese. Phonetics, Grammar and Vocabulary]. *Okinawa gengo kenkyū sentā hōkoku* 3: 245–89.

Teruya, Kikue (1976) Kōkōsei ni okeru hōgen ishiki ni tsuite – Okinawa-ken chūbu chi'iki no ba'ai [Concerning the Dialect Attitudes of High School Students. The Case of Central Okinawa Island in Okinawa Prefecture]. *Sagami kokubun* 3.

Trudgill, Peter (1986) *Dialects in Contact*. Oxford: Blackwell.

UNESCO Ad Hoc Expert Group on Endangered Languages (2003) *Language Vitality and Endangerment*. Available online at: http://unesdoc.unesco.org/images/0018/001836/183699e.pdf (accessed on 3 June 2017).

Weiner, Michael A. (ed.) (1997) *Japan's Minorities. The Illusion of Homogeneity*. London: Routledge.

Yabiku, Hiroshi (1987) Uchinaa yamatuguchi to yamatu uchinaaguchi [Okinawan Japanese and Japanese Uchinaaguchi]. *Kokubungaku – kaishaku to kanshō* 52(7): 119–123.

Yoshimura, Sayaka (2014) Japanese Language Education in the Meiji Period. In: *Language Crisis in the Ryukyus*. Mark Anderson and Patrick Heinrich (eds), 31–53. Newcastle upon Tyne: Cambridge Scholars Publishing.

25
LANGUAGE RIGHTS

Goro Christoph Kimura

The language rights discourse taking roots in Japan

Since the 1980s "language rights" have advanced from an almost unknown term to a common concept in Japanese sociolinguistics and related fields of research.[1] It is now a key term in discussing issues of linguistic inequality in Japan (Kimura 2010a, 2012). Initially heavily influenced by academic and political discourses abroad, the Japanese discourse on language rights has undergone some evolutions that are also relevant for discussions on language rights outside Japan. In this chapter, I will present the main characteristics of the language rights discourse in Japan, examine its spread in the academia, consider some of its practical achievements and finally their implication for discussions beyond the Japanese context.

"Language rights" made its debut in Japanese sociolinguistics as a concept relating to language conflicts outside Japan. It was introduced to a wider range of readers in the 1970s by the work of Tanaka Katsuhiko, who translated and commented texts touching on language rights in Europe (e.g., Tanaka 1975: 37–55). At that time, any issue dealing with multilingual societies was widely believed to be irrelevant for the study of Japanese sociolinguistics – a country that was then perceived to be linguistically homogeneous. Sociolinguistic key topics at the time were related to script problems and the relation between the standard language and Japanese dialects.

The monolingual self-image of post-war Japan was challenged from the mid-1980s onwards. In particular the 1990s saw a remarkable increase of awareness of and concern with old and new linguistic minorities in Japan. With regard to autochthonous minorities, Prime Minister Nakasone Yasuhiro stated in 1986 that Japan was monoethnic, a remark that crucially spurred the Ainu indigenous people movement. In the following years, the Ainu language drew new interest as a marker of a distinctive ethnicity, and in the 1990s, the Ainu Association of Hokkaido began to promote Ainu language programs.

Things also changed with regard to immigrants at the time. The Immigration Control Law was revised in 1990, allowing descendants of Japanese emigrants (*nikkeijin*) to work in Japan. Mainly due to the increase of *nikkeijin* from Latin American countries like Brazil or Peru, the number of foreign residents officially registered in Japan exceeded 1% of the population by 1992. Contrary to the initial anticipation of the government that the *nikkeijin* would smoothly acculturate to their "country of origin", it became soon clear that many *nikkeijin* faced difficulties with regard to linguistic and cultural integration into Japanese society. Especially the education of *nikkeijin* children constituted a veritable challenge.

These developments met with an internationally growing concern for language rights, spurred by the emerging ethnic conflicts after the end of the Cold War in Eastern Europe and elsewhere. Connecting domestic issues with these international discourses, the first Japanese book on language rights was published in 1999 by a group of young sociolinguists (Gengoken Kenkyū-kai 1999). This publication, including previous translations by Tanaka from the 1980s, translations of recent international academic papers and legal documents as well as discussions on language rights issues in Japan, marks the start of more intensive attention on this matter. From 1999 to 2009 more than 190 Japanese publications, including ten books, dealt with "language rights". The total number of contributors amounts to more than 100 individual authors. From this time, publications discussing language rights in relation to Japan outnumbered publications analyzing language rights abroad. This shows that language rights have taken root in the Japanese context. This manifests also with regard to terminology. There was still variation for the English term "language rights" in Japanese in the 1990s. Often, it was referred to as *gengo kenri*, i.e., literally translating "language" (*gengo*) and "rights" (*kenri*). In the twenty-first century, however, the term *gengoken* has been firmly established in analogy to other types of rights such as *sanseiken* (the right to vote) or *seizonken* (the right to live). The term *gengoken* (language rights) is now used without prior explanation or definition, indicating that it is supposed to be known to academic readers.

Why language rights in Japan?

The discourse of language rights is of particular interest to Japanese sociolinguistics because of the comprehensive perspectives it offers. Since the 1990s, five social groups have been at the center of attention – non-native speakers of English, autochthonous linguistic minorities, immigrants, the Deaf and people having difficulties accessing information (see below). Thus, the discourse of language rights involves autochthonous groups as well as immigrants, members of minorities as well as the majority of Japanese society, interlingual as well as intralingual cases.

Language rights have also led to connecting sociolinguistic issues with other academic disciplines, most notably law studies and sociology. The connection with legal studies has led to the founding of the Japanese Association for Language and Law in 2009. With regard to sociology, discussions on language rights have been linked with disability studies, resulting in an original Japanese development in the study of language rights. We will return to this issue further below.

Language rights have also influenced the study of language planning and policy, in particular on questions of how to deal with Japan's linguistic diversity. Enhancing access to the Japanese society by all inhabitants of Japan as well as recognizing specific identities and communicative needs calls for an alternative to the strategy of either assimilation, excluding or ignoring language minorities. Language rights are thus conceived as a contribution to discussions on multicultural "coexistence" (*kyōsei*), a term that is much discussed in contemporary Japan (see e.g., Ueda and Yamashita 2006). All in all, the concept of language rights can thus be said to have played an important role in raising critical language awareness by pointing to issues that have not been identified as "problems" before.

Personality as basis of language rights

Let us next briefly consider the basis of language rights. In Europe and other regions, language rights are closely related to national or ethnic minority rights. Collective rights have been a topic of intense discussion, because they are inevitably intertwined with issues such as self-determination and autonomy of minorities. However, these issues are marginal at best in the Japanese context. In Japan language rights have been conceived to be part of the general human rights of individuals. Thus, pedagogic or human-developmental considerations occupy an important position (Shibuya 2007; Utada 2008: 148). In Japan human personality development (*jinkaku keisei*) and personality rights (*jinkakuken*) have often served as a point of departure for discussions of language rights. In one of the early papers applying language rights on Japan, Suzuki (1992: 48) argued for the right of Koreans residing in Japan to learn their heritage language as part of their personality right. In a similar vein, Katsuragi (2005b: 51) underlines the importance of language rights in Japan for the reason that "it promotes a better understanding of the role of language in the formation of human personality".

A consequence of seeing personality to be the main basis for language rights is that claims for language rights are not dependent on the existence of autonomous languages. Yamada and Shibuya (2011: 54) argue that the protection of minority or endangered languages should not be confined to the protection of an objective, abstract language model. Rather, the most important legal value to ask for language rights lies in the way speakers position themselves through their use of language, including the relationship with the human community and natural environment surrounding them. It is therefore possible to argue for language rights of code-switching among Japanese returnee children from abroad (Kite 2001) or for the language rights of using dialects in courts of law (Fudano 2012). As a matter of fact, all major developments in the Japanese discourse on language rights are related to discussions on "personality" rather than on "ethnolinguistic groups".

Critical view on the role of English in Japan

Let us look next at the five types of social groups on which discourse on language rights is centered in Japan. One specific feature of the Japanese context is its strong concern with English as an international language. Of course, the inclusion of the international dimension on language rights is not unique to Japan. Robert Phillipson, in particular, is widely known for his criticism on linguistic imperialism (Phillipson 1992; Skutnabb-Kangas and Phillipson 2016). However, while language rights are centered on "national language versus minority language" outside Japan, the matter of English is a dominant topic in Japan. About one-fifth of the language rights literature in Japanese deals with the role of English in Japan.

It has been criticized that too much attention (and too many resources) is spent on English and that this undermines the recognition of other languages in Japan. The preoccupation with English often renders problems of linguistic minorities invisible (Terasima 2005; Matsubara 2007). For example, initiatives to include Ryukyuan languages in school are apt to be confronted with objections of preferring English over Ryukyuan languages in school (Karimata 2006: 93). With regard to immigrants, the discourse of language rights has pointed to the fact that the fixation on English deters their fair treatment because most of them do not speak English as their first language. This notwithstanding, Utsunomiya (2007) reports that knowledge of English is used to exclude migrant languages in court documents.

On the other hand, the right of non-native speakers of English has been claimed for the majority of Japanese society. The dominance of native English is thereby seen to result in violations of non-native language rights. According to Tsuda (2006: 238), language rights can be applied as a counter-theory to the international dominance of powerful languages, especially English. Just like the hegemony of national languages infringes on language rights of minorities in nation-states, the global dominance of English undermines the rights of speakers of national languages such as Japanese in international settings.

Adherents of Esperanto in Japan have also addressed the dominance of English. The Esperanto movement in Japan started discussing language rights already in the 1970s, albeit not in academic settings. Note in this context, that the first ever Japanese book on language rights (Gengoken Kenkyū-kai 1999) is actually the result of an Esperanto initiative (Usui 2008). Furthermore, Esperantists remain involved in various aspects of language rights discourses since then by editing books (e.g., Masiko 2006; Kadoya and Masiko 2017) and organizing symposiums (Kimura and Yoshida 2008).

Autochthonous and immigrant minorities

A more typical case of language rights in an international perspective is the claim for language rights by linguistic minorities in Japan. While there are attempts to consider immigrants, legal frameworks for the protection of language rights have been mainly developed for autochthonous minorities. In Europe, for example, where language rights have a long history, traditional minorities have always occupied a central position. The European Charter for Regional or Minority Languages (Council of Europe 1992) explicitly excludes dialects and immigrant languages. The charter aims to support and extend already existing language rights in those states that have signed the charter. In Japan, on the other hand, the focus has initially been on immigrant languages. There was no public discussion on Ainu or Ryukyu language rights before the new wave of immigration to Japan in the 1990s. Hence, language rights developed simultaneously with regard to autochthonous and immigrant languages. There was no discussion whether regional or immigrant languages should be preferred (Shoji 2010: 43). In the 1990s the Ainu language was conceived of as "extinct" by most, and the Ryukyuan languages were classified as "Japanese dialects", while the languages of the immigrants were labeled "foreign". They all entered the discussion on language rights at the same time and with more or less the same level of attention. One of the early documents addressing language rights is the "Recommendation for creating multicultural and multilingual education in Japan" by the Inter-Group Study Association for Minorities (1991). This recommendation does not distinguish the rights of old and new minority groups, stating that "all linguistic and cultural minorities in Japan have the right to share the Japanese language and culture as well as the languages and cultures of their parents or ancestors" (Shōsūsha-mondai Gurūpu-kan Kenkyū-kai 1991). This position was upheld ever since. As an effect, it is difficult to find publications or recommendations that aim to restrict language rights to autochthonous minorities only. This is seen as strong point of the Japanese approach. According to Shoji (2009: 22), the concentration on autochthonous minorities reveals the limits of "Western European language concepts".

Deaf language rights as a precursor

Language rights for the first time were applied to a concrete human rights issue in Japan following an initiative of the movement for bilingual Deaf education.[2] In 2005, the Japan Federation of Bar Associations issued an opinion paper in response to a request by 107 Deaf children and their parents who demanded the right for bilingual education with Japanese Sign Language and written Japanese (Zenkoku Rōji o Motsu Oya no Kai 2006). In dealing with this case, language rights were examined in the light of the Japanese constitution as well as with regard to laws and treaties accepted by the Japanese government.

The Deaf are not a "typical linguistic minority" for which language rights instruments have internationally been developed. The fact that they took the lead in promoting language rights in Japan is however not surprising if we take the Japanese context into account. Japan's autochthonous minorities initially did not single out language as their central concern. In case of the Ainu, concern for social and economic inequality has been regarded to be more important. In Okinawa, the focus has been placed in the high concentration of US military basis there, rather than on the Ryukyuan languages. The concern for political discrimination was more central than cultural and linguistic issues. Among the so-called "oldcomer" immigrants, the Koreans have been quite keen to preserve their heritage language.[3] Their focus was thereby on the right for ethnic education (*minzoku kyōiku-ken*), together with education in Korean culture and history. One reason for this lies in the simple fact the oldcomer rights movement predates the attention on language rights. With regard to the migrants who arrived after 1990 (the so-called "newcomers"), the main political concern was their legal and social integration into the host society. The unstable transmigration pattern of large parts of the *nikkeijin* community adds to the difficulty of claiming language rights.

We now understand that among the potential groups claiming language rights in Japan, the language rights framework fits the interests of the Deaf best. The Deaf case in Japan is also particular in that it has a well-established network of sign language learners among the hearing. After the start of a training program of sign language volunteers by the Ministry of Health and Welfare in 1970, sign language learner circles were established across Japan. By the 1980s, there were more than 1,000 such groups (Yonekawa 2002: 125). As an effect, the Deaf have supporters among the majority and this makes their arguments more acceptable for the hearing. The relative salience of sign language in Japan has certainly favored the relatively rapid development of Deaf language rights.

Merging with disability studies

The case of the Deaf triggered a development that is probably most characteristic of the Japanese discourse on language rights – its entwinement with disability studies. The concept of disability studies originated in the UK in the 1980s. At its center is the so-called "social model", which sees disability not as caused by "shortcomings" of individuals but as being constructed by society. For example, when a person in a wheelchair cannot enter a building due to it having stairs, the problem lies not in the impairment of the person that hinders them to use stairs, but in taking for granted that every member of society can use stairs. This kind of reasoning constitutes a "sociological turn" in the study of disability. Accordingly, the traditional impulse to seek treatment or to cure the impairment of individuals (the medical or individual model) and which "blames the impaired for the way they are" is replaced by a model that encourages society at large to change.

Disability studies were introduced to Japan at the same time as language rights studies. The first book on disability studies in Japanese was published in 1999 (Ishikawa and Nagase 1999), the same year that saw the first Japanese book on language rights. By questioning the modernist ideal of a homogeneous society (Neustupný 2006), language rights and disability studies share many affinities. Both focus on injustices rooted in social conditions rather than concentrating on "catching up", and they are critical of assimilation strategies of minority/dominated members to the majority/dominant part of society. Abe explains the common assumptions between these two fields of study as follows:

> Sometimes people cannot do the things they want. Until now, this has been regarded a matter of individual efforts. [...] But is it really only a matter of will and effort? Is there not rather a problem in society? This question was the starting point of disability studies. The same applies to language abilities. If one cannot speak the language of

> one's parents or grandparents, the responsibility rests not so much on that person as it does on the social situation.
>
> *(Abe 2015: 148)*

This does not mean that both approaches flatly deny integration into the majority society. Learning the language of the wider society is explicitly included in current language right discourses (Kimura 2010b). The same applies for the social model. Despite questioning the medical model, it does not deny medical approaches and rehabilitation itself (Sugino 2007; Kawashima 2013). Another commonality between the two discourses is a concern with legal aspects. That the study of language rights is linked to legal issues is of course self-evident. Disability studies, too, include legal concerns, as non-discrimination laws constitute a part of the realization of the social model (Sugino 2007: 9).

Following years of similar but parallel developments, both approaches became linked in the mid-2000s. Due to its ability to connect existing rights and provisions for disabled persons, disability studies became rapidly popular in Japanese academia. Scholars involved in language rights realized the similarity between the two approaches, and they began to apply the more widely known and accepted terms of disability studies to argue for language rights. For example, the article on "Language and social inequality" in the *Encyclopedia of Applied Linguistics* mentioned people with disability in line with linguistic minorities. Note also the use of "barrier free", originally linked to disability in relation to language.

> It should be acknowledged that "language rights" are innate rights to human beings regardless of national borders. [...] The realization of *linguistic barrier free* in order to enhance language rights of linguistic minorities, including linguistically disabled people and sign language users, speakers of Ainu and Koreans living in Japan, should not be forgotten.
>
> *(Katagiri 2003: 200–201, emphasis mine)*

Another example is Ota (2005: 74–75), who uses the term "universal design", another term from disability studies when discussing education of newcomer immigrant children in Japan.[4] He states that current education practices see the problem located in the migrant children and argues that universal design encourages people to reflect on the empowerment of these children.

> It is not possible to realize universal design without changing the society that causes "disabilities". In a similar vein, it is necessary to change the education system and school itself, in order to enable children with diverse cultural background to participate in learning without feeling "disabled". To insist that children who do not understand Japanese should first learn Japanese is like forcing a person in a wheelchair to climb steps.
>
> *(Ota 2005: 75)*

These initial steps towards linking language rights to disability studies took a decisive step forward though a collection of papers based on presentations at a conference of the Japanese Association of Sociology for Human Liberation (Masiko 2006). The subtitle of this publication, "Liberation of those weak in accessing information from the viewpoint of language rights", explicitly points to a synthesis of the two discourses. "Weak in [accessing] information" (*jōhō jakusha*) is a term referring to those who have difficulties in accessing information, people with information access disability, if you want. Here, the "access to information" (*jōhō hoshō*) discussed in disability studies is connected to language rights. Masiko (2006: 73), the editor of the volume in question, states that with regard to the significance of language rights for sociology, the most important impact comes from its "rapid approach to disability studies". In mentioning rights claimed by the Deaf – which relativizes the link between language rights and ethnicity – Masiko (2006: 76) argues that "the viewpoint of universal design necessitates a discussion on language rights with a perspective from disability studies". Abe (2006), in the same volume, applies *jōhō jakusha* to "those weak in Chinese characters" (*kanji jakusha*). He demonstrates how the kanji used in the Japanese writing system function as barriers for the blind but also for others, including adult persons attending literacy classes, weak-sighted, persons with dyslexia, the Deaf, persons with developmental disability and generally all those who have not gone to Japanese school.

In the following years literacy became one of the core topics in studies combining language rights and disability studies (Kadoya and Abe 2010). In contrast to the traditional literacy movement, which concentrated on raising the literacy rate, this direction of research focused on societal barriers that exclude various people from access to information. According to Kadoya (2010), the discrimination of illiterates has the same structure as the discrimination of minority language users by the majority. He argues that trying to assimilate them by all means will not solve their problems (Kadoya 2010: 27). According to Abe, the objective of literacy movement should therefore be redefined as

> struggling to enhance information services as language rights, and promoting universal design of information in order to construct a society in which "illiteracy" or "reading disabilities" no longer disable social life.
>
> *(Abe 2012: 21–33)*

The "linguocentrism" of the language rights paradigm itself is criticized by Kadoya (2008: 31), who, having communicative disabled in mind, states that "it is necessary to radically reconstitute language rights so as to include communicative problems that have been out of consideration in language rights discourse so far". Abe (2009) includes "language" itself as a possible barrier that can hinder the social participation of those "weak in language". Towards this end he argues for a "universal design of language rights" that also includes liberation from "linguocentrist" ideas and practices.

To sum up, disability studies resulted in the reexamination of the concept of language rights and resulted in a Japanese discourse that differs from that in other countries. While language rights outside of Japan can be typically characterized as "multilingualism oriented language rights", the discourse in Japan can be said to focus on "disability-oriented language rights" (Kimura 2012).

Spread of disability-oriented language rights in the academia

Language rights is a common term in Japanese sociolinguistics today. Let us examine next how well known the recently developed disability-oriented language rights approach is in Japan. In order to assess its scope, I will consider its reception in Japanese sociolinguistic scholarship as well as in neighboring disciplines.

Disability-oriented language rights is an idea that was mainly developed in the journal *Shakai gengogaku* (*Sociolinguistics*). The journal functions as a node in a network of researchers studying language rights and information accessibility. While the idea was initially confined to the small circle of editors of the journal, it gradually expanded into other sociolinguistic journals and associations. Consider as examples two academic societies engaged in sociolinguistics that have their own journals. First, disability-oriented language rights has merged with and become part of "welfare linguistics", an idea proposed by the first president of the Japanese Association of Sociolinguistic Studies, Tokugawa Munemasa (Kimura 2010b; Matsuo et al. 2013). Symposiums and panels at conferences of the association have taken up this topic repeatedly. Second, the Japan Association for Language Policy has also shown increasing concern with policy as a means to enhance accessibility, and it has dealt with this topic in various meetings. Its annual conferences now include a regular session on information accessibility (jōhō hoshō). It is safe to say that the idea of disability-oriented language rights has made its entry into different major sociolinguistic associations and that it represents today an important topic of Japanese sociolinguistics. This can also be seen in the presentation of language rights in a popular textbook on intercultural communication in Japan:

> Language rights are mainly targeting ethnic languages. Yet, blind people, weak-sighted and elderly people who cannot rely on written characters, the users of Japanese Sign Language who cannot rely on voices, are not guaranteed sufficient social life because of language. They can therefore also be regarded as being linguistically discriminated. [Acknowledging] this opens the perspective for guaranteeing language rights to them.
>
> (Maruyama 2010: 63)

Beyond sociolinguistics, discussions on language rights by Japanese jurists are now also including the viewpoint of disability. Sugimoto (2014), for example, mentions people with disability in a paper where he discusses language rights in relation to the Japanese constitution. Oumi (2014: 226–227), dealing with language rights as part of international human rights, states that "there are commonalities, on the one hand, in the problems faced not only by the Deaf and other people with disabilities and in problems of linguistic minorities, on the other hand". She furthermore takes up legal documents on disability and discusses the similarity of rights claims of linguistic minorities and of disabled people.

Such a solid link of language rights to disability studies does not exist in language rights discourses in English, except for the case of language rights discussions on sign languages (e.g., Ball 2011; Trovato 2013). Among sociolinguistic contributions, Wee (2011: 196–197) is exceptional for referring to the disabled. However, the reference here is not the relation of disabled rights and language rights but the contrast between them. Wee, critical of essentialism in conceptions of language, is actually rather essentialist in his conception of disability, which he sees as an impairment of individuals. This viewpoint is quite different from social constructivist disability studies. Also, in law studies outside of Japan, language rights have not been connected to disability studies. For example, in her comprehensive study on language rights, Mowbray (2012) does not mention any documents related to disability.

In Japanese disability studies, information accessibility has been one of its major practical concerns. The Japan Society for Disability Studies seeks to guarantee accessibility not only physically, but also with regard to information for its members, and it has compiled a guideline for its conferences and meetings towards this end. This notwithstanding, it retains little involvement in linguistic accessibility. "Language" as a topic is basically exclusively related to sign language. In disability studies in Japan and outside of Japan, language constitutes an important topic, but it is mainly concerned with terminology and how disability is discussed (Mallett and Slater 2014; Stevens 2013).

In sum, we can say that the language disability rights discourse is now a prominent and well-established topic in Japanese sociolinguistics and juridical discourses on language rights, but that it has not yet spread beyond these disciplines and remains confined to discussions in Japanese.

Japanese possible contributions to international language rights discussions

Let us examine next how the language rights conception informed by disabilities studies can contribute to discussion on language rights on a general level. Language rights are one of the most prominent, but also highly contested notions, in discussions on language and social inequality. While proponents of linguistic human rights see the establishment of universal language rights as essential for protecting linguistic diversity, others are skeptical about the effectiveness of such an approach. Let us consider two recent monographs in English, which highlight the main shortcomings of language rights, namely the tendencies of essentialism and of imposing restrictions (Wee 2011; Pupavac 2012). On the basis of the insights gained thereby, I will then discuss how language rights studies in Japan can contribute to the development of the field in theoretical and methodological terms.

Wee (2011: 71–73) summarizes three problems that are common in language rights discourses (published in English). To start, they focus on discrimination between languages but underestimate discrimination within a given language. Second, they assume that the best way to protect language rights is to elevate its status. Third, language is treated as a bounded entity. Wee (2011: 45) sees the latter assumption as "the most serious problem with the notion of language rights". In short, the principal problem of language rights is that it presupposed fixed ideas on language and identity, ignoring thereby the fluid and hybrid character of language use and identity construction.

The criticism raised by Wee certainly applies to the multilingualism-oriented language rights, which typically seeks to provide a certain status to a certain language. It does not apply to the disability-oriented conception of language rights for two main reasons. The disability-oriented language rights approach deconstructs the homogeneity of language and language users and this allows for discussions of inequality within a language and for addressing extra-lingual issues. Second, the shift to the social model places the focus of attention on the majority. Rather than trying to empower the minority (by granting them or their language a higher status), it seeks to disempower the majority. This direction is clearly present in Plain Japanese (*yasashii nihongo*), which seeks to provide information in a manner comprehensible also to those who are "weak in Japanese" (Iori, Lee and Mori 2013). Furthermore, the concept of universal design calls for more flexibility, and not single solutions, which will always favor some individuals and disfavor others. Disability-oriented language rights results in an "infinite process" of monitoring and correcting discriminations (Kadoya 2010: 61; Abe 2011). Increasing the range of choices is supreme. Third, for the language disability rights discourse, not the existence of a distinct language variety is the basis for rights, but the disablement of persons. From this point of view, Kadoya (2013) criticizes attempts to "prove" that sign language is a proper language in its own rights in order to ensure language rights for the Deaf.

The disability discourse re-conceptualizes language rights, and in so doing, transcends problems of essentialism that are so strongly associated with language rights. The term "language right" acquires a whole different meaning. This is no longer a discourse that "language A should have the status B". Contrary to the claims of Wee (2011), the study of language rights can very well be non-essentialist (see also the above-mentioned rights to code-switching and to dialects).

Yet another critique to the study of language rights is that it is restrictive, because it aims at predefined norms that prohibit liberal expressions (Pupavac 2012). Pupavac claims that institutionalized language rights regimes impose views of (external) experts to local contexts and thereby hinders democratic participation on the local level. This view is also expressed by Wee, who proposes a deliberative democratic model instead of predefined language rights.

Table 25.1 Comparing multilingual and disability-oriented language rights

	Multilingualism-oriented language rights	*Disability-oriented language rights*
Perception of language problems	Inequality among "languages"	Disability of individuals
Prescriptions	Constructing a homogeneous language and providing it with a status	Questioning of the homogeneity of dominant language and offering new choices
Implementation	Defining and enacting unified norms	Gradual changes through deliberation

Wee (2011: 177) states that "problems involving intralanguage discrimination or differences in discourse style and literacy practices can all be opened up for serious discussion within the deliberative democratic model". Note, however, that this has already been realized in the language rights discourse in Japan. Utada (2012) sees deliberative processes not as being opposed to language rights, but as reciprocally helpful. He proposes to utilize language rights as instruments to improve the deliberative process, on the one hand, and to make language rights a matter of deliberative democratic processes, on the other. In this context, the basic consensus of disability studies of "Nothing about us without us", that is, the involvement of the voices of those concerned is essential (Cameron and Moore 2014: 38). Tanaka, Haruhara and Yamada (2012) and Sasaki (2014) are recent examples of studies that include voices of people who are disabled in a linguistic sense.

Disability-oriented language rights transcend the limitations of the multilingual language rights discourse. The contrast between these two approaches can be summarized as depicted in Table 25.1.

There are of course limitations to the international applicability of the language rights discussions that have evolved in Japan. Also, Paulston (2003: 480) has a point in arguing that it is best to conceptualize language rights as emic rather than universal. Due attention needs to be placed on the many different local and cultural contexts. In Japan, for example, the special focus on literacy is beyond doubt an outcome of the Japanese writing system. The so-called "national language and script problem" (*kokugo kokuji mondai*) has been regarded a central issue of language policy for many decades.

Practical achievements

Thus far, we have dealt only with academic discourses. Our final consideration is dedicated to questions of practical impacts. We cannot yet speak of any significant social impact of the language rights discourses to Japanese society at large. For example, for the vast majority of Japanese nationals English is seen to be beneficial for them in a globalizing world, so that language rights claims pointing to the problem of inequality emerging from using English in globalizing contexts have not attracted much support. Yet critical voices addressing linguistic inequalities caused by English as an international language have now spread outside the confined circles of specialists and has been discussed in a popular paperback publication (Se 2015).

There still is no court decision mentioning language rights in Japan. No law exists that explicitly guarantees language rights, and there is no administrative document dealing with language rights. In 1997 the Diet passed a "Law for the promotion of Ainu culture and the dissemination and advocacy of knowledge in respect of Ainu traditions", and in 2006 the Prefectural Assembly of Okinawa approved a regulation to declare 18 September as "Community Language Day". Both include clauses to promote the languages in question. Both cases are achievement of ethnic and linguistic movements, but neither mentions any kind of language rights. Yet we can find that experts have used the notion of language rights in order to argue for new policies on Ainu and Ryukyuan languages (Kimura 2010b). Also, on immigrant language rights, policy papers that include law drafts have been presented (Nihongo Kyōiku Seisaku Masutāpuran Kenkyūkai 2010; Nisihara 2010). Language rights have therefore reached the stage where policies are discussed and made.

With regard to disability-oriented language rights, the above-mentioned request for the right to Japanese Sign Language medium education attracted much public attention. It also resulted in 2008 in the establishment of an officially recognized private Deaf school that uses Japanese Sign Language as medium of instruction. This is the first time that Japanese nationals are educated in a minority language within the education system of modern Japan. It had a strong impact on deaf education in Japan that had so far relied exclusively on auditory-oral methods (Kanazawa 2013: 198–200).

In the process of examining the Deaf case, the legal basis of language rights in Japan was examined. Thereby arguments were elaborated that are also applicable to other linguistic minorities in Japan (Shibuya and Kojima 2007). Kimura (2010b) and Koishi (2012) point out that the experience and arguments of the Deaf case can be fruitfully applied to other minority languages as well. For example, the now practiced splitting of the obligatory school subject *kokugo* (national language) into "sign language" and "Japanese" could be applied also to other minority language aiming at bilingual education.

To turn to another area, the discourse on language rights and disability studies has been taken up by librarians in Japan in order to enhance multicultural services with the same logic in which they have been servicing disabled people in libraries since the 1970s (Abe 2010: 259, 2015: 26). These efforts are grassroots-driven and gradual, which is why they have not drawn much attention so far. We can also see in these efforts a concern to not offend the majority. According to Kadoya (2012: 156), gradualism (*yuruyakasa*) is crucial. He argues that through gradual processes of considering the rights of those weak in accessing information (*jōhō jakusha*) the "happy illusion" of the majority that their power is sustained will remain intact. In such a way, the majority society will change calmly, but radically in the long run.

Outlook

In this chapter, we have seen how language rights have been increasingly adapted to linguistic problems in Japan. In questioning the hegemony of the Japanese language on a national level and that of English on an international plane, the discourses on language rights have been trying to undo what Miura (2000) aptly terms "double monolingualism" in Japanese society. Furthermore, the Deaf case functioned as a trigger to link the language rights discourse with disability studies. This resulted in what we have named here "disability-oriented language rights". It led to an expansion of the range of study, which now also includes individuals linguistically disabled due to social structures and conditions.

The future of this type of language rights is still uncertain. Yet, recent developments suggest that it can be more prevalent, both in Japan and on an international plane. Internationally, the Convention on the Rights of Persons with Disabilities (CRPD), which was adopted by the United Nations General Assembly in 2006 and implemented in 2008, is influenced by the social model and intertwines language rights with accessibility with regard to the Deaf. Departing from individual perspectives, it shows a different model than the "classical" language rights model based on recognition of certain languages (Ball 2011). This development could well lead to reexamining the concept of language rights and to develop it more into the direction of the Japanese discourse.

In Japan, as a result of the CRPD, a revised Basic Act for Persons with Disabilities was approved in July 2011. This is the first law in Japan to acknowledge Japanese Sign Language as a language: "Every person with disabilities, wherever possible, shall be ensured opportunities to choose his or her language (including sign language) and/or other means of communication [...]".[5] Furthermore, Tottori Prefecture approved the first regulation (by-law) on Japanese Sign Language in October 2013. It states that it is the responsibility of the prefecture and other public administrations to enhance the use of sign language. By the end of 2016, 73 prefectures and municipalities in Japan have adopted similar regulations. The number is set to further increase. It is also noteworthy that by March 2016 all local assemblies in Japan have approved that Japan needs to have a sign language law. This is once more demonstrating the vast support for sign language in contemporary Japan.

With regard to disability, the Diet passed an act on the Elimination of Disability Discrimination in 2013 in preparation for the ratification of the Convention on the Rights of Persons with Disabilities in the same year. It will be interesting to see how concepts such as that addressing "reasonable accommodation" can also be applied to language rights issues outside the realm of disability (Oumi 2014; Abe 2015: 32, 134–136). On the other hand, a one-sided reliance on disability studies and the neglect of multilingual aspects in Japan would be problematic. There is criticism to the recent legislations on sign language in Japan, as they often do not distinguish between Japanese Sign Language and manually coded Japanese (Kojima 2012).[6] The question how to connect the multilingual and disability-oriented language rights remains unresolved, and it will become a major challenge for the further development of language rights in Japan.

Notes

1. This chapter is partly based on Kimura (2010a), which presented mainly the development and limits of multilingualism-oriented language rights in Japan, and on Kimura (2015), which focused on the development of disability-oriented language rights.
2. The use of capital D is to mark that the claim here is raised for the Deaf from a socio-cultural point of view.
3. The term "oldcomer" refers to non-ethnic Japanese coming to the Japanese islands before the middle of the twentieth century, especially from the regions colonized or occupied under the Japanese empire.
4. "Universal design" is used for products and buildings that are usable or accessible for everyone, regardless of age, impairment and other distinguishing characteristics.
5. Translation from Japanese Law Translation (www.japaneselawtranslation.go.jp/law/detail/?id=2436&vm=04&re=02).
6. Japanese Sign Language is the language that evolved among the Deaf, while manually coded Japanese is the signed version of the Japanese language. The former has its own structures and expressions whereas the latter follows the grammar and wording of oral Japanese.

References

Abe, Yasushi (2006) Kanji to iu shōgai [Chinese Characters as a Barrier]. In: *Kotoba, kenryoku, sabetsu*. Hidenori Masiko (ed.), 131–163, Tokyo: Sangensha.

——— (2009) Gengo to iu shōgai [Language as a Barrier]. *Shakai gengogaku* 9: 233–251.

―――― (2010) Shikiji mondai no shōgaigaku – shikijikatsudō to kōkyō toshokan o musubu [Disability Studies of Literacy Problems. Bridging Literacy Activities and Public Libraries]. In: *Shikiji no shakai gengogaku*. Hidenori Kadoya and Yasushi Abe (eds), 257–283. Tokyo: Seikatsu Shoin.

―――― (2011) Nihongo hyōki no saikentō – jōhō akusesuken, yunibāsaru dezain no shiten kara [Rethinking Japanese Writing System. From the Viewpoint of the Right to Access to Information and Universal Design]. *Shakai gengogaku* (special issue) 1: 97–116.

―――― (2012) "Shikji" to iu shakai seido ["Literacy" as a Social System]. *Shakai gengogaku* 12: 21–33.

―――― (2015) *Kotoba no bariafurī – jōhōhoshō to komyunikēshon no shōgaigaku* [Barrier Free Language. Disability Studies of Information Accessibility and Communication]. Tokyo: Seikatsu Shoin.

Ball, Andrea R. (2011) Equal Accessibility for Sign Language under the Convention on the Rights of Persons with Disabilities. *Case Western Reserve Journal of International Law* 43: 759–798.

Cameron, Colin and Michele Moore (2014) Disability Studies. In: *Disability Studies. A Student's Guide*. Colin Cameron (ed.), 37–40. Los Angeles: SAGE.

Fudano, Kazuo (2012) *Hōtei ni okeru hōgen – "rinshō kotobagaku" no tachiba kara* [Dialects in the Court. From the Viewpoint of Clinical Linguistics]. Osaka: Izumi Shoin.

Gengoken Kenkyū-kai (1999) *Kotoba e no kenri – gengoken to wa nanika* [Rights to Language. What Are Language Rights?]. Tokyo: Sangensha.

Iori, Isao, Younsuk Lee and Atsushi Mori (eds) (2013) *"Yasashii nihongo wa nani o mezasuka – tabunka kyōsei shakai o jitsugen suru tame ni* [What Does "Plain Japanese" Aim at? To Realize a Multicultural Society]. Tokyo: CoCo Shuppan.

Ishikawa, Jun and Osamu Nagase (eds) (1999) *Shōgaigaku e no shōtai* [Invitation to Disability Studies]. Tokyo: Akashi Shoten.

Kadoya, Hidenori (2008) Gengoken gainen no hihanteki kōsatsu [Critical Thoughts on Language Rights]. (Paper presented at the 10th Conference of the Japanese Association for Language Policy, Nara, 9 November 2008).

―――― (2010) Nihon no shikiji undō saikō [Rethinking the Literacy Movement in Japan]. In: *Shikiji no shakai gengogaku*. Hidenori Kadoya and Yashushi Abe (eds), 25–82. Tokyo: Seikatsu Shoin.

―――― (2012) Shikiji, jōhō no yunibāsaru dezain to iu kōsō – shikiji, gengoken, shōgaigaku [The Concept of Universal Design Applied to Literacy and Information. Literacy, Language Rights and Disability Studies]. *Kotoba to shakai* 14: 141–159.

―――― (2013) Shohyō. Michiko Sasaki (ed.) *Rōsha kara mita "tabunka kyōsei"* [Book Review. Michiko Sasaki (ed.) Multiculturalism from the Viewpoint of the Deaf]. *Shakai gengogaku* 13: 175–186.

Kadoya, Hidenori and Yasushi Abe (eds) (2010) *Shikiji no shakai gengogaku* [Sociolinguistics of Literacy]. Tokyo: Seikatsu Shoin.

Kadoya, Hidenori and Hidenori Masiko (eds.) (2017) *Kōdō suru shakai gengogaku* [Engaged Sociolinguistics]. Tokyo: Sangensha.

Kanazawa, Takayuki (2013) *Shuwa no shakaigaku – kyōiku genba e no shuwa dōnyū ni okeru tōjishasei o megutte* [Sociology of Sign Language. About the Persons Concerned to Introduce Sign Language into School]. Tokyo: Seikatsu Shoin.

Karimata, Shigehisa (2006) Ryūkyūgo no fukken [Revival of the Ryukyuan Language]. In: *Ima sekai no kotoba ga abunai – gurōbaruka to shōsūsha no gengo* [World's Languages are in Danger. Globalization and Minority Languages]. Osahito Miyaoka (ed.), 83–93. Tokyo: Kubapro.

Katagiri, Kuniyoshi (2003) Gengo to shakaiteki fubyōdō [Language and Social Inequality]. In: *Ōyō gengogaku jiten*. Ikuo Koike (ed.), 200–201. Tokyo: Kenkyūsha.

Katsuragi, Takao (2005) Japanese Language Policy from the Point of View of Public Philosophy. *International Journal of the Sociology of Language* 175/176: 41–54.

Kawashima, Satoshi (2013) Kenri jōyaku jidai no shōgaigaku – shakai moderu o ikashi koeru [Disability Studies in the Epoch of the Convention on the Rights of Persons with Disabilities. Applying and Transcending the Social Model]. In: *Shōgaigaku no rihabiritēshon*. Toshiji Kawagoe, Satoshi Kawashima and Ryuji Hoshika (eds), 90–117. Tokyo: Seikatsu Shoin.

Kimura, Goro Christoph (2010a). Language Rights in Japan. What is it Good For? In: *Language Life in Japan*. Patrick Heinrich and Christian Galan (eds), 14–33. London: Routledge.

―――― (2010b) Nihon ni okeru "gengoken" no juyō to tenkai [Adoption and Development of "Language Rights" in Japan]. *Shakai gengokagaku* 13(1): 4–18.

―――― (2012) Gengoken kara mita nihon no gengo mondai [Language Problems in Japan Seen from the Perspective of Language Rights]. In: *Tagengo-shugi saikō*. Yukitoshi Sunano (ed.), 687–709. Tokyo: Sangensha.

––––––– (2015) Shogaigaku-teki gengokenron no tenbō to kadai [Issues and Perspectives of Disability Oriented Language Rights]. *Shakai gengogaku* 15: 1–18.
Kimura, Goro Christoph and Naoko Yoshida (eds) (2008) *Al justa lingvopolitiko en Azio – Aktoj de la 5a Nitobe-Simpozio / Towards Equitable Language Policy in Asia – Proceedings of the 5th Nitobe Symposium.* Tokyo: European Institute at Sophia University and Japana Esperanto-Instituto.
Kite, Yuriko (2001) English-Japanese Codeswitching among Students in an International High School. In: *Studies in Japanese Bilingualism*. Mary Goebel Noguchi and Sandra Fotos (eds), 312–328. Clevedon: Multilingual Matters.
Kojima, Isamu (2012) Gengoken o meguru michinori [The Way towards Language Rights]. In: *Rōsha kara mita "tabunka kyōsei"*. Michiko Sasaki (ed.), 78–92. Tokyo: CoCo Shuppan.
Koishi, Atsuko (2012) Gengo kyōiku no kore kara [Future of Language Education]. In: *Rōsha kara mita "tabunka kyōsei"*. Michiko Sasaki (ed.), 252–283. Tokyo: CoCo Shuppan.
Mallett, Rebecca and Jenny Slater (2014) Language. In: *Disability Studies. A Student's Guide*. Colin Cameron (ed.), 91–94. Los Angeles: SAGE.
Maruyama, Masazumi (2010) Gengoken to tagenshakai [Language Rights and Social Diversity]. In: *Yoku wakaru ibunka komyunikēshon*. Richiko Ikeda (ed.), 62–63. Kyoto: Miverva Shobō.
Masiko, Hidenori (ed.) (2006) *Kotoba, kenryoku, sabetsu [Language, Power and Discrimination]*. Tokyo: Sangensha.
––––––– (2006) Gengoken no shakaigakuteki igi [Sociological Significance of Language Rights]. In: *Kotoba, kenryoku, sabetsu*. Hidenori Masiko (ed.), 65–78. Tokyo: Sangensha.
Matsubara, Koji (2007) Gengoteki mainoritī no tame no gengo seisaku – shōsū gengo washa no gengoken o motomete [Language Policy for Linguistic Minorities. In Search for Minority Language Rights]. *Shōnan Kokusai Joshi Daigaku kiyō* 15: 129–141.
Matsuo, Shin, Akiyoshi Kikuchi, J.F. Morris, Jo Matsuzaki; Ayako Uchinami (Koga), Yasushi Abe, Kazunari Iwata, Katsuichiro Nunō, Yufuko Takashima, Norie Oka, Rie Teshima and IkuyoMorimoto (2013) Shakai sanka no tameno jōhōhoshō to "wakariyasui nihongo" – gaikokujin, rōsha, nanchōsha, chiteki shōgaisha e no jōhōhoshō no kobetsu kadai to kyōtsū-sei [Guaranteeing Equal Access to Information and Plain Japanese as a Means of Equal Participation for Everyone. Specific Problems and Shared Aspects between Foreigners, Deaf and Hard-of-hearing People, and People with Intellectual Disabilities]. *Shakai gengokagaku* 16(1): 22–38.
Miura, Nobutaka (2000) Shokuminchi jidai to posuto-shokuminchi jidai no gengo shihai [Language Dominance in the Era of Colonialism and Postcolonialism]. In: *Gengo teikoku shugi to wa nanika*. Nobutaka Miura and Keisuke Kasuya (eds), 6–24. Tokyo: Fujiwara Shoten.
Mowbray, Jacqueline (2012) *Linguistic Justice. International Law and Language Policy*. Oxford University Press.
Neustupný, Jiří V. (2006) Sociolinguistic Aspects of Social Modernization. In: *Sociolinguistics. An International Handbook of the Science of Language and Society*. Ulrich Ammon, Norbert Dittmar, Klaus J. Mattheier and Peter Trudgill (eds), 2209–2223. Berlin: Walter de Gruyter.
Nihongo Kyōiku Seisaku Masutāpuran Kenkyūkai (2010) *Nihongo kyōiku de tsukuru shakai [Building Society through Japanese Language Education]*. CoCo Shuppan.
Nishihara, Suzuko (2010) Teijū gaikokujin no kyōiku tō ni kansuru seisaku kondankai (dai 4 kai) no tame no shiryō [Paper for the 4th Meeting for Education of Foreigners Living in Japan]. Available online at: www.mext.go.jp/b_menu/shingi/chousa/kokusai/008/shiryou/1292162.htm (accessed 20 September 2017).
Ota, Haruo (2005) Nihonteki monokaruchurarizumu to gakushū konnan [Learning Difficulties in Japanese Monoculturalism]. In: *Gaikokujin no kodomo to nihon no kyōiku – fushūgaku to tabunka kyōsei no kadai*. Takashi Miyajima and Haruo Ota (eds), 57–75. Tokyo: Tokyo University Press.
Oumi, Miho (2014) Kokusai jinken-hō kara miru gengo no kenri [Language Rights from the Viewpoint of International Human Rights Law]. In: *Gurōbarizumu ni tomonau shakai henyō to gengo seisaku*. Reiko Tomiya, Guoyue Peng and Masanori Tsutsumi (eds), 225–249. Tokyo: Hituzi Shobō.
Paulston, Christina Bratt (2003) Language Policies and Language Rights. In: *Sociolinguistics. Essential Readings*. Christina Bratt Paulston and Richard G. Tucker (eds), 472–483. Malden: Blackwell.
Phillipson, Robert (1992) *Linguistic Imperialism*. Oxford: Oxford University Press.
Pupavac, Vanessa (2012) *Language Rights. From Free Speech to Linguistic Governance*. Basingstoke: Palgrave Macmillan.
Sasaki, Michiko (2014) *Mainoritī no shakaisanka – shōgaisha to tayō na riterashī [Social Participation of Minorities. Disabled Persons and Diverse Literacy]*. Tokyo: Kuroshio Shuppan.
Se, Teruhisa (2015) *Eigoka wa guminka [Englishization Means Stupidifying People]*. Tokyo: Shueisha Shinsho.

Shibuya, Kenjiro (2007) Gengoken no rironteki shomondai [Theoretical Problems of Language Rights]. In: *Gengoken no riron to jissen*. Kenjiro Shibuya and Isamu Kojima (eds), 15–101. Tokyo: Sangensha.

Shibuya, Kenjiro and Isamu Kojima (eds) (2008) *Gengoken no riron to jissen* [*The Practice and Theory of Language Rights*]. Tokyo: Sangensha.

Shoji, Hiroshi (2009) Tagengoka to gengo keikan [Multilingualization and Multilingual Landscape]. In: *Nihon no gengo keikan*. Hiroshi Shoji, Peter Backhaus and Florian Coulmas (eds), 17–52. Tokyo: Sangensha.

―――― (2010) "Shisan to shite no bogo" kyōiku no tenkai no kanōsei [Perspectives and Possibilities of Education of "Mother Tongue as an Asset"]. *Kotoba to shakai* 12: 7–47.

Skutnabb-Kangas, Tove and Robert Phillipson (eds) (2016) *Language Rights*. London: Routledge.

Shōsūsha-mondai Gurūpu-kan Kenkyū-kai (1991) Nihon ni okeru tabunka, tagengo kyōiku sōzō ni kansuru sengen [Recommendation for Creating Multicultural and Multilingual Education in Japan]. *RAIK tsūshin* 18: 32.

Stevens, Carolyn S. (2013) *Disability in Japan*. London: Routledge.

Sugimoto, Atsushi (2014) Saikō – gengo to kenpōgaku [Rethinking Language and Constitutional Law]. *Tokyo Kokusai Daigaku ronsō* 20: 53–71.

Sugino, Akihiro (2007) *Shōgaigaku – riron keisei to shatei* [*Disability Studies. Theory Making and Range*]. Tokyo: Tokyo University Press.

Suzuki, Toshikazu (1992) Shōsūgo no kenri ni tsuite – zainichi chōsenjin no gengoken o megutte [Rights of Minority Languages. On Language Rights of Koreans in Japan]. *Risshō hōgaku ronshū* 25(1/4): 25–49.

Tanaka, Katsuhiko (1975) *Gengo no shisō* [*Thoughts on Language*]. Tokyo: NHK Shuppan.

Tanaka, Nozomi; Ken'ichirō Haruhara and Izumi Yamada (eds) (2012) *Ikiru chikara o tsuchikau kotoba – gengoteki mainoritī ga "koe o motsu" tame ni* [*Language for Living. How Linguistic Minorities can "Have a Voice"*]. Tokyo: Taishūkan Shoten.

Terasima, Takayoshi (2005) Shōgakkō "eigo katsudō" no nani ga mondai nanoka [What is the Problem with "English Activities" in Elementary School?]. In: *Shōgakkō de no eigo kyōiku wa hitsuyō nai!* Yukio Otsu (ed.), 55–74. Tokyo: Keio University Press.

Trovato, Sara (2013) A Stronger Reason for the Right to Sign Languages. *Sign Language Studies* 13(3): 401–422.

Tsuda, Yukio (2006) *Eigo shihai to kotoba no byōdō* [*Dominance of English and Linguistic Equality*]. Tokyo: Keio University Press.

Ueda, Koji and Hitoshi Yamashita (eds) (2006) *"Kyōsei" no naijitsu* [*A Critical View on "Multiculturalism"*]. Tokyo: Sangensha.

Usui, Hiroyuki (2008) Interlinguistics and Esperanto Studies in the Social Context of Modern Japan. *Language Problems & Language Planning* 32(2): 181–202.

Utada, Hideto (2008) Shohyō. Kenjiro Shibuya and Isamu Kojima (eds.) Gengoken no riron to jissen [Book Review. Kenjiro Shibuya and Isamu Kojima (eds.) Language Rights. Theory and Practice]. *Shakai gengogaku* 8: 145–156.

―――― (2012) Shohyō. Lionel Wee Language without Rights [Book Review. Lionel Wee Language without Rights]. *Shakai gengogaku* 12: 175–187.

Utsunomiya, Hideto (2007) Minji saiban jitsumu to gengoken no jissen [Language Rights in Civil Trials]. In: *Gengoken no riron to jissen*. Kenjiro Shibuya and Isamu Kojima (eds), 142–170. Tokyo: Sangensha.

Wee, Lionel (2011) *Language without Rights*. Oxford: Oxford University Press.

Yamada, Takao and Kenjiro Shibuya (2011) Gengoken no kanten kara mita kiki gengo mondai [Endangered Languages from the Viewpoint of Language Rights]. In: *Essentials in Ryukyuan Language Documentation*. Patrick Heinrich and Michinori Shimoji (eds), 42–66. Tokyo: ILCAA.

Yonekawa, Akihiko (2002) *Shuwa to iu kotoba* [*Sign Language as Language*]. Tokyo: PHP Shinsho.

Zenkoku Rōji wo Motsu Oya no Kai (2006) *Rō-kyōiku ga kawaru!* [*Deaf Education Will Change!*]. Tokyo: Akashi Shoten.

PART V

Research overviews

26
LANGUAGE LIFE (*GENGO SEIKATSU*)

Patrick Heinrich

Introduction

The study of language life (*gengo seikatsu*) is a well-known example of a precursor of (western) sociolinguistics (*shakai gengogaku*) in Japan. Its development, objective and results remain helpful for understanding Japanese sociolinguistics today. An examination of language life is also important with regard to how cultural-specific (emic) aspects can be put into perspective with universal (etic) aspects of language and society. In this chapter, I first describe the background from which the study of language life emerged. This is followed by an account of the research conducted before 1945, then by a summary of works that are characteristic for language life studies after 1945. The study of language life gave way to the study of sociolinguistics from the 1990s onwards. This notwithstanding, the legacy of language life continues to influence Japanese sociolinguistics to this day, and this chapter concludes with a brief outlook on this and an assessment of the legacy of language life studies in contemporary Japanese sociolinguistics.

Pre-war studies of language life

Following the establishment of linguistics as a modern academic discipline in Japan at the end of the nineteenth century, genealogy, phonology, grammar (*bunpō*) and dialectology became the first focal points of research. These were pressing linguistic issues for the modernization of Japan, which sought to clarify and demystify its relations to other nations (through the study of genealogy) and needed to unify and standardize its language (Doi 1976). A commission was tasked to conduct basic research for the modernization of Japanese. Between 1902 and 1917 the National Language Research Council (*Kokugo chōsa i'inkai*) conducted a number of surveys where methodologies of descriptive linguistics, philology, dialectology and folklore studies were mixed and applied (MKK 1949: 65–68). These studies testify the high level and innovativeness of Japanese linguistics in the early twentieth century. They were seen to be crucial in order to solve existing language problems, at time widely discussed as *kokugo mondai* (national language problems). Before 1945, a total of 71 books were published on *kokugo mondai*, accompanied by 112 books on problems of script and writing (*mojigaku*) (Yamada 1942; Hirai 1998[1948]). These publications amount for 20% of the total book publications on linguistics before 1945. Concern for social and linguistic problems led to large-scale empirical research initiatives by the

National Language Research Council, and these then came to play a fundamental role for the emergence of the Japanese tradition of *gengo seikatsu*.

Language life studies owe much to the study of Japanese dialects. Japanese dialectology initially limited itself almost exclusively to contemporary and synchronic surveys. These studies subsequently led to examinations on who actually spoke dialect (and who spoke Standard Japanese). The interrelation of macro-sociological categories such as age, sex/gender and educational background, on the one hand, and language use, on the other hand, received increasingly more attention. At the same time when Japanese dialectology turned "more social", the concept of *seikatsu* (life, or livelihood) emerged as an important concept in the social sciences in Japan. Reflecting the liberal spirit of the Taishō Period (1912–1926), *seikatsu* complemented the macro-categories of *kokumin* (Japanese national) or *shimin* (citizen). By focusing on life or livelihood as such, Japanese social sciences sought to detach their studies from nation-imagination ideology and the rights and obligations associated with citizenship. The pre-war life studies in Japanese social sciences focused on mundane, everyday activities that were shaping the lives of ordinary people (Takeda 2013). Language was of course an integral part of such activities, and it was therefore only a question of time until linguistics discovered the appeal of *seikatsu* studies for their own discipline. The first linguist to explicitly use the concept of *seikatsu* and to relate it to linguistic issues was Kindaichi Kyōsuke who wrote:

> Life is one harmonious and congruent unity, and just as one can consider analyzing the economic life, the religious life, the social life, the intellectual life, the aesthetic life, the sexual life etc. in a unified way, one can also consider regarding language life (*gengo seikatsu*) as one such abstract entity.
>
> *(Kindaichi 1933: 35)*

By coining the term *gengo seikatsu*, Kindaichi provided for one of the most important key terms of Japanese linguistics of the Shōwa Period (1926–1989). He established in Japan an indigenous tradition of sociolinguistics, one that predated the start of such studies in the US and Europe by three decades. Two factors were decisive for the success and the prominence of language life studies in Japan before 1945. First, a heightened awareness of language problems in Japan – an effect of the unparalleled quick and thorough modernization of Japanese (Heinrich 2012) – and, second, language problems occurring in the Japanese colonies (Yasuda 1998). Both topics crucially involve research into fields that are today part and parcel of the sociolinguistic research agenda, e.g., language standardization and adaptation, language registers, functional diversification, language contact and spread.

One of the early scholars engaging in language life studies was Kikuzawa Sueo. Kikuzawa had spent considerable time studying language problems of written language, as many others did at that time. In his book on the social and modal stratification of Japanese, Kikuzawa (1933) took a whole new direction. He pleaded that Japanese linguists should not simply apply theories and methods developed in the West, but that they should start to independently innovate their research. He called for a unification of the study of language form and function, instead having descriptive linguistics being detached from studies in "meaning" (Kikizawa 1933: 3–9). In order to do so, Kikuzawa proposed to distinguish between the study of *yōsō* (state) and of *yōshiki* (mode) of language. The former approach should be devoted to research on various forms of linguistic realizations (states) within the Japanese speech community. Kikuzawa distinguished thereby between social and local differences but also studied variation due to language change. Kikuzawa devoted most of his attention to the study of language state (*yōsō*) in his book. He also urged linguists to study the differences between written and spoken language along his idea of language mode (*yōshiki*). His call for a differentiated study of written and spoken languages was later picked up by linguists engaging in post-war language life studies, most famously by Tokieda Motoki (1950, 1954). In a later publication, Kikuzawa (1936: 310–388) engaged in the study of language mode in that he collected taboo words used among Shinto priests, and by compiling lists of the specific vocabulary used by merchants, scholars, cosmopolites, prostitutes, former samurai and thieves.

Probably the most remarkable study of language life before 1945 was a study by Kindaichi Haruhiko, the son of Kindaichi Kyōsuke. In his study on the velar plosive in the Tokyo variety, Kindaichi (1967[1941]) studied the variation between the voiced velar stop [g] and the voiced velar nasal [ŋ] by developing what we would call today a variationist approach. In Standard Japanese, we find a complementary distribution between the two variants with the voiced velar stop in work-initial position (e.g., *gin*, silver), whereas the nasalized variant may be used word-internally (e.g., *hiŋasi*, east). In some regional dialects, the voiced velar stop [g] was used in all environments. According to Kindaichi, there were a number of reasons why the nasalized variant in word-internal position had become the standard pronunciation. For one, it was used in the capital city of Tokyo, as well as in a great number of other Japanese local dialects, it was then older of two variants, and it was widely perceived as sounding "beautiful". Kindaichi thought that nobody younger than 30 who had been born and raised in Tokyo would ever use velar stop [g] in word-internal position. To his surprise, however, his little sister started doing exactly this when she entered middle school. Kindaichi therefore expanded his attention to her classmates and found that many were talking in the same way. This was puzzling to him, because all language change that he and everybody else then knew about was the replacement of regional dialects by Standard Japanese, i.e., language change from above.

In order to study the language change in progress he was witnessing, Kindaichi developed a survey through which he sought to clarify how widely this change was currently spread among young Tokyoites, what was motivating this change, what role the social backgrounds of these children were playing. He compiled a list of 13 words and made the children read it out aloud. In addition, he asked them where they currently lived, which schools they had frequented and from where in Japan their parents originated. The results he obtained pointed clearly to language change in progress: 28% used the Standard Japanese pronunciation, 41 fluctuated between [g] and [ŋ] in word-internal positions, and 30% used exclusively the velar plosive [g]. Against his expectation, the origin of the parents played no role in accounting for this result. The only pattern he could find was that those who favored [g] over [ŋ] came from the uptown area of Yamanote, while those from the more working-class neighborhoods of Shitamachi stuck closer to the standard pronunciation. Contrary to what contemporary linguists had predicted, the standard was not spreading everywhere. Quite on the contrary, and somehow shockingly, it was retreating in the most affluent part of the Japanese capital among its youngest speakers. Kindaichi therefore predicted that [g] would replace [ŋ] over time – a prediction confirmed by Hibiya (1988) almost half a century later.

Approaches more centered on the study of society can also be found at this early stage of language life studies. Tanabe Juri published two volumes on the sociology of the Japanese language before 1945 (Tanabe 1936, 1943). The latter book is an expansion and updated version of his first publication on this topic. These publications introduced and familiarized a Japanese readership with works of European linguists such as Marcel Cohen and Charles Bally, in addition to social scientists such as Auguste Compte and Emile Durkheim. Tanabe's work proved an important instructional source for the development of post-war language life studies, as it paved the way for a broader perspective on language. Tanabe (1943: 12) called to expand the range of linguistics and to link it with neighboring fields such as sociology and history. He argued, for example, to study language in relation to illness, to moral or to implied meaning. While such a call might have looked odd to some at the time, such studies are today commonly conducted around the world in fields such as elderspeech, language ideology or pragmatics. In view of the fact that a sociology of Japanese did not exist then, Tanabe promoted works of western scholars, all the while urging his contemporaries to develop their own theories and methodologies on the basis of their studies on Japanese. Tanabe (1943: 152) was keenly aware that methods developed on the basis of western societies and languages could often not be directly applied on the case of Japan. Such systematic studies on Japanese language and society would evolve immediately after 1945, as the disastrous effects of the lost war played a key role in triggering a new wave of attention on the role of language in everyday life.

Post-war studies of language life

It is no exaggeration to say that language life was the most prominent topic of linguistics research in Japan in the 1950s. It was accompanied by research into generative grammar from the 1960s onwards and gradually lost its dominating position in Japanese linguistics. It nevertheless remained a highly influential field of research until the end of the Shōwa Period (1926–1989). *Gengo seikatsu* is today widely remembered as a "popular branch" of Japanese post-war linguistics. This image is largely due to the success of a journal by the name of *Gengo seikatsu*. Published by the National Institute of Japanese Language, the journal had at its peak a circulation of more than 10,000 copies per month. *Gengo seikatsu* was popular to the point that it became unclear to what extent it was addressing a popular readership and to what extent it was actually addressing academics. Dhorne (1983: 69) points out that the majority of the readers of the journal *Gengo seikatsu* were amateurs with an interest in language. Between 1951 and 1988, a total of 436 issues of *Gengo seikatsu* were published, looking at Japanese language and society from every conceivable perspective. It published, for example, special issues on the role and the linguistic properties of memos (volume 192), language on the radio in the age of TV (volume 276), or the language life of New Year's Day (volume 337). Always original, easy to read and moderately priced (300 Yen), the journal was widely popular and crucially contributed to a post-war boom of popular interest on language and linguistics in Japan (Matsumura 1956: 17). The study of language life amounted, however, to much more than this popular branch of "language watching". At its peak in the 1950s and 1960s, the study of *gengo seikatsu* featured two distinct approaches, one being driven by theory, the other focusing on the collection and analysis of data. Let us consider both of these directions.

The theory-driven approach to language life

The post-war study of language life is intricately connected to the National Institute for Japanese Language (*Kokuritsu kokugo kenkyūjo*, today called in English National Institute for Japanese Language and Linguistics). Established in 1948, the institute was tasked by law to "rationalize" the Japanese language in order that it could become the medium of a democratic society (Wenck 1960). To this end, the institute should provide for basic studies on which new and democratic language policies could be formulated, it should collect material and also publish reference works on Japanese. In the first years, there were various ideas how the institute could best realize these ambitious objectives. Yanagita Kunio thought the study of language life should be connected with language didactics (Yanagita 1951: 8), while the institute's first two directors, Nishio Minoru and Iwabuchi Etsutarō, thought it should contribute to a closer convergence of spoken and written language (Neustupný 1974: 72). None of these issues were to become prominent features of the post-war language life studies, though. At first, a theory-driven approach to *gengo seikatsu* took root.

Language life

The initiative to link the study of language life with theory is inseparably linked to the work of Tokieda Motoki. Tokieda had developed a process theory of language (*gengo katei-setsu*), where he proposed a psychological approach to study language. According to Tokieda (1941), language was constituted, first and foremost, by expression acts (*hyōgen kōi*) and by comprehension acts (*rikai kōi*). Tokieda – a staunch critic of Saussure and European structuralism – thought that linguistics should squarely face the heterogeneity of language on the level of *parole* instead of abstracting an empirically non-existent system of homogenous *langue*. The variability of language should be studied by paying attention to the speaker subject (*shutai*), to context (*bamen*) and to the topic of communication (*sozai*). *Gengo seikatsu* should study how these features were responsible for differences and similarities in concrete utterances.

Tokieda's work with regard to *gengo seikatsu* was centered on his ideas of *bamen* (context). Departing from his premise that language was first and foremost an act (*kōi*), he pledged that the study of language should always be linked to the social activities of which these acts were part of (Tokieda 1956: 144). He argued that his process theory of language provided for a theoretical basis to engage in such a kind of study. The individual speakers with their concrete utterances should be the subjects of study. Doing so would require a consideration of the listener, the relation (roles) between the speaker and the listener, the topic of communication, the social situation and the psychological state of all involved. The latter was an important point for Tokieda who distinguished between inner and outer environments of communication. Tokieda was influenced by the work of Husserl and of Humboldt, seeing language as an artifact and as being individually perceived as an activity. The physical and social context aside, Tokieda was therefore also interested in psychology. He claimed that language had an emotional aspect, too, and that this side of communication could be grasped by paying attention to attitudes (*taido*), mood (*kibun*) and emotions (*kanjō*) of individual speakers (Tokieda 1941: 144).

The methods laid out by Tokieda on the basis of his language process theory were applied in a number of studies in the 1950s and 1960s. These works were later collectively seen to be part of a tradition called *bamen-ron* (context studies). An early example of this direction was a work by Uno Yoshikata in which he differentiated between speaker subject, communication topic, listener and the (physical) context of concrete utterances (Uno 1951). Tsukahara Tetsuo studied the relation between speaker and listener by putting the acts of expression in relation to the acts of comprehension, all the while paying consideration to differences between speaking and writing (Tsukahara 1954). Also, in the 1950s, Nagano Masaru summarized the central issues of *bamen-ron* as follows (Nagano 1957: 131): "Who communicates with whom in what circumstances and with what development?" Development (*tenkai*) had developed in another attempt to studying concrete utterances in order to develop a linguistics of *parole*. This approach was then called *bunshō-ron* (discourse studies).

The best-known scholar of *bunshō-ron* was Mio Isago. Mio combined the study of context (called *ba* in his work) with the study of linguistic style. This led him to develop a taxonomy of interactional sentence types (Mio 1948: 81–82). Concretely speaking, he distinguished between *genshō-bun* (phenomena sentence), such as, for example, *ame ga futteiru* (it's raining), *handan-bun* (judgment sentences), such as *Tōkyō wa nihon no shuto de aru* (Tokyo is the capital of Japan), *bunsetsu-bun* (speech tact sentences), such as *Omae wa kono hon o yomeru-ka* (Can you read this book? The person is at the time of utterance not reading it) and *tenkai-bun* (development sentences) such as *Ama da!* (Rain!).[1] Mio claimed that *genshō-bun* would directly refer to the context (*ba*), that *handan-bun* would include the context, that *tenkai-bun* would refer to a limited extent to the context and that *bunsetsu-bun* would be characterized by a reciprocal relation between the utterance and the context. A given speech unit (speech tact) such as *yomeru* (ability to read) could only be understood by considering the context, in this case the observation or knowledge that the person in question had read the book before. Tokieda, too, developed an interest in "developments" beyond the sentence, arguing to consider text or discourse (*bunshō*) as the third fundamental unit other than word (*go*) and sentence (*bun*) in his grammar of spoken Japanese (Tokieda 1950: 21).[2] Accordingly, the task of linguistics should be to identify patterns and constraints on all these levels of analysis. However, this kind of research did not further develop in Japanese linguistics until the 1970s, and it did then under the influence of western discourse studies and text linguistics (e.g., Hinds 1976).

In the theory-driven approach to the study of language life we can recognize the innovative force of post-war language life studies. Driven by a relatively small group of linguists and centered on Tokieda and his work, this tradition completely disappeared after Tokieda's passing in 1967. It is usually not included in historical accounts of "Japanese sociolinguistics" today. Tokieda's work is touched upon in courses on the history of Japanese linguistics, as he remains to this day the most innovative theoretician of Japanese language. He is also remembered for his controversial involvement of Japanese language spread policy in colonial Korea (Yasuda 1998). Mio is sometimes mentioned by Japanese scholars of pragmatics, who are usually familiar with his work. All of these approaches were, however, overshadowed by a data-driven approach to the study of language life. There can be no doubt that *gengo seikatsu* could have very much profited if these two branches would have been linked. However, none of these two post-war approaches to *gengo seikatsu* left any noteworthy influence on the other branch.

The data-driven approach to language life

The data-driven approach to *gengo seikatsu* is intricately linked to the National Institute for Japanese Language. The research of language life launched at the institute sought to study existing language problems of contemporary Japanese society. What was perceived to constitute "a problem" changed over time. Immediately after the establishment of the institute, literacy and the Japanese writing system was conceived as a pressing problem, albeit only for a very short time. In the 1950s and 1960s attention shifted to Standard Japanese language spread, and in the 1970s, when language life studies were already declining, it shifted to issues of urbanization. Few exceptions aside, there was very little "socio-" in this tradition. It is no exaggeration to say that this particular approach to *gengo seikatsu* merely studied linguistic data in correlation to macro-sociological categories such as age, sex/gender, education or birthplace with the help of statistics. As a matter of fact, linguists and statisticians jointly conducted most of the studies we discuss next.

The very first large-scale study of the National Institute is exemplary for the statistical approach that came to dominate its research. Under the direction of Nomoto Kikuo, a survey into literacy was launched in 1948. Nomoto was then working for the Civil Information and Education Section (CI&E) of the American occupational forces. Americans suspected that low levels of literacy and an overtly difficult writing system had caused the rise of fascism in Japan (for a discussion, see Unger 1996). The objective of the study was to find out whether the literacy among the Japanese population was sufficient to fully participate in everyday life (YKNCI 1951). Towards this end, a massive survey was launched, and 17,000 informants from 270 different localities were surveyed. Literacy among adults was never again surveyed in Japan afterwards as the results were seen to indicate that there was no grave literacy problem in Japan. As matter of fact, this survey is often cited to claim that Japanese society enjoys almost total literacy. The survey indeed found that only 1.7% were "illiterate", but at the same time only 4.4% scored more than 90 out of 100 points. What is more, participants had been invited to take part in this survey by postcard. As an effect thereof, illiterates and individuals with little literacy are most likely excluded in large numbers from the sample. The biased realization and interpretation of this investigation notwithstanding, the literacy survey had provided a template for how to study *gengo seikatsu* henceforth, and a great number of studies afterwards employed statistics in the study of language in a similar way.

Language life studies from the 1950s to the 1970s were centered on peripheral areas, seeing the periphery as backwards in development. In particular, the spread of Standard Japanese and the use of honorific language (*keigo*) were studied in rural areas. Hachijojima, a small island located 280 kilometers off the coast to Tokyo, served as the first case for a general language survey that took account of macro-sociological data (KKK 1950). Language standardization was at the time seen to contribute to democratization (Lewin 1979), and researchers were interested both in the state of language standardization in peripheral regions as well as the novel impact of radio and TV broadcast in these regions (see also Shioda 2011). This particular study subsequently functioned as a template for a series of similar large-scale surveys that combined descriptive linguistics and statistics in order to study the standardization process in rural regions across Japan. In this way, aspects of the standardization process across Japan were studied, for example, in Shirakawa City in Fukushima Prefecture (KKK 1951), Tsuruoka City in Yamagata Prefecture (KKK 1953), rural areas in Kanagawa Prefecture (KKK 1954), all the way up to Hokkaido (KKK 1965) in the extreme north of the Japanese Archipelago. These studies paid due attention to the influence of then rapidly spreading TV and radio broadcast in Japan. The boom of American structuralism at the time and its focus on phonology crucially fanned such research, and it ensured that the linguistic descriptions reached a new level of accuracy (Hattori 1951, 1953). Pronunciation and, in particular, accent were studied in great detail.

Another methodological novelty at the time where the so-called "24-hours surveys" (*nijūyon jikan chōsa*). First conducted in Shirakawa (KKK 1951) and later repeated in Tsuruoka City (Yamagata Prefecture) and Iida City (Nagano Prefecture), these surveys used the then new technology of portable recording devices. They reveal the great enthusiasm and methodological boldness of language life studies at the time. They also neatly illustrated that the focus was squarely placed on the collection and statistical analysis of data with very little theoretical foundation or set objectives. The data collected was used to demonstrate the actual situation (*jittai*) of language use and attitudes, and how they differed from a society where everybody would speak standard language, and where all would be confident in their use of Standard Japanese and honorific language. Selecting various localities as case studies, and also the repetition of single surveys such as the case of Tsuruoka City (KKK 1953, 1974, 1994, 2013), served to illustrated how far the standardization process had evolved when and where. The work was interdisciplinary in that it involved researchers from the Institute of Statistical Mathematics (*Tōkei sūri kenkyūjo*). However, we find no consideration of sociological work or theories in these studies. The discussion of "linguistic variation" was one of studying the use of dialect and standard along the lines of sociological macro-categories provided by the statisticians (age, sex/gender, regional background). The use of dialect and standard was simply seen to be caused by these macro-categories. It was thought that one spoke the way one did because one was, for example, "a middle-aged woman from Tsuruoka in 1951". Language life studies saw such characteristics to be inseparably linked to individuals, who therefore inescapably and somehow predictably were believed to produce a specific kind of speech. The surveys engaged in what we call today a "sociolinguistics of distribution" (Blommaert 2010: 5), that is to say, a view that speakers and language occupy a fixed geographic or social space. This orientation towards the study of linguistic variation is unsurprising given the fact that the language life scholars at the Japanese Institute of National Language were trained in dialectology, and dialectology is exactly about the distribution of linguistic variation over time and space. Language life studies were large-scale dialectological surveys that collected data following methods of human statistics and put the data into the context of the standardization process (Hara 2007; Tokugawa 1994). While the collected data was impressive, we find less theorization and less attention to society than in both the pre-war approach and the approach based on Tokieda's process theory.

Attention on and enthusiasm for language life studies started to wane in the 1960s, and the number of studies in language life ceased to grow from that period onwards (Grootaers 1982: 346; Sibata 1985: 84). Many researchers who had formerly been involved in language life surveys now devoted their full attention to the compilation of a new Japanese dialect atlas that evolved at the National Institute for National Language between 1955 and 1975. More importantly, perhaps, the sense of urgency that Japan was plagued by linguistics problems such as a lack of standardization, a difficult writing system or a lack of proficiency in honorific speech had weakened. In accordance with this new sentiment, the study of "language problems" in Japanese society declined. The 1960s and 1970s saw a boom in dialect geography, where insights, experiences and methods of the language life studies proved helpful (e.g., KKK 1966–1974).

The reception of western sociolinguistics

In 1976, the term *shakai gengogaku* (sociolinguistics) was coined and it quickly spread across the Japanese academic world (Grootaers 1982). The introduction of western sociolinguistics coincided with the fading influence of the post-war wave of *gengo seikatsu* studies. Due to the many language life studies that had been conducted, works on western sociolinguistics fell immediately on fertile grounds and received much attention. Already in the 1970, a number of books were translated that stirred Japanese interest, in one way or another, in the reception of *shakai gengogaku*: 1974 saw the Japanese translations of Robbins Burling's *Man's Many Voices* (*Gengo to bunka – gengo jinruigaku no shiten kara*), Peter Farb's *Word Play* (*Kotoba no asobi – hito ga hanasu toki nanika okoruka*), Joshua Fishman's *The Sociology of Language* (*Gengo shakaigaku nyūmon*); in 1975 Peter Trudgill's *Sociolinguistics* (*Gengo to shakai*) was translated; in 1977 Herbert Landar's *Language and Culture* (*Gengo to bunka*); in 1978 John Austin's *How to Do Things with Words* (*Gengo to kōi*); and in 1979 Dell Hymes' *Foundations in Sociolinguistics* (*Kotoba no minzokushi*). These works were widely read and studied, making it difficult to distinguish from the late 1970s onwards what was to be seen as studies in "language life" and what was to be seen as studies in "sociolinguistics".

Students of linguistics who experienced the introduction of sociolinguistics recall the excitement with which the western approach was greeted. Inoue Fumio (personal communication) has talked to me several times about a desire among young scholars at the time to turn to the real problems of contemporary Japanese society – an attitude that had crucially been fanned by the student unrest of the late 1960s. Inoue also recalled Czech-Australian sociolinguist Jiří Neustupný giving a lecture on *shakai gengogaku* at the University of Tokyo in the early 1970s to a packed auditorium. Others have noted the larger scope of sociolinguistics in comparison to language life. Sanada Shinji (2006: 1), who was a student in the 1970s, starts his book on Japanese sociolinguistics by writing that:

> "It is not such a long time ago that the field of sociolinguistic research was established in Japan. [...] It was on an early summer day in 1972 [...] that I saw by accident a flyer of a presentation of a dialectological research circle. Even today, I cannot forget the powerful impact this announcement had on me due to the fact that the subtitle read "seeking a nexus between language and society". [...] Even though the term "geography" existed in linguistic research at this time, "society" did not. Seeking a connection to society was considered a taboo in linguistic research then.
>
> (Sanada 2006: 1)

At the same time, many proponents of language life studies claimed that such a research tradition already existed in Japan, and that sociolinguistics (*shakai gengogaku*) was basically identical with language life (*gengo seikatsu*). Sibata Takesi, for example, stated the following:

> I have already said that sociolinguistics is booming in the United States. Just because it is booming there, must we panic as if to say if we don't hurry we shall be late getting it started in Japan? [...] The reason is that we have had in our backyard; the National Language Research Institute of Japan has since 1949 been steadily engaged in investigations, on large scale of just precisely what is now called sociolinguistics.
>
> (Sibata 1975: 161)

As a result of such claims, we find from the mid-1970s onwards often a synonymous use of the terms *gengo seikatsu* and *shakai gengogaku*, as if they were indeed one and the same tradition. Those engaging most obviously in western approaches, e.g., Hibiya with a PhD thesis under the supervision of William Labov on the velar plosive in Tokyo (Hibiya 1988), but also a number of western sociolinguists active in Japan, e.g., Jiří Neustupný, Leo Loveday or Florian Coulmas, were seen as the "international branch" (*gairai-ha*) of sociolinguistics in a Japanese context.

In hindsight, however, we can notice a number of significant differences between language life and sociolinguistics. The lack of a theoretical foundation in *gengo seikatsu* made it impossible to put its research results in context with insights from other languages and societies. Language life was entirely emic. Language life was also utterly uncritical of the language and power nexus. It was blind to issues of inequality and also to issues of linguistic diversity. We can find no single contribution addressing, for instance, Japan's multilingualism, its often oppressive language polices, or a critical review of its colonial past and its legacy. The short-lived tradition of Tokieda-style language life studies aside, we also do not find research questions derived from theoretical considerations that would develop insights how language and society related to one another. Language life studies were particularistic or "atomistic", simply providing rich linguistic details – and leaving it at this. In particular in this aspect, we can see how similar it was to dialectology. The initial stance that there was nothing to be learned from sociolinguistics proved wrong (Minami 1997: 602), and mainly for this reason the study of language life gradually gave way to the more interdisciplinary, cross-linguistically and theoretically oriented sociolinguistics. Before language life studies would disappear, some calls were made to integrate the skills of collecting and handling data of the language life tradition with the theoretical consideration of sociolinguistics (Ide 1988; Shibuya 1990), but these plans never went beyond the proclamation of good intentions.

Today, there is a clear consensus that *gengo seikatsu* gave way to sociolinguistics at the end of the 1980s. *Gengo seikatsu* was the study of Japanese language and society of the Shōwa Period (1928–1989). In 1988, the last of over 400 issues of the journal *Gengo seikatsu* appeared. The fact that today's leading sociolinguistic journal in Japan claims to engage in the study of the "sociolinguistic sciences" (*shakai gengo kagaku*) underlines how much the field has shifted from emic study of language problems on issues such as democratization and standardization, and later on also urbanization (e.g., KKK 1981, 1982). The indigenous tradition of language life studies was responsible for the collection of a great number of data that is still being discussed in contemporary Japanese sociolinguistics (e.g., Sanada et al. 2010). It also developed a number of methodologies that are still applied today. In this way, there can be no doubt that *gengo seikatsu* has been a success story in the Japanese study of language and society.

Patrick Heinrich

The legacy of language life in Japanese sociolinguistics

All countries in which we find research in sociolinguistics today have a slightly different development and orientation to the study of language and society (Smakman and Heinrich 2015). In European context, sociolinguistics mainly emerged from discussions on the role of the school system reproducing social class differences. It studied the ways in which language was in the service of power and cultural elites, and how it served to sanction and control everybody else (e.g., Ammon 1972). European sociolinguistics also studied the important social functions of non-prestigious language varieties (e.g., Milroy 1979). In the US, sociolinguistics was an emancipative endeavor, restoring the recognition of language varieties such as African-American Vernacular English and showing its systematicity, functionality and creativity (e.g., Labov 1972). Concern for how to maintain linguistic diversity was present in both traditions from the very start (e.g., Fishman 1966 for the US; Gal 1979 for Europe). Both traditions were also predominantly urban. Japan, too, has its very own trajectory in that the study of language in society reflected the concerns of the day. In the case of Japan, these were first the role of language in various forms of everyday life in the pre-war tradition, then the role of variation and style in processes of communication in the Tokieda-tradition, and the social and geographic cartography of the standardization process at the Japanese Institute for National Language. In a word, Japanese society in the Shōwa Period was interested in other issues than the European and US societies at the same time, and we therefore find, unsurprisingly, differences between sociolinguistics and language life studies at that time, too.

While the study of language life is no longer pursued in present-day Japan, we can still see reflections of its tradition in the contemporary research agenda of Japanese sociolinguistics. To this day, language endangerment and revitalization remain marginal fields of study in Japanese sociolinguistics, and so do urban studies. Much emphasis in Japanese sociolinguistics remains on the collection and analysis of data, and it is not an exaggeration to say that too little theorization is conducted on the basis of the many excellent Japanese case studies conducted year after year by Japanese sociolinguists. The study of language and social class has largely remained a taboo. While addressing the linguistically diversifying society (*tagengo shakai*) has now become mainstream in Japanese sociolinguistics, the disparate society (*kakusa shakai*) or the relationless society (*muen shakai*) of the Heisei period (1989–2019) has not, despite the fact that language plays a central role therein. Japanese sociolinguistics remains surprisingly narrow in its scope, even 30 years after the end of the *gengo seikatsu* tradition. Sociolinguistics in Japan could also be socially more engaged. There is no neutral way to approach language in society as all discourse and all interactions are vested with conflict and competing interests. Language plays a central role in social inequality and its continued perpetuation. Conflict and inequality are part and parcel of language diversity and variation, and there exists no way for researchers to step out of this conflicted field. *Laissez-faire* means nothing else but siding with the strong and dominant. Language life was predominantly descriptive and illustrative, and so is Japanese sociolinguistics today. Herein, we probably find the strongest influence of language life studies on contemporary Japanese sociolinguistics.

Notes

1 *Bunsetsu* (literally "speech tact", a syntagmatic unit) is a concept developed by Hashimoto Shinkichi when creating a school grammar (*gakkō bunpō*) of Japanese in the 1930s. It is defined as smallest unit within a sentence (*bun*) that can be identified on the basis of pauses in speech, i.e., on the basis of on "speech tact".

2 Note in this context that the study of phonology was not firmly established in national linguistics (*kokugokaku*) at the time. Scholars still worked with the unit of syllable (*onsetsu*) then. The morpheme was also introduced only afterwards with the reception of American structuralism in the late 1950s.

References

Ammon, Ulrich (1972) *Dialekt, soziale Ungleichheit und Schule*. Weinheim: Beltz.
Austin, John L. (1978) *Gengo to kōi* [*How to Do Things with Words*]. Tokyo: Taishūkan.
Blommaert, Jan (2010) *The Sociolinguistics of Globalization*. Cambridge: Cambridge University Press.
Burling, Robbins (1974) *Gengo to bunka – gengo jinruigaku no shiten kara* [*Man's many Voices*]. Kyoto: Minerva Shobō.
Dhorne, France (1983) "Gengo seikatsu" ou la vie langagière (objectives et méthodes de recherche). *Langages* 68: 63–69.
Doi, Toshio (1976) *The Study of Language in Japan. A Historical Survey*. Tokyo: Shinozaki Shorin.
Farb, Peter (1974) *Kotoba no asobi – hito ga hanasu toki nanika okoru* [*Word Play. What Happens When People Talk*]. Osaka: Yūgakusha.
Fishman, Joshua A. (1966) *Language Loyalty in The United States*. The Hague: Mouton.
——— (1974) *Gengo shakaigaku nyūmon* [*The Sociology of Language*]. Tokyo: Taishūkan.
Gal, Susan (1979) *Language Shift. Social Determinants of Linguistic Change in Bilingual Austria*. San Francisco: Academic Press.
Grootaers, Willem A. (1982) Notes on Japanese Dialectology. *Orbis* 1(2): 517–569.
——— (1982) Dialectology and Sociolinguistics. *Lingua* 57: 327–355.
Hara, Kiyoshi (2007) Tagengo shakai-ron no shatei [The Range of Theories for the Study of Multilingual Societies]. *Kotoba to shakai* 10: 4–24.
Hattori, Shirō (1951) *Onseigaku* [*Phonetics*]. Tokyo: Iwanami Shoten.
——— (1953) Amerika gengogakuha no inshō [My Impression of American Linguists]. *Kokugogaku* 11: 51–54.
Heinrich, Patrick (2012) *The Making of Monolingual Japan. Language Ideology and Japanese Modernity*. Bristol: Multilingual Matters.
Hibiya, Junko (1988) A Quantitative Study of Tokyo Japanese. PhD dissertation, University of Pennsylvania.
——— (1999) Variationist Sociolinguistics. In: *The Handbook of Japanese Linguistics*. Natsuko Tsujimura (ed.), 101–120. Malden: Blackwell.
Hinds, John (1976) *Aspects of Japanese Discourse Structure*. Tokyo: Kaitakusha.
Hirai, Masao (1998[1948]) *Kokugo kokuji mondai no rekishi* [*History of National Language and National Script Problems*]. Tokyo: Sangensha.
Hymes, Dell (1979) *Kotoba no minzokushi – shakai gengogaku no kiso* [*Foundations in Sociolinguistics. An Ethnographic Approach*]. Tokyo: Kinokuniya.
Ide, Sachiko (1988) Shakai gengogaku no riron to hōhōron – nihon to ōbei no apurōchi ni tsuite [Sociolinguistic Theory and Methodology. On the Japanese and the Western Approaches]. *Gengo kenkyū* 93: 97–103.
Kikuzawa, Sueo (1933) Kokugo isō-ron [*The Stratification of Language*]. Tokyo: Meiji Shoin.
——— (1936) *Shinkō kokugogaku no josetsu* [*Introduction of a New National Linguistics*]. Tokyo: Bungakusha.
Kindaichi, Haruhiko (1967[1941]) Ga-gyō bion-ron [A Study of Nasal Sounds]. Republished in: *Nihongo on'in no kenkyū* [*Studies in Japanese Phonology*]. Haruhiko Kindaichi, 168–197. Tokyo: Bungakusha.
Kindaichi, Kyōsuke (1933) *Gengo kenkyū* [*The Study of Language*]. Tokyo: Kawade Shobō.
KKK = Kokuritsu Kokugo Kenkyūjo (1950) *Hachijōjima no gengo chōsa* [*Linguistic Survey in Hachijōjima*]. Tokyo: Kokuritsu Kokugo Kenkyūjo.
——— (1951) *Gengo seikatsu no jittai – Shirakawa-shi oyobi fukin no nōson ni okeru* [*Facts of Language Life. Shirakawa City and its Nearby Rural Areas*]. Tokyo: Kokuritsu Kokugo Kenkyūjo.
——— (1953) *Chi'iki shakai no gengo seikatsu – Tsuruoka ni okeru jittai chōsa* [*Language Life of Local Society. Fact-finding Survey in Tsuruoka*]. Tokyo: Shūei Shuppan.
——— (1954) *Nōson jidō gengo seikatsu no jittai – Kanagawa-ken chūbu chihō no jidō ni tsuite no jittai chōsa* [*Actual Condition of Rural Children's Language Life. Survey on Children in Central Local Districts of Kanagawa Prefecture*]. Tokyo: Kokuritsu Kokugo Kenkyūjo.
——— (1957) *Keigo to keigo ishiki* [*Honorific Language and Honorific Language Awareness*]. Tokyo: Shūei Shuppan.

——— (1965) *Kyōtsūgoka no katei – Hokkaidō ni okeru oyako sandai no kotoba* [Language Standardization Process. Language across Three Generations in Hokkaido]. Tokyo: Kokuritsu Kokugo Kenkyūjo.
——— (1966–1974) *Nihon gengo chizu* [The Linguistic Atlas of Japan] (6 volumes). Tokyo: Kōbun Shohan.
——— (1974) *Chi'iki shakai no gengo seikatsu – Tsuruoka ni okeru 20-nen mae to no hikaku* [Language Life of Local Society. Comparison to the Tsuruoka Survey Conducted 20 Years Ago]. Tokyo: Shūei Shuppan.
——— (1981) *Daitoshi no gengo seikatsu* [Language Life in the City]. Tokyo: Sanseidō.
——— (1982) *Kigyō no naka no keigo* [Honorific Language in the Company]. Tokyo: Sanseidō.
——— (1994) *Tsuruoka hogen no kijutsu kenkyū – dai-3-ji Tsuruoka chōsa* [Descriptive Studies in the Tsuruoka Dialect. The Third Tsuruoka Survey]. Tokyo: Shūei Shuppan.
——— (2013) *Dai-4-kai Tsuruoka-shi ni okeru gengo chōsa* [Fourth Linguistic Survey on Tsuruoka City]. Tokyo: Kokuritsu Kokugo Kenkyūjo.
Labov, William (1972) *Language in the Inner City*. Philadelphia: University of Philadelphia.
Landar, Herbert J. (1977) *Gengo to bunka* [Language and Culture]. Tokyo: Taishūkan.
Lewin, Bruno (1979) Demokratisierungsprozesse in der modernen Sprachentwicklung. In: *Japan nach 1945*. Klaus Kracht (ed.), 87–101. Wiesbaden: Harrassowitz.
Matsumura, Akira (1956) Kokugogaku [National Linguistics]. In: *Kokugo nenkan*, Kokuritsu Kokugo Kenkyūjo (ed.), 14–17. Tokyo: Kokuritsu Kokugo Kenkyūjo.
Milroy, Lesley (1979) Language and Social Network in Belfast. PhD thesis, The Queens University of Belfast.
MKK = Monbushō Kyōkasho-kyoku Kokugoka (1949) *Kokugo chōsa enkaku shiryō* [Materials on the History of Research on the National Language]. Tokyo: Monbushō Kyōkasho-kyoku Kokugoka.
Minami, Fujio (1997) *Gendai nihongo kenkyū* [Studies in Contemporary Japanese]. Tokyo: Sanseidō.
Mio, Isago (1948) *Kokugo-hō bunshō-ron* [National Language Patterns in Discourse Studies]. Tokyo: Sanseidō.
Nagano, Masaru (1957) Bamen to kotoba [Context and Language]. In: *Kōza gendai kokugogaku* (volume 1). Etsutarō Iwabuchi, Ōki Hayashi, Hatsutarō Ōishi and Takesi Sibata (eds), 123–148. Tokyo: Chikuma Shobō.
Neustupný, Jiří V. (1974) The Modernization of the Japanese System of Communication. *Language and Society* 3: 33–50.
Sanada, Shinji (2000) *Nihon ni okeru shakai gengogaku-teki kenkyū bunken risuto* [Bibliography on Literature on Sociolinguistic Research in Japan]. Osaka: Ōsaka Daigaku Bungakubu.
——— (2006) *Shakai gengogaku no kadai* [Tasks of Sociolinguistics]. Tokyo: Kurioshio Shuppan.
Sanada, Shinji, Daniel Long, Yoshiyuki Asahi and Yuehchen Chien (eds) (2010) *Shakai gengogaku zushū* [Japanese Sociolinguistics Illustrated] (second edition). Tokyo: Akiyama Shoten.
Sanada, Shinji and Takesi Sibata (1982) *Nihon ni okeru shakai gengogaku no dōkō* [Trends in Japanese Sociolinguistics]. Private Publication.
Sibata, Takesi (1975) On Some Problems in Japanese Sociolinguistics. In: *Language in Japanese Society. Current Issues in Sociolinguistics*. Fred C. C. Peng (ed.), 159–173. Tokyo: Tokyo University Press.
——— (1985) Sociolinguistic Surveys in Japan. Approaches and Problems. *International Journal of the Sociology of Language* 55: 79–88.
——— (1999) *Sociolinguistics in Japanese Contexts* (translated, edited and introduced by Tetsuya Kunihiro, Fumio Inoue and Daniel Long). Berlin: Mouton de Gruyter.
Shibuya, Katsumi (1990) Gengo seikatsu [Language Life]. *Kokugogaku* 161: 88–100.
Shioda, Takehiro (2011) Constraints on Language Use in Public Broadcasting. In: *Language Life in Japan*. Patrick Heinrich and Christian Galan (eds), 124–139. London: Routledge.
Smakman, Dick and Patrick Heinrich (eds) (2015) *Globalising Sociolinguistics. Challenging and Expanding Theory*. London: Routledge.
Takeda, Tomohiro (2013) *Senzen no seikatsu* [Pre-war Life]. Tokyo: Chikuma Shobō.
Tanabe, Juri (1936) *Gengo shakaigaku* [Sociology of Language]. Tokyo: Jichōsha.
——— (1943) *Gengo shakaigaku josetsu* [An Introduction to the Sociology of Language]. Tokyo: Nikkō Shoin.
Tokieda, Motoki (1941) *Kokugogaku genron* [A General Theory of the National Language]. Tokyo: Iwanami Shoten.
——— (1950) *Nihon bunpō – kōgo-hen* [Japan Grammar. Spoken Language Volume]. Tokyo: Iwanami Shoten.
——— (1954) *Nihon bunpō – bungo-hen* [Japan Grammar. Written Language Volume]. Tokyo: Iwanami Shoten.
——— (1956) *Gendai no kokugogaku* [Modern National Linguistics]. Tokyo: Yūseidō Shuppan.
Tokugawa, Munemasa (1994) Hōgengaku kara shakai gengogaku e [From Dialectology to Sociolinguistics]. *Handai nihongo kenkyū* 6: 1–28.
Trudgill, Peter (1975) *Gengo to shakai* [Sociolinguistics. An Introduction]. Tokyo: Iwanami Shoten.

Tsukahara, Tetsuo (1954) Gengo kodō no tokoro – kōzō jōken [Places of Language Behavior. Structural Conditions]. *Panse* 25: no page numbers.
Unger, Marshall J. (1996) *Literacy and Script Reforms in Occupied Japan*. Oxford. Oxford University Press.
Uno, Yoshikata (1951) Kokugo no bamen [Context of National Language]. *Kokugogaku* 7: 82–94.
Wenck, Günther (1960) Das japanische Staatsinstitut für die Erforschung der japanischen Sprache. *Orientalische Literaturzeitung* 11/12: 566–598.
Yamada, Fusakazu (1942) *Gengo kankei kankō shomoku* [*Language-related Publications*]. Tokyo: Private Publication.
Yasuda, Toshiaki (1998) *Shokuminchi no naka no kokugogaku* [*National Linguistics in the Colonies*]. Tokyo: Sangensha.
YKNCI = Yomi-Kaki Nōryoku Chōsa I'inkai (1951) *Nihonjin no yomi-kaki nōryoku* [*Reading and Writing Proficiency of Japanese*]. Tokyo: Tokyo Daigaku Shuppan.

27
THE STUDY OF JAPANESE LANGUAGE SPEAKERS

Riikka Länsisalmi

Introduction

Discussing "speakers of Japanese" is a challenging task. Already a quick look at the tables of contents of handbooks and introductions to sociolinguistics shows that "speaker" and "language user" usually do not appear as chapter titles. The term "language" dominates instead. Widely used introductions to Japanese language scantly state that "Japanese is the native language of virtually all Japanese nationals" (Hasegawa 2015: 3), or that "Japanese is currently spoken by approximately 127 million people in Japan" (Iwasaki 2013: 1). Iwasaki (2013: 1) further refers to *kokugo* (national language), "especially as the name of a school subject", versus *nihongo* (Japanese language), a term used when Japanese "is contrasted with other languages". Others elaborate that *nihongo* is commonly understood to be "what the Japanese people speak" so that it can be considered equivalent to *kokugo*. In the modern period, Japanese is associated with the standard or common language, "spoken (or speakable) by everyone everywhere in Japan" (Okamoto and Shibamoto-Smith 2016: 27).[1]

In order to sketch an overview of "Japanese and its speakers", one first needs to dismantle the concept of "speaker", and then elaborate on the notion that Japanese is "speakable by everyone everywhere" in Japan. This leads straight to discussions of "non-native" users of Japanese, i.e., second language Japanese learners in Japan (henceforth, J2) and outside Japan (henceforth, JFL).[2] The number of Japanese language learners in Japan was approximately 190,000 in 2015 (Bunkachō 2016: 57–58), while some 3.6 million learners studied the language outside Japan (Japan Foundation 2016a).[3]

Speakers of Japanese: A terminological account

A common-sensical understanding of "native speakers" (henceforth, NS) refers to people speaking their "mother tongue" or "first acquired language". The concept of "native" is thereby contrasted with "non-native". This definition relates to lifetime. Learning a language in early childhood is what makes a speaker "native". Other definitions relate to competence. A NS has a "perfect" command of the language, making NS linguistic authorities in their native tongue.[4] Limiting our discussions to such idealized "Japanese NS" would be misleading. To start, Japanese first language speakers (henceforth, J1) speak Japanese in various ways. Then there are

J1 speakers outside Japan, and those who have learned Japanese side-by-side with another language, in various circumstances. Japanese is also learned as a second language (J2) and a foreign language (JFL). Japanese was also enforced as a *kokugo* (national language) in colonial Taiwan and Korea, where many of the older generation still speak Japanese (Jian and Sanada 2011; Long and Imamura 2013; Loveday 1996; Miyajima 1999; Mühlhäusler and Trew 2000; Sanada 2009; Yim 2001). Forced Japanese language learning also took place within what is currently Japanese territory, namely in Hokkaido and in the Ryukyu Islands (Anderson and Heinrich 2014; Heinrich 2015a; Maher 2014).

Let us consider some of the Japanese terminology used for "language" and for "speaker". Dictionary and encyclopedia definitions of *nihongo* (Japanese language) customarily define it as *kokugo* (national language) or *kōyōgo* (official language). Japanese is said to be the language used across the Japanese Archipelago, mainly by Japanese. The common definition of a "speaker of Japanese" is a person who is monolingual, a native speaker and a Japanese national. Outside linguistics, the term *nihongo washa* (Japanese language speaker) is not commonly used. It usually appears in articles on J1 speakers learning foreign languages. *Nihongo bogo washa* (Japanese mother tongue speaker) tends to be contrasted with *nihongo hi-bogo washa* (Japanese non-native speaker). Also, the loanwords *neitibu* (naitive) and *nonneitibu* (non-native) are used. On the other hand, concepts such as *kokugo washa* (national language speaker) and *kōyōgo washa* (official language speaker) do not exist.[5] *Kokugo* is an essentialist term that departs from an ideological assumption that speakers of *kokugo* are Japanese nationals and native speakers, while *kyōtsūgo* (common language) is a functional variety of Japanese. The latter is too specific to warrant a term designating its speakers. There is also the term *nihongo jun-bogo washa* (semi-native speakers of Japanese), which implies that "speakerhood" is based on deficiencies, rather than on differences. In other words, if one is not a "genuine" NS, one will be labeled as someone requiring an extra prefix that indicates that the language is "incomplete" (*jun-*, semi-/quasi-) or "non-native" (*hi-*, non-). Such speakers are on a quest to reach the unattainable target of "native speakerhood". This shows also in the fact that advanced learners of Japanese (*jōkyū nihongo gakushūsha*) are contrasted with NS, and that there are further categories beyond "advanced" such as super-advanced level speaker (*nihongo chōkyū washa*). There is however no doubt that even "super-advanced" is not "native".

Research on J1 speakers in Japan

What could be termed "regular" J1 speakers were the main object of research in Japanese sociolinguistics up until the 1990s. A number of overviews have summarized these works.[6]

Sociolinguists would not exist if it were not for the speakers. When adopting a speaker-centered perspective (Coulmas 2013), then variability in Japanese is evidenced in speakers' micro-choices regarding, for example, standard and regional dialects, gender-specific/-preferred forms, age-specific forms, occupational jargon, etc. Macro-choices pertain to higher-level units, such as linguistic choices across and functional restrictions on languages (code-switching, bilingualism), and phenomena related to language spread, shift, maintenance and planning. Identity, previously often conceived of in terms of ethnic, social and national identities, is examined as a dynamic and negotiable concept in interaction. Speakers are seen as "active creative agents, able to choose their verbal means", and it consequently becomes the task of sociolinguistics to "explain why they speak the way they do" (Coulmas 2013: 14).

How has Japanese sociolinguistics dealt with this? Heinrich and Masiko (2015) indicate that defining the range of sociolinguistics in Japan is not easy. Social stratification, a core phenomenon examined in Anglo-American "first wave" sociolinguistics (Eckert 2012), is approached in Japan in an emic way through the concept of *zokusei to kotoba* or *kotoba no zokusei* (social variables and language). Japanese studies relate language predominantly to age differences (*nenreisa*) or to sex differences (*seisa*), later reframed as gender and language (*jendā to kotoba*), to specific varieties used at some stage of life such as school slang and youth language, as well as to group language (*shūdango*) (Sanada et al. 2010; Long, Nakai and Miyaji 2001). An overview on applied Japanese sociolinguistics by Long, Nakai and Miyaji (2001) includes language contact in and outside Japan and discussions on immigrants and language under the heading of *zokusei* (literally "attribute"). Numerous studies have dealt with language variation in Japan accounting to social variables such as age, sex/gender and formality in the standard language spoken in Tokyo (e.g., Lauwereyns 2002; Takano 1998; Tomosada and Jinnouchi 2004; Matsuda 1993). Studies such as Hibiya (1995) on "uptown" Yamanote and "downtown" Shitamachi Tokyo Japanese, and variationist sociolinguistics in general, could draw on insights gained in the dialectological studies that predated the first sociolinguistic studies in Japan.[7]

"Second wave" approaches, relying on large-scale empirical surveys to grasp the local dynamics of variation and change, have dominated research on regional speech. Patterns and diversity of honorific expressions, particularly "honorifics-*as*-politeness" (Okamoto and Shibamoto-Smith 2016: 292) is another prominent field of second wave sociolinguistics in Japan (e.g., Ogino, Misono and Fukushima 1985; Ogino 1986). Politeness and honorifics have also been examined from multiple alternative perspectives: e.g., structure and displays of "linguistic femininity", conceptualizations of linguistically polite behavior, consciousness in regional and generational variation, discourse politeness theory and assessment and evaluation of politeness, including in cross-cultural contexts (Dunn 2013; Fukushima 2004; Ide et al. 1986; Okamoto 2013; Usami 2002, 2008, 2015; Yoshioka 2004). The concepts of "power" and "compliance" have been discussed in asymmetrical institutional settings, such as doctor-patient communication and eldercare facilities (Backhaus and Suzuki 2010; Ōtaki 2013). Social constructionist theories have inspired more recent "third wave" investigations of "Japanese politeness" and its varying manifestations. In this research strand, speakers are seen as active agents in actual interaction (Adachi 2016; Cook 2013; Geyer 2013).

Interactional resources used in discourse have also been popular topics, e.g., postpositions and cleft-constructions, laughter, interactional particles and discourse markers used in processes of self-contextualization or the management of information structure (Hayashi 2004; Ikeda 2003; Maynard 1989; Mori 2008; Morita 2008; Onodera 2004; Tanaka 2001, 2005). Heinrich and Masiko (2015) underline the important role of interdisciplinary work in Japanese sociolinguistics. Scholars trained in neighboring disciplines such as sociology, anthropology, political science and historical studies have crucially expanded the field. In English contributions from outside of Japan, speech styles by female NS have attracted much attention (Heinrich 2015b). This has resulted in socio-culturally inspired criticism on "universal models" of politeness (e.g., Ide 1989; Ide et al. 1986; Takahara 1991; Takano 2000; Tsuji 2002) and on the second wave-type focus on "the lexicon and morphology of gendered expression" (Okamoto and Shibamoto-Smith 2016: 292). While studies published in the 1980s rarely went beyond claims of cultural exceptionalism, recent inquiries have shifted attention towards speakers and their stylistic practices. Transgression of normative notions, particularly as displayed by young female speakers (Gagné 2008; Kataoka 1997; Miller 2004, 2011; Tranter 2008) and discourse of older women (Matsumoto 2009, 2011) have been addressed. While the "gap" how female speakers are expected to speak and how they actually speak has been widely explored, Japanese "men's speech" has received much less attention. It has typically been considered unmarked language and as such uninteresting for sociolinguistic research. In folk linguistics, in particular, "female language" has been viewed with respect to a presupposed "male norm" and female speakers resorting to "masculine expressions" have been criticized (Satake 2005).[8] "Manly" speech register by students, "salarymen speech" and "senior speakers" are among the topics covered by SturtzSreetharan (2004, 2006a, 2006b) in her important contributions to close this research gap.

In-between speakers and in-between Japanese

Less typical in Japanese sociolinguistics is the study of "in-between" speakers. The distinction between speakers and in-between speakers is usually drawn on ethnic or on linguistic grounds, but the difference between the two is far from clear. A recent solution is to place language users on a continuum (Takagi 2016). In 2014, the journal *Nihongogaku* (*Studies in Japanese Language*) devoted a special issue to *aida no nihongo* (in-between Japanese). It refrained from applying binary categories such as "young versus old", or "female versus male", placing the focus instead on the fluidity of language use and on varieties that often escape attention.

Notable contributions to *aida no nihongo* studies are works by Abe (2010, 2014), Maree (2014), Okamoto (2016) and Okamoto and Shibamoto-Smith (2004) on gay, *onee* and "new-half" sexual minority varieties, which do not fit traditional categories of women's language (*joseigo*) or men's language (*danseigo*).[9] The loanword *gei* (gay) is used to refer to male homosexuals, "new-half" to "male-to-female transsexuals" and "*onee* language" to "feminine speech associated with (effeminate) gay men" (Okamoto 2016: 15). Okamoto's (2016: 5) observation that "the relationship between linguistic forms and gender is variable, not fixed" is echoed in a number of studies. Contributions by Inoue (2002), Endō (2006), Nakamura (1995, 2001, 2007) and Okamoto and Shibamoto-Smith (2016) demonstrate the construction of gendered speech. Okamoto's (2016) focus on metapragmatic comments on the use of gendered language, and the interpretation of such forms used in local discourse contexts, further expands socio-cultural analyses on the discursive construction of identity. Abe (2014) also points out that exaggerated stereotypical gendered features function as hybrid language acts, simultaneously criticizing the underlying heterosexual-queer dichotomy.

Terms such as *onee* and *onabe* (masculine female homosexual) index possible identity features, but they can also be employed in relation to specific professional roles. Besides investigating how language users deal with dominant perceptions of language, other vantage points consider "gendered" professions from a discourse-analytic angle. In the so-called "water trade" (*mizu shōbai*), i.e., Japan's nightlife entertainment business, skillfully balancing the public and the private, the familiar and the formal, and the relevant speech styles that accompany these acts are part of the professional toolkit (Nakata 2016). *Onabe*, for example, typically work in service profession in bars frequented by female homosexuals attracted to masculine counterparts, in contrast to *rezubian* (lesbians), who identify themselves as female (Abe 2004, 2010).[10]

Another group of the "in-between" category are Japanese repatriate or returnee children (*kikoku shijo*). In schools, the number of returnee pupils has been hovering around 10,000 to 11,000 children (MEXT 2015a). Carroll (2011: 189) observes that these pupils have brought with them "influences from other languages and attitudes from their experiences living in other countries that affect their own language use and may have a wider impact in the longer term". Often lacking (full) exposure to Japan's national school curricula, their command of honorific registers or Japanese script are frequently less solid than that of their Japan-based peers. This notwithstanding, only circa 1,500 of the returnee pupils are seen to require additional "Japanese language guidance" at school (MEXT 2015b).[11] In the literature on returnee children, language education has customarily been discussed in the context of national language education. Studies focusing on (War) Returnees from China (*chūgoku kikokusha*) and on foreign spouses (*gaikokujin haigūsha*), on the other hand, have been related to regional J2 education.

"New speakers" of Japanese

The long-standing "belief in the myth of a classless and monoethnic Japanese society" (Heinrich and Masiko 2015: 256), together with the loss of Japanese colonies, were the main reasons why language diversity did not receive much attention in Japanese sociolinguistics before the mid-1990s (Carroll 2010; Noguchi and Fotos 2001). Speakers, who represent "Otherness" vis-à-vis the "prototypical" J1 speakers in Japan were addressed outside the realm of "mainstream sociolinguistics" (Heinrich and Masiko 2015). Although Ainu, Ruykuyans, Koreans and Chinese have often been referred to as established "minorities" in Japan, the terminology is not entirely clear. Iwama (2007) distinguishes several ways in which the term *mainoriti* (minority) is used in social sciences, newspapers and in popular use to denote either the socially disadvantaged (*shakai jakusha*), ethnic, linguistic and religious minorities (*shōsūsha*), or simply odd people (*kawatta hitobito*) who do not blend in with the "majority". Outside Japanese academia, *mainoriti* tends to be used in reference to the "discriminated and disadvantaged", that is, it refers to issues of disability, age, sexual orientation, race and religion (Takagi 2016). English language scholarship on Japan, by contrast, applied the term "minority" from the mid-1990s onwards to refer to Ainu, Ryukyuans, Koreans, Chinese or *nikkeijin*. Also, *burakumin* have been discussed under the umbrella term of "minority", despite the fact that they do not differ ethnically or linguistically from "majority Japanese".[12] Lumping together such diverse groups has its problems. Hankins (2014: 227) has a point in writing that "[g]roups, the recognition of which has been intended to show diversity in Japan, are, ironically, being homogenized as 'minorities'".

It is now mainstream in Japanese sociolinguistics to turn towards marginalized groups "in a move to dethrone the specter of homogeneity" (Hankins 2014: 222). It must be noted in this context that the number of resident foreigners in Japan represents only 1.8% of the population, a small number compared to other developed economies (Green 2017; Hōmushō 2016). Shibuya (2010) reviews studies related to Japanese in immigration contexts and classifies the types of Japanese in two categories: Japanese used by (1) permanent residents such as *zainichi* Koreans and Chinese, spouses and foreign family members of Japanese nationals, Returnees from China, etc., and (2) others residing in Japan for longer or shorter periods such as most *nikkeijin*, other foreign laborers, and Japanese language learners. People of Ainu and Ryukyuan heritage are now all J1 speakers, and the number of bilingual speakers among these populations is declining. Yamamoto (2001: 28–29) distinguished between four types of bilinguals in Japan: (1) "mainstream Japanese studying a foreign/second language", (2) *kikoku shijo* returnees, (3) "offspring of parents who have different native languages" and (4) "ethnic minorities (born and) residing in Japan". Individuals falling into the first two groups are usually highly educated "elite bilinguals", who choose to acquire another language. Individuals of the third group may be evaluated similarly, if the combination of languages includes Japanese or English. Non-Japanese speakers in the last three groups would be categorized as "folk or circumstantial bilinguals", learning the dominant language (Japanese) in order to adapt to mainstream society. In particular studies on "folk or circumstantial bilinguals" of the second and third category are scarce in Japanese sociolinguistics.

Since Japan saw itself as a monolingual and homogenous nation until the 1990s, and with Japanese sociolinguistics reproducing this belief, it is not surprising to find that issues on former colonial subjects residing in Japan were not addressed. Doing otherwise would have been counter-ideological. In the 1990s, the remnants of the Japanese language (*zanson nihongo*) in the former colonies, together with *nikkeijin* language problems and other migrant language issues became more prominent (Nakamizu 2001). Initially the main attention was directed to identifying "non-native" features in their Japanese. More recently, scholars from neighboring fields of study have expanded their research to also include related macro-level phenomena (Heinrich and Masiko 2015: 260). Sanada and Shoji (2005) or Tagengoka Genshō Kenkyūkai (2013) are useful introductions to this type of research.

In the case of Chinese and Korean residents, "oldcomers" and "newcomers" are customarily distinguished. The distinction is based on the period of time they came to Japan.[13] Forced to hide their mother tongue, oldcomer Koreans acquired Japanese without much notice. Language shift among them proceeded rapidly, so that the second, third, fourth and fifth generations are J1 speakers. The usual pattern is that the second generation is passively bilinguals and from the third generation onwards, descendants are often monolingual J1 speakers (Kim 2005). Newcomer students, trainees, spouses and others, by contrast, have found better conditions to maintain their bilingualism (Long et al. 2002; Sanada, Ogoshi and Yim 2005). About 14% of Korean children are educated in ethnic Korean schools, most of them operated by Chongryun (pro-North-Korea General Federation of Korean Residents in Japan). Though J1 speakers in early childhood, the children frequenting these schools learn Korean within a couple of years (Cary 2001).[14] In general, the situation of residents of Korean background and their language life are better documented than those of the Chinese, *nikkeijin*, and other foreign communities (Huzii 2005; Ryang 2000; Sanada, Ogoshi and Yim 2005).

Oldcomer Chinese tend to maintain bilingualism up until the second generation, but among the third generation bilingual proficiency becomes weaker (Long et al. 2002: 147). Chinese newcomers have been arriving in Japan since the resumption of diplomatic relations with the People's Republic of China in 1972, particularly after the beginning of China's "reform and open door" policy in 1978 (Tajima 2003: 68). One particular group among them are the above-mentioned war orphans (*chūgoku kikokusha*), who lost their parents or remained in China during the Japanese retreat at the end of WWII when they were small children. Some of them have been "repatriated" together with their family members with support of the Japanese government, others came to Japan on their own initiative, and at their own expense. They lack long-established organizations that represent their interest and frequently experience settlement problems due to the complex nature of their ethnic identity (Tomozawa 2001: 137). Much effort has been made to teach them (basic) Japanese. Most research on them has been related to J2 education. Tomozawa, who aptly refers to them as "Japan's hidden bilinguals", states that younger "returnees" and their offspring generally acquire Japanese without difficulty in compulsory education. Maintaining Japanese–Chinese bilingualism is difficult, though. Just like Koreans and *nikkeijin*, bilingual Chinese residents adapt their linguistic resources to their environment and use code-switching in different domains, depending on whom they speak to and about what (Tagengoka Genshō Kenkyūkai 2013; Kawakami 2012).

Reforms of immigration laws from the 1990s onwards have opened the door to South-American *nikkeijin* immigrants of Japanese ancestry and their spouses, down to the third generation (Hirataka, Koishi and Kato 2001: 165). The biggest communities originate from Brazil (184,000) and Peru (48,000) (Hōmushō 2016). The largest number of Nikkeijin residents can be found in Aichi Prefecture and Shizuoka Prefecture where Japan's car industry is mainly located. The Japanese used by *nikkeijin* has attracted interest since the late 1990s (Nakamizu 2005; Shibuya 2010: 13). While older Brazilian *nikkeijin* rely on Portuguese and use the language at home and restricted other domains (e.g., shops run and church frequented by fellow-Brazilians), young children grow up as J1 speakers.

There are few comparative studies of foreign populations in sociolinguistics. Sociologists have been more active. For example, a study by Chiavacchi (2013: 224) identifies the factors that have led to Korean assimilation and to the development of the *nikkeijin* into a "socially detached underclass". Third and fourth generation Koreans are J1 speakers, who often do not speak Korean fluently. Furthermore, mixed Korean-Japanese marriages are now conventional. On the other hand, *nikkeijin* children remain not well integrated in the national school system and, as a consequence thereof, "face very limited opportunities in the Japanese labour market" (Chiavacchi 2013: 224).

Japanese as lingua franca in contemporary Japan remains understudied, too. Most sociolinguistic inquiries on the topic concentrate on the former colonies, most notably on Taiwan (e.g., Jian and Sanada 2011). Saitō (2015) examined Japanese as lingua franca in the domains of "restaurant and drinking establishments", church and in the linguistic landscape in two localities in Gunma Prefecture and Mie Prefecture. Both prefectures have high concentrations of foreign residents. Maher (2004) sketches the history of pidgins and creoles in Japan, including modern varieties such as Japanese–Ryukyu pidgins and Gastarbeiter (*dekasegi*) pidgins among migrant laborers, in existence since the 1980s.[15] Maher (2004: 183–184) supplements these with military base pidgins ("Hamamatsu pidgin" in Shizuoka Prefecture in the 1950s) and "Ogasawara pidgin", concluding that "[p]idgin research in Japan has been long neglected and does not now feature in contemporary linguistic research". This lack of research is of course regrettable, and the topic should be addressed in future sociolinguistic studies.

Besides historical and colonial settings, the study of pidgins falls into the realm of "late modern" sociolinguistic trends in Japan. A novel broad definition of new speakers (*nouveaux locuteurs*) in the era of globalization would, if applied to Japanese contexts, extend from J1-speaking learners of Ainu and Ryukyuan languages to international students, transnational workers, migrants and refugees, and others crossing national or virtual boundaries, adopting and using Japanese and other languages as a result (Guilleux 2015).[16] Short-term foreign residents (students, trainees, laborers, businesspeople, etc.) as well as illegal residents further add to the current situation of nationalities, ethnicities, residence-permit types, language repertoires and proficiencies in Japan.[17] To cater to these diverse populations and to the increasing number of incoming tourists, multilingual information in East Asian languages, English, Portuguese, etc., is now relatively widely available in Japan. These materials and their production have been examined (Shoji, Backhaus and Coulmas 2009; Gottlieb 2011). These developments have prompted Carroll to point to

> the need to strike a balance between ensuring that foreign residents obtain essential information in appropriate languages on one hand, and, on the other, the provision of opportunities for newcomers to learn Japanese language and culture on a long-term basis in order to live together with Japanese people.
>
> *(Carroll 2010: 390)*

J2 speakers in Japan

Providing opportunities for newcomers to learn Japanese has turned into a crucial theme in Japan's super-aged society with too few children. Recent years have seen a surge of interest in and initiatives for J2 education on a local level. At the same time, the national government has been slow to address the needs of immigrants (Green 2014). J2 speakers typically have specific motivations for learning Japanese, e.g., being able to work, study and live in Japan as functional citizens. In this context reference is often made to "children crossing borders" (Kawakami 2012), but in reality children have no choice but to follow their parents who cross borders and move to Japan for one reason or another (Ozeki 2013).

Seibert Vaipae (2001: 186) distinguishes what she terms "language minority students" into three groups depending on who their parents are: "(1) foreign academics and professionals,

(2) working-class immigrants, and (3) Chinese 'war orphans' and their families". Note that Japanese children returning from abroad (*kikoku shijo*) do not fall into this category, because they usually have two Japanese-speaking parents and use Japanese as home language. She points out that the quality of the educational programs and measures targeting this heterogeneous population have not been evaluated for their effectiveness. Educational institutions and government authorities minimize their efforts in dealing with these students, "mainstreaming" them in the absence of a migrant policy. As an effect, newcomer *nikkeijin* children may end up in the very same classes with "elite bilinguals" such as *kikoku shijo*, despite the fact that they have very different linguistic skills (Carroll 2011: 189).

Kawakami (2012: 81) prefers to consider children crossing borders as a concept that represents characteristics of (1) geographical and (2) linguistic mobility, as well as (3) mobility in terms of the type of language education they are immersed in (*kokugo*, JFL, J2, heritage language). Kawakami (2012: 81) focuses on "the relationship between children's language education, identity formation, and citizenship and the kind of society and system of language education needed by children living in a context of increasing mobility". In his view, "plurilinguality" should be "fostered as an reorganized resource" which has meaning for each individual child and is employed in their daily lives (Kawakami 2012: 96). However, it is questionable to what extent this is a sociolinguistic reality in contemporary Japan beyond the small group of students with "elite bilingualism" (Yamamoto 2011).

J2 children and pupils is another concept that has drawn much attention recently. Over 70,000 foreign children are currently enrolled in Japanese public schools, almost 60% in primary school, some 30% in junior high school, and the rest in senior high school. These numbers have remained relatively stable during the past decade (MEXT 2015b). The number of foreign children requiring additional Japanese language guidance (*nihongo shidō*) has increased from less than 30% a decade ago to nearly 40% today. In addition, the number of children with Japanese nationality in need of "guidance" is on the rise, reaching nearly 8,000 pupils according to official statistics. Such children have either one non-Japanese parent or have their "roots abroad" (MEXT 2015a). In 2016, over 34,000 children were reported to be in need of "Japanese language guidance" in primary and middle school (MEXT 2016a). Pupils attending Japanese schools have more than 60 different language backgrounds (Kawakami 2012: 96). Most of these foreign children are speakers of Asian languages (Chinese, Filipino/Tagalog, Vietnamese, Korean, etc.), or speakers of *nikkeijin* languages such as Brazilian Portuguese and Spanish. These children are concentrated in specific schools in the car-manufacturing region of Aichi Prefecture, as well as in Kanagawa Prefecture and Tokyo Prefecture. Nearly 80% of public primary and middle schools in Japan have no such pupils (MEXT 2015b, 2016a).

The organization of J2 education at schools frequented by children of migrant families has not escaped criticism (e.g., Ōtsu 2005), and efforts are currently made to support residents with non-dominant language proficiencies in order to turn them into *seikatsusha* (citizens and consumers) (Kakazu 2011: 69; Kumagai and Satō 2011). Japanese language guidance for foreign children in compulsory education is organized in various ways. It is either included in the curriculum or provided as an extracurricular activity (Miyazaki and Kimura 2014).[18] Various measures targeting Japanese language learning by pupils (and their parents) have been taken, including the deployment of new instructors, the granting of financial assistance, offering training for administrative and teaching personnel at schools, compilation and distribution of instructional booklets on schooling in Japan in multiple languages and the creation of special curricula, materials and learning targets (MEXT 2015b).[19] Academic analyses of learning materials and recommendations for pedagogical practices exist, but the effects of educational efforts are still to be fully explored. The concept itself, *gaikokujin jidō seito* (foreign children and pupils), is oblivious of the diverse backgrounds of these children (Ozeki 2013). It also excludes those going to schools for foreign nationals or those refusing to go to school.[20] The danger of becoming double limited (*daburu rimiteddo*), that is, starting school in Japanese while the mother tongue is still underdeveloped, is another point of concern. In addition, the criteria determining who is "in need of Japanese language guidance" have been criticized for being too vague. Ozeki (2013: 3) claims that the numbers published by the Ministry of Education, Culture, Sports, Science and Technology (MEXT) do not reflect the real scope of language problems that J2 speakers are experiencing in educational settings.

The majority of research activities in this field consists of surveys and case studies targeting localities where the majority of *nikkeijin* or other foreign national children go to school, but also of proposals for J2 assessment, curriculum development, teacher education and reflections on multicultural education and co-living (*kyōsei*). Also, the technical aspects of a bibliographical heritage language education database have been addressed under the umbrella of large research projects (Nakajima, Tanaka and Morishita 2011). This notwithstanding, comprehensive overviews are hard to come by. Part of the problem is that academic publications in Japan do not rigorously separate reports on J2 and JFL education. Established in 2003, a research network entitled "The Mother Tongue, Heritage Language, and Bilingual Education (MHB) Research Association" is divided into interest groups covering "Overseas Heritage Japanese Language", "International School", "Assessment", and "Bilingual Writing" (MHB 2016).

Besides "JSL children", other J2/JFL speaker groups are well represented in Japan. The number of students in language education facilities for foreigners totaled almost 175,000 in 2014, and nearly 190,000 one year later (Bunkachō 2014, 2016). More than 50,000 such students are enrolled in institutions of tertiary education. Roughly 120,000 are learning Japanese in educational institutions. More than 80% of these learners are from Asian countries. Students from the Republic of China (36%) provide for the largest group, followed by Vietnamese (15%). Nepalese, South Korean, Taiwanese and Filipino students represent each about 5%. Roughly 2% of these students have Japanese nationality. The majority of the students (over 60%) are exchange students. Other categories include technical trainees, businesspeople, short-term visitors, spouses of Japanese citizens, *nikkeijin*, "returnees from China", refugees, and others. More than half of the students stay in Japan for a period of one to three years. Most students reside in the Tokyo metropolitan area and the surrounding prefectures. Other large concentrations can be found in the Kansai area, in Fukuoka Prefecture and in Aichi Prefecture.

Ongoing JSL research is reported by the Research Division on Japanese as a Second Language at the National Institute for Japanese Language and Linguistics.[21] There are also a number of specialist periodicals such as *Nihongo kyōiku* (*Journal of Japanese Language Teaching*) or *Nihongo/nihongo kyōiku kenkyū* (*Studies in Japanese Language and Japanese Language Teaching*). The latter journal carries articles on Korean-, Chinese-, Hindi-, Vietnamese-, Malay- and Thai-speaking learners, including contrastive analyses. It concentrates mainly on (contrastive) pragmatics and analysis of selected syntactic or discourse elements and structures. The more established *Nihongo kyōiku* regularly publishes articles and special issues relevant to sociolinguistics (e.g., language minority children, Plain or Easy Japanese, universal communication design, language empowerment, *nikkeijin* laborers, or multilingualization). On the occasion of its 150th edition, Usami (2012) provided for an overview of 610 articles with "sociological perspectives" that were published in the journal. While the earliest issues concentrated on JFL education and its conditions abroad, attention placed on learners in Japan has increased since the late 1980s. Key concepts that reflect sociolinguistic research topics include context and language use (*bamen to gengo un'yō*), culture (*bunka*), as well as social conditions and learning (*shakai jōsei to gakushū*).

JFL speakers

Increasing the number of JFL speakers has been an objective of the Japanese Ministry of Foreign Affairs for many decades now (Gaimushō 2013). Currently, the objective is to have five million JFL learners by 2020. While Japanese still attracts quite a large number of language learners outside of Japan, surveys demonstrate that Japanese is losing ground to Mandarin Chinese.[22]

Compared to J2 education, JFL education abroad has a long history of systematic governmental policies. Learners having mastered and those endeavoring to master Japanese are nowadays often referred to as *nihongo jinzai* (Japanese language human resources). They tend to be seen uniquely as concrete assets for Japan, e.g., *shisan* (property, asset), *jinteki na asetto* (human asset) or *ōkina rieki* (great profit) (Länsisalmi 2016: 222). The Japan Foundation – an independent administrative institution financed by the Japanese government, investment revenues and private donations – has been carrying out surveys on Japanese language education abroad since 1974 (Japan Foundation 2016b). The latest survey reveals that Japanese is studied in 137 countries worldwide, but that the number of overseas learners has decreased by roughly 300,000 after a long period of steady growth. In addition to the current learners, former JFL learners outside educational institutions constitute an important group around the globe, but the size of active Japanese users is hard to guess. Gottlieb (2005: 6) puts the number of current and former learners at an estimated ten million.

Language learning motivations listed in surveys prominently include "interest in Japanese language" (62%), followed by "communication in Japanese" (56%), "interest in *manga, anime,* J-Pop, etc." (54%) and "interest in history, literature, etc." (50%) (Japan Foundation 2012: 4). Knowledge about Japan and its language has been a more important factor than utility-based motivations. "Future employment" (42%) ranks fifth in the survey and "study in Japan" (34%) is in seventh place. The majority of learners, nearly 80%, reside in regions close to Japan in East and Southeast Asia (People's Republic of China, Indonesia, South Korea) where knowledge of Japanese has an instrumental value in the job market. Roughly 10% of the learners live in Australia, less than 5% in the US and only 3% in Europe. The smallest numbers of learners are found in Africa (Japan Foundation 2016a).

Inoue (2007: 98) distinguishes three factors determining the market value of languages: (1) population size (global scale), (2) economic power of the speech community (global and regional scale) and (3) information quantity and cultural elaboration (global, regional and personal scale), and he includes Japanese in all these categories. While the Japan Foundation produces JFL reports on a regular basis, these do not capture the full picture of Japanese language studies outside Japan. Currently available mobile and digital technologies offer unprecedented possibilities and resources to anyone interested in learning Japanese independently. This phenomenon can be evidenced in formal classroom education where JLF teachers nowadays deal with students of increasingly varying proficiencies.[23]

In linguistic research, in particular, Japanese interlanguage produced by NNS learners has been studied. The areas and research interests in JLF and J2 education intersect with many fields of sociolinguistics. However, it is often primarily the specific ways in which NNS use Japanese that capture the interest of scholars. Sasaki (2005) and Mori and Mori (2011) offer extended reviews on J2/JFL research for the period of time from 2000 to 2010, covering both "second language acquisition" and pedagogical practices. In another overview, Nuibe (2007) lists the following main areas of research: teaching Japanese to young children, Japanese for academic purposes, teacher training, teaching methods, second language acquisition and pedagogical grammar. In this overview, sociolinguistics ranks last, covering only about 10% of the reviewed articles and reports. Besides information and publications on JFL by the Japan Foundation, information on the latest trends in Japanese language education is easily available. There are a number of academic associations and research centers that publish journals, newsletters or proceedings. Examples include the Japan Association for Language Teaching (JALT) in Japan, and The Association of Japanese Language Teachers in Europe (AJE) or The American Association of Teachers of Japanese (AATJ) overseas.

In the past decade, identity and language learning has received more attention. It is studied how learners establish "their ability to make their own choices as to how they [want] to present themselves in different social contexts" (Mori and Mori 2011: 459–460). JLF speakers, often a long distance away from Japan, do not necessarily ascribe to idealized linguistic NS models.[24] Critical approaches now address the obvious power imbalances that are inherent in NS versus NNS categorizations (Cook 1999, in Tanaka 2013). Other related areas of interest include Easy or Plain Japanese (*yasashii nihongo* and *wakariyasui nihongo*, respectively), connecting directly to discussions on barrier-free information and *kyōsei nihongo* (co-living Japanese), a language variety created in actual communication situations involving NNS and NS (Yoshinaga 2015; Gottlieb 2012; Matsuo et al. 2013). Besides J2 and JFL education, these topics are often researched in the fields of critical sociolinguistics or welfare linguistics (Murata 2015).

"Virtual speakers" in fiction, translation and real life

There is one more type of speaker – speakers who are "purposefully 'incoherent'" when speaking (Heinrich 2017). There is no label for such speakers yet, but the kind of language they produce is discussed in Japan as *yakuwarigo* (role language), or as *vācharu nihongo* (virtual Japanese). This kind of language use, associated with features of imaginary speakers, has grown in a popular field of cross-disciplinary study. Consumers of Japanese novels, *manga* comics, soap operas, *anime*, TV drama, games, translated literature, etc., regularly come across such language use. Kinsui (2007) notes that speaker characteristics in role language include age, gender, social status or occupation, regional origin, nationality, race or historical period. There is no end to this list. It includes also, for example, imagined alien or robot speech.[25] Teshigawara and Kinsui (2011) state that crafted role language is typically rooted in non-fictional language use, and that Japanese NS audience is well aware of the fictional character of such speakers and such speech. However, only sporadic information is available on the actual abilities to infer the type of role portrayed by virtual speech styles (for both NS and NNS). One of the rare exceptions is Shukuri's (2012) work, which focuses on first person pronouns in "virtual Japanese".[26]

The most typical virtual features are associated with particular speaker first person pronouns, variants of the copula and sentence-final interactional particles. Also, many other features such as honorifics, Sino-Japanese words (*kango*), loanwords (*gairaigo*), interjections, laughter, pidgin-like expressions, accent, intonation, voice quality and particular pragmatic and discourse features are listed in the research literature. This type of research culminates in a role language dictionary, which explains on more than 200 pages lexical items, morphosyntactic features and other expressions that are often linked to fictional characters (Kinsui 2014). Contrastive studies comparing Japanese and (translations into) Korean, Chinese, English, Spanish and Finnish, and reflections on role language in Japanese language education are other additions to the field (Kinsui 2011; Teshigawara and Kinsui 2011). A subfield of role language studies also looks at expressions of non-human characters such as animals or hybrid human-animals (Akizuki 2012; Kawasaki 2015).

Translation, contrastive studies or Japanese language education are other areas, where "hidden" stereotypes incorporated in role language have been studied. Ōta (2009, 2017), for example, investigates how athletics superstar Usain Bolt's "stardom" is reflected in the Japanese translations of his comments (e.g., tough masculine first person pronoun *ore* in edgy katakana) and how Japanese TV subtitles of interviews with foreign athletes reflect their expected roles in "Olympic Stories". Although "role language" is a novel term, similar studies were carried out before the popularization of this field. Examples include dialect use by Japanese romantic heroines in the construction of "authentic femininity" (Shibamoto-Smith 2009), or the manipulation of honorifics in the construction of social identities in Japanese TV drama (Barke 2010). Translated western heroines continue to speak *onna kotoba* (women's language), reflecting a Japanese-inspired normative femininity, while western youngsters resort to frank masculine *otoko kotoba* (male language), and black people are portrayed to speak "dialect", reproducing thereby stereotypes and discriminatory images via translation (Nakamura 2013; Hiramoto 2009).

Japanese language users on the Internet and in social media constitute another area of research. How bloggers write, talk and present themselves to their audiences, how dialectal features and verbal styles are used in messaging, chatting and tweeting are areas that remain little developed at the moment.[27] Rather than approaching such phenomena as "varieties" or "registers" partaking in a "structural system", Heinrich (2017: 221) offers an analysis how such "new presentations of self" by a new generation are now linked to "showing how things are done with words, by doing unexpected things with words, in order to change how things are done with words". Analyzing these phenomena with the customary "first and second wave" sociolinguist's toolkit will prove unsuccessful.

Japanese and its speakers in the future

For the most part, Japan is today an urban society. In such contexts new types of speakers and learners, various degrees of language ownership, poly- and translanguaging and crossing are widely observed. In such settings, the conceptual framework of "speech communities" is taking a backseat to "individual speakers". Diverse groups of speakers are further diversifying, and as an effect sociolinguistic research has to zoom in on individual "linguistic repertoires" (Blommaert and Backus 2013). Such kind of research is not yet prominent in Japanese sociolinguistics. However, in Japan, too, the notion of "speaker" needs to be expanded in order to do justice to the fluidity of urban, globalized and digital life (see Nakane, Otsuji and Armour 2015; Pennycook and Otsuji 2010, 2014, 2015). Any overview of "speaker" needs to consider global communication and mobility, outcomes of personal and socio-political (power-related) histories traced over time, attempts at maintaining and revitalizing languages, efforts of adding or strengthening new languages to the existing repertoire, and how all of this intersects in some way or another with everyday language practices. Sociolinguistics needs to investigate who speaks what kind of Japanese, what it means to them to speak this way, and what they do with language in various local socio-cultural environments around the globe.

Notes

1 In a translator's note to Lee (2010: xiv) Hirano Hubbard explains that the expression "Japanese language" in English corresponds to the Japanese terms *nihongo* and *kokugo*. Symbolic of the nation-state (*kokka*), *kokugo*, including its history and nationalistic connotations with "our language" and development as a scholarly discipline have been widely discussed (e.g., Nishihara 2015; Yasuda 2004). See Galan (2005) on learning how to read and write in Japanese.
2 "Historical speakers" are not discussed here. For overviews, see Takagi, Shibuya and Iyeiri (2015); Frellesvig (2010); Okada (2006).

3 The Agency for Cultural Affairs (Bunkachō 2016: 58) categorizes its policies related to the Japanese language under the headings "Japanese language policy" and "Japanese language education policy", the former covering mainly issues pertaining to L1 Japanese and the latter to those relevant to "Japanese language education for foreigners". It has surveyed the "current status and efforts for the preservation and succession" of Ainu, Hachijo, and the Ryukyuan languages.
4 The concept of "native speaker" has been discussed widely elsewhere (e.g., Meyerhoff and Stanford 2015).
5 *Kokugo* usually refers to Japanese mother tongue education at school. *Kōyōgo* is the de facto Japanese in use. If Japanese is contrasted with other languages, the term *nihongo* is used.
6 For overviews in Japanese sociolinguistics, past and present, see Heinrich and Masiko (2015); Ide (1986); Loveday (1986); Sanada (2006); Sibata (1985); Sibata (1999); Shibamoto (1987).
7 In her study of western middle- and upper-class residential Yamanote and eastern lower-middle-class and blue-collar Shitamachi Hibiya (1995) shows that change and variation pertaining to velar plosive have been particularly influenced by the extra-linguistic factors of age and contact with the socio-economically more affluent Yamanote.
8 Satake (2005) examined discourses on male and female language norms in post-war Japanese newspapers. The majority of comments showed concern about an increasing masculinization, neutralization, or increased "roughness" of language use by women.
9 The latter are usually "characterized in terms of a set of specific linguistic forms involving features such as self-reference and address terms, sentence-final forms, and honorifics, and also in terms of general stylistic features such as politeness, gentleness, and refinement (for *joseigo*) and forcefulness, decisiveness, and roughness (for *danseigo*)" (Okamoto 2016: 10–11).
10 "*[O]nabe* refers, not to female homosexuals in general (*rezu* 'lesbian' serves this function), but specifically to a 'lesbian who dresses and acts like a man' (cf. English nouns *butch, passing woman,* or *dyke*)" (Long 1996: 216).
11 The Clarinet site (Children Living Abroad and Returnees Internet) includes a lengthy manual on Dialogic Language Assessment for Japanese as a Second Language (MEXT 2016b).
12 The *burakumin*, estimated to number circa three million people, are ethnically Japanese. They "remain – albeit less now than formerly – victims of status discrimination" (Gottlieb 2001: 983).
13 Imperial expansion during the colonial period 1905–1945 brought with it an influx of Korean, Chinese and Taiwanese immigrants to Japan referred to as *zainichi*.
14 "For half a century, Japan has permitted ethnic minorities, notably Koreans, to run their own schools while refusing to recognize these schools' graduates by denying their students the right to sit for entrance examinations at national universities. The controversy has centered above all on the rights of graduates of pro-North Korean schools" (Arita 2003: 1).
15 See also Long's (2003) publication on the linguistic heritage of the Ogasawara (Bonin) Islands.
16 See Kawaguchi and Tsunoda (2005) on language ownership. In English language literature "new speakers", as opposed to "traditional speakers" is conventionally employed in the context of minority languages, particularly when discussing language endangerment, maintenance and revitalization.
17 The Ministry of Justice currently puts the number of illegal residents at 60,000 (Hōmushō 2015).
18 One example from Toyohashi City (2016: 53), Aichi Prefecture, schematically describes how an individual study path, stretching from the first six months to two years and beyond, can be composed of "survival", "basic" and "skill-specific" Japanese. This is supplemented by learning Japanese through other school subjects and extra support in them. The Japanese writing system receives some treatment in the instructions, but they also point out that it is difficult to learn to write kanji characters during the time reserved for Japanese language guidance. Thus, assigning daily kanji writing homework or other additional measures of "support" for non-kanji background pupils is necessary (Toyohashi City 2016: 57).
19 For example, the Castanet site includes a collection of extra learning materials in 12 languages for a number of school subjects such as math, society, *kokugo* and *nihongo*. Furthermore, guidelines and tools to help implement special Japanese as a Second Language (JSL) curricula in various subjects have been developed for primary and middle school, and senior high schools in some prefectures have special quota for returnees and foreign students.
20 More than 20,000 students are enrolled in some 200 *gaikokujin gakkō*, i.e., Korean, (English language) international school, Brazilian, Peruvian, Chinese and other ethnic schools. The School Education Act recognizes no more than a handful of these schools, whilst about 120 are accredited as "miscellaneous schools" or "quasi-incorporated educational institutions". The rest of the schools are unaccredited (Miyawaki 2005).

21 NINJAL's JSL Research Division (2009) defines its scope as follows. "In addition to producing purely linguistic descriptions and analyses, it also seeks to clarify the nature of social and cultural problems that non-native learners are likely to face in the process of adjusting themselves to Japanese society."
22 Whilst some surveys on the current and future demand for foreign languages now rank Chinese highest, followed by English, French, German, Italian, Japanese, Portuguese, Russian and Spanish (IALC 2016), others exclude Japanese from the category of the most useful languages when estimated on economic terms. The British Council (2013), to name an example, now ranks Japanese in tenth place, but it is no longer specifically listed as a language needed for economic purposes, neither for cultural, educational and diplomatic ones.
23 A Portal for Learning Japanese maintained by the Japan Foundation (2016), currently lists over 350 links to online sites for learners and teachers of Japanese, and dozens of applications for mobile devices exist.
24 See Mizumoto (2015) on gender, Heinrich (2005) on language ideology in Japanese language learning materials, Kinsui (2011) on role language by Japanese language learners, and Abe (2014) on "universal design" in language learning. Inoue (1995, 2008) notes that Japanese language education does not yet incorporate sociolinguistic perspectives and proposes that it should include attention to variation and discourse.
25 Speech recognition and research and development of social and chat robots are thriving fields in Japan (see Takase, Yoshino and Nakano 2017; Yamazaki 2011).
26 Shukuri (2012) reports that for example the first person pronoun *watashi* used by male characters was associated to gay language by NS but to polite language by NNS.
27 See *vācharu hōgen* (virtual dialect), *nise hōgen* (fake dialect), etc. Okamoto and Shibamoto-Smith (2016: 67–68) note that it is "necessary to place changes in dialect representations in media texts against a non-mediatized social shift".

References

Abe, Hideko (2004) Lesbian Bar Talk in Shinjuku, Tokyo. In: *Japanese Language, Gender, and Ideology. Cultural Models and Real People*. Shigeko Okamoto and Janet S. Shibamoto-Smith (eds), 421–455. New York: Oxford University Press.

—— (2010) *Queer Japanese. Gender and Sexual Identities through Linguistic Practices*. New York: Palgrave Macmillan.

Abe, Hideko Nōnesu (2014) Gei, onee, nyūhāfu no kotoba – danseigo to joseigo no aida [The Language of Gay, onee, New Half Speakers. Between Male and Female Language]. *Nihongogaku* 33(1): 44–59.

Abe, Yasusi (2014) Gengo gakushū no yunibāsaru dezain [Universal Design for Language Learning]. *Nihongogaku* 9(33): 56–67.

Adachi, Chie (2016) Sugoi! Indexicality and Stancetaking in Japanese Compliments. *Language in Society* 45(2): 193–216.

Akizuki, Kōtarō (2012) Dōbutsu kyarakutā no gengogaku [The Language of Hybrid Human-animal Creatures]. *Research Reports of Shokei Gakuin College* 64: 43–57.

Anderson, Mark and Patrick Heinrich (eds) (2014) *Language Crisis in the Ryukyus*. Newcastle upon Tyne: Cambridge Scholars Publishing.

Arita, Eriko (2003) Japanese Discrimination against Korean and other Ethnic Schools. *The Asia-Pacific Journal Japan Focus* 1(4): 1–2. Available online at: http://apjjf.org/-Eriko-ARITA/2137/article.pdf (accessed 5 June 2018).

Backhaus, Peter and Rie Suzuki (2010) Time to Get Up. Compliance Gaining in Japanese Institutional Eldercare. *Shakai gengo kagaku* 13(1): 48–57.

Barke, Andrew (2010) Manipulating Honorifics in the Construction of Social Identities in Japanese Television Drama. Honorifics in Japanese Television Drama. *Journal of Sociolinguistics* 14(4): 456–476.

Blommaert, Jan and Ad Backus (2013) Superdiverse Repertoires and the Individual. In: *Multilingualism and Multimodality*. Ingrid de Saint-Georges and Jean-Jacques Weber (eds), 11–32. Rotterdam: Sense.

The British Council (2013) Languages for the Future. Which Languages the UK Needs Most and Why. Available online at: www.britishcouncil.org/sites/default/files/languages-for-the-future-report.pdf (accessed 16 June 2018).

Bunkachō (2014) Kokunai nihongo kyōiku gaiyō [Overview of Japanese Language Education in Japan]. Available online at: www.bunka.go.jp/tokei_hakusho_shuppan/tokeichosa/nihongokyoiku_jittai/h26/pdf/h26_zenbun.pdf (accessed 24 May 2017).

—— (2016) Policy of Cultural Affairs in Japan. Fiscal 2016. Available online at: www.bunka.go.jp/english/report/annual/pdf/2016_policy.pdf (accessed 7 June 2018).
Carroll, Tessa (2010) Local Government Websites in Japan. International, Multicultural, Multilingual? *Japanese Studies* 30(3): 373–392.
—— (2011) Japanese as an International Language. In: *Language Life in Japan*. Patrick Heinrich and Christian Galan (eds), 186–201. London: Routledge.
Cary, Ann B. (2001) Affiliation, not Assimilation. Resident Koreans and Ethnic Education. In: *Studies in Japanese Bilingualism*. Mary Goebel Noguchi and Sandra Fotos (eds), 98–132. Clevedon: Multilingual Matters.
Chiavacchi, David (2013) Integration and Exclusion of Minorities in Japan. A Comparison of Korean Residents and Nikkeijin. In: *Life Course and Life Style in Comparison*. Akira Tokuyasu, Makoto Kobayashi and Mototaka Mori (eds), 207–230. Tokyo: Hōsei University.
Cook, Haruko Minegishi (2013) A Scientist or Salesman? Identity Construction through Referent Honorifics on a Japanese Shopping Channel Program. *Multilingua* 32(2): 177–202.
Coulmas, Florian (2013) *Sociolinguistics. The Study of Speakers' Choices* (second edition). Cambridge: Cambridge University Press.
Dunn, Cynthia Dickel (2013) Speaking Politely, Kindly, and Beautifully. Ideologies of Politeness in Japanese Business Etiquette Training. *Multilingua* 32(2): 225–245.
Eckert, Penelope (2012) Three Waves of Variation Study. The Emergence of Meaning in the Study of Sociolinguistic Variation. *Annual Review of Anthropology* 41: 87–100.
Endō, Orie (2006) *A Cultural History of Japanese Women's Language*. Ann Arbor: Center for Japanese Studies.
Frellesvig, Bjarke (2010) *A History of the Japanese Language*. Cambridge: Cambridge University Press.
Fukushima, Saeko (2004) Evaluation of Politeness. The Case of Attentiveness. *Multilingua* 23(4): 365–387.
Gagné, Isaac (2008) Urban Princesses. Performance and "Women's Language" in Japan's Gothic/Lolita Subculture. *Journal of Linguistic Anthropology* 18(1): 130–150.
Gaimushō (2013) Kaigai ni okeru nihongo no fukyū sokushin ni kansuru yūshikisha kondankai "saishū hōkokusho" [Expert Panel on the Promotion of Japanese Language Abroad, "Final Report"]. Available online at: www.mofa.go.jp/mofaj/press/release/press24_000013.html (accessed 10 June 2016).
Galan, Christian (2005) Learning to Read and Write in Japanese. A Barrier to Multilingualism? *International Journal of the Sociology of Language* 175/176: 249–269.
Geyer, Naomi (2013) Discernment and Variation. The Action-oriented Use of Japanese Addressee Honorifics. *Multilingua* 32(2): 155–176.
Gottlieb, Nanette (2001) Language and Disability in Japan. *Disability & Society* 16(7): 981–995.
—— (2005) *Language and Society in Japan*. Cambridge: Cambridge University Press.
—— (ed.) (2011) *Language in Public Spaces in Japan*. London: Routledge.
—— (ed.) (2012) *Language and Citizenship in Japan*. London: Routledge.
Green, David (2014) Education of Foreign Children in Japan. Local versus National Initiatives. *Journal of International Migration and Integration* 15(3): 387–410.
—— (2017) As its Population Ages, Japan Quietly Turns to Immigration. *Migration Information Source* (Migration Policy Institute). Available online at: www.migrationpolicy.org/article/its-population-ages-japan-quietly-turns-immigration (accessed 12 March 2018).
Guilleux, Céline (2015) Nouveaux locuteurs dans l'Europe plurilingue du XXIe siècle. *Calenda*. Available online at: https://calenda.org/318429 (accessed 10 June 2016).
Hankins, Joseph D. (2014) *Working Skin. Making Leather, Making a Multicultural Japan*. Oakland: University of California Press.
Hasegawa, Yoko (2015) *Japanese. A Linguistic Introduction*. Cambridge: Cambridge University Press.
Hayashi, Makoto (2004) Discourse within a Sentence. An Exploration of Postpositions in Japanese as an Interactional Resource. *Language in Society* 33(3): 343–376.
Heinrich, Patrick (2005) Language Ideology in JFL Textbooks. *International Journal of the Sociology of Language* 175/176: 213–232.
—— (2012) *The Making of Monolingual Japan. Language Ideology and Japanese Modernity*. Bristol: Multilingual Matters.
—— (2015a) Language Shift. In: *Handbook of the Ryukyuan Languages*. Patrick Heinrich, Shinso Miyara and Michinori Shimoji (eds), 613–630. Boston: De Gruyter Mouton.
—— (2015b) The Study of Politeness and Women's Language in Japan. In: *Globalising Sociolinguistics. Challenging and Expanding Theory*. Dick Smakman and Patrick Heinrich (eds), 178–193. London: Routledge.

––––––– (2017) New Presentations of Self in Everyday Life. Linguistic Transgressions in England, Germany and Japan. In: *Identity and Dialect Performance*. Reem Bassiouney (ed.), 381–407. London: Routledge.

Heinrich, Patrick and Christian Galan (eds.) (2011) *Language Life in Japan*. London: Routledge.

Heinrich, Patrick and Hidenori Masiko (2015) Japanese Sociolinguistics. A Critical Review and Outlook. In: *Contemporary Japan* (Ca' Foscari Japanese Studies) 3: 249–266.

Hibiya, Junko (1995) The Velar Nasal in Tokyo Japanese. A Case of Diffusion from Above. *Language Variation and Change* 7(2): 139–152.

Hiramoto, Mie (2009) Slaves Speak Pseudo-Tōhoku-ben. The Representation of Minorities in the Japanese Translation of "Gone with the Wind". *Journal of Sociolinguistics* 13(2): 249–263.

Hirataka, Fumiya, Atsuko Koishi and Yosuke Kato (2001) On the Language Environment of Brazilian Immigrants in Fujisawa City. In: *Studies in Japanese Bilingualism*. Mary G. Noguchi and Sandra Fotos (eds), 164–183. Clevedon: Multilingual Matters.

Hōmushō (2016) Zairyū gaikokujin tōkei – kyū tōroku gaikokujin tōkei [Statistics on Foreign National Residents. Former Statistics on Registered Foreigners]. Available online at: www.moj.go.jp/housei/toukei/toukei_ichiran_touroku.html (accessed 10 June 2016).

Huzii, Konosuke (2005) Kankoku, chōsenjin [South-, North-Koreans]. In: *Nihon no tagengo shakai*. Shinji Sanada and Hiroshi Shoji (eds), 178–182. Tokyo: Iwanami Shoten.

IALC (=International Association of Language Centres) (2016) News. New Report Compares Current and Future Demand for Nine Foreign Languages. Available online at: www.ialc.org/news/201604-new-report-compares-current-and-future-demand-for-nine-foreign-languages.asp (accessed 1 February 2018).

Ide, Sachiko (1986) Introduction. The Background of Japanese Sociolinguistics. *Journal of Pragmatics* 10(3): 281–286.

––––––– (1989) Formal Forms and Discernment. Two Neglected Aspects of Universals of Linguistic Politeness. *Multilingua* 8(2): 223–248.

Ide, Sachiko, Motoko Hori, Akiko Kawasaki, Shoko Ikuta and Hitomi Haga (1986) Sex Difference and Politeness in Japanese. *International Journal of the Sociology of Language* 58: 25–36.

Ikeda, Tomoko (2003) The Organization and Functions of Laughter in a Japanese Face-to-face Interaction. *Shakai gengo kagaku* 6(1): 52–60.

Inoue, Fumio (1995) Nihongo kyōiku ni okeru shakai gengo gakuteki kiban [Sociolinguistics for Japanese Language Education]. *Monbushō kagaku kenkyūhi sōgō (A) kenkyū seika hōkokusho [MEXT Grants-in-Aid for Scientific Research, General (A), Report on Research Results]*. Tokyo: TUFS.

––––––– (2007) Changing Economic Values of German and Japanese. In: *Language Regimes in Transformation. Future Prospects for German and Japanese in Science, Economy and Politics*. Florian Coulmas (ed.), 95–113. Berlin: Mouton de Gruyter.

––––––– (2008) *Shakai hōgengaku ronkō – shin-hōgen no kiban [Papers in Social Dialectology. Foundations of New Dialect]*. Tokyo: Meiji Shoin.

Inoue, Miyako (2002) Gender, Language, and Modernity. Toward an Effective History of Japanese Women's Language. *American Ethnologist* 29(2): 392–422.

Iwama, Akiko (2007) Nihon ni okeru mainoriti [Minorities in Japan]. In: *Mainoriti to wa nani ka*. Akiko Iwama and Hyo-chong Yu (eds), 25–63. Kyoto: Minerva Shobō.

Iwasaki, Shoichi (2013) *Japanese* (revised edition). Amsterdam: John Benjamins.

Japan Foundation (2010) Nihongo e na, Portal for Learning Japanese. Available online at: http://nihongo-e-na.com/eng/ (accessed 10 January 2016).

Japan Foundation (2012) Japan Foundation Survey Report on Japanese-Language Education Abroad 2012. Available online at: www.jpf.go.jp/j/project/japanese/survey/result/dl/survey_2012/2012_s_excerpt_e.pdf, (accessed 20 August 2016).

––––––– (2016a) 2015-nendo "kaigai nihongo kyōiku kikan chōsa" kekka (sokuhō). [Survey on Japanese-Language Education Abroad 2015. Available online at: www.jpf.go.jp/j/about/press/2016/dl/2016-057-1.pdf (accessed 29 January 2017).

––––––– (2016b) About us. Available online at: www.jpf.go.jp/e/about/index.html (accessed 29 January 2017).

Jian, Yue Zhen and Shinji Sanada (2011) *Taiwan ni watatta nihongo no genzai – ringa furanka toshite no sugata [The Present State of Japanese Language that Crossed Over to Taiwan. Its Status as Lingua Franca]*. Tokyo: Meiji Shoin.

JSL Research Division (2009) National Research Institute for Japanese Language and Linguistics. Available online at: www.ninjal.ac.jp/english/organization/chart/jslrd/ (accessed 15 March 2017).

Kakazu, Katsumi (2011) *Gurōbarizēshon to nihongo kyōiku seisaku* [*Globalization and Japanese-Language Policy*]. Tokyo: CoCo Shuppan.

Kataoka, Kuniyoshi (1997) Affect and Letter-writing. Unconventional Conventions in Casual Writing by Young Japanese Women. *Language in Society* 26(1): 103–136.

Katō, Yoshitaka (2010) *Ibunka sesshoku bamen no intāakushon – nihongo bogo washa to nihongo hibogo washa no intāakushon kihan* [*Interaction in Intercultural Contact Situations. Foundations for Japanese Native and Non-Native Speaker Interaction*]. Tokyo: Tokyo University Press.

Kawaguchi, Ryo and Fumiyuki Tsunoda (2005) *Nihongo wa dare no mono-ka* [*Who Owns Japanese?*]. Tokyo: Yoshikawa Kōbunkan.

Kawakami, Ikuo (2012) Children Crossing Borders and their Citizenship in Japan. In: *Language and Citizenship in Japan*. Nanette Gottlieb (ed.), 79–97. London: Routledge.

Kawasaki, Akemi (2015) Neko kyarakuta no yakuwarigo "nya" ni miru kyara gobi no shiyō [Use of "Role Language Suffix" "nya [meow]" in Feline Characters' Role Language]. *Kanazawa Daigaku ningen shakaigakuiki keizaigakurui shakai gengogaku enshū* 10: 19–43.

Kim, Miseon (2005) Zainichi kankoku-chōsenjin no gengo shiyō [Language Use of Resident South- and North-Koreans]. In: *Nihon no tagengo shakai*. Shinji Sanada and Hiroshi Shoji (eds), 213–238. Tokyo: Iwanami Shoten.

Kinsui, Satoshi (2007) "Yakuwarigo" kenkyū to shakai gengogaku no setten [Crossroads of Research on "Role Language" and Sociolinguistics]. (Paper presented at the 19th Meeting of the Japanese Association of Sociolinguistic Sciences). Available online at: http://skinsui.cocolog-nifty.com/sklab/files/JASS19kinsui_paper.pdf (accessed 25 March 2017).

—— (2011) Yakuwarigo to nihongo kyōiku. [Role Language and Teaching Japanese as a Foreign Language]. *Nihongo kyōiku* 150: 34–41.

—— (ed.) (2014) *"Yakuwarigo" shōjiten* [*Small Dictionary of "Role Language"*]. Tokyo: Kenkyūsha.

Kumagai, Yuri and Shinji Satō (eds) (2011) *Shakai sanka o mezasu nihongo kyōiku* [*Japanese Language Education for Social Participation*]. Tokyo: Hitsuji Shobō.

Länsisalmi, Riikka (2016) Contents and Conceptualisation of Japanese Language Learning. "Charming" or "Arming" Learners? In: *Japanese Language Education in Europe* 21: 221–227. Moers: AJE.

Lauwereyns, Shizuka (2002) Hedges in Japanese Conversation. The Influence of Age, Sex, and Formality. *Language Variation and Change* 14(2): 239–259.

Lee, Yeounsuk (2010) *The Ideology of Kokugo. Nationalizing Language in Modern Japan* (translated by Maki Hirano Hubbard). Honolulu: University of Hawai'i Press.

Long, Daniel (1996) Formation Processes of some Japanese Gay Argot Terms. *American Speech* 71(2): 215–224.

—— (2003) The Unknown Linguistic Heritage of the Ogasawara (Bonin) Islands. Identity and Language Usage in a Japanese Minority Community. *Ogasawara Research* 29: 125–137.

Long, Daniel, Sei'ichi Nakai and Hiroaki Miyaji (eds) (2001) *Ōyō shakai gengogaku o manabu hito no tame ni* [*Introduction to Applied Sociolinguistics*]. Tokyo: Sekai Shisōsha.

Long, Daniel, Miseon Kim, Changsu Shin, Tien-shi Chen, Ichiro Miyamoto and Ellen Nakamizu (2002) Dai 8-kai kenkyū taikai wākushoppu – nihongo to tagengo no tsukaiwake [Workshop of the 8th Congress. Switching between Japanese and other Languages]. *Shakai gengo kagaku* 5(1): 145–150.

Long Daniel and Keisuke Imamura (2013) *The Japanese Language in Palau*. Tokyo: National Institute for Japanese Language and Linguistics. Available online at: www.ninjal.ac.jp/research/project/a/creole/files/creole_Palau.pdf (accessed 15 June 2016).

Loveday, Leo J. (1986) Japanese Sociolinguistics. An Introductory Survey. *Journal of Pragmatics* 10: 287–326.

—— (1996) *Language Contact in Japan*. Oxford: Oxford University Press.

Maher, John C. (2004) A Brief History of Pidgins and Creoles in Japan. *International Christian University publications I-A, Educational Studies* 46: 173–185.

—— (2005) Metroethnicity, Language, and the Principle of Cool. *International Journal of the Sociology of Language* 175/176: 83–102.

—— (2014) Reversing Language Shift and Revitalization. Ainu and the Celtic Languages. *Shakai gengo kagaku* 17(1): 20–35.

Maree, Claire (2013) *Onee kotoba-ron.* [*On onee Language*] Tokyo: Seidosha.

Matsuda, Kenjirō (1993) Dissecting Analogical Leveling Quantitatively. The Case of the Innovative Potential Suffix in Tokyo Japanese. *Language Variation and Change* 5(1): 1–34.

Matsumoto, Yoshiko (2009) Beyond Stereotypes of Old Age. The Discourse of Elderly Japanese Women. *International Journal of the Sociology of Language* 200: 129–151.

—— (2011) Painful to Playful. Quotidian Frames in the Conversational Discourse of Older Japanese Women. *Language in Society* 40(5): 591–616.

Matsuo, Shin, Akiyoshi Kikuchi, J. F. Morris, Jo Matsuzaki, Ayako Uchinami-Koga, Yasusi Abe, Kazunari Iwata, Katsuichirō Nunō, Yufuko Takashima, Norie Oka, Rie Tejima and Ikuyo Morimoto (2013) Guaranteeing Equal Access to Information and Plain Japanese as a Means of Equal Participation for Everyone. *Shakai gengo kagaku* 16(1): 22–38.

Maynard, Senko K. (1989) *Japanese Conversation. Self-Contextualization Through Structure and Interactional Management*. Norwood: Ablex.

MEXT (=Ministry of Education, Culture, Sports, Science and Technology) (2015a) Gakkō ni okeru gaikokujin jidō seitora ni taisuru kyōiku shien ni kansuru yūshikisha kaigi – Heisei 27-nen 11-gatsu 5-nichi kara, dai 1-kai) gijiroku [Support for Foreign Children and Pupils in Schools. Minutes of the First Expert Assembly 5 November 2015]. Available online at: www.mext.go.jp/b_menu/shingi/chousa/shotou/121/gijiroku/1365291.htm (accessed 15 June 2017).

—— (2015b) Gaikokujin jidō seitora ni taisuru kyōiku shien ni kansuru kiso shiryō. [Basic Information on Support for Foreign Children and Pupils in Schools]. Available online at: www.mext.go.jp/b_menu/shingi/chousa/shotou/121/shiryo/__icsFiles/afieldfile/2015/12/22/1365267_01_1.pdf (accessed 15 June 2017).

—— (2016a) Nihongo nōryoku ga jūbun denai kodomotachi e no kyōiku ni tsuite [About Education of Children Who Lack Sufficient Japanese Language Proficiency]. Available online at: www.kantei.go.jp/jp/singi/kyouikusaisei/dai35/sankou1.pdf (accessed 15 June 2017).

—— (2016b) Clarinet e yōkoso [Welcome to Clarinet (Children Living Abroad and Returnees Internet)]. Available online at: www.mext.go.jp/a_menu/shotou/clarinet/main7_a2.htm (accessed 5 June 2017).

Meyerhoff, Miriam and James N. Stanford (2015) "Tings Change, All Tings Change". The Changing Face of Sociolinguistics with a Global Perspective. In: *Globalising Sociolinguistics. Challenging and Expanding Theory*. Dick Smakman and Patrick Heinrich (eds), 1–15. London: Routledge.

MHB (2016) The Mother Tongue, Heritage Language, and Bilingual Education Research Association. Available online at: http://mhb.jp/ (accessed 17 January 2017).

Miller, Laura (2004) Those Naughty Teenage Girls. Japanese kogals, Slang, and Media Assessments. *Journal of Linguistic Anthropology* 14(2): 225–247.

Miller, Laura (2011) Subversive Script and Novel Graphs in Japanese Girls' Culture. *Language & Communication* 31(1): 16–26.

Miyajima, Tatsuo (1999) Gengo seisakushi kenkyū [On the History of Language Policy]. *Shakai gengo kagaku* 2(1): 82–88.

Miyawaki, Hiroyuki (2005) Gaikokujin gakkō [Schools for Foreigners]. In: *Nihon no tagengo shakai [Japan's Multilingual Society]*. Shinji Sanada and Hiroshi Shoji (eds), 128–131. Tokyo: Iwanami Shoten.

Miyazaki, Satoshi and Tetsuya Kimura (2014) Gimu kyōiku katei to kanren suru nihongo kyōiku seisaku [Japanese Language Education Policy and Compulsory Education]. *Waseda Daigaku daigakuin kyōshoku kenkyūka kiyō* 6: 29–40.

Mizumoto, Terumi (2015) *Jendā kara mita nihongo kyōikusho [Japanese Language Education Materials: Gender Perspective]*. Okayama: Daigaku Kyōiku Shuppan.

Mori, Junko (2008) A Conversation Analytic Study of So-called "Cleft construction". *Shakai gengo kagaku* 10(2): 29–41.

Mori, Yoshiko and Junko Mori (2011) Review of Recent Research (2000–2010) on Learning and Instruction with Specific Reference to L2 Japanese. *Language Teaching* 44(4): 447–484.

Morita, Emi (2008) Functions of the Japanese Interactional Particle ne and its Socio-pragmatic Implications. *Shakai gengo kagaku* 10(2): 42–54.

Mühlhäusler, Peter and Rachel Trew (2000) Japanese Language in the Pacific. *Shakai gengo kagaku* 3(1): 24–38.

Murata, Kazuyo (ed.) (2015) *Kyōsei no gengogaku – jizoku kanōna shakai o mezahite [Welfare Linguistics. Toward a Sustainable Society]*. Tokyo: Hitsuji Shobō.

Nakajima, Kazuko, Junko Tanaka and Jun'ya Morishita (2011) Keishōgo kyōiku bunken dētabēsu no kōchiku [Creation of Heritage Language Education Literature Database]. *Bogo, keishōgo, bairingaru kyōiku (MHB) kenkyū* 7: 1–23.

Nakamizu, Ellen (2001) Imin kotoba [Immigrant Languages]. In: *Ōyō shakai gengogaku o manabu hito no tame ni [Introduction to Applied Sociolinguistics]*. Long, Daniel, Sei'ichi Nakai and Hiroaki Miyaji (eds), 100–107. Tokyo: Sekai Shisōsha.

—— (2005) Zainichi burajirujin no gengo shiyō [Language Use by Resident Brazilians]. In: *Nihon no tagengo shakai*. Shinji Sanada and Hiroshi Shoji (eds), 221–224. Tokyo: Iwanami Shoten.
Nakamura, Momoko (1995) *Kotoba to feminizumu* [*Language and Feminism*]. Tokyo: Keisō Shobō.
—— (2001) *Kotoba to jendā* [*Language and Gender*]. Tokyo: Keisō Shobō.
—— (2007) *Onna kotoba* [*Women's Language*]. Tokyo: Hitsuji Shobō.
—— (2013) *Hon'yaku ga tsukuru nihongo – hiroin wa "onna kotoba" o hanashitsuzukeru* [*Japanese Language Created by Translation. Heroines Continue to Speak "Women's Language"*]. Tokyo: Gendai Shokan.
Nakane, Ikuko, Emi Otsuji and Willam S. Armour (eds.) (2015) *Languages and Identities in a Transitional Japan*. London: Routledge.
Nakata, Shion (2016) Sunakku ni okeru gengo komyunikēshon kenkyū – taijin kankei o chōsetsu suru sekkyaku gengo sutorateji [Research on Linguistic Communication in "Snack Bars". Language Strategies that Regulate Interpersonal Relationships with Customers]. PhD dissertation, Sōgō Kenkyū Daigakuin Daigaku.
Nishihara, Suzuko (2015) Kokugo kyōiku to nihongo kyōiku no renkei no igi [The Significance of Links between "kokugo" (J1) and "nihongo" (J2/JFL) Education]. *Nihongogaku* 10(34): 2–10.
Noguchi, Mary G. and Sandra Fotos (eds) (2001) *Studies in Japanese Bilingualism*. Clevedon: Multilingual Matters.
Nuibe, Yoshinori (2007) "Nihongo kyōiku" no kenkyū dōkō to tenbō [Analysis of New Directions of Japanese Language Pedagogy]. *The Bulletin of Japanese Curriculum Research and Development* 30(1): 69–78.
Ogino, Tsunao, Yasuko Misono and Chitsuko Fukushima (1985) Diversity of Honorific Usage in Tokyo. A Sociolinguistic Approach Based on a Field Survey. *International Journal of the Sociology of Language* 55: 23–39.
Ogino, Tsunao (1986) Quantification of Politeness Based on the Usage Patterns of Honorific Expressions. *International Journal of the Sociology of Language* 58: 37–58.
Ōtaki, Sachiko (2013) Asymmetry in Doctor-patient Communication. A Comparison between Japan and the USA. *Shakai gengo kagaku* 16(1): 80–95.
Okada, Kesao (2006) *Edo igengo sesshoku – rango, tōwa to kindai nihongo* [*Language Contact in Edo – Dutch, Chinese and Modern Japanese*]. Tokyo: Kasama Shoin.
Okamoto, Shigeko (2013) Variability in Societal Norms for Japanese Women's Speech. Implications for Linguistic Politeness. *Multilingua* 32(2): 203–223.
—— (2016) Variability and Multiplicity in the Meanings of Stereotypical Gendered Speech in Japanese. *East Asian Pragmatics* 1(1): 5–39.
Okamoto, Shigeko and Janet S. Shibamoto-Smith (2004) *Japanese Language, Gender, and Ideology. Cultural Models and Real People*. Oxford: Oxford University Press.
—— (2016) *The Social Life of the Japanese Language. Cultural Discourses and Situated Practice*. Cambridge: Cambridge University Press.
Onodera, Noriko O. (2004) *Japanese Discourse Markers. Synchronic and Diachronic Discourse Analysis*. Amsterdam: John Benjamins.
Ōta, Makie (2009) Usain Boruto no "I" wa, naze "ore" to yakusareru no ka – supōtsu hōsō no "yakuwarigo" [Why Is Usain Bolt's "I" Translated as "ore" in Japanese? Role Language in Sports Broadcasting]. *Hōsō kenkyū to chōsa* 59(3): 56–73.
—— (2017) Saikō orinpikku hōsō no "yakuwarigo" – nihonjin senshu o shujinkō toshita "monogatari" to iu shiten kara ["Role Language" Used in Olympic Broadcasts. Analyzing Japanese TV Subtitles for Foreign Athletes' Interviews and their Expected Roles in "Olympic Stories"]. *Hōsō kenkyū to chōsa* 67(3): 26–45.
Ōtsu Yukio (2005) Dai-ni gengo kyōiku [Second Language Education]. In: *Nihon no tagengo shakai*. Shinji Sanada and Hiroshi Shoji (eds), 29–31. Tokyo: Iwanami Shoten.
Ozeki, Fumi (2013) *Kodomotachi wa itsu nihongo o manabu no ka – fukusū gengo kankyō o ikiru kodomo e no kyōiku* [*How Do Children Learn Japanese? Language Education for Children in Plurilingual Settings*]. Tokyo: CoCo Shuppan.
Pennycook Alastair and Emi Otsuji (2010) Metrolingualism. Fixity, Fluidity and Language in Flux. *International Journal of Multilingualism* 7(3): 240–254.
—— (2014) Metrolingual Multitasking and Spatial Repertoires. "Pizza mo two Minutes Coming". *Journal of Sociolinguistics* 18(2): 161–184.
—— (2015) *Metrolingualism. Language in the City*. London: Routledge.
Ryang, Sonia (ed.) (2000) *Koreans in Japan. Critical Voices from the Margin*. London: Routledge.

Saitō, Keita (2015) Burajirujin shūjū chi'iki no ringa furanka – Gunma-ken Ōizumi-chō to Mie-ken Iga-shi no hikaku [Lingua Franca in Areas with High Concentrations of Brazilian Residents. A Comparative Study of Oizumi-Town and Iga-City]. *Nihongo kenkyū* 35: 43–57.

Sanada, Shinji (ed.) (2006) *Shakai gengogaku no tenbō [An Outlook on Sociolinguistics]*. Tokyo: Kurosio.

―――― (2009) *Ekkyōshita nihongo – washa no "katari" kara [Japanese that Crossed the Border. Speakers' Stories]*. Tokyo: Izumi Shoin.

Sanada, Shinji, Naoki Ogoshi and Young Cheol Yim (2005) *Zainichi korian no gengosō [Aspects of Resident Koreans' Language]*. Tokyo: Iwanami Shoten.

Sanada, Shinji and Hiroshi Shoji (eds) (2005) *Nihon no tagengo shakai [Japan's Multilingual Society]*. Tokyo: Iwanami Shoten.

Sanada, Shinji, Daniel Long, Yoshiyuki Asahi and Yuehchen Chien (2010) *Shakai gengogaku zushū [Japanese Sociolinguistics Illustrated]* (second edition). Tokyo: Akiyama Shoten.

Sasaki, Yoshinori (2005) Compilation, Publication and Online Distribution of Review Articles on Acquisition of Japanese as a Second Language. Available online at: www.dc.ocha.ac.jp/comparative-cultures/jle/saizensen/kaken02-04/ (accessed 29 June 2017).

Satake, Kuniko (2005) "Onna kotoba, otoko kotoba" – kihan o meguru sengo no shinbun no gensetsu – kokken "kotoba ni kansuru shinbun kiji midashi dētabēsu" kara [The Discourse of Post-WWII Newspapers Involving "Women's/Men's Language" Norm. From the Database of Newspaper Articles Related to Language of the National Institute for Japanese Language]. *Handai nihongo kenkyū* 17: 111–137.

Seibert Vaipae, Sharon (2001) Language Minority Students in Japanese Public Schools. In: *Studies in Japanese Bilingualism*. Mary G. Noguchi and Sandra Fotos (eds), 184–233. Clevedon: Multilingual Matters.

Shibamoto, Janet S. (1987) Japanese Sociolinguistics. *Annual Review of Anthropology* 16: 261–278.

―――― (2009) The Green Leaves of Love. Japanese Romantic Heroines, Authentic Femininity, and Dialect. *Journal of Sociolinguistics* 13(4): 524–546.

Shibuya, Katsumi (2010) Imin gengo kenkyū no chōryū – nikkeijin nihongo henshu no gengo seitairon-teki kenkyū ni mukete [Current Trends in the Study of Immigrant Languages. Toward an Ecolinguistic Study of Nikkeijin Immigrant Varieties of Japanese]. *Machikaneyama ronsō* 44: 1–23.

Shoji, Hiroshi, Peter Backhaus and Florian Coulmas (eds) (2009) *Nihon no gengo keikan [Linguistic Landscapes of Japan]*. Tokyo: Sangensha.

Shukuri, Yukiko (2012) Kyarakuta no taipu to yakuwarigo ni kansuru ishiki chōsa hōkoku – "watashitachi" taipu ni chūmoku shite [Investigation Report on Character Types and Role Language in Modern Japanese in the Real World. Focusing on "watashitachi" Type]. *Gengo kagaku ronshū* 16: 85–96.

Sibata, Takesi (1985) Sociolinguistic Surveys in Japan. Approaches and Problems. *International Journal of the Sociology of Language* 55: 79–88.

―――― (1999) *Sociolinguistics in Japanese Contexts* (translated, edited and introduced by Tetsuya Kunihiro, Fumio Inoue and Daniel Long). Berlin: Mouton de Gruyter.

SturtzSreetharan, Cindi (2004) Students, sarariiman (pl.), and Seniors. Japanese Men's Use of Manly Speech Register. *Language in Society* 33(1): 81–107.

―――― (2006a) Gentlemanly Gender? Japanese Men's Use of Clause-final Politeness in Casual Conversations. *Journal of Sociolinguistics* 10(1): 70–92.

―――― (2006b) "I Read the Nikkei, Too". Crafting Positions of Authority and Masculinity in a Japanese Conversation. *Journal of Linguistic Anthropology* 16(2): 173–193.

Tagengoka Genshō Kenkyūkai (ed.) (2013) *Tagengo shakai nihon – sono genjō to kadai [Japan as Multilingual Society. Present State and Tasks]*. Tokyo: Sangensha.

Tajima, Junko (2003) Chinese Newcomers in the Global City Tokyo. Social Networks and Settlement Tendencies. *International Journal of Japanese Sociology* 12(1): 68–78.

Takahara, Kimiko (1991) Female Speech Patterns in Japanese. *International Journal of the Sociology of Language* 92: 61–85.

Takagi, Chie (2016) Shakai gengo, gengo seikatsu [Language and Society, Language Life]. *Nihongo no kenkyū (tokushū)* 2(3): 91–98.

Takagi, Hiroyuki, Katsumi Shibuya and Yoko Iyeiri (eds) (2015) *Rekishi shakai gengogaku nyūmon [Introduction to Historical Sociolinguistics]*. Tokyo: Taishūkan.

Takano, Shoji (1998) A Quantitative Study of Gender Differences in the Ellipsis of the Japanese Postpositional Particles wa and ga. Gender Composition as a Constraint on Variability. *Language Variation and Change* 10(3): 289–323.

—— (2000) The Myth of a Homogeneous Speech Community. A Sociolinguistic Study of the Speech of Japanese Women in Diverse Gender Roles. *International Journal of the Sociology of Language* 146: 43–85.

Takase, Yutaka, Takashi Yoshino and Yukiko I. Nakano (2017) Taninsū kaiwa ni okeru chōsei kainyū kinō o yūsuru taiwa robotto [Conversational Robot with Conversation Coordination and Intervention Functionality in Multi-party Conversations]. *Jōhō shori gakkai ronbunshi* 58(5): 967–980.

Tanaka, Hiroko (2001) Adverbials for Turn Projection in Japanese. Toward a Demystification of the Telepathic Mode of Communication. *Language in Society* 30(4): 559–587.

—— (2005) Grammar and the Timing of Social Action. Word Order and Preference Organization in Japanese. *Language in Society* 34(3): 389–430.

Tanaka, Rīna (2013) Nihongo kyōiku ni okeru "neitibu/nonneitibu" gainen [Concepts "Native" and "Non-native" in Japanese Language Education]. *Gengo bunka kyōiku kenkyū* 11: 95–111.

Teshigawara, Mihoko and Satoshi Kinsui (2011) Modern Japanese "Role Language" (*yakuwarigo*). Fictionalized Orality in Japanese Literature and Popular Culture. *Sociolinguistic Studies* 5(1): 37–58.

Tomosada, Kenji and Masataka Jinnouchi (2004) On the Diffusion of the Kansai Dialect and the Kansai Way of Speaking among Youth in Japan. *Shakai gengo kagaku* 7(1): 84–91.

Tomozawa, Akie (2001) Japan's Hidden Bilinguals. The Languages of "War Orphans" and their Families after Repatriation from China. In: *Studies in Japanese Bilingualism*. Mary G. Noguchi and Sandra Fotos (eds), 133–163. Clevedon: Multilingual Matters.

Toyohashi City (2016) Nihongo shidō. Nihongo shidō ga hitsuyōna jidōseito [Japanese Language Assistance. Children and Pupils Requiring Japanese Language Assistance]. Available online at: www.gaikoku.toyohashi.ed.jp/kyouikunotebiki/4nihongo.pdf (accessed 16 June 2017).

Tranter, Nicolas (2008) Nonconventional Script Choice in Japan. *International Journal of the Sociology of Language* 192: 133–151.

Tsuji, Kayoko (2002) A Diachronic Study of haru-keigo in the Kyoto City Dialect Female Speech. Focusing on Treatment Expressions Referring to a Third Person. *Shakai gengo kagaku* 5(1): 28–41.

Usami, Mayumi (2002) *Discourse Politeness in Japanese Conversation. Some Implications for a Universal Theory of Politeness*. Tokyo: Hitsuji Shobō.

—— (2008) Frontiers of Studies on Politeness Theories. New Trends in Politeness Studies and Discourse Politeness Theory. *Shakai gengo kagaku* 11(1): 4–22.

—— (2015) On Styles in Japanese Language. Focusing on "Speech-Level Shift" in Japanese Conversation. *Shakai gengo kagaku* 18(1): 7–22.

Usami, Yō (2012) "Shakai" bun'ya ["Society" as a Field of Study]. *Nihongo kyōiku* 53: 55–70.

Yamamoto, Masayo (2001) Japanese Attitudes towards Bilingualism. A Survey and its Implications. In: *Studies in Japanese Bilingualism*. Mary G. Noguchi and Sandra Fotos (eds), 24–44. Clevedon: Multilingual Matters.

Yamazaki, Kei'ichi (2011) Soshiaru robotto to shakai gakuteki kenkyū – esunogurafi, kaiwa bunseki, esunomesodorojī [Social Robots and Sociological Research. Ethnography, Conversation Analysis, Ethnomethodology]. *Nihon robotto gakkaishi* 29(1): 10–13.

Yasuda, Toshiaki (2004) Gakumon to gakumon no aida – kokugogaku to nihongogaku [Between Disciplines. Research on Japanese National Language and Japanese]. *Hitotsubashi ronshō* 131(4): 337–354.

Yim, Young Cheol (2001) Nihongo fukyū seisaku – senzen, kaigai [Policy for Spreading Japanese, Pre-WWII, Overseas]. In: *Ōyō shakai gengogaku o manabu hito no tame ni*. Daniel Long, Sei'ichi Nakai and Hiroaki Miyaji (eds), 193–200. Tokyo: Sekai Shisōsha.

Yoshinaga, Mioko (2015) Nihongo kyōiku to "yasashisa" – nihonjin ni yoru nihongo no manabinaoshi [Japanese Language Education and "Easiness". Japanese People Relearning Japanese]. In: *Kotoba no "yasashisa" to wa nani ka. Hihanteki shakai gengogaku kara no apurōchi*. Mioko Yoshinaga and Hitoshi Yamashita (eds), 19–43. Tokyo: Sangensha.

Yoshioka, Yasuo (2004) Regional and Generational Variation of Politeness Observed in Communication Consciousness and Honorific Behaviour. Comparison of Native Speakers from Metropolitan Areas and Osaka. *Shakai gengo kagaku* 7(1): 92–104.

28
STUDIES OF RYUKYU-SUBSTRATE JAPANESE

Mark Anderson

Language shift in the Ryukyu Islands has led to the emergence of several local varieties of Japanese, each showing trace substratal effects from the now obsolescing Ryukyuan languages. These substrate-influenced Japanese varieties can be referred to collectively as "Ryukyu-substrate Japanese", or individually according to the name of an island group or potentially even a particular settlement (e.g., "Yaeyama-substrate Japanese", "Ishigaki-substrate Japanese", etc.). These varieties used to be stigmatized and Ryukyuans suffering from a linguistic inferiority complex gave them pejorative names such as *uchinaa yamatuguchi* (literally, "Okinawan Japanese") and *ton-futsūgo* (Amamian "Sweet Potato" Japanese) (Nagata 1996: 168). In recent years, however, these names have lost their derogatory connotations, and young people view the varieties positively and use them proactively (Takaesu 2005: 268).

This chapter provides a comprehensive discussion of research on Ryukyu-substrate Japanese to date. After a brief overview of recent changes in its theoretical classification in relation to Standard Japanese and Ryukyuan languages, there will be a detailed discussion of the existing studies in roughly chronological order from 1930 to the present day. The aim of this is to show how increasing sociolinguistic awareness has given rise to changes in attitude towards the value of Ryukyu-substrate Japanese as a marker of identity.

Theoretical classification

For decades, there has been inconsistency in the ways in which scholars classified Ryukyu-substrate Japanese, in part because of a tendency to refer to Ryukyuan languages as *hōgen* (dialects). This tendency has at its root a political motivation to include Ryukyuan languages within the framework of *kokugogaku* (national language studies) so that Japan can be seen as a nation unified under one language.[1] Language shift in the Ryukyus has thus been characterized as dialect leveling towards Standard Japanese, and any mixture of Ryukyuan languages and Japanese has had to be categorized as an "intermediate dialect" between one dialect of Japanese and another.

Consequently, while descriptive analyses and sub-classification of Ryukyu-substrate Japanese varieties to date are excellent and extremely detailed, their theoretical treatment from a broader perspective of worldwide language contact phenomena has been unrealistic. They have been variously described in the literature as pidgins/creoles (Yabiku 1987; Takaesu 1994; Karimata 2006, 2008), new dialects (as opposed to the old, traditional dialects) (Motonaga 1979; Nagata 1996), "reformed" dialects (Nakamoto 1990), neo-dialects (Sanada 1992) and interdialects (Matsumori 1995; Ōno 1995).[2] Long (2010) refuted all of these analyses, concluding that these varieties should be called something else entirely, but Karimata (2010, 2012) took Long's discussion as grounds for using the term "creoloids".[3] By then, however, the issue of classification had already been comprehensively discussed in Anderson (2009), and it had been recognized that these varieties were typical of the kind of substrate-influenced replacing language that has emerged during language shift in other cases worldwide (see Sasse 1992; Batibo 2005; LaPolla 2009; Thomason 2009).[4]

The lack of solid theoretical grounding in studies of Ryukyu-substrate Japanese to date is unsurprising in view of the slow pace of worldwide theoretical development in the area of substratal effects during language shift. As Heffernan (2006: 641) points out, research on the variability that accompanies language shift has focused mainly on the retreating endangered language and, with the exception of a few publications, has neglected variability in the replacing language. Moreover, the terms substratum and superstratum have been underused in studies of language shift, despite their potential for application in this area. Instead, they have generally been associated with historical linguistics as well as contact linguistics in the context of research on pidgins/creoles and dual source so-called "mixed" or "split" languages.[5] Nevertheless, both substratal and superstratal effects attracted the attention of Japanese and Ryukyuan scholars very early in the Ryukyuan language shift process, and scholars' interest has continued to be drawn to Ryukyu-substrate Japanese in bursts over the decades.

Early research on substrative effects: Kuwae and Narita

The earliest mention of substratal interference in the literature is in Kuwae (1930). Based on data collected over a 20-year period, Kuwae notes the use of "erroneous" Japanese among the young Okinawans who constituted the first generation of bilinguals in the early twentieth century. He cites examples such as the following (RSJ = Ryukyu-substrate Japanese; SJ = Standard Japanese):

(1) Collocations
RSJ atama=o   kit-te   ki-ta
     head=ACC   cut-PCP   come-PST
SJ   kami=o   kat-te   ki-ta
     hair=ACC   trim-PCP   come-PST
     I had my hair cut.

(2) Deixis
RSJ kimi=no   ie=ni   asob-i=ni   ku-ru   yo
     2SG=GEN   house=LAT   play-NMLZ=PURP   come-NPST   IP
SJ   kimi=no   ie=ni   asob-i=ni   ik-u   yo
     2SG=GEN   house=LAT   play-NMLZ=PURP   go-NPST   IP
     I'll come and hang out at your house.

(3) Case marker usage
RSJ naha=Ø   it-te   ki-ta
     Naha=Ø   go-PCP   come-PST
SJ   naha=e/ni   it-te   ki-ta
     Naha=LAT   go-PCP   come-PST
     I went to Naha.

(Adapted from Kuwae 1930)

Kuwae claims the above to be examples of Ryukyuan interference, but many of the non-standard features described in the literature, such as reversal of deictic direction or bare case marking, could originate from Kyushu dialects or other varieties introduced into Okinawa by school teachers or other personnel drafted in from mainland Japan during the early Meiji Period (1868–1912). If these features are nonetheless to be considered as Ryukyuan-influenced, the fact that they were noticed as early as 1930 provides evidence that Ryukyu-substrate Japanese has its origins in negative L1 transfer among early consecutive bilingual children (full speakers) when Japanese was being strictly enforced in schools in the early twentieth century. The substrate-influenced variety spoken by this generation could be regarded as an interlanguage of sorts as pointed out by Matsumori (1995: 39) and Long (2013: 87), but since Ryukyuan and Japanese are similarly structured and children became bilingual at school age, it is perhaps more appropriate to conceive of the substrative effects as cross-linguistic transfer or L1 interference.[6]

The next major study of Ryukyu-substrate Japanese was Narita's (1960) paper, written at a time when monolingual speakers of Ryukyuan languages were still common among the older generation. In explicitly noting the existence of "bilingualism" in Okinawan society and acknowledging that language contact also constitutes contact between two cultures on a meta-linguistic level, Narita was in many ways ahead of his time. However, L1 interference is portrayed as a "problem" for primary school classrooms in particular. Narita observes many of the features typical of the Japanese spoken by the same generations of productive bilinguals who constitute today's older generation. These features include: phonological transfer such as (de-)voicing, (de-)palatalization, redistribution of /r/ and /d/, mid-vowel raising and vowel lengthening in single-syllable words; prosodic transfer such as a strong tendency towards accentless pitch patterns; grammatical transfer such as non-standard particle usage; semantic transfer such as double meanings arising from expanded semantic domains and a reversal of yes/no responses to negative interrogatives; and lexical transfer such as direct translations from L1.

Revival in the 1970s and 1980s: Nagata, Motonaga, Yabiku and Kurai

For over a decade after Narita's research, Ryukyu-substrate Japanese attracted little attention among scholars. This was most likely due to the fact that such language contact phenomena were not regarded as worthy subjects of study, given that they were supposedly mere examples of incomplete and erroneous acquisition of the desired standard language. It was not until the late 1970s that interest in Ryukyu-substrate Japanese was revived when Nagata Takashi began to collect data for research on language change in Yonaguni. Nagata interviewed 72 Yonaguni residents across all generations to investigate differences in their phonology, pitch accent, grammar and knowledge of vocabulary. The results were collated and published as the first articles on Yonaguni-substrate Japanese (Nagata 1983, 1984). What is striking about his description of what he referred to as "new Yonaguni dialect" is its phonological and grammatical similarities to Okinawa-substrate Japanese as documented previously by Kuwae and Narita. Nagata would later expand his cross-generational investigation of substratal influences from Yonaguni into the other island groups in the Ryukyu Archipelago.

At around the same time, Motonaga Moriyasu was investigating the substrate-influenced variety spoken by schoolchildren in Shuri and the southeastern part of Okinawa Island (Haebaru, Yonabaru, Chinen). Motonaga's research was no exception to the tendency to regard Ryukyu-substrate Japanese as substandard. While his report is undoubtedly a valuable resource in terms of its findings about young people's language use at the time, its purpose was to raise educators' awareness about the features of young people's problematic "new dialect" for more effective teaching of Standard Japanese (Motonaga 1979: 37). Motonaga constructed a questionnaire using 86 typical expressions in Okinawa-substrate Japanese, mostly taken from Kuwae (1930), and asked children to report whether they used these phrases "often", "sometimes" or "never". The expressions were then ranked according to their frequency of use. Although the survey methods necessitated the omission of items eliciting phonological interference and the sample size was relatively small compared to more recent research (N = 226), Motonaga's (1979) report on the results of this survey provides the first quantitative analysis of the extent to which the Okinawan substratum was evident in the language use of a generation of semi-speaker Okinawans who had not acquired their local language as a mother tongue. His data analysis allowed him to draw up a five-fold typology of non-standard lexical forms present in the new generation's version of Okinawa-substrate Japanese, including various types of direct translation, borrowed forms from mainland dialects and so on. In terms of grammar, he also observed the non-standard particle usage previously reported by Kuwae and Narita, as well as non-standard verb forms such as Okinawan-derived negatives and imperatives, and non-standard adjectival constructions among others.

During the 1980s, interest in Ryukyu-substrate Japanese grew as more people became aware of declining proficiency in – and limited use of – Ryukyuan languages. Motonaga (1984) provides one of the most detailed descriptions of Ryukyu-substrate Japanese to date.[7] He even makes brief mention of substratal features in varieties spoken in island groups other than Okinawa, such as Miyako and Amami. Motonaga offers examples of phonological, pitch accentual, grammatical and lexical features. He also revises his (1979) typology of Okinawa-substrate non-standard lexical forms to a four-fold one, categorizing lexical items according to the extent to which they resemble Standard Japanese (SJ). The categories are as follows:

(a) Items that do not obtain in SJ.
(b) Items that obtain in SJ but differ semantically.
(c) Items that obtain in SJ but idiomatic collocations differ.
(d) Items that obtain in SJ but are used in a "stylistically inappropriate" way.

In a paternalistic tone, which is very much of its time, Motonaga concludes by making the following six recommendations for *kokugo* educators:

- Any corrective approach to standardization must be gradualistic rather than coercive to avoid resistance and the development of an inferiority complex among locals.
- Instruction should focus on appropriacy of language according to situational context, given that the habitual use of certain features (e.g., pronouns, kinship terms, intonation) is difficult to correct.
- Acquisition of Standard Japanese is best achieved via constant repetition and, if possible, immersion, so teachers should create opportunities to use the language in class, school clubs and public-speaking events.
- Language correction in the early years of primary school should focus on correcting high frequency vocabulary so as not to discourage pupils from speaking, while older children should be given explicit instruction contrasting the pronunciation, grammar and vocabulary of their own variety with the standard.
- More use should be made of broadcasts and audio recordings so that children can acquire "correct" pronunciation in the absence of teachers proficient in Standard Japanese.

- A tailor-made curriculum should be designed specifically to correct Ryukyuan phonological, grammatical and lexical interference, and attention ought to be given to spoken language proficiency (e.g., in honorific forms).

Motonaga (1984: 370) is also noteworthy for being the first academic publication to use the term *uchinaa yamatoguchi* to refer to Okinawa-substrate Japanese, defining it as "a regional variety of Standard Japanese retaining certain Okinawan dialectal features".[8] However, the term was also used in Hirayama Ryōmei's (1984: 27) illustrated phrasebook, which brought Okinawa-substrate Japanese to a general readership for the first time. The value of this phrasebook was later recognized by scholars interested in Ryukyu-substrate Japanese, and it should continue to be given attention as it not only provides detailed explanations of the meaning of certain expressions but also traces the history of their use. Additionally, Hirayama points out that many of these expressions are used in other mainland prefectures, and this may indicate that one should be cautious in assuming a Ryukyuan substratal origin without first considering the possibility that the non-standard features have simply been imported from Kyushu, Kansai or eastern regions in mainland Japan.[9]

Inspired by Motonaga and Hirayama, Yabiku (1987) adopted the term *uchinaa yamatuguchi* and expanded its definition, describing it as "diverse linguistic phenomena arising from the process of language shift as Okinawan dialect is replaced by Japanese, including various types of interference or language created as a result thereof" (Yabiku 1987: 119).[10] Since his examples of substrate-influenced features are taken from Motonaga (1984) and Hirayama (1984), Yabiku's paper is much more interesting for its theoretical analysis than for its descriptive value. He introduces for the first time the concept of *yamatu uchinaaguchi* ("Japanese Okinawan"), defining it as "language produced when a speaker with imperfect knowledge of Okinawan takes a Japanese expression and converts only the external form [i.e., phonology and morphology] into Okinawan" (Yabiku 1987: 122). This term appears to denote superstratal influence in the form of inserted direct translations from Japanese within an Okinawan matrix; therefore, the name "Japanese-superstrate Okinawan" would perhaps better capture the concept in English. Yabiku's differentiation between substrate and superstrate influence has never been clearly named as such, but it has far-reaching implications for the study of language contact beyond language shift in the Ryukyus.[11]

In the same year as Yabiku's publication, Kurai (1987) provided the first detailed description of Amami-substrate Japanese (popularly called "*ton-futsūgo*"). Like Motonaga, Kurai saw the substratum as a problem that should be addressed through education in Standard Japanese (SJ), or as he put it, by means of a "medical prescription". He categorizes the reasons for the use of Amami-substrate Japanese as follows:

(a) the speaker does not know the SJ equivalent.
(b) the speaker knows the SJ equivalent but Amami-substrate Japanese comes out accidentally.
(c) the speaker knows the SJ equivalent but deliberately uses Amami-substrate Japanese.

Changing attitudes from the 1990s

Nakamoto (1990) documents some Okinawa-substrate Japanese expressions from Kumejima. He persists with the idea of the standard language from Tokyo as being pleasant-sounding and something to aspire to, in contrast to Okinawan and Okinawa-substrate Japanese, both of which he refers to as "dialects" (*kyūrai* traditional vs. *kaishin* reformed, respectively) that represent a "problem" for education. To the present-day reader, it ought to be obvious from the example sentences he provides that his "reformed dialect" is recognizably a variety of Japanese (Okinawa-substrate) while his "traditional dialect" is another language entirely (Okinawan):[12]

(4)
Traditional dialect: ʔama nu tanmee ya ganjuu shi ʔacchi-misee ga yaa.
Reformed dialect: mukoo no ojii wa genki de aruite iru ka nee.
Standard language: mukoo no ojiisan wa genki deshoo ka.
I wonder if that old guy is well.

Traditional dialect: ʔanmaa ya maa kai ʔnja ga yaa.
Reformed dialect: kaachan wa doko itta ka nee.
Standard language: haha wa doko e itta no ka na.
I wonder where Mum's gone.

(Adapted from Nakamoto 1990: 913)[13]

On the other hand, Nakamoto was one of the first scholars to compare the Ryukyuan situation to Ainu language shift, acknowledging the fundamental differences between research into Ryukyuan language shift and dialect leveling on the mainland (Nakamoto 1990: 918). In addition, he can be credited for recognizing the significance of intergenerational transmission loss in the home domain during the language shift process. Since language is the carrier of culture, he points out, the interruption of mother tongue transmission between generations entails the eventual extinction of its associated culture that has developed over time (Nakamoto 1990: 914). Accordingly, he identifies the need for documentation of the "traditional dialects" before their last speakers die by 2010 (a pessimistic forecast in hindsight) as well as for research into the "reformed dialects" (i.e., Ryukyu-substrate Japanese) to promote greater understanding of the shift process (Nakamoto 1990: 915).[14] Arguably, his vision has since been realized.

Nakamoto's work marked the first stirrings of a change in perspective that would gradually gain traction over the following decade. The documentation and discussion of Ryukyu-substrate Japanese peaked in the mid-1990s with the publication of a number of detailed and influential studies in quick succession (Karimata 1994; Takaesu 1994; Ōno 1995; Nagata 1996; Nohara 1996, 1998).[15] At this time, the foci and methods of research into Ryukyu-substrate Japanese diverged into areas of specialization which still hold to this day. These approaches are summarized and explained below under names that reflect the source of their inspiration in the 1980s:

(a) The Motonaga School: quantitative research documenting changes in substratal effects as well as the use of and attitudes towards substrate-influenced Japanese by means of cross-generational survey questionnaires (Ōno 1995; Nohara 1996, 1998; Kinjō and Shō 2000; Shō, Sasaki and Karimata 2013; Shō and Sasaki 2015).
(b) The Yabiku School: theoretical classification and description of different types of contact phenomena (Karimata 1994, 2006, 2008, 2010, 2012; Takaesu 1992, 1994, 2002, 2004, 2005).
(c) The Nagata School: qualitative research documenting geographical differences in substratal influence from various Ryukyuan languages by means of cross-generational survey interviews (Nagata 1996; Long 2013; Zayasu 2017).
(d) The Conversation Analysis School: detailed analysis of substratal effects and code-switching in context using conversation analysis methods (Anderson 2009, 2015; Miyahira and Petrucci 2014; Sugita 2014).

The Motonaga School: Quantitative research by questionnaire

Quantitative methods similar to those used for Motonaga's (1979) paper became more sophisticated over the years with the development of computer technology. Ono (1995) reports on a 1994 survey conducted in collaboration with Hokama Minako, targeting a sample of elderly people, middle-aged workers and high school students in Naha (N = 214). The questionnaire elicited attitudes towards Okinawa-substrate Japanese vis-à-vis Okinawan and Standard Japanese as well as the respondents' use of typical Okinawa-substrate Japanese phrases such as *tabete nai saa* (… have eaten it all!) and *tabetaaru saa* (… must have eaten it!). While the topic is interesting and under-researched, the sampling method and size is questionable, the data presentation is difficult to follow and no clear conclusions are drawn. However, the idea behind this study, that is, a principal component analysis that reveals factors underlying a positive or negative "image" of language varieties, is a good one that should be revisited using more sophisticated sampling techniques and data reporting.

Subsequent quantitative studies have tended to focus on young people's language (non-speakers and younger semi-speakers), perhaps owing to the relative ease of questionnaire distribution in educational institutions. Nohara Mitsuyoshi, the scholar most often associated with the study of young Okinawans' slang expressions, led a team of researchers from Okinawa International University in producing a series of papers reporting on survey results from elementary, junior high and high schools across Okinawa Island in the early 1990s (summarized in Nohara 1996). Over the previous decade, young people's slang had been discussed informally in the newspapers but had not received scholarly attention (Nohara 1996: 270). It was now recognized that the younger generations of Okinawa-substrate Japanese L1 speakers were not following the expected trajectory of language shift by abandoning Ryukyuan expressions and continuing to standardize their speech but had instead begun to take pride in their own heritage and were actively creating expressions that diverged from both Standard Japanese and the original Ryukyuan source language.

Although Nohara's work is highly regarded among scholars currently studying Ryukyu-substrate Japanese, his early terminology is somewhat confusing. Nohara first referred to young people's expressions as *shin-hōgen* (new dialect), a term coined by Inoue Fumio in the 1980s. However, realizing that his usage of the term could conflict with already established concepts, he later suggested *wakamono kotoba* (young people's language) as an alternative (Nohara 1996: 265). Readers should note that Nohara's use of *shin-hōgen* differs from Nagata's use of the same term to mean "pan-generational Ryukyu-substrate Japanese". Nagata, for his part, admits that his own usage of the term could also cause confusion (Nagata 1996: 13).

Nohara's early research was followed up with a survey of commonly used expressions among university students (N = 43) and older high school students (N < 100) (reported in Nohara 1998). He concludes by categorizing the expressions into the following three types:

Type 1: Okinawan plus Japanese inflection.
Type 2: Japanese plus Okinawan inflection.
Type 3: Other.

The table below shows some examples of commonly used young people's words provided by Nohara. Where kinship terms are separated by a forward slash (/), the word traditionally used by the upper classes appears on the left and the word used by the lower classes appears on the right.

There are, however, problems with Nohara's typology. Firstly, although Nohara cites the items as examples of young people's language, some of the expressions, such as *hingiru* (escape),

Table 28.1 Youth language and Shuri-Okinawan

	Youth language	Okinawan (Shuri dialect)	Standard Japanese	English
Type 1	hingiru	fingiyun	nigeru	escape
	ukiru	ʔukiyun	okiru	rise
	wajiru	wajiyun	okoru	become angry
	hiisai	fiisan	samui	cold
	achisai	ʔachisan	atsui	hot
	maasai	maasan	oishii	tasty
Type 2	karusan	gassan	karui	light
	omosan	ʔnbusan	omoi	heavy
	mijikasan	ʔinchaasan	mijikai	short
	irairaa suru	wajiwajii sun	iraira suru	annoyed
Type 3	arai, haba, sini	ʔippee	totemo	very
	ojii	tanmee / ʔusumee	ojiichan	grandfather
	obaa	ʔnmee / haamee	obaachan	grandmother
	otoo	taarii / suu	otoochan	father
	okaa	ʔayaa / ʔanmaa	okaachan	mother
	niinii	yacchii / ʔafii	oniichan	older brother
	neenee	ʔnmii / ʔangwaa	oneechan	older sister
	yaa	ʔyaa	kimi	you (inf.)
	yattaa	ʔittaa	kimitachi	you (pl. inf.)
	X da baa yoo	X yaru baa yoo	X na no da yo	it's X, you see
	meccha	ʔippee	meccha	really

Source: Nohara (1998), compiled and adapted by the author.

are more commonly used by older bilinguals (Karimata 2006: 51). Unfortunately, it is impossible to tell whether or not the respondents were using these items in their daily lives since Nohara's employment of a questionnaire to elicit students' knowledge of vocabulary does not provide a realistic impression of actual language use. The method is prone to social desirability bias. Students are likely to over-report their use of local expressions since, as Karimata (1994: 96) points out, they know they will be seen as "cool" if they can use them to emphasize group identity.[16] If the respondents were actually using these items on a day-to-day basis then the results show that they were not only creating their own new expressions but also drawing from the Ryukyuan substratum as a resource provided by their elders.

Second, the typology blurs the distinction between *uchinaa yamatuguchi* in general and slang specific to young people's speech. Nohara's Type 3 is a "mop-up" category that includes a range of unrelated features such as phonologically altered Ryukyuan (*yaa*, you), semantically altered Japanese (*arai*, very), and local as well as mainland neologisms unrelated to the substratum (*niinii*, older brother; *meccha*, really). To complicate matters further, the passing of items from generation to generation is by no means a one-way process. Nohara explains that new kinship terms unrelated to the substratum such as *niinii* would have originated in young people's speech and then spread upwards across the generations via the media (Nohara 1998: 247).

Nohara's work has been continued into this century. With a view to raising awareness of young Okinawan people's language among international students and staff, more surveys of high school and university students have been conducted to ascertain which substrate items have been retained in young people's speech: 152 students from all year groups at Okinawa

International University participated in the first survey in 1999, of which the data from 99 respondents were analyzed and reported in Kinjō and Shō (2000). The questionnaire showed 70 items of Okinawa-substrate Japanese embedded in sentences (e.g., *mainichi isogashikute taihen da wake*, I'm busy everyday and it's awful, you see), and students were asked to circle "use", "don't use" or "don't know" as well as respond to other questions about their understanding of certain expressions and their language choices depending on interlocutor. The results were compared to Motonaga's (1979) study, and it was found that some expressions appear to be falling out of use, such as *kasa o kaburu* (SJ: *kasa o sasu*, put up an umbrella), *anta ni kureru yo* (SJ: *anata ni ageru yo*, I'll give it to you), *kazu o yomu* (SJ: *kazoeru*, count [numbers]), and non-standard use of combined particles *ga wa* and *ga mo*. The data were analyzed using *t*-tests to look for significant mean differences by place of origin and sex. However, later studies with larger samples have provided more reliable results.

The next survey, conducted in 2009–2010, investigated the use of Okinawan and Okinawa-substrate Japanese expressions by university students with a view to publishing teaching materials that would allow international students to integrate more easily into the local culture. Students from four different universities on Okinawa Island (N = 432) were asked to fill out a questionnaire eliciting responses to 58 words and expressions on the following scale:

(a) I use it in the same way as the example.
(b) I use it but in a different way from the example.
(c) I don't use it myself but I've heard it before.
(d) I don't use it and haven't heard it before.

Data for 282 students out of the total were analyzed and reported in Shō, Sasaki and Karimata (2013). According to the results, the substrate influence in the students' language tends to manifest in slight semantic and syntactic differences. For example, non-standard usage of Japanese items such as *hazu*, *-kirenai*, *wake*, and *kuru* was reported at a much higher rate (> 80%) than the use of items that do not exist in Standard Japanese or direct translations from Okinawan with very different meanings from the standard (< 20%), such as *yoogaraa* (Okinawan: skinny person), *yasumeru* (make cheaper, SJ: rest) and *aruku* (commute/work, SJ: walk). In a separate participant-generated response section, students were asked to write down any other Okinawan expressions as they might use them in the context of a full sentence. It was found that Okinawan words generally appear as isolated insertions within a Japanese matrix.

In 2011–2012, the same survey was revised and administered to a much larger sample (N = 3,496), this time to first and third year high school students from 47 schools across a wider area in the Okinawa island group. The results were reported in Shō and Sasaki (2015) and were very similar to those of the previous university campus survey, although high school students were found to have an even more depleted substrate repertoire than their elders at university.[17] Statistical analyses using χ^2 and *t*-tests showed greater use of Okinawan and Okinawa-substrate Japanese among those who: (1) intended to work or study in Okinawa in the future; (2) had locally born parents; and (3) came from the southern part of Okinawa Island (excluding Naha). Participant-generated responses yielded many new words in the lexicon that either use elements of Okinawan in creative ways, e.g., *henjiraa* (weird face), or are totally unrelated to the substratum, e.g., *sara* (very). The results were compared with those of Nohara's (1996) study to ascertain what kind of expressions had been retained in the substratum and what might remain in the future, such as Okinawan verbs and adjectives with Japanese inflections, e.g., *kurusu* (hit) and *kashimasai* (noisy); intensifier adverbs meaning "very", e.g., *teegee*, *yakkee*; familiar Okinawan words for food and animals, e.g., *gooyaa* (bitter melon), *gajan* (mosquito); and words with Okinawan -(*y*)*aa* endings for describing people, e.g., *minkaa* (deaf person) and *furaa* (idiot). Shō and Sasaki argue that such substrate-influenced words and expressions are probably learnt at school from older children rather than at home, while Karimata (2006: 53) emphasizes the influence of mass media and celebrity culture.

The Yabiku School: Theoretical classification and description

Although the descriptive work by Narita and Motonaga had a strong influence on later scholars, it was Yabiku who began to make sense of the language shift process by attempting to draw up various typologies from as early as the 1960s (Yabiku 1963). This tradition was picked up and expanded in the 1990s. Karimata (1994) provides a useful overview of the language shift situation as it stood at the time, including more explanations and examples of both *uchinaa yamatuguchi* (Okinawa-substrate Japanese) and *yamatu uchinaaguchi* (Japanese-superstrate Okinawan). Another of Karimata's foci was newly emerging expressions created by young people with no knowledge of Ryukyuan languages (i.e., non-speakers). Karimata refers to these expressions as "uchinaa slang", a term coined by Shinjō Kazuhiro in Mabuigumi (1990).[18]

Inspired by Yabiku (1987), Karimata (2006) went on to promote his Ryukyu Creole hypothesis in relation to young people's Okinawa-substrate Japanese. He makes this claim on the grounds that these varieties have an underlying Ryukyuan grammatical system despite being overwhelmingly Japanese from a lexical point of view. The non-standard usage of -*te aru* and -*te nai* forms are used as supporting evidence. Karimata arrives at a three-fold categorization of young people's expressions which, like Nohara's (1998) typology, lacks sufficient analytical treatment of uchinaa slang in its inclusion of items unrelated to the substratum (Type 3):

Type 1: Items or stems borrowed directly from Ryukyuan.
Type 2: Japanese items or stems with Ryukyuan meaning or inflection.
Type 3: Items appearing in neither Ryukyuan nor SJ.

The Ryukyu Creole hypothesis is further developed in Karimata (2008), this time including Amami-substrate Japanese in the discussion and claiming that the current leveling tendency amounts to decreolization (Karimata 2008: 63). Karimata (2008: 59) traces the birth of a "pidgin Japanese" back to the late nineteenth century but, perhaps realizing that doing so has made his hypothesis indefensible, he abandons the creole hypothesis in his later work and argues instead for Ryukyu Creoloid (Karimata 2010, 2012). Karimata reanalyzes all non-standard, substrate-influenced lexical items and suggests a finer-grained typology than his earlier one:

Type 1: Direct borrowings from Ryukyuan.
Type 2: Direct borrowings from Ryukyuan with Japanese phonology.
Type 3: Japanese items with Ryukyuan meaning.
Type 4: Ryukyuan borrowings with Japanese morpho-phonology.
Type 5: Neologisms using Ryukyuan word formation rules.

Takaesu (1994) is one of the most important papers on Ryukyu-substrate Japanese to date. It documents the phonological, grammatical and lexical features of Okinawa-substrate Japanese, complementing her (1992) descriptive work on pitch accent. Takaesu (2004) builds on her earlier work on grammar and goes into more detail on tense, aspect and mood in the substratum. A more theoretical discussion is resumed in Takaesu (2002, 2005), in which she follows Karimata (1994) in distinguishing between three types of language contact phenomenon

Table 28.2 Ryukyuan Creoloid and Ryukyuan

	Ryukyu Creoloid	Ryukyuan	Standard Japanese	English
Type 1	gooyaa	gooyaa	nigauri	bitter melon
Type 2	yaa	ʔyaa	kimi	you
	hagee	hagëë (Amamian)	aa	ah
Type 3	awateru	ʔawatiin	awateru / isogu	panic / rush
Type 4	hogasu	fugasun	(ana o) akeru	make (a hole)
Type 5	usosaa	yukushimuniisaa	usotsuki	liar

Source: Karimata (2008, 2012), compiled and adapted by the author.

in Okinawa – *uchinaa yamatuguchi, yamatu uchinaaguchi* and *uchinaa slang*. Takaesu returns to Yabiku's original concepts in taking into consideration the matrix language into which items are embedded, rather than analyzing items in isolation. Hence, *uchinaa yamatuguchi* and *yamatu uchinaaguchi* are defined in terms of a speaker's intention to speak utterances of Standard Japanese or Okinawan respectively, while *uchinaa slang* is defined as the use of Okinawan fragments by young people with no knowledge of the language (Takaesu 2002: 152).

The Nagata School: Qualitative research by interview

This strand of research is characterized by a particular method of eliciting detailed data via interviews of very small numbers of participants. In this vein, Nagata (1996) remains one of the most important sources on Ryukyu-substrate Japanese and is the most extensive in geographical terms. The book combines reworked versions of his earlier sociolinguistic and lexical studies with reports on later pan-Ryukyuan surveys of grammatical and phonological substrative features, conducted in 1988 and 1991, respectively. The surveys involved interviews of informants in selected locations across the archipelago. The first survey examined grammatical substrative influence on the Japanese spoken by a small sample (N = 13) of full speakers and rusty speakers (born 1911–1951) in Amami, Miyako, and the Yaeyama Islands of Ishigaki and Iriomote. The second survey of phonological features was more extensive and involved a larger sample (N = 47) and a wider age range of full speakers, rusty speakers and semi-speakers (born 1906–1977) from selected towns and villages in Amami, Okinoerabu, Okinawa, Miyako, Ishigaki, Hateruma and Yonaguni. This was followed by a third survey of vocabulary and pitch accent on Kikai Island (Amami Islands), conducted from 1992 to 1994, with a sample of similar size (N = 50) ranging across the same three generations.

Long (2013) is the most recent study of Amami-substrate Japanese and draws on Kurai's (1987) research. Four university students from Amami were interviewed and the following typology of lexical and grammatical items was drawn up on the basis of the data:

Type 1: Items taken directly from Amamian:

    a: without a change of meaning;
    b: with a change in meaning.

Type 2: Items with Japanese form but changed meaning.

Long finds that Amami-substrate Japanese is more or less similar to Okinawa-substrate Japanese with minor differences in vocabulary and sentence-final particles.

Zayasu's (2017) monograph is the most recent study of Ryukyu-substrate Japanese. He interviewed three people from Tomigusuku in the southern part of Okinawa Island and 12 people from Ishigaki in Yaeyama to investigate cross-generational substrate influence on their Japanese, focusing specifically on non-standard phonology, particle usage and aspect/modality/evidentiality. Participants were chosen from three age groups: elderly (born pre-war), middle-aged (born post-war, pre-reversion) and young (born post-reversion). Unfortunately, this arbitrary way of dividing the generations does not correspond to historical patterns of acquisition and associated language repertoire and behavior. For example, most of Zayasu's "middle-aged" participants were born in the 1950s, which is generally agreed to have been the point at which the intergenerational transmission link was broken (Ōsumi 2001: 73; Karimata 2006: 58; Anderson 2009: 252); therefore, the group may have comprised a mixture of rusty speakers (Ryukyuan L1) and semi-speakers (Japanese L1). Similarly, many of Zayasu's "elderly" cohort were born during the 1930s, a transition period which produced a new generation of bilinguals who became Japanese-dominant. This oversight may have affected Zayasu's conclusions about exactly which language features can be associated with which generation, but the level of linguistic detail in his book nevertheless surpasses that of any other study of Ryukyu-substrate Japanese to date.

The CA School: Transcript analysis

Recorded conversations can capture actual everyday language use in a way that is impossible via questionnaires. Close attention to the detail of transcripts has allowed researchers to tease apart Ryukyu-substrate Japanese as a pan-generational discourse mode from code-switching, which is defined as multi-word stretches of language alternation only available as a resource for speakers with some degree of bilinguality. Previously, scholars had conflated substrate-influenced Japanese and code-switching in order to simplify questionnaire items and avoid the issue of distinguishing between code-switching and borrowing by referring to any simultaneous use of Ryukyuan and Japanese in the same stretch of conversation as *mazari* (mixture [noun]) or *mazaru/majiru* (mix [verb]) (Teruya 1976; Motonaga 1981; Nagata 1984; Kigawa 1986). Although Matsumori (1995: 35) was the first scholar to make explicit reference to code-switching as a separate phenomenon from conventionalized substratal influence, Anderson (2009) investigated this further by analyzing transcripts of informal dialogue between Naha residents. Different generational subgroups were identified according to linguistic behavior by quantifying their proportional use of Okinawan-related words. One problem with Anderson's (2009) method of isolating and quantifying constituent source codes in a text is that it only captures surface forms and does not readily capture and quantify less obvious substrative effects such as semantic transfer, subtle aspectual differences, pitch accent and intonation. The thesis is, therefore, much more valuable for its insights into cross-generational code-switching behavior than it is for its analysis of more subtle characteristics of Ryukyu-substrate Japanese (Anderson 2009: 134–152).

Recent studies have broadened grammatical discussion of Okinawa-substrate Japanese to the pragmatic and discourse levels. Using transcripts of a popular radio drama and task-oriented group discussions among university students, Miyahira and Petrucci (2014) analyze the ways in which interactional particles *sa(a)*, *yo(o)* and *wake* function to construct a participation framework for co-authoring speakership. They conclude that the usage of these particles is more diverse than in Standard Japanese and reflects substrative influence. Sugita (2014) investigates the use of Okinawa-substrate Japanese on local radio in the 1980s, using similar conversation analysis methods and transcribed portions of radio shows. She discusses emotive uses for Okinawa-substrate Japanese as a code for young semi-speakers to emphasize solidarity and intimacy as well as to express anti-mainlander sentiment. An interesting aspect of Sugita's study is the noticeably high proportion of Okinawan use by semi-speakers in her extracts. Compared to transcripts of semi-speaker talk in Anderson (2009), for example, the percentage of Okinawan-related lexemes is relatively high at around 12%. This is perhaps due to the text genre, selective use of text portions or the time period in question.

The future of Ryukyu-substrate Japanese

There is disagreement in the literature as to whether the varieties of Japanese spoken by Ryukyuans will continue to show substratal influence. Nagata (1996: 158) predicts that Ryukyuan words will eventually be phased out and Ryukyu-substrate Japanese may even be replaced by the Tokyo variety. Others believe that some substratal influence (e.g., syntactic, pragmatic) will continue to "stick" across generations (Yabiku 1987: 122). It has also been suggested that the Ryukyu-substrate Japanese spoken by future generations could retain Ryukyuan vocabulary and include neologisms from productive Ryukyuan word formation rules (Shō and Sasaki 2015: 16), or that it could be completely relexified by Japanese while retaining certain substrate-influenced grammatical forms such as *-te aru* (Karimata 2006: 57). While it is impossible to make predictions with any certainty, research has shown that each new generation of Ryukyuans exhibits diminished manifestation of substrative influence compared with the previous generation due to further limitation in exposure to the substratum language, and even the Ryukyu-substrate Japanese spoken by elderly productive bilinguals is leveling towards the standard over time (Nagata 1996: 162). Whatever the case, Nagata (1996: 169) is most likely correct in stating that the future of Ryukyu-substrate Japanese will ultimately depend on whether the Ryukyus retain or lose their regional character.

Research desiderata

This area of Ryukyuan sociolinguistics is generally well researched owing to the diversity in approach, and there are not many obvious gaps in the literature. Nevertheless, there is a need for more surveys on attitudes towards Ryukyu-substrate Japanese. Such research requires the development of questionnaires which have been properly validated via pilot testing and preliminary factor analysis of well-constructed items.

In terms of longitudinal quantitative studies of Ryukyu-substrate Japanese, the valuable research recently conducted by researchers at Okinawa International University and University of the Ryukyus is ongoing, and their surveys need to be repeated in perhaps another decade or so in order that results can continue to be compared longitudinally to track changes in the substratum. Another possible line of investigation in such studies would be the extent to which any elements of the substratum can be used in formal contexts where the use of Standard Japanese is expected.

Acknowledgements

I am grateful to Patrick Heinrich for his comments on early drafts and for sending journals from Hokkaido. I would also like to express my heartfelt gratitude to Hiroshi Sasaki from the Hakushin bookshop for his invaluable service to scholars in supplying publications which are difficult to source elsewhere. Special thanks go to Makiko Shō for taking the time to forward me my online book orders from Japan, along with some rare research reports which I would not otherwise have been able to access.

Notes

1 In recent years, some scholars (e.g., Takaesu 2005; Karimata 2006) have begun to see the value of dropping the term *hōgen* more consistently in favor of *ryūkyūgo* or *ryūkyū shogo* ("Ryukyuan languages"), thereby allowing for somewhat clearer differentiation between local languages and substrate-influenced varieties of Japanese; however, the use of *hōgen* still persists in some circles (e.g., Zayasu 2017).
2 Nagata (1983) was first to highlight the need for more research into pidgins and creoles, and Yabiku (1987) responded to this by trying to apply Hymes' (1971) theory to the Ryukyuan case. Other scholars then adopted this idea in later publications.
3 A "creoloid" is defined as a language that has similarities to a creole but did not develop from a pidgin.
4 The emergence of innovative young people's varieties in the final stages of language shift is well documented in the wider literature, and is by no means unique to the Okinawan case. Sasse (1992: 18) comments that a dead language may "leave a substratum influence (especially lexically) in the dialect of T [the target language] which the former speech community of A [the abandoned language] continues to speak". Batibo (2005: 91) describes the fifth and final phase of his model of language shift, remarking that "some of the linguistic characteristics of L1 [the abandoned language] often remain as residual features in L2 [the target language]. Such phenomena, known as substratum features, may involve prosodic, phonetic, phonological, semantic or lexical elements".
5 The term "mixed language" is usually used in the literature to refer to a very specific and extreme type of language contact phenomenon where a new language evolves from roughly equal input from two "parent" languages. Such languages are comparatively rare, and perhaps the best-known example is Ma'á, spoken in Tanzania, East Africa. Readers are referred to Matras and Bakker (2007) for further information.
6 The term "interlanguage", coined by Selinker (1972), is usually used in the context of L2/foreign language acquisition, in which the interlanguage is a variety of the target L2 that incorporates some degree of interference from the speaker's L1.
7 Motonaga's 1979 and 1984 papers were republished in Motonaga (1994) along with the rest of his life's work.
8 Some scholars follow Motonaga (1984) in spelling this *uchinaa yamatoguchi* (i.e., Japanized with an <o>) while others spell it *uchinaa yamatuguchi* (with a <u>) as pronounced in the Okinawan language.
9 Some islands, such as Kikai and Okinoerabu, have a stronger Kansai influence than others due to out-migration among older generations for work purposes (Kigawa 1986; Nagata 1996: 142).
10 Yabiku's use of *gengo sakuhin* (literally "linguistic composition") is explained on page 122 (1987) as "expression by means of words, phrases and sentences", so I have translated it as "language" in its non-count sense.
11 Karimata (1994, 2012) is the only scholar to have expanded on Yabiku's concept by further exploring phonological, grammatical and lexical superstratal interference from Japanese, not only on Okinawan but also on other Ryukyuan languages. There is a need for more research into Japanese-superstrate Ryukyuan in connection with Ryukyuan language loss and lexical borrowing from Japanese.
12 Note that Nakamoto emphasizes the differences between Standard Japanese and Okinawa-substrate Japanese as the translations are not exactly equivalent and newly coined vocabulary has been included in the "reformed dialect" sentences.
13 Since the standard Hepburn romanization system cannot adequately represent Ryukyuan varieties because of rephonemization, it has been slightly adapted for this chapter. The morae pronounced [ti], [tɕi], [di] and [dzi] in Ryukyuan words are transcribed consistently as <ti>, <chi>, <di> and <ji>. When [ɸ] appears before vowels other than /u/, it is transcribed as <f>.
14 Nakamoto (1990: 916–917) highlights the need for: (1) documentation of new language varieties spoken by children aged under 15; (2) comparative studies of Ryukyuan languages and their corresponding substrate-influenced Japanese varieties; (3) research into intergenerational interaction and transmission; (4) investigations into the role of environmental factors and conservatism/innovation in language shift; and (5) consideration of future developments in the Ryukyuan substratum.
15 Nohara's (1996, 1998) papers were republished as chapters in Nohara (2005).
16 Ōsumi's survey conducted in the same year (1996) has limitations for the same reasons (reported in Ōsumi 2001).
17 Shō and Sasaki (2015) is an abridged version of the full report provided in Sasaki et al. (2014).
18 This came as part of a set of three popular books put together by a large group of young people for general readership: Mabuigumi (1989, 1990) and Haapuudan (2003). Another similar Okinawa-substrate Japanese phrasebook is Fujiki (2004).

References

Anderson, Mark (2009) Emergent Language Shift in Okinawa. PhD thesis, Department of Japanese Studies, University of Sydney.

—— (2015) Substrate-influenced Japanese and Code-switching. In: *Handbook of the Ryukyuan Languages*. Patrick Heinrich, Shinsho Miyara and Michinori Shimoji (eds), 481–509. Boston: de Gruyter Mouton.

Batibo, Herman M. (2005) *Language Decline and Death in Africa. Causes, Consequences and Challenges*. Clevedon: Multilingual Matters.

Fujiki, Hayato (2004) *Haisai! Okinawa kotoba – uchinaa yamatoguchi* [Hello! Okinawan Words – Okinawan Japanese]. Tokyo: Futabasha.

Haapuudan (eds) (2003) *Shin! Okinawa kīwādo* [New! Okinawa Keywords]. Naha: Border Ink.

Heffernan, Kevin (2006) Prosodic Levelling during Language Shift. Okinawan Approximations of Japanese Pitch-accent. *Journal of Sociolinguistics* 10(5): 641–666.

Hirayama, Ryōmei (1984) *Okinawa yamato kotoba no hon* [A Book of Okinawan Japanese]. Naha: Okinawa Shuppan.

Hymes, Dell (1971) *Pidginization and Creolization of Languages*. Cambridge: Cambridge University Press.

Karimata, Shigehisa (1994) Okinawa ni okeru gengo jōkyō (dansō) [The Linguistic Situation in Okinawa (Some Thoughts)]. *Kokubungaku – kaishaku to kanshō* 59(1): 88–98.

—— (2006) Okinawa wakamono kotoba jijō. Ryūkyū kureōru nihongo shiron [The State of Okinawa Young People's Language. The Ryukyu Creole Japanese Hypothesis]. *Nihongogaku* 25: 50–59.

—— (2008) Ton-futsūgo. Uchinaa yamatuguchi wa kureōru-ka. Ryūkyū kureōru nihongo no kenkyū no tame ni [Potato Japanese. Is Uchinaa Yamatuguchi a Creole? In Furtherance of Research into Ryukyu Creole Japanese]. *Nantō bunka* 30: 55–65.

—— (2010) Ryūkyū kureoroido no seikaku [Characteristics of Ryukyu Creoloid]. In: *Okinawa Hawai kontakuto zōn to shite no tōsho*. Masahide Ishihara, Ikue Kina and Shin Yamashiro (eds), 31–42. Tokyo: Sairyūsha.

—— (2012) Ryūkyū rettō ni okeru gengo sesshoku kenkyū no tame no oboegaki [Notes on Research into Language Contact in the Ryukyu Archipelago]. *Ryūkyū no hōgen* 36: 17–38.

Kigawa, Yukio (1986) Okinoerabujima ni okeru kansai hōgen to zenkoku kyōtsūgo no eikyō – ankēto chōsa no kekka kara [The Influence of Kansai Dialect and Standard Japanese in Okinoerabujima. From the Results of a Questionnaire Survey]. *Tōdai ronkyū* 23: 1–18.

Kinjō, Naomi and Makiko Shō (2000) Okinawa no daigakusei no seikatsu gengo no jittai – wakamono no uchinaa yamatuguchi [The Actual Everyday Language of University Students in Okinawa. Young People's Uchinaa Yamatuguchi]. *Southern Review* 15: 25–39.

Kurai, Norio (1987) *Ton-futsūgo shohōsen – shima no hyōjungo o sukkiri saseru hō* [A Medical Prescription for Potato Japanese. A Way to Make the Standard Japanese of the Islands Better Again]. Naze: Private Publication.

Kuwae, Yoshiyuki (1930) *Hyōjungo taishō – okinawago no kenkyū* [A Contrastive Study of Okinawan and the Standard Language]. Naha: Aoyama Shoten.

LaPolla, Randy J. (2009) Causes and Effects of Substratum, Superstratum and Adstratum Influence, with Reference to Tibeto-Burman Languages. In: *Issues in Tibeto-Burman Historical Linguistics*. Yasuhiko Nagano (ed.), 227–237. Osaka: National Museum of Ethnology.

Long, Daniel (2010) Gengo sesshoku-ron kara mita uchinaa yamatuguchi no bunrui [The Classification of Uchinaa Yamatuguchi According to Language Contact Theory]. *Jinbun gakuhō* 428: 1–30.

—— (2013) Amami-Ōshima no ton-futsūgo to Okinawa-hontō no uchinaa yamatuguchi no gengo keishiki ni mirareru kyōtsūten to sōiten [Similarities and Differences in the Linguistic Forms of Potato Japanese in Amami Island and Okinawan Japanese in Okinawa Island]. *Nihongo kenkyū* 33: 87–97.

Mabuigumi (eds) (1989) *Okinawa kīwādo koramu bukku* (jitenban) [Okinawa Keyword Column Book (Dictionary Edition)]. Naha: Okinawa Shuppan.

—— (eds) (1990) *Okinawa kīwādo koramu bukku 2* (nikkiban) [Okinawa Keyword Column Book 2 (journal edition)]. Naha: Okinawa Shuppan.

Matras, Yaron and Peter Bakker (eds) (2007) *The Mixed Language Debate. Theoretical and Empirical Advances*. Berlin: Mouton de Gruyter.

Matsumori, Akiko (1995) Ryūkyuan. Past, Present, and Future. In: *Multilingual Japan*. John C. Maher and Kyoko Yashiro (eds), 19–45. Clevedon: Multilingual Matters.

Miyahira, Katsuyuki and Peter R. Petrucci (2014) Interactional Particles in Okinawan Talk-in-Interaction. In: *Language Crisis in the Ryukyus*. Mark Anderson and Patrick Heinrich (eds), 206–235. Newcastle upon Tyne: Cambridge Scholars Publishing.

Motonaga, Moriyasu (1979) Okinawa ni okeru jidōseito no kotoba [Young People's Language in Okinawa]. *Ryūkyū daigaku kyōiku gakubu kiyō* 23(1): 37–52.

—— (1981) Okinawa ni okeru jidōseito no gengo seikatsu to gengo ishiki [The Language Life and Language Attitudes of Young People in Okinawa]. *Okinawa gengo kenkyū sentā shiryō* 30. University of the Ryukyus.

—— (1984) Nantō hōgen to kokugo kyōiku [The Southern Islands Dialect and National Language Education]. In: *Okinawa/Amami no hōgen*. Ki'ichi Ītoyo, Sukezumi Hino and Ryōichi Satō (eds), 363–386. Tokyo: Kokusho Kankōkai.

—— (1994) *Ryūkyū-ken seikatsugo no kenkyū* [Studies in the Everyday Language of the Ryukyus]. Tokyo: Shunjūsha.

Nagata, Takashi (1983) Yonaguni no gengo henka [Language Change in Yonaguni]. *Gengo no sekai* 1(2).

—— (1984) Yonaguni hōgen no kyōtsūgoka – shakai gengogakuteki kenkyū [Standardization of the Yonaguni Dialect. Sociolinguistic Research]. *Gengo no sekai* 2(1).

—— (1996) *Ryūkyū de umareta kyōtsūgo* [Regional Varieties of Japanese that have Emerged in the Ryukyus]. Tokyo: Ōfū.

Nakamoto, Masachie (1990) *Nihon rettō gengoshi no kenkyū* [A Linguistic History of the Japanese and Ryukyuan Islands]. Tokyo: Taishūkan.

Narita, Yoshimitsu (1960) Okinawa ni okeru bilingualism ni tsuite [On Bilingualism in Okinawa]. *Kokugogaku* 41: 86–93.

Nohara, Mitsuyoshi (1996) Okinawa no wakamono kotoba [Young People's Language in Okinawa]. *Okinawa bunka kenkyū* 22: 265–282.

—— (1998) Ryūkyū shakai hōgengaku e no sasoi – okinawa no wakamono kotoba-kō [Introduction to Ryukyuan Socio-dialectology. Investigation into the Language of Okinawan Youth]. *Okinawa Kokusai Daigaku kōkaikōza* 7: 243–264.

—— (2005) *Uchinaaguchi e no shōtai* [Introduction to Okinawan]. Naha: Okinawa Times.

Ōno, Masao (1995) Chūkan hōgen to shite no uchinaa yamatoguchi no isō [Aspects of Okinawan Japanese as an Interdialect]. *Gengo gekkan* 14(12): 178–191.

Ōsumi, Midori (2001) Language and Identity in Okinawa Today. In: *Studies in Japanese Bilingualism*. Mary Noguchi and Sandra Fotos (eds), 68–97. Clevedon: Multilingual Matters.

Sanada, Shinji (1992) Hōgen no jōkyō to nihongo kyō iku [The Dialect Situation and Japanese Education]. *Nihongo kyōiku* 76: 1–8.

Sasaki, Kayoko, Makiko Shō, Yukiko Karimata and Kanji Tanaka (2014) Kō kō sei no okinawago shiyō ni tsuite no chō sa kenkyū – kiete iku kotoba no naka de nani ga nokotte iku ka? [Survey Research on High School Students' Use of the Okinawan Language. Of the Disappearing Words, Which Ones will Survive?]. 2011–2013 Grants-in-Aid for Scientific Research (C) (Research report).

Sasse, Hans-Jürgen (1992) Theory of Language Death. In: *Language Death: Factual and Theoretical Explorations with Special Reference to East Africa*. Matthias Brenzinger (ed.), 7–30. Berlin: Mouton de Gruyter.

Selinker, Larry (1972) Interlanguage. *International Review of Applied Linguistics (IRAL)* 10(3): 209–231.

Shō, Makiko and Kayoko Sasaki (2015) Kennai kō kōsei no okinawa no kotoba no shiyō ni tsuite – henyō shite iku kotoba, nokotte iku kotoba [Use of the Okinawan Language by High School Students in Okinawa Prefecture. Transforming Words and Surviving Words]. *Okinawa International University Journal of Scientific Research* 18(1): 1–40.

Shō, Makiko, Kayoko Sasaki and Yukiko Karimata (2013) Wakamono no okinawa no kotoba no shiyō oyobi rikai – kennai yondaigaku ni zaiseki suru daigakusei no ba'ai [Young Okinawans' Usage and Comprehension of the Okinawan Language. A Case Study of Students from Four Universities in Okinawa]. *Okinawa Kokusai Daigaku gaikokugo kenkyū* 17(1): 1–25.

Sugita, Yuko (2014) The Discovery of Okinawa-substrate Japanese as a "We-code". The Language of Okinawan Youth in the 1980s and its Impact. In: *Language Crisis in the Ryukyus*. Mark Anderson and Patrick Heinrich (eds), 169–205. Newcastle upon Tyne: Cambridge Scholars Publishing.

Takaesu, Yoriko (1992) Okinawa ni okeru hyōjungo (uchinaa yamatuguchi) no akusento no jittai – 1 mōra/ 2 mōra meishi no ba'ai. [Information about the Accent of Okinawan Japanese (Uchinaa Yamatuguchi). The Case of 1- and 2-mora Nouns]. *Okinawa gengo kenkyū sentā hōkoku* 1.

—— (1994) Uchinaa yamatuguchi – sono onsei, bunpō, goi ni tsuite. [Okinawan Japanese. Its Phonetics, Grammar and Vocabulary]. *Okinawa gengo kenkyū sentā hōkoku* 3, 245–289.

—— (2002) Uchinaa yamatuguchi o megutte [On Okinawan Japanese]. *Kokubungaku – kaishaku to kanshō* 67(7): 151–160.

—— (2004) Uchinaa yamatuguchi – dōshi no asupekuto tensu mūdo [Verb Aspect, Tense and Mood in Okinawan Japanese]. In: *Nihongo no asupekuto tensu mūdo taikei – hyōjungo kenkyū o koete*. Mayumi Kudo (ed.), 302–329. Tokyo: Hitsuji Shobō.

—— (2005) Uchinaa yamatuguchi [Okinawan Japanese]. In: *Jiten nihon no tagengo shakai*. Shinji Sanada and Hiroshi Shoji (eds), 265–68. Tokyo: Iwanami.

Teruya, Kikue (1976) Kōkōsei ni okeru hōgen ishiki ni tsuite. Okinawa-ken chūbu chi'iki no ba'ai [Concerning the Dialect Attitudes of High School Students: The Case of Central Okinawa Island in Okinawa Prefecture]. *Sagami kokubun* 3.

Thomason, Sarah G. (2009) How to Establish Substratum Interference. In: *Issues in Tibeto-Burman Historical Linguistics*. Yasuhiko Nagano (ed.), 319–328. Osaka: National Museum of Ethnology.

Yabiku, Hiroshi (1963) Okinawa ni okeru gengo ten'i no katei ni tsuite [Concerning the Language Shift Process in Okinawa]. *Jinbun shakai kagaku kenkyū* 1: 113–117.

—— (1987) Uchinaa yamatuguchi to yamatu uchinaaguchi [Okinawan Japanese and Japanese Okinawan]. *Kokubungaku – kaishaku to kanshō* 52(7): 119–123.

Zayasu, Hirofumi (2017) *Uchinaa yamatuguchi no kenkyū* [*Research on Okinawan Japanese*]. Tokyo: Shinwasha.

INDEX

Abe, Yasushi 315, 333, 334, 393, 395, 397, 399, 400
accent: Ainu 9; Ryukyuan languages 371, 377; Ryukyu-substrate Japanese 44, 47, 443–444, 450–452; variation 64, 69, 70, 74–75, 83–84, 133, 139, 148, 205, 227, 239, 307, 413, 430
adult 17–18, 176, 206, 219, 273; learner 37–38, 94, 113–114, 211, 340, 344, 365
Ainu 3–21, 63, 65, 84, 129, 136, 139, 144, 146, 162, 172–174, 176–177, 180, 185, 187, 306–307, 310, 315, 332, 335, 343–344, 350, 354–367, 371–372, 389, 392–394, 399, 424, 426, 446
Amami-Ryukyuan 25, 28, 32, 37, 43–46, 48–49, 51–52, 55, 57–59, 65, 71, 82, 172, 370, 373, 376, 378, 380, 383, 441, 444–445, 450–451
American English 117–118, 225, 227, 307; *see also* English
ancestral language 27, 135, 266, 361, 378, 392
Anderson, Mark 28, 44, 45, 50, 54, 58, 59, 307, 375, 377–381, 421–442, 446, 452, 453
anthropology 91, 130, 240, 264, 360, 422
anxiety: foreign language 189–190; kanji 317; new immigrants 188
Aotearoa/New Zealand 80, 85, 365
applied linguistics 93, 97, 122, 175, 177, 178, 305, 394
archive 13–14, 17, 93, 165, 211, 271, 309, 354, 364, 378
Asahi, Yoshiyuki 82, 83–84, 85, 86, 162
assimilation 26, 102, 153, 174, 212, 306, 340, 343–344, 349, 350, 357, 359–361, 365, 373–374, 377, 390, 393, 395, 425
authenticity 130, 134, 136, 225, 431
authority 81, 135, 224, 270, 299, 309, 331
auxiliary verbs 206, 226, 229, 258, 268
awareness 36, 43, 64–65, 69, 83–84, 86, 93, 119, 134, 163, 170, 174–175, 177, 180, 188–190, 192, 208, 220, 226, 228, 244, 255, 274, 280, 282, 291, 301, 306, 310, 324, 340–341, 345, 347–349, 355, 360, 364, 366, 375, 389–390, 408, 410, 430, 441, 444, 448
Azuma, Shoji 210, 219, 221, 270

Backhaus, Peter 28, 110, 114–115, 144, 159, 160, 161, 165, 192, 240, 242, 422, 426
barrier 13, 189–190, 193, 269, 317, 324, 343, 373, 394–395, 430
Beebe, Leslie M. 81, 265
bilingualism 94, 98, 101, 102, 115, 140, 145, 170–182, 186, 209, 218–219, 221–222, 341, 344–345, 350, 355, 371, 382–383, 421; Ainu 14, 20, 354, 364; Chinese 424, 425, 427; education 91, 93, 96, 100, 177, 178, 179, 180, 181–182, 308–309, 372, 374, 382, 392, 428; Korean 221, 424; Miyakoan 171–172; Ryukyuan languages 371–378, 380, 424, 448, 452; Ryukyu-substrate Japanese 45–48, 52–53, 56, 59, 442–443, 453
Blommaert, Jan 29, 31, 145, 149, 151, 163, 301, 413, 431
borrowing 7, 9–13, 35–36, 43, 52, 78–79, 140, 209, 380, 444, 450, 452
Britain, David 80, 201, 210, 211
Brown, Penelope 249–251, 256–258, 266, 270
buraku/burakumin 329–330, 332, 372, 424

capital 114, 121, 152, 328
Carroll, Tessa 91, 173, 299, 302–304, 423, 426–427
child language learning 26–27, 37–38, 71, 81–82, 94, 113–114, 119, 171–172, 174–181, 186, 187–192, 209, 219, 221, 265, 267, 269, 275, 308–309, 326, 329, 330, 333, 348–349, 355–358, 360–363, 365–366, 372–378,

381–382, 390–392, 394, 409, 420, 425–429, 443–433, 450
China 91, 94, 115, 122, 161, 173, 175, 187, 302, 339, 340, 345–346, 348–350, 373, 423–425, 428–429
Chinese language 9, 28, 92–95, 97, 98, 114–115, 160–161, 172–173, 175, 176, 177, 180–181, 185, 188, 191, 192, 206, 226, 227, 283, 285, 307, 344–348, 395, 424–425, 427, 428–430
Chiri, Yukie 9, 16, 361
citizenship 27, 92, 143–144, 173, 188, 308, 331, 340, 343–345, 408, 427
code mixing 68, 79–81, 135, 152, 210, 218, 228
code-switching 45, 59, 69, 79, 93, 97, 100, 102, 135, 145, 148, 177, 209–221, 218–231, 378, 380, 382, 391, 397, 421, 425, 452
colony/colonialism 7, 82, 85, 92, 111, 131, 136–139, 159, 170, 192, 210–212, 300, 302–303, 306–308, 310, 339–341, 343–350, 357–359, 361, 366, 373, 408, 412, 415, 421, 424, 426
common language 45, 67–68, 70–71, 130, 134, 373, 420–421; English in Japan 130; in Ryukyus 35–37; Japanese in Taiwan 131
communicative competence 96, 112, 121, 145, 186, 221, 340, 420
community 26, 78, 80, 82, 86, 91, 113–114, 120, 129, 131, 149–150, 200–201, 206, 208, 211, 222, 248, 256, 272, 274, 283, 304, 330, 370, 374, 391, 408, 429; academic 75, 102; Ainu 354–355, 362, 365; bilingual/multilingual 98, 136, 177, 184, 187–188, 193, 209–210; *buraku* 329; Chichijima 83; Chinese 177; deaf 180; international 94–95, 112, 120, 372; Korean 93, 177, 219, 221; *nikkeijin* 100, 177, 185, 211–212, 393; Okinawa 26–28, 71, 171–172, 374–377, 382, 399; online 271, 273, 366
comparative linguistics 78, 162, 425
contact language 3–4, 7–8, 31, 43, 69, 78–86, 102, 114, 170, 177–178, 181, 184, 186, 188–190, 192–193, 203–205, 209–212, 348, 355, 370, 408, 422, 441–443, 445–446, 450
convergence 79, 81, 92, 144, 150, 153–154, 212, 410
conversation 151, 201, 203–204, 208–210, 218, 220–223, 252, 271, 286–287, 289–290, 330, 333, 356, 373, 374, 378, 380; Ainu 17, 20; English (*eikaiwa*) 110, 113; Ryukyuan languages 35, 37, 59, 171
conversation analysis 221, 239–245, 446, 452
Cook, Haruko Minegishi 250, 422, 430
Corpus 201, 204, 206–208, 213, 269, 300, 302, 305, 308, 382
Correctness 68, 201, 205
Coulmas, Florian 144, 253, 284, 415, 421, 426
Creole 79–80, 83, 131, 185, 222, 426, 442, 450
critical discourse analysis 153, 239, 270

culture 111, 248, 300; academic 239, 244; Ainu 7, 18–21, 354, 358, 362–366; Chinese 192; diversity 153, 182, 185, 241; dominant 97, 131, 135, 138, 146, 137, 189, 229, 302, 305, 347, 359, 360–361, 392, 426, 428; high 284; Korean 192, 393; local 71, 181, 202, 309, 446; *nikkeijin* 99; popular 129, 146, 226, 318; subculture 229, 272–273, 282, 450; traditional 120, 147, 380; western 114, 118, 147
curriculum: Ainu 361, 365; English 111–113, 307; Japanese language 95, 344–345, 427–448; national 120, 137; Ryukyuan languages 38, 373, 445

DeChicchis, Joseph 307, 354–355, 362
decolonization 212, 300, 340, 349
decreolization 450
diachronic 92, 200, 204, 237, 275, 372, 379
dialect: atlas 7–8, 32, 63, 72–73, 175, 201, 210, 414; tag (*hōgen fuda*) 27, 174, 374
dialectology 36, 63–65, 71–72, 75–76, 91, 175, 201, 203, 304, 371, 407–408, 413, 415
diglossia 79
discourse analysis 235, 239–240, 244–245
discrimination 26, 95, 99, 102, 118, 153, 178, 181, 223, 227, 265, 270–271, 303, 306, 309–310, 317–318, 329–331, 333, 355, 358, 366, 374–375, 377, 393–398, 400, 424, 431
documentation: Ainu 3, 7, 13, 366; bilingual/multilingual 101; dialects 63; foreign communities 425; historical 224, 252, 280, 306, 327; Japanese language education 98, 348; language planning and policy 301, 303, 306–307, 310; linguistic landscape 158; Ryukyuan languages 38, 309, 373, 379, 446; Rykyuan-substrate Japanese 59, 443, 445–446, 450
dominant: English; 117, 159; language ideology 28, 65, 283, 288, 330–334, 357, 423; social group 273, 300, 393; variety 82, 98, 139, 370, 398, 416, 424, 427, 452
Dorian, Nancy 211, 370, 372, 381

education 146, 299, 302, 304, 310, 326, 328, 370, 373, 408, 412, 428; Ainu 19, 354, 356, 358–366; bilingual 91–93, 96, 100, 170, 172–175, 178–181, 186, 308–309, 374, 382, 399; endangered language 3, 25–26, 28–29, 36–37, 172–173, 189, 355–357, 366, 370, 372, 379, 391, 442; English 110–114, 118–19, 121, 204, 228, 307; foreign language 111, 116–118, 122, 187, 307; formal Japanese 67, 70–71, 134, 137, 193, 315, 317, 319, 322–324, 326–327, 329, 332–334; internationalization 112–113, 120, 153; Japanese language 91, 94–95, 97–98, 102, 170, 305–306, 339–350, 423, 425–430; Korean 176–177; Okinawa 26, 30, 43, 45, 372, 374, 376, 379;

returnee children (*kikoku shijo*) 178; Ryukyuan languages 38, 349

Endo, Orie 101, 275, 285–286, 288, 290–291, 423

English 110–122, 130–132, 137–140, 143, 148, 150–151, 153, 159–160, 163–164, 173, 189, 244, 306, 430; Ainu teaching material 4, 15; anxiety 189; dominance of 391–392; identity memphasis on 284; gender differences in 283–284, 286–287; identity marker 100; in EPA (the Economic Partnership Agreement) test 101; influence of 228–230; international language 98, 391, 398–399; medium of instruction 98, 180; Okinawan teaching material in 38; publication in 244, 299, 341, 354–355, 396–397, 424; superior language 113, 116–118; varieties 80–81, 212, 225, 227–230, 286, 416 *see also* bilingualism; code-switching; education; immersion; multilingualism

ethnicity; 3, 84–85, 92–95, 100, 102, 111, 120, 129–139, 140, 143–147, 152–153, 161, 170, 172–173, 175–177, 180–182, 184–185, 187, 191–193, 202, 210, 213, 218, 220–223, 226–227, 231, 281, 306, 340–341, 343–344, 347–348, 350, 364, 366, 390, 393, 395–396, 399, 421, 423–426; monoethnic 92, 213, 389; multiethnic 91, 136, 221–222

ethnography 63, 203, 231, 240, 245, 309–310

evidentiality 55, 452

extinct language 4, 5, 25, 32, 68, 79, 83, 163, 310, 379, 392, 446

Fairclough, Norman 239, 270

Fishman, Joshua A. 282, 289, 300, 372, 414, 416

foreign languages education *see* education

formal education *see* education

full speaker 45, 70, 375, 377, 380, 443, 451

Garcia, Ofelia 93, 145–146, 228, 231

gender 86, 114, 136, 143, 201–209, 221, 224, 238, 243, 245, 266, 269, 279–291, 306, 344, 380–381, 383, 408, 412–413, 421–23, 430; Ainu 17; Ryukyuan languages 39, 43

Giles, Howard 81

Globalization 112–113, 115–116, 120–121, 143, 153, 160, 170, 190, 212, 229, 265, 305, 426

Goffman, Erving 221, 241–242, 270, 284

Gottlieb, Nanette 143, 173, 244, 290, 299, 302, 354, 426, 429–430

grammar 26, 29, 38, 64, 93, 112–113, 200, 210, 219, 229, 236, 281, 300, 342, 371, 407, 410, 412, 429, 443–444, 450

grammaticalization 51

Hachijo/Hachijojima 28, 82–83, 172, 315, 413

Hara, Kiyoshi 379, 414

Hattori, Shiro 4–5, 18, 21, 136, 371, 413

Haugh, Michael 249, 254, 256, 265

Heinrich, Patrick 25–26, 29, 31, 35–38, 65, 71, 116, 134, 144, 162–163, 165, 186–187, 213, 222, 236–237, 279, 285, 291, 307, 309, 342, 349, 354, 359, 372–373, 375–379, 408, 416, 421–422, 424–425, 430–431

heritage language 27, 37, 71, 93–95, 133, 178, 212, 381, 391, 393, 424, 427, 428, 447

heterogeneity 160, 165, 184–185, 199, 411

heteroglossia 145

Hibiya, Junko 85, 203–204, 207–208, 409, 415, 422

historical linguistics 442

home language 374, 427

honorifics language (*keigo*) 18, 34–36, 208, 236, 238, 243–245, 248–260, 264, 267, 271, 273, 275, 280, 283–284, 290, 302, 304, 377, 413–414, 422–423, 430–431, 445; *see also* politeness

human rights 329, 362, 391–392, 396–397

hypercorrection 45, 81, 380

Ide, Sachiko 238, 245, 249–251, 283–285, 305, 415, 422

identity 129, 132, 136–138, 140, 149, 187, 192–193, 222, 238, 269, 421, 423, 427, 430; Ainu 255, 366; construction 93, 241–243, 397, 423; cultural 28, 120; disorder 282; dual 122, 130, 308; ethnic 93–94, 129, 133, 135, 425; Japanese 116, 118, 126, 122, 153, 307, 370, 377, 382; linguistic 100, 139, 145–146, 177, 181, 189, 223, 225, 237, 280, 397; local 43, 223; *nikkeijin* 100, 181; Ryukyuan languages 376; Ryukyu-substrate Japanese 441, 448; shift 130, 382; social 182, 254, 281; *zainichi* 181

ideology 120–122, 122; gender 243, 270, 280, 283, 286–290; hegemonic 132, 328; homogenous Japan 341, 374; Japanese 250, 340, 342–350, 421, 424; language 67, 91, 110–111, 113, 116, 119, 122, 143, 149, 154, 176, 184, 187–188, 190, 192, 221, 225, 231, 341, 366, 410; language policy 300–310; literacy 328, 330–332; monolingual 28, 30–31, 144, 163, 187, 218, 374; multilingual 145, 186, 193; nationalist 25, 67, 96–97, 102, 153, 192–193, 319, 408; political 137, 153; ultra-right 122, 193, 228, 302

immersion 37, 444; Ainu 365; English program 176–178, 181

impoliteness 248, 264–275

indexicality 115, 159, 164, 202, 221, 224–225, 228, 241, 248, 251, 259, 289, 367, 423

indigenous language 172, 185, 306–307, 344, 346–347, 361

Inoue, Fumio 67, 73, 75, 130, 160, 203–204, 207, 371, 379, 414, 429, 447

Inoue, Miyako 285, 423

insecurity 102, 193

intercultural communication/interaction 96, 117, 122, 144, 152, 188, 396

intergenerational transmission 370, 372, 376–377, 379, 382, 446, 452
internet 86, 113, 179, 193, 230, 319, 321, 365–366, 371, 431
intonation 31, 47, 52, 56, 148, 227, 246, 430, 444, 452
Ishihara, Masahide 25, 26, 27, 36, 37, 71, 370, 378, 379, 381
Iwasaki, Shoichi 231, 420

Japan: super-aged society 426
Japanese as superior language 189, 361
Japonic 28, 33, 65, 83, 371

Kagoshima 25, 32, 34, 71, 205, 373
Karimata, Shigehisa 33, 38, 44, 55–56, 58, 380, 391, 441–442, 446, 448–453
Kayano, Shigeru 16, 21, 362
Kindaichi, Haruhiko 189, 203, 280, 409
Kindaichi, Kyosuke 4, 16, 361, 408–409
Korea 85, 91, 114, 170, 221; colonial language policy 307, 315, 339–340, 343–350, 412, 421; North Korea 122, 180
Korean 91, 93, 424–425; aggression toward 94, 193, 227–228; code-switching 219, 221; heritage language rights 391–394, 427–428; language 84, 93–94, 111, 114, 116, 129, 131, 136, 139, 160–161, 163, 170, 172–173, 175, 185–186, 188, 192, 221, 372, 426; learners of Japanese 206, 329–330, 428; mock 227, 231; school 176–177, 191; *see also* zainichi
Kubota, Ryuko 111–114, 116–122, 153, 305, 307
Kumejima 33, 46, 445
Kunigami-Ryukyuan 25, 35, 37, 172, 370, 378, 387
Kyushu 46–47, 53–54, 56, 65, 68, 82, 138, 160, 211, 222, 225, 343, 348, 373, 443, 445

Labov, William 130, 199–202, 264, 415–416
Lakoff, Robin T. 265–266, 282–83, 289, 342
language acquisition 119, 177, 180–181, 206, 382; Ainu 365; second 37, 94, 96, 429
language attitude 26, 78, 93, 102, 130–135, 153, 177–193, 201, 205, 280, 324, 348, 370, 413–414, 423; Ainu 3, 20, 174; dialects 63, 67, 138, 162; gendered speech 285–286, 290; honorific 252; literacy 326; old script 319; planning and policy 301–303, 310; Ryukyuan languages 25–30, 36, 211, 377, 379–383; Ryukyu-substrate Japanese 381, 441, 445–447, 453; varieties of English 117
language attrition 177; Okinawan 29; Ryukyuan languages 39, 59, 377, 380, 383
language change 78, 81, 86, 129, 133, 199–213, 212–213, 302, 349, 408–409; in progress 75; Ryukyuan langaues 371, 443; Toyama 72

language choice 93, 114–117, 129, 186, 221, 236, 243; Okinawa 28–29, 36, 370, 377–381, 449
language contact 78, 83, 85, 102, 170, 177, 181, 210, 408, 422; Ainu and Japanese 3, 7–8; Ryukyuan languages and Japanese 31, 43; Ryukyu-substrate Japanese 441–450; Taiwanese and Japanese 348
language death 180, 381; *see also* extinct language
language/dialect vitality: Ainu 19, 356–357; dialects 68, 69, 379; immigrants 100, 144, 177; Ryukyuan languages 30, 370, 381
language diversity 98, 103, 122, 130–131, 415–416; dialects 134, 223; English 118, 121; Japan 162–163, 170, 172–173, 176–177, 182, 188, 190–192, 221, 231, 315, 342–343, 372, 390–397; Japanese 72, 76, 86, 91, 96, 144–147, 152–153, 205, 213, 235, 250, 259, 308, 330, 348, 371, 422–31; Ryukyuan languaes 29, 65, 371
language ecology 92
language education: Ainu 362–64; English 121; Japanese 91, 94–102, 170, 175–176, 180, 304–308; Japanese territories 339–350; national 67, 70; Okinawa 45, 371, 376; other coutnries 187; returnee children 423–430; *see also* education
language maintenance 78–79, 86, 181, 416, 421, 425, 431; Ainu 13, 20, 187, 363–366; immigrants in Japan 93, 94, 96, 100, 179–180; Japanese in Sakhalin 85; returnees 176; Ryukyuan languages 24, 27, 29, 30, 35–37, 187, 191, 373–382; Ryukyu-subsrate Japanese 47; Southeast Asia 346
language planning and policy 71, 173–175, 186–187, 280, 290, 299–310, 322–323, 340–350, 396, 398; Ainu 356; Ryukyuan languages 371; *see also* standardization
language preservation 26–27, 343, 354, 380, 393
language revitalization 180, 416, 431; Ainu 19, 21, 26–27, 176, 354–355, 362–366; local varieties 71, 162; Ryukyuan languages 26–27, 30, 36–38, 70, 309, 371, 379–383
language shift 79, 163, 174; Ainu 19, 354–366; Korean 93–94, 425; Ryukyuan languages 25–26, 31, 34–36, 370–383; Ryukyu-substrate Japanese 43, 59–60, 441–450
language variation 64, 69, 199–213, 422; Ryukyuan languages 26, 32–36, 39, 172
leveling *see* dialect leveling
Levinson, Stephen 249–251, 256–258, 266, 270
Li, Wei 93, 145–146, 173, 182, 228
lingua franca 35, 79, 115, 117, 121–122, 146–147, 151–152, 185, 345–346, 373, 376, 426
linguistic change 72, 79, 170, 199–213
linguistic landscape 18, 26, 28, 93, 110–111, 114–117, 122, 144, 146, 192, 323, 158–165; English 159–160, 163

Index

linguistic relativism 116
linguistic repertoire 19, 29–30, 44–45, 69, 139, 145–147, 149–152, 154, 209, 222–223, 225, 228, 272, 377, 379, 426, 431, 449, 452
literacy 114, 130, 139, 176, 179, 301, 315, 317, 326–335, 346, 375, 382, 395, 398, 412–413
loanword: Ainu and Japanese 3, 7, 9–14, 19–20; from English 204, 228–229, 421–423, 430; Ryukyu-substrate Japanese 44, 46, 59; western 159; *see also* borrowing
Long, Daniel 28, 30, 51–52, 64, 82–85, 158–160, 163, 165, 421–422, 425, 442–443, 446, 451
Loveday, Leo 286, 415, 421

Maher, John C. 86, 91–93, 129, 132, 140, 144, 146–147, 172–179, 182, 189, 213, 231, 307, 354–355, 359, 363, 371–372, 421, 426
mainland Japan 6, 10, 26, 44, 83, 174, 203, 347–349, 374–375, 377, 443, 445
Mandarin Chinese *see* Chinese
Masiko, Hidenori 91, 303, 306, 319, 323, 333, 374, 376–377, 392, 394–395, 421–422, 424–425
Matsumoto, Kazuko 85–86, 201, 210–211, 213
Matsumoto, Yoshiko 251, 422
Matsuo, Shin 25, 100, 396, 430
media 25, 70, 91, 101, 112, 115–116, 134–135, 170, 187, 191–193, 204–205, 218, 222–223, 226, 228–229, 231, 240, 243, 265, 268, 270, 272, 288–290, 302, 333–335, 340, 360, 370, 373, 376, 379, 431, 448, 450
micro-macro distinction 37, 110, 117, 119
minority 28, 32, 37, 81–82, 131–135, 140, 144, 160–161, 170, 173–174, 177–179, 181, 187, 211–212, 221, 224, 315, 329, 339, 341, 343–344, 348, 356–357, 370, 373, 382, 389–399; indigenous 332, 362, 424, 426–428; sexual 423
mixed language 31, 58, 81, 83, 93, 143, 146, 151, 209–210, 229, 442
Miyako-Ryukyuan 25, 33, 36, 38, 43–44, 46–48, 51–53, 56–58, 171–172, 370, 378–379, 383, 444, 451
monolingualism 115, 144, 188, 191, 193, 218, 345, 375, 399
Moseley, Christopher 25–26, 28, 65, 370
mother tongue 45, 78, 96, 139, 173, 178, 182, 187, 189, 191, 374–375, 377, 382, 420–421, 425, 428, 444, 446
motivation: language learning 85, 98, 113, 209, 221, 230, 302, 304–306, 308–309, 342, 363, 384, 426, 429
multilingualism 28, 32, 79, 92, 114, 144–146, 152–154, 173, 176, 179–180, 184–193, 308, 350, 366, 395, 397–398, 415
music: Ainu 365; Okinawan 381
mutual intelligibility 32–33, 68, 79–80, 162, 165, 184, 190, 373

Nakagawa, Hiroshi 5, 7, 9–10, 12, 15–16, 354–364, 366
Nakajima, Tomoko 177–178, 191, 428
Nakamura, Momoko 285, 288, 291, 423, 431
national language 25, 27, 65, 67, 70–71, 73, 115, 133, 137–138, 174–176, 186, 201, 237, 285, 300–306, 309, 322, 340, 342–346, 348–350, 361, 391, 398–399, 407–408, 413–416, 420, 423, 441
National Institute of Japanese Language and Linguistics (NINJAL)/National Language Research Institute (*Kokuritsu Kokugo Kenkyūjo*) 34, 63–64, 67–68, 73, 100, 192, 238, 244, 279, 301, 305, 410
nationalism 102, 111, 120–122, 132, 137–138, 161, 188, 346, 374–376
native speaker 5, 38, 94, 114, 116–118, 122, 131, 193, 205, 212, 251, 286–287, 307, 356, 390–391, 420–421
Neustupný, Jiří V. 301, 393, 410, 414–415
newspaper 16, 27, 49, 224, 271, 288, 290, 373, 424, 447
new speaker 37, 426
new words: in Ainu 12, 20; in Ryukyu-substrate Japanese 449
New Zealand *see* Aotearoa
nonstandard/non-standard 44, 47, 49–53, 56, 59–61, 67, 202, 205, 225, 330, 334, 380, 443–445, 449–450, 452
norm/normative 29, 35, 43, 54, 67, 80, 94, 102, 117–118, 122, 136, 151, 159, 170, 172, 175, 189, 201–202, 209, 222, 243, 249–250, 252, 254, 257, 264, 271–272, 274–275, 283, 289–290, 301–303, 308–309, 333–334, 343, 345, 350, 356
normal language (*futsūgo*) 45, 373–374, 376, 397–398, 422, 431
number of speakers 68, 173, 201, 355

Obana, Yasuko 249–254, 256, 258
Oguma, Eiji 26, 307
Okamoto, Shigeko 68, 129, 133–134, 220, 243, 249–250, 264, 275, 288–289, 308, 420, 422–423
Okinawan-Ryukyuan (*Uchinaaguchi*) 37, 39, 44–45, 58, 69
Orthography 12, 15–16, 29–30, 130, 227, 300, 302, 315, 321–324, 332, 375, 382
Osumi, Midori 36, 44, 375, 377, 452
Otsuji, Emi 92, 129, 139, 143–147, 150–152, 154, 230–231, 431

participant observation 203, 240, 242, 244, 329
pedagogy 178–179, 307, 328
Peng, Fred C. C. 10, 12
Pennycook, Alastair 129, 139, 144–147, 150–152, 165, 230–231, 431
performing arts 381
Petrucci, Peter 25, 28–31, 50, 162, 379, 446, 452

Index

phonetic 43, 47, 28–29, 71, 84, 315–317, 332; change and variation 148, 203, 205, 227, 237; environment 202; interference 3, 14; sociophonetic 205, 281, 286, 290
phonology 8, 47, 64, 84, 93, 211, 407, 413, 443, 445, 450, 452
pidgin 79–80, 83, 130–131, 226, 348, 426, 430, 441–442, 450
pitch 9, 47, 64, 73, 203, 205, 224, 227, 286–288, 291, 443–444, 450–452
politeness 16–17, 39, 210–211, 238, 240–241, 248–261; English 249, 251, 256–260
poverty 25, 100, 291, 360, 377
power 28–31, 97–98, 102, 111, 115–116, 118–119, 122, 132–133, 135, 170, 192, 206, 221, 223, 238–240, 242, 265, 270, 274, 285, 287, 300–310, 326–329, 331, 334, 349, 365–366, 370, 379, 382, 391, 394, 397, 399, 414–416, 422, 428–431
prescriptive 81, 93, 248, 286, 290, 308, 319
prestige 35–36, 94, 130, 163, 201, 223, 346, 364
primary/elementary school 31, 110–112, 119–120, 140, 171, 176–177, 179, 307, 319, 343, 373–374, 427, 443–444
pronunciation 14, 34, 46–47, 84, 117, 148, 172, 204, 227, 302, 304, 318, 321–322, 332, 348, 375–376, 409, 413, 444
punishment 27, 136, 188, 375
purism 93; *see also* language attitude

racism 118, 231
radio broadcasting 37, 133, 288, 290, 363, 410, 413, 452; English medium 176
register 18, 57, 59, 68, 93, 145, 205, 220, 223–224, 284, 374, 377–378, 380, 408, 423, 431
relativism 116
returnee 94–95, 139, 176–177, 192, 221, 423, 425, 428
returnee children (*kikoku shijo*) 176–177, 391, 423–424; *see also* education
reversion (*fukki*) 68, 83, 349, 377–378, 452
rusty speaker 45, 59, 377–378, 380, 382, 451–52
Ryukyu Kingdom 33, 65, 174, 373
Ryukyuan languages 25–27, 29–33, 35–39, 43–45, 47–50, 52, 55–56, 58–59, 65, 69–71, 83, 162, 172–173, 176, 181, 185, 211, 306–307, 309, 315, 332, 343–344, 349–350, 355, 370–381, 391–393, 399, 424, 426, 441–448, 450–453
Ryukyu-substrate Japanese 43–59, 84, 441–453

Sanada, Shinji 69, 72–76, 85, 93, 302–303, 414–415, 421–422, 425–426, 442
second language 3, 19, 26, 37–38, 69, 79, 94, 139, 172, 181, 190, 223, 226, 265, 308, 356, 375, 408, 420–442, 424, 428–429
semi speaker 45, 59, 211, 378, 381, 444, 447, 451–453

Shibamoto, Janet Smith 68, 129, 133–134, 163, 206, 208, 220, 237, 250, 283, 286, 289, 308, 420, 422–423, 431
Shuri variety 34–35, 37, 65, 373, 443, 448
Sibata, Takesi 63, 72, 82, 130, 138–139, 205, 237–238, 240–241, 244, 279, 341, 414–415
social class 33–34, 86, 99, 201, 203, 220, 252, 303, 416
social context 223, 236, 238–240, 243–244, 306, 328, 411, 430
social dialect 76, 86, 135, 273, 284
social identity 182
social meaning 94, 199, 204
social status 178, 238, 252, 430
social structure 121, 300, 399
social variable 72, 422
socialization 93, 96, 98, 114, 275
sociolect 34
sociology of language 175, 279, 414
solidarity 119, 133, 136, 187, 222, 230, 248, 266, 452
sound change 12, 199–200, 203–205, 212
standardization 3, 15, 67, 134, 173–174, 223, 237–238, 300, 304, 306, 408, 413–416
substratum 43–45, 54, 58–59, 371, 377–378, 380, 384, 442, 444–445, 448–450, 453
Sugita, Yuko 59, 309, 378–379, 446, 452–453
superstratum 80, 442
switching *see* code switching
symbolic function 110, 112, 116, 137, 149, 160, 174, 300, 334, 340, 364–365

Taiwan 85, 91, 115, 131, 138, 170–173, 339–340, 343–344, 347–349, 372, 421, 426, 428
Taiwanese language 131, 138, 348–349, 372, 428
Takano, Shoji 205, 208–209, 442
Tanaka, Yukari 68, 86, 130, 134, 160, 222, 223
television broadcasting TV 15, 71, 179, 213, 222, 227–230, 232, 288, 290, 319, 363, 410, 413, 430–431
translanguaging 93, 97, 145–146, 228, 231, 431
transnational 117, 426
Trudgill, Peter 80, 81, 200, 201, 210, 211, 371, 414

Uchinaaguchi (Okinawan–Ryukyuan) 37, 39, 44–45, 58, 69
Uchinaa Yamatuguchi (Okinawan Japanese) 44, 69–70, 380, 441, 445, 448, 450–451
UN (United Nations) 95, 362, 399
urban 29, 83, 132–133, 135, 140, 145–146, 152, 159, 174, 185, 199–200, 209–210, 212–213, 229, 344, 412, 415–416, 431
Usami, Mayumi 250, 422

variation 64, 68–69, 72–73, 81, 91, 134, 161–163, 172, 199–213, 238–239, 245, 254, 287, 319, 330, 342, 390, 408–409,

463

413, 416, 422; Ainu 3, 17, 21; Ryukyuan languages 26, 28, 32–33, 38–39; Ryukyu-substrate Japanese 43–44, 46, 58

Yaeyama-Ryukyuan 25, 33–34, 38, 43–44, 46–50, 52–53, 55, 57, 59, 172, 205, 370, 378, 383, 441, 451–452

Yamashita, Hitoshi 153, 302, 308, 315, 326, 332–333, 390

Yamatu Uchinaaguchi (Japanese Okinawan) 70, 445, 450–451

Yasuda, Toshiaki 153, 175–176, 191, 302–304, 306–308, 342–343, 345, 348, 350, 408, 412

Yonaguni-Ryukyuan 25, 29, 33, 38, 43–44, 46, 59, 172, 370–371, 378, 383, 443, 451

zainichi 131, 136, 139, 180–182, 329–330, 332, 424